THE
TAI-KADAI
LANGUAGES

D1629205

ROUTLEDGE LANGUAGE FAMILY SERIES

Each volume in this series contains an in-depth account of the members of some of the world's most important language families. Written by experts in each language, these accessible accounts provide detailed linguistic analysis and description. The contents are carefully structured to cover the natural system of classification: phonology, morphology, syntax, lexis, semantics, dialectology, and sociolinguistics.

Every volume contains extensive bibliographies for each language, a detailed index and tables, and maps and examples from the languages to demonstrate the linguistic features being described. The consistent format allows comparative study, not only between the languages in each volume, but also across all the volumes in the series.

The Austronesian Languages of Asia and Madagascar
Edited by Nikolaus Himmelmann &
Sander Adelaar

The Bantu Languages
Edited by Derek Nurse &
Gérard Philippson

The Celtic Languages 2nd Edition
Martin J. Ball & James Fife

The Dravidian Languages
Edited by Sanford B. Steever

The Germanic Languages
Edited by Ekkehard Konig &
Johan van der Auwera

The Indo-Aryan Languages
Edited by George Cardona &
Dhanesh K. Jain

The Indo-European Languages
Edited by Paolo Ramat &
Anna Giacalone Ramat

The Iranian Languages
Edited by Gernot Windfuhr

The Khoesan Languages
Edited by Raïner Vossen

The Mongolic Languages
Edited by Juha Janhunan

The Munda Languages
Edited by Gregory D.S. Anderson

The Oceanic Languages
Edited by John Lynch, Malcolm Ross
& Terry Crowley

The Romance Languages
Edited by Martin Harris &
Nigel Vincent

The Semitic Languages
Edited by Robert Hetzron

The Sino-Tibetan Languages
Edited by Graham Thurgood &
Randy J. Lapolla

The Slavonic Languages
Bernard Comrie & Greville G. Corbett

The Tai-Kadai Languages
Edited by Anthony Diller,
Jerold A. Edmondson and Yongxian Luo

The Turkic Languages
Edited by Eva Csato & Lars Johanson

The Uralic Languages
Edited by Daniel Abondolo

THE
TAI-KADAI
LANGUAGES

Edited by

Anthony V. N. Diller,

Jerold A. Edmondson

and

Yongxian Luo

Routledge
Taylor & Francis Group

LONDON AND NEW YORK

First published 2008
First published in paperback 2012
by Routledge
2 Park Square, Milton Park, Abingdon, Oxon OX14 4RN

Simultaneously published in the USA and Canada
by Routledge
711 Third Avenue, New York, NY 10017

Routledge is an imprint of the Taylor & Francis Group, an informa business

© 2008, 2012 Anthony V. N. Diller, Jerold A. Edmondson and Yongxian Luo

This book has been prepared from camera-ready copy provided by the editors

British Library Cataloguing in Publication Data
A catalogue record for this book is available from the British Library

Library of Congress Cataloguing in Publication Data
The Tai-Kadai languages / edited by Anthony V. N. Diller,
Jerold A. Edmondson and Yongxian Luo.
p.cm. – (Routledge language family series)
Includes bibliographical references.
1. Tai-Kadai languages – History. 2. Tai-Kadai languages – Grammar,
Comparative. I. Diller, Anthony Van Nostrand; II. Edmondson, Jerold A.;
III. Luo Yongxian; IV. Series.
PL4113. T35 2008
495.9′1–dc22
2007046237

ISBN: 978–0–7007–1457–5 (hbk)
ISBN: 978–0–415–68847–5 (pbk)
ISBN: 978–0–203–64187–3 (ebk)

CONTENTS

ILLUSTRATIONS

MAPS

TABLES

ABBREVIATIONS

LTBA	Linguistics of the Tibeto-Burman Area
HCT	Handbook of Comparative Tai
ICSTLL	International Conference on Sino-Tibetan Languages and Linguistics
PAL 3	Pan Asiatic Linguistics: Proceedings of the Third International Conference
PAL 4	Pan Asiatic Linguistics: Proceedings of the Fourth International Conference
A	agent
ACHV	achievement
ADV	adverbial
AP	adjective phrase
AQ	audience question
ASEMI	Asie de Sud-Est et Monde Insulindien (Bulletin du Centre de Documentation et de Recherche, Centre National de la Recherche Scientifique, Ecole des Hautes Etudes en Sciences Sociales, Paris)
ASP	aspect
AUX	auxiliary
BA	disposal construction in Chinese
BEFEO	Bulletin de l'Ecole Française d'Extrême-Orient, Hanoi/Paris
BEI	passive construction in Chinese
BEN	benefactive
BENEF	benefactive
C	consonant
CAU	causative
CAUS	causative
CL	numeral classifier
CLA	classifier
CLF	classifier
CLNK	clause linker
CLS	classifier
CM	commenting on developments in story
COMP	complementizer
CONJ	conjunctive; conjunction
CT	class term
CV	action verb
DEM	demonstrative
Det	determiner
DI	demonstrative and interrogative

DIR	directional
DO	direct object
DV	directional verb
EMPH	emphasis/emphatic
EXPR	expressive
FEM	feminine
FOC	focus
FW	functional words
GEN	general
GI	greeting and informational exchange
HP	highlighting particle
IND	inducive
INJ	interjection
INT	intensifier
INTERJ	interjection
INTR	intransitive
IO	indirect object
IP	initial phonemes
IRR	irrealis
MAL	malfactive
MASC	masculine
MOD	modality
MSC	Modern Standard Chinese
MV	modal verb
NEG	negation; negative
NET	noninterventive
NL	non-linguistic instant responses and reactions
NOM	noun phrase conjunctive
NONPROX	non-proximal
NP	noun phrase
NSR	nominalizer
O	object
PAN	proto-Austronesian
PART	particle
PAT	patient
PCL	particle
PEN	personal experience narrative
PER	person
PERF	perfective
PFV	perfective
PFX	prefix
PL	plural
PMP	Proto-Malayo-Polynesian
POSS	possessive
POT	potential
PP	preposition phrase; pragmatic particle
PROG	progressive
PT	Proto-Tai
PURP	purposive
PV	verb-particle

Q	question
QP	quantifier phrase
RCP	reciprocal
RDP	reduplication
RE	reasoning or extensions
REC	reciprocal
REL	relative clause; relative marker; relativizer
RR	rest of the audience's response
S	single direct argument of intransitive clause; subject
SA	speech act
SAP	speech act particle
SFP	sentence-final particle
SG	singular
SLP	sentence linking particle
SPEC	specifier
SUB	supportinative
SUFF	suffix
SUP	suppine
SURF	surface structure
SV	stative verb
SVC	serial-verb construction
T	tone
TAM	tense, aspect and modality
TBU	tone-bearing unit
TOP	topic
TPC	topic
V	verb; vowel
VP	verb phrase
Y.SIB	younger sibling
1/2/3	$1^{st}/2^{nd}/3^{rd}$ person pronoun

PART 1

OVERVIEW CHAPTERS

CHAPTER ONE

INTRODUCTION

Anthony Diller

1.1. TAI-KADAI: PROGRESS AND PROSPECTS

This volume attests to several eventful decades in Tai-Kadai research. The recent past has seen new data become available, substantial analyses completed and larger Tai-Kadai patterns coming into clearer focus. These successes are pointing the way to future projects. The editors hope that this volume not only can stand as a record of current progress but also can provide a stimulus for new field studies and generalizations. The latter may apply to the internal structure and relations of varieties within Tai-Kadai and to relationships with other languages and groupings; also to broader questions of theory and practice.

Further fieldwork is a matter of particular urgency. As elsewhere among the world's major language families, Tai-Kadai's territory is home to speakers of endangered languages. Concern is great that children of those now speaking many Tai-Kadai varieties are substantially modifying and even abandoning their parents' language. This volume documents varieties under threat, pointing to how important it is for more work of this kind to be undertaken while there is still time. Required will be well-trained linguistic researchers, motivated local speakers, appropriate institutional assistance and the acquiescence, if not active support, of governments and local officials. In the past two or three decades Tai-Kadai researchers have been fortunate in that policies of states in the region have generally moved in the direction of facilitating greater access to field sites; the profession's thanks are due to individuals and official units involved in this movement. Gratitude is also due to the funding bodies which have supported Tai-Kadai research. It is hoped that work reported in this volume may encourage others to address these challenges, gain necessary support and pursue further field studies in this critical area.

1.2. ACKNOWLEDGMENTS

Many people and institutions have contributed to the completion of this volume. Gratitude has already been expressed for cooperative support from officials and their units in the Tai-Kadai region; included here in China are the Central University for Nationalities, Beijing, and the Guangxi University for Nationalities. In Thailand, the National Research Council has been helpful. Of course, we owe sincere thanks to the many local language assistants, speakers of Tai-Kadai varieties, whose contributions are the essential basis of analyses presented here.

Themes recurring in this volume have often been points of discussion in a series of stimulating international conferences held in Bangkok. Chulalongkorn, Thammasat and Mahidol Universities have hosted these and thanks are due to Thai colleagues and their linguistics departments for contributing their professional and organizational expertise. The success of these events has helped to bring Tai-Kadai studies to maturity.

Funding agencies have been thanked but double thanks are due. Grants from the Australian Research Council (ARC) have been crucial in bringing this volume together and specifically in enabling work behind chapters 2, 3, 4 and 9. The Research Centre for Linguistic Typology (RCLT) at La Trobe University, Melbourne, provided a most appropriate site for early editorial work. The Centre's inspiring directors also made possible international travel for initial publication arrangements. RCLT provided specific support for work behind chapters 1 and 6. Other tasks have been completed with assistance from the Department of Linguistics of the University of Sydney and final editing has relied heavily on the good offices of the Asia Institute of the University of Melbourne.

Contributors are thanked for their patience with production delays and for their efficiency in responding to requests. The same thanks are extended to staff at Routledge-Curzon.

Production has encountered challenges and many have offered help and advice. Special thanks are due Mr Mike Tianqiao Lu, Ms Haiqing Yu and Mr Phichit Roinil. Further acknowledgements appear in individual chapters.

Finally, in gratitude, the writer would like to call to mind inspiring teachers and other senior colleagues who have shared their many insights, among them: Helen Funnell, James W. Poultney, Mary R. Haas, Robert B. Jones, John U. Wulff, James Gair, David K. Wyatt, Fang-Kuei Li, Paul K. Benedict and William J. Gedney.

1.3. ORGANIZATION

In planning selections for this volume, the editors have kept in mind maximum service to the profession and to the likely readership. They have allocated much space to less-described Tai-Kadai varieties, several treated here in detail for the first time. On the other hand, general and comparative themes are included as well.

Chapter 2 following is by Yongxian Luo and can serve as an introduction to the current state of research, debate and speculation as to Tai-Kadai's ultimate linkages. It also takes a particular stand on the Sino-Tai hypothesis and illustrates how argumentation in the field has been progressing. The chapter should be provocative and we can expect future debate.

Part 2 presents overviews and resources relating to the Tai languages. Thai is the best -described language in the family with many overviews readily available. Rather than offering yet another overview, in chapter 3 the writer selects bibliographic resources and introduces them with commentary, including some impression of how research has developed. Lao is the other national language in the Tai-Kadai grouping but is underrepresented in published research, especially in English. In chapter 4 N. J. Enfield provides a substantial account of Lao verbs and verbal constructions. The extent to which the Lao features he analyzes are found throughout Tai-Kadai suggests a worthwhile direction for future research. Chapter 5 by Jerold A. Edmondson is a survey of Shan and other northern tier Southwestern Tai languages of Myanmar and China. In chapter 6 Stephen Morey describes Tai languages of Assam and includes treatment of their little-known writing system. As for other Southwestern Tai languages, Lue is described in chapter 7 by John F. Hartmann and the Tai dialects of Nghe An, Vietnam, by Michel Ferlus, in chapter 8. Zhuang, a grouping that includes many millions of speakers, spans the Central and Northern branches of Tai and is described in chapter 9 by Yongxian Luo. In chapter 10 phonology of the Northern-branch language Bouyei is outlined by Wil Snyder. Chapter 11, by Wilaiwan Khanittanan, updates the author's earlier work on Saek, a displaced Northern-branch language with archaic features.

Part 3 is given to some special Tai features often overlooked in standard treatments but of undoubted linguistic interest. Chapter 12 by Amara Prasithrathsint considers four-word expressions, taking Tai Lue as a basis, but suggesting a Tai-wide distribution for the phenomena described. Thomas John Hudak in chapter 13 draws on several Tai languages to produce a linguist's guide to Tai aesthetics. In chapter 14 David Holm gives readers an illuminating exegesis of what may well be the first Tai writing system, the Old Zhuang script.

Part 4 is a more tightly-focused set, with four chapters dealing with aspects of diachronic change and grammaticalization, topics of particular relevance as linguistic theory confronts languages of the Tai-Kadai type. In chapter 15 Somsonge Burusphat traces a sequential indicator appearing in a range of Southeast Asian languages and speculates as to etymological connections. Pranee Kullavanijaya in chapter 16 gives a diachronic account of how a Thai (and Tai) functional operator has evolved. More synchronic approaches to grammaticalization are taken up in chapter 17 by Shoichi Iwasaki, analyzing bipolar distribution, and in chapter

18, by Kingarn Thepkanjana and Satoshi Uehara, analyzing directional verbs as success markers.

Part 5 is given to the Kam-Sui languages and provides valuable information on little-described varieties. In one of the more substantial chapters (19) of the volume, Tongyin Yang and Jerold A. Edmondson present a groundbreaking and comprehensive account of Kam (Dong), the numerically dominant member of the Kam-Sui group. This is followed in chapter 20 by a sketch of Sui by James Wei and Jerold A. Edmondson. Chapter 21, by Jinfang Li, is the first description of Chadong available for international readers.

Part 6 treats other little-described varieties, several endangered, but critical for understanding the deeper constituency of Tai-Kadai as a whole and for considering its ultimate relationships. The Hlai (or Li) languages of Hainan are described by Weera Ostapirat in chapter 22. The final chapter (23) by Jerold A. Edmondson describes the Kra group (or Geyang; also Kadai in a sense mentioned in the following section).

1.4. TERMINOLOGY AND ITS INTERPRETATIVE NUANCES

Terminology used by those in Tai-Kadai research still shows flux: usage is not yet entirely uniform and complete professional consensus remains elusive. In some cases terminological variation is simply a matter of alternative names, but in other cases particular claims are presupposed or signaled when specific labels are selected. Specific languages may have multiple names, such as Black Tai, alternating with Tai Dam, Tai Noir, etc., and when transplanted in Thailand, as Lao Song Dam or Lao Song. Also, a single label, such as *Dai*, may subsume what linguistic criteria or speakers themselves might take to be separate languages. Finally some labels, e.g. Red Thai, have been subject of contention (see chapter 8). The editors have not enforced standards in this regard, so readers should keep in mind potential flexibility in usage across chapters. This fluidity applies to transcription systems as well.

By now it is usual for the spelling *Thai* to cover inclusively normative Standard Thai and related colloquial Central Thai varieties, including the more vernacular form sometimes referred to as Bangkok Thai. The spelling *Thai* is also used in regional or local variety names within Thailand's borders such as Southern Thai, Suphanburi Thai, etc. Northern Thai is often called Lanna or Kammueang; Northeastern Thai may be referred to as Isan or local Lao.

Thai in this generally-accepted sense then belongs to the larger *Tai* family of languages, so spelled, as defined by general professional consensus. Most in the field would accept at least as a point of departure Li's (1977) classification of Tai languages, which are spoken over a wide somewhat 'Y-shaped' area stretching from southern China through northern Southeast Asia and on to the northwest into Assam in northeastern India. The reconstructed parent language at this level is *Proto-Tai*. Readers need to keep in mind that *Northern Tai* and *Central Tai* designate major branches in Li's *Tai* family tree, not specific varieties. Languages of these branches are spoken in China and Vietnam. These terms are not to be confused with *Northern Thai* and *Central Thai*, which are regional variety names in Thailand belonging to Li's *Southwestern Tai* branch.

Tai and its Chinese pinyin equivalent Dai also occur in the names of specific varieties, such as *Black Tai*, *Tai-Aiton*, etc. Note also the million-strong *Tày* language of Vietnam, in Li's *Central Tai* branch. This has sometimes been referred to as *Tho*, but that name is now understood to be objectionable. In Chinese usage, *Dai* denotes a nationality unit of Yunnan. This combines speakers of what is elsewhere known as *Lue*, *Lü*, or *Tai-Lue*, along with the markedly different *Dehong* or *Tai-Dehong* (also know as *Chinese Shan* or perhaps *Nuea*, literally 'northern' or 'above', although that term may also refer to a different variety in the general area). In linguistic practice, *Dai* has been used in the sense of *Lue* alone, i.e. in this case excluding Dehong.

One should note that the *Thai/Tai* distinction sketched above has not always been made in way indicated and that this nomenclature pairing is not satisfactory to all. Some scholars, including Benedict (1975), have used *Thai* to refer to a wider (*Tai*) grouping and one sees designations like *Proto-Thai* and *Austro-Thai* in earlier works. In the institutional context in Thailand, and occasionally elsewhere, sometimes *Tai* (and its corresponding Thai-script spelling, without a final –y symbol) is used to indicate varieties in the language family **not** spoken in Thailand or spoken there only as the result of recent immigration. In this usage *Thai* would not then be considered a *Tai* language.

On the other hand, Gedney, Li and others have preferred to call the standard language of Thailand *Siamese* rather than *Thai*, perhaps to reduce potential *Thai/Tai* confusion, especially among English speakers not comfortable with making a non-English initial unaspirated voiceless initial sound for *Tai*, which in any event might sound artificial or arcane to outsiders.

Moreover, Lao scholars I have met are not pleased with Lao being regarded as a Tai language. For some, Thai should instead be considered a member of the Lao language family. One or more Ancient Chinese characters for 'Lao' may be cited in support of this alternative appellation. Enfield (2002) discusses the critical issues here with clarity.

Tai in the sense Li has used it is now so widely accepted as to be the norm. The *Tai* language family in turn is taken as a major sub-branch of *Kam-Tai* within the greater grouping *Tai-Kadai*. Finally, whether *Tai-Kadai* is to be regarded as an isolate or whether it might be placed in some more ambitious macro-family with a designation like *Sino-Tai* or *Austro-Tai* is still a matter of great interest and current professional debate, as papers in this volume will attest.

Kadai as a term raises problems of its own. At least one Thai scholar has objected to *Kadai* (Ostapirat 2000, 2004), noting that it seems to mean 'ladder' in Thai. Another possibility, equally inappropriate, is that given a voiceless rendition of Kadai's second syllable, i.e. to sound something like *Tai*, and given the right vowel-length and tone, *Kadai* could be mistaken for the Thai or Lao noun 'rabbit'. Furthermore, as though to complete a tortoise-and-hare scenario, it seems that *Kra*, Ostapirat's suggested term to replace *Kadai*, in Thai actually sounds like a noun referring to a large maritime turtle, *Chelonia imbricata.* However, in spite of a slow start, Ostapirat's tortoise entry *Kra* may yet overtake the *Kadai* hare and win the terminological race. If so, would *Tai-Kadai* need to become *Tai-Kra* (or could we perhaps settle for something less inventive like *Tai-Gelao*)?

The original rationale for Benedict's (1942, 1975) invention of *Kadai* was apparently to group languages of the Hlai (Li) type on Hainan Island together with the Gelao-Laha type in mainland China and Vietnam, but it would now appear that the case is rather weak for recognizing that particular subgrouping as a unified branch (by whatever name). Reinterpretation of *Kadai* to avoid the subgroup claim is one reasonable approach. *Kadai* in a new sense may be restricted to languages of the Gelao-Laha group (i.e. Kra or Geyang); an opposite possibility is to use it to denote the entire (Tai-Kadai) grouping.

Readers interested in ramifications of these terminology issues and in associated subgrouping proposals, debates and related diagrams might consult Edmondson and Solnit (1988, 1997); Thurgood (1994); Luo (1997, 2007); Diller (2000); Ostapirat (2000, 2004); Matisoff (2001); Edmondson (2007). These sources can be complemented with chapters in this volume. For convenience, one tentative diagram for reference follows but it should not be considered the final picture.

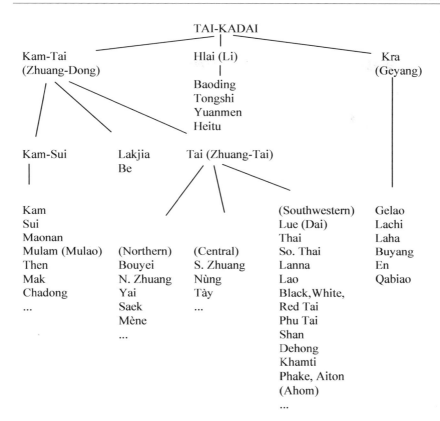

TAI-KADAI

| Kam-Tai (Zhuang-Dong) | Hlai (Li) | Kra (Geyang) |

Baoding
Tongshi
Yuanmen
Heitu

| Kam-Sui | Lakjia Be | Tai (Zhuang-Tai) | |

Kam			(Southwestern)	Gelao
Sui			Lue (Dai)	Lachi
Maonan			Thai	Laha
Mulam (Mulao)	(Northern)	(Central)	So. Thai	Buyang
Then	Bouyei	S. Zhuang	Lanna	En
Mak	N. Zhuang	Nùng	Lao	Qabiao
Chadong	Yai	Tày	Black, White,	
...	Saek	...	Red Tai	
	Mène		Phu Tai	
	...		Shan	
			Dehong	
			Khamti	
			Phake, Aiton	
			(Ahom)	
			...	

REFERENCES

Benedict, Paul K. (1942) 'Thai, Kadai and Indonesian: A New Alignment in Southeastern Asia', *American Anthropologist* 44: 576-601.
— (1975) Austro-Thai Language and Culture with a Glossary of Roots, New Haven: HRAF Press.
Diller, Anthony (2000) 'The Tai Language Family and the Comparative Method', in Khunying Suriya Ratanakul, et al. (eds) *Proceedings of the International Conference on Tai* Studies, *July 29-31 1998*, Institute of Language and Culture for Rural Development, Mahidol University, 1-32.
Edmondson, Jerold A. (2007) 'The Power of Language over the Past: Tai Settlement and Tai Linguistics in Southern China and Northern Vietnam', in Harris, Jimmy G., Somsonge Burusphat, and James E. Harris (eds) *Studies in Tai and Southeast Asian Linguistics*, Bangkok: Ekphimthai Ltd. 39-63.
Edmondson, Jerold A. and David B. Solnit (eds) (1988) *Comparative Kadai: Linguistic Studies beyond Tai*, Summer Institute of Linguistics and University of Texas at Arlington.
— (eds) (1997) *Comparative Kadai: the Tai Branch*. Summer Institute of Linguistics and University of Texas at Arlington.
Enfield, N. J. (2002) 'How to Define 'Lao', 'Thai' and 'Isan' Language? A View from Linguistic Science', *Tai Culture* 7.1: 62-67.
Li Fang-Kuei (1977) *A Handbook of Comparative Tai*, Oceanic Linguistics Special Publications No. 15, Honolulu: University of Hawaii Press.

Luo Yongxian (1997) *The Subgroup Structure of the Tai Languages: A Historical-Comparative Study*, Berkeley, California: Journal of Chinese Linguistics Monograph Series No. 12.

— (2007) 'Sino-Tai Words for "Cut"', in Harris, Jimmy G., Somsonge Burusphat, and James E. Harris (eds) *Studies in Tai and Southeast Asian Linguistics*, Bangkok: Ekphimthai Ltd., 155-181.

Matisoff, James A. (2001) 'Genetic Versus Contact Relationship: Prosodic Diffusibility in South-East Asian Languages', in Alexandra Y. Aikhenvald and R.M.W. Dixon (eds) *Areal Diffusion and Genetic Inheritance: Problems in Comparative Linguistics*, Oxford University Press, 291-327.

Ostapirat, Weera (2000) *Proto-Kra*, Berkeley, California: Linguistics of the Tibeto-Burman Area 23.1 (entire volume).

— (2004) 'Kra-dai and Austronesian: Notes on Phonological Correspondences and Vocabulary Distribution', in Laurent Sagart, Roger Blench and Alicia Sanchez-Mazas (eds) *The Peopling of East Asia: Putting together Archaeology, Linguistics and Genetics*, London: Routledge-Curzon, 107-131.

Thurgood Graham (1994) 'Tai-Kadai and Austronesian: The Nature of the Historical Relationship', *Oceanic Linguistics* 33: 2.

CHAPTER TWO

SINO-TAI AND TAI-KADAI: ANOTHER LOOK[1]

Yongxian Luo

2.1. INTRODUCTION

A key issue in Sino-Tibetan studies is the historical link between Chinese and Tai — whether or not they are genetically related. While there is no question about the status of Tai as a distinct language family (Li 1977), the nature of Sino-Tai relationship is still much debated. Opinions can be divided into three camps: (1) Sino-Tai (De Lacouperie, Maspero, Wulff, Li, Haudricourt, Shafer, Denlinger, Xing, Zhengzhang); (2) Austro-Tai (Schlegel, Benedict);[2] (3) Sino-Tibetan-Austronesian (Sagaart, Reid, Xing). The Sino-Tai hypothesis assumes the membership of Tai under Sino-Tibetan while the Austro-Tai theory argues for a genetic relationship between Tai and Austronesian. The Sino-Tibetan-Austronesian hypothesis proposes a larger phylum that includes Chinese, Tai-Kadai, Miao-Yao, and Austronesian. In addition, there are still others who believe in none of these ideas (Gedney 1976, Thurgood 1994).

Western researchers now generally accept the Austro-Tai theory, but many scholars in China hold the traditional view of Sino-Tai alliance. Some of them consider the Sino-Tai connection to be the result of language shift (Dai and Fu 1995, Luo Meizhen 1992, 1994).

Scholars in the field generally postulate the time depth of Tai to be around 2500 years, and place the homeland of the Tai people somewhere in south China's Guizhou-Guangxi- area (Gedney 1965, Matisoff 1991, Wyatt 1984). Archaeological finds seem to lend support to these arguments.[3] Yet no coherent and systematic account of the history of the Tai people is readily available in early Chinese sources. This is not surprising, as south and southwest China was strange to the early Chinese settlers in the Central Plain. From the fragmented historical records that we can piece together, south China is home to the Bai Yue 百越/百粵 (Hundred Yue), a group of indigenous non-Chinese peoples who inhabited the vast area along the coast as far north as Shandong and south down to the Yangtze basin and west to as far as present-day Sichuan province.

Chinese historical sources indicate that when Qin Shihuang conquered Lingnan in 224 BC, the vast area was inhabited by non-Chinese speaking peoples, some of whom must have been the ancestors of Tai speakers. After Qin and Han dynasties, more systematic accounts were kept of these non-Chinese speaking populations. Barlow (2000a, 2000b) has synthesized these accounts, with an emphasis on the Zhuang people in Guangxi. Several independent studies on this topic have also appeared (Wang 1993, 1998, Xing 1984).

---

1   An earlier version of this paper was presented at a seminar at the Research Centre for Linguistic Typology of La Trobe University in November 2005. The author wishes to thank the participants for useful feedback. This study is supported by a research grant from the Australian Research Council (DP209445).

2   Matisoff (2001: 297) holds a sceptical view about this and other high-order groupings, while in the same paper (p. 316) he is treating it as a supergroup when talking about the Chinese tonal influence on Tai-Kadai, Hmong-Mien and Vietnamese.

3   For a survey on Yueh Neolithic, see Meacham 1983: 147-148.

The linguistic evidence seems to suggest that the Bai Yue were made up of at least two subgroups: one which spoke Austroasiatic-related languages and another that spoke Tai and Hmong-Mien-related languages (Norman and Mei 1976, Li Jingzhong 1995, Pan 1995, La Polla 2001). This has led to the assumption that the Kam-Tai people were generally a subset of the Bai Yue, a view that is gaining increasing acceptance.

The aim of this chapter is to present an update overview of the issue of Sino-Tai connection. It first offers a critical assessment of the different views of the Sino-Tai link, followed by discussions of current progress. More importantly, this study will reassess Li Fang-Kuei's 1976 position paper on Sino-Tai. Some of the issues raised in that paper will be addressed, such as shared morphological features and grammatical processes. Special attention will be paid to Li's comparative method and Benedict's teleo-reconstruction. Some new findings will be presented. The intention is to shed new light on the issue of the nature of historical relationship between Chinese and Tai.

2.2. THE SINO-TAI HYPOTHESIS: A REVIEW OF DIFFERENT THEORIES

2.2.1. Shared typological features between Chinese and Tai

Whatever their ultimate relationship may turn out to be, Chinese and Tai have the following features in common:

1) They share the same number of phonemic tone classes, commonly referred to as A (level), B (departing), C (rising), and D (those ending in final -p, -t, -k); regular correspondence can be established between Chinese and Tai for each of these tonal classes;
2) They share four classes of initials based on type of articulation, i.e. voiceless, half voiceless, voiced, half-voiced;
3) They share correlations between initials and tones, i.e. different initial consonants go with different tones, and the tones in turn affect the voicing of the initial consonants;
4) They share similar rhyme groups (Chinese she 摄);
5) They share a significant number of lexical items, including a considerable amount of 'core vocabulary';[4]
6) They share many typological features in various aspects of grammar, including word order, phrase structure, semantic space and syntactic constructions.[5]

Some of the above features have been used by Denlinger (1989) as 'formal proof' for a Sino-Tai genetic relationship. Particularly important is lexical sharing, which supplies invaluable information for Old Chinese reconstruction. For example, Tai reflexes have been used in the reconstruction of initial clusters for Old Chinese (see discussion in §2.3 and §2.4 below). While some of the above Sino-Tai common traits appear to display areal features (see Matisoff 2001), others are unique to Chinese and Tai. As we shall see below, there is still further evidence that points to a deep Sino-Tai historical connection.

2.2.2. The traditional view on the Sino-Tai link and competing theories

2.2.2.1. De Lacouperie and Wulff

Before the publication of Paul K Benedict's 1942 article, 'Tai, Kadai, and Indonesian: a

---

4   This observation is different from the views held by Benedict (1975) and others (Ostapirat 2005).
5   These include a number of grammaticalised items and functional operators, such as case markers such as 要 *yào* - Tai *ʔau* A1 (instrumental, manner); tense and aspect markers 了 *liǎo* (perfective) Tai *yù* 欲- Tai *yaak* (irrealis), 住/著 *zhù* -Tai *yu* (progressive); 过 *guò* - Tai *kwa* B1 (past, experiential), and many negative words (Luo 1997: 98-99), among others.

new alignment in Southeast Asia', it was taken for granted that Tai was a member of the Sino-Tibetan stock. The traditional view of Sino-Tai alliance was based on the fact that Tai shares with Chinese many typological similarities, both in phonology and grammar, along with a substantial number of lexical items.

De Lacouperie (1883) did pioneering work on Sino-Tai genetic relationship. He put forward over 30 cognate words for what he called the Tai-Shan and Kunlunic (Sino-Tibetan) stock. His thesis set a corner stone for the traditional theory on the Sino-Tai.

Wulff (1934) undertook a systematic study on Sino-Tai connection. This impressive work, using the comparative method, proposed a possible genetic relationship between Chinese and Tai on the basis of over 600 carefully worked-out cognate sets. But Wulff's findings have been interpreted in different ways by scholars. Many researchers, including the present writer, would view them as evidence for a Sino-Tai link, while others, for example, Egerod (1976) and Benedict (1942, 1975), would consider them as evidence for language contact rather than genetic relatedness.

Perhaps the most significant finding of Wulff's work was his discovery of tonal correspondence between Chinese and Tai. Both Chinese and Tai have three tonal categories in open syllables, conveniently labelled as A, B, and C. Regular correspondence can be established between Chinese and Tai for these tone classes, as in Table 2.2.2.1-1:

TABLE 2.2.2.1-1: CHINESE–TAI TONAL CORRESPONDENCES

Chinese tones	Tai tone categories	Thai tones
Ping (p'ing) [level] (unmarked)	A	(unmarked)
Qu (ch'ü) [departing] (marked by -h)	B	mai eek
Shang [rising] (marked by -x)	C	mei thoo
Ru (ju) [entering] (marked by -p -t -k)	D	(unmarked)

Each of these categories is further divided into two allotones, one for high register (A1, B1, C1) and the other for low register (A2, B2, C2). A similar distinction can be observed in syllables with final stop ending (D1, D2). This scheme has been adopted by scholars in the field for comparative work. Xing (1962) expanded these lines of arguments.

2.2.2.2. *Li's position paper on Sino-Tai*

Li made his first pronouncement on the Sino-Tai genetic relationship in 1938, but a full position paper did not appear until 1976. With a sample of over 120 Sino-Tai cognates, Li presented some of the most convincing arguments for a genetic link between Chinese and Tai. Included in his database are sets of regular sound correspondences, and a significant number of core vocabulary items, such as body-part terms (blood, head, eye, arm, neck, shin, skin, flesh, leg), terms for nature and environment (sun, fog, hot), kinship terms (father, mother), everyday words (cut, chop, dig, split, soak, cooked/ripe), among others. These were analyzed and discussed in the context of genetic relationship. Tonal irregularities were considered to be an important feature between Chinese and Tai. In addition, partial correspondences were also proposed as cognate candidates. Thus, a link can be made between Chinese 鼓 'drum' (OC *kag, MC kɔ', and MSC gu³)[6] and Tai *kloŋ, and between Chinese 肚 'stomach' (OC *dag, MC tɔ', MSC du⁴) and Tai *dɔŋ C2, and between Chinese 補 'to mend' (OC *pag, MC pɔ', MSC bu³, Proto Tai *foŋ A1).

It is important to note that Li was employing the standard comparative method in mining Sino-Tai cognates. His methodology is in stark contrast to Benedict's tele-reconstruction (see

---

6   Old Chinese reconstructions are from Li (1971 [1980]); Middle Chinese reconstruction is from Pulleyblank (1991) and Proto-Tai reconstruction is from Li (1977).

2.3 below). Li's identification of cognacy between Chinese and Tai was based on his profound knowledge of the phonological systems of Chinese and Tai. He was well aware of the differences between the tonal, isolating Chinese/Tai languages and the inflectional, non-tonal Indo-European languages. His working criteria are best exemplified in his *Studies on Archaic Chinese Phonology* (1971) and *A Handbook of Comparative Tai* (1977). His methods have served as a model for Chinese and Tai linguistics, with many followers, Chinese and western.

Li's position remains influential among Chinese linguistic circles. His paper has raised many important questions, some of which still await to be answered, a point we shall return to shortly in §2.3 and §2.4.

2.2.2.3. *Haudricourt and Manomaivibool*

Haudricourt's 1974 work appeared as Chapter 29 in the five-part *Introduction to Sino-Tibetan* (1966-1974), edited by Robert Shafer who unequivocally grouped Tai under Sino-Tibetan. With data from 14 Tai dialects, including Siamese, Lao, Shan, Black Tai, White Tai, Tho, Nung, Po-ai, and Wuming, along with data from Sui, Mak, Be and Li, this work represented one of the most serious attempts at the reconstruction of Proto Daïque (Daic). Sound correspondences have been carefully worked out for tones, initials, and finals, using the standard method of comparative linguistics. Frequent reference was made to Chinese, with several dozen good Sino-Tai cognates proposed, indicating the author's agreement with the editor's view on the genetic affiliation of Tai with Sino-Tibetan. Unfortunately, the work is riddled with too many typographical errors, due to the negligence of the type setter/copy editor.

Manomaivibool (1975) is yet another full-scale study on the Sino-Tai link along the lines of Wulff. This impressive work has postulated over six hundred correspondence sets between Chinese and Thai, some of which were also found in Wulff and Haudricourt. But unlike Wulff and Haudricourt, Manomaivibool examined Thai correspondences by comparing them with Karlgren's and Li's reconstructions of Old Chinese and Middle Chinese. The results were revealing: Thai reflexes are found to map in part with Old Chinese (the first half of the first millennium BC) pronunciation and in part with Middle Chinese (6th–11th AD, typically reflected in *Qieyun*) pronunciation. The findings have important ramifications for the reconstruction of Old Chinese, Middle Chinese, and Proto-Tai.

2.2.2.4. *Xing Gongwan: Handbook of Comparative Sino-Tai*

Xing's *Handbook of Comparative Sino-Tai* (1999) is an impressive work on the topic. With over 900 proposed cognates between Chinese and Tai, the book has significantly expanded the Sino-Tai lexicon along the lines of Li (1976). The overwhelming majority of the cognates are found in Li's HCT, indicating that over 70% of Proto-Tai lexicon has Chinese links. A significant number of the shared cognates are proposed for the first time, such as Chinese 霶 (Old Chinese *phjэn) 'rain', Proto-Tai *fon A1; Chinese 眮 (OC *phat) 'blind', PT *ʔbot D1; Chinese 拇 (OC *mэg) 'hand', PT *mue; Chinese 齕 (OC *gэt) 'to bite, gnaw', PT *kat D1. Also worth noting is the fact that Tai often retains earlier meaning of words or forms which are found in Old Chinese but which are now out of use in modern Chinese, eg. Chinese 元 (OC *ŋwjan) 'day', PT *van A2; Chinese 食厄 (OC *ŋɛk) 'hungry', PT *ʔjaak D1; Chinese 盰 (OC *kan) 'night, evening', PT *ɣïɐn A2. For Xing, the existence of words of this kind is testimony to a Sino-Tai genetic relationship.

One is struck by the regular patterns of phonological correspondences Xing has set up for Chinese and Tai. Apart from the comparative method — albeit sometimes a bit loosely applied, Xing also adopts a semantic approach. For him, a deep semantic match can better reveal a deep historical connection. He has summarized three kinds of parallel correspondences between Chinese and Tai: (a) allophones, (b) synonyms, and (c) word families (Xing 1999: 499; see §2.4.3 for more discussion). For instance, Chinese 浸 (OC *tsjэm) 'soak', Dai Ya *tɕum^{B1}* (PT *čum^{B1}*), Chinese 湛 'flood' (OC *drэm), Dai Ya *thum^{A2}*

(PT), Chinese 爛 'boil, cook in water' (OC *dəm), Dai Ya tum^{C1} (PT *tum^{C1}), Chinese 潛 'sink, submerge' (OC *dzjiəm), Dehong tsum^{A1} (PT čem^{A1}) (pp.184-185). Examples of this kind show that Chinese and Tai share extensively in morphological processes, a feature that is less likely to be borrowed.

While Xing's method of semantic differentiation has many merits in it, he probably has stretched it a bit too far in places. For this reason, he has been criticized by a number of scholars (Ting 2000, Nie 2002, Mei 2003). Despite this, this work will remain an important source of reference for scholars in the field.

2.2.2.5. Recent works

Very recently, Gong (2002) built on Manomaivibool's work by reexamining different layers of Sino-Thai cognates — those that correspond to Old Chinese and those that correspond to Middle Chinese. His findings have extended Manomaivibool's thesis. Ting (2002) reevaluated Li's 1976 position, citing supporting evidence from recent progress in Chinese historical linguistics, as did Pan (2002), who considered Sino-Tai link in a wider context. Lan (2003), too, was concerned with different strata of Sino-Tai words. Unlike Gong and Manomaivibool, Lan's focus is on the sound correspondences between Chinese and the Zhuang dialects in South China's Guangxi province, which the largest group of Tai speakers in China inhabit. By comparing Tai forms with Old Chinese and Middle Chinese reconstructions by earlier scholars, he was able to draw a rough picture of the linguistic interaction between Chinese and the Zhuang at different stages in history. Zeng (2004) was tackling a similar issue of the genetic relationship between Chinese and Sui — a member of the Kam-Sui group with which Tai is closely related. Like Manomaivibool, Gong and Lan, she was looking at two types of related words between Chinese and Sui, words that reveal a deeper historical connection and words that point to late contact. The results led her to the belief that Chinese and Sui are genetically related.

At the time of writing, the present writer (forthcoming) has identified some 400 extra putative Sino-Tai cognate words that are not included in Manomaivibool's work. He (Luo 1997b, 1998) has also discovered patterns of regular sound correspondences between Chinese and Tai in the phonetic series of sibilants and liquids as well as sibilants and velars, which lend further support to the xiesheng contact in Old Chinese as also revealed in some of the characters. The Tai correspondences lend strong support to the idea of existence of a sibilant complex in the proto language. In several papers (Luo 2003, 2004, 2005, 2006), he also looked at Sino-Tai sharing in morphological processes. All this was overlooked in the past. Some of his main findings will be discussed below in §2.3 and §2.4.

2.2.3. Benedict's Austro-Tai theory and his method of tele-reconstruction

Benedict's Austro-Thai Studies (1975) was a reaffirmation and expansion of his 1942 paper, which was probably inspired by Schlegel who proposed to separate Tai from Sino-Tibetan. In both works, Benedict vehemently argued for a realignment of Tai-Kadai, first placing it with Indonesian (1942), and later linking it to a larger phylum — Austro-Tai. In his latest theory (1990), Japanese was added to the super stock, forming an even larger alliance.

The Austro-Tai hypothesis has fundamentally challenged the traditional view of the Sino-Tai genetic link. For this reason, it has sparked controversies, and generated heated discussion (see Volume 6 [1976] of Computational Analysis of Asian and African Languages). Authorities have different views on the validity of Benedict's claims. For example, Egerod (1976) supported and accepted Benedict's reconstructions while Haudricourt (1976) was somewhat lukewarm in his reaction. On the other hand, Benedict's approach was strongly criticized by Gedney (1976), who cited evidence from Tai to show that on many occasions Benedict's reconstructions were inadequate. Even Benedict's ardent supporter, Matisoff, had some reservations about such 'megalo-comparison' (Matisoff 1990: 115) and Benedict himself cheerfully admitted himself to be a 'lumper' (Benedict 1990: 169).

One of Benedict's arguments was that the typological similarities between Chinese and Tai are the result of contact rather than genetic inheritance. Yet it must be pointed out that Benedict's thesis was constructed on the basis of tele-reconstruction, which was 'characterized by loose resemblances, semantic leaps and the making up of maximal earlier forms to account for cognate relationship without working out sound correspondences through step-by-step comparison' (Diller 1998: 22). Controversial as it was, Benedict's work opened up new horizons in the field. Its significance was still being evaluated and appreciated (Thurgood 1985, 1990, Reid 1988).

2.2.4. Sino-Tibetan-Austronesian and Kadai-Austronesian

2.2.4.1. *Sagart's Sino-Austronesian hypothesis*

As mentioned in §2.1, Laurent Sagart was a strong proponent of the Sino-Austronesian hypothesis. In a paper published in 1993, he proposed several dozen putative cognates between Chinese and Austronesian, claiming that the two languages are genetically related. Since Tai was viewed as a member of Sino-Tibetan, naturally it belonged to this Sino-Austronesian stock.

In a recent paper Sagart (2005b) has changed his earlier position to connect Tai with Austronesian rather than with Sino-Tibetan, although he still maintains that Sino-Tibetan and Austronesian are genetically related. In his current view, Tai-Kadai is a subgroup of Austronesian. What makes him change his mind is that 'one set of words suffices to show that at least some vocabulary is genuinely shared by Tai-Kadai and AN, not as a result of chance' (2005b: 177). Sagart's set of Kadai-Austronesian cognates is made up of three lexical items (ibid: 178):

	PAN	PMP	Tai	Lakkia
die	maCay	matay	ta:i[1]	plei[1]
eye	maCa	mata	ta[1]	pla[1]
bird	–	manuk	nok[8]	mlok[7]

Furthermore, Sagart provides a piece of supporting evidence that there is a reversal in the singular and plural number with the second person pronouns between Proto-Austronesian and Proto-Tai-Kadai:

	PAN	PKT
2sg	-Su	*məɯ
2pl	-mu	*sou

On the basis of evidence of this kind, Sagart concludes that 'Tai-Kadai has its origin in an early AN language called here 'AAK'. AAK was a daughter language of PAN, and a close relative of PMP.' (ibid: 180)

For his Sino-Tibetan-Austronesian phylum, Sagart offers 61 putative cognate sets between Proto-Austronesian, Old Chinese and Tibeto-Burman. Included in the sets are items such as 'bone', 'elbow', 'breast', 'foot', 'head', 'cloud, cloudy', 'sunlight', 'water', 'cave', 'dig', 'hold in the mouth', 'lick', among others (2005a: 164). In addition, 14 cultural lexical items are also compared (ibid: 165), such as 'paddy', 'chicken', and 'crossbow'.

2.2.4.2. *Kadai-Austronesian*

In an impressive paper, Ostapirat (2005) has made what would appear to a convincing case for a genetic link between Kra-Dai (his term for Tai-Kadai) and Austronesian by gathering new data from the Tai-Kadai languages in China and Vietnam and comparing with Austronesian. 50 carefully selected putative cognate words are cited for Tai-Kadai, of which 20 are on Yahontov's 35 basic word list, and 42 on Swadesh's 100 basic word list. Of these 50 Tai-Kadai core lexical items, 26 are found to have Austronesian connection. Among the 26 possible cognate items, 9 are not on the Swadesh's list.

Ostapirat's proposed Tai-Kadai-Austronesian etyma are listed below.

Gloss	PAN	PKd
eye	maCa	m-ţa A
fart	qe(n)tut	C-tot D
hand	(qa)lima	mja A
leg	paqa	C-ka A
shoulder	qabaRa	*m-ba B
bear (n.)	Cumay	C-me A
louse (head)	kuCu	C-ţu A
sesame	leŋa	l-ŋa A
moon	bulaN	m-djan A
black	tidem	hl/dəm A
eat	kaen	kan A
grandmother	aya	ja C
I	aku	ku A
excrement	Caqi	kai C
grease	SimaR	mal
head	qulu	krai B
nose	ijuŋ	teŋ
tooth	nipen	l-pən
bird	majuk	ŋok D
leaf	(ʔabag)	Hlai beɯ
fire	Sapuy	pui A
water	daNum	ʔuŋ C
live, raw	qulip	(k-)ḍep D
child	aNak	lak D
this	i-ni	ʔ-ni C/B
you	kamu	mə A/B

Having established the lexical correspondence, Ostapirat goes on to discuss Kadai tones in Austronesian roots. Following the theories of tonogenesis by Haudricourt and others, he conjectures that Kadai tones might have some correlations with Austronesian syllable types.

A comparison between Sagart's list and Ostapirat's shows that the correspondences belong to different sets of vocabulary items.[7] A question may now be asked: What is the nature of these lexical items? What can be said about the status of such lexical items? To what extent do they reflect the real picture of genetic relationship? How should we interpret them? In the sections below we shall look at more evidence from the Tai side.

---

7   Sagart (1993) also postulates over 200 possible cognate words between Chinese and Austronesian, including body part terms like 'palm of the hand, sole of the foot' PAn *Da(m)pa, Chinese 跗 [GSR 102] OC *phag, terms for nature and environments; 'open expanse of land or water' PAn *bawaŋ, Chinese 潢 [GSR 707e] *gwaŋ 'lake, pool'; abstract concepts like 'to oppose' PAn *baŋkal, Chinese 奸 [GSR 139cd] *kan or *k-r-an 'treacherous; disobey; violate', among others. Some of Ostapirat's items are also in Sagart's list, eg. 'black', 'sesame', 'to eat'.

2.3. THE ROLE OF TAI IN OLD CHINESE RECONSTRUCTION

Whatever the ultimate relationship between Tai and Chinese may eventually turn out to be, researchers all agree that Tai plays an important role in Old Chinese reconstruction. Scholars in the field are constantly citing Tai materials as supporting evidence (Nishida 1960, Haudricourt 1956, 1974, Li 1970, Benedict 1976, Bodman 1980, Baxter 1992). Indeed, the significance of Tai in OC reconstruction cannot be overestimated, as shall be seen below.

2.3.1. Initial clusters in OC as retained in Tai

It is generally believed that a number of initial clusters should be reconstructed for Old Chinese (Karlgren, Li, Gong, Baxter). The argument behind this is that in Chinese orthography, there are a significant number of *xiesheng* characters where alternations of stop initials (p, b, t, d, k, g) and liquid l- are most common. However, almost no modern Chinese dialect has provided any diachronic link. Much to the comparativists' delight, Tai supplies valuable information.

One of most frequently-cited examples is the word for 'indigo' in Tai. The Chinese cognate of is word, now pronounced with a liquid initial /l/ as 藍 *laan*[A] in modern Chinese, is orthographically associated with a phonetic series 監, with a velar /k/. One would expect to find a velar cluster of some sort (*kl/r- or *gl/r-) in the modern dialects. Yet no modern Chinese dialects are found to retain such an initial. However, many Tai dialects have *graam*[A2] for this item for which Li has proposed a proto cluster *gr- for Tai, thus attesting the existence of the velar cluster in the proto language.

Another example is the reconstruction of labial clusters *pl-, *bl- for Old Chinese. Chinese orthography also suggests that words like 變 'change' (OC, MC MSC biàn) must have derived from an initial cluster involving a labial stop /p/ and a liquid /l/, as the character has the phonetic element 䜌 'luan', pointing to a liquid initial. Kalrgren (1957: 67) has proposed *plian (GSR 178o) for 變. Again no modern Chinese dialects are found to preserve initial *pl-. Much to the comparativist's delight, many Tai dialects have reflexes containing initial /pl-/, for which Li has reconstructed a labial cluster *pl- for Proto-Tai. The Tai form is undoubtedly related to Chinese.

Norman and Mei (1971) observe that in the Chinese Min dialect, there exist a group of words for which a proto *s- cluster may be proposed. Significantly, Tai again supplies supporting evidence, which points to a deep connection between Chinese and Tai, for which Luo (1997a, b) has proposed a sibilant complex for Sino-Tai (see §2.4.1).

2.3.2. Retention of bilabial initials which have developed into labial-dentals in Modern Chinese

In their admirable studies of Old Chinese phonology, the great Qing scholars have made some important discoveries about the phonological system of Old Chinese. One such discovery was that labial-dental initials were lacking in Old Chinese. Reflexes in some modern Chinese dialects such as Cantonese provide supporting evidence. Significantly, a set of cognate words in Tai with labial initials are found to correspond to Modern Chinese labial-dental initials, supplying further evidence for hypothesis of the absence of labial-dental initials in OC.

Gloss	Chrt	Pinyin	GSR	OC	MC	Thai	DH	LM	Yay	FS	HCT
father	父	fù	102a	pjagh	puǒ'	phɔɔB2	po B2	poo B2	po B2	po B2	*bo B2
cooking pot	釜	fǔ	102f	bjag'	buǒ'	mɔɔ C1	mo C1	moo C1	mo C1	mo C1	*hmo C1

bee, beeswax	蜂	fēng	1197s	phjung	phuawŋ	phïŋC1	phɯɯŋ C1	Nung phuɯŋ C1	–	–	(*phǐŋ C1)
skin	膚	fū	69g	pjag	puɔ̌	plïakD1L	pək D1	puɯuk D1L	pyaak D1L	pyaak D1L	*plaak D1L
lungs	肺	fèi	501g	phjadh	puajh	pɔɔt D1L	pɔt D1L	pʏt D1	put D1S	puut D1S	*pǐɔt D1L
fat	肥	féi	582a	bjəd	puaj	phii A2	pi A2	pi A2	pi A2	pi A2	*bi A2
divide	分	fēn	471a	pjiən	pun	pan A1	pan A1	pan A1	pan A1	pan A1	*pan A1

The development of labial sounds into labial-dentals was a feature of late Middle Chinese. The retention of labial initials in Tai indicates a deep historical connection between the two languages.

2.3.3. The reconstruction of final -g for OC: Some supporting evidence

A key feature in Li's Old Chinese reconstruction is that of the final *-g for a group of rhymes that are represented with open-syllables in Middle Chinese. In Li's system, we find codas like *-ag, *-ig, *-əg, and *-ug, with no open syllables in Old Chinese except the *-ar (see below). This has been criticized by a number of scholars (Wang 1985) for being typologically implausible and unusual. However, Li must have some reasons to believe that codas of this kind must have existed in early history. The following examples were cited by him (1976: 41):

Gloss	Chrt	Pinyin	GSR	OC	MC	Thai	DH	LM	Yay	FS	HCT
fog, mist	雾	wù	1109t	mjəgwh	muǎh	mɔk D1	mɔk D1	mookD1	mookD1	mookD1	*hmok D1
hat, cap	帽	mào	1062	məgwh	mawh	muak D1L	WT mok D1	muuk D1L	–	–	*muak D1L
skin, bark	膚	fū	69g	pliag	puɔ̌	plïak D1L	pək D1	puɯuk D1L	pyaak D1L	pjaakD1L	*plïak D1L
forehead	顱	lú	69p	blag	lɔ	phaak D1L	phaak D1L	phaak D1L	pyaak D1L	pjaakD1	phlaak D1L

The first and the second examples are in the traditional Chinese 候部 and 幽部 respectively, and the last two examples in the 魚部. In our data, many more examples of this type are found in Tai, lending support to Li's reconstructions.

Gloss	Chrt	Pinyin	GSR	OC	MC	Thai	DH	LM	Yay	FS	HCT
place, region	處	chù	85a	thjag	tɕʰiəʰ	thïak D2L	–	–	tɯak D2L	tɯak D2L	*dǐek D2L
child	子	zǐ	964a	tsjəg	tsɨ/tsi'	tuuk D2L	luk D2	lok D2	luuk D2	lɯk D2S	*lǐuk D̂2L
base, foundation	基	jī	952g	kəg	kɨ/ki	kok D1S	kok D1S	kuk D1	kok D1S	kɔk D1S	*kok D1S
carry on shoulder	負	fù	1000a	bjag	buw'	bɛɛk D1L	mɛk D1	meek D1L	–	–	*ʔbɛɛk D1L

small	小	xiǎo	1149a	siagw	siaw'	lek D2S	lik D2S	–	–	lɛɛk	*dlek D2S
swaddling clothes	褓	bǎo	1057g	pəgwx	paw'	–	Mok D1L	Mok D1S	–	buk D1S	*ʔbuok D1L[8]
mortar	臼	jiù	1067a	gwjiəg wh	guw'	Khrok D2S	xok D2s	lok D2S	cok D2S	tsok D2K	*grok D2S

These examples show that Li's proposed reconstructions are not groundless speculations.

2.3.4. Unique correspondences: The case of 'five', 'goose', 'gill', 'six'

In his 1976 paper, Li raised a question which has not been seriously addressed until quite recently (Ting 2002). Li's question has to do with a unique sound correspondence between Chinese and Tai in words like 'five', 'six', 'goose', and 'fish gill'. These lexical items take the velar nasal *ŋ- in OC, where Tai correspondences show a laryngeal fricative *h: 'goose' OC *ŋaan, PT *haan B1, 'five' OC *ŋa C, PT *ha C1, and 'gill' Chinese *ŋək, PT *hŋïak.[9] To date no Chinese dialects have been found to display correspondences of this kind. Similarly, 'six' is reconstructed as *ljok in OC with a liquid initial. In Tai it shows a laryngeal fricative in Thai as *hok* D1, and a liquid *lɔk* in Po-ai, reconstructed as *xrok D1 in HCT. These types of sound correspondences are not found in loan words. They are cited by Li as solid evidence in support of Sino-Tai link.

2.3.5. Shared innovation: Finals *-l and *-r

Among the unsettling questions in Old Chinese reconstruction, the reconstruction of finals *-l and *-r is perhaps the most controversial. If these sounds once existed in history, one may expect to find some traces among the modern dialects. But so far, no reflexes among the numerous modern Chinese dialects are found to exhibit traces of these elements.

Two issues are involved here. The first has to do with the development of the traditional *ge* rhymes 歌部 which was reconstructed as *-ar by Li Fang-Kuei (1971). Karlgren also reconstructed part of the *ge* rhymes as *-ar in GSR. The second issue has to do with the reconstruction of final *-r for Old Chinese.

*2.3.5.1. The ge rhymes and *-l*

Li's reconstruction of *-ar for the *ge* rhymes is accepted by Gong (1993) and Pan (2007), who slightly revised it into *-al. Baxter (1993) proposed *-ei for this rhyme on the basis of reflexes from a number of modern dialects as well as Sino-Vietnamese and Sino-Korean forms. Baxter's reconstruction is questioned by Pan (2000, 2007), who believes that it fails to account for the final -i since there were already rhymes that had been reconstructed as such for Old Chinese. For Pan, Li's reconstruction has more explanatory power in that it can elegantly explain -i as lenition of *-l.

If Pan's hypothesis of final *-l lenition is correct, Tai supplies additional evidence. In Tai, a significant number of cognate words with final -i correspond to the traditional 歌 rhyme for Old Chinese. The following examples illustrate:

---

8   Not included in HCT.
9   The majority of Tai dialects take the laryngeal /h/ for this item, except Siamese and Po-ai, which side with Chinese in taking /ŋ-/.

Gloss	Chrt	Pinyin	GSR	OC	MC	Thai	DH	LM	Yay	FS	HCT
hang down, droop	垂	chuí	31a	tjuar	dʑwiɞ dʑwi	yɔɔi A1	–	–	ruay A1	looi A1	*ǰroi A1
beat, hammer	捶	chuí	31i	tjuar	tɕwiɞ, tɕwi	tɔi B1	tɔi B1	–	toy B1	toi B1	*toi B1
spittle, saliva	唾	tuò	31m	thuar	twaʰ	laai A2	laai A2	laai A2	nay A2	naai A2	*mlaai A2
bowl	甀	zhuì	31	thuar	drwiă/ drwi	thuəi C1	–	thuuy C1	tuay C2	tooi C2	*thuai C1
naked, bare	裸	luǒ	351h	luarʼ	lwaʼ	pluai A1	poi A1	Lao pluai A1	Saek puay A1	pjoi A1	*pluai A1[10]
snail, shellfish	蠃	luó	14b	luar	lwa	hɔi A1	hɔi A1	hoy A1	θay A1	θai A1	*srɔi A1[11]
long and narrow mountain	隋	duò	11d	duarx	dwaʼ, dwaʰ	dɔɔi A1	lɔi A1	nooy A2	doy A1	dəi A1	*ʔdl/rɔi A1

These are not confined to the traditional -ar 歌 rhyme. Luo (2006a, 2006b) offers over a dozen more Tai examples that are proposed to be related to several other rhymes in Old Chinese. The forms invariably take final -i in Tai, which cannot be treated as chance occurrence.

2.3.5.2. OC final *-r and Saek -l

From *xiesheng* contact and internal evidence, along with early Sanskrit and Sino-Japanese pronunciations, Pan (2007) postulates a final *-r for Old Chinese, which has developed into -n in the modern dialects.

It is well-known that Saek, a displaced Northern Tai language now spoken in Nakhon Phanom in Thailand, has preserved an archaic final -l. It is worth noting that this final -l is found to correspond to final -n in other Tai dialects. Final -l also occurs in Laha, a member of the Geyang group within Kadai. Characteristically, a significant number of words taking final -l in Saek are found to correspond to the traditional Chinese 元部 (-an) and 文部 (-ən) rhymes. Saek words corresponding to the traditional Chinese *-an rhymes include:

Saek	Thai	Fengshan	HCT	Gloss	Chrt	GSR	OC	MC
saal[1]	saan A1	saanA1	*san A1	fine grain	粲	154b	tsan	tsʰanʰ
khial[4]	ŋɔɔn A1	–	*hŋɔn A1	cock's comb	冠	160a	kwanh	kwanʰ
tlɛl[1]	kron A1	tsɛn A1	*kruɯn A1	snore	鼾	139	han	xan
yual[5]	yɯɯn B2	jian B2	*juɯn B2	pass, extend	延	203a	rjan	jian
nɔɔl[2]	nɔɔn A1	noon A1	*hnɔn A1	worm	蜹	208c	nwanʼ	nwanʼ
sɛl[3]	sen C1	θɛn C1	(*sen C1)	tread, CLF.	线	155r	sjanh	sianʰ
sɛl[6]	san B1	θɛn B1	*san B1	tremble	颤	148s	tjanh	tɕianʰ

---

10 Not included in HCT. Reconstructed by Luo (1997: 244).
11 Not found in HCT. Reconstructed by Luo (1997: 105).

The following are Saek correspondences in OC *-ən rhymes.

Saek	Thai	Fengshan	HCT	Gloss	Chrt	GSR	OC	MC
ɣal⁴	khanA1	hanA2	*ɣan A2	dike	垠	416h	ŋjən	ŋin
buɯl¹	ʔbin	ʔbin	*ʔbin A1	fly, v.	扮	471e	pjən	pʰun
vɯɯl⁴	fuɯɯn A2	fun A2	*vɯɯən A2	burn	焚	474a	bjən	bun
mul⁴	Lao munB2	mɯɯn B2	(*mɯɯən B2)	powder	粉	471d	pjən'	pun'
sɔɔl¹	sɔɔnA1	θoonA1	*sɔn A1	teach	訓	422d	hwjənh	xunʰ

Wider connections can be sought with Tibeto-Burman (Matisoff 2003: 383ff) for final *-r for Proto Sino-Tibetan.

2.4. PROGRESS AND NEW FINDINGS

2.4.1. The sibilant complex

Sibilant clusters have been reconstructed for Old Chinese and Sino-Tibetan by scholars working in the field. In Li's reconstruction of Proto-Tai, consonant clusters have been reconstructed for labials (*pl/r, *phl/r, *vl/r, etc.), dentals (*tl/r, *dl/r, *thl/r, etc.) and velars (*kl/r, *khl/r, *xr, etc.), but no sibilants clusters are proposed by Li.

There is strong evidence that suggests sibilant clusters may have existed in Proto-Tai. A number of consonant clusters have been proposed by Luo (1998) as additions to Li's PT phonemic inventory (*sl-, *sr-, *zl-, etc.). More importantly, regular correspondences can be set up between Chinese and Tai for sibilants and liquids, with several dozen correspondence sets. The sibilant complex points to a deep historical connection between the two languages. Parallel development has been reported from the northern Min dialect of Chinese which displays traces of sibilant clusters (Mei and Norman 1971).

Apart from sibilant + liquid clusters, a parallel sibilant + velar cluster (*sk-, *zg-, etc.) is also found for Chinese and Tai. Luo (1997b) has presented evidence from the Tai side supporting his argument. Some of his Chinese comparisons were used by Li and Benedict in their reconstruction of Old Chinese and Sino-Tibetan, such as 'smell', 'needle', and 'feces'.

2.4.2. The issue of basic vocabulary

One of Benedict's main arguments to keep Tai apart from Sino-Tibetan is that in the area of core vocabulary, the two languages have little in common. The shared lexical items, he argues, are mainly trade terms, numerals and the like, which seem more likely to be loan words. Our data shows that this is not the case. A look at the Proto-Tai lexicon reveals that Tai shares with Chinese quite a large number of basic lexical items, including a sizeable number of body-part terms. Luo (2000) has postulated nearly 70 putative cognates between Chinese and Tai in this lexical field by synthesizing previous works by Wulff, Li and Xing, significantly expanding their inventory. For example:

Gloss	Chrt	PY	GSR	OC	MC	Siamese	Yay	HCT
head	首	shǒu	1102a	skhjəgwx	çuw'	khlaw C1	caw C1	*klau C1
ear	耳	ěr	981a	njɨg'	ɲɨ/ɲi	hu A1	rɯa A2	*xrɯa
neck, throat	喉	hóu	113f	ɣug	ɣəw	khɔɔ A2	ho A2	*ɣɔ A2
bone	骼	gé	766c'	krak	kaɨjk, kɛːjk	duuk D1	dok D1	*ʔdl/ruok D1
flesh	肉	ròu	1033a	njakwh	ɲuwk	nɨa C2	no B2	*nɨa C/B2

One may feel rather reluctant to say that words of this kind are entirely loans, as they are rather stable and are generally resistant to borrowing. If such words were excluded from the Proto-Tai lexicon, more than one third of the Proto-Tai etyma would have to go.

In addition to body-part terms, quite a significant number of basic words are found in early Chinese sources, with good correspondences in Tai. The following examples illustrate:

Gloss	Chrt	PY	GSR	OC	MC	Siamese	Yay	PT
bird	雒	luò	766g	lak	lak	nok D2	nok D2	*nlok D2
black	黮	dàn	658n	tam^h	təm^h / tam^h	dam A1	dam A1	*ʔdam A1
white	皓	hào	1139h	gəkwh	ɣaw'	khaaw A1	haaw A1	*xaau A1
red	赬	chēng	834m	thrjing	tr^{h}iajŋ	ʔdɛɛŋ A1	ʔdiŋ A1	*ʔdiɛŋ A1
dark purple	紺	gàn	606k	kam	kəm' / kam'	klam B1	cam B1	*klam B1
axe	斤	jīn	443a	kjən	kɨn	khwaan A1	vaan A1	*khwaan A1

An interesting thing about these words is that none of them are used in modern standard Chinese in their sense except in certain compounds like *hào yuè* 'the bright moon', found primarily in literary language, indicating that they are residues of early usage. Although the same concepts are now represented in different forms in modern Chinese (particularly the colour terms), the connections between the forms are recognizable. Some of these are obviously the original forms of the concepts designated, such as 'axe', the graphic for which, 斤 *jīn*, apparently a drawing of an axe, was found in oracle bone inscriptions, indicating its antiquity. This graphic serves as the semantic part of current form, 斧 *fǔ*, a form of much later appearance with a different phonetic shape.

Luo (2002, 2004, 2005, 2007, in preparation) has presented an array of basic vocabulary items from everyday words, which has expanded previous works.

2.4.3. Morphological and orthographical evidence

Although consonant and vowel variations as a mechanism of morphological processes are a well-known phenomenon in Chinese and Sino-Tibetan (Karlgren 1933 Matisoff 1978, 1985), comparative work is scarce between Chinese and Tai.[12] A pioneering work was undertaken by Li in 1978 in which he dealt with a parallel morphological processes between Tai and Chinese in the word group 'bent/crooked' and 'dig', where he made the following remarks:

> The genetic relation of Tai and Chinese needs serious study. The general impression that the phonological structure of these two languages is similar may be considered as an areal phenomenon, but is not necessarily so. The resemblance in vocabulary may be due to loans from one language to the other, but it is hard to prove. *The grammatical process of alternating initials may turn out to be an important factor to decide the relationship of Tai and Chinese.* (Emphasis added)
>
> Li Fang-Kuei (1978: 406)

---

12 As an exception, Dong et al. (1984) uses the notion of word families to argue for a genetic relationship between Chinese and Kam-Tai.

Drawing attention to the complexities of the issue of the Sino-Tai link, Li was calling for an in-depth investigation into the phonological and lexical structures of the two languages, proposing morphological processes as a criterion for determining the nature of Sino-Tai historical relationship. By discussing two cognate sets across Tai dialects and comparing them with Chinese, Li has presented evidence for a deep historical connection between these two languages.

In several recent papers (Luo 2002, 2003, 2004, 2005), the present writer has presented further evidence of sharing of morphological processes between Chinese and Tai. Some examples are given below for illustration.

2.4.3.1. 'Soak' ~ 'ooze' ~ 'wet' ~ 'sink' ~ 'submerge'

This group of words are typically represented by sibilant/dental + V + m.

Gloss	Chrt	PY	GSR	OC	MC	Thai	DH	LM	Yay	FS	HCT
to soak	浸	jìn	661m	tsjəmh	tsim^h	čum C1/B1	tsum B1	sam C1	chum C1	sum B1	*čum B1
moisten, wet	沾	zhān	618c	tjam	triam	chum B2	yam A2	–	chom A1/B1	sum C2	*jum C2
dip into	沁	qìn	–	tshjəm^h	ts^{h}im^h	čim C1/B1	tsam C1	cam C1	–	sam C1	*čiam C1
sink	沉	chén	656b-d	djəm	drim	čom A1	tsəm A1	cam A1	cham B1	sam A1	*čam A1
submerge	潛	qián	660n	dzjəm	dziam	dam A1	lam A1	nam A1	dam A1	ʔdam A1	*ʔdam A1

As the above examples show, alternations of historically voiceless vs. voiced initials and tones occur between transitive and intransitive verbs ('soak' vs. 'moisten'; 'dip into' vs. 'sink', 'submerge') for both Chinese and Tai, suggesting the existence of an active morphological process in the proto language.

2.4.3.2. 'Chop', 'cut down', "cut open', 'separate, divide', 'slash'

This word family prototypically takes a dental + V + t/n for both Chinese and Tai.

Gloss	Chrt	Pinyin	GSR	OC	MC	Thai	DH	LM	Yay	FS	HCT
cut fine	剬	tuán	231c	duan	duan	tɔɔn A1	tɔn A1	toon A1	toon A1	toon A1	*tɔn A1
length section	段	duàn	172a	duanh	duan^h	thɔɔn B2	tɔn B2	toon B2	ton B2	ton B2	*dɔn B2
cut off	斷	duàn	170a	duanh	duan	tɔɔn C1	tɔn A2	tan C1	ton C1	ton C1	*ton C1
prune	剟	duān	168e	tuan	tuan	–	taan A1	WT taan A1	taan A1	taan A1	*taan A1
short	短	duǎn	169a	tuanx	tuan'	–	–	tin C1	tin C1	tin C1	*tin C1
cut off	剟	duò	295g	truat	twat	tat D1S	tat D1S	tat D1S	tat D1S	tat D1S	*tat D1

Similarly, we see alternations of initials and tones between verbs and nouns, and between action verbs (cut fine, section, cut off) and adjectival verbs (pruned, short). The variations in finals in Tai (ɔ ~ o ~ a ~i) perhaps point to the effects of lexical diffusion.

2.4.3.3. 'Wide' ~ 'Vast' ~ 'Open'

This group of words takes a (labio-)velar initial plus final -aŋ for both Chinese and Tai.

Gloss	Chrt	PY	GSR	OC	MC	Thai	DH	LM	Yay	FS	HCT
wide	廣	guǎng	707h	kwangx	kwaŋ	kwaaŋ C1	kwaaŋ C1	kwaaŋ C1	kuaaŋ B1	kuaaŋ B1	*kwaaŋ C1
lie athwart	橫	héng	707m	gwang	ɣwaŋ	khwaaŋ A1	xwaaŋ A1	vaaŋ B2	vaaŋ A1	vaaŋ A1	*khwaaŋ A1
expanse of water	潢	huáng	707e	gwang	ɣwaŋ	waŋ A2	waŋ A2	waŋ A2	vaŋ A2	vaŋ A2	*waŋ A2
far apart	曠	kuàng	707o	khwangʰ	khwaŋʰ	haaŋ B1	haaŋ B1	laaŋ B1	luaŋ B1	luaŋ B1¹³	(*xraaŋ B1)
wide	廣	guǎng	707h	kwangx	kwaŋ	kwaaŋ C1	kwaaŋ C1	kwaaŋ C1	kuaaŋ B1	kuaaŋ B1	*kwaaŋ C1
lie athwart	橫	héng	707m	gwang	ɣwaŋ	khwaaŋ A1	xwaaŋ A1	vaaŋ B2	vaaŋ A1	vaaŋ A1	*khwaaŋ A1

The above examples again show regular correspondences in initials and tones between Chinese and Tai. More significantly still, orthography also plays an important role for the Chinese forms which are in the same *xiesheng* series sharing the phonetic element, 黃, which typically takes a labio-velar initial and a final -(a)aŋ. Examples of this kind supply solid evidence for shared morphological derivations between Chinese and Tai. Indeed such structural sharing cannot be easily explained as the results of contact or chance occurrence. If Li Fang-Kuei is right about the postulating morphological processes as an important criterion for genetic relationship, then the above examples supply strong evidence towards understanding the nature of the historical relationship between Chinese and Tai.

2.5. SUMMARY

Tai represents one aspect of the vast historical drama in ST. It is significant to note that the number of shared items between Chinese and Tai is far greater than between Tai and other languages in the surrounding regions such as Miao-Yao and Tibeto-Burman, indicating a close link between the two languages.

Tai and Chinese have been intermingling for centuries. Whatever the ultimate relationship between Chinese and Tai may turn out to be, Tai reflexes provide an invaluable source of information for the reconstruction of Old Chinese. They complement the vast sources of Chinese dialect data now available. They throw new light on our understanding of the linguistic situation in southern China and the surrounding areas.

Throughout this chapter, no attempts have been made to distinguish between loans from cognate words. Surely, no language is immune to loans. While some of the above-discussed comparanda will eventually prove to be loans, it would be unwise to attribute all of them to loan contact. It is sober to realize that it is often exceedingly difficult to distinguish early loans from inherited items. As Li has pointed out: 'We have as yet... no criteria to judge what are loans and what are not.' (1976: 48) A mechanism to separate loans from inherited words is yet to be worked out. More empirical work needs to be carried out before this issue can be resolved.

The following findings can be summarized for this chapter:

(1) There is a significantly large number of shared vocabulary items between Chinese and Tai. Contrary to the claims by some earlier scholars, Chinese and Tai share extensively in basic vocabulary. Many of the shared vocabulary items are included in the Proto-Tai lexicon, which cannot be regarded entirely as loans;

---

13   The Yay form means 'village (larger than *baan⁶*)' (Gedney 1991: 198); the Fengshan form means 'open space in a village; courtyard'.

(2) Derivational morphology is a common feature between Chinese and Tai. It lends strong support to the assumption of a deep historical connection between Chinese and Tai;
(3) The linguistic evidence presented above seems to suggest that the Sino-Tai relationship is a lot deeper than previously thought;
(4) A number of the lexical items in Tai appear to have look-alikes in Austronesian, the nature of which remains to be further examined;
(5) Despite the progress made, the nature of the historical relationship between Chinese and Kam-Tai still remains open.

REFERENCES

Aikhenvald, Alexandra Y. and Dixon, R. M. W. (eds) (2001) *Areal Diffusion and Genetic Inheritance*, Oxford University Press.
Barlow, Jeoffrey G. (2000a) *The Zhuang: Ethnogenesis*. Available on line at: http://mcel.pacificu.edu/as/resources/zhuang/contents.html (accessed 4 December 2006).
Barlow, Jeoffrey G. (2000b, updated 2005) The Zhuang: A Longitudinal Study of Their History and Their Culture, available at:
  http://mcel.pacificu.edu/as/resources/zhuang/index.html (accessed 4 December 2006).
Baxter, William (1992) *Handbook of Old Chinese Phonology*, Berlin/New York: Mouton.
Benedict, Paul K. (1942) 'Thai, Kadai, and Indonesian: A new alignment in Southeast Asia' *American Anthropologists* 44: 576-601.
— (1972) *Sino-Tibetan: A conspectus*, Cambridge: Cambridge University Press.
— (1975) *Austro-Thai Language and Culture*, New Haven: HRAF Press.
— (1976) 'Sino-Tibetan: Another Look', *Journal of the American Oriental Society* 96.2: 167-197.
— (1990) *Japanese/Austro-Thai*, Ann-Arbor: Karoma.
Bodman, Nicholas (1980) 'Proto-Chinese and Sino-Tibetan: Data towards establishing the nature of the relationship', in Coetsem, Frans Van and Waugh, Linda R. (eds.) *Contributions to Historical Linguistics: Issues and Materials*, Leiden: E.J.Brill, 35-199.
Conrady, August (1896) Eine indochinesische causativ-denominativ-Bildung und ihr Zusammenhang mit den Tonaccenten, Leipzig: Otto Harrassovitz.
Dai, Qingxia, and Fu Ailan (1995) 关于汉藏语系语言的分类问题 [On the classification of Sino-Tibetan languages]. Seminar talk given at the meeting of the Chinese Society for Minority Languages on 'The Theories and Methodologies on Sino-Tibetan Studies'. Also available on line at: http://www.wai-yu.com/read.php?tid=3474 (Accessed 10 March, 2007). (In Chinese).
De Lacouperie, Terrien (1883) *Chinese and Siamese*. Academy, August.
— (1887) 'The Languages of China before the Chinese', *Transaction of the Philological Society.* (Reprinted 1969).
Denglinger, Paul B. (1989) 'The Chinese-Tai linguistic relationship: a formal proof', *Monumenta Serica* 38: 167-171.
Diller, A.V.N. (1998) 'The Tai language family and the comparative method', *Proceedings of the International Conference on Tai Studies*, 1-32, Bangkok: Mahidol University.
Diller, A.V.N. (2003) 'Austroasiatic strata in Thai', in Henning Anderson (ed.) *Language Contacts in Prehistory: Studies in Stratigraphy*, Amsterdam: John Benjamins,159-176.
Dong, Weiguang, Cao Guangqu and Yan Xuequn (1984) 'Hanyu he dong tai yu de qinshu guanxi [The genetic relationship between Chinese and Kam-Tai]', *CAAAL* 22: 105-121.
Egerod, Soren (1976) 'Benedict's Austro-Thai hypothesis and the traditional views on Sino-Tai relationship', *CAAAL* 6: 51-63.
Gedney, William J. (1965) 'Review of J. Marvin Brown: *From ancient Thai to Modern Dialects'*, *Social Science Review* (Bangkok) 32: 107-112.

— (1976) 'On the Thai evidence for Austro-Thai', *CAAAL* 6: 65-86.

— (1991) *William J. Gedney's The Yay Language: Glossary, Texts and Translations*, edited by Thomas John Hudak (Michigan Papers on South and Southeast Asian Studies 38), Center for South and Southeast Asian Studies, University of Michigan.

— (1993) *William J. Gedney's The Saek Language: Glossary, Texts and Translations*, edited by Thomas John Hudak (Michigan Papers on South and Southeast Asian Studies 41), Center for South and Southeast Asian Studies, University of Michigan.

Gong Hwang-cherng (1993) 'Cong hanzang yu de bijiao kan hanyu shanggu liuyin yunwei de nice [The reconstruction of final liquid endings in Old Chinese as viewed from Sino-Tibetan comparisons]', in *Xizang yanjiu lunwen ji 4 [Collected Papers on Tibetan Studies] Vol. 4*, Taipei: Tibetan Studies Commission; also in *Hanzang yu yanjiu lunwen ji [Collected Papers on Sino-Tibetan Studies]* (Language and Linguistics Monograph Series C2-2), Taipei: Institute of Linguistics (Preparatory Office), Academia Sinica, 2002, 49-65.

Gong, Qunhu (2002) *Hanyu Taiyu Guanxici De Shijian Cengci [A Study of Sino-Thai Chronological Strata]*, Shanghai: Fudan University Press.

Goodenough, Waugh (1975) Introduction, in Benedict 1975, iv- xi.

Haudricourt, Andre-Georges (1956) De la restitution des initiales dans les langues monosyllabiques: le problème du thai commun. *Bulletin de la Soociété Linguistique de Paris* 52: 307-22.

— (1974) Daic, in Shafer, Robert. (ed.) (1974) *Introduction to Sino-Tibetan*, Part V, Wiesbaden: Otto Harrasowitz, 451-526.

Karlgren, Bernhard (1933) 'Word families in Chinese', *Bulletin of Museum of Far Eastern Antiquities* 5: 5-120.

— (1957) Grammata Serica Recensa, *Bulletin of Museum of Far Eastern Antiquities* 29.

Keightley, David N. (ed.) (1983) *The Origins of Chinese Civilization*, Berkeley/Los Angeles/London: University of California Press.

Lan, Qingyuan (2003) *Zhuanghan tongyuanci jieci yanjiu [A Study of Cognates and Loan Words between Chinese and Zhuang]*. Beijing: Central University for Nationalities Press.

LaPolla, Randy (2001) 'The role of migration and language contact in the development of the Sino-Tibetan Language Family', in Dixon, R.M.W and Aikhenvald, A. Y. (eds.) *Areal Diffusion and Genetic Inheritance*, Oxford: Oxford University Press, 225-54.

Li, Fang-Kuei (1938) 'Language and dialects', *China Yearbook*. (Reprinted in *Journal of Chinese Linguistics* 1973.1: 1-13).

— (1970) 'Some tonal irregularities in the Tai languages', in Jakobson, Roman and Kawamoto, Shigeo (eds.) *Studies in General and Oriental Linguistics*, Tokyo: TEC Corporation for Language and Educational Research, 415-422.

— (1971) '上古音研究 Shangguyin yanjiu [Studies in Archaic Chinese]', *Tsinghua Journal of Chinese Studies*, n.s., 9:1-61. (Shanghu Yinshuguan edition 1980, Beijing: The Commercial Press.)

— (1976) 'Sino-Tai', *CAAAL* 3: 39-48.

— (1977) *A Handbook of Comparative Tai*. (Oceanic Linguistics Special Publications No. 15.) Honolulu: University Press of Hawaii.

— (1978) 'Siamese *khot*', *Monumenta Serica* 33: 403-406.

Li Jingzhong (1995) 语言演变论 *Yuyan yanbian lun [The evolution of language]*, Guangzhou: Huachang chubanshe. (In Chinese)

Luo, Meizhen (1992) 'A second discussion of the genetic classification of the Kam-Tai languages', in Compton, Carol J. and John F Hartmann (eds) *Papers on Tai Languages, Linguistics and Literatures in Honor of William J. Gedney on his 77th Birthday*. (Occasional Paper No. 16, Monograph Series on Southeast Asia, Center for Southeast Asian Studies, Northern Illinois University.

— (1994) 'San lun tai yu de xishu wenti [A third discussion of the genetic classification of the Kam-Tai languages]', *Minzu Yuwen* 6: 1-11.

Luo Yongxian (1996) 'Word families in Tai: a preliminary account', *Pan-Asiatic Linguistics: Proceedings of the Fourth International Symposium on Languages and Linguistics*, Mahidol University, Thailand, Vol. 3, 850-882. (Also in Luo 1997a, Ch.6, 183-224).

— (1997a) *The Subgroup Structure of the Tai Languages: A historical-comparative study.* (Journal of Chinese Linguistics Monograph Series 12.) Berkeley: University of California.
— (1997b) On the Tai evidence for the *sk- hypothesis. Paper presented at the 30th International Conference on Sino-Tibetan Languages and Linguistics, August 23-28, Beijing.
— (1998) 'Evidence for a series of sibilants clusters in Tai and the Sino-Tai relationship', *Journal of Chinese Linguistics* 26.1: 75-125. (Also appeared in as Chapter 4 in Luo 1997a).
— (2000) 'From 'Head' to 'Toe': Sino-Tai lexical correspondences in body part terms,' *Journal of Chinese Linguistics* 28.1: 68-99.
— (2001) Sino-Tai 'Eat', Paper presented at the Annual Meeting of the Southeast Asian Linguistic Society, Bangkok: Institute of Language and Culture for Rural Develop-ment, Mahidol University.
— (2002) Sino-Tai 'Cut', Paper presented at the 35th International Conference on Sino-Tibetan Languages and Linguistics, Tempe: Arizona State University. Also in Jimmy Harris and Songsome Brusphat (eds) (2007) *Studies in Tai and Southeast Asia Linguistics.* Bangkok: Ekphimthai Ltd, 155-182.
— (2003) Sino-Tai 'dike', Paper presented at the 36th International Conference on Sino-Tibetan Languages and Linguistics, La Trobe University, Melbourne.
— (2004) Sino-Tai Cognates for 'Vast/Open' and 'Hollow/Empty', Paper presented at the 37th International Conference on Sino-Tibetan Languages and Linguistics, Lund: Lund University, Sweden.
— (2005) Sino-Tai 'Soak/Moist/Submerge/Sink', Paper presented at the 38th International Conference on Sino-Tibetan Languages and Linguistics, Xiamen: Xiamen University, China.
— (2006a) Sino-Tai correspondence in Old Chinese *-a- finals. Paper presented at the 39th International Conference on Sino-Tibetan Languages and Linguistics, Seattle: University of Washington, September 15-17.
— (2006b) Shanggu hanyu *-l he *-r: Dongtai yu zhengju [On the Tai evidence for Old Chinese *-l and *-r]. Paper presented at the International Conference on East Asia Languages and Linguistics, 24-27 December, Shanghai Normal University. Also to appear in the Conference Proceedings.
— (in reparation) Tai, Sino-Tai: the nature of the relationship.
Manomaivibool, Prapin (1975) *Sino-Thai Lexical Correspondence*, PhD dissertation, University of Washington.
Matisoff, James A. (1978) *Variational Semantics in Tibeto-Burman: The 'Organic Approach' to Linguistic Comparison*, Philadelphia: Institute for the Study of Human Issues.
— (1990) 'On megalocomparison', *Language* 66.1: 106-120.
— (1991) Sino-Tibetan Linguistics: present states and future prospects. *Annual Review of Anthropology* 20: 469-504.
— (2001) 'Prosodic diffusionality and Southeast Asia', in Aikhenvald and Dixon (eds), 291-327.
— (2003) *Handbook of Tibeto-Burman Phonology: System and Philosophy in Sino-Tibetan Reconstruction.* Berkeley/London: University of California Press.
Meacham, William (1983) 'Origins and development of the Yüeh coastal neolithic: a microcosm of culture change on the mainland of East Asia', in David Keightly (ed.), 147-175.
Mei, Tsu-lin (2002) Jianli you zhongguo tese de zhongguo yuyanxue [Building Chinese Linguistics with Chinese characteristics]. *Journal of Chinese Linguistics* 30.2: 211-240.
Mei, Tsu-lin and Jerry Norman (1971) Shilun jige minbei fangyan zhong de laimu s- sheng zi [CL- > S- in some Northern Min dialects]. *Tsinghua Journal of Chinese Studies* 1 & 2: 95-106.
Nie, Hongyin (2002) 'Shenceng duiying xianyi [Comments on 'deep correspondence']', *Minzu Yuwen* 1: 1-7.

Nishida, Tatsuo (1960) 'Common Tai and Archaic Chinese', *Transactions of the Kansai University Institute of Oriental and Occidental Studies* 49: 1-15.

Norman, Jerry, and Mei Tsulin (1976) 'The Austroasiatic in South China: some lexical evidence', *Monumenta Serica* 32: 274-301.

Ostapirat, Weera (2005) 'Kra-Dai and Austronesian', in Laurent Sagart, Roger Blench and Alicia Sanchez-Mazas (eds), 107-131.

Pan, Wuyun (1995) '关于支持澳泰理论的若干材料 Guanyu zhichi aotai lilun de ruogan cailiao [Evidence for Austro-Tai]', in William S-Y Wang (ed.), 113-144.

— (2002) 'On the strata of cognates in Sino-Thai corresponding lexical items', in Ting, Pang-Hsin and Anne O. Yue (eds), 27-55.

— (2007) 'Shanggu hanyu yuwen *-l yu *-r [Consonant Endings *-l and *-r in Ancient Chinese]', *Minzu Yuwen* 1: 1-11.

Ratanakul, Suriya (1990) 'Tai peoples and their languages: a preliminary observation', in Pinit Ratanakul and U Kyaw Than (eds) *Development, Modernization, and Tradition in Southeast Asia: Lessons from Thailand*. Bangkok: Mahidol University, 49-111.

Reid, Lawrence A (1988 [1984-85]) Benedict's Austro-Tai hypothesis: An evaluation. *Asian Perspectives* 26.1: 19-34.

Reid, Lawrence A (2001) Austric: Is it a real language family or not? Seminar talk, Centre for Research on Language Change, Australian National University.

Sagart, Laurent (1993) 'Chinese and Austronesian: evidence for a genetic relationship', *Oceanic Linguistics* 21.2: 1-62.

— (2004) 'The higher phylogeny of Austronesian and the position of Tai-Kadai', *Oceanic Linguistics* 43.2: 411-444.

— (2005a) 'Sino-Tibetan-Austronesian', in Laurent Sagart, Roger Blench and Alicia Sanchez-Mazas (eds), 161-176.

— (2005b) 'Tai-Kadai as a subgroup of Austronesian', in Laurent Sagart, Roger Blench and Alicia Sanchez-Mazas (eds), 177-181

Sagart, Laurent, Roger Blench and Alicia Sanchez-Mazas. (eds) (2005) *The Peopling of East Asia*. London/New York: Routledge/Curzon.

Thurgood, G. (1985) 'Benedict's work: past and present', in Thurgood, G., James Matisoff and David Bradley (eds) *Linguistics of the Sino-Tibetan Area: the State of the Art*, (Pacific Linguistics C 87) Canberra: Australian National University, pp. 1-15.

— (1994) Tai-Kadai and Austronesian: The nature of the historical relationship. *Oceanic Linguistics* 33.2: 345-368.

Ting, Pang-Hsin (2000) '汉藏系语言研究法的检讨 Hanzangxi yuyan yanjiufa de jiantao [A critique of methodologies in Sino-Tibetan linguistic studies]', *Zhongguo Yuwen* 6: 483-489. Also in Ting, Panghsin and Sun Hongkai (eds) *Hanzang yu tongyuan ci yanjiu: Hanzangyu jianjiu de lishi huigu [Cognate Words in Sino-Tibetan Languages]* (vol. 1). Nanning: Guangxi Minzu Chubanshe, 427-442.

— (2002) '论汉语与台语的关系 Lun hanyu yu taiyu de guanxi — Li Fang-Kuei hantai yu tongyuan lun de jiantao [The relationship between Chinese and Tai: a review of Li Fang-Kuei's theory that Chinese and Tai are genetically related]', in Ting, Pang-Hsin and Yue, Anne O. (eds), 9-25.

Ting, Pang-Hsin and Yue, Anne O. (eds) (2002) *Essays in Chinese Historical Linguistics: Festschrift in memory of Professor Fang-Kuei Li on his centennial birthday*, (Language and Linguistics Monograph Series No. W-2), Institute of Linguistics, Academia Sinica and University of Washington.

Wang, Li (1985) 汉语语音史 *Hanyu yuyin shi [Chinese Historical Phonology]*, Beijing: Chinese Academy of Social Science Press.

Wang, Wenguang (1999) 中国南方民族史 *Zhongguo nanfang minzu shi [A history of minority peoples in South China]*, Beijing: Minzu chubanshe.

Wang, William S-Y (ed.) (1995) *The Ancestry of the Chinese Language* (Journal of Chinese Linguistics Monograph Series 8), Berkeley: University of California Press.

Wulff, Kurt (1934) *Chinesisch und Tai: Sprachvergleichende Untersuchungen [Chinese and Tai: Comparative linguistic studies]*, Copenhagen: Levin & Munksgaard.

Wyatt, David (1984) *Thailand: A Short History*, Yale University Press.

Xing, Gongwan (1962) '论调类在汉台语比较上的重要性 Lun diaolei zai hantaiyu bijiao shang de zhongyaoxing [The importance of tones in comparative studies of Chinese and Tai]', *Zhongguo Yuwen* 1: 15-27.

—— (1984) '汉藏系语言及其民族史前情况试析 Hanzangxi yuyan ji qi minzu shiqian qingkuang shixi [A preliminary study of the languages of the Sino-Tibetan family and their prehistory]', *Yuyan Yanjiu* 2: 159-172.

—— (1999) 汉台语比较手册 *Han tai yu bijiao shouce [A Handbook of Comparative Sino-Tai]*, Beijing: The Commercial Press.

Zeng, Xiaoyu (2004) 汉语水语关系论 *Hanyu shuiyu guanxi lun [On the relationship between Chinese and the Sui language]*, Beijing: The Commercial Press. (In Chinese)

Zhengzhang, Shangfang (1995) '汉语与亲属语同源根词及附缀成分比较上的择对问题 Hanyu yu qinshu yu tongyuan gen ci ji fuzhui chengfen bijiao shang de ze dui wenti [The issue of comparison of roots and affixes between Chinese and genetically related languages]', in William S-Y Wang (ed.), 269-282.

—— (2004) 上古汉语音系 *Shanggu hanyu yinxi [Old Chinese Phonology]*, Shanghai: Shanghai Educational Press.

PART 2

TAI LANGUAGES: OVERVIEWS AND RESOURCES

CHAPTER THREE

RESOURCES FOR THAI LANGUAGE RESEARCH

Anthony Diller

3.1. INTRODUCTION

3.1.1. Scope

Thai is spoken, at least as a second variety, by well over half of the total of 80 or 90 million speakers of Tai-Kadai languages. In some respects it reflects features of the greater grouping as a whole, but in other ways it is exceptional. Thai is also by far the most thoroughly described member of the group, with accounts going back several centuries. The purpose of this chapter is to call attention to some five hundred studies of Thai grammar and other aspects of the language. This is no means a comprehensive linguistic bibliography, which would need several times as many entries. Studies are selected here because they are *representative* of ongoing research and because they are useful in providing readers with further bibliography. Some attention is also given to how Thai linguistic research and its subfields have developed historically, including how studies cited relate to broader professional background issues, which also may shift diachronically.

Omitted below are many studies of merit, especially those in languages other than English. In particular, books, theses and journal articles written in Thai have generally not been included even though they contain innovative and revealing linguistic research on the language. Those seriously interested in Thai and in other Tai-Kadai languages will surely need to spend time in Thai university libraries and elsewhere where these illuminating materials are accessible.

The main focus here is on Thai; only a sample of work on Tai, Kam-Tai and Tai-Kadai is included. For further references on the wider family at its different levels, see other chapters in this volume and Huffman (1986a); anthologies edited by Gething, et al. (1976); by Khunying Suriya Ratanakul, et al. (1985, 1998); by Edmondson and Solnit (1988, 1997); and works of Morev (1991); Edmondson (2007); Luo (1997, 2007); Diller (2000); Ostapirat (2000, 2004); Thurgood (2007a). Only selected earlier works of Li, Haudricourt, Gedney, and other pioneers in the field are mentioned here; see Huffman (1986a) for fuller listings.

Thai authors are cited below by family (last) name, with some reluctance. Apologies are due to those who prefer given (first) name citation. As a statistical tendency, last-name citation has been the majority practice among Thai scholars writing for an international linguistics audience, so that is followed here. Such practice is also the norm in scientific and medical writing. Beware however that this contrasts with the humanities where Thai authorities are frequently cited and indexed by given name, a format also followed by many libraries, by Huffman (1986a), and in some other reference works.

Where relevant, several works are mentioned in more than one subsection below for convenience of readers with specific interests. Apologies to readers who find this repetition tedious.

3.1.2. Bibliographies and anthologies

The comprehensive indexical bibliography of Huffman (1986a) includes many works not mentioned here. Bibliographies of Kullavanijaya and Vongvipanond (1984) and of Burusphat (2002) are also of utility.

Many useful papers appear in anthologies and conference proceedings. Of great value and convenience to Thai linguists are collections of papers presented to conferences of the Southeast Linguistics Society (SEALS) and to symposia in the Pan-Asiatic Linguistics series (PAL; see Luksaneeyanawin, et al., 1992; Premsrirat, et al., 1996) and similar symposia (Bamroongraks, et al., 1988). Other anthologies with a strong Thai grammar focus are edited by Bickner, et al. (1986); Abramson (1997); Tingsabadh and Abramson (2001); Harris, Burusphat and Harris (2007). For earlier anthologies, see Huffman (1986a). There is also treatment of Thai in sources where focus is more broadly Tai-Kadai or Southeast Asian (e.g. Ratanakul, Thomas and Premsrirat 1985).

Ongoing resources to keep in mind are the journals *Mon-Khmer Studies*, *Crossroads*, *Linguistics of the Tibeto-Burman Area*, *Journal of the Siam Society* and *Tai Culture*, as well as publications shown on the website of *Pacific Linguistics*. Journals produced in the Thai university context publish linguistic studies of quality in Thai and occasionally in English, among them: *Journal of Language and Linguistics*, *Science of Language Papers*, *Journal of Language and Culture*.

3.1.3. Grammars and overviews

A cogent reason to reign in representation of Thai in this volume is the recent publication by Iwasaki and Ingkaphirom (2005) of a splendid reference grammar of the language. Questions linguists may have about the language's structures and functions will be answered and discussed in this comprehensive and well-indexed volume, with its many examples taken from naturally-occurring speech.

To place Thai grammar in its wider Tai context, I am aware of only one extensive comparative grammar of the Tai languages: the Russian work of Morev (1991). This is a work of insight, fine scholarship and includes an impressive bibliography of Russian sources. Perhaps subsequent research, including that reported in this volume, will stimulate updated comparative Tai or Tai-Kadai grammars.

The earlier reference grammar of Noss (1964), a standard for decades, retains its value with excellent examples and a good index, but today's readers may need some patience in matters of terminology and orientation. Panupong (1970), developing an initiating/ non-initiating distinction, presents an impressive study both of sentence-level syntax and of inter-sentence relations. Her study remains an important milestone for those pursuing structurally-defined relationships. In a rather different linguistic tradition, the Thai grammar (in Russian) of Morev, Plam and Fomicheva (1961) is an earlier landmark analysis also worthy of study. Among grammars written in Thai, my favorite remains Bandhumedha (1979), full of fresh ideas.

For the general reader more comfortable with categories of traditional grammar, a range of pedagogical grammars is available, among which Smyth (2002) is particularly informative, clear and dependable. For a more philological, historical and anthropological account of Thai, consult Anuman Rajadhon (1961, 1981).

For overviews, Haas (1969b) and Li (1974) present concise encyclopedic articles of admirable compactness and lucidity. For more specialized summaries, see Gedney (1967), reviewing Thai research up to that date. More recent overviews, covering the basics of phonology and syntax, include those of Hudak (1987), Bickner (1994), and Diller (2004). Premsrirat (2006) presents a useful sociolinguistic summary.

3.2. PHONETICS, PHONOLOGY AND ORTHOGRAPHY

3.2.1. Distinctive units

The consensus of many authorities would admit the following distinctive (phonemic) units in Thai, although transcription systems vary and individual scholars might have alternative views. Prevoiced and lax stops: b, d; voiceless, unaspirated and tense stops: p, t, c, k ('tense' here perhaps implying also a simultaneous glottal and oral release; c being alveopalatal and affricated); voiceless aspirated stops: ph, th, ch, kh (ch affricated); nasals: m, n, ng [ŋ]; fricatives and aspirates: f, s, h; liquids: r, l (distinguished rather tenuously, with sociolinguistic tendencies towards merger and overcorrection); semivowels w, y [j]. The majority, but not all, scholars in the field admit glottal stop to the consonant inventory but some opt for an analysis in which it becomes predictable; it is generally not shown in the transcription used here. Some consonants show a range of articulations, e.g. as sociolinguistically conditioned. Several initial clusters with second component -r, -l, or -w are permitted but are often simplified in less educated or less careful colloquial speech.

Only voiceless unaspirated stops -p, -t, -k, glottal stop, nasals and semivowels occur in final position. In some systems, final semivowel equivalents are indicated by vocalic diphthongs: [kay[11]] 'chicken' may appear as [kaj[11]] or [kai[11]]. The final stops are unreleased, lacking the tense quality of initial p-, t-, k-. The widely-used Haas transcription represents stop finals as -b, -d, -g, but Abramson's (1972) instrumental studies do not show voicing. Loanwords increasingly introduce finals like -s, -f, etc.

For vowels, nine come in short-long pairs: i i:, u' u': (high back unrounded [ɯ]); u u:, e e:, oe, oe: (mid central or slightly back unrounded [ə] or [ɔ]), o, o:, ae, ae:, a, a:, and o' o': (low back unrounded [ɔ]); three diphthongs ia, u'a and ua occur as phonologically long, with short variants found in a few exclamations or in other marginal vocabulary items. Long vowels can occur finally, as can short vowels plus glottal stop.

The five tones are usually described as mid (33), low (11), falling (52), high (45, 55 or 454) and rising (24). For most speakers, the high tone includes glottal constriction, more salient when vowel is long. (Tone is indicated here in superscripts of these paired numbers, in most cases with lexical rather than phonetic values, e.g. X^{45} represents a contrastive high tone, regardless of its real pitch characteristics; unmarked syllables have so-called neutral tone.)

The preceding phonemic inventory is shown in a romanization differing only in minor respects from the semi-official system prescribed by the Thai Royal Institute. Other systems are encountered, but most approach a one-to-one correspondence with the semi-official system sketched above, including that of Haas (1964, 1969b). Workers in the field soon become used to variation in transcription systems, often merely a matter of symbols used but occasionally indicating more substantial claims as to phonetic detail. More on the phonetic nature of these units and how they are represented follows below.

For general discussion of the Thai inventory, see Tingsabadh and Abramson (1993a, b) and the recent grammars and encyclopedic reviews mentioned above.

Of historical interest is Bradley (1911), apparently the first instrumental analysis of the five Thai phonemic tones, although tones were noted much earlier: La Loubère (1691) counted six. Abramson (1962) marks the professional dawn of modern instrumental research in Thai acoustic phonetics and work of the highest quality by Abramson and colleagues has extended over nearly half a century.

3.2.2. Phonological approaches and overviews

For an overview of studies of Thai phonology up to the mid 1980s, see Rischel (1984). Over several decades, work of L-Thongkum, Luksaneeyanawin, Sutadarat, and other Thai colleagues has contributed significantly to progress in Thai phonetics and phonology and those researching these topics would surely need to attend to the full range of their work. Original phonological approaches are developed in these publications, e.g. Luksaneeyawin (1992) explains 'three-dimensional phonology'. Note also Erikson's and Gandour's phonological contributions. Gandour's work, together with colleagues, spans several decades and constitutes the principal body of neurolinguistic research analyzing how Thai language ability is affected under aphasic or other degenerative neurological conditions.

Redundancy rules constrain tone by patterns of vowel length and whether or not a syllable ends in a stop (referred to as 'closed' or 'open', or in more picturesque Thai-derived terms as 'dead' or 'alive'). Closed syllables occur only with low, falling and high tones. There are also some sandhi-like rules, e.g. tones shift from the values above in fast speech, with some rising tones becoming high; the long vowels in first syllables of certain compounds are shortened. Example: [kha:ng[52]-lang[24]] 'behind', spelling pronunciation; cp. [khang[5]-lang[24]], normal speech. Such rules and debate over some points in the preceding summary are considered in the classic study of Henderson (1949) and in Lodge (1986); also in work of many authorities noted below.

3.2.3. Consonants, vowels and tones

Work of Jimmy G. Harris (e.g. 1972, 1987, 2007) in articulatory phonetics analyzes specifics of the Thai sound system. Exact places and manners of articulation, e.g. of the units transcribed here as [d], [t], [th], [c] and [ch], are established through palatography. Harris provides useful comparisons with other languages and shows how identification of Thai phonetic phenomena has been oversimplified. In an earlier study, Brown (1962, 1965) also makes challenging observations regarding Thai consonant articulations, emphasizing complex articulations and their tonal effects.

Vowels and questions of vowel length are studied from various perspectives in works by Brown, L-Thongkum, Hartmann, Roengpitya, Svastikula and Tumtavitikul. Onsuwan (2000) inspects the stop/vowel interface. Abramson (2001) considers the stability of distinctive vowel length. For pharyngealization, see Henderson (1987); for nasalization, see Beddor, et al., (1999); for states of the glottis such as prephonation and unprephonation, see work of J.G. Harris. Diachronic studies of vowel development are mentioned in 4.5.

Tone and in particular how tone interacts with other phonological elements has stimulated much research in Thai phonetics and phonology. While most authorities concur that citation forms in Thai show five lexical tones, they are also aware that citation values shift in various contexts, leading to different phonological perspectives. In an early study, Leben (1971) argued for a segmental approach to Thai tone. Yip (1982) counters this with a laryngeal tier analysis. An autosegmental approach is outlined by Hoonchamlong (1990). A general overview of Thai tonal issues is given by Erickson (1976), emphasising physiology and by Intrasai (2001), emphasising acoustics; see also Gandour (1976); Robertson (1982). Tone and vowel length are considered by Gandour (1977, 1984), and in a wider comparative context by L-Thongkum and Teeranon and Intajamornrak (2007). Tumtavitikul (1993) studies how consonant onset affects tonal parameters; see also L-Thongkum (1992). Gandour, Potisuk and Harper (1996) discuss stress and vowel length. For tonogenesis, see section 3.4.6.

Questions of pitch/amplitude components of tone and stress and of the interaction of tone, rhythm, sandhi and sentence intonation have been vigorously pursued for decades. A procession of representative studies includes Kroll (1956), Warotamasikkhadit (1968), Whitaker (1969), Hiranburana (1971), Gsell (1972), Noss (1972, 1975), Pantupong (1973), L-Thongkum (1978, 1984), Luksaneeyanawin (1983), Court (1985), Peyasantiwong (1986) and Wong-opasi (1994).

Musical recitation raises interesting research questions. Still of value is List's (1961) study of linguistic tone and song melody. Tumtavitikul and Promkhuntong (2007) present results of an instrumental study of how Thai classical poetry is chanted.

Closely related is how tone, vowel-length and other properties are manifested in speech-act particles, interjections and the like. Perhaps belonging here too is Cooke's (1992) discussion regarding a possible sixth tone in Thai. Do these items show phonological properties somewhat different from other lexical material? Chuenkongchoo (1956) is among the earliest studies; Peyasanitwong (1979, 1981, 1986) further develops the analysis; also Lodge (1986). For conjunctions and linker syllables, consult Bee (1975). Chaimanee's (1994) study of filled hesitation pauses breaks new ground in a related area.

3.2.4. Psycholinguistics and phonology; phonesthesia

Psycholinguistic investigations of tone include work of Abramson (1971) on whispered Thai and of Van Lanker and Fromkin (1978), who report different neural processing for contrastive speech tone and non-lexical musical tone. Psycholinguistic implications of the range publications of Gandour and colleagues deserve attention.

Perception studies using experimental protocols have often involved comparative as well as psycholinguistic issues. Wayland and Guion (2003) investigate tonal perception among native and non-native speakers. For consonant perception, including voicing issues, see the early contrastive studies involving Thai and English of Melamed (1962) and Kanasut-Roengpitya (1965). Other perception studies are by Donald (1978); Carney, et al. (1988). Beach, Burnham, and Kitamura (2001) investigate bilingualism and Thai bilabial stop production and perception. Harris and Bachman (1976) study how Thai speakers perceive consonants in other Tai languages.

General longitudinal and acquisitional studies include Tuaycharoen (1977, 1979) and Imsri and Idsardi (2003). Bilingual acquisition is the topic of Sarawit (1976).

Direct sound-meaning relationships, including sound symbolism, phonesthesia and quasi-morphological or morphophonemic functions of phonological material are the topic of studies by Henderson (1965), Kam (1980) and Chamberlain (1992). These processes seem to be of more importance for Thai than for English, etc., and merit further study.

3.2.5. Orthography and Romanization

For the Thai writing system, Haas (1956), the first complete description in English, remains a useful resource. Danvivathana (1987) presents the system in all of its detail along with historical treatment of how letter shapes and inventories have altered over the centuries. For those simply seeking a practical introduction to Thai orthography, Iwasaki and Ingkapirom (2005) and Smyth (2002) can be recommended, and many pedagogical manuals, CD-ROMs, etc., are available. The encyclopedia entries cited above also contain overviews.

A compact summary of current symbols and basic principles, along with Lao comparisons, can also be found in Diller (1996a). This study includes a historical sound-change rationale for what may seem today like arbitrary and complex system of rules. For more on orthography and diachronic sound change, see section 3.4.6.

Given that the Thai writing system is not only practically efficient but also a longstanding component in the Thai sense of national identity, alternatives have never posed a real threat (Anuman Rajadhon 1961, 1981; Aeosrivongse 1984; Diller 1993, 2002). True, Kings Rama IV and Rama VI each came up with a reformed writing system and a change to romanization was tentatively considered just after political changes of 1932, yet these were never popular options. A few putative simplifications in Thai spelling decreed during the regime of the 1940's were quickly undone and forgotten (Hudak 1986).

King Rama VI (Vajiravudh, r. 1910-1925) proposed different transcription systems for native words and Indic loans in Thai, his own name, pronounced [wachi^{45}rawut^{45}], providing a good example of the latter type. Thai family names are often romanized this way: through transliterating etymological Sanskrit letter values rather than indicating modern sounds. Owners of Indic-component Thai names of this category have reported to me hesitancy to change romanization for a surname that was royally granted both in Thai form and also as romanized in the King's etymological-Sanskritic transcription system. Inconsistent application of this two-fold system also accounts for frequently seen toponym pairs like *Dhonburi, Thonburi; Ubol, Ubon,* etc. (Ronakiat 2007). For more on romanization and transcriptions, including disparagement of the Haas system and apparently phonetics in general, see Prince Dhaninivat (1970).

3.3. SYNTAX AND SEMANTICS

3.3.1. Syntactic typology

Many, but far from all, authorities in the field would concur in a general way with the following first-approximation sketch. Most (including the writer) would also offer qualifications, counter-examples, definitional quandaries and further debate, as is clear from following entries. As to commonly-cited typological parameters, Thai characteristics include basic transitive syntactic order [S + V-trans + O], in more semantic frameworks represented as AVO, and most frequent intransitive order [S + V-intrans]. [V-intrans + S] occurs also occurs in presentational or existential contexts as mentioned below. Understood noun phrases are widely unstated and construed (i.e. are subject to zero anaphora or deletion, etc., depending on analytic framework) and topicalized orders are common. Taken together, these factors give rise to a number of alternative pragmatically- or functionally-determined surface orders in actual discourse.

Nominal modification order in Thai strongly accords with the inherited Tai pattern [nominal head] + [modifier], with possessives and relative clauses also following head nouns. Interestingly, Indic compounds have introduced a contrasting [modifier] + [nominal head] ordering. Some commercial and institutional NP names use the Indic order: compare *Chulalongkorn-mahawithayalay* (Indic compound) and *Mahawithayalay Thammasat* (as though Tai/Thai noun phrase, although components are both Indic); *Ao-Thai Gas* [a:w^{11} thay^{33} kae:s^{45}], 'Gulf-of-Thailand Gas', Indic compounding order for the whole NP, but components are etymologically Thai and English; the 'Gulf-of-Thailand' subcomponent shows Thai/Tai head-modifier order. (This issue is now strictly academic, given Caltex's acquisition.)

Prepositions precede their nominals. Many auxiliaries precede their main verb, but others follow. Positioning of lexical items with semantic functions of auxiliaries in English, or at least with translational similarities, is not clear-cut. Sometimes reinforcing correlative auxiliary components are found on both sides of a verb complex, e.g. the progressive aspect sequence [kam^{33}lang^{33}] X [yu:^{11}] 'to be in process of Xing' (Kullavanijaya and Bisang, 2004); the deontic sequence [sa:^{24}ma:t^{52}] X [day^{52}] 'to be able to X'.

Morphosyntactically, as a tonal language with many typically isolating features, Thai retains a core of basic monosyllabic Tai words. However, in the current lexicon this inherited base is statistically overwhelmed by vocabulary from other sources, often polysyllabic with tonally attenuated or perhaps 'neutral' reduced syllables. Some prefixal syllables show at least a weak semantic content: [ma-] codes a set of fruit-bearing flora such as [ma-muang^{52}] 'mango' and [ma-phra:w^{45}] 'coconut'. This is transparently compound reduction: [ma:k^{11}], now 'areca nut', originally had a wider 'fruit' meaning. Compounding of several types is active and common; some sandhi phenomena apply to compounding. Moderate use is made of full and partial repetition. Derivational processes of several types are mentioned below but no use whatsoever is made of obligatory inflectional morphology to indicate tense, aspect, transitivity, specificity or number. These either are coded lexically, understood from context, or left vague.

Nominal word classes accepted by most scholars are common and proper nouns, including a copious supply of titles and epithets, shading into pronouns; also in the nominal class or else in classes of their own are classifiers, number words (i.e. lexical numerals), and deictics. As modifiers follow head nouns prolifically and endomorphically, rather large noun phrases can be built up. A few nouns are homonymous with verbs, mainly instrumentals as in other languages: [thay^{24}] 'a plow; to plow'; [prae:ng^{33}] 'a brush; to brush'.

Open verbal classes are more controversial. For the protracted debate regarding adjectives and/or adjectival verbs, see section 3.3.6. Progressive grammaticalization is at the bottom of several definitional quandaries: this process not only moves full verbs into preverbal and postverbal auxiliary subclasses, but also into preposition-like coverbs marking semantic case for following nominals. These construction types impinge on wider *serial verb* patterns (3.6). Closed functional classes widely recognized include prepositions (but challenged by Warotamasikkhadit 1988; see also Indrambarya 1994), conjunctions, intensifiers and quantifiers, speech-act and polite particles and interjections. Whether or not one or more additional adverb classes might be needed depends on how generously one defines other classes or on which tests are applied.

Syntactic overviews are presented in the encyclopedic articles mentioned above, with issues developed at greater length in other sources cited. For those interested in how syntactic constructions function in actual speech, an excellent place to go first is Iwasaki and Ingkaphirom (2005). Mention should be made also of many fine theses and other studies in Thai not considered here that describe individual constructions with great insight.

3.3.2. History of Thai syntactic research

Historically, interest in Thai syntactic issues by outsiders is of long standing and in varied frameworks. Progress in understanding the nature of Thai can be traced from the brief but valuable sketch and translated lexical lists of La Loubère (1691), a diplomat-trader, through to the first explicit grammar in English by James Low (1828), an East India Company trader-cartographer. He began by informing readers that Thai has 'no grammar' (meaning inflectional morphology?) but then went on to treat parts of speech with understanding. His book is a technical as well as linguistic milestone: it was printed using the first moveable-type Thai printing-press font, developed by Ann Judson and her missionary colleagues (Winship 1986). Unfortunately the text was replete with myriad typographic errors. Noteworthy here is Smyth (2001), who outlines the early study of Thai by outsiders and provides a useful bibliography and discussion of the early grammars.

A substantial grammar was produced by another missionary, Bishop D. J. B. Pallegoix (1850). He projected the full panoply of Latinate categories onto Thai, including even the future perfect tense. Pallegoix's Latin-Siamese-French-English lexicon, with Thai script and a credible romanization, was an impressive *tour de force*. More importantly, as I suspect, Pallegoix's scholarly friendship and intellectual exchanges with the Buddhist monk Prince Mongkut were influential in promoting the sentiments leading to a vision of Thai as the standard normative language such as we know it today (Diller 2001a). After Mongkut's coronation in 1851 he was subsequently known as King Rama IV. He turned his attention to language reform and to 'correct' Thai, apparently the first time a monarch had pursued normative linguistic interests at that level of detail. He focused not only on lexical issues but even on syntactic minutiae normally of concern only to linguists, such as prescription of different classifier constructions (elephants and horses were to be counted directly, without an idiosyncratic classifier [tua^{33}] 'lit. 'body', since these animals were considered higher in dignity than others). Khanittanan (1987a, b) considers linguistic features in royal writing as they evolved, complemented by the more socio-historical study of Aesrivongse (1984, in Thai), whose insights are behind Diller (1993, 2001a).

Pedagogical grammars and readers, too many to enumerate here, contain insightful discussions of specific constructions and exemplify them in context as well. Especially dependable earlier sources informed by linguistics include Haas (1945); Brown (1967); Anthony, French and Warotamasikkhadit (1967); Jones, Mendiones and Reynolds (1969); Yates and Tryon (1970); Kuo (1982). Landmark syntactic analyses written by those with native-speaker intuitions and reasonably comprehensive in scope include the formidable, influential and abstruse normative grammar of Upakit-Silapasan (1939, in Thai); Warotamasakkhadit (1963), the first grammar written in a generative framework; Panupong's (1970) inter-sentence study mentioned above; Pankhuenkhat (1978) and Bandhumedha (1979, in Thai), well-organized and full of insights.

3.3.3. Theoretical perspectives in syntax

Approaches to Thai syntax have included most of the familiar linguistic frameworks of the mid- to late-20th-century: traditional, structuralist, tagmemic, generative, functional and more discourse-oriented studies. Upakit-Silapasan (1939, in Thai), mentioned above, presents essentially a traditional analysis employing familiar Western Classical grammatical categories, but disguised by neo-Indic nomenclature and making use of several authentically Indic notions, especially *karaka* (semantic deep case) theory. In methodology, Noss (1964) and Panupong (1970) pursue the substitution-frame methodology standard for structural linguistics of their period and are both convincing examples of that approach. As noted above, generative work begins with Warotamasakkhadit (1963) and continues on, as that framework advances, through representative post-Aspects productions such as Bandhumedha (1976) and Surintramont (1979) on deletion, Warotamasakkhadit (1979) on topicalization, Rodman (1977), on coordinating constraints and Wongbiasaj (1980), on movement transformations. Bounding and subjacency are covered by Panpothong (2001). For generative semantics, Stine (1968), on the instrumental case, is a good early example.

Deletion or nominal omission has frequently been a focus of theoretical treatment. As noted above, in terms of the patterns S + Vintrans and S + Vtrans + O, noun phrases S and O are often construed from context. Nominal omission applies to compounding processes as well. In some conventional expressions, head nouns in compounds are optionally or regularly missing: [kho':^{24}-tha:n^{33}] 'request alms', but also 'beggar' with head noun [khon^{33}] 'person' missing. Note also noodle, rice dishes and other culinary productions, e.g. [phat^{11}-thay^{33}] 'Thai-style fried (noodles)'; [phat^{11}- kaphraw^{33} mu:^{24}] '(rice topped with) basil-fried pork', possibly giving rise by analogical formation to [maek^{45}- kaphraw^{33} mu:^{24}] 'Mc(Donald's-style bunned patty with) basil pork'. However, after true prepositions, which are few in the language, nominals resist deletion. Verb-derived coverbs sometimes also reject deletion of following nominal, sometimes not, providing a test for degree of grammaticalization. There are important constraints too, some sentence-internal and some sensitive to macro issues of discourse organization. These are considered with particular insight and cogency by Grima (1978, 1986). For taking missing nominals as empty categories as they were construed in the frameworks of the 1980's, see Lehman and Pingkarawat (1985), Cole (1987), Kobsiriphat (1988) and Pingkarawat (1989). In the post-Government- and-Binding framework, see Hoonchamlong (1991) and Laksinaking (1991) on anaphora. Outsiders may be astonished that grammaticality judgments underpinning generative work of this type are not infrequently contested by native speakers themselves, a topic examined ethnolinguistically by Diller and Khanittanan (2002).

Numerous additional frameworks have been used. Under the institutional aegis of the University of Hawaii's East-West Center, work making reference to case grammar and to the specific format 'lexicase' (see Starosta 2001), includes Kullavanijaya (1974), on word classes; Savetamalya (2001); Clark (1978), with comparisons to Vietnamese coverbs; and Clark and Prasithrathsint (1985), on synchronic lexical derivation. Deep case, that is semantic role relationships rather than those derived from surface syntax, informs the approach of Lekawatana (1970) and also of Vijchulata (1978), who also develops a stratificational analysis. Tagmemic work includes Patamapongse (1971); Phinit-Akson (1972); Punyodyana (1976). Deepadung (1989) exemplifies residential grammar. For Montague grammar, consult Godden (1981). Diller (1997) wonders whether 'subject' is needed in Thai syntax, referring to role and reference grammar. Schiller (1992) produces an autolexical analysis, a framework also used in Wong-Opasi's (1994) treatment of compounding.

3.3.4. Compounding, nominalization and morphological processes

Compounding and questions of complex word formation are treated by Gehr (1951); Fasold (1968); Osipov (1969); Warotamasintop (1975); Vongvipanond (1992); Witayasakpan (1992); Kullavanijaya (1992); Manomaivibool (2000). L-Thongkum (1994) presents a comparative Tai-Kadai study. Vongvipanond (1992) treats doublets with components of related meaning, a type widespread in the Thai lexicon. See also Wong-Opasi (1994), noted above. The astonishingly large set of compounds relating to emotions and personal attributes with component [cay^{33}] 'heart, mind' have attracted much syntactic, semantic and anthropological interest; see the comparative Southeast Asian survey of Matisoff (1986). For Thai data analysed in various ways, see Lee (1987); Diller and Juntanamalaga (1990); Moore (1992). Another common compound type has a component meaning 'head', which Juntanamalaga (1992) convincingly relates to kinesic tabu beliefs relating to heads and feet. Thai nominalization is similar to compounding in some respects. Prasithrathsint (1996), (1997), (2006), (2007) presents a compelling set of diachronic and comparative analyses covering this topic.

Some compounding heads referring to people such as [nak^{45}], [cha:w^{33}] and [phu:^{52}] are in effect bound morphemes. [khon^{33}], another 'person' word, functions as a common noun but also as a generic compounding head and as classifier. Other classifiers do so as well.

Quasi-morphological derivational processes involving vowel ablaut, tonal variation and even some consonantal interchange is sometimes referred to as elaboration and can be found throughout Southeast Asia, surveyed by Henderson (1967), Nacaskul (1976) and Williams (1991). For Thai, Haas (1964) provides many further examples. An early brief analysis of this material along with more straight-forward reduplication is given by Haas (1942). Sookgasem (1997) provides a valuable expansion of reduplication types with discussion of theoretical ramifications. Various patterns of semi-repetition (elaboration or echo-syllables) not only account for common lexical forms but also, for many speakers, show all the signs of active derivation processes. Some patterns of vowel and tone alternation are used to supply vibrancy and emotive wit to informal spoken language. Kullavanijaya (1997) shows how some of these processes are used in intensifying. The deictic system too shows some quasi-morphological paradigmaticity, discussed in Henderson (1967). Iwasaki (2004) shows how topic-marking particles have been derived from such forms. Diller and Juntanamalaga (1988) speculate as to how the current deictic system may be the residue of diachronic reorganization.

Traditional Thai grammatical study (e.g. Upakit-silapasan 1939; Anuman Rajadhon 1981) makes much of morphological processes affecting Indic loanwords borrowed into Thai. Some changes, such as deletion of many Indic final syllables, are simply a matter of assimilation to the Thai phonological system. Other changes, such as those in morphological recombination of Indic roots to create Thai neologisms, may show prefixation, assimilation, etc., that reflect processes in the Indic donor systems. Pali-Sanskrit terminology such as [sama:t[11]] 'samasa compound', [son[24]thi[45]] 'sandhi compound', may be used and are even sometimes applied to compounds non-Indic in provenance. See Gedney (1947); Wan Waithayakorn (1970); Prasithrathsint (1994).

3.3.5. Nominal substitutes and classifiers

Pronouns and nominal substitutes immediately lead into sociolinguistics, as the forms in question are generally more sensitive to such constraints than they are to the more usual pronominal properties of number and even person. The definitional borderline between pronouns, conventionalized epithet-substitutes and ordinary common nouns has been drawn in various ways. Also, classifiers (below) are part of the story as they have anaphoric functions and show other pronominal traits as well. Early studies of note include Cooke (1965), which also compares Vietnamese and Burmese data using distinctive features; Campbell (1969), a useful comprehensive orientation; Palakornkul (1972, 1975) emphasizing sociolinguistic usage; Hatton (1973, 1978), discussing translation; Strecker (1980); Sugamoto (1989). Truwichien (1980) discusses the important topic of address avoidance with great insight, while her longer study (1985) impressively integrates relevant socio-cultural matters. Gething (1986) discusses similar issues. Hatton (1978) and Hoonchamlong (1992) elucidate differences between male- and female-speaker first-person forms and usage. This topic is further developed by Diller and Chirasombutti (2000), who suggest that Thai women are required by the prevailing linguistic system to 'place themselves' through self-reference selections in a more finely-determined social space than that required of male speakers. Chirasombutti (1995) provides further detail and a comparison with Japanese. Wijeyewardene's (1968) contribution at the tabu end of this field is of great anthropological interest.

Hinds (1988) presents a lucid analysis of reflexives, including discourse-based examples. His argument sounds a note of caution for researchers quick to assume that anaphoric properties of reflexives in Thai such as [tua[33]], [e:ng[33]] and [tua[33]e:ng[33]] equate formally to English translational counterparts. Namthammachat (1975) and most theses written in generative frameworks also treat these issues.

Classifiers can claim a respectable store of professional literature. Most classifiers are derived from homonymic common nouns like [tua[33]] 'body'; a few are from verbs, e.g. [phu:k[11]] 'to tie', as a verb; 'bundle' as a classifier for monastic manuscripts. They constitute nearly an open (sub)class, especially if combined with generics like [ya:ng[11]] 'kind, sort' and measure words, both formal, like [ki[33]lo:[33]] 'kilometer; kilogram', and conventional, like [kae:w[52]] '(drinking) glass', as used in a measuring context. These types share many classifier patterns. For many common nouns, classifiers are required in counting expressions, where regular order is [head noun] + [number word] + [classifier]: [no':ng[45] so':ng[24] khon[33]] [younger-sibling two classifier] 'two younger siblings'. Classifiers are also used to suggest definiteness, especially with deictics in the pattern [head noun] + [classifier] + [deictic], but other modifiers can occur in the [deictic] position if they are used to specify, especially contrastively. The counting and definiteness patterns can be combined. In these patterns and elsewhere in the language, head nouns are frequently 'missing': they are construed from discourse context, giving syntacticians room to theorize as to zero anaphora, deletion, empty categories, etc.

Idiosyncratic classifiers are most strongly required for counting items that are discrete, concrete, and part of Thai cultural life. Two or three dozen are used quite commonly in informal conversation, but many more are recognized: McFarland (1944) gives a list of 82; however, it takes the Thai Royal Institute (Ratchabanditsathan 1995) many more than that and a booklet of 128 pages to prescribe the complete system. As items become more abstract or obscure they tend either to be counted with a general classifier [an^{33}], or counted directly with no overt classifier, or else with a 'repeater' construction where a single lexical form occurs in the pattern [head noun] + [numeral] + [classifier] both as head noun and as classifier. A few concrete items, such as several body parts, are also counted in this manner. The system is far from rigid, showing individual and sociolinguistic variation, bureaucratic prescription as above, late acquisition (some items typically learned at school), and, as noted above, diachronic instability both as to the forms used and as to what each classifies (e.g. [tua^{33}], originally for animates with bodies, is now on the rise).

Haas (1942, 1978) was perhaps the pioneer in their analysis along modern linguistic lines and her study remains an admirably concise overview, keeping in mind the passing of time. As a great help both to language learners and to researchers, her dictionary (1964) specifies one or more classifiers for virtually every noun, including indication of those that use the 'repeater' construction. Hiranburana (1978) concentrates on a hierarchical semantic classification, with Placzek (1984, 1985, 1992) providing more detailed studies of this type, with interest in perceptual salience. Plam (1974) supplies a treatment both semantic and syntactic, as do Kölver (1979) and Hundius and Kölver (1983); see also Zhang (1992). Kookiattikoon (2001) looks in depth at their syntax.

Along with pronouns, classifiers are among the Thai word classes highly subject to borrowing and diachronic change, with few forms still shared throughout the language family and, for those that are, some variation in the sets of nouns classified. Palakornkul (1976) and Deepadung (1997) substantiate recent changes or changes in progress, while Jachontov (1971) and Krupa (1978) suggest diachronic dynamics. Gandour, et al. (1984) attend to acquisition issues, as does Carpenter in a series of studies (1986, 1987, 1991, 1992). Gandour, et al., (1985) describe their dissolution in aphasic situations.

For comparative classifier studies, see section 3.4.4.

3.3.6. Verbs, transitivity, predicate constructions and grammaticalization

Thai verbs are a robust class but should a separate class of adjective be recognized? There are good reasons to take adjectives as a subclass of verbs, following Gedney (1947), Haas (1964), Panupong (1970), Hudak (1987) and others who subcategorize these items as a type of verb, perhaps 'adjectival verb'. Such forms do not require (or even admit, in most cases) a copula such as [pen^{33}] or [khu':^{33}] 'to be' to form complete predicates and they interact with auxiliaries, negatives and question/answer patterns mainly in the way full verbs do. But good arguments to the contrary have been advanced too, variously invoking comparative constructions, the ability to occur with certain prefixal formatives, semantic effects of repetition, etc. See Noss (1964); Prapa (1996), Smyth (2002), Iwasaki and Ingkaphirom (2005) and Thai traditional grammar. These authorities, it would seem, would need to acknowledge that complete Thai sentences could lack overt verbs. Nominalizing formatives [ka:n^{33}-] for verbs and [khwa:m^{33}-] have been often been used to distinguish these categories but a number of verbs with cognitive-emotive meanings like 'understand', 'detest', etc. accept both prefixals equally well. To call adjectival verbs 'stative verbs' has been one attack, but one might well wish to call verbs like [yu:^{11}] 'to be located' stative verbs as well and these fail most of the putative adjective tests.

As though to make tightly defining verbs yet more onerous, Thai main verbs are difficult to distinguish absolutely from forms one might wish to take as auxiliaries: markers of timing, aspect and modality. In serial coverb constructions they intrude on prepositions.

As noted, Thai verbs show no formal marking as to transitivity, nor do they overtly indicate finite-nonfinite status. The ability of nominals to be deleted or not to occur overtly presents a moderate challenge to transitivity analysis, but most authorities concur that many lexical verbs are basically in a transitive class, a few like [hay^{52}] 'to give' in a ditransitive one, many more are intransitive and still others alternate in potential transitivity status, perhaps along with other minor semantic effects. Landmark studies of verb classes include Noss (1964), Panupong (1970) and Sindhavananda (1970). More recent discussions are by Sriphen (1982) and Thepkanjana (1992), who develops the useful notion of a transitivity continuum, taking account of verb semantics. Savetamalya (1992), emphasising patient subjects, discusses transitivity using a case-grammar approach. Negation of predicates and elsewhere is considered by Kanasut-Roengpitya (1974) and Lagsanaging (1992).

Semantics and pragmatics interact in transitivity issues. Panupong (1978) and Diller (1997) wonder about how best to analyze single verb forms exhibiting alternating transitivity. Part of the question must include pragmatics: in a rather common construction type, topicalized undergoer or patient/theme object occurs without overt agentive subject: O-undergoer (S-agent) V-trans. Does this merge in a gradient way with S-theme V-intrans? Perhaps related to this problem is a small class of high-frequency verbs such as [mi:^{33}] 'to have; there is/are' and [koe:t^{11}] 'to be born; to happen'. Here a single form appears to have both a transitive use and also to occur intransitively in a pattern of V + S when showing existential or presentative meanings. Sookgasem (1992) clarifies the issues, also considered in the lexicase system by Indrambarya (1996).

This leads to the question of marked passive or pseudo-passive constructions, well-researched topic of long-standing interest (Bergen 1875). Prasithrathsint (1988) documents substantial diachronic change in a range of passive-like constructions. A common issue in the current language involves a verb [thu:k^{11}] 'to come in contact with, touch'. This is widely recognized with a shifted, generalized meaning more like 'to undergo, suffer' and with the function of an adversative passive: [mae:w^{33} thu:k^{11} ma:^{24} kat^{11}] [cat undergo dog bite] 'the cat was bitten by the dog'. In this construction, the form [thu:k^{11}] retains nearly all of the formal syntactic collocational properties of a main verb, if not quite retaining normal verb semantics. This has lead some authorities to resist labelling the construction as 'passive' *per se*, as argued forcefully and entertainingly by Noss (1972b), holding that using 'passive' here would be too much of an imposition of Western grammatical conceptions. (Is it churlish to observe that Noss registers no similar problem with 'subject' and other Western category labels, which his grammar liberally utilizes?)

In any event, as Khanittanan (1979), Prasithrathsint (1988) and others have maintained, the construction has been widely used to translate English and other Western-language passives. Perhaps partly because of resulting translation genres, usage of the [thu:k^{11}] construction is assuredly becoming used in less adversative contexts, especially in Thai technical discourse ('the metal was dissolved in acid') and among middle-class speakers ('I was invited by him to the party'). This recalls Prasithrathsint's (1988) demonstration that earlier Thai 'passive' constructions have been moderately changeable. A syntactically similar, but less common, form [do:n^{33}] 'to be hit by' is more stable in its adversative semantics. The (pseudo-)passive problem is treated structurally and functionally in several doctoral theses and in briefer works, among them: Filbeck (1973a); Lekawatana (1975); Thanyarat (1983); Wongbisaj (1979b) in a generative framework and Savetamalaya (2001) in a lexicase one. Morev (1996) investigates these matters from the perspective of diathesis, which includes consideration of causatives and other transitivity-shifting issues. Gero (1977) and Gsell (1979) are concerned with a similar range of issues.

Serial verb constructions, directionals and causatives have been the focus of much syntactic research. The preceding discussion indicates that the pseudo-passive markers mentioned above have many properties of verbs; as such they may be implicated in the wider phenomenon of serial verb constructions. Definitions have varied but many take this type of construction to consist of two or more verbs or verbal predicates strung together without overt marking of coordination or subordination. In many instances, or in all if so defined, at least one nominal argument is shared, such as subject/agent or object/patient. Usually at least one such nominal is understood, i.e. is an empty category or zero anaphor. Crucial here also is the observation that along with many other serializing languages Thai lacks morphological marking distinguishing finite from non-finite. Also, to assume that the first verb in sequence were in all cases the dominant one leads to quandaries. Constructions of this type are a Southeast and East Asian areal feature, as documented by Clark (1978, 1992) and Clark and Prasithrathsint (1985) in a lexicase framework. Bisang (1996), with grammaticalization and 'great attractors' in mind, analyzes Thai examples in this wider context too, as does Post (2007). Analyses reveal both broad similarities and specific differences with comparable data in nearby languages.

Needleman (1973a) is among the first studies in which a formal post-Aspects generative framework confronts the challenge of the seemingly flat multi-verb structures of Thai verb serialization, followed by Filbeck (1975), Vis (1978) and Sereechareonsatit (1984). Thepkanjana (1986) should be credited, it seems to me, with a notable advance by turning attention to specific semantic subclasses of verbs as a constraint in how longer complexes are contextually built up and strung together, a direction developed by Chuwicha (1993) and in other work. Somewhat similar in orientation, but using the lexicase apparatus with robust use of synchronic derivation, Clark and Prasithrathsint (1985) offer an analysis of verb forms showing context-sensitive differences in sense or structural properties. Working in the same basic framework, Wilawan (1992, 1993) goes on more radically to supply an argument rejecting the 'serial verb' characterization entirely and taking the relevant constructions to be coordinate or subordinate clauses within a system of sentence adjuncts. For more consideration of these matters, further references and a scheme based on symmetrical/asymmetrical properties of these constructions, see Diller (2006a), which also mentions properties of shared arguments, negation, modality and timing.

The verbs [pay[33]] 'to go' and [ma:[33]] 'to come' and similar verbs of motion enter into serial constructions of great frequency, mixing directional, temporal, aspectual and evaluative nuances in intriguing ways that have stimulated much study. These forms are considered in many of the sources cited above, but studies focus on them specifically as well. Gandour (1978a) associates 'come' and 'go' with deictic properties, with Treerat (1990) going on to come (!) to grips with how syntax, predicate semantics and discourse context interact. Temporal-aspectual functions of [pay[33]] offer a particular challenge, with interpretations of timing sometimes suggesting past completive, sometimes future continuative. [khaw[52]] 'to enter', hence inchoative, and some other directionals contribute to the topic as well. Bickner (1985) and Rangkupan (2001) analyze usage of directionals as it indicates psychological perspective in narrative and in other contexts.

The verb [hay[52]] 'to give' in serial constructions promotes a different polysemous complex involving notions like benefactive, causative and complementizer of controlled action. Areal considerations are again relevant; see comparative analyses by Hermann (1979); Pooisrakit (Poo-israkij 1995), Iwasaki and Yap (1998); Post (2007). Vichit-Vadakan (1976) notes differences in intended versus inadvertent causality in constructions with [hay[52]], [tham[33]] 'to do' and the compound [tham[33]hay[52]]. Other studies are by Kumlert (1976), Khamsaen (1978), Indrambarya (1992), with Warotamasikkhadit (1994) offering questions as to prevailing terminology. Grima (1978), while not limited to [hay[52]] constructions, presents an especially cogent discussion of the associated types of zero anaphora. See also chapter 17.

Temporal-aspectual information may be marked by the use of directionals to indicate temporal-aspectual nuances is mentioned above. Other marking of this type, along with modality, can usually be traced back to main-verb sources too, although such verbs may or may not still be in active usage. A problem encountered by those attempting to establish a fixed linear order for lexical forms in auxiliary constructions, e.g. Anthony (1964), Dellinger (1975), is that many of the dozen or more commonly used forms can function in different surface positions with slightly different meanings and collocational dynamics; see critique of Warotamasikkhadit (1979). Thus the form [a:t[11]] can function epistemically as 'apt to, likely to' but also deontically as 'able, capable of'. The epistemic position is more peripheral, preceding positions of irrealis marker [ca^{11}] and negative [may^{52}], with the deontic alternate closer to the verbal core and following positions of such formatives. The favored structuralist solution has been to expand the lexicon: Noss (1964) distinguishes two [a:t^{11}] homonyms in different form classes.

Kimsuvan (1992) considers alternations with [yu:^{11}] 'be located; be happening; at'. This form along with others has been investigated in detail by Kullavanijaya and Bisang (2004) in a selection-theory approach. Similar syntactic and semantic alternations apply to several other forms. [day^{52}] 'can' (and many further possible glosses) is notorious, with functions ranging widely over the epistemic, deontic and temporal-aspectual semantic territory. Enfield (this volume) has given much attention to the counterpart of this form in Lao and much of what he describes in this volume for the Lao would apply to Thai as well. Other approaches involve linkage of semantics to various treatments of phrase structure, an especially well-designed analysis being that of Sookgasem (1990) in Head-driven Phrase Structure Grammar. See also studies of Kanchanawan (1978), with interest in machine translation; Ekniyom (1979), using internal reconstruction; and theses of Kullavanijaya (1968); Scovel (1970); Boonyapatipark (1983). Howard (2000) and Koenig and Muansuwan (2000) inspect perfectivity in detail, e.g. use of the form [lae:w^{45}], originally a verb 'to finish'.

Much of the above discussion relates in one way or another to grammaticalization paths, especially to situations where diachronically prior constructions and senses coexist in the current language along with their evolved alternates, with little or no phonological indication of difference. Enfield (2006) presents a cogent discussion of grammaticalization issues relating to Lao, in most cases with direct application to Thai as well. Not only verbs and derived auxiliaries are at issue, but also other paths like [verb – coverb – preposition], cp. [ca:k^{11}] 'to leave (now very restricted); from' or [noun – preposition], cp. [lang^{24}] 'back (body part noun); in back of (as though preposition or adverb)', with yet another function being classifier for houses. For more on what is essentially grammaticalization, if not explicitly so identified, see work of Clark (from 1978 onwards), Jagacinski (1991), Juntanamalaga and Diller (1992), Bisang (1996), Diller (2001b). Iwasaki (2004) considers the grammaticalization of topic-marking form [nia^{52}]. See Part Four of this volume.

3.3.7. Other parts of speech and constructions

Questions are taken up in work by Kullavanijaya (1980) and Santaputra (1984). A common yes-no question type is coded by a final particle written as though [may^{24}] but usually pronounced [may^{45}]; the ultimate diachronic source is undoubtedly the preverbal negator [may^{42}]. This and other final particles with various speech-act, politeness and discourse functions are analyzed in a number of studies, Cooke (1989) providing a comprehensive orientation, with other studies by Bhamoraput (1972), Peyasantiwong (1981), Kendall, Yoon and Hye-Suk (1986), Horie (Ingkaphirom) and Iwasaki (1996). Phonological reduction of these forms is studied by Peyasanitwong (1979). Bandhumedha (1979) presents a convenient grouping of families of particles and perceptive analyses of functions. For specific treatments, see Cooke (1979) for the [si^{45}] set and Neill's (1989) narrative-based analysis of [na^{45}] and [chay^{52} may^{45}]. Diller and Juntanamalaga (1992) take up the [oe:y^{24}] set. Strings of particles can occur together. Whether such forms are subject to ordering rules is considered by Warotamasikkhadit (1975) and Prasithrathsint (1974).

Conjunctions are considered by Thomas (1979) and by Clark (1994), who presents a comparative study and argument for a topicalizing function. Jagacinski (1991) takes up complementizer [wa:^{52}] and other complement types. For relative clauses and factitive noun clauses marked by formative [thi:^{52}], see Ekniyom (1971); Suktrakul (1975); Sornhiran (1978); Kuno and Wongkhomthong (1981b); Savetamalya (1996) and, for a convincing diachronic analysis, Kullavanijaya, this volume. Comrie (1996) treats clauses of this type comparatively with particular attention to Japanese. Morev (1994) describes possessive constructions. For reciprocals, Bee (1972) comes to grips with the poly-functional [kan^{33}], variously a reciprocal, gathered-plural marker and male first-person pronominal form.

Constructions and their functions of sentences with copular forms or equatives [pen^{33}] and [khu':^{33}] are taken up by Kuno and Wongkhomthong (1980, 1981a). As part of the wider picture, Warotamasikkhadit (1969, 1976a) treats other idiosyncrasies of the verb [pen^{33}] along with verbless sentences.

A postverbal nominal in a construction that might seem SVO superficially on inspection might not be a typical O-type patient semantically: it might turn out to have a locative, manner or instrumental function. Instrumental constructions are described by Warotamasikkhadit (1986). The postverbal position can also accommodate affected body-part terms, e.g. in pain expressions. These introduce the issue of how pain is represented and how this affects construction choice, as discussed by Diller (1980) and by Iwasaki (2002); also in a more comparative anthropological mode by Fabrega and Tyma (1976).

Quantification is taken up by Stine (1981). Whatever the theoretical approach, there can be little doubt that Thai quantificational phrases are prone to occur at the end of predicates, even if this means splitting an earlier noun phrase. Wongbiasaj (1979a) considers this type under quantifier floating. In a related area, Haas (1946) and Kullavanijaya (1997) give examples of a range of intensifying techniques, several of which involve final position as well.

3.3.8. Discourse, conversation and sociolinguistically-based studies

Not a few of the studies cited above consider units greater than single sentences, among them Panupong (1970), Grima (1986) and Hinds (1988b). Iwasaki and Ingapirom (2005), and in their other work, frequently rely on conversation-based examples and cogently take such wider contexts into account. Thomas (1988) argues that Thai grammar needs to recognize the language as 'paragraph-efficient' rather than as based on rules confined to single clauses, with Vongvipanond (1988) arguing for two types of linkage devices: 'macro-cohesive' and 'micro-cohesive'.

An early concern with discourse can be traced in the brief study of Hatton (1975). Vongvipanond (Ekniyom) (1977, 1982) was among the first to consider topicalization in thesis-length detail, along with other discourse-pragmatic phenomena. A similar focus informs Messenger's (1980) dissertation, analyzing theme in discourse. Interest in topic and topic-marking devices continues in the work of Iwasaki, e.g. (2004). Schmidt (1994) is a treatment of aspect in discourse.

1986 was an especially fruitful year for dissertations devoted to Thai discourse by native speakers. Burusphat (1986) presents a comprehensive discourse analysis based on narrative folklore, with texts presented in a convenient appendix, fully transcribed, glossed and translated. Chanawangsa (1986) studies cohesion from several perspectives, while Chodchoey (1986) uses transcribed materials to uncover strategies in oral discourse.

Conversational Analysis (CA) refers to micro-analysis of discourse along sociological lines, including special attention to pauses, repetitions, self-corrections, kinesics, etc., usually ignored in other frameworks. Moerman (1988) presents stunning examples of the insights that this style of analysis can reveal. An extra dimension of complexity in his study is the combination of Northern Thai, Lue and Central Thai in the text material, which is presented in meticulous oral transcriptions. Bilmes (1992) makes similar points. Turn-taking and speaker overlap is of interest in these studies, with Hinds (1988) providing a provocative parallel between Thai driving behavior and informal conversational interaction. While filled pauses are also of interest in CA, Chaimanee (1996) instead devotes attention to them in a comparative study of native and non-native speakers' hesitations.

In other frameworks, an early study considering interpersonal issues in discourse organization is Hatton's (1978) analysis of first-person reference in narratives. Using natural conversation, Hartmann (1993) describes communication in market-places, with the more general thesis-length study of Baron (Meepoe) (2001) analyzing reference to persons in conversation. Patrakom (1977) deals with similar issues from a more philosophical perspective, developing a hermeneutic approach to the characterization of persons. Neill (1989) explicitly develops a synthetic view of discourse as an interaction of grammar, rhetoric and background socio-cultural knowledge.

Khanittanan (1987a, 1987b, 1988b) uncovers diachronic trends in discourse genre and makes a compelling case for the evolution of a more 'autonomous' and abstract type of Thai, partly as the result of different communicative needs arising from modernizing social trends. This genre is less tied to traditional constraints of immediate interpersonal communication, apt to use abstract nominalizations and to make nominal material explicit. In a similar vein, differences between spoken and written discourse are clarified by Chodchoey (1988). Person (1996) turns attention to specialized genre: oral sermons of a Buddhist monk.

For Thai-Japanese comparisons, see Ruetaivan's (1999) study on how motion events are represented in narrative discourse.

3.3.9. Semantics and lexical fields

Several of the syntactic studies already cited show a strong semantic focus. The distinctive feature framework is used by Cooke (1965) in his comparative study of pronominal reference. Hiranburana (1978) develops a related hierarchical-taxonomy approach to classifying Thai classifiers, with several works of Placzek (e.g. 1992) producing a more finely-tuned analysis with particular semantic attention to shape. Gething (1986) discusses the extent to which distinctive features relate to cultural matters. As mentioned above, Thepkanjana's work (e.g. 1986) is notable for uncovering how semantics of verb classes can constrain the makeup of serial verb constructions.

Compounding has attracted semantic attention. The studies cited with regard to compounding [cay^{33}] 'heart, mind' to yield emotional terminology treat semantics as well as syntax. Juntanamalaga's (1992) study classifies the cluster of meanings associated with [hua^{24}] 'head' as it occurs in compounds. Vongvipanond (1992a) presents a substantial semantic and syntactic analysis of compounds where component parts are synonyms.

Additional studies link meaning with syntactic constructions in specific semantic fields. As mentioned, Thai pain terms are described in a comparative context by Fabrega and Tyma (1976) and by Diller (1980), who points to interesting syntactic features of these constructions. Their syntactic analysis is substantially advanced by Iwasaki (2002). A similar topic, traditional Thai disease terminology, is developed in a more ethnographic study by Bamber (1987). Still relating to physiology but in a cheerier subfield, Reed (1976) produces a semantic analysis of Thai gastronomic terms.

Representative thesis-length treatments of semantic topics include Gething (1972) and Terayanont (1988). Varied approaches are attested. Gething (1968, 1972) develops a structural redundancy methodology which he applies to analysis of nominals. His later work (1975, 1979) treats the semantics of locatives and other expressions with comparative reference to Lao. Diller (1994), in a comparative volume, attempts to address issues raised in the 'semantic primitives' enterprise. Folk taxonomy is the focus of studies by Simmonds (1978) and by Stott (1978), describing vernacular forest nomenclature. Historical semantics is taken up by Khanittanan and Placzek (1982), who trace how inherited Tai 'psychic' vocabulary, such as [khwan^{24}] '(roughly) psyche, spirit', has undergone semantic readjustment with the introduction of Indic loans such as [win^{33}ya:n^{33}] '(roughly) soul'. Another historical study of anthropological interest is that of Gething (1977).

Toponyms as a reflection of culture, social organization and environment are treated in impressive studies of Hartmann (2007) and Prasitrathsint (2007b). These link names of villages and other geographical units in Thailand to the wider Tai context, along with consideration of the Southeast Asian ecosystem and socio-political factors.

Kinship: of anthropological merit and impact are studies of Thai kinship terms and their extended usages. Gething (1986a) discusses distinctive features organizing Thai kinship and occupational terms. In a more extended study, Prasitrathsint (2001) presents a componential analysis of the complex system with useful comparative references. For diachronic/comparative development, one could consult also Black Tai (Fippinger, 1971) and check Strecker's (1980, 1984) Proto-Tai reconstructions. Formative studies are by Benedict (1943, 1945), with Chinese comparisons. Also of interest to anthropologists is the fact that Thai speakers appear to enjoy 'disrupting' their lexically normative kinship system in manners exotic (to outsider anthropologists, at least): parental terms [pho':[42]] 'father' and [mae:[42]] 'mother' are used by parents (among others) in referring to or addressing their children: thus, one calls one's daughter 'mother'; but the daughter may call her mother [mae:[42]] too. Also, these terms may precede children's given names or nicknames in the manner of a title. There is yet more: sibling terms are the widely used in address and reference among spouses; see Haas (1969).

3.4. SOCIOLINGUISTIC, COMPARATIVE AND HISTORICAL STUDIES

3.4.1. Sociolinguistic perspectives on Thailand

Studies cited above dealing with pronouns, kinship terms, speech-act particles and discourse are especially likely to be of interest to sociolinguists. In this subsection we note more general descriptions of the rather complex setting in Thailand important in understanding communicative functions of Central Thai in their social setting. For those requiring an overview of Thailand's sociolinguistic situation, Premsrirat (2006) is recommended. The issue of *International Journal of the Sociology of Language* 186 (2007), devoted to Thai sociolinguistics, includes range of current work, some mentioned below. For those interested in the development of the subfield of Thai sociolinguistics, comparisons could be made with the sociolinguistic review of Debyasuvarn (1973) and also with an issue of the journal *Language Sciences* 10 (1988), devoted to papers on Thai sociolinguistics of that era. Roop's (1969) earlier study of language diversity remains useful for perspective.

Beebe (1975, 1976, 1981) presents an impressive set of Labovian studies correlating articulatory alternatives with variables like occupation, age and gender. There is also treatment of these issues a language-learning context by Brown (1967), who usefully distinguishes colloquial 'Bangkok Thai' from the standard language; the former variety shows cluster simplification, substitution of /l/ for /r/, etc.

Multilingualism and language hierarchy in Thailand is the theme of the impressive and informative survey of Smalley (1994), expanding his (1988) introduction. For Smalley, Thailand's local dialects and minority languages are part of a hierarchical structure with standard Central Thai at the top. Speakers tend to become bilingual or multilingual in varieties positioned over them in the hierarchical model.

Following from Smalley's observations, investigators find that local dialects of the Tai family in Thailand are by now most frequently components in speakers' bidialectal (or multilingual) competence: outside of the Central-speaking area virtually all speakers with basic public schooling have at least a functionally passive competence in Central Thai, although active competence and most daily-life communication may be in a local variety. These local varieties are not infrequently mixed with or influenced by the standard language. Chamberlain (1972) and Khanittanan (1973) describe tonal influence of the standard language on Northeastern or Lao varieties. Diller (1979) investigates how tones and segments in Southern and Central Thai are systematically combined in sociolinguistically salient ways. In particular, hybridization is described whereby Southern Thai tones are articulated for what is otherwise Central Thai. This can apply even to the standardized written form. For the north, the interplay of Kam-mueang (Northern Thai), Lue and Central Thai in their sociological context is amply elucidated and documented by Moerman (1965, 1988) in a closely-focused conversational-analysis framework. Similarly, but in a different framework, Premsrirat's (2007) study of endangered languages in Thailand calls attention to this urgent line of research, recalling Bradley's (1992) discussion of the disappearance of Ungong. Morita (2003, 2007) studies the important question of assimilation and language shift among Sino-Thai speakers; her bibliographies are a useful resource for those interested in this issue. From another quarter, Chunsuvimol (1980) considers communicative networks of Thai workers in Singapore.

Dialectology studies of local and regional varieties in Thailand are too numerous to be listed here: many are catalogued and described by Tingsabadh (1984), with leading studies discussed in Smalley (1994). Many fine theses completed in Thai universities describe individual local varieties. Brown (1962) and Hartmann (1980) treat issues of subgrouping. These works and sources mentioned therein can be consulted for Kam-mueang (Northern Thai), Southern Thai and so-called Isan Thai (essentially Lao varieties spoken in Thailand). Chantavibulya (Panupong) (1959) appears to be the first detailed linguistic description of a local dialect (Songkhla, Southern Thai). For comparative reference, a remarkable nearby Southern tonal system is acoustically and physiologically analysed by Rose (1997).

Central Thailand is far from uniform in local speech. For the central-west area, Suphanburi Thai is described by Tingsabadh (1988, 1992), who makes the intriguing and methodologically challenging observation that speakers of this variety really cannot cite their local forms in isolation. Court (1972) describes the unusual tonal system of Traat.

Early landmark comparisons with focus on tone compare varieties within Thailand, and sometimes beyond: Haas (1958); Egerod (1961); Jones (1965). Brown (1962, 1965) is the first book-length work to cover the entire country in detail. It establishes a convenient visual display for comparing tonal systems and remains a valuable dialectology resource. Many later works describe new varieties or provide further analyses, e.g. Strecker (1979); see Tingsabadh (1984).

Sociolinguistic and political commentary on Thai as a standard national language is provided by Aesrivongse (1984, in Thai), whose viewpoint is summarized and extended by Diller (1988, 1991).

3.4.2. Registers, polite speech and special styles

Studies of conversational Thai by Moerman (1977, 1988), Peyasanitwong (1981, 1986), Hinds (1988a), Chodchoey (1986), and by Iwasaki and Ingkaphirom (2000, 2005) elucidate features of colloquial spoken Thai that set it off from the standard written form. Differences are directly confronted by Tiancharoen (1987) and by Chodchoey (1988). Khanittanan (1988b) demonstrates how written Thai has evolved in an 'autonomous' direction not anchored in aspects of personal interaction as regularly encoded in colloquial conversation.

Native speakers of Thai find it easy to characterize samples from written and spoken registers in evaluative terms like [supha:p^{52}] 'polite' or its opposite. In effect this presupposes a diglossic arrangement which includes the distinguishing of lexical pairs that can be described as 'higher' and 'lower' in terms of speech-level, although the relationship among resulting registers is far from a simple binary one. Diller (1985, 1993) suggests that both lexical and syntactic evaluations contribute to this continuum, but it should not be concluded that written Thai always shows 'high' selections and spoken Thai 'low' ones. Sometimes written Thai opts for 'lower' expressions as in journalism: Khanittanan (1994, 2007) shows how styles are manipulated for effects in different segments of news presentation; see also Srinarawat's (2007) informative work on political slang, another use of 'lower' expressions for effect.

Politeness markers and similar indicators of interpersonal dynamics are ubiquitous and especially salient in colloquial Thai. These categories are coded by various means: most obviously by address and reference forms and by final particles such as polite final particles [kha^{45}], [kha^{52}] (female speaker) and [khrap^{45}] (male speaker) and the less polite [ha^{45}], [wa^{45}], etc., (Bandhumedha, 1979; Peyasaniwong 1981; Cooke 1989), but also by various lexical options along the high-low continuum mentioned above. This continuum generally reflects ascribed deference as well as formality. But the system is complex. Lexical selections in formal Thai cannot be taken as necessarily indicative of marking interpersonal deference, e.g. in formal sources high-status and low-status males alike may be referred to as [na:y^{33} X]: 'Mr. X', [na:y^{33} thak^{45}sin^{24}] 'Mr Thaksin' (a former Prime Minister); [na:y^{33} dae:ng^{33}] 'Mr Daeng' (an unemployed unskilled manual worker)'. Compare more colloquial Thai: [na:y^{33} X] seems less deferential than [khun^{33} X] 'Mr. X' (lit. 'honorable X'). Note that [khun^{33} X] is uncommon in formal Thai, e.g. in official reports, etc. Even syntactic choices are implicated in this complex. Khanittanan (1988a) elucidates strategies and issues with great insight, as do Kummer (1992) and Bilmes (2002), while Deephuengton (1992) turns to disagreement strategies. Work of Moerman, Hinds and Iwasaki keep such factors in mind as well.

Thai is remarkable for special registers relating to institutions of royalty and monkhood, although the lexical makeup of these registers shares many selections with the 'high' or 'polite' [supha:p^{52}] level mentioned above. Particularly given the impact of broadcast media, most Thai speakers are at least passively familiar with the hundreds of lexical substitutions these registers prescribe, if not always able to control them actively. Haas (1951) and Jones (1971) lay out the complexity of the system, especially as regards degrees of deference ascribed to ranks of royal persons. Gedney (1961) provides a convenient outline of these registers, while Kanasut-Roengpitya (1973) documents them in greater detail. Diller (2006b) also gives a sketch of 'royal Thai' calling attention to some of its derivational processes and suggesting that functionally it shows some parallels with special avoidance genres in other languages.

Poetic Thai and other literary genres have their own special vocabulary and syntax and show points of contact with the type of language used with royalty and the monkhood. Also, the formal metrical requirements of traditional poetry provide a number of clues both as to abstract phonology and as to how Thai may have developed diachronically. Linguists undertaking work of this type include Warotamaskkhadit (1968a); Bickner (1981, 1992); Chittasophon (1984); Gedney (1980, 1989b); Hartmann (1989); Hudak (1990 and this volume).

3.4.3. Loans, contact and bilingualism

General contact issues are introduced in traditional philological studies, see Anuman Rajadhon (1961, 1981). A linguistic orientation is taken by Warie (1973, 1979). Sometimes overlooked is the importance of foreign language education as an aspect of contact, considered by Chirasombutti (2007).

In the preceding section, lexical items of the higher diglossic registers were noted. These in general are etymologically not inherited Tai vocabulary but are loans introduced over many centuries. Perhaps the most concentrated and conspicuous loan element in Thai is vocabulary from Indic languages Pali and Sanskrit. Gedney (1947), in a work still of great value, presents a formal analysis and catalogue of many hundreds of words of this sort, mainly nouns and verbs. Historically, Indic vocabulary in Thai can be classified into two types: (i) traditional loans, accepted into Thai from the thirteenth to nineteenth centuries; and (ii) coined neologisms created in the twentieth centuries through official institutional action. There are hundreds of both types in current use and distinguishing them is often not a simple matter. Type (i) were typically introduced in pre-modern times through Khmer or Mon intermediaries, subject to assimilation processes in those languages first, or else from Pali Buddhist sources, i.e., terms originally used in religious contexts came be used more generally. Most of these loans are transparent in provenance, but not all. Harris (2007b) convincingly shows how Mon or Khmer mediated Sanskrit *marica* 'hot (capiscum) pepper', borrowed into Thai with sound changes, resulting now in [phrik^{45}].

Type (ii) loans were created by literary and technical authorities in an environment of modernization requiring lexical enrichment, but coupled with nationalistic or esthetic sensibilities disparaging direct loans from English or other Western languages. The solution was to code the Western-based concepts with neologisms constructed from Indic (mainly Sanskrit) morphemes. The neo-Indic forms created also conformed analogically to various assimilated prototypes already established through type (i) forms; for example, there was no attempt to pronounce neo-Sanskrit material the way it would be pronounced in India. Sometimes shifts have occurred in the designated semantics of type (ii) items, especially those of the 1920s or 1930s. Wan Waithayakorn (1970), one of the key figures in the coining process, and Prasithrathsint (1994) discuss the specifics of how these (ii) items were introduced. See also Court (1984).

Austroasiatic, Austronesian and Sino-Tibetan language families have contributed many vocabulary items to Thai at different diachronic periods. Relatively recent loans from Khmer, Malay and southern Chinese varieties like Taeciw are often transparent, while earlier strata feel to Thai speakers like authentic Thai vocabulary and require linguistic scholarship to deduce provenance. Careful analysis and correct differentiation of diachronic strata from various sources of vocabulary now used in Thai can be considered still in the infancy stage. Surely however such studies are a precondition for convincing discussions of remote or ultimate Tai and Tai-Kadai relationships, be they genetic or some form of contact, if that distinction can indeed be maintained.

Contact with Khmer and other Austroasiatic languages is a topic pursued by Khanittanan (2001) and Diller (2002), who both argue for an early period of substantial Thai-Khmer bilingualism. Evidence for this claim lies in the sweep and magnitude of Thai vocabulary that is Khmer-derived (Varasarin 1984). While some occurs at the higher speech-levels, much is basic and currently in every-day usage: [camu:k^{11}] 'nose'; [tapho:k^{42}] 'hip'; [khu':^{33}] 'to be (equivalent)'; [doe:n^{33}] 'to walk'; [koe:t^{11}] 'be born'; [set^{11}] 'to finish'. More tellingly: a number of auxiliaries, conjunctions, prepositions and other grammatical formatives are clearly of Khmer or Mon-Khmer provenance, as is the disyllabic lexical pattern, seen in 'nose' above, now so thoroughly incorporated into Thai that it seems native.

Turning to Austronesian, Suthiwan (1992) focuses on Malay loans into Central Thai. She is able to show several different diachronic strata on the basis of tone assignment and stop devoicing. One Ayudhya-era level is associated with a Thai court adaptation of the Javanese and Malay Panji tales and many of the loans are literary in character, but other strata have toponyms, names of fruits, etc., that are in common usage. Suthiwan also considers Malay loans into Southern Thai, as does Court (1975), who includes insightful diachronic deductions and disussion. More contentious are the earlier levels still. Schlegel (1902) advanced the hypothesis, revived and enhanced (?) by Benedict (1942, 1975, etc.), that Proto-Tai vocabulary shows enough plausible Austronesian cognates to support a standard genetic (hence Austro-Tai) relationship. This topic is pursued in detail elsewhere, whether *pro*, *con* or prevaricating: (e.g., Gedney 1976; Diffloth 1977; Reid 1984; Hartmann 1986b; Matisoff (1990); Thurgood (1994); Diller 2000; Ostapirat 2004).

Another important contact domain concerns Chinese relationships, again a matter of contention. Work of Egerod (1957, 1959b), Manomaivibool (1975, 1976, 2000), Li (1976) and Luo (2000; also this volume and sources mentioned therein) suggest that there are very early, if not genetically inherited, strata of Chinese in the Tai (and Tai-Kadai) languages. Manomaivibool (1976) carefully differentiates early strata, e.g. [plu'ak^{11}] 'peel; bark' versus [phiw^{24}] 'skin', which she takes to be from the same Chinese lexical source 膚, but reflecting different stages. Luo shows the magnitude, basic nature, semantic spread and emphasizes regular correspondence patterns of many items involved. Thurgood (2007a), on the other hand, calls attention to an irregularly-corresponding lexical group taken by Gedney (1979) as evidence for a new set of Proto-Tai initials. Thurgood suggests rather that the items in question represent Chinese loans of various strata, hence the irregularity. This problem is perhaps indicative of more general methodological tensions attending Chinese-Tai (or Tai-Kadai) diachronic research. Whatever the nature of the ultimate Sino-Tibetan relationship, vocabulary of early eras (e.g. terms for numbers, body parts, basic verbs, etc., on at least the Proto-Tai level) is not to be confused with much more recent southern Chinese (mainly Swatow/Taeciw) loans into Central Thai (Egerod 1959a). Unlike the earlier vocabulary, later items are felt by speakers of Thai to be 'Chinese' and sometimes even have phonological properties that effectively mark them as such (e.g., unaspirated initial stops in items with high or rising tones, precluded as a regular possibility for inherited Tai vocabulary). Such vocabulary refers especially to foods, cooking processes, business terms and other transparently Chinese cultural concepts, but also to some pronouns now commonly heard in Thai speech, at least on Bangkok streets. Of relevance here are Morita's (2007) work on Chinese-Thai assimilation and Srinarawat's (1988) on language use of Chinese-background speakers in Bangkok. These are interesting to contrast with Huang's (2007) study of Zhuang-Chinese assimilation.

Portuguese, Persian, Arabic and other languages recalling Indian Ocean pre-modern commerce have brought into Thai designations for grapes, cabbage, roses, soap and other cultural items; see Harris (2007a, 2007b).

English has had a moderate to heavy impact on Thai, explored sociolinguistically by Khanittanan (1979), Nacaskul (1979) and by Chutisilp (1984). Work on the development of the so-called adversative passive marked by [thu:k^{11}] 'to undergo' often notes the use (or misuse) of the construction in translating English passives (e.g. Prasithrathsint 1988; Diller 1993). Lexically, of historical interest is the fact that many English loans like [sathe:^{33}chan^{52}] 'station', commonly used in the nineteenth century, were replaced by Sanskrit neologisms in the early twentieth century, such [satha:^{24}ni:^{33}]. In this case, the Indic neologism even recalls the form of the English prototype as well as its etymological connections (note Proto-Indo-European *sta:* 'stand', appearing in both the Sanskrit and English forms). In a sense then hundreds of such Sanskrit neologisms are an attempt to represent English concepts semantically but through portraying them in neo-Indic phonological guise. This is more in keeping with early twentieth-century nationalistic and literary sensibilities than would have been the simple inclusion of barely assimilated English forms. Nonetheless, sensibilities shift and recent decades have not avoided a substantial influx of direct English borrowing (Senawong 1992). A torrent of such loans now imbues 'pop' culture, teen slang, sports reporting and technology. Commercial establishments like tailor shops frequently display transliterated English names. Human nicknames like 'Nut', 'Golf' and 'Bird' are analyzed by Nacaskul (1987), who clarifies the phonology of such loans; even dogs get English names. The humanities and law, on the other hand, tend to eschew direct English borrowing and such loans are regularly absent from proclamations, constitutions, etc. For the English-to-neoIndic process, see Wan Waithayakorn (1970); Prasithrathsint (1994). Gandour (1979) and Bickner (1986b) discuss the complicated issue of how tone is assigned to English loans. Thai-English bilingualism is studied by Cefola (1981) and by Davis and Schoknecht (1994). Psycholinguistic studies of Burnham, et al. (1992) are of relevance here as well. In reverse, Cohen (1987) provides an entertaining look at expatriate foreigners' acquisition (or not) of Thai in Bangkok.

3.4.4. Comparative studies

Several studies compare standard Central Thai with other Tai varieties of Thailand, some with focus on attitudinal factors: Northern (Lanna) Thai (Pankhuenkhat 1976; Nokaeo 1989); Yong (Davies 1979); Northeastern Thai (Palikupt 1983).

Comparisons with Khmer (Cambodian) include focus on predicates by Martini (1956, 1957); descriptions of remarkable syntactic parallelism by Nacaskul (1971) and by Huffman (1973); study of complement constructions by Poo-israkij (1995); and diachronic lexical analysis Varasarin (1984). Khanittanan (2001) and Diller (2003) develop diachronic proposals related to these comparative studies.

Comparative classifier studies are instructive in several ways. Jones (1970) presents a landmark survey of Southeast systems. It establishes areal patterning of classifier syntax, especially among Tai languages: classifiers follow their head noun as in Thai to the west and south, but precede it, as in Tai varieties like Nung or Zhuang to the east and north. (As for an isogloss, a leading Black Tai linguist, the late Cam Trong, told me that both patterns are used in his language for different purposes. In fact, most speakers of Central Thai admit some flexibility in special contexts, such as the regular [phi: ^{42}-no':ng^{45} so':ng^{24} khon^{33}] 'two siblings' as compared to the more restricted [so':ng^{24} khon^{33} phi: ^{52}-no':ng^{45}] 'both of them, the siblings'. As for particular lexical items, work of Jacob (1965) indicates that Khmer has supplied Thai with several classifiers and vice-versa. Conklin (1981) is a comparative study encompassing Tai (including Thai) and Austronesian classifiers. In a cross-language survey of classifiers and language standardization, Barz and Diller (1985) examine evaluative and normative feelings about classifiers, found to differ across Indo-Aryan and Southeast Asian languages. For Thai especially, sociolinguistic constraints are fine-tuned and crucial in many Thai classifier selections, as established by Juntanamalaga (1988). Thai is placed in a comparative Tai context by Burusphat (2007), who presents a comprehensive treatment of animate classifiers; see also Morev (2000).

Southeast Asian language comparisons including Thai are presented by Downer (1963); Nguyen Dang Liem (1974); Clark (1978, 1992, 1994); Clark and Prasithrathsint (1985). Cooke (1965) considers pronominal reference in Thai, Burmese and Vietnamese.

Interest in Thai-Vietnamese comparison can be traced back at least to Martini (1950) and to Honey and Simmonds (1963). Masuko and and Kiritani (1991) compare Indonesian and Thai consonant articulation. See also Shimizu (1989). Syntactic comparisons of Urak Lawoi, Malay and Thai are presented by Hogan (1978). Chinese and Thai treatments of zero anaphora are compared by Cole (1984). Egerod (1971) includes Thai and Chinese in a study of phonation types. Xing (1955, in Chinese) compares Chinese and Thai 'offspring' compounds. Substantial comparative studies involving Thai and other Asian languages seem regrettably sparse, but include the studies of Japanese and Thai formulaic expressions by Wongkhomthong (1985) and of self-reference in these languages by Chirasombutti (1995).

Thai-English comparisons often have an applied-linguistics focus. Pioneering studies include Kruatrachue (1960) on phonology and Chaiyaratana (1961) on syntax. A sample of others includes studies on pronominalization, considered by Chomaitong (1976); on definiteness, by Lamchote (1971); on aspect, by Noochoochai (1978); and on intonation, by Kanchanathat (1977). For applied studies featuring error analysis, translation problems or difficulties Thai speakers have with specific features of English, representative studies are by Ariyapitipun (1988), Meemeskul-Martin (1984), Palmer (1969), Richards (1968), Schmidt (1988), Suwattee (1981), and by Van Syoc (1964).

3.4.5. Historical and philological studies

Diachronic sources relating to Tai family and to Tai-Kadai are mentioned in section 1.1. This and the next subsection mainly mention works with a focus specifically on (standard and/or Central) Thai, or else the language of Sukhothai; however, controversial hypotheses tracing how Central Thai has developed over the past seven centuries depend crucially on comparative-historical Tai background to provide plausible starting points for presumed Thai-internal diachronic changes. These hypotheses also refer to orthographic history. Even though some may devalue study of written sources as being institutionally 'philology' rather than linguistics, I see no good reasons to disregard orthographic evidence when trying to unravel Thai diachronic sound change.

See Anuman Rajadhon (1961, 1981), Hartmann (1986a), Court (1996) and Diller (1996b 2001a) for historical hypotheses as to how Indic-based orthographies and literary culture, including Thai writing, have developed and spread in the Southeast Asian context. The inventor(s) of Thai writing certainly had Khmer orthography in mind, and perhaps Mon, but significant innovations were introduced as well. These included tone-marking, horizontal rather than vertical representation of clusters, phasing out of redundant vowel-initial graphemes and the creation of new segmental symbols as needed. The latter were usually accomplished through modifications made to existing Khmer-type letters representing similar sounds; thus a new [f] symbol was an enhancement of a given [ph] letter. The impression is strong that the original impetus for Sukhothai script involved great care and attention to Tai sound-system detail along with a semiotic attempt to represent perceived phonetic closeness through graphical similarity. Result: diachronic linguists should take this orthography seriously.

Although it is clear that Thai orthography in general can be traced back to South Indic scripts, intermediate points are still professionally debated. The tradition that Thai writing originated in the reign of King Ramkhaeng of Sukhothai (r. approx. 1279-1298) has been challenged but to date no material evidence of a different origin has been adduced. Also, the historical relations of Thai and Lao scripts are somewhat contentious, although existing material evidence strongly indicates that a Sukhothai-type script had spread east to Lao-speaking areas by the early sixteenth century and constituted the prototype for standard Lao writing. Mon writing, on the other hand, was the basis for Lanna (Northern Thai) script, currently under resuscitation, also known to the east as *tham* (i.e. 'dharma script', as it was used for Buddhist texts). Discussion and further sources are included in Danvivathana (1987) and in Diller (1996a). Hudak (1986) describes official simplifications in Thai spelling during the 1940's, later rescinded.

For those with interest in how lexical, syntactic and semantic aspects of the Thai language has evolved since the Sukhothai era of about seven centuries ago, a good place to start is with the commentaries and texts of Na Nagara and Griswold (1992). They present and discuss key literary sources of the Sukhothai period, although their perspectives are mainly philological and historical. A difficulty encountered in some philological work is the tendency to assume that Sukhothai texts are a direct reflection of earlier stages of Central Thai, or even coincide phonetically with modern Thai, whereas Sukhothai Thai probably stood in a less direct line with it. Note that Brown, 1962, 1965, considers Southern Thai varieties to be the more direct descendants of Sukhothai Thai. To their credit, Na Nagara and Griswold (1992) frequently cite cognate material from non-Central dialects. Weroha (1992) too provides comparisons with local varieties. Mikami (1984) summarizes other features of Thai of the early period, while Bamroograks (1987) makes significant progress in understanding Sukhothai discourse patterns. Prasithrathsint (2007), in a convincing comparative and diachronic study of nominalization, shows that at least the type with prefixal [khwa:m^{A2}]- 'matter (of...);' was present in the language of Sukhothai, with nominalization on the increase in succeeding centuries.

For the complex diachronic development of the pronominal system, Strecker's (1984) treatment of Proto-Tai pronouns is a good place to start, with dialect studies such as Filbeck (1973b) useful to keep in mind. Studies like these indicate that the Thai system is the result of substantial diachronic shifting and innovation. Iamchinda (1992, in Thai) is a seven-hundred year survey covering the period over which written data on pronouns are available.

Jones (1971) makes accessible King Chulalongkorn's important essay on Thai titles and ranks, a study nicely complemented by Tingsabadh and Prasithrathsint (1986, in Thai), who analyze the use of address terms over some centuries.

Etymology, areal contact and comparative-historical semantic shifting are insightfully treated by Matisoff (1986, 1992), who analyzes kinship terms and analogues of Thai 'heart/mind' compounds in [cay ^{33}]. These are considered in the wider Southeast Asian context, however issues are raised that need to be kept in mind when focusing on semantic shifts more specifically in Thai. An especially noteworthy study of the latter type is that of Khanittanan and Placzek (1982), who show how the inherited item [khwan^{24}] 'spirit, soul' underwent semantic reorganization when an Indic term [win^{33}ya:n^{33}] with similar meaning was introduced in Buddhist contexts. For more on etymology, see Burnay and Coedès (1920); Li (1956, 1971, 1977); Anuman Rajadhon (1961, 1981); and Thai-language sources such as Na Nakhon (1973).

Turning to diachronic phonology and phonetics regarding segmentals, we can surmise that the vowel system of Central Thai is an area where Khmer comparisons are merited, but inscriptional Khmer is not without its own interpretive challenges (Jacob 1965, etc.). Tai-internal accounts of earlier vowel inventories and of how they have evolved into the current Central Thai system have led to divergent proposals, especially regarding vowel-length (Sarawit 1973; Hartmann 1976b; Li 1977; Brown 1979; Strecker 1983; Luksaneeyanawin 1992). In any event, Sukhothai orthographic vowel distinctions show affinities both with Angkorian inscriptional Khmer and also with modern Thai, even though the varieties may not be in direct linear relationship. Dhananjayananda (1997) calls attention to one difference: what is now the [e]/[e:] distinction is not marked until the seventeenth century. The same general picture perhaps applies to long-short distinctions in low front and back vowels [ae] and [o'] as well. But does this mean that the distinctions were pronounced earlier but not marked in text until later, or that new contrastive articulations originated subsequently as well? Diachronic aspects of [ay] and [aw] sequences are elucidated in work of Bickner (1992). Finally, as L-Thongkum, Teeranon and Intajamornrak (2007) have convincingly established, diachronic consideration of vowel length change and of tonogenesis, considered below, must be considered as intertwined issues.

Work on Thai syntactic shifts has been less controversial but has a potential contribution to make to typological studies. Analyses of Sukhothai discourse by Bamroograks (1987) and Prasithrathsint (2007) have been mentioned. Grammaticalization, mentioned in 3.6 above, has been an important process in Thai diachronic syntax but I am not aware of a comprehensive text-based study organizing just how all relevant changes have occurred historically. Khanittanan (1987a, 1987b, 1988b) and Prasithrathsint (1988, 1996) have produced leading work in establishing how syntactic patterns of written Thai have shifted in the past two centuries or so, whether qualitatively or quantitatively. Prasithrathsint has traced in great detail the increase of passive-like constructions and nominalizations in written sources. Khanittanan, using a succession of royal prose compositions, identifies a number of features that characterized evolving prose writing of the mid-nineteenth century: zero anaphora of understood subjects; topic-initial sentences; paratactic constructions rather than marking with overt conjunctions; lists with quantifiers in final position. These generally reflect features today associated with spoken Thai (Messenger 1980; Chodchoey 1988; Hinds 1988a).

Over time, a new style of formal written Thai has taken shape, characterized by denser nominalization, clausal embedding and other types of subordination and more overt specification of nominals, rather than leaving zero anaphors to be construed. This has coincided with increased normative interest in specifying what is 'correct' Thai (Diller 1993, 2001a). Lexical selections also play a role here, with higher diglossic choices and technical Indic vocabulary characteristic (Wan Waithayakorn 1970; Prasithrathsint 1994). Resulting in what Khanittanan (1988b) refers to as a more 'autonomous' style, discourse of this type is comparatively depersonalized and even aloof from Thai interpersonal social dynamics. 'Autonomous' Thai does not encode a range of interpersonal communicative factors the way the lower colloquial style typically does with particles, finely calibrated address-reference selections and other choices. This style of written Thai is currently maintained, but as mentioned in subsection 3.4.2 above, written Thai genres also admit a more colloquial type of Thai as well.

Contrasts between these written styles are sometimes manipulated for special effects, such as to produce eye-catching journalistic headlines in a lower more oral style, while providing 'serious' content reporting in the higher more autonomous style (Khanittanan 2007). Also, some Thai authors are adroit in exploiting the difference through stark contrasts in descriptive passages versus dialogue; Chat Kopchitti would be an example. On the other hand, many educated Thai speakers (academics in particular) can, when occasion requires it, produce a spontaneous type of oral discourse showing many features of the higher written style. A methodological consequence of this syntactic vibrancy seems to be that native Thai speakers may disagree with each other as to grammaticality judgments (Diller and Khanittanan 2002). One can hope that future scholarship will contribute to more understanding of these interacting oral and written genres and of their role in the constitution of Thai linguistic competence.

3.4.6. Tonogenesis and its quandaries

In diachronic phonology, one area where an understanding of Tai-wide issues impinges crucially on the more parochial history of Central Thai concerns tonal development. Also, since some of the crucial evidence generally accepted for sound changes is from written texts, matters of orthographic interpretation and development become involved as well.

The Thai writing system has been subject to diachronic phonology in some ways and resistant to it in others. Methodologically, it has been taken as important tool in uncovering and analyzing sound changes relating to tone, thus meriting linguistic concern. Most authorities posit an original (or Proto-Tai) system of three tones for open syllables and limited tonal options for stopped syllables; in general, they took one of the open tones (Li 1977). A sweeping devoicing process is thought to have subsequently occurred affecting voiced obstruents, along with loss of aspiration in formerly aspirated sonorants. For Thai (and Lao), the devoiced stops further acquired aspiration. Lexical items with the newly-arising initials were kept from merger by consonant-induced allophonic tonal distinctions, which then became phonemic. That is, the new unaspirated fully-voiced sonorants (e.g. /m/ < *hm) and aspirated voiceless obstruents (e.g. /ph/ < *b) did not produce homophonic lexical mergers with vocabulary items with the original unaspirated sonorants (e.g. /m/ < *m) and aspirated stops (e.g. /ph/ < *ph). This complex shift is thought occurred after the codification of (Sukhothai) Thai writing, probably in the fourteenth and fifteenth centuries.

Some evidence for this change consists in spelling variation during the period and in environmental loans introduced before the change took place, such as Malay *durian*, *sago*, becoming Thai [thu^{45}rian^{33}], [sa:^{24}khu:^{33}] (Suthiwan 1992). Further evidence is the fact that Thai (following Sukhothai) orthography regularly represents the shifted sonorants with a digraph headed by (now) silent initial *h*- symbol, e.g. as *hm*, *hn*, *hl*; hence [luang^{24}] 'large, grand', written as though *hluang* to reflect the aspirated sonorant initial of the thirteenth century. If the initial sound had been a simple voiced sonorant or something else at the time, it is difficult to explain why that particular digraph was selected for the relevant vocabulary. To clinch the argument, there are also some early Thai loans into nearby Austroasiatic languages that preserve pre-shift initials like /hm/ (Gedney 1965).

In this scenario, the effect was to bifurcate the original tonal system. For Central Thai, devoicing was accompanied not only by aspiration of relevant stops but also by other sound changes in which phonation type of initial consonant affected tone. New tonal mergers took place as well. The result is the three classes of letters referred to as 'high', 'mid', and 'low', with different tonal effects. Central Thai happens to have remerged in such a way as to distinguish five phonemic tones. Since the Thai writing system is widely considered to reflect the situation *before* these major shifts, interpreting its present complexity is in effect a matter of taking into account the results of the complex diachronic sound changes. It also means that the Thai and Lao writing systems are abstract in the sense that they can be interpreted in various ways to accommodate tonal systems of local dialects in Thailand and Laos, a fact with consequences for literacy policy.

A consequence of the changes sketched above is that in the first instance (the Sukhothai period) Thai tone markers [may^{45} e:k^{11}] and [mai^{45} tho:^{33}] would have had direct *phonetic* interpretations, whereas after the changes, their interpretation would become *phonologically abstract* leading to the variable values the markers now exhibit with different groups of consonants. The remaining two tone markers were added after the shifts mentioned above were complete, as can in fact be detected from their restricted distribution, although the physical shape of markers has been subject to shifting (the former cross symbol used for [mai^{45} tho:^{33}] is now used for [mai^{45}cat^{11}awaa^{33}]). Speculations as to the origin of the tone markers and how their interpretation must have shifted are offered in Diller (1996b), who considers Sanskrit chanting marks. Further perspectives range from the earlier work of Brown (1962), Jones (1965, 1966) and recent observations of L-Thongkum, Teeranon and Intajamornrak (2007).

A complication in the preceding model has been known for years, e.g. as discussed by Gedney (1947, sections 175-177), Brown (1965, section 2.3) and others. Not directly accounted for in the tonogenesis-devoicing process sketched above are Indic-provenance items like [bun^{33}] 'merit', ultimately from Pali *puñña*. These items would seem to imply a voicing process for stops $p > b$ and $t > d$ (but not $c > j$ or $k > g$). Note that this would work *in opposition* to the devoicing changes described above. If voicing for 'merit', etc., had originally occurred beforehand in an intermediate language like Old Khmer, why then was 'merit' not caught up in post-Sukhothai tonogenetic devoicing? On the other hand, if it was still pronounced with initial *p*- in Sukhothai times, why is it [bun^{33}] today, while inherited Tai vocabulary like [pa: ^{11}] 'jungle' does not show the same change? Solutions to this have differed. Maybe *puñña* had been previously assimilated in Old Khmer with a preglottalized initial such as [ʔbun^{A}] and it was this that was adopted by Sukhothai (bilingual?) speakers, treating it as having the same initial [ʔb] as in Tai words like [ʔba:n^{C}] 'village'. This escapes the problem for Thai by casting it back onto Old Khmer (why did the Khmers treat Indic p- this way?). The case seems not to be closed.

Many have contributed to the development of the tonogenetic line of research, from earlier scholars such as Bastian (1868), Bradley (1909a, 1909b) and Burnay (1927) on to professional publications more linguistic in orientation of Haudricourt, Gedney, Jones, Li and others. Brown (1962, 1995, 1975), Erikson (1975), Rischel (1984), L-Thongkum (1997), Thurgood (2007b), and L-Thongkum, Teeranon and Intajamornrak (2007) and sources therein present detailed articulatory hypotheses concerning tonogenesis. Anivan (1988) considers phonetic shifts in Central Thai tones in more recent times after establishment of the basic tonogenetic patterns.

Gedney (1985) discusses the vexed question of timing for the main tonogenetic changes. Loan-word evidence from Malay (Suthiwan 1992) was mentioned above for taking the Ayudhya-era fourteenth and fifteenth centuries as the period of changes for Thai. (Malay contact is more convincing for this line of argument than similar indications in Pali and Sanskrit loans, as at earlier stages the latter have come into Thai second-hand through Khmer or Mon, raising extra diachronic possibilities.) If this timing hypothesis is indeed the case, then a troublesome methodological issue arises. The majority of Tai varieties would need to have shared the same basic devoicing and tonogenetic sound changes: a great phonological upheaval over a wide and disparate area in a short a time. Only a few rather isolated varieties of the Sino-Vietnamese frontier area are reported as having escaped systematic devoicing (Haudricourt 1949; Ross 1996; L-Thongkum 1997). Zhuang dialects far removed in time, place and social dynamics from Central Thai would have had to undergo similar shifts. Following a normal application of the Comparative Method, without considering orthographic or loan evidence, one would need to project the changes much further back in time than the fourteenth century (see Jones 1965, 1966; Gedney 1985). Here indeed is an instance where the proto-Tai reconstructions that are accepted are of paramount importance in establishing how (Central) Thai has changed since the Sukhothai period. Is the Sukhothai starting-point positioned before or after the sweeping changes?

To make matters more complex, some, but by no means all, nearby Austroasiatic languages with classical writing systems or relevant evidence of other sorts appear to exhibit similar devoicing shifts, some involving vowel-related and/or phonation-related register phenomena. This includes Khmer, certainly critical in Thai's linguistic history. Further consideration of these sound-change issues is clearly merited. General consideration of the substantial Austroasiatic, and specifically Khmer, impact on Thai has been mentioned: see Nacaskul (1971), Huffman (1973), Varasarin (1984), L-Thongkum (1992), Khanittanan (2001) and Diller (2002). See also chapter 7.

REFERENCES

Abramson, Arthur S. (1962) 'The Vowels and Tones of Standard Thai: Acoustical Measurements and Experiments', *International Journal of American Linguistics* 28.2.3; publ. 20 of the Indiana University Research Center in Anthropology, Folklore, and Linguistics, Bloomington: Indiana University Press.

— (1971) 'Tonal Experiments with Whispered Thai', in A. Valdman (ed.) *Papers in Linguistics and Phonetics to the Memory of Pierre Delattre*, The Hague: Mouton, 31-44.

— (1972) 'Word-Final Stops in Thai', in Jimmy G. Harris and Richard B. Noss (eds) *Tai Phonetics and Phonology*, Bangkok: Central Institute of English Language, 1-7.

— (1978) 'Static and Dynamic Acoustic Cues in Distinctive Tones', *Language and Speech* 21.4: 319-325.

— (2001) 'The Stability of Distinctive Vowel Length in Thai', in M. R. Kalaya Tingsabadh and Arthur S. Abramson (eds), 13-26.

Abramson, Arthur S. (ed.) (1997) *Southeast Asian Linguistic Studies in Honour of Vichin Panupong*, Bangkok: Chulalongkorn University Press.

Abramson, Arthur S. and Ren, Nianqi (1990) 'Distinctive Vowel Length: Duration vs. Spectrum in Thai', *Journal of Phonetics* 18.2: 79-92.

Abramson, Arthur S. and Tingsabadh, K. (1999) 'Thai Final Stops: Cross-Language Perception', *Phonetica* 56.3/4: 111.

Aeosrivongse, Nidhi (1984) 'Phasa Thai matrathan kap kanmu'ang [Standard Thai and Politics]', *Phasa læ Nangsu'* 17: 11-37.

Anivan, Sarinee (1988) 'Evolution of Bangkok Tones', in Bamroongraks, Cholticha, Wilaiwan Khanittanan, et al. (eds), 7-21.

Anthony, Edward (1964) 'Verboid Constructions in Thai', in Albert H. Marwardt (ed.) *Studies in Languages and Linguistics in Honour of Charles C. Fries*, Ann Arbor, Michigan: English Language Institute, University of Michigan, 69-79.

Anthony, Edward M., French, Debora P. and Warotamasikkhadit, Udom (1967) *Foundations of Thai*, Book I, Parts 1 and 2, Ann Arbor, Michigan: University of Michigan Press.

Anuman Rajadhon, Phraya (1961) *The Thai Language* (Thailand Culture Series No. 17), Bangkok: The National Culture Institute.

— (1981) *Essay on Thai Folklore*, Bangkok: Editions Duang Kamol.

Ariyapitipun, Sumon (1988) 'An Analysis of Phonological Errors in the Pronunciation of English Consonants and Vowels by Selected Native Speakers of Thai', unpublished PhD dissertation, University of Georgia.

Arya, Gosa (1976) *Thai Grammar*, Bangkok: Khurusapha Press.

Bamber, Scott (1987) 'Illness Taxonomy in Traditional Thai Medicine', *Proceedings of the International Conference on Thai Studies*, edited by Ann Buller, Vol. 3, Canberra: Australian National University, 605-614.

Bamroograks, Cholticha et al. (1987) 'Sukhothai Thai as a Discourse-Oriented Language: Evidence from Zero Noun Phrases', unpublished PhD dissertation, University of Wisconsin, Madison.

Bamroongraks, Cholticha, Khanittanan, Wilaiwan et al. (eds) (1988) *The International Symposium on Language and Linguistics*, Thammasat University, 9-11 August 1988. Bangkok: Faculty of Liberal Arts, Thammasat University, Thailand.

Bandhumedha, Navavan (1976) 'Noun Phrase Deletion in Thai', unpublished PhD dissertation, University of Washington.

— (1979) *Wayyako'n Thai [Thai Grammar]*, Bangkok: Rungru'angsan Kanphim.

Baron, Amy Meepoe (2001) 'The Interactive Organization of Reference to Persons in Thai Conversations', unpublished PhD dissertation, University of California at Los Angeles.

Barz, R. K. and Diller A. V. N. (1985) 'Classifiers and Standardization: Some South and South-East Asian Comparisons', in David Bradley (ed.) *Language Policy, Language Planning and Sociolinguistics in South-East Asia, Papers in South-East Asian Linguistics*, No.9, Pacific Linguistics A67: 155-184.

Bastian, Adolph (1868) 'Remarks on the Indo-Chinese Alphabets', *Journal of the Royal Asiatic Society of Great Britain and Ireland* 3: 65-80.

Beach, Elizabeth Francis, Burnham, Denis, and Kitamura, Christine (2001) 'Bilingualism and the Relationship between Perception and Production: Greek/English Bilinguals and Thai Bilabial Stops', *International Journal of Bilingualism* 5.2 (June): 221-235.

Beddor, Patrice Speeter and Krakow, Rena Arens (1999) 'Perception of Coarticulatory Nasalization by Speakers of English and Thai: Evidence for Partial Compensation', *Journal of the Acoustical Society of America* 106.5: 2868.

Bee, Peter J. (1972) 'Kan in Modern Standard Thai', *Journal of the Siam Society* 60.2: 87-134.

— (1975) 'Restricted Phonology in Certain Thai Linker-Syllables', in Jimmy G. Harris and James R. Chamberlain (eds) *Studies in Tai Linguistics in Honor of William J. Gedney*, Bangkok: CIEL, 13-42; also in Gething, Thomas W. and Nguyên Dăng Liêm (eds) (1979) *Papers on South-East Asian Linguistics 6: Tai Studies in Honour of William J. Gedney (PL A. 52)*, 11-35, Canberra: Australian National University.

Beebe, Leslie M. (1975) 'Occupational Prestige and Consonant Cluster Simplification in Bangkok Thai', *Linguistics* 165: 42-61.

— (1976) 'Social Conditioning of Grooved and Flat Fricatives in Thai', in Thomas W. Gething et al. (eds) *Tai Linguistics in Honor of Fang-Kuei Li*, Bangkok: Chulalongkorn University Press, 13-27.

— (1981) 'Social and Situational Factors Affecting the Communicative Strategy of Dialect Code-Switching', *International Journal of the Sociology of Language* 32: 139-149.

Benedict, Paul K. (1942) 'Thai, Kadai and Indonesian: A New Alignment in Southeastern Asia', *American Anthropologist* 44: 576-601.

— (1943) 'Studies in Thai Kinship Terminology', *Journal of the American Oriental Society* 63: 168-175.

— (1945) 'Chinese and Thai Kin Numeratives', *Journal of the American Oriental Society* 65: 33-37.

— (1975) Austro-Thai Language and Culture with a Glossary of Roots, New Haven: HRAF Press.

Bergen, F. L. Werner von (1875) *Passive Verb of the Thai Language*, Bangkok: S. J. Smith.

Bhamoraput, Amara (1972) 'Final Particles in Thai', unpublished MA thesis, Brown University.

Bickner, Robert J. (1981) 'A Linguistic Study of a Thai Literary Classic', unpublished PhD dissertation, University of Michigan.

— (1986) 'Thai Tones and English Loan Words: A Proposed Explanation', in Robert Bickner, et al. (eds), 19-40.

— (1989) 'Directional Modification in Thai Fiction: The Use of 'Come' and 'Go' in Text Building', in David Bradley (ed.) *Papers in Southeast Asian Linguistics No. 11, Southeast Asian Syntax*, Canberra: Department of Linguistics, Research School of Pacific Studies, Australian National University, 15-79.

— (1992) 'Some Textual evidence on the Tai sounds *-ay and *-a–u', in Carol J. Compton and John F. Hartmann (eds) *Papers on Tai Languages, Linguistics, and Literatures in Honor of William J. Gedney on His 77th Birthday*, Center for Southeast Asian Studies, Northern Illinois University, 223-230.

Bickner, Robert, Hudak, Thomas J. and Peyasantiwong, Patcharin (eds) (1986) *Papers from a Conference on Thai Studies in Honor of William J. Gedney* (*Michigan Papers on South and Southeast Asian 25*), Center for South and Southeast Asian Studies, University of Michigan.

Bilmes, Jack (1992) 'Dividing the Rice: A Microanalysis of the Mediator's Role in a Northern Thai Negotiation', *Language in Society* 21.45 (Dec): 569-602.

Bilmes, Leela (2002) 'Sociolinguistic Aspects of Thai Politeness', unpublished PhD dissertation, University of Hawaii.

Bisang, W. (1996) 'Areal Typology and Grammaticalization: Processes of Grammaticalization Based on Nouns and Verbs in Mainland South East Asian languages', *Studies in Language* 20.3: 519-97.

Boonyapatipark, Tasanalai (1983) 'A Study of Aspect in Thai', unpublished PhD dissertation, University of London.

Bradley, Cornelius B. (1909a) 'Indications of a Consonant Shift in Siamese Since the Introduction of Alphabetical Writing', *Transactions of the American Philological Association* 38: 19-29.

— (1909b) 'The Oldest Known Writing in Siam', *Journal of the Siam Society* 6.1: 1-64.

— (1911) 'Graphic Analysis of the Tone Accents in the Siamese Language', *Journal of the American Oriental Society* 31: 282-286.

Bradley, David (ed.) (1982) *Papers in South-East Asian Linguistics 8: Pacific Linguistics A62*, Canberra: Australian National University.

— (1992) 'The Disappearance of the Ungong in Thailand', in Nancy C. Dorian (ed.) *Investigating Obsolescence: Studies in Language Contraction and Death*, Cambridge, England: Cambridge University Press, 33-40.

Brown, J. Marvin (1962) 'From Ancient Thai to Modern Dialects: A Theory', unpublished PhD dissertation, Cornell University.

— (1965) *From Ancient Thai to Modern Dialects*, Bangkok: Social Science Association Press of Thailand.
— (1966) 'The Language of Sukhothai: Where Did It Come From? And Where Did It Go?', *Social Science Review* 3: 40-42.
— (1967) *A. U. A. Language Center Thai Course*, Books 1-3, Bangkok: American University Alumni Association Language Center.
— (1976) 'Dead consonants or Dead Tones?', in Thomas W. Gething, Jimmy G. Harris and Pranee Kullavanijaya (eds) *Tai Linguistics in Honor of Fang-Kuei Li*, Bangkok: Chulalongkorn University Press, 28-38.
— (1979) 'Vowel Length in Thai', in Theraphan L-Thongkum, et al. (eds) *Studies in Tai and Mon-Khmer Phonetics and Phonology in Honour of Eugénie J.A. Henderson*, Bangkok: Chulalongkorn University Press, 10-25.
Burnay, Jean (1927) 'Note sur les tones et les initiales du vieux siamois a l'epoque de Sukhodaya', *Journal of the Siam Society* 21.2: 103-117.
Burnay, Jean, and Coedès, Georges (1927) 'Notes d'etymologie tai. 1. Le nom de nombre 'cent'', *Journal of the Siam Society* 20: 49-52.
— (1928) 'The Origins of the Sukhodaya Script', *Journal of the Siam Society* 21: 87-102.
Burnham, D., Webster, D., and Francis, E. (1994) 'The Role of Linguistic context in Perception of Tonal Contrasts', Paper presented at the Asian-Australian Workshop on Cognitive Processing of Asian Languages, University of New South Wales, December.
Burnham, D. and Francis, E. (1997) 'The Role of Linguistic Experience in the Perception of Thai Tones', in T. L-Thongkum (ed.) *South East Asian Linguistic Studies in Honour of Vichin Panupong* (Science of Language Vol. 8.), Bangkok: Chulalongkorn University Press, 29-47.
Burnham, D. (1992) 'Auditory-Visual Perception of Thai Consonants by Thai and Australian Listeners', *PAL 3* 1: 531-545.
Burnham, D., Francis, E., and Webster, D. (1996) 'The Development of Tone Perceptions: Cross-Linguistic Aspects and the Effect of Linguistic Context', *PAL 4* 1: 47-75.
Burnham, Denis, Luksaneeyanawin, Sudaporn, Kirkwood, Kathryn, and Pansottee, Supatra (1992) 'Perception of Central Thai Tones and Segments by Thai and Australian Adults', *PAL 3* 1: 546-560.
Burusphat, Somsonge (1986) 'The Structure of Thai Narrative Discourse', unpublished PhD dissertation, University of Texas at Arlington.
— (2002) 'Discourse Studies in Thailand', *Discourse Studies* 4.4 (Nov): 501-510.
— (2007a) 'The Elision of Negative Morphemes in Tai Languages', in Jimmy G. Harris, et al. (eds), 205-223.
— (2007b) 'Animate Classifiers in Tai Languages', *International Journal of the Sociology of Language* 186: 109-124.
Campbell, Russell N. (1969) *Noun Substitutes in Modern Thai: A Study in Pronominality* (Janua Linguarum Series Practica 65), The Hague and Paris: Mouton.
Campbell, Stuart and Chuan Shaweewongse (1957) *Fundamentals of the Thai Language*, Bangkok: Prachandra Press (reprinted in 1968, London: Paragon Book Gallery).
Carney, Arlene Earley, Jack Gandour, Soranee Holasuit Petty, Amy M. Robbins, Wendy Myers, and Richard Miyamoto (1988) 'The Effect of Adventitious Deafness on the Perception & Production of Voice Onset Time in Thai: A Case Study', *Language & Speech* 31.3 (Jul-Sept): 273-282.
Carpenter, Kathie Lou (1986) 'Productivity and Pragmatics of Thai Classifiers', *Berkeley Linguistics Society* 12: 14-25.
— (1987) 'How Children Learn to Classify Nouns in Thai', unpublished PhD dissertation, Stanford University.
— (1991) 'Later Rather than Sooner: Extralinguistic Categories in the Acquisition of Thai Classifiers', *Journal of Child Language* 18.1 (Feb): 93-113.
— (1992) 'Two Dynamic Views of Classifier Systems: Diachronic Change and Individual Development', *Cognitive Linguistics* 3.2: 129-150.

Cartwright, Basil O. (1907a) *An Elementary Handbook of the Siamese Language*, Bangkok: American Presbyterian Mission Press.

— (1907b) *Siamese-English Dictionary*, Bangkok: American Presbyterian Mission Press.

Caswell, J. (1870) 'Treatise on the Tones of the Siamese Language', *Siam Repository* 2: 93-101.

Cefola, Penchusee L. (1981) 'A Study of Interference of English in the Language of Thai Bilinguals in the United States', unpublished PhD dissertation, Georgetown University.

Chaimanee, Nittaya (1996) 'Communicative Pauses in Thai', in *PAL 4* 1: 174-182.

Chaiyaratana, Chalao (1961) 'A Comparative Study of English and Thai Syntax', unpublished PhD dissertation, Indiana University.

Chamberlain, James R. (1972a) 'The Origin of the Southwestern Tai', *Bulletin des Amis du Laos* 7-8: 233-244.

— (1972b) 'Tone Borrowing in Five Northeastern Dialects', in Jimmy G. Harris and Richard B. Noss (eds) *Tai Phonetics and Phonology*, Central Institute of English Language, Office of State Universities, Bangkok: Prachandra Press, 43-46.

— (1975) 'A New Look at the History and Classification of the Tai Languages', in Jimmy G. Harris and James R. Chamberlain (eds) *Studies in Tai Linguistics in Honor of William J. Gedney*, Bangkok, 49-66.

— (1977) 'An Introduction to Proto-Tai Zoology', unpublished PhD dissertation, University of Michigan.

— (1992) 'Frog Mouths and Mimesis: An Essay on the Relationship between Form and Meaning', in Carol J. Compton and John F. Hartmann (eds), 103-110.

Chanawangsa, Wipah (1986) 'Cohesion in Thai', unpublished PhD dissertation, Georgetown University.

Chantavibulya (Panupong), Vichin (1959) 'The Phonology of the Syllable in Songkhla, a Southern Tai Dialect', unpublished MA thesis, University of London.

Chantavibulya (Panupong), Vichin (1962) 'Inter-sentence Relations in Modern Conversational Thai', unpublished PhD thesis, University of London. See also Panupong (1970).

Chen, Matthew Y. (1992) 'Competing Sound Changes: Evidence from Kam-Tai, Miao-Yao and Tibeto-Burman', *PAL 3 1*: 16-27.

Chirasombutti, Voravudhi (1995) 'Self-reference in Japanese and Thai: a Comparative Study', unpublished PhD dissertation, Australian National University.

— (2007) 'History of Foreign Language Education in Thailand until World War II', *International Journal of the Sociology of Language* 186: 5-12.

Chittasophon, Em-om (1984) 'History and Development of Thai Literary Conventions: A Sociolinguistic Analysis', paper presented to the International Conference on Thai Studies, Thai Studies Program, Chulalongkorn University, Bangkok, August 22-24.

Chodchoey, Supa W. (1986) 'Strategies in Thai Oral Discourse', unpublished PhD dissertation, The Pennsylvania State University.

— (1988) 'Spoken and Written Discourse in Thai: The Difference', in Bamroongraks, Cholticha and Wilaiwan Khanittanan, et al. (eds), 138-149.

Chomaitong, Kannikar (1976) 'A Comparison of Pronominalization in Thai and English', *Pasaa* (Central Institute of English Language, Bangkok) 6.1-2: 200-210.

Chuenkongchoo, Terd (1956) 'The Prosodic Characteristics of Certain Particles in Spoken Thai', unpublished MA thesis, School of Oriental and African Studies, University of London.

Chunsuvimol, Boonruang (1980) 'Language Use and Communicative Networks of Thai Guest Workers in Singapore', unpublished MA thesis, The University of Singapore.

Chutisilp, Pornpimol (1984) 'A Sociolinguistic Study of an Additional Language: English in Thailand', unpublished PhD dissertation, University of Illinois at Urbana-Champaign.

Chuwicha, Yajai (1993) 'Clausehood in Serial Verb Constructions in Thai', paper presented to the Fifth International Conference on Thai Studies, University of London, July.

Clark, Marybeth (1978) *Coverbs and Cases in Vietnamese* (Pacific Linguistics B48), Canberra: The Australian National University.

— (1992) 'Serialization in Mainland Southeast Asia', *PAL 3* 1: 145-168.

— (1991) 'Conjunctions as Topicalizers: More on Southeast Asian Languages', in Martha Ratliff and Eric Schiller (eds) *Papers From the First Annual Meeting of the Southeast Asian Linguistics Society 1991*, Tempe, AZ: Arizona State University, 87-107.

Clark, Marybeth and Prasithrathsint, Amara (1985) 'Synchronic Lexical Derivation in Southeast Asian Languages', in Suriya Ratanakul, et al, (eds) 34-81.

Coedes, Georges (1923) 'Nouvelles notes critiques sur l'inscription de Rama Khamhaeng', *Journal of the Siam Society* 17.3: 113-120.

Cohen, Erik (1987) 'Phut pasaa Thai: Acquisition of Hosts' Language among Expatriates in Bangkok', *International Journal of the Sociology of Language* 63: 5-19.

Cole, P. (1987) 'Null Objects in Universal Grammar', *Linguistic Inquiry* 18: 597-612.

Compton, Carol J. (1992) 'Lao Pronoun Usage as Reflected in Post-1975 Literature', in Martha Ratliff and Eric Schiller (eds) *Papers From The First Annual Meeting of The Southeast Asian Linguistic Society 1991*, Tempe, AZ: Arizona State University, 109-123.

Compton, Carol J. and Hartmann, John F. (eds) (1992) *Papers on Tai Languages, Linguistics, and Literatures in Honor of William J. Gedney on His 77th Birthday* (Occasional Paper No. 16), Center for Southeast Asian Studies, Northern Illinois University.

Comrie Bernard (1996) 'The Unity of Noun-Modifying Clauses in Asian Languages', *PAL 4* 3: 1077-1088.

Condominas, Georges (1976) 'Essai sur l'évolution des systèmes politiques thaïs', *Ethnos* 41: 7-67.

Conklin, Nancy F. (1981) 'The Semantics and Syntax of Numeral Classification in Tai and Austronesian', unpublished PhD dissertation, University of Michigan.

Cooke, Joseph R. (1965) 'Pronominal Reference in Thai, Burmese, and Vietnamese', unpublished PhD dissertation, University of California, Berkeley. Also published in 1969 under the same title by University of California Publications in Linguistics no. 52., Berkeley: University of California Press.

— (1979) 'Forms and Meanings of the Thai Particle *si*', in Nguên Dăng Liêm (ed.) *South-East Asian Linguistic Studies*, Volume 4: *Pacific Linguistics C49*, Canberra: Research School of Pacific Studies, Australian National University, 61-98.

— (1992) 'The Problem of the Sixth Tone in Thai', in Carol J. Compton and John F. Hartmann (eds), 65-76.

— (1989) 'Thai Sentence Particles and Other Topics', *Papers in South-East Asian Linguistics*, No. 12: *Pacific Linguistics A 80*, Australian National University.

— (1992) 'Thai Sentence Particles: Putting the Puzzle Together', *PAL 3*: 1105-1163.

Court, Christopher (1972) 'The Tones of the Traat Dialect', in Jimmy G. Harris and Richard B. Noss (eds), 47-49.

— (1975) The Segmental and Suprasegmental Representation of Malay Loanwords in Satun Thai: A Description with Historical Remarks', in Jimmy G. Harris and James R. Chamberlain (eds), 67-88.

— (1984) 'Some Remarks on Lexical Modernization in Thai', *Proceedings of the International Conference on Thai Studies*, Bangkok: Thai Studies Programme, Chulalongkorn University, Vol. II: 1-13.

— (1985) 'Observations on Some Cases of Tone Sandhi', in Graham Thurgood, James A. Matisoff, and David Bradley (eds) *Linguistics of the Sino-Tibetan Area: The State of the Art* (Canberra: Department of Linguistics, Research Schools of Pacific Studies, ANU), vii. 498: 125-37.

— (1996) 'The Spread of Brahmi Script into Southeast Asia', in Peter T. Daniels and William Bright (eds), *The World's Writing Systems*, Oxford University Press, 445-449.

Coyaud, Maurice (1981) *Contes de Thailande*, Paris: Societe d'Études Linguistiques et Anthropologiques de France.

Cristfield, Arthur G. (1974) 'Lao Final Particles', in Nguên Dăng Liêm (ed.) *South-East Asian Linguistic Studies*, Volumes 1: *Pacific Linguistics C31*, Canberra: Research School of Pacific Studies, Australian National University, 41-46.

— (1978) 'Sound Symbolism and the Expressive Words of Lao', unpublished PhD dissertation, University of Hawaii.

Danvivathana (Ronakiat), Nantana (1987) *The Thai Writing System*, Hamburg: Helmut Buske (Forum Phoneticum 39).

Davidson, Jeremy H. C. S. (1987) 'Another Source for Information on Ayutthaya Thai', in J. H. C. S. Davidson (ed.) *Lai Su' Thai: Essays in Honour of E.H.S. Simmonds*, School of Oriental and African Studies, University of London, 63-72.

— (ed.) (1989) *South-East Asian Linguistics: Essays in Honour of Eugénie J. A. Henderson* (Collected Papers in Oriental and African Studies), School of Oriental and African Studies, University of London.

Davies, Somchit (1979) 'A Comparative Study of Yong and Standard Thai', in Theraphan L-Thongkum, et al. (eds), 26-48.

Davis, Chris and Schoknecht, Colin (1994) 'Lexical Processing in Thai-English Bilinguals', *PAL 4* 4: 1399-1428.

Debyasjvarn, Boonlua M. L. (1973) 'The Sociolinguistic Situation in Thailand', *Report of the Regional Workshop on the Feasibility of a Sociolinguistic Survey of Southeast Asia*, Singapore: SEAMEO Regional Language Center, 78-79.

Deepadung, Sujaritlak (1989) 'The Noun Phrase in Thai in the Residential Grammar Framework', unpublished PhD dissertation, University of Kansas.

— (1997) 'Extension in the Usage of the Thai Classifier /tua/', in Arthur S. Abramson (ed.), 49-55.

Deephuengton, Phawadee (1992) 'Politeness in Thai: Strategies of Refusing and Disagreeing', unpublished PhD dissertation, University of Kansas.

Dellinger, David W. (1975) 'Thai Modals', in Jimmy G. Harris and James R. Chamberlain (eds), 89-99.

Denlinger, Paul B. (1967) 'Chinese and Thai', *Monumenta Serica* 24: 35-41.

— (1989) 'The Chinese-Tai Linguistic Relationship: A Formal Proof', *Monumenta Serica* 38: 167-171.

Dhananjayananda, Puttachart (1997) 'The Emergence of the Length Distinction in Mid-Front Vowels e-ee in Thai', in Jerold A. Edmondson and David B. Solnit (eds), 327-336.

Dhaninivat (Prince) (1970) 'The Transcription of Siamese', in Tej Bunnang and Michael Smithies (eds) *Memoriam Phya Anuman Rajadhon*, Bangkok: The Siam Society, 69-72.

Diffloth, Gérard (1977) 'Mon-Khmer Initial Palatals and 'Substratumized' Austro-Thai', in Philip N. Jenner (ed.) *Mon-Khmer Studies VI*, Honolulu: University of Hawaii Press, 39-58.

Diller, Anthony V. N. (1979) 'Tones, segments and Thai regional society', in L-Thongkum, et al. (eds), 60-93.

— (1980) 'Cross-Cultural Pain Semantics', Pain (Journal of the International Association for the Study of Pain) 9: 9-26.

— (1985) 'High and Low Thai: Views from Within', in David Bradley (ed.) *Language Policy, Language Planning and Sociolinguistics in South-East Asia*, Canberra: The Australian National University, *Papers in South-East Asian Linguistics* No. 9, Pacific Linguistics A67: 51-76.

— (1988) 'Thai Syntax and 'National Grammar'', *Language Sciences* 10: 273-312.

— (1991, 2002) 'What Makes Central Thai a National Language?', in Craig J. Reynolds (ed.) *National Identity and Its Defenders: Thailand 1939-1989*, Monash University Centre of Southeast Asian Studies, Monash Papers on Southeast Asia No. 25; second edition, Chiang Mai: Silkworm Books, 71-107.

— (1993) 'Diglossic Grammaticality in Thai', in William A. Foley (ed.) *The Role of Theory in Language Description*, Berlin: Mouton de Gruyter, 393-420.

— (1994) 'Thai', in Cliff Goddard and Anna Wierzbicka (eds) *Semantic and Lexical Universals, Studies in Language Companion Series Vol. 25*, Amsterdam and Philadelphia: John Benjamins, 149-170.

— (1996a) 'Thai and Lao', in Peter T. Daniels and William Bright (eds) *The World's Writing Systems*, Oxford: Oxford University Press, 457-466.

— (1996b) 'Thai Orthography and the History of Marking Tone', *Oriens Extremus* 39.2: 228-254.
— (1997) 'Does Thai Permit Detransitivity?' in Arthur S. Abramson (ed.), 57-78.
— (2000) 'The Tai Language Family and the Comparative Method', in Khunying Suriya Ratanakul, et al. (eds) *Proceedings of the International Conference on Tai Studies, July 29-31 1998*, Institute of Language and Culture for Rural Development, Mahidol University, 1-32.
— (2001a) 'Thai Grammar and Grammaticality', in Hannes Kniffka (ed.) *Indigenous Grammars Across Cultures*, Frankfurt am Main: Peter Lang, 219-244.
— (2001b) 'Grammaticalization and Thai Syntactic Change', in M. R. Kalaya Tingsabadh and Arthur S. Abramson (eds), 139-175.
— (2003) 'Evidence for Austroasiatic Strata in Thai', in Henning Andersen (ed.) *Language Contacts in Prehistory: Studies in Stratigraphy*, Amsterdam: John Benjamins, 159-176.
— (2004) 'Tai; Thai', in William Frawley (ed.) *International Encyclopedia of Linguistics, Second Edition*, Oxford University Press, volume 4, 128-131.
— (2006a) 'Thai Serial Verbs: Cohesion and Culture', in Alexandra Y. Aikhenvald and R. M. W. Dixon (eds) *Serial Verb Constructions: a Cross-linguistic Typology*, Oxford University Press, 160-167.
— (2006b) 'Polylectal Grammar and Royal Thai', in Felix K. Ameke, Alan Dench and Nicholas Evans (eds) *Catching Language: the Standing Challenge of Grammar Writing*, Trends in Linguistics Monographs 167, Berlin/New York: Mouton de Gruyter, 565-608.
— (2007) '"Cross-eyed Words" in Southern Thai', in Jimmy G. Harris et al. (eds), 25-37.
Diller, Anthony V. N. and Preecha Juntanamalaga (1988) 'Deictic Derivation in Thai', in David Bradley, Eugenie J. A. Henderson and Martine Mauzedon (eds) *Prosodic Analysis and Asian Linguistics to Honour R.K. Sprigg*, Pacific Linguistics C-104: 167-194.
Diller, Anthony V. N. and Preecha Juntanamalaga (1990) 'Full Hearts and Empty Pronominals in Thai', *Australian Journal of Linguistics* 10.2: 231-255.
— (1992) 'Thai Pragmatic Constructions: The oey Paradigm', *Journal of Pragmatics* 18.2-3: 289-301.
Diller, Anthony V. N. and Voravudh Chirasombutti (2000) 'Who am 'I' in Thai? – The Thai First Person: Self-reference or Gendered Self?' in Peter A. Jackson and Nerida M. Cook (eds) *Genders and Sexualities in Modern Thailand*, Chiangmai: Silkworm Books, 114-133.
Diller, Anthony V. N. and Wilaiwan Khanittanan (2002) 'Syntactic Enquiry as a Cultural Activity', in N. J. Enfield (ed.) *Ethnosyntax: Explorations in Grammar and Culture*, Oxford University Press, 31-51.
Dodd, William Clifton (1923) *The Tai Race*, Iowa: Cedar Rapids.
Donald, Susan L. (1978) 'The Perception of Voicing Contrasts in Thai and English', unpublished PhD dissertation, University of Connecticut.
Downer, G. B. (1963) 'Chinese, Thai and Miao-Yao', in H. L. Shorto (ed.) *Linguistic Comparison in Southeast Asia and the Pacific*, London: School of Oriental and African Studies, 133-139.
Edmondson, Jerold A. (1992a) 'A Study of the Tones and Initials in Kam, Lakkja, and Hlai', in Carol J. Compton and John F. Hartmann (eds), 77-102.
— (1992b) 'Some Kadai languages of Northern Guangxi Chaia', *PAL 3* 1: 28-43.
— (1994) 'Change and Variation in Zhuang', in K. L. Adams and T. Hudak (eds) *Papers from the Second Annual Meeting of the Southeast Asian Linguistic Society* 1992, Tempe, AZ: Arizona State University, 147-185.
— (2007) 'The Power of Language over the Past: Tai Settlement and Tai Linguistics in Southern China and Northern Vietnam', in Jimmy G. Harris et al. (eds), 39-63.
Edmondson, Jerold A. and David B. Solnit (eds) (1988) *Comparative Kadai: Linguistic Studies beyond Tai*, Summer Institute of Linguistics and University of Texas at Arlington.
— (eds) (1997) *Comparative Kadai: The Tai Branch.* Summer Institute of Linguistics and University of Texas at Arlington.

Edmondson, Jerold A. and Jinfang Li (1996) 'The Language Corridor', *PAL 4* 3: 983-990.
Egerod, Søren (1957) 'The Eighth Earthly Branch in Archaic Chinese and Tai', *Oriens* 10.2: 296-299.
— (1959a) 'Swatow Loan Words in Siamese', *Acta Orientalia* 23: 137-156.
— (1959b) 'A Note on Some Chinese Numerals as Loan Words in Tai', *T'oung Pao* 47: 67-74.
— (1961) 'Studies in Thai Dialectology', *Acta Orientalia* 26: 43-91.
— (1971b) 'Phonation Types in Chinese and Southeast Asian Languages', *Acta Linguistica Hafniensia* 13.2: 159-71.
Ekniyom, Peansiri (Vongvipanond) (1971) 'Relative Clause in Thai', unpublished MA thesis, University of Washington.
— (1977) 'The Topic/Comment Distinction and Passivization in Thai', *University of Hawaii Working Papers in Linguistics* 9.2: 93-110.
— (1979) 'An Internal Reconstruction of Auxiliaries in Thai', *University of Hawaii Working Paper in Linguistics* 11, 55-56.
— (1982) 'A Study of Informational Structuring in Thai Sentences', unpublished PhD dissertation, University of Hawaii.
Enfield, N. J. (2002) 'How to Define 'Lao', 'Thai' and 'Isan' Language? A View from Linguistic Science'. *Tai Culture* 7.1: 62-67.
— (2003) Linguistic Epidemiology: Semantics and Grammar of Language Contact in Southeast Asia, London: Routledge Curzon.
— (2006) 'Heterosemy and the Grammar-lexicon Trade-off', in Felix K. Ameke, Alan Dench and Nicholas Evans (eds) *Catching Language: the Standing Challenge of Grammar Writing*, Trends in Linguistics Monographs 167, Berlin/New York: Mouton de Gruyter, 297-320.
Erickson, Donna M. (1975) 'Phonetic Implications for an Historical Account of Tonogenesis', in Jimmy G. Harris and James R. Chamberlain (eds), 100-111.
— (1976) 'A Physiological Analysis of the Tones of Thai', unpublished PhD dissertation, University of Connecticut.
— (1993) 'Laryngeal Muscle Activity in Connection with Thai Tones', *Annual Bulletin*, Research Institute of Logopaedics and Phoniatrics, 27: 135-149.
Fabrega, Horacio, Jr and Stephen Tyma (1976) 'Culture, Language and the Shaping of Illness: An Illustration Based on Pain', *Journal of Psychosomatic Research* 20: 323-337.
Fasold, Ralph W. A. (1968) 'Noun Compounding in Thai', unpublished PhD dissertation, University of Chicago.
Filbeck, David (1973a) 'The Passive in Thai', *Anthropological Linguistics* 15: 33-41.
— (1973b) 'Pronouns in Northern Thai', *Anthropological Linguistics* 15: 345-361.
— (1975) 'A Grammar of Verb Serialization in Thai', in Jimmy G. Harris and James R. Chamberlain (eds), 112-129.
Fippinger, Dorothy Crawford (1971) 'Kinship Terms of the Black Tai People', *Journal of the Siam Society* 59.1: 65-82.
Fippinger, Jay and Dorothy Fippinger (1970) 'Black Tai Phonemes, with Reference to White Tai', *Anthropological Linguistics* 12.3: 83-97.
Fischer, Gero (1977) Studien zur Thailändischen Sprache, I. (Zur Formalen Charakteristik des Themas im Thai; Valenztheoretische Untersuchungen zum Thailandischen Verbum Besonderheite Hypersintaktischer Strukturen im Thai), Hamburg: Helmut Buske Verlag.
Foreit, Karen G. (1977) 'Linguistic Relativism and Selective Adaptation for Speech: A Comparative Study of English and Thai', *Perception and Psychophysics* 21.4: 347-351.
Frankfurter, Oscar (1900) *Elements of Siamese Grammar with Appendices*, Bangkok: American Presbyterian Mission Press.
— (1906) 'Secret Writing in Siamese', *Journal of the Siam Society* 3.2: 62-72.
Gandour, Jack T. (1974a) 'Consonant Types and Tone in Siamese', *Journal of Phonetics* 2: 337-350.

— (1974b) 'The glottal stop in Siamese: predictability in phonological description', *Pasaa* 4: 2. Bangkok: Central Institute of the English Language.
— (1976) 'A Reanalysis of some phonological rules in Thai', in Thomas W. Gething, et al. (eds), 47-61.
— (1977) 'On the Interaction between Tone and Vowel Length: Evidence from Thai Dialects', *Phonetica* 34.1: 54-65.
— (1978) 'On the Deictic Use of Verbs of Motion Come and Go in Thai', *Anthropological Linguistics* 20.9: 381-394.
— (1979) 'Tonal Rules for English Loanwords in Thai', in Nguên Dăng Liêm (ed.) *South-East Asian Linguistic Studies*, Volumes 4: *Pacific Linguistics C49*, Canberra: Research School of Pacific Studies, Australian National University, 131-144.
— (1992) 'Neurolinguistic Analysis of Spelling Errors in Thai', *Pan Asiatic Linguistics* 3 1: 561-627.
Gandour, Jack, Buckingham, H. and Dardarandanda, R. (1985) 'The Dissolution of Numeral Classifiers in Thai', *Linguistics* 23.4: 547-566.
Gandour, Jack, et al. (1984) 'The Acquisition of Numeral Classifiers in Thai', *Linguistics* 22: 455-479.
— (1986) 'The Acquisition of the Voicing Contrast in Thai: A Study of Voice Onset Time in Word-Initial Stop Consonants', *Journal of Child Language* 13.3: 561-572.
— (1988) 'Tone in Thai Laryngeal Speech', *Journal of Speech and Hearing Disorders* 53.1: 23-29.
— (1992) 'Stop Voicing in Thai after Unilateral Brain Damage', *Aphasiology* 6.6 (Nov-Dec): 535-547.
— (1994) 'Sequences of Phonemic Approximations in a Thai Conduction Aphasic', *Brain and Language* 46.1 (Jan): 69-95.
— (2002a) 'Neural Circuitry Underlying Perception of Duration Depends on Language Experience', *Brain and Language* 83.2 (Nov): 268-290.
— (2002b) 'A Cross-Linguistic fMRI Study of Spectral and Temporal Cues Underlying Phonological Processing', *Journal of Cognitive Neuroscience* 14.7 (Oct): 1076-1087.
Gandour, Jack T., and Harchman, R. (1978) 'Cross-Language Differences in Tone Perception: A Multidimensional Scaling Investigation', *Language and Speech* 21: 1-33.
Gandour, Jack T., Potisuk, S. and Harper M.P. (1996) 'Effects of Stress on Vowel Length in Thai', *PAL 4* 1: 95-103.
Gandour, Jack T. and Ponglorpisit, Suvit (1990) 'Disruption of Tone Space in a Thai-Speaking Patient with Subcortical Aphasia', *Journal of Neurolinguistics* 5.2-3: 333-351.
Gandour, Jack, and Dardarananda, R. (1982) 'Voice Onset Time in Aphasia: Thai I. Perception', *Brain and Language* 17: 24-33.
Gandour, Jack, Satthamnuwong, N., and Tumtavitikul, A. (1999) 'Effects of Speaking Rate on Thai Tones', *Phonetica* 56.3/4: 123-134.
Gandour, Jack T., Tumtavitikul, Apiluck, and Satthamnuwong, Nakarin (2002) 'Effects of Speaking Rate on the Thai Emphatic Tone', *Asia Pacific Journal of Speech, Language, and Hearing* 7.2: 101-110.
Gandour, Jack, Potisuk, Siripong, and Dechongkit, Sumalee (1994) 'Tonal Coarticulation in Thai', *Journal of Phonetics* 22.4 (Oct): 477-492.
Gedney, William J. (1947) 'Indic Loanwords in Spoken Thai', unpublished PhD dissertation, Yale University.
— (1961) 'Special Vocabularies in Thai', *Mémoires de la Société Finno-Ougrenne* (Helsinki) 14: 109-114.
— (1965) 'Old Tai loanwords in Khmu', paper presented at the Linguistic Society of America, Baltimore.
— (1967) 'Thailand and Laos', in T.A. Sebeok (ed.) *Current Trends in Linguistics*, Vol. 2, The Hague: Mouton, 782-811.
— (1972) 'A Checklist for Determining Tones in Tai Dialects', in M. E. Smith (ed.) *Studies in Linguistics in Honor of George L. Trager*, The Hague: Mouton, 423-437.

— (1976) 'On the Thai Evidence for Austro-Thai', *Ajia Afurikana-go no Keisu Keisan* 6: 65-86.
— (1979) 'Evidence for Another Series of Voiced Initials in Proto-Tai', paper presented at the 12th International Conference of Sino-Tibetan Languages and Linguistics, Paris; also in Gedney (1989a), 229-270.
— (1980) 'A Siamese Invocation', paper presented at the 13th International Conference on Sino-Tibetan Linguistics, University of Virginia; also in Gedney (1989a), 463-478.
— (1985) 'Confronting the Unknown: Tonal Splits and the Geneology of the Tai-Kadai', in Graham Thurgood, James Matisoff, and David Bradley (eds) *Linguistics of the Sino-Tibetan Area: The State of the Art*, Canberra: Department of Linguistics, Research School of Pacific Studies, Australian National University, 116-124.
— (1986) 'Speculations of Early Tai Tones', in John McCoy and Timothy Light (eds) *Contributions to Sino-Tibetan Studies*, Leiden: Brill, 144-56.
— (1989a) Selected Papers on Comparative Tai Studies (Michigan Papers on South and Southeast Asia 29), Center for South and Southeast Asian Studies, University of Michigan.
— (1989b) 'Siamese Verse Forms in Historical Perspective', in Gedney (1989a), 489-544.
— (1991) 'Comment on the Linguistic Arguments Relating to Inscription One', in James R. Chamberlain (ed.) *The Ramkhamhaeng Controversy: Collected Papers*, Bangkok: The Siam Society.
Gehr, E. (1951) 'Affixation in Siamese', *Journal of the Siam Society* 39: 69-82.
Gerini, Gerlamo E. (1904) 'On Siamese Proverbs and Idiomatic Expressions', Journal of the Siam Society 1: 11-168; also in A Tai Festschrift for W.J. Gedney, on the Occasion of his Fifth Cycle of Life Birthday Anniversary (Southeast Asia Studies Working Paper No 8.), Honolulu: University of Hawaii.
Gething, Thomas W. (1968) 'Structural Redundancy in Thai Semantics', *Language* 44.2: 813-18.
— (1972) Aspects of Meaning in Thai Nominals: A Study in Structural Semantics, Janua Linguarum, Series Practica 141, The Hague: Mouton.
— (1975) 'Location in Thai and Lao', in Jimmy G. Harris and James R. Chamberlain (eds), 196-201.
— (1977) 'Polysemy and historical semantics in Thai', *Anthropological Linguistics* 19.3: 99-103.
— (1979) 'Two Types of Semantic Contrast between Thai and Lao', in Thomas Gething and Nguên Dăng Liêm (eds) *Papers in South East Asian Linguistics 6: Tai Studies in Honor of William J. Gedney* (Pacific Linguistics A52), Canberra: Australian National University, 37-41.
— (1986a) 'Selective Development of the Thai Lexicon', *Crossroads* 3.1: 118-122.
— (1986b) 'The Thai Language as a Map of Thai Culture', in Bickner, et al. (eds), 143-148.
Gething, Thomas W., and Nguyên Dang Liêm (eds) (1979) *Papers in South East Asian Linguistics 6: Tai Studies in Honor of William J. Gedney.* (Pacific Linguistics A52.) Canberra: Australian National University.
Gething, Thomas W., Harris, Jimmy G. and Kullavanijaya, Pranee (eds) (1976) *Tai Linguistics in Honor of Fang-Kuei Li*, Bangkok: Chulalongkorn University Press.
Godden, Kurt Sterling (1981) 'Montague Grammar and Machine Translation between Thai and English', unpublished PhD dissertation, University of Kansas.
Grether, H.G. (1957) 'The Use of Honorifics in the Thai Language, the Use of Honorifics in the Present Thai Bible, and the Nature of the Bible as It Relates to the Problem', *Bible Translator* 8: 211-214.
Grierson, George Abraham (1920) 'On the Representation of Tones in Oriental Languages', *Journal of the Royal Asiatic Society*, 453-79.
Grima, John A. Jr (1978) 'Categories of Zero Nominal Reference and Clausal Structure in Thai', unpublished PhD dissertation, University of Michigan.
— (1982) 'A Velar for Alveolar Substitution in Thai Child Language', *Studies in Language* 6.2: 175-192.

— (1986) 'Discourse Factors Contributing to the Understanding of a Zero Pronoun in a Passage from the Phraraatchawicaan', in Bickner, et al. (eds), 159-170.

Gsell, René (1979) 'Sur la prosodie du Thai standard: tons et accents', *Rapport de Recherche*, Institut de Phonétique, Université Paris 3.

— (1979) 'Actants, prédicats et structure du thai', in Catherine Paris (ed.) *Relations prédicat-actant(s) dans les langues de types divers I* (LACITO-Documents Eurasie 2), 147-214, Paris: Société d'Etudes Linguistiques et Anthropologiques de France.

Gutslaff, Carl Friedrich (1832) Remarks on the Siamese Language by the Rev. Mr Gutslaff, communicated through the late Robert Fullerton, London: Cose; also in Siam Repository (1869) 1: 51-58.

Haas, Mary R. (1942a) 'The Use of Numeral Classifiers in Thai', *Language* 18: 201-5.

— (1942b) 'Types of Reduplication in Thai (with some comparisons and contrasts taken from English)', *Studies in Linguistics* 1.4: 1-6.

— (1946) 'Techniques of Intensifying in Thai', *Word* 2: 127-30.

— (1951a) 'Interlingual Word Taboos', *American Anthropologist* 53: 338-343.

— (1951b) 'The Declining Descent Rule for Rank in Thailand: A Correction', *American Anthropologist* 53: 585-587.

— (1954) *Thai Reader*, Washington, DC: American Council of Learned Societies.

— (1955) *Thai Vocabulary*, Washington: American Council of Learned Societies.

— (1956) *The Thai System of Writing*, Washington, DC: American Council of Learned Societies.

— (1957) 'Thai Word Games', *Journal of American Folklore* 70: 173-175.

— (1958) 'The Tones of Four Tai Dialects', *Bulletin of the Institute of History and Philology* 29: 817-826.

— (1964) *Thai-English Student's Dictionary*, Stanford University Press.

— (1969a) 'Sibling Terms as Used by Marriage Partners', *Southwestern Journal of Anthropology* 25: 228-235.

— (1969b) 'The Thai Language', *Encyclopedia Britannica* 21: 934 (The University of Chicago).

— (1978) *Language, Culture and History: Essays by Mary R. Haas*, selected and introduced by Anway S. Dil, Stanford University Press.

Haas, Mary R., and Heng R. Subhanka (1945) *Spoken Thai*, New York: Henry Holt.

Harris, Jimmy G. (1972) 'Phonetic Notes on some Siamese Consonants', in Jimmy G. Harris and Richard B. Noss (eds), 8-22.

— (1986) 'The Persian Connection: Four Loanwords in Siamese', *Pasaa* 16.1: 9-12.

— (1987) Linguistic Phonetic Notes (1969-1979), Bangkok: Craftsman Press.

— (2007a) 'The Origin of the Thai Word "Farang"', in Jimmy G. Harris et al. (eds), 89-91.

— (2007b) 'Nine Loanwords in Thai', in Jimmy G. Harris et al. (eds), 93-103.

— (2007c) 'Notes on Problems in the Phonetic Descriptions of Dental and/or Alveolar Stop Strictures', in Jimmy G. Harris et al. (eds), 105-111.

Harris, Jimmy G. (2001) 'States of the Glottis of Thai Voiceless Stops and Affricates', in M. R. Kalaya Tingsabadh and Arthur S. Abramson (eds), 3-12.

Harris, Jimmy G. and Chamberlain, James R. (eds) (1975) *Studies in Tai Linguistics in Honor of William J. Gedney*, Central Institute of English Language, Office of State Universities, Bangkok: Allied Printers.

Harris, Jimmy G. and Bachman, L. F. (1976) 'The Perception of Some Tai Consonant Sounds by Native Speakers of Siamese', *Pasaa* 6.1-2: 176-185.

Harris, Jimmy G. and Noss, Richard B. (eds) (1972) *Tai Phonetics and Phonology*, Central Institute of English Language, Office of State Universities, Bangkok: Prachandra Press.

Harris, Jimmy G., Burusphat,Somsonge and Harris, James E. (eds) (2007) *Studies in Tai and Southeast Asian Linguistics*, Bangkok: Ekphimthai Ltd.

Hartmann, John F. (1976) 'The Waxing and Waning of Vowel Length in Tai Dialects', in Thomas W. Gething, et al. (eds) *Tai Linguistics in Honor of Fang-Kuei Li*, Bangkok: Chulalongkorn University Press, 142-159.

— (1980) 'A Model of Alignment of Dialects in Southewestern Tai', *Journal of the Siam Society* 68.1: 72-86.
— (1986a) 'The Spread of South Indic Scripts in Southeasat Asia', *Crossroads* 3.1: 6-20.
— (1986b) 'Style, Scope, and Vigor in Comparative Tai Research', in Bickner, et al. (eds), 171-184.
— (1989) 'Lexical Puzzles in an Old Thai Text', *Crossroads: An Interdisciplinary Journal of Southeast Asian Studies* 4.2: 71-85 (Center for Southeast Asian Studies, Northern Illinois University, Dekalb).
— (1993) 'Changing Language and Social Relationships in Thai Food Markets', paper presented at COTSEAL Conference, University of Washington-Seattle, July 23.
— (2007) 'The Power to Name Places: Ban, Muang; Chiang, Viang; Nakon, Krung', in Jimmy G. Harris et al. (eds), 113-137.
Hatton, Howard A. (1973) 'Translation of Pronouns: A Thai Example', *The Bible Translator* 24: 222-234.
— (1975) 'A Thai Discourse Pattern', in Jimmy G. Harris and James R. Chamberlain (eds), 231-251.
— (1978) 'First Person Pronominal Realization in Thai Autobiographical Narratives: A Sociolinguistic Description', unpublished PhD dissertation, University of Pennsylvania.
Haudricourt, Andre-G (1948) 'Les phonèmes et le vocabulaire du thai commun', *Journal Asiatique* 236: 197-238.
— (1949) 'La conservation de la sonorité des sonores du thai commun dans le parler thô de Cao-bang', *Actes due XXIe Congres International des Orientalistes 1948* (1949): 251-252.
— (1950) 'Les consonnes préglottalisées en Indochine', *Bulletin de la Société Linguistique de Paris* 46: 172-182.
— (1952) 'Les occlusives uvulaires en thai', *Bulletin de la Société Linguistique de Paris* 48: 86-89.
Henderson, Eugénie J. A. (1949) 'Prosodies in Siamese: A Study in Synthesis', *Asia Major* (New Series) 1.2: 189-215.
— (1951) 'The Phonology of Loan-words in Some South East Asian Languages', *Transactions of the Philological Society*: 132-158.
— (1965) 'The Typology of Certain Phonetic and Morphological Characteristics of Southeast Asia Languages', *Lingua* 15: 400-434.
— (1967) 'Grammar and Tone in South East Asian Languages', *Language* 6:1-2: 171-178.
— (1975) 'Phonetic Description and Phonological Function: Some Reflections upon Back Unrounded Vowels in Thai, Khmer and Vietnamese', in Jimmy G. Harris and James R. Chamberlain (eds), 259-270.
— (1976) 'Thai Phonetics Sixty Years Ago: Gleanings from the Unpublished Notes of Daniel Jones', in Thomas W. Gething, et al. (eds), 162-170.
— (1987) 'A Phonetic Oddity in Thai', in J. H. C. S. Davidson (ed.), *Lai Su' Thai: Essays in Honour of E.H.S. Simmonds*, University of London, School of Oriental and African Studies., 52-62.
Henry, George (1986) 'A Proposal for a General Computer-based Romanization for Southeast Asian Indic-derived Scripts', *Crossroads* 3.1: 62-79.
Hermann, Karen (1979) 'Coping with Complex Polysemy: A Comparison of Dative/Benefactive Constructions in Mandarin and Thai', *Proceedings of the 5th Annual Meeting of the Berkeley Linguistics Society*, 106-113.
Hinds, John (1988a) 'Conversational Interaction in Central Thai', in Cholticha Bamroongraks, et al. (eds) (1988), 150-162.
— (1988b) 'Reflexives in Thai', *Phasa lae Phasasat: Journal of Language and Linguistics* (Thammasat University, Bangkok) 1: 2-24.
Hiranburana Samang (1971) 'The Role of Accent in Thai Grammar', unpublished PhD dissertation, University of London.
— (1972) 'Changes in the Pitch Contours of Unaccented syllables in Spoken Thai', in Jimmy G. Harris and Richard B. Noss (eds), 23-27.

— (1979) 'A Classification of Thai Classifiers', in Nguyên Dang Liêm (ed.) *South-East Asian Linguistic Studies, Volume 4:Pacific Linguistics C49*, Canberra: Research School of Pacific Studies, Australian National University, 39-54.

Hogan, David (1978) 'Urak Lawoi, Malay and Thai: Some Syntactic Comparisons', *Te Reo* 21: 15-33.

Honey, P. J. and Simmonds, E. H. S. (1963) 'Thai and Vietnamese: Some Elements of Nominal Structure Compared', in H. L. Shorto (ed.) *Linguistic Comparison in Southeast Asia and Pacific*, London: School of Oriental and African Studies, University of London, 71-78.

Hoonchamlong, Yuphapann (1990) 'Tones in Thai: An Autosegmental View' *Phasa lae Phasasat: Journal of Language and Linguistics* (Thammasat University, Bangkok) 9.1: 1-31.

— (1991) 'Some Issues in Thai Anaphora: A Government and Binding Approach', unpublished PhD dissertation, University of Wisconsin at Madison.

— (1992) 'Some Observations on phom and dichan: Male and Female First Person Pronouns in Thai', in Carol J. Compton and John F. Hartmann (eds) (1992), 186-204.

Horie, Preeya Ingkaphirom and Iwasaki Shoichi (1996) 'Register and Pragmatic Particles in Thai Conversation', *PAL 4* 4: 1177-1196.

Howard, Kathryn (2000) 'The Notion of Current Relevance in the Thai Perfect', *Linguistics* 38.2: 373-407.

Huang, Pingwan (2007) 'Sinification of the Zhuang People, Culture and their Language', in Jimmy G. Harris et al. (eds), 139-153.

Hudak, Thomas J. (1986) 'Spelling Reforms of Field Marshall Phibulsonkram', *Crossroads* 3.1: 123-133.

— (1987) 'Thai', in Bernard Comrie (ed.) *The World's Major Languages*, London and Sydney: Croom Helm, 757-776.

— (1990) 'The Indigenization of Pali Meters in Thai Poetry', *Monographs in International Studies, Southeast Asia Series No. 87*, Athens, Ohio: University of Ohio Press.

— (2001) 'Limericks and Rhyme in Thai', in M. R. Kalaya Tingsabadh and Arthur S. Abramson (eds), 41-50.

Huffman, Franklin E. (1973) 'Thai and Cambodian: A Case of Syntactic Borrowing?', *Journal of the American Oriental Society* 93.4: 488-509.

— (1986a) Bibliography and Index of Mainland Southeast Asian Languages and Linguistics, New Haven and London: Yale University Press.

— (1986b) 'Khmer Loanwords in Thai', in Bickner, et al. (eds), 199-210.

Hundius, Harald and Kolver, Ulrike (1983) 'Syntax and Semantics of Numeral Classifiers in Thai', *Studies in Language* 7.2: 165-214.

Iamchinda, Meechai (1992) 'Wiwatanakarn khong rabob burutsapphanam thai tangtae samai Sukhothai – samai patchuban [Change in Thai Pronominal System from Sukhothai Period – Present]', unpublished MA thesis, Thammasat University.

Imsri, Patcharee and Idsardi, William J. (2003) 'The Perception of Stops by Thai Children and Adults', *Proceedings of the Annual Boston University Conference on Language Development* 27.1: 321-333.

Indigenous Languages of Thailand Research Project (1977) *Bibliography of Tai Language Studies*, Bangkok: Central Institute of English Language, Office of State Universities.

Indrambarya Kitima (1992) 'The Grammatical Function of "HAY" in Thai', *PAL 3* 1: 1163-1236.

— (1994) 'Are there prepositions in Thai?' in Mark Alves (ed.) *Papers from the Third Annual Meeting of the Southeast Asian Linguistics Society* (1993), Tempe: Arizona State University Program for Southeast Asian Studies, 101-117.

— (1996) 'On Impersonal Verbs in Thai', *PAL 4* 2: 505-521.

Intrasai, Jiraporn (2001) 'Topics in Thai Tonology: An Acoustic Investigation and Some Pedagogical Applications', unpublished PhD dissertation, University of Delaware.

Ishii, Yoneo (1977) *A Glossorial Index of the Sukhothai Inscriptions*, Kyoto: Shoukadoh Publishing.

Iwasaki, Shoichi (2002) 'Proprioceptive-state Expressions in Thai', *Studies in Language* 26.1: 33-66

— (2004) 'What is /nîa/ doing /nîa/?: Grammaticalization of topic in Thai', paper presented to 14th Annual Conference of the Southeast Asian Linguistics Society (SEALS XIV), Bangkok, 19-21 May.

— (1996) 'The Syntactic and Functional Structures of Intonation Unit in Thai', *PAL 4* 2: 750-761.

Iwasaki, Shoichi and Horie, Preeya Ingkapirom (2000) 'Creating Speech Register in Thai Conversation', *Language in Society* 29.4: 519-554.

Iwasaki, Shoichi and Ingkapirom, Preeya (2005) *A Reference Grammar of Thai*, Cambridge University Press.

Iwasaki, Shoichi and Yap, Foong-Ha (1998) '"Give" constructions in Thai and Beyond: A Cognitive Grammaticalization Perspective', in Khunying Suriya Ratanakul, et al. (eds), 371-382.

Jachontov, S. E. (1971) 'O proiskhozhdenie tajskich cislitel'nych', *Voprosy filologii stran Azzi i Afiki*, Leningrad University 1: 93-99.

Jacob, Judith M. (1965) 'Notes on the Numerals and Numeral Coefficients in Old, Middle and Modern Khmer', *Lingua* 15: 143-162.

Jagacinski, Ngampit (1991) 'Waa and Complement-Taking Predicates in Thai', in Martha Ratliff and Eric Schiller (eds) *Papers from the First Annual Meeting of the Southeast Asian Linguistics Society* (1991), Tempe, AZ: Arizona State University Program for Southeast Asian Studies, 205-223.

— (1986) 'Tai Lue Scripts: The Old and the New', *Crossroads* 3.1: 80-96.

— (1992) 'The 'au usages in Thai', in Compton and Hartmann (eds), 118-138.

Jataputra, Nuntika (1981) 'Orthographic Reform in the Thai Language', unpublished PhD dissertation, Northwestern University.

Jones, Robert B. (1965) 'On the Reconstruction of Proto-Thai', *Lingua* 14: 194-229.

— (1966) 'Comparative Thai Studies: A Critique', in Ba Shin, Jean Boisselier, and A. B. Griswold (eds) *Essays Offered to G. H. Luce by his Colleagues and Friends in Honour of his Seventy-fifth Birthday*, Volume 1, Ascona: Artibus Asiae, 160-3.

— (1970) 'Classifier Constructions in Southeast Asia', *Journal of the American Oriental Society* 90.1: 1-12.

— (1971) 'Thai Titles and Ranks', Cornell University Southeast Asia Program Data Paper No. 81.

— (1976) 'Tone Shift in Tai Dialects', in Thomas W. Gething, et al. (eds), 171-178.

Jones, Robert B., Mendiones, Ruchira C. and Reynolds, Craig J. (1969) *Thai Cultural Reader, Book I*, Cornell University Southeast Asia Program.

Jones, Robert B., and Mendiones, Ruchira C. (1969) *Thai Cultural Reader, Book II*, Cornell University Southeast Asia Program.

— (1970) *Introduction to Thai Literature*, Cornell University Southeast Asia Program.

Jonsson, Nanna L. (1991) 'Proto Southwestern Tai', unpublished PhD dissertation, State University of New York at Albany.

Jumsai, M. L. Manich (1984) 'Thai Language and Writing', *Proceedings of the International Conference on Thai Studies*, Bangkok: Thai Studies Programme, Chulalongkorn University, Vol. II 'Language and Literature', 1-5.

Juntanamalaga, Preecha (1988) 'Social Issues in Thai Classifier Usage', *Language Sciences* 10: 313-330.

— (1992) 'On the Semantics of Thai Compounds in hua "head"', in Compton and Hartmann (eds), 168-178.

Juntanamalaga, Preecha and Diller, Anthony, V. N. (1992) 'Thai Pragmatic Constructions: The oey Paradigm', *Journal of Pragmatics* 18.2-3: 289-301.

Kam, Tak Him (1980) 'Semantic-tonal Processes in Cantonese, Taishanese, Bobai, and Siamese', *Journal of Chinese Linguistics* 8.2: 205-240.

Kanasut-Roengpitya, Kanita (1965) 'The Perception of the Occlusives of Thai and English: A Contrastive Study', unpublished MA thesis, University of Hawaii.

— (1973) 'A Semantic Study of Royal and Sacerdotal Usage in Thai', unpublished PhD dissertation, University of California, Berkeley.

— (1974) 'Negation in Thai: A Study in semantic relationships', *Bulletin of the Faculty of Arts* (Chulalongkorn University) 8: 93-146.

Kanchanathat, Narumon (1977) 'An Instrumental Study of Thai Speakers' English Intonation', unpublished PhD dissertation, University of Michigan.

Kanchanawan, Nitaya (1978) 'Expression for Time in the Thai Verb and Its Application to Thai-English Machine Translation', unpublished PhD dissertation, University of Texas, Austin.

— (1984) 'Thai-English Machine Translation', *Proceedings of the International Conference on Thai Studies*, Bangkok: Thai Studies Programme, Chulalongkorn University), Vol. II 'Language and Literature', 1-23.

Karnchana Nacaskul (1971) 'Parallelism in the Use and Construction of Certain Grammatical and Lexical Items in Cambodian and Thai: A Typological Comparative Study', unpublished PhD dissertation, University of London.

— (1976) 'Types of Elaboration in Some Southeast Asian Languages', *Austroasiatic Studies* 2: 873-889.

Kendall, Sue Ann and Yoon, James Hye-Suk (1986) 'Sentence Particles as Evidence for Morphosyntactic Interaction with Pragmatics', *Studies in the Linguistic Sciences* 16.1: 53-77.

Kessakul, Ruetaivan (1999) 'Two Faces of Linguistic Encoding in Thai Motion Events: Evidence from Thai Spoken Narrative Discourse Compared with Japanese', in Graham W. Thurgood (ed.) *Papers From the Ninth Annual Meeting of the Southeast Asian Linguistics Society*, Tempe, AZ: Arizona State University Southeast Asia Program, 73-89.

Khamsaen, Jarida P. (1978) 'Causative Construction in Thai', *Bulletin of the Deccan College Research Institute (Poona)* 38.1-4: 123-135.

Khanittanan Wilaiwan W. (1973) 'The Influence of Siamese on Five Lao Dialects', unpublished PhD dissertation, University of Michigan.

— (1994) Raingan wichai laksana phasa thi chai phan su'muanchon thorathat [Report of research into features of language used in television media], Bangkok: National Research Council.

Khanittanan, Wilaiwan (1983) 'Kamti Thai: From an SVO to SOV Language', in B. H. Krishnamurti, Colin P. Masica and Anjani K. Sinha (eds) *South Asian Linguistics: Structure, Convergence and Diglossia*, Delhi: Motilal Barnarsidas.

— (1979) 'How Much is English Influencing the Language of Educated Bangkok Thais?', in Nguên Dăng Liêm (ed.), *South East Asian Linguistic Studies, Pacific Linguistics* C-49: 55-59

— (1987a) 'Phasa nai nangsu' Sam Somdet [Language in the book Three Princes]', *Thammasat University Journal* 15: 35-49.

— (1987b) 'Some Aspects of Linguistic Change in the Language Usage of King Rama IV, Rama V and Rama VI', in Ann Buller (ed.) *Proceedings of the International Conference for Thai Studies* (Canberra) 3: 53-70.

— (1988a) 'Some Observations on Expressing Politeness in Thai', *Language Sciences* 10.2: 353-362.

— (1988b) 'Thai Written Discourse: A Change toward a More Autonomous Style?', in Bamroongraks, Cholticha and Wilaiwan Khanittanan, et al., (eds), 120-127.

— (2001) 'Khmero-Thai: the great change in the history of the language of the Chao Phraya Basin', paper presented at the Ninth Annual Meeting of the Southeast Asian Linguistic Society, Bangkok.

— (2007) 'Language of the News Media in Thailand', *International Journal of the Sociology of Language* 186: 29-42.

Khanittanan Wilaiwan, and Placzek, Jim (1982) 'Historical and Contemporary Meanings of Thai khwan: The Use of Lexical Meaning Change as an Indicator of Culture Change', in Bruce Matthews and J. Nagata, (eds) *Religion, Values and Development in Southeast Asia*, Singapore: Institute of Southeast Asian Studies.

Kimsuvan, Anek (1992) 'The Pragmatical Use of / yuu/', *PAL 3 1*: 169-243.

Kobsiriphat, Wissanu (1988) 'Empty Categories in Thai', unpublished PhD dissertation, University of Washington.

Koenig, J. P. and Muansuwan, N. (2000) 'How to End Without Ever Finishing: Thai Semi-Perfectivity', *Journal of Semantics* 17.2: 147-184.

Kölver, Urike (1979) 'Syntaktische Untersuchung von Numeral-klassifikationen im Zentral-Thai', *Arbeiten des Kölner Universalienprojekts* 34, Cologne.

Kookiattikoon, Supath (2001) 'The Syntax of Classifiers in Thai', unpublished PhD dissertation, University of Kansas.

Kroll, Mary E. (1956) 'Suprasegmental Phonemes of Thai (Bangkok Dialect)', unpublished MA thesis, Georgetown University.

Kruatrachue, Foongfuang (1960) 'Thai and English: A Comparative study of Phonology for Pedagogical Applications', unpublished PhD dissertation, Indiana University.

Krupa, Victor (1978) 'Classifiers in the Languages of Southeast Asia: Evolution of a Lexico-Syntactic Category', *Asian and African Studies* (Bratislava) 14: 119-124.

Kullavanijaya, Pranee (1968) 'A Study of Preverbs in Thai', unpublished MA thesis, University of Hawaii.

— (1974) 'Transitive Verbs in Thai', unpublished PhD dissertation, University of Hawaii.

— (1980) 'A Question or not a Question: This is a Question', paper presented at the 13th International Conference on Sino-Tibetan Languages and Linguistics, Charlottersville: University of Virginia.

— (1992) 'A Study of Some Two-Syllabled Words in Thailand', *PAL 3* 1: 651-664.

— (1997) 'Verb Intensifying Devices in Bangkok Thai', in Arthur Abramson (ed.), 147-152.

— (2001) 'A Study of Lexical variation in Seven Zhuang Dialects', in M. R. Kalaya Tingsabadh and Arthur S. Abramson (eds), 229-258.

Kullavanijaya, Pranee and Bisang, Walter (2004) 'Another Look at Aspect in Thai', paper presented to the Thirteenth Annual Meeting of the Southeast Asian Linguistics Society (SEALS XIII), Bangkok, May.

Kullavanijaya, Pranee and Thepkanjana, Kingkarn (2001) 'Devices for Forming Entity-Denoting Signs in Thai Sign Language', in M. R. Kalaya Tingsabadh and Arthur S. Abramson (eds), 139-175.

Kullavanijaya, Pranee and Vongvipanond, Peansiri (1984) *Bibliography of Thai Grammar and Phonology*, Bangkok: Chulalongkorn University.

Kumlert, Duangporn (1976) 'Causative Sentences in Thai', unpublished MA thesis, University of the Philippines.

Kummer, Manfred (1992) 'Politeness in Thai', in Richard J. Watts et al. (eds) *Politeness in Language: Studies in its History, Theory and Practice*, 325-336, Berlin: Mouton de Gruyter.

Kuno, Susumu, and Wongkhomthong, Preya (1980) 'Two Copulative verbs in Thai', *Harvard Studies in Syntax and Semantics* 3: 243-315.

— (1981a) 'Characterizational and Identificational Sentences in Thai', *Studies in Language* 5.1: 65-109.

— (1981b) 'Relative Clauses in Thai', *Studies in Language* 5.1: 195-226.

Kuo, William (1982) *Teaching Grammar of Thai*, University of California at Berkeley, Center for South and Southeast Asian Studies.

La Loubère, Simon de (1691) *Du Royaume de Siam*, 2 vols, Paris: Jean Baptiste Coignard.

Lafont, Pierre-Bernard (1962) 'Les écritures du Pali au Laos', *Bulletin de l 'Ecôle Française d'Extrême-Orient* 50: 395-405.

Lagsanaging, Dhirawit (1991) 'The Syntax and Semantics of Anaphors in Thai', *Phasa lae Phasasat: Journal of Language and Linguistics* (Thammasat University, Bangkok) Jan-Mar: 42-57.

— (1992) 'Pragmatics of Negation in Thai', *PAL 3* 3: 1427-39.

Lamchote, Duangta (1971) 'The Definite and Indefinite Articles in English and their Thai Equivalents', unpublished MA thesis, Chulalongkorn University.

Leben, W. R. (1971) 'On the Segmental Nature of Tone in Thai', *M.I.T. Res. Lab. of Electronics, Quarterly Progress Report* 101: 221-4.

Lee, Chotiros K. (1987) 'Heart Language', in Ann Buller (ed.) *Proceedings of the International Conference on Thai Studies*, Vol. II, 149-194, Canberra: Australian National University.

Lehman, F. K. and Pingkarawat, Namtip (1985) 'Missing Nominals, Nonspecificity and Related Matters, with Especial Reference to Thai and Burmese', *Studies in the Linguistic Sciences* 15.2: 101-121.

Lekawatana, Pongsri (1970) 'Verb Phrases in Thai: A Study in Deep-Case Relationships', unpublished PhD dissertation, University of Michigan.

— (1975) 'The so-called Passive in Thai', in Thomas W. Gething (ed.), 1-12. Also in Thomas W. Gething and Nguên Dăng Liêm (eds) (1979) *Papers in South East Asian Linguistics 6: Tai Studies in Honor of William J. Gedney (Pacific Linguistics A52)*, Canberra: Australian National University, 1-10.

Levy, Annick (1972) 'Mission Ethno-linguistique en Thailande', *Asie du Sud-est et Monde Insulindien* 3.2: 51-55.

Li Fang-Kuei (1944) 'The Influence of the Primitive Tai Glottal Stop and Pre-glottalized Consonants on the Tone System of Po-ai', *Bulletin of Chinese Studies* 4: 59-68.

— (1945) 'Some Old Chinese loan words in the Tai languages', *Harvard-Yenching Journal of Asiatic Studies* 8: 333-342.

— (1954) 'Consonant Clusters in Tai', *Language* 30: 368-379.

— (1956) 'Siamese wan and waan', *Language* 32: 81-82.

— (1959) 'Classification by Vocabulary: Tai Dialects', *Anthropological Linguistics* 1: 15-21.

— (1960) 'A Tentative Classification of Tai Dialects', in Stanley Diamond (ed.) *Culture in History, Essays in Honour of Paul Radin*, New York: Columbia University Press, 951-959

— (1970) 'Some Tonal Irregularities in the Tai Languages', in Roman Jakobson and Shigeo Kawamoto (eds) *Studies in General and Oriental Linguistics*, Tokyo: TEC Corporation for Language and Educational Research, 415-22.

— (1971) 'On Siamese jaai', *BIHP* 42.3: 337-40.

— (1974) 'Tai Languages', *Encyclopedia Britannica*, 15 ed., Macropaedia 17: 989-992.

— (1975) 'Some Words for Thai Dialectology', in Jimmy G. Harris and James R. Chamberlain (eds), 271-273.

— (1976) 'Sino-Tai', Computational Analysis of Asian and African Languages 3: 39-48.

— (1977) 'A Handbook of Comparative Tai', *Oceanic Linguistics Special Publications* 15, Honolulu: University of Hawaii Press.

— (1977-78) 'Siamese Khot', *Monumenta Serica* 33: 403-406.

— (1983) 'Proto-Tai *kh- and *x-', *Min Zu Yu Wen* 6: 7-9.

— (1992) 'The Tai Languages', in Compton and Hartmann (eds), 1-4.

Lisker, Leigh and Abramson, Arthur (1964) 'A Cross Language Study of Voicing in Initial Stops: Acoustical Measurements', *Word* 20.3: 384-422.

List, George (1961) 'Speech Melody and Song Melody in Central Thailand', *Ethnomusicology* 5: 16-32.

Lodge, Ken (1986) 'Allegro Rules in Colloquial Thai: Some Thoughts on Process Phonology', *Journal of Linguistics* 22.2: 331-354.

Low, James (1828) *A Grammar of the T'hai or Siamese Language*, Calcutta: Baptist Mission Press.

L-Thongkum, Theraphan (1976) 'Relative Durations of Syllables in Siamese Connected Speech', in Thomas Gething, et al. (eds), 225-232

— (1978) 'Rhythm in Thai', unpublished PhD dissertation, University of Edinburgh.

— (1984) 'Rhythmic Groups and Stress Groups in Thai', *Proceedings of the International Conference on Thai Studies*, Bangkok: Thai Studies Programme, Chulalongkorn University, Vol. II 'Language and Literature', 1-10.

— (1992) 'The Raising and Lowering of Pitch Caused by a Voicing Distinction in Sonorants (Nasals and Approximants): an Epidemic Disease in SEA Languages', *PAL 3 1*: 1079-1104.

— (1994) 'The Lexicalization and Conceptualization of Some Noun Compounds in Tai-Kadai Languages', *Acta Linguistica Hafniensia* 27.2: 353-358.

— (1997) 'Implications of the Retention of Proto-Voiced Plosives and Fricatives in the Dai Tho Language of Yunnan Province for a Theory of Tonal Development and Tai Language Classification', in Edmondson and Solnit 1997: 191-220.

L-Thongkum, Theraphan, Teeranon, Phanintra and Intajamornrak, Chommanad (2007) 'The Interaction between Vowel Length and Pitch in Southeast Asian (SEA) Languages: Implications for Tonogenesis', in Jimmy G. Harris et al. (eds), 225-239.

L-Thongkum, Theraphan, Panupong, Vichin, Kullavanijaya, Pranee and Tingsabadh, M. R. Kalaya (eds) (1979) *Studies in Tai and Mon-Khmer Phonetics and Phonology in Honour of Eugénie J.A. Henderson*, Bangkok: Chulalongkorn University Press.

— (1992) 'Three-Dimensional Phonology: A Historical Implication', *PAL 3 1*: 75-90.

Luksaneeyanawin, Sudaporn (1983) 'Intonation in Thai', unpublished PhD dissertation, University of Edinburgh.

— (1984) 'Some Semantic Functions of Reduplication in Thai', *Chiangmai Symposium on Languages and Linguistics*.

— (1992) 'Three-dimensional Phonology, A Historical Implication', *PAL 3 1*: 75-90.

Luksaneeyanawin, Sudaporn, Prasithrathsint, Amara et al. (eds) (1992) *Pan Asiatic Linguistics: Proceedings of the Third International Conference on Language and Linguistics*, Bangkok: Chulalongkorn University. (=*PAL 3*.)

Luo Yongxian, (1996) 'Word Families in Tai: A Preliminary Account', *PAL 4 3*: 850-882.

— (1996) 'Tonal Irregularities in Tai Revisited', *Mon-Khmer Studies* 25: 69-102.

— (1997) *The Subgroup Structure of the Tai Languages: A Historical-Comparative Study*, Berkeley, California: Journal of Chinese Linguistics Monograph Series No. 12.

— (2000) 'From "Head" to "Toe": Sino-Tai Lexical Correspondences in Body Part Terms', *Journal of Chinese Linguistics* 28:1: 67-99.

— (2001) 'The Hypothesis of a New Branch for the Tai Languages', in M. R. Kalaya Tingsabadh and Arthur S. Abramson (eds), 177-188.

— (2007) 'Sino-Tai Words for "Cut"', in Jimmy G. Harris et al. (eds), 155-181.

Manomaivibool, Prapin (1975) 'A Study of Sino-Thai Lexical Correspondences', unpublished PhD dissertation, University of Washington.

— (1976) 'Layers of Chinese Loanwords in Thai', in Thomas W. Gething, et al. (eds) *Tai Linguistics in Honor of Fang-Kuei Li*, Bangkok: Chulalongkorn University Press, 79-84

— (2000) 'Tracing the Meanings of Thai Disyllabic Words', in Marlys Macken (ed.) *Papers from the Tenth Annual Meeting of the Southeast Asian Linguistics Society*, Tempe: Arizona State University Program Southeast Asian Studies, 285-295.

Martini, François (1950) 'L'opposition nom et verbe en vietnamien et en siamois', *Bulletin de la Société Linguistique de Paris* 46: 183-196.

— (1956) 'Les expressions de 'être' en siamois et en cambodigien', *Bulletin de la Société Linguistique de Paris* 52: 289-306.

— (1957-8) 'La distinction du prédicat de qualité et de l'epithète en cambodgien et en siamois', *Bulletin de la Société Linguistique de Paris* 53: 295-305.

Maspero, Henri (1911) 'Contribution à l'étude du systèms phonétiques des langues thai', *Bulletin de l 'Ecôle Française d'Extrême-Orient* 11: 153-169.

Masuko, Yukie and Kiritani, Shigeru (1991) 'The Duration of Geminate Consonants in Indonesian and in Thai', *Annual Bulletin, Research Institute of Logopedics and Phoniatrics* 25: 81-89.

Matisoff, James A. (1986) 'Hearts and minds in Southeast Asian languages and English: An essay in comparative lexical semantics of psycho-collocations', *Cahiers de Linguistique Asia Orientale* (Paris) 15.1: 5-57.

— (1990) 'On Megalocomparison', *Language* 66.1: 106-120.

— (1992) 'Siamese jaai Revisited, or ¡Ay, Madre!: A Case Study in Multiple Etymological Possibilities', in Compton and Hartmann (eds), 111-117.
McFarland, George B. (1944) *Thai-English Dictionary* (2nd edition), Stanford University Press.
Meemeskul-Martin, Ruchirawam (1984) 'Towards a Descriptive Model of Thai-English Translation', unpublished PhD dissertation, Georgetown University.
Melamed, Judith T. (1962) 'An Experiment in Sound Discrimination in English and Thai', unpublished PhD dissertation, Indiana University.
Messenger, Scribner A. (1980) 'Theme as a Stylistic Parameter in Thai Prose', unpublished PhD dissertation, Cornell University.
Mikami, Naomitsu (1984) 'Some Observations on the Thai Language in the Sukhothai Inscriptions', *Proceedings of the International Conference on Thai Studies*, Bangkok: Thai Studies Programme, Chulalongkorn University, Vol. II 'Language and Literature', 1-20.
Minnigerode, B., and Vichapun, A. (1969) 'Informationstheoretische Untersuchungen an der thailändische Sprache', *Phonetica* 20.1: 46-56.
Miyamoto, Tadao (1992) 'Truncation of Sanskrit and Pali Loanwords in Thai', *PAL 3* 1: 869-882.
Moerman, Michael (1977) 'The Preference for Self-correction in a Tai Conversational Corpus', *Language* 25.4: 872-882.
Moerman, Michel (1965) 'Ethnic Identification in a Complex Civilization: Who are the Lue?' *American Anthropologist* 67.5: 1215-30.
— (1988) *Talking Culture: Ethnography and Conversation Analysis*, Philadelphia: University of Pennsylvania Press.
Moore, Christopher (1992) *Heart Talk*, Bangkok: White Lotus.
Morev, L. N., Plam, I. I. and Fomicheva, N. F. (1961) *Taiskii iazyk [The Thai Language]*, Moscow: Publishing House for Oriental Literature.
Morev, Lev N. (1964) Osnovy sintaksia taiskogo iazyka [Fundamentals of Thai Syntax], Moscow, Nauka.
— (1991) Sopostavitel'naya grammitika taiskikh yazikov [Comparative grammar of the Tai languages], Moscow: Nauka, Glavnaya Redaktsiya Vostochnoi Literaturi.
— (1994) 'Possessive constructions in Tai', in Hajime Kitamura, Tatsuo Nishida and Yasuhiko Nagano, (eds) *Current Issues in Sino-Tibetan Linguistics* (26th International Conference on Sino-Tibetan Languages and Linguistics, 13-17 September 1993), Osaka: National Museum of Ethnology, 890-905.
— (1996) 'Diathesis in the Tai Languages', *PAL 4* 3: 1109-1117.
— (2000) 'Some Afterthoughts on Classifiers in the Tai Languages', *Mon-Khmer Studies* 30.2: 75-82.
Morey, Stephen (2005) *The Tai Languages of Assam: A Grammar and Texts*, Canberra: Pacific Linguistics 565.
Morita, Liang (2003) 'Language Shift in the Thai Chinese Community', *Journal of Multilingual and Multicultural Matters* 26.6: 485-495.
— (2007) 'Discussing Assimilation and Language Shift among the Chinese in Thailand' *International Journal of the Sociology of Language* 186: 43-58.
Na Nagara, Prasert and Griswold, A. B. (1992) *Epigraphic and Historical Studies*, Bangkok: The Historical Society under Royal Patronage of H.R.H. Princess Maha Chakri Sirindhorn.
Na Nakhon, Pluang (1973) *Panha Phasa Thai [Thai Language Problems]*, Bangkok: Ruam San.
Nacaskul, Karnchana (1962) 'A Study of Cognate Words in Thai and Cambodian', unpublished M. A. thesis, University of London.
— (1976) 'Types of Elaboration in Some Southeast Asian Languages', *Austroasiatic Studies* (Oceanic Linguistics Special Publications No. 13) 2: 873-889.
— (1979) 'A note on English loanwords in Thai', in Theraphan L-Thongkum, et al. (eds), 151-162.

— (1987) 'The Phonology of Thai Pet Names', in Jeremy H. C. S. Davidson (ed.) *Lai Su' Thai: Essays in Honour of E. H. S. Simmonds*, School of Oriental and African Studies, University of London, 41-51.

Namthammachat, P. (1975) 'Reflexivization in Thai', unpublished PhD dissertation, Syracuse University.

Nguên Dăng Liêm (1974) 'Clauses and cases in English and Southeast Asian languages (Burmese, Cambodian, Cantonese, Lao, Thai and Vietnamese) in contrast', in Nguên Dăng Liêm (ed.) *South-East Asian Linguistic Studies*, Volume 1: *Pacific Linguistics C31*, Canberra: Research School of Pacific Studies, Australian National University, 129-155.

Nguên Dăng Liêm (ed.) (1974, 1976, 1979a, 1979b) *South-East Asian Linguistic Studies, Volumes 1, 2, 3, 4 (Pacific Linguistics C31, C42, C45, C49)*, Canberra: Research School of Pacific Studies, Australian National University.

Needleman, Rosa M. (1973a) 'Tai Verbal Structures and Some Implications for Current Linguistic Theory', unpublished PhD dissertation, University of California at Los Angeles.

Neill, Catherine Ray (1989a) 'Sources of Meaning in Thai Narrative Discourse: Grammar, Rhetoric, and Socio-Cultural Knowledge (Volumes I and II)', unpublished PhD dissertation, Georgetown University.

— (1989b) 'Final Particle ná' and châj máj in Thai Oral Narrative', *Phasaa* 19.1: 61-76.

Nokaeo, Preeya (1989) 'Central Thai and Northern Thai: A Linguistic and Attitudinal Study', unpublished PhD dissertation, University of Texas, Austin.

Noochoochai, Ponlasit (1978) 'Temporal Aspect in Thai and English: A Contrastive Analysis', unpublished PhD dissertation, New York University.

Noss, Richard B. (1964) *Thai Reference Grammar*, Washington, DC: US Government Printing Office.

— (1972a) 'Rhythm in Thai', in Jimmy G. Harris and Richard B. Noss (eds), 33-42

— (1972b) 'The ungrounded transformer', *Language Sciences* 23: 8-14.

— (1975) 'How Useful are Citation Form in Synchronic Thai Phonology?', in Jimmy G. Harris and James R. Chamberlain (eds), 274-284.

Onsuwan, Chutamanee (2000) 'Temporal Relations between Thai Initial Stops and Vowels: Acoustic and Perceptual Studies', in Marlys Macken (ed.) *Papers From the Tenth Annual Meeting of the Southeast Asian Linguistics Society*, Tempe: Arizona State University Program in Southeast Asian Studies, 271-283.

Osatananda, Varisa (1996) 'An Analysis of Tonal Assignment on Japanese Loanwords in Thai', *PAL 4* 1: 198-210.

Oshika, Beatrice R. T. (1973) 'The Relationship of Kam-Sui-Mak To Tai', unpublished PhD dissertation, University of Michigan.

Osipov, Ju. M. (1969) Voprosy Slavoobrazovaniji V Sovrennom Tajskom Jazyke [Questions of word formation in modern Thai], Moscow: Nauka.

Ostapirat, Weera (2000) *Proto-Kra*, Berkeley, California: Linguistics of the Tibeto-Burman Area 23.1 (entire volume).

— (2004) 'Kra-dai and Austronesian: Notes on Phonological Correspondences and Vocabulary Distribution', in Laurent Sagart, Roger Blench and Alicia Sanchez-Mazas (eds) *The Peopling of East Asia: Putting together Archaeology, Linguistics and Genetics*, London: Routledge-Curzon, 107-131.

— (2007) 'Proto-Tai Velars and Postvelars', in Jimmy G. Harris et al. (eds), 293-299.

PAL 2, see Bamroongraks, Cholticha, Wilaiwan Khanittanan, et al., (eds) (1988).

PAL 3, Pan-Asiatic Linguistics 3 = Pan-Asiatic Linguistics: Proceedings of the Third International Conference on Languages and Linguistics, edited by Lukasneeyanawin, Sudaporn, Amara Prasithrathsint, et al. Bangkok: Chulalongkorn University, 1992.

PAL 4, Pan-Asiatic Linguistics 4 = Pan Asiatic Linguistics: Proceedings of the Fourth International Conference on Languages and Linguistics, edited by Premsrirat, Suwilai, et al., Institute of Language and Culture for Rural Development, Mahidol University at Salaya, Bangkok, 1996.

Palakornkul, Angkab (1972) 'A Sociolinguistic Study of Pronominal Strategy in Spoken Bangkok Thai', unpublished PhD dissertation, University of Texas at Austin.
— (1975) 'A sociolinguistic study of pronominal usage in spoken Bangkok Thai', *International Journal of the Sociology of Language* 5: 11-42.
— (1976) 'Some observation on variation and change in the use of classifiers in Thai', *Pasaa* 6.1-2: 186-199.
Palikupt, Deeyoo (1983) 'Central Thai and Northeastern Thai: A Linguistic and Attitudinal Study', unpublished PhD dissertation, University of Texas at Austin.
Pallegoix, Jean B. (1850) *Grammatica Linguae Thai*, Bangkok: Assumption College Press.
Palmer, Adrian S. (1969)' Thai tone variants and the language teachers', *Language Learning* 19.3-4: 287-299
Pankhuenkhat, Ruengdet (1976) 'A Synchronic comparative Study of Modern Thai and Modern Lanna', unpublished PhD dissertation, Deccan College, Poona, India.
— (1978) *An Introduction to Thai Syntax*, Bangkok: Mahidol University Southeast Asia Center.
Panpothong, Natthaporn (2001) 'Is there wh-movement in Thai?', in M. R. Kalaya Tingsabadh and Arthur S. Abramson (eds), 53-62.
Pantupong, Woranut (1973) 'Pitch, stress and rhythm in Thai', *Pasaa* 3.2: 41-63.
Panupong, Vichin (1970) Inter-Sentence Relations in Modern Conversational Thai, Bangkok: The Siam Society.
— (1978) 'Some basic problems of semantics concerning certain types of homophonic-graphic words in Thai', in W. U. Dressler and W. Meid (eds) *Proceedings of the Twelfth International Congress of Linguists* (Vienna), Innsbrucker Beitrage zur Sprachwissenschaft, 217-221.
Patamapongse, Patamaka (1971) 'A Tagmemic Approach to Certain Thai Clauses', unpublished PhD dissertation, University of Pittsburgh.
Patrakom, Nopawan (1977) 'The Hermeneutics of Listening: Thai Responses to the Characterization of Persons', unpublished PhD dissertation, University of Colorado at Boulder.
Person, Kirk R. (1996) 'Thailand's "Straight-Talking" Monk: A Discourse Analysis of the Hortatory Speech of Phra Phayom Kalayano', *PAL 4* 2: 767-792.
Peyasanitwong, Patcharin (1979) 'Phonological Reduction of Some Final Particles in Modern Thai', in Nguên Dăng Liêm (ed.) *South-East Asian Linguistic Studies*, Volume 4: *Pacific Linguistics C49*, Canberra: Research School of Pacific Studies, Australian National University, 99-115.
— (1981) 'A Study of Final Particles in Conversational Thai', unpublished PhD dissertation, University of Michigan.
— (1986) 'Stress in Thai', in Bickner, et al. (eds), 211-230.
Phinit-Akson, Vinit (1972) 'A Tagmemic Contrastive Analysis of Some English and Thai Question Constructions', unpublished PhD dissertation, University of Pittsburgh.
Pingkarawat, Namtip (1989) 'Empty Noun Phrases and the Theory of Control, with Special Reference to Thai', unpublished PhD dissertation, University of Illinois at Urbana-Champaign.
Placzek, James A. (1984) 'Perceptual and Cultural Salience in Noun Classification: the Puzzling Case of Standard Thai lêm', unpublished PhD dissertation, University of British Columbia.
— (1985) 'The Missing "long things" in the Thai Noun Classifier System', *Journal of the Siam Society* 73: 162-175.
— (1992) 'The Perceptual Foundation of the Thai Classifier System', in Compton and Hartmann (eds), 154-167.
Plam, Youri (1972) 'Sur la classification des noms dans la langue thai (siamoise)', in Jacques Barraum, et al. (eds) *Langues et Techniques, Nature et Societe, Vol. I: Approache Linguistique*, Paris: Klincksieck, 195-202.
Poo-israkij, Orawan (1995) 'Verbal Complementation in Khmer', unpublished PhD dissertation, Australian National University.

Post, Mark (2007) 'Grammaticalization and Compounding in Thai and Chinese : A Text-Frequency Approach', *Studies in Language* 31.1 : 117-176.

Prasithrathsint, Amara (1974) 'Coocurrences of Final Particles in Thai', *Chulalongkorn University: Bulletin of the Faculty of Arts* 8: 74-79.

— (1988) 'Change in Passive Constructions in Written Thai from 1802 to 1982', *Language Sciences* 10: 363-393.

— (1994) 'Borrowing and Nominalization of Technical Terms in Standard Thai', in Istvan Fodor and Claude Hagege (eds) *Language Reform, History and Future, Vol. VI.*, Hamburg: Helmut Buske Verlag, 9-24.

— (1996) 'Stylistic Differentiation of /kaan/ and /khwaam/ Nominalization in Standard Thai', *PAL 4* 4: 1206-1216.

— (1997) 'The Emergence and Development of Abstract Nominalization in Standard Thai', in Arthur S. Abramson (ed.), 179-190.

— (2000) 'Adjectives as Verbs in Thai', *Linguistic Typology* 4: 251-271.

— (2001) 'A Componential Analysis of Kinship Terms in Thai', in M. R. Kalaya Tingsabadh and Arthur S. Abramson (eds), 261-276.

— (2006) 'Nominalization and Categorization of Verbs in Thai', in Paul Sidwell (ed.) *Papers from the Fifteenth Meeting of the Southeast Linguistics Society*, Canberra: Australian National University.

— (2007a) 'a Comparison of Ways of Talking in Dehong Tai, Ahom Thai, and Sukhothai Thai with a Focus on Nominalization', in Jimmy G. Harris et al. (eds), 1-9.

— (2007b) Principles of Thai Place-name Formation: a Reflection of Natural and Cultural Heritage', *International Journal of the Sociology of Language* 186: 59-74.

Premsrirat, Suwilai (2006) 'Thailand: language Situation', in K. Brown (ed.) *Encyclopedia of Language and Linguistics, Vol. 2*, Amsterdam: Elsevier, 642-644.

— (2007) 'Endangered Languages of Thailand' *International Journal of the Sociology of Language* 186: 75-95.

Premsrirat, Suwilai, et al. (eds) (1996) Pan Asiatic Linguistics: Proceedings of the Fourth International Conference on Languages and Linguistics. Bangkok: Mahidol University. (=PAL 4.)

Punyodyana, Tasaniya (1976) 'The Thai Verb in a Tagmemic Framework', unpublished PhD dissertation, Cornell University.

Rama VI (Vajiravudh), King of Siam (1912) 'The Romanization of Siamese words', *Journal of the Siam Society* 9: 1-10.

Rangkupan, Suda (2001) 'Linguistic Characteristics of Psychological Perspective in Thai Narrative Discourse', unpublished PhD dissertation, New York State University at Buffalo.

Ratanakul, Khunying Suriya, Thomas, David and Premsrira, Suwilai t (eds), (1985) *Southeast Asian Linguistics Presented to A.-G. Haudricourt*, Bangkok: Mahidol University.

Ratanakul, Khunying Suriya, Burusphat, Somsonge et al., (eds) (1998) *Proceedings of the International Conference on Tai Studies, July 29-31, 1998*, Bangkok: Institute of Language and Culture for Rural Development, Mahidol University.

Reed, Tipawan Truong-Quang (1976) 'A Study in Semantics: The Meaning of Gastronomy in Thai Culture', M. A. thesis, Northern Illinois University.

Reid, L. (1984) 'Benedict's Austro-Tai Hypothesis', *Asian Perspectives* 26: 19-34.

Richards, Jack (1968) 'Pronunciation Features of Thai Speakers of English', *Te Reo* 10-11:67-75.

Rischel, Jørgen (1984) 'Achievements and Challenges in Present-Day Thai Phonetics', *Proceedings of the International Conference on Thai Studies*, Bangkok: Thai Studies Programme, Chulalongkorn University, Vol. II 'Language and Literature', 1-35.

Robertson, Jack F. (1982) 'Bangkok Thai Tones', unpublished PhD dissertation, University of Southern California.

Rodman, Robert (1977) 'Constraints on coordination in Thai, Korean and Mandarin Chinese', *Linguistica Antverpiensia* 11: 143-154.

Roengpitya, Rungpat (2000) 'A Historical and Perceptual Study of Vowel Length in Thai' in Marlis Maklin (ed.) *Papers from the Tenth Annual Meeting of the Southeast Asian Linguistics Society*, Tempe: Arizona State University Program Southeast Asian Studies, 353-365.

Ronakiat, Nantana (Danvivatana) (2007) 'A Survey of Attempts to Write Thai Street Signs in Romanization', in Jimmy G. Harris et al. (eds), 183-203.

Roop, D. H. (1969) 'The Problem of Linguistic Diversity in Thailand: An Approach to a Solution', in Peter Hinton (ed.) *Tribesmen and Peasants in North Thailand*, Chiangmai: Tribal Research Centre, 100-107.

Rose, Phil (1997) 'A Seven-tone Dialect in Southern Thai with Super High: Pakphanang Tonal Acoustics and Physiological Inferences', in Arthur S. Abramson (ed.), 191-209.

Ross, Peter A. (1996) 'Archaic Features of Baan Ha Thai', *Phasa lae Phasasat: Journal of Language and Linguistics* (Thammasat University, Bangkok) 14.2: 53-46.

Santaputra, Sirinee (1984) 'Structure and Function of Questions in Thai', unpublished PhD dissertation, University of Hawaii.

Sarawit, Mary E. (1973) 'The Proto-Tai Vowel System', unpublished PhD dissertation, University of Michigan.

— (1975) 'Some Changes in the Final Component of the Tai Syllable', in Jimmy G. Harris and James R. Chamberlain (eds), 316-328.

— (1976) 'Assimilation in child language acquisition', in Thomas W. Gething, et al. (eds) 205-213.

Savetamalya, Saranya (1996) 'Verbal relative clauses as adnominal modifiers in Thai', *PAL 4* 2: 627-646.

— (2001) 'A Categorization of thùuk in Thai: Lexicase Analysis', in M. R. Kalaya Tingsabadh and Arthur S. Abramson (eds), 117-136.

— (1992) 'Patient Subject Constructions in Thai', *PAL 3* 1: 244-281.

Schiller, Eric (1992) 'Parts of Speech in Southeast Asian Languages: An Autolexical View', *PAL 3* 1: 777-803.

Schlegel, Gustave (1902) 'Siamese Studies', *T'oung Pao, Supplement to Series 2* 2: 1-128.

Schmidt, Anne Marie (1988) 'The Acquisition of Some American English Duration Parameters by Nonnative Speakers of English', unpublished PhD dissertation, University of Florida'.

Schmidt, Todd P. (1994) 'A Non-Linear Analysis of Aspect in Thai Narrative Discourse', in Karen L. Adams and Thomas Hudak (eds) *Papers From The Second Annual Meeting Of The Southeast Asian Linguistics Society*, Tempe: Arizona State University Program in Southeast Asian Studies, 327-342.

Scovel, Thomas S. (1970) 'A Grammar of time in Thai', unpublished PhD dissertation, University of Michigan.

Scupin, Raymond (1988) 'Language, Hierarchy and Hegemony: Thai Muslim Discourse Strategies', *Language Sciences* 10: 331-351.

Senawong, Pornpimol (1992) 'Sociolinguistic Aspects of Phonological Transference from English to Thai', *PAL 3 1*: 972-1078.

Sereechareonsatit, Tasanee (1984) 'Conjunct Verbs and Verbs-in-a-series in Thai', unpublished PhD dissertation, University of Illinois at Urbana-Champaign.

Shimizu, Katsumasa, (1989) 'A Cross-Language Study of Voicing Contrasts of Stops', *Onsei Kagaku Kenkyuu, Studia Phonologica* 23: 1-12.

Shorto, H. L. (ed.) (1963) *Linguistic Comparison in South-East Asia and the Pacific*, London: School of Oriental and African Studies, University of London.

Simmonds, E. H. S. (1978) 'Observations on Folk Taxonomy in Thailand', in Phillip A. Stott (ed.) *Nature and Man in South-East Asia*, School of African and Oriental Studies, University of London, 128-141.

Sindhavananda, Kanchana (1970) 'The Verb in Modern Thai', unpublished PhD dissertation, Georgetown University.

Smalley, William A. (1988) 'Thailand's Hierarchy of Multilingualism', *Language Sciences* 10.2: 245-261.

— (1994) Linguistic Diversity and National Unity in Thailand, Chicago: University of Chicago Press.

Smyth, David (2001) 'Farangs and Siamese: A Brief History of Learning Thai', in M. R. Kalaya Tingsabadh and Arthur S. Abramson (eds), 277-285.

— (2002) *Thai: An Essential Grammar*, London: Routledge.
Sookgasem, Prapa (1990) 'Morphology, Syntax and Semantics of Auxiliaries in Thai', unpublished PhD dissertation, University of Arizona.
— (1996) 'The Predicative-Adjective Construction in Thai', *PAL 4* 2: 579-607.
— (1997) 'A Complicating Distortion of Syntactic Categories: the Case of Reduplication in Thai', in Arthur S. Abramson (ed.), 253-272.
— (1992) 'A verb-subject construction in Thai: an analysis of the existential verb "mii"', *PAL 3* 1: 282-307.
Sornhiran, Pasine (1978) 'A Transformational Study of Relative Clauses in Thai', unpublished PhD dissertation, University of Texas at Austin.
Srinarawat, Deeyu (1988) 'Language Use of the Chinese in Bangkok', in Bamroongraks and Khanittanan, et al., (eds), 275-283.
— (2007) 'Thai Political Slang: Formation and Attitudes towards Usage', *International Journal of the Sociology of Language* 186: 95-107.
Sriphen, Salee (1982) 'The Thai Verb Phrase', unpublished PhD dissertation, University of Michigan.
Starosta, Stanley (2001) 'The Identification of Word Classes in Thai', in M. R. Kalaya Tingsabadh and Arthur S. Abramson (eds), 63-90.
Stein, Mark J. (1981) 'Quantification in Thai', unpublished PhD dissertation, University of Massachusetts.
Stine, Philip C. (1968) 'The Instrumental Case in Thai: A Study of Syntax and Semantics in a Generative Model', unpublished PhD dissertation, University of Michigan.
Stott, Philip A. (1978) 'The Red Forest of Thailand: A Study in Vernacular Forest Nomenclature', in Phillip A. Stott (ed.) *Nature and man in South-East Asia*, School of African and Oriental Studies, University of London, 165-75.
Strecker, David (1979) 'A Preliminary Typology of Tone Shapes and Tonal Sound Changes in Tai: The Lan Na A-tones', in Theraphan L.-Thongkum, et al. (eds), 171-240.
— (1980) 'Absolute vs Relative Meaning: The Case of the Thai Pronouns', in Robert S. Haller (ed.) *Papers from the 1979 Mid-America Linguistic Conference*, University of Nebraska, 259-268.
— (1983) 'Proto-Tai Vowels Revisited: A Comparison and Critique of the Work of Sarawit and Li', *Linguistics of the Tibeto-Burman Area* 7.2: 33-74.
— (1984) 'Proto-Tai Personal Pronouns', unpublished PhD dissertation, University of Michigan.
Sugamoto, Nobuko (1989) 'Pronominality: A Noun-pronoun Continuum', in Roberta Corrigan, Fred Eckman, Michael Norman (eds) *Linguistic Categorization*, Amsterdam and Philadelphia: J. Benjamins Publish Co, 267ff.
Suktrakul, Suthinee (1975) 'A Contrastive Analysis of Relative Clauses in Thai-English', unpublished PhD dissertation, Rutgers University.
Surintramont, Aporn (1979) 'Some Deletion Phenomena in Thai', unpublished PhD dissertation, University of Illinois at Urbana-Champaign.
Sutadarat, Suntana Gungsandan (1978) 'A Phonological Description of Standard Thai', unpublished PhD dissertation, University of Wisconsin-Madison.
Suthiwan, Titima (1992) 'Malay Loanwords in Thai', *PAL 3 1*: 1358-1366.
Suwattee Duangduen (1981) 'A Linguistic Analysis of the Difficulties in the English Verbal System Encountered by Native Speakers of Thai', unpublished PhD dissertation, University of North Carolina.
Svastikula, M. L. Katyanee (1986) 'A Perceptual and Acoustic Study of the Effects of Speech Rate on Distinctive Vowel Length in Thai', unpublished PhD dissertation, University of Connecticut.
Terayanont, Vachira (1988) 'Semantic Analysis of the Thai Language', unpublished PhD dissertation, Oklahoma State University.
Terwiel, B. J. (1978) 'The Origin of the T'ai Peoples Reconsidered', *Oriens Extremus* 25.2: 239-258.
Thanyarat, Panakul (1983) 'A Functional Analysis of English and Thai Passive Constructions', unpublished PhD dissertation, Northwestern University.

Thepkanjana, Kingkarn (1986) 'Serial Verb Constructions in Thai', unpublished PhD dissertation, University of Michigan.
— (1992) 'Transitivity Continuum in Thai', *PAL 3* 1: 308-338.
Thomas, David (1979) 'Coordinate Conjunctions in Thai', in Theraphan L-Thongkum, et al. (eds), 60-93.
— (1988) 'Clause-Efficient vs. Paragraph-Efficient Languages', *PAL 2*: 52-56.
Thongkum, Luangthongkum: see L-Thongkum.
Thurgood, Graham (1994) 'Tai-Kadai and Austronesian: The Nature of the Historical Relationship', *Oceanic Linguistics* 33: 2.
— (2007a) 'A Comment on Gedney's Proposal for Another series of Initials in Proto-Tai Revisited', in Jimmy G. Harris et al. (eds), 241-261.
— (2007b) 'Tonogenesis Revisited: Revising the Model and the Analysis', Jimmy G. Harris et al. (eds), 263-291.
Thurgood, Graham, Matisoff, James and Bradley, David (eds) (1985) *Linguistics of the Sino-Tibetan Area: The State of the Art* (Pacific Linguistics C 87), Canberra: Department of Linguistics, Research School of Pacific Studies, Australian National University.
Tiancharoen, Supanee (1987) 'A Comparative Study of Spoken and Written Thai: Linguistic and Sociolinguistic Perspectives', unpublished PhD dissertation, Georgetown University.
Tingsabadh, Kalaya M. R. (1984) 'Thai Dialectology up to the Year 1984', Paper presented to the International Conference on Thai Studies, Bangkok, August 22-24, Thai Studies Program, Chulalongkorn University.
— (1988) 'Loss of Preeminence of Citation Forms in the Study of Tones in Thai Dialects', in Bamroongraks, Cholticha and Wilaiwan Khanittanan, et al., (eds), 224-27.
— (1992) 'Tonal Overlapping: An Instrumental Study of Suphanburi Thai', *PAL 3* 1: 804-851.
— (2001) 'Thai Tone Geography', in M. R. Kalaya Tingsabadh and Arthur S. Abramson (eds), 205-228.
Tingsabadh, Kalaya M. R. and Abramson, Arthur S. (1993a) 'Thai', *Haskins Laboratories Status Report on Speech Research* 113: 131-134.
— (1993b) 'Thai', Journal of the International Phonetic Association 23: 24-28.
Tingsabadh, Kalaya M. R. and Prasithrathsint, Amara (1986) Kanchai kham riakkhan nai phasa thai samai krung rattanakosin [The Use of Address Terms in Thai during the Rattanakosin Period], Bangkok: Chulalongkorn University Press.
Tingsabadh, M. R. Kalaya and Arthur S. Abramson (eds) (2001) *Essays in Tai Linguistics*, Bangkok: Chulalongkorn University Press
Treerat, Wipha (1990) 'On the Deictic Use of 'Coming' and 'Going' in Thai', unpublished MA dissertation, Australian National University, Canberra.
Truwichien, Aim-on (1980) 'Address Avoidance in Thai', *Language and Linguisitcs, Journal of Humanities [Warasan Manutsayasat]* (Chiangmai University) 10.3: 31-39.
— (1985) 'Address and Reference in Thai: Sociocultural Significance of Variation in Meaning Attribution', unpublished PhD dissertation, State University of New York at Buffalo.
Tuaycharoen, Pintip (1977) 'The Phonetic and Phonological Development of a Thai Baby: From Early Communicative Interaction to Speech', unpublished PhD dissertation, School of Oriental and African Studies, University of London.
— (1979) 'An Account of Speech Development of a Thai Child: From Babbling to Speech', in Theraphan L-Thongkum, et al. (eds) 261-77.
Tumtavitikul, Apiluck (1993) 'Consonant Onsets and Tones in Thai', unpublished PhD dissertation, University of Texas at Austin.
— (2001) 'Thai Poetry: A Metrical Analysis', in M. R. Kalaya Tingsabadh and Arthur S. Abramson (eds), 29-40.
— (1996) 'The Mid Central vowel in Thai', *PAL 4* 1: 11-24.
Tumtavitikul, Apiluck and Promkhuntong, Sayweeworn (2007) 'Thai Poetry Reading: Phonetics and Phonology', in Jimmy G. Harris et al. (eds), 11-23.
Upakit-Silapasan, Phraya (Nim Kanchanachiwa) (1939) *Lak phasa Thai [Principles of the Thai Language]*, republished 1979, Bangkok: Thai Wattanaphanit.

Van Lancker, D. and Fromkin, V. (1978) 'Cerebral Dominance for Pitch Contrasts in Tone Language Speakers and in Musically Untrained and Trained English Speakers', *Journal of Phonetics* 6.1: 19-23.

Van Syoc, Bryce (1964) 'Teaching English /r/ and /l/ with Special Reference to Speakers of Thai', *Language Learning* 14.3-4: 137-146.

Varasarin, Uraisi (1984) *Les éléments khmers dans la formation de la langue siamoise* (Langues et civilizations de l'asie du sud-est et du monde insulindien, 15), Paris: SELAF.

Vichit-Vadakan, Rasami (1976) 'The Concept of Inadvertence in Thai Periphrastic Causative Constructions', *Syntax and Semantics* 6: 459-476.

Vijchulata, Boosakorn Tanticharusthum (1978) 'The Surface Syntactic Structure of the Simple Clause in Thai: A Stratificational Model with (Deep) Case Hypothesis', unpublished PhD dissertation, University of Florida.

Vis, Joan (1978) 'Aspects of Verb Serialization in Thai', unpublished PhD dissertation, School of Oriental and African Studies, University of London.

Vongvipanond, Peansiri (Ekniyom) (1988) 'Macro- and Micro-Cohesive Devices in Thai Expository Discourses', in Cholticha Bamroongraks and Wilaiwan Khanittanan, et al. (eds), 129-137.

— (1992a) Lexical Significance of Semantic Doublets in Thai', in Compton and Hartmann (eds), 139-153.

— (1992b) 'A Model of a Discourse Grammar for the Analysis Thai', *PAL 3* 1: 339-354.

Wan Waithayakorn (Naradhiph-Bongsprabandh), Prince (1970) 'On Coining Thai Words', in Tej Bunnag and Michael Smithies (eds) *In Memoriam Phya Anuman Rajadhon*, Bangkok: Siam Society, 33-38.

Warie, Pairat (1973) 'Some Aspects of Code-mixing in Thai', *Studies in the Linguistic Sciences* 7.1: 21-40.

— (1979) 'Some Sociolinguistic Aspects of Language Contact in Thailand', unpublished PhD dissertation, University of Illinois.

Warotamasikkhadit, Udom (1963) 'Thai Syntax: An Outline', unpublished PhD dissertation, University of Texas. [Revised and published, The Hague: Mouton, 1972.]

— (1968a) 'A Note on Internal Rhyme in Thai Poetry', *Journal of the Siam Society* 61.2: 269-272.

— (1968b) 'Stress and Tones Rules in Thai', in Joseph K. Yamagiwa, (ed.) Papers of the CIC Far Eastern Language Institute, Ann Arbor, Panel on Far Eastern Language Institutes of the Committee on Institutional Cooperation, 169-175.

— (1969) 'Verbless Sentences in Thai', *Linguistics* 47: 74-79.

— (1975) 'Dependency of Underlying Structure and Final Particles in Thai', in Jimmy G. Harris and James R. Chamberain (eds), 342-354.

— (1976a) 'Peculiarities of the Thai Substantive Verb *pen*', in Thomas W. Gething, et al., 233-241.

— (1976b) 'Dependency of the Underlying Structure and Final Particles in Thai', *Asie du Sud-Est Continentale* 3: 252-263.

— (1979) 'Complications in Temporal Preverbs and Their Semantic Interpretation', in Nguên Dăng Liêm (ed.) *South-East Asian Linguistic Studies, Vol. 4, Pacific Linguistics C49*, Canberra: Research School of Pacific Studies, Australian National University, 145-153.

— (1979) 'Thai Sentence Focus', in Theraphan L-Thongkum, et al. (eds), 313-324.

— (1986) 'Peculiarities of Instrumental Nouns in Thai', in Robert Bickner, et al. (eds), 239-245.

— (1988) 'There are no Prepositions in Thai', in Cholticha Bamroongraks and Wilaiwan Khanittanan, et al., (eds), 70-76.

— (1994) 'Is *hay* Really a Benefactive-Causitive in Thai?' in Karen L. Adams and Thomas John Hudak (eds) *Papers from the Second Annual Meeting of the Southeast Asian Linguistics Society 1992*, Tempe: Arizona State University, 383-388.

Warotamasintop, Worawut (1975) 'N + V Compound Nouns in Thai', *Publications of the Berkeley Linguistics Society* 1: 445-459.

Wayland, Ratree and Guion, Susan (2003) 'Perceptual Discrimination of Thai Tones by Naive and Experienced Learners of Thai', *Applied Psycholinguistics* 24.1: 113-129.

Weroha, Seree (1992) 'Semantic Considerations in Interpreting Inscriptions: Illustrations from Lue, Lao, and Kammuang', in Compton and Hartmann (eds), 179-185.

Whitaker, H.A. (1969) 'Stylistic Tone-changing Rules in Spoken Thai', *Glossa* 3.2: 190-197.

Wijeyewardene, Gehan (1968) 'Address, Abuse and Animal Categories in Northern Thailand', *Man N.S.* 3: 76-93.

Wilawan, Supriya (1993) 'A Reanalysis of So-Called Serial Verb Constructions in Thai, Khmer, Mandarin Chinese and Yoruba', unpublished PhD dissertation, University of Hawaii.

— (1992) 'The So-called Serial Verb Constructions', *PAL 3* 3: 1237-1293.

Williams, Jeffrey P. (1991) 'A Note on Echo Word Morphology in Thai and the Languages of South and South-East Asia', *Australian Journal of Linguistics* 11.1: 107-111.

Winship, Michael (1986) 'Early Thai Printing: The Beginning to 1851', *Crossroads* 3.1: 45-61.

Witayasakpan, Sompong (1992) 'The Amazing Morphology of Thai', *PAL 3 1*: 355-456.

Wongbiasaj, Soranee (1979a) 'Quantifier Floating in Thai and the Notions of Cardinality/Ordinality', *Studies in the Linguistic Sciences* 9.2: 189-199.

— (1979b) 'On the Passive in Thai', *Studies in the Linguistic Sciences* 9.1: 207-216.

— (1980) 'On Movement Transformations in Thai', unpublished PhD dissertation, University of Illinois at Urbana-Champaign.

Wongkhomthong, Preya (1985) 'A Preliminary Investigation of Thai and Japanese Formulaic Expressions', unpublished PhD dissertation, University of California, Berkeley.

Wong-opasi, Uthaiwan (1994a) 'The Interplay between Tone, Stress and Syllabification in Thai', in Martha Ratliff and Eric Schiller (eds) *Papers from the First Annual Meeting of the Southeast Asian Linguistics Society 1992*, Tempe: Arizona State University, 441-481.

— (1994b) 'An Autolexical Syntax vs. Noun Incorporation Analysis of Thai Compounds', in Hajime Kitamura, Tatsuo Nishida and Yasuhiko Nagano (eds) *Current Issues in Sino-Tibetan Linguistics, 26th International Conference on Sino-Tibetan Languages and Linguistics, 13-17 September 1993*, Osaka: National Museum of Ethnology, 861-868.

Xing Gongwan (1955) 'Hàn yu zi, er he tai yu zhù cí luk shi xi [A tentative comparison of Chinese erh and tzu and Tai luk]', *Zhong guo yu wen chan kao zi liao xuan ji*, Peking: Zhong hua shu ju, 143-53.

Yates, Warren G. and Tryon, Absorn (1970) *Thai Basic Course*, Washington, DC Foreign Service Institute.

Yip, Moira (1982) 'Against a Segmental Analysis of Zahao and Thai: A Laryngeal Tier Proposal', *Linguistic Analysis* 9.1: 79-94.

Zhang, Gongjin (1992) 'Measure Words in Tai: Their Syntactic Function, Word Order, and the Problem of Deletion', in Compton and Hartmann (eds), 205-222.

CHAPTER FOUR

VERBS AND MULTI-VERB CONSTRUCTIONS IN LAO

N. J. Enfield

4.1. INTRODUCTION

The following Lao sentence shows six verbs in a row, in a single prosodically integrated unit, with no inflection or explicit marking of the grammatical relationship between them.[1]

(1) caw^4 $l\grave{o}\grave{o}ng^2$ $m\grave{e}\grave{e}^4$ qaw^3 paj^3 $h\hat{e}t^1$ kin^3 $beng^1$
     2SG   try.out   PCL   take   go   make   eat   look
     'You go ahead and take (them) and try cooking (them)!'(38.12)

This sentence – the words of a merchant giving a sales pitch for her sausages – is no mere 'string of verbs'. Such sequences in Lao can be analysed in terms of nested (usually binary) relationships. In example (1), a left-headed complement-taking adverbial $l\grave{o}\grave{o}ng^2$ 'try out' combines with a right-marking adverbial $beng^1$ 'look' in bracketing a complex verb phrase consisting of a 'disposal' construction expressing focus on manipulation of an object (with the combination qaw^3-$h\hat{e}t^1$ 'take (and) do/make'), incorporating paj^3 'go' as an inner directional particle, in a purposive clause chain with kin^3 'eat'. The surface string of six contiguous verbs in (1) is highly structured, yet there is little if any surface indication of such structure in the language.

As in the grammar of Tai languages generally, almost every problem in Lao clausal grammar demands an understanding of the range of possible relationships between verbs or verb phrases in unmarked sequences. Tai languages are strongly isolating, and provide little overt marking of the grammatical associations between words in syntactic combinations. The aim of this chapter is to portray the kind of grammatical structure one finds at the heart of a typical Tai language, by describing the wide and varied range of structures which may underlie any given 'V1-V2' sequence in one sample language, namely, Lao.[2] The structures vary in a number of ways, including the specific semantic relation between verbs, and the status as 'head' of either V1, V2, both, or neither. A range of grammatical and semantic tests can help to establish the range of covert categories.

Table 4.1-1 lists a range of distinct grammatical relationships underlying unmarked V1-V2 sequences. Each of the constructions is discussed in this chapter. Each of the strings in the 'Example' column is a possible independent surface utterance, with the meaning given in the 'Meaning' column.

The chapter is structured as follows. I begin in Section 4.2 with some observations about the defining properties of verbs in Lao along with a semantic sub-classification of verbs. In Section 4.3, I turn to problems in argument structure, and conditions for variation in surface realization of arguments. There is heavy use of argument ellipsis as well as movement, both

---

1   See appendix for information on the language and the source of text examples, along with a list of abbreviations used in interlinear glosses.
2   I use 'V1-V2' to refer to such sequences generally, and I intend for 'V' to be vague as to the distinction between 'verb' and 'verb phrase'.

TABLE 4.1-1: SOME V1-V2 SEQUENCES WITH DIFFERENT UNDERLYING STRUCTURES

Construction	Example	Gloss	Meaning
Pre-V asp-mod marking	$kheej^2\ paj^3$	'accustomed' 'go'	'(S/he) has (ever) been/gone.'
Post-V asp-mod marking	$paj^3\ l\grave{e}\grave{e}w^4$	'go' 'finish'	'(S/he) has gone.'
'Despatch' 3-place constr.	$qaw^3\ haj^5$	'take' 'give'	'(S/he) gave (it) to (him/her).'
'Disposal' constr.	$qaw^3\ thim^5$	'take' 'discard'	'(S/he) threw (it) out.'
Complex motion	$long^2\ paj^3$	'descend' 'go'	'(S/he) went down.'
Rsltv, simple, same-subj	$tok^2\ taaj^3$	'fall' 'die'	'(S/he) fell and died.'
Rsltv, simple, diff-subj	$\tilde{n}ing^2\ taaj^3$	'shoot' 'die'	'(S/he) shot (it) dead.'
Advbl compl., r-head stv.	$kin^3\ k\hat{e}ng^1$	'eat' 'adept'	'(S/he)'s good at eating.'
Advbl compl., r-head actv	$nang^2\ lin^5$	'sit' 'play'	'(S/he)'s sitting for fun.'
Advbl compl. l-head	$faaw^4\ khian^3$	'hurry' 'write'	'(S/he) wrote (it) in a hurry.'
Advbl compd., l-mrking	$lak^1\ kin^3$	'steal' 'eat'	'(S/he) secretly ate (it).'
Advbl compd., r-marking	$khaap^4\ qaw^3$	'mouth.grab' 'take'	'(S/he) took (it) away in mouth.'
Causative, simple	$haj^5\ paj^3$	'give' 'go'	'(S/he) let (him/her) go.'
Causative, complex	$sang^1\text{-}haj^5\ paj^3$	'order-give' 'go'	'(S/he) ordered (him/her) to go.'
Compl, contrl, same-subj	$jaak^5\ paj^3$	'want' 'go'	'(S/he) wants to go.'
Compl, contrl, diff-subj	$h\hat{e}n^3\ maa^2$	'see' 'come'	'(S/he) saw (him/her) come.'
	$jaak^5\ haj^5\ maa^2$	'want' 'give' 'come'	'(S/he) wants (him/her) to come.'
Compl, non-control	$khit^1\ vaa^1\ paj^3$	'think' 'say' 'go'	'(S/he) thinks (he has) gone.'
Verb chain	$paj^3\ maa^2\ ...$	'come' 'go' ...	'(S/he) came and went and....'
	$maa^2\ hian^2$	'come' 'study'	'(S/he) came to study.'
Verb compound	$nii^3\ paq^2$	'flee' 'abandon'	'(S/he) abandoned (him/her).'
Oblique	$h\hat{e}t^1\ nam^2$	'do' 'accompany'	'(S/he) did (it) with (him/her).'
	$h\hat{e}t^1\ haj^5$	'do' 'give'	'(S/he) did (it) for (him/her).'

conditioned by discourse-sensitive information structure factors. This interacts with versatility in lexical valency and transitivity. Also discussed here are fundamental grammatical problems of how arguments are added and subtracted from clauses where necessary. Section 4.4 forms the body of the chapter, presenting a range of different kinds of underlying form that an unmarked V1-V2 sequence can conceivably have (as listed in Figure 4.3.4.1-1). Section 4.4.5 summarizes and concludes.

4.2. VERBS, VERB CLASSES, ASPECT-MODALITY MARKING

The term 'verb' is used for members of the class of words accessible to a defined set of grammatical markings and processes associated with words denoting semantically prototypical actions/events (e.g. tii^3 'hit', $lèèn^1$ 'run'). This category in Lao includes words denoting not only actions and events, but also words denoting concepts confined to a distinct 'adjective' class in some languages (e.g. $suung^3$ '(be) tall', $dèèng^3$ '(be) red').

Canonical main verbs such as tii^3 'hit', vaw^4 'say', or $hên^3$ 'see' in simple clauses have the following definitive properties:

- may be directly marked (preverbally) by aspect-modality elements such as
  - negator $bòò^1$
  - irrealis markers si^0 and ca^0
  - attainment marker daj^0
  - progressive markers $kamlang^2$ and $phuam^2$

- may be used alone in affirmative responses to polar questions ('yes-answers')

- may (in combination with their complements) form nominal modifiers in combination with the relativizer $thii^1$;

- may be nominalized using either of the nominalizers $kaan^3$ or $khuam^2$.

The differential accessibility of Lao verbs to more subtle grammatical possibilities may be used as a basis for sub-categorization of the verb class, along the lines of traditional logical/aspectual classes such as *state, activity, achievement, accomplishment,* and *semelfactive* (Vendler 1967, Dowty 1979, Smith 1997).[3] Table 4.2-1 outlines some formal properties of the main logical/aspectual verb subclasses (with the addition of a category 'gradable states', corresponding in functional terms roughly with adjectives in English):

TABLE 4.2-1: FIVE LAO VERB CATEGORIES BASED ON LOGICAL/ASPECTUAL DISTINCTIONS

	1. 'VP at t' entails 'sth. hpnd at t'?	2. 'VP-PFV' entails 'VP now'?	3. 'prog-VP' entails 'VP-PFV'?	4. 'begin to V' grammatical?	5. 'almost V' ambiguous?	6. reduplication grammatical?
Achievement *('meet sb.')*	+	−	−	−	−	−
Accomplishment *('build a house')*	+	−	−	+	+	−
Semelfactive *('knock sth.')*	+	−	−	−	−	−
Activity *('walk')*	+	−	+	+	−	−
State *('have sth.')*	−	+	−	−	−	−
Gradable state *('be tall')*	−	+	−	+	−	+

---

3   Note that these semantic classes as applied to Lao do not neatly match those established for English. The subtleties are beyond the scope of our discussion.

Notes: - In column 4, iterative readings are not included.

- The ambiguity referred to in column 5 is that of English *He almost built a house* – i.e. it could mean that almost *finished* or that he almost *began*.

- The reduplication referred to in column 6 is one of two types, in which stress is on the second element only.

While it has often been noted that aspect/modality distinctions in languages such as Lao need not be explicitly marked, there are nevertheless many options for explicit aspect/modality marking. Most of them are preverbal. Such 'left aspect-modality marking' almost always occurs only once per clause. It does not usually appear on a lower verb of a tight complement construction, since the aspect-modality properties of a tightly subordinated lower clause are determined by the matrix verb and the semantics of the particular type of complementation involved.[4] Lower clauses of loose complement constructions (e.g. speech and cognition complements) may take left aspect-modality marking independently of the main complement verb. In some types of serialization, such as verb compounding or chaining, again no such marking may appear on any non-initial verb. However, right-headed resultative and adverbial V1-V2 constructions are equivocal in this respect – i.e. they can take aspect-modality marking on either V1 or V2 (but not both). See §4.4.2, below, for further discussion.

4.3. ARGUMENT STRUCTURE IN SINGLE-VERB CLAUSES

I now raise some preliminary issues concerning the realization of arguments in simple Lao clauses (i.e. clauses with only one verb), including widespread ellipsis of arguments, the role of information structure features such as topic and focus in determining constituent order, and lexically specified patterns in transitivity and valency of verbs.

4.3.1. Ellipsis

Ellipsis is the normal form of anaphora for referents which are contextually retrievable (i.e. known and active or semi-active; Chafe 1994). It is just one of a number of factors contributing to difficulties in decisively analysing surface strings in Lao. Lean expressions of the following kind are typical Lao sentences:

(2)   *ñaaw²*
      long
      '(It was) long.' (891.2)

(3)   *lùùm²*
      forget
      '(I have) forgotten (it).' (1354.9)

(4)   *hên³*
      see
      '(I) saw (it).' (3.8)

---

4   An occasional exception concerns irrealis markers *si⁰* and *ca⁰* on lower verb complements of future-oriented or irrealis verbs like *jaak⁵* 'want', and *tòòng⁴.kaan³* 'require'. Thus: *man² jaak⁵ (ca⁰) paj³* [3SG want (IRR) go] 'He wants to go' vs. *man² ca⁰ jaak⁵ paj³* [3SG IRR want go] 'He will want to go'.

In each case, referents of the ellipsed arguments are active in the discourse context, and as the free translations show, zero anaphors correspond to pronominal anaphors in languages like English.

While the *option* of ellipsis is widespread, there are situations in which it is obligatory. For example, same-subject control complement constructions (as in *want* complement constructions, see §4.4.9.1.1 on page 163) stipulate that the lower complement subject (coreferential with the matrix subject) cannot be overtly expressed. In other cases, by contrast, ellipsis is ruled out. For example, a relativized-upon argument to which a relative clause is attached must be phonologically realized:

(5) *khòòj⁵*   *hên³*   **(maa³)*   *(thii¹)*   *kin³*   *kaj¹*   *caw⁴*
     1SG   see   dog   REL   eat   chicken   2SG
     'I saw the dog which ate your chicken(s).'

There is no syntactic control of ellipsis across conjoined clauses in Lao, in contrast to languages like English or Dyirbal which have 'pivot' type grammatical relations. In English, the following examples unambiguously describe bizarre situations:

(6) *He dropped the melon and burst.*

(7) *The schoolmaster spanked the little boy and ran home crying to his mother.*

Analogous expressions in Lao are ambiguous, since the ellipsed second clause subject may be coreferential with either the subject or object of the first clause. They are thus given the pragmatically most expected meaning. The strongly preferred readings of these two examples in Lao would be the pragmatically obvious ones (i.e. '...and it [the melon] burst...', '...and he [the boy] ran home...').

Ellipsis is in general completely open to pragmatic interpretation, as the following example (after Foley and Van Valin 1984: 194) shows.

(8) *tam³*   *khuaj²*   *taaj³*
    crash.into buffalo   die
    i. '(S/he) crashed into a buffalo and died.'
    ii. '(S/he) crashed into a buffalo and it died.'
    iii. '(S/he) crashed into a buffalo and (the car) died (i.e. stalled).'

However, in a small number of complement constructions (most notably involving the verb *jaak⁵* 'want') there is syntactic control of coreference under obligatory ellipsis. In these cases, the complement clause subject must be ellipsed, and must be coreferential with the main clause subject:

(9) *laaw²*   *jaak⁵*   *khaa⁵*   *kaj¹*
     3SG   want   kill   chicken
     'S/he wants to kill a chicken.'

(10) **laaw²* *jaak⁵* *caw⁴* *khaa⁵* *kaj¹*
      3SG   want   2SG   kill   chicken
      (S/he wants you to kill a chicken.)

If a different subject is to be expressed in the lower clause of a *want* construction, the verb *haj⁵* 'give' is used to signal that the subject of the complement is non-coreferential with the main subject (and the lower subject then may or may not be ellipsed):

(11)   *laaw²*   *jaak⁵*   *haj⁵*   *(caw⁴)*   *khaa⁵*   *kaj¹*

    3SG   want   give   2SG   kill   chicken

'S/he wants (you) to kill a chicken.'

The ubiquity and freedom of nominal ellipsis in Lao discourse makes it difficult (for both grammarian and child) to be sure about underlying patterns of argument structure. Seemingly simple questions such as whether a verb is transitive or intransitive are complex here, and increase in complexity when we look at the great versatility of verbs in their patterns of transitivity and valency.

4.3.2. Transitivity and valency

Almost no Lao verb is restricted to a single argument structure construction. Most Lao verbs may appear with either one or two arguments (i.e. they are 'ambitransitive'; Dixon 1994).[5] Given that nominal ellipsis is so common, one ideally has to distinguish between cases in which an argument is 'there' but ellipsed, and cases in which it is simply 'not there' (cf. Mosel 1991). The distinction hinges on contextual retrievability of an absent argument as specifically known (or not) to both speaker and listener, and assumed by each to be known to the other. (In practice, this means that the distinction is often unverifiable.)

Rather than simply classifying Lao verbs as 'transitive', 'intransitive' and 'ambitransitive' of various sub-types, it is more useful to list a number of important argument structure constructions and classify verbs according to their accessibility to these constructions. We first list three constructions involving just one noun phrase:[6]

(12)   *Resultant state intransitive construction* $S^{TH/PAT}$-V

    Agent-controlled verbs, usually telic, with patient/theme as subject and where agent is unexpressed and not contextually retrievable (e.g. *kaang³* 'to be hoisted', *pia³* 'to be platted', *tom⁴* 'to be boiled').

---

5   For present purposes, an 'argument' is a syntactic-semantic entity, defined as a participant which is contextually retrievable and referential, and which corresponds to and elaborates a participant specified in the semantics of a relational element such as a verb. An argument need not have surface realisation (e.g. in Lao it may be ellipsed), and a surface nominal expression need not be an argument (e.g. it may be incorporated and thus non-referential; e.g. fox in John went fox-hunting). A 'participant' is any entity which the semantics of a verb or a whole sentence specifies as being involved. Thus, the sentence John painted his house has two arguments ('John' and 'his house') but at least three participants (i.e. one must understand that 'paint' is also involved).

6   Abbreviations in this sections are as follows. 'A' denotes arguments treated grammatically like prototypical agents, 'O' denotes arguments treated grammatically like prototypical patients, and 'S' denotes the single argument of an intransitive clause (after Dixon 1994). A and O are defined by language-specific formal grammatical behaviour, with reference to semantic prototypes ('someone who does something to something', 'something to which something is done'). S is a different kind of entity—semantics do not enter into the definition of S at all. Abbreviations for semantic roles are AGT (agent), TH (theme), PAT (patient), EXP (experiencer), EFF (effector), MVR (mover).

(13) *Stative-inchoative intransitive construction* **STH-V**
Expresses the meaning 'S is in (or enters into) state V'; these are typical 'adjectives' (e.g. *laaj²* 'striped', *hòòn⁴* 'hot', *dii³* 'good'); inchoative reading is rare, encouraged by irrealis or progressive marking.

(14) *Active intransitive construction* **S$^{AGT/TH}$-V**
Meaning: 'S does V'; includes typical active intransitives (e.g. *caam³* 'sneeze', *lèèn¹* 'run', *san¹* 'shake').

These three one-place constructions may be differentiated in terms of a range of grammatical distinctions, as summarized in Table 4.3.2-1:[7]

TABLE 4.3.2-1: GRAMMATICAL DISTINCTIONS BETWEEN THREE ONE-PLACE CONSTRUCTIONS

Test	Res-state-intr	Stv-incho-intr	Actv-intr
Meaning	'S is in (or enters into) state V (because something is done to it)'	'S is in (or enters into) state V (not because anything is done to it)'	i. 'S does V' ii. 'V happens to S (not because anything is done to it)'
Reading of *bò⁰*- negation	n/a *(introduces trackable agent, thus no longer intransitive)*	i. 'will not enter state' ii. 'is not in state'	i. 'will not happen' ii. 'is not happening'
Reading of *bò⁰-daj⁰*- negation	'not-in-state-now' (='has not been V-ed')	i. 'did not enter state' ii. 'was not in state'	i. 'did not happen'
Transitive counterpart?	Transitive, S = A	Caused-state, S = O	no
Reading of progressive *kamlang²*-	n/a *(introduces trackable agent, thus no longer intransitive)*	'entering state now'; or 'temporarily in state'	'happening now'
Reading of perfective *lèèw⁴*	i. 'in state now' ii. 'already entering into state now'	i. 'in state now' ii. 'already entering into state now'	'happening now' *(endpoint – e.g. of motion verbs – not entailed)*

Now, compare these three one-place constructions with five two-place constructions:

(15) *Transitive construction* **A$^{AGT/EFF}$-V-O$^{PAT/TH}$**

Expresses the meaning 'A does V to O (which causes O to be in some state)' (e.g. *tom⁴* 'boil', *pia³* 'plat', *khaa⁵* 'kill', *puk²* 'waken').

(16 *External possessor construction* **A$^{POSS'R}$-V-O$^{POSS'D}$**
Expresses the meaning 'The O of A is V'; includes many expressions of referring to body parts and bodily processes (e.g. *tèèk⁵* 'be broken (e.g. of one's hair ends)').

---

7   Space restrictions in this chapter prevent detailed discussion of the points made in Table 4.3.2-1 and Table 4.3.2-2.

(17) *Experiencer subject construction*   **A^{EXP}-V-OTH**

Expresses the meaning 'A has the experience of V due to the stimulus of O'; includes 'applied stimulus' expressions (e.g. *sèèp^4* '(find something) delicious', *nak^2* '(find something) heavy', *tùùn^1* 'be startled (by something)').

(18) *Caused state construction*   **A^{EFF}-V-OTH**

Expresses the meaning 'A causes O to be in state V' (e.g. *laaj^2* '((cause to) become) striped', *dam^3* '((cause to) become) black', *hòòn^4* '((cause to) become) hot'). (These are usually not agentive – exceptions include *qun^1* 'warm (something) up'.)

(19) *Applied effector construction* **ATH-V-O^{EFF}**

Expresses the meaning 'A is in state V because of O'; includes (e.g. *vaan^3* 'be sweet (because of something)', *phêt^2* 'be spicy (because of something)', *taaj^3* 'die (from something)').

Notice that external possessor construction, the experiencer subject construction, and the applied effector construction can show some overlap. In many external possessor constructions the A is an experiencer, but in these cases the O is a *locus* not an *effector*. While the subject of the following two examples – *khòòj^5* 'I' – is an experiencer, in (20) the O argument is not the cause of the itch, while in (21) it is.

(20) *khòòj^5*   *khan^2*   *khaa^3*

1SG   itch   leg

'I have an itch in my leg'; 'My leg's itchy.' (external possessor)

(21) *khòòj^5*   *khan^2*   *song^5*   *nii^4*

1SG   itch   pants   DEM.GEN

'I am itchy (from) these pants.' (applied effector)

External possessor constructions can take applied effector arguments:

(22) *khòòj^5*   *khan^2*   *khaa^3*   *song^5*   *nii^4*

1SG   itch   leg   pants   DEM.GEN

'I am itchy (in) my leg (from) these pants.'

(23) *man^2*   *lùam^5*   *taa^3*   *còò^4*   *tholathat^1*

3SG   glary   eye   screen   television

'S/he's glary (in) the eyes (from) the television screen.'

In these two examples, the body parts *khaa^3* 'leg' and *taa^3* 'eye' are loci of experience in external possessor constructions, each then taking applied effector arguments which refer to the cause of the experience in the possessed body part (*song^5 nii^4* 'these pants' and *còò^4 tholathat^1* 'television screen', respectively).

Some grammatical distinctions between the five constructions are summarized in Table 4.3.2-2:

TABLE 4.3.2-2: GRAMMATICAL DISTINCTIONS BETWEEN FIVE TWO-PLACE CONSTRUCTIONS

Test	Transitive	Ext-pssr	Exp-subj	Causd-st	Appl-eff
Meaning	'A does (V) to O; causes O to be in certain state'	'A's O is V'	'A feels something (V) because of O'	'Because of A, O enters and/or is in state V'	'because of O, A enters and/or is in state V'
Reading of $bò^0$- negation	'A doesn't V O'	'A's O isn't V'	'A's O isn't V'	'A doesn't/ won't V'	'A isn't in state V bcs. of O'
Reading of $bò^0\text{-}daj^0$- negation	'A hasn't / didn't V O'	"	"	'A hasn't V-ed'	"
Intransitive counterpart?	Res-state-intr. O as S	i. with 'A's O' as S ii. %A as S	stative-inch. intransitive, O as S (often with 'I' as understood A)	stative-inch. intransitive, O as S	stative-inch. intransitive, A as S
***A hêt¹-haj⁵ O V* paraphrase OK?**	%	no	no	yes	no
***O hêt¹-haj⁵ A V* paraphrase OK?**	no	no	yes	no	yes
O trackable as ø?	yes	no	yes	% (often A is V also)	no
O trackable as pronoun?	yes	no	yes	%	no
Reading of progressive *kamlang²-*	doing it now	happening now	feeling it now	becoming V now	becoming V now
Reading of perfective *-lèèw⁴*	not doing it now, O now in state V	O now in state V	feeling it now	in state V now, nothing happening	in state V now, nothing happening

Almost every verb can appear in more than one of these constructions, and this provides speakers with many possibilities for manipulating argument structure in discourse without the use of morphological marking. For example, suppression of an agent or effector can often be achieved by use of the intransitive construction:

(24)   *khòòj⁵   pia³   phom³   phen¹*

   1SG   plat   hair   3SG

   'I platted her hair.'

(25)   *phom³   phen¹   pia³*

   hair   3SG   plat

   'Her hair is/was platted.'

To add a causer argument to a stative-intransitive verb, speakers may use the caused state construction:

(26)   *kon⁴   mòò⁵   laaj²*

   bottom   pot   striped

   'The bottom of the pot is striped.'

(27)   *phaa⁵   nan⁴   ca⁰   laaj²   kon⁴   mòò⁵*

   cloth   DEM.NONPROX   IRR   striped   bottom   pot

   'That cloth will cause there to be lines on the bottom of the pot.' (attested)

An effector can be added to a stative-inchoative intransitive clause by the applied effector construction:

(28)   *kapaw³   nii⁴   nak²*

   bag   DEM.GEN   heavy

   'This bag is heavy.'

(29)   *kapaw³   nii⁴   nak²   kòòng⁴*

   bag   DEM.GEN   heavy   camera

   'This bag is heavy (from the) camera (in it).'

Some verbs are quite restricted in their accessibility to different constructions, such as intransitives like *tèèk⁵* 'break' and *fot²* 'boil'. *Tèèk⁵* 'break' only appears in the intransitive and external possessor constructions:

(30)   *paaj³   phom³   tèèk⁵*

   tip   hair   break

   'The tips of the hairs are/have broken.'

(31)   *phom³*   *tèèk⁵*   *paaj³*

      hair   break   tip

      'The hairs (have) broken (their) tips.'

To add a causer to an expression involving *tèèk⁵* 'break', one cannot simply use the verb in the transitive construction (*à la* English *break*), but must use a syntactic causative construction (as described in §4.4.8, below). There are many verbs of breaking in Lao which are more semantically specific than *tèèk⁵* 'break', and which do occur in the transitive construction (often involving *tèèk⁵* 'break' as an intransitive resultative V2; cf. §4.4.6.2 on page 134).

In the case of *fot²* 'boil$_{INTR}$', only the intransitive construction is available:

(32)   *nam⁴*   *nii⁴*   *fot²*

      water   DEM.GEN   boil

      'This water is (now) boiling.'

To add a causer to the clause, a different lexical item is selected, namely *tom⁴* 'boil$_{TR}$':

(33)   **khòòj⁵*   *fot²*   *nam⁴*   *nii⁴*

      1SG   boil$_{INTR}$ water   DEM.GEN

      (I boiled this water.)

(34)   *khòòj⁵*   *tom⁴*   *nam⁴*   *nii⁴*

      1SG   boil$_{TR}$ water   DEM.GEN

      'I boiled this water.'

In turn, *tom⁴* 'boil$_{TR}$' itself may be used in the stative-inchoative intransitive construction, but with a different meaning to its counterpart *fot²* 'boil$_{INTR}$' in (32) – i.e. where there is a focus on resultant state rather than on an ongoing event:

(35)   *nam⁴*   *nii⁴*   *tom⁴*

      water   DEM.GEN   boil$_{TR}$

      'This water is boiled.' (Probably not boiling now.)

Another verb which may not appear in the transitive construction is *tùùn¹* 'awaken', shown here in the intransitive construction and experiencer subject construction, respectively:

(36)   *khòòj⁵*   *tùùn¹*

      1SG   awaken

      'I woke up/got a start.'

(37)   *khòòj⁵*   *tùùn¹*   *caw⁴*

      1SG   awaken   2SG

      'I got a start/surprise (from) you.'

With this verb, expression of a causer in subject position requires a syntactic causative such as *hêt¹-haj⁵* [make-give] 'cause' (38), otherwise one may select a different verb, namely *puk²* 'waken', which is accessible to the transitive construction (39):

(38) *caw⁴*   *hêt¹-haj⁵*   *khòòj⁵*   *tùùn¹*

     2SG   make-give   1SG   awaken

     'You caused me to wake up (i.e. woke me up unintentionally).'

(39) *caw⁴*   *puk²*   *khòòj⁵*

     2SG   waken   1SG

     'You woke me up (intentionally).'

By contrast with these more restricted verbs, a few verbs are highly versatile. Consider the following examples involving *nak²* 'heavy':

(40) *kapaw³*   *nii⁴*   *nak²*

     bag   DEM.GEN   heavy

     'This bag is heavy.' (Stative-inchoative intransitive construction)

(41) *khòòj⁵*   *nak²*   *tiin³*

     1SG   heavy   feet

     'My feet are heavy.' (External possessor construction)

(42) *khòòj⁵*   *nak²*   *sùa⁴*

     1SG   heavy   jacket

     'I'm heavy from the jacket.' (Applied effector construction)[8]

(43) *kapaw³*   *nii⁴*   *nak²*   *kòòng⁴*

     bag   DEM.GEN   heavy   camera

     'The bag is heavy from the camera (inside it).' (Applied effector construction)

(44) *khòòj⁵*   *nak²*   *kapaw³*   *nii⁴*

     1SG   heavy   bag   DEM.GEN

     'I find this bag heavy.' (Experiencer subject construction)

Context determines what the precise semantic relations between arguments are. With the ever-present possibility of ellipsis, multiple interpretations become even more likely. Just to give one example, *khòòj⁵ nak²* [1SG heavy] could be an intransitive construction meaning 'I'm

---

8   This sentence could be used, for example, when weighing oneself while wearing a heavy jacket.

heavy' or an experiencer subject construction meaning 'I'm finding (it) heavy' (i.e. where O is ellipsed and retrievable in the context).

The use of these different constructions with certain labile verbs gives the impression that different verbs have different 'derivational properties'. For example, consider the following two caused state constructions with stative verbs *mùaj¹* 'tired' and *baw³* 'light' each taking two arguments:

(45) *bik²   qan⁰-nii⁴   mùaj¹   mùù²khòòj⁵*

      pen   CLF-DEM.GEN   tired   hand   1SG

      'This pen tires my hand.'

(46) *keep⁵   khuu¹   nii⁴   baw³   tiin³*

      shoe   pair   DEM.GEN   light   foot

      'This pair of shoes is light (on) the foot.'

In intransitive constructions involving these two verbs, the mapping of arguments is not the same. In the case of *mùaj¹* 'tired', for example, the O of the caused state construction becomes the S of the intransitive construction, while for *baw³* 'light' transitive, the new S argument is the erstwhile *A*:

(47) *mùù²   khòòj⁵   mùaj¹*

      hand   1SG   tired

      'My hand is tired.'

(48) *keep⁵   khuu¹   nii⁴   baw³*

      shoe   pair   DEM.GEN   light

      'This pair of shoes is light.'

Finally, there are verbs which lack strong asymmetry in the semantic role of arguments, resulting either in single sequences having two different truth-conditional interpretations (49), or a single truth-conditional situation being describable by sequences of opposite ordering (50a, b, where the difference in order is related to an information structure distinction):

(49) *man²   bang³   hùan*

      3SG   block.from.view   house

      i. 'He's blocked from view by the house'.

      ii. 'He's blocking the house from view.'

(50) (a) *sùa⁴   nii⁴   tit³   nam⁰-mùk²*

           shirt   DEM.GEN   touch/attach   CT.LIQUID-ink

           'This shirt has got ink on it.'

      (b) *nam⁰-mùk²   tit²   sùa⁴   nii⁴*

           CT.LIQUID-ink   touch/attach   shirt   DEM.GEN

           'Ink has got on this shirt.'

The alternative argument structure frames for single verbs described in this section are familiar cases of 'ambitransitivity' or 'dual transitivity' (Dixon 1991: 286ff, 1994). A notable aspect of the Lao verbal lexicon is its versatility in this regard, found across Tai languages in general. In keeping with the typological profile of these languages, there is no overt morphological marking of the alternatives. Some have claimed that the alternative argument structure frames are 'derived' by 'zero morphemes' (Clark and Prasithratsint 1985). A simpler (although perhaps not significantly different) solution is to describe the verbs as being accessible to more than one argument structure construction, as suggested here.

The details of verbal argument structure and grammatical relations in Lao cannot be explored further in this context, as this section is intended to cover preliminaries to our examination of multiple verbs in combination.

4.3.3. Formal mechanisms for valency-changing

The previous section described a number of alternative constructions which allow speakers to manipulate the valency of verbs without formal morphological marking. There are also limited formal mechanisms for valency-changing derivation, and these all involve multiple verb constructions.[9] They will each be discussed in detail in §4.4, below. §4.4.8 describes causative constructions which use complement-taking verbs to add causers or effectors to simple clauses. The most common verbs are *haj⁵* 'give', *hêt¹* 'make/do', and *qaw³* 'take', each of which often appear in compound combinations with other causative or resultative verbs. There is also a so-called 'passive' construction involving the verb *thùùk⁵* 'strike' as a complement-taking predicate, whose subject is coreferential with an argument (usually but not always O) of the lower predicate. See §4.4.9.4 on page 171, for details.

4.3.4. Constituent structure and information structure: subject, topic, focus

Lao is a strongly head-initial language, in which verbs precede objects, prepositions precede noun phrases, possesseds precede possessors, heads of relative clauses come first, and nominal heads precede modifiers. Most Tai languages are like this, but many Northern Tai and Kadai languages have some head-final patterns in the noun phrase (especially with relativization) apparently under influence of Sinitic languages (Gedney 1989: 122, Wang and Zheng 1993, Long and Zheng 1998). In only a few cases does the head apparently come to the right (for example, as a modal meaning 'can', *daj⁴* is postverbal; Enfield 2002a: Ch. 3).

At the core of the Lao clause is a simple right-branching NP VP structure, realized as either A-V-O, or S-V. Here are some examples:

(51) *saam³*   *khon²*   *taaj³*
     three   person   die
     'Three people died.' (11.9)

(52) *khaw³*   *khon³*   *khon²*
     3PL   transport person
     'They transported people.' (686.1)

---

9   Note that Lao, like other Tai languages, lacks morphological causativity. By contrast, many of the Mon-Khmer languages with which Tai languages have been in extensive contact over the last 2000 years or more do have morphological causativisation (involving prefixes and/or infixes). Influence in this regard has been from Tai to Mon-Khmer rather than the other way around. For example, Kmhmu has apparently developed syntactic causatives on the model of Thai (Suwilai 1987: 25ff), while Thai has no productive causative morphology.

(53) *kuu³*   *jaan⁴*   *mùng²*
     1SG   afraid   2SG
     'I was afraid of you.' (1274.6)

(54) *phu⁰-pên³-mia²*   *khòòng³*   *thaaw⁴*   *nan⁴*   *hên³*   *qavaj²ñavaq¹*
     person-be-wife   of   young.man   DEM.NONPROX   see   organ

     khòòng³   *faaj¹*   *coon³*
     of   side   bandit
     'That young man's wife saw the bandit's organ (i.e. genitals).' (889.11)

While these examples show the 'unmarked' constituent order, there are many ways to vary the formal structuring of a single set of predicate-argument relations to express distinctions in information structure (Lambrecht 1994). Outside the clausal core there are robust outer slots into which arguments may be placed for discourse-related purposes.

Lao is a 'topic-prominent' language, a fact with significant consequences in the grammar (Li and Thompson 1976; see below).[10] I do not claim, however, that Lao lacks a grammatical relation 'subject'. Some processes are sensitive to the grouping of S and A arguments (for example the coreference constraint under 'want' complements mentioned in §4.3.1, above), and the basis of these, I regard 'subject' as an established (but not necessarily central) notion in Lao grammar.[11]

The following subsections describe possible permutations and markings of the clause and sentence related to distinctions in information structure.

4.3.4.1. *Sites for 'movement' – left and right position*

The simple subject-predicate strings shown in (52-54), above, are ideal examples of A-V-O structure, but such examples are in rare in discourse. Beyond the core, the Lao clause contains a topic-like *left position* (LP) and an afterthought-like *right position* (RP). These are common sites for non-default placement of core nominals as well as verbs and verb phrases.[12]

(LEFT POSITION) · SUBJ · AM-[V (OBJ)]-AM   FINAL.PARTICLES · (RIGHT POSITION)

FIGURE 4.3.4.1-1: CONSTITUENTS OF THE LAO CLAUSE, IN ORDER

For example:

(55) *qaa³haan³*   *lèèng²*   / *caw⁴*   *si⁰*   *saj¹*   *mak⁰-phêt¹*   *qiik⁵*   *vaa³*   *mùù⁴*   *nii⁴*
     food   evening   2SG   IRR   put   CT.FRUIT-chilli   more   PCL   day   DEM.GEN
     'Dinner, are you going to put chilli in (it) again, today?'

Note firstly that the object cannot be abandoned in position as a result of movement of other elements of the verb phrase:

---

10   'Topic-prominence' should not be construed as a 'type' on a par with 'subject-prominence'. LaPolla (1997) has rightly pointed out that while 'subject-prominence' arises from a set of structural constraints, 'topic-prominence' such as that famously found in Modern Standard Chinese arises from plain lack of constraints rather than from constraints of a different kind.

11   I also find it convenient to refer to 'object' — there is evidence of a verb phrase in Lao, such that nothing can be inserted between the verb and its immediate complement (the 'object').

12   In Figure 4.3.4.1-1, 'AM' refers to aspect-modality marking, deliberately left vague here—in fact there are a number of 'AM' slots; see §4.4.2, below for further discussion of aspect-modality marking.

(56)   *si^0 saj^1 / caw^4 mak^0-$phêt^1$ $qiik^5$ vaa^3 \$mùù^4$ nii^4

      IRR   put   2SG   CT.FRUIT-chilli   more   PCL   day   DEM.GEN

      (Will put in, you chilli again, today?)

Similarly, V cannot be removed leaving its left aspect-modality marking in place:

(57)   *saj^1 /caw^4 si^0 mak^0-$phêt^1$ $qiik^5$ vaa^3 \$mùù^4$ nii^4

      put   2SG   IRR   CT.FRUIT-chilli   more   PCL   day   DEM.GEN

      (Put in, are you going to chilli again, today?)

In other words, if V moves, its object and aspect-modality markings move with it. The object, however, can be moved on its own into other positions, as required:

(58) mak^0-$phêt^1$ /caw^4 si^0 saj^1 $qiik^5$ vaa^3 \$mùù^4$ nii^4

      CT.FRUIT-chilli   2SG   IRR   put   more   PCL   day   DEM.GEN

      'Chilli, are you going to put (some) in again, today?'

Due to the ubiquity of nominal ellipsis and the possibility for expression of either subject or object arguments in both left position and right position, naturally occurring sentences often cannot be removed from their original context without confusion arising as to the basic predicate-argument relationships being expressed. Consider the following examples:[13]

(59)   Surface sequence: V NP NP
      Underlying structure: [t_A V O] \RP$_A$

      qaw^3 mia^2 \ haw^2 ni^0
      take   wife   1SG   TPC.PCL
      'Took a wife, I (did),' (375.2)

(60)   Surface sequence: NP NP V
      Underlying structure: LP$_O$ / [A V t_O]

      lot^1 / haw^2 la^0 $bò^0$ mii^2
      vehicle   1SG   PCL   NEG   have
      'A car, I didn't have.' (371.1)

---

13 The notations 't' and 'ø' are used in these examples for convenience. They both mark sites in which a nominal could be expressed—and would be expressed in a 'pragmatically neutral' context—but is not. I use 'ø' to signify the default syntactic position of a trackable argument which is not phonologically realized anywhere in the sentence, and 't' to signify the default syntactic position of an argument which does appear in the sentence, but in a pragmatically more marked position (i.e. left position or right position). The terms 'deletion' and 'movement' are handy metaphors in this context. '/' marks the border between left position and the main clause, '\' marks the border between the main clause and right position. These generally correspond to intonational cues in speech (especially '\', which is accompanied by significant lowering of intensity and pitch).

(61)   Surface sequence: V NP
Underlying structure: $[t_S \text{ V}] \setminus \text{RP}_S$

taaj³   lèèw⁴   \phòò¹   han⁰
die   PFV   father   TPC.PCL
'(He)'d be dead, the father.' (177.6)

In each case, the 't' slot could include an overt argument, coreferential with the argument subscripted. Compare the following to (61):[14]

(62)   Surface sequence: NP V NP
Underlying structure: $[\text{NP}_i \text{ V}] \setminus \text{RP}_i$

phen¹   taaj³   lèèw⁴   \phòò¹   han⁰
3SG   die   PFV   father   TPC.PCL
'He'd be dead, the father.'

The combination of ellipsis and movement may create structural ambiguity (again, the 't' slot could be filled), such as the following in which the sentence-initial noun phrase could be interpreted as either an A in subject position, or an O in left-position:

(63) Surfacesequence: NPV_{tr}
Underlying structure i.: $\text{LP}_O/[\text{ø}_A\text{Vt}_O]$
Underlying structure ii.: $[\text{AVø}_O]$

phuak⁴   juu¹   nam²   thaang²   ka⁰   qaw³
group   be.at   accompany   road   FOC.PCL   take
i. 'Thoseᵢ along the road, (they_j) took øᵢ.' (actual reading, 654.10)
ii. 'Those along the road took (them/it).' (possible reading)

In the next example, remarkable in showing surface OVA order in what is basically an AVO language, we can infer from the presence of the postverbphrasal particle *dêj²* (which forms a right border to the core of the clause; cf. Figure 4.3.4.1-1 above), that the nominal *phu⁰-saaw³* 'girl(s)' is in Right Position (i.e. is postposed, and not in a pragmatically neutral position in the verb phrase).

(64)   Surfacesequence: NPVtrPCLNP
Underlyingstructurei.: $\text{LP}_O/[t_A\text{Vt}_O\text{PCL}]\setminus\text{RP}_A$
Underlyingstructureii.: $[\text{AVt}_O\text{PCL}]\setminus\text{RP}_O$

tamluat⁵/mak¹   dêj²   \   phu⁰-saaw³   tòòn³   nan⁴
police   like   PCL girls   time   DEM.NONPROX
i. 'Policeᵢ, (they_j) liked (themᵢ) you know, the girls_j back then.' (actual reading, 375.4)
ii. 'Police liked (them) you know, the girls back then.'

---

14 Note that there are 'binding' restrictions here, with respect to relative placement of pronouns and coreferential NPs — thus, **phòò¹ taaj³ lèèw⁴, phen¹* (The father'd be dead, he).

A third parameter, namely 'dual transitivity' due to accessibility of a verb to both transitive and intransitive constructions (cf. §4.3.2, above), intersects with these constituent order options to create even further surface ambiguity. In the following examples of 'NP V' sequences, the sentence-initial noun phrase may be taken as either (i) an S, (ii) an A in subject position, with O ellipsed, or (iii) an O in left position, with A ellipsed (cf. Chao 1968: 72, 701 on the same alternation in Modern Standard Chinese):

(65)   Surface sequence: NPV

Underlying structure i.: $[S_O V]$

Underlying structure ii.: $[A V \emptyset_O]$

Underlying structure iii.: $LP_O / [\emptyset_A V t_O]$

(a)   *kaj¹*   *kin³*   *lèèw⁴*

chicken   eat   PFV

i. 'The chicken has been eaten.'

ii. 'The chicken has eaten (it).'

iii. 'The chicken, (they) have eaten.'

(b)   *khèèw⁵*   *bò⁰*   *than²*   *mii²*

tooth   NEG   be.on.time   have/there.is

i. 'There were not yet any teeth.' (possible reading)

ii. 'The teeth didn't yet have (it/them).' (possible reading)

iii. 'Teeth, (it/they) didn't yet have.' (actual reading, 853.8)

These are typical examples of the context-dependency of Lao grammar. There are no overt, surface means for disambiguation in examples such as (63-65). Such vagueness causes few problems in real use, since it is usually clear to interlocutors, given features of the semantic/pragmatic context, just which discourse participants are involved, and in what ways. The structures underlying the alternative analyses described here can be diagnosed by various syntactic tests such as insertion of overt arguments, and reversal of 'movement' to check if semantics are significantly altered.

4.3.4.2. *The focus particle ka⁰*

An important element of the Lao clause is the focus particle *ka⁰*, appearing immediately before the main verb phrase (including its left aspect-modality marking), and immediately after the sentential subject.[15] It is a sentence-level marker, and cannot appear inside clauses which are tightly subordinated, such as relative clauses or controlled complement clauses. The grammatical constraints on *ka⁰* make it useful in diagnosing certain structural relationships in multi-verb constructions, as will become clear later in the chapter. The following examples are typical:

---

15   The *ka⁰* slot (between subject and predicate) is a common site for hesitation/pausing, and *ka⁰* itself is often prosodically extended (as *kaa*; cf. Tagalog *sa*, Himmelmann 2002). It may also appear as *kò⁰/kòò¹*, although less commonly (despite the fact that it is always written in the Lao orthography as if it should be pronounced *kòò¹*).

(66) *man²*   *ka⁰*   *bò⁰*   *mèèn¹*   *phii³*   *dêj²*

3SG   FOC.PCL   NEG   be   spirit   PCL

'And so she was not a spirit, you know.' (198.10)

(67) *tèè¹*   *khòòj⁵*   *ka⁰*   *bò⁰*   *cùù¹*   *khak¹*   *paan³-daj³*

but   1SG   FOC.PCL   NEG   remember   clear   extent-which

'But I can't remember very clearly.' (247.9)

(68) *lèèw⁴*   *hòòt⁴*   *mùù⁴-maj¹-mùù⁴-lun¹*   *haw²*   *ka⁰*   *si⁰*   *ma⁰*   *thaam³*

PFV   reach   day-new-day-after   1SG   FOC.PCL   IRR   come   ask

qiik⁵   *vaa¹-san⁴*

more   say-thus

'"And so when it comes to the new day [i.e. tomorrow], then I will come and ask further", he said.' (142.10)

I describe *ka⁰* as having a 'focussing' function, but this is not supported by a resolved analysis and should be considered a working description. The precise meaning of *ka⁰* is elusive, and it clearly has a function associated with discourse-oriented notions such as 'givenness', 'contrastiveness' and 'focus' (Chafe 1994, Lambrecht 1994). It makes reference to prior discourse or assumed information, and requires that what immediately precedes it be given. Thus, for example, when it directly marks a subject entity (such as the pronominal subjects in (66-68)), that entity cannot be an interrogative pronoun (see (73-74), §4.4.1.6, below).

The import of *ka⁰* often emerges in English translations as 'so/then' (see (68), above) or 'too/also':

(69) *khan²*   *mùng²*   *paj³*   *kuu³*   *ka⁰*   *paj³*

if   2SG   go   1SG   FOC.PCL   go

'If you go, then I go.'

(70) *qaaj⁴*   *khòòj⁵*   *suup⁵*   *jaa³*   *khòòj⁵*   *ka⁰*   *suup⁵*   *jaa³*

O.BRO   1SG   smoke   medicine   1SG   FOC.PCL   smoke   medicine

'My brother smokes; I smoke, too.'

In sentences isolated from context, the import of *ka⁰* can be entirely untranslatable. (For example, I am unable to render into English the subtle 'focussing' meaning of *ka⁰* in (67).)

I use the term 'focus particle' for *ka⁰* throughout this work, and it is beyond the scope of this study to say more than this about exactly what it means.[16] The important point for our purposes is that *ka⁰* has particular properties with respect to the clause and the sentence and

---

16 This element has analogues in virtually all the surrounding languages, and the problem of describing it has vexed scholars. The matter deserves further attention, in Lao, and across the mainland Southeast Asia area.

the verb phrase, and is useful in grammatical tests for diagnosing some (covert) features of clausal organization. See §4.4.1.6, below.

That ka^0 is a pre-VP marker (in constituent structure terms) is demonstrated by the fact that it cannot appear between left position and subject. In a simple transitive sentence with the object fronted, in left position, ka^0 must appear between the subject (if expressed) and the verb, not after the topicalized first noun phrase (thus the ungrammaticality of (71b)):

(71)   (a) pa^0-$dèèk^5$ ($khòòj^5$) ka^0 kin^3

           CT.FISH-jugged.fish   (1SG)   FOC.PCL   eat

           'Jugged fish, (I) eat.'

       (b)   *pa^0-$dèèk^5$ ka^0 $hòòj^5$ kin^3

           CT.FISH-jugged.fish   FOC.PCL   1SG   eat

A significant function of ka^0 is in marking off clausal topics from the predications that follow and scope over them, with a result often translationally equivalent to the English 'for to' construction:

(72) haw^2 ca^0 $patisêêt^5$ ka^0 $bò^0$ $pên^3$ $kaan^3$-$som^3khùan^2$

       1SG   IRR   refuse   FOC.PCL   NEG   be   NSR-appropriate

       'For me to refuse would not be appropriate.' (85.6)

A clue to the 'focussing' semantic function of ka^0 emerges from its interaction with the pronoun $phaj^3$ which may normally either mean 'who' (in a WH-question), or 'whoever/anyone' (in a declarative sentence). The following example, without ka^0, is ambiguous:

(73) $phaj^3$ $bò^0$ kin^3 $siin^4$ dip^2

       who/anyone   NEG   eat   meat   raw

       i. 'Who doesn't eat raw meat?'

       ii. 'No-one eats raw meat.' (i.e. 'Anyone/everyone doesn't eat raw meat.')

Insertion of ka^0 after the subject $phaj^3$ 'who/anyone' disallows the interrogative reading 'who?' (by its requirement that the preceding constituent be 'given'), forcing the declarative (73ii) reading:

(74) $phaj^3$ ka^0 $bò^0$ kin^3 $siin^4$ dip^2

       who/anyone   FOC.PCL   NEG   eat   meat   raw

       'No-one at all eats raw meat.' (i.e. 'Anyone/everyone doesn't eat raw meat.')

       (NOT: 'Who doesn't eat raw meat?')

That ka^0 is a sentence-level marker is further supported by the fact that it cannot appear in a clause which has been relativized, and which therefore functions as a modifier in a noun phrase:

(75) $khòòj^5$ $bò^0$ mak^1 $[phaj^3$ $[(*ka^0)$ kin^3 $siin^4$ $dip^2]_{\text{REL.CLS.}}]_{\text{NP}}$

     1SG   NEG   like   who/anyone   (FOC.PCL)   eat   meat   raw

     'I don't like anyone who eats raw meat.'

The predication in the relative clause does not say anything on the sentence level at all. What is being said in this sentence is said by the main verb $bò^0$ mak^1 [NEG like] 'don't like', and accordingly, just before this verb (including its left aspect-modality marking) is the only place where ka^0 could be inserted in (75).

4.3.4.3.   Disposal constructions

The 'disposal construction' (see §4.4.4, below for details) can be regarded as a syntactic permutation available for two-argument predicates whose transitivity (in the sense of Hopper and Thompson 1980) is high. More specifically, the construction is a permutation available only to two-argument clauses which constitute 'Transitive constructions', as described in §4.3.2, above. Thus, example (76a), describing a controlled agentive event in which the object argument is highly affected, is accessible to the 'disposal' alternation (76b). Example (77a), by contrast, describes a situation in which there is no action, in which the subject is not a controller or agent, and in which the object is not affected. Accordingly, the 'disposal' alternation is not available (77b):

(76)   (a) kuu^3 $khaa^5$ paa^3

          1SG   kill   fish

          'I kill (the) fish.'

     (b) kuu^3 qaw^3 paa^3 ma^0 $khaa^5$

          1SG   take   fish   come   kill

          'I kill (the) fish.' (= 'I take (the) fish and kill (it/them).')

(77)   (a) kuu^3 $khiw^3$ paa^3

          1SG   smelly   fish

          'I find (the) fish smelly.'

     (b) $*kuu^3$ qaw^3 paa^3 ma^0 $khiw^3$

          1SG   take   fish   come   smelly

          (I take the fish and find (it/them) smelly.)

Conditions for use of the disposal construction are related to information structure, but the facts are not yet clearly understood. (See §4.4.4, below, for further discussion; also Enfield 2002b: 23-25.)

4.3.5. Summary

This concludes our preliminary discussion of argument structure properties of basic (i.e. single-verb) clauses in Lao. Lao clauses are characterized by widespread ellipsis of retrievable arguments, widespread ambitransitivity of verbs, with a range of different variations in possibilities for alternation of semantic role of arguments, and widespread possibility for movement of arguments into pragmatically sensitive extra-clausal positions. The combination of these three features of Lao clause structure results in many situations in which the fundamentals of predicate-argument relations cannot be read off from the surface form of Lao sentences, but must be resolved by reference to contextual information. We now turn to the domain of multi-verb constructions, in which the scope for structural ambiguity becomes even greater.

4.4. MULTI-VERB CONSTRUCTIONS

To understand how Lao speakers package information in clauses, including management of arguments in various roles and levels of functional, structural and informational status in the clause, as well as subordination and coordination of predicates, one has to understand multi-verb constructions. The same goes for any Tai language. In investigating the most basic issues of grammatical relations and argument structure in Lao, one immediately comes across unmarked V1-V2 sequences, and these conceal a great many structural distinctions (cf. Table 4.1-1 above). This section, making up the body of this chapter, describes a range of the most important structural categories of multi-verb constructions.[17]

4.4.1. Headship, 'main verb properties', and constituency tests

Lao speakers do not use case-marking or cross-referencing morphology, and seldom explicitly mark relationships of subordination (e.g. as speakers of other languages might do by infinitive verb forms or the like). There are few simple ways for grammarians to work out which element is the 'head' in compounds or complex predicates, and in addition there are ambiguities with respect to the distinction between coordinate and subordinate relationships between verb phrases which appear in surface sequence. Figuring out how various verbs are related in various kinds of unmarked multi-verb sequences dominates the task of describing Lao grammar. In this section, we consider some phenomena helpful in devising tests for discovering these relations.

In the rest of this section, I outline headship properties as defined by the following aspects of grammatical behaviour:

i.   Grammatical features of canonical main verbs
ii.   Clause separability
iii. Yes-answers
iv.   Ellipsibility of object complements (in main and relative clauses)
v.   Insertability of left aspect-modality marking
vi.   Insertability of the focus particle ka^0

These are the topics of the following sub-sections.

4.4.1.1. *Grammatical features of canonical main verbs*

In assessing the respective roles of different verbs in multi-verb sequences, the question arises as to whether either of the two verbs is more or less accessible than the other to the normal grammatical features of main verbs. As discussed in §4.2, the class of verbs in Lao consists of words which may take: (a) direct negation with prefixed $bòò^1/bò^0$, (b) direct irrealis marking with prefixed si^0, (c) marking of attainment with prefixed daj^4/daj^0, (d) marking of currently relevant state with postverbal $lèèw^4$ (among other possibilities of aspect-modality marking). Another property of verbs in Lao is that they may be used as nominal attributives in noun

---

17 Note that in referring to 'multi-verb constructions', I restrict this in general to sequences which normally form prosodically integrated units. Also, I do not use the term 'serial verb construction', although many of the constructions discussed here might be referred to by that term. The term 'serial verb construction' has been used in a range of ways in the literature (cf. Lord 1993, Durie 1997, Aikhenvald and Dixon 2006), and may be too suggestive of certain specific types of construction which form only a subset of the broader set of expressions described in this chapter.

phrases (comparable to adjectives, gerundive attributives and relative clauses in other languages; cf. *khon² suung³* [person tall] 'tall person', *khon² lèèn¹* [person run] 'running person', *khon² paj³* [person go] 'person (who) goes'), and in this role may be linked overtly to the modified noun by the relativizer *thii¹*. Verbs in secondary or subordinate function often are not accessible to some or all of these properties.

4.4.1.2. *Clause separability of multi-verb constructions*

A multi-verb construction shows *clause separability* if it can be paraphrased with insertion of overt marking which forces a reading of the verbs as each belonging to an independent clause, and where this causes no significant change in the basic semantic relationship between those verbs (although, of course, certain pragmatic effects may arise).

One way to clause-separate a multi-verb construction is to insert between verbs a marked pause, and/or an adverbial expression such as *lang³-caak⁵ nan⁴* 'after that', *nòòk⁴-caak⁵ nan⁴* 'apart from that; as well as that', *phùa¹* 'in order to', or *lùù³-vaa¹* 'or'. Another is to insert the clause-linker *lèka⁰* 'and then' (a reduced form of the perfective *lèèw⁴* 'finish' in combination with the VP-marking focus particle *ka⁰*; see §4.3.4.2, above; §4.4.1.6, below). In general (although not exclusively), the perfective *lèèw⁴* 'finish' marks the previous clause, and the focus particle *ka⁰* refers to the coming clause, whose subject being coreferential with that of the previous clause, and being tracked across these clauses, is naturally ellipsed. The result is that *lèka⁰* routinely signals (but does not entail) consecutivity and subject coreferentiality between conjoined clauses. Other functions of *lèka⁰* include distributive enumeration of actions which are not necessarily performed consecutively (cf. §4.4.10.1, below).[18] While these various ways of clause-separating multiple verbs in a single construction alter the semantic content of the original string, what is important for clause-separability as a grammatical test is whether or not the insertion upsets the basic semantic relation between verbs.

Thus, the sequence 'return come study' in (78a) – not subordinating, apart from iconic temporal sequence – is clause-separable, as shown by the acceptability (with negligible change in semantic relationship between V1 and V2) of (78b) and (78c):

(78) (a) *kap²-khùùn²*   *maa²*   *tòò¹*   *pathêêt⁴*   *hian²*

   back-return   come   continue   country   study

   '(They came) back to (their) country to continue (their) studies.' (1202.2)

   (b) *kap²-khùùn²*   *maa²*   *pathêêt⁴*   *phùa¹*   *hian²*   *tòò¹*

   back-return   come   country   in.order.to   study   continue

   '(They came) back to (their) country in order to continue (their) studies.' (= (78a))

   (c) *kap²-khùùn²*   *maa²*   *tòò¹*   *pathêêt⁴*   *lèka⁰*   *hian²*

   back-return   come   continue   country   CLNK   study

   '(They came) back to (their) country and (they) continued (their) studies.' (= (78a))

In contrast, (79a) – a subordinating complement construction – is *non* clause-separable, as shown by the significant change of semantic relationship between V1 and V2 in the clause-separated permutations (79b) and (79c):

---

18 Note that there are other linkers which seem at first glance very similar to *lèka⁰* (such as *la⁰*, *lèèw⁴*, and *loot⁴*), but which certainly play subtly different functions in linking clauses in discourse. The issues are beyond the scope of the present discussion.

(79) (a) *phuak⁴*   *khòòj⁵*   *hên³*   *man²*   *ñing²*   *baan⁴*

group   1SG   see   3SG   shoot   village

'We saw them bomb the village.' (1157.7)

(b) *phuak⁴* *khòòj⁵* *hên³* *man²* - *nòòk⁴* *caak⁵* *nan⁴* *man²* *ñing²* *baan⁴*

group   1SG   see   3SG   out   from   that   3SG   shoot   village

'We saw them – as well as that, they bombed the village.' (≠(79a))

(c) *phuak⁴*   *khòòj⁵*   *hên³*   *man²*   *lèka⁰*   *ñing²*   *baan⁴*

group   1SG   see   3SG   CLNK   shoot   village

'We saw them and then bombed the village.' (≠(79a))

Clause-separability as a grammatical test reveals differences in relationships between verbs in multi-verb constructions. In general, verb combinations involving relationships of subordination are not clause-separable.

4.4.1.3. *The yes-answer*

Polar questions in Lao are formed by taking a declarative sentence and adding one of a set of interrogative sentence-final particles, the most general or default being *bòò³* (related to the negative *bòò¹/bò⁰*):

(80)   *caw⁴*   *si⁰*   *paj³*   *talaat⁵*   *bòò³*

2SG   IRR   go   market   PCL(Q)

'Will you go to the market?'

One way of yes-answering a polar question is to use an affirmative particle such as the very polite *dooj³*, the standard polite *caw⁴*, or the informal *qee⁴/qee⁵*. Another common method of affirmative answer is to repeat some portion of the question, typically the main verb alone:

(81)   (*khòòj⁵*)   (*si⁰*)   *paj³*   (*talaat⁵*)   (**bòò³*)

1SG   IRR   go   market   PCL(Q)

'(Yes, I will) go (to the market).'

Thus, as a yes-answer to (80), *paj³* 'go' could appear alone or in combination with any of the other elements in the question (apart from the interrogative particle itself). The important thing here with respect to the yes-answer as a test for main-verbhood is that in answering (80) by means of repetition of some portion of the question, the main verb *paj³* 'go' is necessary and sufficient as a yes-answer. Also importantly, preverbal aspect-modality markers such as irrealis *si⁰*, preverbal *daj⁰*, and inner directional particles, can never appear alone.

The following complement construction shows the verb *suup⁵* 'suck/smoke' subordinate to the main complement-taking predicate *haam⁵* 'to forbid':

(82)   *khaw³*   *haam⁵*   *suup⁵*

3PL   forbid   smoke

'They forbid (people) to smoke (it).' (117.10)

A question is formed by adding the interrogative particle $bòò^3$:

(83)   *khaw³   haam⁵   suup⁵   bòò³*
       3PL   forbid   smoke   PCL(Q)
       'Do they forbid (people) to smoke (it)?'

Only the matrix verb *haam⁵* 'forbid' can appear alone as a yes-answer here:

(84) *haam⁵*

    forbid

    '(Yes, they) forbid (people to smoke it).'

On the other hand, in the case of 'want' complement constructions, the usual yes-answer includes both the matrix verb *jaak⁵* 'want' and its equi complement verb:

(85)   Q: *caw⁴   jaak⁵   paj³   bòò³*
           2SG   want   go   PCL(Q)
           'Do you want to go?'

     Ai: *jaak⁵   paj³*
        want   go
        '(Yes, I) want to go.'

However, it is also possible to answer the question using either the main verb *jaak⁵* 'want' alone:

(85) Aii   *jaak⁵*

       want

       '(Yes, I) want (to go).'

or the equi complement alone:

(85) Aiii   *paj³*

        go

        '(Yes, I want to) go.' (or – '(Yes, I'll) go.')

The difference between these two replies is that (85)Aiii is arguably not a straight answer to (85)Q (i.e. in that it does not directly respond to the sentence-meaning of the question – cf. English *I'll go* as an answer to *Do you want to go?*).

Other complement-taking predicates which are borderline between full complement-taking verbs and preverbal aspect-modality markers similarly show varying yes-answer properties. A notable example is *kheej²* 'accustomed to, have ever', which allows 'V1', 'V2', or 'V1-V2' as yes-answers to a question 'V1-V2?', but differs from *jaak⁵* 'want' in that the preferred yes-answer is V1 alone (rather than 'V1-V2'):

(86) Q: *caw⁴*   *kheej²*   *paj³*   *bòò³*
            2SG   ever   go   PCL(Q)
            'Have you ever been?'

      Ai: *kheej²*
             ever
             '(Yes, I have) ever (been).' (preferred)

      Aii: *kheej²*   *paj³*
             ever   go
             '(Yes, I have) ever been.'

      Aiii: *paj³*
             go
             '(Yes, I have ever) been.' (or – '(Yes, I) go.')

Again, it is arguable whether *paj³* 'go' in (86Aiii) is a straight answer (i.e. a direct response to the sentence-meaning of the original question). Otherwise, it is unclear what the communicative difference between these responses is.

In contrast, for right-headed adverbial complement constructions (§4.4.6.3, below), yes-answer status is unequivocally with V2:

(87) Q: *caw⁴*   *paj³*   *viang²-can³*   *muan¹*   *bòò³*
            2SG   go   Vientiane   fun   PCL(Q)
            Did you have fun going to Vientiane?'

      Ai: *muan¹*
             fun
             '(Yes, I had) fun.'

      Aii: **paj³*
             go
             ((Yes, I) went.)

(88) Q: *faaj¹*   *viang²-can³*   *sanaq¹*   *dii³*   *bòò³*
            side   Vientiane   win   good   PCL(Q)
            '(Would it be) good (if) the Vientiane side won?'

      Ai: *dii³*
             good
             '(Yes, it would be) good.'

      Aii: **sanaq¹*
             win
             ((Yes, it would) win.)

Compare these with cases in which the verbs in sequence are coordinated/compounded – as in the synonym compound (89) (cf. §4.4.10.2, below), or the left-marking adverbial compound (90) (cf. §4.4.6.4.1, below) – and cannot be separated in a minimal straight yes-answer:

(89) Q: *man²*   *nii³-paq²*   *naang²*   *qan⁰-nii⁴*   *bòò³*

3SG   flee-abandon young.woman CLF-DEM.GEN PCL(Q)

'Did he abandon that young woman?'

Ai. *nii³-paq²*

flee-abandon

'(Yes, he) abandoned (her).'

(90) Q: *lak¹-khaam⁵* *saaj²-dèèn³* *bòò³*

steal-cross   border   PCL(Q)

'(Did they) secretly cross the border?'

A: *lak¹-khaam⁵*

steal-cross

'(Yes, they) secretly crossed (it).'

In sum, three types of yes-answer behaviour can be determined for a given V1-V2 combination:

TABLE 4.4.1.3-1: THREE TYPES OF V1-V2 COMBINATION, BY YES-ANSWER BEHAVIOUR.

Preferred yes-answer	**V1**	**V2**	**V1-V2**
Examples	Cognitive complements 'see', 'forget', 'hear', and phase complements such as 'begin' and 'cease'.	Complement structures with adverbials or resultatives in V2 position.	Verb compounds (coordinative and adverbial).

4.4.1.4. *Ellipsibility of object complements*

4.4.1.4.1. *Ellipsibility of object complements in main clauses*

As already mentioned, ellipsis of nominal complements is normal and widespread in Lao. Any main verb in a simple clause can be expressed without accompanying phonological material referring to its arguments (cf. examples (2-4), above):

(91)   *kuu³*   *kin³*   *maak⁵*   *nii⁴*   *tèè¹*   *mùng²*   *bò⁰*   *kin³*   *ø*

1SG   eat   fruit   DEM.GEN   but   2SG   NEG   eat

'I eat this fruit, but you don't eat (it).'

Also, many (but not all) verb-prepositions – i.e. verbs marking non-core participants – may ellipse their complements:

(92)   *mùng²   paj³,   kuu³   jaak⁵   paj³   nam²*   ø
       2SG   go   1SG   want   go   accompany
       '(If) you go, I want to go with (you).'

It is less clear whether the verb phrase or sentence complements of complement-taking main verbs can in general be ellipsed, and in many cases it would seem impossible:

(93)   *??mùng²   jaak⁵   paj³   tèè¹   kuu³   bò⁰   jaak⁵*   ø
        2SG   want   go   but   1SG   NEG   want
        ('You want to go, but I don't want to.')

Clearly, however, main complement-taking predicates cannot normally be ellipsed. Thus, the following example does not mean 'You want to go, but I don't want to' (i.e. where *jaak⁵* 'want' is ellipsed from the second clause):

(94)   *mùng²   jaak⁵   paj³   tèè¹   kuu³   bò⁰   paj³*
        2SG   want   go   but   1SG   NEG   go
        'You want to go, but I'm not going.'

Moreover, the effect cannot be achieved by removing the whole verb complex (i.e. *jaak⁵ paj³* 'want to go') under identity with that of the previous clause:

(95)   **mùng²   jaak⁵   paj³   tèè¹   kuu³   bò⁰*
        2SG   want   go   but   1SG   NEG
        (You want to go but I not.)

(96)   **mùng²   jaak⁵   paj³   tèè¹   bò⁰   kuu³*
        2SG   want   go   but   NEG   1SG
        (You want to go but not me.)

4.4.1.4.2. *Ellipsibility of object complements in relativization*

An exception to the general rule in Lao that any noun phrase can be ellipsed under contextual retrievability is the requirement that in a relative clause some phonological material corresponding to the argument being relativized upon must appear (i.e. as the nominal modified by the relative clause).[19] Consider the following examples, showing a simple transitive clause in (97a), and in (97b) this clause relativized, in object function, with the erstwhile subject as head (using *khon²* 'person'):[20]

---

19 Occasional exceptions are noted, but these are not really relative clauses, rather sentences in left/right position, with ellipsed subjects. I heard and noted the following example (Oudom Xay, September 1999): *tok² vang⁰-kii⁴ ni⁰, caw⁴ kêp² lèèw⁴ vaa³* [fall just.now, 2SG collect PFV PCL] 'Did you pick up (the thing that) fell just now?', in which the string *tok² vang⁰-kii⁴ ni⁰* 'fell just now' could be mistaken for a relative clause with no head noun being modified. However, unlike a regular (headed) relative clause, it cannot appear with this meaning in a core argument slot: **caw⁴ kêp² tok² vang⁰-kii⁴ ni⁰ lèw⁰-vaa³* (Did you collect what fell just now?). I suggest that a more faithful translation of the original example would be '(It) fell just now, did you pick (it) up?'.

20 Note that (97b) is in fact a multi-verb sequence, with the verbs *hên³* 'see' and *mak¹* 'like' adjacent. Such sequences are not discussed further in this chapter.

(97)   (a) qi^0-dam^3 mak^1 bak^0-$dèèng^3$
                CLF.FEM-D.   like   CLF.MASC-D.
                'Dam likes Deng.'

        (b) kuu^3 $hên^3$ *($khon^2$) mak^1 bak^0-$dèèng^3$
                1SG   see   person   like   CLF.MASC-D.
                'I saw the person who likes Deng.'

These examples, showing that a relative clause cannot appear without an explicit nominal head to modify, involve a simple transitive verb mak^1 'like'. Now we consider relative clauses derived from clauses containing multi-verb constructions, and the question arises as to whether one or the other verb can be ellipsed. The possibilities are different for different constructions.

For example, the following head-final adverbial construction includes the verb $muan^1$ 'enjoyable' in V2 position:

(98) $laaw^2$ lin^5 $kitaa^3$ $muan^1$
        3SG   play   guitar   enjoyable
        'S/he plays guitar nicely (i.e. her playing sounds good).'

While the adverbial V2 $muan^1$ 'enjoyable' is head for yes-answer purposes, it cannot stand alone in a relative clause and retain its adverbial function. Instead, if it appears alone (as in (99b, 100b), below), it is taken for a main verb (in this case 'adjective') in itself:

(99) (a) $khòòj^5$ $hên^3$ [$khon^2$ lin^5 $kitaa^3$ $muan^1$]
        1SG   see   person   play   guitar   enjoyable
        'I saw the person who plays guitar nicely.'

    (b) $khòòj^5$ $hên^3$ $muan^1$]   [$khon^2$
        1SG   see   enjoyable   person
        'I saw the enjoyable/fun person.' (not entailed by (99a))

(100)   (a) $khòòj^5$ $hên^3$ [$kitaa^3$ lin^5 $muan^1$]
                1SG   see   guitar   play   enjoyable
                'I saw the guitar that is enjoyable to play.'

        (b) $khòòj^5$ $hên^3$ [$kitaa^3$ $muan^1$]
                1SG   see   guitar   enjoyable
                'I saw the enjoyable/fun guitar.' (not entailed by (100a))

In contrast, V2 complements of left-head complement-taking predicates such as $haam^5$ 'forbid' or huu^4 'know' are optional in relative clauses:

(101)   (a) $khòòj^5$ $haam^5$ $suup^5$ jaa^3 $hên^3$ $khon^2$
                1SG   forbid   smoke   medicine   see   person
                'I saw the person who forbade (you) to smoke.'

(b) *khòòj⁵*   *hên³*   *khon²*   *haam⁵*
     1SG   see   person   forbid
     'I saw the person who forbade (you).' (entailed by (101a))

(102) (a) *khòòj⁵* *hên³* *khon²* *huu⁴* *vaa¹* *caw⁴* *juu¹* *han⁵*
            1SG   see   person know   COMP   2SG   be.at   there
            'I saw the person who knows you were there.'

       (b) *khòòj⁵*   *hên³*   *khon²*   *huu⁴*
            1SG   see   person   know
            'I saw the person who knows.' (entailed by (102a))

In sum, while a relative clause must attach to a nominal head, there is a logical possibility in the case of multi-verb constructions that one of the verbs can be omitted. Left- and right-headed V1-V2 structures behave differently with respect to this possibility, due to the contrasting status of V1, and V2, respectively, as head.

4.4.1.5. *Insertability of left aspect-modality marking*

Certain aspect-modality marking appears immediately before the verb, a fact which allows for distinction between certain types of multi-verb construction. Thus, in a V1-V2 sequence, we may ask whether an aspect-modality marking such as *bò⁰* 'NEG' or *si⁰* 'IRR' appears before V1, V2, either, or neither. For example, in the case of verb compounds (§4.4.10.2, below), no marking of V2 is possible (103), while in resultative constructions (§4.4.6.2, below) it is usually possible for either V1 or V2 to be directly marked (104):

(103) (a) *man²*   *bò⁰*   *daj⁰*   *nii³-paq²*
            3SG   NEG   ACHV   flee-abandon
            'He didn't abandon (her).'

       (b) *man²*   *nii³*   *bò⁰*   *daj⁰*   *paq²*
            3SG   flee   NEG   ACHV   abandon
            (NOT: 'He didn't abandon (her).')
            Possible reading: 'He fled, he didn't abandon (her).'

(104) (a) *man²*   *bò⁰*   *daj⁰*   *piing⁴*   *suk²*
            3SG   NEG   ACHV   grill   cooked
            'It did not, by grilling, get cooked.'

       (b) *man²*   *piing⁴*   *bò⁰*   *daj⁰*   *suk²*
            3SG   grill   NEG   ACHV   cooked
            'It, by grilling, did not get cooked.'

4.4.1.6. *Insertability of focus particle ka⁰*

In §4.3.4.2, above, we encountered the focus particle *ka⁰*. We now consider how it is useful in understanding grammatical properties of different multi-verb constructions. We begin with tight complementation structures (see §4.4.9, below, for discussion of different complement types), a permissive and a causative, respectively:

(105) *phen¹   bò⁰   haj⁵   ø   paj³*
       3SG   NEG   give   go
       'He wouldn't let (me) go.'

(106) *baang³-thùa¹   ø   hêt¹   kèèw⁴   tèèk⁵*
       some-occasion   do/make   glass   break
       'Sometimes (I) might break a glass.'

The following text examples show *ka⁰* appearing immediately after the main subject slot of these constructions:

(107) *phen¹   ka⁰   bò⁰   haj⁵   ø   paj³*
       3SG   FOC.PCL   NEG   give   go
       'So, he wouldn't let (me) go.' (332.2)

(108) *baang³-thùa¹   ø   ka⁰   hêt¹   kèèw⁴   tèèk⁵*
       some-occasion   FOC.PCL   do/make   glass   break
       'So, sometimes (I) might break a glass.' (1001.9)

If *ka⁰* appeared after the lower subject slot in these examples (i.e. before *paj³* 'go' and *tèèk⁵* 'break', respectively), the embedded complement readings would not be possible at all. Thus, with *ka⁰* after the lower subject slot, marked by '*ø*' in (107), as follows, the verb *paj³* 'go' and its subject would no longer be embedded under *haj⁵* 'give/make/let', but as the translations reveal, the two verbs would belong to distinct clauses (note that further readings are possible, as indicated by '...'):

(107') *phen¹   bò⁰   haj⁵   ø   ka⁰   paj³*
       3SG   NEG   give   FOC.PCL   go
       i. '(So, even if) they don't give (it to me), (I'll) go (anyway).'
       ii. '(If) they don't give (it to me), (so then I'll) go.'

The verbs *haj⁵* 'give' and *paj³* 'go' are interpreted in (107') as heads of separate clauses, coordinated. *Paj³* 'go' functions as an independent verbal head, with the result that *haj⁵* 'give' is not interpreted in its causative complement-taking sense 'give/make/let', and instead is interpreted as a regular main verb, literally, 'give'. The overall expression, with two separate clauses, may then take on a conditional meaning (arising from the need to interpret a relevant link between the juxtaposed clauses).

Similarly, to take example (108) and move the focus particle *ka⁰* to the point immediately before V2 would again disallow a reading in which the lower clause (i.e. *kèèw⁴ tèèk⁵* ['glass break']) were subordinate to the higher verb *hêt¹* 'do/make', and would instead force a biclausal coordination reading (again, readings other than (i) and (ii) are possible):

(108') *baang³-thùa¹*   *ø hêt¹*   *kèèw⁴ ka⁰*   *tèèk⁵*
some-occasion   do/make   glass FOC.PCL break
i. 'Sometimes (I) might make a glass, and (it) will (also) break.'
ii. 'Sometimes (when) (I) do (it), the glasses (also) break.'

Insertion of *ka⁰* before V2 in the preceding examples causes a radical change in interpretation, depending on the nature of the relationship between V1 and V2. In other cases, however, there is more than one option for *ka⁰*-insertion. Consider the following two right-marking adverbial constructions (cf. §4.4.6.3- 4.4.6.4, below):

(109)   (a)   *laaw²*   *tèèm⁴*   *huup⁴*   *lin⁵*
              3SG   paint   picture play
              'S/he paints pictures for fun.'

        (b)   *laaw²*   *tèèm⁴*   *huup⁴*   *kêng¹*
              3SG   paint   picture   adept
              'S/he's good at painting pictures.'

These naturally both allow insertion of *ka⁰* immediately after the main subject *laaw²* 's/he', marking off the whole verb sequence in each case as a predication about the focussed initial nominal:

(110) (a) *laaw² ka⁰*   *tèèm⁴ huup⁴   lin⁵*
          3SG   FOC.PCL paint picture play
          'S/he also paints pictures for fun.'

      (b) *laaw² ka⁰*   *tèèm⁴ huup⁴   kêng¹*
          3SG   FOC.PCL paint picture adept
          'S/he's also good at painting pictures.'

However, only (109b) allows insertion of *ka⁰* before V2:

(111) (a) **laaw² tèèm⁴ huup⁴   ka⁰*   *lin⁵*
          3SG   paint picture FOC.PCL play
          (S/he also paints pictures for fun.)

      (b) laaw² tèèm⁴ huup⁴ ka⁰   kêng¹
          3SG   paint picture FOC.PCL adept
          'S/he'salsogoodatpaintingpictures.'

The issue here is how the post-*ka⁰* verb in a construction such as (111b) (here, it is *kêng¹* 'adept') relates semantically to what precedes it, e.g. whether the main subject has a semantic role with respect to V2, and if so, what role it is. In (109-111), *kêng¹* 'adept' is a gradable state verb ('adjective'), which may be construed in this case as either predicating a property of the main subject 's/he', or (adverbially) of a whole predication 'S/he paints pictures'.
    The unacceptability of (111a) suggests that *lin⁵* 'play' in (109a) does not have the same outer scope as *kêng¹* 'adept', and belongs in an inner clause layer, where it directly marks the

verb phrase only, not the subject alone, and not the sentence as a whole. This distinction between the behaviour of (109a) and (109b) relates to a distinction between compounding versus complementation in right-headed adverbial constructions, and active versus stative aspectual structure of an adverbial V2 head (compare stative *kêng¹* 'adept' versus active *lin⁵* 'play'). See §4.4.6.3- 4.4.6.4, below, for further discussion.

The focus particle *ka⁰* belongs in a post-subject/pre-VP slot *on the sentence level*. It cannot appear in the post-subject/pre-VP slot of an embedded clause, or a relative clause (as noted in §4.3.4.2, above). That it can appear before certain V2 resultative/adverbials suggests that the latter can be structurally main-predicate like, more so than the verbs in their sentential 'subjects'. This structural distinction is helpful in working out distinctions between various types of V1-V2 sequences.

4.4.1.7. *Comment*

This finishes our preview of various structural tests which help to distinguish between different types of V1-V2 strings. The remainder of §4.4 is concerned with describing the various V1-V2 constructions, and the grammatical distinctions between them. (See Table 4.5.2-1, at the end of the chapter, for a summary of the constructions.)

4.4.2. Deverbal aspect/modality marking

A number of regular verbs have secondary roles as aspect-modality markers. Whether one takes this to mean that they are polysemous (have multiple meanings, i.e. as a verb in one context and an aspect-modality marker in another context), or monosemous (have single abstract meanings applicable in all their uses), or subject to derivational processes (marked by a zero morpheme), they are nonetheless relevant to our theme in that they present us with sequences of more than one lexical item identifiable as a 'verb' together in a single clause.

Most aspectual/modals appear immediately before the verb, and some appear after the object. (Only a few – e.g. *daj⁴* 'acquire, attain, can', *than²* 'be on time, (not) yet' – may appear either before or after the verb, and in each case their meaning is different in the two positions.) The relative order, roughly speaking, of the preverbal aspect/modality categories to be discussed here is as follows ('ASP/MOD' are less restricted aspect-modality slots; this figure is an expansion of 'AM-[V (OBJ)]-AM' in Figure 4.3.4.1-1, above):

ASP/MOD · IRR · NEG · ASP/MOD · *daj⁰* · DIR.PCL · [VERB (OBJ)] · ASP/MOD

FIGURE 4.4.2-1: ELEMENTS OF THE LAO VERB PHRASE, IN ORDER

The Lao clause shows a tight bond between the verb and its immediate complement, and there is no syntactic slot available for intervening material. Many aspectual/modals are transparently related to existing verbs, and as such are of transitional or grammaticalising status (e.g. from complement-taking main verbs to simple preverbal markers).

There are also some non-deverbal aspect-modality markers, which we now preview. Two preverbal irrealis markers *si⁰* and *ca⁰* are mutually substitutable, the occasional difference being stylistic, or associated with idiomatic combinations with other grammatical elements (e.g. the complex relativizer *thii²-ca⁰*; cf. ungrammatical **thii²-si⁰*).[21] These commonly have the effect of marking future tense, as follows:

---

21 Speakers of neighbouring Thai use *ca⁰* alone for much the same range of functions as *ca⁰* and *si⁰* together in Lao. This, like other uses more idiomatic in Thai, sometimes carries a more formal feel in Lao—correspondingly, *si⁰* is considered 'more Lao'.

(112)   *phò⁰-tuu⁴*   *si⁰*   *fang²*
        grandfather   IRR   listen
        'I[grandfather]'ll listen.' (50.3)

(113)   *lèèw⁴*   *mùù⁴*   *nii⁴*   *si⁰*   *vaw⁴*   *qan⁰*   *kaw¹*   *han⁵*   *lèq⁵*
        PFV   day   DEM.GEN   IRR   speak   CLF   old   TPC.PCL   PCL
        'And so today (I)'ll tell the old one (i.e. the old story).' (35.5)

They may also have a 'relative future tense' function, i.e. marking temporal posteriority, but not necessarily with respect to the speech event itself:

(114)   *mù⁰-vaan¹*   *nii⁴*   *khòòj⁵*   *si⁰*   *paj³*   *talaat⁵*   *tèè¹*   *bò⁰*   *mii²*   *vêlaa²*
        yesterday   DEM.GEN   1SG   IRR   go   market   but   NEG   have   time
        'Yesterday, I was going to go to the market, but I didn't have time.'

A subjunctive/conditional meaning is also common:

(115)   *si⁰*   *khap²*   *lot¹*   *ka⁰*   *bò⁰*   *tòòng⁴*   *kin³*   *law⁵*
        IRR   drive   vehicle   FOC.PCL   NEG   must   consume   liquor
        '(If you)'re going to drive, (you) needn't drink liquor.'

Another non-deverbal left-marking aspectual/modal is the negation marker *bòò¹/bò⁰*. It follows irrealis marking (*si⁰/ca⁰*), as in the following two examples:

(116)   baang³-thii²   man²   ka⁰   si⁰   bò⁰   mòq²   paan³-daj³
        maybe   3SG   FOC.PCL   IRR   NEG   appropriate   extent-which
        'Maybe it wouldn't be very appropriate [i.e. to have too many chickens, when making a chicken coop].' (20.9)

(117)   *khòòj⁵*   *si⁰*   *bò⁰*   *hian²*   *nangsùù³*   *tòò¹*   *qiik⁵*
        1SG   IRR   NEG   study   writing   connect   more
        'I wasn't going to study any further.' (608.14)

In the following sections, we look at deverbal aspect-modality markers, and we consider their relation to full verb functions. We begin with those which appear before the verb.

4.4.2.1. *Preverbal deverbal aspectual/modals*

Most left aspectual/modals are related to verbs in complement-taking functions. The relative ordering of these is fairly fixed, with most coming after the irrealis 'IRR' and negation 'NEG' slots in Figure 4.4.2-1.

    A number of aspectual/modals may appear directly after negation, some idiomatically restricted to negated contexts only. For example, *suu¹* and *khòòj¹* must always be negated (yielding *bò⁰-suu¹-V* 'not tending to V' and *bò⁰-khòòj¹-V* 'not particularly V'):

(118)   *ngen²*   /khaw³   *bò⁰*   *suu¹*   *daj⁰*   *saj⁴*   *laaj³*
        money   3PL   NEG   tend.to   ACHV   use   much
        'Money, they didn't tend to use much (then).' (246.14)

(119) *khòòj⁵*   *bò⁰*   *khòòj¹*   *mii²*
       1SG   NEG   particularly   have
       'I haven't particularly had (money).' (638.1)

These are surely related to the verbs *khòòj¹* 'gradual' and *suu¹* 'reach, towards'.
    Another example of deverbal left aspect-modality marking which only appears with
negation is *than²*, which as a main verb means 'be on time for (something)', and as a
preverbal aspectual/modal means 'yet' (but always explicitly negated, as *bò⁰ than²* meaning
'not yet'):

(120) *tòòn³*   *nan⁴*   *qisalaq²*   *bò⁰*   *than²*   *mii²*   *ñang³*   *dêj²*
       time   that   I.   NEG   yet   have   anything   PCL
       'At that time, the Issara (freedom fighters) didn't yet have anything, you know.'
       (411.13)

A left aspectual/modal which appears in the post-negation slot, but which does not require
negation, is *tòòng⁴*, meaning 'must' (and as a main verb meaning 'touch, strike'):

(121) *tòòng⁴*   *haj⁵*   *laaw²*   *khit⁰*   *khak⁰-khak¹*   *khian³*   *vaj⁴*   *sakòòn¹*
       must   give   3SG   think   RDP-clear   write   fix.in.place   PCL
       '(We) have to get him to think hard about it, and write some (stories) down.' (211.3)

(122) *qan⁰*   *nii⁴*   *ni⁰*   *bò⁰*   *tòòng⁴*   *qaw³*   *ma⁰*
       thing   DEM.GEN   TPC.PCL   NEG   must   take   DIR.PCL(come)
       peet⁵   *juu¹*   *pathêêt⁴*   *laaw²*
       open   be.at   country   Lao
       'This (recording) here, you needn't bring (it and) play (it) in Laos.' (642.13)

It is possible to combine *tòòng⁴* as an aspectual/modal with *tòòng⁴* as a main verb:

(123) *bò⁰*   *tòng⁴*   *tòòng⁴*   *dee⁴*
       NEG   must   touch   PCL
       'There's no need to touch (it)!'

Immediately before the main verb, and after all other left aspect-modality marking, the
directional particles *paj⁰* 'go' and *ma⁰* 'come' may appear (cf. full verbs *paj³* 'go' and *maa²*
'come'). These denote directionality of the action – literally or figuratively – with respect to
the subject. These 'inner directionals' are always unstressed and atonal in this position:

(124) *haw²*   *phu⁰-nùng¹*   *veej⁴*   *si⁰*   *paj⁰*   *sòòj¹*   *kan³*
       1SG   CLF.PERSON-one   PCL   IRR   DIR.PCL(go)   help   RCP
       'I alone will go and help them.' (165.16)

(125) *lèèw⁴*   *hòòt⁴*   *mùù⁴-maj¹-mùù⁴-lun²*   *haw²*   *ka⁰*   *si⁰*   *ma⁰*
      PFV   reach   day-new-day-after   1SG   FOC.PCL   IRR   DIR.PCL(come)

      thaam³   *qiik⁵*   *vaa¹-san⁴*
      ask   more   say-thus

      '"And so when it comes to the new day, I will come and ask further", (he) said.' (142.11)
As a left aspectual/modal, *daj⁴*, elsewhere a main verb meaning 'come to have', has a slot of its own, after post-negation aspectual/modals, and before inner directionals. It has a meaning glossed here as 'ACHV' (with interpretations ranging from 'achievement' to 'must' to 'get to' to 'manage to'; cf. Enfield 2003: Chapter 3):

(126) *tòò¹*   *paj³*   *nii⁴*   *si⁰*   *daj⁰*   *sanee³*   *law¹*   *nithaan²*
      connect   go   DEM.GEN   IRR   ACHV   introduce   tell   tale

      lùang¹   *sin³saj²*
      story   S.
      'Now, (I must) introduce the tale of Sinsay.' (152.6)

(127) *haw²*   *bò⁰*   *daj⁰*   *kin³*   *khaw⁵*   *dêj²*
      1SG   NEG   ACHV   eat   rice   PCL
      'I didn't (get to) eat, you know.' (390.13)

(128) *khian³*   *qan⁰-nan⁴*   *phen¹*   *vaj⁴*   *vaa¹*   *si⁰*   *bò⁰*   *daj⁰*   *maa²*
      write   CLF-DEM.NONPROX   3SG   keep   say   IRR   NEG   ACHV   come
      '(I) write a whatdoyoucallit [lit. a "that thing"] (to) them, telling (them I) won't (be able to) come (back).' (551.5)

(129) *tamluat⁵*   *bò⁰*   *than²*   *daj⁰*   *maa²*   *tòòn³*   *nan⁴*
      police   NEG   on.time   ACHV   come   time   DEM.NONPROX
      'The police hadn't yet arrived at that time.' (3.13)

(130) *haw²*   *ka⁰*   *daj⁰*   *paj³*   *fang²*
      1SG   FOC.PCL   ACHV   go   listen
      'I did (get to) go and listen.' (368.13)

Examples in this section have shown that a main verb may be left-marked by a string of morphemes with aspectual and/or modal function, in a reasonably fixed order (as specified in Figure 4.4.2-1). Only those morphemes that fill the irrealis and negation slots are not deverbal (i.e. they are the only ones not transparently related to full verbs).

The greater verbiness of the pre-irrealis and post-negation aspect-modality slots shows up in stress/intonation patterns. These elements normally take stress. The *daj⁰* and directional slots are seldom if ever stressed, and negation also is usually not. However, if negation appears with a left aspectual/modal (apart from 'irrealis'), the modal takes stress, and the negative marker goes unstressed. Pre-irrealis aspectual/modals are also usually stressed.[22]

Note that elements which go in the more verby pre-irrealis and post-negation slots tend

---

22 Intonation is an important component of the grammar of Lao, about which little is yet known.

also to be more freely movable around the verb complex. Thus, some post-negation aspectual/modals may appear after daj^0, as in the following example, derived from (118) above (repeated below example (131) for convenience):

(131) $ngen^2/$ $khaw^3$ $bò^0$ daj^0 suu^1 saj^4 $laaj^3$
        money   3PL   NEG   ACHV   tend.to   use   much
        'Money, they didn't tend to use much (then).'

(118) $ngen^2/$ $khaw^3$ $bò^0$ suu^1 daj^0 saj^4 $laaj^3$
        money   3PL   NEG   tend.to ACHV   use   much
        'Money, they didn't tend to use much
        (then).' (246.14)

There is apparently no difference in meaning between these two examples. Some pre-irrealis aspectual/modals, being adverbial in nature, may appear sentence-initially (i.e. before the subject), as the following examples of $kùap^5$ 'almost' illustrate:

(132) $kùap^5$ $khòòj^5$ lom^4
        almost   1SG   fall.over
        'I almost fell over.'

(133) $khòòj^5$ $kùap^5$ lom^4
        1SG   almost   fall.over
        'I almost fell over.'

Note that placement of the focus marker ka^0 is always before *all* the left aspectual/modals described here (see examples (116), (125), and (130), above). In every example discussed so far in this section, ka^0 is insertable immediately before the leftmost verbal marker. Given the known properties of ka^0 (cf. §4.3.4.2, §4.4.1.6, above) we may conclude from this that the first left aspectual/modal is the leftmost element of the sentence-level verb phrase.

Examples with all the slots in the verb complex shown in Figure 4.4.2-1 filled are rare. None occur in my corpus, but the following constructed example is considered by informants to be a natural sounding sentence:

(134) $laaw^2$ $khùù^2$ si^0 $bò^0$ $khòòj^1$ daj^0 paj^3 kin^3
      3SG   probably IRR NEG particularly ACHV DIR.PCL(GO) consume

      $kafèê^2$ $lèèw^4$
      coffee PF

      'S/he probably doesn't tend to get to go and drink coffee anymore.'

These and other details of the internal complexities of preverbal aspect-modality marking need not be discussed further here. We now consider their relevance to the topic of this chapter, namely their status as 'verbs' in surface strings involving other verbs.

4.4.2.2. *Preverbal aspectual/modals or complement-taking predicates?*

Given that certain preverbal aspectual-modals double as verbs, then in certain apparent V1-V2 strings, the V1 element may be interpreted as either a complement-taking predicate with a V2 verbal complement, or as a left aspect-modality marker of a single main verb to its right. It is often difficult to make a decisive analysis one way or the other, since the path of grammaticalization is from complement-taking predicate to preverbal marker, with accompanying semantic change. It is not always possible to say when a V1 element has become 'grammatical' and is no longer 'lexical', but there are illustrative cases in which the V1 element is clearly polysemous, with one aspectual-modal meaning and one full verb meaning. We consider the two examples of *mak¹* 'like, tend to' and *jaak⁵* 'want, somewhat'.

4.4.2.2.1. *mak¹* 'like, tend to'

As a complement-taking predicate, *mak¹* means 'like to', as illustrated in the following examples:

(135) *bɔ̀⁰*   *mak¹*   *hêt¹*   *ka⁰*   *taam³*   *caw⁴*
      NEG   like   do/work   FOC.PCL   follow   2SG
      '(If you) didn't like working, then that was up to you.' (773.11)

(136) *tèè¹*   *vaa¹*   *khɔ̀ɔ̀j⁵*   *mak¹*   *paj³*   *beng¹*   *paj³*   *som²*
      but   COMP   1SG   like   go   look   go   spectate
      'But I like to go and watch, to spectate.' (282.12)

Elsewhere, *mak¹* functions as an aspectual/modal, referring to something 'tending to' happen. The next two examples have non-desirable predications in the lower verb phrases — 'catching disease', and 'getting arrested' – showing clearly that these are not things the main subject literally 'likes':

(137) *man²*   *ka⁰*   *si⁰*   *hêt¹*   *haj⁵ kaj¹*   *haw²*   *han⁰*   *bɔ̀⁰*
      3SG   FOC.PCL   IRR   make   give chicken   1SG   TPC.PCL   NEG

      mak¹   *tit²*   *phañaat⁴*
      like   attach   disease

      'It will cause those chickens of ours not to tend to catch disease.' (14.9)

(138) *phu⁰-ñing²*   *nùng¹*   *sakeet⁵ vêlaa²*   *nan⁴*   *han⁰*   *mak¹ ca⁰*
      person-female   wear   skirt   time   DEM.NONPROX TPC.PCL   like   IRR

      thùùk⁵   *cap²*
      suffer   catch

      'Women who wore skirts at that time would tend to get arrested.' (281.9)

Note that in (137), *mak¹* appears in the post-negation slot, while in (138) it is in the pre-irrealis slot (cf. Figure 4.4.2-1, above). This reveals a structural distinction, which may need to be further explored. Consider the following contrasts, involving the same alternations with other preverbal aspectual/modals *qaat⁵-ca⁰* 'might' and *naa⁵-ca⁰* 'should':[23]

---

23 It seems here that *ca⁰* and the aspectual-modal form a unit, with the effect that NEG and IRR can occur
    in the non-canonical order, as in the (b) examples.

(139) (a) *qaat⁵*   *ca⁰*   *bò⁰*   *paj³*
            Might   IRR   NEG   go
            'might not go'

       (b) *bò⁰*   *qaat⁵*   *ca⁰*   *paj³*
            NEG   might   IRR   go
            'not likely to go'

(140) (a) *naa⁵*   *ca⁰*   *bò⁰*   *hêt¹*
            should   IRR   NEG   do
            'should not do it' (or: 'should have not done it')

       (b) *bò⁰*   *naa⁵*   *ca⁰*   *hêt¹*
            NEG   should   IRR   do
            'shouldn't do it' (or: 'should not have done it')

That preverbal *mak¹* is polysemous is decisively demonstrated by the following jocular expression, in which one of the meanings of *mak¹* is asserted, and one meaning is negated:

(141) *khòòj⁵* *mak¹* *lùùm²* *tèè¹* *khòòj⁵* *bò⁰* *mak¹* *lùùm²*
        1SG   tend   forget   but   1SG   NEG   like   forget
        'I tend to forget (things), but I don't like to forget things.'

Some examples show bridging contexts in which both readings are possible (i.e. they are communicatively equivalent):

(142) *suan¹-laaj³*   *kaan³-hêt¹*   *khòòk⁴*   *kaj¹*   *ni⁰*   *khaw³*   *mak¹*
        part-much   NSR-make   coop   chicken   TPC.PCL   3PL   like

       hêt¹   *juu¹*   *bòòn¹*   *suung³*
        make   be.at   place   high

        'Mostly, (in) making chicken coops, they like?/tend? to make them in high places.' (13.8)

(143) *khaw³* *mak¹* *khaaj³* *tòòn³* *saw⁴*   *naa³*
        3PL   like   sell   time   early.morning   PCL
        'They like?/tend? to sell (stuff) in the early morning,
        you know.' (220.8)

In its complement-taking predicate usage, *mak¹* is a main verb, as demonstrated by the fact that a 'like to' interpretation is forced when *mak¹* is used as a yes-answer:

(144) Q: *khaw³* *mak¹* *khaaj³* *tòòn³* *saw⁴*   *bòò³*
             3PL   like   sell   time   early.morning   PCL(Q)
             'Do they like?/tend? to sell (stuff) in the early morning?'

A: *mak¹*

like

'Yes, they like to.' (NOT: 'Yes, they tend to'.)

Similarly, if the clausal object of *mak¹* is postposed, in right position, *mak¹* is left on its own, and again may only be interpreted as a main verb, meaning 'like to':

(145)   *mak¹*   *dêj²*   \ *khaaj³*   *tòòn³*   *saw⁴*

like   PCL   sell   time   early.morning

'They like it, you know – selling in the early morning.'

(NOT: 'They tend to...')

In both cases, if *mak¹* and the following verb (phrase) were not separated, the ambiguity between 'tend to V' and 'like to V' would remain. Compare the following examples to (144A) and (145), respectively:

(146)   *mak¹*   *khaaj³*

like   sell

i. '(Yes, they) tend to sell (them).'

ii. '(Yes, they) like to sell (them).'

(147)   *mak¹*   *khaaj³*   *dêj²*   \   *tòòn³*   *saw⁴*

like   sell   PCL   time   morning

i. '(They) like selling, you know, in the morning.'

ii. '(They) tend to sell, you know, in the morning.'

4.4.2.2.2. *jaak⁵* 'want, somewhat'

Now consider *jaak⁵* 'want', which in V1 position may be interpreted as a complement-taking predicate 'want to', or as a preverbal modal/adverbial marker 'somewhat', as the ambiguity of the following example demonstrates:

(148)   *khon²*   *hùan²*   *nii⁴*   *jaak⁵*   *kêng¹*

people   house   DEM.GEN   want   adept

i. 'People of this house are somewhat clever.'

ii. 'The people of this house want to be clever.'

In the following examples, *jaak⁵* 'want' receives the aspect-modality interpretation 'somewhat' (note that in all cases the lower verbs are stative):

(149)   *diaw.nii⁴*   *ka⁰*   *jaak⁵*   *thaw⁵*   *nòòj⁵-nùng¹*   *lèèw⁴*

now   FOC.PCL   want   be.aged   small-one   PFV

'Now (they) tend to be a little bit aged already.' (767.4)

(NOT: 'Now they want to be a little bit aged already.')

(150) *jaak⁵*   *kham¹-mùùt⁴*   *dèè¹*   *lèèw⁴*   *san.na⁰*

      want   twilight-dark   PCL   PFV   PCL

      'It had already become twilight-ish and somewhat dark.' (941.5)

      (NOT: 'It already wanted to become twilight and dark.')

(151) *hêt¹*   *ka⁰*   *bò⁰*   *jaak⁵*   *dii³*   *paan-daj³*

      make   FOC.PCL   NEG   want   good   extent-which

      'It was not very well made.' (932.10)

      (NOT: 'It didn't want to be well made.')

(152) *jaak⁵*   *qòòn¹*   *hèèng²*   *lèèw⁴*   *sùa³*   *na⁰*

      want   weak   strength   PFV   tiger   PCL

      '(He) was somewhat weak already, the tiger.' (938.3)

      (NOT: '(He) wanted to be weak already, the tiger.')

In these cases, *jaak⁵* alone as a yes-answer would not be acceptable, and the complement of *jaak⁵* could not be postposed into right position leaving *jaak⁵* on its own as a main verb. The following ungrammatical examples are modelled on (149) and (150), above:

(153) **diaw.nii⁴*   *ka⁰*   *jaak⁵*   *lèèw⁴*   *dêj²*   \   *thaw⁵*   *nòòj⁵-nùng¹*

      now   FOC.PCL   want   PFV   PCL   be.aged   small-one

      Does not mean: 'Now (they) tend to be already – a little bit aged.'

(Interpretable if *jaak⁵* is taken as a simple main verb 'to be hungry', and the two verbs head separate clauses: 'Now (they)'re hungry – (they)'re a bit old.')

(154) *jaak⁵   *lèèw⁴*   *san.na⁰*   \   *kham¹-mùùt⁴*   *dèè¹*

      want   PFV   PCL   twilight-dark   PCL

      Does not mean: 'It had already somewhat become – twilight and dark.'

      (Interpretable as: '(I'm) hungry – it's getting late.')

If a [*jaak⁵* + complement] expression is rephrased with the complement moved into right position (as in (153) and (154)), the verb *jaak⁵* on its own cannot be interpreted as an aspect-modality marker. The only available interpretation in these cases is to regard *jaak⁵* as playing yet another role, i.e. acting as a separate main verb 'to be hungry (for something)'.

Note finally that we can make explicit the contrast between these two senses of *jaak⁵* due to the combinatoric constraint whereby the aspect-modality sense 'somewhat' only appears with stative verb complements. The following examples show that while *jaak⁵* is ambiguous with a stative verb such as *suung³* 'tall' (as in (155)), the 'somewhat' meaning is not available when the complement of *jaak⁵* is a *non*-stative verb such as *paj³* 'go' (as in (155)):

(155) *laaw²*   *jaak⁵*   *suung³*

      3SG   want   tall

      i. 'S/he wants to be tall.'

      ii. 'S/he is somewhat tall.'

(156)   *laaw²*   *jaak⁵*   *paj³*
        3SG   want   go
        'S/he wants to go.'
        (NOT: 'S/he somewhat goes.')

4.4.2.2.3. *Summary*

We have observed in this section the close relationship between preverbal aspect-modality marking and head-initial complementation structures. The distinction between the two is demonstrated by grammatical effects associated with differences in headedness. For a V1-V2 combination, two possibilities are that (a) V1 is head, taking subordinate V2 as a complement, or (b) that V2 is head, modified aspectually/modally by the preceding V1. These are obviously beginning and end points on a path of reanalysis in grammatical change (Harris and Campbell 1995: 61ff). This section has shown that for some combinations of verbs these patterns compete, producing semantic (and subsequent behavioural) distinctions.

4.4.2.3. *Postverbal aspectual/modals*

Postverbal aspect-modality marking is different in nature to the preverbal marking observed in the previous section. Right aspectual/modals include both some unstressed morphemes (e.g. *la⁰/le⁰* 'PFV'), as well as some fully stressed and main verb-like elements (e.g. *lèèw⁴* 'PFV', *daj⁴* 'can', *than²* 'on time', and others which may be impossible to distinguish from resultative/adverbials), and a number of non-deverbal adverbial/aspectual morphemes (e.g. *qiik⁵* 'more', and other right-compounding adverbials). Postverbal aspect-modality marking seldom intervenes between verb phrases. Most postverbal aspect-modality markers behave grammatically like resultative V2s (§4.4.6.2, below; cf. Enfield 2003: 117ff).

4.4.2.4. *Postverbal aspectual/modals or right-head resultative/adverbials?*

Other sections in this chapter provide details on resultative constructions and adverbial constructions, in which the clausal head is the resultative/adverbial V2 (cf. §4.4.6, below). Certain V2 elements have taken on aspectual modal functions, becoming distinct in meaning, while more or less retaining the grammatical behaviour of the resultative/adverbial V2 elements. The following example shows the verb *daj⁴* in V2 position, ambiguous as to a modal reading 'can' and a resultative verb reading 'succeed':

(157)   *sêng³*   *daj⁴*
        sit.exam   can/succeed
        i. '(I) can sit the exam.' (V2 as modal)
        ii. '(I) passed the exam.' (V2 as verb)

Sections §4.4.6.2- 4.4.6.4, below, give further details on resultative and adverbial expressions. We now turn to multi-verb constructions for the expression of three-participant events.

4.4.3. 'Despatch' expressions for hosting three arguments in a single clause

Some verbs describe events which involve three participants (e.g. transfer verbs like *haj⁵* 'give' and placement verbs like *saj¹* 'put').[24] There are three basic strategies in Lao for associating three participants with a single verb in a clausal predication, namely (1) zero anaphora (i.e. simply omitting explicit reference to one or more participants, as in *I gave John* when it is understood in the context that 'the money' is the theme), (2) using the Left Position

---

24 This section is based on Enfield (forthcoming), and the issues are covered in more detail there.

to host a third argument (as in *The money, I gave John*), and (3) incorporation of a theme argument with the verb (*I money-gave John*). See Enfield (forthcoming) for details.

Most commonly, however, when a verb describes an event in which three participants are involved, an additional verb will share the work of hosting three arguments in a single clause. The basic pattern is as follows:

(158) NP_{AGENT} — V1 — NP_{THEME} — V2 — NP_{GOAL}

where V2 is a verb of 'despatch' (i.e. expressing some kind of transfer or placement), and V1 may be either a despatch verb or a 'handling' verb (i.e. a verb describing the way in which something is handled, usually *qaw³* 'take in hand', but also including verbs such as *ñok¹* 'lift' and *cap²* 'grab'). The two variations on this basic pattern are accordingly termed the 'handling-despatch' and 'despatch-despatch' patterns.

The 'handling-despatch' construction typically describes transfer or placement (i.e. where the verb specifying three participants is a 'give' or 'put' verb, as V2).

(159)   'Handling-despatch' construction
         NP_{SOURCE} — $V_{HANDLING}$ — NP_{THEME} — $V_{DESPATCH}$ — NP_{GOAL}

The following examples all feature *qaw³* 'take' as the handling verb, with three-participant despatch verbs in V2 position (*vaj⁴* 'put/place/fix', *song¹* 'send', *haj⁵* 'give' and *saj¹* 'put/put in', respectively).

(160) *qaw³*   *kiaw¹*   *vaj⁴*
      take   cutter   place/fix
      '(S/he) put the cutter away.' (929.1)

(161) *qaw³ vèèn¹-taa³*   *ma⁰*   *song¹ cêk²*   *khùùn²*
      take mirror-eye('spectacles') DIR.PCL(come) send chinaman   return
      '(He) took the spectacles back to the Chinaman.' (57.8)

(162) *qaw³ ngaaw⁴ maa²*   *haj⁵ qaaj⁴ nèè¹*
      take sword   DIR.PCL(come)   give O.BRO PCL
      'Please give me the sword.' (891.15)

(163) *tamlaa²ᵢ*   *khaw³*   *ka⁰*   *qaw³*   *ø*ᵢ *maa²*   *saj¹ thong³-sùa⁵*
      recipe   3PL   FOC.PCL   take   come   put bag-shirt
      'The recipe, he put in his shirt pocket.' (40.10)[25]

The next examples feature different handling verbs (*ñok¹* 'lift', *hòòp⁵* 'carry in the arms', and *nam²* 'lead, take with', respectively) in V1 handling-verb position:

(164) *dang³*   *faj²*   *lèka⁰*   *saj¹*   *taw⁴-faj²*   *mòò⁵-kèèng³*   *ñaj¹*   *ñok¹*
      light   fire   CLNK   put   stove-fire   pot-soup   big   lift
      '(He) lit the fire, and then put the big soup pot on the stove.' (925.7)

_____

25 This example shows fronting of the theme *tamlaa²* 'recipe'.

(165) bak^2 $ñak^1$ kum^3phan^2 $hòòp^5$ $phuu^2$ $pên^3$ $nuaj^1$

      CLF.MASC   ogre   K.   carry.in.arms   mountain   be   CLF

      ma^0 $thim^5$ saj^1 ø

      DIR.PCL(come)   discard   put

      'The ogre Kumphan carried the mountain whole (and) dropped it (on that place).' (201.6)

(166) ca^0 $tòòng^4$ nam^2 $saan^3$ nii^4 haj^5 $sêê^3naa^2.qaa^3maat^4$

      IRR   must   lead   official.letter   DEM.GEN   give   military.forces

      '(We) will have to take this official letter to the military forces.' (89.11)

In the 'despatch-despatch' construction, both V1 and V2 are three-participant verbs, both expressing some kind of 'giving', 'transfer', or 'placement':

(167) 'Despatch-despatch' construction

      NP_{SOURCE} — $V_{DESPATCH}$ — NP_{THEME} — $V_{DESPATCH}$ — NP_{GOAL}

The second despatch verb is normally haj^5 'give' or saj^1 'put', with the first verb expressing a more specific notion of 'despatch', such as $mòòp^4$ 'hand over' or $song^1$ 'send' in the following examples:

(168) $phon^3$ $thii^2$-$sut^2ø$ ka^0 $mòòp^4$ $mùang^2$ haj^5 sin^2saj^2

      result   at-extreme   FOC.PCL   hand.over   kingdom   give   S.

      'The final result (was that he) handed over the kingdom to Sinxay.' (205.10)

(169) $khòòj^5$ si^0 $song^1$ lot^1-cak^2 haj^5 $phòò^1$

      1SG   IRR   send   CT.VEHICLE-motorcycle   give   father

      'I'm going to deliver the motorcycle to Dad.'

Verbs of 'communication' such as vaw^4 'say', law^1 'relate, tell', and $saaj^3$ 'screen (e.g. a film)' allow addition of a final verb of 'reception' (typically $fang^2$ 'listen' or $beng^1$ 'look') to the two-verb structure sketched in (158) using the simple despatch verb haj^5 'give' in V2 position as follows:[26]

(170) 'Communication-despatch-reception' construction

      NP_{SOURCE} —$V_{COMMUNICATION}$ —NP_{THEME}—$V_{DESPATCH}$('give')—NP_{GOAL}—$V_{RECEPTION}$

Here are some examples:

(171) $khòòj^5$ daj^0 $vaw^4ø$ haj^5 caw^4 $fang^2$ $nòòj^5$-$nùng^1$ $mèèn^1$ $bòò^3$

      1SG   ACHV   say   give   2SG   listen   a.little   be.so   PCL

      'I did tell you (this joke) a little, right?' (35.2)

---

26 This type of construction is found across languages of mainland Southeast Asia, including Vietnamese, Khmer, and Cantonese (cf. e.g. Matthews and Yip 1994: 138).

(172) *khòò³   haj⁵   vaw⁴   ø   haj⁵   qaaj⁴   fang²*
     request give say   give O.BRO listen
     'Please tell (it) to me.' (199.12)

(173) *man²   saaj³   nang³   haj⁵   kuu³   beng¹*
     3SG   screen   movie   give   1SG   look
     'S/he screened a movie (for) me (to) watch.'

Similar constructions to those we have seen so far in this section are also used for descriptions of three-participant events in which no single verb specifies three participants. The following examples illustrate the structure in (158), where V1 is *qaw³* 'take', and the theme argument is an instrument:

(174) *qaw³   nèèw²-visaa²   maj¹   ma⁰*   *khèèng¹khan³   kap²   haw²   na⁰*
     take   manner-plan   new   DIR.PCL(come) compete   with 1SG   PCL
     'They will fight us with a new strategy, you know.' (150.3)

(175) *bèèp⁵   ø   qaw³   hua³-laan⁴   son²*   *kan³*
     style   take   head-bald   make.collide RCP
     '...(in the) manner (of) butting each other with bald heads.' (72.6)

(176) *man²   qaw³   sòòn³   ma⁰*   *cam⁴   kacèè³   fong⁴*   *leej²*
     3SG   take   arrow   DIR.PCL(come) ram   lock   come.apart   altogether
     'He broke the lock apart with an arrow.' (176.17)
     (i.e. 'He took an arrow and rammed the lock – it came apart completely.')

The following examples also illustrate the structure in (158), where V1 is *qaw³* 'take', but in these cases the theme argument is a causee:[27]

(177) *qaw³   siang²-miang⁵   ma⁰*   *suaj¹*
     take   S.M.   DIR.PCL(come)   help
     '(He would) get Siang-Miang to (come and) help (him).' (93.16)

(178) *qaw³   khon²   paj⁰*   *khut¹   hêt¹   khòòng².mùang³*
     take   people DIR.PCL(go)   dig   make   canal
     'They got the people to dig the canals.' (267.9)

---

27 In the first two of these examples it is conceivable that the theme arguments are 'instruments', but I think this would be metaphorical—the idea of an 'instrument' (at least as a semantic role in grammatical constructions) should not be stretched to include entities which are not 'things'.

(179) qaw³   pasaason²   paj⁰   hian² juu¹   vat¹   naa³ lèka⁰
       take   common.person   DIR.PCL(go)   study be.at temple PCL   CLNK

       qaw³   khon²   paj⁰   sòòn³
       take   person   DIR.PCL(go)   teach

'They got the common people to (go and) study at the temples, you know, and they got people to (go and) teach them.' (255.1)

See also sections below (§4.4.8) for further description of causative constructions.

4.4.4. Disposal constructions

So-called 'disposal constructions'[28] take the same basic form as 'despatch' constructions examined in the previous section, but the difference is that the addition of a second verb does not bring an extra participant into the clause (Enfield 2002b: 23-25).

Here are three examples of the disposal construction:

(180) phen¹   ka⁰   qaw³   to⁰-nii⁴   paj³   hian²   khùù²-kan³
       3SG   FOC.PCL   take   CLF-DEM.GEN   DIR.PCL(go) study   same-RCP
'They also did study this.' (270.6)

(181) [saj⁵-kòòk⁵ nii⁴]ᵢ   caw⁴   qaw³   øᵢ paj³   cùùn³
       sausage   DEM.GEN 2SG   take   DIR.PCL(go) fry
'These sausages... you go and fry.' (39.10)

(182) pasaason²   qaw³   vithañuq¹   ma⁰   fang²
       common.person   take   radio   DIR.PCL(come)   listen
'The people would listen to radios.' (233.6)

In the third example, the noun phrase vithañuq¹ 'radio' is patient/object of both the preceding, and following, verbs. The example describes the same event as the following, in which only one verb appears:

(183) pasaason²   fang²   vithañuq¹
       common.person   listen   radio
'The people would listen to radios.'

A notable feature of these constructions is their inclusion of a directional particle (either ma⁰ 'come' or paj⁰ 'go') before V2. Does the directional verb particle attach to the preceding verb phrase, or to V2? The two directionals are not symmetrical in their semantics: ma⁰ 'come' is less suggestive of literal motion on the figure's part, and instead suggests merely self-directed action, while paj⁰ 'go' is more suggestive of real motion on the figure's part. Compare the following two examples:

---

28 The term 'disposal construction' is one of a number of equivalent terms (including also 'pretransitive' construction) which have arisen mostly in the study of Sinitic languages (Li and Thompson 1981: Chapter 15, Matthews and Yip 1994: 144), and other Southeast Asian languages such as Lue (Jagacinski 1987) and Bouyei (Zhou 2000). These terms are far from ideal, however.

(184) *qaw³*   *khanom³*   *ma⁰*   *kin¹*
      take   sweet   DIR.PCL(come)   eat
      '(S/he) picked up the sweets to eat.' (or: '(S/he) picked up the sweets and ate (them).')

(185) *qaw³*   *khanom³*   *paj⁰*   *kin³*
      take   sweet   DIR.PCL(go)   eat
      '(S/he) picked up the sweets to go and eat.' (or: '(S/he) picked up the sweets and went
      and ate (them).')

I am unable to specify the exact conditions under which a structure like (182) is preferred to
one like (183). While other 'take'- and related constructions function to add an extra argument
to a clause (Enfield 2002b, forthcoming; §4.4.3, above), this 'disposal' or 'pretransitive'
construction has no such function. Although there are two transitive verbs in (182), there
remain only two arguments, both shared by the two verbs. The function of the construction
clearly relates to information structure distinctions, but this is not yet well understood for Lao
(Enfield 2002b: 23-25).[29]

4.4.5. Complex motion expressions

Expression of complex motion events involves a number of complexities which pose
challenges to the capacity of the clause to package information (Talmy 1985, 2000). I have
investigated the expression of complex motion in Lao using video stimuli, including a set of
schematic animations (Bohnemeyer and Caelen 1999) and a set of video clips with real actors
(van Staden et al 2001). These stimuli were designed to manipulate a number of parameters of
potential linguistic importance including number and type of non-figure objects in a motion
scene, variation of manner and path combinations, and number of separate vector changes in a
single motion scene.

4.4.5.1. *Consecutive vector motion*

One way in which a motion event may be complex is due to a mover changing direction of
motion a number of times. Description of such 'multi-vector' events demands separation of
each vector description into distinct clauses, and thus does not make use of the kind of tight
V1-V2 strings which are the focus of this chapter. 'Consecutivising' constructions separate
out *parts* of a complex motion event (e.g. different vectors, *temporally distinct*, and not of the
same kind). Basically, these are clause-chains (see §4.4.10.1, below), which remain
clause-separable by partition into distinct intonation units, with or without morphological
material such as conjunctive particles.

   One of the scenes in the set of animated stimuli (Bohnemeyer and Caelen 1999) shows a
complex path in which a moving figure (a red ball) sitting at the bottom of a tall blue
container rolls to the side of the container, up the inside wall to the top, across the rim of the
container wall, and down the outside to the outer base of the container, then continuing along
the ground going away from the base of the container, to a small green pyramid, rolling
finally up the side of the pyramid and coming to a halt at its peak. The following spontaneous
description of this scene shows each separate clause (separated by '–') expressing one distinct
vector at a time (note that a number of the vectors in the scene are not included in the
description at all):

---

29 See research on this problem in other Tai-Kadai languages Lue (Jagacinski 1987) and Bouyei (Zhou
    2000), as well as Sinitic languages (Chao 1968, Li and Thompson 1981, Matthews and Yip 1994).

(186) *sii³-dèèng³*   *king⁴*   *khùn⁵*   *paj³*   *paaj³*   *sii³-thalêê²*   –   *king⁴*

colour-red   roll   ascend   go   tip   colour-sea   roll

long²   *maa²*   *phùùn⁴*   *din³ -*   *lèèw⁴*   *long²*   *paj³*   *haa³*

descend   come   floor   ground   PFV   descend   go   seek

sii³-khiaw³ -   khùn⁵   còòm³   *sii³-khiaw³*

colour-green   ascend   peak   colour-green

'The red thing rolls up to the tip of the sea-coloured thing – (it) comes rolling down to
– the ground – then (it) goes down towards the green thing – (and) goes up to the peak
(of) – the green thing.'

The aspects of this example most relevant for present purposes are contained within single
clause units. These are the manner-path-direction constructions in which combinations of
manner and path of motion and/or presence of multiple non-figure objects are expressed by
more than one verb together in a single clause. We now turn to these.

4.4.5.2. *Manner-path-direction constructions*

In events with a single motion vector, three distinct facets of motion can be distinguished,
namely *manner* (i.e. by what action the motion is conducted, e.g. 'walk', 'roll', 'fly'), *path*
(i.e. with respect to spatial coordinates intrinsic to the non-figure entities in the scene, e.g.
'ascend/up', 'enter/into', 'cross/across') and *direction* (i.e. with respect to some relative
deictic anchor, e.g. 'go/away', 'come/here').

1	2		3	4
FIG mover	**verb of** **MANNER**		**verb of** **PATH**	**verb of** **DIRECTION**
	DOZENS OF VERBS:		10 VERBS:	3 VERBS:
	lèèn¹, 'run' *ñaang¹* 'walk' *king⁴* 'roll' *lùan¹* 'slide' *tên⁴* 'jump' *lòòj²* 'float' *etc. ...*	*khii¹* 'ride' *bin³* 'fly' *khaan²* 'crawl' *taj¹* 'creep' *com¹* 'sink' *doot⁵* 'leap' *etc. ...*	*khùn⁵* 'ascend' *long²* 'descend' *khaw⁵* 'enter' *qòòk⁵* 'exit' *khaam⁵* 'cross.over' *lòòt⁴* 'cross.under' *taam³* 'follow' *phaan¹* 'pass' *liap⁴* 'go along edge' *qòòm⁴* 'go around'	*paj³* 'go' *mùa²* 'return' *maa²* 'come'

FIGURE 4.4.5.2-1: SLOTS IN THE 'MANNER-PATH-DIRECTION CONSTRUCTION'

Two representative examples of this construction can be found in the first two clauses of (186),
above:

(187) (a)   *king⁴*   *khùn⁵*   *paj³*
             roll   ascend   go

       (b)   *king⁴*   *long²*   *maa²*
             roll   descend   come
             '...roll down coming...'

It is impossible to reflect in the English translation the fact that the three elements are each unmarked verbs of similar status.[30]

Due to the fact that these constructions express 'overlay' of multiple facets of motion in a single 'happening', they are not clause-separable. Thus, while the three verbs in (188), below, describe simultaneous and overlaid facets of a single event, the insertion of the linking particle *lèka⁰* in subsequent examples (189) and (190) encourages an interpretation by which the different verbs express temporally separated events, where the resulting meaning is very different to the non clause-separated example:

(188) *man²*   *ñaang¹*   *qòòk⁵*   *paj³*
       3SG   walk   exit   go
       'He walked out away.'

(189) *man²*   *ñaang¹*   *lèka⁰*   *qòòk⁵*   *paj³*
       3SG   walk   CLNK   exit   go
       'He walked and went out away.'

(190) *man²*   *ñaang¹*   *lèka⁰*   *qòòk⁵*   *lèka⁰*   *paj³*
       3SG   walk   CLNK   exit   CLNK   go
       'He walked and went out and went.'

4.4.5.3. *Multi-participant motion events*

The 'path' and 'direction' verbs in the manner-path-direction construction may take complements referring to non-figure participants. These can be simple nominals or oblique phrases headed by 'deverbal prepositions' such as *haa³* 'seek'/'towards', *theng³* 'reach'/'to', *hòòt⁴* 'reach'/'to', or *caak⁵* 'leave'/'from'. By the term 'non-figure participants' I mean the participants in a motion event which have semantic roles such as 'source', 'goal', 'path', etc. (e.g. *house* in *He ran from/to/past the house*; Jackendoff 1983, Talmy 2000).

The following examples, based on example (188), above, show the addition of non-figure participants – in the first case as simple nominals (*khòòj⁴* 'hill' and *hùan²* 'house'), and in the second case as adjuncts headed by deverbal prepositions (*taam³ thaang³* [follow path] 'along the path' and *haa³ hùan²* [seek house] 'towards the house'):

(191) *man²*   *ñaang¹*   *khùn⁵*   *khòòj⁴*   *paj³*   *hùan²*
       3SG   walk   ascend   hill   go   house
       'He walked up the hill away to (his) house.'

---

30 Thus, Lao and similar languages do not fit Talmy's (1985, 2000) popular typology which assumes a clear distinction between 'verb' and 'satellite' in a clause.

(192) *man² ñaang¹ khùn⁵ taam³ thaang² paj³ haa³ hùan²*
       3SG   walk   ascend follow path   go   seek   house
       'He walked up along the path towards (his) house.'

Descriptions of complex motion events can combine these manner-path-direction constructions with chains of deverbal adjuncts (see §4.4.7, below). The following example is one speaker's description of an animated scene in which motion of a red figure along a single vector is accompanied by the presence of numerous non-figure objects (a blue 'source', a yellow 'path', a red 'via', and a green 'goal'):

(193) *sii³-dèèng³ king⁴ qòòk⁵ caak⁵ sii³-faa⁴ – taam³ sên⁵*
       colour-red   roll   exit   from   colour-blue   follow line

       sii³-lùang³ kaaj³ sii³-dèèng³ maa² haa³ sii³-khiaw³
       colour-yellow pass colour-red come seek colour-green

       'The red thing rolls out from the blue thing – (and) follows the yellow line, passing the red thing, coming towards the green thing.' (B5)

4.4.6. Secondary predication constructions

Secondary predication constructions are V1-V2 constructions in which one of the verbs (in most cases V2) makes a secondary predication in addition to that of the main verb phrase. There are three semantic subtypes: resultative, adverbial, and depictive, with subtypes of each. In contrast to the constructions we have seen so far, negation (by the negative marker *bò⁰*) may appear on *V2* in many of these constructions, and indeed usually does.[31]
   Semantically, I make the following distinctions among secondary predications:[32]

Resultative:
The secondary verb expresses something that happens or is the case *because* the primary predication happens or is the case. Typical examples are *She licked the platter clean* and *He broke it in half*.

Adverbial:
The secondary verb says something about the *manner* of the primary predication, as in *He ate fast* and *She spoke hesitantly*.

Depictive:
The secondary verb expresses an incidental and transient state of one of the participants in a primary predication. There is no connection of cause, result, or manner between the two predications. Stock examples are *She ate the fish raw* and *He gave the lecture nude*.

The following examples, differing only with respect to the identity of the verb in second position, illustrate the three types, respectively:

(194) *man² kin³ paa³ nii⁴ met²*
       3SG   eat   fish DEM.GEN finished
       'S/he ate this fish up.'

---

31 With respect to a V1-V2 string, I refer to negation of V1 as initial negation, and negation of V2 as medial negation—when either pattern is possible, there is a corresponding semantic distinction.
32 These three categories are not always neatly separable from each other. Also, while I describe these distinctions as 'semantic', some of the meaning referred in these three categories may be derived from pragmatic implicature. I leave this question open for further exploration in another context.

(195) *man²*   *kin³*   *paa³*   *nii⁴*   *vaj²*
       3SG   eat   fish   DEM.GEN   fast
       'S/he ate this fish fast.'

(196) *man²*   *kin³*   *paa³*   *nii⁴*   *dip²*
       3SG   eat   fish   DEM.GEN   raw
       'S/he ate this fish raw.'

The following subsections survey these three subtypes of descriptive complement construction, and also include some semantically related, but grammatically distinct, constructions (namely, left-headed constructions described in §4.4.6.3.4 and §4.4.6.4.1). First, however, a note on a general aspectual property of these constructions.

4.4.6.1. *Potential/actual ambiguity in descriptive complement constructions*

In the absence of explicit marking, descriptive complement constructions may be ambiguous as to whether they predicate the actuality of the descriptive V2 being realized with respect to a given V1 (e.g. when referring to a particular occasion of a certain event having a certain result), or predicating the *potential* for the descriptive V2 to be realized with respect to the given V1. Thus, the following example of a resultative construction has two interpretations (the first of which was intended in the original context):

(197) *baang³*   *khon²*   *ka⁰*   *paj³*$_{V1}$ *vit²*$_{V2}$
       some   people   FOC.PCL   go   avoid/escape

       baang³   *khon²*   *ka⁰*   *paj³*$_{V1}$ *bò⁰*   *vit²*$_{V2}$
       some   people   FOC.PCL   go   NEG   avoid/escape

       i. 'Some people made it through, some people didn't make it through.' (755.3)

       ii. 'Some people would/can make it through, some people wouldn't/can't make it through.'

The (ii) interpretation expresses the *potential* for a particular event (here 'going') to enable and actually result in, a second event (here 'escaping'). This is expressible as an 'if-then' inference: 'Some people, if they went, would make it through; some people, if they went, wouldn't make it through.' I use the term *non-finite* to refer to cases in which the V2 element is not asserted (Enfield 2003: 100).

This is a typical example of semantic and/or pragmatic effects cohering around a grammatical structure of simple V1-V2 juxtaposition, or 'associative organization' (Diller 1988, Bisang 1991, 1996). Thus, due to the high level of pragmatic dependency in Lao grammar, a modal meaning may emerge naturally out of this resultative V1-V2 structure.[33]

In certain sections below, it will be convenient to disregard 'potential' or non-finite readings of these constructions.

---

33 Enfield (2003: 125-128) shows that this 'actual'/'potential' opening licences a path in semantic change of the verb *daj⁴* 'succeed' in V2 position, to mean 'can', related to both the general lack of morphological expression of relationships among predicates in combination, and the heavy reliance on context in determining relationships among expressions with 'associative' organisation.

4.4.6.2. *Resultative constructions*

Resultative constructions are phonologically tight (i.e. they naturally fall under single intonation units), consisting of a verb (phrase) V1, followed by a verb V2 which predicates a result of V1. No morphology encodes the resultative relationship between verbs:[34]

(198) *laaw² ñing² nok¹ taaj³*
       3SG   shoot bird   die
       'S/he shot a bird dead.'

(199) *caw⁴ qat² patuu³ nèn⁵ bòò³*
       2SG   close door   tight PCL(Q)
       'Did you close the door tight?'

(200) *laaw²   doot⁵   khua³   taaj³*
       3SG   leap   bridge die
       'S/he leapt from a bridge and died.'

The yes-answer properties of examples (198-200) are not unequivocal, and if either verb is available alone as a yes-answer, it is usually V2. This is a marked contrast with left-headed complement structures such as those described in §4.4.6.3.4, below. In examples (198-200), it is less obvious which of the two verbs is head, and V2 seems more likely. This is perhaps an odd fact for an otherwise strongly head-initial language.

We now consider some general facts about the semantics of resultative constructions, before going on to discuss some sub-types.

4.4.6.2.1. *Semantics of cause-result expressions: lexicalization versus syntax*

Many events or situations which we want to put into words seem conceptually unitary, yet involve distinct subcomponents. Imagine a man killing a duckling by cutting its neck open. It is natural to think of this as a unitary scene, and describe it with simple grammar, such as the following single-verb transitive clause:

(201)   *He killed a duckling.*

But this event can easily be thought of as having more than one component – (a) the man cuts a duckling's neck open; (b) the duckling dies (or becomes no longer alive). While the verb *kill* does not specify *what* the agent does, it does contain in its semantic structure reference to these two separate sub-events: 'the man did something to the duckling, and because of this, after this, it was not alive any more'. This single-verb two-component expression can be represented as $[p_{\text{EVENT}}+q_{\text{RESULT}}]$, with a single set of square brackets representing the single verb form (i.e. *kill*), and the sign '+' representing the relation of cause specified in the verb's internal semantics.

In Lao, as in other languages with widespread use of multi-verb constructions, it is common to explicitly spell out the multi-component structure of events, as follows:

(202)   *man²   paat⁵   khòò²   taaj³*
        3SG   slice   neck   die
        'He killed (it) by slicing (its) neck.' ('He sliced (its) neck (and it) died.')

---

34 Throughout this section, the discussion is restricted to 'finite' construals of resultative constructions (i.e. in which V1 and V2 are interpreted as having been attained; cf. §4.4.6.1, above).

The separate expression of those event components by two different verbs can be represented as $[p_{\text{EVENT}}]+[q_{\text{RESULT}}]$, each component in its own set of square brackets (representing two separate verb forms).

A large class of such conceptually unitary yet multi-component event descriptions may (on semantic grounds) be termed *resultative*, because they predicate a relationship of *result* between sub-components (as in our example 'cut-neck-and-then-because-of-this-be-dead').[35] As just shown, semantically resultative expressions sometimes contain *explicit* reference to more than one event component (*He pounded it flat*), while sometimes the event components are still phonologically separate but bound in morphology (*He flatt-en-ed it*), or are hidden away in the semantics of a single verb (*He squashed it*).

4.4.6.2.2. *Same-subject resultatives*

In same-subject resultatives, the logical subjects of V1 and resultative V2, subscripted for convenience in the following examples, are coreferential (see also (197), above):

(203) *ñang²*   *daj⁰*   *kin³*ᵥ₁   *qiim¹*ᵥ₂   *juu¹*
       still   ACHV   eat   satiated   PCL
       'One still could eat one's fill (at that time).' (741.1)

We may note three important properties displayed by these constructions. First, V1 may appear with its own direct object complement, showing that the first element is a VP and not just a V (using as our example the V1-V2 combination *kin³ qiim¹* 'eat be.satiated' from example (203)):

(204) *khòòj⁵*   *kin³*   *mak⁰-muang¹*   *qiim¹*   *lèèw⁴*
       1SG   eat   CT.FRUIT-mango   full   PFV
       'I've eaten my fill of mangoes.'

Second, V2 may be directly negated:

(205) *khòòj⁵*   *kin³*   *mak⁰-muang¹*   *bò⁰*   *qiim¹*
       1SG   eat   CT.FRUIT-mango   NEG   full
       'I've not (yet) eaten my fill of mangoes.'

Third, with the medial negation shown in (205), V1 is entailed. Thus, (205) entails 'I've eaten mangoes'. Schematically (assuming a finite reading):

(206) [ᵥ₁ *bò⁰* ᵥ₂] 'ᵥ₁-NEG-ᵥ₂' entails [ᵥ₁ *lèèw⁴*] 'ᵥ₁ PFV'.

Same-subject resultatives are like VP chains (§4.4.10.1., below) with subject of V2 ellipsed under coreference with that of V1, and with further tightness due to the semantic relationship between V1 and V2. V2 is not simply conceptually associated or temporally connected to V1, but has a more specific relation of condition or consequence. (Unlike these resultative constructions, sequential or distributive VP chains may not be medially negated; cf. 4.4.10.1., below.)

These facts suggest the following constituent structure analysis of same-subject resultatives (dotted line connects verbs with their common subject):

---

35 It is possible that the Lao resultative constructions do not mean 'V1 happened, and then because of this V2 happened', but something more along the lines of 'V1 happened; V2 happened; V2 happened (or could happen) because V1 happened before this'. Of course, it is also possible that the element of causation is pragmatically inferred. Further work is necessary to clarify the matter.

(207)

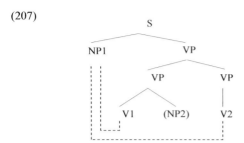

The two verbs have the same subject, as demonstrated by the following entailment property of these structures:

(208)   NP1-V1-NP2-V2 entails NP1-V1-NP2 and NP1-V2

Thus, (204) [1SG eat mango full] entails both [1SG eat mango] and [1SG full] (with a close temporal connection implied by the fact that V2 is caused by V1).

In further support of this analysis, note that these constructions are clause-separable, like VP chains (§4.4.10.1, below). Compare (204) with the following:

(209)   *khòòj⁵*   *kin³*   *mak⁰-muang¹*   *naa³*   –   *khòòj⁵*   *qiim¹*   *lèèw⁴*
        1SG   eat   CT.FRUIT-mango   PCL   –   1SG   full   PFV
        'Hey, I ate mangoes – I'm full.'

(210)   *khòòj⁵*   *kin³*   *mak⁰-muang¹*   *lèka⁰*   *qiim¹*   *lèèw⁴*
        1SG   eat   CT.FRUIT-mango   CLNK   full   PFV
        'I ate mangoes and (so I'm) full.'

Consider now insertability of the focus particle *ka⁰*, which may appear in one of two places. First, as would be expected, it may appear marking the highest VP in (207), between matrix subject and predicate (cf. (205)):

(211)   *khòòj⁵*   *ka⁰*   *kin³*   *mak⁰-muang¹*   *bò⁰*   *qiim¹*
        1SG   FOC.PCL   eat   CT.FRUIT-mango   NEG   full
        'I've also not (yet) eaten my fill of mangoes.'

However, a second possibility is for *ka⁰* to appear immediately before the resultative V2 (and any accompanying aspect-modality marking such as negation):

(212)   *khòòj⁵*   *kin³*   *mak⁰-muang¹*   *ka⁰*   *bò⁰*   *qiim¹*
        1SG   eat   CT.FRUIT-mango   FOC.PCL   NEG   full
        'I don't/didn't even get full from eating *mangoes*.'

This second possibility supports an analysis in which the resultative V2 is a higher predication about the whole of what precedes it – i.e. with an alternative constituent structure to (207) above, in which V2 is head of the highest sentential VP, and what precedes it is a kind of sentential subject:

(213)

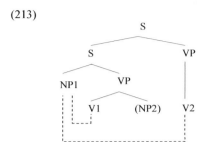

In relativization of the main subject of a different-subject resultative construction, the initial verb must be overtly mentioned. Consider the following different-subject resultative (214), and its relativized form (215) with both VPs present:

(214) *man²* *ñing²* *nok¹* *taaj³*
      3SG   shoot   bird   die
      'He shot the bird dead.'

(215) *kuu³* *hên³* *khon²* *ñing²* *nok¹* *taaj³*
      1SG   see   person   shoot   bird   die
      'I saw the person who shot the bird dead.'

The first VP is not omissable without changing the meaning:

(216) *kuu³* *hên³* *khon²* *taaj³*
      1SG   see   person   die
      'I saw the person who died' (not entailed by (215))

The situation for a same-subject resultative, in which the main subject is necessarily also the subject of the second verb (cf. (208), above), is different. Here is a same-subject resultative (217), and in (218) the full construction in a relative clause:

(217) *man²* *tok²* *khua³* *taaj³*
      3SG   fall   bridge   die
      'He fell off the bridge and died.'

(218) *kuu³* *hên³* *khon²* *tok²* *khua³* *taaj³*
      1SG   see   person   fall   bridge   die
      'I saw the person who fell off the bridge and died.'

In this case, the first VP *is* omissable from the relative clause:

(219) *kuu³* *hên³* *khon²* *taaj³*
      1SG   see   person   die
      'I saw the person who died' (entailed by (218))

This is because the same-subject resultative pattern entails NP1-V2.

4.4.6.2.3. *Projected resultatives*

'Accomplishment' verbs have been described by Dowty as having a structure in which an activity leads to and causes a change of state (Dowty 1979: 91ff; cf. Foley and Van Valin 1984: 38). The similar but distinct class of *projected accomplishment* verbs (e.g. *samak¹* 'apply.for', *haa³/sòòk⁴* 'look for', *hian²* 'study', *sòòp⁵/sêng³* 'sit an exam', *fang²* 'listen'), also refer to an activity leading up to a resultant event or change of state, but instead of entailing the successful result of that ensuing event, the entailment is that in undertaking the activity, the subject's *purpose* is to achieve that result. (Cf. Quine's 'intentional object verbs', 1960: 219-22.) For example, the aim entailed by 'seeking' is 'finding', of 'sitting an exam' is 'passing an exam', of 'listening' to someone is 'understanding' what they are saying. But unlike true accomplishments, none of 'seek', 'sit an exam', nor 'listen' entail those projected results.

Compare entailments of accomplishments with those of projected accomplishments:

(220)   Accomplishment

   '*knit a scarf*'

   entails ACTIVITY 'knit'

   entails PURPOSE 'want there to be a scarf'

   entails RESULT 'birth of scarf'

   (i.e. change of state from 'there is not a scarf' to 'there is a scarf')

(221)   Projected accomplishment

   '*look for a scarf*'

   entails ACTIVITY 'look for scarf'

   entails PURPOSE 'want to find scarf'

   IDEAL RESULT of activity is achievement of purpose 'find scarf'

   (i.e. change of state from 'do not have scarf' to 'have scarf')

   does not entail 'find scarf'

In a projected resultative construction, a projected accomplishment verb in V1 position makes reference to an *intended* result, and the realization of this result is expressed by the resultative V2:

(222)   *man²*   *haa³*   *kacèè³*   *hên³*   *lèèw⁴*

   3SG   seek   key   see   PFV

   'He's found the key.'

Here, *haa³* 'seek' projects – and does not entail – a result such as 'seeing' or 'encountering' or 'finding' something. Its internal structure may be expressed as '[p_{EVENT}-'seek'($>q_{\text{RESULT}}$-'find')]' (cf. Table 4.4.6.2.5-1, below). Addition of the separate verb *hên³* 'see' as a resultative V2 overtly expresses the projected result '($>q$)'. The overall structure is '[p_{EVENT}-'seek'($>q_{\text{RESULT}}$-'find')]+[q_{RESULT}-'see']'.

In these projected resultative constructions, medial negation is permissible, whereby V1 is entailed (once again, assuming a finite reading):

(223)   *man²*   *haa³*   *kacèè³*   *bò⁰*   *hên³*
        3SG   seek   key   NEG   see
        'He hasn't found (or: can't find) the key.'

Example (223) entails that he has looked for the key.

4.4.6.2.4. *Reiterative resultatives*

As discussed in §4.4.6.2.1, above, sometimes the complexity of multi-component resultative events is encompassed in the semantics of a single verb:

(224)   *man²*   *khaa⁵*   *pêt²*   *to⁰*   *nan⁴*
        3SG   kill   duck   CLF   DEM.NONPROX
        'He killed that duck.'

The verb *khaa⁵* 'kill' contains a complex structure [p_{EVENT}+q_{RESULT}] (specifically, ['do something to x'$_{EVENT}$ + 'x is not alive any more'$_{RESULT}$]).

A similar resultative event can be explicitly spelt out in Lao with a multi-verb resultative construction:

(225)   *man²*   *tii³*   *pêt²*   *to⁰*   *nan⁴*   *taaj³*
        3SG   hit   duck   CLF   DEM.NONPROX   die
        'He hit that duck dead.'

Here, the subcomponents [p_{EVENT}] and [q_{RESULT}] are separately lexicalized, and the resultative relationship emerges from the construction itself.

It is possible for these two options to combine, in a construction I call the 'reiterative resultative construction', of the form '[p+q]+[q]':

(226)   *man²*   *khaa⁵*   *pêt²*   *to⁰*   *nan⁴*   *taaj³*
        3SG   kill   duck   CLF   DEM.NONPROX   die
        'He killed that duck dead.'

In this example, a single RESULT event component – 'die' – is specified twice. It appears first in the internal semantic structure of *khaa⁵* 'kill', and is then explicitly reiterated by *taaj³* 'die' in resultative V2 function, as follows:

(227) ['do something to x'$_{EVENT}$+'x is not alive any more'$_{RESULT}$]+['x is dead'$_{RESULT}$]

More abstractly, the structure of a reiterative resultative construction is as follows:

(228)   [p_{EVENT}+$q_{RESULTi}$]+[$q_{RESULTi}$]

While for regular and projected resultatives V1 is entailed under medial negation (see (206), §4.4.6.2.2, above), in the case of V1-V2 'reiterative resultative' combinations, medial negation is acceptable, but V1 is not entailed:

(229) (a) *khaa⁵*   *taaj³*
          kill   die
          '(I) killed (it) dead.'

(b) *khaa⁵*   *bô⁰*   *taaj³*

kill   NEG   die

'I couldn't/can't/didn't kill it.' (NOT: I killed it but/and it didn't die.)

(230) (a) *paj³*   *theng³*

go   reach

'(He) reached (there).'

(b) *paj³*   *bô⁰*   *theng³*

go   NEG   reach

'(He) couldn't/can't/didn't didn't reach there.' (NOT: He went there but/and didn't reach there.)

The medially negated example (229b) does not entail V1. One possibility is that *khaa⁵* 'kill' may in fact differ from its English translation in not entailing that the undergoer dies. However, it is difficult, if possible at all, to paraphrase example (229b), in the manner of regular resultatives, as '(I) killed it, (but) it didn't die'. The V1-V2 example (229a) is not a straightforward resultative construction, because V1 *khaa⁵* 'kill' already contains the result 'die' (the meaning of V2) in its semantics. In contrast, the V1 elements of simple resultatives do not contain results in their semantics, and those of projected resultative constructions do contain reference to a result, but do not *entail* that result.

Like resultatives in general, these reiterative resultatives lend themselves easily to potential readings (e.g. (229b) as '(It) can't be killed dead', (230a) as 'It can be reached'; see §4.4.6.1, above).

4.4.6.2.5. *Summary*

The last few sections have illustrated some ways in which semantic structures expressed in lexicon and syntax may co-occur and interact. Three types of resultative construction are recognized, defined by the internal semantics of V1. These are illustrated in Table 4.4.6.2.5-1:

TABLE 4.4.6.2.5-1:   THREE TYPES OF RESULTATIVE CONSTRUCTION, ACCORDING TO SEMANTIC STRUCTURE OF V1

	Expression	**Semantic structure**	**Example**	**Semantic structure of example**
	Simple verb	$[p]$	*hit*	['hit']
a.	Simple resultative construction	$[p]+[q]$	*hit-die* ('kill')	['hit']+['dies']
	Resultative verb	$[p+q]$	*kill*	['do-something-to' + 'dies']
b.	Reiterative resultative construction	$[p+q]+[q]$	*kill-die* ('kill dead')	['do-something-to' + 'dies']+['dies']
	Projected accomplishment verb	$[p(>q)]$	*seek*	['seek'(>'find')]
c.	Projected resultative construction	$[p(>q)]+[q]$	*seek-find*	['seek '(>'find')]+['acquire']

Notation: '(>q)' *means 'with the purpose of having q happen', not entailing q*

'[ ]' *represents a single verb form*

'+' *represents a resultative relationship between semantic components.*

4.4.6.3. *Adverbial complementation*

Adverbial complementation, either left- or right-marking, shows relatively loose syntactic organization. In adverbial complementation of the right-marking type, an adverbial V2 follows a main VP, whereby headship properties are split between V1 and V2. In adverbial complementation of the left-marking type, certain verbs (for example *faaw⁴* 'hurry' and *lòòng²* 'try out') behave grammatically like control complement-taking predicates (cf. §4.4.9.1, below), but have adverbial scope (in semantic terms) over their subordinate predicates. Adverbial complement constructions of the right-marking type allow either initial or medial negation, as well as initial or medial insertion of the focus particle *ka⁰*. This choice appears to be associated with two alternative underlying structures (just as shown for resultatives, above).

4.4.6.3.1. *Right-headed stative adverbial complementation*

In right-headed stative adverbial complement constructions, V2 is a stative verb with semantic scope over preceding material, making a predication – some evaluation of manner or style – about the phrase headed by V1. An example involves the (gradable stative) verb *kêng¹* 'adept, clever, good at things', given as a main verb in the following example:

(231) *laan³*   *caw⁴*   *ni⁰*   *man²*   *bò⁰*   *kêng¹*   *bò⁰*
       nephew/niece   2SG   TPC.PCL   3SG   NEG   adept   PCL(Q)
       'Is your nephew not adept?' (178.6)

In the following examples, *kêng¹* 'adept' appears immediately after a verb phrase over which it has adverbial scope, giving the meaning 'does VP well, is good at VP':

(232) *son²*   *kêng¹*   \   *faaj¹*   *son²*
       fight   adept   side   fight
       '(They) fought well, the fighting team.' (72.6)

(233) *kin³*   *kêng¹*
       eat   adept
       '(Geese) are good at eating (vegetables).' (216.5)

(234) *haaj⁴*   *kêng¹*   *juu¹*
       angry   adept   PCL
       '(She's) good at being angry.' (999.11)

(235) *khòòj⁵*   *lom²*   *kêng¹*
       1SG   speak   adept
       'I'm good at talking.' (1100.12)

In each case, the focus particle *ka⁰* may be inserted in either of two different positions: immediately before the right-marking adverbial *kêng¹* 'adept', or between main subject and predicate (i.e. after the subject noun phrase, and before V1). Compare the following, based on (235):

(236) (a) *khòòj⁵ ka⁰   lom²   kêng¹*
          1SG   FOC.PCL speak   adept
          '*I'm* also good at talking.'

      (b) *khòòj⁵ lom²   ka⁰   kêng¹*
          1SG   speak   FOC.PCL adept
          'I'm also good at *talking*.'

Further, it is *kêng¹* 'adept' which is head for yes-answer purposes:

(237) Q: *khòòj⁵ lom²   kêng¹   bòò³*
         1SG   speak   adept   PCL(Q)
         'Am I good at talking?'

      A: (*lom²*) *kêng¹*
         speak   adept
         '(Yes, you're) good at (talking).'

Now let us consider *ñaak⁴* 'difficult', shown here as a main verb (in a relative clause):

(238) *phaa²saa³ soo²viat⁴ ka⁰   pên³ phaa²saa³ thii¹ ñaak⁴*
      language   Soviet   FOC.PCL be   language   REL   difficult
      'Russian is a language which is difficult.'
      (1349.12)

The following examples show *ñaak⁴* 'difficult' as head of a right-marking adverbial complement construction:

(239) *nam⁰-man²   ni⁰   haa³   ñaak⁴   dêj²*
      CT.LIQUID-oily TPC.PCL seek   difficult PCL
      'Oil was hard to find, you know.' (311.2)

(240) *puuk⁵   ñaak⁴*
      plant   difficult
      '(They) are difficult to cultivate.' (1041.9)

(241) *man²   kêp²   ñaak⁴*
      3SG   gather   difficult
      'It [coffee] is difficult to harvest.' (1047.2)

(242) *lot¹   paj³   ñaak⁴*
      vehicle go   difficult
      'It's difficult for cars to go (there).' (1060.7)

Different right-marking adverbial complements show different negation tendencies, such that speakers find negation preferable on V1 for some verb-adverb combinations, and on V2 for others. (It seems that the nature of the V2 adverb can condition these judgements.) Negation of example (242), for instance, is more idiomatic medially than initially (for the meaning given in the free translation):

(243)   *lot¹*   *paj³*   *bò⁰*   *ñaak⁴*
     vehicle   go   NEG   difficult
     'It's not difficult for cars to go (there).'

(244)   *lot¹*   *bò⁰*   *paj³*   *ñaak⁴*
     vehicle   NEG   go   difficult
     'It's not difficult for cars to go (there).' (less idiomatic than (243))

On the other hand, the combination *cêp² nak²* [be.hurt heavy] 'seriously hurt/ill', in the following example, is more naturally negated initially:

(245)   *bò⁰*   *cêp²*   *nak²*
     NEG   hurt   heavy
     '(They) weren't seriously hurt.' (2.7)

Clearly, the scope of adverbial modification by V2 (*nak²* 'heavy') is different in (245) to that of V2 (*ñaak⁴* 'difficult') in (242-243). A paraphrase into English along the lines given for the preceding examples with *ñaak⁴* 'difficult' would not be felicitous – i.e. *nak²* 'heavy' modifies *cêp²* 'hurt/ill' only, and a translation 'For them to be injured would be heavy' is unacceptable. This difference may account for the fact that medial negation in this example is unidiomatic, similar in awkwardness to the English translation given:

(246)   *?cêp²*   *bò⁰*   *nak²*
     hurt   NEG   heavy
     '(They were) hurt not seriously.'

Medial negation would be natural with some intonational distancing between V1 and V2, such that they would no longer be in a tight single-unit construction:

(247)   *cêp²*   –   *bò⁰*   *nak²*
     hurt   NEG   heavy
     'They were hurt – not seriously.'

Consider another example of initial negation, this time with the noun phrase object of V1 present between the two verbs:

(248)   *khan²*   *khòòj⁵*   *bò⁰*   *kam³*   *bêêk⁵*   *cam³*   *laq¹*
     if   1SG   NEG   clasp   brake   reach.limit   PCL
     'Had I not put on (the) brake hard...' (788.2)

There may well be semantic reasons for some combinations to prefer initial negation. For example, it may be observed that with the right-marking adverbial *khak¹* 'clearly', a range of cognition/perception verbs almost always take left negation (e.g. *bò⁰ cùù¹ khak¹* [NEG remember clear] 'can't remember clearly', *bò⁰ hên³ khak¹* [NEG see clear] 'can't see clearly', *bò⁰ daj⁴.ñin² khak¹* [NEG hear clear] 'can't hear clearly', *bò⁰ huu⁴ khak¹* [NEG know clear] 'don't know clearly').

Grammatical behaviour of right-headed stative adverbial complement constructions (exactly as for same-subject resultative constructions; §4.4.6.2.2., above) suggests that these right-headed structures have more than one underlying constituent structure analysis.

Consider the following expression – not a tight adverbial construction – involving *ñaak⁴*
'difficult' in a main-verb function:

(249)   *vaw⁴*   *phaa²saa³*   *qang³kit²*   *man²*   *ka⁰*   *ñaak⁴*
        speak   language   English   3SG   FOC.PCL   difficult
        'Speaking English, it's difficult!'

Here, the stative adverbial *ñaak⁴* 'difficult' is immediately preceded by the focus particle *ka⁰*.
The predication over which it has scope is *vaw⁴ phaa²saa³ qang³kit²* 'speak English', which is
referred to by the third-person pronominal subject *man²*. The following structure may be
posited for (249):

(249') [*vaw⁴*   *phaa²saa³*   *qang³kit²*]ₗ.ₚ,ᵢ   [*man²*_SUBJ,i   *ka⁰*   <*ñaak⁴*>_VP]
        speak   language   English   3SG   FOC.PCL   difficult
        'Speaking English, it's difficult!'

In (249'), the verb *ñaak⁴* 'difficult' is the main verb of a simple clause whose subject is *man²*
'it'. This subject is coreferential with a verb phrase occupying the topic-like left position. The
adverbial interpretation of the overall predication emerges pragmatically from semantic
relations between the particular predicates involved (i.e. 'speak' and 'difficult').

The right-headed stative adverbial complement construction provides a way to express the
same idea with tighter grammatical cohesion, as follows:

(250)   *vaw⁴*   *phaa²saa³*   *qang³kit²*   *ñaak⁴*
        speak   language   English   difficult
        'Speaking English is difficult.' (or: 'It's difficult to speak English.')

Now, consider what kind of grammatical structure is entailed by this tighter adverbial
construction. Recall the alternative constituent structures suggested for resultative
constructions ((207) and (213), above), closely related to the right-headed adverbial
constructions discussed here. The following are alternative analyses of (250) (using only the
direct English glosses, for convenience), along the same lines:

(251)   (a)

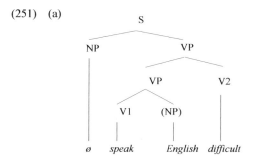

(b)

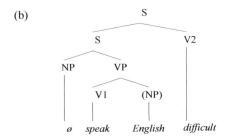

What arguments may be used to select one or other of these possible structures for right-headed adverbial complement structures?

First, irrealis marking (the preverbal si^0) on V1 has scope over both verbs:

(252) *khaw⁵*   *thaang²*   *nii⁴*   *man²*   *ka⁰*   *si⁰*   *khaw⁵*   *ñaak⁴*   *lèq⁵*
       enter   way   DEM.GEN   3SG   FOC.PCL   IRR   enter   difficult   PCL
       'Coming in this way, it would be difficult for it [a tiger] to enter.' (933.12)

In this example, initial irrealis marking on *khaw⁵ ñaak⁴* [enter difficult] 'difficult to enter' results in an interpretation that it *would be* (or in another context *will be*) difficult for the tiger to enter (i.e. both the 'entering' and the 'difficulty' are situated, by si^0, in the future or the irrealis mode). If scope of aspect-modality marking is a function of constituent structure organization, then (251a) is the likely structure underlying (252), since the aspect-modality prefix si^0 would attach to the highest level VP, which dominates both V1 and V2.

The next issue is negation. As already noted, with right-headed stative adverbial complements, as with resultative constructions generally, negation is possible either preceding V1, or preceding V2. Negation properties of right-headed stative adverbial complement constructions, discussed in §4.4.6.3.1., above, are revealing. The following sentence (repeated from (244) above) is ambiguous, which may be taken as resulting from ambiguous scope of modification by the adverb, and diagnostic of alternative constituent structures:

(253) *lot¹*   *bò⁰*   *paj³*   *ñaak⁴*
       car   NEG   go   difficult
       i. 'For cars it is/would not be difficult to go (there).'
       ii. 'For cars not to go (there) is/would be difficult.'

The (253i) reading has *ñaak⁴* 'difficult' scoping over *paj³* 'go' only, with the resultant adverbial construction – meaning 'difficult to go' – under the scope of negation. For this I suggest a constituent structure like (251a) in which negation attaches to the highest VP, such that adverbial modification is complete within the scope of negation. Thus, the (253i) reading suggests the following structure:

(254)

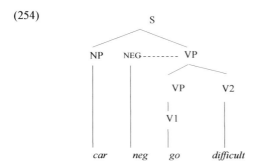

The (253ii) reading, however, has negation scoping over *paj³* 'go' only, with *ñaak⁴* 'difficult' scoping over this negated predicate. If these scope distinctions emerge from differences in constituent structure, we may assume that the (253ii) interpretation has a structure along the lines of (251b), as follows:

(255)

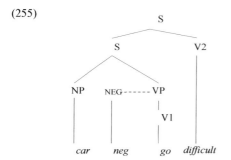

This analysis is supported by the fact that insertion of the focus particle *ka⁰* before *ñaak⁴* 'difficult' *forces* the (253ii) reading (and is indeed the most idiomatic way of expressing the meaning given in (253ii)). I suggest that it does this by preventing V1 and V2 from having a single dominant VP node whose all-in-one-go negation could otherwise result in the (253i) reading:

(256)   *lot¹*   *bò⁰*   *paj³*   *ka⁰*   *ñaak⁴*

      car   NEG   go   FOC.PCL   difficult

      'For cars not to go (there) would (also) be difficult.'

      (NOT: 'For cars it's not difficult to go (there).')

Consider now a verb – *dii³* 'good' – which due to its semantics does not have the same possibility as, say, *ñaak⁴* 'difficult' to vary in adverbial scope, and accordingly shows different behaviour in its role as a right-headed stative adverbial complement V2. *Dii³* 'good' is a gradable stative verb which can be used to comment adverbially on a whole predication ('It is good that S'). The following structure, with the focus particle *ka⁰* directly marking *bò⁰ dii³* 'no good' and putting V2 'good' alone into the highest VP node (*à la* (251), above), is allowed:

(257) *khaw³* *kin³* *mak⁰-muang¹*   *ka⁰*   *bò⁰*   *dii³*
      3PL   eat   CT.FRUIT-mango   FOC.PCL   NEG   good
      'It's (also) no good that s/he eats mangoes [or: ate the mangoes].'

However, *dii³* 'good' does not function adverbially at a lower level, and cannot be used with a meaning akin to English 'well'. (Other verbs and constructions are used for this.) The following example is ungrammatical because the focus particle *ka⁰* forces a reading in which 'eat mangoes' combines with 'good' under a single highest VP node (i.e. barring *dii³* 'good' from having its required sentential scope):

(258) **khaw³* *ka⁰*   *kin³*   *mak⁰-muang¹*   *bò⁰*   *dii³*
      3PL   FOC.PCL   eat   CT.FRUIT-mango   NEG   good
      (S/he also ate (the) mangoes no good.)

The constituent structure alternatives shown in (251) (cf. (207) and (213), above) account for the variant grammatical behaviours of both adverbial and resultative constructions shown here.

4.4.6.3.2. Comparison with resultative constructions

Now, let us compare these properties of right-headed stative adverbial complement constructions with same-subject resultative constructions such as the following, repeated with original number from above:

(200) *laaw²* *doot⁵* *khua³* *taaj³*
      3SG   leap   bridge   die
      'S/he leapt from a bridge and died.'

In the next example (259), verb-initial aspect-modality marking (e.g. the string *khùù² si⁰ bò⁰ daj⁰* 'probably hasn't') on V1 *doot⁵* 'leap' results in an ambiguity parallel to that of the English translation, namely that while *taaj³* 'die' is clearly under the scope of the aspect-modality marking (i.e. entailing that 's/he probably hasn't died'), *doot⁵* 'leap' may or may not be:

(259) *laaw²* *khùù²* *si⁰*   *bò⁰*   *daj⁰*   *doot⁵* *khua³*   *taaj³*
      3SG   like   IRR   NEG   ACHV   leap   bridge   die
      'S/he probably hasn't leapt from a/the bridge and died.'

In other words, (259) entails nothing about whether a 'leaping from the bridge' event has occurred. It is ambiguous between 'S/he leapt off the bridge, but probably didn't die from it' and 'It's probably not the case that s/he leapt off the bridge (to her death)'. That this aspect-modality marking scopes specifically over V2 supports the claim that V2 is head. (Also, only *taaj³* 'die' is necessary and sufficient as a yes-answer.) For this construction, I suggest a structure like that in (251a), above, where the right-most V is head, as follows:

(260)

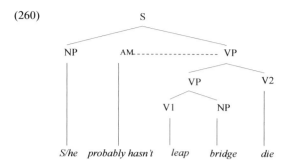

Accordingly, the interpretation with this structure only allows insertion of the focus marker *ka⁰* immediately after the main subject, and not in the position before V2:

(261) *laaw²*   *ka⁰*   *khùù²*   *si⁰*   *bò⁰*   *daj⁰*   *doot⁵*   *khua³*   *taaj³*
       3SG   FOC.PCL   like   IRR   NEG   ACHV   leap   bridge   die
       'S/he (too) probably hasn't leapt from the bridge and died.'

(262) **laaw²*   *khùù²*   *si⁰*   *bò⁰*   *daj⁰*   *doot⁵*   *khua³*   *ka⁰*   *taaj³*
       3SG   like   IRR   NEG   ACHV   leap   bridge   FOC.PCL   die
       (S/he probably hasn't leapt from the bridge and then died.)

Now, compare (259) to the following, in which the same aspect-modality marking appears not on V1, but on V2:

(263) *laaw²*   *doot⁵*   *khua³*   *khùù²*   *si⁰*   *bò⁰*   *daj⁰*   *taaj³*
       3SG   leap   bridge   like   IRR   NEG   ACHV   die
       '(When) s/he jumped off the bridge, s/he probably didn't die.'
       (Also: 'If s/he were to jump off the bridge, she probably wouldn't die.')

This has a kind of topic-comment style, such that the translation could also be 'Speaking of her leaping off the bridge, she probably didn't/wouldn't die'. In contrast to (259), this suggests a constituent structure like (251b), as follows:
    Accordingly, the focus particle *ka⁰* is insertable before V2 (and its attendant aspect-modality marking):

(264) *laaw²*   *doot⁵*   *khua³*   *ka⁰*   *khùù²*   *si⁰*   *bò⁰*   *daj⁰*   *taaj³*
       3SG   leap   bridge   FOC.PCL   like   IRR   NEG   ACHV   die
       '(When) s/he jumped from the bridge, s/he probably didn't die.'
       (also: '(Even if) s/he jumped off the bridge, s/he probably wouldn't die.')

Furthermore, the subject *laaw²* 's/he' may be repeated before V2, as follows:

(265) *laaw²*   *doot⁵*   *khua³*   *laaw²*   *khùù²*   *si⁰*   *bò⁰*   *daj⁰*   *taaj³*
       3SG   leap   bridge   3SG   like   IRR   NEG   ACHV   die
       'S/he jumped off the bridge, s/he probably hasn't died.'

This, indeed, is ruled out by the structure shown in (259-260), above:

(266) *laaw² khùù² si⁰ bò⁰ daj⁰ doot⁵ khua³ laaw² taaj³
       3SG   like   IRR NEG ACHV leap   bridge 3SG   die
       (S/he probably hasn't jumped off the bridge and then she died.)

4.4.6.3.3. *Right-headed active adverbial complementation*

Another type of right-headed adverbial complementation involves an *active* verb – such as *lin⁵* 'play' – in V2 position, as shown in the following example:

(267) man² qaan¹ pùm⁴ lin⁵
       3SG   read   book play
       'He's reading a book for fun.'

These constructions contrast grammatically with right-headed stative adverbial complementation in that they allow neither medial negation nor insertion between V1 and V2 of the focus particle *ka⁰* (§4.4.1.6, above):

(268) *man² qaan¹ pùm⁴ bò⁰ lin⁵
       3SG   read   book NEG play
       (He's not reading a book for fun; He's reading a book not for fun.)

(269) *man² qaan¹ pùm⁴ ka⁰   lin⁵
       3SG   read   book FOC.PCL play
       (He's reading a book for fun.)

Right-headed active adverbial complementation is not especially productive, with fewer verbs available to fulfil the role performed by *lin⁵* 'play' in (267).

4.4.6.3.4. *Left-headed adverbial complementation*

Some verbs may appear as V1 complement-taking predicates with a semantically adverbial function, behaving grammatically like same-subject complement constructions (§4.4.9.1.1, below). Consider the following uses of the otherwise intransitive active verb *faaw⁴* 'to hurry':

(270) faaw⁴   khian³   nangsùù³   teen³
       hurry   write   letter   announce
       '(They) hurriedly wrote a letter of announcement.' (86.7)

(271) faaw⁴   ñap²   saphaw³   khaw⁵   maa²
       hurry   shift.across boat   enter   come
       '(They) hurriedly shifted their boats across in (to the shore).' (134.13)

(272) faaw⁴   lèèn¹   kap²   khùùn²
       hurry   run   return   go.back
       'They hurriedly ran back.' (148.11)

The initial verb *faaw⁴* 'hurry' is head of the expression, and may appear alone as a yes-answer. Other properties of adverbial complementation are not observed, since the headedness is opposite to that which we have seen so far.

4.4.6.4. *Adverbial compounds*

In contrast to these adverbial complement constructions (both left- and right-headed), multi-verb adverbial *compounds* are syntactically more tightly bound, allowing in the medial position neither negation nor insertion of the focus particle *ka⁰*. Neither verb alone appears to be grammatical head. Adverbial compounds may be either left-marking (mostly expressing posture and manner) or right-marking (mostly expressing manner and purpose).

4.4.6.4.1. *Left-marking adverbial compounds*

In left-marking adverbial compounds, neither verb may appear alone as a yes-answer, and no material such as negation, focus marking, or aspect-modality marking may appear in the slot between the adverbial and the following VP. An example involves the verb *lak¹* 'steal', which appears as a regular transitive verb in the following example:

(273)   *haw²*   *bò⁰*   *daj⁰*   *lak¹*   *ñang³*   *phaj³*   *naa²*
       1SG   NEG   ACHV   steal   anything   anyone   PCL
       'Hey, I didn't steal anything of anyone's!' (674.6)

In the next three examples, *lak¹* 'steal' appears in V1 position of a V1-V2 left-marking adverbial compound, giving the meaning 'secretly/stealthily V2':

(274)   *fang²*   *ka⁰*   *daj⁴*   *juu¹*   *tèè¹*   *tòòng⁴.daj⁰*   *lak¹*   *fang²*
       listen   FOC.PCL   can   PCL   but   must   steal   listen
       'One could listen to (the radio), but one had to listen secretly.' (233.4)

(275)   *lak¹*   *khaam⁵*   *saaj²-dèèn³*
       steal   cross   border
       '...crossed the border secretly.' (1227.1)

(276)   *jaan⁴*   *khaw³*   *paj³*   *lak¹*   *tii³*
       afraid   3SG   DIR.PCL(go)   steal   hit
       '(They) were afraid (he) would secretly attack.' (148.13)

Using (276) as an example, we may show that medial negation in this kind of adverbial construction is ungrammatical (277), and that clause separation by the linker *lèka⁰* changes the semantic relation between the verbs, ruling out an adverbial reading, and forcing a simple transitive-verb reading for *lak¹* 'steal', with the two verbs predicating separate events (278):

(277)   **jaan⁴*   *khaw³*   *paj³*   *lak¹*   *bò⁰*   *tii³*
       afraid   3SG   DIR.PCL(go)   steal   NEG   hit
       ((They) were afraid (he) would secretly not attack.(?))

(278)   *jaan⁴*   *khaw³*   *paj³*   *lak¹*   *lèka⁰*   *tii³*
       afraid   3PL   DIR.PCL(go)   steal   CLNK   hit
       'They were afraid he would steal (it) and attack.'

In examples (274-276), *lak^1* 'steal' by itself does not have headship properties at all (in particular it cannot appear alone as a yes-answer), and it seems instead that the V1-V2 compound as a whole is the head of the expression.

While this contrasts with the less restricted behaviour of left-marking adverbial complementation (e.g. involving *faaw^4* 'hurry'; see §4.4.6.3.4., above), *semantically* it is hard to tell in what way the modification is different. It is notable that the adverbial complement-taking predicate *faaw^4* 'hurry' is not essentially a transitive verb – appearing either as a complement-taking predicate, or an intransitive verb – while the adverbial compounding verb *lak^1* 'steal' is common as a transitive verb. The only behavioural difference between left-headed complementation and left-marking adverbial compounds seems to be that left-headed complement V1s (such as *faaw^4* 'hurry') can appear alone as yes-answers.

A productive area of left-marking adverbial compounding involves posture verbs such as *nòòn^2* 'lie', *jùùn^3* 'stand', and *nang^1* 'sit' in V1 position (see Enfield 2002b, 2004):[36]

(279) *mè^0-paa^4*   *nan^4*   *laaw^2 ka^0*   *nang^1 khaaj^3*
        CT.MOTHER-aunty   DEM.NONPROX   3SG   FOC.PCL   sit   sell

        saj^5-kòòk^5   *juu^1*
        sausage   PCL

        'So that aunty, she sat selling sausages.' (38.3)

(280) *nang^1*   *lom^2*   *kan^3*   *lin^5*   *juu^1*   *naj^2*   *paa^1*
        sit   chat   RCP   play   be.at   in   forest
        'We'd sit and chat together for fun in the forest.' (1080.9)

(281) *laaw^2 ka^0*   *paj^3*   *jùùn^3 lòò^2-thaa^5*   *lot^1.mèè^2*   *juu^1*
        3SG   FOC.PCL   DIR.PCL(go)   stand   wait   CT.VEHICLE-bus   PCL
        'Sohewentandstoodwaitingforthebus.' (40.11)

Another productive area of left-marking adverbial compounding involves regular combination of a set of activity verbs with the reciprocal particle *kan^3*, forming a complex V1 adverbial element:

(282)   *phaa^2-kan^3 V* 'V together' (*phaa^2* 'to lead someone along in doing something')
e.g.   *phaa^2-kan^3*   *khù*
        lead.along-RCP   ascend
        '(They) went up (the bank) together.' (80.7)

(283)   *sòòj^1-kan^3 V* 'help each other to V' (*sòòj^1* 'help')
e.g.   *khaw^3*   *sòòj^1-kan^3*   *tèèng^1*   *kin^3*
        3PL   help-RCP   prepare   eat
        'They helped each other to prepare the meal.'

---

36 Note that if both verbs in such a construction are postural, then either order is possible. Thus, compare *mùùn^2 taa^3 nòòn^2* [open eye lie/sleep] with *nòòn^2 mùùn^2 taa^3* [lie/sleep open eye], both of which mean 'sleep with one's eyes open'.

(284)   *ñaat⁴-kan³* V 'compete with each other in V-ing' (*ñaat⁴* 'snatch something away, fight over something')

e.g.   *khaw³*   *ñaat⁴-kan³*   *kin³*   *khaw⁵*

         3PL   snatch-RCP   eat   rice

         'Theyfoughtwitheachothertoeatthemeal.'

Note that the left-marking adverbial element marks the whole VP which follows it, not just the following verb (i.e. the structure is [V1$_{\text{ADVERBIAL}}$]-[V2-NP], rather than [V1$_{\text{ADVERBIAL}}$-V2]-[NP]). This is clear from the pattern of entailment of these sentences:

(285)   NP1 V1 V2 NP2 → NP1 V2 NP2

         (≠ NP1 V1 NP2)

Thus, the following left-marking adverbial compound construction entails 'I watched television', and does not entail 'I lay down on the television'.

(286)   *khòòj⁵*   *nòòn²*   *beng¹*   *thoo²lathat¹*
         1SG   lie   watch   television
         'I watched television lying down'

4.4.6.4.2. *Right-marking adverbial compounding*

In right-marking adverbial compounding, V2 is a semantically general active verb whose meaning is subsumed by a V1 element with more specific semantics. The following examples show *qaw³* 'take' in V2 position, and in each case, V1 can be interpreted as a more semantically specific way of 'taking/getting' something (i.e. *lòòk⁴* 'peel off', *cap²* 'grab, catch', *khaap⁴* 'take/carry in the mouth'), with direct translations along the lines of 'take by V1-ing':

(287)   ...*lòòk⁴*   *qaw³*   *nang³*...
         peel.off   take   hide
         '...(they) peeled off the (tiger's) hide...' (944.7)

(288)   *naang²* *nan⁴* *ka⁰*   *lèèn¹* *paj³* *cap²* *qaw³* *ngaaw⁴* *thii¹* *tok²* *juu¹*
         girl   that   FOC.PCL   run   go   grab   take   sword   REL   fall be.at

         taam³ *deen¹*
         along   ground

         'The girl ran off, and grabbed the sword which had fallen on the ground.' (892.1)

(289)   *hên³* *maa³* *to⁰* *nùng¹* *khaap⁴*   *qaw³* *saj⁵-kòòk⁵* *laaw²* *lèèn¹*
         see   dog   CLF one   carry.in.mouth   take   sausage   3SG   run
         paj³ *lèèw⁴*
         go   PFV
         '(He) saw a dog running away, carrying his sausages in its mouth.' (41.10)

In these examples, V1 and V2 combine as effectively a single verb, taking a single set of core arguments, and neither ka^0-insertion nor medial negation between these verbs is allowed, as shown by the following ungrammatical examples (based on example (287)):

(290)   *...$lòòk^4$ ka^0 qaw^3 $nang^3$...
        peel.off   FOC.PCL   take   hide
        (...(they) also peeled off the (tiger's) hide...)

(291)   *...$lòòk^4$ $bò^0$ qaw^3 $nang^3$...
        peel.off   NEG   take   hide
        (...(they) peeled not off the (tiger's) hide...)

In these examples, it is as if the V2 element classifies V1 (as an instance of 'taking'), in analogous fashion to the relationship between nominal classifiers and the nouns to which they correspond.

4.4.6.5. Depictive secondary predication

Depictive secondary predication involves an adjunct or similar non-core element which describes a property of one core participant in a clause, which holds at the same time as the main predication, but where that property is independent of the main predication (Schultze-Berndt and Himmelmann in press). Stock examples from English include *He served the fish raw* and *He left the party nude*, where the adjectives *raw* and *nude* supply information about the state of one core argument of the clause during the time at which the main clause action takes place. There is a range of ways in which depictive secondary predications can be expressed in Lao, and these mostly involve multi-verb expressions. I mention just two basic strategies here (see Enfield forthcoming b for detailed discussion).

First, a depictive secondary predication may be made by V2, as in the following example:

(292) man^2 kin^3 $siin^4$ nii^4 dip^2
        3SG   eat   meat   DEM.GEN   raw
        'S/he eats this meat raw.'

The crucial point here is that the secondary predicate dip^2 'raw' appears outside the noun phrase to which it refers (which has its right border at the demonstrative determiner nii^4), and thus is not a regular modifier, but instead performs the depictive function described at the start of this section, making an assertion about the state of the direct object argument ($siin^4$ 'meat') during the time at which the main predicate action takes place (i.e. when it is eaten).

In other cases, it is V1 which performs the depictive function, such as in the case of verbs of posture and wearing. Here are two examples of V1 depictive expressions:

(293) man^2 $nang^1$ $qaan^1$ $pùm^4$
        3SG   sit   read   book
        'He sat reading a book.' (or: 'He read a book sitting.')

(294) man^2 maw^2 maa^2 $hùan^2$
        3SG   drunk   come   house
        'He came home drunk.'

These have been described above, under the rubric of left-marking adverbial compounds (§4.4.6.4.1, above). The following section describes another construction which can perform a secondary predication, but which has other functions too.

4.4.6.6.   *Adverbial/depictive/resultative adjuncts marked by pên³ 'be'*

The copula verb *pên³* 'be' can combine with a nominal complement to form a descriptive complement adjunct, with a range of semantic functions. The following example shows the numeral classifier *nuaj¹* (used with nouns referring to round things and assembled 'units', including mountains) as the complement of *pên³*, in an adjunct to the verb phrase *hòòp⁵ phuu²* 'carry a mountain':

(295)   *bak²*   *ñak¹*   *kumphan²*   *hòòp⁵*   *phuu²*   *pên³*   *nuaj¹*
        CT.MASC   ogre   K.   carry.in.arms   mountain   be   CLF
        'The Ogre Kumphan carried the mountain whole.' (201)

In example (295), *nuaj¹* is a classifier used for mountains, and the complete phrase *pên³ nuaj¹* is a depictive adjunct meaning 'whole' or 'as a unit'. The use of sortal classifiers in *pên³*-adjuncts with the meaning 'whole, as a unit' is productive. The following two examples have similarly depictive semantics (in that the adjuncts describe the form or state of the main clause complement at the time of the main verb event taking place, without relations of manner or cause being predicated):

(296)   *khaw³*   *kin³*   *siin⁴*   *pên³*   *tòòn¹*
        3PL   eat   meat   be   chunk
        'They ate (the) meat in chunks.'

(297)   *man²*   *hèèng⁵*   *lè⁰*   *kèq²*   *qòòk⁵*   *pên³*   *phèèn¹*   *cia⁴*
        3SG   dry   PCL   scrape/peel   exit   be   CLF.SHEET   paper
        '(When) it's dry, then peel it off in/as paper sheets.' (113)

Other examples involving *pên³*-adjuncts have resultative meaning, where the predication in the adjunct results from, and is true *after*, the V1 predication. The adjuncts in the following four examples express the physical form of the nominal complement of V1 which results from the event described in V1, due to physical transformation or modification (298-299), a transformation in status or social role (300), or coming into existence (301):

(298)   *ma⁰*   *paat⁵*   *pên³*   *sii¹*   *liam¹*
        DIR.PCL(come)   slice   be   four   sides
        'Bring (the wood and) cut (it) into four sided (pieces).' (114)

(299)   *liaw³*   *beng¹*   *sùak⁴*   *khanaat⁵*   *nii⁴*   *pùaj¹*   *pên³*   *phong³*
        turn   look   rope   size   DEM.GEN   dissolved   be   powder
        '(They) turned (and) looked (and saw) a rope of such size dissolved into powder.' (133)

(300)   *phen¹*   *leej²*   *haj⁵*   *buat⁵*   *pên³*   *phaq¹*
        3SG   then   give   ordain   be   monk
        'Then he had (me) ordained (as) a monk.' (321)

(301) *can³thaa²*   *mè⁰-khaw⁴*   *keet⁵*   *luuk⁴*   *pên³*   *sat²*

     C.   CT.MOTHER-queen   born   child   be   animal

'Chantha the queen gave birth to children (in the form of) animals.' (153)

Further cases are comparable to 'predicative complements' (cf. English *John considers me a friend*):

(302) *kuu³*   *thùù³*   *khon²*   *nii⁴*   *pên³*   *qaaj⁴*

     1SG   regard   person   DEM.GEN   be   O.BRO

?'I regard this person (as a) brother.'

In this last example, unlike the examples we have seen so far in this section, the *pên³*-adjunct is not omissable without changing the meaning of the main verb. In the construction shown in example (302), the meaning of *thùù³* is 'regard, consider'. If the *pên³*-adjunct were removed, the meaning would become 'hold, carry', and the sentence would mean 'I carried this person' (cf. English *I regarded John a friend* versus *I regarded John*).

4.4.6.7. *Temporal, quantifying, extent, and manner complements marked by daj⁴ 'acquire'*

The verb *daj⁴* 'acquire, come to have' has a range of functions in combination with other verbs (Enfield 2003: Chapter 3). One of its regular duties is to link clauses with adverbial complements of various different semantic types. These complements may express a period of time since the main predication has been the case:

(303) *qaw³*   *paj³*   *daj⁴*   *sòòng³-saam³*   *mùù⁴*   *ni.lèq⁵*

     take   go   'acquire'   two-three   day   PCL

'(They) had taken (the child) away for two or three days.' (965.6)

They may include a numeral classifier phrase expressing the extent to which the main predication is achieved:

(304) *puuk⁵*   *phoon²*   *khùn⁵*   *daj⁴*   *cêt²*   *nuaj¹*

     plant   hillock   ascend   'acquire'   seven   CLF

'(They) planted up seven hillocks.' (112.6)

(305) *laaw²*   *kin³*   *khaw⁵*   *daj⁴*   *sòòng³*   *thuaj⁵*   *lèèw⁴*

     3SG   eat   rice   'acquire'   two   bowl   PFV

'S/he has (already) eaten two bowls of rice.'

They may include a gradable stative verb expressing the extent or manner to which the main predication is achieved:

(306) *haw²*   *hêt¹*   *daj⁴*   *nòòj⁴*   *tam⁰-tam¹*

     1SG   make   'acquire'   small   low-RDP

'I built (the house) small, quite low.' (90.9)

(307)   sùang¹   bò⁰   daj⁴   kaj³
        conceal   NEG   'acquire'   far
        '(They) hid (him) not far away.' (183.1)

(308)   com¹   thòòng¹.khùn⁵.caj³   daj⁴   lian¹.laj³   kua¹   muu¹
        mutter 'by-heart'   'acquire'   flowing   more.than   peer
        '(I) could/would mutter (the chants) by heart more fluently than the others.'(321.2)

(309)   man² lèèn¹ daj⁴   vaj²
        3SG   run   'acquire' fast
        'S/he runs fast.'

These constructions are discussed in detail in Enfield (2003: 133-140).

4.4.7. Oblique phrases/adjunction

In Lao, translational equivalents of English prepositional phrases are basically verb phrases which, rather than being coordinated with other verb phrases (as in the verb phrase chains discussed in §4.4.10.1, below; cf. also the motion expressions discussed in §4.4.5.3, above), are adjoined to the main predicate. In this position, they perform the usual functions of prepositional phrases in other languages, namely to add non-core arguments – such as locatives, comitatives, benefactives, and the like – to clauses.

Lao has two kinds of 'preposition' type elements, denominal and deverbal. Denominal prepositions appear elsewhere as regular nouns, and these include locatives such as *naa⁵* 'face, in front of', *lang³* 'back, behind', *khaang⁵* 'side, beside'. Denominal prepositions express stative relations of location, and can also express more abstract relations (e.g. *lùang¹* 'matter, story' as a preposition meaning 'about'). Relevant to this chapter are deverbal prepositions, which appear elsewhere as main verbs, including *khaw⁵* 'enter, into', *nam²* 'accompany, with', and *haj⁵* 'give, for' (Durie 1988). Verbs 'become' deverbal prepositions when they appear in a certain grammatical slot. Clark and Prasithrathsint (1985; cf. Clark 1989: 192) have described this transformation of verb to preposition in Southeast Asian languages as 'zero derivation', marked not by morphological material but by syntactic position.[37] Deverbal prepositions cannot take overt subject arguments, are not clause-separable, and cannot be given aspect-modality marking separately from the main verb. Let us now consider their properties in some more detail.

Deverbal prepositional phrases (in square brackets in the following examples) appear after the main clause:

(310)   laj¹   ñaat⁴   qaw³   tòòn¹   siin⁴   [nam²   maa³]
        chase grab   take   lump   meat   with/from   dog
        '(She) chased (the dog) to grab the lump of meat from the dog.' (911.5)

(311)   khan²   haw²   juu¹   [nam²   mè⁰-thaw⁵]
        if   1SG   be.at   accompany   CT.MOTHER-old
        'If we live with mother-in-law...' (392.4)

---

37 There are problems with the 'synchronic derivation' analysis (à la Clark and Prasithrathsint 1985), because such an analysis assumes firstly that the verb meaning is the primary one, and secondly that some kind of real-time active derivation underlies the deverbal preposition uses.

A deverbal preposition marks arguments which are both semantically and syntactically peripheral. Importantly, the notion embodied in the preposition is not predicated as an event (or, as Harrison 1992 puts it, is 'atemporalized' or 'not temporally profiled'). Rather, it provides a way of adding an argument to the core of a clause (in the sense of Foley and Van Valin, 1984, 1985). A deverbal preposition cannot be marked by an overt clause linking particle (such as the clause coordinating particle *lèka⁰*, or subordinating particles like *phùa¹* 'in order to'), since the preposition is not at the core of any clause, subordinate or otherwise. The following examples, based on (311), force separate clausehood on the two verbs, and the basic meaning of the V1-V2 sequence is completely changed:

(312) *khan²   haw²   juu¹   lèka⁰   nam²   mè⁰-thaw⁵*

        if   1SG   be.at   CLNK   accompany   CT.MOTHER-old

        'If we stay, and then accompany mother-in-law...'

        (*'If we stay and then with mother-in-law...')

(313) *khan²   haw²   juu¹   phùa¹   nam²   mè⁰-thaw⁵*

        if   1SG   be.at   in.order.to   accompany   CT.MOTHER-old

        'If we stay in order to accompany mother-in-law...'

        (*'If we stay in order to with mother-in-law...')

Note also that while various aspect-modality markers may appear on the main verb *juu¹* 'be (somewhere)' in example (311), they may not appear on the deverbal preposition *nam²* 'with'. This is consistent with their 'oblique' status; i.e. their adjunction to the main VP constituent. The following examples show that preverbal aspect-modality markers (the experiential marker *kheej²* and the irrealis marker *ca⁰*) cannot occur adjacent to verbs in 'preposition' function:[38]

(314) (a) *khan²   haw²   kheej²   juu¹   nam²   mè⁰-thaw⁵*

            if   1SG   EXP   be.at   accompany   CT.MOTHER-old

            'If we ever lived with mother-in-law...'

    (b) **khan²   haw²   juu¹   kheej²   nam²   mè⁰-thaw⁵*

            if   1SG   be.at   EXP   accompany   CT.MOTHER-old

            (If we lived ever with mother-in-law...)

(315) (a) khan²   haw²   ca⁰   juu¹   nam²   mè⁰-thaw⁵

            if   1SG   IRR   be.at   accompany   CT.MOTHER-old

            'If we were to live with mother-in-law...'

    (b) **khan²   haw²   juu¹   ca⁰   nam²   mè⁰-thaw⁵*

            if   1SG   be.at   IRR   accompany   CT.MOTHER-old

            (If we were to live with mother-in-law...)

---

38 Matthews and Yip (1994: 60-61) show that coverbs in Cantonese (analogous to what I refer to here as 'deverbal prepositions') may take aspectual/modal marking. Lao and nearby languages do not allow such patterns at all. An important difference is that placement of the coverb phrase in Cantonese is preferred before the main verb.

The non-core status of the deverbal preposition is also evident in its phonological weakness, being normally de-stressed, and atonal. Indeed, stress alone can distinguish between a verb's function as either a main verb or an adjoined preposition. An example concerns the verb *juu¹*, meaning either 'be/live somewhere' (as a main verb) or 'at' (as a deverbal preposition). In the following examples, the status of *saw²* 'cease' as either an intransitive verb 'stop (e.g. for the night)', or a same-subject control complement verb 'cease', corresponds to a distinction between the two meanings of *juu¹* (where stress is marked by '*'*'):

(316)   (a)   *ca⁰*   *"saw²*   *juu¹*   *'vang²-'viang²*
                IRR   stop   be.at   V.
                'We'll stop at Vang Viang.'(171.4)

          (b)   *ca⁰*   *'saw²*   *'juu¹*   *'vang²-'viang²*
                IRR   stop   be.at   V.
                'We'll stop living in Vang Viang.'

In example (316a), the deverbal preposition *juu¹* 'at' is de-stressed, and the whole example has a single peak (on *saw²* 'stop'). To get the (316b) reading, *juu¹* 'live' would bear tone and take full stress, and there would be two intonation peaks, on *saw²* 'stop', and *juu¹* 'be/live somewhere', respectively.

Despite the restricted verb properties of deverbal prepositions, they nevertheless remain fundamentally verbs. Thus, most deverbal prepositions, like regular verbs, allow ellipsis of their nominal complements:

(317)   *khan²*   *haw²*   *juu¹*   *nam²*   ø
          if   1SG   be.at   accompany
          'If we live with (her)...'

(318)   *khaw³*   *ñaang¹*   *khaam⁵*   *(thanon³)*   *lèèw⁴*
          3PL   walk   cross   (street)   finish
          'S/he has walked across (the street) already.'

An exception is *caak⁵* 'separate from, from', which does not allow ellipsis of the complement:[39]

(319)   *khaw³*   *qòòk⁵*   *caak⁵*   **(hùan²)*   *lèèw⁴*
          3PL   exit   from   house   finish
          'S/he has come out of the house.'

The following examples show more than one deverbal prepositional phrase adjoining a single core clause (the second example showing the same preposition – *haj⁵* 'give, for' – used twice):

---

39 *Caak⁵* differs from other deverbal prepositions in that in its role as a verb it is both rare and semantically specific, meaning 'depart/separate from someone or something with likely lasting separation' (e.g. when leaving home to move to another village).

(320) *phen¹*   *kin³*   *khaw⁵*   *juu¹*   *talaat⁵*   *nam²*   *khòòj⁵*
       3SG   eat   rice   be.at   market   with   1SG
       'He ate (rice) at the market with me.'

(321) *sêt¹*   *toq²*   *haj⁵*   *luuk⁴*   *haj⁵*   *khòòj⁵*   *nèè¹*
       wipe   table   give   child   give   1SG   PCL
       'Wipe the table for (my) child for me, would you?'

A final point to note is that it seems impossible in some cases to distinguish a deverbal preposition construction from a directional serial verb construction (cf. §4.4.5.2, above; also, example (318), earlier in this section). The square-bracketed strings in the following examples could be analysed either as deverbal prepositions or as components of serial verb constructions in which path, manner, and/or direction are overlaid as facets of a single event:

(322) *kap²*   *[khùùn²]*   *paj³*   *haa³*   *sùa³*
       go.back   return   go   seek   tiger
       '(We'll) go back and look for the tiger.' (855.3)

(323) *nam⁴*   *nan⁴*   *fong⁴*   *[khùn⁵*   *mùa²*   *hòòt⁴]*   *bòòn¹*
       water   DEM.NONPROX   splash   ascend   go   reach   place

       lang³khaa²   *phun⁴*   *lèq⁵*
       roof   yonder   PCL
       'That water splashed up all the way onto the roof.' (937.10)

It is not clear whether a distinction should be made, and it may be that these two analyses amount to essentially the same thing.

4.4.8. Causative constructions

In Lao, as in any language, notions of causation are expressed in a range of ways. The one typologically common strategy which is not found in Lao (nor in Tai languages generally) is morphological causativization.[40] Causation may be expressed lexically, in verbs containing a notion of 'cause' in their internal semantics (e.g. *khaa⁵* 'kill'; including at least the semantic components 'do', 'because' and 'die'), as well as by selection of different argument structure constructions involving the same verb, allowing transitivity alternations which differ as to the presence or absence of a 'causer' in the argument structure:

(324) *kafêê²*   *nan⁴*   *qun¹*
       coffee   DEM.NONPROX   warm
       'That coffee is warm.'

(325) *phen²*   *qun¹*   *kafêê²*   *nan⁴*
       3SG   heat   coffee   DEM.NONPROX
       'He warmed that coffee.'

---

40 Indeed, this property of Tai languages has apparently contributed, via areal diffusion, to a demise of morphological strategies in Mon-Khmer languages (e.g. Khmer and Khmu, Enfield 2003: 54-55; cf. Suwilai 1987: 25ff, Clark 1989: 200-202).

Note that this strategy is not available for all comparable verbs. Compare *hòòn⁴* 'hot', which does not enter into the 'caused state' construction (cf. §4.3.2, above):

(326)   *kafêê²*   *nan⁴*   *hòòn⁴*
        coffee   DEM.NONPROX   hot
        'That coffee is hot.'

(327)   *phen²   *hòòn⁴*   *kafêê²*   *nan⁴*
        3SG   hot   coffee   DEM.NONPROX
        (He heated that coffee.)

For *hòòn⁴* 'hot', only a periphrastic strategy is available for expressing controlled/intentional causation:

(328)   *man²*   *hêt¹*   *(haj⁵)*   *kafêê²*   *hòòn⁴*
        3SG   make   give   coffee   hot
        'He made the coffee hot.'

This periphrastic strategy is relevant in the present context, as it involves no overt marking of the relationship between the main causative verb and its complement. There are three productive causative complement constructions, involving the verbs *hêt¹* 'do/make' and *haj⁵* 'give', along with some variations involving verbs with more specific semantics. We now survey the main types.[41]

4.4.8.1. *Causative constructions in haj⁵ 'give'*

The verb *haj⁵* 'give' is widespread in descriptions of interpersonal causation, translatable in different contexts with English causative verbs *have*, *let*, *make*, and *get*:

(329)   *man²*   *haj⁵*   *nòòj⁴*   *paj³*   *talaat⁵*
        3SG   give   N.   go   market
        'He had/let/made/got Noi (to) go to the market.'

The idea common to these various translations is that the causer (i.e. the main subject) does or says something (usually *to* the causee – i.e. the lower clause subject), because of which the causee does something – in addition, the main subject knew that as a result of his action, the complement event would happen. This is compatible with a wide range of kinds of interpersonal causation including 'allowing', 'forcing', and 'ordering' – in each case, the complement event happens because of what the main subject has done (or said), and this is under the control of the main subject, in the sense that s/he is aware that the complement event will happen as a result of his or her action (cf. Wierzbicka's 2002: 171-177 analysis of German *lassen*). Accordingly, these constructions only involve animate arguments, and thus cannot be used to express equivalents of, say, *The wind made the door close* or *Pepper makes me sneeze*.

4.4.8.2. *Causative constructions in hêt¹ 'do/make'*

The verb *hêt¹* 'do/make' is used as a main verb in a causative construction with more restricted use than constructions involving *haj⁵* 'give':

---

41   The present description of the semantic content of these three basic syntactic causative constructions, and the distinctions between them, is preliminary. Further work is required to establish a comprehensive account.

(330) *man²*   *hêt¹*   *kèèw⁴*   *tèèk⁵*
       3SG   do/make   glass   break
       'He broke the glass.'

This example would be a typical description of a situation in which somebody has bumped or dropped the glass, and as a result it has fallen and broken. In this case, the main subject does something (usually *to* the 'causee' participant), and because of that the complement event occurs. An important difference between this and the *haj⁵* 'give' construction is that here the complement event must specify something that happens *to* the lower clause subject (not something that the lower clause subject *does*). Hence, it cannot be used in the kinds of interpersonal causation typical of the *haj⁵* 'give' construction:

(331) **man²* *hêt¹*   *nòòj⁴*   *paj³*   *talaat⁵*
       3SG   do/make   N.   go   market
       (He made? Noi (to) go to the market.)

The *hêt¹* 'do/make' causative construction is never used with an animate causee (and, indeed, never with an inanimate causer).

4.4.8.3. *Causative constructions in hêt¹-haj⁵ 'make-give'*

The verbs *hêt¹* 'do/make' and *haj⁵* 'give' are combined in a third common syntactic causative construction:

(332) *man²*   *hêt¹-haj⁵*   *kèèw⁴*   *tèèk⁵*
       3SG   make-give   glass   break
       'He caused the glass to break.'

(333) *man²*   *hêt¹-haj⁵*   *kuu³*   *met²*   *ngen²*   *laaj³*
       3SG   make-give   1SG   finish   money   much
       'He caused me to lose a lot of money.'

The meaning of this construction is more general than that of the previous two types, similar in meaning to the *haj⁵* 'give' construction, but apparently lacking the component of main subject control (i.e. it is not necessarily the case the main subject was aware that his or her action would result in the complement event occurring). An important difference between this and the previous two constructions is that there seems to be a specification that what the main subject does is not done *to* the lower subject. Further, there is no restriction with regard to animacy of the causer and causee arguments.

4.4.8.4. *Other verbs as causative complement-taking predicates*

Verbs of more specific meaning than *hêt¹* 'do/make' and *haj⁵* 'give' can be used as complement-taking predicates with causative meaning:

(334) *laaw²*   *phaa²/khii¹/suaj¹*   *maa⁴*   *tên⁴*   *khaam⁵*   *hua⁴*
       3SG   lead/ride/help   horse   jump   cross.over   fence
       'He led/rode/helped the horse to jump over the fence.'

Many verbs combine obligatorily with *haj⁵* 'give' (in the same slot as *hêt¹* 'do/make' in the *hêt¹-haj⁵* 'make-give' construction), as shown for *bangkhap¹* 'force' in the following example:

(335)   *laaw²   bangkhap¹   *(haj⁵)   maa⁴   tên⁴   khaam⁵   hua⁴*
        3SG   force   give   horse   jump   cross.over   fence
        'He forced the horse to jump over the fence.'

The next example shows *haam⁵* 'forbid' in this structure, with the added feature of obligatory negation on *haj⁵* 'give', due to the nature of the causation expressed (i.e. 'causing something not to happen'):

(336)   *laaw²   haam⁵   *(bò⁰   haj⁵)   maa⁴   tên⁴   khaam⁵   hua⁴*
        3SG   forbid   NEG   give   horse   jump   cross.over   fence
        'He forbade the horse to jump over the fence.'

Structures such as these are discussed further in §4.4.9.1, below, on control complementation structures.

4.4.8.5. *Other periphrastic strategies for expressing causation*

For completeness, I now briefly mention three more strategies for description of causation in Lao, although they are not cases of 'multi-verb constructions' in the sense pursued in this chapter (cf. Enfield 2002c).

Suppose that a situation of 'being cold' causes a person to 'shiver'. This could be expressed by a *hêt¹-haj⁵* 'make-give' construction, as described in §4.4.8.3, above:

(337)   *khuam²-naaw³   hêt¹   haj⁵   laaw²   san¹*
        NSR-cold   do/make   give   3SG   shiver
        'The cold is making him shiver.'

Three alternatives for expressing this causative relation are as follows. First, the preposition-like element *con³* 'until' (not a verb) can host an adverbial/resultative complement which describes a situation or event that the main event gives rise to:

(338)   *laaw²   naaw³   con³   san¹*
        3SG   cold   until   shiver
        'He is (so) cold that he is shivering.'

Second, the two causally connected situations – 'cold' and 'shivering' – can be expressed in separate clauses and linked by *ñòòn⁴* 'because' (which precedes the logical protasis; i.e. the causing event):

(339)   *laaw²   san¹   ñòòn⁴   laaw²   naaw³*
        3SG   cold   because   3SG   shiver
        'He is shivering because he is cold.'

Third, the two distinct clauses can be linked by marking the logical apodosis (i.e. the *caused* event) with *kòò¹*, elsewhere a verb meaning 'construct, create':[42]

---

42 The element *kòò¹* here takes full stress, and is distinct from the focus particle *ka⁰*, discussed in §4.3.4.2. and §4.4.1.6., above.

(340) *laaw²   naaw³   kòò¹   laaw³   si⁰   san¹*
       3SG   cold   create   3SG   IRR   shiver
       'He is cold, that's why he is shivering.'

4.4.9. Complementation

There are a number of basic categories of complementation in Lao, and in none of them is the relationship between the main and subordinate predicate morphological marked in an overt way. In each case, V1 is the clausal head, and accordingly has certain associated grammatical properties (e.g. typically functioning as a yes-answer). A basic division is between 'control' and 'non-control' complements, referring to the extent to which the temporal or argument structure properties of the complement-taking predicate will determine those of the lower predicate.

4.4.9.1. *Control complementation*

In control complementation, there is control by the main verb of argument coreference as well as temporal relation across the two predicates. The two patterns discussed here are same-subject, and different-subject, respectively.

4.4.9.1.1. *Same-subject control complements*

In same-subject control complements, the matrix verb specifies a verb phrase as its complement, where the subject of the subordinate verb phrase (a) must be understood as coreferential with the main subject, and (b) cannot overtly appear immediately prior to the lower verb. I suggest a constituent structure for this construction as follows:

(341)

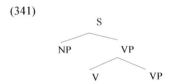

One piece of evidence for this right-branching structure in which the main verb takes a VP complement is that the complement of a same-subject control complement verb such as *jaak⁵* 'want to' can be a complex verb phrase, such as a complement construction, a compound verb, or a verb phrase chain. This suggests that the complement of the main V is an expandable VP, and not, say, a V and an NP in a flat structure (i.e., [NP_SUBJ <V_SSCC V NP>]). Here are some examples of same-subject control complement constructions using the main verb *jaak⁵* 'want', with various kinds of complex VP complements (in square brackets), including a *haj⁵* 'give' causative construction:

(342) *bò⁰   jaak⁵   [haj⁵   nòòng⁴   qòòk⁵   caak⁵   vang²]*
       NEG   want   give   Y.SIB   exit   from   palace
       'I don't want you to leave the palace.' (160.8)

a distributive clause chain:

(343) *jaak⁵   [qòòk⁵   paj³   som²   suan³   paj³   qaap⁵   nam⁴]*
       want   exit   go   appreciate garden   go   bathe   water
       'She wanted to go out and appreciate the garden, and bathe.' (159.9)

a cognition complement with overt complementizer:

(344) *khaw³*   *jaak⁵* *fang²*   *phòq¹* *khaw³*   *jaak⁵* *[huu⁴* *vaa¹*
       3PL   want   listen   because 3PL   want   know COMP

       sathaan³akaan³ *man²* *pian¹-pèèng³* *paj³* *jaang¹-daj³]*
       situation   3SG   change-fix   go   way-which

       'They wanted to listen (to the radio) because they wanted to know how the situation
       had changed.' (234.1)

a complex 'disposal' construction:

(345) *muu¹*   *haw²*   *jaak⁵* *[ñok¹-qaw³* *lùang¹* *nithaan²* *siang²-miang⁵*
       group   1SG   want   lift-take   story   tale   S.M.

       ma⁰   *lom²]*
       DIR.PCL(come)   discuss

       'We want to raise the story of Siang Miang for discussion.' (67.1)

or a right-headed adverbial/resultative construction:

(346) *mii²*   *laang²* *qan³*   *man²* *jaak⁵* *saj⁴* *haw²* *lùù³* *jaak⁵*
       there.is   some   CLF   3SG   want   use   1SG   or   want

       [khom¹ *haw²* *long²]*
       press   1SG   descend

       'There are some things (with regard to which) they [i.e. women] want to "use" ['take
       advantage of'] us or want to oppress us.' (581.10)

Same-subject control complement verbs include typical equi verbs like *jaak⁵* 'want' and
various other verbs (many of which include 'want' in their internal semantics), such as *sòòk⁴*
'look to', *còòp⁵* 'stalk in order to', *haan³* 'dare to' (=*kaa⁴* 'dare to'; cf. example (366), below),
ñòòm² 'agree to', *lùùm²* 'forget to', as well as phase complements like *leem¹* 'begin to'.[43]
These are illustrated in the following examples:

(347) *bò⁰*   *jaak⁵*   *caaj¹*   *ngen²*
       NEG   want   pay   money
       '(He) didn't want to pay.' (814.12)

(348) *sòòk⁴*   *ñing²*   *nok¹*   *ñing²*   *nuu³*
       look.for   shoot   bird   shoot   rat
       '(We'd) look to shoot birds and rats.' (1172.4)

---

43 These verbs can take different-subject subordinate clauses only if *haj⁵* 'give' is used to mark the
    switch of reference (cf. §4.3.1, above).

(349) *còòp⁵*   *baaj¹*   *tèè¹*   *haang³*   *maa⁴*
       stalk   stroke   only   tail   horse
       'All (they) do is look to stroke horse's tails.' (103.12)⁴⁴

(350) *khòòj⁵*   *bò⁰*   *haan³*   *hêt¹*   *ñang³*
       1SG   NEG   dare   do   anything
       'I didn't dare to do anything.' (1189.3)

(351) *maa³*   *ka⁰*   *bò⁰*   *ñòòm²*   *vaang²*
       dog   FOC.PCL   NEG   yield   release
       'The dog wouldn't yield to release (the sausages).' (42.4)

(352) *khòòj⁵*   *lùùm²*   *law¹*   *suu¹*   *caw⁴*   *fang²*
       1SG   forget   tell   reach   2SG   listen
       'I forgot to tell you.' (1240.3)

(353) *khòòj⁵*   *leem¹*   *huu⁴-cak²*   *mia²*   *khòòj⁵*
       1SG   begin   know   wife   1SG
       'I began to get to know my wife (at that time).' (1224.7)

In general, separate marking of aspect-modality cannot appear in the lower complement of these constructions, but some future-oriented verbs such as *jaak⁵* 'want' occasionally allow preverbal marking of the lower verb by either of the irrealis particles *si⁰-* or *ca⁰-* (e.g. *man² jaak⁵ ca⁰ paj³* [3SG want IRR go] 'S/he wants to go').

4.4.9.1.2. *Different-subject control complements*

In different-subject control complement constructions, the matrix verb takes a sentential complement whose subject may or may not be ellipsed. The complement cannot be given independent aspectual-modal marking, and its subject, if ellipsed, cannot be coreferential with the main subject.⁴⁵ Usually, aspectual-modal marking cannot appear at all in the lower clause – for example, in a structure like *Someone saw John send the letter*, the lower clause *John send the letter* occurs at the same time as the main event of someone seeing it. Thus, tense of the lower verb remains controlled by that of the upper verb. However, certain

---

44 This sentence is a jocular remark about balding men who grow their hair long at the back.
45 In cases where upper and lower subjects are coreferential (e.g. when one sees oneself do something in a mirror, or help oneself do something in a dream), a logophoric pronoun *qêêng³* (usually preceded by the classifier *too³* 'body, self', or an appropriate pronoun) can be used as the higher-clause-object/lower-clause-subject, as in the following example:

lèèw⁴   *khon²*   *laaw³*   *ni⁰*   *si⁰*   *song¹*   *to⁰-qêêng³*   *paj³*   *qùt²-hiiw³*
PFV   person   Lao   TPC.PCL   IRR   send   CLF-self   go   starve-be.hungry

nam²   *khaw³*   *ka⁰*   *bò⁰*   *jaak⁵*   *hêt¹*   *nòq¹*
accompany   3PL   FOC.PCL   NEG   want   do   PCL

'And so for Lao people to send their own (i.e. 'themselves') to go and starve with them is not something they want to do, right?' (1348.7)

aspectual marking (such as the progressive marker *kamlang²*) is occasionally possible.

The relationship between upper and lower predicates in different-subject control complement constructions is tight, such that the lower clause is strongly dependent on the main verb. V2 cannot appear as a yes-answer, nor, importantly, is internal insertion of the focus particle *ka⁰* (i.e. between the lower subject and predicate) possible. These facts both indicate that the lower verb does not head an independent verb phrase.

The following two structures show possible constituent structure analyses of these types of constructions:

(354)   (a)   (b)

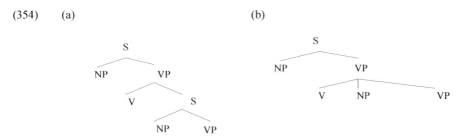

The structure in (354a) appears to be appropriate for describing different-subject control complement constructions in which the upper verb clearly takes the lower clause as a whole complement, as in direct perception-of-event complements like those of *hên³* 'see' or *daj⁴.ñin²* 'hear', such as the following (the sentential complement is given in square brackets):

(355) *laaw²   daj⁰   ma⁰   hên³   [phò⁰-luung²   phu⁰-nùng¹*
        3SG   ACHV   DIR.PCL(come) see   CT.FATHER-uncle CLF.PERSON-one

        saj¹   vèèn¹-taa³   qaan¹   nang⁰sùù³]
        put.on   spectacles   read   writing

       'He saw an old man put on glasses to read.' (52.8)

(356) *phuak⁴ khòòj⁵   hên³   [man²   ñing²   baan⁴]*
        group   1SG   see   3SG   shoot   village
       'We saw them bomb the village.' (1157.7)

WH-questions may be formed from these constructions by substituting *ñang³* 'what' for the whole lower NP-VP structure. Thus, (356) could be an answer to the following:

(357) *phuak⁴ caw⁴   hên³   ñang³*
        group   2SG   see   what
       'What did you see?'

Note, however, that the complement clause cannot be freely moved into left position or right position in the same way that noun phrases and other less tightly dependent constituents can be.

A yes-answer to a polar question formed from (356) would simply be the matrix verb *hên³* [see] '(I) saw (it)', showing that this is the head with respect to the whole construction.

I describe constructions of the form shown in (354a) as S-COMP different-subject contro601 complement constructions. Note that one difference between these and the 'flat' different-subject control complement constructions we are about to discuss is that S-COMP different-subject complement clauses tend not to allow their subjects to be ellipsed.

Other different-subject control complement constructions are better analysed as having the structure in (354b). I refer to these as 'flat' different-subject control complement constructions, due to the main verb phrase being flat with respect to the relatedness of the upper verb and lower verb phrase, namely that they appear as constituent structure sisters. One important point about this structure is that it directly reflects the ambiguity of the lower noun phrase as either object of the upper verb, or subject of the lower verb, or, better, simultaneously both. A typical instance involves haj^5 'give' in its causative function (see §4.4.8.1, above):

(358) haj^5 $to^0\text{-}mên^2$ $taaj^3$
       give   CT.CREATURE-louse   die
       '...to make the lice die.' (1185.11)

Unlike the S-COMP different-subject control complement construction described above, here the lower subject and predicate cannot be replaced in a WH-question by $ñang^3$ 'what?':

(359) haj^5 $ñang^3$
       give   what
       ($\neq$'to do/cause what?')

Another difference, again related to contrasting headship properties emerging from different constituent structures, concerns the kind of yes-answer which would be elicited by a polar question based on a flat different-subject control complement construction. Thus, with reference to (358), neither haj^5 'give' (the matrix causative verb), nor $taaj^3$ 'die' (the lower verb) would suffice as a yes-answer on its own, suggesting that neither is an unequivocal head of the overall expression:

(360) Q: haj^5 $to^0\text{-}mên^2$ $taaj^3$ $bòò^3$
            give   CT.CREATURE-louse   die   PCL(Q)
            'to make the lice die?'

       A: haj^5 $taaj^3$
            give   die
            '(Yes,) to make (them) die.'

Flat different-subject control complement verbs typically include verbs of causation such as haj^5 'give', $hêt^1$ 'make', $haam^5$ 'forbid', and $suaj^1$ 'help', as shown, respectively, in the following examples (cf. §4.4.8., above):

(361) $phen^1$ ka^0 $bò^0$ haj^5 paj^3
       3SG   FOC.PCL   NEG   give   go
       'He wouldn't let (me) go.' (332.2)

(362) $baang^3\text{-}thùa^1$ ka^0 $hêt^1$ $kèèw^4$ $tèèk^5$
       some-occasion   FOC.PCL   make   glass   break
       'Sometimes (I) might break a glass.' (1001.9)

(363) *khaw³*   *haam⁵*   *suup⁵*
      3PL   forbid   smoke
      'They forbid (people) to smoke (it).' (117.10)

(364) *Khòòj⁵ paj³ suaj¹ mè⁰-tuu⁴*   *khòòj⁵ hêt¹ viak⁴*
      1SG   go help CT.MOTHER-grandparent 1SG do work
      'I went to help my grandmother to work.' (1073.5)

Also, note that the lower VP can be structurally complex. In the following example, the main different-subject control complement verb is *haj⁵* 'give', the lower subject is *khon²* 'person', and the lower VP (in square brackets) is a 'disposal' construction involving *qaw³* 'take' (§4.4.4., above):

(365) *haj⁵*   *khon²* *[maa² qaw³ khùang¹ thaj²-haw² ni⁰*
      give   person come take stuff   people-1PL FOC.PCL

      paj³   *tom⁴]*
      DIR.PCL(go) boil

      '(They'd) get someone to come and take our clothes and boil them.' (1185.7)

Semantically, these involve causation, whereby the 'object' of the first verb is affected by action of the main subject, and as a result of that main subject action, the first verb 'object' is the lower verb 'subject' with respect to the lower VP. (This particular example (365) would have a constituent structure along the lines of [NP₁<V NP₂ (V NP₃ VP)$_{VP}$>$_{VP}$], where NP₂ *khon²* 'person' is the main 'causee', and is the 'subject' of the action predicated in the lower complex clause.)

Finally, note that the two kinds of complement construction described in this section and the previous one may be combined in single complex clauses. The following example shows a flat different-subject control complement (in square brackets) subordinate to a same-subject control complement verb (with the whole same-subject control complement construction in angle brackets), such that the whole sentence has a structure along the lines of (NP<V$_{SSCC}$[V$_{DSCC}$ NP VP]$_{VP}$>$_{VP}$):

(366) *thaang² khan⁵ theng² ka⁰*   *<bò⁰ kaa⁴ [khom¹-hêng³ ø·ᵤₛ· long²]>*
      way   level upon   FOC.PCL NEG dare oppress   descend
      'The upper administration <didn't dare [to force (us) to come down]>.' (592.1)

4.4.9.2. *Non-controlled complementation*

A final class of complements, involving verbs of speech and cognition, and usually marked with an overt complementizer *vaa¹* 'say', is loosely subordinating, whereby the lower clause retains many of the properties of an independent sentence. The structure of such sentences resembles that of (354a), proposed for S-COMP different-subject control complement constructions described in §4.4.9.1.2, above – namely where the whole lower clause is properly a complement of the main verb.

Here are some examples of non-controlled complementation, involving verbs of speech and cognition *bòòk⁵* 'tell', *haaj⁴* 'berate', *khùt¹* 'think', *huu⁴* 'know', and *jaan⁴* 'afraid', respectively, all requiring that the complement be overtly marked by *vaa¹* 'say' in its role as a complementizer:[46]

(367) | *naj²* | *vêlaa²* | *nan⁴* | | *siang²-miang⁵* | *bòòk⁵* | | *vaa¹* | *sùak⁴* |
|---|---|---|---|---|---|---|---|---|
| in | time | DEM.NONPROX | | S.-M. | tell | | COMP | rope |

sii¹	*sên⁵*	*haj⁵*		*dùng³*		*khêng¹*		*samee³*	*kan³*
four	CLF	give		pull		tightly.stretched		evenly	RCP

'At that time, Siang Miang told them that the four ropes were to be pulled to an even tightness.' (125.1)

(368) | *haaj⁴* | | *vaa¹* | | *qaw³* | *ñon²* | | *vaan¹* | | *qan⁰-nii⁴* |
|---|---|---|---|---|---|---|---|---|---|
| berate | | COMP | | take | aeroplane | | scatter | | CLF-DEM.GEN |

'(He) was angry [i.e. 'berated me'] that I took an aeroplane and scattered these (flowers).' (551.13)

(369) | *khùt¹* | | *vaa¹* | | *man²* | *taaj³* | | *lèèw⁴* |
|---|---|---|---|---|---|---|---|
| think | | COMP | | 3SG | die | | PFV |

'(He) thought that it had died.' (187.7)

(370) | *Khaw³* | *ñang²* | *bò⁰* | | *huu⁴* | *vaa¹* | | *si⁰* | *song¹* | *paj³* | *bòòn¹* | *daj³* |
|---|---|---|---|---|---|---|---|---|---|---|---|
| 3PL | still | NEG | | know | COMP | | IRR | send | go | place | which |

'They didn't yet know where they'd send (us).' (1171.3)

(371)	*jaan⁴*	*vaa¹*	*khòòng³*	*haw²*	*ni⁰*		*hên³*
afraid	COMP	of	1SG	TPC.PCL		see

'(We're) worried our (man) will see (him).' (121.1)

Let us now consider some grammatical properties of these constructions, with reference to the following example, whose main complement-taking verb is *laaj²-ngaan²* 'report':

---

46 The roles of *vaa¹* 'say' are many and varied, but further discussion is beyond the present scope. Note that *vaa¹* is common as a main complement-taking predicate in itself, meaning 'utter', 'say':

(a)	*muu¹*	*vaa¹*	*qooj⁴*	*jaan⁴*	*man²*	*taaj³*	*lèèw⁴*
group	say	INTJ	afraid	3SG	die	PFV

'The others said, 'Oh, we suspect it's dead!'.' (186.1)

(b) | *phuak⁴* | *ñuan²* | *vaa¹* | *caw⁴-naaj²* | *phen¹* | *pòòj¹* | *kuu³* | *loot⁴* |
|---|---|---|---|---|---|---|---|
| group | Vietnamese | say | authorities | 3SG | release | 1SG | right.away |

'The Vietnamese said 'The authorities let me/us go right away'.' (506.14)

(372) *man²*   *laaj²-ngaan²*   *vaa¹*   *khon²*   *baan⁴*   *nii⁴*   *ñaaj⁴*   *paj³*
       3SG   report   COMP   person   village   DEM.GEN   move   go

       juu¹   *baan⁴*   *nan⁴*
       be.at   village   DEM.NONPROX

'(They) reported that the people of this village had moved to that village.' (1158.4)

First, (372) fails the clause separability test, since the lower predicate is dependent on the upper predicate in a particular way. The whole sentence is not simply an assertion of the two clauses, and in particular the lower clause is not entailed – thus, (372) does not entail that 'the people of this village had moved to that village', since this describes an event which constitutes the content of someone's report, and is not an *assertion* of that event. Example (372) merely entails that someone reported something. Second, due to the relative grammatical independence of the lower clause, insertion of the focus marker *ka⁰* is possible either between the higher subject and matrix predicate (i.e. immediately after *man²* 'it'), or inside the complement, between the lower subject and its predicate (i.e. immediately after the subject *khon² baan⁴ nii⁴* 'people of this village').

(373) *man²*   *laaj²-ngaan²*   *vaa¹*   *khon²*   *baan⁴*   *nii⁴*   *ka⁰*   *ñaaj⁴*
       3SG   report   COMP   person   village   DEM.GEN   FOC.PCL   move

       paj³   *juu¹*   *baan⁴*   *nan⁴*
       go   be.at   village   DEM.NONPROX

'They reported that the people of this village also moved to that village.'

Third, in this kind of construction, the aspect-modality marking on the lower verb phrase is independent of the aspect-modality properties of the matrix verb. Thus, the following example, inserting complex aspect-modality marking (cf. Figure 4.4.2-1 above) on the lower verb of (372), is grammatical (cf. also (370), above):

(374) *man²*   *laaj²-ngaan²*   *vaa¹*   *khon²*   *baan⁴*   *nii⁴*   *khùù²*   *si⁰*
       3SG   report   COMP   person   village   DEM.GEN   probably   IRR

       bò⁰   *than²*   *daj⁰*   *ñaaj⁴*   *paj³*   *juu¹*   *baan⁴*   *nan⁴*
       NEG   yet   ACHV   move   go   be.at   village   DEM.NONPROX

'They reported that the people of this village have probably not yet moved to that village.'

Finally, the whole lower clause, including or not including the complementizer *vaa¹*, may be replaced by *ñang³* 'what?' in a WH-question, as follows:

(375) *man²*   *laaj²-ngaan²*   *(vaa¹)*   *ñang³*
       3SG   report   COMP   what
       'What did he report?'

4.4.9.3. *Verbs appearing in both controlled and non-controlled complementation*

Some complement-taking predicates, like *hên³* 'see' or *daj⁴.ñin²* 'hear', may act either as S-COMP different-subject complement verbs (without overt complement marking, cf.

§4.4.9.1.2, above) or may head non-controlling constructions whose lower complements are overtly marked (by *vaa¹*). Compare the (a) and (b) examples in the following pairs:

(376) (a) *phuak⁴*   *khòòj⁵*   *hên³*   *man²*   *ñing²*   *baan⁴*
             group   1SG   see   3SG   shoot   village
             'We saw them shoot (i.e. bomb) the village.' (1157.7)

        (b) *phuak⁴*   *khòòj⁵*   *hên³*   *vaa¹*   *man²*   *(si⁰)*   *ñing²*   *baan⁴*
             group   1SG   see   COMP   3SG   IRR   shoot   village
             'We saw that they shot (i.e. bombed) the village.'

(377) (a) *laaw²*   *daj⁰.ñin²*   *caw⁴*   *khaa⁵*   *man²*
             3SG   hear   2SG   kill   3SG
             'S/he heard you kill it.'

        (b) *laaw²*   *daj⁰.ñin²*   *vaa¹*   *caw⁴*   *(si⁰)*   *khaa⁵*   *man²*
             3SG   hear   COMP   2SG   IRR   kill   3SG
             'S/he heard that you killed it (/will kill it).'

In the (a) examples, the complement must be read as co-temporal with the main verb. Thus, for example, in (376a) the 'seeing' and the 'bombing' happened at the same time. However, in the (b) examples, in which the lower clause is separated from the main verb by the complementizer *vaa¹*, the lower verb is not temporally dependent on the main verb, as shown by the possibility of inserting independent aspect-modality marking on the lower verb. There is a difference in evidential status between the (a) and (b) examples, such that in the (a) examples the main subject has had direct perceptual access to the event predicated in the lower clause, whereas in the (b) examples the subject infers the truth of the lower clause predication, either by visual evidence of the results (376b), or by hearsay (377b).

4.4.9.4. *So-called 'passive': the undergoer complement construction*

A final type of complement construction is the 'undergoer complement construction', marked by the verb *thùùk⁵* 'strike, come into contact with', which has traditionally been regarded as a 'passive' marker. Cross-linguistically, the term 'passive' normally refers to a construction type in a language with an S/A pivot ('subject') with the syntactic function of removing an 'A' from a transitive clause, and putting the 'O' into intransitive subject (S) position, often allowing the erstwhile A to be expressed in an oblique phrase (Foley and Van Valin 1985, Dixon 1994, inter alia). Motivations for having such a construction in a 'subject-prominent' language relate to argument management in discourse, providing speakers with a way to background A arguments, foreground O arguments, and otherwise manipulate grammatical relations where strict constraints on functional structure apply (e.g. due to control of cross-clausal co-reference of ellipsed arguments). In Lao, however, there is little need for a dedicated passive construction, since the functions just discussed are taken care of by ellipsis, freedom of pragmatically-determined argument movement, and great versatility in verb argument structure (cf. §4.3, above). Co-reference of ellipsed subjects in conjoined clauses is not under strict syntactic control (i.e. Lao has no 'pivot').

Let us then consider what the so-called passive marked by *thùùk⁵* 'strike' actually does. First, the following examples show *thùùk⁵* as a transitive verb meaning 'strike, come into contact with':

(378) khòòj⁵   thùùk⁵   toq²
       1SG   strike   table
       'I bumped into the table.'

(379) nang³ to⁰   nii⁴   thùùk⁵   nam⁴   man²   bò⁰   mii²   khun²naphaap⁴
       hide   CLF   DEM.GEN   strike   water 3SG   NEG   have   quality
       '(If) this hide comes into contact with water, it doesn't have (the) quality [to stay in tact].' (131.9)

(380) phuak⁴ khèèng¹   phuak⁴ ñang³   ni⁰   thùùk⁵   ka⁰   daj⁴
       group   lower.leg   group   whatever   TPC.PCL   strike   FOC.PCL   can
       'It's okay for (the ball) to come into contact with the lower leg and whatever.' (289.10)

The 'contact' meaning of thùùk⁵ may be extended beyond literal physical contact, as the following examples show:

(381) bò⁰   khùan²   thùùk⁵   laat⁴sakaan³
       NEG   should   strike   royal.service
       '(They) shouldn't be selected for royal service.' (104.5)

(382) thùùk⁵   khòò⁵-haa³   vaa¹   pên³   khon²   bò⁰   dii³
       strike   accusation   COMP   be   person   NEG   good
       '(You'd) get an accusation that you were a bad person.' (232.7)

The next set of examples show thùùk⁵ in the context in which it is most likely to be labeled as a 'passive' marker. In these cases, it takes a verb phrase or sentence complement, where the subject of thùùk⁵ is coreferential with the *object* of the lower complement:

(383) qaat⁵   ca⁰   thùùk⁵   cap²   ka⁰   pên³   daj⁴
       might   IRR   suffer   catch   FOC.PCL   be   can
       'It was possible that (you) might even get caught.' (273.1)

(384) ka⁰   thùùk⁵   khaw³   ñing²   taaj³
       FOC.PCL   suffer   3PL   shoot   die
       '(And then they'd) get shot dead by them.' (755.5)

(385) phu⁰-thii¹-sòòng³   paj³   ka⁰   thùùk⁵   paa³   kin³
       CLF.PERSON-ORD-two   go   FOC.PCL   suffer   fish   eat
       'The second person went, and he (also) got eaten by fish.' (969.3)

(386) caw⁴   ca⁰   thùùk⁵   pòòj¹   tua³   naj²   mùa¹   daj³
       2SG   IRR   suffer   release   body   in   time   which
       'When would you be released?' (273.8)

It is easy to see why one might label these examples as 'passive'. If we view thùùk⁵ as simply a grammatical marker here, its function would seem to be to put an O argument (a patient) of the verb it marks into main subject position (cf. the English translations). However, not all uses of thùùk⁵ as a complement-taking predicate follow this pattern. The following examples show thùùk⁵ taking same-subject VP complements, meaning that it 'fell to' the subject to do something; the subject had to do something:

(387) *thùùk⁵ nêê²lathêêt⁴ paj³ han⁰*
       suffer exile   go   PCL
       '(He) was exiled.' (155.2)

(388) *nèè¹-nòòn²*   *haw²*   *tòòng⁴*   *thùùk⁵*   *son²*
       definitely   1SG   must   suffer   fight
       'I will definitely have to fight.' (i.e. 'Definitely I must be made to fight'.) (98.9)

These are clearly not 'passive' by any description (since the main subject is subject, not object, of the lower verb), but they are indeed 'adversative' in meaning.

Further, in the next three examples, the main subject of *thùùk⁵* is not an argument of the lower clause at all, but a *possessor* of an argument of the lower clause (in a rather more abstract sense in the second and third examples):

(389) *thùùk⁵*   *ñak¹*   *hak²*   *khèèn³*   *hak²*   *khaa³*   *qiik⁵*
       suffer   troll   snap   arm   snap   leg   more
       '(They) got (their) arms, and (their) legs too, snapped by a troll.' (974.13)

(390) *lùù³*   *vaa¹*   *thùùk⁵*   *phu⁰-khon²*   *lom⁴*   *taaj³*   *sia³*   *haaj³*
       or   COMP   strike   CLF.PERSON-person   fall   die   lose   disappear
       '...or (if you) suffer anyone (of your people) falling over and dying...' (125.13)

(391) *phen¹*   *thùùk⁵*   *phua³*   *paj⁰*   *nòòn²*   *kap²*   *phu⁰-saaw³*
       3SG   strike/suffer   husband   go   sleep   with   CLF.PERSON-girl
       'She suffered her husband sleeping with (another) girl.'
       (or: 'She was slept-with-another-girl by her husband.')

Thus, while *thùùk⁵* in one of its common functions seems analogous in grammatical function to a 'passive' marker, it is not a passive marker in the usual sense. The main subject may correspond to subject or object or even neither argument of the lower clause. The relationship between simple transitive sentences and undergoer complement constructions marked by *thùùk⁵* is not a simple one of syntactic permutation, but involves addition of specific semantic content (meaning essentially 'have a (usually adverse) experience of VP, not by one's choice or control').

4.4.10. Coordinating constructions

4.4.10.1. Verb (phrase) chaining

A verb (phrase) chain is a string of verb phrases with no overt linking morphology, usually with a single understood subject, which may or may not be overtly expressed. The following examples are typical (chained verb phrases are each square-bracketed):

(392) *paj³* [*cap² nok¹*] [*cap² nuu³*] [*cap² puu³*] [*cap² paa³*] [*ma⁰*   *kin³*]
       go   catch bird   catch rat   catch crab   catch fish   DIR.PCL(come)   eat
       '(We'd) go and catch birds, and rats, and crabs and fish to eat.' (1172.6)

(393) *khan²* *phu⁰-daj³*   *dùù⁴*   *paj³* [*qaap⁵* *nam⁴*] [*sak¹* *khùang¹*]
       if   CLF.PERSON-any   naughty   go   bathe   water   wash   clothes
       'If anyone was naughty and went to bathe or wash their clothes...' (1189.13)

(394)   [*kap²-khùùn²*   *maa²*   *pathêêt⁴*]   [*hian²*   *tòò¹*]
       go.back-return   come   country   study   continue
       '(They) returned to their country (to) continue (their) studies.' (1202.2)

Different semantic relationships between clauses may hold. In (392) and (393), the chained clauses are in a parallel or distributive relationship – there is no dependence among the bracketed verb phrases in terms of temporal, consequential, conditional, causative, or purposive relation. In (394), however, there is a purposive relationship between the two clauses, such that the second VP describes the purpose of the first VP, and the truth of the whole sentence entails the truth of the first VP, but not necessarily the second (i.e. it only means that 'the purpose of the first VP was the second VP'). These different kinds of semantic relationships can be hierarchically combined in a single sentence, as follows:

(395)   [<*tùk²*   *hèè³*>   <*haa³*   *hòòj³*>]...[<*saj¹*   *mòòng²*>   <*haa³*   *paa³*>]
       cast   fish.net   seek   shells   put   fish.net   seek   fish
       'We'd cast *hèè³* nets for shells, and put out *mòòng²* nets for fish.' (1066.1)

The two constituents in square brackets are VPs in parallel. Both of these complex VPs consist of two chained VPs (in angled brackets), where the second VP describes the intended purpose of the first.

A second kind of relationship between chained verb phrases is a 'sequential' one – i.e. where the events listed in the chain are understood to happen one after the other. In clause chains where the actions predicated are to be interpreted as distinctly separated events, this separation is often overtly marked by the clause linker *lèka⁰* (see §4.4.1.2, above), which is almost always followed by a zero anaphor coreferential with the subject of the previous clause. In the following example, *ø*'s refer to *tamluat⁵* 'police', and other ellipsed arguments are unmarked:

(396)   *khan²*   [*tamluat⁵*   *hên³*]   *han⁰*   [ø   *qaw³*   *paj³*]   [ø   *kêp²*
       if   police   see   TPC.PCL   take   go   collect

       paj³]   *lèka⁰*   [ø   *pap²-maj³*]   *lèka⁰*   [ø   *pòòj¹*   *ma⁰*
       go   CLNK   fine   CLNK   release   DIR.PCL(come)

       kin³   *law⁵*   *khùù²*   *kaw¹*]
       consume   liquor   like   old
       'If the police see (them), (they) would take (them) away, pick (them) up, and then fine (them), and then release (them) to come and carry on drinking like before.' (1294.4)

Here, the linker *lèka⁰* overtly partitions the string of verb phrases into the three separate events of (i) 'police taking them, picking them up', (ii) 'police fining them', and (iii) 'police releasing them to carry on drinking'. Here is another example, with numerous chained clauses (all with subject ellipsed), and just one overt linking of clauses using *lèka⁰*:

(397)   [*kap²*   *maa²*]   [*ma⁰*   *laang⁴*   *tiin³*][*laang⁴*   *mùù²*]
       return   come   DIR.PCL(come)   wash   foot   wash   hand

       [*qanaa²maj²*]   *lèka⁰*   [*khùn⁵*   *tiang³*]   [*tii³*   *kalèèng¹*]   [*nòòn²*]
       clean.up   CLNK   ascend   bed   hit   bell   sleep

       '(We'd) come back and wash (our) feet, (and) wash (our) hands, clean up, and then get into bed, (when they'd) ring the bell (for us) to go to sleep.' (1242.8)

Here, the first chain ['return' + 'wash hands' + 'wash feet' + 'clean up'] shows no overt marking between VPs. These actions are habitually linked together in a normal daily complex event (given the context of boarding school life for children), and so are conceptually unitary, relatively speaking. This complex (but monoclausal) chain is then connected by the clause linker *lèka⁰* to another unmarked chain of VPs, ['get into bed' + 'hit the bell' + 'sleep'], again a series of action habitually linked in the daily flow of events, although not necessarily normally directly linked to those of the first chain.[47]

Such strings are typical in narratives. The following example is illustrative, from one speaker's elicited description of a series of events acted out in a video stimulus designed to explore the cross-linguistic packaging of complex series of events (van Staden et al. 2001). The clause linker *lèka⁰* (shown in boldface) occurs seven times:

(398)

phu⁰-saaj²	*khon²*	*nii⁴*	*nòòn²-lap²/*	*juu¹*	*la⁰*	*laaw²*
CLF-male	CLF	DEM.GEN	lie-sleep	be.at	PCL	3SG
ka⁰/	*huu⁴.mùa¹*	*khùn⁵*	*maa²/*	*sii³*	*taa³*	***lèka⁰/***
FOC.PCL	become.conscious	ascend	come	rub	eye	CLNK
luk¹	*khùn⁵/*	*nang¹*	*juu¹*	***lèka⁰***	*hêt/*	*jiat⁵/*
arise	ascend	sit	be.at	CLNK	do	stretch.out
qèèw³/	*jiat⁵-khaan⁴/*	***lèka⁰***	*kaw³*	*hua³*	***lèka⁰/***	*luk¹*
lower.back	stretch.oneself	CLNK	scratch	head	CLNK	arise
ñaang¹	*paj³*	*cap²*	*qaw³*	*saam²/*	*ñaang¹*	*paj³*
walk	go	grab	take	bowl	walk	go
qaw³	*nam⁴*	*juu¹*	*kakhuq¹/****lèka⁰***	*thêêk⁵*	*nam⁴*	*saj¹*
take	water	be.at	bucket CLNK	pour.out	water	put
saam²/	***lèka⁰***	*thùù³*	*saam²*	*kap²*	*khùùn²*	*maa²*
bowl	CLNK	carry	bowl	go.back	return	come

'This man is sleeping – and then he – wakes up – rubs (his) eyes and then – gets up – sits there and then does – stretches – his back – stretches (him)self – and then scratches (his) head and then – gets up (and) walks (to) get a bowl – and then walks (to) get water in a bucket – and then pours the water into the bowl – and then carries the bowl back.' [NV137 05.086]

4.4.10.2. *Verb compounds*

Two or more verbs can be compounded, resulting in what is effectively a single verb, with a single subject and a single object. These usually involve a pair of near synonyms. This may be interpreted as lexical compounding or syntactic coordination of verbs under V', under VP.

Here are a few examples, with the compound verb in square brackets (in the third example the clause is relativized):

---

47 Notably, the subject of *tii³ kalèèng¹* 'ring the bell' is non-coreferential with the subject of the prior and subsequent verb phrases, *khùn⁵ tiang³* 'get into bed', and *nòòn²* 'lie down/sleep', respectively. This is an exception to the rather strong tendency for verb phrases in such series to have coreferential subjects.

(399) *man²*   *ka⁰*   [*nii³*   *paq²*]   *naang²*   *qan⁰-nii⁴*
     3SG   FOC.PCL   flee   abandon young.woman CLF-DEM.GEN
     'He ran away from and abandoned that girl.' (903.11)

(400) *baat⁵*   [*phop¹*   *hên³*]   *tòòn³*   *nan⁴*   *khòòj⁵*   *jaak⁵* *mùa²*
     moment   meet   see   time   DEM.NONPROX 1SG   want   return
     'When (I) met (them) at that time, I wanted to go back.' (1175.13)

(401) *phuak⁴*   *thii¹-vaa¹*   [*pun⁴*   *cii⁴*   *khaa⁵*]   *khaw³*
     group   REL-COMP   hold.up stick.up kill   3PL
     'those who hold up and stick up and urder people' (824.3)

In each of these cases, the verbs in compound are clause-separable. Semantically, they involve simple synonymic reiteration (as in (399), (400)). Thus, a verb compound V1-V2 entails both V1 and V2.

4.5. CONCLUSION

4.5.1. Ambiguity and complexity

The very wide range of possible relationships between verbs and/or verb phrases in Lao means that many decontextualized surface sequences are ambiguous. Consider the following example, in which *haj⁵* 'give' has three possible structural and semantic roles (as full verb in a verb phrase string, as subordinate verb in a purposive complement, and as deverbal preposition with benefactive meaning):

(402) *laaw²*   *nùng¹*   *khaw⁵*   *haj⁵*   *khòòj⁵*
     3SG   steam   rice   give   1SG
     i. 'S/he steamed rice (and then) gave (it) to me.'
     ii. 'S/he steamed rice to give me.'
     iii. 'S/he steamed rice for me.' (either 'for my benefit', or 'on my behalf')

The (i) and (ii) readings in (402) may be forced with overt marking by the clause-coordinating marker *lèka⁰* and the subordinating marker *phùa¹* 'in order to', respectively:

(403) *laaw²*   *nùng¹*   *khaw⁵*   *lèka⁰*   *haj⁵*   *khòòj⁵*
     3SG   steam   rice   CLNK   give   1SG
     i. 'S/he steamed rice and then gave (it) to me.'
     ii. (*S/he steamed rice to give me.)
     iii. (*S/he steamed rice for me.)

(404) *laaw²*   *nùng¹*   *khaw⁵*   *phùa¹*   *haj⁵*   *khòòj⁵*
     3SG   steam   rice   in.order.to give   1SG
     i. (*S/he steamed rice (and then) gave (it) to me.)
     ii. 'S/he steamed rice to give me.'
     iii. (*She steamed rice for me.)[48]

---

48 Clearly, the reading in (i) allows 'She steamed rice for me', if we only consider the benefactive reading of this English gloss. What is important here is that (404) cannot permit the usual broader reading of the benefactive *haj⁵* in Lao, namely the one that includes 'on my behalf'.

Such ambiguities are common, but are easily resolved by the constraints of grammatical and/or pragmatic context.

The many different patterns reviewed in this chapter may be nested together to form more complex constructions. Consider the following example, taken from (398), above, showing four verbs in sequence:

(405) *ñaang¹ paj³ qaw³ nam⁴ juu¹ kakhuq¹*
       walk   go   take water be.at bucket
       '(He) walks (to) get water in a bucket.'

Here, *ñaang¹* 'walk' and *paj³* 'go' form a 'manner-direction' motion construction, where their respective motion semantics are overlaid facets of a single event. As a unit, these combine with *qaw³* 'take' in a verb phrase chain. Finally, the verb *juu¹* 'be at' serves as a 'prepositional' marker, hosting the oblique nominal *kakhuq¹* 'bucket' as a modifier of the object argument of *qaw³* 'take', namely *nam⁴* 'water'.

Here is another example, with five verbs in sequence:

(406) *bŏ⁰ jaak⁵ haj⁵ nii³ kaj³ caak⁵   phòò¹-mèè¹*
       NEG want   give flee far   separate.from father-mother
       '(They) don't want (their children) to go far from (their) parents.' (295.10)

The verb *jaak⁵* 'want' is here a same-subject control complement verb. In the complement clause, *haj⁵* 'give' is performing a switch-reference function to accommodate the different subject in the lower verb. The central verb of the lower complement is *nii³* 'flee', followed by *kaj³* 'far' as a right-marking (adverbial/resultative) descriptive complement, and finally with *caak⁵* 'separate.from, from' as a deverbal preposition heading the adjunct meaning 'from (their) parents'.

Finally, recall the example with six verbs in sequence described at the opening of this chapter, repeated here:

(1) *caw⁴ lòòng²   qaw³ paj³ hêt¹ kin³ beng¹ mèè⁴*
     2SG   try.out take go   make eat   look   PCL
     'You go ahead and take (them) and try cooking (them)!' (38.12)

The verb *lòòng²* 'try out' acts here as a left-marking complement-taking adverb, and combines with *beng¹* 'look', a right-marking adverbial, to bracket a four-verb phrase containing a 'disposal' construction (*qaw³ hêt¹* 'take (and) do/make'), with *paj³* 'go' as a directional particle, and forming purposive clause chain with *kin³* 'eat'.

While the details of possibilities for combining the range of constructions described throughout §4.4 are complex and not yet well understood, the examples just discussed should give a sense of the way in which surface strings of verbs are not mere 'strings of verbs', but hierarchically structured (usually binary) nestings of V1-V2 constructions. (See Table 4.1-1, above, and Table 5.4.2-1, below, for summary of the available constructions, as described in this chapter.)

4.5.2. Summary

This chapter has surveyed a significant portion of the complex clausal grammar of Lao, exemplifying the kind of system one can expect to find in a Tai language. Notable if not amazing is the great variety of complex syntactic-semantic configurations which can underlie a sequence of verbs or verb phrases lacking overt marking of their interrelationship. A no doubt rich topic for further research concerns the combinatorial productivity of each of these constructions, an issue requiring particular attention to their semantics.

Table 4.5.2-1 summarizes a range of distinguishing features of the different constructions surveyed in §4.4, above.

TABLE 4.5.2-1: GRAMMATICAL PROPERTIES DISTINGUISHING A RANGE OF LAO V1-V2 STRUCTURES

	Yes-answer head?	Clause-separable?	Which V omissible in relative clause?	Medial negation OK?	With medial negation, V1 entailed?	*Ka* insertable w/o major semantic change?
Left aspect-modality markers, deverbal (§4.4.2)	*V2*	*no*	*V1*	*%*	*no*	*no*
'Despatch' 3-place expressions (§4.4.3)	*V2*	*%*	*V1*	*no*	*n/a*	*no*
'Disposal' constructions (§4.4.4)	*V2*	*%*	*V1*	*no*	*n/a*	*no*
Manner-path-direction constructions (§4.4.5.2)	*V1-V2-V3*	*no*	*neither*	*no*	*n/a*	*no*
Different subject resultatives (§4.4.6.2)	*V2*	*yes*	*%V2*	*yes*	*yes*	*yes*
Same-subject resultatives (§4.4.6.2.2)	*V2*	*yes*	*%V1*	*yes*	*yes*	*yes*
Projected resultatives (§4.4.6.2.3)	*V2*	*yes*	*%*	*yes*	*yes*	*yes*
Reiterative resultatives (§4.4.6.2.4)	*V1*	*%yes*	*%*	*yes*	*no*	*yes*
Right-headed stative adverbial complements (§4.4.6.3.1)	*V2*	*no*	*V2*	*yes*	*yes*	*yes*
Right-headed active adverbial complements (§4.4.6.3.3)	*V1-V2*	*no*	*neither*	*no*	*n/a*	*no*
Left-headed adverbial complements (§4.4.6.3.4)	*V1*	*%*	*%V2*	*no*	*n/a*	*no*
Left-marking adverbial compounds (§4.4.6.4.1)	*V1-V2*	*no*	*neither*	*no*	*n/a*	*no*
Right-marking adverbial compounds (§4.4.6.4.2)	*V1-V2*	*no*	*either*	*no*	*n/a*	*no*
Depictive complement constructions (§4.4.6.5)	*V1*	*no*	*V2*	*yes*	*yes*	*yes*
pên³-adjunct constructions (§4.4.6.6)	*V1*	*no*	*V2*	*no*	*n/a*	*no*
daj⁴-complement constructions (§4.4.6.7)	*V1 or V2*	*no*	*V2*	*yes*	*yes*	*yes*
Oblique phrase constructions (§4.4.7)	*V1*	*no*	*V2*	*no*	*n/a*	*no*
'Give', 'make', 'make-give' causative constructions (§4.4.8.1-4.4.8.3)	*V1-V2*	*no*	*neither*	*yes*	*yes*	*no*
Control complements, same-subject (§4.4.9.1.1)	*V1*	*no*	*%V2*	*no*	*n/a*	*no*
Control complements, different subject (§4.4.9.1.2)	*V1*	*no*	*V2*	*yes*	*yes*	*no*
Non-control complements (§4.4.9.2)	*V1*	*no*	*V2*	*yes*	*yes*	*no*
VP chains (§4.4.10.1)	*V1-V2*	*yes*	*neither*	*no*	*n/a*	*no*
Verb compounds (§4.4.10.2)	*V1-V2*	*%*	*neither*	*no*	*n/a*	*no*

ACKNOWLEDGEMENTS

I thank Tony Diller and Nick Evans for their generous and significant contributions of time and ideas to this chapter. For discussion of various issues raised, and/or for comments on specific points made herein, I thank Sasha Aikhenvald, Felix Ameka, Peter Austin, Walter Bisang, Jürgen Bohnemeyer, Bob Dixon, Martina Faller, Cliff Goddard, Steve Levinson, Stephen Matthews, John Newman, Gunter Senft, Kingkarn Thepkanjana, Satoshi Uehara, and Anna Wierzbicka. I also thank Anouk Diederen for expert assistance in preparation of the original submission, and Luo Yongxian for handling the final version. The research reported on here was supported at various times by an Australian Research Council grant (A59601467 'Thai-Lao linguistic interaction', chief investigator Anthony V. N. Diller), an Australian Postgraduate Award, the University of Melbourne Faculty of Arts fieldwork grant, and the Max Planck Society. Some of the tables and examples appear in Enfield (2003, 2005).

NOTE

The main research and writing of this chapter was done between 1998 and 2001. Since this chapter was completed, several publications have appeared which treat related issues in detail, and which provide further information on the situation of languages and linguistics of Laos:

Enfield, N. J. (2002) 'How to define "Lao", "Thai", and "Isan" language? A view from linguistic science'. *Tai Culture* 7.1: 62-67.
Enfield, N. J. (2003) 'Demonstratives in space and interaction: data from Lao speakers and implications for semantic analysis', *Language* 79.1: 82-117.
Enfield, N. J. (2004a) 'Adjectives in Lao' in *Adjective classes: a cross-linguistic typology*, edited by R. M. W. Dixon and A. Y. Aikhenvald, Oxford: Oxford University Press, 323-347.
Enfield, N. J. (2004b) 'Nominal classification in Lao: a sketch', *Sprachtypologie und Universalienforschung* (Special Issue on Nominal Classification, edited by A. K. Aikhenvald) 57.2/3: 117-143.
Enfield, N. J. (2006a) 'Lao body part terms', *Language Sciences* 28.2/3: 181-200.
Enfield, N. J. (2006b) 'Laos - Language situation', in *Encyclopedia of Language and Linguistics, 2nd Edition*, edited by Keith Brown. Cambridge: Cambridge University Press, Volume 6, 698-700.
Enfield, N. J. (in press, 2007) 'Lao separation verbs and the logic of linguistic event categorization', *Cognitive Linguistics*.
Enfield, N. J. (in press, 2007) 'Lao linguistics in the 20th century and since', In *Nouvelles recherches sur le Laos*, edited by Yves Goudineau and Michel Lorrillard, Paris, Vientien : Ecole Francaise d'Extrême-Orient, collection 'Etudes thématiques'.
Enfield, N. J. (in press, 2007) 'Language and culture in Laos: an agenda for research', *Proceedings of 1st International Conference on Lao Studies*, DeKalb, Illinois.

APPENDIX

Lao is the national language of Laos, spoken by over four million people there (Enfield 1999). Dialects of Lao are also spoken by a minority in Northeast Cambodia, and a large minority (at least ten million) in Northeast Thailand (i.e. in areas bordering lowland Laos). There are also scattered Lao-speaking villages in Western Cambodia and Central and Eastern Thailand. The dialects spoken in Thailand are currently undergoing rapid change under the influence of central Thai (Diller 1988, 1991; for Thai influence on Lao in Laos, see Enfield 1999).

Many examples provided in this paper are from a corpus of spontaneous spoken language collected in Laos in 1996-1997. This corpus contains several hours of material, on a range of topics and styles (procedural descriptions, jokes, informal conversation, myths, fables, life-story narratives), from a range of speakers (both male and female, ages from teenage to octogenarian). Examples from this corpus have a reference number in brackets after the English translation. A number of examples are taken from recordings made in September – October 2000 and July 2001, using semi-experimental materials – these are noted as they appear. Remaining examples are constructed and/or elicited, and checked with native speaker consultants.

Abbreviations used in glosses are as follows:

1/2/31st/2nd/3rd	person pronoun	NONPROX	non-proximal
ACHV	achievement	NSR	nominalizer
CLF	classifier	O.BRO	older brother
CLNK	clause linker	ORD	ordinator
COMP	complementizer	PCL	particle
CT	class term	PFV	perfective
DEM	demonstrative	PL	plural
DIR	directional	PROG	progressive
EXPR	expressive	Q	question
FEM	feminine	RCP	reciprocal
FOC	focus	RDP	reduplication
GEN	general	REL	relativizer
IRR	irrealis	SG	singular
MASC	masculine	TPC	topic
NEG	negation	Y.SIB	younger sibling

Small caps are used for grammatical morphemes, italics for emphasis and mentions, single capital letter with period (e.g. D.) for gloss of proper names, period between morphemes to indicate semantically unanalysable morphology. The symbols *(x) and (*x) indicate that the example is ungrammatical if x is excluded, and included, respectively. Note that in interlinear glossing in this chapter I do not mark distinctions between pronouns used at different 'levels' of speech, since it is irrelevant to the topic at hand. Thus, among first person singular pronouns, both kuu^3 and $khòòj^5$ are glossed as '1SG', despite the distinction in social level between the two forms (kuu^3 being the bare form for 'I', $khòòj^5$ being a general polite form; Enfield 2002a: 147-149).

There is no standard romanization of Lao. The system used in this chapter (like the Lao orthography itself) does not feature sentence-based punctuation such as capital letters and periods. This is primarily to index their spoken (not written) source. Examples are transcribed according to the following conventions:

Consonants					Vowels			Tones
b	d				i	u		1./32/
p	t	c	k	q(glottalstop)	ù(unrounded)			2./35/
ph	th		kh		ê	e	o	3./13/
m	n	ñ	ng					4./51/
f	s		h		è	a	ò	5./31/
w	l	j						0./unstressed/

REFERENCES

Aikhenvald, Alexandra Y, and Dixon, R. M. W. (eds) (2006) *Serial Verb Constructions: A Cross-Linguistic Typology*, Oxford: Oxford University Press.

Andrews, Avery D. and Manning, Christopher D. (1999) *Complex Predicates and Information Spreading in LFG*, Stanford: CSLI.

Bisang, Walter (1991) 'Verb serialization, grammaticalization and attractor positions in Chinese, Hmong, Vietnamese, Thai and Khmer', in Hansjakob Seiler and Waldfried Premper (eds) *Partizipation: das Sprachliche Erfassen von Sachverhalten*, Tübingen: Gunter Narr Verlag, 509-562.

Bisang, Walter (1996) 'Areal typology and grammaticalization: processes of grammaticalization based on nouns and verbs in South-east Asian languages', *Studies in Language* 20.3: 519-597.

Bohnemeyer, Jürgen and Caelen, Martijn (1999) 'The ECOM clips: a stimulus for the linguistic coding of event complexity', in David Wilkins (ed.) *'Manual' for the 1999 Field Season*, Typescript, Max Planck Institute for Psycholinguistics, Nijmegen.

Chafe, Wallace (1994) *Discourse, Consciousness, and Time: The Flow and Displacement of Conscious Experience in Speaking and Writing*, Chicago: University of Chicago Press.

Chao, Yuen Ren (1968) *A Grammar of Spoken Chinese*, Berkeley: University of California Press.

Clark, Marybeth (1989) 'Hmong and Areal Southeast Asia', in David Bradley (ed.) *Southeast Asian Syntax*, Pacific Linguistics, A-77, 175-230.

Clark, Marybeth and Prasithratsint, Amara (1985) 'Synchronic lexical derivation in Southeast Asian languages', in Suriya Ratanakul, David Thomas, and Suwilai Premsrirat (eds) *Southeast Asian Linguistic Studies Presented to Andre-G. Haudricourt*, Bangkok: Mahidol University, 34-81.

Diller, Anthony V. N. (1988) 'Thai syntax and "national grammar"', *Language Sciences* 10(2): 273-312.

— (1991) 'What makes Central Thai a national language?', in Craig J. Reynolds (ed.) *National Identity and its Defenders*, Chiang Mai: Silkworm Books, 87-132.

Dixon, R. M. W. (1991) *A New Approach to English Grammar, on Semantic Principles*, Oxford: Clarendon Press.

Dixon, R. M. W. (1994) *Ergativity*, Cambridge: CUP.

Dowty, David R. (1979) *Word Meaning and Montague Grammar: The Semantics of Verbs and Times in Generative Semantics and in Montague's PTQ*, Dordrecht: Kluwer Academic Publishers.

Durie, Mark (1988) 'Verb serialisation and "verbal prepositions" in Oceanic languages', *Oceanic linguistics* 2: 1-23.

— (1997) 'Grammatical structures in verb serialization', in Alex Alsina, Joan Bresnan, and Peter Sells (eds) *Complex predicates*, Stanford: CSLI, 289-354.

Enfield, N. J. (1999) 'Lao as a national language', in Grant Evans (ed.) *Laos: Culture and Society*, Chiang Mai: Silkworm Books, 258-290.

— (2001) 'On genetic and areal linguistics in Mainland Southeast Asia: parallel polyfunctionality of "acquire"', in Alexandra Aikhenvald and R. M. W. Dixon (eds) *Areal diffusion and genetic inheritance*, Oxford: Oxford University Press, 255-290.

— (2002a) 'Combinatoric properties of natural semantic metalanguage expressions in Lao', in Cliff Goddard and Anna Wierzbicka (eds) *Meaning and universal grammar*, Amsterdam: John Benjamins, 87-199.

— (2002b) 'Semantics and combinatorics of "sit," "stand," and "lie" in Lao', in John Newman (ed.) *The Linguistics of Sitting, Standing, and Lying*, Amsterdam: Benjamins, 25-41.

— (2002c) 'Biclausal expressions of "cause" in mainland Southeast Asia', paper presented at the 28th Meeting of the Berkeley Linguistics Society, University of California at Berkeley, February 15.

— (2003) *Linguistic Epidemiology: Semantics and Grammar of Language Contact in Mainland Southeast Asia*, London: Routledge.
— (2004) 'Cultural logic and syntactic productivity: associated posture constructions in Lao', in N. J. Enfield (ed.) *Ethnosyntax: Explorations in Culture and Grammar*, Oxford: Oxford University Press, 231-258.
— (2005a) 'Functions of "give" and "take" in Lao complex predicates', in Robert S. Bauer (ed.) *Collected Papers on Southeast Asian and Pacific Languages*, Canberra: Pacific Linguistics, 13-36.
— (2005b) 'Depictive secondary predicates in Lao', in Nikolaus P. Himmelmann and Eva Schultze-Berndt (eds) *Secondary Predication and Adverbial Modification: The Typology of Depictives*, Oxford: Oxford University Press.
— (forthcoming) 'Encoding three-participant events in the Lao clause', *Linguistics* (scheduled for publication in 2007).
Foley, William A. and Van Valin, Robert D. Jr (1984) *Functional Syntax and Universal Grammar*, Cambridge: Cambridge University Press.
— (1985) 'Information packaging in the clause', in Timothy Shopen (ed.) *Language Typology and Syntactic Description (Volume 1, Clause Structure)*, Cambridge: Cambridge University Press, 282-364.
Foley, William A. and Olson, Mike (1985) 'Clausehood and verb serialisation', in J. Nichols and A. C. Woodbury (eds) *Grammar inside and outside the Clause: Some Approaches to Theory from the Field*, Cambridge: Cambridge University Press, 17-60.
Gedney, William J. (1989) *Selected papers on comparative Tai studies*, Michigan: Ann Arbor.
Harris, Alice C. and Campbell, Lyle (1995) *Historical syntax in cross-linguistic perspective*, Cambridge: Cambridge University Press.
Harrison, Colin J. (1992) *The grammar of directional serial verb constructions*, dissertation, Australian National University Department of Linguistics Honours.
Himmelmann, Nikolaus P. (2002) 'Asymmetries in word architecture: another look at the suffixing preference', formal colloquium talk, Max Planck Institute for Psycholinguistics, Nijmegen, February 26.
Hopper, Paul J. (1991) 'On some principles of grammaticization', in Elizabeth Closs Traugott and Bernd Heine (eds) *Approaches to Grammaticalization*, Amsterdams: John Benjamins, vol. 1, 17–35.
Hopper, Paul J. and Thompson, Sandra (1980) 'Transitivity in grammar and discourse', *Language* 56: 251-99.
Jackendoff, Ray (1983) *Semantics and cognition*, Cambridge, Mass.: MIT Press
Jagacinski, Ngampit (1987) 'The Tai Lue of Xipsongbanna in China's Yunnan Province: description and a study of the OV order in the AU construction', unpublished PhD thesis, Ohio State University, Ann Arbor: UMI Microfilms.
Lambrecht, Knud (1994) *Information Structure and Sentence Form: Topic, Focus, and the Mental Representation of Grammatical Relations*, Cambridge: Cambridge University Press.
LaPolla, Randy (1997) 'Grammaticalization as the development of constraints on the search for relevance', paper presented at Departmental Seminar, Department of Linguistics, the University of Melbourne, August 15.
— (2001) 'The role of migration and language contact in the development of the Sino-Tibetan language family', in Alexandra Aikhenvald and R. M. W. Dixon (eds) *Areal Diffusion and Genetic Inheritance: Problems in Comparative Linguistics*, Oxford: Oxford University Press, 225-254.
Li, Charles N. and Thompson, Sandra A. (1976) 'Subject and topic: a new typology of language', in Charles N. Li (ed.) *Subject and Topic*, New York: Academic Press, 457-489.
— (1981) *Mandarin Chinese: A Functional Reference Grammar*, Berkeley: University of California Press.
Long, Yaohong and Zheng Guoqiao (1998) *The Dong Language in Guizhou Province, China*, Texas: SIL/UTA.

Lord, Carol (1993) *Historical Change in Serial Verb Constructions*, Amsterdam/ Philadelphia: John Benjamins.

Matthews, Stephen and Yip, Virginia (1994) *Cantonese: A Comprehensive Grammar*, London: Routledge.

Mosel, Ulrike (1991) 'Towards a Typology of Valency', in H. Seiler & Premper, W. (eds) *Partizipation: Das sprachliche Erfassen von Sachverhalten*, Tübingen: Gunter Narr Verlag, 240-251.

Quine, W. V. O. (1960) *Word and Object*, Cambridge, Mass.: MIT Press.

Schultze-Berndt, Eva and Himmelmann, Nikolaus P. (2004) 'Depictive Secondary Predicates in Crosslinguistic Perspective', *Linguistic Typology* 8.1: 59-131.

Smith, Carlota S. (1997) *The Parameter of Aspect*, Dordrecht: Kluwer.

Suwilai Premsrirat (1987) *Khmu, a Minority Language of Thailand*, Pacific Linguistics A-75, Canberra: ANU.

Talmy, Leonard (1985) 'Lexicalisation patterns: semantic structure in lexical forms', in Timothy Shopen (ed.) *Language Typology and Syntactic Description (Volume 3, Grammatical Categories and the Lexicon)*, Cambridge: Cambridge University Press, 57-149.

— (2000) *Toward a Cognitive Semantics* (2 volumes), Cambridge, Mass.: MIT Press.

van Staden, Miriam, Senft, Gunter, Enfield, Nick and Bohnemeyer, Jürgen (2001) 'Staged Events', in Steve Levinson and Nick Enfield (eds) *'Manual' for the field season 2001*, Nijmegen: Max Planck Institute for Psycholinguistics, 100-110..

Vendler, Zeno (1967) *Linguistics in Philosophy*, Ithaca, New York: Cornell University Press.

Wang, Jun and Zheng Guoqiao (1993) *An Outline Grammar of Mulao*, trans. Luo Yongxian, Canberra: National Thai Studies Centre, Australian National University.

Wierzbicka, Anna (2002) 'English causative constructions in an ethnosyntactic perspective: focusing on LET', in N. J. Enfield (ed.) *Ethnosyntax: Explorations in Grammar and Culture*, Oxford: Oxford University Press, 162-205.

Zhou, Guoyan (2000) 'The origin and development of the "disposal" form in Bouyei language', in Somsonge Burusphat (ed.) *Proceedings of the International Conference on Tai Studies*, Bangkok: Institute of Language and Culture for Rural Development, 443-456.

CHAPTER FIVE

SHAN AND OTHER NORTHERN TIER SOUTHEAST TAI LANGUAGES OF MYANMAR AND CHINA: THEMES AND VARIATIONS

Jerold A. Edmondson

5.1. BACKGROUND

This paper reports on the themes and variations in the northern tier of SW Tai languages found in Myanmar and to a lesser extent that found in adjoining areas of China.[1] The term *northern tier of SW Tai* was used in Edmondson and Solnit 1997 to describe those languages whose historical lineage goes through the root of Tai settlements on the Shweli River between Myanmar and China as early as the 6th c. and who then began to expand to the west, south, and north, reaching a high point of migration in the 13th c. The analysis to be presented below will investigate how contemporary linguistic data can help determine the various subgroups within the northern tier languages and, at the same time, my analysis will contrast northern tier languages to those from a few nearby SW Tai groups, which in regard to history, culture, and in the eyes of the speakers themselves, are regarded as not belonging to northern tier language. I will claim that none of these non-northern tier groups participates in the same polylectal, historical, cultural, and social lineage descended from the Shweli culture of the 13th century I call *Shan*. If one is trying to determine who belongs to the Shan and how non-Shan languages of the area differ, then the autonym is not helpful, as all these people call themselves simply *Tai* plus some modifier designating a geographic places or a distinctive feature. The exonym for the people and language, *Shan*, has become more distinctive, as this is the term used by the Burmese ရှမ်း and Chinese 掸 *shàn* 'an old name for a group associated with contemporary Dai people of Yunnan' to refer to just these groups. In English as well, *Shan* has specialized to refer to the Tai groups of Burma and western China, since Cushing's dictionary and handbook (1888a and 1888b). As for the subgroupings within

---

1   The author wishes to recognize the significant help of Ms. Chang Yi-ming of Bangkok, Thailand for arranging my first trips to Myanmar. Chang Yi-ming was the sole field worker on the second and third trips to Myanmar in 1995 and 1996. The author also wishes to express his profound thanks to Professor Than Tun ဒေါက်တာသန်းထွန်း, U Sai Aung Tun စိုင်းအောင်ထွန်းကြည်, U Sai Kham Mong, and especially to U Tun Aye ဦးထွန်းအေး of Myitkyina Degree College, Myitkyina and Daw Ah Nan ဒေါ်အာနန်, Mandalay University, Department of History for accompanying and assisting us on the expedition and most of all for teaching us the meaning of the Burmese expression ဦးနှောက်မစားပါနဲ့ 'Don't let it eat your brain!' or 'Take it easy.' Also my appreciation goes to Dr Stephen Morey of La Trobe University, Professor †Jørgen Rischel of the University of Copenhagen for helpful comments on a draft version of this paper, and Ms. Nance Cunningham, a field worker among the Shan, for proofing the Burmese and Shan spellings and for other content help. Last but not least, we also wish to thank the forty or fifty Shan informants who welcomed so warmly outsiders into the circle of their linguistic lives at a time when everyone was in stress.

Shan, this present work must be considered a first step as much greater bodies of linguistic data, information from local monasteries and archives, and social history of the Shan in various places would be required. I begin this task by discussing where the data for this paper were collected.

The data for this analysis represent speech samples from: (1) 德宏傣 Dehong Dai as spoken in 芒市 Mangshi (in Shan known as Mong Kwan မိူင်းၶွၼ်), just up the 瑞丽 Ruili River (pronounced *Shweli* in Yunnanese and known in Shan as the Nam Mao or ၼမ်ႉမၢဝ်း) – from a native speaker official, 郭玉平 Ms. Guo Yuping, who was attending a meeting in Sichuan Province in 1990; (2) Shan, Khamti, and Phake, collected during three linguistic fieldwork expeditions to the Union of Myanmar, and (3) non-northern tier languages studied during a trip in 2002 to 新平 Xinping County in Yunnan Province, China. My longest visit to Kachin State and Shan State was in December 1994, with subsequent trips to Singkhaling in October 1995 and Putao-O of Kachin State in June 1996. These trips allowed us to sample the Shan language across a wide range of the Shan and Khamti homeland in a breadth not possible for many years. As there was only limited time, I restricted my data gathering mostly to northern Shan venues, though I also interviewed several speakers from Taunggyi, Pan Long, and other locations near Yangon. Altogether I examined forty-three locations (about 50 speakers), including urban, semi-urban, and villages settings. I include here as well data gathered earlier from Shan speakers in Thailand and China. I have studied the vocabulary of the groups that call themselves: Tai Long, Tai Mao, Tai Liang, Tai Lɯa, Tai Taɯ, Tai Man, Tai Khamti, Tai Phake, Tai Manthi, Tai Tung, Tai Ting, Tai Lui, Tai Yay, Tai Saʔ, and Tai Loi. At each location I elicited and recorded about 500 words for later computer analysis of tone and voice quality contrasts. In many cases the groups lived in separate villages within the same close geographic area.

The locations I studied in 1994 took the Shweli River Valley on the China- Myanmar border as their point of focus, where the Shan Chronicles and historical documents tell us the Shan people first entered Burma from China, established their capital at Mong Mao, and then spread in the subsequent centuries to the southwest over present Southern Shan State, to the north into Khamti areas, and to the west to the Irrawaddy and Chindwin basins, and finally to Manipur and Assam in India (Elias 1876, Scott and Hardiman 1900). The Shweli River is regarded as the seat of Shan history, culture, and language. The southern areas, such as those at Taunggyi and Keng Tung, have perhaps come in for more intensive study in previous work, but these areas were settled much later and were brought much earlier under Burman suzerainty. I visited locations near larger towns and settlement areas such as: Myitkyina, Bhamo, Hsen Wi, and Lashio. I also incorporated data from various locations at Pan Long, Keng Tung, and Namhkam-Mu-se, as well as Mangshi and Xinping County of Yunnan Province, China, in order to compare my data with examples from SW Tai groups in China, but usually not regarded as northern tier languages cf. Luo 1993. In addition, I spent about 16 hours on an Ayeyarwady ferry traveling from near Katha to Bhamo. My fellow sojourners were mostly Shan traders and travelers from nearby territory. I was able to interview quite of number of them and include their data, but it was often not possible to locate their villages precisely from the names they provided. Lastly, I included some data gathered in Yangon from Shan informants from Kut Kai and Taunggyi.

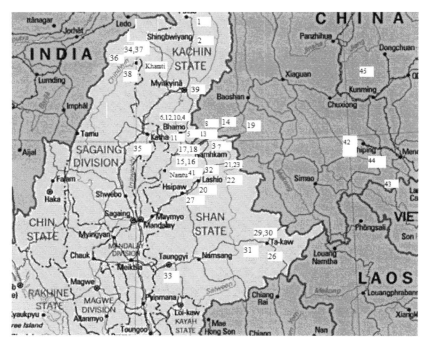

MAP 5.1-1: AREAS STUDIED, SHOWING THE APPROXIMATE LOCATION OF THE DATA SITES

On the visit to Singkaling on the upper reaches of the Chindwin River in the northwest part of Myanmar in Sagaing Division I interviewed Khamti speakers in a village south of the city at Manpang. In this area I also found speakers of Tai Phake originally from Assam in India, a monk (I had earlier obtained data from a Tai Phake woman in Bangkok), as well as other Shan speakers on the Chindwin further south at Homalin (in Shan called Hom Maak Leng), and at Tamanthi.[2] The visit in 1996 focused on Putao-O in Kachin State, which was settled by Khamti speakers. There several different speakers were interviewed and word lists taken.

Tai comparativists believe that there was a powerful principle underlying the relationship between the initials and tones in languages of the Tai branch active in the proto-language. While this relationship has been formulated in many ways, perhaps the most popular account is found in Wm J. Gedney's Checklist for Tai tones (1972). This system requires a division of the old initial consonants and tones into a grid of five columns and four rows that is generally called a *Gedney diagram*. The columns Gedney labels A, B, C, DL, and DS (A, B, and C being names for the proto-tone shapes in open syllables and DS and DL being those originally found in short and long closed syllables, respectively). The first three, A, B, and C are assumed to have been linguistically distinctive, whereas DL and DS, are thought to have been originally different only in length. The rows represent properties of the consonant initials in the proto-language; the first Row Gedney labeled 1, *voiceless friction*, including voiceless aspirated stops such as *ph, voiceless fricatives such as *f, and voiceless sonorants such as *hn; the second was called 2, *voiceless unaspirated stops* such as *p; the third was called 3, *glottal stop* *ʔ and *preglottalized consonants*, e.g., *ʔb; and the fourth was called 4, *voiced consonants* such as *b. At various places and times then, new tonal categories developed with

---

2   We were not able to gather any data on languages from Assam other than Phake.

the consonant initials causing small changes in pitch that ultimately led to new tonal categories. If every consonant split its tones – with DL and DS the first to differentiate based not on consonants but vowel length – then there could be maximally twelve tones (not counting the D tones). No Tai language has ever been found with so many splits. Generally, splitting or merging takes place between rows in a fashion that keeps contiguous boxes in the same category. For example, A1, A2, and A3 are distinct as a group from the tone found in vocabulary with original A4 initials, but according to the principle of *contiguity in splitting.* A1 and A3 could not ally to contrast to A2 and A4. While there are at times developments that blend a tone value in one column with the tone value in another, these are, generally speaking, more resistant to collapse than rows. One good example of splitting is the rule for the Northern Tai language subgroup (and in many other places as well), which generally divides between rows 3 and 4 so that 1, 2, and 3 consonant initials yielded the *High or Series 1* set of contrastive tones, one each for the columns A, B, C, DL, and DS, on the one hand, whereas Row 4, the voiced initials, engendered the *Low or Series 2* set of contrastive pitches, on the other. Usually, there was a concomitant loss of voicing contrast of the original stops and fricatives in Row 4 displacing the contrast from the initial consonant to the tone. The result was a language with five tones in Series 1 and five tones in Series 2; in each series there are three tone categories on open syllables, one on the short closed syllable, and one on the long closed syllable. Furthermore, the pitch trajectories of closed syllable tone categories were assumed to have assumed the pitch trajectory of open syllables, since the tone shapes of DL and DS resemble those of the open syllable tone categories, whereby the correspondence pattern between a D column and an A, B, or C column has been taken as evidence of different genetic subdivisions within a branch.

	A	B	C	DL	DS
1. voiceless friction					
2. voiceless unaspirated					
3. preglottalized					
4. voiced					

FIGURE 5.1-1: GEDNEY DIAGRAM OF TAI TONES

The major finding of my investigation is that the Shan nation is cloven linguistically into two major subtypes according to the pattern of tone splitting and consonant development. The system in the north of Shan territory has six tones, which may be described using the system of Gedney (1972) as: A1-A4; A23=B4, B123, C123-C4. The system in the south of Shan territory has five tones with tonal development: A123-A4, B123, B4=C123, and C4. These characteristic patterns are leitmotif identifiers for Northern Shan and Southern Shan, respectively, and these must be of some age, for – despite secondary mutations of the tonal system in Khamti and Phake, Shan tones conform well to one of these two prototypes.[3] It is to be noted, moreover, that the pattern of merger of B4 and C123 appears to be relatively wide-ranging, being found in Central Thai, Tai Kha, Tai Padi (China and Vietnam) and some kinds of Red Tai. One other feature of Shan is also strongly diagnostic, the change of initial ʔd → l or n that seems to have occurred at all Shan locations. But, as before, the loss of plosive articulation in favor of a sonorant is also found in younger Black/White Tai speakers as well as in SW Tai locations to the northeast of Shan territory in Yunnan, China at 元江 Yuanjiang, 武定 Wuding and other places, cf. Luo (1993: 7-8). Moreover, there is considerable variation in the pattern of 'dead' D-tone splitting. In sum, the tonal splitting has been emphasized in descriptions by Edmondson and Solnit (1997) as well as Robinson (1994)

---

3   Morey (2004, this volume) and later sections of this paper discuss Khamti and Phake, which may be examples of subsequent developments of the Northern Shan system.

as a necessary feature of the northern tier of Southwestern Tai. I am now able to confirm that this division is in fact a major watershed throughout Shan varieties.

The Shan language has also employed a writing system for some centuries. The older system was that used by Cushing in the late 19th century in his works. Since that time a new simplified script has been developed based upon Southern Shan sounds, which has been used for vernacular writing, cf. *Shan Magazine* and the *Shan New Testament* 1994, cf. Sao Tern Moeng 1995 for description in detail. Tones are indicated after each syllable with the following diacritics: A123 – no diacritic is added; A4 – the diacritic ꞉ is used; B123 – the diacritic ˌ is used; B4=C123 the diacritic ꞉ is used. For the sixth tone, A23=B4, in Northern Shan and for the 'Emphatic Tone…to put emphasis on any word' in Southern Shan the diacritic ꞊ is used. The twenty initials are: ၵ[k-], ၶ [kh-], င [ŋ-], ၸ [tɕ-], သ [s-], ၺ [ɲ-], တ [t-], ထ [th-], ၼ [n-], ပ [p-], ၽ [ph-], ၾ [f-], မ [m-], ယ [j-], ရ [r-], လ [l-], ဝ [w-], ႁ [θ], ႇ [h-], ဢ [ʔ-]. The nuclear vowels of the syllable are represented (if we use a randomly picked initial မ) as follows: မ [ʔɐ] (this nuclear vowel is often called the 'short a'), မႃ [ʔa] (this nuclear vowel is often called the 'long a'), မိ [ʔi], မေ [ʔe], မႄ [ʔɛ], မု [ʔu], မူဝ် [ʔo], မေႃ [ʔɔ], မိုဝ် [ʔɯ], and မႂ်ဝ် [ʔə]. There are slightly modified graphs for cases in which the vowel is in a closed syllable. The codas of syllables are formed from the graph of an initial plus a *vowel killer*, which is the graph[c], for example in the word လဵၵ်း [lek[DSi]]. Readers wishing to know more about the new Shan orthography and lexicon should consult Sao Tern Moeng (1995).

This paper is concerned with the patterns of sound changes I have discovered and their geographic distribution. These include the changes: (1) $f \rightarrow ph$, (2) the merger of *ʔd, n*, and *l* $\rightarrow l$, (3) the palatalization of k before i, to $tɕ$, (4) the breaking of $ɔ$ and $ɛ$ to $ɔa$ and $ɛa$ respectively, and (5) $kh \rightarrow x$. As has been found before, the five changes once splayed out on the geography of Shan locations in the form of isoglosses did not result in one sharply defined division between the various Shan villages, but showed instead *a pattern of implicational overlapping variation* in wave-like fashion across geographic space. For other changes there was a kind of *lectal fragmentation* without an obvious pattern of wavelike spread from an origin to the periphery. The lack of patterning for some changes suggests very extensive interdialectal mixing and interleaving from migration among groups originally speaking different form of the language. This phenomenon is characteristic especially of the area between Bhamo and Namhkam, which suggest an intrusion of speakers from outside into an area that was otherwise characterized by gradual change from place-to-place. This lack of pattern is compatible with the claim that the Tai Lua of this area have moved west from Yunnan into this area at a time in the not too distant past.

5.2. LOCATIONS STUDIED

In order to be able to refer to locations rapidly, I have assigned each place a number that corresponds approximately to the order in which the data were elicited from north to south. The speakers were interviewed in a variety of settings: at home, in a hotel room, in a village setting.

TABLE 5.2-1: SPEAKERS AND LOCATIONS STUDIED

	Location Autonym	Location	Number of speakers	Lg group
1.	Tai Khamti	Putao	two males; one female	Tai
	Tai Khamti	Hukawng	one female	Tai
3.	Tai Mao	Namhkam	two males	Tai
4.	Tai Lua	Namtieng	one speaker	Tai
5.	Tai Tau	Namlieng	one female speaker	Tai
6.	Tai Man	Nampha	two female speakers	Tai

7.	Tai Mao	Hamtɛ	three speakers	Tai
8.	Tai Long	Muang Wan	one female	Tai
9.	Tai Saʔ	Longchuan, China	one male	T-B
10.	Tai Luua	Myute	three speakers	Tai
11.	Tai Long	Lɔai tɕe	one speaker	Tai
12.	Tai Mao	Namhkam	two speakers	Tai
13.	Tai Man	Nampha	three speakers	Tai
14.	Tai Tauu	Mangshi	one female	Tai
15.	Tai Saʔ	Namhkam	one male	T B
16.	Tai Loi	Namhkam	one speaker	M-K
17.	Tai Luua	Mu-se	three males	Tai
18.	Tai Mao	Mu-se	two males	Tai
19.	Tai Tauu	Hsen Wi	one female	Tai
20.	Tai Long	Hopang	one female	Tai
21.	Tai Mao	Lashio	one female	Tai
22.	Tai Ting	Kunlong	one female	Tai
23.	Tai Loi	Namhsan	one female	M-K
24.	Tai Lɛng	Namhsan	one male, one female	Tai
25.	Tai Khuun	Keng Tung	one male	Tai
26.	Tai Tauu	Hsipaw	one male	Tai
27.	Tai Man		one male	Tai
28.	Tai Nui	Keng Tung	one female	Tai
29.	Tai Luua	Keng Tung	one female	Tai
30.	Tai Yay	Pan Long	one male/one female	Tai
31.	Tai Long	Kutkai	one female	Tai
32.	Tai Long	Taunggyi	one female	Tai
33.	Tai Khamti	Khamti	two male speakers	Tai
34.	Tai Liang	Banmauk	one female	Tai
35.	Tai Ho	Homalin maaklang	one female	Tai
36.	Tai Tong	Singkaling	one male	Tai
37.	Tai Phake	Man Phake	one male	Tai
38.	Tai Lɛng	Man Maxo	one male; one female	Tai
39.	Tai Sau	Sambaiyue	two female speakers	Tai
40.	Tai	Namtu	one female	Tai
41.	Tai Kha, Ya	Xinping, China	three male	Tai
42.	Tai Dam, Don	Jinping, China	Luo 1993, Dao 2000, Chen and Zhang	Tai
43.	Tai	Yuanjiang	Luo 1993	Tai
44.	Tai	Wuding	Luo 1993	Tai

Before turning to the empirical analysis, however, I provide some of the social history of the Shan ethnicity stressing their dynastic succession and sense of ethnic identity and ethnic division.

5.3. A GLIMPSE AT SHAN SETTLEMENT HISTORY

As can be seen in Table 5.2-1, there are a large number of autonyms and subgroups among the Shan according to traditional taxonomy. The Shan call themselves *Tai* plus a noun or adjective of restriction, *Tai Lɯa* (the Upper Tai), *Tai Long* (the Great Tai), *Tai Man* (the Burmese Tai), etc. This situation is the natural result of the Shan hereditary system of local autonomy, as the Shan were, for many centuries, governed by a local noble or *saopha* 'prince' (Burmese and English *Sawbwa*) and lesser Sawbwa were tributary to greater Sawbwa, but there remained in the majority of their history a relatively large degree of local autonomy and a sense of identification with a geographic location. Elias reports that the Shan settlements in Myanmar were first established at Mong Mao on the Shweli by the Mao Shan '13 miles east of Namhkam and close to the frontier' (Scott and Hardiman I.195) (tradition says in AD 569 but probably later).

Although there was no continuous and sustained seat of central power among the Shan, there are periods in which the Shan were annexing territory and periods of contraction and finally great suffering and loss of independence under siege from the Chinese (in the early days), from the Burmese (esp. in the 17th and 18th centuries), and the Kachin (in the 19th century). The maximum extent of the Mao Kingdom was reached in the early 13th century under the Conquistador Sam Long Pha (in Shan သၢမ်လူင်ၽႃႉ), the first Sawbwa of Mong Kawng (Burmese Mogaung). The Mogaung court outlasted Mong Mao by one hundred fifty years. Sam Long Pha ruled over 99 lesser Sawbwas whose territory reached up to the western border of Burma and beyond into Assam in India. These included the provinces of: Khamti, Singkaling Khamti on the Chindwin River, Huhkawng, and several others. The lack of a constant central authority and a governing capital resulted in a rather large number of subgroups or ethnicities within a larger Shan nation or Confederation.

Shan society shows another distinctive feature of Highland Burma in that their political, social, and ethnic networks display *categories*, cf. the discussion in Leach 1954 of how people's ethnicity can change as they move down the mountain to places of lower elevation. People groups that were once not linguistically and culturally *Shan* are now regarded as *Shan* and they often are accepted as members of the Shan confederation and legitimate participants in the hydrological system needed for wet paddy rice cultivation. This phenomenon seemed especially common around Namhkam, where I encountered two groups, the *Tai Saʔ* and the *Tai Loi*. The languages spoken by these two proved to be Achang 阿昌 (Tibeto-Burman or TB) and De'ang 德昂 (Mon-Khmer or MK) respectively, but the groups partake in Shan society and government, speak the local language, celebrate the local feast days, and wear a variation on the local dress. This kind of system, as Leach reports, is also well established among the Kachin of Kachin State to the north, a confederation made up of the core group, the Jingphaw, and groups of lesser size, the Maru, Zaiwa, and Langsu etc. Similarly, around Namhkam the groups called Tai Saʔ and Tai Loi are original non-Shan ethnicities who are today members of the Shan category, (Leach 1954: 29-30), who still speak their original Tibeto-Burman and Mon-Khmer languages as well as Shan. As Leach reports, the most important feature of belonging to the *Shan* category is *being Buddhist* and the second feature is being *engaged in wet paddy rice cultivation*. He noted in the 50's that the Achang met both these tests, but though the 'Palaung' were Buddhists, they lived in the mountains and cultivated tea and not rice, so they were excluded.[4] It is unclear to us whether the Tai Loi today are the same as Leach's 'Palaung' and whether they are now regarded as belonging to

---

4   The Palaung are a MK language of this general area. The Tai Loi speak another MK language, however.

the Shan category. I would note that they were identified to us by other Shan and they identified themselves as 'Tai' and thus they may have crossed the ethnic line of demarcation into full membership in the Shan confederation since the 1950s.

5.3.1. Tai Khamti

One group, once ruled by the Mogaung Shan, are the Tai Khamti, who have traditionally been regarded as a group distinct from the Shan. It appears that originally they were quite unlike the Shan. At least Dr Cushing talks about the Khamti and the Burman Shan as if they were different groups (1888a, 1888b). There is some basis for this view, as the Khamti are thought to have had an independent existence until the time of Sam Long Pha (Elias 1876: 39f). He was the brother and general of the Mong Mao Emperor (Chaukwam Pha), who in AD 1220 conquered much of Upper Burma and the territory to the west of the Chindwin including Manipur and Assam. Later, however, the Khamti areas were ruled by the Mao Shan Kings and sought their protection, for later they were virtually driven out Huhkawng Valley by Kachin raiding. So at the turn of the century there were Shan only 100 miles north of Mogaung (Scott and Hardiman I.201) 'and their rulers were always tributary to the power that held Mogaung, and it cannot be said that the population retains more direct Tai characteristics than their Mogaung and Mohnyin neighbors.' Still, even today Shan scholars feel an ethnic difference between Shan and Khamti, attaching an adjective to their moniker. As Sao Tern Moeng (1995: xi) says, '... K.S. (for Khamti Shan) which is the language of the Shans of the northwestern part of Burma.' While I found phonological, lexical, and orthographical differences in Khamti, it was on linguistic grounds closely related to Burman Shan.

The Tai Khamti live today in the northernmost and westernmost settlement areas where Shan are found, e.g., in the community at Putao-O, which is located in Kachin State about 75 km due north of Myitkyina in the valley of the Mali Hka, the major tributary of the Irrawaddy. This valley extends almost to the three-way border between, Myanmar, China, and India. I also studied the Khamti of the Huhkawng Valley to the west of Putao-O. According to Scott (1900) this area was once populated exclusively by Shan but they were gradually replaced by the Kachin until only a few settlements remained at the end of the 19th c. The largest of these was at Mong Khwan (Maing Kwan). The final area of Khamti settlement is at Singkaling Khamti at the northern end of the valley of the Chindwin. People there claim ancestry from Putao-O via Huhkawng Valley.

5.3.2. Tai Mao

The second group among the Shan nation I studied live in Mong Mao or မိုင်းမောင်း This is the group who dwell on the banks of the Shweli or Nam Mao. They acquired the name Mao at the time they established Mong Mao on the Shweli River opposite the current city of Namhkam. They are the ones referred to by the Chinese as the *Baiyi* 白夷 or 百夷 and by the Burmese as the *Shan gji* or Great Shan. According to Elias (1876), 'they sometimes speak of themselves as Tai-Lung or Great Shan. But this is no real distinction. The Siamese speak of them as Tai *güt* or left-behind Tais (those that did not come in Ayudia and form a kingdom). To the Assamese they are known under the name Sam; to the Munnipuris as Kapo (Kabbo) or Pong, etc &.' I found, however, that today the terms *Tai Mao* and the *Tai Long/Lung* are not completely coextensive. The usual distinction was that the term Tai Mao designated those Shan who live directly on the Shweli; those not found on the Shweli were the Tai Long. To the north and west around Bhamo and to the east in Dehong Prefecture in China are the people groups known as *Tai Nwa/Lwa*.

5.3.3. Tai Long

The third designation, Tai Long, is more difficult to identify with a location, as tradition asserts that the Shan of Upper Burma (Scott and Hardiman 195) 'are always spoken of by other branches of the Tai family as the Tai Long, Great Shans, while the other branches call themselves Tai Noi, or Little Shans.' But during my trip speakers categorize themselves as Tai Long as opposed to Tai Mao or Tai Lwa, even at Namhkam and Mu-se. So, they seem to be saying that the Tai Long are also a subbranch of the Tai. Scott opines that Tai Long may also refer to the Shan-Tayok or Shan-Chinese, those coming from China. I did not find the autonym Tai Long among speakers much north of the Shweli, in Chinese territory. But south of there to Lashio that was a common appellative.

5.3.4. Tai Nɯa/Lɯa

If we count the Tai Long as a third group, then the Tai Lɯa/Nɯa are a fourth. In Shan *Nɯa* means 'upper on the course of a river; above; or north'; among the Tai Nɯa speakers the term *Nɯa* is usually pronounced *Lɯa*. They are generally found north of the Shweli and make up the majority of the Shan found in Chinese territory. It can also mean 'north'. But both *north* and *upper* cry out for a reference point 'north of what' and 'above what'. The answer is probably north of Mong Mao or above it on the Shweli River.

5.3.5. Tai Man

The fifth group call themselves Tai Man. The modifying term *Man* or မန်; in Shan script means 'Burma, Myanmar; Burma Proper, the region inhabited by the Burmese, as distinguished from the ethnic minorities'. It is presumably a borrowing from the Burmese language [mjan] or မြန်. It is said that the Tai Man are the descendents of mixed Shan and Burman ethnicity. Though I found just as Scott surmised 'The people, whether they are called Shan-Burmese, Kadu, Pwon (or Hpon), have certainly more of the Tai than of the Burman about them.' (201). Anderson (1876) says that the population of Bhamo consisted mostly of Shan-Burmese in 1868. I found them today in a separate village, Nampha, but their language seems to have no larger number of Burmese loanwords than are found in other kinds of Shan. It is, however, phonologically not identical to other kinds.

5.3.6. Tai Laing

A sixth group among the Shan are the Tai Laing. This group probably constitutes the descendants of the Shan who lived under the Sawbwaship of Mong Lɛng, Burmese Mohlaing). That was one of the territories ruled from the Mogaung when it rose to importance after Sam Long Pha, the Shan conqueror of Assam. In the late 1880s this territory caused British rule perennial trouble under the rebellious Hkam Leng (Burmese Kan Hlaing). As a result, their district was divided and assigned to Mong Mit (Scott and Hardiman 1900 I.340ff). I was helped by two informants, Mr Sai Tshun Sing, born 1934, and Ms. Haɯ Pjenmen, born 1956. They are resident in the village called Man Maxo, very near to Myitkyina. I studied a group of them in a village north of Myitkyina on the banks of the Ayeyarwady (Irrawaddy). I was told there were other villages on the other side of the river as well. Some reports also suggest that they also dwell west of Katha Town west of the Ayeyarwady near the village of Banmauk. However, the language of Banmauk was not identical that of Man Maxo as I discovered when I interviewed speakers from there. Features are: *ʔd, *n → l, *kh → x, *f → f. Tones are: A1-A23-A4, B123, B4=A23, C123-C4. They call themselves [tai^{A4} laiŋ^{A3}] 'Red Tai', which Proto-Tai *iɛ → ɛ → ai demonstrating a change found widely in Burmese, e.g. Mohlaing for Mong Lɛng and Burmese influenced Shan varieties. Many lexical items in this kind of Shan are bisyllabic.

5.3.7. Tai Ting

The seventh group I studied call themselves Tai Ting, presumably because they live on the Ting River where it joins the Thanlwin (Salween). It is situated in territory just to the west of 耿马傣族佤族自治县 Gengma Dai-Wa Autonomous County in China.

5.3.8. Tai Taɯ

The eighth group represented in my corpus is the Tai Taɯ. In Shan *Taɯ* means 'space beneath; south', presumably from being lower on the Shweli or simply south. I found that people as far north as Hsen Wi used this autonym. This term may apply to all the Shan in Southern Shan

State except the Tai Khun near Keng Tung.

Perhaps a variety of Tai Tauu is the group I studied calling itself Tai Sau. I interviewed two women from the village of Sambaiyue, exact location unknown, but presumably not far from the Ayeyarwady as they were passengers on the ferry. This kind of Shan had five tones A123-A4, B123, B4=C123, C4 with other changes *ʔd → l, *kh → x, and *n and *nl and *f were preserved unchanged as [n] and [f]. The diphthong [auu] had not changed to [ai]. As described above for Southern Shan, /s/ contrasted with /sɦ/ with the former deriving from /tɕ/ and the latter from /s/.

5.3.9. The Tai Khun and Tai Nui

The ninth and tenth groups I examined, the Tai Khun and Tai Nui are located much further south and east than the others at Keng Tung in the Golden Triangle. They were rather different phonologically and lexically from the varieties of Shan west of the Thanlwin (Salween). For instance Tai Nui demonstrated a variant of six tone Shan with the system A1-A23-A4, B123, B4=A23, C123-C4. Also *ʔd → l and a few *nl → l, *f → f and even *ph → f (perhaps a case of hypercorrection, as e.g. fak^{DS1} 'vegetable' has replaced the historical form $phak^{DS1}$.

5.3.10. Tai Phake

I was able to elicit data from a monk originally from Assam in India. He had been living in Singkaling in NW Myanmar on the Chindwin for about 15 years. I also obtained data from a woman originally from Dibrugarh District in Assam. At the time of the interview in November 1995 I estimated his age to have been 70. Linguistically speaking, Tai Phake is quite close to Khamti with slight tone differences. It shows the important diagnostic ʔb → m and ʔd → n like Khamti, e.g. $*bin^{A3}$ → min^{A3} 'to fly' and $*ʔdoi$ → noi^{A3} 'mountain'. This sound change must have occurred after the arrival of the Ahom in Assam Province, as many of the place names said to be of Ahom origin and, indeed, the original Ahom script do not show this change. With regard to the change kh → x Tai Phake is in the middle ground. It has an affricate kx instead of kh.

5.3.11. Tai Saʔ

The group known as Tai Saʔ also speak a tonal language, but it is not a Tai language. Instead this group speaks a variety of Ngochang, known in China as *Achang*. The phonology I found in their speech was similar to that described for Longchuan 陇川 County in Dehong Prefecture. The Shan historian Professor U Sai Aung Tun has told us that the Tai Saʔ originally came from China to work as blacksmiths among the Shan. They are also mentioned by Luce (1985: 104), who calls them the Maingtha, dwellers in ancient homes along the middle Ta-p'ing River, which enters the Irrawaddy at Bhamo, parallelling the river on the China side of the frontier in two small towns called Hu-sa and La-sa. Thus, the area is called in Shan Muung Saʔ and in Burmese, Maingtha. Luce accounts that there were less than 500 in Burmese territory in 1931. The population in China according to the 阿昌语简志 *Achangyu jianzhi* is 13,000.

5.3.12. Tai Loi

Tai Loi are the Tai of the mountain loi^{A3}. The data from Tai Loi proved to be a non-tonal language resembling De'ang, in the past called Benglong 崩龙; a comparison of some Tai Loi showed it to resemble the Bulei subtype of De'ang in Chinese sources. It is reported to be similar to Silver Palaung, a Mon-Khmer language of Myanmar.

5.3.13. Tai Dam and Don

Tai Don is the autonym of the relatively well-known White Tai of Vietnam, Laos, and China. Here I provide data from Jinping County of southern Yunnan. According to Dao Jie (2000: 204), Tai Don retains *ʔb and *ʔd in $ʔbau^{33}$ 'thin' and $ʔdu^{33}$ 'to see', unlike the northern tier of SW Tai languages, which have *ʔb → m or v and *ʔd → l or n. It does share with the northern tier of SW Tai the change *kh → x, cf. xa^{33} 'leg', $xwaan^{33}$ 'axe', $xwaa^{33}$

'right', and xwaai[42] 'water buffalo'. Other rules described above for northern tier languages are not found in Tai Don.

5.3.14. Tai Kha, Tai Xa, and Tai Ya.

The Tai Kha, Tai Xa, and Tai Ya of Xinping County of Yunnan Province on the 红河 or Red River are known as the 花腰傣 'Flowery-waisted Tai' for their elaborate and unique style of women's clothing. Their language has five tones A1, A234, B123, B4 = C123, C4. It has several features in common with Shan, for example: $*\text{?da}\text{ŋ}^A \rightarrow la\text{ŋ}^{43}$ 'nose', $*\text{ɣwaa} \rightarrow xaai^{A4}$ 'buffalo' $*\text{khwaa A} \rightarrow xa^{A1}$ 'right'.

5.4. COMPARATIVE RESULTS

5.4.1. Shan phonological basics

Shan has five or six tones in open syllables and typically three or four tones in closed syllables. The writing system is based on southern forms of Shan centered at Taunggyi. An example of the tonal pattern for the northern areas of Shan, which I will call Type 1 Shan, as spoken in Mangshi would be:

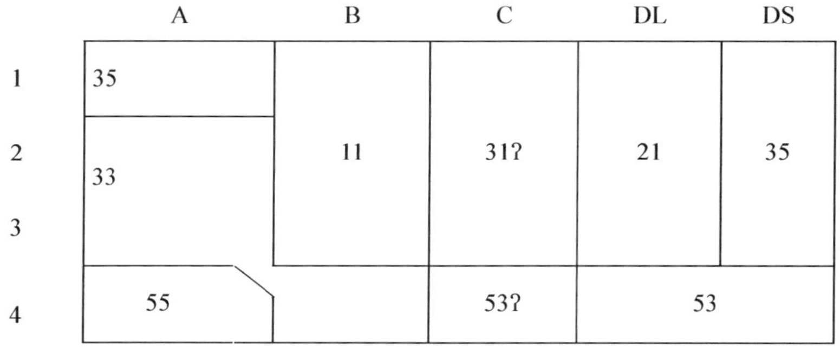

	A	B	C	DL	DS
1	35	11	31?	21	35
2	33				
3					
4	55		53?	53	

FIGURE 5.4.1-1: NORTHERN SHAN TONE VALUES AS A FUNCTION OF PROTO-TAI TONE CATEGORIES AND INITIAL CONSONANTS

Tai Khamti of Putao in extreme northern Myanmar has a very similar system except that, in addition to the system in Figure 5.4.1-1, A1 and B123 have merged. The principle informants for this data were Mr Soi Kwoi, born 1924, Ms. Soi Noi Sieng, born 1932, and Mr Saw New Sar Daw, born 1927. All were originally from Putao but lived at the time in Myitkyina, Kachin State.

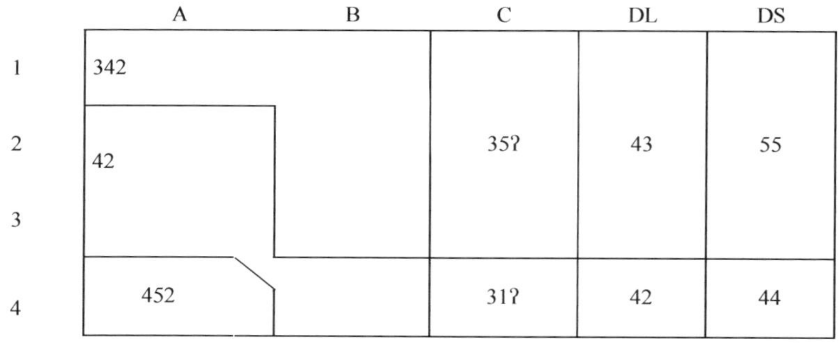

	A	B	C	DL	DS
1	342		35?	43	55
2	42				
3					
4	452		31?	42	44

FIGURE 5.4.1-2: KHAMTI TONE VALUES AS A FUNCTION OF PROTO-TAI TONE CATEGORIES AND INITIAL CONSONANTS

The tones of Southern or Type 2 Shan should be contrasted with those of northern Shan and Khamti. The tone data here is from Taunggyi, as is found in the speech of Daw Nang Vo Khang, Assistant Librarian of the Shan State Library.

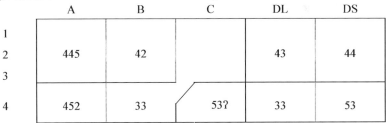

FIGURE 5.4.1-3: SOUTHERN SHAN TONE VALUES AS A FUNCTION OF PROTO-TAI TONE CATEGORIES AND INITIAL CONSONANTS

Southern Shan has five tones in open syllables and four tones in closed syllables as follows:

Tone	category	Tone value
Tone 1	(A123)	445
Tone 2	(A4)	55
Tone 3	(C123)=Tone 6 (B4)	33̲
Tone 4	(C4)	53?
Tone 5	(B123)	42̲
Tone 7L	(DL123)	43
Tone 8L	(DL4)	33
Tone 7S	(DS123)	44
Tone 8S	(DS4)	53

It is noteworthy that B123 as well as B4=C123 have creaky voice. The tone categories C4 shows a falling pitch trajectory and ends in glottal constriction. The closure for several tokens averaged about 70 milliseconds and should be contrasted to the creaky voice quality that ends the B123 syllable, which takes nearly twice as long (average 150 msec.) and makes a very different audio impression. The division between the five tone and six tone types of Shan runs surprisingly far north. Daw Saw Khin Gyi from Kut Kai demonstrates the five tone type even though Kut Kai is only 60 km south of Mu-se on the Shweli. Five tone systems are found also at Kunlong and Ho-pang to the east of Kut Kai on the Nam Ting near the Chinese border.

One final language deserves special mention, namely Tai Phake. Most of these people live in Northeast India as Morey reports. There are a few in Myanmar near the border. I was able to gather data from one of these speakers. The tonal analysis I obtained is identical to that in Morey 2004.

In the A1 tone category the pitch starts at mid level and drops a very little before rising to the highest level (about 60 semitones). The A234 category begins mid (about 58 semitones) rises slightly and the falls to about 52 semitones. I record these as 335 and 342 respectively. The B tones are level with the upper one slightly higher. The C tones for this speaker differ a little from the report in Morey. The C123 tones fall from 58 to 55 semitones (but for some words they fall more). Often there is a slight rise before the creaky voice, value 32̲, but sometimes this tone may end lower than C4. The C4 tone ends in glottal constriction in this speaker. The dead tones are not distinguished for length; the DL123 and DS123 have a value of 58 semitones; where the DL4 and DS4 are falling with value 31.

	A	B	C	DL DS
1	335			
2		33	3$\underset{\sim}{2}$	33
3	342			
4		22	21?	31

FIGURE 5.4.1-4: PHAKE TONE VALUES AS A FUNCTION OF PROTO-TAI TONE CATEGORIES AND INITIAL CONSONANTS

5.4.2. Consonant changes in Shan

There are roughly seven changes in initial consonants in the kinds of Shan I have studied. Some of these represent changes that are far advanced to the point of being nearly complete; others are rather restricted in application and may represent incipient change. In northern locations the original wide groove fricatives and affricates become the affricate *ts-*, whereas in Southern Shan the reflex is *s-*. On the other hand, original *s is retained in Northern Shan but become aspirated *s* in Southern Shan. They are kept separate in the Shan writing system ∞ is /ts/ and ∞ is /s/. For many speakers in the south, *ts* has become *s* and the sound signified by ∞ in Shan script is aspirated /sɦ/. The two can be exemplified by *sa⁴* 'angry' and *sɦa⁴* 'basket'. In the south there is a definite burst of air before the *s* in 'basket' not found in 'angry'. Northern Shan seems not to have this contrast. Thus, I can compare Northern and Southern Shan sibilants as follows (proto-forms from Li 1977):

Source	Gloss	Northern	Southern
*dʑ	boy, male	tsaai²	saai²
*dʑ	elephant	tsaaŋ⁴	saaŋ⁴
*dʑ	artisan	tsaaŋ⁶	saaŋ⁶
*tɕh	prince, lord	tsau³	sau³
*s	three	saam¹	sɦaam¹
*s	four	si⁵	sɦi⁵
*s	unmarried girl	sau¹	sɦau¹
*z	wash (hands)	sak⁸	sɦak⁸
*z	wash (surface)	suk⁸	sɦuk⁸
*s	tiger	suɯ¹	sɦuɯ¹
*s	pillar	sau¹	sɦau¹
*s	tall, high	suŋ¹	sɦuŋ¹

It is quite evident that in both forms of Shan the original contrast is maintained, but it is maintained in different manners. Southern Shan seems to evidence peculiar sound shift like phenomenon in which *s/z → /sɦ/ and *tɕh/dʑ - > /s/. In the figure below I give an airflow diagram of a minimally contrasting Southern Shan pair *sɦa^{A1}* 'basket' (top) vs. *sa^{A1}* 'angry'. Both waves are plotted on the same time scale. The upper track shows a period of strong airflow during the production of fricative air stream /sɦ/ in comparison to the much lower air stream of /s/. This sound change is strong reminiscent of developments in the history of Burmese. The modern standard language of Yangon, for example, also makes a distinction between s/sɦ. An informal look at the airflow of several Burmese speakers and Shan speakers pronouncing Burmese vocabulary demonstrates diagrams (not presented here). Bradley (1978) suggests an identical pattern of change has occurred with proto-Burmic *s becoming aspirated and *ts becoming /s/.

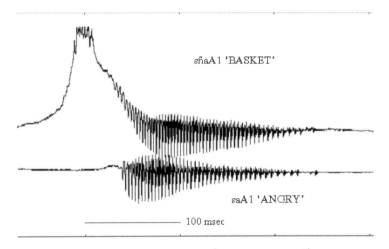

FIGURE 5.4.2-1: TAUNGGYI SHAN *Sɦa^{al}* 'BASKET' VS *sa^{al}* 'ANGRY'.

Sound changes in several locations are presented in Table 5.4.2-1:

TABLE 5.4.2-1: A COMPARISON OF SOUND CHANGE IN SHAN LOCATIONS

Site	Tone	*kh,	*f	*v	*?d/ *?dl	*l	*n, *nl	*?b/ *?bl	m	kw	ɔ/ɛ	ki	auɯ	ŋ
1	1	x~kx	ph	ph	l/n	l/n	n	n	m	k, x	ɔa/ia	tɕi	auɯ	ŋ
2	1	kh	ph	ph	n/l	l	n	m/l	mb	khw	ɔa/iɛ	tɕi	auɯ	ŋ
3	1	x	f	f	l	l	l	m/l	m	k	ɔ/ia	tɕi	auɯ	ŋ
4	1	x, kx	f	f	l	l~ld	l	m/l	m	k	ɔ/iɛ	tɕi	auɯ	ŋ
5	1	x	f	f	l	l	l	m	m	k	ɔ	tɕi	auɯ	ŋ
6	1	x~kw	ph	f	l	l	n	m	m	kw	ɔa/ia	tɕi	auɯ	ŋ
7	1	x~k	ph	ph~f	ld	ld	l	mb	mb	x	ɔa/ia	tɕi	auɯ	ŋg
8	1	x	f	f	ld/nd	nd	ld/nd	mb/l	mb	x	ɔa/ia	tɕi	auɯ	ŋg
11	1	x	f	f	ld/l	ld	ld	m/ld	mb	x	ɔa/ia	ki	auɯ	ŋg

12	1	x	ph	f	l	n	n	m	m	xw	ɔa	tɕi	aɯ	ŋ
14	1	x	ph	f	ld	ld	l	mb	mb	k	ɔa	ki	aɯ	ŋ
17		kh~x	f	f	l	l	n~l	m	m	k	ɔ	ki	aɯ	ŋ
18			ph	f	l	l	n~l	m	m	k	ɔ		aɯ	ŋ
20	2	khw ~kw	ph	f	l~n	l	n	m/l	m	kw	ɔ/ɛ	ki	aɯ	ŋ
21	2	kh	ph	ph	l	l	n	mb/l	m	k	ɔ	ki	ai	ŋ
22	1	x	f	f	l	l	n	m/l	m	x	ɔ	ki	aɯ	ŋ
23	2	x~kh	f	f	l	l	n	m/l	m	k	ɔ	ki	aɯ	ŋ
25	1	x	ph	fh	l	l	l	m	m	xw	ɔa/ai	tɕi	ai	ŋ
26	2	kh	ph	f	l	l	n	w	m	k			ai	ŋ
27	2		ph	f	l	l	m	m					aɯ	ŋ
29	2	kh~x	ph	f	l	l	ld	v/l	m	k	ɔ/ia	ki	ai	ŋ
31	2	kh	ph	f~ph	l	l		m/l	m	kw	ɔ/iɛ		aɯ	
32	2	kw			l	l	n	m	m	kw	iɛ	tɕi		
33	2	kh~x			l	l	n	v/m	m	kw	/ia	ki		
34	1	x.	ph	ph	n	l	n	m/l	m	kw		tɕi	aɯ	
35	1	x	f~ph	f	l/l	l~n	n	m	m	x	/ia	tɕi	aɯ	ŋ
36	1	kh	f~ph	f	n		n	m/l	m	k	ɔa/ɛ	ki	ai	ŋ
37	1	kh	ph	ph	n~l	n	n	n/l	m	kw~k	ɔa/ɛ	tɕi	aɯ	ŋ
38	1	x~kx	ph	ph	n	l	n	m/n	m	xw	ɔa/iɛ		aɯ	ŋ
39		x	f	f	l	l	l			x~xw	ɔa/ia	çi	aɯ~ai	ŋ
40		xw	f	f	l	l	n	/l	m	xw	ɔa/iɛ	tɕi	aɯ	
41	2	kh	ph	ph	l/n	l	n	m/m	m	kw	ɔa /ia	tɕi	ai	ŋ
42	2	x			n~l	l								ŋ
43	Not1 or 2		ph	ph	ʔd~l	l	n	ʔb~v/l		k				ŋ

5.4.3. Deplosivization

There is one sound change that seems to be found in all kinds of Shan, both north and south. That change involves deplosivization, the stop component, a preglottalized *d* (written /ʔd-/) changes to /l/ and preglottalized *b* (written /ʔb-/) changes to *m* or *v*. Some examples of deplosivization are: *mi^1 mu^1* 'bear' (Tai Laing of Maan Maxo). Deplosivization in some places near the China border may widen the class of candidates for this rule by extending the change having /n/ change to /l/ (in syllable initial position; there are no instances of syllables with coda -*l*; only -*n* is found). In the north and west in Tai Khamti deplosivization travels another path, namely /ʔd/ becomes /n/; and predictably then a few case of /l/ become subject to this rule and develop into /n/ as well.

There is a tendency of n to follow in the wake of *ʔd* in deplosivization showing the forces of patterning in sound change. In fact, the propensity of /ʔb ʔd/ to disappear in favor of *m* or *w* and *l* or *n* respectively, is widespread in the northern tier of SW Tai. Indeed, Luo (1993: 8) provides data that shows these changes are found outside Shan to include many non-Shan northern tier languages. The White and Black Tai of Jinping County 金平县 are currently undergoing this change. Older speakers have /ʔb ʔd/, whereas speakers of the middle years have partially changed these to /v l/ respectively, and younger speakers use /v l/ to a very high degree. The Tai Hongjin varieties, cf. Luo 1993, (at all but one or two locations) show the same developments /ʔb/ -> /v/ and /ʔd/ -> /l/. For example, an *l* initial is found in *ʔdam^1

'black' and *ʔdaau[1] 'star', but only Mangshi, Namtieng, Namlieng, Nampha, and Lashio have the $n \to l$ development, e.g. in *nlam[C] 'water' becoming lam[4]. These areas run from the very southeastern reaches of Yunnan Province to trans-Chindwin Burma and from Chiangrai Province, Thailand to Sichuan Province China. This change is even found outside the SW Tai branch, as some forms of Zhuang in Guangxi Province also have this change.

Lc	*n	*ʔd/ʔdl	*l	*ʔb	*ʔbl	*m
4	l	l	l~ld	m	l	m
3	l	l	l	l	l	m
5	l	l	l	m		m
7	l	ld	ld	mb		mb
25	l	l	l	m		m
14	l	ld	ld	mb		mb
11	ld	ld/l	ld	mb	ld	mb
8	ld	ld/nd	nd	mb	l	mb
29	ld	l	l	v	l	m
39	l	l	l			
17	n~l	l	l	m		m
18	n~l	l	l	m		m
22	n	l	l	m	l	m
40	n	l	l		l	m
6	n	l	l	m		m
41	n	l/n	l	m	m	m
Hongjin	n	l	l			
21	n	l	l	mb	l	m
23	n	l	l	m	l	m
26	n	l	l	w		m
43	n	l	l	v		l
30	n					
31	n	l	l	m	l	m
35	n	l/l	l~n	m		m
32	n	l	l	m		m
33	n	l	l	v|m		m
12	n	l	n	m		m
20	n	l~n	l	m	l	m
2	n	n~l	l	m	l	mb
42		n~l	l			
34	n	n	l	m	l	m
37	n	n	l	m	l	m
38	n	n	l	m	n	m
1	n	l~n	l~n	n		m
36	n	n	n	m	l	m

FIGURE 5.4.3-1: DEPLOSIVIZATION OF /ʔd/ → /l/, /ʔb/ → /m/, /ʔbl/ → /l/, AND VARIABLY /n/ → /l/

The changes begin with the rule ʔd → l and then the subsequent spread of this rule to encompass the change n → l. These mutations are, of course, variable, occurring in overlapping patterns. As can be seen in areas from Mangshi to Bhamo along the Myanmar-China border the *ʔd in the SWT parent language has changed to l virtually everywhere. To the south in Southern Shan territory, in the west, and in the east only ʔd is changed. The only exceptions are the territory of the Khamti in the far north, where *ʔd → n and then *l → n. Indeed, this irregular phonological correspondence is (along with lexical differences) the most significant linguistic shibboleths for Khamti, e. g. *nuuan^A3* 'moon' from *ʔduuan^A3* and *pha^C2 nuŋ^C2* 'sky-screams, thunder' from *faa^C2 ruŋ^C2*. There are still many examples of Khamti *l* from *l, e.g. *lum^A4* 'wind' from *lom^A4*; the change of *l*. But, concentrating on the non-Khamti forms for the moment, I also see evidence in location 38 of a sound change that began by mutating *ʔd* to *l*, as in most places, and then at a later time *n* also changed to *l*. According to Grierson (1928) Ahom had *ʔd-*. We know, moreover, from reports in Chinese sources, such as Wang (1984: 212-14) that the *l* reflex is characteristic for large areas of Dehong Prefecture in Yunnan to the east. My own study of Guo Yuping from Mangshi also found the *l* reflex (Edmondson and Solnit 1994). The change n → l is not universal in Myanmar and is strongest in territory between Bhamo and Namhkam. It is most clearly associated with groups that refer to themselves as Tai Luua [lə¹], although others now have it as well. This pattern seems to be the result of immigration of Tai Luua speakers in relatively recent times and does not seem to be the result of a pattern of wavelike change.

A clue to the mechanism of deplosivization is also in evidence on the Sino-Myanmar border area. At Mangshi and other locations studied by Ed Robinson (Mau Hong Tai Mao from tape recorded August 1994), my own recordings of speakers from a place called Nam Kha, and Jimmy G. Harris (pc) realize /m/ as a very short prenasalized voiced stop [m̃b] and lateral /l/ as a very short lateral or nasal plus d, i.e. [ld n̆d], *mbe^B4* 'mother' and *m̃bu^A1* 'pig' and *n̆din^A4* 'tongue'. Edmondson et al. (2004) show from laryngoscopic study of Sui, a Kam-Sui language of Guizhou, China, that preglottalization involves a moderate glottal stop articulation released into a voiced stop. If the sphincteric gesture for the glottal stop were to involve the velic valve above the glottal aperture and then to transfer entirely to the velic area, the change of ʔb → m̃b would be complete. This development is not of great age, since it has now started to operate on *m* and *l/n* segments irrespective of whether they are from the historical sources *m̥*, *ʔb*, or *m*, and similarly with *l*, as Table 5.4.2-1 shows.

5.4.4. Lenition of /kh/ to /x/

The velars in SWT are known to be especially subject to change. In some cases it appears as if the *kh* is in reality *kx* or *kx̱* in variation with *kh*.

Loc	*kh	Loc	*kh
14	kh	12	x
29	kh	22	x
2	kh	23	x
21	kh	30	x
26	kh	6	x
Hongjin	kh	25	x
17.	kh/x	7	x
		1	x
		18	x
		39	x

FIGURE 5.4.4-1: CHANGE OF /kh/ TO /x/ IN SHAN BY REGION

This change is especially noticeable in Tai Lə territory of Yunnan Province at Dehong Prefecture, but also it is found in Bhamo. It has spread to Putao-O in the far north among that kind of Khamti, but it is not found in the Khamti found in the Huhkawng Valley to the west. The unchanged *kh* is found south of line passing east-west through Lashio.

5.4.5. Fortition of /f/ to /ph/.

This change must have occurred early in the history of Shan. It is one of the changes characteristic of wide areas inhabited by Shan. However, for a long time these speakers have been in contact speakers of the original *f*. There are even cases of hypercorrection found along the Shweli. Thus, I found some speakers who produce *fak*[7] 'vegetable'. This item of native Tai vocabulary originally had *ph. But, these speakers have become accustomed to reversing the rule f → ph to ph → f. In some cases lexical items are caught in the reversal or hypercorrection.

5.4.6. Variation of fortition (f to ph) by location

Loc	*f	Loc	*f
4	f	6	fh
5	f	25	fh
8	f	7	ph/f
11	f	17	ph/f
12	f	31	ph/f
14	f	1	ph
22	f	2	ph
23	f	18	ph
29	f	21	ph
30	f		

FIGURE 5.4.6-1: FORTITION OF /f/ TO /ph/

The original *f* has come into most areas with only a few scattered residues of *ph* remaining, for instance, in the far north in Khamti areas and in a few places in the territory north of the Shweli River. I found some cases of *ph* in southern Shan areas also. This kind of pattern suggests contamination of Shan in Myanmar by the Tai Lua of Yunnan.

5.4.7. Loss of secondary articulation

The loss of clusters or simplification of a complex consonant is very widespread in the Tai family. There are indeed only a few places in the entire family where clusters are preserved without exception. The second stage in the process of loss is the formation of initial consonants with secondary articulations. Prominent among these are palatalizations, such as *pj- kj-*, and *mj-* and labializations *kw-* and *khw-*. Palatalization are not found in Shan and labialized velars are also being replaced by simple velars.

Loc	*k(h)w	Loc	*k(h)w
14	k	1	x
29	k	21	kw
4	k	12	kw
5	k	23	kw
8	x	6	kw
11	x	2	khw
22	x	25	xw
30	x	31	kw
7	x	32	kw

FIGURE 5.4.7-1: LOSS OF SECONDARY ARTICULATION

The loss of labialization is a change that again seems to have started in Chinese Shan territory of Yunnan and has spread. Possibly this change is the result of migration.

5.4.8. Vowel changes

I give here the vowel changes without further analysis for the moment. I am currently still analyzing these.

Loc	*ɔ	*ɛ	*aɯ
1	ɔa	ɛ a	aɯ
2	ɔa	ai	aɯ
4	ɔ	iɛ	aɯ
5	ɔ	iɛ	aɯ
6	ɔa	iɛ	aɯ
7	ɔa	iɛ	aɯ
8	ɔa	iɛ	aɯ
11	ɔ	ɛ	aɯ
12	ɔa	iɛ	aɯ
14	ɔ	iɛ	aɯ
17	ɔ	ia	aɯ
18	ɔ	ia	aɯ
21	ɔ	ɛ	ai
22	ɔ	ɛ	aɯ
23	ɔ	ɛ	ai
25	ɔa	iɛ	ai aɯ
26			
27			
28			
29		iɛ	ai
30	ɔ	ɛ	aɯ
31			ɔ
32			ai

FIGURE 5.4.8-1: VOWEL DIPHTHONGIZATION CHANGES

5.4.9. Palatalization

In Shan locations there is also a variable rule of palatalization showing the original *ki* and the changed form *tɕi* variably.

Location	pronunciation	Location	pronunciation
36	ki	4	tɕi
11	ki	5	tɕi
14	ki	6	tɕi
17	ki	7	tɕi
21	ki	8	tɕi
22	ki	12	tɕi
23	ki	25	tɕi
29	ki	32	tɕi
33	ki	34	tɕi
20	ki	35	tɕi
1	tɕi	39	ɕi
2	tɕi	40	tɕi
3	tɕi	41	tɕi

FIGURE 5.4.9-1: PATTERN OF PALATALIZATIONS

5.5. CONCLUSION

My research question at the beginning was whether there is linguistic evidence to support the traditional divisions with the Shan community. I conclude that there indeed are three rather clearly defined groups that correspond to the autonyms: Tai Khamti, Southern Shan, and Northern Shan. Although I have only limited data on Tai Tauu, it is still easily separated from the other two by virtue of having a five tone system instead of six tones. Moreover, the tonal organization is sufficiently different within the five and six tones to make a natural development from one to the other quite unlikely. The key tonal category is B4, which allies with A23 in the north and with C123 in the south. This division is for that reason not of recent origin. The age of the difference is further underlined by being geographically rather distinct.

Also geographically and linguistically distinct is Tai Khamti. It shows a unique pattern of deplosivization in that both *ʔd* and *l* (in part) become *n*. That change is not attested elsewhere and thus also probably dates from a time when the Khamti were a group distinct from the northern Shan. There are also some lexical correspondences that appear to be different between Shan and Khamti that support this division. In recent centuries the Khamti have been governed by the Shan Sawbwas of Mogaung and their language has no doubt been mingled with that of their southern lieges.

As for the Tai Long (I use it in its historical sense), there is a striking similarity to all the patterns of variation at various geographic locations. It can be characterized as the 'background' and the 'intrusion'. The intrusion is the area roughly from Bhamo to Namhkam/Muse. The background comprises the areas in Myitkyina and northward, on the one hand, and the areas south of Muse. It appears that the Bhamo/Shweli area around Namhkam/Muse is an area where there has been considerable in-migration from the east in Yunnan Province by the Tai Luua. In these areas the traditional names are not very accurate predictors of linguistic forms. Virtually every sound change shows Tai Luua contamination and, thus, I feel that movement is the cause and not innovation within a sedentary population. Taken as a whole, Northern Shan, Southern Shan, and Khamti are certainly enough alike to share a common writing system and sense a common identity. The mixing of varieties along the Shweli River basin should not really come as a surprise, as it is in this place from the earliest times, through the British annexation of Upper Burma, and up to the present that there has been the greatest concentration of Shan history and the densest lines of communication. This area was favored over the southern route near Hsen Wi and the northern route along the Nam Taping north of Bhamo. It was in these places that in times of conflict Chinese, Burmese, and Shan warriors marauded and in times of peace Shan traders and immigrants trekked.

REFERENCES

Anderson, John (1876) 'Mandalay to Momien', in Edward B. Sladen and Colonel Horace Brown (eds) *A narrative of two expeditions to Western China of 1868 and 1875*, London: Macmillan.

Boruah, Bhim Kanta (1992) 'Thai languages in India: a linguistic analysis', in *Proceedings of the Third International Symposium on Language and Lingusitics, Pan Asiatic Linguistics II*, Bangkok: Chulalongkorn University, 852-60.

Bradley, David (1978) *Proto-Loloish* (Scandinavian Institute of Asian Studies Monograph Series, 4), London: Curzon Press.

Brown, J. Marvin (1965) 'From Ancient Thai to modern dialects', reprinted in Brown, J. Marvin (1985). *From Ancient Thai to modern dialects and other writings on historical Thai linguistics*, Bangkok: White Lotus Press.

Chamberlain, James R. (1975) 'A New Look at the History and Classification of the Tai Languages', in Jimmy G. Harris and James Chamberlain (eds) *Studies in Tai Linguistics in Honor of William J. Gedney*, Bangkok: Central Institute of the English Language, 49-66.

Cushing, Josiah Nelson (1888a) *Elementary Handbook of the Shan language*, Rangoon. Reprinted (1971) Westmead, Farnborough, Hants, England: Gregg International Publishers Limited.

— (1888b) *A Shan and English dictionary*, 1st ed, Rangoon. Reprinted (1971) Westmead, Farnborough, Hants, England: Gregg International Publishers Limited.

Dao Jie (2000) '金平傣语和泰国语的音系比较 Jinping Daiyu he Taiguoyu de yinxi bijiao [A comparison of the sound systems of Jinping Dai and Standard Thai]', in Xi Weining (ed.) 傣族文化论 Daizu wenhualun [Essays on Dai culture], Kunming: Yunnan Minzu Chubanshe.

Dhonge, R. V. and Phramaha Wiliaisak (1992) 'A comparative study of standard Thai and Tai-Phake spoken in Assam (India)', in Proceedings of the Third International Symposium on Language and Linguistics, Pan Asiatic Linguistics, Bangkok: Chulalongkorn University, 735-46.

Diller, Anthony (1992) 'Tai languages in Assam: Daughters or Ghosts?', in C. J. Compton and John F. Hartmann (eds), Papers on Tai languages, Linguistics, and Literatures (Occasional Paper No. 16), Northern Illinois University: Center for Southeast Asian Studies, 5-43.

Edmondson, Jerold A. and Solnit, David B. (1994), 'The northern tier of SW Tai', paper presented at the 4th Annual meeting of the Southeast Asian Linguistics Society, Bangkok/Chiangmai, Thailand.

Edmondson, Jerold A. and Solnit, David B. (1997), 'Comparative Shan', in Jerold A. Edmondson and David B. Solnit (eds) Comparative Kadai: the Tai branch, Dallas: SIL/UTA Series in Linguistics.

Edmondson, Jerold A., Esling, John H., Harris, Jimmy G. and Wei, James (2004), 'A phonetic study of Sui consonants and tones', Mon Khmer Studies 33: 1-20.

Egerod, Søren (1957) 'Essentials of Shan phonology and script', in Bulletin of the Institute of History and Philology, Academia Sinica 29: 121-9.

Elias, Ney (1876) Introductory sketch of the history of the Shan in Upper Burma and Western Yunna, Calcutta: Printed at the Foreign Department Press.

Enriques, Major C. M. (1933) Races of Burma (Handbooks for the Indian Army), Delhi: Manager of Publication.

FitzGerald, Charles P. (1972) The Southern Expansion of the Chinese People, New York: Praeger. Reprinted (1993) Bangkok and Cheney: White Lotus Press.

Gedney, William J. (1972) 'A checklist for determining tones in Tai dialects', in Smith, M. Estellie (ed.) Studies in Linguistics in Honor of George L. Trager (Janua Linguarum, Ser. Maior, 52), The Hague: Mouton, 423-37. Reprinted in William J. Gedney (1989) Selected Papers on Comparative Tai Studies, ed. by Robert Bickner, John F. Hartmann, Thomas J. Hudak, and Patcharin Peyasanitwong), Michigan Papers on South and Southeast Asia Center for South and Southeast Asian Studies 29), Ann Arbor: Center for South and Southeast Asia Studies, University of Michigan, 191-206.

Gedney, William J. (1976) 'Notes on Tai Nuea', in Thomas, Gething, Jimmy Harris, and Pranee Kalluvanijaya (eds) Tai Linguistics in honor of Fang-Kuei Li, Bangkok: Chulalongkorn University Press.

Glick, Irving and Sao Tern Moeng (1991) Shan for English Speakers: Dialogues, Readings, and Vocabulary, Wheaton: Dunwoody Press.

Gohain, Aimya Khang (1992) 'The Tai language as spoken by the Tai-Phakes', in Proceedings of the Third International Symposium on Language and Linguistics, Volume 1, Pan Asiatic Linguistics, Bangkok: Chulalongkorn University, 44-59.

Grierson, G. A. (1928) Linguistic survey of India, Vol. II, Mon-Khmer and Siamese-Chinese families (including Khassi and Tai), Dehli, Varanasi, and Patna: Motilal Banarsidass.

Hall, D.G.E. (1991) A history of South-East Asia, Houndmills, Basingstoke, Hampshire and London: Macmillan Education Ltd.

Hallett, Holt S. (1885) 'An historical sketch of the Shans', in A.R. Colquhoun Amongst the Shan, London: Field & Tuer; Simpkin, Marshall & Co.; Hamilton, Adams & Co. and New York: Scribner & Welford.

Harris, Jimmy G. (1975) 'A comparative word list of three Tai Nuea dialects', in Jimmy G. Harris and James R. Chamberlain (eds) Studies in Tai Linguistics in Honor of William J. Gedney, Bangkok: CIEL.

Harris, Jimmy G. (1976) 'Notes on Khamti Shan', in Thomas W. Gething et al. (eds) Tai Linguistics in Honor of Fang-Kuei Li, Bangkok: Chulalongkorn University Press.

Haudricourt, André-Georges (1975) 'Du nouveau sur le tai neua', *ASEMI* VI.4: 163-7.

Leech, Edmund R. (1954) *Political System of Highland Burma: A Study of Kachin Social Structure*, Cambridge: Harvard University Press.

Li, Fang-kuei (1977) *A Handbook of Comparative Tai*, Honolulu: The University Press of Hawaii.

Liamprawat, Suwathana (1985) 'Sound Correspondences among Tai Mao, Tai Khamti, and Lanna', *Journal of Language and Culture* 5.2: 27-45. In Tai.

Lowis, C. C. (1919) *The Tribes of Burma* (Ethnographical Survey of India, Burma No. 4), Rangoon: Office of the Superintendent, Government Printing, Burma.

Luce, Gordon H. (1985) *Phases of Prepagan Burma*, Oxford: Oxford University Press.

Luo, Meizhen (1984) 'The changes and developments of vowel length and consonant finals in Dai languages', *Minzu Yuwen* 6: 20-25.

— 1993 '论方言－兼谈傣语方言的划分 Lun Fangyan: Jiantan Daiyu fangyan de huafen (Discourse on language varieties in general: Concurrent discussions about the divisions among Dai local languages)', *Minzu Yuwen* 3: 1-10. In Chinese.

Ma Khin Myo Thant. (n.d.) *Road map of the Union of Myanmar*, Yangon: Aungtagon Press.

Mix, H. W. (1920) *A English and Shan Dictionary*, Rangoon: American Baptist Mission Press, F. D. Phinney Supt.

Morey, Stephen (2004) 'Tonal Change in the Tai Languages of Northeast India', paper presented at the 12th meeting of the SE Asian Linguistics Society, Bangkok.

Needham, J. F. (1894) *Outline Grammar of the (Khamti) Language*, Rangoon: Superintendent Government Printing.

Ningombe, M. S. (1996) 'Tai-elements in the place names of Assam', in *Proceedings of the Fourth International Symposium on Language and Linguistics*, Pan Asiatic Linguistics, Volume III, Bangkok: Mahidol University, 1001-17.

Robinson, Edward (1994) 'Features of Proto-Nɯa-Khamti', paper presented at the 27th ICSTLL, October, Paris.

Sao Saimong Mongrai (1965) 'The Shan States and British Annexation', Cornell Data Paper 57, Ithaca: Department of Asian Studies, Cornell University.

Sao Tern Moeng. (1995) *Shan-English Dictionary*, Hyattsville, MD: Dunwoody Press.

Scott, James George and Hardiman, J. P. (1900) *Gazetteer of Upper Burma and Shan State*, Rangoon: The Superintendant, Government Printing (5 Vols).

Seidenfaden, Erik (1958) 'The Thai peoples', in *The Origins and Habitats of the Tai Peoples with a Sketch of Their Material and Spiritual Culture*, Bangkok: The Siam Society.

Shan New Testament with Psalms and Proverbs: A new translation in Common Language, ထမ်,မႃႇၵျမ်းလိၵ်ႈၵၢင်မ့်, ပႃး ၵျမ်းသႂ်,လၢမ်,တင်း ၵျမ်းသုၵ်ႇတၢမ်, ၵၢင်ပႃးၶႂ်ႈ သမ်,မႃႇၵျမ်းလိၵ်ႈထႂ်ႇဝၢႆၵြႃး ၶႂ်းၸၢမ်းတၢ်းပၢၼ်မ့် (1994), The Bible Society of Myanmar.

Shan State Magazine (2000) 'The Shan settlements in Myanmar', Taunggyi. Available at www.shanland.org/History/shan_settlements_in_myanmar.htm.

Solnit, David, B. and Edmondson, Jerold A. (1994) 'The northern tier of Southwestern Tai', paper presented at the Fourth Annual meeting of the Southeast Asian Linguistics Society, Bangkok/Chiangmai, Thailand.

Terrien de Lacouperie, Albert Etienne Jean Baptiste (1885) 'Cradle of the Shan Race', in Colquhoun, A. R. *Amongst the Shan*, London: Field & Tuer; Simpkin, Marshall & Co.; Hamilton, Adams & Co. and New York: Scribner & Welford.

Thakur, G. C. Sharma (1982) *The Tai Phakes of Assam*, Belhi: B. R. Publishing Corporation.

Tint Hswei, Colonel တင့်ဆွေ (1992), ပြည်ထောင်စုမြန်မာနိုင်ငံ၏တိုင်းရင်းသားလူမျိုးများ. *National races of the Union of Myanmar*, Yangon: Security Publishing House. In Burmese.

Wang, Jun (ed.) (1984) 壮侗语族语言简志 *Zhuang-Dong Yuzu Yuyan jianzhi [Outline Grammar of the Kam-Tai Languages]*, Beijing: Nationalities Publishing House.

Weidert, Alfons (1971) *Tai Khamti phonology*, Wiesbaden: Franz Steiner Verlag.

Xing Gongwan (1989) '红河上游傣雅语 Honghe shangyou dai ya yu [Introduction to the Tai-ya language on the Upper reaches of the Hong He (Red River)]', *Minzu Yuwen* 3: 40-46.

Young, Linda (1985) *Shan Chrestomathy: An Introduction to Tai Mau Language and Literature*, Center for South and Southeast Asia Studies, University of California, Berkeley; Lanhan/New York/London: University Press of America.

Yu, Cuirong (1986) 'Some phenomena of sound change in Daila Dai', *Minzu Yuwen* 2: 29-33.

— (1990) 'Phonetic character of Daila vernacular', *Minzu Yuwen* 1: 50-62.

Zhou Yaowen (1982) 'Yunnan Dehong Daiwen Gaijin zhong de jige wenti (Questions regarding the reform of the Dehong Dai script of Yunnan)', paper presented at the 15 ICSTLL, Beijing.

— (1983) 'The phonology and writing system of Mengding Dai', *Minzu Yuwen* 6: 10-15.

CHAPTER SIX

THE TAI LANGUAGES OF ASSAM[1]

Stephen Morey

6.1. THE TAI PEOPLE IN ASSAM

More than a million people in the Northeast of India claim Tai ethnicity. However, over 99% of these are Tai Ahoms who no longer maintain Tai as a spoken language. In addition to the Ahoms, there are a number of other groups, the Aiton, Khamti, Khamyang, Nora, Phake and Turung, who also claim Tai ethnicity. Tai language is spoken, to varying extents, in all of these communities.

This chapter will briefly outline each of these groups and discuss some of the salient features of the languages spoken by these groups.

6.1.1. Tai Ahom

According to traditional accounts, a group of Tai, led by a prince named Sukhapha (ᨶᩣᩴᩅ᩠ᩓᩢ *sɯ kaa phaa*)[2], arrived in Assam in 1228 from what is now South West China. Sukapha founded the kingdom that is now known as the Ahom, which ruled in the Brahmaputra valley for 600 years. During this time, the Ahom gradually assimilated with the local Hindus and lost their language and culture. It seems that by early in the nineteenth century, everyday usage of Ahom language had ceased and that Ahom people all spoke Assamese as their mother tongue.

Nevertheless, the Ahom language remains in vestigial use as a ritual language in religious ceremonies, such as the Ahom Soklong wedding which includes the chanting of prayers that are said to be based on ancient Ahom religious practices (see Terwiel 1996 and Morey 2002, 2005). There is also an enthusiastic program of Ahom language revival. Two Ahom dictionaries, G. C. Barua (1920) and B. K. Baruah and Phukan (1964) have been produced. These are in a large part based on a late eighteenth century manuscript word list, known as the

---

1   I am very grateful to Dr Anthony Diller for reading and commenting on this chapter, the final version of which gained much from his comments. During the writing of this chapter I have been employed as a postdoctoral fellow at the Research Centre for Linguistic Typology, La Trobe University, and I particularly wish to acknowledge Prof. Alexandra Aikhenvald from RCLT who read through the manuscript and made many valuable suggestions. The data on Tai Aiton comes largely a historical narrative told to me by Nang Wimala Thoumoung and from the translations of Aiton historical texts undertaken with Sri Nabin Shyam Phalung. I also acknowledge Ong Cham, Chow En Lai (Chaw Sangea Phalung), who helped with the translation of Ong Cham's story, and Sa Cham Thoumoung, the teller of many tales. The fieldwork on Tai Phake was undertaken in Namphakey Village, Naharkatia, Dibrugarh District in March 2001 and February 2002. I would particularly like to thank Ai Chanta Gohain, and Aithown Che Chakap who have provided a great deal of information about the phenomena described here and patiently cooperated with repeated requests for further information. I am also indebted to the Khamyang informants, particularly Chaw Sa Myat Chowlik, and Chaw Deben Chowlik, who have been so patient in the process of giving me information about their seriously endangered language. I am, of course, responsible for any inconsistencies or inaccuracies contained in this chapter.
2   Nothing is known of the Ahom tonal system, and therefore no tones are marked. Nabin Shyam Phalung states that the meaning of this King's name is 'tiger-equal to-sky', and is pronounced *sɯ¹ kaa² phaa³* in Aiton.

Bar Amra. This manuscript, written entirely in Ahom script, gives definitions for several thousand Ahom words in Assamese.

In addition to words attested in the *Bar Amra*, there are a large number of other words included in these two dictionaries. Some of these were added by members of the Ahom priesthood, called Deodhais. Of particular interest to scholars have been those words in both dictionaries that have initial consonant clusters, particularly with /r/ as the second member. Some of these do appear in Ahom manuscripts, but it seems that many do not. The reliability of these clusters cannot thus be ensured, and as a consequence, historical reconstructions which rely on G. C. Barua (1920) or B. K. Barua and Phukan (1964) should be closely re-examined.

There is also an *Ahom Primer* (G. C. Barua 1936), which includes some grammatical information about Ahom. Much of this information, however, was provided by a Tai Aiton speaker, Mohendra Shyam Phalung, who lived with G. C. Barua in the early 1930s.

The extent to which this modern use of the Ahom language can be regarded as a continuation of the ancient Ahom language has been disputed, and is discussed by Terwiel (1996) and Morey (2002, 2005).

In addition to the *Bar Amra* mentioned above, there are a large number of Ahom manuscripts, some of which have been carefully analysed (Terwiel and Ranoo Wichasin 1992, Ranoo Wichasin 1996).

6.1.2. Other Tai groups in Assam

At least six other groups of Tai have entered Assam since the arrival of the Ahom, bringing with them distinctive varieties of language. Of these languages, Ahom and five others, Aiton, Khamti, Nora, Phake and Turung, were referred to in the *Linguistic Survey of India* (Grierson 1904), the work through which the various Tai languages in India became best known. A seventh group, Khamyang, which may be the same as Nora, is still spoken in a single village in Tinsukia District, Assam, but only by older adults.

Aiton, Khamti and Phake are each spoken by over a thousand people, and are still being learned by children. In Khamyang and Nora villages (except for Pawaimukh village), only Assamese is spoken, although some men who have trained as monks in other Tai speaking areas have acquired an adult-learners ability in Tai.

The speech of the Turungs, who now speak a variety of Singpho (Tibeto-Burman), is discussed below in section 6.1.2.5.

6.1.2.1. *Tai Aiton*

Aiton is spoken in about 10 villages in the Dhonsiri river valley on the south side of the Brahmaputra River. The Dhonsiri forms the boundary between Golaghat district and Karbi Anglong autonomous district, and Aiton villages are found on both sides of the river.

It is not clear how long the Aitons have been in Assam. The traditional view is that the Aiton, Khamti, Khamyang, Phake and Turung all entered Assam between the middle of the eighteenth century and the early nineteenth century, having migrated from Burma and bringing with them Theravada Buddhist religion and scripts which are closely related to the Shan of Burma.

This view is not uncontroversial. Diller (1992: 8-11) discusses the evidence suggesting that at least some of these groups arrived in Assam with Sukapha, some 500 years before the traditional date. Even today, Aiton villagers can recite by heart stories of the arrival of Sukapha in Assam. If it is not their own history, why is it such an important part of their culture?

Aiton stories also refer to contact with later kings of the Tai Ahom. One text mentions the Ahom King Suhungmung or Dehingia Raja (1497 – 1539), who conquered the Dhonsiri valley in which the Aitons now live. If the Aitons were already living in the Dhonsiri valley in the time of Suhungmung, we might expect them to record the event.

On the other hand, the Aitons also tell stories and sing songs about their ancestral home, *muŋ² maau²*, in what is now Southwestern China, suggesting that their migration to India may be a more recent phenomenon.

As Diller (1992: 11) points out, if we accept that the other Tai groups arrived at any date earlier than the eighteenth century, 'their (Burmese-linked) Buddhism and relative lack of Indo-Aryan assimilation would then remain to be explained'.

Several Aiton informants have stated that until about five generations ago, the Aitons did not follow Theravada Buddhism, but rather worshipped spirits (sun^2 $phii^1$) and sacrificed animals. The Aitons were then converted to Theravada Buddhism in the mid nineteenth century by a Burmese monk, Pi En Duin Sayadaw (pii^1 εn^1 dun^2).

It is also worthwhile to note Grierson's statement on the Aitons, namely that they were

... also called Shām Doāniyās, or Shān interpreters, are said to have been a section of the Shāns at Mūng Kâng which supplied eunuchs to the royal seraglio, and to have emigrated to Assam to avoid the punishment to which, for some reason, they had been condemned (1904: 65).

The Aitons that I have interviewed all reject this suggestion by Grierson. However the statement about interpretation may be significant, given that the Aiton language is demonstrably closer to what the original Ahom seems to have been than any of the other spoken Tai languages are (see below section 6.2.2.2). Perhaps the Aiton speech of today does contain some echoes of the original Ahom speech.

If indeed the Aitons have been in the Dhonsiri valley since the fifteenth century, and if they were not followers of Theravada Buddhism at that time, then perhaps their language and cultural practises were closer to that of the Ahoms.

Among the present day Aitons, there are estimated to be about 1,500 speakers, almost all of whom are bilingual in Assamese, and perhaps 10% of whom are also speakers of Turung (Tibeto-Burman). The language is still being learned by children.

There are large collections of manuscripts in the village temples and some in private hands. There are, however, only a small number of people who can read these manuscripts.

Grierson (1904: 193-211) includes some brief grammatical notes, texts and a comparative word list in Aiton. The data in Grierson does not accord with the findings of Aiton phonology reported below in sections 6.3.1 and 6.3.2, and it appears that Grierson's analysis is based entirely on a transcription of Tai written materials, rather than any attempt to represent the spoken language.

More recently both Diller (1992) and Morey (2005) have presented data on Aiton.

6.1.2.2. *Tai Khamti*

Most of the Tai Khamti live in Arunachal Pradesh state of India, or in northern Burma. In Assam, there is one small Khamti village near Margherita in Tinsukia district and several villages on the north bank of the Brahmaputra at Narayanpur, in North Lakhimpur district. So far as I know, no linguistic work has been done in Narayanpur. In addition to Grierson (1904), Robinson (1849), Needham (1894), Harris (1976), Weidert (1977), Wilaiwan (1986) and Chaw Khouk Manpoong (1993) have all examined the Khamti language.

There are probably fewer than 600 Khamti speakers in Assam and perhaps between five and ten thousand in Arunachal Pradesh.

6.1.2.3. *Tai Khamyang*

Of the various groups of Tai who reside in Assam today, the Khamyang are the only group not mentioned by Grierson in the *Linguistic Survey of India* (1904).

Grierson did, however, mention and exemplify the language of the Nora (1904: 179-191). It is said by some Tai in India that Nora and Khamyang are the same (see Diller 1992: 12), although I have never heard the remaining Khamyang speakers refer to themselves as Nora. In his description of Nora, Grierson stated that there were around 300 speakers in his time. He provided some phonological notes which suggest some similarities with present day Khamyang, and also two texts, including some riddles.

Boruah (2001: 41) lists several Khamyang villages in Jorhat and Golaghat districts. Tai Khamyang is not spoken in any of these villages, a situation which parallels that of the Ahom. In some of the Tai communities of Northeast India, self-identification is not necessarily based on language usage.

Of the origin, language and history of the Khamyang, very little has been written. Muhi Chandra Shyam Panjok[3] (1981) discusses the origin of the Khamyangs. He does not cite any sources, but presumably his pamphlet is based on historical Tai manuscripts.

According to Panjok's account, a group of Tai, identified as Khamyangs, were sent into Assam by the Tai King Sukhanpha to search for his brother Sukapha who had earlier founded the Ahom Kingdom in the Brahmaputra valley. The traditional date for the latter event is 1228. After being welcomed by Sukapha, the Khamyangs set out to return to King Sukhanpha in what is now the Shan States. The history states that the Khamyang then settled at Nawng Yang lake and lived there for about 500 years.

Leach (1964: 33) places Nawng Yang Lake in a location to the south of the Tirap River, probably just immediately south of the Burma-India border. It is from this lake that the name Khamyang was derived.

The Khamyangs then ventured back into Assam, commencing from 1780. Caught up in the various troubles that accompanied the final years of the Ahom Kingdom, the Khamyangs fought both with and against the Ahoms and were divided. One group eventually settled in Dibrugarh district and from there migrated to Pawaimukh in 1922. Chaw Sa Myat Chowlik, born in about 1920, has confirmed to me that the village was founded when he was two, and that his parents brought him there from Dibrugarh district.

A second group of Khamyangs settled in Dhali in 1798 and these were the ancestors of the Khamyangs who now live in Golaghat and Jorhat districts, mentioned by Boruah (2001) above.

Today Tai Khamyang is only spoken in the single village of Pawaimukh, near Margherita in Tinsukia district. Only older adults are full speakers of the language. The bi-dialectal linguistic situation in Pawaimukh is described in more detail in Section 6.6.

6.1.2.4. *Tai Phake*

There are 11 Phake villages in both Assam and Arunachal Pradesh. There are perhaps 2000 speakers and the language is still being learned by children. There are large collections of manuscripts in every village, and a significant number of people can read and write the Tai script.[4]

Although Phake was mentioned by Grierson (1904), he provided no information about the number of speakers and no data on the language. The Thai linguist Dr Banchob Bandhumedha spent a great deal of time in the Phake community and published a dictionary (Banchob 1987). The language has also been studied by Wilaiwan (1983), Banchob (1987), Diller (1992), Gogoi (1994), Aimya Khang (1997) and Morey (2005).

6.1.2.5. *Tai Turung*

The history of the Turung is a matter of some dispute. The Turung themselves believe that they were originally a Tai speaking group who migrated from place to place in Northeast India and the surrounding areas, eventually settling in Jorhat and Golaghat districts of Assam. In Turung villages there are historical manuscripts, written in Tai, which detail the history of their migrations. The name Turung is interchangeable with Tairung or Tailung in these manuscripts. Tailung would be rendered in Aiton as *tai² luŋ¹* and means 'great Tai'. Because the Turung were in contact with the Singpho for a long period, they eventually adopted the

---

3   Muhi Chandra Shyam Payok is from Chalapathar and is not a speaker of Tai. It must be presumed that a Tai speaker, possibly not a Tai Khamyang speaker, conveyed the meaning of the old Tai MS to him.

4   The Tai writing system is described in detail in Morey (2005: 179-207).

Singpho language (Jinghpaw subgroup of Tibeto-Burman).

British records from as early as the mid 19th century suggest that the Turung, which he calls Tairong, were a Tai speaking group who were captured by the Singpho and held as slaves for a period of years.[5] Grierson explains that they were taken prisoner by the Singphos or Kachins and

> made to work as slaves.... They were released by Captain Neufville ... in 1825, and continued their journey to the Jorhat Subdivision, where they now live. During their servitude to the Kachins they entirely forgot their own language, and now only speak that of their conquerors, Singpho. (1904: 64)

Grierson goes on to note that the Tairong still had books in their own language, and his study of Tairong includes a translation of the *Story of the Prodigal Son* in Tairong, which suggests some knowledge of Tai language by at least some members of the community. This translation contains some curious features and it is possible that Grierson's informants were second language learners of Tai, as the Tai speakers in Turung villages are today. Grierson (1904: 167) states that 'about 150 of them are said to speak their own language' by which he means a Tai language.

A number of recordings of Tai Turung made by Dr Banchob Bandhumedha in the 1960s have recently come to light.[6] These recordings were made in Tai language in the Turung village of Titabor. At least one of the informants, Soi Lendro, was clearly a fluent Tai speaker who was also able to read from manuscripts. When the writer visited Titabor in September 2003, Soi Lendro was still alive. He confirmed that he had been raised speaking Turung (Tibeto-Burman) and had learned Tai as a young adult, when living in a Khamti Buddhist monastery as a monk. The other two of Banchob's informants who were still living, Nang Ee Hom and Nang Ai Mii, both confirmed that they could not speak Tai, but had learned some Tai prayers from a visiting monk, and it was these prayers that Dr Banchob recorded.

A survey of six Turung villages in 2003 established that Turung, as a Tai language, is no longer spoken. Apart from those Turungs, who, like Soi Lendro, have learned Tai as monks, the other Tai speakers in Turung villages are all Aitons who have married Turungs and moved to live there. One village, Balipathar (*baan³ saai²* in Aiton), is a half-Turung, half-Aiton village.

Turung today is a Tibeto-Burman language of the Jinghpaw sub-family, and is called Turung by its speakers. In this Turung language, the large majority of words are Tibeto-Burman. Some kinship terms are Tai, as are some terms for religious or material culture. The Turung themselves regard their language as a mixture of Tai and Singpho (Jinghpaw/Tibeto-Burman). The language of younger Turungs is shifting to Assamese, the language of wider communication. Even older speakers code switch into Assamese very frequently.

The word Turung is taken from the name of a river in Upper Burma where the Turungs lived several centuries ago. The term appears to have become conflated with the term *tai² loŋ¹* 'great Tai' (in Aiton pronunciation). Grierson (1904: 167) stated that 'The Tairongs (or great Tais) ... are also called Turung or Sham (i.e. Shan) Turung ...'. The term 'great Tai' is first encountered in Buchanan (1798), who says of them that they are:

> ... a people called, by the *Burmas*, *Kathee Shawn*, to themselves they assume the name of *Tai-loong*, or great Tai. They are called *Moitay Kabo* by the *Kathee*, or people of *Cussay*. They inhabit the upper part of the *Kiaynduayn* river, and from that west to the *Erawade*.

---

5   Aiton oral histories also state that the Turungs were held as slaves of the Singpho for a time.

6   I am very grateful to Dr Nawawan Bandhumedha, niece of the late Dr Banchob, for making these recordings available to me.

This, however, would appear to refer to the Khamtis who reside in what is now Burma. Of the several groups mentioned in Aiton manuscript, *The Treaty between the Aitons and the Turungs*,[7] we find Takum, Tarung and Tarai. Each of these words is pronounced in Aiton with an initial syllable of [tə], an example of the sesqui-syllabic structure so frequently encountered in the Jinghpaw languages.

Perhaps Turung was the name of a smaller group of Tibeto-Burman speakers, and when the Turung came to live with the Aiton, the name was re-interpreted as a Tai word, because of its chance similarity to the words for 'great Tai'. Perhaps the Turungs were never speakers of a Tai language. This is the view is held by Singpho speakers living in Margherita subdivision of Tinsukia district in Upper Assam. The Singpho regard the Turung as one of four Singpho groups of *hkawng*[8] 'river bank'. These groups are named after the rivers near which they live, as Tieng Hkawng, Diyun Hkawng, Num Hpuk Hkawng and Tarung Hkawng. The first two are named for rivers in Arunachal Pradesh and the third, Num Hpuk, refers to the Dihing river. Further research on the grammar and history of Turung is in progress.

6.2. NOTES ON THE PHONOLOGY OF THE TAI LANGUAGES OF ASSAM

6.2.1. Consonants

Tai Phake, Khamti and Khamyang all appear to have the same inventory of initial consonants, which is given in Table 6.2.1-1, although cognate words do not necessarily have the same initials (see below Table 6.6-1 which compares Khamyang with Phake and Khamti).

TABLE 6.2.1-1: CONSONANT PHONEMES IN PHAKE, KHAMTI AND KHAMYANG

	Bilabial	Dental/ Alveolar	Palatal	Velar	Glottal
Voiceless unaspirated stops	p	t	c	k	(ʔ)
Voiceless aspirated stops	ph	th		kh	
Nasals	m	n	ñ	ŋ	
Voiceless fricative		s			h
Semi vowel	w		y		
Lateral Approximant	l				

Each of the seventeen consonants represented in Table 6.2.1-1 corresponds to a single letter in the Tai orthography.

In Aiton, on the other hand, there are three additional phonemes, /b/, /d/ and /r/. The stops /b/ and /d/ are usually shown in writing by the homorganic nasal stops /m/ and /n/ respectively, although sometimes the Burmese letters for <b> and <d> are used. Many words which have initial consonants that are reflexes of proto *ʔm or *ʔn (realized as /b/ and /d/ respectively in Standard Thai) are in variation between voiced stops and their corresponding nasals in Aiton (as exemplified by *nai⁻³/dai⁻³* 'get' in Table 6.4.3-1 below).

The rhotic /r/ is realized as an approximant with fairly strong retroflexion. It would be best phonetically described as either [ɹ] or [ɻ]. It is shown in writing by the symbol r, which is the symbol for /l/ and the symbol for a subscripted /r/ in combination.

In addition to these additional phonemes, there are some consonant weakenings that are observed in Aiton. Both the bilabial and velar voiceless aspirated stops (/ph/ and /kh/) are usually realized with fricativization, as [ɸ] and [χ]. The semivowels (/y/ and /w/) are also usually released as voiced fricatives ([ʒ] and [β]). The voiceless fricative /s/ is often

7   Dated to the late 19th century, this manuscript is translated in Morey 1999b.
8   The spelling *hkawng* and the names of the various groups follows the spelling system devised for the Jinghpaw language in Kachin State, Burma.

palatalized. None of these processes appears to be related to linguistic environment.

It is possible that the weakening of voiceless aspirates to voiceless fricatives and the strengthening of semi vowels to voiced fricatives has so changed the phoneme inventory that it might be better to express it as in Table 6.2.1-2:

TABLE 6.2.1-2: REALIGNED AITON PHONEME CHART

	Bilabial	Dental / Alveolar	Palatal	Velar	Glottal
Voiced Stops	b	d			(?)
Voiceless unaspirated stops	p	t	c	k	
Voiceless aspirated stops		th			
Nasals	m	n	ñ	ŋ	
Voiceless fricative	ɸ		ʃ	x	h
Voiced fricative	β		ʒ		
Rhotic Approximant		r			
Lateral Approximant		l			

However a more cautious approach to the Aiton consonant phonemes would present an inventory like Table 6.2.1-3 with the addition of /b/, /d/ and /r/. This more conservative inventory tallies better with the writing system of the Aitons which lists the letters in groups of stops and nasals, viz: /k/, /kh/, /ŋ/, /c/, /s/ /ñ/, /t/, /th/, /n/, /p/, /ph/, /m/ and then the semivowels /y/, /r/, /l/, /w/, and finally /h/ and vowel initial words.

As for Ahom, by examination of the surviving Ahom manuscripts, and assuming that there is a one to one correspondence between the glyphs for the initial consonants and their phonemes, the following phoneme table can be presented:

TABLE 6.2.1-3: POSSIBLE CONSONANT PHONEMES IN AHOM

	Bilabial	Dental/ Alveolar	Palatal	Velar	Glottal
Voiceless unaspirated stops	p	t	c	k	(?)
Voiceless aspirated stops	ph	th		kh	
Voiced stop	b	d			
Nasals	m	n	ñ	ŋ	
Voiceless fricative		s			h
Semi vowel			y / ʒ [9]		
Rhotic Approximant	r				
Lateral Approximant	l				

6.2.1.1. *Consonant clusters*

Consonant clusters are occasionally found with borrowed words in Phake, Khamti and Khamyang. In Aiton, on the other hand, they are very common in three types of words: borrowed words, onomatopoeic words and words for which initial clusters are reconstructed

9   In Assamese the proto phoneme /*y/ is realized as [z] or [ʒ]. It is possible that this was also the case in Ahom.

for proto-Tai.

In the 1970s, the Thai linguist Banchob Bandhumedha wrote a manuscript *Aiton–English–Thai Dictionary*. This records the following initial clusters for Aiton, mainly in onomatopoeic words:

1) br   pr   phr   dr   pl
    cr   sr   kr   khr   gr
    kl

Several of these clusters appear to occur only in two syllable words where the first syllable is unstressed and probably pronounced with an unstressed schwa. For example Banchob records *srā⁸* 'Buddhist monk', which is written ꩬ꩟ꩳ which I have phonemicized as *sa¹ rā¹*. Many of the other clusters are found only in onomatopoeic words.

Diller (1992: 15) mentions only four clusters, namely:

2) pr phr kr khr

From the word list of 2000 items collected from Bidya Thoumoung, the following clusters were recorded:

3) pr   phr   tr   khr
    pl
    py   ky

Of these, several such as /tr/, /py/ and /ky/ are only found with words that are obviously borrowed from Pali or Burmese. The cluster /kr/ was also recorded in some texts, but only in the borrowed word *krii¹* 'big' (from Burmese).

6.2.2. Vowels

In terms of vowel quality, most of the Tai languages of Assam have a nine vowel contrast, with a tenth phoneme provided by the length contrast between /a/ and /aa/. Table 6.2.2-1 gives the vowel phonemes in Phake. The forms in brackets show the orthography used by Banchob (1987) which is maintained here for the sake of consistency.

TABLE 6.2.2-1: VOWEL PHONEMES IN PHAKE

i	ɯ (ü)	u
e	ɤ (ə)	o
ɛ		ɔ
	a, aa	

Both Banchob (1987) and Diller (1992) reported a regular process of diphthongization of the mid-low vowels before velar consonants.

4)   /ɛ/   →   [ai] / __ velar
     /ɔ/   →   [au] / __ velar

Other diphthongizations may be occurring among Phake speakers. Diller (1992: 17) notes that 'the vowel -ɔ- in other non-final environments shows the same [-uɔ-] or [-wɔ-] variant noted by Harris for Khamti (1976: 120); there is most frequently a contiguous labial *p* or *m*: *kɔp⁶* [kwɔp] 'scoop'; *pɔt¹* [pwɔt] 'to scrub'...'

In February 2002, the Phake informant Yehom Buragohain was recorded speaking the second of Diller's examples. The word (*pɔt⁴* in Banchob's system) seems to clearly show diphthongization, with a shift in the vowel shape at the end of the vowel, not at the beginning.

This word might better be phonetically expressed as [pɔɔt].

6.2.2.1. *Vowel merger in Aiton*

In terms of vowel quality there appear to be only six vowel contrasts in Aiton, with a seventh provided by the length distinction between /a/ and /aa/, as in Table 6.2.2.1-1:

TABLE 6.2.2.1-1: VOWEL PHONEMES IN AITON

i	ɯ	u
ɛ		ɔ
	a, aa	

The relation between Aiton and Phake vowels is shown in (5)

5) Phake [i,e]   >   Aiton [i]
    Phake [ɛ]   >   Aiton [ɛ]
    Phake [ɯ,ɣ]   >   Aiton [ɯ]
    Phake [a,aa] >   Aiton [a,aa]
    Phake [u,o]   >   Aiton [u]
    Phake [ɔ]   >   Aiton [ɔ]

The symbols <ɛ> and <ɔ> have been chosen for the Aiton mid vowels rather than <e> and <o>, because <ɛ> and <ɔ> in Aiton correspond with <ɛ> and <ɔ> in Phake.

This merger of mid-open and open vowels is at least several generations old. It was clearly notated in Banchob's manuscript *Aiton–English–Thai Dictionary*, as is shown in the following table:

TABLE 6.2.2.1-2: EXAMPLES OF PROTO */i/ AND */e/ RECORDED BY BANCHOB (MS) AND (1987) AND COMPARED WITH THE PROTO FORMS AFTER LI (1977)

Aiton (Banchob MS)	Phake (Banchob 1987)	Putative proto form (after Li 1977)	Gloss
cit[1]	cēt[1]		'seven'
cip[1]	cēp[1]	*cepD2	'to be ill'
pīk[1]	pik[1]	*pi(i)kD2	'wing'
pit[1]	pɛt[1]	*petD2	'duck'
bit[1]	mit[1]	*ʔbitD3	'to twist'
bit[1]	met[1]	*ʔbetD3	'fishhook'
cit[4]	cēt[4]	*chetD4	'to wipe'

There is also some orthographic evidence that the merger is much older. One early example of the merger of /e/ > /i/ in open syllables is provided in the *Treaty between the Aitons and the Turungs*, where the word ꮳ *ʒii³* '1st daughter' is found. This word is *ye³* in Phake. The manuscript was written about 1950 and was copied in the 1980s before it was damaged by insects. The vowel -ᷟ [ii] can still clearly be seen, even though the consonant has been eaten by ants.

6.2.2.2. *Possible reconstruction of Ahom vowel system*

Both in Ahom script and in the scripts used by the other Tai groups in Northeast India, only six vowels are distinguished in the orthography. As discussed above, in Tai Phake, there are clearly 9 vowels and thus the script underspecifies for the vowel contrasts. However, in Aiton, there has been a merger of mid-open vowels and open vowels.

The underspecification of contrast in the script is particularly problematic with the marking of front vowels in open syllables. In Phake, where there are three contrastive front vowels, words like ye^2 'granary' and me^2 'wife' are written with initial soi^1 tho^2 (c-), just as words with the rhyme /-ɛ/ would be. The same symbol is used for both vowels. In Aiton, on the other hand, where /e/ and /i/ have merged, the words for 'granary' and 'wife' are written with $luŋ^1$ $k\bar{i}^5$ $tɛŋ^1$ (-°) [ii].

The Aiton pattern is also found in Ahom, at least in the *Bar Amra*, where the word for 'granary' is written as ဟ (yii), as in (6):

6)   ဟ   vẟ   ဂ   ✓ဤၚဳၜဿၚႄ

yii   cam   baa   phrɔralɔk

yii   PRT   say   granary (Assamese bʰɔral)

' *ʒii* means 'a granary'.'

(*Bar Amra*, p 13 third line)

From this evidence, it is possible to draw the conclusion that the Ahom vowel system, at least in the final stages of the language, was the same as Aiton, given below in Table 6.2.2.2-1:

TABLE 6.2.2.2-1: POSSIBLE VOWEL PHONEMES IN AHOM

i	ɯ	u
ɛ		ɔ
	a, (aa)	

In modern Aiton, there is a length contrast between /a/ and /aa/ in closed syllables. This contrast is not marked in the Aiton orthography. It is assumed that this contrast was present in Ahom.

6.2.3. Tones

The tonal system for Khamti has been discussed by Harris (1976) and Weidert (1977). The tonal systems for Phake, Khamyang and Aiton are presented below in the tables that follow:

6.2.3.1. *Phake tones*

Table 6.2.3.1-1 presents the Phake tones including an analysis of the contours, based on examples elicited from Ee Nyan Khet, a female speaker born in 1939. In this elicitation, all the tones were collected using the sequence [maa], except for tone 5, which was $mɛ^5$ 'mother'. It is possible that as a result of $mɛ^5$ having a higher vowel than the other words elicited, the pitch of tone 5 is slightly higher than it would have been if a word with the rhyme [aa] had been recorded.

TABLE 6.2.3.1-1: TONES IN PHAKE

	A	B	C	DL	DS
1	6	1	3	1	
2	2				
3					
4		5	4		

Tone no.	contour (Hz)	key feature(s)	description
1	200-190	level	mid to high level tone with slight final fall
2	225-250-150	high level then falling	mid to high onset, with rise then sharp fall
3	160-120	glottal constriction	mid falling or level tone with strong glottal constriction
4	175-125	falling	mid to high onset with immediate sharp fall
5	180-160	low	mid to low onset with slight gradual fall
6	220-200-275	rising	low to mid onset with slight fall before sharp rise

In addition to these citation tones, there are other tones which occur in Phake in questions, commands and negative sentences. These are discussed below in Section 6.5.

6.2.3.2. *Khamyang tones*

The Khamyang tonal system has six tones with a different distribution from the six tones of the Phake. The tone box in Table 6.2.3.2-1 is based on an interview with Chaw Deben Chowlik.[10] This tone box differs from the Phake, where A2-3 is merged with A4, and B4 is a separate tone. It also differs from Khamti where A1 is merged with B1-3.

TABLE 6.2.3.2-1: TONES IN KHAMYANG

	A	B	C	DL	DS
1	6	1	3	1	
2	5				
3					
4	2	5	4	4	

Tone		
	1	mid level with slight fall
	2	high with a slight rise then falling
	3	low, falling and glottalized
	4	high with a slight rise then falling with glottal ending
	5	low falling
	6	level, with possible rise at the end

Of particular interest in the Khamyang tonal system is the contrast between the second and fourth tones. Both have identical contours, with the final glottal in Tone 4 being the only way of contrasting them. Because both tones have the same contour as the Phake second tone, Phake informants hear the Khamyang Tone 4 as the Phake Tone 2.

6.2.3.3. *Aiton tones*

Contemporary Aiton appears to have only three contrastive tones. In late 1999, the Aiton informant Bidya Thoumoung produced the following five tones:

---

10 I am very grateful to Jerrold Edmondson for discussing these tones with me.

TABLE 6.2.3.3-1: TONES PRODUCED BY BIDYA THOUMOUNG FOR AITON

1. mid/high level
2. high level then falling
3. mid falling
4. mid rising
5. mid falling glottalized

Subsequently a word-list of around 2000 items was collected from Bidya Thoumoung. It quickly became clear that there were only three contrastive tones, as shown in Table 6.2.3.3-2:

TABLE 6.2.3.3-2: AITON TONE BOX

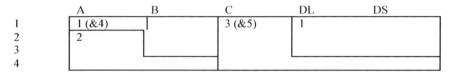

	A	B	C	DL	DS
1	1 (&4)		3 (&5)	1	
2	2				
3					
4					

Description of Tones:
1. mid/high level
2. high level then falling
3. mid falling
(4. mid rising)
(5. mid falling glottalized)

Eliciting the Aiton tonal system was not straightforward, unlike the Phake and Khamyang. This experience of difficulty with the Aiton tonal system was shared with Banchob Bandhumedha, in whose manuscript *Aiton–English–Thai Dictionary* there are no fewer than 10 tones marked. Some of these are clearly allotones, but it is also clear that Banchob never completed her analysis of Aiton tones.

Diller (1992: 18) reported two different systems for Aiton, one similar to Table 6.2.3.3-2 and the other somewhat similar to the Phake system as described in Table 6.2.3.1-1. Despite considerable effort, I have not been able to find any Aiton speaker who uses a tonal system like that reported by Diller and called Aiton$_2$.

6.2.3.4. *Ahom tones*

Almost nothing is known of the original tonal system of the Ahoms. Grierson, having indicated that there should be tones in Ahom, adds:

'Moreover, in the one word, the tones of which I have been able to ascertain, they differ from those of the Khāmtī and Shān. This is the word *mā*, which, when it means 'a horse, has in Āhom a long tone, and in Khāmtī and abrupt tone, while *mā*, 'a dog', has in Āhom an abrupt tone, but in Khāmtī and Shān a rising inflection.' (1904: 90)

It would be most curious if this statement reflected the situation. The abrupt tone referred to is presumably a glottalized or creaky tone, a feature of words with C tones (such as the word for 'horse'), but rarely if ever of A tones (such as the word for 'dog'). Grierson gives no information about his source for this claim, and it must be treated with some caution.

The only recent attempt to reconstruct Ahom tones has been Weidert (1979), who compared the Shan, Standard Thai and Khamti tonal systems in order to make a reconstruction of the Ahom tonal system. I do not believe that his methodology was valid. First of all it fails to take into account the tonal systems of the other Tai languages remaining in Assam, the Aiton, Khamyang and Phake. Secondly, Weidert's methodology gave equal weight to each of the three languages, even although Standard Thai is not part of the Shan group of languages and on linguistic grounds has been separated from Ahom for a long time.

Future attempts to reconstruct the original Ahom tone system might involve:

- Exploring foreign sources, particularly from China, which have data about the Ahom. It is likely that Chinese missions visited Assam over the centuries, and if they did, they may have collected some linguistic information about Ahom. Any recording of the Ahom language in Chinese would encode information about the Ahom tones.

- Comparing the tonal systems of the existing Tai languages of Assam and trying to explain how they came about. Existing tone systems in Assam are quite different from those in, for example, Shan state of Burma. This may be due to the influence of the Ahom.

6.3. NOTES ON THE MORPHOSYNTAX OF THE TAI LANGUAGES OF ASSAM

6.3.1. Morphology

In common with many languages of Southeast Asia, the Tai languages are isolating in structure and share a common propensity for monosyllabic morphemes (Edmondson and Solnit 1997: 7). Both 'content words' and 'function words' are generally expressed by such monosyllabic morphemes, as in (7):

7)
hā¹	nɛ⁴	luk⁴ ɔn¹	nɛ⁴	pɛ⁴	kün²	kā¹	trā²	nɛ⁴
time	DEF	child	DEF	win	RECIP	GO	case	DEF

'So the boy won the case.'
(Phake Story, *Story of the kum bird*, told by Ee Nyan Khet)

As will be discussed below in section 6.4, some grammatical functions such as Tense, Aspect and Modality (TAM) are expressed by morphemes which while also functioning as independent words, sometimes behave like bound morphemes. This can be seen in example (7) with *kā¹* 'go', which is here realized with initial consonant lenition as [ŋā¹], with assimilation to the previous nasal. In some cases where *kā¹* follows a verb, the articulation of the two morphemes approaches that of a single phonological word. This initial consonant lenition is found only in Phake, and not in the other Tai varieties.

The Tai varieties in Assam are not exclusively isolating; nor is the vocabulary exclusively monosyllabic. Compounds are commonly formed, such as *luk⁴ ɔn¹* in (7), which is formed from two monosyllabic morphemes, *luk⁴* 'child' and *ɔn¹* 'small'. There are also polysyllabic morphemes which cannot be analysed as a compound of two monosyllables. Some of these arise due to borrowings from Burmese, Assamese and Pali/Sanskrit or due to reduction of initial syllables, so that in Phake the word for 'brinjal' (eggplant) is *ma¹ khɔ⁶*, from two Tai words *maak¹ khɔ⁶* (fruit-brinjal).

Even clearer examples of non-isolating morphology are found with the use of changed tone in Phake to express negation, imperatives and questions, discussed below in section 6.5, a phenomenon which appears to be unique in the Tai-Kadai languages.

6.3.2. Syntactic structure

The Tai languages of Assam exhibit a basic constituent order of Subject Verb Object (SVO) as exemplified in (8):

8)
kon²	mɔŋ²	khau⁶	kā¹	pam³	mai⁴	nan⁴	sɛ⁶
person	city	3PL	go	fell	tree	that	PRT
'These city people went and cut that tree down.'							
(Phake Story, *Story of the foolish king*, told by Ee Nyan Khet)							

Sentences with a different constituent order very frequently occur in Tai. Since the expression of noun phrases is not obligatory in any of these languages, if a participant has already been introduced, it is not necessary to express it either by a full noun phrase or by a pronoun. Therefore a sentence such as (9) would be as grammatical as (8), provided that the agent had already been introduced into the discourse.

9)   ကၞ   ၒ   ၓ   ၶၮၵ   ၸၺ ။
      kā¹   pam³   mai⁴   nan⁴   se⁶
      go   fell   tree   that   PRT
      '(They) cut that tree down.'

If there is only one noun phrase, there is a preference for this noun phrase to be expressed before the verb. In some cases, this would see a surface constituent order of OV realized. Even when two NPs are present, the object NP may be topicalized, leading to realizations of either SOV or OSV. This phenomenon, combined with the fact that these languages are spoken in an area where most of the other languages (Assamese and the various Tibeto-Burman languages) have fixed SOV constituent order, has led some scholars to propose that constituent order in the Tai languages is shifting towards SOV.

For example, Greenberg (1966: 109) listed Khamti, uniquely among the Tai family, as having a basic 'word' order of SOV, the norm for Tai being SVO. It appears that Greenberg's observation was based on Grierson's conclusions, which are themselves based on Needham's *General Rules of Syntax* for Khamti (1894: 81), restated here:

TABLE 6.3.2-1: GENERAL RULES OF SYNTAX FOR KHAMTI (NEEDHAM 1894: 81)

a)	The adjective follows the noun it qualifies
b)	Numerals sometimes precede, at others follow, the nouns they qualify. When a numeral particle is used, they invariably follow the noun they qualify.
c)	Demonstrative pronouns are generally placed immediately after the nouns they qualify, except in relative clauses when they may either be put at the beginning or at the end of the sentence.
d)	Relative clauses should stand before antecedent clauses
e)	Interrogative pronouns rarely ever stand first in a sentence.
f)	Adverbs are generally placed after a verb.
g)	Prepositions precede their nouns
h)	The order of words in a predicative sentence are (1) subject, (2) direct object, (3) indirect object, and (4) verb. In an interrogative sentence the order is (1) subject, (2) indirect object, (3) direct object, and (4) verb.

Needham appears to have derived his *General Rules of Syntax* from elicited sentences. When Diller (1992) examined more closely the data in Needham (1894), he identified examples showing a wide range of constituent orders – with both OV and VO being represented – and concluded that

'The general impression, especially from connected text, is of very "pragmatically" controlled configuration: issues such as topicality, specificness, and so forth, appear to play a crucial role on how sentence constituents are ordered' (1992: 27).

On the other hand, Wilaiwan, who has undertaken fieldwork among the Khamti, reported that 'SOV is the dominant word order in Kamti while in other known Tai dialects SOV is the dominant one. We may conclude that Kamti has developed from SVO to SOV' (1986: 178).

My own limited fieldwork among the Khamti speakers in Assam and some from Arunachal Pradesh, has not confirmed Wilaiwan's conclusion. When asked to provide a translation into

Khamti for 'the tiger ate the deer', the traditional Khamti chief Chaw Khamoon Gohain, immediately produced (10):[11]

10) ꠅ꠰ꠅ   ꠌꠛ   ꠌꠛꠇ ॥
     suɯ⁴   kaap¹   phaan³
     tiger   bite   barking deer
     'The tiger ate the barking deer.'

On further questioning, he stated that (11) could also be used – where the O argument is marked by a 'postposition' *mai⁵*.

11) ꠅ꠰ꠅ   ꠌꠛꠇ   ꠗ   ꠌꠛ ॥
     suɯ⁴   phaan³   mai⁵   kaap¹
     tiger   barking deer to   bite
     'The tiger ate the barking deer.'

I was also able to record a small amount of text from Chaw Khamoon, and in those texts, most of the sentences did have the verb in final position, with the animate object marked with *mai⁵*. On the basis of this, we might tentatively conclude that SOV is possible in Khamti if the O is marked by the word *mai⁵*. Only further research, including the collection and analysis of substantial corpus of Khamti texts, will be able to further illuminate this issue.

All the Tai varieties in India show considerable variation in the ordering of the arguments around the verb. Nevertheless, it is at least arguable that SVO remains the basic word order.[12] There seems to be a preference that if there is only one noun phrase argument, with the exception of an NP incorporated with a verb, it will be placed before the verb.[13] In practise, therefore, sentences with objects are often not SVO.[14] A more detailed discussion of constituent order is found in Morey (in press).

The core arguments of a predication are expressed either as noun phrases or as prepositional phrases. Noun phrases are headed by nouns or pronouns, the former of which can be postmodified in a variety of ways, such as in example (12) which shows a noun modified by an adjective and example (13) which shows a noun modified by a possessor:

---

11 The tones are numbered after Harris (1976).
12 The late Aimya Khang Gohain, of the Tai Phake, insisted that these languages were SVO and made corrections to stories and other texts given to me by other villagers so that they reflected this proscription.
13 A good example of this is seen in the following sentence:

hauu²	kin²	dii²	ʒau³	haŋ²		mɛ²	kɔ³	hauu³	kin²
or	eat	good	FINISHED	to		mother	also	for	eat

haŋ²	man²	kɔ³	hauu³	kin²
to	3SG	LINK	GIVE	eat

'They fed them well, both his mother and him.'

(Aiton story, *The twelve questions*, told by Sa Cham Thoumoung)

14 Diller (1992: 20 fn44) wisely reminds us that 'the question of a viable characterization of SUBJECT for Tai languages is not above theoretical interest, but here we must be content with 'pretheoretic' S, O, and so forth'. Diller's advice will be followed in this chapter.

12) ကွန်ꩬ်   ဆုင်ႆ ॥
    kon²   suŋ⁶
    person   tall
    'a tall person'
    (Phake sentence)

13) ပꩰ်လိက်   လုက်ꩰ်ꩫ်   ꩫꩫ် ॥
    pāp⁴ lik⁴   luk⁴ ɔn¹   nan⁴
    book   child   that
    'the child's book'
    (Phake sentence)

As mentioned earlier, some arguments are marked in prepositional phrases. Animate core participants which are not agents (anti-agentive) are frequently found in prepositional phrases marked by the preposition *haŋ²* 'to', as in (14).

14) ꩧ   ꩫ   သꩫ်   ꩫ   ကꩰ်   ꩬꩫ်   ꩾꩫ်   ꩫꩫ်   ꩤ   ꩫ ॥
    hā¹ nɛ⁴ sɔ̄⁶ nɛ⁴ kāp⁴ tüŋ¹ wɔt⁴ haŋ² mū⁶ nɛ⁴
    time DEF tiger DEF bite all PRT to pig DEF
    'The tiger ate the pig up.'
    (Phake Story, *Story of deception*, told by Ee Nyan Khet)

The use of the prepositional phrase in (14) might be a type of non-obligatory case marking, used both with objects and with indirect objects and sometimes with a subject when it is in the role of experiencer. Pragmatic and discourse factors determine when it is used. This 'preposition' *haŋ²* and the Khamti postposition *mai⁵*, illustrated above in (11), appear to have exactly the same function – the marking of animate non-agents.

    Adjectives can also appear as the intransitive predicate, as in (15):

15) ပꩰ်သꩫ်ꩬ်   ꩫ   ဆꩫ်   သꩫ် ॥
    pa¹ sāu⁶   nɛ⁴   sɔp¹   phɛu⁶
    girl   DEF beautiful excessive
    'That girl was very beautiful.'
    (Phake Story, *Story of the foolish king*, told by Ee Nyan Khet)

Like other languages of the Tai-Kadai family, the Tai languages of Assam have classifiers for counting most nouns. Several hundred specific classifiers have been recorded, but are very infrequently encountered in texts or everyday conversation. The most common classifiers are the general classifier *an²*, the classifier for person *kɔ⁴* and the classifier for animals, *to²/tuu²*. Their use is exemplified in (16):

16) ꩤ   ꩧ   ꩬ ॥
    muu¹   haa³   tuu²
    pig   five   CLF
    'Five Pigs'
    (Aiton sentence)

6.4. THE DEVELOPMENT OF BOUND TAM MARKERS IN TAI AITON

6.4.1. Areal influence on the Tai languages of Assam

Given that the Tai languages of Assam have been in close contact with languages of the Tibeto-Burman family for many centuries, and more recently have come into contact with some Indo-European languages, particularly Assamese, we might expect areal influence on the Tai languages. Furthermore, since the first arrival of Tai people in India in the thirteenth century, they have also become gradually separated from those who speak other languages of the Tai family.

Considerable word borrowing from both Burmese and Assamese is found among the Tai languages.[15] Both Burmese and Assamese are much more widely spoken and more prestigious than the Tai varieties. On the other hand, there is very little borrowing from other Tibeto-Burman languages spoken in Northeast India, despite the Tais having been in contact with these groups for many years.

Syntactic change is also occurring in the Tai languages, with constituent order change and the apparently related phenomenon of the development of bound TAM markers discussed in this chapter.

Grierson (1904) was probably the first to explicitly suggest an origin of this influence. Basing his claims about Khamti on Needham (1894) and about Shan on Cushing (1888), he discussed constituent order (which he calls 'order of words'), as follows:

> In the different members of the Tai languages customs differ as to the order of words. ... Shan and Khamti appear to have been influenced by Tibeto-Burman languages in this respect. ... In Siamese, the order of words is as in English, subject, verb, object. ... In Shan the rule about the object following the verb is not imperative, whereas in Khamti (which at the present day stands isolated amid a sea of Tibeto-Burman languages), the order is as in them, subject, object, verb ...' (1904: 75-6)

Diller (1992: 20-21) also discussed this, categorising the 'shifting from what was undoubtedly original Tai S-V-O order to the "Brahmaputra areal" S-O-V order' as being of 'more than passing interest'.

However, as exemplified above in section 6.3.2, there is a considerable variation in the ordering of the core arguments in Khamti and in all the Tai varieties in Assam. Whilst it appears that this variation is an indication of a gradual shift to a verb final syntax, it would not be appropriate to describe these languages as having a fixed constituent order. One of the factors that influences constituent order appears to be the TAM marking described below.

6.4.2. Position of TAM markers in Tai languages

In all the Tai languages, there are TAM markers that precede the verb, such as Aiton ta^1 'WILL' and those that follow the verb. This section discusses only the TAM markers that follow the verb. In other languages of the Tai family, if the object is expressed, these TAM markers will be separated from the verb and placed utterance final, as in (17), an example from Standard Thai:

17) chán   súː   khâːw   maːléːw
     I   buy   rice   COME-ALREADY
     S V_t–   O   (–V_t)
(Standard Thai sentence, after Panupong 1970: 20)

This is called a discontinuous constituent by Panupong. She marked this constituent V_t– ... (–V_t), showing that there was a transitive verb (V_t) complex, interrupted by the object. Vichin adds that it is possible to antepose the object, thus making the discontinuous constituent 'continuous' (1970: 20).

We can typify the pattern of (17) in (18):

---

15 Burmese borrowing into Tai has yet to be comprehensively studied. It appears that a large proportion of the Burmese vocabulary in Tai are words borrowed and pronounced by the Tais according to the written Burmese form rather than the current standard Burmese pronunciation.

18) S V O TAM marker

If the object is topicalized, or elided for any reason, the TAM marked will end up immediately following the verb, leading to the patterns in (19) or (20) – where only (20) is possible in standard Thai:

19) S (O) V TAM marker

20) (O) S V TAM marker

Examples of both of these are found in Tai Aiton, as in (21), which is an example of (19), and (22), which is an example of (20). Both examples are from the same speaker and the same text.

21)

လၟ	လုၵ်	လၢန်	မန်	ၸ်	မန်	ၸေႃ ||
lai^3	luk^3	laan^1	man^2	khau^1	man^2	cau^3
so	child	grandchild	3SG	1PL	3SG	self

မိုင်	သီ	အၼ်	ၶူ	ၵႃ ||
muɳ^2	sii^1	an^2	khuu^2	kaa^1
country	four	CLF	build	GO

'Then his descendents, themselves, founded four countries.'

22)

ၸႃ	မန်	ၵေႃ	ၵုၼ်	သိုင်	ၵုၼ်	မိုင် ||
caa^2	man^2	kɔ^3	kun^2	suɳ^1	kun^2	muɳ^2
to	3SG	LINK	person	country	person	country

သၟတ်	လၟ	ႁဝ်	ၵႃ ||
sɔt^1	phai^2	hau^3	kaa^1
burn	fire	GIVE	GO

'The countrymen burned his body.'
(Aiton Historical Manuscript read by Nang Wimala Thoumoung)

In both (21) and (22), *kaa^1*, a marker indicating that the event is past and gone, is adjacent to the main verb. This occurs because the objects, *muɳ^2 sii^1 an^2* 'four countries' and *caa^2 man^2* 'him' in (21) and (22) respectively, have been anteposed.

A further development is shown in (23), where the order of subject, verb and object is the common Tai SVO, but the TAM marker is no longer in final position, being now adjacent to the verb in the middle of the sentence.

23)

မန်	အႃ	ပၢၵ်	ၼွၵ်	မန်	ၸ	ၵပ်	ၵႃ
mɔn^2	aa^3	paak^1	nɔi^3	mɔn^2	pai^2	kap^3	kaa^1
3SG	open	mouth	PRT	3SG	go	bite	GO

ၵွၼ်	ၼိုဝ် ||
kɔn^3	nɯ^3
piece	meat

'He opened his mouth to grab that piece of meat.'
(Aiton Story, *Story of the crow and the fox*, No. 56, told by Ong Cham.)

This sentence is of the pattern:

24)   S   V   TAM marker   O

Diller (2001) has described seven different grammaticalized uses of *kaa¹*, the proto Tai
*kwaːɓ₁, which originally meant 'to pass beyond'. Of these, describing the phenomenon we
are observing here, he stated: 'An extreme development ... is in the Assamese variety Aiton,
where the item has become a postclitic on main verbs. The direct object, if any, follows.'

As a consequence of the frequent topicalization of objects, the verb is frequently observed
adjacent to at least some of its TAM morphology. It appears that the speakers are in the
process of reinterpreting this TAM morphology as being attached to the verb. In such a
circumstance, a sentence such as (23) can then arise.

We will now examine the historical development of this phenomenon.

6.4.3. TAM markers in Tai Aiton

Table 6.4.3-1 lists seven Tense/Aspect/Mood markers frequently recorded in Aiton texts:

TABLE 6.4.3-1: TAM MARKERS IN AITON TEXTS

Marker	Gloss	Grammaticalized meaning
kaa¹	GO	Marker of past time
maa²	COME	Marker of past time, used when the scope of the process indicated by the verb is in some way towards the speaker.[16]
wai³	KEEP	Marker of past time, used when the process indicated by the verb had or has some continuation.
ai³	PRT	Possibly a grammaticalized reduction of *wai³* 'KEEP'
ʒau³	FINISHED	Indicates that the process of the verb is complete, or that a section of the text has been completed
ta¹, tak¹, ti¹	WILL	Marker of future action, or action which should be undertaken
nai³ / dai³	GET	In preverbal position, indicates that the process has been or will be accomplished

The interpretations assigned to each of these must be regarded as tentative. None of these
words have been fully bleached of their original verbal meanings, except for *ai³*. In particular
kaa¹, *maa²*, *wai³* and *nai³/dai³* are all commonly found as full verbs in their original meaning.

As we shall see, the phenomenon of the attachment of the TAM morphology to the verb
that is exhibited in (23) above is widespread in Aiton narrative texts. For the time being these
morphemes will be described as TAM markers without attempting to further characterize
them, and they will be glossed as in Table 6.4.4.3-1.

6.4.4. Development of bound TAM morphemes in Aiton narrative texts

The study of Aiton texts has allowed a degree of time depth in examination of this
phenomenon. Three manuscripts will be compared below: a text which is perhaps 200 or more
years old and which shows few signs of this phenomenon (see 4.4.1), a text which is perhaps
100 years old and shows some signs of the phenomenon (see 4.4.2), and a text which was
probably complied within the last 50 years which shows marking on almost every sentence
(see 4.4.3). These will then be compared with contemporary spoken practise (4.4.4).

---

16   See, for example, Appendix 1, sentence 6.

6.4.4.1. *The oldest historical Aiton MS: (ca. eighteenth/nineteeth century)*

The *Creation of the World* is written on one side of a manuscript now kept in the village of Ban Lung (Bargaon), Karbi Anglong District, Assam. It is one of the oldest surviving Aiton manuscripts. On the reverse side of this manuscript, several later MSS are written, including the *Book of history (from) the time of the ancestor Chaw Tai Lung up until Sukapha*, which is discussed in 4.4.2.

The *Creation of the World* contains very few examples of the use of *kaa¹*, either as a TAM marker or as a full verb. Example (25) is one case where it is arguably acting as a TAM marker.

25)					
	တင်ကႃ	ၼံ	လိက်	ၼံ	ၼွိ ။
	taŋ¹ kaa¹	nam³	lik³	nam³	nɔi¹
	all	river	small	river	small
	ႁိင်	ꩡိုမ်	ကႃ	ꩡံ	ယွ် ။
	hɛŋ³	cɯm²	kaa¹	cam³	ʒau³
	dry	evaporate	GO	PRT	FINISHED

'All the small rivers have dried up and evaporated.'
(*Creation of the World* No. 8)

This example suggests that the process by which *kaa¹* is becoming a TAM marker began several centuries ago. This sentence is also important because it may give some clues as to where this process began. It is usually believed the Aitons came into Assam around 300 years ago from Burma; possibly bringing this manuscript with them, or at least bringing an older copy of it. If so, that would suggest that this innovation began before the Aitons had any contact with the Assamese language.

6.4.4.2. *Late nineteenth century MS*

The word *kaa1* is found rather more frequently in the *Book of history (from) the time of the ancestor Chau Tai Lung up until Sukapha* (Morey 1999b) which although written on the back of *The Creation of the World*, is in a different hand and was clearly written somewhat later.

Example (26) shows the use of *kaa¹* immediately following the verb. It could be argued that this use of *kaa¹* is a serial verb structure indicating direction, or that it is a sentence of the form of (23) above, an SVO sentence in which *kaa¹* is a TAM marker directly adjacent to the verb. If it is the latter, it is the oldest example of such a sentence yet identified. It should be noted that the object of this sentence is a prepositional phrase. There is no example in the text of a sentence showing verb-*kaa¹*-object NP:

26)[17]								
	ယင်	ꩡွ်ယိုမ်ꩭၼ်	ဝ	ၼို	တူ	ၼင်	မိုင်	ကွိ ။
	ʒaŋ²	cau³ sɯ¹ khan	wai³	naɯ²	tuu²	naaŋ²	mɯŋ²	kɔi³
	have	Chaw Su Khan	keep	in	body	lady	country	PRT
	ယွတ်ၸြႃမွက်ꩭံၼိင်			ပွက်	ကႃ	တံ	မိုင်ၸြိ	ယွ် ။
	ʒɔt³ phaa³ mɔk¹ kham² nɛŋ²			pɔk³	kaa¹	tam²	mɯŋ² phii¹	ʒau³
	Yot Pha Mok Kham Naeng			return	GO	to	heaven	FINISHED

17 I was not able to establish the correct tones for several words in this sentence. The Tai script does not mark tone, so proper names are a particular problem, as their original meaning tends to get lost and several interpretations become possible.

'At the time when Chaw Su Khan was still in the Queen's womb, the God Yot Pha Mok Kham Naeng returned to heaven.'

(*Book of history (from) the time of the ancestor Chaw Tai Lung up until Sukapha* No. 22)

This example is important because it shows the particle ka *kaa*^{1}, as a TAM marker, directly following the verb, whereas the TAM particle *ʒau*^{3}, which marks completion, is utterance final.

However, in this particular text, the word *kaa*^{1} is only found five times in a text that has 79 sentences and runs for four pages of manuscript. Several of the other examples show *kaa*^{1} as a TAM marker, but its position is sentence final, as in (18) above:

27)

cau^3 sɯ^1 khan phaa^3	caŋ^2 tii^2	maa^2
Chaw Su Khan Pha will come		

au^2	luk^3	caai^2	cau^3 sɯ^1 ʒɔt^3 phaa^3	kaa^1	hɔ^1 ‖
take	son	male	Chaw Su Yot Pha	GO	PRT

'Chaw Su Khan Pha came and took the son of Chaw Su Yot Pha.'

(*Book of history (from) the time of the ancestor Chaw Tai Lung up until Sukapha* No. 41)

One sentence in the text, here given as example (28), has not only the order of (23), but also gives indication as to the scope of the marker.

28)

haɯ^3	kaa^1	kin^2	tai^2 pɔŋ^2	kɔi^3 ‖
give	GO	eat	Tai Pong	PRT

'He was given Tai Pong (country) to rule.'

(*Book of history (from) the time of the ancestor Chaw Tai Lung up until Sukapha* No. 34)

This is not translated as 'He was given Tai Pong and ruled it', because it is the verb *haɯ*^{3} which bears the TAM marking rather than the verb *kin*^{2} 'eat' – here metaphorically extended to mean 'rule'.

Perhaps at the time of the composition of this manuscript, only one verb in a sentence could carry this marker. In contrast, in (29), from a contemporary speaker, both *haɯ*^{3} and the verb that follows it (a compound verb meaning 'kill', which Sa Cham Thoumoung mistakenly gave as *taai*^{2} *au*^{2} 'die-take' rather than the more usual *au*^{2} *taai*^{2}) are marked by *kaa*^{1}.

29)

cit^1	wan^2	nai^3	khau^1	ma^1	dai^3
seven	day	this	3PL	NEG	get
haɯ^3	taai^2	au^2	kaa^1	ʒau^3 ‖	
give	die	take	GO	FINISHED	

'If they have not got (the answer) in these seven days, let them be killed.'

(Aiton Story, *Story of the twelve questions* No. 31, told by Sa Cham Thoumoung)

Further cross-linguistic examination of texts in the Tai languages across a range of time will be needed to add to our understanding of this phenomenon.

6.4.4.3. *Mid twentieth century text*

A further development of *kaa¹* can be seen in a story told by Nang Wimala Thoumoung, who said of this story that:

30) ပုင်   ကာၤ်   ၜၢင်ၜ   ꩫꧤ   ꧯꧤꩬꧥ   ꩮ   ꩩ   ꧠ ။
     puŋ¹   an²   ʒaa² sii¹   naaŋ² kɔi³   phaa³ luŋ¹   khai²   wai³   kaa¹
     story   CLF   nun   Nang Koi   Phalung   tell   KEEP   GO
     'The nun Nang Koi Phalung told this story.'

It is not known whether Nang Koi Phalung possessed a old manuscript of this history, or whether she learned the story from reading manuscripts or listening to other people. The version discussed here was read in January 2000 by Nang Wimala Thoumoung from a Tai language manuscript written in Assamese script. A copy of the MS, in Tai script, was made by Bidya Thoumoung and this was used as the basis for an analysis. The analysis was then rechecked with Nang Wimala in April 2001. She compared the version in Bidya Thoumoung's MS with her own MS in Assamese script, and any differences were noted.

The first 15 lines of the text are reproduced in Appendix 1. In examining these sentences, and taking lines 1 & 2 as a single sentence, we can see that the main verb in each line is usually marked with some kind of TAM marker, as follows:

TABLE 6.4.4.3-1: SENTENCE ANALYSIS IN NANG WIMALA'S HISTORICAL STORY

Line	TAM Marker	Example	Gloss	Translation
1-2	kaa¹	hit¹ kaa¹	make-GO	'made'
3	ta¹ nai³ .... wai³	ta¹ nai³ pai² khup¹ paai³ wai³	WILL-GET-go-kneel-pray-KEEP	'went to pray'
4	ai³	khup¹ paai³ ai³	kneel-pray-PRT	'prayed', 'kept praying'
5	kaa¹	duut¹ kaa¹	hot-GO	'was hot', 'became hot'
6	maa²	nuu² lɛm² maa²	look-see-COME	'looked towards'
7	maa²	nuu² han¹ maa²	look-see-COME	'saw'
8	kaa¹	hɔŋ³ kaa¹	call-GO	'called'
9	kaa¹	hɔŋ³ kaa¹	call-GO	'called'
9	maa²	thin¹ maa²	send-COME	'sent'
9.1	kaa¹	khai² sup¹ khai² khaam² kaa¹	tell-mouth-tell-word-GO	'discussed'
9.2	kaa¹	hɔŋ³ kaa¹	call-GO	'called'
10	maa² ... wai³	maa² suŋ¹ wai³	COME-send-KEEP	'sent'
10.1	kaa¹	kaai¹ khuu¹ lai¹ maa²	erect ... COME	'erected (a ladder)'
10.1	maa²	luŋ² maa²	down ... COME	'came down'
10.2	kaa¹	taŋ³ ... kaa¹	set up ... GO	'founded'
11	kaa¹	tɛ¹ ... kaa¹	make ... GO	'made'
12	kaa¹	taŋ³ ... kaa¹	set up ... GO	'founded'
13	kaa¹	kaaŋ³ kaa¹ laai¹ kaa¹	wide-GO-many-GO	'increased'
14	-			
14.1	wai³	khai² wai³	tell-KEEP	'told'
14.2	kaa¹	pin² kaa¹	be-GO	'was'
15	kaa¹	pin² kaa¹	be-GO	'was'

In every sentence in Table 6.4.4.3-1 except for those numbered (9.1), (11), (12), (14) and (15.1), the main verb is marked by either *kaa¹*, *maa²* or *wai³* immediately following the verb, following the patterns in (19), (20) or (23) above.

In (9.1) from Table 6.4.4.3-1, the nouns *sup¹* 'mouth' and *khaam²* 'word' are part of an elaborated four syllable expression. These two nouns are arguably behaving syntactically as if they were incorporated nouns, in which case the TAM marker would not be regarded as following the object.

In sentences (11) and (12) from Nang Wimala's story, the direct object of the verb intervenes. Sentence (11) is here reproduced as (31):

31)
a¹ luk³	pa¹ nan³	khau¹	sɔŋ¹	pii²	nɔŋ³
from	there	3PL	two	elder	younger

sɔŋ¹	caai²	tɛ¹	muŋ²	kaa¹	tii²	nan³
two	male	make/begin	country	GO	place	that

'Then those two brothers made a kingdom/country there.'
(Nang Wimala's *Historical Story* No. 11)

It might be argued that this too is a case of object incorporation, where *tɛ¹ muŋ²* is analysed as a single grammatical word, meaning 'found a country'. However, example (32), from the same text, also has the object (and adjective) between the verb and *kaa¹*, and here it seems less likely to be an object incorporation meaning 'to live tiger catch'. It must be added, however, that the question of how we establish what is clear incorporation and what is not still remains to be explored for the Tai varieties in India.

32)
aai³ tɔn³	khau¹	sɛu³	suɯ¹	nip¹ /dip¹	maa²
Aiton	3PL	catch	tiger	alive	COME

'The Aitons caught a live tiger.'
(Nang Wimala's *Historical Story* No. 79)

The case of (14) from Nang Wimala's story - here reprinted as (33) - is interesting. It is a negative sentence and perhaps indicates that there is some restriction on the use of these TAM particles with negatives, or alternatively some restriction on the use of TAM markers when there are final modal particles like *pɛ³* and *dai³* which mark ability.

33)
naŋ¹ nai³	waa²	kau³	pa³	hui¹	thuu¹	kau³	mun¹	mɔ³
like that	say	9	basket	seed	bean	9	10000	pot

khau³	kau³	pɛ²	mai³	saaŋ²	aan¹	pa¹	pɛ³
rice	9	bundle	wood	bamboo	count	NEG	can

tak³	pa¹	dai³/nai³	phan²	tai²	ʒaŋ²
count	NEG	get	tribe	Tai	be

'It was said that there were as many Tai people as nine baskets of seeds, ninety thousand pots of rice and nine bundles of bamboo, so many that they could not be counted in voice or on paper.'
(Nang Wimala's *Historical Story* No. 14)

To summarize the TAM marking in this text, we can construct the following frame:

34) Subject   (WILL)   verb   (TAM₁)   (Object) (TAM₁)(TAM₂)

In (34), TAM$_1$ stands for those markers like *kaa^1* 'GO', *maa^2* 'COME' or *wai^3* 'KEEP' that can stand either before or after the object, and TAM$_2$ stands for utterance final aspect markers like *yau^3* 'FINISHED'.

Furthermore, as (35) below will show, it is not necessary to overtly mark time when a temporal adverbial is added.

6.4.4.4. *Contemporary spoken texts*

Having analysed Nang Wimala's manuscript in some detail, an argument can be made out for the gradual development of almost obligatory marking of past time in narrative texts, using one of a number of (near-) bound morphemes, of which *kaa^1* is the most frequent.

However, in a number of contemporary stories, we do not find this phenomenon as frequently as in Nang Wimala's story.

Appendix 2 presents the first twelve lines of a text told by Ong Cham in January 1998. Following the methodology of Table 6.4.4.3-1 above, we will examine each sentence in turn. Sentence 1, which names the text, is omitted.

TABLE 6.4.4.4-1: ANALYSIS OF SENTENCES IN ONG CHAM'S *STORY OF THE CROW AND THE FOX*

Line	TAM Marker	Example	Gloss	Translation
2	ta^1	ta^1 khai^2	WILL-tell	'will tell'
3	–			
4	dai^3	uɯŋ^1 dai^3 kin^2	NEG-GET-eat	'didn't get to eat.'
5	–			
6	kaa^1	pai^2 kaa^1	go-GO	'went'
7	-			
8	kaa^1	pai^2 ... kaa^1	go ... GO	'went'
9	–			
10	–			
11	–			
12	kaa^1	pai^2 thuɯŋ^1 kaa^1	go-reach-GO	'went up to, reached'

A number of the sentences in Ong Cham's story have the existential verb *ʒaŋ^2* as the main verb. Although there are sentences recorded with this verb and the TAM markers under discussion, they seem to be less frequently found with the existential verb than with other verbs.

Ong Cham's story also contains several negative sentences, such as (4) and several sentences like (5) – here reprinted as (35) – which are marked by temporal adverbs which indicate the time relationship, making the marking of past time redundant, although still possible and found in some other examples:

35) ၌ၜ   ဃၜ်   ၢၢ်   ကၤ   ၢၢၤ်   ကၦ   ၡၤၢ်   ၜၒ   ၡၤၢၣ် ॥
     muu^2 ʒaam^2 nan^3 kaa^2 an^2 uu^1 luk^3 tii^2 tun^3 mai^3
     time   time   that   crow   CLF   live   from   at   tree
     'At that time the crow was living in a tree.'
     (Ong Cham's *Story of the crow and the fox* No 5)

However, there are also sentences in Ong Cham's story which have no TAM marking of any kind, and yet are clearly past time, such as (10) – here reprinted as (36).

36) ဖော်   ၀   ၂ဟန်   ၌ဖ်   ၇ာ၇ဖ် ။
     mɔn²   pai²   han¹   nɯ³   an²
     3SG   go   see   meat   CLF
     'She went to look at that meat!'
     (Ong Cham's *Story of the crow and the fox* No 10)

This sentence would also be acceptable with *kaa¹* following the verb *han¹* 'see', but Ong Cham chose not to use it. Clearly *kaa¹* is not obligatory for marking past time in situations like this.

In some contemporary stories, the use of the TAM marker is somewhat more widespread. Example (37) consists of two sentences spoken by Sa Cham Thoumoung. They are part of a story in which two brothers go out hunting. The first shoots and misses, but the second gets his prey:

37.1) ၁ှ်ဖ   ကၣ   ၀ှ   ၈ၣ၇ဖ်   ကၣ ။
       ʒɯ²   kaa¹   ma¹   thuk¹   kaa¹
       shoot   GO   NEG   touch   GO
       'He shot but didn't hit it.'

37.2) ၁ှ်ဖ   ကၣ   ၀   ၈ၣ၇ဖ်   ကၣ ။
       ʒɯ²   kaa¹   pai²   thuk¹   kaa¹
       shoot   GO   go   touch   GO
       'He shot and hit it.'

It was stated above in the discussion of (33) that it appeared that the time marking with *kaa¹* might not apply when the sentence was negative. This however is not the case in (37.1) in which the second verb is clearly negative, and clearly marked with *kaa¹*.

6.4.4.5. *Conversation*

Conversation is even less likely to mark verbs in this way – even when past time is being talked about - because conversation relies much more on context. The various particles listed in Table 6.4.3-1 occur very infrequently in any of the conversations which have so far been analysed, at least in part because much of the text is in the present tense, and therefore unmarked by those particles; and much of what remains was negative.

However, whenever the future time was intended, the future particle *ti¹* or *ta¹* is obligatory.

The following is an exchange clearly in past time. It is an extract of a conversation[18] between myself and Nabin Shyam Phalung:

Stephen Morey

38.1) Anthony Diller   ၈ၣ   ၀ၥ် ။
                             waa²   saŋ¹
       Anthony Diller   say   what
       'What did Anthony Diller say (about it)?'

---

18   The topic of the conversation is the difficulty of the tones in the Aiton Tai variety!

Nabin Shyam

38.2)   လဲကောၵ္ပို   ၵ္ဍ   ဎပ်   ဎၵ္ဎ   ⋯⋯ ॥
    lai³ kɔ³ pɯ²   waa²   ʒaap¹   luŋ¹   ai³
    therefore   say   difficult   much   PRT

    Anthony Diller   ၵ္ဍ   ⋯⋯   ⋯ ॥
    waa²   caa²   hau²
    Anthony Diller   say   to   1PL

    ၵ်   ⋯⋯   ⋯⋯   ကွယ်ၜြၥၵ္ဎၵ္ဍ   ⋯⋯ ॥
    mu²   hau²   kaa¹   ɔs¹ trɛ¹ lii¹ yaa¹   naa³
    time   1PL   go   Australia   PRT
    '"It is really difficult", Anthony Diller said to us when we went to Australia.'

Example (38.2) is in three sections: in the first line, the verb is marked by *ai³*, a particle which appears to be a grammaticalization of *wai³* 'KEEP'. The second line is not marked by any TAM marker, and the last line, added as an afterthought, contains a temporal adverbial which clearly indicates past time, and incidentally contains a non-grammaticalized usage of *kaa¹* in its full verbal meaning of 'go'.

6.4.5. Is *kaa¹* a past tense marker?

It has been shown that *kaa¹* is widely used in Aiton narratives to indicate past time, but can it be called a past tense marker, given that Tai languages are usually categorized as not having tense marking?

    Comrie (1985: 9) defined tense as a 'grammaticalized expression of location in time', and added that:

> Indeed, given that no restrictions are placed by the definition on what kind of location in time is to be considered, it is probable that most of the world's languages will turn out to have tense... (Comrie 1985: 9)

In discussing the difference between tense marking, that is grammaticalization, and lexicalization, he stated that 'grammaticalization refers to integration into the grammatical system of a language, while lexicalization refers merely to integration into the lexicon of the language' (1985: 10). Full grammaticalization requires two criteria, obligatory expression and morphological boundedness. As he concluded: 'The clearest instances of grammaticalization satisfy both these criteria (they are obligatory and morphologically bound), the clearest instances of lexicalization satisfy neither, while there will be many borderline cases which the criteria do not assign unequivocally to grammaticalization or lexicalization'.

    By this definition, *kaa¹* is neither a clearly grammaticalized tense marker, nor a simple lexicalization. It is often bound to its verb, although not in all cases, and it is not obligatory, although it may be becoming obligatory, at least in narrative texts.

    Foley (1986: 142) said of tense 'Tense delimits the whole sentence by situating it in time with regard to the present moment of speaking: does it precede, overlap with or follow the moment of speaking?' By this definition, in most of the cases seen above, such as examples (37.1) and (37.2), *kaa¹* is behaving as a past tense marker.

    However, as indicated in Table 6.4.3-1 above, *kaa¹* is not the only morpheme that is arguably a past tense marker in Aiton. It can be supplanted by *maa²* 'come' if the action is referring towards the speaker or the place where the speaker is, as in (39.2).

39.1)   ⋯⋯   ⋯   ⋯⋯   ⋯⋯   ⋯⋯   ⋯⋯   ⋯⋯   ⋯ ॥
    wan²   luŋ²   cau³ phaa³   sik¹ kyaa²   kam¹pa¹laa¹   mɔn²   dut¹   kaa¹
    day   one   king   Sikkya   throne   3SG   hot   GO
    'One day, the throne of Lord Sikkya was very hot.'

39.2)   ဖြစ်   ဝၵ်   ႒   ဝၵ်   ဧၵ   ၒၵ်� ။
       mɔn² cau³ nuu² lɛm² maa² muɯŋ² kaaŋ²
       3SG RESP look look at COME the earth
       'He looked (down) at the earth.'

39.3)   ႒   ၵၼ်   ဧၵ   ဝၵ်ဝၵ   ဝၵ်   ဝၵ်   ကၼ်   ဝၵ် ။
       duu²   han¹   maa²   cau³ phaa³   ʒaau²   taŋ¹   kun²   suɯŋ³
       look   see   COME   king   Yau   all   person country

       ကၼ်   ၵၼ်   ဝၵ်ဝၵ်   ၒ   ကၵ်   ၒ   ဝၵ ။
       kun²   muɯŋ²   suu² tɔŋ²   hau²   kaaŋ³   hau³   laai¹
       person country pray   GIVE   wide   GIVE   many
       'He saw that king Yau and all the people were praying for more people.'

There are several versions of this text. In one of these alternative versions, the manuscript written by Nang Wimala, the first three words of (39.3) are given as (40):

40)   ႒   ၵၼ်   ကၵ
       duu²   han¹   kaa¹
       look   see   GO
       'He saw ...'

The use of *kaa¹* and *maa²* here is not aspectual. There is a perfective aspect marker *yau³/yau⁴* in Phake and Aiton, which can co-occur with *kaa¹* and *maa²*. However it would not be appropriate in (39) because the Lord Sikkya has not finished looking at the earth when the sentences are uttered. In (39) and (40), *kaa¹* seems simply to mean that the action referred to was in the past.

Diller (1992: 24) categorized this morpheme as occurring 'postverbally to indicate several time-related factors, most commonly past time or possibly perfective aspect ... In this function, articulation sometimes approaches postclitic status'. In the story printed as an appendix to his article, Diller glosses *kaa¹* as 'PAST'.

It should also be mentioned that the *wai³* 'keep' can be used in a similar position to both *kaa¹* and *maa²*, that is either immediately after the verb or utterance finally. It appears to be used to mark past time, where there is some long or medium term result, as in (41):

41)   ဝၵ်   ၒ   �0ၵ်   ၵၼ်   ၒ   ၒၵ်   ၒ   ၒၵ် ။
       ʒau³   huu¹   man²   an²   pai²   khɛn¹   wai³   nuu¹
       FINISHED head   3SG   CLF   go   hang   KEEP   above

       ၵၵ်ၒ   ဝၵ် ။
       tun³ mai³   suŋ¹ suŋ¹
       tree   very tall
       'Then he hung the head (of Ngi Ra Ngi Reu Reu) on a very tall tree.'
       (Historical Manuscript read by Nang Wimala Thoumoung No. 60)

Because of these other TAM markers, at least part of whose function is to mark past time, I have not glossed *kaa¹* as 'PAST', but rather as 'GO', with the capitalization indicating that it is a grammaticalized morpheme. This word is not fully bleached of its original meaning, and so would be best not described as the Aiton past tense marker. It indicates that the action of the verb to which it is attached is gone. It may well develop into a fully grammaticalized and bound past tense marker.

6.4.6. Coda

It appears that Tai Aiton is quite far down the path towards the development of grammaticalized bound markers to express tense and aspect functions.

It should not be surprising that these phenomena have been observed. They were noticed some time ago, as this quote from Grierson indicates:[19]

> It is a common belief that these isolating, monosyllabic, languages are examples of the infancy of speech. It is sometimes said that they are in the 'radical' stage, and that they may be expected to develop gradually into agglutinative and finally into synthetic tongues. So far, however, are they from being in their infancy, that the exact reverse is the case. They are languages in the last stage of decrepitude. That they will all pass, and that some of them are now passing, through the agglutinative stage, may be admitted, but they have been there before. These monosyllabic words are worn down polysyllables, and these polysyllables were formed, just as we see polysyllables formed at the present day in other languages, by prefixes and suffixes (1903: 69).

6.5. CHANGED TONE IN PHAKE

Although Tai Phake is closely related to, and largely mutually exclusive with, the Aiton, Khamti and Khamyang varieties, the speech of many Tai Phake informants exhibits a number of changed tones, most noticeably in interrogative, negative and imperative situations. These changed tones are rarely if ever observed in the speech of the other Tai communities.

6.5.1. The Tai Phake questioning tone

The standard way to ask a polar question in Tai Phake is to state the proposition, and then to add a particle $n\jmath^6$ which questions the entire proposition, and which by itself is translated as 'is it?', as demonstrated in (42), which is literally 'You have become a housewife, haven't you?'

42)
    ဧ   ၓႃ   ၝ႑ႃ   ၵ႑   ၵ႑ ॥
    maü²   pen²   hɔn²   kā¹   nɔ⁶
    2SG   be, become   house   GO   PRT.QN
    'Are you married?' (asked to a woman)
    (Phake sentence elicited from the late Aimya Khang Gohain)

However, Banchob (1987) lists a number of common words, in which alteration of the tone to the rising or sixth tone would express a question. In example (43), the word ik^1 'more', which is spoken with the first tone in its citation form, is spoken with the sixth tone in example (43):

43)
    ၒ႑   ၯ   ၟၵႃ ॥
    ta¹   au²   ik⁶
    WILL   take   more.QN
    'Will you take some more?'
    (Banchob 1987: 433)

Banchob's data was collected in the 1960s and 1970s. Today, many of the Phake informants use a special questioning tone on the last lexical item of the sentence. This questioning tone first rises and then falls, and here arbitrarily notated as –7.

---

19 Grierson's note: 'Most of the following is based on Conrady's Eine indochinesische Causativ-Denominativ- Bildung und im Zusammenhang mit den Tonaccenten.'

44) ဖွင့်   ကဲ့   ကွ   ဆူ   ဟန် ။
     mauk¹   kɔ²   kau²   sū⁶   han⁷
     pipe   salt   1SG   2PL   see
     'Did you find my pipe of salt?'
     (Phake Story, *Story of the dolphin, crow and mosquito* No. 41, told by Aithown Che
     Chakap.)

Aithown Che explained that 'generally when there is a question, this type of tone is found.'

Recordings of this tone have been analysed and compared with the second tone. The second tone is a high tone which rises slightly and then falls, whereas the questioning tone clearly rises and then falls, as shown in Table 6.5.1-1, the informant for which was a male speaker, Ai Chanta:

TABLE 6.5.1-1: COMPARISON OF QUESTIONING TONE AND HIGH FALLING TONE IN PHAKE

Word	Tone	Frequency at start	Frequency at middle	Frequency at end
kin2	high level falling	160Hz	160Hz	100Hz
kin7	rising falling	140Hz	180Hz	115Hz

Aithown Che gave further examples, such as (45), which was the question to which (46) was the answer:

45) ဆူ   ကင်   ဆူ ။
     sū⁶   kin²   sū⁷
     2PL   eat   PRT.QN
     'Are you eating?'

46) ကွ   ကင်   ဆူ ။
     kau²   kin²   sū¹
     1SG   eat   TOWARDS
     'I am eating.'
     (Phake Sentences, elicited from Ai Chanta)

As mentioned above, the questioning tone is found on the final lexical item of an utterance, regardless of its word class. Although it seems most often to be found with verbs, it can be found with nouns. Example (47) is a question that was asked when making a tour of a village and observing that an old house had been demolished and a new one was about to be erected:

47) ဟန်   နင် ။
     hɔn²   nin⁷
     house   earth
     '(Will it be) a house built on the ground?'[20]
     (Phake Sentences, spoken by Ai Chanta.)

There seems to be some restriction on the use of the questioning tone. It is not used if the question particle nɔ⁶ is used. The following two sentences were elicited from Ai Chanta:

---

20 Traditional Tai houses are built on stilts and called *hɔn² hāŋ³* in Phake. Many Tai people are now demolishing their traditional style houses and building brick houses at ground level. These are called *hɔn² nin².*

48) ၽၵ် ၼႆ ၵိၼ် ၼီ ။
phak¹ nai³ kin² nī⁷
vegetables/dishes this eat good.QN
'Is this dish good to eat?'[21]

49) ၵိၼ် ၼီ ၼေႃ ။
kin² nī² nɔ⁶
eat good PRT.QN
'Is it good to eat?'

In (48), the questioning tone is found on the word *nī²* 'good', producing *nī ⁷*, whereas in (49), because the question particle *nɔ⁶* is present, the word maintains its citation tone.

The questioning tone may have arisen from the tone of the question particle, *nɔ⁶*, merging with the falling second tone of words like *nī²* to produce a rising falling tone. It appears that it is now generalising to words which were not originally second tone.

For a word that in citation form has the first tone, such as *kā¹* 'GO', the questioning form is simply a rising tone, as in (50). In this case, because the tone on *kā⁶* is identical to one of the citation tones, it will be marked as if it were one of those citation tones, a practice that will be followed whenever a changed tone corresponds to one of the citation tones:

50) မႂ် ၼွၼ် ၼီ ၵႃ မႃၼႆ ။
maü² nɔn² nī² kā⁶ ma¹ nai⁴
2SG sleep good GO.QN today
'Did you sleep well last night?'
(Phake sentence elicited from Ai Chanta)

The various tone combinations so far observed are summarized in Table 6.5.1-2:

TABLE 6.5.1-2: THE QUESTIONING TONE IN PHAKE

Word in Citation form	Question morpheme	Word in question form	Tone change process
kin²	$_^{6}$	kin⁷	$_^{2} + _^{6} = _^{7}$
nī²	$_^{6}$	nī⁷	$_^{2} + _^{6} = _^{7}$
kā¹	$_^{6}$	kā⁶	$_^{1} + _^{6} = _^{6}$

6.5.2. The Tai Phake negative tone

In addition to a questioning tone, Banchob (1987) also gives examples of a negative tone, which is also expressed with the sixth tone. One of her examples is given here as (51), to which an interlinear gloss has been added.

51) မႃ ၵႃ လႃလႃ ။
mā⁵ kā⁶ lā² lā²
NEG go.NEG PRT
'Not to go at all.'
(Banchob 1987: 359)

21 The Tai word *phak¹* literally means 'vegetable', but has come to mean the dishes that are eaten with rice. It can include meat dishes.

Diller (1992: 19) also discusses this phenomenon[22], described as 'a morphophonemic tone sandhi rule', indicating that it operates on words with the second tone after 'the preclitic negative marker [*m-*]' but not after *mau¹*.

This negative tone is common among the Phakes, as in (53), the answer to (52). In both sentences the verb *kin²* 'eat' has an altered tone:

52)   ဗ္ဂ   ဧၢ   ၶ၈ၷ ॥
       khau³   ta¹   kin⁷
       rice   will   eat
       'Will you eat rice?'

53)   ဧ   ၶ၈ၷ ॥
       ma¹   kin⁶
       NEG   eat.NEG
       '(I) won't eat.'
       (Phake sentences elicited from Ai Chanta)

There appear to be some constraints on the use of this negative tone, just as there were on the questioning tone. It was not used in (54):

54)   ကဗ္ဂ   ဧ   ၒ   ၶ၈ၷ ॥
       kau²   ma¹   pai¹   kin²
       1SG   NEG   not yet   eat
       'I haven't eaten yet.'
       (Phake sentence elicited from Ai Chanta)

There are two negatives words in (54) and it appears be that the negative tone can only be used immediately following the negative particle *ma¹*. In (55), the modal verb *khaü³* 'want' intervenes and the negative tone cannot be used.

55)   ဧ   ဗ္ဂ   ၮြ ॥
       ma¹   khaü³   au²
       NEG   want   take
       '(I) don't want to take (it).'
       (Phake sentence elicited from Yehom Buragohain)

The negative tone is also found very frequently in narratives, as in (56). The word for 'wet' is *yam²* in citation form.

56)   ဗ္ဂ   ဧၢ   ဧ   ၯ   ၛ   ၵ္ဂ   ၲ ॥
       hau²   ta¹   ma¹   yam⁶   wā⁵   nüŋ¹   nai⁴
       1PL   WILL   NEG   wet.NEG   say   like   this
       '"We will not get wet", he spoke like this.'

       (Phake Story, *The birth and early life of Chaw Mahosatha* No. 39, told by Ee Nyan Khet)

Although it is apparently an innovation in Tai Phake, in all of the examples discussed so far it is redundant, in that it seems never to occur without the negative particle *ma¹*, or to carry any meaning that would be lost if it were not present. This is in contrast to the questioning tone, the absence of which in a sentence like (48) above would change the illocutionary force from an interrogative to a declarative sentence.

Example (57), spoken by Ngo Ong, a Phake speaker from Ningkam village, appears to show a semantic difference, where the negative tone is used only for the habitual negative in (57.2) and not when the action is non-habitual, as in (57.3).

---

22 In discussing Diller's findings, I have used the tone numbering in Banchob (1987), to avoid confusion.

57.1)   ေ   က်ိၵ   လ ॥
        ma¹   kin⁶   yɛ⁴
        NEG   eat.NEG   PRT
        'As to *ma¹ kin⁶*.'

57.2)   ကၠ   ဝၵ   ကၟ   ေ   က်ိၵ   က   ေ   က်ိၵ ॥
        kū⁵   wan²   kau²   ma¹   kin⁶   nɛ⁴   ma¹   kin⁶
        every   day   1SG   NEG   eat.NEG   DEF   NEG eat.NEG
        '(If I) don't eat fish every day, I would say *ma¹ kin⁶*.'

57.3)   ၆်ိၵ   ကၟ   ၵ်ိ   ကိ်ၵ ॥
        mɔ⁵ nai⁴   kau²   üm¹   kin²
        today   1SG   NEG   eat
        '(If I didn't eat) today, I would say *üm¹ kin²*.'
        (Phake sentences spoken by Ngo Ong)

An alternative explanation would appear to be that the negative tone can only be used following the negative marker *ma¹*, and not when it follows the negative marker *üm¹*.

Ee Nyan Khet offered a different explanation for why the tone sometimes does not change. In the case of (58), the words were spoken in anger, and therefore the pronunciation was, as Ee Nyan Khet put it *cɔn² nüŋ⁵ haiŋ²* 'a little strong.'

58)   ၵ်ိ   ဝၟ   လုၵ်   ၆ ॥
       üm¹   yaŋ²   luk⁴   maü²
       NEG   have   child   2SG
       'You shouldn't have our child!'
       (Phake Story, *The story of the kum bird* No. 55, told by Ee Nyan Khet)

From (57) and (58), it is not clear whether the use of the negative marker *ma¹* triggers the negative tone, whilst *üm¹* does not, or whether the decision not to use a negative tone in (58) and (57.3) then leads to the use of the marker *üm¹*.

Sometimes the negative tone is not spoken in oral texts, as the contrast between examples (59) and (60) indicates.

59)   ၅   ၈   ေ   ၆ ॥
       pū¹   nai⁴   ma¹   haü⁶
       grandfather   that   NEG   give.NEG
       '(But), the old man didn't give (them) the food.'
       (Phake Story, *The story of the two brothers*, No. 8, told by Ee Nyan Khet)

60)   ၅   ၈   ေ   ၆   ၆်ၵ॥
       pū¹   nai⁴   ma¹   haü³   wɔt⁴
       grandfather   this   NEG   give   PRT
       '(and so) the old man did not give (them the food).'
       (Phake Story, *The story of the two brothers* No. 10, told by Ee Nyan Khet)

In example (59), the negative tone is clearly present, whereas it was not in example (60), from the same text a few moments later. The negative tone is most frequently found with verbs that have the second (high falling) tone. Its generalization to use with words such as *haü³*, which has the third tone in citation, may be a process which is ongoing, and may explain why the negative tone is not used on all occasions.

The Phake negative tone is probably a fairly recent innovation among the Phake community. However there is one word for which tone alterations may occur not just among the Phakes. The existential verb *yaŋ²* 'have' is realized as *ñaŋ⁵* in Khamyang, but according to Deben Chowlik, it can be pronounced in Khamyang with both a questioning tone and a negative tone, just as in Phake. As discussed below in section 6.6, the Khamyangs are bidialectal and the tonal alteration on this word in Khamyang may be due to the influence of Phake, rather than an example of true Khamyang usage.

It is interesting to note, in the light of the fact that there is tonal variation on the word *yaŋ²*, even in Khamyang, that this word can have both positive and negative meanings in written texts where tonal differences are not notated. In (61) it is negative, whereas in (62) it is positive:

61) ဃ္ဒ   ၃   ဃၟ   ဃၟ   ?ၟ ||
     yaŋ⁶   nai³   yū¹   sau²   hüŋ⁶
     have.NEG   get   live at   stay   long in time
     'I will not get time to remain here for a long time.'
     (Phake Manuscript, *Grandfather Teaches Grandchildren*, Introduction No. 6)

62) ဃ္ဒ   ဃၟ   ၜ္ဒ   ဒၟ   ?ၟ   ၑ   ၜ္ဒ   ဃ္ဒၟ   ၜ
     sün⁶   sū⁶   thɔm¹ tün²   nam⁴ khām²   wā⁵   kau²   sɔn⁶   cam⁴
     if   2PL   listen to   words   say   1SG   teach   PRT

     ဃ္ဒ   ဒၟ   ၃   ?ၟ   ၑ   ?ၟ   ၑ   ?ၟ ||
     yaŋ²   tak¹   nī²   pen²   cɔ⁵   sɛn⁶   khā¹   kan⁵nā³
     have   will   good be   time/life many period of time   future
     'If you listen to the words that I teach, you will have many good lives in the future.'
     (Phake Manuscript, *Grandfather Teaches Grandchildren*, Introduction No. 25)

6.5.3. The Tai Phake imperative tone

One further example of tone alteration has been observed. In Phake, as in Aiton (see above section 6.4, the verbs *kā¹* 'go', *mā²* 'come' and *wai⁴* 'keep', can appear in postverbal or utterance final position as grammaticalized markers of past time.

In example (63), however, the word whose citation form is *kā¹* is pronounced with a different tone, and marks an imperative:

63) ၜ္ဒ   ၑ   ?ၟၜ္ဒ   ၜ   ?ၟ   ၜ   ?ၟၜ္ဒ   ၜ   ?ၟ ||
     au²   ka⁸   nüŋ¹ kau¹   kɔ⁴   nüŋ⁵   me²   nüŋ¹ kau¹   kɔ⁴   nüŋ⁵
     take   GO.IMP again   CLF   one   wife again   CLF   one
     'Take another one, take another wife!'
     (Aiton Story, *The widow* No 12, told by Aithown Che)

When translating this text, Aithown Che explained that each of the three TAM markers that could express past time (*kā¹* 'GO', *mā²* 'COME' and *wai⁴* 'KEEP') also had an imperative form, spoken with a high short vowel and with a tone that exhibited glottal constriction and creaky voice. This tone will be marked *ka⁸* as in (63). None of these imperative markers is bleached of its original meaning and native speakers would gloss *ka⁸* as 'go'.

The word *wai⁸* is used in commands when the action will have some long term result, so that in (64), where a stepmother is commanding her stepdaughter to spin, the yarn thus spun will be kept and sold to feed the family. If, on the other hand, the words *pan¹ ka⁸* has been used, this implication would be absent.

64) ?ၟၜ္ဒ   ၜ   ၃ ||
     cüŋ¹ nai⁴   pan¹   wai⁸
     now   spin   KEEP.IMP
     'Now spin!'
     (Aiton Story, *The widow*, told by Aithown Che.)

When the action is towards the speaker, *ma⁸* can be used as an imperative as in *kin² ma⁸* (eat-COME.IMP), which might be said to a child who was another location and would need to come towards the speaker to eat.The use of these imperative marks is even found with a first person singular agent, as in (65):

(65)

ဗွန်⁵	ဗၟ²	ကာ¹	လ⁴	ကာ¹	pai²	kau²	၁¹	ta¹	khyā²	ka⁸
pɔn⁵	pɔ²	kā¹	lɛ¹	kā¹	pai²	kau²	ɔ¹	ta¹	khyā²	ka⁸
other	enough	go	roam	go	go	1SG	PRT	WILL	finish	GO.IMP

'Others may go roaming but I will need to finish.'
(Discussion of *Rice Pounding Song*, by Ee Nyan het)

The usage of imperative particles is summarized in Table 6.5.3-1:

TABLE 6.5.3-1: IMPERATIVE MARKERS IN PHAKE AND AITON

	TAM₂ as markers of imperative
ka⁸	General imperative marker
ma⁸	Marker of imperative - used when the scope of the process indicated by the verb is in some way towards the speaker
wai⁸	Marker of imperative, used when the process indicated by the verb is intended to have long term results.

An analogous process is also found with 1st person non-singular reference (Hortative). Here, the word *sɔ¹* 'to persuade' is recorded with the same short tone and a hortative meaning as in (66). Unlike the markers of imperative for second person, it is utterance initial. In this example it co-occurs with an imperative particle *ta⁴*, and with the 1st person plural pronoun.

(66)

sɔ⁸	hau²	ān¹	nāu²	ta⁴	wā⁵	nüŋ¹ nai⁴
let's	1PL	count	star	PRT	say	like that

'Let us count the number of stars.'
(Phake Story, *Story of deception*, told by Ee Nyan Khet)

Even when there is no 1st person plural pronoun and no imperative particle, *sɔ⁸* has the same hortative meaning, as in (67):

(67)

sɔ⁸	kā¹	tī⁵	naü²	thɔn¹
let's	go	place	in	forest.

'Let's go to the forest.'
(Phake Story, *Story of the foolish king*, told by Ee Nyan Khet)

As far as I know, no other Tai languages of the southwestern group of the Tai family exhibit these characteristics which have been demonstrated for Phake.

6.6. BI-DIALECTALISM IN THE TAI KHAMYANG SPEECH COMMUNITY

As discussed above in section 6.1.2.3, the Khamyang variety of Tai is now only spoken in one remaining village, Pawaimukh, near Margherita in Tinsukia district, Assam.

Pawaimukh is a small village on the Burhi Dihing River about seven miles downstream of Margherita, situated near a large bend in the river. The community has around 40 houses, stretched along a single road running more or less north-south. In the middle of the village is the Buddhist temple, in front of which is the small sand pagoda (kqng2 muu2 saai2), illustrated by Terwiel (1980: 123).

There are now no more than fifty older adults in Pawaimukh who speak Tai Khamyang as a mother tongue. They use the Tai language in communicating with each other, in certain religious and ritual circumstances, and when they come into contact with other Tai speaking people from one of the eight nearby Tai Phake villages,[23] or from further afield. There has also been considerable intermarriage between the Khamyangs in Pawaimukh and the Phakes.

Only two of the villagers can read the Tai language. One of these, my principal informant Chaw Sa Myat Chowlik, was born around 1920. His enormous knowledge of Tai culture, literature, religion and ceremonies makes him one of the most important informants about the Tai in all Assam.

In addition to the older generation of full speakers, there is a middle generation of what may be described as semi-speakers. Their Tai language usage has not been thoroughly investigated.

Even children in Pawaimukh have some patchy knowledge of the Tai language. In early 2001 one teenage boy sang a Tai song for me, and although he did not know the meaning of the song, he knew it was Tai.

A meeting of the Khamyang elders was held in 2001, and a decision taken to actively promote the language in the village. By early 2002, Chaw Sa Myat's brother, Chaw Mihingta Chowlik, had begun teaching the Tai language to the younger children in Pawaimukh village. Every evening after school, primary school age children would gather to practise writing – which Chaw Mihingta is himself learning – and Tai vocabulary, as well as some simple Tai dialogues that Chaw Mihingta has written. Some of these children can now communicate in simple Tai sentences and in March 2002 they practised their Tai with me.

Over several years, covering several field trips to Pawaimukh, I have recorded a significant amount of the speech of Chaw Sa Myat Chowlik. Although an excellent informant, he is not easily able to assist with the work of transcribing and analysing those texts.

For this task, I have worked with Chaw Deben Chowlik, otherwise known as Chaw Kyun, who was born around 1940 and never learned to read Tai, although he is fully proficient in reading Assamese and also knows some English. His spoken forms are quite distinct from Phake forms, and he claims that they represent a more 'authentic' Khamyang.

When analysing some of Chaw Sa Myat's texts, Chaw Deben often pointed out that Chaw Sa Myat was actually speaking Phake to me, rather than Khamyang. A good example of this is (68), where Chaw Sa Myat spoke line (68.1) with Phake phonology and then repeated it as (68.2) with Khamyang phonology:

68.1) ꩬ ꩬ ꩬ ꩬ ꩬ ꩬ ꩬ ॥
       cau³   khau⁶   yɛ⁴   thauu⁶   ta¹   kā¹   nai³
       RESP   3PL   PRT   where   WILL go   get
       'His father said: "Where will you get (them)?"'

68.2) ꩬ   ꩬ   ꩬ   ꩬ
       thauu⁶   ti¹   kaa¹   lai³
       where   WILL   go   get
       'Where will you get it?'
       (Khamyang story, *Story of the child and the king*, Nos. 8 & 9, told by Sa Myat Chowlik)

The differences between the two relate to the pronunciation of the tones and the use of initial /l/ in (68.2), for the reflex of proto Southwestern Tai ɯʔd and ɯʔdl which is always /n/

---

23 As an indication of the extent to which Pawaimukh is regarded as part of the Phake, In January 2000, I was presented by the Tai Phakes with a document listing all the Phake villages, and Pawaimukh was included as one of them.

in Phake, but is often /l/ in Khamyang. In addition, in the word *thauu⁶* 'where', there is a full realization of [ɯ], the second element of the diphthong, in Phake, whereas [ɯ] is hardly audible in the Khamyang pronunciation. These phonological features seem to mark out the Khamyang from the Phake.

The differences in the distribution of /b/, /l/ and /m/ in the Khamyang as spoken by Chaw Deben and other Tai varieties are shown in Table 6.6-1:

TABLE 6.6-1: COMPARISON OF KHAMYANG INITIAL /b/, /l/ AND /m/

English	Khamyang	Phake (Banchob 1987)	Aiton (Morey 2005)	Khamti (Harris 1976)	proto initial
good	lii⁵	nī²	dii²	ni¹	*ʔd
star	laau⁵	nāu²	daau²	naaw¹	*ʔdl
cold	laau⁶	nāu⁶	naau¹	naaw⁴	*hn
speak	baa⁵	wā⁵	waa²		*w
comb	bii⁶	wī⁶	wii¹	wi⁴	*hw
fan	bii²	wī²	wii²		*w
shoulder	maa¹	mā¹	baa¹		*ʔb
village	maan³	mān³	baan³	maan⁵	*ʔb

The use of initial /b/, rather than /w/ for the words listed in Table 6.6-1 and presumably for all words with reflexes of initial *w and *hw in proto Southwestern Tai, follows the patterns which have been reconstructed for Ahom (see Diller 1992: 14 fn).

However, Deben Chowlik appears the only Tai Khamyang informant who regularly uses [b] for the initial consonant in these words. Other Khamyang informants pronounce this consonant as [w], which is the form found in Tai Phake. It is not clear whether Deben Chowlik's use of [b] represents original Khamyang speech standards from the time when the language was more widely spoken, or whether it is an idiosyncratic usage.

Significantly, Grierson (1904: 179) noticed that in Nora, which is usually supposed to be the same as Khamyang, 'the letter w is sometimes *ba*, but more usually *wa*.'

If this use of [b] is indeed preserving the original Khamyang pronunciation, then this seems to be a case of bi-dialectalism, where Khamyang speakers use both the Khamyang [b] and Phake [w] for the reflexes of initial *w and *hw.

The use of initial /l/ for words which are reflexes of initial *d in Proto Southwestern Tai, is similar to that found in modern Shan. However there are a number of words which are now pronounced with initial [l] in Khamyang that had initial *n in Proto Southwestern Tai, such as *laau⁶* 'cold'. The present situation among the Khamyang seems to be that most words whose initial consonants are reflexes of either initial *d or initial *n, can be realized with either initial /l/ or initial /n/, in relatively free variation. On the other hand, there is no evidence that words whose initial consonants are reflexes of *l are pronounced with initials other than /l/.

Both this usage of initial /b/ and initial /l/ is under pressure in the Khamyang village from the Phake norm to use /w/ and /n/ respectively. Chaw Sa Myat Chowlik often uses /w/ and /n/, following the Phake pattern, even when he is using Khamyang tones.

Recently, some recordings of Tai Khamyang speakers made in the 1960s by Dr Banchob Bandhumedha have come to light. Banchob's informant was Chaw Kyen Chowlik, and he read a list of words, the initial consonants of which are reflexes of proto ɯɯ, including [naau⁵] 'star', [nɔi⁵] 'hill' and [dɛŋ⁵] 'red'. This use of initial [d] is more typical of Aiton phonology than Phake or Khamyang. It is not yet clear what the status of this material is.

A second feature of Khamyang speech is vowel reduction, found frequently in the speech of Chaw Deben Chowlik, particularly with grammatical words. For example, the word (/luk⁴/ in Phake) 'from' is pronounced by him as [lʊk], and is distinguished from the word for 'child', (also /luk⁴/ in Phake). These two were analysed for their formant structure, and this is reported in Table 6.6-2:

TABLE 6.6-2: VOWEL REDUCTION/CENTRALIZATION IN KHAMYANG

Khamyang word	Gloss	1st formant	2nd formant	phonetic
luk^4	from	400	1600	[ʊ], [ɤ]
luk^4	child	380	1000	[ʊ]

Centralizations have been observed in Phake on words such as *haŋ^2* 'to', and other very frequent grammatical words, so much so that the Phakes are now writing these words as if they had the vowel [ɯ]. It is unlikely that we will ever find the word *luk^4* 'from' written ဢုက် (l - ɯ - k - final consonant) in Khamyang, because Chaw Sa Myat would follow the traditional spelling and there is no younger generation of people literate in Khamyang to set new norms.

There is also a process of reduction of the second member of the diphthong[24] /auɯ/. The latter was already commented above in the speech of Chaw Sa Myat (see above example (68)), and is one of the more noticeable differences between Phake and Khamyang.

The words *thauɯ^6* 'where' and *hauɯ^3* 'give' occur quite frequently but in each case the final /ɯ/ is barely audible. This could be notated phonetically as [aaᵊ]. This is so striking that a casual observer might initially hear the vowels as simply [aa], particularly in comparison with Phake where the final /ɯ/ is so clear.

In addition to these phonological features of Khamyang, there are also grammatical features of Chaw Deben's speech that are not found in Phake. In April 2001, I elicited the following sentence from him:

69)   luk^4 thauɯ^6 maaŋ$^{2(1)}$
      from   where   come.?
      'Where have you come from?'

In (69), there is an affix /-ŋ/ attached to the word *maa^2* 'come'. The tone shape of the word is not the same as when the word 'come' appears in citation form. It is somewhat longer and may be a combination of the tone shape of tone 2 and tone 1, here notated as -2 (1). Table 6.6-3 compares the tones of the citation forms of tone 1 and 2 with the tone on *maaŋ^{2}1$^)$*.

TABLE 6.6-3: COMPARISON OF KHAMYANG TONES

	Hz at commencement	Hz at highest point	Hz at end of word	contour	length
tone 2	180Hz	210Hz	110Hz	falling then rising	0.42"
tone 1	140Hz	140Hz	120Hz	level then falling	0.49"
the tone on maaŋ$^{2(}$1$^)$	170Hz	200Hz	150Hz	rising then slowly falling	0.86"

---

24   These are often treated as final offglides -*w*, -*y*, -*ɯ*. As Diller (1992: 16) points out, 'an alternative diphthong treatment' is possible. The phenomena being reported here would seem to support the diphthong hypothesis, at least synchronically.

At first, it seemed that this /-ŋ/ suffix may be a kind of questioning particle, but example (70) makes it clear that it is not.

70) ɯ²   kau²   uu¹   liiŋ⁵
     Yes   1SG   stay   good
     'Yes, I am well.'

Since Deben Chowlik does not know how to write Tai script, it was not possible to ask him how to write this, and, hence to establish whether final /-ŋ/ would be present in writing. However, Chaw Cha Seng, who also knows Tai script, was present when this was done and wrote ᨣᨰᨈᨩᨵ ᩬ *liŋ*. This does suggest that the final /-ŋ/ is present. Unfortunately it has not yet been possible to categorize this final /-ŋ/ accurately, although it does appear to be some sort of bound morpheme.

Another feature of the Khamyang speech, as exhibited by Deben Chowlik, is the merging of two words into a single syllable, especially when the second word is a grammatical one. This is illustrated in (71), where the words *mɤ⁵* 'time' and *nan⁴* 'that' are merged to be *mɤn⁴*, whilst the words *kɔ⁴* 'CLF-persons' and */ɤŋ⁵* 'one' are merged to become *kɔŋ⁴*.

71) mɤn⁴   cau³ phaa⁴   kɔŋ⁴   ñaŋ⁵   bai⁴
     time-that   king   CLF-one   have   KEEP
     'At that time there was a king.'
     (Khamyang story, *The hunter's parrot* No. 1, told by Deben Chowlik)

In both cases the very prominent fourth tone (high rising then falling with glottal final) is adopted by the whole merged word, overtaking the fifth tone (mid level then falling).

Several other merged words of this type were observed, making the transcription and translation of a text very difficult without the informant being present.

These various phonological and syntactic features mark Khamyang as a distinct linguistic variety, one that would be called dialect if mutual intelligibility were the criteria for determining the boundary between language and dialect.

However, many and perhaps most Khamyang speakers do not use these Khamyang norms, at least not with me. All Tai Khamyang speakers are at least bi-dialectal. Several people informed me that it was necessary for them to converge to the speech standards of other Tais when talking to Phake or Khamti speakers, because Khamyang would be difficult for other Tai speakers to understand. That they are able to do this can be seen in examples (68) above and (72) below. Most of the Khamyangs also use what they regard as Phake when speaking to me, because they perceive that I am more competent in Phake than Khamyang. This has made the collection of data on Khamyang more difficult than the other Tai varieties. The exception is Chaw Deben Chowlik who has worked very hard to provide 'authentic' Khamyang forms.

This use of Phake standards by Khamyang speakers extends to the use of Phake consonant and vowel phonology (see (68) above), and, less commonly, Phake tones. In example (72), the sentence is repeated, first in Phake and then in Khamyang.

72) ᨣᩫ᩠   ᨠᩥ᩠ᨶᩮ   ᨶᩣ᩠   ᨣᩫ᩠   ᨠᩥ᩠ᨶᩮ   ᨶᩣ᩠ ॥
     khauɯ³   kin²   nɤ⁴   khauɯ³   kin⁵   lɤ⁴
     want   eat   meat   want   eat   meat
     'Want to eat meat.'
     (Khamyang Story, *Of children and kings*, told by Sa Myat Chowlik)

In Phake, the word for 'eat' is pronounced with a high rising then falling tone (Tone 2), whereas in Khamyang it is pronounced with a mid level then falling tone (Tone 5). The word for 'meat' is on a mid falling tone in Phake (Tone 4), but on a high rising then falling tone with glottal final in Khamyang (Tone 4). Tone 4 in Khamyang has almost exactly the same contour as tone 2 in Phake, but with a final glottal constriction. The effect is that the tone on 'eat' in Phake is higher than that on 'meat', but the reverse is true in Khamyang.

In March 2002 several texts collected in previous years were checked through by Deben Chowlik. When listening to Chaw Sa Myat speak on tape, Deben Chowlik gave what he regarded as 'pure Khamyang' version for every Phake-ism.

Subsequent to my field research in Pawaimukh, tapes of the Khamyang were played to Phake and Aiton speakers, who commented that whilst understanding the language, it was clearly different from their own varieties and not entirely straightforward.

Unfortunately, this unique speech of the Khamyang is being lost. Only a small fraction of the speech norms, literature and culture has so far been recorded. It is hoped that this will progressively be analysed and made available to scholars.

As mentioned several times above, one of the interesting issues in the analysis of the Tai varieties of Northeast India is constituent order. Sentences with fronted objects are common, but various other constituent orders are possible, such as V-S.

This latter order is exemplified in (73) below, where it is the forgetting of the Khamyang variety by younger people that Chaw Deben wants to stress, and so the verb appears before the subject of the sentence. This example is presented both for its grammatical interest, and also for the message that its content conveys about the future of the Tai Khamyang language:

73) ꩴꩰꩦ   ꩪꩪ   ꩮꩦꩳ   ꩤꩳ   ꩫ   ꩵ
    nan⁴ kɔ¹   luum²   caŋ¹ nai³   luk⁴   nɛ⁴   khau⁶
    moreover   forget   now   child   DEF   3SG

    ꩤꩳꩳ   ꩵ   ꩶ   ꩲꩳ   ꩷   ꩸ ॥
    luk⁴ ɔn¹   khau⁶   uŋ¹   taan³   haai⁶   aa⁴
    child   3PL   NEG   speak   disappear   PRT(GO)
    'Moreover, they've forgotten, those children now, (because) those children can't speak (Khamyang), it's all gone.'

REFERENCES

Aimya Khang Gohain (1991) 'The Tai language as Spoken by the Tai-Phake', in *Pan Asiatic Linguistics: Proceedings of the Third International Symposium on Language and Linguistics*, Bangkok: Chulalongkorn University, 44-59.
— (1997) *Elementary Tai Primer*, Dibrugarh University: Department of Assamese. (In Assamese and English)
Banchob Bandhumedha (1987) *Phake-Thai-English Dictionary*, manuscript, published by the author (In English and Thai)
— (undated) *Aiton-Thai-English Dictionary*, manuscript. (In English and Thai)
Barua, Bimala Kanta and N.N. Deodhari Phukan (1964) *Ahom Lexicons, Based on Original Tai Manuscripts*, Guwahati: Department of Historical and Antiquarian Studies.
Barua, Ghan Kanta (1936) *Ahom Primer*, Guwahati: Department of Historical and Antiquarian Studies in Assam. (In Assamese and English)
Bauer, Robert S. and Benedict, Paul K. (1997) *Modern Cantonese Phonology*, Berlin: Mouton de Gruyter.
Boruah, Bhimkanta (2001) 'Tai Language in India: An Introduction', *Indian Journal of Tai Studies* 1: 30-33, Moranhat, Assam: Institute of Tai Studies and Research.
Buchanan, Francis (1798) 'A comparative vocabulary of some of the languages spoken in the Burma empire', *Asiatick Researches* 5: 219-40.
Chau Khouk Manpoong (1993) *New Tai Reader*, Chongkham, Arunachal Pradesh: Tai Literature Committee. (2 volumes in Khamti)
Comrie, Bernard (1985) *Tense*, Cambridge: Cambridge University Press.

Cushing, Rev. J. N. (1888) *Elementary Handbook of the Shan Language*, Rangoon: American Baptist Missionary Press.

Diller, Anthony (1992) 'Tai Languages in Assam: Daughters or Ghosts?', in Carol J. Compton and John F. Hartmann (eds) *Papers on Tai Languages, Linguistics and Literatures*, Northern Illinois Center for Southeast Asian Studies. (Paper #C)

— (2001) 'Grammaticalization and Tai Syntactic Change', in M. R. Kalaya Tingsabadh and Arthur S. Abramson (eds) *Essays in Tai Linguistics*, Bangkok: Chulalongkorn University Press, 139-175.

Edmondson, Jerold A. and Solnit, David B. (1997) 'Introduction', in Jerold A. Edmondson and David B. Solnit (eds) *Comparative Kadai-The Tai Branch*, Arlington: University of Texas, 1-27.

Foley, William A. (1986) *The Papuan Languages of New Guinea*, Cambridge: Cambridge University Press.

Gedney, William J. (1972) 'A Checklist for Determining Tones in Tai Dialects', in M. Estelle Smith (ed.) *Studies in Linguistics in Honor of George L. Trager*, Mouton: The Hague, 423-37.

Gogoi, Nomal Chandra (1994) *Morphological Study of the Tai Phake Language*, unpublished PhD dissertation, Dibrugarh University.

Greenberg, Joseph H. (1966) 'Some Universals of Grammar with Particular Reference to the Order of Meaningful Elements', in J. H. Greenberg (ed.) *Universals of Language* (2nd edition), Cambridge, Mass.: MIT Press.

Grierson, Sir George (1904) *Linguistic Survey of India* (Vol. 2 of *Mon-Khmer and Siamese-Chinese Families*), Calcutta: Office of the Supt. of Govt. Print. Reprinted in 1966, Delhi: Motital Banarsidass.

Harris, Jimmy G. (1976) 'Notes on Khamti Shan', in *Thai Linguistics in honour of Fang Kuei Li*, Bangkok: Chulalongkorn University.

Heine, Bernd (2001) 'On word order change without word order change', paper presented at the Fifteenth International Conference on Historical Linguistics, La Trobe University.

Leach, E. R. (1964) *Political Systems of Highland Burma*, London: London School of Economics.

Morey, Stephen (1999a) *Book for teaching the Tai Language: Tai Aiton Primer*, Dibrugarh: Triograph Press. (In Tai Aiton and Assamese)

— (1999b) *Tai Aiton History*, Dibrugarh: Triograph Press. (In Tai Aiton, Assamese and English)

— (1999c) *Book for Teaching the Tai Language: Tai Phake Primer*, Dibrugarh: Triograph Press. (In Tai Phake and Assamese)

— (2001a) *Book of Calling the Khon*, Dibrugarh: Triograph Press. (In Tai Khamyang and English)

— (2001b) *Grandfather Teaches Grandchildren*, Dibrugarh: Triograph Press. (In Tai Phake and English)

— (2001c) 'The literature of the Tai of Assam', *Melbourne Papers in Linguistics and Applied Linguistics* 1.1: 37-46.

— (2002) 'Tai languages of Assam, a progress report: Does anything remain of the Tai Ahom language?', in David Bradley and Maya Bradley (eds) *Language Maintenance for Endangered Languages: An Active Approach*, London: Curzon Press, 98-113.

— (2005) *The Tai Languages of Assam: A Grammar and Texts*, Canberra: Pacific Linguistics.

— (in press) 'Constituent order change in the Tai languages of Assam', to appear in *Linguistic Typology*.

— (in preparation) *The Turung language of Assam*, manuscript.

Needham, J. F. (1894) *Outline Grammar of the vj (Khâmtî) Language: As Spoken by the Khâmtîs Residing in the Neighbourhood of Sadiya*, Rangoon: Superintendent of Government Printing, Burma.

Panjok, Muhi Chandra Shyam (1981) 'History of Tai Khamyang Group of Great Tai Race', paper presented at the International Conference of Tai Studies, New Delhi, February.

Phukan, Punaram Mohan (1998) *Tai Ahom Vocabulary*, Dibrugarh: Professor Girin Phukan. (In Assamese)

Ranoo Wichasin (1996) *Ahom Buranji*, Bangkok: Amarin Printing & Publishing. (In Thai)

Robinson, W. (1849) 'Notes on the languages spoken by the various tribes inhabiting the Valley of Assam and its mountain confines', *Journal of the Bengal Asiatic Society* xviiii: 310-42.

Terwiel, B. J. (1980) *The Tai of Assam and Ancient Tai Ritual, Volume I, Life Style Ceremonies*, Gaya: Centre for South East Asian Studies.

— (1981) *The Tai of Assam and Ancient Tai Ritual, Volume II, Sacrifices and Time-reckoning*, Gaya: Centre for South East Asian Studies.

— (1996) 'Recreating the Past: Revivalism in Northeastern India', *Bijdragen – Journal of the Royal Institute of Linguistics and Anthropology* (Leiden) 152: 275-292.

Terwiel, B. J. and Ranoo Wichasin (eds & trans.) (1992) *Tai Ahoms and the Stars: Three Ritual Texts to Ward off Danger*, Ithaca: Cornell University SEAP.

Vichin Panupong (née Chantavibulya) (1970) *Inter-Sentence Relations in Modern Conversational Thai*, Bangkok: The Siam Society.

Weidert, Alfons (1977) *Tai-Khamti Phonology and Vocabulary*, Wiesbaden: Franz Steiner Verlag.

Wilaiwan Kanittanan (1986) 'Kamti Tai: From an SVO to an SOV Language', in B. H. Krishnamurti (ed.) *South Asian Linguistics: Structure, Convergence and Diglossia*, Delhi: Motilal Barnarsidas, 174-178.

— (1983) 'Language of the Tai Phakes', in *Linguistics along Historical Lines: The Evolution of Thai and English*, Bangkok: Thammasat University. (In Thai)

APPENDIX 1

History of the Aiton, told by Nang Wimala Thoumoung, reading from a manuscript copied from the nun Nang Koi Phalung.

This story was initially told by Nang Wimala in January 2000. It was transcribed into Tai script by Bidya Thoumoung and translated by Stephen Morey on return to Australia. This transcription forms the basis of the following analysis. The translation was checked together with Nang Wimala in April 2001, and compared with her own copy of the manuscript, which in Tai language but using Assamese script.

There are thus three versions of the text, that in Bidya Thoumoung's manuscript, that in Nang Wimala's manuscript and the readin recorded in January 2000. Some of the lines differ from one version to the next. These alternate versions have been presented below.

1)

a¹ khiŋ¹	luɯ̃ŋ²	cau³ phaa³	yaau²
time	one	king	Yau

'At one time there was a king (called) Yau.'

2)

man²	cau³	wi³ nɛ²	an² luɯ̃ŋ²	hit¹	kaa¹	tii²	muŋ²	khau¹
3SG	RESP	Vinaya*	CLF one	make	GO	at	city/country	3PL

'He was a just ruler who founded the country.'

3)

lai³ pɯ² nai³	cau³ phaa³	cau³ phɔi³	kup¹ taŋ¹	kun²	suɯ̃ŋ³
therefore	king	EUPH	with	person	country

kun²	muŋ²	tii²	dɔi²	tau¹ san³	nai³
person	city	at	hill	Tau San	this

ဣ	၁	၁	၁	၁	၁ ॥
ta¹	dai³	pai²	khup³	paai³	wai³
will	GET	GO	kneel	pray	KEEP

၁	၁	၁	၁	၁	၁ ॥
caa²	phii¹	luŋ¹	phii¹	taŋ³	kam¹ phaa³
to	ghost	big	ghost	set up	world

'The king, together with all the people of the country, went to Mount Tau San in order to pray to the great spirit who had made the world.'

4)

၁	၁	၁	၁	၁	၁	၁ ॥
muuŋ² kāŋ²	ai³	lai³	cau³ phaa³	luŋ¹khup³	paai³	ai³
the earth	PRT	thus	king big	kneel	pray	PRT*

'So the great king (and his people) prayed.'

5)

၁	၁	၁	၁	၁	၁	၁ ॥
wan² luɯ²	cau³phaa³	sik¹ kyaa²	kam¹pa¹laa¹	mən²	duut¹	kaa¹
day one	king	Sikkya	throne	3SG	hot	GO

'One day, the throne of Lord Sikkya was very hot.'

6)

၁	၁	၁	၁	၁	၁ ॥
mən²	cau³	nuu²	lɛm²	maa²	muuŋ² kaaŋ²
3SG	RESP	look	look at	COME	the earth

'He looked (down) at the earth.'

7)

၁	၁	၁	၁	၁	၁	၁	၁ ॥
duu²	han¹	maa²	cau³ phaa³	ʒaau²	taŋ¹	kun²	suuŋ³
look	see	COME	king	Yau	all	person	country

၁	၁	၁	၁	၁	၁	၁ ॥
kun²	muuŋ²	suu² tɔŋ²	hauu²	kaaŋ³	hauu³	laai¹
person	country	pray	GIVE	wide	GIVE	many

'He saw that king Yau and all the people were praying for more people.'

Notes: Nang Wi's manuscript has ၁ 'PRT' at the end of the first line, and ၁ for ၁ and has ၁ kaa¹ 'GO', in place of ၁ maa² 'COME' in the first line. She stated that the meaning was the same.

8)

၁	၁	၁	၁	၁	၁	၁	၁ ॥
lai³ pu² nai³	cau³	sik¹ kyaa²	hɔŋ³	kaa¹	haŋ²	yaa²	siŋ¹ phaa²
therefore	RESP	Sikkya	call	GO	to	grandmother	Singpha

'So Lord Sikkya called to grandmother Singpha.'

9)

ဗိ	ဃပ်	ဗိ	ဗ္ဒ	လာင်	ကူ	ဗ္ဒိ	ရွင်	ကူ ။
khai²	sup¹	khai²	khaam²	kan²	kaa¹	nɔi³	hɔŋ³	kaa¹
tell	mouth	tell	word	RECIP	GO	PRT*	call	GO

လာင်	ဗိ	မာင်	၌	ကော	ဗိင်	မ	၆င်္မ၆/
laan¹	caai²	man²	sɔŋ¹	kɔ³	thin¹	maa²	muŋ² kaaŋ²
grandchild	male	3SG	two	CLF	send	COME	earth

'They discussed together and then called their two grandchildren and sent them to earth.'

Notes: * Nang Wi translated *kaa¹ nɔi³* as 'afterwards'. Nang Wi stated that in her MS, the first words were ရှၤၤဃၤဃၤ *mun³ sup¹ mun³ khaam²* 'speak-mouth-speak-word'. *mun³* is a word only used in written language version.

On the recording, Nang Wimala read the following two lines:

9.1)

ဗ္ဒ	ဗိ	ဗိ	ဃပ်	ဗိ	ဗ္ဒ	လာင်	ကူ ။
ʒau³	ai³	khai²	sup¹	khai²	khaam²	kan²	kaa¹
FINISHED	PRT	tell	mouth	tell	word	RECIP	GO

'When he had done that they iscussed together.'

9.2)

ဗိ	ဃပ်	ဗိ	ဗ္ဒ	လာင်	ဗ္ဒ	ရွင်	ကူ ။
khai²	sup¹	khai²	khaam²	kan²	ʒau³	hɔŋ³	kaa¹
tell	mouth	tell	word	RECIP	FINISHED	call	GO

လာင်	ဗိ	မာင်	၌	ကော ။
laan¹	caai²	man²	sɔŋ¹	kɔ³
grandchild	male	3SG	two	CLF

After discussing he called his two grandsons.'

10)

ကူ	ဗိင်ကော	ဗိ	ဗ္ဒ	ဗ္ဒိင်	ဗ္ဒ	ဗိ ။
yaa²	siŋ¹ phaa²	kaai¹	khuu¹ lai¹	sɛŋ¹	khuu¹ lai¹	kham²
grandmother	Singpha	erect	ladder	diamond	ladder	gold

ဗ္ဒိ	မ	ဗ္ဒင်	၌	ဗိ	၆င်္၆င်္၆င်္ ။
nɔi³	maa²	suŋ¹	wai³	tii²	muŋ² hu³ muŋ² ham³
PRT	COME	send	keep	to	Muang Heu Muang Ham

'Grandmother Singpha erected a diamond and golden ladder and sent them to Muang Heu Muang Ham.'

On the recording, Nang Wimala said:

10.1)

ကူ	ကော	..	ကူ	ဗိင်ကော	ဗိ	ကာပင်	၌
ʒaa²	ɔ¹	...	ʒaa²	siŋ¹ phaa²	kaai¹	ɛ¹ haŋ¹	wa²
grandmother	HESIT	...	grandmother	Singpha	erect	HESIT	say

ဗိ	ဗ္ဒ	မ	ကင်	မ	၌	၆င်ကော ။
kaai¹	khuu¹ lai¹	maa²	luŋ²	maa²	dɔi²	tau¹ san³
erect	ladder	COME	down	COME	mountain	Tau San

'Grandmother Singpha set up a ladder for them to come down to Mount Tau San.'

10.2)

ကင်	၌	၆င်ကော	ကင်	မ	ဗ္ဒ
luk³	dɔi²	tau¹ san³	luŋ²	maa²	ʒau³
from	mountain	Tau San	down	COME	FINISHED

ဧ၊   ၜၭ   ၿၭ   ကၟ   ၕ   ၿၭ်ၿၭ်ၿၭ်ၿ် ॥
maa²   taŋ³   muɯŋ²   kaa¹   tii²   muɯŋ² huɯ³ muɯŋ² ham³
COME   found   country   GO   to   Muang Heu Muang Ham
'From Mount Tau San they came down and founded Muang Heu Muang Ham.'

11) ကၟၭၭ်ၭ်   ၮၭၭ်   ၿ   ?   8   ၿၭ်
     a¹ luk³   pa¹   khau¹   sɔŋ¹   pii²   nɔŋ³
                 nan³
     from   there   3PL   two   elder   younger

     ?   ၿ   ၜၭ   ၿၭ   ကၟ   ၕ   ၭ်ၭ် ॥
     sɔŋ¹   caai²   tɛ¹   muɯŋ²   kaa¹   tii²   nan³
     two   male   make/begin country GO   place   that
     'After that, those two brothers made a kingdom/country there.'

12) ကၟၭၭ်ၭ်   ၕ   ၭ်ၭ်   8   ၿ   ၿၭ်
     a¹ luk³   tii²   nan³   pii²   caai²   mɔn²
     from   place   that   elder   male   3SG

     ဧ၊   ၜၭ   ၿၭ   ကၟ   ၕ   ၿၭ်ၿၭ်ၿၭ်ၿၭ်   ॥
     maa²   taŋ³   muɯŋ²   kaa¹   tii²   muɯŋ² khuɯ¹ muɯŋ²   ʒaau²
     come   set up   country   GO   at   Muang Kheu Muang   Yaau
     'Then the elder brother founded (his) kingdom at Muang Kheu Muang Yaau.'

13) ကၟၭၭ်ၭ်   ၮၭ်ၭ်   ၿ   ၜၭ်   ကၟ   ၕ   ကၟ
     a¹ luk³   pa¹ nan³   khau¹   kaaŋ³   kaa¹   laai¹   kaa¹
     from   there   3PL   wide   GO   many   GO*

     ၭ်ၭ်   ၕး   ၕၐ   ၜၭ်ၭ်   ၕး   ၿ ॥
     aan¹   pa¹   pɛ³   tak³   pa¹   dai³/nai³
     count   NEG   can   count   NEG   get
     'Then the numbers increased so much that no one could count them.'

Notes: * Nang Wi stated that ၜၭ်ကၟၕၿၭ kaaŋ³ kaa¹ laai¹ kaa¹ means 'increase in numbers', and that ၭ်ၭ် aan¹ means 'count with the mouth' and ၜၭ်ၭ် tak³ means 'count with writing'.

14) ၿၭ်   ၕ   ၿ   ၕၟ   ၮၭၭ်   ၕ၊   ၿ   ၕ်   ၜၭ
     naŋ¹nai³   waa²   kau³   pa³   hui¹   thuu¹   kau³   mun¹   mɔ³
     like that say   9   basket   seed   bean   9   10000   pot

     ၿ   ၿ   ၕ   ၿ   ၜၭ်   ၭ်ၭ်   ၕး   ၕၐ   ၜၭ်ၭ်
     khau³   kau³   pɛ²   mai³   saaŋ²   aan¹   pa¹   pɛ³   tak³
     rice   9   bundle   wood   bamboo   count   NEG   can   count

     ၕး   ၿ   ၜၭ်   ၕ   ၜၭ်
     pa¹   dai³/nai³   phan²   tai²   ʒaŋ²   ॥
     NEG   get   tribe   Tai   be
     'It was said that there were as many Tai people as nine baskets of seeds, ninety thousand pots of rice and nine bundles of bamboo, so many that they could not be counted in voice or on paper.'

On the recording, Nang Wimala said:

14.1)

ɛ¹ haŋ¹	an²	ȝaa² sii¹	naaŋ² kɔi³	khai²	wai³	khaam²	kɔ³
HESIT	PRT	nun	Nang Koi	tell	KEEP	word	LINK

uŋ¹	cauu²	naa¹	kau²	mat³
NEG	be	QN	1SG	remember

'The nun Nang Koi told these words, and isn't it so that I remember them.'

14.2)

phan²	tai³	pin²	kaa¹	kau³	pa³	hui¹	thuu¹	kau³	mun¹	mɔ³
tribe	Tai	be	GO	9	basket	seed	bean	9	10000	pot

khau³	kau³	pɛ²	mai³	saaŋ²	aan¹	pa:	co	tak³	pa:	dai³
rice	9	bundle	wood	bamboo	count	NEG	can	count	NEG	get

'There were as many Tai people as nine baskets of seeds, ninety thousand pots of rice and nine bundles of bamboo, so many that they could not be counted in voice or on paper.'

15)

nauu²	muk³	nan³	aai³ tɔn²	pin²	kaa¹	phan²	aai³
in	gather	that	Aiton	be	GO	tribe	1st son

khun¹	luŋ¹	luk³	caai²	man²	kɔ³	aai³
prince	big	child	male	3SG	CLF	1st son

'In that group, the Aitons were of the first son, (because) Khun Lung was the first son.'

16)

khun¹ lai¹	ŋii²
Khun Lai	2nd son

'And Khun Lai was the second son.'

APPENDIX 2

The Story of the crow and the fox, told by Ong Cham on October 1, 1998, Bargoan Village (baan³ luŋ¹), Karbi Anglong District, Assam; translated into English with the help of Chaw Sangea Phalung.

1)

an²	luuŋ²	puŋ¹	an²	luuŋ²
CLF	one	story	CLF	one

'A Story'

2)

ta¹	khai²	khaam²	aai³ tɔn²	tai²	aai³ tɔn²	puŋ¹	aai³ tɔn²
WILL	tell	word	Aiton	Tai	Aiton	story	Aiton

'I will tell an Aiton story.'

3) ka   ဂူ   လုံင်   ဝင်း   ဇာ   ဦ   ထွန်း   အာန် ။
kaa² tuu² luɯŋ² ʒaŋ² uu¹ tii² thuɯn¹ an²
crow CLF one to be live at forest CLF*
'There was a crow living in the forest.'

Note: * This is probably a merging of a final unstressed *nan³* 'that' with *an²* 'CLF'.

4) ဝန်   နာန်   မုန်   တုံင်မဲ   ကာဝင်   ကော   ဦ   ဒဲ   ကင် ။
waɯn² nan³ muɯn² tɔŋ³ mai³ ka¹ saŋ¹ kɔ³ uɯm¹ dai³ kin²
day that 3SG hungry what LINK NEG get eat
'One day she was hungry, and she didn't get to eat anything.'

5) မုဝ်   ဇမ်   နာန်   ကာ   အာန်   ဦ   လုက်   ဦ   တွန်မဲ ။
muɯ² ʒaam² nan³ kaa² an² uu¹ luk³ tii² tun³ mai³
time time that crow CLF* live from at tree
'At that time the crow was living in a tree.'

Notes: * these two words are spoken so quickly together that it sounds like [kaan²].

6) ဝန်   ပဲ   ကာ   ပဲ   ဟာန်   ခွန်   ဖဲ ။
muɯn² pai² kaa¹ pai² han¹ khɔn² phai²
3SG go GO go see smoke fire
'She went out and saw some smoke.'

7) ပွန်   ပဲ   ဖဲ ။
puɯn² pau¹ phai²
other burn/blow fire
'Someone was making a fire.'

8) မုဝ်   ဇမ်   နာန်   ပဲ   ကွ်   ကာ   ဦ   ခွန်   ဖဲ ။
muɯ² ʒaam² nan³ pai² kaɯ³ kaa¹ tii² khɔn² phai²
at that time go near GO at smoke fire
'Then she went near to the fire.'

9) ပဲ   ဟာန်   မုက်ဆုဝ   ခဲ   ဒဲ   ဖာန်   တူလုံင်
pai² han¹ muk³ suɯ²   khau¹ dai³ phaan² tuu² luɯŋ²
go see hunter 3PL get deer CLF one

ဦဲ   ကာန်   ဆဲ   ကာန် ။
tɛp¹ kan² sɔi²   kan²
cut RECIP cut to pieces, to slice RECIP
'She saw that the hunters had got a deer, and were slicing it up.'

10) ဝန်   ပဲ   ဟာန်   နုဲ   အာန် ။
muɯn² pai² han¹ nuɯ³ an²
3SG go see meat CLF
'She went to look at that meat!'

11) ဝန်   ခဲ   ကင်   နမ်ရိဲ   ဝန်   ဆဲ ။
muɯn² khaɯ² kin² nam³ rit¹ muɯn² cɔi³
3SG want eat saliva 3SG come out
'She wanted to eat and her saliva was running.'

12)

မူဝ်	ယၟ	နၟၜ်	မၟၜ်	၀	ၜုၚ်	ကၜ	ၼိဝ်	ၦၼ်ၜသုဝ်	ၜၒ ॥
mu²	ʒaam²	nan³	muun²	pai²	thuuŋ¹	kaa¹	him²	muk³ suɯ²	khau¹
time	time	that	3SG	go	reach	go	near	hunter	3PL

'Then, she approached close to the hunters.'

CHAPTER SEVEN

THE LUE LANGUANGE

John F. Hartmann

7.1. LUE AND NEIGHBOURING DIALECTS

Lue[1] is one of the dialects of the Tai language family, which in its totality stretches from the island of Hainan,[2] through much of the north of Vietnam and areas of southern China (chiefly Guangxi, Guizhou and Yunnan), through Laos and Thailand, across the northern reaches of Burma and finally into Assam[3] in India. A division of the entire family into three branches — Northern, Central and Southwestern — has been proposed by F. K. Li (1959) based on comparative lexicon. More recently, Gedney (1973) suggests a two-way division by combining the Central and Southwestern branches. The dialects of the Northern branch are found in the Guangxi-Guizhou region. The Central branch of dialects covers the border areas between China and the more easterly portions of the north of Vietnam. The Southwestern branch covers the remaining area of the Tai-speaking domain, by far the largest in terms of geographic area. The last is under consideration here, as it includes Lue and the related dialects of Lao, Shan, Khuen, Northern Thai, Siamese, White Tai, Black Tai, and Red Tai.

The old Lue capital of Chieng Rung, 'City of the Dawn', sits on the west bank of the Mekong River one thousand kilometers due north of Bangkok.[4] One of the few historical

---

1   Lue is also spelled Lu or Lü. In Siamese, it is pronounced /lìi/ with a high level tone. The Lue of Chieng Rung pronounce /lìi/ with a low level tone that has a slight fall at the terminus. Contrary to common belief among many Thais and westerners, the Lue are not hill tribe people. They are lowland, wet rice producers who practice Buddhism and speak a Tai dialect closely related to Siamese, or standard Thai. U. S. I. S. (The United States Information Service) has produced a film for distribution in Thailand where the Lue are classed as hill tribes (*chaawkhǎw*), clearly an error.

2   Many western scholars of comparative and historical Tai include Ong, Be and Li speech of Hainan in their studies. (See Benedict 1942, 1975; Haudricourt 1967 and Chamberlain 1971, for example.) The data on these languages appear to be very sketchy. Their similarity to other Tai languages is found in a handful of words, which may be fortuitous borrowings. In his study of 'National languages', Chang Kun (1967) shows Li as an intermediary language between Mia-Yao and Kam-Tai, a classification that I would favor, at least until better data are available. The possibility exists that these languages are Pidgins or Creoles. Mantaro Hashimoto (1980) has published the most reliable data on Be to date.

3   Ahom, the Tai language of Assam, India, died out about 1800 (Gedney 1974). An Ahom-Assamese-English Dictionary by Borua was published in Calcutta in 1920. Other materials include Ahom Lexicons, 1964, Ahom Buranji (Chronicles), an 1872 publication by Dalton of a descriptive ethnography of Bengal. A Thai university professor, Dr Banjob Phantumeetha has written, in Thai, a popular account of her travels in Assam. Grierson (1904) also refers to Ahom in his survey. Anthony Diller (personal communication 1981) reports that he found, during a recent visit of Assam, 'several older men who could chant historical texts and ceremonial things for hours'. The chanting is apparently done from written texts with an Assamese pronunciation (phonology) and without preservation of the tonal distinctions of the original Ahom texts. Except for vestige phrases used for fun, 'no one uses Ahom for daily life purposes'.

4   The exact location of Chieng Rung in Yunnan is 1000-101031' east longitude and 21031' north latitude (just below the Tropic of Cancer). Many maps show this to be part of an 'autonomous region' of which there are several in The People's Republic of China. In the case of Chieng Rung, it is the capital of the Tai Autonomous Region of Sipsongpanna (Wade-Giles: Hsishuangpanna; Pinyin: Xishuangpanna).

references to this city-state comes from Coedes (1968), who reports that at about the time Assam was captured by the Tais in 1229, the Tai chiefs of Chieng Rung and Ngoen Yang (the site of Chieng Saen) on the upper Mekong arranged a marriage between their children as part of forming an alliance. Phinith (1977) has published an annotated translation of a Chieng Rung Chronicle written originally in Siamese and covering the period 1836-1858.

Today, Lue settlements exist in relative close proximity in Moeng Yong, Burma; Chiengrai and Chiengmai provinces in Thailand; and in and around Muang Sing and Luang Prabang in northern Laos. In the north of Vietnam, Lue reside in the area of Binh Lue and along the border of China just west of the Black River (LeBar, et al. 1964). Close by, to the west and just inside the border of Vietnam is the community of Cheng Tung (not to be confused with Kengtung, Burma), the source of an article on Lue phonology published by F. K. Li (1964). The total population of the Lue in the five-nation region probably does not exceed 500,000, with the major concentration around Chieng Rung.

Detailed information on Lue speech and writing has been published in Chinese (Fu Mao-Chi, et al. 1956).[5] Entitled 'The phonemic system of Chieng Rung, Sipsongpanna in Yunnan Province', it is an extensive piece of fieldwork and analysis done by a team over a period of four years. More recently the Chinese have revised the traditional Lue script to facilitate literacy.

Data, in the form of unpublished field notes of Lue of Moeng Yong, Burma and Chieng Rung are available from Gedney (1968-69). Some notes on various aspects of Lue phonology and discourse can be found in Hartmann (1975, 1976a). Weroha (1974), a native speaker of the Chiengkham variety of Lue, has compiled an extensive lexicon and written several papers on his own phonological system. Moerman (1972, 1977) has published an analysis of a segment of a conversation in Chiengkham Lue. Many older and minor works on Lue and neighboring dialects are found in the literature. They will be listed at the conclusion of this chapter. For the moment, we shall deal with the more important, reliable publications.

Li (1964) makes note of the existence of several dialects in Lue. He concludes in his own study of the Cheng Tung variety of Lue that it is simply a 'close dialect variant' of the nearby White Tai analyzed by Minot (1940, 1949). The Lue of Chieng Rung recorded by Gedney (1968) displays tonal splits and other phonological similarities which link it to the Lue of Cheng Tung and White Tai just mentioned. On the other hand, the even more recent data on Lue of Moeng Yong (Gedney 1968-69) has a tonal array parallel to Khuen spoken in adjacent areas to the west of Kengtung Province in Burma as well as to Yuan (or Northern Thai) spoken directly to the south (Egerod 1959).

We can begin to see that these relationships and overlaps of varieties of Lue speech as one moves from east to west show the dynamics of a dialect pattern of 'almost continuous Variation' (Moerman 1965) among the Tai peoples of this northern geographic region. The unreality of absolutely discrete dialects cannot be overemphasized. Gedney (1967) describes the linguistic situation as 'gradual transition throughout much of the Tai-speaking domain, except perhaps for the boundary between Northern Tai and the others'.

The *Linguistic Survey of India*, which includes a sizeable portion of the Lue found in the western geographical regions – i.e., the Shan State – indicates that Lue might be closely related to Khuen, Shan, Lao and Siamese. In his introduction to the survey Grierson (1928) states that Lue and Khuen are varieties of 'Lao' which is 'spoken throughout the country situated between the 19th parallel of north latitude and the northern boundary of the kingdom of Siam'. We must realize that he is describing conditions as he saw them at the beginning of the 20th century. The Siamese kingdom did not incorporate the Chiengmai region until the reign of Rama I. Historically, Chiengmai, Chiengrai and other cities of the north were Lao in the sense that they were founded by Mengrai, a Lao prince (Coedes 1968). The Thais of the Central Plains (or 'middle Menam') were known by their neighbors as Syām, i.e., Siam.

---

5   The original article is, of course, in Chinese. I have used a copy which is a translation by Mrs James Dew, generously provided by Professor Gedney.

Grierson's divisions appear to reflect these older historic states. To confuse the issue even more, the term Yuan is often used to refer to the language of the same area – northern Thailand. Again, Coedes tells us that the label Yuan is derived from YonaraÚtha or YonakaraÚtha, 'kingdom of the Yuan'. Chiengmai, 'the new city', founded by Mengrai in 1296, was its capital. Yuan (or Yon) has also been used by American missionaries (Dodd 1923) to refer to the alphabet used in the north, varieties of which extended beyond Chiengmai into Kengtung (Khuen) and presumably Chieng Rung (Lue). Egerod and others likewise use the term Yuan to designate the dialect of northern Thailand and its centre at Chiengmai. The Siamese (Bangkok Thais) have another ethnic term of the same shape, Yuan, referring usually to the Vietnamese or, occasionally, to the Mongo dynasty in China.

To return to Grierson's early study, he considers Lue and Khuen to be a link or transitional dialect area between what he designates as the Northern group – the extinct language Ahom, plus Khamti and Shan – on the one hand, and Siamese, Lao and 'Southeastern Shan' (Tai speech east of the Salween River) on the other. In this connection, it is interesting to note the comment made more recently by Gedney (1967):

> the speech of those villages and towns in the extreme northeast of Burma where the people refer to themselves and their language as 'Lue' seems to be closer linguistically to the Shan and Khuen spoken to the west and the dialects of northern Thailand to the south than it is to the dialect of the Lue capital city of Chieng Rung in Sipsongpanna.

Cushing (1881), in the preface to his Shan-English dictionary, reflects a similar viewpoint in stating that the Khuen of Kengtung and the Lue of Chieng Rung are both dialects of Shan. Still another authority on the Tai dialects of the more northwestern reaches of the Tai domain is the linguist Søren Egerod, who states (1959):

> Khun is a sister language of Tai Yuan spoken in the Lanna or Phayap region of Thailand (capital Chiengmai) and Tai Lu spoken in the Sipsong Panna area (capital Kenghung) of Yunnan, China. The three languages of Khun, Yuan, and Lu are closely related and use very similar systems of writing based on the Mon-Burmese tradition as far as the form of letters go, but in usage closer to Siamese than to Shan, especially as far as borrowing of vocabulary is concerned.

Lanna Thai, the alternate term used by Egerod and many others for Northern Thai, was historically used by the Siamese to refer to their northern neighbors (Coedes, op.cit.). Yuan, the general label preferred by Egerod, is used interchangeably with the term Lao by LeBar et al. (1964). Haas (1958) names the same dialect after the chief city in which it is spoken - the Chiengmai dialect. Still another label for the same general dialect is *Muang* (Mundhenk 1967) following the local custom of the natives calling themselves 'people of the *muang*' (Moerman 1967). The term *muang* (or *mueang*) is often translated *town*, but in some instances it can indicate an area as large as a kingdom or nation. In the case of *Kam Muang* (language of the *mueang*), the speaker is probably identifying his speech with that of Meuang Lanna (see maps).[6]

---

6   The interplay between 'city talk' and rural speech is dealt with interestingly by Leonard Bloomfield (1927). Here it is doubtful that kam muang means city talk. Looking at the Mission Pavie map at the end of this chapter, we see the label Muang Lan Na 'country of a million fields' to cover the old kingdom that had its center at Chiengmai. To translate khon muang simply as people of the muang is really incomplete. Relying on cartography and historical information, the fuller reference is more properly made to the people and the language of Muang Lanna Thai 'the kingdom of Lanna'.

Finally, more recent works on the language of this region use the term Northern Thai, referring to the dialects of the northern part of Thailand proper. Earlier we have seen the use of Northern Thai in speaking of the branch of the Tai language family found in Guangxi and Guizhou, China.

Clearly, the best works on Northern Thai phonology and lexicon are the volumes by Hope and Purnell (1962) and Purnell (1963). The first work, *A Colorful Colloquial*, is subtitled, 'An introduction to the study of spoken Northern Thai...' and is based on the speech of Chiengrai province. A further note on the cover of this work states 'Adaptation of Chiengmai dialect...', an indication that we are dealing with a mixed phenomenon. Purnell's introductory comments are a further recognition of linguistic diversity within Northern Thai itself.

The Northern Thai presented in this volume is that of Chiengrai province. There are seven provinces in northern Thailand, each with a slight though generally mutual intelligible variation of speech... Even in Chiengrai province there are many differences between rural and urban speech, the latter being in the process of assimilation with Central Thai...

At least one of the Tai peoples in Chiengrai province would be some of the Lue. It is estimated that 50,000 Lue live in the Chiengkham district of Chiengrai. The work of an urban Lue from Chiengkham has been cited (cf. Weroha).

Brown (1965) lists Northern Thai as one of the seven Thai dialects dealt with in his study of modern dialects used in his historical reconstruction. He claims that while there are several different dialects, the differences are 'relatively minor'. He then lists the five dialects of Northern Thai as: Chiengrai, Chiengmai, Phrae, Nan, Lampang. Missing from his list are Maehongson and Tak. His informants were all from the five provincial capitals (*amphur mueng*), and, as such, would probably show less diversity than rural speakers from the same broad region.

Two studies written in Thai are the Master's thesis on Chiengmai speech by Suntharagul (1963) and a monograph on Lanna Thai by Phayomyong (1968). The latter deals with the Yuan script. Another short work designed to teach the Northern Thai writing system is that of Davis (1970) who did his work in Nan province.

Further impressions of the relationship of Lue to other dialects concern the problem of mutual intelligibility. Seidenfaden (1925) comments, 'The Lu tonque is – as anyone conversant with colloquial Thai will easily detect – for all purposes a mere dial of the latter, and is practically identical with the language spoken in Chiengmai'. The Lue he refers to is most likely spoken by Lue who have resided in northern Thailand in Chiengkham and around Chiengmai province as long ago as one hundred years when they were moved as a result of skirmishes between Thailand and Burma. Moerman (1965),[7] an American anthropologist who lived among the Lue of Chiengkham, a district in the northeastern part of Chiengrai province, made these remarks based on fourteen months of living there:

---

7   Moerman (1965) has attempted to deal with the confusing array of ethnic terms. He notes:

The Chinese *Pai-i*, for example, includes some, but not all, of China's Thai people. The term *Yang* is used by the Siamese for the Karen, by the Eastern Lao for the Lue (Archer 1892: 346), and by the Lue of Ban Ping for non-Buddhist Thai in China. The term Yuan is used by the Lue, the Shan (Archer 1892: 346), and the Lao (Mouhot 1864 II: 129) for the Thai of Lannathai, who call themselves 'people of the *myang*' (*khon myang*). The Siamese call the Yuan *Lao* and reserve the term *Yuan* for the Annamese (i.e. Vietnamese).

Although I am not a linguist, it is perhaps worth recording that my own observations, both in speaking and listening to native speakers, indicate that the Lue, Lao, Yuan and Yong are all mutually intelligible. Chiengkham (Thailand) Lue informants report that their speech was easily understood in the Burmese and Chinese Shan States during World War II. Although speakers of Northern dialect often seem to understand speakers of another dialect more easily than they can understand Siamese (Central Thai), the genetic significance of this relative intelligibility is difficult to evaluate since Northern speakers react to and discuss solely in terms of lexicon. The comparative unintelligibility of Siamese results from its Cambodian and Sanskrit borrowings rather than from differences of tonal structure which might be of greater genetic significance. Differences of tone among the Northern dialects are ignored or 'automatically' compensated for by native listeners.

Of the four dialects named by Moerman, two require some explanation. By 'Yong' he probably means Lue of Moeng Yong, Burma. This Burmese-based community of Lue speakers appears to be quite large and influential. There is a great deal of communication and cultural contact between Moeng Yong and the Lue communities of Northern Thailand. It is not surprising that they speak mutually intelligible dialects. As for the 'Lao' that Moerman mentions, again we do not know if this label is being used in the older historical sense of referring to Northern Thai in general or if it should be reserved for the speech of nearby Lao communities just across the Mekong River at Ban Houei Sai. Without place names such as 'Lao of Luang Prabang', we do not know what the intended point of comparison is. There are also Yong speakers in and around Chiengmai (Davies 1979).

The claim made by Simmalawong (1972) is much more specific in this respect. She described the Lao and Lue spoken at Muang Sing, Laos as nearly indistinguishable. Historically, Muang Sing was once part of the Lue circle of 'twelve (*sipsong*) cities'.

Another point brought up by Moerman is that of tonal differences among mutually intelligible dialects. He claims that they are ignored or 'automatically' adjusted to by speakers of these dialects. It will be shown later that if we examine the tonal splits, i.e., the system of distribution of contrasting tonemes, we find that for Lue of Moeng Yong and the varieties of Northern Thai mentioned, the tonal array is identical even though there may be phonetic differences in the actual shapes. Speakers from Nan, Phrae, Chiengmai, Chiengrai, Lampang or even Khuen from Kengtung all have the same underlying system of tones. We cannot say for certain what the case is for Lue speakers from Chiengkham. It appears that older, more conservative speakers, like the older Lue at Mae Sai, Thailand, have a tonal array identical to that of Chieng Rung in Sipsongpanna. Younger speakers who still identify themselves as Lue but live in Chiengkham district probably have the tonal splits of Northern Thai. Siamese (Central Thai) has a system of tonal splits that is clearly different from the general array for Northern Thai. It is this factor which impedes intelligibility between Siamese and Northern Thai on the one hand and facilitates communication between a speaker of Northern Thai and Lue of Moeng Yong on the other. The system of tonal splits for various dialects will be illustrated in the next chapter.

The coexistence of apparently disparate dialects at the same geographic point, a major city, is not uncommon. Kengtung (Chieng Tung), Burma is the capital of the Khuen, a sister dialect of Lue. At the same time, the city is considered by many to be a Shan-speaking area. After all, it is in the area designated as the Shan State. As far as I could determine from interviewing a single Khuen speaker, his was the major urban dialect. As one moved out into the suburbs and nearby rural areas, the dialects were different, i.e., presumably more like Shan. Until quite recently, the Khuen community supported a powerful chief (or petty prince). For generations, they have maintained close contacts with Chiengmai, which in part explains the closeness of those two dialects. In addition, the Khuen (and Lue) alphabet is nearly identical to the older Yuan script of Chiengmai, which, in turn, is similar to Shan orthography. Of course, all of these alphabets, including Burmese, Siamese, etc., can be traced to their source of Indian script (Coedes, 1968).

From the Shan standpoint, then, Khuen and Lue are subdialects of Shan (Cushing 1914). Brown (1965) divides Shan into three subgroups, which do not include Khuen and Lue, dialects which he does not mention in his work at all.

Shan is spoken in the Shan State of Burma by about two million people. There are apparently three main dialects; northern (centered at Lashio), southern (centered at Taunggyi), and eastern (centered at Chiang Tung, sometimes written Kengtung).

Cushing's great Shan-English dictionary uses the speech of Laikha and Mongnai, two cities roughly midway between Kengtung and Taunggyi.

The preceding discussion of ethnolinguistic groups suggests a picture of not only gradual transition from one geographic point to another, but also pockets of great diversity at key points like Kengtung (Khuen and Shan), Muang Sing (Lue and Lao), Vientiane (Lao, Black Tai, etc.) and Bangkok (Central Thai, Lao and non-Tai languages). Within each group, subdivisions can be made along the lines of social class differences (Beebe 1974). These are centers of economic and political power which attract linguistically diverse peoples from great distances, especially in politically unstable times. The fluidity of movement of Tai peoples is consequently greater than dialect labels now show. For example, the presence of Saek speakers near Nakorn Phanom, Thailand is one illustration of an extreme geographic movement of Tai people out of southern China into Laos and adjacent areas of Thailand (Gedney 1970a). A group called Lao Song who live outside of Bangkok at Petburi are actually Black Tai who originally came from northeastern Laos (Gedney 1974).

Still another factor that complicates efforts to distinguish people along ethnolinguistic lines is the apparent ease with which some Tai groups (e.g., Shan) can move in and out of unrelated language communities (e.g., Kachin). Leach (1954) has shown how groups in Burma interact and coexist through shifts in language affiliation:

It can easily be established that most of these supposedly distinct 'races' and 'tribes' intermarry with one another. Moreover it is evident that substantial bodies of population have transferred themselves from one language group to another even within the last century.

Realising that languages change as a function of time, space, political and other forces, we can see that it is somewhat difficult to identify anyone speaker in absolute terms either linguistically or ethnically. In other words, there is no necessary isomorphism between language, culture and race. So, to answer the question, 'Who is Lue?' (cf. Moerman 1965), the answer is simply, whoever says he is. To answer the question, 'What is Lue speech?' requires an examination of all of the linguistics dimensions of the several varieties of Lue already cited. Such will be part of the task of the next chapter.

Before concluding the discussion of the place of Lue in the Southwestern branch of the Tai family, brief mention should be made of the Tai dialects spoken to the north and west of the Lue communities in Sipsongpanna. Gedney (1965a) suggests that there is a connection between Chinese Shan, Tai-Neua and Lue, dialects which he believes are in their present geographical location in Yunnan as a 'result of northward movement rather than the reverse'. That is, in arguing against the traditional homeland of Proto-Tai in Yunnan itself (cf. Brown 1965 and the opposing view of Mote 1964, Gedney 1966a and Burling 1965), the parent of the Tai family is now placed in the area along the border separating Vietnam and southern Guangxi province in southeastern China. Of the daughter languages that developed over time and a change of location, White Tai, Lue, Khuen, Northern Tai and possibly some varieties of Shan might be conceived of as one fairly uniform group which took part in a westward migration or what Coedes (1968) describes as a 'gradual engulfing' of the region.

For the sake of balanced argument, certain geographical and political factors can also be brought into account for the surprising degree of linguistic unity suggested in the preceding paragraph. Using ethnographic information, LeBar (1964) places these dialects in a region designated as the 'central Mekong area, from Luang Prabang north to Sip Song panna, and including northern Thailand and easternmost Burma'. Similarly, Simmonds (1965) comments on geographic factors promoting 'remarkable homogeneity of the Yuan dialects and of the dialects of the Middle Mekong'. From reading the early travel accounts of American missionaries (Dodd 1923) and the French imperialists (Mission Pavie), the impression is gained that, despite the lack of modern amenities, there are no great barriers to travel in the region. That is not to say that natural geographic boundaries do not exist. The very fact that the Tai live at low riverine elevations has had an impact on their linguistic and cultural development. Indeed Tai peoples monopolize the middle Mekong River area today. Another geographic index is the division between the decidedly flat Central Plains of much of Thailand and the more hilly north beginning approximately at Uttaradit, a demarcation that marks a dialect boundary as well.

While nothing more than a supposition at this point, there is also the factor of political domination to be considered. It is conceivable that the exercise of power by northern kingdoms such as the ones centered at Chiengmai and Chieng Rung was great enough at one time to promote the spread of a metropolitan (mueang) dialect. Certainly today we find the compelling reach of Bangkok speech into areas that until recently were more Lao-like (Khanittanan 1973). The thesis of linguistic homogeneity as a function of political control might also be used to explain the reverse situation. That is, linguistic diversity would be traced to macro-political disunity which mayor may not be accompanied by geographical discontinuities.

Another indicator of the relationship of Lue to neighbouring dialects comes from comparative lexicon. In the course of translating the two texts used in this study, use was mad of vocabularies and dictionaries compiled by Donaldson (1970) for White Tai, Egerod (1971) Purnell (1963) for Northern Thai and Cushing (1914) for Shan. The younger, more creative singer used a 'literary' vocabulary that often could be traced to sources in both White Tai and Shan.

Both singers had a core vocabulary that was 90% like Northern Thai and 70% (by their own estimates) like Siamese. No dictionary of Lue has been published to date. Until such time, we can do no more than make guesses about shared vocabularies. Still it is clear that Lue is, as its geographic position would indicate, a dialect that overlaps both White Tai and Shan and is close to Northern Thai.

Additional references to varieties of Lue can be found in the work of the following: Carthew (1952), Deydier (1954), Dodd (1910), Embree and Dotson (1950), Finot (1917), Grierson (1904, 1928), Henry (1903), Lefèvre-Pontalis (1892), LeMay (1925), Rispeaud (1933), Schrock (1970), Srisawat (1955), Brun (1976), Davies (1979), Gainey and Thongkum (1977), Hsieh (1978), Lafont (1962), F. K. Li (1977), Morev (1978), Phinith (1977), Pramoj (1980), Sarawit (1979), Siam Society (1966), T'ung (1958), Tao (1958), Weroha (1975), and Moerman (1977).

Finally, maps are shown at the end of this chapter in order to put the Lue and neighbouring dialects into clear perspective linguistically and historically.

Map 7.1-1, hand-drawn, highlights the three points from which the data for the following chapters will be taken. For Lue of Cheng Tung (Sipsongpanna) we have the monograph of Li (1964); for Lue of Chieng Rung (Sipsongpanna), there is the publication of Fu Mao-Chi et al. (1956), the unpublished fieldnotes of Gedney (1968) and my own field data. Likewise, for Lue of Moeng Yong (Burma), we have relied on the unpublished fieldnotes of Gedney (1969) and my own data. The more recent Russian work on Lue (Morev 1978) appears to be in close agreement with the earlier work of Fu Mao-Chi et al. (1956), but has not been utilized here.

Map 7.1-2, from the 1904 Linguistic Survey of India shows the relationship of Lue to Khün and varieties of Shan.

Map 7.1-3 shows the small but distinct Lue enclave in Binh Lu', Vietnam. The source is Deydier (1954).

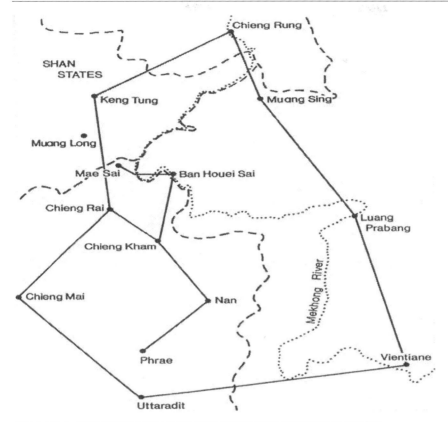

MAP 7.1-1: SHOWING AREAS OF GREATEST LUE CONCENTRATION

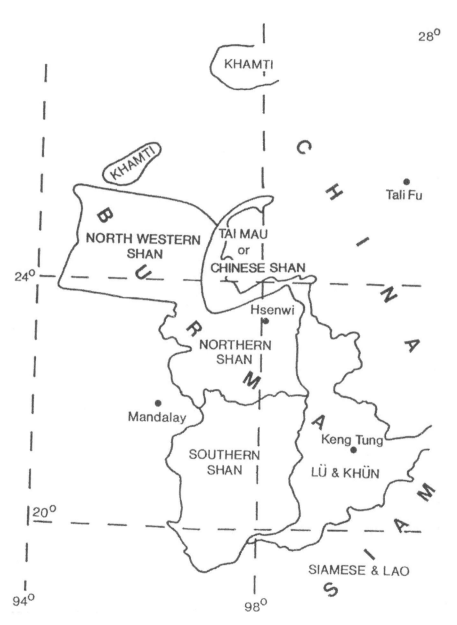

MAP 7.1-2: SHOWING THE LOCALITIES IN WHICH THE TAI LANGUAGES OF BRITISH INDIA ARE SPOKEN

RÉPUBLIQUE POPULAIRE DE CHINE

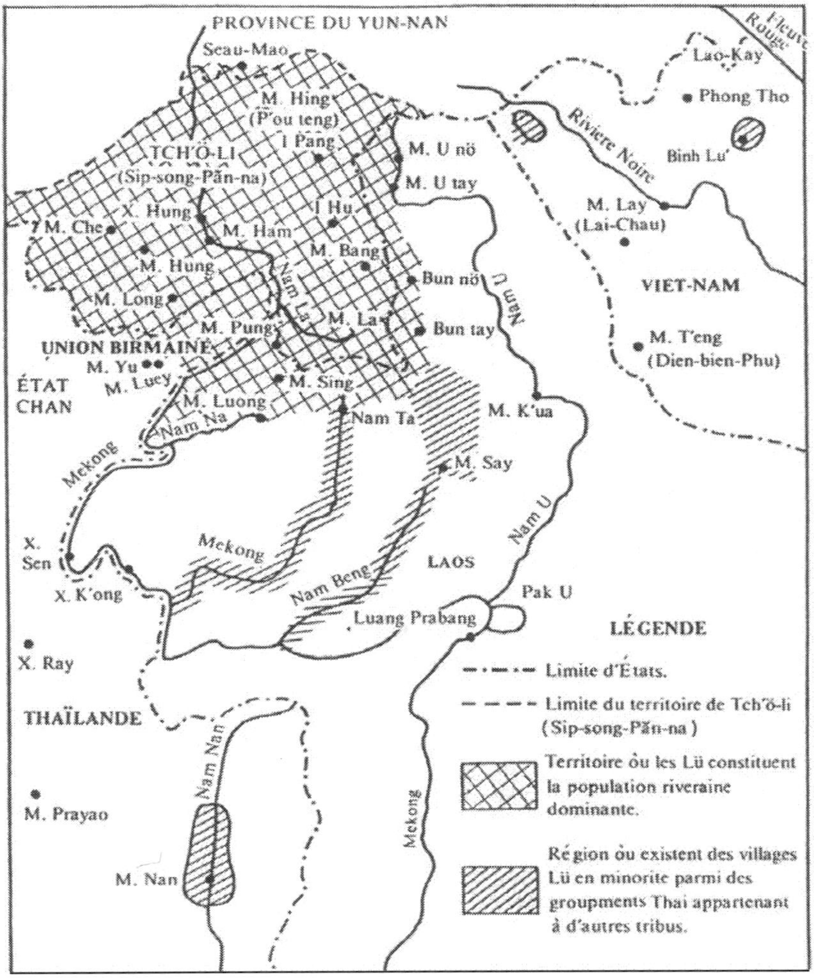

MAP 7.1-3: SHOWING THREE MAJOR LUE SPEECH AREAS PREVIOUSLY STUDIED BY GEDNEY (1964) AND LI (1964)

7.2. PHONOLOGY

In the preceding section, a survey of data from both published and unpublished sources indicated in general terms the close relationship between three varieties of Lue and the following: Shan, Khuen, Northern Thai, Lao and White Tai. In this chapter, we shall proceed to examine the phonological structure of the syllable in these dialects using Siamese as a reference point in the comparisons.

Most discussions of Tai, comparative or otherwise, begin with a description of the syllable, the Tai languages being basically monosyllabic. Tai is also tonal, and the syllable is the unit of tone placement (Abramson 1962). Depending on the phonemic analysis used – whether the glottal stop or vowel length are given the status of phonemes – the structure of the Tai syllable can be schematized as shown.

INITIAL	TONE	
C_1 (C) (C)	V_1 (V) VOCALIC NUCLEUS	(C_2) FINAL

Giving the glottal stop phonemic status, it then follows that every syllable has an obligatory initial consonant. One or two consonants may follow to form a two or three consonant cluster. In the Southwestern branch, double consonant clusters are the rule with the sonorants r, l, w, y as the second member. A vowel or vowel cluster will follow, and, optionally, a final consonant or semivowel. The possibilities for finals are limited to the stops p, t, k, ʔ (glottal stop), the nasals m, n, ŋ and the semi-vowel w, y, ɏ. The tone, which may be a register or contour (cf. Pike 1948), extends over the voiced portion of the syllable. The unvoiced segments do not carry tone; nevertheless they do have a conditioning effect on the final output of the tone on any particular syllable.

As part of the conditioning effect of finals on the shape of tones, syllables are further categorized as *free* (or smooth) and *dead* (or checked). In Siamese the terms are *khampen* and *khamtaay* respectively. Checked syllables end in the stops p, t, k, ʔ; a smooth syllable ends in a vowel or the sonorants m, n, ŋ, w, y, ɏ (ɏ = ɨ as final offglide).

The conditioning effect of initial consonants is explained not in terms of syllable types but in a taxonomy of the phonetic characteristics of the reconstructed initials of the parent language. For Lue of Chieng Rung and White Tai of Muang Te, for example, it suffices to know whether or not an initial consonant was voiced or unvoiced in the parent, which, in the case of Proto-Southwestern Tai may not go back in time much farther than 1,000 years. For dialects where the distribution of tones is much more complex, a finer four-way grid for classifying the initials is needed. The grid used here is taken from Gedney (1964). The tones A, B, C, D are designations for proto-tones. The D-short and D-long are the tones for the checked syllables with long and short vowel nuclei respectively. The length of the vocalic nucleus in checked syllables is the third variable governing the shape of syllable tone. In analyzing the tone of anyone dialect, the usual procedure is to find minimal pairs in the smooth syllables. Whatever tones then emerge for the checked syllables can be matched up with the closest smooth counterparts. This is not always easily done, especially with knowledge of only one or two dialects. The difficulties in applying this procedure of mapping the tones from checked syllables onto the tones for smooth ones in the Northern Tai dialect is a case in point (cf. Purnell).

Initials \ Tones	Smooth syllables			Checked syllables	
	A	B	C	D-short	D-long
HIGH Voiceless friction sounds					
MID Voiceless unaspirated stops					
Glottal stop & pre-glottal sound					
LOW Voiced sounds					

The preceding chart covers the salient phonetic features of initial consonants as they govern the historical development of tone in the Central and Southwestern branches. The Northern branch of the Tai family goes further in dividing the High class initials (or proto-voiceless friction sounds) along the lines of a *hm vs. *kh difference affecting the development of tones in the proto-A category (Gedney 1972b, 1974). This fine distinction does not concern Lue. Lue development is one of the simplest among the Tai languages.

If we go back to the time of the parent language, it is assumed that only three tones could be associated with smooth syllables, designated here as A (unmarked or neutral tone), B (Siamese *máy ʔèek*) and C (Siamese *máy thoo*). This condition of three simple tones is traced back to Proto-Tai, the period antecedent to the partition of the parent (or more homogeneous original model) into more diverse daughter dialects.[8]

It is not clear what the case is when the time depth is pushed back even further to include the distantly related speech group called Kam-Sui-Mak (Li 1965, Oshika 1973). The shape of this older family tree can be found in a comparison of models suggested by Gedney (1970a, 1974) and Haudricourt (1967). The general presumption is that the opening stage of tonal splitting was simultaneous if not sudden in its effects on several languages in South-east Asia.

It is interesting to note in both of the models that Saek, classified elsewhere as a dialect of the Northern Tai (Guangxi-Guizhou region), is seen by both scholars as diverging somewhat sooner than its sister dialects. The first scheme is from Gedney, the second from Haudricourt. The latter combines the so-called Tai-Kadai configuration. Haudricourt prefers the single label 'Kadai'.

At any rate, we are concerned here with the differentiation of the three tones A, B, C into double that number in Lue in the southwestern branch. Using information provided by the Siamese writing system which was reformed by Ram Khamhaeng in 1283 (Coedes 1968) and which uses only the three undifferentiated tones, we can say, as does Gedney (1972b):

This tonal system lasted at least until after the time (about 1300 AD) when alphabetic writing systems were devised for some of the languages of the southwestern part of the Tai-speaking domain, including Siamese.

---

8   The tones *ABC were distinguished by pitch registers and syllable-final characteristics. Thus according to Brown (1965), tone A was high, B mid, C low. Correspondingly, syllable endings were whispered, voiced and glottalised. Haudricourt (1961/1972) is in basic agreement with the phonetics of the endings except that he posits a final -*h* for syllables with the A tone. It is often found that the tones in the C column have a creaky or glottalised quality. There are numerous exceptions, however. See Strecker (1979) for a more recent attempt at reconstruction of tones *ABC.

It is not clear from this whether or not tones began to break up earlier in the Northern branch.

This splitting of the tones which occurred some time after 1300 AD in at least the Southwestern branch resulted in Lue, White Tai and many other Tai dialects being left with six tones in place of the original three. The division is what Haudricourt described as a 'bipartition' of the three proto-tones along the lines of voicing of the initial consonant at the time of the split. The tonal splits of Lue at Chieng Rung can be diagrammed with a simple two-way division rather than the more complex four-way grid shown earlier.

A.   (Gedney)

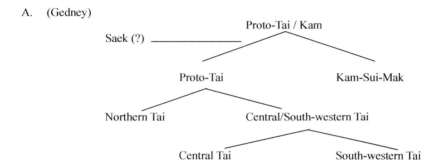

B.   (Haudricourt)

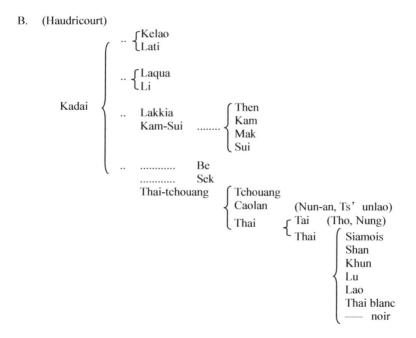

PROTO-TAI TONES (SMOOTH SYLLABLES)

	A	B	C
Voiceless	1	2	3
Voiced	4	5	6

The general shape of the tones of Chieng Rung are shown in the following diagram using both a system of numbered tones and their description in words along with the scheme used often in phonological description of Chinese tones. In the latter system, a pitch level of 5 is high and 1 is low; 3 would be in the mid range. (* = proto-; vl = voiceless, vd = voiced).

	*A	*B	*C	*D-long	*D-short
*vl (yin)	1 high-level ⌐ 55	2 mid-rising ⟋ 35	3 low, glot., slt. rise ⌐ 13	= 2	= 1
*vd (yang)	4 falling |	5 mid-level ⊣	6 low, level, slt, rise ⌐⌐	= 5	= 5

| Smooth syllables | Checked syllables |

In this matrix, the maximum number of six tones is found on the smooth syllables. The tones on the checked syllables are matched up with their nearest counterparts in the class of smooth syllables. As explained earlier, the tones of the smooth and checked are conditioned by different variables so that they stand in complementary distribution. The tones shown here, then, are phonemic, not phonetic. In some works, e.g., Purnell (1963), it is not always clear whether the tones which are enumerated are phonemic or not. Closer examination reveals that the seven tones of Northern Thai, for example, are phonetic; only six can be isolated on free syllables.

Recalling the information from the four-way division of initials of Proto-Tai as they influenced tonal development, we can plot the tonal similarities and differences in the three varieties of Lue along with Khuen, Shan and White Tai.

Shan: Keng Tung City   Khuen: 5 miles east of Keng Tung

    A   B   C   A   B   C

*vl friction
*vl unaspir. stops
*glott.stop. & pre-glott. snd.
*vd

*vl
*vd

Lue: Moeng Yong, Burma   Lue: Chieng Rung

    A   B   C   A   B   C

Lue: Chieng Tong   White Tai: Tung Ngia, N. Vietnam

    A   B   C   A   B   C

*vl

*vd

The data for the tonal charts shown above come from the unpublished fieldnotes of Gedney except for his Publication on White Tai (1964) and F. K. Li's article on Lue of Cheng Tung (1964). The charts illustrate the nearly identical tonal contours for corresponding tones in Shan and Khuen of Keng Tung and Lue of Moeng Yong. This tonal isomorphism is obscured by the three different ethnic labels. On the other hand, Lue of Chieng Rung is much different from Lue of Moeng Yong or nearby White Tai.

On the following pages, the tonal shapes of Khuen of Keng Tung and Lue of Chieng Rung are compared to dialects studied by Brown (1965) such as Shan, varieties of Lao, and the dialects of Thai spoken at Bangkok, northeastern and southern and northern Thailand. Again, it can be seen that Lue of Chieng Rung is closest to Shan, Khuen and the Northern Thai spoken at Chiengrai and Nan. But the Shan and Lue are closest in exhibiting the simple *voiced-voiceless split. Brown's Shan informant was located in Chiengrai. It would be informative to know his exact origins. The Shan of Keng Tung from Gedney's unpublished fieldnotes has tonal splits identical to Khuen of Keng Tung and Lue of Moeng Yong. However, he has Shan data from Hsi Paw, Burma and Chefang, Yunnan with tonal splits identical to the *vd - *vl one seen in Brown's charts. Another dialect spoken at Hsen wii has six tones, making it even closer to Lue of Chieng Rung. Most dialects of Shan have only five tones due to coalescence of tones, as in Siamese.

By contrast, Lue does not participate in any of the tonal splits found in the Lao of our data. A glance at the charts reveals that the Lao column C invariably has a split at the top conditioned by the High class initials (proto-voiceless friction).

The shapes of the Bangkok tones seem to share something in common with both the north and the northeast. They appear to mark something of a transitional zone.

Haas (1958) finds that the Siamese and Chiengmai tonal systems are very close, the former being a reduction of the latter. (She presumably means a reduction in the number of tones.) Brown (1965: 113) claims that the Khorat[9] and Bangkok dialects are mutually intelligible, presumably on the basis of tone his major interest. To further complicate the picture of the relationship of Siamese (Central and Bangkok Thai included) to other dialects, Haas (op.cit. fn. 4) states: 'In most other respects, Siamese and Nakhonsithammarat are much closer together than Siamese and Chiengmai.' The other aspects are not detailed.

The relationship of Bangkok Thai to other dialects is best illuminated by a closer comparison of more data. We recall that the typical pattern of tonal splits for the dialects of northern Thailand showed a division between A12-A34 or the *voiceless friction and *voiceless unaspirated sounds vs. the *pre-glottalized and *voiced initials. In other words, the Mid class initials of the Siamese alphabet are divided, e.g. in Chiengmai. Yet Bangkok Thai splits A column slightly higher – above, not through, the Mid class initials, or at A1-A234.

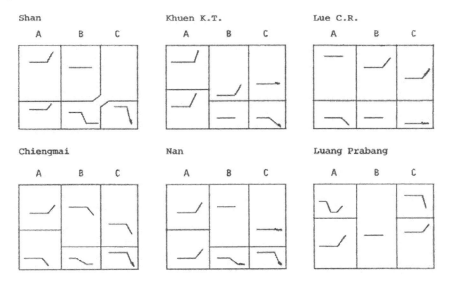

---

9   In Brown's chart for Khorat note that only four tones exist. This is something of a surprise and means that, unless an error has been made, Khorat has the fewest number of tones of any Tai dialect.

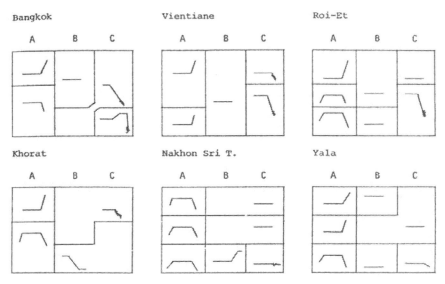

(Data from Brown 1965, except for Khuen and Lue)

If the Bangkok system is seen as a reduction of the Northern Thai system, the question is, why does it make the split in the A column at the point it does? Why does Bangkok Thai avoid dividing the Mid class initials? The answer comes from Haudricourt's astute observations concerning the use (functionalism) of tonal splits as a means of avoiding confusion that would result in homophony if tonal differences were not re-employed. His explanation underscores the basic tenet of de Saussure which says that in language there are only differences. When, in Thai, differences are lost in the classes of initials, the burden is taken up elsewhere: in tones, vowel splits (e.g., the Southern Thai dialects) or vowel lengthening perhaps. In this instance, the Bangkok split, the unique division of column A can be traced to the merging of the High and Low series in ph, th, ch, kh. To quote Haudricourt himself (court translation in Harris and Noss 1972):

> Thus the 'high' letters and the 'low' letters represent the two ancient series of initials - the voiceless aspirates and voiced consonants - which fell together in pronunciation and so caused the tones of the following vowels to split. The 'mid' letters on the contrary represent the voiceless, non-aspirated stops, or glottalized consonants. These 'mid' consonants were neither modified nor confused with the 'high' and 'low' series in the course of the change; the three old tones, A, B, and C thus had no reason to be modified phonetically after 'mid' initials, but since the confusion of the 'high' and 'low' initials had given rise to a system of six tonemes for the vowels in the environment following 'high' and 'low' consonants, then the three tones in the environment following 'mid' initials become phonemically speaking three architonemes, each of which tended to be confused phonetically with one or other of its corresponding tonemes...

Haudricourt's notions of the tripartition and the resulting architonemes in Bangkok and Lao dialects is well illustrated as a real process in Brown's data. In the dialects of Roi-Et and Ubon, for example, the A-Mid and A-Low tones are nearly identical in shape (rising-falling) contour. They differ only in height. They seem to be remarkably close to coalescing, or coming near to the stage of being an architoneme (A-Mid and A-Low being phonetically identical). The Roi-Et and Ubon charts are adapted from Brown (1965). Special note should be made of the A column which shows the tripartition and the near-coalescence that would result in a Bangkok-like A split if completed.

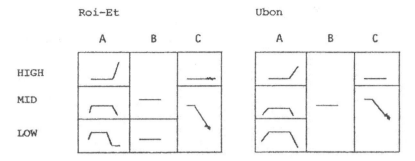

Haudricourt goes on to explain the A12-A34 split in Khuen and Yuan as another manifestation of tripartition. I prefer to view it simply as a bipartition of the A column due to the merger of *b, d, g (Low) with *p, t, k (Mid). There is no evidence for a three-way split in the Band C columns of the other dialects with the same A12-A34 division. In effect, in these dialects (Khuen, Yuan) the two-way split simply functions to move the Mid class p-, t-, k- out of the Mid class tonal category. The remaining items in the Mid class initial series can have the same tone as the Low class p-, j-, k- and the other members of their series. Again, the idea is to use tonal partition to avoid general homophony.

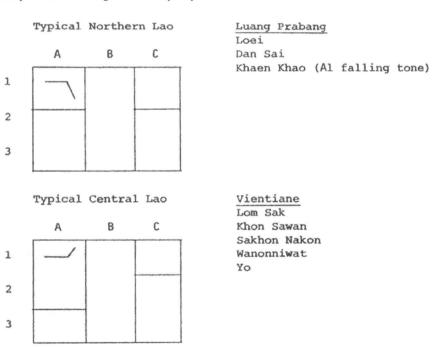

Typical Southern Lao[10]/North-eastern Thai

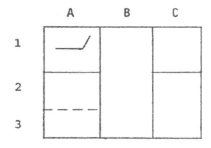

Roi Et
Nong Khai
Ubon
Bua Yai
Khon Kaen
Udon

Transitional Lao/North-eastern-Central Thai

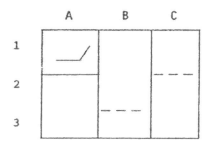

Khorat
Si Saket
Tha Tum

---

10   Compton (1975) has 'Southern Lao' data from Sithadone, Laos. In analysing her data (mohlam), I have found that it fits my scheme previously devised for what I have called Southern Lao: a 3-way split in column A between High-Mid-Low initials. As usual in Lao dialects, the C column shows a High-Mid/Low split. My chart for Compton's Southern Lao data appears as follows with approximations of tonal shapes and pitch levels. Ideally, one should have data from Bassac (Champasak), the third, or Southern Lao capital, historically speaking.

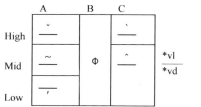

˘ mid rising
~ low, mid, slight
   rise and fall
Φ mid level
ˋ low level
ˆ mid falling
ˊ high falling

In her study of Lao dialects, Panka (1980) provides a quotation from the work of Chit Phumisak (1976) where he points to the historical-political divisions of Laos into the kingdoms of Luang Prabang, Vientiane, and Champasak. Panka uses these three points and ethnographic evidence to set up areas called Northern, Central and Southern Lao. See Hartmann (1981) for further discussion.

Haudricourt's observations allow us to understand not only Bangkok Thai, but the Lao dialects (including Northeastern Thai) and those of southern Thailand as well. These three areas have all participated in tripartition because all of them have undergone the same change of *voiced > voiceless > aspirate initials in the Low series. As a result, the Low and High initials must be distinguished along tonal lines at all cost. But the Mid series in these dialects is free to coalesce tonally with either High or Mid.

Dialects of Lao take all three options for fusion or separation of tones along with lines of tripartition. Again looking at Brown's charts and rearranging them in a new classification, three patterns of Lao dialect differences emerge. First is the Lao dialect around Luang Prabang where the split is A1-A23. (It may be significant that the A1 tone is falling.) Dialects typified by Vientiane have an A12-A3 split. Typical of the Roi-Et group is the three way A1-A2-A3 split with the tendency to coalesce A23. The fusion is complete in typical Khorat-type dialects.

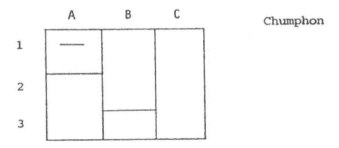

The grouping of Lao dialects along the lines of preference for coalescence after tripartition suggests three regional dialects: Northern, Central and Southern Lao. A fourth group called transitional is part of the Southern Lao group shown on the preceding page. It is separated out to show the transition toward the same A1-23 split found in Bangkok Thai and its similarity to a transitional Southern Thai found in Chumphon in peninsular Thailand. The A1 tonal contour rises for Khorat and Bangkok, but falls for the Chumphon dialect indicating another significant difference between Central and Southern speech.

It is even more interesting to note that Saek, a dialect from the Northern Tai branch which has relocated in the Lao area around Nakhon Phanom, has undergone the change of merging the High and Low aspirates and the resulting tripartition. The other Northern Tai dialects pattern differently. Wuming, Zhuang, Puyi (cf. Sarawit 1973: dialect points 11, 12, 37, 38, 31, 36) have the simple *vl-*vd split. Yay, Po-ai, and Puyi (dialect points 7-9, 1-6, 10, 13-30, 32-35, 39, 40), also Northern Tai dialects, have tonal splits which parallel the divisions shown in the charts for Khuen and Northern Thai in general. We could say that with Saek we have an isolated instance of a Northern Tai dialect (Gedney 1970a) that has acquired Lao features due to contact factors which override genetic subgrouping.

On the other hand, it is equally interesting to note that Red Tai spoken in Laos is not typical of the Lao dialects. That is, following Gedney's data (1964) Red Tai does not have the Lao-like tripartition nor do the aspirates replace the *b, d, g... series. Instead, Red Tai has the features of White and Black Tai and other Tai dialects. The Lao-Central-Southern Thai features do not extend as far north as Red Tai which is spoken just south of the Black Tai community of Son La and north of Sam Neua, Laos. The latter point may well be the north-eastern frontier for the two features of the Lao, Central and Southern Thai dialects we have been considering. Simmonds (1965) states:

> The dialect of Sam Neua, if it is to be considered valid as a dialect of Lao, appears in a somewhat anomalous position in that the tonal pattern resembles that of Black Tai while aspirated plosives occur on all tones, which is a feature of Lao.

This dialect could be considered a transitional point between the bipartite and tripartite groups as they have been classified up until now. The divisions of Sam Neua, adapted from Simmonds' information,[11] appear in the following chart. Note the A1 tone is rising as in the majority of Lao and Central Thai dialects.

Sam Neua

	A	B	C	
1				*vl
2				
3				*vd

In order to summarize in a more general way the discussion of the last several pages, reference is made to the charts below showing bipartition (and its variant) contrasted to tripartition. The correlation of the two-way and three-way split with different initials is shown in synchronic terms.

---

11 I cite these Sam Neua data with some hesitation. Strictly speaking, it is not a Lao dialect because it does not have the H-M/L split in the C column that is characteristic of Lao. Then too, the data Simmonds has for other dialects do not agree with the work of Brown, for example.

Here is a suggested alignment of dialects in Southwestern Tai into three major subdivisions: upper, middle, and lower Southwestern Tai.

A. Bipartition: *vl vs *vd. Found in: Shan
                                           Tai Neua
                                           Lue C. Rung
                                           Lue C. Tung
                                           White Tai
                                           Black Tai
                                           Red Tai
                                           Sam Neua (?)
                                           Cao Bang
                                           Wuming

	A	B	C	
ph				HIGH
p,b				MID
p				LOW

        Variant Bipartition: *vl fr & unasp. vs *Pre-glot. &
                             vd. Found in: Shan Keng Tung
                                            Khuen Keng Tung
                                            Lue Moeng Yong
                                            Chiengrai
                                            Chiengmai
                                            Nan
                                            Phrae
                                            Phayao
                                            Tak

	A	B	C	
ph				HIGH
p				MID
b				
p				LOW

B. Tripartition: High vs Mid vs Low.
                             Found in: Luang Prabang
                                        Loei
                                        Vientiane
                                        Roi-Et
                                        Ubon
                                        Khorat
                                        Bangkok
                                        Chumphon
                                        Saek

	A	B	C	
ph				HIGH
p,b				MID
ph				LOW

A cartogram suggesting an alignment of these dialects is given below.

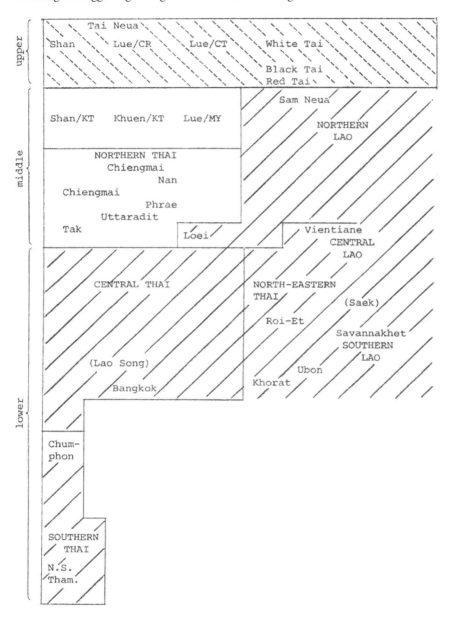

For the dialects of the Central branch, Sarawit (1973) has five points. In this very small area between White, Black and Red Tai to the west and the Zhuang dialects around Wuming there is a line of continuity. The Central dialects of Lung Chow, Nung, W. Nung and Ning Ming (Gedney 1973) have the *vl - *vd split. Lung Ming shows a tonal split identical to Po-ai, to which it is fairly close geographically, and identical to the Chiengmai split. The remaining dialect, Lei Ping, is aberrant. It has the three-way splits of Lao and Saek, indicating a displacement or unusual history. The schematic diagram below suggests a grouping of the dialects of the northern reaches of the Tai speaking domain along the dimension of bipartition. The largest and most continuous group starts from the east with Wuming and the southeastern segment of the Puyi group and continues across to Shan.

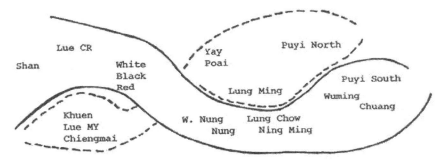

The continuous line indicates simple *vl-vd bipartition. The dotted line encloses dialects where partition is through the center of the so-called Mid initials or rows 12-34.

Comparisons with the tonal splits of the other two branches enlarges our understanding. First the Northern Tai. Southeastern Area: Wuming, Zhuang, Puyi 11, 12, 31, 36-38.

	A	B	C	
	1	2	3	HIGH
*vl				MID
*vd	4	5	6	LOW

North-eastern Area: Yay, Poai, Puyi 1-10, 13-30, 32-35, 39, 40

A. Puyi 7-9

	A	B	C	
	1	2	3	HIGH
				MID
	4	5	6	LOW

B.   Remaining Puyi and Yay

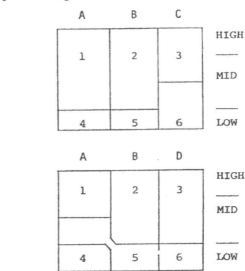

C.   Poai

Gedney (1967) advises students of Tai linguistics to advance our understanding of the Tai dialects by preparing an atlas showing various isoglosses. In Sarawit (1973) we find an admirable beginning for the vocalic changes. Our investigation of bipartition and tripartition clearly shows an east to west isogloss for the phenomenon. A map on page 277 shows the *vl-*vd split connecting Wuming in the east to Shan in the west.

Still another isogloss which separates the more southerly dialects where the High and Low class aspirates merge (Lao, Central and Southern Thai) from the long northern band can be sketched, although with some uncertainty. Brown (1965: 14) would draw a line for this purpose from Luang Prabang 'down to Mekong to (and including) the Thai province of Loei'. Adding to this the information found in Simmonds (1965), the boundary for the High ph/Low ph merger can be drawn through Tak. The question is, where does it cross northern Laos? The following map suggests a line connecting Luang Prabang and Sam Neua. From this we predict that the Lue and Lao dialects at Muang Sing, Laos – for which we have no data – will not have the tripartite tonal splits typical of Lao dialects.

If the notion of bipartition is allowed to cover the dialects of northern Thailand, then the isogloss for tonal splits separating bipartition from tripartition and the isogloss separating the aspirated low class initials (So.) from the unaspirated low class initials (No.) are identical.

In this discussion of the classification of dialects based on common patterns of tonal splits, it is worth recalling that F. K. Li (1959) based his categories on lexical groupings. He appears to be following the lead of Leonard Bloomfield who contrasted the differences between the Germanic languages and other European languages first on the basis of vocabulary and then, secondarily, on phonological criteria. However, Li is careful to point out, 'It is not claimed that lexical distribution is the sole, or even necessarily the best criterion for the classification of languages'. Later he continues, 'If a classification based on lexical elements is supported by phonological criteria, or vice versa, it will have more validity'. We have chosen the reverse approach, using the phonological dimensions of tone and their relationship to classes of initial consonants. As for lexical comparisons, earlier it was pointed out that Lue and Northern Tai shared as high as 90% of their vocabulary in common according to estimates of native speakers. The proportion for Lue and Siamese was put at 70%. A thoroughgoing study of comparative lexicon would doubtless prove extremely interesting, if not exhausting, and would shed further light on the subgrouping of dialects within Southwestern Tai.

For the moment, we shall continue phonological comparisons of the contoids, ignoring variation, which shall be detailed later. The chart (A) directly below takes the data of Fu (1956) and compares it to Siamese (S). Three gaps denoted by a dash require an explanation. First, the glottal stop is not given phonemic status in the Fu analysis. Secondly, Siamese (c) and (ch) merge in Lue of Chieng Rung /ts/. Lastly, Siamese /r/ is Lue /h/ in illiterate speech. Following the comments on the next page, lexical citations (Chart B) are given showing changes from Siamese to Lue, or vice versa.

A. Siamese and Lue (C. R.) initials compared

		Bilabial		Dental		Palatal		Velar		Glottal	
		(S)	Lue	(S)	Lue	(S)	Lue	(S)	Lue	(S)	Lue
Stops:											
	vd unasp.	(b)	b	(d)	d						
	vl unasp.	(p)	p	(t)	t	(c)	ts	(k)	k	(?)	-
	vl asp.	(ph)	ph	(th)	th	(ch)	-	(kh)	x		
Spirants:											
	vl unasp.	(f)	f	(s)	s					(h)	h
Sonorants:											
	vd semi-vowels	(w)	v			(j)	j				
	vd nasals	(m)	m	(n)	n			(n)	ŋ		
	vd lateral			(l)	l						
	vd trill/retro-flex			(r)	-						

The preceding chart requires additional elaboration. The symbol /ts/ used by Fu is later described as having [tɕ] as its actual pronunciation. If such is the case, then this sound must be close if not identical to the /c/ of Siamese, Northern Thai and White Tai. Cognates from Lue of Moeng Yong invariably have /s/ in place of /c/. Perhaps the reason for using /ts/ is the difficulty in analyzing its exact articulation. Fu does not give a description of the mechanics of its production.

Harris (1972) has tackled the description of this troublesome sound with rigor. In the opening paragraphs of his article he takes exception to previous descriptions:

> The Siamese syllable initial consonant sounds represented by the symbol ꜟ have been described as frontal palatal (Kruatrachue, 1960); palatalized apical dental (Thaweesomboon 1969); palatoalveolar (Richards 1966); and voiced palatal (Fowler and Israsena 1952). I have not observed any of these pronunciations of ꜟ either in Siamese or in other Thai dialects. In fact, the description of Siamese as a palatal stop or affricate is misleading.

Later we read his own description, which would appear to cover Lue of Chieng Rung.

> tɕ represents a voiceless unaspirated alveolopalatal glottalized stop. The fricative release of this sound usually is quite short in duration and not very perceptible. This sound only occurs syllable initially in Siamese. This is a very common pronunciation in Siamese.

tɕa:n 'dish'

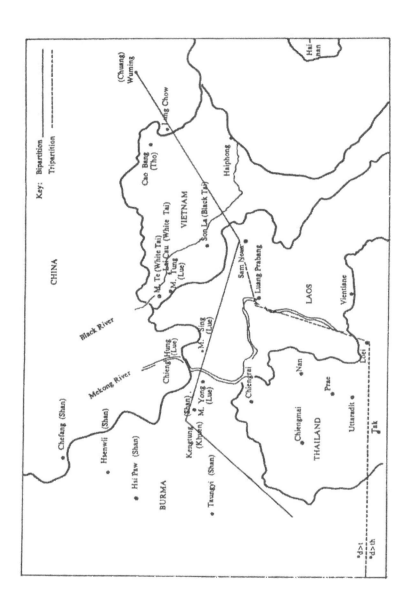

MAP 7.2-1: SHOWING THE ISOGLOSSES OF CHANGE FROM PROTO-TAI
*d TO MODERN t AND th RESPECTIVELY

B. Siamese and Lue initials are compared below:

	Siamese	Lue Chieng Rung	Gloss
(b)/b	bàa	baa²	*shoulder*
(p)/p	pen	pin¹	*to be, alive*
(ph)/ph	phàk	phak¹	*vegetable*
(f)/f	fǎa	faa¹	*plank wall*
(w)/v	wan	van⁴	*day*
(m)/m	maa	maa⁴	*to come*
(d)/d	dàa	daa²	*to scold*
(t)/t	taa	taa¹	*eye*
(th)/th	thàk	thak¹	*to knit*
(s)/s	sǐŋ	siŋ¹	*lion*
(n(/n	naa	naa⁴	*rice field*
(1)/1	laa	laa⁴	*donkey*
(r)/-	rian	heen⁴	*to learn*
(c)/ts	càk	tsak¹	*machine*
(ch)/-	chiaŋ	tseŋ⁴	*city*
(j)/j	yaa	yaa¹	*medicine*
(k)/x	khaa	xaa⁴	*long, dry grass*
(n)/n	ŋaa	ŋaa⁴	*ivory*
(?)/-	kɔ?	kɔ¹	*island*
(h)/h	hàk	hak¹	*to break*

On the following pages a comparison of Lue to six other dialects in the Southwestern branch with which it has varying degrees of contact is shown. The listing follows Sarawit's reconstruction (1973). In the case of Khuen and Lue of Cheng Tung, educated guesses had to be made due to the lack of citation forms.

Proto-SW	Siamese	Shan	Khuen	N. Thai	Lue MY	Lue CR	White
High class initials (proto-voiceless friction sounds)							
*ph	ph	ph	ph	ph	ph	ph	ph
*th	th	th	th	th	th	th	th
*kh	kh	kh	kh	kh	kh	kh	kh
*ch	ch	sh	s	s	s	ts	c
*nm	m	m	m	m	m	m	m
*hn	n	n	n	n	n	n	n
*ñ	y	y	y	ñ	y	y	ñ
*ŋ	ŋ	ŋ,h	ŋ	ŋ	ŋ,h	ŋ	h
*f	f	ph	f	f	f	f	f

Proto-SW	Siamese	Shan	Khuen	N. Thai	Lue MY	Lue CR	White
High class initials (continued)							
*s	s	š	s	s	s	s	s
*xh	kh	kh	kh	kh	kh̥	x	x
*hw	w	w	w	w̥	v	v	v
*h	h	h	h	h	h	h	h
*hl	l	l	l	l	l	l	l
Mid class initials (proto-voiceless unaspirated stops)							
*p	p	p	p	p	p	p	p
*t	t	t	t	t	t	t	t
*c	c	s	c	c	c	c	c
*k	k	k	k	k	k	k	k
Mid class initials (glottal stop and pre-glottalised sounds)							
*ʔb	b	m,w	b	b	b	b	b
*ʔd	d	n,l	d	d	d	d	d
*ʔy	y	y	y	y	y	y	y
*ʔ	ʔ	ʔ	ʔ	ʔ	ʔ	ʔ	ʔ
*ʔl	d	l,m	d	d	d,b	d	b
Low class initials (proto-voiced sounds)							
*b	ph	p	p	p	p	p	p
*d	th	t	t	t	t	t	t
*j	ch	s	c	c	c	c	c
*g	kh	k	k	k	k	k	k
*m	m	m	m	m	m	m	m
*n	n	n	n	n	n	n	n
*ñ	y	y	y	ñ	ñ	y	ñ
*ŋ	ŋ	ŋ	ŋ	ŋ	ŋ	ŋ	ŋ
*y	y	y	y	y	y	y	y
*w	w	w	w	w	v	v	v
*l	l	l	l	l	l	l	l
*r	r,l̥	h	h,r	h	h	r,h,hr,l	h
*v	f	ph	f	f	f	f	f
*z	s	sh	s	s	s	s	s
*ɣ	kh	kh	kh	kh	kh̥	x	x

In the chart above, one is struck by the similarity of the Lue of Chieng Rung to Siamese. It has not followed the pattern of *ʔl changing to d, b and b, and *ñ remaining *ñ as in Lue of Moeng Yong and White Tai, for example. Neither has Lue of Chieng Tung for that matter. The replacement of Siamese /kh/ by Lue of Chieng Rung /x/ is a matter of variation which will be described later. The presence of /w/ in Lue of Cheng Tung (Li 1964), /v/ in Lue of Chieng Rung and Moeng Yong, /v/ in White Tai and /w/ in Khuen, Shan and Northern Thai calls for an explanation. At first glance, it seems that an isogloss would separate the /v/ of White Tai and Lue from the /w/ of Khuen, Shan and Northern Thai, or the eastern dialects from the western. But a closer look is not so convincing.

The reason for the puzzlement over the v-w isogloss may lie in varying conventions, theoretical reasons, or uncertainties of perception. In his phonemic analysis of Lue, Li (1964) chooses /w/ which he describes as 'labio-dental with no or little friction when it stands alone as an initial, otherwise it means simply lip rounding'. This seems to accord very closely with Harris's (1972) description of Siamese w̵ and w.

w represents a voiced labio-velar approximant. This sound occurs syllable initially in Siamese:

wa: *to say*

W̶, a voiced labio-velar fricative, is a common pronunciation in emphatic speech. The friction is not very heavy put is perceptible.

To continue, in his article on White, Black and Red Tai, Gedney (1964) describes the White Tai /v-/ as a 'voiced labiodental fricative like English v'.

Similarly, in his unpublished fieldnotes on Lue dialects, Gedney shows a /v-/ for both Chieng Rung and Moeng Yong. In syllable final position a /-w/ is used, as solution to the problem, which is quite like that of the Fippingers (1970), whose phonemic chart of Black Tai phonemes reads, in part:

Labial

Liquid   v-

        -w

Classical phonemic theory, of course, forces the use of either /v/ or /w/ but not both. In other transcriptions we find w- and -u. Fu (op. cit), for example, uses v-, xv- and -u in his citations.

From the standpoint of phonemic theory, the ideal solution is the one used by Li (1964) where he uses /w/ as his general symbol even though it usually approximates /v/ in syllable initial positions. Still it is intriguing to find that Li uses /w/ in his study of Wuming but /v/ for his analysis of Po-ai and Zhuang. A similar shift is seen in Gedney, who has /v/ in Yay and Saek as well as /v/ in Shan of Chefang, Tai Neua, Khuen and Shan of Keng Tung but /w/ for Shan of Hsi Paw: woo¹, *ox*, wii⁴ *fan* (fieldnote citations).

Egerod consistently uses w in his phonemic charts for Shan, Khuen, Northern Thai and other Thai dialects. Purnell uses w in his Northern Thai dictionary. Davis has w for his description of the Nan dialect. We cannot be sure if they are merely following the 'Haas tradition' of using w for Siamese, if they are seeking an ideal phonemic solution to the problem, or if the w rather than v reflects linguistic reality for those dialects.

Up to this point in the comparison of Lue initial consonants with those of surrounding dialects, it is clear that the differences are not great except for Shan. Compared to Siamese, Shan has several changes which are unique among the dialects in the S.W. branch: Siamese b > Shan m, w; Siamese d > Shan *n, l;* Siamese f > Shan ph; Siamese ch and c > Shan sh. What we have seen and said of Lue initials thus far indicates its dissimilarity to Shan. However, when we examine variation in Lue in greater depth in the next chapter, we will see that Lue points in the western half of Sipsongpanna have Shan initials: m, w and n, l and ph. The Mekong River, which bisects the Lue area of Sipsongpanna, is a major isogloss for these features in Yunnan at least. This does not appear to hold true for vocalic changes which we shall presently examine.

First we shall briefly compare consonant clusters. In spoken Lue of Chieng Rung, the only clusters found in the description of Fu (1956) are kv- and xv-. Otherwise the only other significant development of clusters from Proto-Tai is that *br and *gr appear as ph and kh, x aspirates in the modern Lue low class initial series.

Despite the general observation that only two clusters are found in contemporary Lue and most of the surrounding dialects, other data include some more rarely spoken and literary clusters. The following chart has been prepared showing possible ones. No attempt is made to trace their historical development.

Siamese	Shan	Khuen	N. Thai	Lue	Lao	White Tai
	py		py			
	phy		phw			
	pw					
pr	pr					
pl				pl		
phr	phr			(ph)		
phl						
	my	my	my			
	mr					
	tw	tw	tw,cw	tw		
tr	tr			thr		
				thl		
	thw	thw	thw			
	lw		lw,ʔw			
	sr	sr				
	shr		sw,sy	sw	sw	
kw	kw	kw	kw,ky	kw	kw	kw
			w(n)y			xw
khw	khw	khw	khw	xw	khw	khw
kr	kr					
kl						
khr	khr			(x)		
khl						
						nw

Comparing different sets of data leads to the conclusion that the status of clusters in various dialects is quite uncertain. The 17 clusters for Shan come from Egerod (*op. cit*). Contrast this with only three in the Shan study by Phanthumetha (1961): pr, kw, and khw. To the Northern Thai clusters shown (Egerod 1961), adds jw and sl. Roffe (1946) has, for Lao of Luang Prabang, cw, kw, thw, khw, sw, nw, lw, ha. It is clear that many of these more exotic clusters are literary only. The final certainty is that the clusters kw and khw are stable everywhere and comprise the main clusters in the northern geographic points of the Southwestern branch. As we move south toward Bangkok and Southern Thailand, the number of clusters increases, especially those with l or r as a second member. Suffice it to say that in spoken Lue in general, we can expect to find only xw, khw (xw ~ khw) and kw. Sarawit (1973) shows the historical development of clusters using data based on speech rather than literary sources.

When we turn our attention to systems of vocoids, the link between Lue, Shan, Khuen and White Tai is confirmed even more. Unlike Northern Thai, Siamese and Lao which all have the diphthongs [ia], [ia], [ua], these four more northerly dialects have none at all. We find instead that they have been lowered and shortened in length to [e], [ə], and [o] respectively.

A second feature is vowel length. In every dialect in the Tai language family, there is a length distinction between [a/aa]. The former is higher and farther back, the latter lower and more central. By using the distinctive feature of height rather than length, length does not need to be considered phonemic in those systems that do not have length contrast in the other vowels. This is the case with respect to Lue of Cheng Tung (Li 1964). That system is shown below.

Front Unrounded	Back Unrounded	Back Unrounded
/ i	ɨ	u
e	ə	o
ɛ	ɤ	ɔ
	a	/

Finally, we turn to the compendious work of Brown (1965) as arbiter. Surprisingly, he undoes the work of most of the scholars just mentioned. He shows a v all the way from Shan and Chiengmai dialects down through Bangkok. Haas (1964) and most concerned linguists show a w initial for Siamese (Central or Bangkok). Even Brown (1969) himself later opts for w in his A. U. A. Thai language series. Still, in his comparative work (1965), only the Southern Thai dialects starting at Chumphon exhibit a [w]. The possibility exists that Brown's earlier (1965) solution for v and w is linked to initial clusters involving [w/v] as the second element. In his Bangkok chart, no clusters appear; a v is convenient there as an initial. On the other hand, for Yala and Satun we find a few clusters and the necessary initial [w].

If we were to attempt to draw an isogloss separating v from w, in the Southwestern branch at least, it would be an impossible task using the data we have. Taking a temporary stand, it seems safe to assume that [v] and [w] vary quite widely throughout most of the Southwestern region. In Cambodian, v and w also vary, suggesting a regional feature (Ehrman 1972).[12] In general, the data suggest that v be reserved for the dialects of the northern geographic reaches (White Tai, Lue, Shan, Khuen, Tai Neua) and [w] for the lower portions (Lao, Siamese, Southern Thai). It may turn out that the Northern Thai region is a transitional zone for [v] and [w], as it appears to be for [kh] and [w].

This same description applies to Shan (Egerod 1957), White and Black Tai (Gedney 1964). In most of Lue of Sipsongpanna (Fu 1956) the situation can be considered the same. In a small district of Sipsongpanna, vowel length does appear to be phonemic in the speech of speakers of all age groups. In some other areas, older speakers in Sipsongpanna maintain the length distinction, while the younger do not. As we move southward into the Lue community of Moeng Yong, it appears that vowel length is phonemic. But again, it may depend on the age and personal history of the speaker. The Lue in Thailand likewise may be preserving an older distinction or may have acquired it through contact with Standard Thai taught in the schools and reinforced by the Siamese alphabet.

The map in the following page displays an isogloss separating the northern region, where vowel length is not phonemic, from the southern portions where vowel length contrasts are more common but still not of great significance in terms of functional load.

To illustrate the transition from absence of phonemic vowel length to partial, examine Khuen. While the Khuen system is generally viewed as having phonemic vowel length, the three central vowels – [e, ə, o] – are short only before a final glottal stop, clearly non-phonemic. For a fuller discussion of vowel length see Sarawit (1973) and Hartmann (1976a).

Similarly, Lue of Moeng Yong analysed by Sarawit (1973) shows an absence of vowel length contrasts on the high vowels on live syllables. We assume from her rule that these same

---

12 Ehrman (1972) says: 'The Cambodian /v/ varies from speaker to speaker. Some speakers pronounce it like English w but others pronounce it like English v but with both lips rather than the upper lip and lower teeth as in English'. The same appears to be true in Tai dialects in contact with Cambodian at one time or another, but, in particular, those of more recent contact, such as Lao and Northeastern Thai. In Cambodian, it could probably be shown to be a sociolinguistic variable; v appears to be the prestige form.

vowels contrast on dead syllables. We can schematize the transition or gradual change of vowel length contrast below the isogloss shown on the following chart using the Khuen and Lue data.

Lue M.Y.   only short in Lue M.Y. (long in Khuen)

Khuen   only short in Khuen (long in Lue M.Y.)

ɛ,ɛɛ a,aa ɔ,ɔɔ   short/long in both Khuen and Lue Moeng Yong

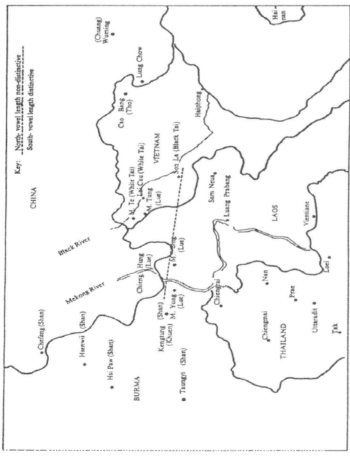

MAP 7.2-2: SHOWING VOWEL LENGTH DISTINCTIONS BETWEEN NORTH AND SOUTH

In addition to the general absence of vowel length and the lowering of diphthongs to single vowels, a unique vowel raising phenomenon called *nasal umlaut* by Li (1964) exists in all varieties of Lue and White Tai. Defined as a raising of vowels corresponding to Siamese /e/ and /u/ before a final nasal, Li gives the following examples:

Siamese /khon/ person   Lue /kun^2/
       /pen/ to be   /pin/
       /doə/ forest   /duə/
       /phom/ hair   /phum/

The debate over the historical development of vowel length is discussed further in Hartmann (1976a), F. K. Li (1977) and Brown (1979). Brown's solution is for Proto-Thai (Siamese); Li's is for Proto-Tai, as it is commonly known (three branches).

Final nasal environments shorten the front and back low vowels in the Lue of Moeng Yong. The rules according to Sarawit are as follows:

$$*\varepsilon{:}\varepsilon \quad / \text{———————} \quad \left\{ \begin{array}{l} \text{Nasal} \\ \text{Glide} \\ \text{[+labial]} \end{array} \right.$$

$$*\text{ɔ}{:}\text{ɔɔ} \quad / \text{———————} \quad \left\{ \begin{array}{l} \text{Nasal} \\ \text{Glide} \\ \text{[+palatal]} \end{array} \right.$$

We might note that in other White Tai, Lue and Shan data, there appears to be a raising of Siamese /ə/ to /i/, completing the raising of all mid vowels to high in the environment of final nasals. For example, in the speech of some informants we find /ŋîn/ silver. Until more data are available, it is best to treat these items as exceptions.[13]

Quite possibly the most exclusively Lue feature is the raising of Siamese /a/ to Lue /ɛ/ when 'flanked by a dental or prepalatal initial and a dental final'. Li (1964) gives the following examples.

Siamese /tat/ 'to cut'   Lue CT   /tɛt/
       /sat/ 'animal'   /sɛt/

Sarawit (1973) shows the same phenomenon for Lue of Moeng Yong in her rule:

$$*a \quad a, \quad \varepsilon \, / \quad \underset{\text{[+dental]}}{C} \text{—————————} \underset{\text{[+dental]}}{C}$$

Up to this point we have been considering the difference between the vocalic nucleus of Tai Lue and other dialects. The only bothersome issue is whether or not vowel length should be considered phonemic in Lue, or even if the emic/etic distinction is a useful notion.

For White Tai, Shan and Lue of Cheng Tung, it was possible to argue conclusively that vowel length was not distinctive. With those three dialects, then, the emic statement captures a very important generalization. But when we turn to other dialect areas and the speech of different age groups, the emic notion is more difficult to apply. For one thing, vowel length does not always cover the whole vocalic array as illustrated in the Khuen of Keng Tung, and Lue of Cheng Tung data that are available. When it comes to Northern Thai, the situation is

---

13 Conversely, in Northern Thai, Hope and Purnell (1962) report:
    Frequently, /y/ before /k,n/ becomes /ə/ in Northern. In Lue too, we find /dɔ́k/ 'late at night' and /sɔ́k/ 'war' for Siamese /dìk/ and /sìk/. (Lue citations - high tone; Siamese - low tone.)

more difficult to describe in emic terms. In a brief footnote to his work on Northern Thai, Mundhenk (1967) appears to deny any length distinction whatsoever – except [a, aa]. Contrariwise, in the glossary to his translation of a Northern Thai poem based on two oral renditions, Egerod (1971) shows length variation for all of the vowels except [i], and that single exception may be an oversight. Either this means that a conclusive statement about phonemic length cannot be made for Northern Thai or that the distinction is being lost. This unclear picture serves as a cautionary note to anyone doing further fieldwork in Tai dialects.

Certainly for the majority of Lue speakers, vowel length is not distinctive, based on all of the information at our disposal. Variation does exist, however. In the next section, we shall deal with several aspects of variation in Lue in detail.

7.3. VARIATION

The focal point of this chapter will be the dialect map adapted from the admirable work of Fu et al. (1956) referred to in the previous chapters. A copy of their map follows on page 289. On it I have summarized the information on differences in initials found in the three subdialect areas of Sipsongpanna, the area covered by the map. It is this region which has been traditionally regarded as the home of the Lue, the place where they are found in largest concentrations. The capital, Chiang Rung, is shown on the map on the left bank of the Mekong River where it flows out of Yunnan, and into adjoining Burma, Thailand and Laos. This city and the dialect region it dominates naturally have all of the features identifiable as typical Lue speech as outlined in the preceding chapter. In abstracted form, the map shows how the lower half of Sipsongpanna has strictly Lue-like features, while the upper half shows distinct signs of Shan-like features.

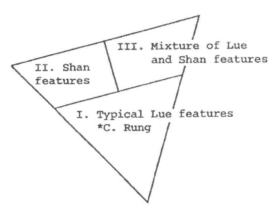

Perhaps the most interesting free variant is the /x/ ~ /kh/ oscillation reported throughout all of Sipsongpanna. Apparently this same variation extends into Northern Thai as well. In their language instruction text for Northern Thai, Hope and Purnell (1962) indicate that /kh/ can also be pronounced as '/x/ (voiceless velar fricative) or /khx/ combination of the two'. In the preceding chapter, it was seen that /x/ contrasts with /kh/ in White Tai, while /kh/ alone appears in Lao and Siamese.

Similarly, region II in Sipsongpanna has the noticeable free variant /ph/ ~ /f/, showing a transition to the unique Shan feature of /ph/ where other dialects use /f/ only. There is no indication in any publications on these dialects that these are socially conditioned variations. From an anthropological standpoint, it would be enlightening to find out if the speakers in region II or III regard themselves as Lue or Shan or perhaps even Tai Neua.

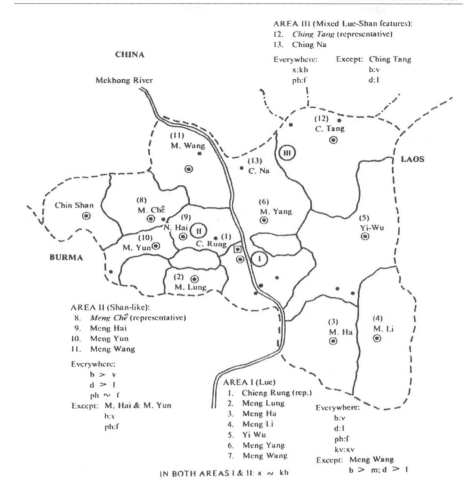

AREA III (Mixed Lue-Shan features):
12. *Ching Tang* (representative)
13. Ching Na

Everywhere: Except: Ching Tang
x:kh   b:v
ph:f   d:l

CHINA

Mekhong River

(11)
M. Wang

(13)
C. Na

III

(12)
C. Tang

LAOS

Chin Shan

(8)
M. Chê

(9)
N. Hai

(6)
M. Yang

(5)
Yi-Wu

(10)
M. Yun

II

(1)
C. Rung

I

BURMA

(2)
M. Lung

AREA II (Shan-like):
 8. *Meng Chê* (representative)
 9. Meng Hai
10. Meng Yun
11. Meng Wang

Everywhere:
    b > v
    d > l
    ph ~ f
Except: M. Hai & M. Yun
    b:v
    ph:f

(3)
M. Ha

(4)
M. Li

AREA I (Lue)
 1. Chieng Rung (rep.)
 2. Meng Lung
 3. Meng Ha
 4. Meng Li
 5. Yi Wu
 6. Meng Yang
 7. Meng Wang

Everywhere:
    b:v
    d:l
    ph:f
    kv:xv
Except: Meng Wang
    b > m; d > l

IN BOTH AREAS I & II: x ~ kh

(Adapted from Fu Mao-Chi et al., 1956)

MAP 7.3-1: THREE MAJOR DIALECT AREAS WITHIN SIPSONGPANNA

There is a socially conditioned variant report by Fu (op. cit.) for Lue of Chieng Rung. It mirrors exactly the same phenomenon found in Bangkok speech by Beebe (1974). In the Lue case, the conditioning factor is literacy. For those who are literate a h:l distinction can be found in Siamese h:r cognates. For the illiterate the contrast merges to /h/.

The following list shows the conditioning effect of literacy on the speech of the Lue. No reference is made to socioeconomic class differences. It is probably the case that the former and present ruling classes are of necessity more literate than the peasantry. The comparisons are between standard written Thai and Lue of Chieng Rung. The data are taken from Fu (op. cit.).

Standard Thai	Lue Chieng Rung (Hung)	
	Illiterate	Literate
rûup	hop[5]	h~lop
rúu	huu[6]	h~luu
rák	hak[5]	h~lak
raw	haw[4]	h~law
rɛɛŋ	hɛɛŋ	h~lɛɛŋ

In an additional note, the authors state that the illiterate change *r to h- completely, but the literate confuse *r with r-, hr- or hl in addition to l ~ h. It is not clear whether or not a reading pronunciation is meant here. That is, it may be the case that subjects were asked to read from texts and gave all of these variant pronunciations for r- cognates. By the same token, it is even more remarkable to note that Li (1964) has /hr/ as a phoneme in his analysis of Lue of Cheng Tung. He reports:

> The phonemic status of /hr/ is interesting. It often alternates with /h/ in tone 2, 4, and 6 ..., /hr/ being the literary and more formal pronunciation, and /h/ being the common form. Thus a word like /hray[2]/ chicken flea, is likely to be pronounced with /h/, while a word like /hra[2]-ca[4] ma[2]ta/ mother of a prince, is likely to be pronounced with /hr/.

When we turn our attention to variation in vowel length, diversity is not as great as it was for initials. In the previous chapter, it was stated that, in general, vowel length is not phonemic for Lue of Cheng Tung (Li, 1964) or for Lue of Chieng Rung (Fu, 1956.). For Lue of Moeng Yong, Burma and Lue of Chiengkham, Thailand, length distinction varies depending on the vowel height, the age or location of the speaker or other incompletely studied variables. Here we wish to demonstrate only that phonemic vowel length is not to be found throughout most of Sipsongpanna. Again we refer to the map adapted from a translation of the work of Fu (1956). In only one small pocket southeast of Chieng Rung is vowel length phonemic for all age groups (See Map 7.3-2). A generational difference does appear at two points: Chieng Rung and Meng-Hai. There, the older speakers maintain a u:uu and ɛ:ɛɛ contrast. Otherwise vowel length differences are phonetically conditioned. In dead syllables with a rising tone, all vowels are lengthened (cf. Li 1964). In another case reported in unpublished notes, Gedney found that his chief Chieng Rung informant has a length distinction between ɛ:ɛɛ and o:oo, before nasals. Along the same lines, Sarawit's (1973) rules for Lue of Moeng Yong show an absence of phonemic contrast for the high vowels.

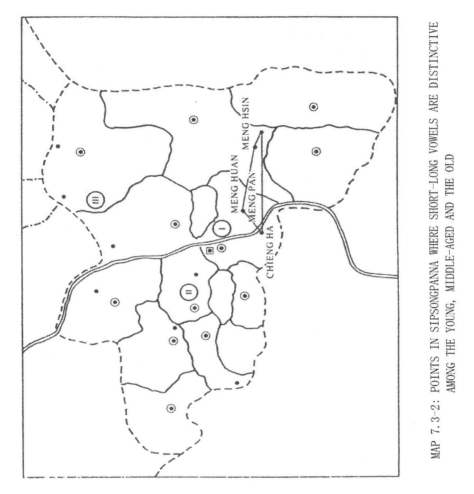

MAP 7.3-2: POINTS IN SIPSONGPANNA WHERE SHORT-LONG VOWELS ARE DISTINCTIVE AMONG THE YOUNG, MIDDLE-AGED AND THE OLD

These geographical and generational differences in vowel length distinctions appear to be somewhat idiosyncratic. Or quite possibly they argue well for the theory of lexical diffusion as put forth most recent by Chen and Wang (1975). In that theory of linguistic change, systems are transformed not by sudden and wholesale replacements or alterations of rules. Instead, change is selective and enters the language partially, though regularly, with a preference for naturalness conditions that are not always easy to explain. Thus in Siamese, there is a definite preference for vowel length with the low series: aa, ɛɛ, ɔɔ, and the high central vowel ii. In the tonal category *C, vowel length is promoted or at least preserved in Siamese. These detail and supporting data are presented at length by Hartmann (1976a), Li (1977) and Brown (1979).

It is certainly clear that in most Tai dialects, vowel length is not phonemic. In the Proto-Tai reconstructions of both Brown (1965) and Sarawit (1973) vowel length is clearly distinctive. One assumes that the loss of length contrast, along with the loss of distinctions in the initials was absorbed by the development of tonal distinctions resulting from the two- and three-way splits. Similarly for Chinese, Chen and Wang found that of 600-odd dialects they studied, vowel length was phonemic only in Guangzhou and a few Mandarin dialect of Hebei province.

The loss of vocalic length contrasts in the other Chinese dialects apparently was compensated for by the development of tonal differences. The following quote from Chen and Wang (1975) might well parallel what has happened to vowel length in Tai, historically speaking:

> A comparative study of a fairly representative sample of Chinese dialects suggests that the phonemic contrast of vowel duration either quickly disappear, being highly unstable, or was re-interpreted as a distinctive pitch contour.

A final variant in Lue worth commenting on, if only for its unusualness, is syllabic m̩. Because it varies chiefly with the full or partially reduced forms for the negative baw1,2 or ba-5, it might be considered a lexical variant as well. But here we take the theoretical stand of Pike (1967) which asserts the obvious overlap of phonology, grammar (syntax) and lexicon (semantics). Because the negative in Lue is in a syntactically weak position typical of function words, it is, as in English, subject to reduction in stress – a phonological phenomenon – and is realized by three apparently different lexical forms.

By way of comparison, syllabic m̩ is found in Northern Thai (Hope and Purnell 1962) as a variant of ba-, a prefix used to indicate fruit and some other roundish, lumpy objects. In Shan, mk is used, as in Lue, to express negation (Cushing 1914; Egerod 1957). Likewise, Cantonese and Cambodian use syllabic mk in negation. In Lue, however, m̩ represents at least four other different morphemes. The details are presented in Hartmann (1975).

From the standpoint of phonology, the syllabic m̩ in Lue is remarkable in that it has two tones depending on the tonal category of the following morpheme. Accordingly, m̩ ^{2} (mid-rising) is followed by syllables bearing tones 1 or 4, the tones of the A column in the charts of historical development of tones. Syllabic m̩ ^{1} (high-level) is followed by syllables bearing tones 2, 5 (column B), 3, 6 (column C). In synchronic terms, the difference between the A tonal environment on the one hand, and the combined B-C category on the other, is that the former has a higher entry point for the tones (1 & 4) than the latter (2, 3, 5, 6).

Assuming that a reduction of stress precedes the reassignment of tone 1 or 2 to m̩, a final polarization rule can be used to explain the bitonal nature of the syllable.

$$\overset{\text{m̩}}{} \longrightarrow [\alpha \text{ H}] / \underline{\hspace{3cm}} [-\alpha \text{ H}]$$

Or in more concrete terms this means

$$\overset{\text{m̩}}{} \text{ (unstressed)} \rightarrow \begin{Bmatrix} \text{m̩}^2 \text{ (low) } / \underline{\hspace{1.5cm}} \text{+high pitch} \\ \text{m̩}^1 \text{ (high)} / \underline{\hspace{1.5cm}} \text{-high pitch} \end{Bmatrix}$$

It should be understood that the actual shape of tone 2 is mid-rising. But for purposes of polarization, it is relatively low with respect to tone 1, which is, in fact, high level.

As a phonological/lexical innovation, then, syllabic m̩ is presented as a variant of Lue *baw²* 'not', *maak²* 'fruit', *bak¹* 'prefix used for young males, informal', *mii⁶* 'day (linear time) ', the vocative prefix as in *m̩¹ pɔɔ* 'father dear' and in the forms *m̩ tuu¹* 'door' and *m̩ saŋ¹* 'what'. Because the syllabic mk is found in neighboring Shan and Northern Thai, though to a lesser extent perhaps, and in words of high frequency, this would be an important lexical/phonological isogloss showing the lines of communication among these dialects and the direction of change in Lue towards these more dominant speech communities.

Syllabic mk in Lue must be said to be a feature of ordinary speech. As for the 'elevated speech' of the sung narrative, only /baw²/ *not* appears. One informant, the 70 year old Caw Mom Laa, the last son of the former Prince of Chieng Rung, vehemently denied the existence of mk in any form of Lue. He, of course, was highly literate in Lue and was considered the final authority on all linguistic matters concerning Lue. The innovation of m̩ certainly is not that recent, as the study by Fu et al. shows. But again, it shows that Lue has participated in changes developing in Shan and Northern Thai, both of which have the syllabic mk.

The same tendency of Lue to reduce the syllable to a syllabic (as in m̩) is found in polysyllabic words where the reduction results in *phonetic* 'clusters' that resemble the list of exotic *phonemic* clusters reported by Egerod for Shan and Northern Thai. Such Lue clusters would include sl-, sn-, phy-, sb-, pl-, ky-, xn-, phl-, kl-, none of which were reported earlier as genuine initial consonant clusters in the array of Chieng Rung phonemes.

Syllables involved in the reduction have the short central vowels /a/ and /i/ followed by the glottal stop when pronounced in isolation. In a context of reduced stress in rapid speech, the tone of the syllable (1- high level or 5- mid level) is neutralized and the vowel reduced to zero. Fu (1956) lists the following forms as illustration.

$sa^1-la^1-?at^2$ is read as $sa-la^1-?at^2$ or $sla^1-?at^2$ *grandeur*
sa^1-nam^1 is read as $sa-nam^1$ or $snam^1$ *government*
sa^1-nat^1 is read as $sa-nat^1$ or $snat^1$ *secret*
sa^1-mut^1 is read as $sa-mut^1$ or $smut^1$ *sea*
pha^1-yaa^1 is read as $pha-yaa^1$ or $phyaa^1$ *wisdom*
$suk^1-sa^1-bay^4$ is read as $suk^1-sa-bay^4$ or suk^1-sbay^4 *good fortune*
$saa^1-sa^1-naa^4$ is read as $saa^1-sa-naa^4$ or saa^1-snaa^4 *religion*

pha^5-yaa^4 is read as $pha-yaa^4$ or $phyaa^4$ *a title, rank*
pa^5-laat^5 is read as $pa-laat^5$ or $plaat^5$ *to slip, fall*
pha^5-yaat^5 is read as $pha -taat$ or $phyaat$ *sickness*
$sa^5-na?^5$ is read as $sa-na?^5$ *effect, influence*
$pa^5-ya?^5$ is read as $pa-ya?$ or $pya?$ *performance*
$xa?^5-na?^5$ is read as $xa-na?^5$ or $xna?^5$ *suppress*
phi^5-liin^6 is read as $phi-liin^6$ or $phliin^6$ *scared and disperse, as a flock of birds*

ka^5-liin^6 is read as $kaliin^6$ or $kliin^6$ *noise of a cannon firing*
$pa^5-yɔɔ^2$ is read as $pa-yɔɔ^2$ or $pyɔɔ^2$ *comfort*

REFERENCES

Abramson, Arthur S. (1962) 'The vowels and tones of Standard Thai: acoustical measurements and experiments', *International Journal of American Linguistics* 28.3: 2.

Beebe, Leslie (1974) 'Socially conditioned variation in Bangkok Thai', unpublished PhD dissertation, University of Michigan, Ann Arbor.

Benedict, Paul K. (1942) 'Thai, Kadai, and Indonesian: A new alignment in Southeast Asia' *American Anthropologists* 44: 576-601.

— (1975) *Austro-Thai Language and Culture with a Glossary of Roots*, New Haven: Human Relations Area Files Press.

Brown, J. Marvin (1965) *From Ancient Thai to Modern Dialects*, Bangkok: Social Science Association Press of Thailand.

— (1969) *A. U. A. Language Center Thai course*, Bangkok, Thailand: The American University Alumni Association Language Center.

— (1979) 'Vowel length in Thai', in Thongkum et al. (eds), 10-25.

Brun, Viggo (1976) (trans.) *Sug: the Trickster Who Fooled the Monk*, Lund: Studentlitteratur.

Burling, Robbins (1965) *Hill Farms and Padi Fields: Life in Mainland Southeast Asia*, Englewood Cliffs, N.J.: Prentice-Hall.

Carthew, M. (1952) 'The history of the Thai in Yunnan', *Journal of the Siam Society* 40.1: 1-38.

Chamberlain, James R. (1971) *A Workbook in Comparative and Historical Tai Linguistics*, Bangkok: Central Institute of English Language.

Chang, Kun (1967) 'China: National Languages', in Sebeok, Thomas A. (ed.) *Current Trends of Linguistics II*, The Hague and Paris: Mouton, 151–76.

Chen, Matthew Y. and Wang, William S.-Y. (1975) 'Sound change: actuation and implementation', *Language* 51.2: 255-281.

Coedes, G. (1968) *The Indianized States of Southeast Asia*, Honolulu: University Press of Hawaii. (An English version of the 1944 French edition)

Cushing, J. N. (1914) *A Shan and English Dictionary*, Rangoon: American Baptist Mission Press. (Second printing of 1881 edition)

Davies, Somchit (1979) 'A comparative study of Yong and Standard Thai', in Thongkum et al. (eds), 26-48.

Davis, Richard (1970) *A Northern Thai Reader*, Bangkok: The Siam Society.

Deydier, Henry (1954) 'Dans les Sip-Song P'an-na', *France Asie* 98: 825-834.

Dodd, Rev. Clifton W. (1910) 'Tour through South China, among the Tai race', *The China Recorder* December Issue.

— (1923) *The Thai Race*, Cedar Rapids, Iowa: Torch Press.

Donaldson, Jean and Chính Nhìm Biêu (1970) *Tai-Vietnamese-English vocabulary*, Saigon: Bộ Giáo-Dục Xuất Bản.

Egerod, Søren (1957) 'Essentials of Shan phonology and script', *Bulletin of the Institute of History and Philology* I: 121-129, Taipei: Academica Sinica.

— (1959) 'Essentials of Khün phonology and script', *Acta Orientalia* 24.3-4: 123-146.

— (1961) 'Studies in Tai dialectology', Acta *Orientalia* 26: 43-91.

— (1971) *The Poem in Four Songs*, Lund, Sweden: Studentlitteratur.

Ehrman, Madeline E. (1972) *Contemporary Cambodian: Grammatical Sketch*, Washington, DC: FSI, Department of state.

Embree, John F. and Dostson, Lilian O. (1950) *Bibliography of the Peoples and Cultures of Mainland Southeast Asia*, New Haven: S. E. A. Studies, Yale University.

Finot, Louis (1917) 'Recherches sur la littérature Laotienne', *Bulletin de l'Ecole Française d'Extrême-orient* 17.5: 5-220.

Fippinger, Jay and Fippinger, Dorothy (1970) 'Black Tai phonemes with reference to White Tai', *Anthropological Linguistics* 12.3: 83-97.

Fowler, Murray and Isarasena, Tasaniya (1952) *The Tonal Distribution of the Sounds of Siamese*, Madison: University of Wisconsin Press.

Fu, Mao-Chi, Tao, Shi-Shun, Wei T'ung and Tao Chung Ch'ian (1956) 'The phonemic system of Chieng Rung, Sipsongpanna in Yunnan province', *Yü-Yen Yen-Chiu* 1: 223-264, Peking. In Chinese (An unpublished English translation by Mrs James Dew, 1973)

Gainey, Jerry and Thongkum, Theraphan (1977) *Language Map of Thailand Handbook*, Bangkok: Office of State Universities. Indigenous languages of Thailand research project, Central Institute of English Language.

Gedney, William J. (1964) 'A comparative sketch of White, Black and Red Tai', *Social Science Review*, Special Publication No.1: 1-47, Bangkok: Social Science Association Press.

— (1965a) 'Review of Marvin J. Brown: from Ancient Thai to modern dialects', *Social Science Review* 3.2: 107-112.

— (1966a) 'Linguistic diversity among Tai dialects in Southern Kwangsi', paper presented at the 41st L.S.A. meeting.

— (1967) 'Future directions in comparative Tai linguistics', manuscript, University of Michigan.

— (1968) 'Lue of Moeng Yong and Chieng Rung', unpublished data.

— (1969) 'Lue of Moeng Yong and Chieng Rung', unpublished data.

— (1970a) 'The Saek language of Nakhon Phanom Proyince', *Journal of the Siam Society* 58.1: 67-87.

— (1972b) 'A checklist for determining tones in Tai dialects', in M. Estellie Smith (ed.) *Studies in linguistics in honor of George L. Trager*, The Hague: Mouton, 423-437.

— (1973) 'Notes on the Tai dialect of Ning Ming: Pt. I.', paper presented at the 6th International Conference on Sino-Tibetan Linguistics.

— (1974) 'Notes from a seminar on comparative-historical Tai', ms.

Gething, Thomas W., Harris, Jimmy G. and Kullavanijaya, Pranee (eds) (1976) *Tai Linguistics in Honor of Fang-Kuei Li*, Bangkok: Chulalongkorn University Press.

Grierson, G. A. (1904) 'An Ahom cosmogony, with a translation and a vocabulary of the Ahom language', *Journal of the Royal Asiatic Society* (1904): 181-232.

—— (1928) *Linguistic survey of India, vol.1, part 2: Comparative vocabulary*, Calcutta, India: Government of India Central Publication Branch.

Haas, Mary R. (1958) 'The tones of four Tai dialects', *Bulletin of the Institute of History and Philology* 29: 817-826, Taipei: Academia Sinica.

—— (1964) *Thai-English student's dictionary*, Standford, California: Stanford University Press.

Harris, Jimmy G. (1972) 'Phonetic notes on some Siamese consonants', in Jimmy G. Harris and Richard B. Noss (eds) *Tai phonetics and phonology*, Bangkok: Central Institute of English Language, Mahidol University, 8-22.

Harris, Jimmy G. and Richard B. Noss (eds) (1972) *Tai phonetics and phonology*, Bangkok: Central Institute of English Language, Mahidol University.

Hartmann, John F. (1975) 'Syllabic m̩ in Tai-Lue and neighboring Tai dialects', in Gething, Thomas W. (ed.) *A Tai Festschrift for William J. Gedney* (Southeast Asia Studies Working Paper 8), Honolulu: University of Hawaii Southeast Asian Studies Program. Also in Gething, Thomas W. and Nguyên Đăng Liêm (eds) (1979) *Papers on South-East Asian Linguistics 6: Tai Studies in Honour of William J. Gedney* (PL A52), Canberra: Australian National University, 97-107.

—— (1976a) 'The waxing and waning of vowel length in Tai dialects', in Gething et al.(eds): 142-159.

—— (1981) *Conversing in Lao: A handbook for US sponsors of Lao-speaking refugees and medical personnel*, DeKalb: Northern Illinois University.

Hashimoto, M. (1980) *The Be Language : A classified lexicon of its Limkow dialect (Asian and African Lexicon 11)*, Tokyo, ILCAA.

Haudricourt, André-G. (1961) 'Bipartition et tripartition des system de tons dans quelques langues d'Extrême-Orient', *Bulletin de la Société Linguistique de Paris* 56.1 : 163-80. (1967) 'La langue Lakkia', *Bulletin de la Société Linguistique de Paris* 62.1: 165-182.

—— (1972) 'Two-way and three-way splitting of tonal systems in some Far Eastern languages' (English translation of Haudricourt (1961) by Christopher Court, in Jimmy G. Harris and Richard B. Noss (eds) *Tai Phonetics and Phonology*, Bangkok : Central Institute for English Language: 55-86.

Henry, M. A. (1903) 'The Lolos and other tribes of Western China', *Journal of the Royal Anthropological Institute of Great Britain and Ireland* 33: 96-107.

Hope, E. R. and Purnell, H. C. (1962) *A colorful colloquial*, Chiengmai, Thailand: Overseas Missionary Fellowship.

Hsieh, Pei-chich (1978) 'Changes and continuity in Southwest Yunnan: the Xishuangbann Tai autonomous prefecture', *Bulletin of Concerned Asian Scholars* 10.3: 29-37.

Khanittanan, Wilawan Wichienrot (1973) 'The influence of Siamese on five Lao dialects', unpublished PhD dissertation, University of Michigan, Ann Arbor.

Kruatrachue, Foongfuang (1960) 'Thai and English: a comparative study of phonology for pedagogical applications', unpublished PhD Dissertation, University of Indiana, Bloomington, IN.

Lafont, Périe Bernard (1962) 'Les écritures tay du Laos', *BEFEO* 50: 376-393.

Leach, E. R.(1954) *Political systems of Highland Burma*, London: LSE Press.

LeBar, Frank M., Hickey, G. C. and Musgrave, J.K. (1964) *Ethnic groups of Mainland Southeast Asia*, New Haven, Conn.: Human Relations Area Files Press.

Lefèbre Pontaliss, Pierre (1892) 'Etude sur quelques alphabets et vocabulaires thaïs', *T'oung Pao* 3: 39-64.

LeMay, R. S. (1925) 'The Lue', *Journal of the Siam Society* 19.3: 159-184.

Li, Fang-Kuei (1959) 'Classification by vocabulary: Tai dialects', *Anthropological Linguistics* 1.2: 15-21.

— (1964) 'The phonemic system of the Tai-Lü language', *Bulletin of the Institute of History and Philology* 35: 7-14, Academia Sinica.

— (1965) 'The Tai and the Kam-Sui languages', *Lingua* 14: 148-179.

— (1977) *A handbook of comparative Tai*, Oceanic Linguistics Special Publication 15, Honolulu: The University Press of Hawaii.

Minot, Georges (1940) 'Dictionnaire Tay-Blanc Français avec transcription latine', *Bulletin de l'Ecole Française d'Extrême-Orient* 40.1: 1-237.

— (1949) *Vocabulaire Français-Tay Blanc et elements de grammaire*, 2 vols, Paris: EFEO.

Moerman, Michael (1965) 'Ethnic identification in a complex civilization: who are the Lue?', *American Anthropology* 6: 1215-1230.

— (1967) 'A minority and its government: the Thai-Lue of Northern Thailand', in Peter Kundstadter (ed.) *Southeast Asian tribes, minorities, and nations*, Princeton, N.J.: Princeton University Press, 401-424.

— (1972) 'Analysis of Lue conversation', in David Sudnow (ed.) *Studies in social interaction*, New York: Free Press, 170-228.

— (1977) 'The preference for self-correction in a Tai conversational corpus', *Language* 53.4: 872-882.

Morev, Lev Nikolaevich (1978) *Jazyk Li (The Ly (Lue) language)*, Moscow: Nauka: Institute of Oriental Studies. (In Russian.)

Mote, F. W. (1964) 'Problems of Thai prehistory', *Social Science Review* 2.2: 100-109.

Mundhenk, Norman A. (1967) 'Auxiliary verbs in Myang of Northern Thailand', unpublished MA thesis, Hartford Seminary Foundation, Chiengmai, Thailand.

Oshika, Beatrice R. T. (1973) 'The relationship of Kam-Sui-Mak to Tai', unpublished PhD dissertation, University of Michigan, Ann Arbor.

Panka, Kanchana (1980) The Phonological Characteristics of Lao Dialects in Amphoe Muang, Nakhon Pathom Province, M.A. thesis, Chulalongkorn University.

Phanthumetha, Banchop (1961) *Kalemantai*, Bangkok: Samkhom Phasa Læ Nangsue.

Phayomyong, Mani (1968) *Tamra Rian Nansyy Lanna Thai*, Thailand: University of Chiengmai.

Phinith, Saveng (1977) 'Un text siamoise relatif a l'histoire du sud des Sipsongpanna (de 1836 à 1858 E.C.)', *BEFEO* 64: 116-150.

Phumisak, Chit (1976) *The Origin of the Words Siam, Thai, Lao and Khom, and Their Social Contexts*, Bangkok: Sociology and Anthropology Textbook Foundation, Sociology Association of Thailand.

Pramoj, Khukrit (1980) 'Souy Suan Phlu', *Siam Rath* (newspaper) 7 articles in a series from 26 August – 6 September. (In Thai)

Purnell, Herbert (1963) *A short Northern Thai-English dictionary*, Chiengmai, Thailand: Overseas Missionary Fellowship.

Richards, Jack (1966) 'Pronunciation features of Thai speakers of English', unpublished MA thesis, Victoria University of Wellington, New Zealand.

Rispeaud, Jean (1933) 'Notes sur les alphabets Lüe du Yün-nan et les denominations ethniques données aux T'ăy', *The Journal of the Royal Asiatic Society, North China Branch* 64: 143-150.

Roffe, G. Edward (1946) 'The phonemic structure of Lao', *Journal of the American Oriental Society* 66: 289-295.

Sarawit, Mary E. (1973) 'The Proto-Tai vowel system', unpublished PhD dissertation, University of Michigan, Ann Arbor.

— (1979) 'Syllabic m̩ in two Yoong dialects', in Thongkum et al, (eds) 163-170.

Schrock, Joan, et al. (1970). *The Lu*, Department of the Army Pamphlet no. 550-107, Washington, DC: HQ Department of the Army.

Seidenfaden, Erik (1925) 'Supplementary note', *Journal of the Siam Society* 19.3: 185-190.

Siam Society (1966) *The Kamthieng house*, Bangkok: The Siam Society.

Simmanlawong, Pinkham (1972) Personal communication.

Simmonds, E. H. S. (1965) 'Notes on some Tai dialects of Laos and neighboring regions', *Lingua* 14.1: 133-147.

Srisawat, Boonchuay (Srisavasdi, Boon Chuey) (1955) *Thai Sipsongpannaa: lue khon Thai nay pratheet ciin* (2 vols.), Bangkok: Rong Phim Rap Phim.

Strecker, David S. (1979) 'Higher falls more: A tonal sound change in Tai', *CAAAL* 11: 30-84.

Suntharagul, Benchawan (1963) 'Nuay siang phaasaa Chiengmai', unpublished MA thesis, Chulalongkorn University, Bangkok.

Tao, Yu-lian (1958) 'The experience in improving and promoting the writing of Sip-song--pan-na', *Shao-shu Min-tsu Yü-wen Lun-chi* 1: 78-81. (In Chinese)

Thaweesomboon, Sanit (1969) *An analysis of Thai students' problems in pronouncing the vowels and consonants of American English*, Bangkok: N. I. D. A. (In Thai)

Thungkum, Theraphan L., Panupong, Vichin, Cullavanijaya, Pranee and Tingsabadh, M. R. Kalaya (eds) (1979) *Studies in Tai and Mon-Khmer Phonetics and Phonology in Honour of Eugénie J. A. Henderson*, Bangkok: Chulalongkorn University Press.

T'ung Wei and Tao Hsiao-chung (1958) 'An outline of the personal pronouns in the Tai language of Sip-song-pan-na', *Shao-shu Min-tsu Yü-wen Lun-chi* 1: 56-63. (In Chinese)

Weroha, Seree (1974) 'Tai Lue-English dictionary', manuscript.

— (1975) 'Tones in Tai Lue', in Jimmy G. Harris, and James R. Chamberlain (eds) *Studies in Tai Linguistics in Honor of William J. Gedney*, Bangkok: Central Insitute of English Language, Office of State Universities, 387-419. (In Thai)

CHAPTER EIGHT

THE TAI DIALECTS OF NGHỆ AN, VIETNAM (TAY DAENG, TAY YO, TAY MUONG)

Michel Ferlus

8.1. INTRODUCTION

Il convient tout d'abord d'apporter quelques précisions sur la terminologie utilisée. Le groupe des langues *thai*, tel qu'il est défini ici, correspond aux langues du *thai commun* de A. G. Haudricourt (1948), ou encore au *southwestern tai* de Li Fangkuei (1977). A côté de ce groupe *thai*, on distingue le groupe des langues *tay*, ou *central tai*, et le groupe des langues *yaay*, ou *northern tai*. Ces trois groupes, *thai*, *tay* et *yaay* forment la branche *thai-yaay* (la branche *tai* de Li Fangkuei) de la famille *tai-kadai* (selon la graphie anglo-saxonne). La terminologie que nous utilisons ici ne fait que suivre les usages de A. G. Haudricourt et se différencie donc sensiblement de celle de Li Fangkuei reprise par la plupart des auteurs, en particulier Edmondson & Solnit (1997). Il nous a paru plus normal en effet de se conformer aux auto-désignations des locuteurs de ces langues, *yaay* (et ses variantes) est l'autonyme des populations du groupe *northern tai*, tandis que *tai/thai* (ou *tay/thay*) est l'autonyme des populations des groupes *central tai* et *southwestern tai*.

Les formes écrites *tai*, *tay*, *thai* et *thay* proviennent toutes du même étymon *daj^A 'population, êtres humains'. Le sens de 'homme libre' qu'on lui attribue parfois est probablement postérieur et lié aux anciennes structures féodales développées par ces populations. En dehors de son emploi d'ethnonyme, le sens primitif s'est bien préservé dans des expressions comme *thay ban* [tʰaj^{A2} baːn^{C1}] 'les villageois' (même s'ils ne sont pas d'ethnie *thai*). Cet étymon *daj^A a évolué vers la prononciation [tʰaj^{A2}] en siamois et en lao, et vers [taj^{A2}] dans les autres langues des groupes *thai* et *tay*. Normalement donc, la forme thai (*ou thay*) [tʰaj^{A2}] devrait, en raison de sa prononciation, être réservée au siamois et au lao. Cependant, dans les écrits linguistiques et ethnographiques, son usage a été étendu aux autres langues, bien que ce vocable y soit prononcé [taj^{A2}], pour former le groupe nommé *thai commun* (ou *southwestern tai*). Au Vietnam, dont la langue nationale est romanisée, les auteurs ont retenu le terme *Thái* pour désigner globalement les ethnies du groupe des langues *thai* localisées au sud et au sud-ouest du Fleuve Rouge, et le terme *Tày* pour couvrir les ethnies du groupe des langues *tay*, *thô* et *nung* (en viet: *tày*, *thô* et *nùng*) des provinces du nord. La cohabitation de toutes ces variantes phonétiques, orthographiques et sémantiques d'une même notion est une cause permanente de confusion et il faut une solide habitude aux spécialistes pour en maîtriser l'utilisation. Dans les limites de cette étude nous garderons *thai* (viet: *thái*) pour désigner l'ensemble des langues parlées par des populations Thai au sud et sud-ouest du Fleuve Rouge, mais nous utiliserons *tay* pour désigner chaque langue en particulier (tay noir, tay daeng, tay yo, etc.).

298

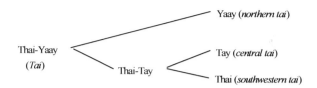

FIGURE 8.1-1: LA BRANCHE DES LANGUES THAI-YAAY (TAI) DE LA FAMILLE TAI-KADAI

Le groupe des langues (désormais dites) *thai* forme un vaste ensemble qui couvre une partie de l'Asie du Sud-Est, depuis le Nord Vietnam jusqu'en Assam et vers la Péninsule Malaise. Toutes les langues thai sont très proches les unes des autres et il est très facile de reconstruire un *proto thai* (PT), autrement dit le *thai commun* de A. G. Haudricourt, ou encore un *proto southwestern tai* extractible des reconstructions de Li Fangkuei, quoique non exprimé en tant que tel.

Ici, nous traiterons des trois dialectes parlés dans la province du Nghệ An, le tay daeng, le Tay Yo et le tay muong. Il faut bien insister sur le fait que les états de langue décrits ici ne sont représentatifs que du lieu de l'enquête (publiée ou inédite, récente ou ancienne) et ne doivent en aucun cas être considérés comme une norme.

8.2. LES THAI ET LES DIALECTES THAI DU NGHỆ AN

Les Tay Daeng [dɛːŋ^{A1}] (écrit aussi Dèng) sont appelés Tay Thanh ou Man Thanh par les Viet. Chez les auteurs occidentaux, ils sont souvent dénommés Tai/Tay rouges d'après la signification du mot 'daeng' et ce nom leur est encore fréquemment attribué dans la littérature. Toutefois, selon l'administrateur R. Robert (1941) qui leur a réservé une excellente et célèbre description ethnographique, leur ethnonyme proviendrait de Muong Daeng (aujourd'hui Yên Khương sur le haut Sông Mã), province de Thanh Hóa, d'où ils sont originaires et qui reste leur région par excellence. Nous pensons qu'il faut retenir cette explication et proscrire l'appellation de Tay rouge dans toutes les langues. Le terme thanh, plus particulièrement utilisé au Nghệ An, est la forme vietnamisée de theng [tʰɛːŋ^{A1}], du nom de l'ancien Muong Theng des récits historiques, localisé dans la plaine de Điện Biên et considéré comme le berceau de la plupart des populations Thai du Nord-Laos et surtout du Nord-Vietnam. Dans les siècles passés, une forte expansion des Tay Daeng les a conduit dans la province de Sam Neua (Laos), où ils constituent aujourd'hui le fond de la population, et dans les districts de l'ouest du Nghệ An. Ils sont parfois nommés Tay Meuy [məːjC^1] dans la langue de leurs voisins Tay Yo où ce terme signifie 'groupe, gens', et c'est par cet ethnonyme qu'ils sont également connus au Laos.

Les Tay Yo [jɔː^{C2}] sont principalement localisés dans les trois districts de Quỳ Hợp, Quỳ Châu et Quế Phong, province de Nghệ An, qui semblent constituer leur région d'origine. On les rencontre également dans le district voisin de Tương Dương et dans la province de Thanh Hóa. Dans les siècles passées, ils ont essaimé dans le centre du Laos et de là dans le Nord-Est de la Thaïlande. Dans ces deux pays, ils sont connus sous les noms de Tay Nyo [ɲɔː^{C2}] (écrit aussi Nho), prononciation lao de Tay Yo. Au Nghệ An, l'autonyme Tay Yo semble plus particulièrement en usage dans le district de Quỳ Châu. Au Laos, les Tay Maen [mɛːn^{A2}] (écrit aussi Mène), ainsi nommés d'après leur lieu d'origine dans le district de Tương Dương, sont linguistiquement des Tay Yo bien qu'ils n'avouent pas cet ethnonyme. Au risque d'embrouiller encore un peu plus la situation, il faut savoir que les Tay Yo sont fréquemment désignés comme des Tay blanc par leurs voisins Thai et Viet. Le dialecte des Tay Yo n'a jamais été décrit in situ.

Les Tay Muong [mɨəŋ^{A2}], ou Tay Pao [paːw^{C1}] d'après le nom thai, Nam Pao, du fleuve Sông Cà, sont principalement localisés dans le district de Tương Dương, d'ancien chef-lieu

Cửa Rào, où se rejoignent les deux rivières Nam Neun [nən^{A2}] et Nam Mô [mo:^{C2}] pour former le Sông Cả. Ils sont appelés Thái Hàng Tổng par les Vietnamiens. Les Tay Muong ont été signalés pour la première fois par Albert Louppe (1934) qui en a laissé une description ethnographique. Cet ethnonyme peut également couvrir les locuteurs Tay Maen ou Tay Yo (à l'exception des Tay Thanh) localisés dans les districts du bassin du Sông Cả. Le dialecte tay muong décrit ici est plus précisément du tay pao. Ce dialecte, à l'instar du tay yo, n'a jamais été décrit.

Au cours de leurs migrations vers d'autres provinces et des pays voisins, ces populations ont pu recevoir d'autres ethnonymes, ainsi les Phou Thai de la province de Savannakhet (Laos) proviennent des régions Tay Muong et Tay Yo du Nghệ An. Les Tay Tac (viet: Tày Tắc) (Donaldson & Edmondson 1997) de la province de Sơn La (Vietnam) sont reconnus comme des Tay blanc quoique leur langue et leur écriture soient du type tay daeng. Pour avoir des éclaircissements sur ces problèmes embrouillés de dénominations ethniques et de migrations on peut se reporter à certains passages de Chamberlain (1991) et à Vi Văn An (1996).

Nos enquêtes de terrain ont été menées grâce à la collaboration de M. Trần Trí Dõi, professeur à l'Université de Hanoi, et de Mme Võ Thị Thường, ethnologue au Musée d'Ethnographie du Vietnam.

8.3. GÉNÉRALITÉS PHONÉTIQUES

La structure du mot de base dans les trois dialectes, tay daeng (tay thanh), Tay Yo et tay muong, est strictement monosyllabique: **CV(C)/T**, (C: consonne; V: voyelle; T: ton).

Les trois systèmes d'initiales sont globalement les mêmes, mise à part la particularité du tay daeng où p^h n'est pas représenté (à la suite de sa confusion récente avec f). Cependant, si l'on envisage les unités de chaque système, non du point de vue strictement phonétique, mais du point de vue de la phonétique historique, on constate que certaines initiales reconstruites du proto thai peuvent, dans les correspondances lexicales, attester des réflexes différents selon les dialectes. Ces divergences concernent principalement les initiales *x *ɣ *ɟ (aussi *gr>*ɟ). Par ailleurs, les trois dialectes ont connu le même phénomène de dévoisement des anciennes occlusives sonores en sourdes non aspirées (*b- *d- ...> p- t-...).

Les systèmes vocaliques présentent des différences portant sur la longueur pertinente; le Tay Yo et le tay muong n'attestent que a:~a, tandis que le tay daeng possède en plus l'opposition dans les voyelles fermées i:~i, i:~ɨ et u:~u. En revanche et contrairement aux consonnes initiales, les correspondances vocaliques dans le vocabulaire commun entre les trois dialectes et le proto thai sont assez univoques. Ils ont en outre préservé la voyelle finale -ə du proto thai, voyelle qui, rappelons-le, est devenue -aɨ en tay noir et tay blanc, et s'est confondue avec -aj en siamois et en lao.

Les trois dialectes ont développé un même système tonal de base à six tons. Le nombre des tons a pu ultérieurement se réduire à cinq, suite à des confusions qui peuvent varier selon les dialectes. Nous suivrons les usages en vigueur dans la notation des catégories tonales: A B C (finales sonores), DL (finales sourdes, voyelles longues) et DS (finales sourdes, voyelles brèves), en combinaison avec les chiffres 1 (série haute) ou 2 (série basse). Dans les reconstructions du proto thai, seules les catégories A B C, qui indiquent les trois tons primordiaux, sont indiquées, les autres catégories DL et DS, ainsi que les séries 1 et 2, se déterminent par la simple observation du consonantisme de la forme reconstruite. Dans les listes comparatives on se contentera d'indiquer les catégories tonales (A1, A2, etc.) des correspondances. S'il y a disharmonie tonale dans une correspondance, la catégorie sera précisée après chaque terme. La mélodie des réalisations phonétiques des tons dans chaque dialecte est indiquée par un nombre composé de deux ou trois chiffres allant de [^{1}], son le plus bas, à [^{5}], son le plus haut, auquel peut s'ajouter une constriction glottale [^{ʔ}]. Dans cette étude, la manière de noter les tons dépendra des besoins. Dans les tableaux, la notation des tons sera la plus précise possible. Dans le vocabulaire des dialectes, la notation des tons sera allégée de la constriction glottale en raison de son rôle distinctif phonologiquement très faible.

Le proto thai utilisé ici a été élaboré sur la base du *thai commun* de A. G. Haudricourt (1948), modifié par les suggestions ultérieures de l'auteur lui-même (1952, 1972). On a pris en compte les reconstructions implicites de Li Fangkuei (1977) sur le *southwestern tai* et divers autres apports, A. Diller (1988) et M. Ferlus (1994). Le travail de Luo Yongxian (1997), qu'il convient de citer, a été publié plus tard. Il ne nous est pas possible, dans les limites de cette étude, de justifier notre reconstruction, mais il faut noter que le tay blanc de Phong Thổ (province de Điện Biên, ex Lai Châu) est la langue clé sans laquelle le proto thai ne pourrait être reconstruit. Se reporter au tableau: *Du proto thai aux dialectes actuels: évolution des initiales*.

8.4. TAY DAENG (OU TAY THANH)

Les données proviennent de sources écrites, publiées (Gedney 1964, Robert 1941) ou manuscrites (Fénard 1920), et de données personnelles recueillies ces dernières années au Vietnam. Nos principaux informateurs ont été: M. Vi Văn An de Con Cuông (Nghệ An), ethnologue au Musée d'ethnographie de Hanôi; MM. Hà Anh Đức, Hà Công Tín et Khà Văn Tiến de Mai Châu (Hòa Bình).

8.4.1. Système consonantique

	initiales					finales		
		tʰ		kʰ				
p	t	c	k	ʔ		p	t	k
b	d							
m	n	ɲ	ŋ			m	n	ŋ
f	s			h				
v	j					w	j	
	l							

L'absence d'un pʰ est le fait notoire du système des initiales du tay daeng (et aussi du tay noir). Cela est dû à la confusion, probablement récente, de pʰ attendu (issu de PT *pʰ et *pʰr >pʰ) avec f (issu de PT *f et *v >f). Donnons quelques exemples par comparaison avec le Tay Yo qui n'a pas connu cette confusion:

	tay daeng	*tay yo*	
A1	fi:	pʰi:	'génie'
A1	fum	pʰom	'cheveux'
A1	fon	fin/fɔn	'pluie'
C2	fa:	fa:	'ciel'

A Mai Châu (Hòa Bình), on observe une tendance à la confusion de b avec v, au profit de l'un ou de l'autre, et pareillement de d avec l, parmi les locuteurs adultes. Curieusement, les distinctions sont rétablies dans la jeune génération, peut être sous l'influence du vietnamien.

8.4.2. Système vocalique

Le système comprend dix-sept unités phonétiques (sept longues, trois diphtongues et sept brèves) qui s'organisent en seize unités phonologiques.

i:	i	ɨ:		u:	u
	e	ə:	/ ə		o
ɛ:				ɔ:	
ia		ɨa		ua	
		a:	a		

Les brèves n'apparaissent qu'en syllabe fermée. Les longues peuvent apparaître dans tous les types de syllabe à l'exception de ɔ: qui ne se trouve qu'en syllabe ouverte dans un nombre limité d'exemples: bɔ:ᴬ¹ 'feuille', cɔ:ᴬ¹ 'coeur', sɔ:ᴮ¹ 'poser', mɔ:ᴮ¹ 'nouveau'... Rappelons que cette voyelle, préservée telle quelle du proto thai, est devenue aɨ en tay noir (et tay blanc), et s'est confondue avec aj en siamois (et en lao). Comparons:

proto thai		tay daeng	tay noir	siamois	
*^{h}mɔ:^{B}	B1	mɔ:	mai	maj	'nouveau'
*maj^C	C2	maj	maj	maj	'végétal'

Les emprunts au vietnamien en -ɔ- tendent à introduire l'opposition ɔ:~ə en syllabe fermée.

8.4.3. Système tonal

Le tay thanh (tay daeng du Nghệ An) parlé à Con Cuông atteste un système tonal à cinq unités, les tons B2 et C1 s'étant confondus. D'après d'autres sources disponibles (Gedney 1964, Robert 1941, Fénart 1920) cette situation caractérise également les dialectes tay daeng parlés au Thanh Hóa et au Laos.

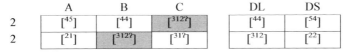

	A	B	C	DL	DS
2	[^{45}]	[^{44}]	[^{312ʔ}]	[^{44}]	[^{54}]
2	[^{21}]	[^{312ʔ}]	[^{31ʔ}]	[^{312}]	[^{22}]

FIGURE 8.4.3-1: TONS DU TAY THANH (Con Cuông, Nghệ An)

Signalons le cas intéressant des deux sous dialectes tay daeng à six tons parlés à Mai Châu (Hòa Bình), région excentrée aux limites de la zone proprement tay daeng et au contact des Muong (langue viet-muong).

A Mai Châu Thượng (Mai Châu 'haut') les tons B2 et C1 sont nettement distincts.

	A	B	C	DL	DS
1	[^{53}]	[^{31}]	[^{35ʔ}]	[^{21}]	
2	[^{11}]	[^{33}]	[^{313}]	[^{33}]	[^{33}]

FIGURE 8.4.3-2: TONS DU TAY DAENG (Mai Chau Thượng, Hòa Bình)

En revanche, à Mai Châu Hạ (Mai Châu 'bas'), limitrophe du précédent mais orienté vers le Thanh Hóa, les tons B2 et C1 ont la même mélodie et ne se différencient que par une légère constriction glottale qui n'est réellement audible que dans une prononciation soignée. On peut penser que ces deux tons sont sur le point de se confondre.

	A	B	C	DL	DS
1	[^{54}]	[^{45}]	[^{213ʔ}]	[^{45}]	
2	[^{22}]	[^{213}]	[^{31ʔ}]	[^{213}]	[^{22}]

FIGURE 8.4.3-3: TONS DU TAY DAENG (Mai Châu Hạ, Hòa Bình)

Le fait le plus remarquable des deux variantes dialectales de Mai Châu reste la confusion les tons DS1 et DS2, fait assez rare dans le groupe thai. Ainsi, les mots issus de PT *lak 'voler, dérober' et *^{h}lak 'poteau' ont la même prononciation, [lak^{33}] à Mai Châu Thượng et [lak^{22}] à Mai Châu Hạ.

8.4.4. Notes grammaticales

Les différences dialectales sont minimes et ne semblent dues qu'à l'influence des langues voisines (lao, tay yo). Les tons des particules et des exemples sont ceux du tay thanh de Con Cuông; les tons des extraits de texte sont ceux du tay daeng de Mai Châu Hạ.

Groupe verbal:
Marques et modalités placées avant le verbe: saːŋ^{45} si:^{21} action en cours, 'en train de'; ɲaŋ^{21} 'en train de, encore'; daj^{312} passé; ci:^{312} [ci] futur; mom^{31} passé, 'terminé de'; bɔ:^{312} /

baw³¹² négation; ɲa:²¹ impératif négatif; hɔ:³¹² 'faire que'. Placées après le verbe: lɛ:w³¹ passé; daj³¹² / daj³¹² lɛ:w³¹ possibilité; baw³¹² interrogation; la:⁴⁵ expressif de politesse (en fin de phrase).

Exemples: kʰɔ:j³¹² sa:ŋ⁴⁵ si:²¹ kin⁴⁵ 'je mange, je suis en train de manger'; ɲaŋ²¹ kin⁴⁵ kʰaw³¹² 'encore en train de manger'; kʰɔ:j³¹² paj⁴⁵ lɛ:w³¹ 'je suis parti'; kʰɔ:j³¹² daj³¹² paj⁴⁵ 'je suis déjà parti/allé'; kʰɔ:j³¹² daj³¹² paj⁴⁵ lɛ:w³¹ 'id.'; man²¹ ci mia²¹ ba:n³¹² 'il rentrera au village'; hɔ:³¹² ta:n²¹ sɔ:k³¹² 'cherchez!'; law²¹ mom³¹ 'déjà mangé'; mia²¹ mom³¹ 'de retour, une fois rentré'; kʰɔ:j³¹² ʔet⁵⁴ daj³¹² 'je peux le faire'.

Interrogatifs:
lɔ:²¹ interrogatif en général; pʰu: lɔ:²¹ / kun²¹ lɔ:²¹ 'qui, lequel'; to:⁴⁵ lɔ:²¹ 'quel, lequel' (animal); cɔ:⁴⁵ lɔ:²¹ 'quand'; fɔ:⁴⁵ 'qui'; ʔan⁴⁵ lɔ:²¹ / nɛ:w²¹ lɔ:²¹ / jo:ŋ²¹ lɔ:²¹ 'quoi, lequel'; maŋ⁴⁵ 'quoi, quel' (dialecte de Mai Châu); ka-lɔ:²¹ 'où'; ti:³¹² lɔ:²¹ 'où, quel endroit?'.

Exemples: paj⁴⁵ lɔ:²¹ la:⁴⁵ – paj⁴⁵ cɔ:³¹² 'où vas-tu? – je vais au marché'; sɛ:⁴⁵ ju:⁴⁴ ti:³¹² lɔ:²¹ 'où est la voiture?'; ʔoŋ⁴⁵ luk²² ti:³¹² lɔ:²¹ ma:²¹ la:⁴⁵ 'd'où viens-tu donc!'; miŋ²¹ mi:²¹ ki:⁴⁴ kun²¹ lu:k³¹² la:⁴⁵ 'combien as-tu d'enfants?'; miŋ²¹ het²² maŋ⁴⁵ la:⁴⁵ 'que fais-tu?'.

Pronoms personnels:
ku:⁴⁵ 'je'; kʰɔ:j³¹² 'je' (poli); miŋ²¹ 'tu'; ta:n²¹ 'tu' (poli); man²¹ 'il, elle'; haw²¹ 'nous'; su:⁴⁵ 'vous'; kʰaw⁴⁵ 'ils, elles'; piən³¹² 'ils, elles, on'. L'expression tiŋ²¹ la:j⁴⁵ 'tous' rajoutée à un pronom singulier sert à former le pluriel: haw²¹ tiŋ²¹ la:j⁴⁵ 'nous tous'; ta:n²¹ tiŋ²¹ la:j⁴⁵ 'vous tous'.

Démonstratifs:
ni:³¹ 'ce...ci' (rapproché); nan³¹ 'ce...là' (distance moyenne). Exemples: kun²¹ ni:³¹ / fu:³¹² ni:³¹ 'celui/celle-ci'; kun²¹ nan³¹ / fu:³¹² nan³¹ 'celui/celle-là'; ʔan⁴⁵ ni:³¹ 'ceci'; ʔan⁴⁵ nan³¹ 'cela'.

Nombres et classificateur:
L'ordre le plus usité est *nom–nombre–class.* (ma:³¹ sɔ:ŋ⁴⁵ to:⁴⁵ 'deux chevaux'), mais l'ordre *nombre–class.–nom* (sa:m⁴⁵ bɔ:⁴⁵ tʰuaj³¹² 'trois tasses') est également très fréquent.

Principaux classificateurs: kun²¹ / fu:³¹² personnes; ʔoŋ⁴⁵ personnes importantes; to:⁴⁵ et mɛ:³¹² animaux; ʔan⁴⁵ objets en général; kɔ:⁴⁵ arbres; bɔ:⁴⁵ objets plats, feuilles, assiettes; ma:k⁴⁴ couteaux, manches; ma:k³¹² fruits, formes rondes; nuaj⁴⁴ objets ronds, oeufs, noix d'arec; mit⁵⁴ grains, pilules; hua⁴⁵ tubercules; lam²¹ objets longs, tubes, bateaux; laŋ⁴⁵ maisons; fin⁴⁵ étoffes, nattes; kɔ:n⁴⁵ morceaux; tʰɛ:ŋ⁴⁵ lingots; sen³¹² ficelle; toŋ³¹² terrains, rizières; kʰaw⁴⁵ armes à feu; ham²¹ rouleaux; pap⁵⁴ livres.

Phrases diverses:
Extraits d'un texte de rituel des funérailles, psalmodié pour guider les âmes du défunt vers le pays des ancêtres. Les tons sont ceux du sous dialecte de Mai Châu Hạ.

ɲim⁵⁴ ŋɔ:²¹³ tʰa:ŋ⁴⁵ ci:n⁴⁵ ha:²¹³ kʰam²¹³ 'Année du cheval (Nhâm Ngọ), neuvième mois, cinquième jour [14 octobre 1942]'; ke:⁵⁴ bian⁵⁴ sac⁴⁵ paj⁵⁴ ta:ŋ²² ja:w²² 'j'écris le texte *Suivre le long chemin*'; ...ka:j⁵⁴ nan³¹ loŋ²² tok²² sɔ:²¹³ na:ŋ²² ɲɔ:⁴⁵ pa:n²¹³ nam³¹ ɲɔ:⁴⁵ pen⁵⁴ fɔ:ŋ²² 'Après cela, descendre à l'endroit où la princesse a barré le fleuve, [les eaux passent] en vague'; kɔ:ŋ²² du:⁵⁴ tɔ:²¹³ hia²² luaŋ⁵⁴ laj⁵⁴ '[elle] attend de voir les grands bateaux descendre' taw³¹ faw²¹³ du:⁵⁴ tɔ:²¹³ hia²² ɲɔ:⁴⁵ laj⁵⁴ loŋ²² 'pour surveiller les grands bateaux qui descendent [et se saisir des âmes]'; ...ka:j⁵⁴ nan³¹ loŋ²² tok²² sɔ:²¹³ fa:²¹³ taŋ²¹³ fa:⁵⁴ tɔ:⁴⁵ fa:⁵⁴ 'Après cela, descendre à l'endroit où les falaises se dressent face à face'; bɔ:⁴⁵ ŋɔn²² bɔ:⁴⁵ kʰam²² la:²¹³ nam³¹ '[il y a] des mines d'argent et d'or sous l'eau'; ...ka:j⁵⁴ nan³¹ tok²² mia²² huaj³¹ bɔ:k⁴⁵ bua⁵⁴ ti:²¹³ kaw⁴⁵ 'Après cela, arriver à l'ancien ruisseau aux fleurs de lotus'; ...ka:⁵⁴ ni:³¹ kʰin⁵⁴ hian²² ca:w²² cet²² sip²² ca:m³¹ 'jusqu'ici, monter à la maison [des ancêtres] du clan, [il y a eu] soixante-dix haltes'; kʰɔ:j³¹² ni:³¹ caŋ⁴⁵ kʰin²² hian²² tʰɛ:n⁵⁴ 'sortant d'ici, monter vers la maison des Then [divinités célestes]'.

(Traduit par M. Khà Văn Tiến avec la participation de Mme Võ Thị Thường).

8.5. TAY YO

Le Tay Yo est principalement parlé dans les trois districts de Quỳ Hợp, Quỳ Châu et Quế Phong de la province de Nghệ An. On ne dispose pas de publication sur ce dialecte in situ. La très intéressante étude de J. R. Chamberlain (1991) sur le tay maen (mène) du Laos concerne un dialecte originaire du district de Tương Dương et est malheureusement assez influencé par le lao. On a pu profiter des notes inédites laissées par Henri Maspero (Ferlus 1993) qui a travaillé dans la région vers 1920. Nos informateurs ont été MM. Lang Văn O et Lang Văn Doãn son fils, M. Vi Ngọc Chân et Mme Lang Thị Hồng, tous des environs de Quỳ Châu.

8.5.1. Système consonantique

	initiales				finales		
p^h	t^h		k^h				
p	t	c	k	ʔ	p	t	c /k
b	d						
m	n	ɲ	ŋ		m	n	ɲ /ŋ
f	s			h			
v	j (z)				w	j	
	l						

L'influence du vietnamien se fait fortement sentir sur la prononciation du tay yo. L'initiale palatale j est fréquemment prononcée z. Les finales palatales c-ɲ se sont développées sous l'influence des finales *ch-nh* du viet.

Le Tay Yo (et aussi le tay muong) se singularise par une évolution originale des fricatives vélaires initiales du proto thai: *x >h et *ɣ >k :

proto thai		*tay daeng*	*tay yo*	
*xɛːn^A	A1	k^hɛːn	hɛːn	'bras'
*xaw^C	C1	k^haw	haw	'entrer'
*xon^A	A1	k^hun	hon	'poil'
*xaːt	DL1	k^haːt^DL1	haːt^{DL1/2}	'déchiré'
*ɣwaːj^A	A2	k^hwaːj	kwaːj	'buffle'
*ɣam^A	A2	k^ham	kam	'or'
*ɣɛːŋ^B	B2	k^hɛːŋ	kɛːŋ	'mollet'
*ɣɛːp	DL2	k^hɛːp^{DL2}	kɛːp^{DL1/2}	'étroit'

Tandis que PT *k^h >k^h et *g >k comme dans les autres langues thai (excepté en siamois et en lao où *g >k^h):

*k^haw^C	C1	k^haw	k^haw	'riz'
*k^hɛːŋ^A	A1	k^hɛːŋ	k^haɲ	'dur'
*gon^A	A2	kun	kon	'fils'
*gem^A	A2	kem	kem	'salé'

8.5.2. Système vocalique

Le système comprend dix-neuf unités phonétiques (neuf longues, trois diphtongues et sept brèves) qui s'organisent en treize unités phonologiques.

```
i:  /  i   ɨ:  /  ɨ   u:  /  u
e:  /  e   ə:  /  ə   o:  /  o
ɛ:                    ɔ:
ia         ɨa         ua
           a:    a
```

Dans le système vocalique du tay yo, la paire a:~a est la seule opposition de longueur. Les termes de chacune des six paires i/i, ɨ/ɨ, u/u, e/e, ə/ə, et o/o sont en distribution complémentaire, les longues n'apparaissant que dans les syllabes ouvertes, et les brèves dans les syllabes fermées. Pour éclairer ces problèmes de distribution, nous donnons ci-dessous les sous systèmes vocaliques selon les contextes.

```
finales p-m et t-n          finales c-ɲ / finales k-ŋ
i       ɨ       u       i           ɨ       u
e       ə       o                   ə       o
ɛ:              ɔ:                           ɔ:
ia      ɨa      ua      ia          ɨa      ua
        a:      a       a       a:          a
```

```
finale Ø            finale w            finale j
i:  ɨ:  u:          i:                              u:
e:  ə:  o:                              ə:          (o:)
ɛ:  ɔ:              ɛ:                               ɔ:
ia  ɨa  ua          ia                  ɨa          ua
    a:                  a:    a         a:          a
```

La rime -o:j n'apparaît que dans des emprunts. Les finales palatales c-ɲ sont en distribution complémentaire avec les vélaires k-ŋ à l'instar de finales *ch-nh* par rapport à *c-ng* en viet. Les rimes -ic/-ac (et -iɲ/-aɲ) du Tay Yo correspondent aux rimes -i:k/-ɛ:k (et -i:ŋ/-ɛ:ŋ) des autres langues du groupe thai. Donnons quelques exemples:

proto thai		tay daeng	tay yo	
*pi:k	DL1	pi:k^{DL1}	pic($=$DS2)	'aile'
*li:ŋ^{A}	A2	li:ŋ	liɲ	'singe'
*tɛ:k	DL1	tɛ:k^{DL1}	tac($=$DS2)	'cassé'
*kʰɛ:ŋ^{A}	A1	kʰɛ:ŋ	kʰaɲ	'dur'

Dans quelques mots, on a pu observer des variantes plus fermées de la voyelle a (longue ou brève), comme par exemple: pa:/pɐ:/pə/pɔ:^{A2} 'aller', sa:/sɐ:^{A2} 'il, elle', man/mɐn^{A2} 'tubercule'. Ce phénomène, très limité, est lié au ton A2.

8.5.3. Système tonal

	A	B	C	DL	DS
1	[^{13}]	[^{11ʔ}]	[^{33ʔ}]		[^{55}]
2	[^{55}]	[^{31}]	[^{53ʔ}]	[^{11}]	[^{11}]

FIGURE 8.5.3-1: TONS DU TAY YO (Quỳ Châu, Nghệ An)

La caractéristique la plus remarquable de ce système tonal réside dans la confusion des tons

DL1 et DL2. Ce fait, que le Tay Yo partage avec le tay muong, est unique dans toute la famille des langues tai-kadai. Ainsi les deux vocables 'exposer au soleil' et 'sangsue de terre', distincts en proto thai et en tay daeng (ici Mai Châu Hạ), sont homophones en tay yo.

Proto thai		tay daeng	tay yo	
*taːk	DL1	taːk^{45}	taːk^{11}	'exposer au soleil'
*daːk	DL2	taːk^{213}	taːk^{11}	'sangsue de terre'

La rareté de ce type de confusion permet de l'utiliser comme traceur linguistique pour suivre les migrations vers le Laos et le nord-est de la Thaïlande. Elle est, par exemple, attestée dans la langue des Phou Thai du Centre-Laos, ce qui permet de confirmer que cette population est bien originaire du Nghệ An. Il en est de même pour les Tay Mène et les Tay Nyo.

La détermination des tons dans les mots comportant les brèves fermées i ɨ u devant les occlusives finales p t c/k dépend de la qualité longue ou brève de la voyelle dans les mots correspondants en proto thai et dans les autres langues thai ayant préservé cette distinction. Ces faits nous amènent à penser que le Tay Yo (et aussi le tay muong) possédait autrefois l'opposition de longueur pour les voyelles fermées devant les occlusives finales. A la suite de la confusion générale des tons DL1 et DL2, les mots Tay Yo en voyelles brèves fermées, correspondant à des longues en proto thai et en tay daeng, se retrouvent à la suite de l'abrégement vocalique au ton DS2, quelle que soit la qualité sourde ou sonore de l'initiale en proto thai. L'abrégement vocalique a donc eu lieu après la confusion des tons. Cette situation n'est qu'en apparence contraire au schéma de la tonogénèse.

proto thai	tay daeng	tay yo (*DL1/2>DS2)	
*piːk	piːk^{DL1}	pic^{DS2}	'aile'
*siːk	siːk^{DL1}	sic^{DS2}	'déchirer'
*cuːt	cuːt^{DL1}	cut^{DS2}	'allumer (un feu)'
*^{h}ruːk	huːk^{DL1}	huk^{DS2}	'métier à tisser'
*puːk	puːk^{DL1}	puk^{DS2}	'planter'
*ɗuːk	duːk^{DL1}	duk^{DS2}	'os'
*miːt	miːt^{DL2}	mit^{DS2}	'couteau'
*gɨːp	kɨːp^{DL2}	kɨp^{DS2}	'empan'
*vuːk	fuːk^{DL2}	fuk^{DS2}	'natte'

En revanche, dans les mots en voyelles fermées originellement brèves, les correspondances tonales attestent régulièrement la distinction entre DS1 et DS2.

proto thai	tay daeng	tay yo	
*sip	sip^{DS1}	sip^{DS1}	'dix'
*tɨk	tɨk^{DS1}	tɨk^{DS1}	'pêcher (à la ligne)'
*kup	kup^{DS1}	kup^{DS1}	'chapeau (de pluie)'
*suk	suk^{DS1}	suk^{DS1}	'mûr, cuit'
(*luːk)	luːk^{DL2})	lik^{DS2}	'fils'
*luk	luk^{DS2}	luk^{DS2}	'se lever'

On peut penser que la perte de l'opposition de longueur pour les voyelles fermées i ɨ u est la conséquence de l'influence directe des unités homologues i ɯ u du vietnamien pour lesquelles cette opposition n'existe pas.

Le système tonal du tay maen (mène) donné par J. R. Chamberlain (1991: p. 108) représente un état intermédiaire entre celui du Tay Yo de Quỳ Châu et celui du tay muong de Tương Dương. Il confirme la confusion des tons DL1 et DL2 mais s'en différencie par la confusion des tons B1 et B2, confusion également attestée en tay muong. En quelque sorte, le tay maen assure la transition entre le Tay Yo et le tay muong, ces derniers n'étant, il faut le rappeler, que des sous dialectes d'une même langue. Notons que le lieu d'origine des Tay Maen est justement située dans le nord-est du district de Tương Dương en direction de Quỳ Châu.

8.5.4. Notes grammaticales

Ces notes proviennent pour l'essentiel des écrits inédits laissés par Henri Maspero. Les extraits de textes sont tirés de manuscrits en écriture Tay Yo traditionnelle.

Groupe verbal:
Marques et modalités placées avant le verbe: ca:^{11} / ca- et ca-ha:^{13} futur; da:^{13} passé (du viet *đã*); paj^{11} 'pas encore'; bɔ:^{11} négation; ɲa:^{11} négation impérative; hɔ:^{33} 'faire que'; kʰam^{33} 'avoir l'intention de'. Placées après le verbe: lɛ:w^{53} passé (en fin de phrase); mom^{53} 'terminé de'.
   Exemples: mia^{31} na:^{33} ku:^{55} ca-mia^{55} ba:n^{33} 'demain, je rentrerai au village'; kʰɔ:j^{33} ca-ha:^{13} ki:^{55} 'je mangerai'; miŋ^{55} ki:^{55} kʰaw^{33} bɔ:^{11} 'est-ce que tu manges?'; bɔ:^{11} ki:^{55} kʰaw^{33} mange pas'; ki:^{55} kʰaw^{33} paj^{11} 'as [-tu] mangé?'; ki:^{55} lɛ:w^{53} bɔ:^{11} 'as [-tu] fini de manger?'; kʰɔ:j^{33} ki:^{55} lɛ:w^{53} 'j'ai mangé'; ki:^{55} mom^{53} 'terminé de manger'; paj^{11} ki:^{55} kʰaw^{33} 'pas encore mangé'; mi:^{55} bɔ:^{33} 'y [en] a-t-il?'; bɔ:^{33} mi:^{55} 'il n'y [en] a pas'; paj^{11} mi:^{55} 'il n'y [en] a pas encore'.

Interrogatifs:
lə:^{55} interrogatif; ka:^{31}lə:^{55} / ka-lə:^{55} 'où'; ʔa-lə:^{55} 'quoi, lequel'; pia^{53} 'qui'; tua^{53} 'quoi, quel'; cə:^{55} lə:^{55} 'quand'; ɲa:m^{55} lə:^{55} 'quand, quel moment'; ki:^{11} 'combien de'.
   Exemples: miŋ^{55} pɛ:^{55} ka-lə:^{55} 'où vas-tu?'; pɛ:^{55} ta:ŋ^{55} lə:^{55} 'où vas-tu?' (quelle direction?); pɔ:^{31} me:^{31} sa:^{55} zu:^{11} ka-lə:^{55} 'où sont ses parents?'; zu:^{11} ka-lə:^{55} ma:^{55} ni:^{53} 'd'où arrive [-t-il] ici?'; ʔa:j^{33} pɛ:^{55} cə:^{55} lə:^{55} 'quand êtes-vous allé?'; mi:^{55} ki:^{11} lik^{11} 'combien avez [-vous] d'enfants?'; ʔa:j^{33} (daj^{33}) ki:^{11} tuaj^{31} 'quel âge avez-vous?'; miŋ^{55} ki:^{55} tua^{53} 'que manges-tu?'; miŋ^{55} ten^{13} lə:^{55} 'comment t'appelles-tu?'; ten^{13} tua^{53} 'quel [est ton] nom?'; sa:^{55} ʔe:^{55} tua^{53} 'que fait-il?'; pia^{53} ni:^{53} 'qui [est celui-] ci?'; pia^{53} ʔa:^{33} 'qui [est celui-] là?'.

Pronoms personnels:
ku:^{55} 'je'; kʰɔ:j^{33} 'je (poli)'; miŋ^{55} 'tu'; ɲa:j^{55} 'tu (poli)'; sa:^{55} / sɛ:^{55} 'il, elle'; mə:j^{33} haw^{55} et tu:^{13} kʰɔ:j^{33} 'nous tous (inclusif)'; mə:j^{33} tu:^{13} 'nous tous (exclusif)'; mə:j^{33} su:^{13} 'vous tous'; mə:j^{33} sa:^{55} 'ils, elles'.

Démonstratifs:
ni:^{53} 'ce...ci' (rapproché); ʔa:^{33} 'ce...là' (moyen); na:^{33} 'ce...là' (loin devant, en face); ʔu:n^{31} / ʔi:n^{31} 'ce...là' (loin, autre); han^{53} 'ce....là (autre). Les démonstratifs se placent toujours après le déterminé.
   Exemples: pɔ:^{55} ni:^{53} 'cette personne-ci'; pɔ:^{55} ʔa:^{33} 'cette personne-là'; pɔ:^{55} ʔu:n^{33} 'cette personne-là (là-bas), l'autre'; nɔ:^{31} hian^{55} ni:^{53} 'cette maison-ci'; nɔ:^{31} hian^{55} na:^{33} 'cette maison-là'; nɔ:^{31} hian^{55} ʔu:n^{31} 'cette maison-là (là-bas)'; pia^{53} ni:^{53} 'qui [est celui-] ci?'; pia^{53} ʔa:^{33} 'qui [est celui-] là?'; ka-ni:^{53} 'ici'; ka-han^{53} 'là'. cə:^{55} ni:^{53} 'maintenant'; cə:^{55} han^{53} 'à ce moment-là'.

Nombres et classificateurs:
Comme dans toutes les langues thai, l'usage des classificateurs est très répandu. En Tay Yo l'ordre est *nombre–class.–nom* (sip^{55} kɔ:^{13} maj^{53} 'dix arbres'), sauf dans le cas où le nombre est 'un' (*class.–nom–'un'*, kɔ:n^{33} hin^{13} niŋ^{31} 'une pierre'). Selon Maspero, on peut avoir l'ordre *nom–nombre–class.* dans le cas d'une réponse à une interrogation (mi:^{55} ki^{11} ʔan^{13} mit^{11} – mi:^{55} mit^{11} sɔ:ŋ^{13} ʔan^{13} 'combien de couteaux? – il y a deux couteaux').
   Principaux classificateurs: kon^{11} personnes; ʔoŋ^{13} fonctionnaires; to:^{55} / me:^{31} animaux; nɔ:^{31} objets, outils; ʔan^{13} objets en général; pʰən^{13} tissus, vêtements; sen^{33} fils, cordes; bɔ:^{13} objets en feuille; pe:n^{33} planches; laŋ^{13} maison; ma:k^{11} fruits, oeufs; kɔ:n^{33} morceaux, pierres; lem^{33} bâteaux; to:j^{13} paire (viet *đôi*); ne:n^{33} bâtonnets; kɔ:^{13} arbre.
   Exemples: ʔoŋ^{13} kwa:n^{13} niŋ^{31} 'un fonctionnaire'; sɔ:ŋ^{13} kon^{55} lik^{11} 'deux fils/filles'; sa:m^{13} ma:k^{11} saj^{11} 'trois oeufs'; si:^{11} laŋ^{13} hian^{55} 'quatre maisons'; ha:^{33} me:^{31} kwa:j^{55} 'cinq buffles'; hok^{55} bɔ:^{13} cia^{33} 'six feuilles de papier'.

Phrases diverses:

1: kʰɔːj⁵⁵ məːj⁵⁵ ʔoŋ¹³ ʔaː³³ maː⁵⁵ hian⁵⁵ lɛːw⁵³ 'J'ai invité cette personne-là, [elle] est arrivée chez moi'.

2: man⁵⁵ mia⁵⁵ hian⁵⁵ faːŋ¹³ viː⁵⁵ man⁵⁵ miː⁵⁵ viak¹¹ kaːn¹³ 'Il rentre à la maison parce qu'il a du travail'.

3: pʰaːj¹³ puk¹¹ kɔː¹³ maj⁵³ niŋ³¹ kɨː⁵⁵ sɔː¹¹ kɔː¹³ baː¹³ 'Il faut planter un arbre comme arbre [banian] aux génies'; niː⁵³ puk¹¹ kɛːm⁵⁵ baːn³³ 'il est planté à la lisière du village'; kɔː¹³ baː¹³ han⁵³ miː⁵⁵ taːj¹³ pʰaːj¹³ puk¹¹ laːj³¹ '[Si] ce banian meurt, il faudra [en] replanter de nouveau'. (Extraits du Fonds Maspero)

4: ŋwian³³ piː¹³ haːm¹¹ ŋiː³³ pua¹³ tiː³¹ mɔːj⁵⁵ tʰian³³ haː⁵³ 'Au début des années [du règne] Hàm Nghi, le roi qui gouverne son monde'; fuː¹¹ kwiː⁵⁵ cuː¹³ mian⁵⁵ puː⁵⁵ kwaːj⁵⁵ mak⁵⁵ ʔaw¹³ sək⁵⁵ saː³³ '[dans] le district de Quỳ Châu, muong de Pu Koai, [on] a subit les pirates'; pʰaː³³ cut¹¹ paj³¹ taj⁵⁵ niː¹³ sam⁵³ '[ils] ont brûlé [semé la destruction], les villageois se sont tous enfui'. (Extrait du manuscrit *Les rébellions*).

5: caw³³ vaː³¹ hɔː³³ tɛːŋ¹¹ caːŋ³³ daː¹³ kaŋ¹¹ tuː¹³ vian⁵⁵ 'Les chefs ordonnent de disposer les éléphants près des portes, [à l'intérieur] des remparts de la cité'; bak⁵⁵ haː¹³ saːm¹³ pan⁵⁵ maː⁵³ toː⁵⁵ dam¹³ ʔaːn¹¹ sɛːt¹¹ '[on] concentre trois mille chevaux noirs à selle orange'; law¹³ pan⁵⁵ maː⁵³ ʔaːn¹¹ siːw³³ bɔːk¹¹ tɔːŋ⁵⁵ 'avec mille chevaux à selle verte [mouchetée] de fleurs *tong*'. (Extraits du manuscrit *Chuang*).

(*Traduit par M. Lang Văn O avec la participation du Professeur Trần Trí Dõi*).

8.5.5. Situation linguistique du Tay Yo:

Le vocabulaire Tay Yo contient des mots dont le phonétisme est en disharmonie avec celui des autres langues thai, la différence pouvant porter sur le consonantisme, le vocalisme ou le ton. Donnons quelques exemples en comparaison avec le proto thai et le tay daeng:

	proto thai		*tay daeng*	*tay yo*	*(disharmonie)*
'éventail'	*wiː^A	A2	viː	piː	*initiale*
'près de'	*klɔː^C	C1	kɔː	kʰɔː	*initiale*
'creuser'	*kʰut	DS1	kʰut	kut	*initiale*
'chanter'	*xap	DS1	kʰap	kap	*initiale*
'porter'	*tʰɨːA	A1	tʰɨː	tɨː	*initiale*
'feu'	*vaj^A	A2	faj	fɨː	*voyelle*
'fils'	*luːk	DL2	luːk^{DL2}	lik^{DS2}	*voyelle*
'je'	*kuː^A	A1	kuː^{A1}	kuː^{A2}	*ton*
'ventre'	*puːm^A	A1	puːm^{A1}	pum^{A2}	*ton*
'corps'	*tua^A	A1	toː^{A1}	toː^{A2}	*ton*

Les correspondances suivantes s'expliquent très bien par l'évolution générale de la fricative vélaire *x >h dans le cas particulier de *xw >hw (identifié à PT *ʰw>v):

	proto thai		*tay daeng*	*tay yo*	*(disharmonie)*
'hache'	*xwaːn^A	A1	kʰwaːn	vaːn	*initiale*
'âme'	*xwan^A	A1	kʰwan	van	*initiale*
'suspendre'	*xwɛːn^A	A1	kʰwɛːn	vɛːn	*initiale*

La correspondance suivante ne concerne qu'une liste partielle de mots:

	proto thai		*tay daeng*	*tay yo*	*(disharmonie)*
'avoir peur'	*klua^A	A1	-	koː	*voyelle*
'rire'	*hua^A	A1	hua	hoː	*voyelle*
'clôture'	*rua^C	C2	hua	hoː	*voyelle*

Par ailleurs, le Tay Yo atteste du vocabulaire sans correspondance dans les autres langues de la branche thai:

tay yo		*tay yo*	
kɛːt$^{DL1/2}$	'malade'	nɔː^{A2}	'personne'
saː/sɐ̯ː^{A2}	'il, elle'	nɔː^{B2}	'class. d'objet'
mɔːj^{C1}	'groupe, Tay Meuy'	kiː^{A2}	'manger'
lɔː^{A1}	'rêver'	ʔɛː^{A2}	'faire'
lɔː^{A2}	'interrogatif'	ʔaː^{A2}	'prendre'
kaː^{A2}	'réciproque'		

Le mot pɐ̯ʔpaː^{A2} 'aller', parfois placé dans cette liste, est en fait attesté dans d'autres langues thai avec le sens de 'accompagner'.

Quelques uns de ces mots, comme fiː^{A2} 'feu' et lɨk^{DS2} 'fils, enfant', sont régulièrement attestés dans la branche yaay. J. R. Chamberlain (1991), à qui ces problèmes n'ont pas échappé, en a conclu un peu hâtivement à propos du tay maen que cette langue devait être classée dans le *northern tai*. Il faut objecter que, mis à part une courte liste de mots, le vocabulaire du Tay Yo relève bien de la branche thai selon des correspondances régulières. L'évolution de la fricative vélaire *x >h, commune au Tay Yo et aux langues yaay, n'est pas la preuve d'une parenté proche car la liste des mots attestant ce changement n'est pas la même dans les deux branches. Toutefois, le vocabulaire atypique contenu dans le Tay Yo pose un réel problème qu'il faut tenter d'élucider. Récemment, Weera Ostapirat (1998) a mis en évidence dans le dialecte chinois de Jízhào, sur la côte sud-ouest du Guangdong, une strate de vocabulaire apparentée au tai en général et plus particulièrement au bê de Hainan. Parmi les dix-sept mots qui nous sont donnés, on relève (notations de l'auteur) vi^{31} (A2) 'feu', nam^{11} (C2) 'eau', man^{31} (A2) 'il, elle', et surtout ky^{11} (C2) 'manger', forme que l'on ne peut s'empêcher de comparer au Tay Yo kiː^{55} (A2) en dépit des différences de voyelle et de ton. Il est vraisemblable que ce substrat tai-bê du dialecte chinois de Jízhào est la survivance d'une langue disparue qui était le chaînon reliant les langues thai-yaay du Guanxi et le bê de Hainan. La situation géographique de Jízhào corrobore tout à fait cette vue.

Comment dans ce cas expliquer la présence d'une strate similaire dans le Tay Yo dont la localisation actuelle ne s'insère pas dans le continuum géographique qui relie la région des langues thai-yaay et celle du bê? L'hypothèse d'une ancienne répartition de la branche yaay (*northern tai*) sur une zone allant du Guizhou au Thanh Hòa et au Nghệ An, a été avancée par Chamberlain (1991: 120). Cette hypothèse est recevable, mais elle présente l'inconvénient d'escamoter le berceau des langues viet-muong pourtant bien ancré dans le nord du Vietnam. Je pense, quant à moi, qu'il s'agit plutôt d'un ancien déplacement de population, comme il y en a eu beaucoup à l'époque de la domination chinoise, dans le but d'installer des populations fidèles pour mieux contrôler le pays. Par la suite, cette langue déplacée aurait été recouverte par la langue d'une partie des Thai venus du Muong Theng en donnant naissance à ce qui devait devenir le Tay Yo (et le tay muong), ne laissant subsister qu'un substrat réduit. L'autre partie de cette expansion des Thai aurait donné les Tay Daeng actuels.

8.6. TAY MUONG

Le tay muong, le Tay Yo et le tay maen peuvent être considérés comme des sous dialectes d'une même langue. Le tay muong se différencie cependant du Tay Yo par une influence moindre de la prononciation du vietnamien, et surtout par une influence du lao, aussi bien dans le vocabulaire que dans certains changements phonétiques. On ne dispose d'aucune publication ni de donnée sur le dialecte tay muong, sinon quelques mots inclus dans le dictionnaire *Laotien-Français* du Père Guignard (1912). Nos informateurs ont été: MM. Lô Văn Mai Liễu, Lô Văn Thoại et Lô Văn Bình, tous des environs de Hòa Bình, Tương Dương (Nghệ An).

8.6.1. Système consonantique

```
      initiales                    finales
pʰ    tʰ        kʰ
p     t     c   k    ʔ           p     t   k
b     d
m     n     ɲ   ŋ               m     n   ŋ
f     s              h
v     j                          w     j
      l
```

Le système consonantique est fondamentalement le même que celui du tay yo, l'influence du viet en moins. L'évolution des fricative vélaires du proto thai y est la même: *x >h et *ɣ >k. Le tay muong, sous l'influence du lao, se différencie cependant du Tay Yo par le changement irrégulier *ɟ >s/c (en Tay Yo *ɟ >c) qui interfère avec la confusion *z >s.

proto thai		lao	tay muong	tay yo	
*ɟaːŋᶜ	C2	saːŋ	s/caːŋ	caːŋ	'éléphant'
*ɟiːᴮ	B2	sɨː	s/ciː	ciː	'nom'
*ɟaːjᴬ	A2	saːj	s/caːj	caːj	'homme'
*zaːjᴬ	A2	saːj	saːj	saːj	'sable'
*ziːᶜ	C2	sɨː	sɨː	sɨː	'acheter'
*ziːᴮ	B2	sɨː	sɨː	sɨː	'droit'

Les nombreux emprunts au lao ont parfois créé des doublets, paires de mots issus d'un même étymon.

proto thai		tay muong	emprunt lao
*ɓlɨanᴬ	A1	bɨan 'lune'	dɨan 'mois'
*xɔːjᶜ	C1	hɔːj 'serf, vassal'	kʰɔːj 'je, moi (poli)'

8.6.2. Système vocalique

```
iː   /   i    ɨː   /   ɨ    uː   /   u
eː   /   e    əː   /   ə    oː   /   o
ɛː                          ɔː
ia            ɨa            ua
              aː       a
```

Le système vocalique est fondamentalement le même que celui du tay yo. Seule particularité, partagée avec le tay maen, les diphtongues se sont simplifiées devant les semi voyelles finales.

	tay yo	tay muong	
A1	hiaw	hɛːw	'vert'
B1	niaw	neːw	'(riz) glutineux'
C1	ʔɨaj	ʔəːj	'soeur aînée'
C1	kuaj	koːj	'banane'

8.6.3. Système tonal

	A	B	C	DL	DS
1	[¹³]		[³³ʔ]		[⁵⁵]
2	[⁵⁵]	[³¹]	[⁵³]	[¹¹]	[¹¹]

FIGURE 8.6.3-1: TONS DU TAY MUONG (Tương Dương, Nghệ An)

En plus de la confusion de DL1 avec DL2, on note la confusion de B1 avec B2. Ce système semble être également celui du tay maen bien que ce dialecte soit plus proche du Tay Yo par l'évolution du consonantisme initial.

8.6.4. Texte

Nous manquons de données consistantes sur la syntaxe du tay muong. Nous donnons ci-dessous la transcription et la traduction d'un texte manuscrit en écriture *Lai Pao*, détaillant une opération de restitution de terre communale.

tiaŋ¹³   diaŋ¹³   fu:³¹   ho:j³¹   ŋian³³   vian⁵³   ŋa:⁵⁵   mi:⁵⁵   soŋ³¹

Tương   Dương   arrond.   Hội   Nguyên   district   Nga   Mi   canton

Arrondissement de Tương Dương, district de Hội Nguyên, canton de Nga Mi, ...

ŋa:⁵⁵   mi:⁵⁵   sa:³¹   │   kʰɔ:j³³   ʔoŋ¹³ li:⁵³

Nga   Mi   commune   │   moi   chef

... commune de Nga Mi. Je soussigné [l'ancien] chef, ...

mi:⁵⁵   tə:⁵⁵   ni:⁵³   hə:³³   ʔɛ:ŋ¹³   tu:n⁵⁵   dɔ:³¹   │

avoir   papier   ce   pour   monsieur   Tun   là

... j'ai ce document [contrat] que je restitue à monsieur Tun.

tɛ:³¹ kɔ:n¹³ han³³   ha:ŋ⁵⁵ sa:³¹   kɔ:³¹   kəm⁵⁵   mɛ:ŋ³¹   din¹³   nam⁵³   ha:ŋ³¹

autrefois   conseil   #   céder   parcelle   terre   Năm   Hạng

Autrefois, le conseil communal a cédé en location la parcelle de terre Năm Hạng ...

hə:³³   ʔɛ:ŋ¹³   soŋ³³   ko:¹³   mi:⁵⁵   sa:m¹³   nɛ:n³³   │

pour   monsieur   Sông   Cô   avoir   3   barre   │

... à monsieur Sông Cô pour [le prix de] trois barres [d'argent].

ma:⁵⁵ hɔ:t¹¹   tiaj³³   ŋa:⁵⁵   haw⁵⁵   kɨaŋ⁵⁵   ciŋ³¹ ma:⁵⁵   kəm⁵⁵

arriver   à   époque (?)   Cương   à présent   céder

Arrivé à la génération de Cương [fils de Sông Cô]', alors, [Cương] a mis en gage ...

hə:³³   kʰɔ:j³³   mi:⁵⁵   ŋən⁵⁵   sɔ:ŋ¹³   nɛ:n³³   │ ma:⁵⁵   ʔə:n¹³ ni:⁵³

à   moi   avoir   argent   2   barre   │ arriver   aujourd'hui

...chez moi [cette terre] pour deux barres [d'argent].   Aujourd'hui, ...

kʰɔ:j³³   kɔ:³¹   kʰon³³   bɔ:³¹   mi:⁵⁵   ʔan¹³ lə:⁵⁵   tiaw¹³   │

je   #   difficulté   nég.   avoir   quoi   dépenser   │

... j'ai des difficultés [je manque d'argent], je n'ai plus rien à dépenser.

kʰɔ:j³³   ciŋ³¹   daj³³   kəm⁵⁵   hə:³³   ʔɛ:ŋ¹³   tu:n⁵⁵

je   alors   gagner   gage   à   monsieur   Tun

Alors, je reprends à Monsieur Tun [du conseil] ...

mi:⁵⁵	ŋən⁵⁵	sɔːŋ¹³	nɛːn³³	ciŋ³¹ daj³³	mi:⁵⁵	tə:⁵⁵	ni:⁵³
avoir	argent	2	barre	conséquence	avoir	document	ce

... deux barres [d'argent].   *En conséquence, par ce document, ...*

ja:w¹³	sa:k¹¹	din¹³	kaw³¹	hə:³³	ŋa:j⁵⁵	
confier	abornement	terre	ancien	pour	lui	

... je lui restitue [le contrat de] l'ancien abornement.

mɨa³¹ na:³³	ba:n³³ mɨaŋ⁵⁵	cuak¹¹	daj³³	ɲa:m⁵⁵	lə:⁵⁵
désormais	communauté	reprendre	gagner	temps	quel

A l'avenir, la communauté pourra reprendre [ce terrain], n'importe quand ...

hə:³³	ma:⁵⁵	cuak¹¹	nam⁵⁵	kʰɔ:j³³	
pour	venir	reprendre	avec	moi	

... et lever le gage avec moi [qui me lie au Conseil].

kʰɔ:j³³	ciŋ³¹	cuak¹¹	nam⁵⁵	ʔɛ:ŋ¹³	tu:n⁵⁵
je	alors	rendre	par	monsieur	*Tun*

Je restituerai [la terre], par [l'entremise de] Monsieur Tun ...

hə:³³	ba:n³³	hə:³³	mɨaŋ⁵⁵	ti:¹³	tə:⁵⁵	ja:w¹³
à	village	à	région	notifier	document	confier

au conseil [village et région]'.   *C'est notifié dans ce procès-verbal.*

tʰɛ:ŋ⁵⁵	tʰa:j¹¹	tʰəp¹¹	nian¹³	tʰət⁵⁵	ŋwa:t¹¹	tʰə:³³	kɨw¹³	ɲət¹¹
Thành	Thái	10	année	7	mois	-ième	9	jour

Dixième année, septième mois, neuvième jour [du règne de] Thành Thái (1899).

(*Traduit par M. Lô Văn Mai Liễu avec la participation du Professeur Trần Trí Dõi et de Mme Võ Thị Thường*)

8.6.5. Texte

Nous manquons de données consistantes sur la syntaxe du tay muong. Nous donnons ci-dessous la transcription et la traduction d'un texte manuscrit en écriture *Lai Pao*, détaillant une opération de restitution de terre communale.

tɨaŋ¹³	dɨaŋ¹³	fu:³¹	ho:j³¹	ŋian³³	vian⁵³	ŋa:⁵⁵	mi:⁵⁵	soŋ³¹
Tương Dương		arrond.	Hội Nguyên		district	Nga Mi		canton

Arrondissement de Tương Dương, district de Hội Nguyên, canton de Nga Mi,

ŋa:⁵⁵ mi:⁵⁵	sa:³¹	/	kʰɔ:j³³	ʔoŋ¹³ li:⁵³	mi:⁵⁵	tə:⁵⁵	ni:⁵³	hə:³³
Nga Mi	commune	/	moi	chef	avoir	document	ce	pour

commune de Nga Mi. Je soussigné [l'ancien] chef, je restitue ce document [contrat] à

ʔɛ:ŋ¹³	tu:n⁵⁵	dɔ:³¹	/	te:³¹ kɔ:n¹³ han³³	ha:ŋ⁵⁵ sa:³¹	kɔ:³¹	kəm⁵⁵	mɛ:ŋ³¹
monsieur	Tun	là	/	autrefois	conseil	#	céder	parcelle

Monsieur Tun. Autrefois,   *le Conseil Communal a cédé en location la parcelle de*

din¹³   nam⁵³ ha:ŋ³¹   hə:³³   ʔɛ:ŋ¹³   soŋ³³ ko:¹³   mi:⁵⁵   sa:m¹³   nɛ:n³³   /
terre   Nặm Hạng   pour   monsieur   Sông Cô   avoir   3   barre   /
terre [dite] Nặm Hạng à Monsieur Sông Cô pour [le prix de] trois barres [d'argent].

ma:⁵⁵ hɔ:t¹¹   tɨaj³³   ɲa:⁵⁵ haw⁵⁵   kɨaŋ⁵⁵   ciŋ³¹ ma:⁵⁵   kəm⁵⁵
arriver   à   époque (?)   Cương   à présent   céder
Arrivé à la génération de Cương [fils de Sông Cô], alors   [Cương] a mis en gage

hə:³³   kʰɔ:j³³   mi:⁵⁵   ŋən⁵⁵   sɔ:ŋ¹³   nɛ:n³³   /   ma:⁵⁵   ʔə:n¹³ ni:⁵³
à   moi   avoir   argent   2   barre   /   arriver   aujourd'hui
chez moi [cette terre] pour deux barres [d'argent]. Aujourd'hui,

kʰɔ:j³³   kɔ:³¹   kʰon³³   bɔ:³¹   mi:⁵⁵   ʔan¹³ lə:⁵⁵   tiaw¹³   /
je   #   difficulté   NÉG   avoir   quoi   dépenser   /
j'ai des difficultés [je manque d'argent], je n'ai plus rien à dépenser.

kʰɔ:j³³   ciŋ³¹   daj³³   kəm⁵⁵   hə:³³   ʔɛ:ŋ¹³   tu:n⁵⁵   mi:⁵⁵   ŋən⁵⁵
je   alors   gagner   gage   à   monsieur   Tun   avoir   argent
Alors, je reprends à Monsieur Tun [du Conseil] le prix [sous forme] de

sɔ:ŋ¹³   nɛ:n³³   /   ciŋ³¹ daj³³   mi:⁵⁵   tɔ:⁵⁵   ni:⁵³   ja:w¹³   sa:k¹¹
2   barre   /   conséquence   avoir   document   ce   confier   abornement
deux barres. En conséquence, par ce document, je lui restitue [le contrat de]

din¹³   kaw³¹   hə:³³   ŋaj⁵⁵   /   mɨa³¹ na:³³   ba:n³³ mɨaŋ⁵⁵   cuak¹¹
terre   ancien   pour   lui   /   désormais   communauté   reprendre
l'ancien abornement.   A l'avenir, la communauté pourra reprendre [ce terrain]

daj³³   ɲa:m⁵⁵   lə:⁵⁵   hə:³³   ma:⁵⁵   cuak¹¹   nam⁵⁵   kʰɔ:j³³   /
gagner   temps   quel   pour   venir   reprendre   avec   moi   /
n'importe quand   et lever le gage avec moi   [qui me lie au Conseil].

kʰɔ:j³³   ciŋ³¹   cuak¹¹   nam⁵⁵   ʔɛ:ŋ¹³   tu:n⁵⁵   hə:³³   ba:n³³   hə:³³   mɨaŋ⁵⁵ /
je   alors   rendre   par   monsieur   Tun   à   village   à   région   /
Je restituerai [la terre] par [l'entremise de] M. Tun au Conseil [village et région].

ti:¹³   tɔ:⁵⁵   ja:w¹³   /
notifier   document   confier   /
C'est notifié dans ce document [procès-verbal].

tʰɛ:ŋ⁵⁵   tʰa:j¹¹   tʰəp¹¹   nian¹³   tʰɔt⁵⁵   ŋwa:t¹¹   tʰɔ:³³   ki:w¹³   ɲɔt¹¹   /
Thành   Thái   10   année   7   mois   -ième   9   jour   /
Dixième année, septième mois, neuvième jour [du règne de] Thành Thái (1899).

(Traduit par M. Lô Văn Mai Liễu avec la participation du Professeur Trần Trí Dõi et de Mme Võ Thị Thường)

8.7. LE PROTO THAI ET LES DIALECTES

Résumons, à l'aide d'exemples précis, les évolutions des initiales du proto thai (pʰr- pʰ- 6l- ɟ-
x- ɣ- g- kʰr- et gr-) responsables des différences dialectales, en comparaison avec les
évolutions uniformes de quelques initiales significatives (f- ɓ- ɗ- c- s- z- et kʰ).
    Abréviations: sm (siamois); t. nr (tay noir); t. bl (tay blanc); t. dg (tay daeng); t. yo (tay
yo); t. mg (tay muong).

*PT		sm	lao	t. nr	t. bl	t. dg	t. yo	t. mg	
pʰriː^A	A1	pʰ-	pʰ-	f-	pʰ-	fiː	pʰiː	pʰiː	esprit
pʰuː^C	C1	pʰ-	pʰ-	f-	pʰ-	fuː	pʰuː	pʰuː	mâle
faː^A	A1	f-	f-	f-	f-	faː	faː	faː	cloison
ɓəː^A	A1	b-	b-	b-	b-	bəː	bəː	bəː	feuille
ɗaŋ^A	A1	d-	d-	d-	d-	daŋ	daŋ	daŋ	nez
6lɔːk	A1	d-	d-	b-	b-	bɔːk	bɔːk	bɔːk	fleur
cəː^A	A1	c-	c-	c-	c-	cəː	cəː	cəː	coeur
ɟaːŋ^C	C2	cʰ-	s-	c-	c-	caːŋ	caːŋ	s/caːŋ	éléphant
saːk	DL1	s-	s-	s-	s-	saːk	saːk	saːk	pilon
ziː ^C	C2	s-	s-	s-	s-	siː	siː	siː	acheter
xɛːn^A	A1	kʰ-	kʰ-	kʰ-	x-	kʰɛːn	hɛːn	hɛːn	bras
kʰaw ^C	C1	kʰ-	kʰ-	kʰ-	kʰ-	kʰaw	kʰaw	kʰaw	riz
ɣam^A	A2	kʰ-	kʰ-	k-	x-	kʰam	kam	kam	or
gem^A	A2	kʰ-	kʰ-	k-	k-	kem	kem	kem	salé
kʰrajᴮ	B1	kʰ-	kʰ-	s-	cʰ-	saj	saj	saj	oeuf
grok	DS2	kʰr-	kʰ-	c-	c-	cok	cok	sok	mortier

RÉFÉRENCES BIBLIOGRAPHIQUES

Baccam Don & als (1989) *Tai Dam-English, English-Tai Dam Vocabulary Book*, Summer
    Institute of Linguistics. [tay noir]
Chamberlain, James R. (1991) 'Mène: A Tai Dialect Originally Spoken in Nghê An (Nghê
    Tinh), Vietnam', *The Journal of the Siam Society* 79.2.
Điêu Chính Nhìm & Jean Donaldson (1970) *Tai-Vietnamese-English Vocabulary*, Saigon,
    Department of Education. [tay blanc]
Diller, Anthony V. N. (1988) 'Consonant Mergers and Inscription One', *The Journal of the
    Siam Society* 76: 161-77. Repris dans J. R. Chamberlain (ed.) (1991) *The Ramkhamhaeng
    Controversy: Collected Papers*, Bangkok: The Siam Society.
Donaldson, Jean & Jerold A. Edmondson (1997) 'A Preliminary Examination of Tay Tac',
    Jerold A. Edmondson and David B. Solnit (eds) *Comparative Kadai: The Tai Branch*, The
    Summer Institute of Linguistics and the University of Texas at Arlington, 235-266.
Edmondson, Jerold A. & David B. Solnit (eds) (1997) *Comparative Kadai: The Tai Branch*,
    The Summer Institute of Linguistics and the University of Texas at Arlington.
Fénard, Père Emmanuel (vers 1920) 'Lexique Tay-Français', manuscrit. [tay daeng]
Ferlus, Michel (1990) 'Remarques sur le Consonantisme du Proto Thai-yay', paper distributed
    for circulation at the 23rd International Conference on Sino-Tibetan Languages and
    Linguistics, University of Texas at Arlington, October 5-7.
— (1993) 'Phonétique et écriture du Tai de Qui Châu (Vietnam)', *Cahiers de Linguistique
    Asie Orientale* 22.1: 87-106.

— (1994) 'L'évolution des fricatives vélaires *x et *γ dans les langues Thai', *Cahiers de Linguistique Asie Orientale* 23 (Hommages à Alexis Rygaloff): 129-139.

— (1999) 'Les dialectes et les écritures des Tai (Thai) du Nghệ An (Vietnam)', *Treizièmes Journées de Linguistique d'Asie Orientale*, Paris (EHESS-CNRS), 10-11 juin.

Gedney, William (1964) 'A Comparative Sketch of White, Black and Red Thai', *The Social Science Review*, special number: 1-47, Bangkok. Repris dans *Selected Papers on comparative Tai Studies*, 1989: 415-62.

— (1989) *Selected Papers on Comparative Tai Studies* (Robert J. Bickner et als eds), Michigan Papers on south and southeast asia n° 29, University of Michigan.

Guignard, Père Théodore (1912) *Dictionnaire Laotien-Français*, Hong Kong: Imprimerie de Nazareth.

Haudricourt, André G. (1948) 'Les Phonèmes et le Vocabulaire du Thai Commun', *Journal Asiatique* 236: 197-238. Repris dans (1972) *Problèmes de Phonologie diachronique*, 85-118.

— (1952) 'Les Occlusives Uvulaires en Thai', *Bulletin de la Société de Linguistique de Paris* 48: 86-9.

— (1961) 'Bipartition et tripartition des systèmes de tons dans quelques langues d'Extrême-Orient', *Bulletin de la Société de Linguistique de Paris* 56.1: 163-80. Traduit en anglais et annoté par Christopher Court dans (1972) *Tai Phonetics and Phonology*, eds. Jimmy Harris & Richard B. Noss, Central Institute of English Language, Office of State Universities, Bangkok: Prachandra Press, 58-86.

— (1972) *Problèmes de Phonologie Diachronique*, Paris: SELAF.

Li, Fang-Kuei (1977) *A Handbook of Comparative Tai*, The University Press of Hawaii.

— (1989) 'Proto Tai *kh and *x', in J. H. Davidson (ed.) *South-East Asian Linguistic Studies, Essays in Honour of Eugénie J. A. Henderson*, London, SOAS, 143-46.

Louppe, Albert (1934) *Muongs de Cua-Rao*, Hanoi: Imprimerie d'Extrême-Orient.

Luo, Yongxian (1997) *The Subgroup Structure of the Tai Languages: A Historical-comparative Study*, Journal of Chinese Linguistics Monograph Series N° 12.

Robert, R. (1941) *Notes sur les Tay Dèng de Lang Chánh (Thanh-Hoá, Annam)*. Institut Indochinois pour l'Etude de L'Homme, n° 1, Hanoi: Imprimerie d'Extrême-Orient.

Vi Văn An (1996) 'Supplementary Material about the Names and the History of Settlement of the Tai Groups in the Region of Highway N° 7: Province Nghe An (Central Vietnam)', *Tai Culture* 1.1: 30-40.

Weera Ostapirat (1998) 'A Mainland Bê Language?', *Journal of Chinese Linguistics* 26.2: 338-44.

Du proto thai aux dialectes actuels: évolution des initiales

*PT	siam	lao	t. nr	t. bl	t. dg	tay yo	t. mg
pʰ	pʰ	pʰ	f	pʰ	f	pʰ	pʰ
p	p	p	p	p	p	p	p
b	pʰ	pʰ	p	p	p	p	p
tʰ	tʰ	tʰ	tʰ	tʰ	tʰ	tʰ	tʰ
t	t	t	t	t	t	t	t
d	tʰ	tʰ	t	t	t	t	t
c	c	c	c	c	c	c	c
ɟ	cʰ	s	c	c	c	c	s/c
kʰ	kʰ	kʰ	kʰ	kʰ	kʰ	kʰ	kʰ
k	k	k	k	k	k	k	k
g	kʰ	kʰ	k	k	k	k	k
ʔ	ʔ	ʔ	ʔ	ʔ	ʔ	ʔ	ʔ
ɓ	b	b	b	b	b	b	b
ɗ	d	d	d	d	d	d	d
ʔj	j	j	j	j	j	z	j
f	f	f	f	f	f	f	f
v	f	f	f	f	f	f	f
s	s	s	s	s	s	s	s
z	s	s	s	s	s	s	s
x	kʰ	kʰ	kʰ	x	kʰ	h	h
ɣ	kʰ	kʰ	k	x	kʰ	k	k
h	h	h	h	h	h	h	h
m	m	m	m	m	m	m	m
ʰm	m	m	m	m	m	m	m
n	n	n	n	n	n	n	n
ʰn	n	n	h	n	n	n	n
ɲ	j	ɲ	ɲ	ɲ	ɲ/j	ɲ	ɲ
ʰɲ	j	ɲ	ɲ	ɲ	ɲ/j	ɲ	ɲ
ŋ	ŋ	ŋ	ŋ	ŋ	ŋ	ŋ	ŋ
ʰŋ	h	ŋ/h	h	h	h	h	h
w	w	v	v	v	v	v	v
ʰw	w	v	v	v	v	v	v
j	j	ɲ	j	j	j	ɲ	ɲ
r	r	h	h	h	h	h	h
ʰr	h	h	h	h	h	h	h
l	l	l	l	l	l	l	l
ʰl	l	l	l	l	l	l	l
pʰr	pʰ	pʰ	f	pʰ	f	pʰ	pʰ
kʰr	kʰ	kʰ	s	cʰ	s	s	s
br	pʰr	pʰ	p	p	p	p	p
gr	kʰr	kʰ	c	c	c	s	c
pl	pl	p	p	p	p	p	p
kl	kl	k	k	k	k	k	k
ɓl	d	d	b	b	b	b	b
ml	ml/l	m	m	m	m	m	m

CHAPTER NINE

ZHUANG

Yongxian Luo

9.1. INTRODUCTION

9.1.1. Geographic setting

Zhuang is the language of the largest minority group in the People's Republic of China, with approximately 18 million speakers.[1] The majority of Zhuang speakers live in Guangxi in Southern China, between 20° 54' and 26° 20' north latitude on the southeastern corner of the Yunnan-Guizhou Plateau. A small number of them are scattered in adjacent areas of Guangdong, Hunan, Guizhou and Yunnan provinces (see Map 9.1.2-1). The name Zhuang is not an indigenous cover term, but more of an administrative term, from which the province of Guangxi, the administrative area of Zhuang, acquired its name – Guangxi Zhuang Autonomous Region. Although Zhuang speakers spread all over Guangxi, the majority of them concentrate in four prefectures: Nanning, Baise, Hechi and Liuzhou along the Xi River system. A passage to Southeast Asia, the Zhuang area is also inhabited by a number of tribal groups such as the Kam, Sui, Mulao and Maonan, as well as the Miao, Yao, Lakkja, along with Hakka, Yue and many varieties of the local Chinese.

9.1.2. Language and its speakers

Zhuang is an important member of the Tai language family, which is divided into three branches – Northern, Central and Southwestern, according to a generally accepted classification (Li 1977; see also the editor's Introduction to this volume). Chinese linguists divide Zhuang into two dialect groups: Northern and Southern, with the You (Yu) River as the diaglossal line. As the name indicates, Northern Zhuang is located on the north side of the river, north of the provincial capital city Nanning; and Southern Zhuang, the south side, in areas south of Nanning. The two groups belong to different branches of the Tai family under Li's scheme. Northern Zhuang is in the Northern Branch, while Southern Zhuang, the Central Branch. Northern Zhuang makes up two-thirds of the entire Zhuang population.

The Zhuang are primarily lowland dwellers, who are traditionally an agricultural people. They grow rice in both plains and steep terraces and they raise livestock. They have a well-developed art and handicraft style. They are very musical, capable of composing impromptu verses in songs, to be sung in festivals or in courtships. They have a very rich oral literature. One of the most important pieces is the *Baeu-ro-do* epic song, which has been the subject of a detailed anthropological study (Holm 2004).

In religion, the Zhuang are basically animistic, with a strong belief in the power of spirits in nature. Witchcraft, shamanism, and ancestor-worship are practiced in the Zhuang area. Buddhism has not had much impact among the Zhuang, unlike in Southwestern Tai, such as the Dai of Sipsongpanna and Dehong. In comparison, Daoism and Confucianism have had

---

1   The exact figure of Zhuang speakers is unknown. This figure is projected from a population growth of 16.7% for minority people in China between 1990 and 2000, according to the latest population census. In the 1990 government census, Zhuang population was 15.5 million.

more success. Christian missionaries were present in Zhuang areas in the late 19th century, but their impact was minimal.

MAP 9.1.2-1: ZHUANG SPEAKING AREA

9.1.3. Change and variations

It would be correct to assume that linguistically the Zhuang are a homogenous group. However, there is a high degree of variations in the phonological and grammatical structures between Northern and Southern Zhuang. One of the most striking differences between Northern and Southern Zhuang is that Northern Zhuang lacks aspirated stops, while Southern Zhuang possesses them. Also, over 60 distinct tonal systems have been reported, ranging from 5 to 11 tones among individual dialects. These may roughly fall under 13 regional groupings (Zhang et al 1999: 29-31).

Lexical and grammatical variations are common. Northern and Southern Zhuang each possess a set of vocabulary items that are foreign to the other group. For example, the word for 'moon' is *ʔdɯan¹* in Northern Zhuang, *ha:i¹* in Southern Zhuang. 'Tiger' is *kuk⁷* in Northern Zhuang, and *sə¹* in Southern Zhuang. In grammar, for descriptive clauses, Northern Zhuang uses the construction N + Clause + Deictics, while in Southern Zhuang, the same clause is structured as N + Relative pronoun + Clause + Deictics. Such differences have caused problems for mutual intelligibility between speakers of the Northern and Southern groups. Edmondson (1993) has offered a perceptive discussion of change and variations in Zhuang.

In terms of mutual intelligibility, Northern Zhuang and Buyi are much closer. In fact it would be linguistically more appropriate to treat Northern Zhuang and the Buyi as a dialect continuum. Indeed the division of Northern Zhuang and Buyi is entirely a matter of administration.

9.1.4. Autonyms and ethonyms

If ethnonyms are important to understand a particular speech community, the name Zhuang does not reflect a wide range of self-address terms used by different groups of Zhuang speakers. Over a dozen such terms have been recorded (Zhang et al. 1999: 3-4, 318). Some of them are toponyms referring to the locality. Others carry ethnographic information.

Of the common autonyms for Zhuang, the term pu^6 $tsu:\eta^5$ ('person-Zhuang') appears to be used mainly by Northern Zhuang speakers. Another common Zhuang self-reference term is pu^6 $\jmath ai^6$, which is used by those who live further north near Guizhou.[2] This term is also shared by the Buyi (Bouyei) people as self-designation. Southern Zhuang speakers generally call themselves pu^6 to^4 (or tho^4 in some dialects) or pu^6 $no\eta^4$ who are clearly the same or closely related to the Tho and the Nung in Vietnam. A small number of speakers in the County of Wenshan and Malipo in southeastern Yunnan refer to themselves as pu^6 dai^4 or pu^6 $thai^4$.

9.1.5. Early history

Chinese historical records on Zhuang are curiously fragmented. Little systematic account is available in standard historical books on the settlement and movement of the Zhuang people. In view of the reconstructed materials, Zhuang ancestors are believed to have inhabited southern China since ancient times. They are generally thought to be a member of Baiyue or A Hundred Yue, which comprises Luoyue, Dongyue, Dianyue, Nanyue, Shan, Xi'ou, Yelang, among others. All these are designations for the various groups of Yue (Viet) people who spread over a vast territory in what is now Fujian, Zhejiang, Hunan, Guangdong, Guangxi, Guizhou, and Yunnan provinces. The Yue must include some varieties of Han Chinese such as Cantonese as well as the non-Han peoples of the south.

Proto-Zhuang (Tai) is estimated to have a time depth of about 2500 years old, according to authorities in the field (Matisoff 1991, Wyatt 1984). The Zhuang must have had contact with the Han Chinese quite early in history, particularly after Emporor Qin Shihuang conquered Lingnan (modern Guangdong and Guangxi) in 204 BC. Yet the term Zhuang did not appear in Chinese sources until the Song dynasty (960 – 1280 AD).[3]

Some important events unfolded during this time. Nong Zhigao, a Zhuang hero, led a fierce attack against the Song rulers in 1052 from a base in Guangyuan in what is now Jingxi and surrounding areas in Guangxi. The revolt ended in Nong Zhigao's total defeat in 1055. Then followed a period of relative stability in Yuan and Ming times as the Yuan and Ming rulers adopted a policy of employing local headmen to be in charge of local affairs. This system of *tusi* or local chieftain system of administration was continued by the Central court through to the beginning of the Manchu or Qing era (early 17th century).

A new frontier policy was introduced soon after the Qing rulers took power. The policy, known as *gai tu gui liu*, was aiming to bring the autonomous chieftaincies into the regular bureaucratic system. *Gai tu gui liu* was often implemented through military repression. By the late 18th century, the majority of local chieftains were replaced by Han officials. This was the period when there were massive migration movements of Han Chinese into the area. Luo (1996: 34-65) has synthesized Chinese textual evidence that are pertinent to the issues

---

2   A small number of these speakers have moved from Guizhou to north Vietnam, which has been the subject of a study by Gedney (1991).

3   The current Chinese character for Zhuang, literally meaning 'robust', was adopted in 1958 at the suggestion of the late Premier Zhou Enlai when the Guangxi Zhuang Autonomous Region was founded, possibly because of the somewhat derogatory meaning of the original character, 'house boy'.

discussed here. Barlow (2001) is perhaps the most comprehensive account of Zhuang history from ancient to modern times, although some of his arguments need to be substantiated or verified.

9.1.6. Language contact, convergence and divergence, Chinese influence

The linguistic situation in Zhuang area is complex. As a 'language corridor' (Edmondson and Li 1996), Guangxi is an ideal laboratory for linguistic investigation in language contact, language convergence and divergence, being home to over a dozen languages from different language stocks. Zhuang is found to share a number of typological similarities with neighbouring languages in being tonal, basically monosyllabic, and having an SVO order. But what did ancient Zhuang look like? Did Zhuang inherit its tones from its parent language? If not, how did it acquire them? Questions of this kind still remain to be answered.

It seems reasonable to assume that before Qin Shihuang's southern expansion (q.v), Guangxi was predominantly inhabited by non-Han peoples, among whom were the Zhuang. Intermarriages must have taken place between local women and Han soldiers who settled down in the area, resulting in language mixing in this region. The language of Qin's army must have left its traces in Pinghua, a kind of local Chinese dialect unique to Guangxi area which possess a number of archaic features of Old Chinese. Pinghua has characteristically absorbed many Zhuang elements and vice versa.

Migration movements of the Han people into Zhuang areas at different times in history had profound impact on Zhuang language and culture. They contributed to different layers of loans into Zhuang. Some of these loans provide valuable clues for the reconstruction of Old Chinese (Bodman 1980). Others raise questions. Attempts have been made to sort out the connections (Zhang 1988, Lan 1999, 2001), but opinions are divided on the directions of borrowing (Zhang 1988, Lan 2001).

Despite close contact with the local Chinese, the Zhuang still retain many distinct traditions and cultural traits of their own. In Zhuang areas, the Zhuang language is alive and well. It seems premature to assume that the Zhuang have been heavily Sinicized.

9.1.7. Zhuang writing

One thing that distinguishes Zhuang from other dialects of the Tai family is its unique writing system. Anthropologists, ethnographers, and historians working in Southern China would not fail to notice a type of Chinese-based writing system used by the Zhuang people in Guangxi and the surrounding regions. This kind of writing system is used by shamen or village headmen to record songs, for account keeping, calendrical reckonings, and other important things and events. Fan Chengda, a scholar official and a travellor in the Song dynasty (date), was credited with the discovery of this type of writing (Fan 1175), which was already nearly 300 years older than the Thai writing system. One can assume that such a writing system must have existed before Fan's times. For example, *Yupian*, a dictionary compiled shortly after Han times, contains several dozen words like 鸭, 'duck'. This is obviously a Zhuang (Tai) word, which is not found in any Chinese dialect. This character is now still used in Zhuang area. Mention must also be made of a little song, *Yue Ren Ge*, included in *Shuo Yuan* by Liu Xiang of the Han dynasty. The song was decyphered by a Zhuang linguist Wei Qingwen, and by Zhengzhang (1991), who believed it to be of Zhuang (Tai) origin, recorded in Chinese characters. In a way, this could be seen as early attempts at Zhuang writing.

The Chinese character-based Zhuang writing was modeled on principles of the Chinese writing system, where each character consists of two components: a meaning part and a phonetic part. The meaning part often takes the form of radicals while the phonetic part is represented by certain recurrent and phonetically stable graphs. In some cases, two meaning components are put together to form a character, with no clue of phonetic readings at all, as in the case of 不+长, 'short', whose meaning resides primarily in the two composite semantic elements, 'not' and 'long', as neither of the two ideographs was employed to signal any phonetic content. Such items are only decypherable to trained scholars or shamen who knew both Zhuang and Chinese well. They would not be understood by outsiders. The chapter by David Holm in this volume treats this issue in greater detail.

In the late 1950s, after the founding of the People's Republic of China, a new Zhuang writing system was introduced using the Roman alphabets. The system was devised by Chinese linguists with the help from some Russian scholars. The Zhuang dialect of Wuming was taken as the norm for Standard Zhuang. It was promoted in Zhuang areas through to the early 1960s before the Cultural Revolution, with some success. The Romanised Zhuang writing system was reintroduced, with minor revisions, in the early 1980s. A number of dictionaries have been printed using this writing system.

9.2. PHONOLOGY

As mentioned in §9.1.3, substantial differences exist in the phonological systems of Northern and Southern Zhuang. In addition to the absence of aspirated stops in Northern Zhuang, and their presence in Southern Zhuang, Northern Zhuang has a group of /r/ sounds, represented as ɣ, r, ð, j and l according to dialects. These correspond to an array of forms in Southern Zhuang. The following examples illustrate this.

TABLE 9.2-1: NORTHERN ZHUANG /r/ AND THEIR SOUTHERN ZHUANG COUNTERPARTS

	Northern Zhuang				Southern Zhuang				
Gloss	Wu-ming	Nan-dan	Yishan	Du'an	Daxin	Ning-ming	Long-an	Debao	Guang-nan
'tail'	$\gamma i\partial\eta^1$	$ri\partial\eta^1$	$hj\mu\eta^1$	$r\mu\eta^1$	$ha{:}\eta^1$	$ha{:}\eta^1$	$th\mu{:}\eta^1$	$tha{:}\eta^1$	$tha{:}\eta^1$
'stone'	γin^1	jin^1	$hjin^1$	rin^1	hin	$th\partial n^1$	$thin^1$	$th\partial n^2$	$thin^1$
'fart'	γot^7	rat^7	$hjot^7$	$r\mu t^7$	$t\mu t^7$	$th\partial t^7$	$th\mu t^8$	tat^7	$t\eta t^7$
'water'	γam^6	ram^4	$hjam^6$	ram^6	nam^3	nam^6	nam^6	nom^6	nam^6
'ear'	$\gamma \mu^4$	ri^4	$hj\mu^4$	$r\mu^4$	hu^1	$khj\partial u^4$	$hl\mu^4$	$khjou^4$	$t\varphi hu^1$
'sieve'	$\gamma a\eta^1$	$ra\eta^1$	$hja\eta^1$	$ra\eta^1$	$s\mu\eta^1$	$khja\eta^1$	$hla\eta^1$	$khja\eta^1$	$t\varphi ha\eta^1$
'ear (of rice)'	$\gamma i\partial\eta^4$	$ji{:}\eta^1$	$hja{:}\eta^1$	$j\mu{:}\eta^1$	$\hbar u\eta^4$	$lu{:}\eta^4$	$hlu{:}\eta^4$	$ru{:}\eta^4$	$lu{:}\eta^4$
'nest'	$\gamma o{:}\eta^4$	$ro{:}\eta^4$	$hjo{:}\eta^4$	$ro{:}\eta^4$	$\hbar u{:}\eta^4$	$la\eta^4$	$hlo{:}\eta^4$	$ru{:}\eta^4$	Wenma $zu{:}\eta^4$
'to bark'	γau^2	rau^2	$hjau^2$	rau^5	hau^2	hau^2	$hlau^5$	hau^6	hau^2
'sesame'	γa^4	ra^4	hja^4	ra^4	ha^4	ηa^4	ηa^4	ηa^4	ηa^4

In Finals, Northern and Southern Zhuang also exhibit variations:

TABLE 9.2-2: SOME VARIATIONS IN RHYMES BETWEEN NORTHERN AND SOUTHERN ZHUANG

	Northern Zhuang				Southern Zhuang				
Gloss	Wu-ming	Nan-dan	Yishan	Du'an	Long-zhou	Ning-ming	Longan	Debao	Guang-nan
'bed bug'	$\gamma u\vartheta t^8$	$ri\vartheta t^8$	$hj u t^8$	$\gamma u t^8$	$l\vartheta t^8$	$li{:}t^8$	$hl u t^8$	$lu{:}t^{10}$	$l u t^8$
'bite'	hap^8	hap^8	hap^8	hap^8	$khup^7$	$kh u p^7$	hap^8	$kh\vartheta p^7$	$kh\vartheta p^7$
'house'	$\gamma a{:}n^4$	$ra{:}n^4$	$ra{:}n^4$	$ra{:}n^4$	$l\vartheta n^4$	$l u m^4$	$hla{:}n^4$	$ru{:}n^2$	$lo{:}n^2$
'long'	γai^4	rai^4	$hjai^4$	rai^4	$l i^4$	$l\vartheta i^4$	$hlai^4$	rei^4	li^4
'sleep'	nin^4	nin^4	nin^4	nin^4	$no{:}n^4$	$no{:}n^4$	nin^4	$no{:}n^4$	$n\vartheta{:}n^4$

In the Zhuang dialect of Wenshan, a southern Zhuang variety, final -p -t -k were dropped. A number of syllables with final nasals -m, -n, and -ŋ are also undergoing similar sound change, giving rise to the emergence of nasalized vowels.

TABLE 9.2-3: COMPARISON OF SOME WENSHAN ZHUANG AND WUMING ZHUANG FINALS

Gloss	'bedbug'	'bite'	'six'	'carry'	'fish bone'	'yam'	'skin'	'grand-child'	'three'
Wenshan	$lu\varepsilon^5$	$kh\varepsilon^4$	$tsha^4$	tha^2	$k\tilde{\varepsilon}^3$	$m\tilde{a}^4$	$n\tilde{\varepsilon}^1$	$l\tilde{a}^4$	$s\tilde{a}^4$
Wuming	$\gamma u\vartheta t^8$	hap^8	γok^7	$\gamma a{:}p^7$	$ka{:}\eta^3$	$ma{:}n^4$	$na\eta^1$	$la{:}n^1$	$\theta a{:}m^1$

Like the initials, tonal variations are noticeable. The tonal pitches of a number of dialects differ substantially from those of Wuming, the speech of Standard Zhuang. Table 9.2-4 contrasts the tones among six Zhuang dialects.[4]

TABLE 9.2-4: TONE CONTRAST IN SIX ZHUANG DIALECTS

GLOSS / PHONETICS	'dog' ma	'rice field' na	'grow' ma	'horse' ma	'soak' ma	'river' ta
Wuming	24	31	55	42	35	33
Sanjiang	55	121	54	24	33	11
Yangshuo	42	231	53	35	55	213
Daxin	55/53	21	13	44	42	33
Ningming	343	32	35	43	54	21
Jingxi	54	31	2323	13	45	214

Below we briefly describe the phonology of Fengshan Zhuang, the author's native dialect, which will be used for a grammatical sketch of Zhuang in the following sections.

---

4   The numerics in the box indicate the tonal pitch using Chao's 5-scale notation.

9.2.1. Fengshan Zhuang phonology

9.2.1.1. *Consonants*

Table 9.2.1.1-1 lists the nineteen segmental consonant phonemes in Fengshan Zhuang.

TABLE 9.2.1.1-1: FENGSHAN ZHUANG CONSONANTS

	Labial	Alveolar	Palatal	Velar	Glottal
Stops vls. unaspirated	p	t	ts	k	ʔ
Voiced	ʔb	ʔd	ʔj		
Nasals	m	n	ɲ	ŋ	
Fricative vls	f	θ	ç		h
Voiced	v (w)		j		
Lateral		l			

All 19 consonants may appear in initial position. Permited initial consonant clusters include labial pj, mj. Depending on methods of analysis, labialized tʷ, ʔdʷ, lʷ, çʷ, sʷ, tsʷ, jʷ, ɲʷ, kʷ, ŋʷ can be proposed. Only p, t, k, m, n, and ŋ can occur final position. No consonant clusters are permitted in final position.

9.2.1.2. *Vowels*

Table 9.2.1.2-1 lists the eight vowel phonemes in Fengshan.

TABLE 9.2.1.2-1: FENGSHAN ZHUANG VOWELS

	Front	Back unrounded	Back rounded
High	i	ɯ	u
Mid	e		o
Low	ɛ	a	ɔ

[a] is inherently long as [a:] when occurring in open syllables, as in pa^3 [pa:³], ma^6 [ma:⁶], ta^1 [ta:¹], ka^3 [ka:³]. There is no length contrast in this environment. However, there is a length contrast when [a] is followed by another element, as in [ai] vs. [a:i], [au] vs. [a:u], [am] vs. [a:m], [an] vs. [a:n], [at] vs. [a:t], [ak] vs. [a:k], [ap] vs. [a:p]. Short [a] is phonetically realized as [ɐ].

[o] is phonetically long as [o:], while [ɔ] is short. Since there is no length contrast for each of these phonemes, they are simply written as [o] and [ɔ]. The same holds for [e] (long) and [ɛ] (short).

All the eight vowels may occur as vocalic neclei, with an initial consonant, with a final consonant or with an initial and final consonant.

9.2.1.3. *Diphthongs and triphthongs*

There are 14 diphthongs: /ie/, /ɯa/, /ua/, /ua:/, /a:i/, /ai/, /oi/, /ui/, /əi/, /a:u/, /au/, /eu/, /ɛu/, /iu/, along with 4 triphthongs: /ieu/, /ua:i/, /uai/, /ua:u/. In this study, /ua:/ is written as /wa/ to distinguish from /ua/, which is phonetically [uɐ]. All the simple vowels can take final consonants. But no diphthongs or triphthongs can take final consonants except for /ie/, /ɯa/ and /ua:/, eg. $liet^5$ 'run', $lɯat^5$ 'blood', $lua:t^5$ 'snatch'. There are no combinations like /aip/, /a:it/, /oip/, or /auk/.

Finals that take /u/ as the first element, namely /-ua/, /-uaː/, /-uaːi/, /-uai/, /-uaːu/, /-uaːm/, /-uam/, /-uaːŋ/, /-uaŋ/, /-uaːp/, /-uaːt/, /-uat/, /-uaːk/ and /-uak/ can combine with initials /t-/, /ʔd-/, /ts-/, /θ-/, /l-/, /k-/, /ŋ-/, and /ʔ-/ only. These finals do not occur with labial initials /p-/, /ʔb-/, /f-/, /v-/, nor the laryngeal fricative /h-/.

9.2.1.4. *Tones*

Each syllable in Fengshan carries one of six phonemic tones, as illustrated in Table 9.2.1.4-1.

TABLE 9.2.1.4-1: TONES IN FENGSHAN

Tone mark	Pitch contour	Numeric values					
1	Rising	24	ʎ	ma^1	'dog'	na^1	'thick'
2	high level	55	˥	ma^2	'soak'	pa^2	'wilderness'
3	mid low level	22	˧	ma^3	'grow'	ka^3	'kill'
4	Low level	11	˩	na^4	'rice field'	lum^4	'wind'
5	mid level	33	˧	ta^5	'river'	$na{:}m^5$	'soil'
6	high fall	41	˥	ma^6	'horse'	lam^6	'water'

Checked syllables occur in tone 2, tone 4 and tone 5. Historically voiceless initials combine with tone 2, while historically voiced initials occur with tone 4 for short vowels, and tone 5 for long vowels. Examples: pak^2 'to plant', $pa{:}k^2$ 'mouth', lap^2 'dark', $la{:}p^2$ 'carry with shoulder poles', tat^2 'to cut (small plants), $ta{:}t^2$ 'waterfall'; tak^4 'male (animal)', $ta{:}k^5$ 'to measure'; lak^4 'steal', $la{:}k^5$ 'root'.

Syllables taking the glottal stop /ʔ/and the preglottalized stops /ʔb/, /ʔd/ and /ʔj/ merge with historical low tones in the tone B, C and D (long) categories, that is, they merge with tone 5 and tone 6. Eg. $ʔbuŋ^6$ 'water spinach', $ʔba{:}n^6$ 'village', $ʔda^5$ 'to scold', $ʔda{:}t^5$ 'hot', $ʔɔŋ^5$ 'jar', $ʔa{:}p^5$, 'bathe in river', $ʔju^5$ 'live, stay', $ʔjiaŋ^6$ 'to dry over fire'. Such syllables take the historical high tones in other dialects.

9.3. WORD CLASSES AND BASIC SYNTACTIC PATTERNS

9.3.1. Word classes

The following word classes can be recognized, for Zhuang:

1) Noun, with subclasses: common noun, place name, personal name, and question word
2) Pronoun
3) Classifier
4) Numeral
5) Demonstrative
6) Time word
7) Verb, with subclasses: common verb, adjectival verb, auxiliary verb
8) Adverb
9) Preposition
10) Conjunction
11) Speech act particle
12) Interjection

9.3.2. Word structure

The majority of words in Zhuang are monosyllabic. Examples:

hun⁴ 'human being', *mu¹* 'pig', *po¹* 'hill', *lam⁶* 'water', *la:n⁴* 'house', *ʔbɯt²* 'pluck', *kat²* 'bite', *lɛn¹* 'see', *la:u¹* 'fear', *tɔk²* 'fall', *ʔdi¹* 'good', *hom¹* 'fragrant', *mo²* 'new', *ʔbɯk²* 'great'.

Disyllabic words are not uncommon. Some of the disyllabic words are bound morphemes. Others are compound morphemes. Examples of bound disyllabic compounds include *ʔda:u¹ ʔdi⁵* 'star', *pi⁵ pieŋ⁴/pieŋ⁴ pi⁵* 'dragonfly', *ʔbuŋ⁵ ʔba⁶* 'butterfly', *fam⁴ fɯk⁴* 'all of a sudden', *lu⁶ liŋ⁵* 'drop and roll', *kuŋ³ kiŋ²* 'to roll, trundle', *len⁶ tsen⁶* 'mean, stingy', *ŋɔk⁴ ŋak⁴* 'zigzag', *tsum⁵ tswa:⁶* 'feel/scope in the dark', *ŋɔn⁵ ŋwa⁶* 'dizzy'. Note the alliterating and rhyming devices of these examples.

9.3.2.1 Compounding

Compounding in Zhuang accounts for a large number of nouns, adjectives and verbs. In most cases, the part of speech of the compound can be determined from the first element of the compound. The meaning of the compound is more or less related to its components. Compounds in Zhuang are generally patterned as follows:

A. Noun compounds

(i) Noun + Verb

(1) *ʔda:ŋ¹ tɛn³* 'body + wear = clothing'
      tsau³ tok² 'head + hammer in = headache'
      ŋan⁴ ni³ 'money + owe = debt, debt money'
      hau⁶ naŋ³ 'rice + steam = steamed rice'

(ii) Noun + Noun

This group is the most productive and most versatile. Various semantic links can be observed between the head noun and the modifying noun.

(2) *hau⁶ hɔn¹* 'grain + seeds = grain seeds' (head-purpose)
      lam⁶ ʔbo⁵ 'water + spring/well = spring water' (head + source)
      tin¹ fɯŋ⁴ 'foot + hand = techniques, skills' (coordinate compounding)
      la:n⁴ fai⁶ 'house + timber = timber house' (head + material)
      naŋ¹ pa:k² 'skin + mouth = lips' (head + location)

B. Verb/Adjectival Compounds

(iii) Coordinating verb compounds

(3) *tɔk² θɛt²* 'drop + jump = startle'
      jop⁵ jua⁶ 'instigate + abet = instigate, abet'
      hɯm³ lɔŋ⁴ 'descend + ascend = communicate, be in contact, have connections'
      ka:i¹ ɕɯ⁶ 'selling + buying = (to do) business, trade'
      tɯk⁴ lam⁶ 'be + tumble = fall, tumble'

(iv) Verb + Noun

Many of this kind of compound appear to have a Verb-Object relationship between the verb and the noun.

(4) lo^6 na^3 'know + face = to know, recognize'

  $la{:}u^1$ hi^2 'fear + breath = to fear'

  $tsai^4$ ho^4 'love + throat = be concerned about'

But this is not always the case. The noun after the verb may indicate the subject of the verb, or the cause, or be metaphorical, among others.

(5) $ta{:}i^1$ la^2 'die + epidemic = to die of pestilence' (cause)

  $\mathfrak{2}ok^5$ $\mathfrak{n}u^5$ 'to urinate' (exit + urine = to urinate) (subject)

  $luan^4$ $va{:}i^4$ 'crawl + buffalo = (of baby) to crawl' (metaphorical, to (walk) on all fours like a buffalo)

  $la{:}i^5$ $m\mathfrak{d}t^4$ 'creep + ant = feel numb' (metaphorical, to have the feeling as if ants were creeping on you)

  pan^4 hum^4 'become + night = to dream' (metaphorical)

  $va{:}n^1$ $tsua^1$ 'sweet + salt = tastes like salt' (metaphorical)

  (v) Noun + Adjective

(6) na^3 $mo\eta^1$ 'shy' (face + grey)

  $\theta i\eta^2$ han^1 'quick-tempered' (temper + strong)

  $\theta a{:}u^1$ $\mathfrak{2}di^1$ 'beautiful' (girl + good)

  $\mathfrak{2}da{:}\eta^1$ $pjiet^2$ 'sad' (body + depart)

  ho^4 $\mathfrak{2}da{:}t^5$ 'angry' (throat + hot)

  (vi) Resultative Verb Compounds

 The second verb in the compound denotes the resulting state of the first verb.

(7) tum^2 ςuk^4 'boil + cooked = cooked as a result of boiling'

  tup^4 tek^2 'hit + broken = broken from being hit'

  $\mathfrak{2}ut^2$ ko^4 'bend + crooked = crooked as a result of being bent'

  $kuak^5$ pan^4 'do + accomplished = achieved through working'

Quite a significant number of compounds are formed with prefixes or suffixes. For details, see §9.4.1.1.

9.3.3. Basic word order

Subject-verb-object is the preferred word order in Zhuang.

(8) *Me⁶ ʔdam¹ pjak².*

'Mother plants vegetables'.

Modifiers follow the head.

(9) *no⁵ va:i⁴* 'meat + buffalo = beef'

lau³ va:n¹ 'wine + sweet = sweet wine'

9.3.4. Demonstrative adjectives

The generic demonstrative adjectives in Zhuang are *ni⁶* 'this' and *te¹* 'that'. They are seldom used alone to function as demonstrative pronouns. *ni⁶* and *te¹* often combines with other elements to form compound deictic expressions:

(10) *tsie⁴ ni⁶* 'here, this place', *tsie⁴ te¹* 'there, that place, yonder'

ten⁵ ni⁶ 'this place, here', *ten⁵ te¹* 'that place, there'

mɯa⁵ ni⁶ 'now, this time', *mɯa⁵ te¹* 'then, that time'

ŋɔn⁴ ni⁶ 'today, this day', *ŋɔn⁴ te¹* 'that day'

taɲ³ ni⁶ 'this way, like this', *taɲ³ te⁶* 'that way, like that'

ka:u⁵ ni⁶ 'this much', *ka:u⁵ te¹* 'that much'.

te¹ has other functions, such as third person singular pronoun and a relative marker, which will be discussed later.

9.3.5. Pronouns and other pronominal items

9.3.5.1. *Personal pronouns*

The Zhuang pronoun system is quite simple, compared with Thai and other Southwestern Tai dialects such as Sipsongpanna Dai Lue. There are no honorific pronouns in Zhuang of the sort found in Thai and Lue. But it doesn't mean that Zhuang pronouns can be used freely without any constraints. The choice of pronouns in Zhuang is sensitive to social factors such as age, social position and attitude of the speaker towards the addressee.

As a general rule, the use of the first and second person singular pronoun is to be avoided, in polite conversation with strangers and acquaintances, between relatives or when speaking to a superior. In such situations, a kinship term is used for the addressee and the term **hoi²**, literally 'slave', is used for self reference by the speaker.

Parents would use kinship terms to refer to themselves when they speak to their children. The use of first person plural (inclusive) is considered polite.

Table 9.3.5.1-1 lists the personal pronouns in Fengshan Zhuang.

TABLE 9.3.5.1-1: PERSONAL PRONOUNS IN FENGSHAN ZHUANG

First person			Second Person		Third Person	
Singular	Plural (excl.)	Plural (incl.)	Singular	Plural	Singular	Plural
ku¹	*tu¹, po⁴ tu¹*	*lau⁴*	*mɯŋ⁴*	*θu¹, po⁴ θu¹*	*te¹*	*po⁴ te¹*

In Wuming, there is a plural marker, $kjo\eta^2$, which is used to form second and third plural pronouns: $kjo\eta^2 mu\eta^4$ 'you (plural)'; $kjo\eta^2 te^1$ 'they'. In Southern Zhuang, such as the dialects of Jingxi, Lungzhou, and Lungming, first person singular is ηo^5 (ku^1 is also used) and second person singular is ni^5, which appear to have been borrowed from Chinese.

No dual personal pronouns are found in Zhuang. To express this concept, $\theta o\eta^l pu^6$ 'two-person' is to be used along with the pronouns, as in $\theta o\eta^l pu^6 lau^4$ 'both of us, the two of us', $\theta o\eta^l pu^6 \theta u^1$ 'both of you, the two of you', $\theta o\eta^l pu^6 te^1$ 'both of them, the two of them'.

9.3.5.2. Interrogative and indefinite pronouns

The most common interrogative pronominal stem in Zhuang is lau^4, which is used to form a paradigm of interrogative pronouns.

TABLE 9.3.5.2-1: INTERROGATIVE AND INDEFINITE PRONOUNS

Form	Meaning
$pu^6 lau^4$	'which person, who'
$tsie^4 lau^4$	'what/which place, where'
$ten^5 lau^4$	'what/which place, where'
$pai^5 lau^4$	'which side/direction, what side/direction'
$mwa^5 lau^4$	'what time (long period), when'
$ku^2 lau^4$	'what time (short period), when'
$kuak^5 lau^4$	'how (to do), what (to do)'
$pan^4 lau^4$	'how'
$vi^5 lau^4$	'for what (reason), why'
$ka{:}u^5 lau^4$	'what amount, how many, how much'

The element lau^4 generally does not occur alone as an interrogative pronoun, except in utterances like $mu\eta^4 pai^l lau^4 le^4$ 'where are you going?', which is a short form of $mu\eta^4 pai^l tsie^4 lau^4 le^4$. Other interrogative and indefinite pronouns include ma^4 'what', which also functions as a stem in $kai^2 ma^4$ 'what'; $kuak^5 ma^4$ 'what (to do)', $tua^4 ma^4$ 'what (animals)', $jia\eta^5 ma^4$ 'what kind, what sort'.

Two items may be included under this category, fwa^6 and $?un^5$, both roughly translatable into English as 'other', with different pragmatic functions. They both function as adjectives. Examples:

(11) $tsie^4 fwa^6$ 'other (people's) place' (as opposed to $tsie^4 lau^4$ 'our place')

$pwa\eta^4 fwa^6$ 'other/foreign country' (as opposed to $pwa\eta^4 lau^4$ 'our country')

$pu^6 ?un^5$ 'other people, someone else' (not this person)

$kai^2 ?un^5$ 'other things, something else' (not this piece/item, but something else)

$mwa^5 ?un^5$ 'other times, a different time' (not this time/moment)

9.3.5.3. Reflexives

The following reflexive pronouns can be recognized for Zhuang:

TABLE 9.3.5.3-1: REFLEXIVES

Form	Meaning
la^3 le^2	'self' (colloquial)
la^3 $?da{:}\eta^1$	'self' (lit. 'below-body')
fan^5 -	'-self (lit. 'share')
pon^3 fan^5	'self' (in Standard Zhuang, 'original share')
$?da{:}\eta^1$ kau^2	'self' (lit. 'body-old – the old body')

The first three items are bare reflexives, which are indefinite. They can be qualified by other pronouns to form compound reflexive pronouns, as in la^3 le^2 hoi^2 / ku^1 '(I) myself (polite / equal)', la^3 le^2 lau^4 '(we) ourselves', la^3 le^2 $m\,u\,\eta^4$ '(you) yourself ', la^3 le^2 te^1 '(he/she) him/herself ', fan^5 ku^1 'myself', fan^5 $m\,u\,\eta^4$, fan^5 θu^1 'yourselves', and so on. The first two reflexives can be used alone as subjects and objects, while fan^5 needs to be used in conjunction with the pronoun, as ku^1 pai^1 fan^5 ku^1, $m\,u\,\eta^4$ pai^1 fan^5 $m\,u\,\eta^4$ 'I go by myself/on my own and you go by yourself/on your own.' Of these two, la^3 le^2 may also function as a qualifier, as in $la{:}n^4$ la^3 le^2 'one's own home, our own home', na^4 la^3 le^2 'one's own field, our own field'. pon^3 fan^5 is mainly used in Wuming area and is normally used alone in the sense of an impersonal reflexive pronoun. Similarly, $?da{:}\eta^1$ kau^2 is often used alone without a qualifier, unlike la^3 le^2 and la^3 $?da{:}\eta^1$.

9.3.5.4. *Reciprocal:* $to\eta^6$/to^6

Two reciprocal prefixes, which are free variants of one another, are used in Zhuang to form reciprocal expressions.

(12) $to\eta^6$/to^6 $tsai^4$ 'love each other'

$to\eta^6$/to^6 $\text{\textctc}uan^1$ 'meet with each other'

$to\eta^6$ θi^3 'have sexual intercourse with each other' (vulgar)

$to\eta^6$/to^6 hut^2 'to abuse each other verbally'

9.3.6. Classifiers and quantifiers

9.3.6.1. *Numbers*

9.3.6.1.1. *Cardinals*

The cardinals for Zhuang from 'one' to 'ten' are listed below.

TABLE 9.3.6.1.1-1: CARDINALS

$?deu^1$	$\theta o\eta^1$	$\theta a{:}m^1$	θi^2	ha^3	$l\,\mathit{o}k^2$	$\text{\textctc}\varepsilon t^2$	pet^2	ku^3	$\text{\textctc}ip^4$
one	two	three	four	five	six	seven	eight	nine	ten

In Wuming, there is a cardinal $n\,u\,\eta^5$, 'one'.

'Eleven' to 'nineteen' are formed by putting an appropriate number after 'ten', with the exception of 'eleven' and 'twelve', which are formed respectively by adding $?it^2$ 'one' and ji^5 'two' after 'ten'.

TABLE 9.3.6.1.1-2: 'ELEVEN' TO 'NINETEEN'

$çip^4 \,\text{?}it^2$	$çip^4 \,\text{p}i^5$	$çip^4 \,\theta a{:}m^1$	$çip^4 \,\theta i^2$	$çip^4 ha^3$	$çip^4 lok^2$	$çip^4 \,çet^2$	$çip^4 \,pet^2$	$çip^4 ku^3$
eleven	twelve	thirteen	fourteen	fifteen	sixteen	seventeen	eighteen	nineteen

'Twenty' to 'ninety' are formed by reversing the word order of each of the numbers from 'twelve' to 'nineteen':

TABLE 9.3.6.1.1-3: 'TWENTY' TO 'NINETY'

$\text{p}i^5 çip^4$	$\theta a{:}m^1 çip^4$	$\theta i^2 çip^4$	$ha^3 çip^4$	$lok^2 çip^4$	$çet^2 çip^4$	$pet^2 çip^4$	$ku^3 çip^4$
twenty	thirty	forty	fifty	sixty	seventy	eighty	ninety

Other units of numbers in Zhuang include $pa{:}k^2$ 'hundred', $çien^1$ 'thousand', and $fa{:}n^5$ 'ten thousand'.

Note the use of $\text{?}it^2$ and $\text{p}i^5$ with these numbers:

(13) $pa{:}k^2 \,\text{?}it^2$ 'one hundred and ten' Cf. $pa{:}k^2 \,\text{?}deu^1$ 'one hundred'
  $pa{:}k^2 \text{p}i^5$ 'one hundred and twenty' Cf. $\theta o{:}\eta^1 pa{:}k^2$ 'two hundred'
  $fa{:}n^5 \,\text{?}it^2$ 'eleven thousand' Cf. $fa{:}n^5 \,\text{?}deu^1$ 'ten thousand'
  $fa{:}n^5 \,\text{p}i^5$ 'twelve thousand' Cf. $\theta o{:}\eta^1 fa{:}n^5$ 'twenty thousand'

9.3.6.1.2. *Ordinals*

Ordinals are formed by adding the ordinal prefix $ta{:}i^5$ to a cardinal, except for 'first' and 'second', in which case the forms $\text{?}it^2$ 'one' and $\text{p}i^5$ 'two', rather than $\text{?}deu^1$ and $\theta o{:}\eta^1$, are used.

(14) $ta{:}i^5 \,\text{?}it^2$ 'first', $ta{:}i^5 \,\text{p}i^5$ 'second', $ta{:}i^5 \,\theta a{:}m^1$ 'third', $ta{:}i^5 \,çip^4$ 'tenth'.

For ordinals over ten, $ta{:}i^5$ is generally omitted, probably for prosodic reasons.

9.3.6.1.3. *Approximates and other number-related concepts*

Approximate numbers can be expressed by using θak^2 before a numeral: $\theta ak^2 pa{:}k^2$ 'about a hundred', $mi^4 \,\theta ak^2 ha^3 lok^2 pu^6$ 'there are about five or six people'. The concept of 'exceeding, over' can be expressed by putting $tu\eta^6 hu\textit{w}m^3$ after the numeral-classifier phrase, as in $çip^4 pu^6 tu\eta^6 hu\textit{w}m^3$.

In the case of ten, or ten folds, the element $la{:}i^1$ or tsi^3 is used after the numerals, as in $çip^4 la{:}i^1 tua^4 pit^2$ 'over ten ducks', $\text{p}i^5 \,çip^4 tsi^3 pu^6 hek^2$ 'over twenty guests', $pa{:}k^2 la{:}i^1 \,(OR{:} tsi^3) man^4 \,\text{p}an^4$ 'over a hundred dollars'. Other terms related to numbers are $ti\eta^4$ 'half', $fua\eta^5$ 'half, part, portion (of an object)', θin^6 'quarter'. Examples: $ti\eta^4 \,\text{?}deu^1$ 'a half', $ti\eta^4 la{:}i^1$ 'a bigger half, over a half', $\theta o\eta^1 fua\eta^5$ 'two halves', $\theta a{:}m^1 fua\eta^5$ 'three parts'; $\theta in^6 \,\text{?}deu^1$ 'a quarter'.

Fractions and percentages are expressed by $çi\eta^4$ '10%', $ka{:}i^2$ X 'one-Xth', eg. $t\text{ɔ}^1/\theta iet^5 \,\theta o\eta^1 çi\eta^4$ 'increase/decrease by twenty percent', $çip^4 çi\eta^4$ 'one hundred percent', $ka{:}i^2 \,\theta a{:}m^1$ 'one-third'.

9.3.6.1.4. *Names of the month*

Zhuang has two sets of names of the month, one native, and the other, loans from Chinese. The native names are formed by putting the number after and the head word, $\text{?}d\textit{w}an^1$ 'month', while in the case of the Chinese loans, the order is reverse, that is, the number comes before the head word, *ŋuat⁵*. Table 9.3.6.1.4-1 lists these names.

TABLE 9.3.6.1.4-1: NAMES OF THE MONTH

	Native name	Chinese Loan
January	*ʔduan¹ ɕieŋ¹*	–
February	*ʔduan¹ ɲi⁵*	*ɲi⁵ ŋuat⁵*
March	*ʔduan¹ θa:m¹*	*θa:m¹ ŋuat⁵*
April	*ʔduan¹ θi²*	*θi² ŋuat⁵*
May	*ʔduan¹ ha³*	*ha³ ŋuat⁵*
June	*ʔduan¹ lɔk²*	*lɔk² ŋuat⁵*
July	*ʔduan¹ ɕɛt²*	*ɕɛt² ŋuat⁵*
August	*ʔduan¹ pet²*	*pet² ŋuat⁵*
September	*ʔduan¹ ku³*	*ku³ ŋuat⁵*
October	*ʔduan¹ ɕip⁴*	*ɕip⁴ ŋuat⁵*
November	*ʔduan¹ ʔit¹*	*ɕip³ ʔit² ŋuat⁵*
December	*ʔduan¹ la:p⁵*	–

It is interesting to note that no numerals are used for January and December in both systems. This seems to be an indication that a ten-month calendar was once used by the Zhuang.

9.3.6.1.5. *Questions seeking numbers as answers*

Questions seeking numbers or quantities as answers usually have the following elements: *tsi³* 'how many (where the answer is expected to be a concrete number lesser than 'ten'), *tsi³ la:i¹* 'how many, how much', *ka:u⁵ lau⁴* 'how much, how many'. Examples:

(15) *ɕɔm¹*   *tsi³*   *tua⁴*   *va:i⁴*?
      missing   how many   CL   buffalo
      'How many buffalos are missing?'

(16) *nam⁴ niŋ⁴*   *muɯŋ⁴*   *pai¹*   *kwa²*   *tsi³ la:i¹*   *ʔba:t⁵*
      Nanning   2sg   go   ASP   how many   time
      'How many times have you been to Nanning?'

(17) *ʔba:n⁶*   *lau⁴*   *mi⁴*   *ka:u⁵ lau⁴*   *hun⁴*?
      village   1pl   have   how many   person
      'How many people are there in our village?'

9.3.6.2. *Numeral-classifier constructions*

9.3.6.2.1. *Basic structure*

Numeral-classifier constructions in Zhuang have the structure 'Numeral + Classifier + Noun':

(18) *θoŋ¹ tua⁴ va:i⁴* 'two buffalos'

    θa:m¹ pu⁶ hun⁴ 'three people'

However, if the numeral is 'one', the construction is: Classifier + Noun + Numeral:

(19) *tua⁴ va:i⁴ ʔdeu¹* 'one buffalo'

    pu⁶ hun⁴ to:k⁵ 'one person only'

This is different from Thai and other Southwestern Tai dialects, where the construction is: Noun + Numeral + Classifier. In Zhuang, such construction is permitted for pragmatic purposes:

(20) | *la:n⁴* | *lau4* | *mi⁴* | *mu¹* | *θoŋ¹* | *tua⁴,* | *kai²* | *θa:m¹ çip⁴* | *tua⁴* |
|---|---|---|---|---|---|---|---|---|
| house | 1sg | have | pig | two | CL, | chicken | thirty | CL |

'Our family has two pigs and thirty chickens.'

The unmarked counterpart of the above construction is:

  (21) *la:n⁴ lau4 mi⁴ θoŋ¹ tua⁴ mu¹, θa:m¹ çip⁴ tua⁴ kai²*

The reduplication of classifiers has the meaning of 'every…, all':

(22) | *mu¹* | **tua⁴** | **tua⁴** | *pi⁴.* |
|---|---|---|---|
| pig | CL | CL | fat |

    'These pigs are all fat/every pig is fat.'

(23) | *pɔ⁴ te¹* | **pu⁶** | **pu⁶** | *pai¹.* |
|---|---|---|---|
| 3pl | CL | CL | go |

    'They all went.'

When a classifier is used without a numeral, its function is to categorize. Examples:

(24) *lɯk⁴ ʔit²* 'grapes (fruit), *ko¹ ʔit²* 'grape plants', *kau¹ ʔit²* 'grape vine';

    kau¹ kwa¹ 'pumpkin vine', *lɯk⁴ kwa¹* 'pumpkin (the fruit)', *ʔbaɯ¹ kwa¹* 'pumpkin leaf';

    tua⁴ kuk² 'tiger', *tua⁴ ʔdɯan¹* 'earthworm', *tua⁴ tsua:u¹* 'spider

Without the use of classifiers, the meaning of some of the above examples is still comprehensible, such as *kuk²* 'tiger'. For others, such as *kwa¹*, the use of classifiers specifies the type, rather than the prototypical meaning of the noun in question.

9.3.6.2.2. *Commonly used classifiers*

Below is a list of some of the most commonly used classifiers in Zhuang.

A. Noun classifiers

(25) *ʔen¹* – general classifier for inanimate things, big or small objects, eg. *θi² ʔen¹ tsoi³* 'four bananas', *ha³ ʔen¹ la:n⁴* 'five houses'.

tua^4– general classifier for animals, children, eg. $\theta o\eta^{l}$ tua^4 ma^{l} 'two dogs', $\theta a{:}m^{l}$ tua^4 $l\mathit{u}\mathit{u}k^4$ 'three children'.

pu^6 – general classifier for human being, eg. tsi^3 pu^6 hek^2 'several guests',

ko^{l} – general classifier for plants eg. $\theta a{:}m^{l}$ ko^{l} $fa\mathit{i}^6$ 'three trees'.

$\theta\mathit{æ}n^3$– classifier for long, thin, stiff objects such as sticks, eg. $\theta o\eta^{l}$ $\theta\mathit{æ}n^3$ $t\mathit{u}\mathit{u}\eta^3$ 'two sticks'.

$n\mathit{æ}t^4$ – classifier for grains, eg. lok^2 $n\mathit{æ}t^4$ hau^6 'six grains'.

$ka{:}i^2$ – classifier for things conceptualised as 'piece', eg. $\theta o\eta^{l}$ $ka{:}i^2$ no^5 'two pieces of meat'.

la^2 – classifier for winds, rains, eg. la^2 hun^{l} $\mathit{?}deu^{l}$ 'a shower'.

$kon^{3/1}$ – classifier for stones, eg. tsi^3 kon^3 hin^{l} 'several stones/rocks'.

$ho\eta^2$ – measure for rooms, eg. ha^3 $ho\eta^2$ $la{:}n^4$ 'five rooms'.

$fa{:}k^5$ – classifier for tools, eg. $fa{:}k^5$ mit^4 $\mathit{?}deu^{l}$ 'a knife'.

$\mathit{?}ba^{l}$ – classifier for flat and relatively big objects such as quilt, blankets, land, eg. $\theta a{:}m^{l}$ $\mathit{?}ba^{l}$ li^5 'three upland field'.

$\mathit{?}ba\mathit{u}\mathit{u}^{l}$– flat, thin, relatively small objects (derived from 'leaf'), eg. $\theta o\eta^{l}$ $\mathit{?}ba\mathit{u}\mathit{u}^{l}$ $f\mathit{ɔ}t^4$ 'two leaves'.

B. Measures of events

In addition to things and objects, actions and events can also be measured.

(26) $\mathit{?}ba{:}t^5$, pai^4 – measure for actions or events

$ta{:}u^2$ – measure for events involving trips

C. Derivational measures

A number of measure words are derived from verbs, indicating 'an instance of V-ing':

(27) $la{:}p^2$ 'load' (from 'to carry on shoulder poles')
kam^{l} 'a handful' (from 'to hold')
kop^2 'handful (from 'to scoop')
loi^6 'bundle, string of' (from 'to string')

D. Measures of length and weight

The following are some common measures of length and weight in Zhuang:

(28) hup^4 'a length span between thumb and middle finger'
$\theta\mathit{ɔ}m^{l}$ 'a span of arms-spread'
$pa{:}n^2$ 'a span of one arm'
$\varsigma a{:}\eta^4$ 'a measure of weight, 50 grams'
kan^{l} 'a measure of weight (from Chinese jin) = 500 grams'
$tieu^5$ 'a measure of weight, 5 kilograms'

E. Aggregate classifiers/measures

A number of aggregate classifiers/measures are found in Zhuang. Some are for animate things and others, inanimate things.

(29)   *fɔn²* 'flock, group', eg. *fɔn² lɔk⁴ ʔdeu¹* 'a flock of birds'
       pa:ŋ¹ 'group, gang (of people)', eg. *pa:ŋ¹ hun⁴ ni⁶* 'this group of people'
       toi⁵ 'team (of people)', eg. *tsi³ toi⁵ luik⁴ ha:k⁵* 'several teams of school children'
       toi² 'pair (of animate things)', eg. *toi² luik⁴ va¹ ʔdeu¹* 'a twin'
       ku⁵ 'pair of (inanimate things)', eg. *θa:m¹ ku⁵ tui⁵* 'three pairs of chopsticks'
       mɔŋ³ 'pile, heap', eg. *θoŋ¹ mɔŋ³ tau5* 'two piles of ash'

9.3.7. Closed functional classes

9.3.7.1. *Auxiliaries*

A number of auxiliaries can be found in Zhuang. These can take another verb as their argument.

(30)   *jieu²*   *jiaŋ⁵*   *pi¹*   *ni⁶*   **ʒ̑a:k⁵**   *pan⁴*   *loŋ⁴.*
       Look   manner   year   this   AUX   become   flooded
       'It seems that there is going to be a flood this year.'

(31)   *kɔ¹*   **lo⁶**   *kuak⁵*   *ça:ŋ⁵ fai⁶*
       elder brother   know   do   carpentry'
       'Elder brother knows how to do carpentry work'.

(32)   *pi⁶*   **ça:ŋ⁵**   *ɲɛn²*   */ pan⁴*   *na:i²*
       sister-in-law   AUX   be moody   / get   sick.
       'Sister-in-law tends to be moody / is easy to get sick.'

Auxiliaries that can fill this slot include *ʔbau⁵ jɔŋ⁵* 'no need to', *ʔbau⁵ çɛ³* 'no need to, unnecessary to', *ɕun³* 'allow to', *haui³* 'let, allow to, permit to', *ŋa⁵* 'crave to, wish to', *ɲien⁵* 'be willing to', *ma:i³* 'like to, love to', *mi⁴ na³* 'have the cheek to, dare to', *ʔbau⁵ mi⁴ na³* 'dare not, too shy to (do); *ʔbau⁵ ʔdi¹* 'no good (doing sth.)', *ka:m³* 'dare to', *la:u¹* 'fear to', *ʔdai⁶* 'succeeded in, got to', *ʔbau⁵ ʔdai⁶ ʔbau⁵* 'have to, cannot but (do sth.)', among others. See §9.5.2 below for a discussion of syntactic properties of modal-auxiliaries.

9.3.7.2. *Negatives*

Negative words in Zhuang include *ʔbau⁵, ʔam⁶* and *çaŋ⁴. ʔbau⁵* is the most general, which is found across the Tai language family.

(33)   *te¹*   *ʔbau²*   *lo⁶*   *na³*   *ku¹*
       he/she   not   know   face   1sg
       'He/She doesn't know me.'

ʔbau⁵ can have an emphatic form, *ʔbau⁵ ... na:u²*, translatable into English as 'not ... at all'.

(34)   *muŋ⁴*   *tau³*   *ku¹*   *ʔbau⁵*   *lo⁶ ʔde⁵*   *na:u²*
       you   come   1sg   NEG   know   EMPH
       'I knew nothing about your arrival.'

ʔam⁶ can be used interchangeably with *ʔbau⁵*. This form is mainly found in Northern Zhuang.

çaŋ⁴ carries tense/aspect meanings. It designates that an event or situation expressed by the verb in question has not eventualized at the time of speaking.

(35) *me⁵*   *pai¹*   *huɯ¹*   *çaŋ⁴*   *ta:u²*.

     mother   go   market   NEG   return

     'Mother went to the market, and has not returned yet.'

A mild negation may be expressed by *ʔbau⁵* / *ʔam⁶* / *çaŋ⁴* … *ka:u⁵ laɯ⁴·* meaning 'not … too much, not very…'.

(36) *te¹li⁶*   *nom³*,   *çaŋ⁴*   *lo⁶jieu³*   *ka:u⁵laɯ⁴*

     3sgstill   young   NEG   sensible   much

     'He/she is still young; hence he/she is not very sensible.'

There are a few negative imperative markers in Zhuang. See §9.3.7.2 for discussion.

9.3.7.3. *Prepositions, locative words*

Prepositions. Genuine prepositions in Zhuang are few. Most prepositions in Zhuang are derived from verbs.

(37) *te¹*   **ʔdi⁶**   *ʔa:u¹*   *ta³çua⁶*

     3sg   **with**   uncle   talk

     'He/she is talking to/with his/her uncle.'

(38) *kɔ¹*   *ta:i⁵ θa:ŋ¹*   *tɔ¹*   *kɔ¹*   *ɲi⁵*

     brother first   tall   **MORE THAN** brother second

     'First elder brother is taller than second elder brother.'

(39) *te¹*   *pan⁴*   *na:i² nin⁴*   **ʒu⁵**   *ʔbon⁵*

     3sg become sick sleep **in**   bed

     'He/she is sick, and is lying in bed.'

(40) **ʔok⁵** *pi¹*   *tau¹*   **taŋ⁴** *pi¹*   *ni⁶ te¹*   *pai¹tsie⁴ lok⁵*   *kuak⁵ θuan²*

     from years before **to**   year this 3sggo place   outside do   work

     'From the year before till this year he went out to work.'

(41) *lak⁴*   *θwi¹*   **haɯ³**   *te¹*

     don't tell   **to**   3sg.

     'Don't tell (this) to him.'

Prepositions of this kind may be analysed as coverbs. Other examples include *ta:u²* 'towards', eg. *jiau² ta:u² laŋ¹* 'look back'; *kwa²* 'comparative marker', eg. *θa:ŋ¹ kwa² muɯŋ⁴* 'taller than you'; *num³* 'like, as', eg. *kan⁶ num³ me⁵* '(as) hardworking as mother'); *luaŋ⁴* 'along', eg. *luaŋ⁴ vi³ pja:i³* 'walk along the stream'; *çо⁵* 'facing, towards', eg. *pja:i³ çо⁵ ʔba:n⁶* 'walk towards the village'.

Locative words. Zhuang has a set of locative or direction words to express the concepts like 'above', 'below', 'inside', 'outside', 'beside', 'in the middle of' and the like. Table 9.3.7.3-1 lists the locative words in Zhuang.

TABLE 9.3.7.3-1: LOCATIVE WORDS

kum^4	'on top of, above'
la^3	'under, below'
$?dau^1$	'in, inside'
lok^5	'out, outside'
$?den^1$	'beside'
$tsa{:}\eta^1$	'in the centre of'
na^3	'front, in front of'
$la\eta^1$	'back, behind'

Locative words can take nouns as their arguments.

(42) $?dau^1\ \theta uan^1$ 'inside the garden'
 $?den^1\ la{:}n^4$ 'beside the house'
 $kum^4\ \varphi o\eta^4$ 'on the table'
 $tsa{:}\eta^1\ hu^1$ 'in the centre of the market'

They can also function as modifiers. Thus there is a distinction between:

(43) $kum^4\ la{:}n^4$ 'on (top of) the house'   cf. $la{:}n^4\ kum^4$ 'the house above'
 $lok^5\ ba{:}n^6$ 'outside the village'   cf. $ba{:}n^6\ lok^5$ 'the other village'
 $?den^1\ \varphi o\eta^4$ 'on the side of the table' cf. $\varphi o\eta^4\ ?den^1$ 'the table nearby'

Directional phrases involving locative words can be formed by putting a directional particle $pa{:}i^5$ before the locative words, except for $tsa{:}\eta^1$ 'in the centre of'.

(44) $pa{:}i^5\ kum^4$ 'above, up'
 $pa{:}i^5\ la^3$ 'below, beneath'
 $pa{:}i^5\ ?dau^1$ 'inside'
 $pa{:}i^5\ lok^5$ 'outside'
 $pa{:}i^5\ ta^1\ \eta on^4\ ?ok^5$ 'the east (lit. 'the side/direction where the sun comes out')
 $pa{:}i^5\ \theta oi^6/kwa^4$ 'the left/right side'

To describe different part of a vertical object, such as a mountain, or a tree, Zhuang uses the concepts tin^1 'foot, bottom', kok^2 'base', $tsa{:}\eta^1$ 'middle' and $pja{:}i^1$ 'tip, top'. Eg. $kok^2\ fai^6$ 'the base of a tree', $pja{:}i^1\ fai^6$ 'tree top'; $tin^1\ ?da{:}i^1$ 'the foot of a mountain', $tsa{:}\eta^1\ ?da{:}i^1$ 'the middle of a mountain – half way up the mountain', $pja{:}i^1\ ?da{:}i^1$ 'the top of the mountain'.

For syntactic behaviours of locative and directional phrases, see §9.5.1.3 for discussion.

9.3.7.4. *Adverbials and adverbial phrases*

Adverbials and adverbial phrases in Zhuang can be divided into two types: **preverbal** and **post-verbal**. They denote degree, frequency, time and place.

9.3.7.4.1. *Preverbal adverbials*

Most adverbials are preverbal. Examples of preverbal adverbials are *li⁶* 'still', *ɕam⁵* 'together', *ɕam⁵ ɕai⁵* 'all together', *ɕaŋ³ la:i²* 'fortunately', *lak⁴ liem⁴* 'quietly, secretly', *pa:i⁴ la:ŋ⁴* 'nearly, almost', *nai⁵ niem⁴ tem¹* 'on the verge of', *tau³ fa:n²* 'on the contrary', *fam⁶ fɯk⁴* 'suddenly', *ka:k⁵* 'only, alone', *jiet²… jiet²…* 'the more…the more', *kɘ³… kɘ³…* 'the more… the more…', *mi⁴ nai⁵* 'a little bit, somewhat…', *… ma:n⁵* '…then'.

(45) *tsuɱ²te¹*   **ɕam⁵**   *pai¹   hɯi¹*

    3pl   together   go   market

    'They went to the market together.'

(46) *va:i⁴*   *tɔk²*   *la:k²*   **pa:i⁴ la:ŋ⁴**   *ta:i¹*

    buffalo   drop   fall   nearly   die

    'The buffalo nearly died from falling over the cliff.'

(47) *te¹*   **ka:k⁵**   *kɯn¹*   **ka:k⁵**   *ʨu⁵*.

    3sg   alone   eat   alone   live

    'He lives on his own and does his own cooking.'

The majority of preverbal adverbs are non-movable. They do not occur anywhere else in the sentence other than right before the verb they modify. Thus, examples (45), (46) and (47) will become unacceptable if the adverbs are moved to other places:

(45') **ɕam⁵ tsuɱ² te¹ pai¹ hɯi¹*.

(46') **pa:i⁴ la:ŋ⁴ va:i⁴ tɔk² la:k² ta:i¹*.

(47') **te¹ kɯn¹ ka:k⁵ ʨu⁵ ka:k⁵*.

9.3.7.4.2. *Post-verbal adverbials*

These include adverbials of frequency, as well as adverbials degree, among others. They, too, are non-movable. Examples:

(48) *kuak⁵ θoŋ¹ ʔba:t⁵* 'do twice'

(49) *θwa⁵ tsi³ ta:u²* 'wash several times'

(50) *tup⁴ θa:m¹ pai⁴* 'strike/hit three times'

Other post-verbal adverbs include *kon²* 'first', *laŋ¹* 'later', *tem¹* 'in addition', *pja:ŋ⁴* 'wrongly, adversely'.

(51) *ku¹ pai¹* **kon²**,   *mɯŋ⁴ ma:n⁵ lɯaŋ⁴* **laŋ⁵**

    1sg go   before,   you   slowly follow later

    'I go first. You follow.'

(52) *te¹   ŋa⁵   kuak⁵   **pja:ŋ⁴***

   3sg love do   wrong

   'He/she likes to tell lies.'

(53) *mɯɯŋ⁴   nau⁴   tsie⁴   ni⁶   tsai¹   ha,   tsie⁴   te¹   fa⁶   tsai¹   **tem¹**.*

   you   say   place   this far   PART,   place   that   even far   evenmore

   'You said this place is quite far away (from town), that place is even further.'

In Standard Zhuang, *la:i¹* can be used both pre-verbally and post-verbally, with a difference in meaning. Preverbal *la:i¹* is translatable into English as 'quite, rather', while post-verbal *la:i¹* means 'very, excessively', eg. *la:i¹ ʔdiŋ¹* 'quite red', *ʔdiŋ¹ la:i¹* 'very red'.

9.3.7.5. *Temporal adverbs, time words*

Temporal adverbs in Zhuang typically immediately precede the verb phrase. Examples of common temporal adverbs include: *lien⁴* 'just', *ŋam³ ŋa:m²* 'just, just now', *ŋa:m² lian⁴* 'just now, right at this moment', *ɕaŋ⁴* 'not yet', *ʔiŋ⁵* 'already', *mo² na³* 'later, in the future'. Examples:

(54) *te¹   **lien⁴** / **ŋam³ŋa:m²** taŋ⁴*

   3sg just   /justnow   arrive

   'He just arrived.'

(55) *ku¹   **ʔiŋ⁵**   kɯn¹   ʔie⁵   le⁵*

   1sg already eat   finish PART

   'I've already eaten.'

Like other preverbal adverbs, temporal adverbs are non-movable.

   Time words in Zhuang are prototypically compounds of disyllabic words. Common time words in Zhuang are formed by compound heads *ku²* 'moment' and *mɯɯa⁵*, as well as monosyllabic words like *ŋɔn⁴* 'day', *hat²* 'morning', *ham⁵* 'evening, night' and *pi¹*, plus the demonstrative adjectives *ni⁶* 'this' and *te¹* 'that' and so on.

(56) ***ku²** ni⁶* 'now, at the moment', ***ku²** pan⁵* 'just now, a while ago', ***ku²** tem¹* 'in a minute'

   ***mɯɯa⁵** kon²* 'before, previously, formerly', ***mɯɯa⁵** ni⁶* 'now, at present'; ***mɯɯa⁵** te¹* 'then, in those times', ***mɯɯa⁵** ʔdu⁶* 'previous times', ***mɯɯa⁵** laŋ¹* 'later times'.

   ŋɔn⁴** kon²* '(several) days ago', ***ŋɔn⁴** ni⁶* 'today', ***ŋɔn⁴** lɯan⁴* 'yesterday', ***ŋɔn⁴** ɕok⁵* 'tomorrow', ***ŋɔn⁴** lɯ¹* 'the day after tomorrow', ***ŋɔn⁴** lɯaŋ⁵* 'in three days', ***ŋɔn⁴** mo²/na³*, 'later, later on, in the future', ***ŋɔn⁴** ʔdu⁶* 'previous day', ***ŋɔn⁴** laŋ¹* 'next day'. ***hat² 'morning' and ***ham⁵*** 'evening, night' can take the same modifiers as ***ŋɔn⁴***.

   ***pi¹** kwa²* 'last year', ***pi¹** tau¹* 'two years ago, the year before last', ***pi¹** ni⁶* 'this year', ***pi¹** mo²* 'next year', ***pi¹** na³* 'in two years, the years ahead'.

The locative word ***tsa:ŋ¹*** 'in the centre of', discussed earlier in §9.3.7.3 above, can also be used to form temporal expressions in Zhuang, as illustrated below.

(57) *tsa:ŋ¹ hat²* 'in the morning'

   tsa:ŋ¹ ŋɔn⁴ 'during the day, in the afternoon'

   tsa:ŋ¹ ham⁵ 'in the evening'

   tsa:ŋ¹ hɯm⁴ 'late at night, at midnight'

   tsa:ŋ¹ ɕieŋ¹ 'during Spring Festival'

Time words are movable adverbials. They can occur at the beginning of a sentence. They can also occur before or after the verb phrase. Thus the sentence 'he came home **yesterday**' can be said in Zhuang as:

(58) *ŋɔn⁴ lɯan⁴ te¹ ta:u² la:n⁴* (yesterday-3sg-return-home)

   te¹ ŋɔn⁴ lɯan⁴ ta:u² la:n⁴ (3sg-yesterday-return-home)

   te¹ ta:u² la:n⁴ ŋɔn⁴ lɯan⁴ (3sg-return-home- yesterday)

where the time word *ŋɔn⁴ lɯan⁴* 'yesterday' can occur freely in the initial, middle or final position of the sentence. This is different from adverbials of duration and of frequency, which can occur post-verbally only:

(59) *pai¹ ha³ ŋɔn⁴*   'go-five-day – go for five days'

   ʝu⁵ ɕip⁴ pi¹   'live-ten-year – live for ten years'

   ʔdoŋ¹ θa:m¹ ʔdɯan¹ 'pickle-three-month – to pickle for three months'

where change of the order of the time phrase will render the sentence unacceptable.

9.3.7.6. Imperative and negative imperative markers

There is no special marker for positive imperatives in Zhuang. However, a number of negative imperative markers are found in Zhuang, with different shades in meaning. These include *ʔbau⁵ lak⁴* 'don't', *ʔbau⁵ pa⁵* 'don't do…yet (but do it later)', *taŋ⁶ pa⁵* (same as *ʔbau⁵ pa⁵*).

(60) *ʔbau⁵ lak⁴ ɕua⁶ taŋ³ te¹*

   don't   speak way   that

   'Don't talk like that.'

In fast speech, *ʔbau⁵ lak⁴* can be shortened as *ʔblak⁴* or simply *lak⁴*.

(61) *ʔbau⁵ pa⁵ pai¹*   OR: *taŋ⁶ pa⁵ pai¹*

   don't   go   don't go

   'Don't go now (but go later).'

ʔbau⁵ pa⁵ and *taŋ⁶ pa⁵* can be shortened as *pa⁵*.

In Wuming, the negative imperative markers fore the above are *kai²* 'don't' and *kai² pa⁵* 'don't do … yet.'

9.3.7.7. *Particles and interjections*

Zhuang has a number of sentence particles for discourse purposes. They indicate the speaker's attitude in the utterances. The tones of these particles are not fixed. They may vary from speaker to speaker, and the degree of intensity of the utterances. Some examples follow.

(62) *hun¹   tɔk²   lo.*
rain   fall   PART
'It is raining.' (assertive)

(63) *te¹   ʔba:ŋ⁶   θa:i⁵   ɟu⁵   la:n⁴   pa.*
3sg   perhaps   stay   home   PART
'S/he is probably at home.' (assumption)

(64) *le¹   pu⁶ lak⁴   nə*
guard   thief   PART
'Keep an eye on thieves.' (warning, suggestion)

(65) *ka:i²   ni⁶   ʔdi¹   na*
piece   this   good   PART
'This one is good, isn't it?' (seeking affirmation)

(66) *pai¹   ʔam⁶   pai¹   le?*
go   not   go   PART
'Are you going (or not)?' (question)

(67) *ɟa!   la:i⁵   na⁴   ni⁶   mi⁴   non¹   lə!*
INTERJ.   CLF.   field   this   have   insect   PART
'Oh God, there are pests in this field!' (alarmed, surprise)

(68) *ne,   ʔau¹   ka:i²   ni⁶   pai¹.*
INTERJ.   take   piece   this   go
'Take this, then/Here you are.' (impatience)

It must be pointed out that there is a wide range of particles and interjections available in each dialect, whose usages and functions need to be further investigated.

9.3.7.8. *Intensifiers*

A small set of words in Zhuang function as intensifiers to describe the degree of intensity of a state or situation. These include *la:i¹* 'excessively, too', *ta⁶ la:i⁶* 'indeed', *pan⁴ ma⁴* 'very', *tem¹* 'also, in addition', and *ɟa:k⁵ ta:i¹* 'extremely, ... to death (vulgar)', among others. Intensifiers in Zhuang follow the adjectival verb they modify. Examples: *tsai¹ **la:i¹*** 'too far away', *tin³ **la:i¹*** 'too short', *hun⁴ la:i¹ **la:i¹*** '(there are) too many people'; *ʔdi¹ ta⁶ **la:i⁶*** 'very good indeed', *θeu² **pan⁴ ma⁴*** 'extremely/really clean', *fa⁶ lai⁴ **tem¹*** 'even longer'; *ʔdi⁶ la:u¹ **ɟa:k⁵ ta:i¹*** 'extremely scared, scared to death', *ham⁴ **ɟa:k⁵ ta:i¹*** 'exceptionally/extremely bitter'.

9.3.8. Elaborate expressions

Elaborate expressions are four-syllabled idiomatic expressions, often carrying rich cultural connotations.

(69) $\theta i^2 ka^1 la^3 tu\eta^6$ 'fond of moving around, tend not to stay in one place'

 $pi^6 nua\eta^6 pau^2 \textit{?}a{:}u^1$ 'relatives'

 $hun^1 t\mathfrak{o}k^2 pja^3 lai^4$ 'bad weather'

 $tsau^3 tsiet^2 ta^1 la{:}i^4$ 'adversity, times of misfortune'

 $hai^1 li^5 \varphi a{:}u^6 na^4$ 'to open up new land'

9.3.9. Colour terms

Basic colour terms in Zhuanginclude $\textit{?}di\eta^1$ 'red', $ha{:}u^1$ 'white', and fon^6 'black' ($\textit{?}dam^1$ in Wuming and a number of other dialects). To 'black' we may add mi^3 'soot' (the colour of charcoal) and fot^5 'black (of wound)'. Related to 'red' are non^5 'pink' and $tsam^2$ 'purple'. 'Green' is heu^1. There are two words for 'blue', $l\mathfrak{o}k^4$ and φep^5. $l\mathfrak{o}k^4$ appears to be related to Chinese lu^4, which means 'green' and φep^5 is a native word. Also, there are two items for 'yellow', hen^3 and $l\textit{w}an^2$, with different shades of meaning. hen^3 is the general term for 'yellow', while $l\textit{w}an^2$ specifically refers to orange colour, or the colour of fruits about to ripen.

To describe a specific type of colour, Zhuang often associates it with a prototypical object that it best represents, very much like the English expressions such as 'snow-white' and 'sky-blue'. Examples are $\textit{?}di\eta^1 l\textit{w}at^5$ 'red (as) blood — blood-red', $hen^3 tsoi^3$ 'yellow (as) banana — banana-yellow', and $\varphi ep^5 lom^3$ 'blue (as) indigo — indigo-blue', among others.

9.3.10. Emotional concepts

Like many other cultures, Zhuang make heavy use of body part terms in expressing emotional concepts. The majority of emotional concepts in Zhuang are associated with the face, the throat, and the heart. Colour, taste, dimension, touch, direction and so on also play an important role in the formation of concepts of this kind.

Concepts with na^3 'face'. As with English, concepts involving 'face' typically describe visible facial expressions. Examples: $na^3 nom^3$ ('young') 'shy, stand on ceremony', $na^3 \textit{ɲ}e^5$ ('shy') 'embarrassed', $na^3 na^1$ ('thick') 'unashamed, thick-skinned', $na^3 \textit{?}ba{:}\eta$ ('thin') 'shy', $na^3 mo\eta^1$ ('grey') 'shy', $na^3 \textit{?}di\eta^1$ ('red') 'blushed', $na^3 heu^1$ ('green') 'stern-faced', $na^3 hu\textit{w}^2$ ('dry') 'worried, panic', $na^3 \textit{?}b\mathfrak{o}\eta^1$ ('fluffy') 'relieved', θiet^5 ('diminish') na^3 'lose face', mi^4 ('have') na^3 'glorious, feel honoured'.

Concepts with ho^4 'throat'. These are typically associated with inner feelings. It is interesting to see that Zhuang uses 'throat' as the locus of emotions that are cross-linguistically related to the mind. Examples: $ho^4 han^4$ ('itchy, the taste/feel of uncooked taro') 'jealous', $ho^4 \textit{ɲ}a{:}p^2$ ('itchy') 'irritated', $ho^4 ta\eta^3$ ('erect') 'grudged', $ho^4 lai^4$ ('long') 'good tempered', $ho^4 lu\eta^2$ ('slack') 'good-tempered, gentle-hearted', $ho^4 h\textit{w}m^3$ ('ascend') 'angry', $ho^4 l\mathfrak{o}\eta^4$ ('descend') 'convinced', $ho^4 \textit{?}do\eta^6$ ('stiff') 'hard-lined, cruel'; $ho^4 \textit{?}un^5$ ('soft') 'soft, not strict'; mai^4 ('happy') ho^4 'happy, glad (not shown on the face)', $tsai^4$ ('love') ho^4 'concerned', $tsen^5$ ('stuck') ho^4 'to have grievance, feel uncomfortable with', $lua\eta^5$ ('suspend') ho^4 'keep in suspense, uneasy'.

Concepts with θam^1 'heart'. Many languages use 'heart' as the locus of emotion, and Zhuang is no exception. Examples: $\theta am^1 \theta o^5$ ('straight') 'honest', $\theta am^1 \textit{?}di^1$ ('good') 'kind-hearted', $\theta am^1 \textit{?}duk^2$ ('rotten') 'black-hearted'; $\varphi a{:}u^3$ ('fry') θam^1 'worried (about), anxious', nak^2 ('heavy') θam^1 'concentrated, determined'.

Other related concepts. In addition to the above, Zhuang uses the eye, stomach, body and breath to describe emotions. Examples: *ta¹ ʔdiŋ¹* ('eye-red') 'jealous, envy', *ta¹ θa:ŋ¹* ('eye-high/tall') 'arrogant, snobbish'; *tuɲ⁶ ɟja:k⁵* ('stomach-bad') 'evil-hearted'; *ʔda:ŋ¹ pjiet²* ('body-separate') 'sad'; *tɔk² ɕuɪ¹* ('drop-breath') 'pity'. There are also concepts that do not involve the use of body part terms, such as *mai⁴* 'happy', *ʔa:k²* 'joyful, hilarious', among others.

9.4. GRAMMATICAL PROCESSES

9.4.1. Grammar and grammatical processes

Zhuang is a non-inflexional language. It has no inflections for case, gender, tense or number. Affixing and reduplicating represent the major morphological processes.

9.4.1.1. Affixing

There are more prefixes than suffixes in Zhuang. Some commonly-used prefixes are listed below.

A. Noun prefixes:

(70) **pu⁶** – general prefix for human beings:

pu⁶ hek²	'guests'
pu⁶ nɔŋ⁴	'the Nung people'
pu⁶ jieu⁴	'the Yao people'

(71) **pau²** – prefix for adult male person:

pau² ta¹	'father-in-law'
pau² luŋ⁴	'father's elder brother'
pau² mo¹	'shaman'

Nouns taking the above prefixes are generally used as reference terms, and not as address terms.

(72) **la:u⁶** – honorific prefix for people:

la:u⁶ θai²	'teacher'
la:u⁶ ʔdo:ŋ¹	'relative by the marriage of one's children'
la:u⁶ tɔŋ⁴	'friends who is the same age'

Nouns with *la:u⁶* can be used as address terms.

(73) **ta⁶** – prefix for kinships of seniority:

ta⁶ ta¹	'maternal grandpa'
ta⁶ po⁵	'father'
ta⁶ pa³	'father or mother's elder sisters'

(74) **ta⁵** – prefix for girls:

ta⁵ nuaŋ⁶	'younger sister'
ta⁵ θa:u¹	'girl'

(75) **pɔ⁴** – plural prefix for human beings:

pɔ⁴ lau⁴   'us, we'

pɔ⁴ θu¹   'you (plural)'

pɔ⁴ te¹   'they, those (people)'

(76) **na³**– prefix for abstract nouns indicating position in the social or family hierarchy:

na³ po⁵   'father's generation'

na³ pi⁶   'elder siblings' generations'

na³ la:n¹   'grandchild's generation'

(77) **lɯk⁴** – prefix for fruits, small objects:

lɯk⁴ pɯak²   'taro'

lɯk⁴ ma:n⁵   'chilli pepper'

lɯk⁴ ta¹   'pupil, eyeball'

(78) **ka:i²** – prefix for things, attached to verbs to form a noun, nominalizer:

ka:i² kɯn¹   'things to eat – food'

ka:i² tɕn³   'things to wear–clothing'

ka:i² jɔɲ⁵   'things to use – spending money, utensil'

(79) **tin¹** – compounding head for 'seedlings':

tin¹ ma:k²   'seedlings of fruit plants'

tin¹ pjak²   'vegetable seedlings'

tin¹ pɯak²   'taro seedlings'

(80) **tsau³** – compounding head for 'source, end':

tsau³ ta⁵   'source of a river'

tsau³ ʔba:n⁶ 'the front of the village'

tsau³ ha:n⁴   'the ends of a shoulder pole'

(81) **ten⁵** – compounding head for 'site, place, location':

ten⁵ la:n⁴   'house site'

ten⁵ θɯan¹   'garden site'

ten⁵ ʑu⁵   'address, residence'

B. Verb/adjectival prefix

The form **pan⁴** merits special attention. This item is polysemous. It can be used as a lexical verb, meaning 'to become, to be'. It can also function as an aspectual marker to denote an achieved result. As a prefix, it has two meanings.

(i) Verb/adjectival prefix, detransitiviser, whose meaning may be described as '-able'. All activity verbs can take this prefix.

(82) *pan⁴ kɯn¹* 'edible'
  pan⁴ kuak⁵ 'workable'
  pan⁴ ɟu⁵ 'livable'
  pan⁴ pai¹ 'goable'
  pan⁴ nin⁴ 'able to be slept on'

(ii) Prefix for disease terms. The majority of disease terms in Zhuang are formed with this prefix. Some common disease terms are given below.

(83) *pan⁴ ʔai¹* 'to caugh'
  pan⁴ ʔda:t⁵ 'have a fever'
  pan4 mɯ² 'have asthma'
  pan⁴ pa:k⁵ 'be insane'
  pan⁴ pai⁴ 'have a skin ulcer'

9.4.1.2. *Suffixing*

Suffixes in Zhuang mainly occur with nouns and verbs. Noun suffixes function like noun qualifiers. Verb suffixes express certain aspectual meaning.

A.   Diminutive suffix *lɯk⁴*:

(84) *mu¹ lɯk⁴* 'piglet'
  va:i⁴ lɯk⁴ 'calf, veal'
  ma¹ lɯk⁴ 'puppy'
  pit² lɯk⁴ 'duckling'

B.   Gender suffixes *tak⁴* 'male (animals), *pu⁶* 'male' (birds); *me⁵* 'female':

(85) *va:i⁴ tak⁴* 'bull, (male) buffalo'
  ma¹ tak⁴ '(male) dog'
  ma⁶ tak⁴ 'horse'
  kai² pu⁶ 'rooster'

(86) *va:i⁴ me⁵* 'cow'
  ma¹ me⁵ '(female) dog, bitch'
  ma⁶ me⁵ 'hare'
  kai² me⁵ 'hen'

C.   Verb + C + *ɯa⁵* (Standard Zhuang C + *aɯ²*): do something quickly, or casually. In this pattern, the initial consonant of the verb is copied, plus the final /-*ɯa⁵*/.

(87) *kɯn¹ kɯa⁵* 'eat straight away'
  ʔdam¹ ʔdɯa⁵ 'plant (it) straight away'
  lɔk² lɯa⁵ 'just pull (it) out'
  mɔk² mɯa⁵ 'simply bury (it)'
  fan⁴ fɯa⁵ 'just slash (it), cut randomly'
  hɯat⁵ hɯa⁵ 'tie up quickly'

D.   Verb + *jɔ⁵*: do something tentatively, try to do

(88) *kuak⁵ jɔ⁵* 'do (something) tentatively'
    çim⁴ jɔ⁵ 'try to taste (it)'
    tɯ⁴ jɔ⁵ 'try to harness'
    ʔdam¹ jɔ⁵ 'try to plant'
    lua:m¹ jɔ⁵ 'try to carry (by two or more people)'

E.   Suffix for disease terms: Noun + *tsiet²*

This is quite a productive pattern. The suffix *tsiet²* is obviously derived from the lexeme *tsiet²*, meaning 'ache'.

(89) *ʔda:ŋ¹ tsiet⁷* 'feel pain all through'
    hɯat⁵ tsiet⁷ 'have a back pain'
    ta¹ tsiet⁷ 'have a sore eye'
    tuŋ⁶ tsiet⁷ 'have a stomach ache'
    tsau³ tsiet² 'have a headache'

9.4.2. Reduplication

Reduplication in Zhuang occurs with verbs, adjectives, nouns and classifiers. Reduplication of verbs prototypically refers to repeated action. Reduplication in Zhuang takes the following forms:

9.4.2.1. *Reduplication of verbs*

Only simple verbs, i.e. phonologically monosyllabic verbs, can be reduplicated. Reduplication of verbs takes the following forms.

A. AABB

This occurs with verbs of opposite polarity. Examples:

(90) *hau³ hau³ ʔok⁵ ʔok⁵* 'keep coming in and out'
    pai¹ pai¹ ta:u² ta:u² 'come and go, keep passing by'
    hɯm³ hɯm³ lɔŋ⁴ lɔŋ⁴ 'keep in close contact'; 'keep going up and down'

B. A ***pai¹*** A ***ta:u²*** (lit. 'A go A come'). Examples:

(91) *çua⁶ **pai¹** çua⁶ **ta:u²*** 'keep persuading/talking for a long time'
    *pja:i³ **pai¹** pja:i³ **ta:u²*** 'keep walking; walk back and forth'
    *la¹ **pai¹** la¹ **ta:u²*** 'keep searching for a long time'

C. A ***hɯm³*** A ***lɔŋ⁴*** (lit. 'A ascend A descend'). Examples:

(92) *θuan² **hɯm³** θuan² **lɔŋ⁴*** 'keep counting'
    *ʔdiap⁵ **hɯm³** ʔdiap⁵ **lɔŋ⁴*** 'keep thinking'(also as *ʔdiap⁵ pai¹ ʔdiap⁵ ta:u²*)
    *kam⁵ **hɯm³** kam⁵ **lɔŋ⁴*** 'try hard to convince'

D. A *la:i¹* A *ta:i⁵* – do too much/excessively. Examples:

(93) *ka:ŋ³ la:i¹ ka:ŋ³ ta:i⁵* 'talk too much, talk excessively'
  lɛn¹ la:i¹ lɛn¹ ta:i⁵ 'see a lot, see too much'
  pai¹ la:i¹ pai¹ ta:i⁵ 'go too often'
  ham² la:i¹ ham² ta:i⁵ 'ask too much'

9.4.2.2. Reduplication of adjectives

Reduplication of adjectives designates the high degree of tensity of the situation described by the adjective in question. Only gradable adjectives are permitted to undergo this process.

(94) *na³ ʔding¹ ʔding¹* 'very red face'
  θak⁴ θeu² θeu² 'wash extremely clean'
  pja:i³ ɲam⁴ ɲam⁴ 'walk very fast'
  ʔdam¹ ti⁵ ti⁵ 'plant very close together'

A number of preverbal adverbs can be reduplicated this way.

(95) ***ma:n⁵ ma:n⁵*** *pja:i³* 'walk **very slowly**' (*ma:n⁵* 'slow')
  na:n⁴ na:n⁴ *pai¹* 'go **occasionally**' (*na:n⁴* 'long (time)')
  ŋa:m² ŋa:m² *taŋ⁴* '**just** arrived' (*ŋa:m²* 'suitable, just')
  liam⁴ liam⁴ *ʔua:k⁵* 'dodge **quietly**' (*liam⁴* 'quietly')

9.4.2.3. Reduplication of nouns and classifiers

Reduplication of nouns and classifiers has the meaning 'all, every'.

(96) ***la:n⁴***   ***la:n⁴***   *mi⁴*   *mu¹*   *çieŋ¹*
  house   house   have   pig   Spring Festival
  'Every household has a pig for the Spring Festival.'

(97) ma:k²   ***ʔɛn¹***   ***ʔɛn¹***   *va:n¹*
  fruit   CLF   CLF   sweet
  'All the fruits are sweet.'

Sometimes, two nouns can be reduplicated in AABB form.

(98) *ʔdaɯ¹ ʔdaɯ¹ lok⁵ lok⁵* (inside + outside) 'inside and outside, every corner'
  pi⁶ pi⁶ nuaɲ⁶ nuaɲ⁶ (elder sibling + younger sibling) 'all the relatives'
  pit² pit² kai² kai² (duck + chicken) 'ducks and chickens, all domestic fowls'

9.4.3. Lexical nominalization

As mentioned in §9.4.1.1, the element ***ka:i²*** can function as a nominalizer in Zhuang. It can be combined with verbs, adjectives and pronouns to form nominal compounds.

(99) *ka:i² kɯn¹* 'things to eat – food'

  ka:i² tən³ 'things to wear – clothing'

  ka:i² jɔŋ⁵ 'things to use – spending money; utensil'

  ka:i² ʔdi¹ 'things good – good things, things of superior quality'

Items with similar function include **tua⁴** and **ʔdən¹**. *tua⁴* is used for animals and *ʔdən¹*, utensils.

(100) *tua⁴ ʔbin¹* 'flying insects/birds/animals' (*ʔbin¹* 'to fly')

  tua⁴ tɯ⁴ 'beasts of burden' (*tɯ⁴* 'to harness, hold')

  tua⁴ çieŋ⁶ 'domesticated animals' (*çieŋ⁶* 'to raise')

  tua⁴ pɯaŋ² 'untamed domestic animals' (*pɯaŋ²* 'untamed, set free')

  tua⁴ ka:i¹ 'animals for sale' (*ka:i¹* 'to sell')

(101) *ʔdən¹ ʔdi⁵* 'utensils, tools' (the meaning of *ʔdi⁵* is unknown. It also occurs in the compound for *ʔda:u¹ ʔdi⁵* 'star'.)

  ʔdən¹ jɔŋ⁵ 'utensils' (*jɔŋ⁵* 'to use')

  ʔdən¹ tsaŋ¹ 'containers' (*tsaŋ¹* 'to contain')

  ʔdən¹ kɔm⁵ 'cover (noun)' (*kɔm⁵* 'to cover')

9.5. SIMPLE MAIN CLAUSES

Simple clauses in Zhuang may be divided into two types: transitive and intransitive. As mentioned in §9.3.3, Zhuang is an SVO language, with Subject-Verb-Object as the preferred word order. However, V-S order occasionally occurs.

(102) *tɔk² hun¹ le.*

  drop rain PART

  'It is raining.'

(103) *pi² pai¹ ha³ tua⁴ va:i⁴ lo.*

  escape go five CL buffalo PART

  'Five buffalos escaped.'

See §9.6.2.3 for treatment of related phenomena.

9.5.1. Types of predicate arguments

9.5.1.1. *Double-subject/topic-comment sentences*

One type of sentences in Zhuang structurally involves two subjects, a typological feature also found in Chinese. This type of constructions may be referred to as 'double-subject sentences' (Chao 1968: 67-104) or 'Topic-comment sentences' (Li and Thompson 1981: 92-108), depending on the type of analysis one chooses to adopt. There is some kind of semantic relationship between the two subjects, such as 'part' vs. 'whole'. In the following examples, the topic noun phrases are underlined in bold.

(104) $la:i^5$ na^4 ni^6 hau^6 pan^4
       CLF   field   this   rice   grow well
       'This piece of land, rice grows well in it.'

(105) $\text{?}ba:n^4$ te^1 hun^4 $la:i^1$
       village   that   people   many
       'That village has a lot of people/There are a lot of people in that village.'

(106) $nuaŋ^6$ $\text{?}daŋ^1$ tau^3 $luat^5$
       y. sibling   nose   come   blood
       'Younger brother's nose is bleeding/Younger brother has got a bleeding nose.'

(107) tua^5 $miɐu^4$ $laŋ^1$ ngt^4 $fa:k^5$
       Bean   season   late   grain   plump
       'Late-season beans, they have plump grains./The grains of late-season beans are plump.'

(108) $ha^3\ tua^4\ kai^2\ me^5\ ni^6$ tua^4 tua^4 $\text{?}ok^5$ $tsai^2$.
       Five CLF chicken female this   CLF   CLF   lay   egg
       'These five chooks, all (of them) are laying eggs.'

9.5.1.2. *Direct vs. indirect objects*

It is important to recognize in Zhuang a number of verbs that can take two objects, a direct object (DO) and an indirect object (IO). Some of these verbs require the preposition or co-verb hau^3 (derived from the lexical verb 'to give') before the indirect object. The word order is: V + DO + hau^3 + IO. Examples:

(109) a. $çe^1$ 'leave, save': $çe^1\ hau^6\ hau^3\ te^1$ 'leave (some) rice to him'

     b. $çie^2$ 'lend': $çie^2\ ŋan^4\ hau^3\ ku^1$ 'lend some money to me'

     c. $jien^5$ 'pass on to': $jien^5\ \text{?}ien^1\ hau^3\ kɔ^1$ 'pass a cigarette to elder brother'

     d. $ka:i^1$ 'sell...(to)': $ka:i^1\ va:i^4\ hau^3\ muŋ^4$ 'sell the buffalo to you'

     e. pan^1 'allocate': $pan^1\ hau^6\ hɔn^1\ hau^3\ pɔ^4\ te^1$ 'allocate some seeds to them'

     f. $θui^1$ 'tell': $θui^1\ tɔ^4\ hau^3\ nuaŋ^6$ 'tell younger brother/sister a story'

The use of hau^3 is obligatory in constructions of this kind. Note that the direct object can be fronted, as in $hau^6\ çe^1\ hau^3\ te^1\ le$ 'food, (we have) left him', but not the indirect object, as utterances like $*te^1 hau^6\ çe^1\ hau^3\ le$ are not acceptable. In addition, when the contexts are clear, the direct object can be omitted, as in $lak^4\ çe^1\ hau^3\ te^1$ 'Don't leave (it) to him.'

    Unlike the above, some verbs take optional hau^3. These include lok^2 'give for free, bestow', poi^4 'pay back, return', $θɔŋ^2$ 'send, present'. These have the pattern: V + (hau^3) + IO + DO.

(110) lok^2 (hau^3) te^1 tai^5 hau^6 $θa:n^1$ $\text{?}deu^1$
       give   H   3sg   bag   rice   husked   one
       'Give him a bag of rice for free'

(111)   poi⁴ (hauɯ³)   ku¹   θa:m¹   pa:k²   man⁴   ŋan⁴
      pay back H   1sg   three   hundred   dollar   money
      'Pay me back three hundred dollars'

Sentences like (110) and (111) can be rearranged into the 'V + DO + hauɯ³ + IO' construction just discussed above, in which case the use of hauɯ³ is obligatory.

(110') lok² tai⁵ hau⁶ θa:nᵀ deu¹ hauɯ³ te¹   'give him a bag of rice'

(111') poi⁴ θa:m¹ pa:k² man⁴ ŋan⁴ hauɯ³ ku¹ 'pay back three hundred dollars to me'

It is worth pointing out that sentences like (109a) do not have a parallel construction 'V + IO + DO' unless the direct object is specified or quantified. In other words, specification/quantification plays a role in the syntax of Zhuang. Thus, (109a′) is unacceptable as the direct object is unspecified and unquantified while (109a″) is OK with a quantified direct object.

(109a′) *çe¹ hauɯ³ te¹ hau⁶   'leave him some rice'

(109a″) çe¹ hauɯ³ te¹ θoŋ¹ tai⁵ hau⁶ 'leave him two bags of rice'

The main verb 'to give' hauɯ³ does not allow 'Verb + hauɯ³ + IO + DO':

(112) *ku¹ hauɯ³ hauɯ³ te¹ θa:m¹ man⁴ ŋan⁴. 'I gave him three dollars.'

but rather 'Verb + IO + DO' or 'Verb + DO + hauɯ³ + IO':

(113) ku¹ hauɯ³ te¹ θa:m¹ man⁴ ŋan⁴.   'I gave him three dollars.'

(114) ku¹ hauɯ³ θa:m¹ man⁴ ŋan⁴ hauɯ³ te¹. (same as above)

Quantification also interacts with aspect in Zhuang, a point we will pick up later.
    Furthermore, some verbs never take hauɯ³. Verbs of this kind allow 'V + IO + DO' pattern only. Examples:

(115)   te¹   ham²   ku¹   tsi³   çɔn⁴.
      3sg   ask   1sg   several   utterance
      'He asked me several questions.'

(116)   pau²   kuak⁵   puuan²   ʑam¹   te¹   çip⁴   man⁴   ŋan⁴.
      CL   do   trade   rip   3sg   ten   dollar   money
      'The vender ripped him off 10 dollars.'

9.5.1.3. Locative and directional phrases

9.5.1.3.1. Locative phrases

Locative expressions in Zhuang are typically introduced by the locative marker ʑu⁵.
Locative expressions can occur before or after the verb, depending on event types.

(116) a. *ɟuˑ⁵ kɯn⁴ lauˑ⁴ ninˑ⁴*   (OR: *ninˑ⁴ ɟuˑ⁵ kɯn⁴ lauˑ⁴*) 'to sleep upstairs'

    b. *ɟuˑ⁵ ʔdaɯ¹ la:n⁴ naɲ⁵* (OR: *naɲ⁵ ɟuˑ⁵ ʔdaɯ¹ la:n⁴*) 'to sit inside the house'

    c. *ɟuˑ⁵ kɯn⁴ heɲ¹ lon²*   (OR: *lon² ɟuˑ⁵ kɯn⁴ heɲ¹*) 'to chop on the chopping board'.

If the event is a volitional, and if the action is involves a purpose, the locative phrase comes before the verb phrase.

(117) *ɟuˑ⁵ la:n⁴ tɯ¹ lɯk⁴*   'to look after children at home/to stay at home to look after children'

(117′) ?? *tɯ¹ lɯk⁴ ɟuˑ⁵ la:n⁴*   'to look after children at home'

But if the action is non-volitional, or if the verb is one of placement, the locative comes after the verb. Consider the following pairs:

(118) *hɔm³ ɟuˑ⁵ tsa:ŋ¹ la:n⁴*   'to fall in the centre of the house'

(118′) ?? *ɟuˑ⁵ tsa:ŋ¹ la:n⁴ hɔm³*   'to fall in the centre of the house'

(119) *ta:i¹ ɟuˑ⁵ la³ ʔba:n⁶*   'to die (on the road) down the village'

(119′) ?? *ɟuˑ⁵ la³ ʔba:n⁶ ta:i¹*   'to die (on the road) down the village'

(120) *ɕe¹ ɟuˑ⁵ kɯn⁴ ɕoŋ⁴*   'leave on the table'

(120′) *ɟuˑ⁵ kɯn⁴ ɕoŋ⁴ ɕe¹*   'leave on the table'

(121) *tɔk² ɟuˑ⁵ tin¹ ʔdɔ:i¹*   'drop at the foot of the hill'

(121′) *ɟuˑ⁵ tin¹ ʔdɔ:i¹ tɔk²*   'drop at the foot of the hill'

When locative expressions occur in the slots of a subject, or of an object of a transitive verb, *ɟuˑ⁵* is not used.

(122) *ʔdaɯ¹ θɯan¹ ʔdam¹ mi⁴   ha:u²la:i¹ pjak².*
    inside garden plant have many   vegetable
    'There are a lot of vegetables in the garden.'

(123) *mɯŋ⁶   ta:ɯ⁴ lok⁵   la:n⁴, ku¹ jieu² ʔdaɯ¹ la:n⁴*
    2sg   guard outside house, 1sg search inside   house
    'You guard outside the house, and I'll search inside.'

(124) *ham⁵ luan⁴   nuaŋ⁶   nin⁴   **kɯm⁴   lau⁴***
Last night   y. sibling sleep above   building'
'Younger brother slept (in the room) upstairs last night.'

9.5.1.3.2. *Directional phrases with pai¹ and ma¹*

Directional phrases in Zhuang proto-typically involve the use of the directional verbs *pai¹* 'go'
and *ma¹* (OR: *tau³*) 'come', which function like co-verbs. Like locative phrases, directional
phrases can occur both pre-verbally and post-verbally.

(125) *tsuŋ² te¹   pai¹   na⁴   θiu¹   hau⁶.*
3pl   go   field   harvest   crops
'They went to the field and harvested crops.'
'They went to the field to harvest crops.'

(126) *tua⁴   kai² me⁵   ni⁶   ŋɔn⁴   ŋɔn⁴   tau³   la:n⁴   la¹   kɯm¹.*
CL   hen   this   day   day   come   house look for eat
'This hen comes into the house to look for food every day.'

In post-verbal usage, the directional phrase has selectional restrictions. It can occur with verbs
that involve destination. The choice of *pai¹* and *ma¹* depends on whether the arrival point is
towards or away from the speaker.

(127) *va:i⁴   çiaŋ²   pai¹   pa²   le.*
buffalo   release go   pasture PART
'The buffalos were released to pasture land.'

(128) *te¹   ŋɔn⁴   laɯ⁴   ta:u²   pai¹/ma¹?*
3sg   day   which   return   go/come
'What day will he return (away from speaker/towards speaker)?'

9.5.1.4. *Manner and instrumental adjuncts*

One of the most common ways in which manner and instrumental adjuncts are introduced in
Zhuang is through the use of the construction 'Verb + *ʔau¹*', roughly translated as 'do sth. by
way of V-ing'.

(129) *no⁵kai²   ni⁶   tum²   **ʔau¹**   ʔdi¹   kɯm¹,   ça:u³   **ʔau¹***
meatchicken this   boil   SUFF.   good   eat,   fry   SUFF.

ʔam⁶   ʔdi¹   kɯm¹.
not   good   eat

'This chicken tastes good if it is boiled, it doesn't taste good if stir fried.'

(130) *ka:i²*   *tɔŋ⁴ jieŋ⁵*   *ni⁶*   *lua:m¹*   **ʔau¹**   *naŋ⁵*   *pan⁴*
       CLF   thing   this   carry   SUFF.   then   do
       'This thing will have to be carried by more than two people.'

In the above examples, **ʔau¹** functions like a suffix or a clitic. This pattern is quite characteristic of Zhuang.

ʔau¹ can also be used as a lexical verb meaning 'take, use', which can introduce the instrument with which an act is carried out.

(131) *kɔ¹*   **ʔau¹**   *lo:k²*   *tak²*   *lam⁶*.
       elder   take   ladle   scoop   water
       brother
       'Elder brother scooped water with a ladle.'

Similar items with this function include *tɯ⁴* 'hold, carry', and *jɔŋ⁵* 'use'.

(132) *ta:i²*   *tɯ⁴/jɔŋ⁵*   *lap²*   *tsaŋ¹*   *pit²*.
       grandma   use   coop   hold   duck
       'Grandma used the coop to hold ducks.'

(133) *ʔa:u¹*   *tɯ⁴*   *ɕa:k⁵*   *la:m⁵*   *ma⁶*.
       uncle   take   rope   tie   horse
       'Uncle tied the horse with a rope'.

9.5.1.5. 'Missing' arguments

It is a salient feature of Zhuang grammar that noun phrases do not need to be specified when they are understood from contexts. This is not unique to Zhuang. Many languages have this property. Utterances like the following are very common in Zhuang daily conversation.

(134) *pai¹*   *ʔam⁶*   *pai¹*?   — *pai¹*.
       go   not   go   go
       'Are (you/we) going?'—'Yes.'

In narrative discourse, the information chain characteristically requires only the actions to be specified. The following is an instruction on division of labour during a planting season:

(135) *ŋɔn⁴ni⁶*   *tsa:ŋ¹hat²*   *lwai²*   *na⁴,*   *tsa:ŋ¹ŋɔn⁴*   *pa:t⁵*
       today   morning   rake   field,   afternoon   reinforce

       va:i¹.   *ŋɔn⁴ɕok⁵*   *hat²lom⁵*   *lɔk²*   *tsa³,*
       dam   tomorrow   morning-early   pull   rice seedling,

       lieu⁶   *ɕi⁴*   *ʔdam¹*   *na⁴,*   *kɯm¹*   *ŋa:i⁴*   *ʔjie⁵*
       finish   then   plant   field,   eat   lunch   finish

       tai⁵   *pɯm⁵,*   *ŋɔn⁴lɯ⁴*   *tsa:ŋ¹hat²*   *θiu¹*   *tua⁵,*
       carry   manure   day after tomorrow   morning   harvest   bean

tsa:ŋ¹ ŋɔn⁴   *çoi⁵*   *m ɯaŋ¹.*
afternoon   repair   ditch

'(We'll) rake the field in the morning today. In the afternoon, (we'll) reinforce the dam. Tomorrow morning (we'll) pull the rice seedlings. Then (we'll) plant the field. After lunch (we'll) deliver manure to the field. The day after tomorrow, (we'll) harvest beans in the morning. In the afternoon, (we'll) repair the ditch.'

This is true also of proverbs or other similar construction types, where impersonal pronouns are involved, which do not need to be specified.

(136)   *kuak⁵*   *na⁴*   *ʔbau⁵*   *la:u¹*   *la:i¹,*   *kuak⁵*   *va:i¹*   *ʔbau⁵*
         Make   field   not   worry   many   make   dam   not

         la:u¹   *lai⁴*
         worry   long

'When (one) opens new fields, (one) doesn't need to be worried about the quantity being too large; when (one) makes dams, (one) doesn't need to be concerned about them being too long.' (proverb)

A number of complement taking verbs in Zhuang display 'pro-drop' properties. In languages like English, such pronouns need to be supplied.

(137)   *lɯk⁴*   *ha:k⁵*   *ni⁶*   *lo⁶ʔde⁵*   *lwa²*   *leu.*
         Child   school   this   know   wrong   PART
'The student knows that (s/he) is wrong.'

(138)   *nuaŋ⁶*   *ʔdiep⁵*   *nau⁴*   *ɟa:k⁵*   *pai¹*   *to:k⁵*   *nai⁵*   *sɯ¹*   *tem¹*
         y.sibling think   say   want   go   read   some   book   more
'Younger sister/brother thought (s/he) would want to go to do some more studies.'

(139)   *te¹*   *lum³*   *pu⁶*   *laɯ⁴*   *nau⁴*   *mi⁴*   *ma⁴*   *ɟu⁵*   *ʔdaɯ¹*   *ho⁴.*
         3sg   like   who   say   have   sth.   at   inside   throat
'S/he looks as if (s/he) has something in her/his mind.'

9.5.2. Modality: irrealis and epistemic

As mentioned in §9.3.7.1, a closed class of modal-auxiliaries in Zhuang express irrealis and epistemic meanings. Modal-auxiliaries in Zhuang display a number of syntactic properties found in their counterparts in other languages. They retain some characteristic of verbs.

9.5.2.1. Irrealis *ɟa:k⁵*

When used with non-volitional subject, this item characteristically marks future meaning.

(140)   *hau⁶*   *ɟa:k⁵*   *lieu⁶*   *lo.*
         Rice   IRR   finished   PART
'Rice is running out.'

(141)   *na⁴*   *ta:n¹*   *ʒa:k⁵*   *ʒie⁵*   *le.*
        field   harvest   IRR   accomplish   PART
        'The harvest of this field is about to accomplish.'

ʒa:k⁵ in sentences like (140) and (141) cancels the truth conditions of the event described by the verb phrase. Without the use of *ʒa:k⁵*, (140) and (141) mean 'rice has run out' and 'the harvest has been accomplished' respectively.
With volitional subject, *ʒa:k⁵* expresses the intention of the subject in question.

(142)   *te¹*   *ʒa:k⁵*   *pai¹*   *ʔau¹*   *fɯm⁴.*
        3sg   IRR   go   take   firewood
        'He is going to/wants to go to collect firewood.'

Not only can *ʒa:k⁵* modify main verbs, it can also take other modal-auxiliaries that express irrealis,eg.:

(143)   *nau⁴*   *pai¹*   *nau⁴*   *ta:u²*,   *tɔk²laŋ¹*   *te¹*   *ʒa:k⁵*   **ɲien⁵**   *kuak⁵*   *leu*
        talk   go   talk   come   finally   3sg   IRR   **willing**   do   PART
        'Having been persuaded for some time, finally he was about to be willing to do the job.'

(144)   *ta:i²*   *ʔbau⁵*   *ʔdi¹ ʒu⁵*,   *ʒa:k⁵*   **ŋa⁵**   *kɯm¹*   *nai⁵*   *θu⁵*   *θeu²*   *ʔdeu¹.*
        grandma   not   well,   IRR   **crave**   eat   bit   porridge   clear   one
        'Grandma is feeling unwell. She would like to have a bit of thin porridge.'

9.5.2.2.   *'Must', 'should', and 'have to'*

The concepts of 'must', 'should' and 'have to' in Zhuang can be expressed through double negative constructions like '*ʔbau⁵* + Verb + *ʔbau⁵ pan⁴*', or '*ʔbau⁵* + *ʔdai⁶* + *bau⁵* + Verb'. They may also be expressed through the construction 'Clause + *naŋ⁵ pan⁴*'.

(145)   *çɔn⁴ ha:u²*   *ni⁶*   *mɯŋ⁴*   *ʔbau⁵*   *çua⁶*   *ʔbau⁵*   *pan⁴*
        remark   this   you   not   speak   not   AUX
        'This remark you have to/must speak out.'

(146)   *mɯŋ⁴*   *la¹*   *te¹*,   *te¹*   *ʔbau⁵*   *ʔdai⁶*   *ʔbau⁵*   *pa:ŋ¹*
        2sg   lookfor   3sg   3sg   not   AUX   not   help
        'If you go to him, (I think) he'll have to help.'

(147)   *ka:i²*   *sɯan²*   *ni⁶*,   *tsi³*   *pu⁶*   *hun⁴*   *kuak⁵*   *naŋ⁵*   *pan⁴¹*
        CLF   thing   this   several   CL   people   do   then   AUX
        'This matter should be dealt with/done by several people.'

9.5.2.3. *Compound verbs with nau⁴ 'to say'*

A set of compound verbs in Zhuang take the verb *nau⁴* 'to say' as head. These describe certain psychological state or activities that are associated with a range of modal meanings such as counter-factual, supposition, assumption and so on. Examples:

(148) *ku¹*   *lwa² nau⁴*   *mɯŋ⁴*   *ʔam⁶*   *lo⁶.*

  1sg   thought   2sg   not   know

  'I thought you didn't know (but I was mistaken).' (counterfactual)

(149) *ku¹*   *ʔbau⁵*   *ɲi⁴nau⁴*   *te¹*   *pan⁴*   *hun⁴*   *taŋ³*   *ni⁶.*

  1sg   not   doubt   3sg   become   person   kind   this

  'I didn't realize that s/he should have become a person like this.' (contrary to what was expected)

(150) *te¹*   *ɲi⁴nau⁴*   *tsuɲ²te¹*   *nau⁴*   *haɯ³*   *ku¹*   *lo⁶ʔde⁵*   *le.*

  3sg   suspect   3pl   tell   give   1sg   know   PART

  'S/he thought/suspected that they had already told me.' (supposition)

(151) *te¹*   *lum³ pu⁶*   *nau⁴*   *ʔiɲ⁵*   *lo⁶ ʔde⁵*   *le.*

  3sg   seem/look   as if   already   know   PART

  'It seems that he already knew about it.' (supposition)

Other verbs in this category include *la:u¹ hi² nau⁴* 'fear (that)…', *lo⁶ ɲie¹ nau⁴* 'hear say (that)…', *ʔdiep⁵ nau⁴* '(I/she/he/we…) was thinking that…', *pa:k² nau⁴* 'verbally say that…(but think or do otherwise)…', *ŋa⁵ tsie⁴ nau⁴* 'hope/wish that…, desire that…', among others.

(152) *te¹*   *la:u¹hi²nau⁴*   *mɯŋ⁴*   *lum⁴,*   *vi⁵naŋ⁵*   *haɯ³*   *ku¹*   *tau³*   *heu⁵.*

  3sg   fear   2sg   forget   therefore   let   1sg   come   call

  'Fearing that you might forget, s/he asked me to come and call you.'

(153) *ku¹*   *lo⁶ɲie¹*   *nau⁴*   *la:n¹*   *te¹*   *kɯm¹lau³*   *ŋɔn⁶lɯan⁴.*

  1sg   hear   say   grandchild   3sg   get married   yesterday

  'I was told that his/her grandson/granddaughter got married yesterday.'

(154) *te¹*   *pa:k²*   *nau⁴*   *tau³*   *pa:ŋ¹,*   *ʔdaɯ¹*   *ho⁴*   *ʔbau⁵*   *ɲien⁵*   *pa:ŋ¹*

  1sg   mouth   say   come   help   inside   throat   not   willing   help

  'S/he said s/he would like to come and help but in fact s/he was unwilling to.'

(155) *pa³*   *ŋa⁵tsie⁴*   *nau⁴*   *haɯ³*   *mɯŋ⁴*   *pai¹*   *jieu²*   *te¹*

  aunt   crave   say   let   2sg   go   see   3sg

  'Aunty would very much hope that you go and visit her.'

9.5.2.4. *Scope of negation with modal-auxiliaries*

The scope of negation with modal-auxiliaries in Zhuang is determined by the position of the negator. If the negator occurs before the auxiliary, it has scope over the entire verb phrase. If the negator follows the auxiliary, only the clause outside the auxiliary is affected.

(156) $m\, \textit{uuŋ}^4$ heu^5 te^1 pai^1, te^1 $\textit{ʔbau}^5$ $ka{:}m^3$ pai^1.
         you   call   3sg   go,   3sg   not   dare   go
         'If you tell him to go, he doesn't dare to go (ie. he is scared to).'

(157) $m\, \textit{uuŋ}^4$ heu^5 te^1 pai^1, te^1 $ka{:}m^3$ $\textit{ʔbau}^5$ pai^1?
         you   say   3sg   go   3sg   dare   not   go
         'If you tell him to go, how dare he not go? (i.e. he has to go).'

Note that unlike other modal auxiliaries, the irrealis marker $\textit{ʒa{:}k}^5$ does not allow a negator to occur before it. It can only take a negator after it.

(158) $\textit{ʒa{:}k}^5$ pai^1 $\textit{ʔbau}^5$ $\textit{ʔdi}^1$, $\textit{ʒa{:}k}^5$ $\textit{ʔbau}^5$ pai^1 je^5 $\textit{ʔbau}^5$ $\textit{ʔdi}^1$.
         IRR   go   not   good   IRR   NOT   go   also   NOT   good
         'It is not good planning to go; it is equally no good not to go.'

9.5.2.5. *Auxiliaries in serial verb constructions*

While auxiliaries typically occur before a verb phrase, they can also occur in the middle of a clause that involves serial verb constructions.

(159) ku^1 mi^4 nai^5 $\theta uuan^2$ $\textit{ʔdeu}^1$ $\textbf{\textit{ŋa}}^5\textbf{\textit{tsie}}^4$ $\textit{ça{:}m}^1$ $m\, \textit{uuŋ}^4$ $pa{:}ŋ^1$.
         1sg   have   bit   thing   one   IRR   request   2sg   help
         'I have something on which I would like to seek your help.'

In such cases, the scope of modification is for the events or situations expressed by the verbs that come after the auxiliary, not the entire serial verb constructions.

9.5.3. Interrogative sentences

Interrogative sentences in Zhuang can be divided into yes-no questions, alternative questions and substantive questions, as illustrated below.

9.5.3.1. *Yes-no questions*

Yes-no questions in Zhuang take the form of 'A-not-A' or 'A-not', like Mandarin Chinese. A positive answer is given by repeating the verb. A negative answer is provided by repeating the negator.

(160) $m\, \textit{uuŋ}^4$ $kuak^5$ $\textit{ʔbau}^5$ $kuak^5$?   – $kuak^5$.
         2sg   do   NOT   do   –   do
         'Are you going to do it?'– 'Yes, I am.'

(161) pa^3 $k\, \textit{uum}^1$ $\textit{ŋa{:}i}^4$ $ça\textit{ŋ}^4$?   – $ça\textit{ŋ}^4$
         Aunt   eat   lunch   NOTYET   –   not yet
         'Have you eaten your lunch yet, aunty?' – 'No, not yet.

Alternatively, yes-no questions can also be formed by adding a question marker *mi² le⁴* (short form: *mi²* or *mia²*) at the end of a sentence:

(162) *te¹*   *tau³*   *mi²*?   – *tau³*.
       1sg   come   PART   come
       'Will he be coming?' – 'Yes, he will.'

(163) *mɯɯŋ⁴*   *lo⁶na³*   *te¹*   *mi²le⁴*?   – *lo⁶na³*
       2sg   know   3sg   PART   know
       'Do you know him/her?' – 'Yes, I do.'

9.5.3.2. *Alternative questions*

Alternative questions are formed by putting the conjunction *lo⁶ nau⁴* 'or' in between the two clauses or phrases in question.

(164) *lau⁴*   *pai¹*   *lo⁶nau⁴*   *pɔ⁴te¹*   *tau³*?
       1pl   know   OR   3pl   come
       'Are we going or are they coming?'

(165) *mɯɯŋ⁴*   *ʔau¹*   *ka:i²*   *ni⁶*   *lo⁶nau⁴*   *(ʔau¹)*   *ka:i²*   *te¹*?
       2sg   take   CL   this   OR   take   CL   that
       'Do you take this one or that one?'

(166) *θu¹*   *pai¹*   *lo⁶ nau⁴*   *ʔbau⁵*   *pai¹*?
       2pl   go   OR   NOT   go
       'Are you going or not?'

9.5.3.3. *Substantive questions*

Substantive questions are formed by using interrogative pronouns or adverbs 'who, what, when, which/what…, how, why/how come…'.

(167) **pu⁶ laɯ⁴**   *nau⁴*   *haɯ³*   *mɯɯŋ⁴*?
       who   tell   give   2sg
       'Who told you (that)?'

(168) *pu⁶*   *te¹*   **pu⁶ laɯ⁴**?
       CL   that   who
       'Who is that person? '

(169) *mɯɯŋ⁴*   *ŋɔn⁴ lɯɯan⁴*   *ʝu⁵*   *la:n⁴*   *kuak⁵*   **ma⁴**?
       2sg   yesterday   stay   home   do   what
       'What were you doing at home yesterday?'

(170) te¹ **mɯɯa⁵laɯ⁴** ta:u² tau³?
     3sg when return come
     'When did he/she come back?' OR 'When is he/she coming back?'

(171) luŋ⁴ ham⁵ lɯan⁴ **kuak⁵ laɯ⁴** ʔbau⁵ tau³?
     uncle last night why not come
     'Why didn't uncle come last night?'

(172) ve⁵ **taŋ³laɯ⁴** te¹ ʔam⁶ pai¹ le?
     For what 3sg not go PART
     'Why didn't s/he go?'

(173) ku¹ **kuak⁵ taŋ³laɯ⁴** ham² te¹ le?
     1sg how ask 3sg PART
     'How shall/should I ask him/her?'

Questions may occur in indirect speech, where more than one element can be asked.

(174) ta¹ ŋa⁵tsie⁴ lo⁶ **pu⁶laɯ⁴ vi⁶taŋ³laɯ⁴** ʔbau⁵ tau³
     grandpa like know who forwhat not come
     'Grandpa wanted to know who didn't come and why.'

9.5.3.4. *Negative questions/rhetorical questions*

Negative questions or rhetorical questions in Zhuang do not seek any information. They are discourse-oriented, expressing the speaker's intense feeling or expectation in seeking agreement or confirmation from the listener.

(175) te¹ mɯŋ⁴ to³ ʔbau⁵ lo⁶ na³?
     3sg 2sg PART NOT know
     'Don't you even know him?'

(176) mɯŋ⁴ kuak⁵ laɯ⁴ ʔbau⁵ pai¹ ham² te¹
     2sg why NOT go ask 3sg
     'Why don't you go and ask him?'

(177) ku¹ to³ ʔbau⁵ ho⁴hɯn³, mɯŋ⁴ ɲɛn² kuak⁵ma⁴ le?
     1sg even NOT angry 2sg moody forwhat PART
     'I am not even angry. Why should you be in a bad mood, then?'

9.5.4. Comparative sentences

Comparisons in Zhuang are formed with comparative markers. The three degrees of universal comparison are present in Zhuang: similarity, comparative, and superlative.

9.5.4.1. *Similarity*

The generic comparison marker for similarity is **lum³**, which is derived from the lexical verb 'resemble, to be like'.

(178)   *te¹   θaːŋ¹   **lum³**   po⁵*.
        3sg   tall   LIKE   father
        'He/she is as tall as his/her father'.

Sentences like (178) can be said in a different way as (179):

(179)   *te¹   θaːŋ¹   ʔdi⁶   po⁶   tuŋ⁶   lum³*
        3sg   tall   with   father   reciprocal   resemble
        (same as above)

To make sentences like (178) into a negative, the construction is: 'Noun 1 + *ʔbau⁵/ʔam⁶* + adjective + *kaːu⁵* + Noun 2'.

(178')   *te¹   ʔbau⁵/ʔam⁶   θaːŋ¹   kaːu⁵   po⁵*.
         3sg   NOT   tall   AS   father
         'He/she is not as tall as his/her father'.

9.5.4.2. *Comparative*

The comparative degree is formed by *kwa²* (from the lexical verb 'pass') or *tɔ¹* (from the lexical verb 'more').

(180)   *te¹   θaːŋ¹   kwa²/tɔ¹   po⁵*.
        3sg   tall   COMP   father
        'He/she is taller than his/her father'.

(181)   *pi¹ ni⁶   ʔdaːt¹   tɔ¹   pi¹ kwa²*.
        This year   hot   COMP   last year
        'This year is hotter than last father.'

(182)   *tsi³   ʔɐn¹   ni⁶   ʔɐn¹   lauɯ⁴   ʔdi¹   tɔ¹?*
        Several   CL   this   CL   which   good   COMP
        'Of these, which is one is better?'

In some dialects, the comparative marker *laːi¹* 'more' is used before the verb or adjective in question.

(183)   *luɯk⁴   ʔbaːu⁵   ni⁶   laːi¹   kuɯaŋ⁶*.
        CL   boy   this   COMP.   smart
        'This boy is smarter.'

9.5.4.3. *Superlative*

There are several ways in which the superlative degree can be expressed in Zhuang. The concept 'he is the tallest in his family' can be said in the following ways:

(184)   *la:n⁴*   *te¹*   *te¹*   *θa:ng¹*   *tɔ¹*   *pu⁶*   *ʔɯn⁵*.
         family   3sg   3sg   tall   COMP   CL   other
         'He/she is taller than anyone else in his/her family.'

(185)   *la:n⁴*   *te¹*   *te¹*   *θa:ŋ¹*   *ta:i⁵*   *ʔit².*
         family   3sg   3sg   tall   the   first
         'He/she is the tallest in his/her family (lit. he/she is the number one in body height.'

(186)   *la:n⁴*   *te¹*   *te¹*   *θuai³*   *θa:ŋ¹*
         family   3sg   3sg   SUP   tall
         (as above)

The superlative marker *θuai³* in (186) appears to be a recent loan from Chinese.

9.5.5. Existential sentences and copula sentences

Zhuang has a number of devices for making existential assertion and statements that would require a copula sentence to express in English. Some of these constructions have typological implications while others appear to be characteristic of Zhuang.

9.5.5.1. *The mi⁴ 'there + be' constructions*

Sentences with **mi⁴**. Existential assertion can be made in Zhuang using the generic existential verb *mi⁴* 'to have, to exist'. *mi⁴* displays a number of syntactic properties which deserve attention. It can be used as a main verb taking a subject and an object. It can introduce an indefinite NP, and it can occur after another verb, indicating a situation expressed by the verb in which the entity indicated by the NP is in.

When used as a main verb, *mi⁴* takes an object which denotes an entity that exists or is located in a place expressed by the subject NP, very much like the English 'There + Be' construction.

(187)   *ʔdaɯ¹*   *ta⁵*   *ni⁶*   *mi⁴*   *pja¹*   *la:i¹.*
         inside   river   this   have   fish   many
         'There's a lot of fish in this river.'

(188)   *la:n⁴*   *li⁶*   *mi⁴*   *ka:u⁵ laɯ⁴*   *hau⁶*?
         house   still   have   how much   rice
         'How much rice do we still have in our house?'

An important function of *mi⁴* is to introduce an indefinite NP.

(189)   *mi⁴*   *pu⁶ hek²*   *tau³*   *la:n⁴.*
         have   guest   come   house
         'We have visitors to our house.'

(190) *mi⁴*   *ha:u²la:i¹*   *hun⁴*   *ɟu⁵*   *ta⁵*   *tɯk²*   *pja¹*
have   many   people   stay   river   huntfor   fish
'There are a lot of people fishing in the river.'

A more characteristic use of *mi⁴* is to co-occur with a transitive verb to form a verb compound. It describes a situation in which an entity exists.

(191) *la³*   *lɯaŋ⁵*   *ɕieng⁶*   *mi⁴*   *mu¹*.
below   animal pen   raise   have   pig
'Raised in the pen are some pigs.'

(192) *ʔdaɯ¹*   *θɯan¹*   *ʔdam¹*   *mi⁴*   *pjak²*
inside   garden   plant   have   vegetable
'Planted in the garden are some vegetables.'

(193) *ha:m⁵*   *kuŋ⁶*   *tu¹*   *ʔdoŋ¹*   *mi⁴*   *la:ŋ⁴*   *θɔm³*
jar   corner   door   pickle   have   bamboo shoot   sour
'In the jar behind the door there are some pickled bamboo shoots.'

9.5.5.2. *Sentences with tɯk⁴ and other copula verbs*

What is usually expressed in English with the copula 'be' can be said in various ways in Zhuang. Apart from the generic copula verb **tɯk⁴** 'be', a number of copula verbs are available in Zhuang with similar syntactic functions and semantic content.

(194) *te¹*   **tɯk⁴**   *la:u⁶θai¹*

3sg   BE   teacher

'He/she is a teacher.'

(195) *la:n¹*   *te¹*   **ʔdai⁶**   *θo:ŋ¹*   *ho:p²*   *leu.*
grandchild   3sg   achieve   two   anniversary   PART
'His/her grandchild is two years old now.'

(196) *ʔba:u⁵*   *te¹*   **heu⁵**   **kuak⁵**   *ɕo⁵*   *ma⁴* ?
Boy   that   call   do   name   what
'What's that boy's name?'

(197) *θo:ŋ¹*   *pu⁶*   *te¹*   **pan⁴**   *tsau³ ja⁵*
two   CL   that   BE   husband-wife
'The two of them are husband and wife.'

(198) *hau⁶*   **va:n⁴**   *hau⁶,*   *pjak²*   **va:n⁴**   *pjak²*
rice   BE   rice   vegetable   BE   vegetable
'Rice is rice; vegetable is vegetable. (They should be kept apart).'

9.5.5.3. *Nominal predicates*

Copula sentences in Zhuang very often take the form of nominal predicates, that is, the predicate is made up of only a noun phrase, without a verb.

(199) $ta:i^2$ $pi^1 mo^2$ $pet^2 \,\varsigma ip^4$
        grandma   next year   eighty
        'Grandma will be eighty next year.'

(200) $\eta\jmath n^4 \,\varsigma ok^5$ $\eta\jmath n^4$ hu^1
        tomorrow   day   market
        'Tomorrow is market day.'

(201) tua^4 mu^1 ni^6 $\theta o:\eta^1$ $pa:k^2$ kan^1
        CL   pig   this   two   hundred   MEASURE-WEIGHT
        'This pig weighs two hundred kan (= a hundred kilograms).' (1 kan^1 = 500g)

(202) pau^2 mo^1 hun^4 pu^6 $n\jmath\eta^4$
        CL   shaman   person   CL   Nung
        'The shaman is a Nung speaker.'

(203) $ka:i^2$ ni^6 $ka:i^2$ ku^1, $ka:i^2$ te^1 $ka:i^2$ $mu\t{u}\eta^4$
        CL   this   CL   1sg,   CL   that   CL   2sg
        'This one is mine/belongs to me, and that one is yours/belongs to you.'

(204) te^1 (pan^4) na^3 na^6, $mu\t{u}\eta^4$ (pan^4) na^3 $la:n^1$
        3sg   be   face   uncle/aunt   2sg   be   face   niece/nephew
        '(In the family linear order), he/she is your uncle/aunt, and you are his/her niece/nephew.'

As (204) has shown, a copula verb can often be supplied for sentences of this kind.

9.5.6. Passive and pseudo-passive

Passive in Zhuang is formed with **$tu\t{u}k^4$** and **$\eta a:i^6$**, the former being a native word, the latter appearing to be a Chinese loan.

(205) $lu\t{u}k^4$ ni^6 **$tu\t{u}k^4$** $\varsigma a\eta^4$ $la:i^1$.
        child   this   PASS   hate   much
        'This child is most hated.'

(206) te^1 $mu\t{u}a^5$ ςo^4 $\varsigma a:\eta^6 \varsigma u^4$ **$tu\t{u}k^4$** $\t{?}da^5$
        3sg   when   young   often   PASS   scold
        'He/she was often scolded when young.'

(207) te^1 $\eta\jmath n^4 lu\t{u}an^4$ **$\eta a:i^6$** $\eta u\t{u}a^4$ hap^4
        3sg   yesterday   PASS   snake   bite
        'He/she was bitten by a snake yesterday.'

In Wuming and some other dialects, *teŋ¹* is used alongside with *tɯk⁴*, with similar function.

Like many other languages in the region, the Zhuang passive often carries 'adversative' meaning, an areal feature which is shared by languages like Mandarin. In Zhuang this feature was probably inherent in the meaning of lexical verbs, 'to undergo, to suffer, to endure', as reflected in some lexical compounds: *tɯk⁴ liaŋ⁴* 'suffer from a cold', *tɯk⁴ leŋ⁴* 'tiring (lit. 'endure strength/effort)'.

When no 'adversative' meaning is involved, 'pragmatic passive' or what might be called 'pseudo passive' is used, depending on how 'passive' is defined. In examples (208) and (209), the subject of the sentence is the patient of the predicate verb, which is characteristic of a passive construction.

(208)   *pjak⁴*   *ʔdam¹*   *le.*
         vegetable   plant   PART
         'The vegetables were planted.'

(209)   *kai²*   *ka³*   *leu.*
         chicken   kill   PART
         'The chicken was killed.'

The auxiliary *ʔdai⁶* may also be used as a passive marker, with non-adversative meaning.

(210)   *te¹*   *ʔdai⁶*   *ha ɯ³*   *kuak⁵*   *pau² mo¹*   *ta:u²*   *poi⁴.*
         3sg   PASS   allow   do   shaman as   before
         'He was allowed to practice shamanism as before.'

9.5.7. Tense and aspect

Zhuang has no markers of tense. However, it has a number of aspect markers. These include *ʔja:k⁵* — futurity/irrealis (see also §9.5.2.1 above); *çiŋ², tɯk²* — progressive/durative; *lieu⁶, ʔjie⁵, pan⁴, pai¹* — completive/perfective; *pan⁴* — accomplishment; and *kwa², va:i³* — experiential. All are post-verbal aspect markers with the exception of *ʔja:k⁵* and *çiŋ²*. As will be seen below, the aspectual system of Zhuang is quite sensitive to quantification and other semantic considerations.

9.5.7.1. *Futurity / irrealis: ʔja:k⁵*

This item is widely distributed across all the Zhuang dialects. Some examples have already been given in §9.5.2.1.

(211)   *jieu²*   *jieŋ⁵*   *ʔja:k⁵*   *tɔk²*   *hun¹.*
         look   manner   FUT   drop   rain
         'It looks as if it is going to rain.'

9.5.7.2. *Progressive/durative/continuative: çiŋ² and tɯk²*

These two markers have different syntactic properties. *çiŋ²* is a preverbal aspectual marker, while *tɯk²* is a postverbal marker, which is mainly used in Wuming and surrounding regions. Both can be used as lexical verbs, *çiŋ²* meaning 'straight (not off the mark)' and *tɯk²*, 'to fetch, to do V-ing'.

(212)   *pai¹   ɲam⁴   nai⁵,   hun⁴ la:i¹   ɕiŋ²   ɕa³   muɯŋ⁴.*
     go   quick   a bit   everybody   PROG   wait   2sg
     'Hurry up. Everybody is waiting for you.'

(213)   *luɯk⁴   θa:u¹   ni⁶   tai³   tuɯk²   taŋ⁴   ŋɔn⁴*
     CL   girl   this   cry   PROG   all   day
     'The girl kept crying for a whole day.'

(214)   *ta⁶po⁵   ʔdi⁶   ta¹   ʔju⁵   kuɯn⁴   ɕa:n⁵   naŋ⁵   tuɯk²   ta³ɕua⁶.*
     father   and   grandpa   stay   up   veranda   sit   PROG   talk
     '(While) sitting on the veranda, father talked with grandpa.'

9.5.7.3. Completive/accomplishment lieu⁶, ʔjie⁵, pan⁴, pai¹

These items are put together as a class because of their similar function. However, each of these has preference over a particular type of verbs.
    lieu⁶ typically goes with consumption verbs.

(215)   *ŋan⁴   jɔŋ⁵   lieu⁶   le.*
     money   use   ASP   PART
     'Money has been used up.'

Without *lieu⁶*, (215) would have different readings, as (215').

(215')   *ŋan⁴   jɔŋ⁵   le.*
     'Money is being used.'
     'Money has been used.'

With verbs of change, the use of *lieu⁶* describes a quantified event, and requires a plural subject.

(216)   *ha³   tua⁴   kai²   ta:i¹   lieu⁶.*
     five   CL   chicken   die   ASP
     'Five chickens (have) all died.'

Even if the subject is not quantified, plurality is still implied.

(217)   *kai²   ta:i¹   lieu⁶   le.*
     chicken   die   ASP   PART
     'All chickens (have) died.'

If the above two conditions are violated, the use of *lieu⁶* will be ruled out.

(218)   *tua⁴   kai²   te¹/ʔdieu¹   ta:i¹   lieu⁶.

        CL   chicken   that/one   die   ASP

        *'That/one chicken has all died.'

Like *lieu⁶*, *pai¹* also marks a quantified event. It typically occurs with verbs of disappearance.

(219)   ka:i¹   pai¹   θoŋ¹   tua⁴   mu¹   le

        sell   ASP   two   CL   pig   PART

        'Two pigs have been sold.'

Note that in sentences like (219), only indefinite and quantified NPs can occur in that position. Definite NPs with sentences of this kind must occur in subject position. (219a) and (219b) are both unacceptable they violate these conditions:

(219a)   *ka:i¹   pai¹   θoŋ¹   tua⁴   mu¹   te¹   le

         sell   ASP   two   CL   pig   that   PART

         'Those two pigs have been sold.'

(219b)   *ka:i¹   pai¹   mu¹   le

         sell   ASP   pig   PART

         'Pigs have been sold.'

(219a,b) will be acceptable if the NP occurs in subject position, as in (219c):

(219c)   (θoŋ¹   tua⁴)   mu¹   (te¹)   ka:i¹   pai¹   le

         two   CL   pig   that   sell   ASP   PART

         '(Those two) pigs have been sold.'

pan⁴ goes with achievement verbs.

(220)   pjak²   kuak⁵   **pan⁴**   çaŋ⁴?

        vegetable   do   ASP   not yet

        'Has the vegetable been cooked (ready) yet?'

Without the use of *pan⁴*, (220) will have two readings: 'Is the vegetable/dish being cooked?' or 'Has the vegetable/dish been cooked?'. No meaning of achievement is implied.

    ʒie⁵ does not express the type of aspectual meaning as *lieu⁶* and *pan⁴*. It simply means that an action or event was brought to an end at the time of speech event. Very often another event is expected to follow. Thus *ʒie⁵* typically functions as event punctuator.

(221) *lau⁴*   *kwn¹*   *hau⁶*   ***ȵie⁵***   *pai¹*   *pa:t⁵*   *va:i¹*

1pl   eat   meal   ASP   go   reinforce   dam

'After we have had our lunch, we'll go and reinforce the dam.'

9.5.7.4. *Experiential: kwa², va:i³*

These two are used to mark what is generally known as the experiential aspect. Both are derived from their use as lexical verbs meaning 'pass', which is quite iconic.

(222) *ku¹*   *pai¹*   **kwa²**   *na:m⁴niŋ⁴*   (OR: *ku¹*   *pai¹*   *na:m⁴niŋ⁴*   **kwa²**)

1sg   go   ASP   Nanning   1sg   go   Nanning   ASP

'I've been to Nanning before.'

With change-of-state verbs, *kwa²* marks an unbounded event.

(223) *te¹*   *ka¹*   *lak²*   **kwa²**

3sg   leg   break   ASP

'S/he broke her/his leg before.'

(223) does not mean that the person's leg was still in a state of being broken at the time of speech event. The sentence simply means that some sort of effect is being felt as a result of the event in question. Similarly, sentences like (224) doesn't imply a natural consequence of the event. In other words, it does not mean that the speaker is still in debt. Rather, some pragmatic meaning is conveyed.

(224) *te¹*   *çie²*   *ŋan⁴*   *ha ɯ³*   *lau⁴*   **kwa²**.

3sg   lend   money   give   1pl   ASP

'S/he once lent us money before.' (We know her/his ersonality).

va:i³ is not so widely distributed as *kwa²*. It mainly occurs in the Zhuang dialects in the northwest.

(225) *ten⁵*   *ni⁶*   *mi⁴*   *hun⁴*   *taŋ⁴*   **va:i³**

place   this   have   people   arrive   ASP

'This place has been frequented before.'

9.6. COMPLEX CONSTRUCTIONS

Complex constructions in Zhuang are divided into two types: subordinate constructions and co-ordinate constructions.

9.6.1. Subordinate constructions

Subordinate constructions in Zhuang include relative clauses, conditionals, concessions, cause-effect, resultative/change of state, and so on.

9.6.1.1. *Relative clauses*

Relative clauses in Zhuang are introduced by a classifier and a deictic word *te¹*, which is also used as a third personal singular pronoun. The classifier and the deictic word together function like relative clause markers.

(226)

pu⁶	ku²pan⁵	lau⁴	ɕuaŋ¹	**te¹**	ɕeu³	tɯk⁴	**pu⁶**
CL	just now	1pl	meet	**that**	just	BE	**CL**

ŋɔn⁴lɯan⁴	ku¹	ʔdi⁶	mɯŋ⁴	tɯan¹	te¹
yesterday	1sg	with	2sg	mention	that

'The person we met a while ago is just the person I mentioned to you yesterday.'

(227)

tua⁴	la ɯ⁴	tɯk⁴	**tua⁴**	pi²	ŋɔn⁴lɯan⁴	lau⁴
CL	which	BE	CL	escape	yesterday	1pl

ʔja:k⁵	tɯ⁴	pai¹	ka:i¹	ŋɔn⁴ni⁶	te¹
want	carry	go	sell	today	that

'Which (pig) is the one that escaped yesterday and which we want to sell today?'

Nested relative clauses are possible, as (227) shows. In nested relative clauses, only one relative marker is used, unlike English.

(228)

ku¹	ŋaʔ⁵tsie⁴	pai¹	jieu²	**pu⁶**	pau²mo²	mɯŋ⁴
1sg	wish	go	see	**CL**	doctor	2sg

tɯan⁴	ŋɔn⁴kon²	tsiu²	lɯk⁴ʔba:u⁵	ja:k⁵	tau³	ham²
mention	daybefore	save	boy	want	com	propose

la:n¹	lau⁴	**te¹**
niece	1pl	**that**

'I might as well want o see the doctor whom you mentioned to me the other day and who saved the boy who was proposing for the hand of our niece.'

9.6.1.2. *Conditionals*

Conditionals in Zhuang are introduced by *ta:ŋ⁵ nau⁴...ɕi⁴...* 'if...then...', *... naŋ⁵* '(only by...)...then...', *ʔbau⁵ lɯm⁵ nau⁴...tu³...* 'no matter...'. The order of the clauses cannot be reversed.

(229)

ta:ŋ⁵ nau⁴	ŋɔn⁴ ɕok⁶	ʔbɯn¹	leɳ⁶,	lau⁴	**ɕi⁴**	kwa⁶	tua⁶
if	tomorrow	sky	sunny	1pl	then	weed	bean

'If the weather is fine tomorrow, we will weed the bean field.'

(230)   *kan⁶*   *ɕo²*   *puɯŋ⁵*,   *pjak²*   ***naŋ⁵***   *ma³*

diligent   put   fertiliser   vegetable   then   grow

'Only by applying fertiliser more often will the vegetables grow.'

(231)   *ʔbau⁵luɯŋ⁵nau⁴*   *ku¹*   *nau⁴*   *taŋ³*   *lauɯ⁴*,   *te¹*   ***tu³***   *bau⁵*   *ha:n¹*

no matter   1sg   say   kind   which   3sg   CONJ   not   answer

'No matter what I said, he just wouldn't answer.'

Sometimes, no conditional marker is used. The conditional meaning is inferred from the contexts.

(232)   *muɯŋ⁴*   *ʔbau⁵*   *pai¹*   *heu⁵*,   *ta¹*   ***ɕi⁴***   *ʔbau⁵*   *tau³*

2sg   not   go   call   grandpa   then   not   come

'If you don't go call grandpa, he won't come.'

9.6.1.3. *Concessions*

Concession is expressed by ***jien⁴ nau⁴***… 'although…', …***hoŋ¹*** 'but', ***ha:n⁴*** …***ko³*** … 'even though'. ***hoŋ¹*** and ***ha:n⁴*** …***ko³*** … are used mainly in Wuming and surrounding regions.

(233)   *ta¹*   ***jien⁴nau⁴***   *pi¹nien⁴*   *tse²*,   *kuak⁵*   *hoŋ¹*   *li¹*   *han¹*

grandpa   although   age   old   do   work   still   strong

'Although he is already old, grandpa is still pretty strong at work.'

(234)   *te¹*   *mi⁴*   *ŋan⁴*   *la:i¹*,   ***hoŋ¹***   *pan⁴*   *hun⁴*   *tset⁵*.

3sg   have   money   much   but   be   person   mean

'He is very rich, but he is very mean.'

(235)   ***ha:n⁴***   *nuaŋ⁶*   *kuak⁵*   *ʔbau⁵*   *tiu⁴*,   *muɯŋ⁴*   ***ko³***   *ʔbau⁵ɕe³*   *ho⁴ʔda:t⁵*

even   y.sibling   do   not   right   2sg   CONJ   no-need   angry

'Even if younger brother/sister was wrong, you shouldn't flare up.'

9.6.1.4. *Cause-effect*

Cause-effect is expressed through ***vi⁵ nau⁴***… 'because…', and ***ɕi⁵ nau⁴***…***ɕi⁴***… 'since… then…'

(236) **vi⁵nau⁴** *pi¹*   *kwa²* *leŋ⁶* *la:i¹*,   *hau⁴*   *ʔbau⁵* *pan⁴*

because   last   year   dry   much   crop   not   develop

'Because there was a bad draught, arvest was not good last year.'

(237) *mɯŋ⁴* **çi⁵nau⁴** *pan4*   *piŋ⁵*, **çi⁴**   *ʒu⁵*   *la:n⁴*   *jiet²na:i²*

2sg   since   become   sick   then   stay   home   rest

'Since you are unwell, you might just as well stay at home for a rest.'

9.6.1.5. Resulative/change of state

Like resultative compounds, resultative clauses describe change of state as a result of an action or event happening. Resultative clauses typically have the syntactic frame: [N1 + V1] + [*taŋ⁴* (OR: *tɯk²*) + [RESULTN2 + V2] + *pai¹*].

(238) *te¹*   *ʔai¹*   **taŋ⁴**   *ho⁴*   *lɛ²*   **pai¹**

3sg   cough   reach   throat   coarse   go

'He/she coughed so much that his/her throat became coarse.'

(239) *pja³*   *lai⁴*   **taŋ⁴**   *la:n⁴*   *lien⁴*   **pai¹**

thunder   roar   reach   house   tremble   go

'The thunder roared so loud that the house trembled.'

9.6.2. Coordinate clauses

Coordinate clauses in Zhuang are of two types, overt and covert coordination. In overt coordination, a coordinate marker or conjunction is used, while in covert coordination, there is no such marker. Only overt coordination is discussed here.

9.6.2.1. Forms of conjunction and disjunction

Conjunction. At the sentential level, conjunctions in Zhuang express the following semantic contents:

(i) Listing

(240) *mɯŋ⁴* **ʔdi⁶** *kɔ¹*   **ʔdi⁶** *pi⁶*   **ʔdi⁶** *la:n¹*   *pai¹*   *hɯ¹*

2sg   and   brother and   sister-in-law   and   nephew   go   market

'You, your brother, your sister-in-law and your nephew go to the market.'

(ii) Juxtaposed references

(241) *kɔ¹*   **ʔdi⁶**   *pi⁶*   *tuŋ⁶*   *çeŋ¹*

elder brother   and   sister in law   recip.   argue

'Elder brother and sister-in-law argued./E. brother argued with sister-in-law.'

(242) *lau⁴*   **peŋ⁴**   *kɯm¹*   **peŋ⁴**   *ta³ çua⁶.*
       1pl   as   eat   as   talk
       'Let's eat while we talk./Let's eat and talk.'

(iii) Correlative

(243) *lau³*   *ʔdo:ŋ¹*   **kɯa³**   *na:n⁴*   **kɯa³**   *hom¹*
       wine   brew   the more   long time the more fragrant
       'Wines, the longer you brew them, the more lavour they have.'

(244) *mɯŋ⁴*   *pai¹*   *ku¹*   **je⁵**   *pai¹*
       2sg   go   1sg   also   go
       'You go, and I also go.'/ 'If you go, I'll go, too.'

(245) *te¹*   **ʔbau⁵ta:n⁵nau⁴**   *lo⁶*   *kuak⁵*   *ça:ŋ⁵fai⁴*   **li⁶**   *lo⁶*
       3sg   not only   know   do   carpentry   also   know

       tam³lo:k²   **tem¹**
       weave   in addition

       'He not only can do carpentry work, but also knows how to weave.'

(246) *pu⁶*   *lau⁴*   *lɛn¹*   *pu⁶*   *te¹*   (*çi⁴*)   *mi⁴*   *fan⁵*
       CL   which   see   CL   that   then   have   share
       'Whoever spotted (the game) will have a share.' (As a saying in hunting.)

(iv) Temporal succession

(247) *lau⁴*   *hat²lom⁵*   *lwai²*   *na⁴,*   **lieu⁶ çi⁴**   *ʔdam¹*   *na².*
       1pl   morning   rake   field   then   plant   field
       'We'll rake the field in the morning, and then we'll transplant rice seedlings.'

(248) *θu¹*   *kɯm¹*   *hau⁶*   *kon²,*   **ʒie⁵ naŋ⁵**   *tuŋ⁶ ʔan⁵.*
       2pl   eat   food   first   after that   together discuss
       'You have your meal first. After that we'll have a talk.'

Disjunction. Disjunctions in Zhuang include *ʔbau⁵ ʔdəi¹* 'or else', *ʔbau⁵ mi⁴* 'otherwise' and *lo⁶ nau⁴* 'or'. These all occur clause or phrase initially. *ʔbau⁵ ʔdəi¹* and *ʔbau⁵ mi⁴* are used in declarative sentences while *lo⁶ nau⁴* only occurs in alternative questions.

(249) lau⁴ ȵa:k⁵ kuak⁵ muɯaŋ¹ kon², **ʔbau⁵ʔdəi¹** çi⁴ kwa² miau⁴.

1pl want make ditch first or-else then pass season

'We got to make the ditch first, or else it will be too late.'

(250) kuak⁵ çi⁴ kuak⁵ kuak⁵ ʔdi¹, **ʔbau⁵mi²** çi⁴ lak⁴ kuak⁵.

Do then do PURP well otherwise then don't do

'If you want to do it, do it well; otherwise don't do it.'

9.6.2.2. Coordinate serialization

Among coordinate clauses in Zhuang, perhaps most notable are what is generally known as serial verb constructions (SVC), constructions that involve multiple clauses in one single verb complex without overt coordinate markers. According to the event types, these can be grouped into stance-activity sequence and parallel action sequence. The sequences may be concurrent, consecutive, alternative, purpose-result, causative, and so on. In some cases, ambiguities exist.

(251) te¹ ça:ŋ⁶çi⁴ çiŋ³ vai⁶tsi² kɯn¹ lau³.

3sg often invite friends eat wine

'He/she often invites friends for a drink'. (consecutive)

(252) ʔdɔt² ʔɔm⁵ lau³ ʔdeu¹ lau³ ʔda:ŋ¹ kon²

drink mouthful wine one warm body first

'Have a little wine first and it will warm you up.' (cause-effect)

'Have a bit of wine to warm yourself up first.' (purpose)

'Warm yourself up first by drinking a little wine.' (manner)

(253) tsuŋ²te¹ kɯn¹ lau³ kuak⁵ vɯan¹

3pl eat wine make folk song

'They drank and sang.'(alternative)

'They drank in order to sing.' (purpose)

'They sang while drinking.'(comitative)

(254) nuaŋ⁶ kəi⁵ ma⁶ ka¹ lak²

y.sibling ride horse leg broken

'Younger brother broke his leg from riding a horse.' (cause-result)
'Younger brother rode a horse and broke his leg.' (consecutive)
'Younger brother rode a horse that had a broken leg.' (descriptive)

(255)   *luŋ⁴*   *ʔau¹*   *ça:k⁵*   *la:m⁵*   *va:i⁴*

         uncle   take   rope   tieup   buffalo

         'Uncle tied the buffalo with a rope.'(instrumental)
         'Uncle used a rope to tie the buffalo.' (consecutive)

(256)   *kuŋ¹*   *pja:i³*   *lɔn¹*   *ma:i³*   *ka:k⁵*   *ʔdi¹*   *la³le²*   *ta³çua⁶*

         grandpa   walk   road   love   alone   with   self   talk

         'Grandpa likes to talk to himself when he goes for a walk.' (descriptive)

(257)   *ʔa:u¹*   *naŋ⁵*   *çɛ¹*   *pai¹*   *hɯ¹*

         uncle   sit   bus   go   market

         'Uncle
went to the market by bus.'(manner)

         'Uncle took a bus to the market.'(instrument)

(258)   *pa³*   *ʔdam¹*   *θa:m¹*   *ko¹*   *kwa¹*   *pan⁴*   *ʔɛn¹*   *la:u⁶*.

         Aunt   plant   three   CL   pumpkin   bear   CL   big

         'Aunt planted three pumpkin plants, (and they) produced big pumpkins.' (descriptive)

(259)   *ŋɔn⁴luan⁴*   *mɯŋ⁴*   *çɯ⁶*   *ʔdai⁶*   *tsi³*   *ʔɛn¹*   *ma:k²*

         yesterday   2sg   buy   obtain   several   CL   fruit

         ta:i²   *ma:i*   *³kɯm¹*

         grandma   like   eat

         'You bought some fruits yesterday that grandma enjoyed eating.' (descriptive)

         'You bought some fruits yesterday and grandma liked (to eat) them.'(consecutive)

(260)   *ta¹*   *çieŋ⁶*   *pan⁴*   *ha³*   *tua⁴*   *ma⁶*   *ŋa⁵tsie⁴*

         grandpa   raise   ASP   five   CL   horse   wish

         haɯ³   *hun⁴*   *ʔau¹*   *va:i⁴*   *tau³*   *vuan⁵*

         let   people   take   buffalo   come   exchange

         'Grandpa has raised five horses that he would like someone to exchange for buffalos.' (descriptive)

(261)   *la:u⁶θai¹*   *haɯ³*   *lɯk⁴ha:k⁵*   *ʔju⁵*   *la:n⁴*   *to:k⁵*   *θɯ¹*

         teacher   let   student   stay   home   read   book

         'The teacher allowed the students to stay at home to read.' (benefactive/purposive)
         'The teacher made the student work at home.' (causative)

9.6.2.3. *Simplex clauses*

In addition to the above-discussed clause types, there is a distinctive type of clause in Zhuang which syntactically looks like a simple clause but which expresses the same meaning as a complex clause. Clauses of this type have only one subject NP and a VP consisting of two conjoining VPs. Prosodically, there are no pauses in between the two VPs as there are in complex clauses. But semantically, some sort of subordinate relationship can be accounted for between the two VPs in clauses of this kind. In most cases, a simplex clause can readily be paraphrased into a complex clause containing two clauses — a main clause and a subordinate clause. Quite often, the subject NP may function both as A and O of the two verbs respectively, which provides insight into ergativity-related issues.

(262) tua^4 $la\,\omega^4$ pi^4 $\wp i^4$ ka^3.

      CL   which   fat   CONJ   kill

      'Whichever one that is fat will be killed.'

(263) te^1 $\textrm{?}bau^5$ θon^1 je^5 lo^6.

      3sg   NEG   each   CONJ   know

      'He/she knows (what to do) even though he/she is not taught.'

(264) hau^6 $lu\eta^1$ $\textrm{?}dai^4$ $hau^2\,la{:}i^1$ $na{:}n^4$ li^6 $\textrm{?}dip^2$.

      Rice   cook   get   a lot   long   still   raw

      'Although cooked for quite a while, the rice was still not ready.'

(265) te^1 $lian^4$ hau^3 $\textrm{?}bon^5$ nin^4 $\wp i^4$ $ts\varepsilon n^1$.

      3sg   just   enter   bed   sleep   CONJ   snore

      'As soon as he went to bed he started snoring.'

(266) $luk^4\! pe^4$ $jiet^2$ $\textrm{?}da^5$ $jiet^2$ $\textrm{?}bau^5$ $ta\eta^3 l\,\omega a^4$

      child-small   themore   scold   themore   not   listen

      'As for children, the more you scold them, the more disobedient they would become.'

(267) $m\,\omega\eta^1$ $\!pa\eta^2$ $ma^6 la\,\omega^4$ je^5 $\!\eta a{:}k^5$ pai^1 $jieu^2$ $\textrm{?}do{:}\eta^1$.

      2sg   busy   howmuch   CONJ   AUX   go   see   relative

      'Even though you are very busy, you'll have to go and visit our relatives.'

9.6.3. Anaphora and binding

Zhuang appears to follow some principles of government and binding proposed by Chomsky (1981).

(268) $kuŋ^1$ lo^6 $ʔde^5$ la^3 le^2 $ʔda{:}ŋ^1$ jai^6.
Grandpa know   self   body   weak
'Grandpa$_i$ knows that he himself$_i$ is failing.'

(269) $na^6pa\textit{u}^6$ nau^4 pa^3 $ta{:}i^5$ $ŋa^5$ la^3le^2 $ka{:}k^5$ pai^1.
mother'sb.swife say aunt great crave self   lone go
'Aunty$_i$ said great aunt$_j$ would like to go by herself*$_{i/j}$.'

(270) $nua\textit{ŋ}^6$ nau^4 la^3le^2 te^1 $ka{:}k^5$ $çie\textit{ŋ}^6$ la^3le^2 $ʔdai^6$ $va{:}i^3$
y.sibling say self 3sg alone support self   able pass
'Younger brother$_i$ says he$_{i/*j}$ can support himself$_{i/*j}$ OK.'

However, bare reflexives in Zhuang exhibit long-distance binding in cases like the following, which apparently violate the binding principle that an anaphor is bound in its governing category.

(271) $jɛ^6{}_i$ nau^4 $pa^3{}_j$ $çieu^5$ hun^4 $ʔbau^5$ han^5 la^3 $le^2{}_{i/j}$.
uncle say aunt lifetime   not   praise self
'Uncle said that aunty never praised himself/herself.'

(272) $jɛ^6{}_i$ $ʔda\textit{u}^1$ ho^4 nau^4 $pa^3{}_j$ $ʔbau^5$ ku^2 la^3 $le^2{}_{i/j}$.
uncle inside   throat   say   aunt not   care self
'Uncle thought/felt that aunty never cared about himself/herself.'

Such long-distance binding is subject to the condition that the remote antecedent of la^3 le^2 must agree with all its closer potential antecedents in person (and number). If this condition is not met, then only local binding is allowed.

(273) $jɛ^6{}_i$ nau^4 $hoi^2{}_j$ $ʔbau^5$ ku^2 la^3 $le^2{}_{*i/j}$.
uncle say slave not   care self
'Uncle said that I never cared about myself.'

(274) $te^1{}_i$ $ʔda\textit{u}^1$ ho^4 nau^4 $mu\textit{ŋ}^4{}_j$ $ʔbau^5$ ku^2 la^3 $le^2{}_{*i/j}$.
3sg inside throat say you   not   care self
'S/he thought/felt that you never cared about yourself.'

Like English, Zhuang exhibits the specificity effects. (275) and (276) illustrate.

(275) $mu\textit{ŋ}^4$ kum^1 kwa^2 $pjak^2$ pu^6 $la\textit{u}^4$ $lu\textit{ŋ}^1$ le?
2sg   eat   ASP   dish   who   cook   PART
'Who$_i$ have you eaten the dish cooked by t$_i$ before?'

(276) *mɯɯŋ⁴ kɯm¹ kwa² pa:n⁴ pjak² pu⁶laɯ⁴ luŋ¹ te¹ le
  2sg   eat   ASP plate dish who   cook that PART
  *'Whoᵢ have you eaten that plate of dish cooked by tᵢ?'

It, too, displays weak cross-over effects. Thus, the subject and the predicate NPs in (277) cannot have the same reference.

(277) pu⁶   ɕaŋ⁴   te¹   te¹   tɯk⁴   pu⁶ laɯ⁴?
  CL   hate   3sg   REL   BE   who
  *'Whoᵢ is the person that hates himᵢ?'
  'Whoᵢ is the person that hates himⱼ?'

For the so-called donkey sentences, Zhuang exhibits interesting paradigms.

(278) a. mɯɯŋ⁴   ŋa⁵   ʔau¹   tua⁴   laɯ⁴,   ku¹   haɯ³   mɯɯŋ⁴
       2sg   desire want   CL   which   1sg   give   2sg

       tua⁴   laɯ⁴
       CL   which

       'I'll give you whichever one you like.' (Lit. 'You like which one, I'll give you which one.')

    b. mɯɯŋ⁴   ŋa⁵   ʔau¹   tua⁴   laɯ⁴,   ku¹   haɯ³   mɯɯŋ⁴
       2sg   desire want   CL   which   1sg   give   2sg

       tua⁴   te¹.
       CL   that
       (same as above)

(279) a. *pu⁶laɯ⁴   pa:ŋ⁴   hoi²   kwa²,   hoi²   ʔbau⁵   lum⁴   pu⁶laɯ⁴
       who   help   slave   ASP   slave   not   forget   who
       *'Whoever has helped me before, I won't forget whom.'

    b. *pu⁶laɯ⁴   pa:ŋ⁴   hoi²   kwa²,   hoi²   ʔbau⁵   lum⁴   te¹
       who   help   slave   ASP   slave   not   forget   3sg
       'Whoever has helped me before, I won't forget him.'

    c. pu⁶laɯ⁴   pa:ŋ⁴   hoi²   kwa²,   hoi²   ʔbau⁵   lum⁴   pu⁶   te¹
       who   help   slave   ASP   slave   not   forget   CL   that
       'I won't forget those who have helped me before.'

The unacceptability of (279a) and (279b) indicates that sentences of this kind behave quite differently from those like (278).

9.7. ACKNOWLEDGEMENTS

Parts of this study were carried out with support from the Australian Research Council Grant DP0209445. Some of the ideas were developed during the author's study leave in 2001 and early 2002. The author records his thanks to Dr Anthony Diller for useful comments and suggestions.

REFERENCES

Early work on Zhuang was carried out by Li (1940, 1956). Ramsey (1987: 234-243) has offered a succinct survey of Zhuang. Edmondson (1994, 2001) has undertaken important phonological studies of a number of Zhuang dialects. Gedney (1991, 1993) has provided excellent data for comparative work. Substantial work on grammar was done by Chinese linguists (Wei 1985, and Guangxi Language Reform Committee 1989) and Russian linguists (Moskalev 1971, Seduchenko 1961). Luo (1991) is an in-depth study of the tense-aspect system in Zhuang, where a sketch of Zhuang grammar is offered. A comprehensive treatment of the history and culture of the Zhuang is offered by Barlow (2001).

Barlow, Jeoffery (2001) *The Zhuang: A Longitudinal Study of Their History and Their Culture*, on-line publication, last updated Jan. 22, 2001, (accessed February, 2002).
    http://mcel.pacificu.edu/as/resources/zhuang/
Bodman, Nicholas (1980) 'Proto-Chinese and Sino-Tibetan: Data towards establishing the nature of the relationship', in Coetsem, Frans Van and Waugh, Linda R. (eds.) *Contributions to Historical Linguistics: Issues and Materials*, Leiden: E.J.Brill, 35-199.
Chao, Yuen-Ren (1968) *A Grammar of Spoken Chinese*, Berkeley and Los Angeles: University of California.
Chomsky, Noam (1981) *Lectures in Government and Binding*, Dordrecht, Floris.
Edmondson, Jerold A. (1994) 'Change and Variation in Zhuang', in K. L. Adams and T. Hudak (eds) *Papers from the Second Annual Meeting of the Southeast Asian Linguistic Society* 1992, Tempe, AZ: Arizona State University, 147-185.
— (2001) 'Zhuang-Bouyei', in Garry, Jane, and Carl Rubino (eds) *Facts About the World's Languages: An Encyclopedia of the World's Major Languages: Past and Present*, New York/Dublin: H. W. Wilson Press, 356-359.
Edmondson, Jerold A, and Solnit, David (eds) (1997) *Comparative Kadai: The Tai Branch*, Dallas: SIL and University of Texas at Arlington.
Edmondson, Jerold, and Li Jinfang (1996) 'The Language Corridor', *Pan-Asiatic Linguistics IV*, 3: 981-89.
Fan, Chengda. *Guihai Yuhengzhi* [Records of an official posting in Guangxi].
Gedney, William J. (1991a) *William J. Gedney's the Yay Language*, edited by Thomas John Hudak (Michigan Papers on South and Southeast Asia No. 38), Ann Arbor: Center for South and Southeast Asia Studies, the University of Michigan.
— (1991b) *William J. Gedney's The Tai Dialect of Lungming*, edited by Thomas John Hudak (Michigan Papers on South and Southeast Asia No. 39), Ann Arbor: Center for South and Southeast Asia Studies, the University of Michigan.
— (1993) *William J. Gedney's the Saek Language*, edited by Thomas John Hudak (Michigan Papers on South and Southeast Asia No. 41), Ann Arbor: Center for South and Southeast Asia Studies, the University of Michigan.

Guangxi Language Reform Commission, Language Research Centre (1989) *Wuming Zhuangyu Yufa [A grammar of the Zhuang dialect of Wuming]*, Nanning: Guangxi Ethnic Publisher.

Holm, David (2004) *Recalling Lost Souls: The Baeu Rodo Scriptures, Tai Cosmogonic Texts from Guangxi in Southern China*, Bangkok: White Lotus.

Kullavanijaya, Pranee (1986) *Chon chat thai nai Satharnarat Prachachon Chin [Zhuang, a Tai group in the People's Republic of China]*, Chulalongkorn University Press.

Lan, Qingyuan (1999) 'Zhuang-Han Guanxici de lishi cengci [Layers of Related Words between Chinese and Zhuang]', unpublished PhD dissertation, Shanghai Normal University.

Lan, Qingyuan (2001) 'Zhuangyu zhonggu hanyu jieci ji hanyueyu yu pinghua de guanxi [Loan words between Middle Chinese and Zhuang and their relationships with Pinghua]', *Minzu Yuwen* 3: 48-61.

Li, Charles and Thompson, Sandra (1981) *Mandarin Chinese: A Functional Reference Grammar*, Berkeley and Los Angeles: University of California Press.

Li, Fang-Kuei (1940) *The Tai Dialect of Lungchow*, Institute of History of Philology, Academia Sinica, Monograph Series A, No. 16, Shanghai: The Commercial Press.

Li, Fang-Kuei (1956) *The Tai Dialect of Wuming*, Institute of History of Philology, Academia Sinica, Monograph Series A, No. 19, Shanghai: The Commercial Press.

Li, Lianjin (2000) *Pinhua Yanjiu [Studies on Pinghua]*, Nanning: Guangxi Ethinic Publisher.

Luo, Yongxian (1991) 'Tense and Aspect in Zhuang: A Study of a Set of Tense and Aspect Markers', unpublished MA thesis, Australian National University.

— (1996) 'The Subgroup Structure of the Tai Languages: A Historical Comparative Study', PhD dissertation, Australian National University; also published with the same title as Monograph 12 of *Journal of Chinese Linguistics*, University of California, Berkeley, 1997. (Chapter 2 of the dissertation, 'Chinese Textual Evidence Bearing on Non-Han Chinese of the South', was not included in the 1997 version.)

Matisoff, James (1991) 'Sino-Tibetan Linguistics: Present States and Prospects', *Annual Review of Anthropology*: 469-504.

Moskalev, A. A. (1971) *Grammatica iazyka chzhuan [A Grammar of Zhuang Language]*, Moscow: Nauka.

Ramsey, S. R. (1987) *The Languages of China*, Princeton University Press.

Saul, Janice E. and Wilson, Nancy Freiberger (1980) *Nung Gramm*, Summer Institute of Linguistics and University of Texas at Arlington

Serduchenko, G. P. (1961) *Chuangtskii iazyk [The Chuang Language]*, Languages of Asia and Africa, Moskow: Nauka.

Wei, Qingwen (1985) *Zhuangyu Yufa Yanjiu [Studies on Zhuang Grammar]*, Nanning: Guangxi Ethnic Publisher.

Wyatt, David (1984) *Thailand: A Short History*, Yale University Press.

Zhang et al. (1999) *Zhuangyu fangyan yanjiu [Studies on Zhuang Dialects]*, Chengdu: Sichuan Minzu Chubanshe.

Zhang, Junru (1988) 'Guangxi pinhua dui dangdi zhuangdong yuzu yuyan de yingxiang' [The influence of Pinghua of Guangxi on the local Zhuang-Dong languages], *Minzu Yuwen* 3: 51-56.

Zhengzhang, Shangfang (1991) 'Decipherment of the Yue-Ren-Ge (Song of the Yue Boatman)', *Cahiers de linguistique Asie Orientale* 22: 159-68.

CHAPTER TEN

BOUYEI PHONOLOGY

Wil C. Snyder

10.1. INTRODUCTION

The Bouyei are a relatively populous people of Guizhou province, China. According to the 1990 government census, there were almost two and a half million Bouyei living in Guizhou at that time. The largest percentage of Bouyei resides in the Qiannan Bouyei-Miao autonomous prefecture, the Qianxinan Bouyei-Miao autonomous prefecture, the Anshun region, the Liupenshui city area and the Guiyang city area. In addition, a small percentage of Bouyei reside in the Zunyi area, the Bijie area, the Qiandongnan Miao-Dong autonomous prefecture, and Yunnan province.

The Bouyei language is classified as a Northern Tai language, part of the Kadai language family. It is very similar to the Zhuang language of Guangxi province. Actually, southern Zhuang, northern Zhuang and Bouyei can be viewed as a continuum of dialects. In many ways, Bouyei and northern Zhuang are linguistically closer than northern Zhuang and southern Zhuang. The Bouyei language itself has various dialects, many dialects being mutually unintelligible to a significant degree in vocabulary and semantics. However, the grammar and basic vocabulary of the various dialects is quite similar. According to the Bouyei language survey done in the 1950's, there are three major dialectal areas. Geographically, the first dialectal area covers the southern part of the Bouyei language area, and is comprised of Wangmo, Ceheng, Luodian, Dushan, Libo, Duyun, Pingtang, Zhenfeng, Anlong, Xingren and Xingyi counties. The second dialectal area is made up of Longli, Guiding, Qingzhen, Pingba, Kaiyang counties, the Guiyang city area, and the Anshun area, and covers the northeastern part of the language area. Zhenning, Guanling, Ziyun, Qinglong, Pu'an, Liuzhi, Panxian, Shuicheng, Bijie, and Weining counties make up the third dialectal area, in the western part of the language area. In general, with regard to the phonologies of the various dialects, the 2000 survey [Wu, Snyder, Liang] bore these results out as well, though intelligibility groupings differed somewhat.

Historically, the Bouyei have no script of their own. In many Bouyei areas, some Bouyei songs and scriptures have been written with a kind of modified Chinese character script, though the script is often different in each place. In 1956, under the direction of the government of the People's Republic of China, a roman script was created for the Bouyei language. The Bouyei language is spoken by virtually all Bouyei people in the rural parts of these areas, and by many in the towns and cities as well. Many Bouyei can also communicate in the local variety of Mandarin to some degree, and some are completely bilingual.

10.2. PHONOLOGY OF WANGMO BOUYEI

Based on the 1950's Bouyei language survey, the Chinese government chose the Bouyei variety of Wangmo county as the standard, or representative dialect of Bouyei. Based on the survey published in 2000, Wangmo still makes a good choice for a representative dialect. In doing intelligibility analysis, the Bouyei of Ceheng, Wangmo and Luodian counties came out to be the main 'center of communication' for the entire Bouyei language, 'center of communication' being the dialectal area most intelligible to all other dialects. In addition, the Bouyei population is heavily concentrated in these areas, and there is less Chinese influence in these counties than most other Bouyei areas. Wangmo county is on the Guizhou-Guangxi border, and has many of the characteristics of northern Zhuang. The basic phonology of Wangmo (Fuxing county) is outlined below. Some of its characteristics are then compared with other Bouyei dialects. This article is based on the data from the more recent survey published in 2000, which used a 500 item word list.

Below are the phoneme charts for the Bouyei dialect of Fuxing town, Wangmo county. Allophones are listed in square brackets [].

10.2.1. Initial consonants

		BiLab	LaDe	InDe	Alv	AlPal	Pal	Vel	Glo
Plos.	vl	p, pj			t			k, kw	ʔ, ʔj, [ʔw]
Pregl.		ʔb			ʔd				
Aff.	vl					tɕ			
Fric.	vl		f	θ	[s], [s̢]	ɕ		x,[xw]	[h]
	vd		v	ð,[ðw]	[z̢] ,[ʐ]				[ɦ]
Nas.	vd	m			n		ɲ	ŋ	
Lat.	vd				l				
App.	vd						j		

10.2.2. Final consonants

p, t, k, m, n, ŋ

10.2.3. Vowels

	Front	Central	Back
	unrd	unrd	rd
Close	i	[ɨ]	u
Near-Close	[I]		[ʊ]
Close-mid	[e]		o,[o:]
Mid		ə	
Open-mid	ɛ		ɔ
Near-open		ɐ	
Open	a,a:		

10.2.4. Tones

Category	1	2	3	4	5	6	7	8
Pitch value	24	42	52	31	35	33	35	34

The phoneme inventory of this dialect is quite typical of Bouyei. There is a series of voiceless unaspirated stops /p, t, k, g/, and a series of pre-glottalized stops /ʔb, ʔd/ (there is no instance of a velar pre-glottalized stop anywhere in Bouyei). There is an alveo-palatal affricate /tɕ/ (there are dialects with alveolar and even palatal affricates in addition to the alveo-palatal). The fricatives include the bi-labial fricatives /f/ and /v/, a series of voiced and voiceless interdental/alveolar fricatives (some dialects have both interdental and alveolar fricatives which are phonemic), an alveo-palatal /ɕ/, and the velar fricative /x/. Nasals include /m/, /n/, /ɲ/ and /ŋ/, and there is one lateral /l/, and the palatal approximate /j/.

[f] and [v] often occur in complimentary distribution, but not exclusively. The instances of [f] in the data corresponds mainly to *mw and *v of proto-tai, and [v] corresponds to *v, *ɣw, *w, *hw, *f and *xw. [v] occurs mainly with odd numbered tones, and [f] only occurs with an odd tone once, all other instances being with even numbered tones. Examples:

[va^5] 'pants', [fa^2] 'iron', [viəŋ^1] 'mend', [fiəm^2] 'dark'

[s], [s̠] and [θ] are all variants of one phoneme. The degree of dental fronting on any lexical item varies from person to person within the village, and for any one speaker can vary on a single lexical item depending on the phonological environment. Some words are most often pronounced with say, [s], but if pronounced with [θ] they are never confused with any other word. Similarly, [z] and [ð] are both variants of a single phoneme. [ʐ] only occurs in the data once, following a closely bound open syllable morpheme. This is also a variant with [ð] and [z]. All these alveolar and dental fricatives seem to be in a state of flux, with a large degree of variation allowed over each phoneme. Examples:

[ʐ]: [xo^6 ʐau^2] 'we (inclusive)'
[z]: [zɐi^2] 'long', [za^6 fai^4] 'root'
[ð]: [ðwa:u^5 ðum^2] 'yawn', [ðiŋ^4] 'afternoon', [ðam^4] 'water', [ðɔn^1] 'road'
[s]: [sɐi^3] 'intestines', [so:ŋ^1] 'two', [so^6] 'straight'
[s̠]: [s̠i^5] 'four', [s̠aŋ^1] 'tall', [s̠ɐi^1] 'clean'
[θ]: [θoɐi^5] 'garlic', [θat^7] 'mat', [θa^1] 'paper'

[n̠] is phonemic, occurring before low vowels as well as high, as in [n̠a^1] 'grass'. [x], [h] and [ɦ] are all variants, [h] only occurring once in the data, and [ɦ] twice.

[ʔj], [ʔw], [pj], [kw], [ðw] and [xw] are listed among the initial consonant inventory, but whether the palatalization and labialization are phonemic or not is difficult to tell from simply eliciting word lists. See Section 10.3.3 for discussion of using word games to distinguish C + i from Cj, and C + u from Cw.

Kadai languages have length distinction on some vowels, and Bouyei is no different. In the 2000 survey, the vowel lengths for each dialect were measured computationally. The Wangmo Fuxing variety has phonemic /a:/, /a/ and /o:/, /o/. Each of [a], [ɐ] and [a:] are all phonemic, and occur many times.

In this variety, [e]/[ε], [i]/[I], and [u]/[ʊ] are allophone pairs. [ə] and [ɨ] are allophones, according to the following rule:

/ə/ → [ɨ]   in the environments /C(V) #; /C ə (C)#.

Each Bouyei dialect has a number of diphthongs and a few triphthongs. On open syllables Wangmo has the following diphthongs and triphthongs:

ia, iε, iu, iə, ua, uε, uə, ai, au, aɨ, ɐi, ɐu, ɐɨ, iə, εu, εi
iai, iεu, uai, uəi, uεi, uau, oɐi

On syllables ending in a nasal, Wangmo has the following diphthongs:

iε, io, iə, uə, ua, uo, ɨə

Finally, Wangmo has the following diphthongs on syllables closed by a stop:

iu, ia, iε, iə, uə, ɨə

This dialect has six open tones corresponding to the historical voiced/voiceless split of the A, B and C tones. The D tone split into voiceless and voiced sets (but not long and short sets). So tone 7 has words from the 7th and 9th categories, and tone 8 has words from the 8th and 10th categories. Looking at the pitch values, we can see that the odd numbered tone category pitch values are generally high or rising, and the even numbered category values are lower or falling. Each tone category therefore follows the voiced-low principle in this dialect. The pitch of tone category 3 is listed as falling [53], but is not a true falling tone. The fall only occurs in isolation or at the end of an utterance, otherwise the pitch is [55].

10.3. COMPARISON WITH OTHER DIALECTS

10.3.1. Aspiration

The Wangmo dialect, like most Bouyei dialects, has no aspirated stops or affricates. The only dialects with phonemic aspiration are in Shuicheng (Fa'er), Zhenning (Shitouzhai) and Ziyun (Nonghe), which are western dialect areas. Both Zhenning (Banle) and Ziyun (Huohua) are in this western area, but have no aspirated stops, and seem to be phonologically closer to the first dialectal area. Zhenning (Shitouzhai) and Ziyun (Nonghe) both have phonemic /ph, th, kh/, the occurrence of aspiration on certain words is regular and constant. Shuicheng (Fa'er), on the other hand, has many instances of aspiration, but the aspiration is quite often sporadic. Only [ph] occurs regularly on particular words. However, there are instances of [pfh, th, kh, tsh, tɕh].

Qinglong (Zitang), also considered a western dialect, has very little evidence of aspiration on stops. In the data are recorded a total of five instances of [th], [tsh] or [tɕh], but the aspiration that occurs is sporadic and non-phonemic. Anshun (Huangla), another western dialect, only has phonemic aspiration on the alveolar affricates, [tsh] and [tɕh], with no instances of [ph, th, kh]. The Huishui (Danggu) dialect and the Longli (Yangchang) dialect are in the second or northeast dialectal area, and there are a few instances of aspiration [th, tsh, tɕh] in these two dialects, but again the aspiration is sporadic and not phonemic.

In each of these dialects with aspirated stops or affricates, though, very few of the items match with aspirated proto-forms. For example, in the Zhenning (Shitouzhai) data, [ph] occurs on six lexical items, but only two of these lexical items have aspiration on the proto-form. [th] occurs on eleven items, but only one out of those eleven has an aspiriated proto-form. In each dialect with aspirated stops or affricates, the preponderance of aspiration occurs on lexical items which don't often evidence aspiration in other Kadai languages, and so have unaspirated proto-forms. Oddly though, many of the aspirated items are aspirated in each of the third dialectal area dialects. For example, there are six items with initial [ph] in the the Zhenning (Shitouzhai) data, five in Ziyuan (Nonghe), and four in Shuicheng (Fa'er) (one with [pf]). Each of the five Ziyuan (Nonghe) examples are also aspirated in Zhenning (Shitouzhai), though only one of the Shuicheng (Fa'er) items is also aspirated in Zhenning (Shitouzhai). However, the Longli (Yangchang) and Huishui (Danggu) aspirated items do not overlap with those of Zhenning (Shitouzhai), Ziyun (Nonghe), or Shuicheng (Fa'er). So it seems that in the Bouyei dialects with aspiration, the occurrence of aspiration on most lexical items is not often due to historical aspiration on those same items, but due to some other process. See examples in chart below.

Lexical items	Zhenning (Shitouzhai)	Ziyun (Nonghe)	Shuicheng (Fa'er)	Proto-Tai[1]
thunder	pha³	pha³	pha?⁴	*phl/ra C1
mountain	puə¹	po¹	pu¹	*b/puo A1
navel	phoə⁴ lɐi⁶	pho³ ?duɯ¹	phɔŋ¹ ?dəŋ¹	*gbl/rɯɯ A1
swell up	pha:u²	pha:u¹	pɐu⁴	*bɔŋ A2
walk	phɛ³	phɛ³	jaŋ¹	*phl/rai C1
flat	phaŋ³	pha:m³	?bɛn¹	*pɛn A1
blow	*	puə⁵	pfo⁶, phu¹	*p– C1
father	pue⁶	pu⁵	pfu⁶, pvu⁶	*bɔ B2

1   The Proto-Tai data is taken from Li Fang-Kuei (1977).

10.3.2. Dental and alveolar fricatives

As discussed above, in the Wangmo (Fuxing) dialect there is a fair degree of synchronic variation on the dental/alveolar fricatives. This variation is very common over the whole language. Also, in many dialects, this set of fricatives tends toward the dental point of articulation, while in others it tends more toward alveolar/alveo-palatal. For example, we see that Wangmo (Fuxing) generally tends toward the dental point of articulation, but the Changshun (Guyang) dialect shows [s, ʒ]. However, regardless of whether this set of fricatives is more dental or alveolar/alveo-palatal, each dialect always has the alveo-palatal voiced fricative [ɕ]. The point of articulation for this phoneme is constant throughout each dialect, with few exceptions.

In many dialects, the variation is sporadic and doesn't depend on the phonological environment to any significant degree. Sometimes though, the variation is influenced most often by environment. For example, in the Anlong (Pingle) dialect, the lexical item 'bird' was pronounced with [r], [ð] and [ʒ] on three different examples, with the environment being different on each occasion.

'bird' [tu² rɔk⁷] 'bird nest' [ðoŋ² ðɔk⁷] 'owl' [ʒɔk⁷ tɕɐu³ mɐu⁵]

In many dialects, [ʒ] occurs most often before rounded vowels. But the Dushan (Nanzhai) dialect shows [s/s̺, ɕ], and [z/z̺, ʒ], both [z] and [ʒ] being phonemic.

'root' [za⁶], 'pull, to' [ʒa⁶] 'go down, to' [zoŋ²], 'bird nest' [ʒoŋ² ʒo³]

In addition to the alveolar and dental fricatives, two of the western dialects, Zhenning (Shitouzhai) and Ziyun (Nonghe) also have a lateral fricative [ɬ]. This sound corresponds to dental/alveolar sounds in other dialects. Below are some items from these two dialects with the lateral fricative, compared with Wangmo (Fuxing).

lexical item	Zhenning (Shitouzhai)	Ziyun (Nonghe)	Wangmo (Fuxing)
fly (insect)	nian² ɬa¹	n̠iɐŋ² ɬa⁵	nɛŋ² θa⁵
intestines	ɬai³	ɬai³	sɐi³
sour	ɬaŋ³	ɬam³	θɔm³
paper	ɬa¹	ɬa¹	θa¹

To summarize, within most dialects Bouyei varies widely with respect to the point of articulation of dental and alveolar fricatives. For the voiceless dental/alveolar fricative, point of articulation can range from [θ] to [ɕ], and the voiced dental/alveolar fricative can range from [ð] to [ʒ]. These fricative sounds may be in a state of flux, but this can only be ascertained by future survey work.

10.3.3. Palatalization and labialization

Each of the dialects have many instances of palatalization and labialization on stops (and sometimes on other initial consonants). Traditionally, these palatalized and labialized initials have been considered phonemic. However, whether the palatalization and labialization is phonemic or not is difficult to ascertain. For example, the word for vegetable is most often something like [pjɐk⁷]. In many dialects, the palatalization seems quite strong, the high semi-vowel closely bound to the initial stop. In other dialects, the pronunciation seems closer to initial stop plus high vowel [i]. Analyzing the sounds on the computer verifies these observations. In some dialects, the palatal or labial part of the initial is relatively long, much like a high vowel. In others, it is very short. Judging the phonemic status of these sounds by ear is of course subjective and most often inaccurate. But even if the palatalization (or labialization) is tightly bound phonetically to the initial stop, the phonemic status is still in question. In the Luodian (Luokun) dialect, we used a word game to ascertain the phonemic status of these initials. In this dialect, a sort of 'pig latin' involves saying a word and following it with the initial of the word + [in] + the tone of the word. So dog [ma¹] would be [ma¹min¹], and 'bird' [ðɔk⁸] would be [ðɔk⁸ ðin²]. Here are some samples of words, as spoken in the word game, with the initials [pj, kw, ʔj, ʔw, ŋw].

'stupid' [ʔwa⁴ʔwin⁴]	'wipe' [ʔwɐt¹⁰ʔwin⁶]
'difficult' [ʔjaˤʔjin⁶]	'live/stay' [ʔjuˤʔjin⁶]
'vegetable' [pjɐk⁷pin⁵]	'fish' [pja¹pin¹]
'right' [kwa:²kin²]	'kneel' [kwiˤkin⁶]
'seed' [ŋwihˤŋwin⁶]	'roof tile' [ŋwa⁴ŋwin⁴]

The labialization on [ʔw] and [ŋw] moves with the initial onto the second syllable, indicating it is part of the phoneme, whereas the labialization of [kw] does not, indicating that 'right' is [kua:³¹] phonemically and 'kneel' is [kui⁶] phonemically. Similarly, [ʔj] is phonemic (/ʔj/), whereas [pj] is actually /p/ + /i/. Luodian (Luokun) is the only dialect where this kind of word game has been used to analyze the phonemic status of labialized and palatalized stops. Most likely similar analysis of other dialects would give sometimes similar and sometimes divergent results.

Although for [kw] and [pj] the labialization and palatalization are not phonemic, they are clearly a result of historical processes, as shown by the reflexes for some of the items above.

Lexical item	Luodian (Luokun)	Proto-Tai
wipe	ʔwɐt¹⁰	*kw _t D1 L
live/stay	ʔju⁶	*ʔju B1
vegetable	piak⁷	*phl/rək D1S
right	kwa:²	*kw/gwa A1/2

10.3.4. Vowels

Vowel length is a common phonological feature of Kadai languages, but whether length is phonemic, or whether a phonemic distinction is based on quality rather than length, needs careful evaluation. Most Bouyei dialects have a phonemic length distinction on [a], /a/ and /a:/, though not all. For example, in the Dushan (Nanzhai) and Guiding (Gugong) dialects, [a:] occurs only a few times, always in the environment C_i#. In the data, many dialects have instances of length on other vowels, but these are not phonemic. The data was analyzed on the computer to check vowel length. In the Ceheng data, for example, there were some instances of [o:] and [ɔ:], but their occurrence was sporadic, and always preceding a nasal. Dushan (Shuiyan) also had some instances of [o:], always preceding a nasal. In the Wangmo (Fuxing) data, [o:] occurs in a total of nine items, again always preceding a nasal. In the Xingyi (Bajie) dialect, [ɔ:] occurs on five items. In most other dialects, four of these five items are diphthongs. The length on [ɔ:] in Xingyi (Bajie) is possibly becoming phonemic due to loss of diphthong.

[æ] occurs phonemically (separate from both [a] and [ɛ]) in Anshun (Huangla), Qinglong (Zitang), Shuicheng (Fa'er), Zhenning (Shitouzhai), and Ziyun (Nonghe). The occurrence of this vowel is one of the characteristics of western dialects. Of these few dialects, Anshun (Huangla) and Ziyun (Nonghe) each have about 30 or more instances of [æ] within the data, with many of these lexical items being the same. Zhenning (Shitouzhai) has only about a dozen or so instances, and only a few of these also have [æ] in Anshun (Huangla) and Ziyuan (Nonghe). Finally, Shuicheng (Fa'er) only has about half a dozen instances, with only one item, 'rice', also having [æ] in the other three dialects. Comparing items from Anshun (Huangla), Ziyun (Nonghe), and Zhenning (Shitouzhai) with Wangmo (Fuxing), we see that /æ/ in western dialects corresponds with /a/ in most other Bouyei dialects.

Lexical item	Anshun (Huangla)	Ziyun (Nonghe)	Zhenning (Shitouzhai)	Wangmo (Fuxing)
dirt	n/æm⁶/ næm⁶	næ:m⁶	naŋ⁶	nam⁶
spider	kæu¹	ko¹	ko¹	kuau¹
body	ʔdæŋ¹	ʔdaŋ¹	ʔdaŋ¹	ʔdaŋ¹
mouth	pæk⁷	pa⁵	pa¹	pa⁵
chest	ʔæ⁵	ʔak⁷	ʔak⁷	ʔak⁷
ghost	væŋ²	væŋ²	vaŋ²	faŋ²
dry (in the sun)	tæk⁷	ta⁵	ta⁵	ta⁵
rope	tsæk⁸	tsa⁶	tsaʔ⁸	ça⁶
three	θæm¹	ɬam¹	ɬæm¹	sam¹
hundred	pæk⁷	pa⁵	pa¹	pa⁵
tall	θæŋ¹	ɬæŋ¹	ɬaŋ¹	s̪aŋ¹
white	ɣæ:u¹	xo¹	xo¹	xau¹

With regard to mid vowels, some dialects have a symmetrical distribution of /e/, /ɛ/, /o/ and /ɔ/. Luodian (Luokun) has the following minimal pairs:

'flying insect' [neŋ²],   'top, crest' [nɛŋ²]
'cat' [meu²],   'hair' [mɛu²]
'early' [ðom⁶],   'eagle' [ðɔm⁶]
'cut (meat)' [ðon⁵],   'road' [ðɔn¹]

We've seen that Wangmo (Fuxing) has /ɛ/ (with the allophone [e]), /o/ and /ɔ/. Some other dialects have only two mid vowel phonemes, sometimes with allophones. Anshun (Huangla), for example has /ɛ/ and /o/, with allophones [e] and [ɔ] respectively.

10.3.5. Tones

The pitch value pattern of the Libo (Fucun) dialect is an example of a common pattern among the Bouyei dialects.

Libo (Fucun)

Category	1	2	3	4	5	6
Pitch value	13	21	33	53	35	55

The pitch value pattern is symmetric, two rising pitches (one low one high), two falling (one high and one low), and two level pitches. However, there are many divergent patterns among the various dialects, almost a dozen different patterns out of 24 dialects.[2] For example,

Duyan (Fuxi)

Category	1	2	3	4	5	6
Pitch value	24	33	31	41	44	35

---

2   For each dialect, Gedney boxes were used to chart the pitch values of each tone, and the computer was used to visualize the pitch values

Guiding (Gonggu)

Category	1	2	3	4	5	6
Pitch value	35	23	14	32	44	42

Luodian (Luokun)

Category	1	2	3	4	5	6
Pitch value	24	423	33	31	35	41

Xingyi (Bajie)

Category	1	2	3	4	5	6
Pitch value	33	52	25	35	24	41

The majority of Bouyei dialects have six tones on open syllables, with the exception of four dialects with only five tones.

Pingtang (Xiliang)

Category	1	2	3	4	5,6
Pitch value	13	31	33	42	35

Shuicheng (Fa'er)

Category	1	2	3,4	5	6
Pitch value	44	33 or 31	41	55	24

Zhenning (Shitouzhai)

Category	1	2	3,4	5	6
Pitch value	44	31	42	34	24

Ziyun (Nonghe)

Category	1	2	3,4	5	6
Pitch value	33	31	41	35	24

The third and fourth tones have merged in three of these dialects, with the fifth and sixth tone having merged in Pingtang (Xiliang).

Like other Kadai languages, Bouyei exhibits evidence of a four way split among the closed (checked) syllable lexical items. Only four of the twenty-four dialects in the data retain all four checked tones.

Duyan (Fuxi)

Category	7	8	9	10
Pitch value	45	33	44	25

Guiding (Gonggu)

Category	7	8	9	10
Pitch value	45	13	33 or 34	44

Longli (Yangchang)

Category	7	8	9	10
Pitch value	45	24	34	55

Xingyi (Bajie)

Category	7	8	9	10
Pitch value	24	44	23 or 22	31

The seventh tone always tends to be high rising, the eighth either low rising or mid level, the ninth tone mid or mid rising. The tenth tone varies most widely, from high rising, to high level, to low falling.

Most common are dialects where the seventh and ninth tones have merged, and the eighth and tenth tones have merged. These tones are labled 7 and 8 respectively. About half the dialects in the data fall into this category. In these dialects, the seventh tone is again always high rising, but the eighth tone varies widely, from mid level (several dialects), to high level (Ceheng (Huarong), Pingtang (Xiliang)), to high falling (Zhenfeng (Mingu)), and mid rising (four of the dialects).

In several dialects, the seventh and ninth tones have merged, but the eighth and tenth have been retained. The seventh tone is always high rising, and the eighth is either low falling or mid level. The tenth tone again varies most widely, from mid level, to high falling, to high level. Finally, each of the D tones in Shuicheng (Fa'er) have merged into a high level tone.

The phonemic pitch of most Kadai languages follow the voiced-low voiceless-high principle. That is, on words with original, historic voiced initials, the pitch tends to be lower or falling, whereas on words with original voiceless initials, the pitch tends to be higher or rising. In general, Bouyei holds to this principle as well, though there are numerous exceptions. The exceptions are generally distributed over most of the dialects, with no dialectal area standing out. As noted above, the Libo (Fucun) dialect has a common pitch value pattern over its six open tones. However, the third tone is a mid level tone, whereas the sixth tone is high level. The Duyun (Fuxi) dialect has a low falling third tone, and a high rising sixth tone. In Xingyi (Bajie), the fourth tone is high rising. Many other dialects have exceptions as well. Among the checked tones, the seventh tone is amazingly consistent as a high rising pitch. In the four dialects with a separate ninth tone, the values are high level, mid level or rising, which is more or less consistent with the voiced-voiceless principle. In the dialects with separate eighth and tenth tones, the eighth tone is most often low falling or mid level, but in Guiding (Gonggu) and Longli (Yangchang) the eighth tone is low but rising, and in Xingyi (Bajie) it is high level. Where the eighth and tenth tones have merged, four dialects have a mid rising pitch, and two have a high level pitch.

We can see that the different patterns of pitch value are distributed over each major dialectal region, with no apparent correlation of any one pattern to any one major dialectal area. However, concerning checked tones, each of the western dialects have merged the seventh and ninth tones, and the eighth and tenth tones, but several other dialects in both the southern and northeastern dialectal areas fall into this pattern as well. Also, of the four dialects with less than six tones on open syllables, three are western area dialects (Shuicheng (Fa'er), Zhenning (Shitouzhai) and Ziyun (Nonghe)). So the western dialects have somewhat of a trend to merge tones, as compared to the southern and northeastern dialects.

10.3.6. Finals

The majority of Bouyei dialects have the nasal finals /m, n, ŋ/. Few of the dialects seem to be losing these sounds. There are very few occurrences of vowel nasalization in any of the dialects, none of it phonemic. Only Shuicheng (Fa'er) and Zhenning (Shitouzhai) have lost any of the final nasals, both dialects having lost final /m/. The finals /n/ and /ŋ/ still occur in these dialects.

Most dialects have the final stops [p, t, k, ʔ]. Some of the dialects are losing final /k/, with these dialects having fewer instances of final /k/ compared to other dialects. Where final /k/ has been lost, most often final /ʔ/ occurs instead, though sometimes the syllable has become completely open. Four of the dialects have lost final /k/ completely. Three of these four are in the northeastern dialectal area, Changshun (Guyang), Dushan (Shuiyan), and Guiding (Gonggu), the other being Pingtang (Xiliang) in the south. Finally, Zhenning (Shitouzhai) has lost the final /p/, the final /p/ being replaced by final /k/. Below we compare three items with final /p/ in Ziyun (Nonghe) with Zhenning (Shitouzhai).

	Zhenning (Shitouzhai)	Ziyun (Nonghe)
'claw'	jik^8	jip^8
'liver'	tak^7	tap^7
'bamboo hat'	kak^7	kap^7

10.3.7. Summary

The phonology of Bouyei is fairly typical for a Kadai language, with relatively few initial consonants, a relatively large number of vowels, diphthongs and some triphthongs, normally six open tones and up to four checked tones.

In general, the phonemes and tones of most lexical items match up well with Proto-Tai, though we can see some small tendencies within Bouyei for phonological change. For example, in some western dialects aspiration is occurring on items with no aspiration on the proto-form. Only Zhenning (Shitouzhai) and Ziyun (Nonghe) have a fairly consistent inventory of aspirated initials. Also, the point of articulation of dental and alveolar fricatives seems to be unstable, this phenomena occurring over most Bouyei dialects.

With regard to vowels, there is no significant difference among the phonemic inventory of the various Bouyei dialects, with the exception of /æ/, which is a characteristic of the western dialects. Each dialect has numerous diphthongs as well as some triphthongs.

Most Bouyei dialects have six open tones, though some have only five. Most dialects have at least two D tones, some having up to four D tones. Whether there is a tendency among Bouyei dialects to merge tones or not is unclear, future survey will need to be done to see any tendency. Tone sandhi does not appear to be a phenomenon in Bouyei, which is surprising since it occurs in some Zhuang dialects. However, extensive research in the many various dialects may well turn up tone sandhi in some areas.

The finals are typical of a Kadai language, having only nasal and stopped finals. In some dialects, loss of final [k] is occurring.

In each of the dialects investigated so far, very few phonological rules are in evidence, and virtually all of these involve vowels. Many dialects have rules such as /i/ assimilating to [I], or /i/ assimilating to [ɯ] or [ə], but there is very little assimilation or other kinds of processes going on with the consonants, and no known tone sandhi. In light of this, we would predict very little change in the phonology of Bouyei in the near future.

REFERENCES

Chinese Academy of Social Sciences Nationalites Research Department (1959) *Bouyei Language Survey Report*, Beijing: Sciences Press.

Hyman, Larry M. (1975) *Phonology: Theory and Analysis*, New York: Holt, Rinehart and Winston.

Li Fang-Kuei (1977) *A Handbook of Comparative Tai* (Oceanic Linguistics Special Publications Number 15), Honolulu: The University Press of Hawaii.

Snyder, Donna M. (1995) 'Variation in Bouyei', unpublished MA thesis, University of Texas at Arlington.

Snyder, Wil C. and Lu Tian Qiao (1997) 'Wuming Zhuang Tone Sandhi: A Phonological, Syntactic and Cognitive Investigation', in Jerold A. Edmondson, and David B. Solnit (eds) *Comparative Kadai: The Tai Branch*, Dallas: UTA/SIL, 107-137.

Wu, Wenyi, Wil Snyder, and Liang Yongshu (2000) *Zhongguo Buyi yu duibi yanjiu [Bouyei Comparative Research]*, Guiyang: Guizhou People's Publishing House.

CHAPTER ELEVEN

SAEK REVISITED

Wilaiwan Khanittanan

Saek in Nakhon Phanom has been referred to by those who study it as a 'displaced' language. It shows basic features of the Northern branch of Tai, including many characteristic Northern lexical items, but is undergoing substantial contact-induced change from nearby Southwestern varieties. It is endangered (Boltz 1991; Wilaiwan Khanittanan 1976; Gedney 1970, 1993) but there are efforts to preserve it (see below). The purpose here is to follow up and briefly to update earlier more extensive descriptions of Saek (Gedney 1970, 1993; Wilaiwan Khanittanan 1976). The reader is referred to these studies for further detail and for diachronic discussion.

Earlier observations on Saek (Wilaiwan Khanittanan 1976) indicated that at that time there were many consonant and consonant cluster variations in the language. A prediction was made that under Siamese and Lao influence Saek would lose consonant clusters, the sound /r/ would merge with /l/ or /h/, and that /f/ would be added to the sound system. Thirty years have passed and the results of the present study show that some of the predictions have come true while others have not. For this study, the same list of 1300 words used in 1976 has been used to collect data. Ban Bawa was selected for the site of the update study, some 90 kilometers from Ban Atsamart of the first study. The main informant of this study is a 23-year-old male university student, in contrast to a 45-year-old female school teacher of the first study. Below is the comparison between Saek in 1976 (henceforth Saek 1) and Saek in 2006 (henceforth Saek 2).

The comparison in this study is limited to consonants as the most salient indicators of language contrast. Sets on Table 11-1 overleave illustrate the initial consonants, final consonants, and consonant clusters of Saek 1 (Wilaiwan Khanittanan 1976) and of Saek 2.

/f/ is analyzed as a new sound in the system though it occurs only twice in the word list, as in /fii^1/ 'boil' (noun) and /faay^1/ 'cotton'. Saek 1 has /phay^4/ and /paay^1/ respectively for these words. /f/ in /fii^1/ contrasts with /vii^4/ 'fire' and /vii^6 gaw^6/ 'to fan', as does /faay^1/ with /vaay^4/ 'buffalo'. Besides many new words with the initial /f/ from Siamese have come into use, for example /fay^6-faa^4/ 'electricity' and /fan^6 phleen^6/ 'listen to a song'.

The voice velar stop /g/, which is not found in Lao and Siamese, is stable in Saek. Of the 50 words for which Saek 1 has /g/ as initial, Saek 2 has the same in 48 words. The two words for which Saek 2 has other initials are /keen$^{1'}$ arm' and /kheep^5/ 'narrow'. The sound /g/ in both Saek 1 and Saek 2 corresponds to Proto-Tai voiceless fricative *x, unaspirated voiceless stop *k, and voiced fricative *ɣ.

TABLE 11-1: COMPARISON OF SAEK PHONEMES AS SPOKEN BY ONE SPEAKER IN 1976 AND ANOTHER IN 2006

Saek 1	Saek 2
(i) Initial consonants	(i) Initial consonants

Saek 1

(i) Initial consonants

b d	g			
p t	c	k	?	
ph	th	kh		
m	n	ñ	ŋ	
v s	h			
l	y			
r				

(ii) Final consonants:

-p	-t	-k	-?
-m	-n	- ŋ	
-w	-y		
-l			

(iii) Consonant clusters:

bl-		
pl-	tl-	kw-
pr-	tr-	
phl-	thl-	khw-
phr-	thr-	
ml-		

(iv) Tones

Tone 1	rising
Tone 2	low
Tone 3	mid falling
Tone 4	high falling
Tone 5	high rising-falling
Tone 6	mid

Saek 2

(i) Initial consonants

b	d	g		
p	t	c	k	?
ph	th	kh		
m	n	ñ	ŋ	
v s	h			
(f) l	y			
r				

(ii) Final consonants:

-p-t	-k	-?
-m	-n	- ŋ
-w	-y	

(iii) Consonant clusters:

bl-	
pl-	tl-
pr-	tr-
phl-	thl-
phr-	thr-

(iv) Tones

Tone 1	rising
Tone 2	low
Tone 3	mid falling
Tone 4	high
Tone 5	high falling
Tone 6	mid

	Saek List 2	Li's Proto-Tai
'rice'	gaw^2	*xau C2
'to bite'	gat^4	*kat D15
'neck'	gɔɔ^2	*ɣɔɔ A2

/r/ is a clear trill in both Saek 1 and Saek 2. Of the 88 words with the initial /r-/ in the word list in Saek 1, Saek 2 uses /r/ in 72 words. Of the 16 words which Saek 2 differs, four substitute /r/ with /l/. Some words have dropped out of use. Other items are replaced by Siamese or Lao words with different initials, in some cases etymologically distinct.

Gloss	Saek 1	Saek 2
'matter, affairs'	rɯaŋ³	lɯaŋ²
'to receive'	rap³	lap²
'car'	rot²	lot²
'school'	rooŋ⁴-rian⁴	looŋ⁴-lian⁴
'to tighten, to pull'	rat²	dɛt¹
'thread'	raay³	daay⁵
'eczema'	reet²	hit⁴
'underneath'	reek⁵	thaaʔ⁴-tɤɤ³
'rim, edge'	rim⁴	khɔɔp³
'raw'	rip⁴	dip⁴
'fast'	riw⁴	ñam⁴
'place, land'	rii⁶	boo³
'to remove'	ruk⁴	thuut²
'mountain'	rɔɔy¹	phuu⁴
'to string'	rɔɔy⁶	hɔy⁶
'personal pronoun for the third person'	raw²	(not in use)

Consonant clusters

Saek 2 does not have /ml-/, /kw-/, and /khw-/ clusters. Otherwise it has all other clusters that Saek 1 does. Some clusters are retained in only one or two words. /bl-/ is used only in the word in the corpus: /blɛt⁴/ 'to modify a form'. The /ml-/ cluster is simplified to /m/. /kw-/ and /khw-/ become /kua/ and khua. This particular sound shift, characteristic also of Lao, has put an Isan or Northeastern touch on Saek. Examples:

	Saek 1	Saek 2
'more'	kwaa²	kua⁴
'mad'	kwaa³	kua³
'scratch'	kwaaw⁴	kaw¹
'to sell'	kwaay¹	kuay¹
'to sweep'	kwaat⁶	kuat²
'slippery'	mlɯɯl⁵~ mlɯɯn⁵	mɯɯn⁵
'meat'	mlɔɔ³	mɔɔ³
'to open one's eyes'	mlɔɔn⁴	mɔɔn⁴

Clusters with /-r-/ and /-l-/ are numerous in both Saek 1 and Saek 2. They are apparently used interchangeably in most words. Contrary to the /-ua-/ sound, these clusters mark Saek off from other Northeastern dialects.

	Saek1	Saek2
'a kind of fish'	praa^2-three^2	praa^6-tree^5
'broken'	preek^3	preek^3
'leech'	plin^1	pin^1
'to set free'	prii^6	plii^6
'forehead'	phraak^6	phaak^6
'all gone'	phreek^3	phreek^3
'betel leaf'	phluu^4	phluu^4/phuu^4
'thin'	phrɔɔm^6	phrɔɔm^2
'almost'	thram^2	thram^2
'hair'	phram^2/phlam^2	phram^2/
'middle'	tlaaŋ^1	tlaaŋ^1
'drum'	tlɔɔŋ^1	trɔɔŋ^1
'to get married'	trɔɔŋ^1	trɔɔŋ^1
'clear'	trɔm^2	rɔŋ^3
'lat in the morning'	thlaa^4	thraa^4
'half'	thrɯɯŋ^5	thrɯɯŋ^5
'hard'	thriaŋ^5	thiaŋ^5
'toslip'	thrɤɤt^5/thlɤɤt^5	thlɤɤt^5

Structurally Saek 1 and Saek 2 are very much alike. Saek 2, of the younger generation, shows more variation in all the sounds above. With new ways of life and new subjects to talk about it is natural for the younger generation of Saek speakers to be more open to the new vocabulary coming into the language. They have added the new sound /f/ to their language but they still retain the old Saek words such as /kuuk^2/ 'tiger', /maaŋ^4/ 'ghost', and /ŋiaŋ^5/ 'finger'. In Ban Bawa, there has been a campaign to keep Saek alive and it has worked well. Precha Chaipanha, father of our main informant, is the head of this successful campaign. It appears that Saek is not going to be extinct in the near future.

REFERENCES

Benedict, Paul K. (1997) 'Linguistic Prediction: The Case of Saek', in Jerold A. Edmondson and David Solnit (eds) *Comparative Kadai: The Tai Branch*, Summer Institute of Linguistics/University of Texas at Arlington, 161-187.

Boltz, William G. (1991) 'The Old Chinese Terrestrial Rames in Saek', in William G. Boltz and Michael C. Shapiro (eds) *Studies in the Historical Phonology of Asian Languages*, Amsterdam and Philadelphia: John Benjamins, 53-66.

Gedney, William J. (1970) 'The Saek Language of Nakhon Phanom Province'. *Journal of The Siam Society* 58: 67-87.

— (1993) *William J. Gedney's The Saek Language: Glossary, Texts and Translations*, edited by Thomas John Hudak, Michigan Papers on South and Southeast Asia Number 41. University of Michigan: Center for South and Southeast Asian Studies.

Li, Fang-Kuei (1977) *A Handbook of Comparative Tai* (Oceanic Linguistics Special Publications 15), Honolulu: University of Hawaii Press.

Wilaiwan Khanittanan (1976) *The Saek Language* (in Thai), Bangkok: Thammasat University Press..

PART 3

TAI LANGUAGES: SPECIAL TOPICS

CHAPTER TWELVE

FOUR-WORD ELABORATE EXPRESSIONS IN YUNNAN TAI LUE: A PAN-TAI CULTURAL TRAIT?[1]

Amara Prasithrathsint

12.1. INTRODUCTION

A four-word elaborate expression is an idiom that is composed of four monosyllabic words; thus, it is named a 'four-syllable word' or a 'four-syllable compound' by some linguists.

Examples of four-word elaborate expressions in Standard Thai are as follows:

(1)   yùu dii   kin dii
        stay good eat good
        'to be well-off'

(2)   kin khâaw kin plaa
        eat rice   eat fish
        to eat (rice)

(3)   tham rây   thǎy   naa
        make farm   plough rice paddy
        'to do rice- farming'

(4)   yùu   yen   pen   sùk
        stay cool   stay happy
        'to live happily'

---

1   The earlier version of this paper was presented at the International Conference on Hua Yao Dai Culture of Upper Red River in Xin Ping County, Yunnan Province, People's Republic of China, January 3-8, 2001. All the data on which this study is based was from Wu Ling Yun and his book while he was in Thailand in 1987. He often encouraged me to write a paper on this topic, but it took me very long to finish writing the paper as he wished. I am very grateful to him and dedicate this paper to him. I would also like to thank Dr Pranee Kullavanijaya, an expert in Tai linguistics, for her valuable advice and suggestions, which have helped me improve this paper.

(5)   hěn   nâa   hěn   taa
       see   face   see   eye
       'to see (somebody's face)'

(6)   chaay   ciŋ   yǐŋ   thέε
       man   true   woman   real
       'a real man or woman'

(7)   bùk   pàa   fàa   doŋ
       invade forest go through   forest
       'to go through a forest; to brave danger or hardship'

(8)   khǒn   lúk   khǒn   phɔŋ
       hair   get up   hair   swell
       'to have hair stand on end; to be frightened'

(9)   cèp   thɔ́ɔŋ   khɔ́ɔŋ   cay
       hurt   stomach   irritate   heart

       'to be hurt'

(10)   cèp   khây   dâay   pùay
       hurt   fever   get   illness
       'to be sick'

Expressions shown above are labeled differently by different scholars. Haas (1964: xvii) named them 'elaborate expressions'. According to her, such expressions

> are frequently based on compounds… and are expanded by repeating a part of the compound and adding a new part, by inserting a syllable for the sake of rhyme, or by inserting a syllable with some vague semantic relation to one of the original parts.

Karnchana Nacaskul (1976) in her paper entitled 'Types of elaboration in some Southeast Asian Languages' maintains that four-word expressions are a type of *elaboration* called 'compound elaboration', which is commonly found in Khmer and Thai. According to her, compound elaboration is derived from elaboration of various kinds; for instance, /khâw-òk-khâw-cay/ (enter-chest-enter-heart) 'to understand' is derived from /khâw/ 'to enter' + /òk cay/ (chest + heart) with the repetition of the word /khâw/. Such four-word expressions marked by repetition of some parts are labeled 'reduplicatives' (=/kham-sám/ in Thai) by Bandhumetha (1977, cited in Thongdaeng 1998: 18-20). As for those which do not have repetition but in which components have similar meanings, Bandhumetha labels them 'doublets' (=/kham-sɔ́ɔn/ in Thai). Both *reduplicatives* and *doublets* which are composed of four monosyllabic words are called 'four-syllable words' in Bandhumetha 1984 (cited in Thongdaeng 1998: 20).

In addition to Thai, some other Tai languages are also found to have four-word expressions. Examples of such words in Debao Zhuang are given by Meng Wen Piao (1986, cited in Thongdaeng 1998: 25). Those in Tai Nuea, Tai Mao, and Dehong Tai are treated by Banchob Bhandhumetha (1985), Young (1985) and Wu Ling Yun (1990), respectively.[2] Thongdaeng's thesis (1998) shows a detailed analysis of 'four-syllable words' in Tai Mau. She defines a four-syllable word as a word formulated by arranging four syllables or four words successively; all the syllables are related phonologically or semantically. Functionally, the whole word is a single unit. She found four patterns of the structure of the four-syllable words in Tai Mau. They are as follows (ordered from the most frequently used to the least frequently used):

Pattern 1: ABAC (The first and third syllables repeat each other.)

Example: (11) paaj tin   paaj mǐ

                      end foot end hand   'easy'

Pattern 2: ABCD (All four syllables are different.)

Example: (12) khǎt   tsai sāi hɛ́ŋ

                     obstruct heart put strength   'to try hard'

Pattern 3: AABB (the second syllable repeats the first and the fourth repeats the third)

Example: (13) hǐŋ hǐŋ láan láan

                     long long long long   'long (time)'

Pattern 4: ABCB (the second and fourth syllables repeat each other.)

Example: (14) kāa ŋaaj máa ŋaaj

                     go easy come easy   'go easily'   (Thongdaeng 1998: 42-54)

In this study, I will analyze the structure of the four-word expressions in Tai Lue in the light of the previous studies on the same phenomenon in other Tai languages. I will also argue that syntactically, a four-word expression is a word, not a phrase or a clause.

12.2. EXAMPLES OF FOUR-WORD EXPRESSIONS IN TAI LUE

Four-word expressions are abundant in Tai Lue. The following are examples from the data. The gloss of each word and the meaning of the whole expression are provided for each example.

(15)   púk   hay   dám   nâa[3]
        grow farm transplant rice paddy
        'to do rice farming.'

---

2   All of these are cited in Thongdaeng (1998: 25-30)

3   Tai Lue has 6 tones. They are: 1. Mid (3-3), 2. High (4-4), 3. Falling (4-2), 4. Rising (2-4), 5. Low (1-1) and 6. Low-mid (2-1-3). In this paper the mid tone will not be marked. All the rest will be marked as follows: ´ for high, ^ for falling, ˇ for rising, ` for low, and ˜ for low-mid.

(16)   pho   săŋ   mɛ   sɔ́n
         father   command   mother teach
         'to be taught by parents; to   be well brought up'

(17)   xăaw   náa   páa   thók
         rice   much   fish   cheap
         'to be abundant;   to be fertile'

(18)   fàa dét   dáw dĭ
         sky sunny   star good
         'The weather is fine'

(19)   páak   dăy   waa   pén
         speak   able   say   able
         'to be able to speak but unable to do'

(20)   sì   thók   kháy fêŋ
         buy cheap sell expensive
         'to cheat; to be dishonest'

(21)   yŭ   dĭ   kĭn   wáan
         stay good   eat   sweet
         'to be well; to be well-off'

(22)   dĭk   dám kam   kĭn
         late at night dark night start
         'nightfall, to become dark'

(23)   kĭn xăaw kĭn nàm
         eat rice eat water
         'to eat (rice)'

(24)   tsîŋ   nàm tsîŋ   dĭn
         snatch away   water snatch away soil
         'to take away land from others'

(25)   kǐn yǎy kǐn lúŋ
         eat big eat big
         'to be greedy'

(26)   sì nók sì núu
         buy bird buy mouse
         'to buy birds'

(27)   xāw káat xāw lî
         enter market enter market
         'to go to a market'

(28)   māy tsáy māy khɔ́
         burn heart burn neck
         'to be unhappy'

(29)   nə̂n sǐp nə̂n sâw
         money ten money twenty
         'little money'

(30)   wáan sóp wáan páak
         sweet lip sweet mouth
         'to speak nicely'

(31)   kàm fàa kàm dǐn
         hold up sky hold up earth
         'to be brave'

(32)   tsáy dǐ tsáy wáan
         heart good heart sweet
         'to be kind-hearted'

(33)   hú tsɛ̄ŋ táa tsɛ̄ŋ
         ear bright eye bright
         'to be wise'

(34)   páy páy mâa   mâa
        go   go   come come
        'to go back and forth'

(35)   nɔ̌y nɔ̌y yǎy yǎy
        small small big big
        'small and big'

12.3. THE STRUCTURE OF THE FOUR-WORD EXPRESSIONS IN TAI LUE

The above examples shows that the structure of the four-word expressions in Tai Lue exhibits five characteristics: 1) components: 4 monosyllabic words (ABCD); 2) reduplication: ABAC, ABCB, or AABB; 3) rhyme: ABB'D; 4) semantic parallelism. The four words can be split into two parallel sets of semantic units (AB~CD); and 5) Idiomatic meaning: The meaning of a four-word expression must be learned as a whole. These will be discussed below.

12.3.1. Components: A four-word expression is composed of four monosyllabic words

A four-word expression in Tai Lue is composed of four isolating or monosyllabic words, as can be seen in the examples above. There are some words in Tai Lue that are similar to a four-word expression in the pronunciation because they have four syllables, but they are composed of only two or three words. In this study I do not treat them as four-word expressions, as in the following examples.

(36)   manôo hó-tsáy   (2 words)
        heart heart   'heart'

(37)   pi   nɔ̌ŋ   wɔ̂ŋsáa   (3 words)
        elder sibling   younger sibling   relative   'kin'

Also, it should be noted that the four words that are components in the four-word expression can be different or reduplicative. If they are different, the structure of the expression will be ABCD, following Thongdaeng's analysis of Tai Mau (Thongdaeng 1998: 54). If they are reduplicative, the structure will be ABAC, ABCB, or AABB, as shown below.

12.3.2. Reduplication: A four-word expression may have reduplication

Most of the four-word expressions in Tai Lue have repetition of some components. Two patterns of repetition are found: 1) the first and third words repeat each other (ABAC) as in Examples (23)–(32) ; 2) the first and second words repeat each other, and the third and fourth repeat each other (AABB), as in Examples (34)–(35). It may be interesting to note that in Pattern ABAC, B and C or the second and third words are related semantically (See detail in 3.4) or derive from two-word compounds in the language. For example, in (25) /yǎy/ and /lúŋ/ derive from a common compound /yǎy-lúŋ/ meaning 'big'. Also, /tsáy/ and /khɔ̌/ in (28) correspond to /tsáy-khɔ̌/ 'mood, disposition, character', which is a common two-word compound in Tai Lue (and also in Standard Thai too).

Another pattern that has reduplication is ABCB, in which the second and fourth words repeat each other. This pattern is very rare. There is only one in the list of examples–Example No. 33 /hú tsɛ̃ŋ táa tsɛ̃ŋ/ (ear-bright-eye-bright) 'to be wise'.

As for the pattern AABB, each reduplicative pair is a two word compound; for example, /nɔ̌y nɔ̌y yǎy yǎy/ in (35) is composed of two pairs of reduplicatives – /nɔ̌y-nɔ̌y/ 'small', and /yǎy-yǎy/ 'big'.

12.3.3. Rhyme: In most four-word expressions, the second and third words rhyme or alliterate

As can be seen in Examples (17) and (22), the second and third words rhyme, forming the pattern ABB'C (the symbol ' signifies the rhyme). In (17) the words /náa/ and /páa/ rhyme. In Example (18), the second and third words alliterate, forming the pattern ABB"C (" signifies alliteration). Alliteration means the condition whereby two or more words have the same initial sound. The words /dét/ and /dáw/ begin with the same consonant sound. There is also alliteration between the second and fourth words – ABCB", for example in (26) and (29) – the words /nôk/ and /núu/ alliterate, and so do /sǐp/ and /sâw/.

12.3.4. Semantic parallelism: The four words can be split into two parallel sets of semantic units (AB~ CD)

In each four-word expression there are two semantic units: one unit is composed of the first and second words, and the other is composed of the third and fourth words – AB~CD. The two semantic units (AB and CD) are parallel (the sign ~ signifies parallelism.); that is, the meaning of the first unit is the same, similar, opposite or somewhat related to that of the second unit. All the examples (15)–(35) show this characteristic. In (15), /púk hay/ 'to do farming' and /dám nâa/ 'to do rice-farming' parallel–both have similar meanings. In (16), /pho sǎŋ/ 'Father commands' and /mɛ sɔ́n/ 'Mother teaches' are also parallel because the concepts 'father' and 'mother' contrast with each other. Both words normally form a compound meaning 'parents'. The words for 'command' and 'teach' in Tai Lue (and also in Thai) have some features in common, such as implying power on the part of the performer of the action. Also, both words form a compound meaning 'to teach and bring up somebody'. In (27), /xãw káat/ and /xãw lĭ/ mean exactly the same ('to go to a market'). The words /káat/ and /lĭ/ are synonymous, both meaning 'market'.

12.3.5. Idiomatic meaning: The meaning of a four -word expression must be learned as a whole

A four-word expression is an idiomatic word; i.e., its meaning must be interpreted as a whole. The whole meaning is not derived directly from the meanings of the four words put together. Even the denotative meaning is idiomatic; for example, the meaning of (26) ('to buy birds') is not predictable from the meanings of the four words put together ('buy birds and mice'). Also, in (22), the meaning of the whole word ('to eat rice) is not the same as the meanings of the fourth word ('to eat rice and water').

Most four-word expressions have figurative or metaphorical meanings. Almost all of the examples support this. For instance, in (30) /wáan sóp wáan páak/ 'sweet lips' means 'to speak nicely'. Also, in (33) the denotative meaning is 'to have good ears and bright eyes' but the figurative meaning of this expression is 'to be wise.' Therefore, it is clear that a four-word expression is an idiom. Its meaning has to be learned as a whole through cultural transmission.

12.4. THE GRAMMATICAL STATUS OF FOUR-WORD EXPRESSIONS

I maintain that four-word expressions are words, not phrases or clauses for several reasons. First, the positions of the four parts cannot be shifted. For example, in (15) if we shift the parts and get /dám nâa púk hay/, which mean exactly the same (to do rice-farming'), instead of the original one–/púk hay dám nâa/, it would no longer be acceptable as a four-word expression. Second, none of the parts can be omitted; for example, if we change /hú tsɛ̃ŋ táa tsɛ̃ŋ/ ('ear-bright-eye-bright') 'to be wise' into /hú táa tsɛ̃ŋ/, it would not be an expression any more, but would be interpreted as a clause meaning 'the ears and the eyes are bright or clear.' Third, the expression cannot be interrupted; i.e., we cannot insert any word inside it. For example, if we put the conjunction meaning 'and' between the two parallel units: /hú tsɛ̃ŋ AND táa tsɛ̃ŋ/, this string of words would become a co-ordinate sentence, not a four-word expression any more. Lastly, a four-word expression is used as a single word, mostly as a verb. It can replace a single verb in a clause, as in the following examples in Thai:

(38)   khǎw *ruay*

        he   rich   'He is rich.'

(39)   khǎw *yùu dii kin dii*

        he   well-off   'He is well-off.'

As can be seen, /*ruay*/ and /*yùu dii kin dii*/ behave exactly the same syntactically. Both of them are the verbs of the two clauses.

12.5. CONCLUSION

In the preceding pages, I have shown the structure of the four-word expressions in Tai Lue. Concerning the components, a four-word expression is composed of *four monosyllabic words*. Phonologically, it is marked by *repetition, rhyme* and *alliteration*. Semantically, each four-word expression can be split into *two parallel semantic units*, and the whole meaning of the expression is *idiomatic*. I have also argued that syntactically, four-word expressions are *words*, not phrases or clauses.

The result of my analysis suggests that the structure of four-word expressions in Tai Lue is the same as that in Thai and other Tai languages. It seems very likely that the occurrence of four-word expressions is a common feature in Tai language and culture. Since four-word expressions are marked by characteristics of verse, idiomaticity, and redundancy, it is safe to say that *Tai people value rhetoric ability, metaphor, and wordiness* in their speech. These are characteristics of oral communication. Can we conclude that Tai society is more like an oral society than a literate society? Why is the use of four-word expressions persistent in Tai culture? The persistence is evident in Tai Lue, which has been in contact with Chinese for a long time but still maintains this feature, which is missing in Chinese. Can we say that it is an inherent feature in Tai culture or a Pan-Tai cultural trait? In order to make a definite conclusion about this, we need more evidence from more Tai languages.

REFERENCES

Bhandhumetha, Banchob (1985) 'Tai Nuea (/tai-nɨa/)', in Princess Kalayani Wattana (ed.) *Yunnan*, Bangkok: Thai Watana Phanich, 204-218.
Bhandhumetha, Nawawan (1977) *Language Use* (/kaan-cháy phaasǎa/), Bangkok: Kaanphim Satrisaan.
— (1984) 'On four-syllable words (/rîaŋ khɔ̌ɔŋ kham-sìiphayaan/)', *Journal of Thai Language and Literature* 3: 8-13.
Haas, Mary R. (1964) *Thai-English Student's Dictionary*, Stanford: Stanford University Press.
Kullavanijaya, Pranee (1985) 'Two Tai dialects in Yunnan', *Science of Language* 5: 1-13.
Meng Wen Piao (1986) 'Reduplicatives in Debao Zhuang', In Pranee Kullavanijaya (ed.) *Zhuang: The Tai in the People's Republic of China*, Bangkok: Craftsman Press, Ltd., 56-76.
Nacaskul, Karnchana (1976) 'Types of elaboration in some Southeast Asian languages', in Philip N. Jenner, Laurence C. Thompson, and Stanley Starosta (eds) *Austroasiatic Studies, Part II (Oceanic Linguistics Special Publication No. 13)*, Honolulu: University of Hawaii Press, 873-889.
Thongdaeng, Wityada (1998) 'Four-syllable words in Tai Mau', unpublished M. A. thesis, Chulalongkorn University.

Wu Ling Yun (1990) 'On phonetic characteristics of the four-syllable constructions in Dehong Dai language', *Proceedings of the Fourth International Conference on Thai Studies*, Institute of Southeast Asian Studies, Kunming, China.

Young, Linda Wai Ling (1985) *Shan Chrestomathy: An Introduction to Tai Mau Language and Literature*, (Monograph Series No. 28), Berkeley, California: Center for South and Southeast Asian Studies, University of California.

CHAPTER THIRTEEN

TAI AESTHETICS

Thomas John Hudak

The Tai family of languages and dialects extends across Southeast Asia from the island of Hainan in the east, through northern Vietnam, Laos, Thailand, Myanmar (Burma), and into Assam in the west, and from the Chinese provinces of Yunnan, Guizhou (Kweichow), and Guangxi (Kwangsi) in the north to the northern border of Malaysia in the south. Following Fang-kuei Li (1960), linguists generally divide this family into three main branches: the Northern (N), the Central (C), and the Southwestern (SW). Representative members include Bouyei (Pu-Yi), Saek, and Yay in the Northern Branch; Tày (Thô), Western Nung, the dialects at Lungming, Lungchow, and Wuming in the Central; and Thai (or Siamese), Lao, Shan, and Lue in the Southwestern.

Traditionally, literature, both oral and written, in these languages has been equated with poetry; and it has only been recently, primarily in Thai and Lao literature through western influence, that poetry has turned to the lyric and to expressions of social concern. Outside of Thailand and Laos, poetry is more often than not referred to as songs. And this more traditional poetry has been and remains the vehicle for myths, epics, princely accolades, courting songs, and didactic lessons, with the type of song (or poem) often recognized more by the content than by the melody. In addition to poetic topics and themes, these languages share a common aesthetic that is most clearly defined for Thai where poets and critics have viewed poetry from an analytical perspective. Highly esteemed and valued poetry is described as *phay¹rɔʔ⁴* – sweet, melodious, musical, harmonious, worth listening to. Scholars talk about Thai poetry as resembling music (Mosel 1959: 28; 1961).[1] Gedney (1989: 489) elaborates in greater detail when he claims, 'the paramount importance of form [of poetry] is reminiscent of eighteenth-century Western music; in both cases, in Siamese poetry as well as, say, in minuets by Haydn and Mozart, one feels that the main purpose was not so much to produce something basically new and different as to exploit existing patterns in elegant and graceful ways'. Young (1985: 169) claims that Tai Mau Shan has 'unique rhythmic and reduplicative techniques.' Compton (1979; 1992) explores the techniques used to create the melodiousness found in the Lao mohlam. And in a less literary vein, the Thai cultural scholar Phya Anuman Rajadhon (1968: 77) discusses how new Thai compounds are created with musicality and melodiousness in mind: '... there is an unconscious selection of sounds. A word with a prominent or more musical sound is selected as the second of two words.' Sound, and more precisely pleasing sound, is the common overriding aesthetic that pervades all of the Tai languages. To achieve this goal, one must select the appropriate word for the appropriate situation and topic; and at the same time select words that do not jar or disturb the ear (*khat² huu⁵*).

13.1. LINGUISTIC TECHNIQUES FOR THE CREATION OF *phay¹rɔʔ⁴*

Forms that contribute to the aesthetics of *phay¹rɔʔ⁴* occur in everyday language; and when formalized, they constitute the requirements for poetic composition. When Phya Anuman talks about more musical sounds, he means sounds produced through alliteration and vocalic rhyme, two techniques highly exploited in everyday speech as well as in more formal poetic

---

1 Thai or Siamese, Southwestern Branch, has the following tonal system: 1 - mid level, 2 - low level, 3 - falling, 4 - high level, 5 - rising (Haas 1964).

compositions. A glance through any Tai language dictionary will reveal any number of compounds that are linked by either consonantal or vocalic rhyme:[2]

biat⁶bian¹ – to crowd, Saek (N)
hap³haw³ – to bite into, close, Yay (N)
cii¹ceen⁴– to owe money, Lungming, (C)
buk²baŋ³ – tube, Western Nung, (C)
caa²maa⁶ – packhorse saddle, Lue (SW)
dam¹nam⁶ – to dive into water, Thai (SW)

Many of these compounds result from what Haas (1942; 1946; 1964: xviii-xix) describes for Thai as reduplicative techniques that involve qualitative, quantitative, and tonal aspects of the lexical items. For example, in the creation of Thai compounds, front and back vowels may alternate. Thus, in *yuŋ³yiŋ³* – to be confused, confusing, the back vowel [u] alternates with the front vowel [i]; in *soo¹see¹* – to stagger, the back vowel [o] alternates with the front vowel [e]; and in *ŋɔɔ¹ŋɛɛ¹* – fussy or childish, the back vowel [B] alternates with the front vowel [e]. In addition, any vowel may alternate with [a]: *chiŋ¹chaŋ¹* – to hate. Quantitative changes also occur, *put⁴puut⁴* – sound of car honking, as do tonal: *krasip⁴krasaap³* – to whisper. Increasing evidence suggests that sound symbolism is closely related to these reduplicative techniques. In a study of vowels in modifiers and intensifiers found in the northeastern dialect of Thai (Northeastern Thai or Isaan), Theraphan (1979: 254) notes than rounded and unrounded back vowels [u ɯ o ɤ] '... suggest a larger size or a higher degree of intensity' whereas [i ɛ ɔ] '... suggest a smaller size or lower degree of intensity.' Young (1985: 19) in her work with Tai Mau Shan records reduplicated or rhyming syllables that when combined with adjectives and intensifiers indicate good or bad connotations. Generally the vowels [i e ɛ ɔ] induce pleasant associations and the vowels [u o aa] unpleasant ones: *ʔon⁴ yɔm³-yɔm³* - soft with a good connotation and *ʔon⁴ yum³-yum³* - soft with a bad connotation.[3] Scovel (1975) in his study of Northern Thai (Chiengmai dialect), on the other hand, finds it difficult to substantiate the claim that sound symbolism exists.

Based upon compounding and reduplicative patterns and occurring throughout the Tai languages, as well as other unrelated languages in the region, are elaborate expressions. An elaborate expression is a four-syllable compound which has an idiomatic meaning. Expansion of the original compound or word occurs in a number of ways: by repeating a part of the compound, by inserting a syllable for rhyme, or by inserting a syllable that has some semantic relationship to one of the other syllables. When rhyme occurs, as it does frequently, it is between the second and third syllables. Examples include the following:

1. repetition of part of a compound, from Thai:
   nam⁶ taa¹ nam⁶ huu⁵
   water-eye-water-ear
   'tear'

---

2   Saek, Northern Branch, has the following tonal system: 1 - mid with a rise on the end, 2 - low level, 3 - mid-falling to low, 4 - high rising-falling, 5 - high-falling, 6 - mid with a slight fall (Hudak 1993). Yay, Northern Branch, has the following system: 1 - level, slightly lower than mid, 2 - low level, 3 - rising, 4 - high level, 5 - falling, 6 - higher than mid with a slight rise toward the end (Hudak 1991a). The dialect of Lungming, Central Branch, has the following system: 1 - high level, 2 - high-rising, 3 - mid level, 4 - low-falling, from mid-low to low, 5 - low level, 6 - falling from mid-low to low and then rising to mid-low (Hudak 1991b). Western Nung, Central Branch, has the following system: 1 - low-rising, 2 - low-falling, 3 - mid-low, 4 - mid-high, 5 - mid-falling, 6 - falling (Hudak 1995). Lue, Southwestern Branch, has the following system: 1 - high level, 2 - low-rising, 3 - low level, 4 - low-falling, 5 - mid level, 6 - falling (Hudak 1996).

3   Tai Mau Shan, Southwestern Branch, has the following tonal system: 1 - high level, 2 - high-falling, 3 - mid level, 4 - mid-falling, 5 - low-rising, 6 - low level (Young 1985).

2. insertion of syllable for rhyme, from Yay:
$rak^1 ma^6 ka^3 hun^4$
steal-horse-kill-people
'expression for the worst crime'

3. insertion of syllable with semantic relation, from Saek:
$rim^2 luaŋ^5 rim^2 sɔɔŋ^4$
fill-space below the house-fill-couplet with no meaning
'to fill the space below the house'

Cushing (1914: 13) describes another variation of these expressions. In Shan, he finds what he calls 'phonetic couplets' in which meaningless syllables are joined to words for the euphonic sound they create. These added syllables usually have the same consonant and tone as the base word with only the vowels differing. While infrequent, the couplets are used by children or old women to express anger or to create an atmosphere of fun. In many cases used alone, these couplets also appear in elaborate expressions, as in the following:[4]

$shuk^5 shi^3 shuk^5 shak^5$
confused-redundant syllable-confused-phonetic couplet
'confused, disordered'

The base word in this expression is $shuk^5$ with $shak^5$ the meaningless syllable that forms the couplet. The complete expression is created by following the base word with a nonsense syllable consisting of the initial of the base word [sh] plus the high front vowel [i]; to this is added the full phonetic couplet (the base word plus the euphonic syllable). A slightly different variation occurs with $maak^2 keŋ^4$ – tamarind. In this case, the first syllable is repeated with the phonetic couplet then added: $maak^2 keŋ^4 maak^2 kaaŋ^4$.

Since these expressions exist in large numbers throughout the Tai languages, as well as in other languages in the region, Gedney (1989: 536) has suggested that they are part of the language and that, regardless of their phonetic structure, they are not something that has been created for formal poetic composition by poets. Roffe (1975: 288) in the conclusion to his study of Lao four-syllable expressions summarizes their contribution to the production of $phay^1rɔʔ$: 'Without them the speaker or writer will make himself understood, but will prove to be rather dull and pedestrian. With them, he enthralls his audience with both lilt and light, making his message both meaningful and melodious.'

Proverbs, also common to the Tai languages, incorporate both rhyming and reduplicative techniques to create pleasing sounds. But added to these phonological techniques are parallel structures and similar or identical syllable number per line to create a cohesive and tightly structured unit. While the number of syllables per line varies, five is a fairly common number, probably because Tai phrases tend to fall into phonological and syntactic groups of five syllables. The number of lines per proverb also varies but in a large number of cases two lines predominate with the end syllable of the first line rhyming with either the second or third syllable of the following line, effectively creating a rhyming couplet, which as we will see later is a basic component in the creation of formal verse. The following Bouyei proverb (Snyder 1998: 69) has unequal lines of four and five syllables linked by the optional rhyming syllables ($ʔdi^1$ and pi^1). The original spelling recently created and used in the proverb has been changed to a phonetic transcription to show the rhyme:[5]

---

4   Shan, Southwestern Branch, has the following tonal system: 1 - rising, 2 - low level, 3 - mid level, 4 - high level, 5 - falling (Cushing 1914; Hudak 2000).
5   Other than Snyder's and Hartmann's all translations are mine. Bouyei, Northern Branch, has the following tonal system: 1 - low-rising, 2 - low-falling, 3 - mid level, 4 - high-falling, 5 - high-rising, 6 - high (Snyder 1998).

pu⁴ ka³ pian⁵   ʔdi¹
classifier-kill-change-good

ʔaw¹ pi¹ mɛw² cip³ ha³
want-year-cat-ten-five

'It's impossible to change a bad character. [lit., For a murderer to change, one must wait for the fifteenth year of the cat.]'

In the following Lue example from Muong Yong[6] (Hudak 1996: 1344), the cohesion is even tighter with each line having five syllables and identical syntactic structures, linked with the rhyming pair law¹ and kaw⁴:

yaa² pay⁴ cok¹ huu¹law¹
don't-go-take out-deep pit

yaa² pay⁴ kaw⁴ kun⁴ bay³
don't-go-talk to-person-stupid

'Don't dig deep pits.
Don't go and talk to a stupid person.'

The following five-syllable Red Tai example[7] (DeGeorge 1928: 912) exemplifies the use of alliteration as well as rhyme between the second and third syllable, the scheme typical to the elaborate expressions:

kay² say² kay² katak¹
chicken-lay egg-chicken-crow
'It's the chicken with eggs that crows.'

Comparable patterns of parallelism and rhyme can be found in puns (Manas 1972; Aporn 1973), limericks (Hudak 1996; 2001), riddles and tongue-twisters (Hudak 1996).

13.2. *phay¹rɔʔ⁴* AND POETIC CONSTRAINTS

In poems and songs, the aesthetic-producing techniques used in everyday language to create interest and melodiousness have been formalized and over time canonized. Almost all of the Tai languages favor the five-syllable line so common to the proverbs. These lines are arranged in couplets with the end syllable of the first line rhyming with another syllable, usually the second, in the second line:

O O O O O̲
O O̲ O O O

---

6   Muong Yong Lue, Southwestern Branch, has the following tonal system: 1 - high-rising, 2 - low-rising, 3 - low level, 4 - mid, with slight rise and fall, 5 - mid level, 6 - falling (Hudak 1996).

7   DeGeorge's transcription of the Red Tai tones was largely impressionistic. To indicate them, he used the symbols from Vietnamese orthography; hence they should be treated as approximate at best. Red Tai, Southwestern Branch, has the following tonal system: 1 - rising, 2 - low level, 3 - falling, 4 - mid level, 5 - low-rising, 6 - high level,

This syllabic couplet arrangement forms the most basic stanzaic pattern upon which longer poems are built. Thus a poem may consist of an unlimited number of couplets linked to one another by rhyme. Two syllables rhyme when they share the same final vowel or vowel plus consonant. Prior to the tonal changes that swept through the Tai languages, the two syllables also had to have the same tone in order to rhyme. While the five-syllable line is the ideal, a more common pattern is to show various lengths with the rhyme sometimes omitted. Both of these characteristics appear in the following selection from a Lue oral narrative (Hartmann 1992: 268):

say^1 mɤn^1 nam^6 ʔaaŋ^2 kɛw^3
clear-like-water-jar-glass

mɤn^1 vɛn^5 yɛɛŋ^4 taa^1
like-mirror-shine-eye

pii^5 maa^4 phit^{5}ca ʔ^{1}ra ʔ^{6}naa^4
older sibling-come-investigate

'As clear as water in a glass jar
Like a mirror shining into the eye
I have studied the story'

The Lue narrative is an example of oral literature that has been handed down from one generation to another. But the same characteristics that define these examples as literature also occur in pieces that are created extemporaneously. While doing fieldwork with the speakers of Western Nung, William J. Gedney asked for some sample texts. Having seen two older women sitting along side the road singing, he asked for them to sing their songs. The result was a 226 line song based on the five-syllable couplet. From the topics covered in the song, Gedney realized that much of it was created extemporaneously. And while parts of the song violated the requirements of syllable number and rhyme scheme, as in the Lue narrative, large sections of the song followed the requirements exactly as in these four lines (Hudak 1995: 787):

pan^4 dew^1 mat^4 pii^1 kaa^2
be-one-is-year-past

lum^3 cii^2 chaa^2 pii^{1}caay^1
like-I-old-year before last

cɯɯɯ^4 cin^1 nam^6 too^2 baw^3
when-eat-water-with-water dipper

chaa^2 ɲaak^5 khaw^3 too^2 peŋ^4
old-eat-rice-with-teapot

'It is the same as the year gone by.
I, formerly, in the year before last,
When I drank water from a dipper,
I ate rice with a teapot.'

For elaborations on this basic couplet arrangement, one must look to Thai and Laotian poetry. In both Thai and Lao there exist handbooks known as *chan^{5}tha^{4}lak^4* which describe and prescribe each verse form in terms of the number of syllables required per line, the number of lines per stanza, and the required rhyme scheme. To each of these schematic descriptions is added an example that sometimes fulfills the requirements exactly and at other times only approaches fulfillment. In the *chan^{5}tha^{4}lak^4*, there is a verse form known as *raay^3 yaaw^1*

which is identical to those described above for Lue and Western Nung and used throughout the Tai family. This meter consists of any number of syllables per line with the end syllable of that line usually rhyming with the second syllable of the next line; any number of lines can complete a stanza. Found throughout the Tai family, it probably can be regarded as the oldest and the original Tai verse form (Gedney 1989; Hudak 1990; Hartmann 1992). While line lengths in *raay³ yaaw¹* are not set and tend to vary, the five-syllable length appears to be the underlying structure. In both Thai and Lao, other types of *raay³* also occur. There has not been enough research on the oral literatures of the other Tai languages to see whether or not this may also be the case for them.

While the syllabic *raay³ yaaw¹* with its end rhyme and occasional alliteration has remained the favored verse form of most of the Tai languages, Thai and Lao, by contrast, show a far richer development and elaboration of types and aesthetic techniques. Thai, for example, has five classical verse forms used for poetry composed before 1932: *raay³*, *khlooŋ¹*, *kaap²* borrowed from Cambodian, *chan⁵* borrowed from Pali, and *klɔɔn¹*. The stanzas of these verse forms, with various numbers of lines per stanza, are all based upon the five-syllable line, with the borrowed forms modified to fit this syllabic constraint (Hudak 1990). At the same time, the rhyme schemes used for the stanzas fall into three general patterns, each dependent upon the number of lines in the stanza (Hudak 1986; see Apiluck 2001 for a slightly different interpretation). But what becomes apparent is the explosion of rhyming techniques. The rhyme as prescribed for the *raay³* forms remains but another between the end syllables of two lines, termed external or outer rhyme (*sam⁵phat² nɔɔk³*), has been added to help define the various new stanzas. The following example from the eighteenth century *Bun¹noo¹waat³ kham¹ chan⁵* shows both types of rhymes: *hɔɔy³* and *yɔɔy⁴* represent the original rhyme scheme while *raŋ¹* and *daŋ¹* the new one:

bay¹ phoo¹ su²wan¹ hɔɔy³
leaf-Bo tree-gold-hang

ra⁴yaa⁴ yɔɔy⁴ bɔ² ruŋ¹raŋ¹
pendant-hang loosely-not-ragged

lom¹ phat⁴ kra²dɯŋ¹ daŋ¹
wind-blow-bell-sound

sa²nɔ² sap²tha⁴ ʔon¹la⁴weeŋ¹
melodious-sounds-agreeable to the ears

'The leaves of the golden Bo hang down,
Loose pendants moving freely.
The wind blows sounding the bells
Making melodious and agreeable sounds'

Even more numerous are the alliterative and vocalic patterns, termed internal or inner rhyme (*sam⁵phat² nay¹*), that occur between syllables within a line. Rhyme can occur between two adjacent syllables, three adjacent syllables, four adjacent syllables, and two syllables with one or two intervening non-rhyming syllables (Hudak 1987). In addition, syllabic, phonological, and syntactic parallelism become increasingly important as components of verse. At the same time, variations in syntax, frequently employed to accommodate metrical requirements, remain common (Udom 1992). Compton (1979; 1992) and Koret (1995; 2000) outline and describe in depth comparable patterns for Lao.

All of the verse forms, as defined in Thai, have some requirements for tonal placement, with those for *khlooŋ¹*, known as *ʔeek² thoo¹*, the most complicated (Cooke 1980). Originally Thai had a three tone system with one group of words unmarked, a second with the tone marker known as *may⁴ ʔeek²*, and the third with *may⁴ thoo¹*. In the original *khlooŋ¹*, certain syllables required the first tone marker and others the second, which Gedney (1989: 499) hypothesizes may have given the verses a lilting or rocking sensation. Composition of these verse forms when Thai had a three tone system was probably relatively easy, all based on the actual pronunciation of the words with no confusion as to which tone belonged where. However, after the tone splits had occurred in Thai, as well as in the other Tai languages, composition became more difficult. Because of merging of tones, each of the tone markers now represented two tones, not one – low and falling for *may⁴ ʔeek²*, falling and high for *may⁴ thoo¹*. With this change, the poets had to decide whether to follow the actual pronunciation, which now offered choices, or to ignore it and follow the spelling. In modern Thai with its emphasis on the written form, poets have focused on the spelling of the word rather than its actual pronunciation. Bickner (1991) provides a detailed and convincing argument for the development of *raay³* and *khlooŋ¹* when Thai had a three tone system.

With the borrowing of *chan⁵* from Pali, the Thai poets were forced to redefine the syllable since the phonological concept of the Pali syllable differed from that of the Thai. The Pali *chan⁵* forms were based on two types of syllables, light and heavy, with syllable and word boundaries ignored in defining the syllable. Light syllables consisted of a short vowel followed by not more than one consonant. By contrast, a heavy syllable contained a long vowel or any vowel followed by two or more consonants. Once redefined, the Thai light syllable (*la⁴hu ʔ²*) consisted of a short vowel with no final consonant and the unwritten final glottal stop ignored; a heavy syllable (*kha⁴ru ʔ²*) terminated in a long vowel or any vowel plus a final consonant. This redefinition of the syllable conformed to the possible syllable types in Thai: CVC, CVVC, CCVC, CCVVC, and CCVV (with VV indicating a long vowel). By ignoring the unwritten glottal stop, the distinction between the two syllable types remained; otherwise all the syllables would be heavy. Of the 108 possible Pali meters, only eighteen were used by the poets, six for compositions prior to 1913 and twelve for those after 1913. Those finally chosen were probably selected because the light and heavy sequence closely fit the phonological structure of Thai (see Hudak 1985 and 1990 for a complete discussion.)

Even with the redefinition of the syllable, the poets encountered problems fulfilling the requirements if only because Thai syllables lack large numbers of light syllables, particularly in sequence. To remedy this situation, a number of unwritten conventions for reciting the meters were devised that altered the pronunciation of words. The results were twofold. First, an application of the conventions fulfilled the requirements demanded by the meter. Second, the techniques used to recite the meters contributed to the production of *phay¹rɔʔ⁴* while at the same time created a more complicated and sophisticated meter. Sound remained important but what constituted an appropriate and melodious sound had expanded to include words that were no longer pronounced in the usual way. To meet the demands of the light and heavy syllable requirements more and more Indic loanwords were used. As a result, the *chan⁵* meters came to be regarded as difficult and erudite, meters understood and enjoyed only by the educated and the intelligentsia. There are six main conventions.

1) *syllable substitution and addition*. In Thai, Indic loanwords, which were heavily used in the *chan⁵* forms, generally have two forms, a shorter form which was the usual pronunciation and a longer form which was used as a combining form. Thus, *soŋ⁵*, the usual word for 'monk', would fulfill a heavy syllable sequence. However, if a heavy-light sequence was needed the longer alternant, *soŋ⁵kha⁴*, would be used.

2) *syllable breaking*. To obtain two light syllables a monosyllabic heavy syllable could be divided: *khot⁴* – 'elephant' could be rewritten as *kho⁴cha⁴*. In this case, the second syllable begins with [ch] because the final sound of *khot⁴* is spelled with the orthographic symbol for [ch] which is pronounced as [t] when in the final position.

3) *syllable crossover*. With this convention a word could be divided between two lines. For *khat²ti²ya⁴* – 'king', *khat-²*, a heavy syllable, ends the first line with *-ti²ya⁴*, two light syllables, beginning the second line.

4) *syncopation*. In this case, a short vowel usually pronounced is muted; *sa²dɛɛŋ¹* becomes *sdɛɛŋ¹*, a light-heavy sequence becomes a single heavy syllable.

5) *vowel reduction.* In natural speech, unstressed long vowels in polysyllabic words are reduced to short vowels, although the reduced vowel may not be as short as a natural short vowel: *daa¹bot²* – 'hermit', which consists of two heavy syllables when the syllables are given equal stress, becomes *dăbot²*, a light-heavy sequence, when recited.

6) *alternate pronunciations.* A number of words have a variety of pronunciations, the choice dependent upon the metrical requirements: cave – *khuu¹haa⁵, khu⁴haa⁵*; lion – *siŋ⁵, sii⁵, sii⁵ha²*.

While these conventions are most common in the *chan⁵* meters, they can also be found in the other classical verse forms (Hudak 1992).

With the proliferation of verse types and rhyming techniques, poetry written in Thai, particularly in the nineteenth century, became more and more a showcase for sound, with *kloon¹* becoming the favored meter (Kuo 1980; Bofman 1984; Gedney 1997). Over time, sound has seemingly become more important than content. One genre still popular today, *kon¹la⁴bot²*, gave strict emphasis to alliterative and vocalic patterns, resulting in a wide variety of tongue-twisters. In the 1940s, 1950s, and 1970s, the aesthetics of sound came under heavy criticism from poets and critics alike who claimed that this type of verse had no importance for the people. Content dealing with social concerns became paramount. But looking closely at much of this social realism, one can still find all of the techniques that were used to produce *phay¹roʔ⁴*. Over time, this criticism subsided and poets once again consciously turned their attention to the production of melodious verse even though the content had changed. Today's contemporary poetry, and even jingles used in advertising, continues to use these same techniques.

A final question concerns how far an analysis of *phay¹roʔ⁴* can be taken. All of the techniques discussed above are used in the poetry. But what about patterns that are not formally recognized by the poets as in the following examples from the classic nineteenth century *kloon¹* narrative poem *ʔi²naw⁵* (Hudak 1987):

1)   *pra²saan⁵ siaŋ⁵ phiaŋ¹ phin¹phaat³ khɔɔŋ⁴*

    unite-sound-as-orchestra-ring

    '[The bees] unite their sounds like the sounds of an orchestra.'

2)   *suŋ³ meek³ mɔɔk³ muɯɯt³mua¹ thua³ thaa¹trii¹*

    which-clouds-mist-overcast-everywhere-earth

    'Gloomy clouds and mist covered the earth everywhere.'

In the first example, all but two of the syllables end in a nasal, the difference being in the point of articulation. This is an example of semi-consonance, which Mark and Li noted for the dialect found at Wuming. In the second example, *meek³* and *mɔɔk³* have the same initial and final consonants, which is para-rhyme. Neither of these two techniques is attested by the poets, but they do occur on a regular basis in all forms of poetry. Do these two techniques then and others such as semi-assonance and consonance, contribute to the aesthetics of *phay¹roʔ⁴* or are they merely the result of a western-orientated poetic analysis?   Speaking from a strictly Thai perspective, the author of the most respected *chan⁵tha⁴lak⁴*, Phya Uppakit Silpasarn (1968: 353-54), maintains that these are not true examples of rhyme and should be avoided. Nevertheless, an examination of highly valued compositions (i.e., melodious), such as those by Rama II or Sunthorn Phu, reveals these techniques in great number whereas in less melodious pieces they are lacking.

13.3. CONCLUSION

Throughout the Tai family of languages, those who can use the language in creative and, most importantly, melodious ways are held in great esteem. These may be farmers and merchants who can use a clever turn of speech or professional poets and storytellers. For their production of pleasing speech, the farmer and merchant can look to the language they use on a daily basis with intensifiers; limericks; proverbs; elaborate expressions; puns and word play; and consonantal and vocalic rhyme found in compounds. The poets and professional storytellers can utilize the same techniques as well as those formalized and canonized into patterns to create an expressive and pleasing oral and written literature. In both cases, what is said is important. But how something is said may be even more significant. To make and carry a point, the language must be *phay¹rɔʔ⁴*.

REFERENCES

Anuman Rajadhon, Phya (1968) 'The Nature and Development of the Thai Language', in *Essays on Thai Folklore*, Bangkok: The Social Science Association Press, 75-102.
Apiluck Tumtavitikul (2001) 'Thai Poetry: A Metrical Analysis', in M. R. Kalaya Tingsabadh and Arthur S. Abramson (eds) *Essays in Tai Linguistics*, Bangkok: Chulalongkorn University Press, 29-40.
Aporn Surintramont (1973) 'Some Aspects of Underlying Syllable Structure in Thai: Evidence from *khampuan* – A Thai Word Game', *Studies in the Linguistic Sciences* 3 (Spring): 121-42.
Bickner, R. J. (1991) 'An Introduction to the Thai Poem "Lilit Phra Law" (The Story of King Law)', *Monograph Series on Southeast Asia, Special Report No. 25*, DeKalb, IL: Center for Southeast Asian Studies, Northern Illinois University.
Bofman, T. H. (1984) *The Poetics of the Ramakian, Monograph Series on Southeast Asia, Special Report No. 21*, DeKalb, IL: Center for Southeast Asian Studies, Northern Illinois University.
Compton, C. J. (1979) *Courting Poetry in Laos: A Textural and Linguistic Analysis, Monograph Series on Southeast Asia, Special Report No. 18*, DeKalb, IL: Center for Southeast Asia, Northern Illinois University.
— (1992) 'Lao Poetics: Internal Rhyme in the Text of a Lao Sithandone Performance', in Carol J. Compton and John F. Hartmann (eds) *Papers on Tai Languages, Linguistics, and Literatures: In Honor of William J. Gedney on His 77th Birthday*, DeKalb, IL: Center for Southeast Asia, Northern Illinois University, 231-61.
Cooke, J. R (1980) 'The Thai *Khlong* Poem: Description and Examples', *Journal of the American Oriental Society* 100 (4): 421-37.
Cushing, J. N. (1914) *A Shan and English Dictionary*, Rangoon: American Baptist Mission Press.
DeGeorge, J. B. (1928) 'Proverbes, Maximes et Sentences Tays', *Anthropos* 23: 596-616, 911-32.
Foret, P. (1994) 'Whispered so Softly it Resounds in the Forest, Spoken so Loudly it can Hardly be Heard: The Art of Parallelism in Traditional Lao Literature', unpublished PhD Thesis, School of Oriental and African Studies, University of London.
Gedney, W. J. (1989) 'Siamese Verse Forms in Historical Perspective', in Robert J. Bickner, John Hartmann, Thomas John Hudak, and Patcharin Peyasantiwong (eds) *Selected Papers on Comparative Tai Studies, Michigan Papers on South and Southeast Asia No. 29*, Ann Arbor, MI: Center for South and Southeast Asian Studies, University of Michigan, 489-544.
— (1997) 'The Rise and Decline of a Siamese Verse Form', in Thomas John Hudak (ed.) *William J. Gedney's Thai and Indic Literary Studies, Michigan Papers on South and Southeast Asia No. 46*, Ann Arbor, MI: Center for South and Southeast Asian Studies, The University of Micihigan, 101-18.

Haas, M. (1942) 'Types of Reduplication in Thai', *Studies in Linguistics* I: 1.4.1-1.4.6.
— (1946) 'Techniques of Intensifying in Thai', *Word* 2: 127-30.
— (1964) *Thai-English Student's Dictionary*, 2nd edition, Stanford, CA: Stanford University Press.
Hartmann, J.F. (1992) 'Tai Dam Poetics and Proto-Tai Tone Categories', in Carol J. Compton and John F. Hartmann (eds) *Papers on Tai Languages, Linguistics, and Literatures: In Honor of William J. Gedney on His 77th Birthday, Monograph Series on Southeast Asia, Occasional Papers No. 16,* Dekalb, IL: Center for Southeast Asian Studies, Northern Illinois University, 262-77.
Hudak, T.J. (1985) 'Poetic Conventions in Thai *chan* Meters', *Journal of the American Oriental Society* 105.1: 107-19.
— (1986) 'Meta-rhymes in Classical Thai Poetry', *Journal of the Siam Society* 74: 38-61.
— (1987) 'Internal Rhyme Patterns in Classical Thai Poetry', *Crossroads* 3.2-3: 94-105.
— (1990) *The Indigenization of Pali Meters in Thai Poetry, Monograph in International Studies, Southeast Asia Series, No. 87,* Athens, OH: Ohio University.
— (1991a) *William J. Gedney's The Yay Language: Glossary, Texts, and Translations, Michigan Papers on South and Southeast Asia No. 38,* Ann Arbor, MI: Center for South and Southeast Asian Studies, The University of Michigan.
— (1991b) *William J. Gedney's The Tai Dialect of Lungming: Glossary, Texts, and Translations, Michigan Papers on South and Southeast Asia No. 39,* Ann Arbor, MI: Center for South and Southeast Asian Studies, The University of Michigan.
— (1992) 'Further Observations on the Thai *chan* Poetic Conventions', in Carol J. Compton and John F. Hartmann (eds) *Papers on Tai Languages, Linguistics, and Literatures: In Honor of William J. Gedney's 77th Birthday, Monograph Series on Southeast Asia, Occasional Papers No. 16,* DeKalb, IL: Center for Southeast Asian Studies, Northern Illinois University, 278-85.
— (1993) *William J. Gedney's The Saek Language: Glossary, Texts, and Translations, Michigan Papers on South and Southeast Asia No. 41,* Ann Arbor, MI: Center for South and Southeast Asian Studies, The University of Michigan.
— (1995) *William J. Gedney's Central Tai Dialects: Glossaries, Texts, and Translations, Michigan Papers on South and Southeast Asia No. 43,* Ann Arbor, MI: Center for South and Southeast Asian Studies, The University of Michigan.
— (1996) *William J. Gedney's The Lue Language: Glossary, Texts, and Translations, Monographs on South and Southeast Asia No. 44,* Ann Arbor, MI: Center for South and Southeast Asian Studies, The University of Michigan.
— (2000) *Cushing's Shan-English Dictionary: A Phonetic Version,* Monograph Series Press, Tempe, AZ: Program for Southeast Asian Studies, Arizona State University.
— (2001) 'Limericks and Rhyme in Thai', in M. R. Kalaya Tingsabadh and Arthur S. Abramson (eds) *Essays in Tai Linguistics,* Bangkok: Chulalongkorn University Press, 41-49.
Koret, Peter (1995) 'The Art of Parallelism in Traditional Lao Literature', in Manas Chitakasem (ed.) *Thai Literary Traditions,* Bangkok: Chulalongkorn University Press, 265-98.
— (2000) 'Books of Search: Convention and Creativity in Traditional Lao Literature', in David Smyth (ed.) *The Canon in Southeast Asian Literatures,* Cornwall, GB: Curzon Press, 210-33.
Kuo, W. (1980) 'The Prosodic Structure of Rama II's *klɔɔn*', *Journal of the Siam Society* 68.2: 15-33.
Li, F. K. (1960) 'A Tentative Classification of Tai Dialects', in S. Diamond (ed.) *Culture in History: Essays in Honor of Paul Radin,* New York: Columbia University Press, 951-9.
Manas Chitakasem (1972) 'The Emergence and Development of the *Nira* Genre in Thai Poetry', *Journal of the Siam Society* 60.2: 135-68.
Mosel, J. N. (1959) 'Sound and Rhythm in Thai and English Verse', *Phaasa lae Nangsue* [*Language and Books*] 1 (December): 29-34.

— (1961) *Trends and Structure in Contemporary Thai Poetry*, Southeast Asia Program, Data Paper 43, Ithaca, NY: Department of Far Eastern Studies, Cornell University.

Roffe, G. E. (1975) 'Rhyme, Reduplication, etc. in Lao', in Jimmy G. Harris and James R. Chamberlain (eds) *Studies in Tai Linguistics in Honor of William J. Gedney*, Bangkok: Central Institute of English Language, Office of State Universities, 285-315.

Scovel, T. (1975) 'Some Observations on Restricted Intensifiers in Northern Thai', in Thomas W. Gething (ed.) *A Tai Festschrift for William J. Gedney, Southeast Asian Studies Working Paper No. 8*, Honolulu: Southeast Asian Studies Program, University of Hawaii, 96-111.

Snyder, D. (1998) 'Folk Wisdom in Bouyei Proverbs and Songs', in Somsonge Burusphat (ed.) *Proceedings: The International Conference on Tai Studies, July 29-31, 1998*, Bangkok: Institute of Language and Culture for Rural Development, Mahidol University, 61-87.

Theraphan L. Thongkum (1979) 'Iconicity of Vowel Qualities in Northeastern Thai Reduplicated Words', in Theraphan L. Thongkum, Pranee Kullavanijaya, Vichin Panupong, and M. R. Kalaya Tingsabadh (eds) *Studies in Tai and Mon-Khmer Phonetics and Phonology In Honour of Eugénie J. A. Henderson*, Bangkok: Chulalongkorn University Press, 247-60.

Udom Warotamasikkhadit (1992) 'Syntactic Variations in Thai Poetry', in Carol J. Compton and John F. Hartmann (eds) *Papers on Tai Languages, Linguistics, and Literatures: In Honor of William J. Gedney's 77th Birthday, Monograph Series on Southeast Asia, Occasional Papers No. 16*, DeKalb, IL: Center for Southeast Asian Studies, Northern Illinois University, 293-300.

Uppakit Silpasarn, Phya (1968) *Làk Phaasa Thay* [*Principles of the Thay Language*], Bangkok: Thay Wátthanaa Phaanít.

Young, L. W. L. (1985) *Shan Chrestomathy: An Introduction to Tai Mau Language and Literature*, Center for South and Southeast Asian Studies, University of California - Berkeley; New York: University Press of America.

CHAPTER FOURTEEN

THE OLD ZHUANG SCRIPT

David Holm

The Chinese writing system reigned supreme throughout East Asia until the European incursions of the last two centuries. The Chinese character script was employed not only in China itself, and in Japan, but also in Korea and Vietnam. Korea and Vietnam have since gone their separate ways, but even now, the Chinese character script continues to be used by literati, poets, and religious practitioners to write Korean and Vietnamese. For minority peoples inside the Chinese empire and within this wider ambit – the Sinosphere, the Chinese script was for many centuries the only writing system available, and was widely regarded as one of the sources of Chinese power and prestige. The script itself is regarded as a national treasure and a source of spiritual power as well as cultural prestige.

'Zhuang' is the current designation for the largest Tai-speaking national minority living in the south of China, mainly in the province of Guangxi (currently designated the Guangxi Zhuang Autonomous Region), but also in contiguous provinces. The term includes a number of recognisable sub-groups, and includes speakers of both Northern Tai and Central Tai dialects. They are arguably indigenous to sub-tropical southern China, and are closely related linguistically and culturally to the Bouyei of Guizhou and to the Nùng, Thổ and Tài in the northernmost part of Vietnam. They are also by far the largest minority in China, with a population of around 17 million. The Zhuang and their forebears have been in close contact with the Chinese state since the invasion of Chinese armies under Qin Shihuang in 219 BCE, a history of over two millennia. They remain today linguistically, ethnically, and culturally distinct from Han Chinese. How they have maintained this identity is a question of considerable interest. While ethnic conflict may be endemic elsewhere in the world, symbiosis as well as conflict has characterized inter-ethnic relations between the Zhuang and the Han, at least in recent centuries.

The Old Zhuang Script is a key instance of this symbiosis. Although there is a romanised script for the Zhuang language (called *Zhuangwen* 壮文), officially promoted by the People's Government since the 1950's, many literate people in Zhuang society continue to use a modified version of the Chinese character script for writing in the Zhuang language. Indeed, we have good evidence that they have done so since at least the Song dynasty a thousand years ago (Holm 2003: 39). This character script, called *gu Zhuang zi* 古壮字 ('old Zhuang characters') in Chinese and *sawndip* ('uncooked script') in Zhuang, is rather like the vernacular scripts used for writing southern dialects of Chinese, such as Cantonese, Hakka and Hokkien.[1] In the vernacular scripts of such dialects, most of the characters are the same as standard Chinese graphs, such as one would find in a Chinese dictionary, but dialect words which have no counterpart in Standard Chinese are written by making up new characters out of the same graphic elements, radicals, and phonetic graphs as are available in the graphic repertoire of the Chinese script. The ways in which new characters are composed follow mostly the same 'rules' of composition – the *liu shu* 六書, 'six ways of writing' – as found in the standard Chinese script.[2] Thus, for example (and most commonly), a semantic determinative ('radical'), may be combined with a phonophoric element ('phonetic'), a

---

1   The script is called *ndip* 'uncooked' because it is unstandardised, and graphic renderings of Zhuang words are made in a 'raw', that is, unmediated and impromptu fashion. 'Uncooked' when applied to subject peoples of the Chinese empire also tended to mean 'uncivilized'.

2   On the *liushu* see William Boltz (1994: 144–149).

graphic element indicating the pronunciation of the word in question. Less commonly, the semantic meaning of a word is formed by the combination of graphic elements.

Characters in the Old Zhuang Script for the most part obey the same graphic rules, but the script differs from the vernacular dialect scripts because the language it represents is Tai rather than Han Chinese. This means that there is much less overlap with standard Chinese in both lexicon and phonology than is the case with Chinese dialects. This has a number of important consequences. Firstly, in terms of the lexicon: even though there are a good many Han Chinese loan-words in Zhuang, most of the words found in Zhuang are not cognate with those of Chinese, or at least are not recognized as such by those who use the script. The consequence is that for most words in the Zhuang lexicon, there is an initial choice between borrowing a Chinese character for its sound (a phonetic reading), and borrowing a Chinese character for its meaning (a semantic reading). Logically, of course, only in the case of recognisable Han Chinese loan-words is it possible to adopt a character for both its sound and its meaning at the same time. Then, as processes of secondary elaboration, semantic elements may be added to characters being read phonetically, in order to designate their semantic field; and phonophoric elements may be added to characters read semantically.

Secondly, in terms of phonology: while Zhuang, like Chinese, is in the main an isolating language in which morphemes (basic units of meaning) are monosyllabic, the repertoire of initial consonants, vowels, codas and tones is different. Most dialects of Zhuang tend to be less phonetically impoverished than Standard Chinese, at least, and some Zhuang initial consonants, vowels, and tonal contours are not found in Chinese at all. For Chinese characters borrowed for their sound (and read phonetically), then, the phonetic match between the original Chinese word and the Zhuang word is more or less approximate.

Unlike the Chinese script itself, which was standardised by the First Emperor of Qin over 2000 years ago and in principle is the same all over China, the Old Zhuang Script has never been subject to full-scale standardization at the hands of a centralised political authority.[3] There is therefore a great deal of variation in the script, both from place to place and even from person to person. There is variation in terms of which Chinese characters have been borrowed to represent which Zhuang words, and in the ways in which Chinese characters used as phonetic signs are read in Zhuang. Thus, for instance, the common Chinese character er^2 而 'then, and; you, your' is used to write as many as ten different morphemes (see Table 14-1 below). Not only are particular characters used to write more than one Zhuang morpheme, but the converse is also true: the same Zhuang morpheme can be written in more than one way, even in a single text.[4] This is quite unlike written Chinese, where by and large (and at least in principle) there is a one-to-one correspondence between character graph and morpheme.

TABLE 14-1: ZHUANG READINGS OF 而 er^2 (SOURCE: *GU ZHUANGZI ZIDIAN*)

Zhuangwen	IPA	gloss
rox	γo^4	'to know'
rieg	$\gamma i{:}k^8$	'to change (clothes)'
ra	γa^1	'to look for'
raep	$\gamma \varepsilon p^7$	'to plait (straw)'
raet	$\gamma \varepsilon t^7$	'mushroom'
roiz	$\gamma o{:}i^2$	classifier for male human beings
rwz	$\gamma \text{ɯ}^2$	'ear'
lawz	$\gamma \varepsilon \text{ɯ}^2$	'what'

---

3   The possible role of Zhuang local chieftains in promoting standardised scripts within their domains is a question that has yet to be investigated. On local chieftaincy in Guangxi during the Ming and Qing dynasties, see Jennifer Took (2005).

4   Indeed, cases can be found where the same word in Zhuang has been written with two different Chinese characters in successive lines of text. A number of instances are discussed in Holm (2003).

riuz	ɣiːu^2	'to flow'
heux	heːu^4	'to twine, wind round'

The old Zhuang script was commonly used as the main written medium for a variety of literary forms in the Zhuang language, including cosmogonic songs, ritual texts used by vernacular priests (*mogong* 麽公), ritual masters (*shigong* 師公), and Taoist priests (*daogong* 道公), song-texts used in the annual springtime 'song markets' and on other ceremonial occasions such as weddings and funerals, moral homilies in verse such as the *Cienzyiengzgo* 傳揚歌 (Song of Civilization), cheap novelettes and story-teller's tales such as *Dangzvuengz* 唐皇 (Emperor of the Tang), and playscripts for the marionette theatre, ritual masters' plays (*shigongxi* 師公戲), and Zhuang opera. These materials circulate in the form of manuscripts, rather than printed books (see Ouyang Ruoxiu 1986 vols.1–2 and Holm 2003: 182–6). They come from different strata in regional cultures: ritual texts often contain the oldest material, and circulate in a very limited fashion from masters to disciples; story-teller's tales are often Zhuang adaptations of Chinese chapbook materials, and probably date mostly from the Qing and early Republican periods; while song-texts have much wider circulation in rural communities, and may in many cases represent first-generation transcription of what were originally orally-transmitted lyrics. Many of these materials are still in circulation today, though song markets have been transformed since the 1980s by the introduction of Canto-pop and lavish sponsorship by local and regional governments.

The high degree of variability in the Old Zhuang Script often makes it difficult to read. Zhuang speakers who are literate in Chinese can puzzle out the meaning of more popular texts and works of literature from their own dialect area. For older texts, such as ritual and cosmogonic texts, it is impossible to read the script without the assistance of the traditional owners of the manuscript. For vernacular priests, at least, the script serves as a mnemonic device for recitations and other forms of religious performance which include special religious vocabulary and archaic words and phrases. Like the texts themselves, the script is lineage property and is not intended to be read by outsiders.

Little is known for certain about the history of the Old Zhuang Script. Pre-modern Chinese sources confine themselves to short lists of non-standard characters and their meanings. Basic questions about the age of the script have to be pieced together from internal evidence and from indirect evidence on the cultural history and historical geography of the Zhuang in Guangxi (Holm 2003: 159–71). The internal evidence is abundant, but to analyze it requires a systematic approach that encompasses Chinese historical phonology, dialectology, and comparative and historical Tai phonology. To provide a firm basis for such analysis, the readings of texts written in the Old Zhuang Script have first to be established, and this is no easy matter, as I will explain below.

There are some signs that the Old Zhuang Script is finally attracting the attention of scholars internationally. Robert Bauer has written a preliminary study (2000), based on the readings given in the only published dictionary of the old Zhuang script, the *Gu Zhuang zi zidian* 古壯字字典 (Su Yongqin et al. 1989). A recent study of Zhuang identity politics (Kaup 2000) has mentioned the prevalence of the old Zhuang script in Zhuang society, and, by contrast, noted the resistance officials have encountered in propagating Zhuangwen, the official romanised script. In China itself, there have been a number of article-length studies devoted to the old Zhuang script in specific localities (see e.g. Zheng Yiqing 1988, and Huang Ge 1982), and more general overviews (e.g. Zhang Yuansheng 1990).

None of these studies so far has been based on a text corpus. Most have looked at relatively small samples of characters, and concentrated attention on examples of the more exotic non-standard Zhuang characters found in particular localities. Thus they have tended to overlook the much more basic question of how the script actually works. In fact, in any particular Zhuang text, standard Chinese characters outnumber the specially made-up Zhuang characters by a large margin, in some cases by a factor of at least 10 to 1. The Old Zhuang

Script dictionary, likewise, concentrates on the non-standard 'invented' characters, and is relatively poor as a guide to the readings of regular Chinese characters in Zhuang texts.[5]

14.1. METHODOLOGY

The elements of a more constructive approach to the old Zhuang script are already exemplified in the work of Li Fang-Kuei. In his *The Tai Dialect of Wu-ming* (1956), Li edited a number of song texts from his target area, Matou village in the eastern part of Wuming, transcribing the contents of song-books and providing transcriptions in the local lect, glosses in Chinese, translations in Chinese and English, and a concordance. The way forward to more substantial breakthroughs, and an appropriate methodology and set of protocols, can be developed on this basis. Over the last decade, I have edited two major corpuses of ritual texts belonging to vernacular priests (*mogong*) from two different localities, Donglan county in the northwest of Guangxi (Holm 2001a and 2003), and the area along the Tianyang-Bama border in the central-west (Holm 2004). I have also edited the text of a ritual play from eastern Bama performed at funerals by Taoist priests (2001b). In the course of this work I have developed a methodology for transcribing, glossing, translating and annotating traditional Zhuang texts, and for tracking the underlying morphemes where these have been obscured by processes of synonym substitution (very common in recitations of texts of the oldest stratum). The methodology (described fully in Holm 2003: 36–41) ensures a high degree of accuracy in the identification of Zhuang morphemes represented in the script, and thereby provides a base for the reliable collation of textual readings and comparisons between texts cross-regionally.

Briefly, this methodology involves recording complete recitations of manuscripts by their original owners or by others trained by the same master; lengthy and systematic interviews with them covering the semantic and pragmatic aspects of texts in performance; investigations of local Zhuang dialect and local history, including village and family history; comparisons with similar bodies of song and narrative song from other parts of Guangxi, Yunnan and Guizhou; comparisons of readings with pronunciations in Middle Chinese, Old Chinese, the *Pinghua* dialect (the dialect spoken by the older strata of Han Chinese settlers in Guangxi), Cantonese, and Southwestern Mandarin; and identification of Tai morphemes by reference to a growing body of lexical material on Zhuang and other Tai languages.[6] Some priests know very little about the texts they recite, except how to recite them, and very few of them have the meta-linguistic skills needed to isolate and identify the meaning of individual words. The process of establishing a text (and investigating all possible variant readings) can be a lengthy one, involving a reiterative process.

This work is still in progress. In the rest of this chapter, I will present first a sample text, then some of our preliminary findings.

14.2. A SAMPLE TEXT

The following example comes from a manuscript from Laiman village in the south of Bama county, and is the opening passage from a *mogong* scripture on the creation of fire. The passage we will be examining here starts with the third column from the right, beginning with the characters 三盖:

---

5   Also, and most unfortunately, it gives no information about the geographical provenance of any of its entries, designating characters found in areas other than Wuming county (the home of the standard Zhuang lect) simply as *fang* 方 'dialect'.

6   Most notably Li Fang-Kuei's researches on Lungchow (1940), Wuming (1956) and Po-ai (1988, 1990), and Thomas Hudak's edited versions of William J. Gedney's material for Yay (1991a), Lungming (1991b), and other languages.

Plate 1 Scripture on the creation of fire

The first eight lines may be translated into English as follows (see Holm 2004: 126):

The Three Realms were established by the Three Kings,
The Four Realms were created by the Four Kings.
In times of yore fire had not yet been created,
In times of yore fire had not yet been established.
People ate their meat raw like crows,
People ate their fish raw like otters.
People ate their grain in the ear like monkeys,
People ate their meat red like tigers.

The transcription into IPA in the interlinear glosses below represents the local pronunciation, while the lines below provide Standard Zhuang equivalents (in Zhuangwen) and glosses in English:

三	盖	三	皇	至		1
ła:m˩	ka:i˩	ła:m˩	βuəŋ˩	ci:˩		
sam	gaiq	sam	vuengz	ciq		
three	realm	three	king	establish		

四	盖	四	皇	造		2
ł⁽ᵛ⁾i:˩	ka:i˩	ł⁽ᵛ⁾i˩	βuəŋ˩	ca:u˧˥		
seiq	gaiq	seiq	vuengz	cauh		
four	realm	four	king	create		

召	礶	增	造	燬		3
ce:u˧˥	kɔːˀn˧	cɐŋ˩	ca:u˧˥	fi:˩		
ciuh	gonq	caengz	cauh	feiz		
generation	before	not yet	create	fire		

召	貫	增	至	火	4
ceːuᴧ	koːˀn˧	cɐŋ˨	ciː˥	ho˩	
ciuh	gonq	caengz	ciq	hoj	
generation	before	not yet	establish	fire	

哏	臄	垃	貧	鴉	5
kən˨	no˥ᴧ	ʔdɪp˥	pɐn˨	ʔaᴧ	
gwn	noh	ndip	baenz	a	
eat	meat	raw	become, like	crow	

哏	魿	垃	貧	猺	6
kən˨	tɕa˨	ʔdɪp˥	pɐn˨	naːk˧	
gwn	bya	ndip	baenz	nag	
eat	fish	raw	become, like	otter	

哏	糇	角	貧	猵	7
kən˨ᴧ	hɐu˥ᴧ	kaːk˥	pɐn˨	lɪŋˀ˨	
gwn	haeux	gak	baenz	lingz	
eat	grain	unhusked	become, like	ape	

哏	臄	関	貧	庲	8
kən˨	no˥ᴧ	ʔdɪŋ˨ᴧ	pɐn˨	kʊk˥	
gwn	noh	nding	baenz	guk	
eat	meat	red	become, like	tiger	

The following information is pertinent to these readings:[7]

三 *sam* 'three' Ch. MSC *san*¹ 'three'; EMC, LMC and EM sam; PT *sam A1

盖 *gaiq* 'realm' MSC *gai*⁴ 'cover, canopy', used for 界 MSC *jie*⁴ 'realm'; EMC kəijʰ/kɛːjʰ, LMC kjaːj`.

皇 *vuengz* 'king' MSC *huang*² 'august, sovereign', EMC ɣwaŋ, used for 王 MSC *wang*² 'king'; EMC wuaŋ, LMC yuaŋ.

至 *ciq* 'establish' MSC *zhi*⁴ 'arrive', EMC tɕiʰ, LMC tʂiì, used for either 治 MSC *chi*² 'put in order', EMC driʰ/dri, LMC trɦii; or 置 MSC *zhi*⁴ 'set in place', EMC triʰ/tri, LMC trì.

四 *seiq* 'four' Ch. MSC *si*⁴ 'four', EMC siʰ; PT *si B1.

造 *cauh* 'create' Ch. MSC *zao*⁴ 'construct, create', EMC dzaw`, LMC tsɦaẁ, EM tsaẁ.

召 *ciuh* 'generation' MSC *zhao*⁴ 'summon', EMC driawʰ, LMC trɦiaẁ, EM tsaẁ.

礶 *gonq* 'before' graphic variant for 罐 MSC *guan*⁴ 'jar, pot', EMC kwanʰ, LMC kuaǹ; PT *k- B1.

增 *caengz* 'not yet' MSC *zeng*¹ 'add', EMC tsəŋ, LMC tsəăŋ.

燬 *feiz* 'fire' Zhuang graph composed of 'fire' radical 火 plus phonetic   derived from 微 MSC *wei*¹ 'small, minute', EMC muj, LMC ʋjyj/ʋji; Pinghua (w)uøi⁵⁴ (Tiandong), fei⁵⁴ (Mashan Qiaoshang);   PT *vɛi A2.

貫 *gonq* 'before' MSC *guan*⁴ 'pass through', EMC kwanʰ, LMC kwaǹ.

---

7 Sources of information: Pulleyblank (1991), Li Lianjin (2000), Liu Cunhan (1998), Li Fang-Kuei (1977), Holm (2004).

火 *hoj*   'fire'   Ch. MSC *huo*[3] 'fire'; EMC xwa', LMC xua´; SwM ho[54].

跟 *gwn*   'eat'   graphic variant of 跟, MSC *gen*[1] 'heel; follow'; EMC and LMC kən; PT *k- A1.

胬 *noh*   'meat, flesh' Zhuang graph composed of 'meat, flesh' radical 肉 plus phonetic 奴, MSC *nu*[2] 'wife and children; slave', EMC nɔ, LMC nuă; PT *nȉo C2.

垃 *ndip*   'raw'   Zhuang graph composed of 'fire' radical 火 plus phonetic 立, MSC *li*[4] 'stand up, set up', EMC and LMC lip; PT *ʔdl/rip D1S.

貧 *baenz*   'become'   MSC *pin*[2] 'poor'; EMC bjin, LMC pɦjin; Pinghua pɐn[42].

鴉 *a*   'crow'   Ch. MSC *ya*[1] 'crow'; MSC ʔai/ʔɔː, LMC ʔja; Pinghua a[54]/jia[54]; cf. PT *ka A1.

哏 *gwn*   'eat'   MSC *gen*[2] 'comical', read as 'mouth' radical 口 plus phonetic 艮, MSC *gen*[4], EMC kən[h], LMC kən`.

鲃 *bya*   'fish'   Zhuang graph composed of 'fish' radical 魚 plus phonetic 巴, Zh. *bya* 'karst peak'; 岜 in turn composed of 'mountain' radical 山 plus phonetic 巴, MSC *ba*[1], EMC pai/pɛː, LMC paː; PT *pla A1.

獀 *nag*   'otter'   Zhuang graph composed of 'dog' radical 犭 plus phonetic 匿, MSC *ni*[4] 'hide', EMC nrik, LMC nriˬk; Pinghua (j)ak[33] (Tian-dong) but initial varies: most locations have initial n-, ŋ-, or zero initial; PT *n- D2L.

粩 *haeux*   'rice'   Zhuang graph composed of 'grain' radical 米 plus phonetic 厚, MSC *hou*[4], EMC ɣəw`, LMC xɦəw`; PT *xəu C1.

角 *gak*   'spikey'   Ch. 角 MSC *jiao*[3] 'horn, corner', EMC kaɨwk/kɛːwk, LMC kjaːwk.

猄 *lingz*   'monkey'   cf. 狑, MSC *ling*[2], name of ancient minority people; graph composed of 'dog' radical 犭 plus phonetic 灵 (靈), MSC *ling*[2] 'numinous', EMC lɛjŋ, LMC liaŋ; PT *liŋ A2.

閞 *nding*   'red'   MSC *lin*[4] 'like fire in appearance'; PT *ʔdl/riɛŋ A1.

膔 *guk*   'tiger'   Zhuang graph composed of 'tiger' radical 虎 plus phonetic 谷, MSC *gu*[3] 'valley', EMC kəwk; PT *k- D1S.

A number of typical phenomena are evident in this short passage:

* Readings of characters in northern Mandarin (also called Modern Standard Chinese or *Putonghua*) are irrelevant. They are given here for reference only.

* Readings that are most pertinent are those of Middle Chinese and Pinghua.

* Words like *sam* 'three', *seiq* 'four', and *gak* 'horn; spikey' (written here as 三, 四 and 角), which are found in all branches of the Tai family and are best deemed 'common morphemes' rather than Chinese loan words.

* Chinese loan-words written with a borrowed character that is homophonic in MC or Pinghua, such as 盖 (for 界), 皇 (for 王), and 至 (for 治 or 置).

* Zhuang morphemes written with Chinese characters homophonic in MC or Pinghua, e.g. 召 and 確.

* Zhuang graphs composed of a semantic determinative (radical) plus phonophoric element, e.g. 胬. The number of these graphs in this sample is higher than average because of the density of animal names. In one case, the phonophoric graph comes not from Chinese, but from a well-established Zhuang graph.

* Existing Chinese characters reinterpreted graphically as a radical plus phonetic, of which there is one instance, 哏.

* Close inspection of the manuscripts will confirm that there are quite a number of graphic variations of standard Chinese characters. Such variants are sometimes called 土俗字 *tusuzi* 'local and vernacular characters'. While not found in modern Chinese printed material, they are commonly found in Chinese manuscripts, and are primarily a feature of the Chinese graphic tradition rather than a specifically Zhuang phenomenon. A number of the variants evident here – e.g. 微 for 微 – can be shown to date back to at least the Northern Wei period (386–534 CE).

* Zhuang morphemes can appear written with different characters in the same text, and even in successive lines. There are two instances of that here: 礶 in line 3 for *gonq* is followed by 貫 in line 4; and 跟 for *gwn* 'eat' in line 6 is followed by 哏 in line 7.

* A number of words in this passage beginning with initial c- [ɕ] are written with characters that were and are pronounced with alveolar or retroflexive affricate initials (*ciq, cauh, ciuh*, and *caengz*). Affricated stop initials are not found in the Bama-Tianyang lect or in standard Zhuang based on the dialect of Wuming; they are however found in other Zhuang dialects. *Caengz* 'not yet', for example, is pronounced with initial tɕ- in Hengxian and initial ts- in Liujiang, Rong'an, Longsheng, Laibin, Guigang, Lianshan, southern Yongning, Debao, Jingxi, and Wenzhou-Malipo (Zhang Junru et al., 807).[8]

Phonetically, most Zhuang readings will be seen to be most closely aligned with Middle Chinese, with Pinghua, or with both. The reading of 鴉 as *a* for 'crow' and 貧 as *baenz* can be seen as closer to Pinghua readings. In other cases sound changes in Zhuang (Tai) seem to have run broadly parallel to sound changes in Chinese, as with *feiz* 'fire' and 微.

14.3. RELATIVE FREQUENCY OF CHARACTER TYPES AND READINGS

When one examines a typical Zhuang manuscript, ones first impression is of a text written in standard Chinese characters. The proportion of made-up characters peculiar to Zhuang and not found in Han Chinese manuscripts is quite low, even if the presence of such characters is salient to readers literate in Chinese.

In order to test this impression, I have calculated the proportion of standard Chinese graphs to non-standard Zhuang characters for a number of ritual texts from Donglan and Bama. Each character in the text was classified as a character read phonetically, a character read semantically, as a Han loan-word, or as a common morpheme (a so-called *guanxici* 关系词, a word which, whatever its origins, has been part of a common Han-Tai lexical stock for so long that it is difficult to judge whether it is a Han borrowing into Tai or a Tai borrowing into Han), or as a Zhuang creation.[9] The texts chosen were two ritual texts from Donglan and two texts from the Tianyang-Bama border area.[10] The results are given in the following table:

---

8   There is more than one source for affricate initials in Zhuang. See Zhang Junru (1983).

9   Such *guanxici* include words like *gaeq* 'chicken' (cf. 鷄 MSC *ji¹*) and many of the numbers below ten. Such words are tallied in the table below as phonetic/semantic readings.

10 These were texts 1–2 in *Killing a Buffalo for the Ancestors*, a total of 152 + 466 = 618 lines, and texts 1 and 2 from *Recalling Lost Souls*, a total of 194 + 125 + 95 = 414 lines.

TABLE 14.3-1: TYPOLOGY OF GRAPHS AND READING IN ZHUANG

Type of reading	Donglan	%	Tianyang-Bama	%
phonetic	2303	71.3	1147	55.3
semantic	78	2.4	88	4.2
phonetic/semantic	40	1.2	25	1.2
Han loans	708	21.9	598	28.8
Zhuang characters	97	3.0	187	9.0
doubtful	5	0.2	29	1.4
Total number of characters	3231		2074	

The impression of a preponderance of standard Chinese characters in Zhuang manuscripts is borne out by this survey. Only 3% of the graphs in the Donglan text, and 9% of the graphs in the Tianyang-Bama texts, were found to be *sawndip*. All the others – 97% and 91% respectively – were found to be either standard Chinese characters or vernacular characters in common use in Han Chinese manuscripts.[11] The table also indicates that phonetic reading is by far the most common way of reading ordinary Chinese characters in Zhuang texts – at least texts of this type.[12] Semantic readings of Chinese characters, such as reading 月 (MSC *yue*[4] 'moon') as *ndwen* 'moon' or 里 (MSC *li*[3] 'inside') as *ndaw* 'inside', account only for 2.4% and 4.2% respectively of the total. By contrast, the relatively high percentages of Chinese characters read as Han loan words and common morphemes will come as no surprise, given the long period of contact between the Zhuang and the Chinese state.

14.4. PHONETIC READINGS

In employing the Chinese script, phonetic correspondences with Zhuang morphosyllables are often only approximate. Indeed, correspondence can only be approximate, given that Chinese and Zhuang differ in their inventories of initial consonants, rhymes, and tones. Lacking entirely from Chinese are sounds like Zhuang initial r- (realized as [ɣ] in many areas), pre-glottalized initials [ʔb] and [ʔd], geminate consonant initials like pl- and ngv-, and high back vowels like [ɯ]. It is often assumed by Chinese scholars that approximate and partial correspondence (correspondence of initials only, or of finals only) is fairly common, and that the latitude is fairly wide. The inference that seems to be drawn is that phonetic correspondences are too idiosyncratic to be worth careful investigation. Thus correspondences between Chinese and Zhuang readings have not yet been worked out systematically. When this is done, we often find that the phonetic match is actually quite close.

What I have found thus far, briefly, is this: that Zhuang phonetic readings of Chinese characters often evince a range of different pronunciations reflecting the pronunciation of Chinese at different historical periods. While isolated readings reflect the pronunciation of modern Southwestern Mandarin, many more correspond quite closely to reconstructions of Early Middle Chinese – that is, the language of the *Qieyun* 切韻, a rhyme book completed in

---

11   An example of the latter would be the character 觧 instead of the standard character 解 for MSC *jie*[3] 'to release'. Both of these have the semantic classifier 'horn' (角) on the left-hand side of the character, but the vernacular character has the graph for 'sheep, goat' (羊) on the right-hand side, rather than a graph for 'knife' (刀) over the graph for 'cattle' (牛). On the phenomenon of vernacular characters in Han Chinese texts, see especially Zhang Yongquan (1995).

12   The content of these texts was old non-Chinese material probably derived from orally-transmitted 'ancient song' (*fwengeq*). In ritual texts translated from Chinese originals, such as the Taoist-derived 'Thirty-six Passes' (Sanshiliu guan 三十六關) texts from Jingxi in the Melbourne collection, the proportion of semantic readings is much higher.

601 CE (see Baxter 1992: 35–8). For example, the character for 'ant' (蟻, pronounced yi^3 in Modern Standard Chinese) is used in Zhuang texts from Bama and Tianyang to represent *nyi* 'to hear'. The actual pronunciation of *nyi*, with a palatalized nasal initial and a short 'a' offglide after the central -i- vowel (ɲiă¹), is very close phonetically to the Early Middle Chinese pronunciation of 'ant', ŋiă (as reconstructed by Pulleyblank 1991: 367). Such examples abound (Holm 2001a, 2003, and 2004, passim). This might suggest a date for the early layers of the script to around the time of the Sui-Tang transition, if not earlier. This would be exciting enough in itself, but other readings can be shown to correspond more closely to reconstructions of Old Chinese, a still older layer (see especially Baxter 1992). One example will have to suffice: the character 貫, now read as $guan^4$ in MSC, meaning 'pass through; string of cash', is frequently read as the common word *gonq* (koːn⁵) 'first, before' in Zhuang texts. This reading corresponds closely to Old Chinese *kons, but less well to Middle Chinese kwanH (Baxter 1992: 761; cf. Pulleyblank 1991: 114), to say nothing of Southwestern Mandarin. What this seems to suggest is that Zhuang readings of Chinese characters might be used to check the validity of reconstructions of Middle Chinese and Old Chinese, just as other foreign-language borrowings have been so used.[13]

Such readings need to be checked against their pronunciations in *Pinghua*. We often find that Zhuang readings could equally well come from more recent reading pronunciations in *Pinghua*, and this means they do not necessarily represent older layers of borrowings. The word for 'ant' in the *Pinghua* of the Tianyang-Bama area is pronounced variously as (j)i¹³ (Tiandong) and n̩i¹³ (Bose); a majority of other locations in Guangxi also have the pronunciation n̩i or ŋi (with various tonal contours).[14] The Bose pronunciation is very close to the Zhuang pronunciation, both in initial ([n̩] and [ŋ] being very close in articulation and hard to distinguish), final rhyme, and in tonal contour (the Tianyang-Bama first tone having a 213 contour). There is therefore no need to assume that the reading *nyi* 'to hear' must have been borrowed from Middle Chinese. The close correspondence of the Zhuang reading with both MC and *Pinghua*, and the close correspondence of MC and the modern *Pinghua* reading, mean that the borrowing could have taken place at any time during the last 1400 years. The character 貫, on the other hand, has *Pinghua* readings like kun⁵⁴ (Tiandong and Bose), and kun (with various tonal contours) in most other places. Lingui near Guilin, which has koŋ³³, is one of the few exceptions.[15] Lingui belongs to the oldest historical layer of *Pinghua*. In this case, there is a *prima facie* case for supposing that the Zhuang reading is quite old. Of course, in order to be fully convincing, we would need many more examples of this type.

Secondly, the script often reflects local dialect words and local pronunciations of standard Zhuang words. These reflections often serve as clues to the geographic provenance of texts, and also diachronically the movement of textual traditions. In some cases, characters used to render particular Zhuang words may have come from elsewhere, and may therefore correspond best to the pronunciation of the word in a different dialect or sub-dialect. For example, in the Donglan manuscripts the Zhuang word *youq* (ʔju⁵) 'to stay, be at' is represented by the character 係 MSC xi^4 'to be'.[16] This is a very common usage in a number of Donglan manuscripts, and is very well-attested. The problem is that 係, as pronounced in any Chinese dialect, is a poor phonetic fit for *youq* (ʔjou⁵ or ʔjuː⁵).[17] However, in certain Bouyei dialects of Guizhou we find the morpheme ʔju⁵ is pronounced as ji⁵ (Libo

---

13   On the evidence of Tibetan, Sino-Vietnamese, Sino-Korean, and Uighur inscriptions, see Hashimoto (1984), 63–139 and 190–206.
14   Li Lianjin (2000), 94, item 931.
15   Ibid. 236, item 2357.
16   See Donglan 1: 48 in Holm (2003), 79.
17   係 is not included in Pulleyblank (1991). a closely related character, 系, is reconstructed as EMC *γɛiʰ*, LMC *xɦjaj`*, and Early Mandarin *xî* (p. 332); see also Karlgren (1957) 876c. The Cantonese pronunciation for 係 is *hɐi²²*, though this does not help very much either; nor do Pinghua readings (Li Lianjin 2000, 76, item 758).

county, Weng'an village), jie⁵ (Dushan county, Nanzhai village), or juɯ⁵ (Libo county, Chaoyang village).[18] In Zhuang dialects the same word is pronounced as juɯ⁵ in the Liujiang-Yishan area, ji⁵ in Nandan, and juɯ⁵ in Longsheng, all places near the Guizhou border.[19] Any one of these pronunciations would be a much better phonetic fit than the local pronunciation in Donglan, which is ʔjuː⁵. In fact, in this case these indications are corroborated by what is known of the history of the priestly lineage. The Donglan manuscript tradition originated further to the north and east, in the Libo-Huanjiang area, and the use of 係 for *youq* has been transported southwards along with that tradition.

Similarly, a character used to render a Zhuang word may occasionally provide evidence of diachronic sound change. For example, in a manuscript from Shanglin county in the central part of Guangxi, there is the line *Mbwn miz fwnz raq daeuj gou lwg* ('In the sky there is a gust of wind coming, my child'), in which the word for 'gust (of wind), bout (of illness)' *raq* (ɣa⁵) is written with the character 迦 MSC *jia*¹, a character commonly used in Chinese for the transliteration of the Sanskrit syllables [ka] and [kā].[20] Pulleyblank's reconstruction of this character in Middle Chinese is kia (or kai) for EMC, and kia for LMC. The initial does not correspond well with the initial of this morpheme in most Northern Zhuang dialects, including Shanglin.[21] By contrast, Jingxi and Debao in the far southwest of Guangxi have initial khj-, which is a much closer fit.[22] Li Fang-Kuei constructs an initial *xr- for this item in Proto-Tai.[23] While it is not entirely impossible that the text may incorporate graphic renderings borrowed from the Jingxi area, it is much more plausible in this case to suppose that 迦 represents an older pronunciation, now long since obsolete in the Shanglin area.

14.5. REGIONAL VARIATION

For all their obvious variability, most manuscripts tend to use only one (or at most two or three) characters for the most common words in the lexicon (words like 'come', 'go', 'up', 'down', etc.). Colleagues and I are currently engaged in a survey of regional variations in the 50 or so Zhuang-speaking counties of Guangxi and contiguous provinces. By mapping which characters are used for a core vocabulary (of, say, 60 commonly-used words), we expect to gain a preliminary idea of the likely degree of underlying similarity between the scripts of different areas. It will also be possible to develop a statistical measure for the relative age of the script in different areas, based on the age of individual borrowings among the core vocabulary items (Holm, forthcoming). For ritual and literary texts, a preliminary survey I have conducted suggests that historically there were several geographical areas where initial generation of the Old Zhuang Script took place. Also, it is interesting to note that Middle Chinese readings are found in considerable numbers in most Old Zhuang Script locations in Guangxi, while Southwestern Mandarin readings predominate in the old Bouyei scripts of Guizhou, the province to the north of Guangxi. This in turn suggests that the Old Zhuang Script in Guangxi is – at least in most places – considerably older than the Bouyei script.

14.6. ZHUANG CHARACTERS

When Chinese scholars say of the Old Zhuang Script that the composition of graphs conforms to *liushu* principles, this is usually understood in a very general sense. Namely, that (1) graphic components are arranged within a square matrix so as to form a 'square character'

---

18 See Zhongguo kexueyuan Shaoshu minzu yuyan yanjiusuo (1959), 310.
19 Zhang Junru et al. (1999), 724.
20 'Ciengq Sunzngeih' [The song of Shun as a boy], in Zhang Yuansheng et al. (1992), 291 (line 67b).
21 Also, initial *r*- is usually represented by Chinese characters with initial *l*- or *j*-.
22 Zhang Junru et al. (1999), p. 597 (item 15).
23 Li Fang-Kuei (1977), 233-234. Haudricourt (1974: 467, 471) reconstructs the initial of this morpheme in proto-Daic as *sr-.

(*fangkuaizi* 方块字), with graphic elements arranged in a balanced left-right and up-down fashion; (2) all of the graphic elements used are either Chinese characters themselves, or are elements found in Chinese characters; (3) graphic elements are used for their phonetic value or their semantic value, or both in some cases; (4) traditional Chinese radicals are used frequently as semantic determinatives, in preference to other graphs.

One of the earliest attempts to classify Zhuang characters on the basis of a corpus of texts was by Li Fang-Kuei (1957: 20–24). Li's classification into ten types of graph is summarized in Holm (2003: 45–47). Li himself only made oblique reference to the *liushu*, labelling his third category *xieshengzi* 諧聲字 ('graphs which harmonize the sound'). His categories 3–10 apply to *sawndip*. In his third category, phonetic compounds, he distinguishes between characters which employ a semantically borrowed character for their semantic element (e.g. ċ for *ok* 'to emerge, come or go out') those which indicate the general semantic field by means of one of the traditional 214 radicals, and those which employ the mouth radical to indicate that the other component is to be read phonetically.

The characters in a number of Li's categories can be considered to be in conformity with the *liushu* only in the broadest possible sense. From a Chinese point of view, a double-phonetic character such as 屺 *san* (θan^1) 'white rice (already pounded)' may appear to have 山 'mountain' as a radical (semantic determinative); a double-semantic character such as 睭 *gaeuj* (kau^3) 'to look' may appear to have 目 'eye' as a radical, but in fact, as Li's analysis makes clear, a different mechanism is in operation. In other cases meaning and word identification is indicated by purely graphic means. In 冇 *ndwi* (ʔdwi^1) 'not; empty', the meaning is derived from a host character 有 'to have, to exist' by removal of two horizontal strokes.[24] The character 冫 *mbiengj* (ʔbwaŋ^3) 'side' is produced by removing one side from the common graph 門 *men^2* 'door' (Li p.23). Li calls such characters *biaoyizi* 表意字 'graphs which exteriorise the meaning'. The two examples given are subtractive; that is, they involve the elimination of brushstrokes or graphic elements.

In other cases I have discovered, meaning is generated by an innovative reinterpretation of graphic elements. For example, in a text from Bama, the character 晶 is used to represent the Zhuang word *canz* (ça:n^2) 'drying platform' (Holm and Meng, forthcoming, line 1502). This character is composed of three symmetrically arranged 正 graphs, the meaning of 正 *zheng^4* being 'straight, upright; correct'. None of these elements either alone or in combination is phonophoric. Rather, the three characters represent graphically the way in which firewood is stacked neatly under the drying platform of Zhuang farmhouses, and hence (metonymically) represent the drying platform itself. In Chinese, by contrast, the character script continues to exhibit this kind of graphic creativity only within the context of folk poetry, Taoist-inspired word games, and riddles based on the graphic composition of characters.

14.7. CONCLUSION

Zhuang texts exhibit a pattern of combined phonetic and semantic readings of standard Chinese characters, with special Zhuang characters occupying an important but largely supplementary role. The creation of new characters follows *liushu* principles, but not exclusively. Each graph, representing a monosyllabic morpheme in Chinese, is also used in Zhuang to represent a single monosyllabic morpheme. Literacy in the Old Zhuang Script is heavily dependent on literacy in Chinese.

Phonetically, representation of Zhuang morphosyllables is often approximate, but investigation will often indicate that the phonetic match at the point of borrowing is much closer than has often been supposed. By and large, readings correspond most frequently to *Pinghua* and Middle Chinese readings of Chinese characters, and much less frequently to Southwestern Mandarin pronunciation. While it is not always possible to distinguish between

---

24 This character is found in Pinghua as well as in Cantonese. For the latter, see Cheung and Bauer (2002).

Pinghua and the reconstructed pronunciation of Middle Chinese, Zhuang readings of Chinese characters occasionally provide evidence of even older strata of borrowings.

Graphically, the script shows signs of close integration with the Chinese world of signs, but also shows signs of innovation.

Historically, it is likely that the Chinese script has always had the capacity to represent languages other than Chinese, and the development of the Old Zhuang Script may have begun very early in the contact period. Given the likely age of the Old Zhuang Script, it is not unlikely that the remote ancestors of the Thai and Lao used a character script like the Old Zhuang Script during the period before they migrated southwards.

REFERENCES

Bauer, Robert S. (2000) 'The Chinese-based Writing System of the Zhuang Language, *Cahiers de Linguistique Asie Orientale* 29.2: 223–253.

Baxter, William H. (1992) *A Handbook of Old Chinese Phonology*, Berlin and New York: Mouton de Gruyter.

Boltz, William G. (1994) *The Origin and Early Development of the Chinese Writing System*, New Haven: American Oriental Society.

Cheung Kwan-hin and Bauer, Robert S. (2002) *The Representation of Cantonese with Chinese Characters*, Berkeley: Journal of Chinese Linguistics Monograph 18.

Hashimoto, Mantaro J. (1984) *Phonology of Ancient Chinese*, 2 vols, Tokyo: Institute for the Study of Languages & Cultures of Asia & Africa.

Haudricourt, Andre-G. (1974) 'Explication et Commentaire', in Robert Shafer (ed.) *Introduction to Sino-Tibetan*, Part V, Wiesbaden: Otto Harrassowitz, 453–525.

Holm, David (2001a) 'The Ancient Song of Doengving: A Zhuang Funeral Text from Donglan, Guangxi', *Monumenta Serica* XLIX: 71–140.

— (2001b) 'Aspects of Funerals among the Zhuang: The Horse Play', *Proceedings of the International Conference on Society, Ethnicity and Cultural Performance*, Taipei: Center for Chinese Studies, 215–259.

— (2003) *Killing a Buffalo for the Ancestors: A Zhuang Cosmological Text from Southwest China*, DeKalb: Southeast Asian Publications, Northern Illinois University.

— (2004) *Recalling Lost Souls: The Baeu Rodo Scriptures, Tai Cosmogonic Texts from Southern China*, Bangkok: White Lotus Company Ltd.

— (forthcoming) 'Regional Variation in the Old Zhuang Script: A Statistical Approach'.

Holm, David, and Meng Yuanyao (forthcoming) *Hanvueng, The Goose King and the Ancestral King: An Epic from Guangxi in Southern China*.

Huang Ge (1982) 'Shanglin diqu Zhuangzu fangkuaizi de gouzao' [The Construction of Zhuang Characters in the Shanglin Area], *Minzu yuwen [Languages of the Nationalities]* 2.74: 54.

Hudak, Thomas John (1991a) *William J. Gedney's The Yay Language: Glossaries, Texts and Translations*, Ann Arbor: University of Michigan Center for South and Southeast Asian Studies.

— (1991b) *William J. Gedney's The Tai Dialect of Lungming: Glossaries, Texts and Translations*, Ann Arbor: University of Michigan Center for South and Southeast Asian Studies.

Karlgren, Bernard (1957) *Grammata Serica Recensa*, Stockholm: The Museum of Far Eastern Antiquities.

Kaup, Catherine (2000) *Creating the Zhuang: Ethnic Politics in China*, Boulder and London: Lynne Rienner, Publishers.

Li Fanggui [Li Fang-Kuei] (1940) *Longzhou tuyu The Tai Dialect of Lungchow* (Texts, Translations, and Glossary), Shanghai: Shangwu yinshuguan. Repr. Taipei: Zhongyang yanjiuyuan Lishi yuyan yanjiusuo, 1993.

— (1956) *Wuming tuyu The Tai Dialect of Wu-ming* (Texts, Translations, and Glossary). Taipei: Zhongyang yanjiuyuan Lishi yuyan yanjiusuo.

— (1977) *A Handbook of Comparative Tai*, Honolulu: University of Hawaii Press.

— (1988, 1990) *Bo'ai tuyu The Tai Dialect of Po-ai* (Texts, Translations, and Glossary), 2 vols., Taipei: Zhongyang yanjiuyuan Lishi yuyan yanjiusuo.

Li Lianjin (2000) *Pinghua yinyun yanjiu [Research on the Phonology of Pinghua]*, Nanning: Guangxi renmin chubanshe.

Liu Cunhan (1998) *Liuzhou fangyan cidian [Dictionary of Liuzhou Dialect]*, Nanjing: Jiangsu jiaoyu chubanshe.

Ouyang Ruoxiu (1986) *Zhuangzu wenxue shi [History of Zhuang Literature]*, 3 vols, Nanning: Guangxi renmin chubanshe.

Pulleyblank, Edwin (1991) *Lexicon of Reconstructed Pronunciation in Early Middle Chinese, Late Middle Chinese, and Early Mandarin*, Vancouver: University of British Columbia Press.

Su Yongqin et al. (1989) *Sawndip sawdenj: Gu Zhuangzi zidian* [Dictionary of the Old Zhuang Script], Nanning: Guangxi minzu chubanshe.

Took, Jennifer (2005) *A Native Chieftaincy in Southwest China: Franchising a Tai Chieftaincy under the Tusi System of Late Imperial China*, Leiden and Boston: Brill.

Zhang Junru (1983) 'Zhuang-Dong yuzu saicayin de chansheng he fazhan' [The Emergence and Development of Affricated Stops in the Zhuang-Kam Language Group], *Minzu yuwen* 1.

Zhang Junru et al. (1999) *Zhuangyu fangyan yanjiu [Research on Zhuang Dialects]*, Chengdu: Sichuan minzu chubanshe.

Zhang Yongquan (1995) *Hanyu suzi yanjiu [Research on Demotic Characters in Chinese]*, Changsha: Yuelu shushe.

Zhang Yuansheng (1990) 'Fangkuai Zhuangzi' [The square Zhuang script], in Zhongguo minzu gu wenzi yanjiuhui (ed.) *Zhongguo minzu gu wenzi tulu [Illustrated Record of the Ancient Scripts of China's Minority Peoples]*, Beijing: Zhongguo shehui kexue chubanshe, 227–232.

Zhang Yuansheng et al. (1992) *Gu Zhuangzi wenxian xuanzhu [A Selection of Annotated Texts in the Old Zhuang Script]*, Tianjin: Tianjin guji chubanshe.

Zheng Yiqing (1988) 'Jingxi fangkuai Zhuangzi shixi', *Minzu yuwen* 4: 41–47.

Zhongguo kexueyuan Shaoshu minzu yuyan yanjiusuo (1959) *Buyiyu diaocha baogao [Report on Surveys of the Bouyei Language]*, Beijing: Kexue chubanshe.

PART 4

GRAMMATICALIZATION AND HISTORICAL SYNTAX

CHAPTER FIFTEEN

AN ETYMOLOGICAL SPECULATION ON THE SEQUENTIAL INDICATOR *kɔɔ³* IN THAI NARRATIVE

*Somsonge Burusphat**

15.1. INTRODUCTION

This paper aims to study a selected discourse feature in Southeast Asian narrative and its areal diffusion to determine its source. This feature serves as a sequential indicator highlighting a chronological theme-line or storyline of the narrative. The focus will be on the preverbal auxiliary *kɔɔ³* in Thai narrative in comparison with the preverbal auxiliaries of other Southeast Asian languages having the same function in order to determine the historical implication of *kɔɔ³*.

The data are drawn from various documents such as theses, articles, and books. Some data, i.e. Black Tai, Kam, Sgaw Karen, and Kui are collected by the author. The total number of Southeast Asian narratives used for this study is 23. All these narratives are compared as to forms of the preverbal auxiliary functioning as the sequential indicator. The preverbal auxiliary may be truly absent in particular languages or it may exist in the languages but does not appear in the data due to the shortness of the narratives or the style of the narrator.

15.2. SEQUENTIALITY AS A SIGNIFICANT FEATURE OF NARRATIVE DISCOURSE

Longacre (1996: 8-9) classifies all possible discourses in all languages according to two basic etic parameters: contingent temporal succession and agent orientation. Both parameters are defined as follows:

> Contingent temporal succession (henceforth contingent succession) refers to a framework of temporal succession in which some (often most) of the events or doings are contingent on previous events or doings. Agent orientation refers to orientation towards agents with at least a partial identity of agent reference running through the discourse.

Narrative discourse is plus in respect to both parameters. This study will focus on the concept of contingent succession or more concretely chronological linkage as characteristic of Southeast Asian narrative. The event-series which are reported in chronological succession in the narrative constitute the main line or storyline of the narrative. The storyline is a generic term to include any happenings that push the story forward. The important characteristics of these happenings are punctuality, sequentiality, and (most often) volition (Longacre 1990). Punctiliar happenings include actions and events that are well articulated as to inception, terminus, or both. The sequential happenings involve the regular chronological succession of actions and events; volitional happenings are actions or events that are conscious or planned.

---

*   I would like to extend my thanks to Prof. Anthony Diller for editing the final draft of this paper and Megan Sinnott for editing the first draft of the paper. I also thank Sophana Srichampa for providing me with useful information on the sequential indicator in Vietnamese.

Longacre (1996) asserts that each surface type of discourse has characteristic tense/aspect/voice features in the verbs that occur on its mainline in discourse in a particular language. Hence narrative (story) discourse has some sort of nondurative preterit, or historical present. In languages with tense-aspect systems such as English, successive actions and events which advance the story are reported in simple past tense forms. The Southeast Asian languages examined in this paper do not have verbal inflection and therefore the storyline cannot be characterized on the basis of verb forms as in English. The storyline in these languages is realized by a conspiracy of various devices, that is, the use of aspectual auxiliaries to mark the completeness of actions or events; the use of temporal auxiliaries, expressions, or adverbial clauses to indicate the temporal succession of actions and events; and simple juxtaposition of chronological successive clauses in iconic order, i. e. prior clauses referring to prior actions or events in a reported event sequence.

The major concern of this chapter is the preverbal temporal auxiliary which marks the chronological succession of actions and events. The languages of the Southeast Asia area use this sequential indicator characterized by various forms to move the story forward as illustrated in languages of various language families below.

15.2.1. Austroasiatic language family

Vietnamese: *thì* 'then'

(1)
Ngöô	*øi*	*em*	*vaøo*	*nhaø*	*tröôùc*	*chaøng*	*vöøa*	*böôùc*
person	younger	brother	comein	house	first	3rd per	just	step

chaân	*qua*	*ngöıngcöœa*	***thì***	*ngöôøi*	*chòdaâu*	*ôœ*	*trong*	*buoàng*
foot	across	doorstep	then	person	sister-in-law	at	in	room

chaïy	*ra*	*laàm*	*chaøng*	*laô*	*choàng*	*mình*	*voäi*	*oâmchaàm*	*laáy*
run	out	mistake	3rd per	be	husband	oneself	hurry	embrace	take

'The younger brother entered the house first. When he had just walked pass the doorstep, his sister-in-law came out. She thought that he was the elder brother then embraced him with sudden haste.' (Suksiri ms)

Kammu: *kɔɔ* 'then'

(2)
lɛɛ	*kɔɔ*	*dɛɛ*	***kɔɔ***	*yɔh*	*yaam,*	*sat,*	*pɛ*	*kɔɔ*
and	then	also	then	go	cry,	animal,	goat	then

yɔh	*yaam*	*taam*	*pasaa*	*pɛ*	*ni*	*lɛ:*
go	cry	follow	language	goat	that	perf:

'And then other animals as well came to bewail him. The goat wailed in the goat language: …' (Lindell 1989: 32)

So: *ka:* 'then'

(3)
mi:	*ʌ:t*	*muay*	*ci.ŋay*	*wak*	*an*	*ba:r*	*tɔ:*	***ka:***	*pia*
have	exist	one	day	group	3psg	two	CLSF_body	then	invite

ra.nɤ	*pʌ*	*cu:ay?*	*ne:w*	*cia*	*nuŋ*	*tru:ŋ*	*ki:*
together	go	search	something	eat	in	forest	there

'It happened one day, the two of them invited each other to go searching for something to eat in the forest. ' (Migliazza 1998: 191)

15.2.2. Tai-Kadai Language Family

Southwestern Tai

Khün: *kɔ³* 'then'

(4) *pho¹man²* **kɔ:⁵** *khaw⁴ paj² naj²weŋ² paj² ha:¹ sɯ⁵ khaw⁴ sa:n¹*
father   then enter   go   in town   go   find buy   milled rice
'One day the husband went into town to buy some milled rice.' (Rasi 1978: 118)

Northern Tai

Zhuang: *cou⁶* 'then'

(5) *kjoŋ² vun²* **cou⁶** *pai¹ heu⁶ te¹ ma¹   pa:ŋ¹*
CLS   man then go   call he come   help
'So people turned to the almighty god Pauloktau for help.' (Somsonge and Sinnott 1998: 182)

Kam: *ɕu:³³* 'then'

(6) *ja:¹¹ mau³³* **ɕu:³³** *laŋ¹   ju:³³ ta³³ ja:¹¹ maŋ⁵³ ɲa⁵⁵ pai⁵⁵ ja:¹¹ qe³⁵*
two he/she then at once again from two side river go   two CLS
'They went separately to the banks of the river.' (Somsonge and Sinnott 1998: 152)

Hlai (Li): *fan⁵³* 'then'

(7) *ɬu:k⁵⁵khau¹¹* **fan⁵³** *tsau¹¹   ʔe:ŋ⁵⁵ ko:ŋ⁵⁵ tha⁵⁵   kɯ⁵⁵ ʔje:ŋ⁵³*
elder sister   then put down jar   food   to have a look
'The elder sister then put down the jar of food for her brother to take a look.' (Somsonge and Sinnott 1998: 94)

15.2.3. Sino-Tibetan language family

Chinese: *jiu* 'then'

(8) *ta   bu   you   fenshuo,* **jiu**   *jiao   ren   ba neige tuhao*
he   not   let   explain, then   order person ba That local-thu
tuhao   tuidao   shui   li.
local-thug   push -into water   inside
'Accepting no further explanation [from the thug], he immediately ordered to have him pushed into the water.' (Chauncey 1998: 384)

Moken: *ka?* 'particle'

(9) *pe: ɲu: ɲa:* **ka?** *meta? tʰu: ʔenoŋ   ɲa: ɲa: lakaw tʰu:*
turn   that she par. ask for with mother she she go   with
bujaŋ   ɲu: la:

young man   that   par.
'Therefore, she asked for mother to go with the young man.' (Veena 1980: 278)

Mien: *ʔɛʔ⁴* '*topic marker*'

(10) *taʔ²ɲe:²*   *nɔːj¹*   *nin³*   *ʔɛʔ⁴*   *dzuən⁶*
    second   day   he   topic marker   return
    'The next day he then returned.' (Kasamaporn 1990: 147)

The sequential indicators in the illustrated clauses mark the storyline status of the clauses. However, not all the storyline clauses are flagged with these sequential indicators since there are other devices used to mark the storyline as well. The choice of each device or a combination of devices is varied according to the strands of discourse information. Some languages may use a particular device to distinguish the more important happenings in the storyline from the lesser, routine, and somewhat predictable happenings. For example, in Sui narrative the more important happenings are reported in clauses, which are marked with the temporal word *lən²* 'after that.' Furthermore, a device may be chosen depending on the style of the narrator.

In Thai narrative the preserial auxiliary *kɔɔ³* is of considerable importance. It has multiple functions as described by Yajai (1985). However the major concern of its functions here is as a sequential indicator. The great majority of storyline clauses in Thai narrative are introduced by *kɔɔ³* functioning to introduce a new sequence of actions and events. Functioning as a sequential indicator it is usually glossed as 'link, then, or particle'.The preserial verb *kɔɔ³* will be compared with other sequential indicators of Southeast Asian languages having the same function in order to determine its source.

15.3. COMPARISON OF THE SEQUENTIAL INDICATORS IN SOUTHEAST ASIAN LANGUAGES

The pre-verbal auxiliary functioning as the sequential indicator in the same manner as *kɔɔ³* in Thai is realized by various forms in the Southeast Asian languages as listed below with sources and locations. Some languages may not have the pre-verbal auxiliary as a sequential indicator or the pre-verbal auxiliary does exist but it does not appear in the texts used for this study. Thus the X mark will be used to indicate the absence of this form in the languages. The Southeast Asian languages illustrated below are grouped by language family as follows:

15.3.1. Austroasiatic language family

Diffloth (1976) classifies the languages of the Austroasiatic language family into two main branches, namely, the Munda and Nicobarese of India and Mon-Khmer of the Southeast Asian mainland. The Mon-Khmer branch is divided into Northern Mon-Khmer, Eastern Mon-Khmer, and Southern Mon-Khmer. Vietnamese, Kammu and Pray are used as representatives for the Northern Mon-Khmer sub-branch; Khmer, Northern Khmer, So, and Kui for the Eastern Mon-Khmer sub-branch; and Mon and Chaobon (ɲahkur) for the Southern Mon-Khmer sub-branch.

Languages	Sources	Locations	Forms
Northern Mon-Khmer			
Vietnamese	Suksiri (ms)	Hanoi, Vietnam	*thì*
Kammu	Lindell (1989)	Luangprabang, Laos	*kɔɔ*
Pray	Mingkwan (1989)	Nan, Thailand	*kɔ*
Eastern Mon-Khmer			
Khmer	Uraisri et al (1997)	Cambodia	*kɔ*
Northern Khmer	Somkiet (1982)	Buriram, Thailand	*kə?¹*
So	Migliazza (1998)	Sakonnakorn, Thailand	*ka:*
Kui	Somsonge (1992b)	Srisaket, Thailand	*kʌ?*
Southern Mon-Khmer			
Mon	Orathai (1992)	Rangoon, Burma	*X*
Chaobon (ɲahkur)	Payau (1979)	Chaiyapoom, Thailand	*kɔ*

15.3.2. Tai-Kadai language family

Edmondson and Solnit (1998) classify the Tai-Kadai or Kadai language family into three main branches, i. e. Hlai (Li), Kam-Tai, and Gelao. The Hlai language is used for comparison in this study. The Kam-Tai branch is further divided into Tai and Kam-Sui. Li (1960) proposes three sub-branches of the Tai group, i. e. Southwestern Tai, Central Tai, and Northern Tai. Thai, Lao, Thai Song Dam (Black Thai), Tai Dam (Black Tai),[2] Phuan, Dai (Tai Lue), Khün, and Ai-ton represent the Southwestern Tai. Northern Zhuang and Bouyei are representatives for the Northern Tai. There are no data from the Central Tai. Kam and Sui represent the Kam-Sui branch.

Languages	Sources	Locations	Forms
Southwestern:			
Thai	Wiyada (1981) Yajai (1985) and Somsonge (1991)	Bangkok, Thailand	*kɔɔ³*
Lao	Vitalee (1988)	Vientiane Laos	*kɔ*
Thai Song Dam	Sunan (1985)	Petchaburi, Thailand	*kɔ*
Tai Dam	Somsonge[3]	Dien Bien Phu, Vietnam	*kɔ*
Phuan	Chaluay (1982)	Suphanburi Thailand	*kʌ?⁴*
Khün	Rasi (1978)	Kengtung, the Shan State of Burma	*kɔ:⁵*
Dai (Tai Lue)	Somsonge and Sinnott eds (1998)	Sipsongbanna, China	*kɔ:⁴*
Ai-ton	Diller (1992)	Assam, India	*kɔ*
Northern:			
N. Zhuang	Somsonge and Sinnott eds. (1998)	Guangxi, China	*cou⁶*
Bouyei	Somsonge and Sinnott eds. (1998)	Guizhou, China	*ɕi³*

---

1   Somkiet (1982) treats kə? in the Northern Khmer language as a lexical linker frequently co-occurring with *nɛɛh* as *nɛɛh kə?* glossed as 'then.'

2   Thai Song Dam or Black Thai and Tai Dam or Black Tai are originally the same ethnic group. The former whose data are drawn reside in Suphanburi, Thailand whereas the latter live in Dien Bien Phu, Vietnam.

3   The Tai Dam (Black Tai) narrative was collected at Dien Bien Phu, Vietnam in May 2000 by the author.

Languages	Sources	Locations	Forms
Kam-Sui:			
Kam	Somsonge and Sinnott eds. (1998)	Guizhou, China	$\wp u^{33}$
Sui	Somsonge and Sinnott eds. (1998)	Sandu, China	X
Hlai (Li):	Somsonge and Sinnott eds. (1998)	Hainan, China	fan^{53}

15.3.3. Sino-Tibetan language family

Benedict (1972) classifies the Sino-Tibetan language family into two major groups, i. e. Tibeto-Karen and Chinese. Mandarin Chinese is used as a representative of the Chinese branch. The Tibeto-Karen is sub-divided into Tibeto-Burman and Karen groups. Burmese and Lawa represent the Tibeto-Burman group. Sgaw Karen and Tavoyan Sgaw Karen represent the Karen group.

Languages	Sources	Locations	Forms
Mandarin Chinese	Chauncey (1998)	China	jiu
Burmese	Language Institute (1995)[4]	Rangoon, Burma	lɛ:
Lawa	Jiranan (1985)	Maehongsorn, Thailand	X
Sgaw Karen	Somsonge (1992a)	Maehongsorn, Thailand	X
Tavoyan Sgaw Karen	Chaiyathip (1993)	Tavoyan, Southeastern Burma	X

15.3.4. Austronesian language family

Moken, Urak Lawoi' and Malay are used as representatives of the Austronesian language family.

Languages	Sources	Locations	Forms
Moken	Veena (1980)	Phuket, Thailand	ka?
Urak Lawoi'	Amon (1979)	Satul, Thailand	pot
Malay	Amon (p. c.)	Malaysia	pun

15.3.5. Hmong-Mien language family

Languages	Source	Locations	Forms
Green Hmong	Somroedee (1998)	Chiangmai and Tak, Thailand	le
Mien	Kasamaphorn (1990)	Chiangrai, Thailand	?ɛ?⁴

The list of grammatical forms of the sequential indicator above shows that in the Austroasiatic language family, Kammu and Pray of the Northern Mon-Khmer group; Khmer, Northern Khmer, So and Kui of the Eastern Mon-Khmer group; and Chaobon (ɲahkur) of the Southern Mon-Khmer group share similar forms to $kɔɔ^3$ in Thai. This form does not show in Vietnamese of the Viet-Muong sub-group of the Northern Mon-Khmer and in Mon of the Southern Mon-Khmer branch.

All the languages of the Southwestern group of the Tai-Kadai language family have cognates of $kɔɔ^3$. The Northern Tai group has forms which are different from $kɔɔ^3$. Most

---

4   The Burmese data is based on the Burmese folktale entitled 'The crow that wanted to be beautiful' transcribed into phonetic symbols and translated into English for the purpose of this study by May Myat Khaing and Sarinya Khammuang.

forms are similar to Chinese *jiu*. This indicates that the languages of this group have had an influence from Chinese. The sequential indicator of any form does not exist in Sui. However this does not mean that Sui does not have it. The absence of this form may be due to the shortness of the texts used for the analysis.

The cognates of *kɔɔ³* do not appear in the Sino-Tibetan language family. Some languages of this family do not use the preverbal auxiliary as a sequential indicator but use other means to express the sequentiality of the events. For example, the Sgaw Karen uses the post-verbal aspectual auxiliaries *wɛ́* to report events.

In the Austronesian language family, the Moken has the cognate of *kɔɔ³*. Since Moken has some Mon-Khmer affinities, it must have some link with the Mon-Khmer. Luce and Bohmu Ba Shin (1961) mention the history of Moken as sea people under constant pressure on the Tongkin plain from East and North where the original homeland of Malayan peoples was. Perhaps under double pressure between the Yüeh (Viêt) of Kuangtung and the Mon-Khmer of Tongkin, they migrated to the South along the coast ranging from Tongkin to the mouth of the Irrawaddy. During the interpersonal contact with Khmer in their original homeland, the Moken might have adopted some linguistic features such as the sequential indicator *kaʔ*.

Green Hmong and Mien languages have the preverbal auxiliaries *le* and *ʔɛ⁴* respectively instead of the cognate *kɔɔ³*.

15.4. THE SEQUENTIAL INDICATOR *kɔɔ³* AS AN AREAL FEATURE

Henderson (1965) lists a number of phonetic features which are typologically characteristics of the Southeast Asian area. In Southeast Asia there are areal features that language families share. Emeneau (1980) gives an example of area features in Southeast Asia. The 'attenuation' in Thai is carried by simple reduplication; e. g. *kàw* 'old (of things),' *kàw kàw* 'oldish'; *dii* 'good, well,' *dii-dii* 'rather good, rather well.' In Vietnamese the same meaning is carried by simple reduplication in the case of three of the tones. The Tibeto-Burman languages of this area also show this type of construction.[5]

As seen in the previous section, the sequential indicator *kɔɔ³* is found throughout the languages of the three language families, i.e. Austroasiatic, Tai-Kadai, and Austonesian language family of the Southeast Asian area regardless of language frontiers. Therefore the sequential indicator *kɔɔ:³* can be regarded as an areal feature in this linguistic area.[6]

Map 15.4-1 displays the geographical distribution of the sequential indicator in the languages of Southeast Asia. The word *kɔɔ³* has spread throughout the areas of Thailand, Laos, Cambodia, Northwestern Vietnam, Shan of Burma and Assam of India.

---

5   See the occurences of this areal feature in Lahu (Matisoff 1973), Karen (Jones 1961) and the comparative treatment of Southeast Asian and Malay phenomena, including Burmese data in Karnchana (1976)

6   Emeneau (1980: 1) defines linguistic areas as 'areas in which languages belonging to more than one family show traits in common which do not belong to the other members of (at least) one of the families.'

MAP 15.4-1: GEOGRAPHICAL DISTRIBUTION OF THE SEQUENTIAL INDICATOR IN THE SOUTHEAST ASIAN AREA

15.5. HISTORICAL IMPLICATIONS

This section aims to determine the historical implication from the geographical distribution of forms of the sequential indicator using a comparative method supported by orthographic evidence. The major issues are the origin of the sequential indicator $k\jmath\jmath^3$ and its direction of diffusion throughout the languages of the Southeast Asian area.

The presence of $k\jmath\jmath^3$ in the Southwestern Tai group and Mon-Khmer group points to the possibility that diffusion has proceeded from Khmer into Thai or vice versa. According to Hall (1968) the Shans, the Laotians and the Siamese or Thai have made their first historical appearance in Southeast Asia in the sixth century BC under Chinese suzerainty, but made many attempts to assert their independence. They moved along rivers and in the valleys of central Indo-China. Small groups of them settled among the Khmers, the Mons, and the

Burmese. During that time the Khmer empire was at the zenith of its civilization. The Siamese therefore had been influenced by the well-established Khmer group as George Cœdès (1964: 370) put it: 'From Cambodia the Siamese assimilated its political organization, material civilization, writing and a considerable number of words.'

According to Trudgill (1974: 223), certain innovations started from an urban area as cited below:

> Diffusion patterns are also mediated through a system of urban centers in any given area, 'where diffusion is primarily dependent on individuals in one central place communicating with those in another.' The innovation can be seen spreading from a center to surrounding areas. Central places have been recognized in dialect theory as the source of *focal area*.

The Angkor kingdom in Cambodia was the setting in which diffusion could take place and in which linguistic areal relationship develops. Having the Angkor kingdom as the focal area and the Siamese as the newcomers, it can be concluded that *kɔɔ³* has spread from Khmer to Thai. The interpersonal contacts seem to play an important role on the diffusion.

The conclusion is further supported by the comparison of forms of the sequential indicator. Only the Southwestern Tai group who moved from China to the present locations have the cognates of *kɔɔ³* whereas the form is absent in the Northern Tai group who are still residing in China and present in all languages of Mon-Khmer groups except Mon.

The form has not spread to Burmese, Mon and Vietnamese for the following reasons. Burmese and Mon have their established states in Burma as focal areas and do not acquire the form in question. Vietnamese were under Chinese rule from 111 BC to AD 939 and were subjected to intensive sinicization (Hall 1968) and thus far from the influence of either Khmer or Thai. Since the development of the form was confined to the areas of the kingdoms with their great concentrations of population, and that the influences did not reach the more inaccessible, jungly, tribal areas, the form did not spread to the small Tibeto-Burman groups such as Lawa and Sgaw Karen. As for the ethnic groups of Mon-Khmer branch such as Chaobon (ɲahkur), Pray, they have the cognates of *kɔɔ³* since they are genetically related to Khmer.

The sequential indicator *kɔɔ³* not only has a close pronunciation to the word *kɔɔ* in Khmer but the writing of *kɔɔ³* in Thai is similar to *kɔɔ* in Khmer. The modern Thai writing of *kɔɔ³* is ก็   whereas the modern writing of *kɔɔ* in Khmer is on the next page. The spelling of this word always puzzles Thai language learners and the word has to be memorized as a special spelling. However, there should be a historical explanation of this spelling.

Wiyada (1981) studies the meanings and the etymology of *kɔɔ³* in Thai by using spoken language, stone inscriptions and documents classified by periods starting from Sukhothai period to the present time. The word *kɔɔ³* was written in the First Stone Inscription of King Ramkhamhaeng as ก. However, she cannot conclude that the word was first used in the period of Sukhothai since other stone inscriptions older than the First Stone Inscription of King Ramkhamhaeng may be discovered in the future. Though the word *kɔɔ* in Khmer does not appear in the Khmer inscriptions that she has studied, it cannot be concluded that *kɔɔ* in Khmer was borrowed from Thai. There are still other Khmer inscriptions in which *kɔɔ* may be found.

The writing of *kɔɔ³* with the low tone marker *may⁴ eek²* may be used as more evidence to support the Khmer origin of this word. Diller (1991) studies documents of Sukhothai and Ayutthaya period other than the First Stone Inscription of King Ramkhamhaeng. He finds a sporadic use of the tone marker which enables him to reach a conclusion that the First Stone Inscription of King Ramkhamhaeng was written before the full development of tone writing. There is a sociolinguistic explanation to this conclusion. The interpersonal contact with Khmer and Tai dialect mixing around Chao Praya River Basin during the 14-15ᵗʰ century caused the phonological change especially the tones; therefore the old writing system does not match the tones. As a consequence, a new writing system was introduced from Khmer. This new writing system writes vowel on a consonant whereas the writing of Ramkhamhaeng Period has tone marker on a consonant.

Since the Thai writing during Ramkhamhaeng Period had been influenced by the Khmer writing system especially in the writing of tones, I am convinced that the writing of the low tone marker on the consonant ꞃ is an attempt to write the word $kɔɔ^1$ which was borrowed from Khmer. Writing Thai words in that period might not need a tone marker. Cam Cauông (1992) studied Black Tai in Vietnam and found out that there were two series of tones, the high and the low. Each tone series has three tones. There was no marker of these tones in the ancient Black Tai orthography. The three tones in each series were written in the same way. The readers could read the tone values from their context. Early this century the two tone markers similar to may^4 eek^1 and may^4 $thoo$ in Thai and Lao have been introduced. However Black Tai people still use the old writing system without the tone markers because Black Tai is not the national language and there is no need for accuracy of the writing system. The old Black Tai writing seems to support the claim made above. There might be no need to write tones of Thai words during Ramkhamhaeng Period as well and the low tone marker was intended to write loanwords such as $kɔɔ^3$.

As to the question why $kɔɔ^3$ in Thai and $kɔɔ$ in Khmer are presently written in a similar way, a comparative study of Tai orthography may clarify this matter. The list below shows the writing of $kɔɔ^3$ in other Tai languages with phonetic values in comparison with the Thai and Khmer writing.

Languages	Orthography	Phonetic values
Modern Thai	ก๊	$kɔɔ^3$ (falling)
Khmer	ก	$kɔɔ$ (mid)
Black Thai	𑄋	$kɔ^1$ (low)
Khon	ก๊	$kɔ^5$ (high falling)
Lao	ກໍ	$kɔ$ (mid)
Ai-ton	ꩬꩴꩱ	$kɔ$ (mid)

It seems that the mid tone is unmarked as for the case of Khmer, Lao, and Ai-ton. The falling tone in Thai is unmarked as well and the vowel shortening symbol appears instead. The question is what is the phonetic value of the ancient Thai writing of $kɔɔ^3$, i. e. ꞃ   and how it develops to the present writing ก๊.

A comparison of the orthography above gives a clue that ꞃ should be pronounced as $kɔ^1$ with the short vowel ɔ and the low tone since the phonetic values of the writing in other related languages have the short vowel ɔ. The word ก๊ is always pronounced with the short vowel ɔ in connected speech. Only in citation form is the vowel lengthened. The original writing and pronunciation of ꞃ is still preserved in Black Thai. The Black Tai people in Vietnam also keep this form and pronunciation. The original writing ꞃ was transmitted from the Sukhothai Kingdom to the Lanna and Lanchang Kingdom through the dissemination and propagation of Buddhism. The Lanna Kingdom had Chiangmai as the center. The Lanchang Kingdom covered the areas of Sipsongbanna in China, Sipsongjuthai in Vietnam and Luang Prabang in Laos (Suree 1999). In the Lao language, the word $kɔ$ (mid tone) is written with the long vowel symbol ꞃ but pronounced with the short vowel ɔ. The same thing has occurred with the Lik-Tai orthography of Ai-ton in which the long vowel symbol ꞃ is used for the short vowel pronunciation. Nantana (1992) has found that the Thai Noi orthography, which is used for writing Lao and Isan Thai, has the system that the writing of short and long vowels is interchangeable. This indicates that the vowel length was not contrastive in the distant past.

The replacement of ñ with ก̃ has to do with the vowel length. Sarawit (1973) posits the proto form of the vowel ɔɔ as *oo. The additional short vowel ɔ occurs in loanwords and in native words which have undergone irregular or specially conditioned phonological developments. If we believe in this reconstruction of the vowel system of Proto-Tai, it may be used to support the claim that ñ is pronounced with a short vowel because it is a Khmer word.[7] The short vowel ɔ was not written until the mid Ratanakosin Period. Puttachart (1992) compares the documents of Sukhothai, Ayuthaya and Ratanakoson periods with other Tai dialects and has found that the vowel length of the pair *e-ee* is not contrastive. It is conditioned by the syllable structure. In the mid Ratanakosin Period, this pair of vowels became contrastive and the symbols <ı-> <ı-#> <เı̃#> and <ı-ะ> were added to the writing system. Since ñ was pronounced with a short vowel, the symbol ี่ called *may⁴tay²khuu⁴* in Thai was used to indicate the short vowel. The low tone marker has been replaced by the vowel shortening symbol ี่.. I believe that the low tone has changed to a contour tone during this period of time and thus the low tone marker was no longer used. The contour tone later on has caused the length of the vowel ɔ and hence ก̃ is pronounced with long vowel in citation form in the modern Thai.[8] In sum, the development of ก̃ is as follows:

Sukhothai Period	Mid Ratakosin Period	recent
ก̀	ก̃	ก̃
kɔ² (low tone)	*kɔ³* (falling tone)	*kɔɔ³* (falling tone)

The similarity of Thai and Khmer writings of this word is due to the influence of Thai language on Khmer in the Ratanakosin Period. According to Hall (1968) in the thirteenth century the decline of Khmer power on the one side and the disappearance of a strong Burma on the other provided the T'ais with an unrivalled opportunity for expansion. When the western parts of the Khmer empire were controlled by T'ai, the majority of Rama Khamheng's subjects must have been Mons and Khmers. From his subjects he adopted the script which he used for writing the T'ai language in 1283. He aimed to set up an official language that could be used also by his Mon-Khmer-speaking subjects. His Sukhothai script was adopted throughout Siam and had a strong influence upon the development of writing in the Laos states.

Furthermore, Huffman (1986) points out the influence of Thai on Khmer as follows: In the fifteenth century Cambodia fell into its lowest point. In the Ratanakosin Period Khmer borrowed from Thai the language, culture, literature and other items which Thai had borrowed from Khmer during the eighth to twelfth century. In the eighteenth and nineteenth centuries, the Thai language influenced the Khmer language to such an extreme that Khmer grammar was modified according to Thai grammar. Therefore there are a large number of words shared by Thai and Khmer and it cannot be determined which words are native of which language.

Since the vowel shortening symbol ี่ was introduced to the Thai writing system during Ratanakosin Period in which the Thai language had much influence on Khmer, I believe that this symbol[9] was borrowed from Thai to Khmer. This conclusion agrees with Wiyada (1981). She points out that there are only two words written with this symbol in Khmer, that is, ก̃ 'then' and ฎ̃ 'which, that' pronounced as kɔɔ and dɔɔ respectively whereas this symbol is productive in Thai. Therefore the symbol ก̃ must have been invented by Thai and transmitted to Khmer later on.

---

7   See further discussion on the reconstruction of the vowel system of Proto-Tai in Li (1977) and Strecker (1983).

8   See further discussion of the effect of contour on the development of the contrastive vowel length in Hartmann (1976).

9   According to Karnchana (1981), the *may⁴tay¹khuu⁴* symbol is called *lek-as-sa-da* เลขอัสฎา in Khmer.

15.6. CONCLUSION

This chapter studies the preverbal auxiliary $k\jmath\jmath^3$ as a sequential indicator highlighting a chronological theme-line or storyline of the narrative. This preverbal auxiliary is compared with other Southeast Asian languages to determine its source of areal diffusion. It has been found that all languages of Mon-Khmer language family except Mon have cognates of $k\jmath\jmath^3$. The languages of the Southwestern group of the Tai-Kadai language family possess similar forms whereas the Northern group has different forms. This form is absent in languages of Sino-Tibetan language family and in Urak Lawoi' and Malay of the Austronesian language family. Only the Moken language has the cognate of $k\jmath\jmath^3$.

As the sequential indicator $k\jmath\jmath^3$ appears in most Southeast Asian language families, it can be regarded as an area feature in Southeast Asian linguistic area. Based on the areal diffusion of this discourse feature, it is concluded that this form is originally a Khmer word. When Thai people migrated from China to the south, they adopted this form from Khmer during the time that the Khmer empire was at the zenith of its civilization. Not only the pronunciation of this word is similar in Thai and Khmer but also its spelling. Based on a comparative study of Tai orthography, it has been found that this word was originally pronounced with a short vowel [a] so the vowel shortening symbol ◌ั was used to indicate this short vowel. The similarity of Thai and Khmer spelling of this word is due to the influence of Thai language on Khmer in the Ratanakosin Period. The vowel shortening symbol must have been invented by Thai and transmitted to Khmer.

REFERENCES

Amon Saengmani (1979) 'Phonology of the Urak Lawoi' Language: Adang Island', unpublished MA thesis, Mahidol University, Thailand.

Benedict, Paul K. (1972) *Sino-Tibetan: A Conspectus*, Cambridge: Cambridge University Press.

Câm Cường (1992) 'Studying of Vietnamese Thai's Script: Its Comparison with the Script of Thailand', in *Pan Asiatic Linguistics: Proceedings of the Third International Symposium on Language and Linguistics II*, Bangkok: Chulalongkorn University Printing Press House, 614-627.

Chaiyathip Katsura (1993) 'An Analysis of Cohesion in Sgaw Karen Folk Narratives', unpublished MA thesis, Payap University, Thailand.

Chaluay Boonprasert (1982) 'Discourse Structure in Phuan', unpublished MA thesis, Mahidol University, Thailand.

Chauncey C. Chu (1998) *Discourse Grammar of Mandarin Chinese* (*Berkeley Models of Grammars, Vol. 6*), Bern, Berlin, Bruxelles, Frankfurt am Main, New York, Oxford, Wien: Peter Lang Publishing Group.

Cœdès, George (1964) *Les États Hindouisés d' Indochine et d' Indonésie*, Paris (1948).

Diffloth, Gérald (1976) *Proto-Mon-Khmer Final Spirants*, Discussion Paper Number 88, Kyoto: Center for Southeast Asian Studies, Kyoto University.

— (1991) 'Katuic languages', notes from Forum Talk at Mahidol University on 2 July, Bangkok, Thailand.

Diller, Anthony (1991) 'Sukhothai Superscript [ə̀]: Tone Mark or Vowel Sign?', paper presented at the XXIV International Conference on Sino-Tibetan Languages and Linguistics, Ramkhamhaeng and Chiangmai University, October.

— (1992) 'Tai Languages in Assam: Daughters or Ghosts?' in Carol J. Compton and John F. Hartmann (eds) *Papers on Tai Languages, Linguistics, and Literatures: In Honor of William J. Gedney on his 77th Birthday*, DeKalb: Center for Southeast Asian Studies, Northern Illinois University, 5-43.

Emeneau, Murray B. (1980) *Language and Linguistic Area*, Stanford, California: Stanford University Press.

Hall, D. G. E. (1968) *A History of South-East Asia*, London: The Macmillan Press Ltd.

Hartmann, John F. (1976) 'The Waxing and Waning of Vowel Length in Tai Dialects', in Thomas W. Gething et al (eds) *Tai Linguistics in Honor of Fang Kuei Li*, Bangkok: Chulalongkorn University Press, 142-159.

Henderson, Eugénie J. A. (1965) 'The Topography of Certain Phonetic and Morphological Characteristics of South East Asian Languages', in G. B. Milner and Eugénie J. A. Henderson (eds) *Indo-Pacific Linguistics Studies (Lingua 14-15)*, *Vol. 2 : Descriptive Linguistics*, Amsterdam, North Holland Publishing Co., 400-434.

Huffman, Franklin E. (1986) 'Khmer Loanwords in Thai', in Robert J. Bickner, Thomas J. Hudak and Patcharin Peyasantiwong (eds) *Papers from a Conference on Thai Studies in Honor of William J. Gedney*, Ann Arbor: University of Michigan, 199-210.

Jiranan Komonkitiskun (1985) 'Some General Characteristics of Lawa Grammar (La-up dialect)', unpublished MA thesis, Mahidol University, Thailand.

Jones, Robert B., Jr. (1961) *Karen Linguistic Studies*, Berkeley and Los Angeles: University of California Publications in Linguistics, no. 25.

Karnchana Nacsakul (1976) 'Types of Elaboration in Some Southeast Asian Languages', *Austroasiatic Studies (Oceanic Linguistics Special Publication 13)*: 873-89.

Karnchana Nacsakul (1981) *Reading Khmer*, Bangkok: Chulalongkorn University Book Center.

Kasamaphorn Manikhaw (1990) 'Referents for Participants in Mien Narrative Discourse', unpublished MA thesis, Chulalongkorn University, Thailand. (In Thai)

Language Institute (1995) *Burmese Language: Intermediate Level*, Burmese Language Department, Language Institute, Burma.

Li, Fang-Kuei (1977) *A Handbook of Comparative Tai*, Oceanic Linguistics Special Publications 15, Honolulu: University Press of Hawaii.

Lindell, Kristina (1989) *Folk Tales from Kammu-IV*, London: Scandinavian Institute of Asian Studies Monograph Series.

Longacre, Robert E. (1990) *Storyline Concerns and Word-order Typology in East and West Africa, Studies in African Linguistics Supplement 10*, Los Angeles: The James S. Coleman African Studies Center and the Department of Linguistics, University of California at Los Angeles.

— (1996) *The Grammar of Discourse*, New York and London: Plenum Press.

Luce, G. H. and Shin, Bohmu Ba (1961) 'Pagán Myinkaba Kubyankgyi Temple of Rāhajynār (1113 AD) and the Old Mon Writings on its Walls', *Bulletin of the Burma Historical Commission* II: 277-416.

Matisoff, James A. (1973) *The Grammar of Lahu*, Berkeley and Los Angeles: University of California publications in linguistics, no. 75.

Migliazza, Brian (1998) 'A Grammar of So: A Mon-Khmer Language of Northern Thailand', unpublished PhD dissertation, Mahidol University, Thailand.

Mingkwan Malapol (1989) 'Pray Grammar at Ban Pae Klang, Thung Chang District, Nan Province', unpublished MA thesis, Mahidol University, Thailand.

Nantana Ronnakiet (1992) 'Evidence of the Thai Noi Alphabet Found in Inscriptions', in *Pan Asiatic Linguistics: Proceedings of the Third International Symposium on Languages and Linguistics* III, Bangkok: Chulalongkorn University Printing Press, 1326-1334.

Orathai Saijampa (1992) 'Participant Reference in Mon Narrative Discourse (Literary Mon)', unpublished MA thesis, Mahidol University, Thailand.

Payau Memanas (1979) 'A Description of Chaobon (ɲahkur): An Austroasiatic Language in Thailand', unpublished MA thesis, Mahidol University, Thailand.

Puttachart Dhananjayananda (1992) 'The Emergence of Lenth Distinction of Mid-front Vowel e-ee in Thai', in *Pan Asiatic Linguistics: Proceedings of the Third International Symposium on Language and Linguistics* III, Bangkok: Chulalongkorn University Press, 1294-1304.

Rasi Petsuk (1978) 'General Characteristics of the Khün Language', unpublished MA thesis, Mahidol University, Thailand.

Sarawit, Mary Elizabeth Sautter (1973) 'The Proto-Tai Vowel System', unpublished PhD dissertation, The University of Michigan.

Somkiet Poopatwiboon (1982) 'Discourse Level Cohesion in Northern Khmer', unpublished MA thesis, Mahidol University, Thailand.

Somroedee Dej-amorn. 1998. 'Discourse Functions of Particle 'le' in Green Hmong', unpublished MA thesis, Chulalongkorn University, Thailand. (In Thai)

Somsonge Burusphat (1991) *The Structure of Thai Narrative*, Dallas and Arlington: Summer Institute of Linguistics and University of Texas Arlington.

— (1992a) 'Highlighting through the Particle *swe?* in Sgaw Karen Narrative Discourse', in Martha Ratliff and Eric Schiller (eds) *Papers from the First Annual Meeting of the Southeast Asian Linguistics Society 1991*, Program for Southeast Asian Studies, Arizona State University, 47-63.

— (1992b) 'The functions of *kʌ?* in oral Kui narrative', *Mon-Khmer Studies* XVIII-XIX: 223-231.

Somsonge Burusphat and Megan Sinnott (eds) (1998) *Kam-Tai Oral Literatures*, Bangkok: T&D Printing Ltd.

Strecker, David (1983) 'Proto-Tai vowels revisited: a comparison and critique of the work of Sarawit and Li', *Linguistics of the Tibeto-Burman Area* 7.2: 33-74.

Suksiri Danthanavanich (2000) 'Cohesion Devices in Vietnamese Folktales', unpublished MA thesis, Mahidol University, Thailand.

— (ms) Vietnamese folktale data.

Sunan Udomwech (1985) *An Annotated Collection of Thai Song Dam Folktales*, Department of Thai Language, Petchaburi Teacher College. (In Thai)

Suree Thongkhongharn (1999) *Thai Song Dam Culture and Custom Part 1: Thai Song Dam Orthography*, Nakornpatom, Thailand: National Agricultural Training Center, Kasetsart University. (In Thai)

Trudgill, Peter (1974) 'Linguistic Change and Diffusion: Description and Explanation in Sociolinguistic Dialect Geography', *Language in Society* 3: 215-246.

Uraisri Worasarin et al. (1997) *Kulabphaylin*, trans. ลุก แ ถ ม , Bangkok: Jongjalearnkanphim Ltd. (In Thai and Khmer).

Veena Chantanakomes (1980) 'A Description of Moken: A Malayo-Polynesian Language', unpublished MA thesis, Mahidol University, Thailand.

Vitalee Beyondkee (1988) *Banpa*, Mudsaku: Raduka.

Wiyada Sa-anwong (1981) 'The Use of the Expression 'kɔ:[3]' in the Thai Language', unpublished MA thesis, Silpakorn University, Thailand. (In Thai)

Yajai Chuwicha (1985) 'The Multi-purpose Marker in Oral Narrative: A Discourse Analysis', paper presented at the 18th International Conference on Sino-Tibetan Language and Linguistics, Bangkok.

CHAPTER SIXTEEN

A HISTORICAL STUDY OF /thîi/ IN THAI

Pranee Kullavanijaya

16.1. THE AIM OF THE STUDY[1]

The aim of the present study of /thîi/ is three-fold. The first is to study the various occurrences of /thîi/ in modern Thai so as to identify its various functions. The second is to investigate the historical development of /thîi/ in four periods: Sukhothai, Ayutthaya, Mid-Ratanakosin covering the reigns of King Rama IV and V, and the present day Thai, henceforth, modern Thai. This leads to the third aim, that is to see whether the historical development agrees with the grammaticalization pathway of /thîi/ proposed by W. Bisang in his important paper on processes of grammaticalization of nouns and verbs in east and mainland South East Asian languages (Bisang, 1996). The last section of the paper surveys the use of equivalent words of /thîi/ in two other Tai languages.

16.2. SOURCES OF DATA

The data for modern Thai are based on 800 lines of text randomly drawn from the Chulalongkorn University electronic corpus and a 21line column from a daily newspaper. These are supported by the writer's knowledge as a native speaker of Thai.

For the study of earlier Thai, the data are from various sources. The Sukhothai data are based on twelve inscriptions from BE. 1835-1960, which appear in *Charuek Samai Sukhothai* (Sukhothai Inscriptions, National Library of Thailand, 1983). Altogether the Sukhothai data are 1128 lines long. The Ayutthaya data are from Kosaapaan's Memoirs (1987) and are 925 lines in length. The data reflect the Thai language around the year 1658, more or less in the last part of the Ayutthaya period. The Mid-Ratanakosin data, covering language in the reigns of Kings Rama IV and V, are based on randomly selected letters, notes and announcements during the two reigns (1964, 1998) and comprise 983 lines of text. The two reigns marked the beginning of changes in Thai ways of thinking and living and thus should reflect language changes. It should be pointed out that data from earlier eras, as with any historical documents, cannot be said to be absolute representative of their time. However, the writer is certain that the study based on the data mentioned above reveal, to a significant extent, the historical pathway of /thîi/ in Thai.

16.3. /thîi/ IN MODERN THAI

In modern Thai the word /thîi/ illustrates a variety of both meanings and functions. This is discussed below.

16.3.1. /thîi/ as a simple noun

As a simple noun, /thîi/ means 'a piece of land' and can be modified by /din/ 'soil' as in /thîi din/. It is used with classifiers such as /phǔɯn/ in /thîi din phǔɯn níi/, 'this piece of land' or

---

1 I would like to express my deep appreciation to Martin Haspelmath, Matthew Dryer and Orin Gensler, for giving valuable comments when I presented the first draft of my paper at the Max Planck Institute in Leipzig during my short visit as a DAAD researcher in October 2001. I am especially grateful to Bernard Comrie and Walter Bisang for sharing their knowledge of attributive clauses in other languages.

/plɛɛŋ/ in /thîi din sɔ̌ɔŋ plɛɛŋ/ 'two pieces of land'. /thîi/ as a simple noun is rarely found in my data mostly because the texts under study are not related to the matter of land, although it is well used in spoken Thai.

16.3.2. /thîi/ as a class noun

Bisang (1996) used 'class noun' to account for the high level abstraction of /thîi/ which appears in the head position of a noun phrase usually ending with postnominal determiners (1996: 547). From his examples, /thîi/ as a class noun is usually followed by a verb or verb phrase. I will adopt Bisang's 'class noun' with some modification. I make the distinction between a /thîi/ in a compound and a /thîi/ referred to hence as the /thîi/ class noun. Principally, a class noun /thîi/ is a type of compounds but the 'class noun' /thîi/ still denotes a location, while /thîi/ in a compound does not denote a location but a person or an instrument. Thus, to me, the /thîi/ class noun is closer in meaning to the /thîi/ simple noun than the /thîi/ in a compound or hence the /thîi/ compound which has the meaning of /thîi/ far detached from 'land'. Examples of the /thîi/ class noun are:

(1)   thîi tàak ʔaakàat   'resort'
       (place – exposed- air)

(2)   thîi wâa kaan ʔamphəə   'district head quarter'
       (place- tell- affairs-district)

(3)   thîi khǎay tǔa   'ticket booth'
       (place- sell- ticket)

(4)   thîi bambàt náam sǐa   'polluted water section'
       (place- treat-water- waste)

(5)   thîi phák phûu dooy sǎan 'passenger area / booth'
       (place-rest-passengers)

It should be observed that the /thîi/ class noun is an active word formation process in modern Thai.

16.3.3. The /thîi/ compound

As has already been mentioned, /thîi/ in a compound denotes a person, group of persons, an instrument, a state or other meanings but not a location. The /thîi/ compound may be a compound noun (6a) and (6b) or a compound verb (6c). If it is a verb, it usually has a metaphorical sense. The compounds in (6d.) are adverbials functioning as discourse markers. Some examples of the /thîi/ compound are given below:

(6) a.   thîi prùksǎa   *(thîi - to consult)*   'a consultant'
          thîi pràʔchum[2]   *(thîi - to meet)*   'a committee'
          thîi phuîŋ   *(thîi -to depend)*   'a patron'
          thîi bâan   *(thîi - house)*   'a husband/wife'

---

2   *thîi pràʔchum* can also mean 'a meeting hall', in which case it is considered a class noun.

b. thîi yép krà?   *(thîi - to sew- paper)*   'a stapler'
    dàat
    thîi pàw phǒm   *(thîi - to blow - hair)*   'a hair dryer'
    thîi nɔɔn   *(thîi - to sleep)*   'a mattress'

c. kin thîi   *(to eat - thîi)*   'to consume space'
    khoŋ thîi   *(to maintain - thîi)*   'to be stable'
    thǔŋ thîi   *(to arrive- thîi)*   'to die'

d. thîi thέε   *(thîi - real)*   'in fact'
    thîi ciŋ   *(thîi - true)*   'in fact'

As can be seen from the examples, /thîi/ has shifted its concrete meaning into an abstract one. Here, /thii/ does not denote a piece of land or any location.

16.3.4. /thîi/ as a classifier

Although hardly found in the written data, /thîi/ as a classifier is not uncommon in spoken Thai:

(7) a. khɔ̌ɔ   náamchaa   sɔ̌ɔŋ   thîi

         ask for   *tea*   *two*   *clf.*

         'May I have two teas?'

     b. cɔɔŋ   thîi   wáy   hây   sɔ̌ɔŋ   thîi   dûay.

         reserve   *seat*   *keep* *give* *two*   *clf.* *also*

         'Reserve two seats for me.'

16.3.5. /thîi/ as an ordinal numeral marker

As an ordinal numeral marker, /thîi/ is found preceding the numerals denoting ordinal numbers, for examples:

(8) a. lûuk   khon   thîi   sɔ̌ɔŋ   khɔ̌ɔŋ   khǎw   kèŋ
         child   *clf.*   *numeral marker*   *two*   *of*   *he*   *smart*
         'His second child is smart.'

     b. khraaw   thîi   lέεw   khǎw   mâydâay   maa
         time   *numeral marker*   *past*   *he*   *not*   *come*
         'Last time he did not come.'

16.3.6. /thîi/ as a preposition

When /thîi/ is a preposition, it can be left out particularly when the verb is a locative verb or implies location for example, one may say /khǎw yùu rooŋrian/ as well as /khǎw yùu thîi rooŋrian / 'He is at school'.

(9) a. dèkdèk   thîi   bâan   khǎw   mây   sǝbaay   bɔ̀y

         children   *at*   *house*   *he*   *not*   *well*   *often*

         'The children at his house often fell ill.'

b. man dâay   ráp   chɔɔn   pay   ʔɔ̀ɔk   ŋaan   thîi   chiəŋmaày

    it   get   receive   invite   go   out   work   at   Chiengmai

'It was invited for a show in Chiengmai.'

16.3.7. /thîi/ as a relative clause marker

In modern Thai when an embedded clause modifying the antecedent noun which usually precedes it, /thîi/ is placed at the head of the clause. In this position /thîi/ functions as a marker[3] linking the embedded clause to the preceding noun. The noun or as referred to as an antecedent noun before /thîi/ must have the syntactic relation with the verb in the embedded clause as a subject or an object of the verb if the /thîi/ embedded clause is a relative clause. My data shows that the /thîi/ relative clause occurs with the highest frequency compared to /thîi/ in other functions.

(10) a. hùn   láʔkhɔɔn   lék   thîi   kǎw   lǒŋlǎy

          puppet   drama   small   that   he   obsessed

          'The small puppet drama that he felt obsessed with.'

      b. dèk   thîi   mii   ʔaakaan   daŋ   klàaw   tôŋ   rîip   phaa   pay   hǎa   mɔ̌ɔ

          child   that   has   symptom   like   said   must   hurry   take   go   find   doctor

          'The child who has this symptom must be taken to see a doctor as soon as possible.'

16.3.8. /thîi/ as a complementizer

As a complementizer /thîi/ heads an embedded clause the preceding noun of which does not have any grammatical relation with the verb in the embedded clause. I will call such an embedded clause a /thîi/ complement, with /thîi/ as a complementizer. The /thîi/ complement has two functions: it modifies the preceding noun, in which case it will be referred to as the /thîi/ noun complement, or it complements the preceding verb in which case it is called the /thîi/ verb complement. The /thîi/ noun complement will be dealt with first.

16.3.8.1. *The /thîi/ noun complement*[4]

In the following examples, the head noun of the /thîi/ noun complement is underlined.

(11) a. <u>rûaŋ</u>   thîi   khǎw   mây   phûut   kàp   khray   ləəy   pen   rûaŋ   kàw

          story   that   he   not   speak   with   who   atall   is   story   old

          'The fact that he did not speak with anyone at all was an old story.'

---

3   Comrie (1998) uses the term 'subordinator' in state of 'complementizer'. For him, the embedded clause functions as the attributive to the noun. He has also shown that in several languages of South East Asia, there seems to be no need to differentiate between a relative clause and a noun complement clause. Although this is interesting, I will maintain the difference between the two since it is still arguable whether Thai is like Japanese in having only modifying clauses; also, the recognition of both seems to show a better picture of /thîi/ historical development.

4   The term fact-S construction is also used as for example, in Comrie (1998). I use the term noun complement since the head noun can be an abstract noun as well as a lexical noun.

b.   thǔɯŋ <u>weelaa</u> thîi krà?suaŋsùksǎa   cà?   tɔ̂ŋ   thópthuan ruîaŋ níi

     each   time   that ministry of education will   must review   story this

    'It's time for the Ministry of Education to review this matter.'

c.   panhǎa   sǎmkhan   thîisùt   khɯɯ   <u>panhǎa</u>   <u>sètthà?kìt</u> thîi

     problem   important most   is   problem   economy   that

    prà?chaachon wǎŋ cà?   hây   ràtthà?baan plòt   nîi

     people   hope will   cause government remove debt

    prà?thêet   dâay   dooyrew

     country   can   quickly

    'The most important problem is the economy one which the Thai people hope that the government will remove the country's debts in no time'

It should be noted that the antecedent noun can be a lexical noun, as in (11b) or (11c) or an abstract noun as in (11a). The abstract nouns often found are /kaan/ 'work', /sìŋ/ 'thing' and /ruîaŋ/ 'matter'.

16.3.8.2. *The /thîi/ verb complement*

The /thîi/ embedded clause which complements the preceding verb is called here the /thîi/ verb complement. It usually occurs with /cà?/ 'will' preceding the verb in the clause and usually denotes an action which has not yet occurred but will occur or is likely to occur, for examples:

(12) a. khǎw khít   thîi   cà?   ?ɔ̀ɔk càak   ŋaan

     she   think   that   will   out   from   work

    'She thinks that she will resign from work.'

b. dèk   ní?yom   thîi   cà?   khâw   rian   sǎay   sǎaman

     a student prefer   that   will   enter learn line   common

    'School students prefer going to academic schools.'

c. phûu   còp   pɔɔwɔɔchɔɔ   sǎamâat thîi   cà?

     person finish lower vocation school can   that   will

    ?ɔ̀ɔk   pay   thamŋaan   dâay   lέεw

     out   go   work   can   already

    'One who finishes lower vocational education can start working already.'

It should be noted that the verb phrase with /thîi/ as a complementizer can occur after a preverb such as /nâa/ and /khuan/ 'should' :

d. khǎw   nâathîi   cà?   pay   sɔ̀ɔp

    he   *had better* *will* *go*   *take an examination*

    'He had better take the examination.'

e. khǎw   khuanthîi   cà?   pay   sɔ̀ɔp

    she   *had better* *will* *go*   *take an examination*

    'She should take the examination.'

Such occurrences are very recent but have gained more frequency in spoken Thai, although they are rarely seen in written Thai. It is interesting to observe that only some preverbs can take the verb phrase with /thîi/ complementizer. This might be a piece of evidence supporting that these preverbs were verbs before, although this requires a much deeper study to confirm this observation.

16.3.9. /thîi/ as a nominalizer

/thîi/ as a nominalizer makes the clause a nominal which may function as a subject of a verb. In this function, the /thîi/ clause nominal is considered different from the /thîi/ verb complement which complements the verb. Such a differentiation is observed by many linguists in generative grammar (Hurford, 1994) and also by Bisang (1996). For a clear comparison between Bisang's pathways of grammaticalization and the historical study in this paper, the same differentiation is adopted.

(13) a. thîi   krà?suaŋsùksǎa   mii   ná?yoobaay

      that *ministry of education* *have* *policy*

      daŋ   klàaw   nâacà?   tɔ̂ŋ   thópthuan

      as *said*   *should* *must* *review*

      'That the ministry of education has given the aforementioned policy should be reviewed'

    b. nákrian   yǐŋ   khon   nán   yɔɔmráp   thîi   thəə   hǔarɔ́?

      student *girl* *clf.* *that* *accept* *that* *she* *laugh*

      daŋ   kwàa   khray

      loud *more* *who*

      'That girl student accepted that her laughing was louder than those of others'

    c. thîi   khǎw   mây   thǐaŋ   thamhây   thəə   kròot

      that *he* *not* *argue* *make* *she* *angry*

      'That he did not talk back made her angry.'

It can be seen from the above that /thîi/ in modern Thai displays a variety of functions. Whether /thîi/ in these functions occurs in other periods or not will be studied in the following sections.

16.4. A HISTORICAL DEVELOPMENT OF /thîi/

In this section a study of occurrences of /thîi/ in the Sukhothai, Ayutthaya and Mid-Ratanakosin periods will be made. Then in the following section, these occurrences will be considered with those in modern Thai to give the historical development of /thîi/. After that it will be shown whether the historical development agrees with the grammaticalization pathway proposed by Bisang in 1996.

16.4.1. /thîi/ in the Sukhothai period

Although the Sukhothai scripts were found late into the Ayutthaya period, our data will cover only the inscriptions written within the year 1399, approximately 50 years after the generally accepted end of the Sukhothai period in 1350. This is to conform to the historical period rather than the type of scripts. The data reveal /thîi/ with the following functions.

16.4.1.1. */thîi/ as a simple noun*

In the Sukhothai data, /thîi/ as a simple noun denotes a piece of land or land and is found usually followed by a demonstrative *nîi* 'this', *nán* 'that', *day* 'any', for examples:

(14) a. ʔùpəmaa   daŋ   riaŋ   thɔ́n   ʔɔ́ɔy   wáy   mâak[5]

         compare   *as*   *arrange*   *chunk*   *sugarcane* *keep*   *many*

         daam   dàat   tem   thîi   səthǎan   nán   lɛɛ

         cover   *cover*   *full*   *land*   *place*   *that*

         'As if (one) arranges chunks of sugarcane covering the whole land'

    b. …thîi nán   kɔ̀ɔ   práʔthantathâatsukhontháʔceedii

      land   *that*   *build* *stupa*

      mii   sǎam   ʔan

      have   *three* *clf.*

      '…that place, build three stupas.'

There are few occurrences of /thîi/ followed by a place name which make it possible to interpret them as prepositions:

(15) a. ʔan   nùŋ   pràʔdìtsathǎan   wáy   nǔa   cɔɔm   khǎw

         clf.   *one*   *to place*   *keep* *above* *top*   *hill*

         thîi   pàakpráʔbaaŋ

         land   *name of place*

         'One was placed at the top of a hill of Paak Phrabang'

---

5   Transcription Note: For the transcription of examples in the earlier periods, a comparison to the modern Thai phonemic system is used, i.e. the earlier script is read with the modern Thai pronunciation and since phonetic detail is not at issue in this paper, a broad transcription is used.

b.   phɔ́ɔkhǔnphǎamɯaŋ   câw   mɯaŋrâat   ʔaw   phon

King Phaa Mueng   *king*   *Mueng Ratt Town*   *bring*   *soldiers*

maa   tòp   kan   thîibaaŋkhlǒoŋ

come   *join*   *together*   *place name of place*

'King Phaa Mueng, the king of Raat led his soldiers to meet (with another group) at Baang Khloong   place'

However I have interpreted such occurrences of /thîi/ as a noun, for the following reasons:

First, the data in the Sukhothai period show that when a specification of the location is needed, a relational noun such as /nay/ 'in' or /bon/ 'on' is used:

c.   cɯŋ   ʔaw   fǎŋ   loŋ   nay   klaaŋ   mɯaŋ

then   *get*   *bury*   *down*   *in*   *heart*   *city*

'bury in the heart of the city'

If no specification or description of the location is required, only the land or /thîi/ is mentioned:

d.   kɔ̀ɔ   práʔthantàʔthâat   thîi   nán

build   *stupa*   *place*   *that*

'build the stupa at that place'

Second, it is observed that in the data, occurrences of a place name do not usually occur alone without a specification that it is a town, for example:

e.   khon   ʔan   mii   nay   mɯaŋ   thay

man   *clf.*   *have*   *in*   *town*   *Thai*

'people in Thailand'

In the data, the occurrence such as /*khon ʔan mii nay thay/ is hardly found, while such occurrence is common in modern Thai:

f.   pàa   thîi   sǒmboon   nay   chiəŋmày

forest   *that*   *complete*   *in*   *Chiangmai*

'Untouched forest in Chiangmai'

Thus, it is possible to say that when a place is not a town but a site or a location /thîi/ is used. Therefore, /thîi/ in (15a) and (15b) may well be interpreted as a noun meaning place. However, I do not deny that such a usage is most likely to give the direction for a preposition /thîi/ later on.

An occurrence of /thîi/ in the following sentence gives a more abstract sense of /thîi/, that is, 'a position':

(16) a.   ...dâay   sàwɔ̌ɔyrâat   thɛɛn   thîi   pùu   yâa
       get   reign   replace place grandfather grandmother
       '...get to reign in place of the grandparents'

16.4.1.2. */thîi/ as a class noun*

In the Sukhothai data, few occurrences of a class noun were found:

(17) a.   thîi   sǎŋsà?kaan
       place   worship
       'a place to worship (something)'

    b.   laaŋ   hɛ̀ŋ   thîi   chumnum phrá?má?hǎathâat... pen pàa   pen doŋ
       some place place meet   Buddha's relics   is   forest is   forest
       'Some places, the places where Lord Buddha's relics are plenty... are dense
        with trees...'

There are few occurrences of /thîi/ followed by a clause. Together the construction occurs as a noun in apposition or a genitive attribute to a preceding noun. In all these occurrences, the meaning of a location of an action is conveyed.

    c.   cuŋ   câk   hɔ̌?   pay nay   tôn phrá?sǐimá?hǎaphoo
       then   will   fly   go   in   tree Bhodhi tree
       thîi   phrá?phút   pencâaw   tràt kɛɛ sǎnphétyú?tà?yaan
       place   LordbBuddha say   to   enlightenment
       '(The relics) rose to the Bhodhi tree, the place Lord Buddha was enlightened'

    d.   khùt   ?aw   din   thîi   má?hǎasǐisàtthaarâatcù?nii   yìap
       dig   take   soil   place   name   step on
       'Dig the soil, the place Mahaasrisattharaatculamunee steps on.'

An examination of the Sukhothai data shows that when a relative clause occurred, /?an/ was commonly used as a relative marker, for examples:

    e.   buuchaa   prá?sà?thùpceedii   phrá?sǐimá?hǎaphoo
       worship   stupa   Bodhi tree
       ?an   sá?mɔ̌ə   daŋ   ton   phrá?câaw   raw
       which   equal   as   body   Buddha   we
       '...worship the stupas and the Bodhi tree which are equivalent to the Lord
       Buddha himself.'

    f.   phrá?thâat.   tháŋlǎay   ?an   mii   nay   phɛ̀ndin   nîi...
       relics   all   which   have   in   land   this
       'All the Buddha's relics which are in this land'

Since /?an/ was a common relative marker in the Sukhothai period, I would interpret /thîi/ in (17c). and d. not as a relative marker but as a class noun. Again, this may mark the beginning of /thîi/ as a complementizer or a relative marker.

16.4.1.3. *The /thîi/ compound*

A compound noun is identified as one unit where /thîi/ does not denote any meaning of location or place. The Sukhothai data showed a few examples of such compounds:

(18)   a.   thîi   chìp   thîi   hăay
            place   *lost*   *place*   *lost*
            'peril'

       b.   thîi   lóm   thîi   taay
            place   *fall*   *place*   *die*
            'death'

There were few occurrences of /thîi/ before /lέεw/ 'finish' and /sùt/ 'end' which might be interpreted as a unit marking a type of numerals, for examples:

(19)   a.   muîa   pii   ?an   càk   sîn   sàatsà?năa   phrá?phútpencâaw
            time   *year*   *which*   *will*   *end*   *religion*   *Lord Buddha*
            thîisùt   tháŋlăay   ?an   pii   chûat
            end   *all*   *that is* *year*   *rat*
            'The time the Buddhist religion ends will be the year of the rat.'

       b.   thŏŋ   wiaŋcan   wiaŋkham   pen   thîi   lέεw   buîaŋhŭanɔɔn...
            reach   *Vientianne*   *Viengkham* *is*   *the*   *last*   *the south*
            fàŋ   thá?lee má?hăasà?mùt   pen   thîilέεw
            sea   *ocean*   *is*   *the end*
            'To Vientianne (and) Viengkham as the last (point). To the south, the sea shore is the end.'

Example (19b) shows that /thîi lέεw/ occurs as a unit meaning 'the end'. Since there was no evidence of /thîi/ as a numeral marker in the Ayutthaya   period. I will interpret   /thîisùt/ and /thîilέεw/ as compounds.

It can be concluded that the Sukhothai data revealed three functions of /thîi/: a simple noun, a class noun, a compound noun. /thîi/ as a simple noun occurred most frequently. It is observed that some occurrences of /thîi/ as a simple noun followed by a place name may be the beginning of /thîi/ as a preposition. Also, there is an evidence of /thîi/ as a class noun followed by a clause which makes it likely to be the beginning of /thîi/ as a complementizer or a relative marker.

16.4.2. /thîi/ in the Ayutthaya period

The Ayutthaya data illustrate functions of /thîi/ as follows:

4.2.1 /thîi/ as a simple noun

Similar to the Sukhothai data, /thîi/ as a simple noun in Ayutthaya denotes a piece of land or place. It is also usually followed by a demonstrative /nîi/, /níi/ 'this', /nán/ 'that':

(20) a. dûay   thîi   nán   pen   mɯaŋ   nɔ́ɔy
          because   land   that   is   city   small
          'Because that place is a small city'

      b. sùt   tɯ̀k   nán   pen   thîi   plàaw
          end   building that   is   land   vacant
          'To the end of the building is a vacant piece of land.'

16.4.2.1. */thîi/ as a class noun*

/thîi/ functioning as a class noun is found with the highest frequency in my Ayutthaya data in comparison to other functions of /thîi/. Again, the Ayutthaya data display cases where a /thîi/ class noun occurring as a noun in apposition to the preceding noun: /maa duu tɯ̀k thîi khâa pra̠ʔcâw yùu/ (*come – see – building – place –I- stay*) 'Come to see the building, the place I stay.' Also, the /thîi/ class noun can be followed by a clause as in (21b).

(21) a. lɛɛ   pen   thîi   tham   thǎŋ   lɛɛ   thǔŋ
          and   is   place   make   pail   and   bag
          'And is the place for making pails and bags.'

      b. lɛɛ   chán   sǎam   nán   pen   thîi   naay   kampàn   yùu
          and   storey   three   that   is   place   master   ship   stay
          'And the third storey is the ship captain's place'

When the /thîi/ class noun followed by a clause occurs after a noun as in (21c), a question can be asked whether /thîi/ is functioning as a relative clause marker.

      c. lɛɛ   phûu   mii   chɯ̂ɯ   sɯ̂ŋ   kin   dûay   khâaphá̠ʔcâw
          and   person   have   name   which   eat   with   I

          nán   taam   maa   sòŋ   thǔŋ   tɯ̀k   thîi   khâaphá̠ʔcâw   yùu
          that   follow   come   send   arrive   building place   I   stay
          'And the important people who had dinner with me, walked me to the building, the place I stayed'

I will interpret /thîi/ here as a class noun similar to the cases in the Sukhothai period (see 4.1.2) for the same reason that the data show /sɯ̂ŋ/ or /ʔan/ as a relative marker in this period, for example:

      d. lɛɛ   naay   kampàn   nam   khâaphá̠ʔcâw   pay   duu
          and   master   ship   lead   I   *go   see*

          thîi   sɯ̂ŋ   tèŋ   wáy   sǎwkrà̠ʔdooŋ
          place   which   arrange   keep   mast
          'And the ship captain took me to see the place which was arranged to keep the masts.'

16.4.2.2. */thîi/ as a compound noun*

/thîi/ as a compound noun in the Ayutthaya period can be found although such occurrences are not many.

(22)   thîi   taw   phlɔɔŋ   'a fireplace'

         place   fireplace   fire

(23)   thîi   yùu   'aresidence'

         place   live

In sum, the Ayutthaya data illustrate three functions of /thîi/: as a simple noun, a class noun and a compound noun. The occurrences of simple noun followed by a class noun in this period have already indicated the direction for /thîi/ to develop into a relative marker later on.

16.4.3. /thîi/ in the Mid-Ratanakosin period

The Mid-Ratanakosin period in this article covers the reigns of King Rama IV and V. It will be seen that the function of /thîi/ has greatly multiplied in this period:

16.4.3.1. */thîi/ occurs as a simple noun denoting a piece of land or a place, for example:*

(24)   a.   tháŋ   thîi   tháŋ   bâan(RamaIV)

               both   land   and   house

               'Both land and house'

         b.   mii   thîi   ŋaam   hèŋ   nɯ̀ŋ(RamaV)

               have   land   nice   clf.   one

               'There is a nice piece of land.'

In addition, the Rama V data give another meaning of /thîi/ as a simple noun, ie. 'seat', as in /plìan thîi kan sǎam khráŋ/ 'Change seat three times.'

16.4.3.2. *The /thîi/ as an ordinal numeral marker*

In this period, there was evidence for the first time that /thîi/ occurred before numeral words.

(25)   lɛ́ɛw   cɯŋ   fǎŋ   phlɔɔy   kâaw   yàaŋ   thîi   nɯ̀ŋ

         then   so   engrave   jewel   nine   kinds   one

         phét   thîi   sɔ̌ɔŋ   thápthim   .(Rama IV)

         diamond   two   ruby

         'Then engrave nine kinds of jewels; first, diamond ; second, ruby...'

16.4.3.3. */thîi/ as a class noun*
Examples of /thîi/ as a class noun are:

(26)   a.   thîi   tâŋ   phráʔbàʔrommáʔthâat
            place   set   Lord Buddha's relics
            'the place to put Lord Buddha's relics'

       b.   thîi   sǒŋ
            place   bath
            'the place for bathing'

16.4.3.4. *The /thîi/ compound*
The data in the reign of King Rama V gave a large number of the /thîi/ compounds:

(27)   a.   thîi   pràʔchum   'a committee'

       b.   thîi   rúu thîi hěn   'publicly known'

       c.   thîi   thέɛ   'in fact'

       d.   thîi   sùt   'finally; last'

The last two compounds illustrate that the /thîi/ compounds can also function as a discourse marker.

16.4.3.5. */thîi/ as a relative clause marker*
A study of /thîi/ in the Sukhothai and Ayutthaya periods above has shown that the closest case of /thîi/ as a relative clause marker was the construction in which a head noun denoting a location was followed by a /thîi/ class noun (17c, 17d and 21c). The data in the Mid-Ratanakosin period, however, show that /thîi/ in the following examples has been grammaticalized into a full relative clause marker. As can be seen here, the /thîi/ relative marker can follow not only a locative noun but other types of noun.[6] Moreover, it shows a grammatical relation to the verb in the embedded clause as either a subject or an object. These occurrences indicate that /thîi/ has been fully grammaticalized as a relative marker. Also, /ʔan/ which used to be the relative clause marker was hardly found in this period.

(28)   a.   thân   thîi   pen   câwkhǒoŋ   dɔɔm   thîi   hây
            one   that   is   owner   old   that   give

            sâaŋ   phráʔphútháʔrûup...
            build   Buddha's image

            'The one who was the old owner, who has the Buddha's image built'

---

6   Diller (2001) has made the same observation for the relative marker /thîi/. He quoted Givon who, based on a study of the evolution of dependent clause morpho-syntax in Biblical Hebrew, gave the development line of 'place' to 'locative' and to 'general relative'.

b. ...câawnaay   nán   dâay   rápphráʔrâatcháʔthaan bâaŋ mây
     royalfamily   *that* *get*   *receive*   *some* *not*

   dâay   rápphráʔrâatcháʔthaan bâaŋ   dâay   ráp   tɛ̀ɛ   *thîi*
   get   *receive*   *some* *get* *receive* *only* *that*

   dâay   khâw   maa   fâw   nay   phráʔrâatcháʔwaŋ   (Rama IV)
   get   *enter* *come* *watch* *in*   *palace*

'As for the royal family, some received (the King's gift), some did not. Only (those) that were granted to come into the palace received (the gift).'

The example (26b) shows that the relative clause /thîi/ can be far apart from the antecedent noun. It is likely that such occurrence helps accelerating the /thîi/ nominals which were found also in this period.

16.4.3.6. *thîi* as a complementizer

The clause beginning with /thîi/ as a complementizer or the /thîi/ complement was found commonly and could function as a complement of a noun or a verb:

(29) a. thâa   kaansùɯɯp   pay mii   weelaa thîi   càʔ   dâay   tham
     if   *continue*   *go*   *have* *time*   *that* *will* *get*   *do*
     khɯ̂n   ...(RamaIV)
     up

     'If in the future there is the time (chance) to do (this ceremony)...'

  b. ...kɔ̂ɔ mák   phɔɔcay   thîi   càʔ   làwwâa bâan   nán   mùaŋ nán
     then *tend* *prefer*   *that* *will* *tell*   *house* *that* *city* *that*
     pen   khɔ̌ɔŋ phráʔʔin   loŋ   maa   sǎaŋ   (RamaIV)
     is   *thing* *name of diety* *down* *come* *build*

     '...will usually prefer to say that a house or a city was built by diety.'

  c. phrɔ́ʔ   nâataa   kɔ̂ʔ   làwníi   chân mɔ̀ʔthîi phûak   nán
     because *face*   *is*   *land*   *these* *very* *suitable* *that those*
     càʔ   tiikanchiaŋ sǐaciŋciŋ (RamaV)
     will   *swim*   *really*

     'Because the island looks really suitable for those (people) to swim'

  d. kaan   thîi   khâaphráʔphútthácâw càʔ   càt   hây   mii   rooŋrian
     matter *that*   *I*   *will* *arrange* *cause* *have* *school*
     sɔ̌ɔn   nǎŋsɯ̌ɯ ʔaŋkrìt   khɯ̂n nán...
     teach *book*   *English*   *rise* *that*

     'The (idea) that I would like to have an English school set up...'

Sentences (29a) and (29d) are examples of /thîi/ complementizer of a noun complement where as the other sentences illustrate /thîi/ as a complementizer of a verb complement. It is noted that a sentence such as (29d), where /thîi/ modifies an abstract head noun /kaan/ 'content, matter', occurred with a high frequency in the time of Rama V. The other abstract noun equally used was /khwaam/ 'matter'. Since /kaan/ and /khwaam/ are abstract in meaning, they may be left out. Such an optionality is hypothesized as an important factor for a /thîi/ nominalizer.

16.4.3.7. *thîi/ as a nominalizer*

In the Mid-Ratanakosin data, the use of /thîi/ as a marker of a clause nominal, or called here a nominalizer, has also been found:

(30) a. thîi dâay sà?dètphrá?râatchá?damnɔɔn maa sùu sa?thǎanthîi…
          that *get* *come*   *come* *to* *place*

          náp   wâa   pen   sà?mǎymoŋkhon…
          count   *that*   *to be*   *auspicious time*
          'That (the King) came to the (exhibition) place is considered the auspicious time'

      b. bɔɔk hây   sâap wâa thîi cà? khâw ráp   tamnèŋ   nán
          wâa
          tell *make* *know* *say* *that* *will* *enter* *receive* *position* *that*

          cà?   tham kaan   daŋ   níi   (RamaV)
          will *work*   *like* *this*
          'Tell (him) that in taking the position, (you) will work this way.'

      c. tɛ̀ɛ taam thîi wâa lɛ́ɛw chǎn cà? lâw châ?phɔ́? thîi dâay hěn
          but follow   *say* *past* *I*   *will* *tell* *only*   *that* *get* *see*
          'But accordingly to what was said, I would tell only what I saw.'

All examples above are from the data in the time of Rama V. It is observed that /thîi/ nominals in this period occurred quite commonly.

16.4.3.8. *thîi/ as a preposition*

Data in the reign of Rama V show many occurences of /thîi/ between two nouns or noun phrases as in /ruu thîi fàŋ khlɔɔŋ/ (hole-thîi-bank-canal) 'hole on the canal bank' or /sôm thîi ʔiiden/ (orange-thîi-Eden) 'oranges-at-Eden'. These data seem to show that there has been a rebracketting of /thîi/ as a noun and that /thîi/ has become a preposition. In /thîi khùt din klaaŋ khlɔɔŋ mii rɯa lamliaŋ pay thǒm thîi thá?leesàap/ (thîi-dig-soil-middle-canal-have-boat-transport-fill up-thîi-lake) '(From) the soil digging machine in the middle of the canal, there is a boat to take the soil and dump it into the lake', the /thîi/ in /thîi thá?leesàap/ does not mean 'land' and should be interpreted a preposition meaning 'at'. Here one may omit /thîi/ and the meaning of the sentence is still understandable and accepted. The possible omission of /thîi/ shows that /thîi/ is not a noun but a preposition.

In sum, the Mid-Ratanakosin data displayed new functions of /thîi/: a relative clause marker, a complementizer, a nominalizer and a preposition.

16.4.4. Summary of the functions of /thîi/

In this section, all functions of /thîi/ from the Sukhothai period to the present time will be listed for clarity.

(i) */thîi/ as a simple noun.* Here, /thîi/ occurs by itself or can be modified by noun, an adjective or a demonstrative for example, /thîi din/ (a piece of land), /thîi plàaw/ (a vacant piece of land), /thîi nîi/ (this land). The use of /thîi/ as a simple noun prototypically denoting a piece of land, land or place is found in all periods studied.

(ii) */thîi/ as a class noun.* In this usage, /thîi/ does not convey the meaning of 'land'; rather, it designates the location for a certain action. This function differs from that as a simple noun in that it is followed by a verb or a verb phrase, for example, /thîi kèp khɔ̌ɔŋ/ 'place for keeping things'. In this function, /thîi/ may occur alone or in apposition to the preceding noun. This usage is found in all periods.

(iii) *The /thîi/ compound.* The /thîi/ compound does not denote the location but a person, a state or an instrument, for example, /thîi prà? chum/ 'a committee', /thîi chìp thîi hǎay/ 'peril', /thîi yép krà?dàat/ 'a stapler'. This usage is frequently found in our data from the Mid-Rattanakosin period and modern Thai, where /thîi/ carries a wide range of meanings, eg. a person, as in /thîi phuîŋ/ 'a patron', an instrument, as in /thîi yép krà? dàat/ 'a stapler'. Also, in these periods, some /thîi/ compounds are found to function as discourse makers such as //thîi/ thɛ́ɛ/ 'in fact'. It can be said that in the latter two periods the /thîi/ compounds /thîi/ has lost its meaning of 'land'. But such /thîi/ compounds rarely occurred in the Sukhothai data where they signified a situation or state, for example, /thîi chip thîi hǎay/ 'peril'.

(iv) */thîi/ as a preposition.* Data from all periods show that /thîi/ occurs before a locative noun or a place name. /thîi/ in these usages may be analysed as a preposition or a noun. In the Sukhothai period, it was not a preposition but a noun. In the Mid-Rattanakosin period and modern time, it has become a preposition linking a locative noun as well as non-locative noun to the preceding noun or verb.

(v) */thîi/ as a relative clause marker and a complementizer.* Although the function of */thîi/* as a relative clause marker was found to start in the Sukhothai period, it is argued here that /thîi/ developed into a full relative clause marker in the Mid-Ratanakosin period. As a relative clause marker it has been found with high frequency since Rama V period, and at present, it can be found in any one-hundred word passage.

The /thîi/ noun complement was also found first in the Mid-Ratanakosin period frequently occurred after the abstract head noun such as /kaan/ (see 29d). These occurrences are proposed to be the origin of the /thîi/ nominals.

As for the /thîi/ verb complement, modern Thai data show much more occurrences than those in the Mid-Ratanakosin period.

(vi) */thîi/ as a nominalizer.* From the data, the /thîi/ nominalizer first occurred in the Mid-Ratanakosin period[7] and since has been found used with a considerably high frequency. The /thîi/ nominal occurs as a subject of the verb.

(vii) */thîi/ as a classifier.* My data show that this function of /thîi/ appears only in modern Thai.

(viii) */thîi/ as an ordinal numeral marker.* /thîi/ before a numeral was found first in the Mid-Ratanakosin period.

Table 16.4.4-1 is a summary of the functions of */thîi/* in the four periods under study.

---

7   An unpublished study of emergence and development of nominalization in Thai by Prasithrathasint (1994) showed that a /thîi/ nominal occurred during the time of Rama I to Rama IV. Her study confirms that the syntactic development of /thîi/ as a nominalizer did not occur earlier than the Ratanakosin period.

TABLE 16.4.4-1: OCCURRENCES OF NINE FUNCTIONS OF /thîi/ IN THE FOUR PERIODS

Function/ Periods	1	2	3	4	5	6	7	8	9
Sukhothai	√	√-	√-						
Ayutthaya	√	√	√-						
Mid-Ratanakosin	√	√	√	√	√	√	√		√
Modern Thai	√	√	√	√	√	√	√	√	√

1 = a simple noun   4 = a preposition   7 = a nominalizer
2 = a class noun   5 = a relative clause marker   8 = a classifier
3 = a compound   6 = a complementizer   9 = a numeral marker
√- rarely occurs

16.5. A COMPARISON OF A GRAMMATICALIZATION PATHWAY OF /thîi/ AND A HISTORICAL DEVELOPMENT OF /thîi/

In this section, a brief summary of the grammaticalization pathway of /thîi/ given by Bisang (1996) will be given first followed by a proposed historical development of /thîi/. In the last sub section a comparison of the two will be made.

16.5.1. Bisang's grammaticalization pathway of /thîi/

Bisang (1996) used the term 'pathways of grammaticalization' to describe the possible transitions from one word category to another. His study is a synchronic study and for him, the transitions may coincide with the historical developments in several cases. It is the purpose of this section to see how much of the coincidence there is in the case of /thîi/.

Bisang (1996: 555) gave three types of pathways of grammaticalization for nouns. The first is a pathway between nouns and classifier for which he proposes two subtypes:

N → CN (class noun)   → Q (quantifier) → CL (classifier) and N → Q → CL. The second type of pathways of grammaticalization for nouns illustrates the transition from nouns to conjunctional nouns or relative markers. Bisang proposed N → CN → Nom (nominalization) → CONJN (conjunctioner noun) or to REL (relative marker). The third type of pathways of grammaticalization for nouns shows the transition from nouns to conjunctional nouns or to demonstrative adverbials. Bisang gave N → CN → RELN (relational nouns) →CONJN or to DEMA (demonstrative adverbials). Since /thîi/ is an example Bisang gave for the second type of pathways of grammaticalization, I will therefore not talk about the first and the third types any further.

Bisang (1996: 557) gave an example of /thîi/ as a noun in a verb compound /kin thîi/ 'take up space'. According to him /thîi/ is rarely used as a noun in Thai. This might be a misunderstanding due to a lack of /thîi/ as a noun in the written data which I have already made the observation (see 3.1). In fact, /thîi/ as a noun is commonly used in everyday spoken Thai.

Bisang proposed that /thîi/ as a nominalizer occurred as an extension of a class noun. That is to say, instead of having a noun, a verb of a verb phrase as its attribute, /thîi/ takes a clause or a sentence as an attribute instead. /thîi/ then becomes a nominalizer. He gave the following as an example of /thîi/ in the function of a nominalizer (Bisang 1996: 559):[8]

(31)   thîi   khǎw tham nǐi   mâj dâaj phǒn
        Nom he   do   here NEG bear fruit
        'That he did it is of no use.'

From a nominalizer, /thîi/, according to Bisang, can either develop to a conjunctional noun or a relative marker. By conjunctional noun, Bisang meant a complementizer or an adverbial subordinator. His examples (Bisang 1996: 550) for a conjunctional noun and a relative marker are given here:

(32)   phǒm jindii thîi   khun maa hǎa
        I   beglad CONJN you   come see/visit
        'I'm glad you come to see me.'

(33)   còdmǎaj thîi phǒm jàag-cà   khǐan hâj khun
        letter REL I   want write COV. give you
        'The letter which I wanted to write to you.'

Here in the first example, /thîi/ is a complementizer of a verb complement. It can be seen therefore that according to Bisang's grammatical pathway of /thîi/, the transition line is from a noun to a class noun, to a nominalizer and then to a conjunctional noun or a complementizer and a relative marker. The following diagram is mine illustrating Bisang's transition of /thîi/:

thîi   ⟶   thîi   ⟶   thîi   ⟶   thîi CONJN (complementizer)

N   CN   NOM   thîi REL

My study of a historical development of /thîi/ shows that there is a reverse order of nominalizers and complementizers/relative markers as will be discussed below (see 5.2)

Bisang did not mention /thîi/ as a preposition, a classifier or a numeral marker. It is likely that his written data lacked the evidences for /thîi/ in these functions. Besides, Bisang did not mention a /thîi/ compound although he gave an example of /kin thîi/ 'to take up room/space' as a 'VO compoun'.

16.5.2. Historical development of /thîi/

Table 16.4.4-1 illustrating the nine functions in the four periods shows that /thîi/ as a simple noun, a class noun and a compound noun occurs in every period. However, the distributions of these three types of /thîi/ differ. While /thîi/ class nouns and /thîi/ compounds occurred commonly in the Mid-Ratanakosin and Modern Thai period, they occurred rarely in Sukhothai. In the Ayutthaya period, although /thîi/ class nouns occurred frequently, /thîi/ compounds were rare. These distributions therefore illustrate the gradual shift from a /thîi/ simple noun to a /thîi/ compound. Semantically, this also shows a shift from a concrete meaning of /thîi/ as 'land' to a generalized meaning of /thîi/ as person, instrument, or an abstract meaning as a discourse marker.

---

8   The transcription in Bisang's examples follows what was given in his article.

Based on the data of the four periods, it is seen that /thîi/ as syntactic markers, that is, a relative clause marker, a complementizer, a nominalizer[9] and a preposition appeared first in the Mid-Ratanakosin period. The complementizer seemed most likely to begin to form itself in the Sukhothai period where the /thîi/ class noun modified the preceding noun as a noun in apposition. In the Mid-Ratanakosin period, the study reveals that in Rama IV data, the /thîi/ noun complement often occurred after the abstract head noun /kaan/ or /sìŋ/. This abstract head noun could be omitted or in other words, the /thîi/ noun complement could be headless. Observe that this is possible only with /kaan/ or /sìŋ/. Such a headless noun complement most probably gave birth to the /thîi/ nominalizer which has come into a wider use in the reign of King Rama V and later on. It is also observed that the antecedent nouns occurring far apart from their /thîi/ relative clauses were often found in Rama IV data. This made these relative clauses similar to the /thîi/ nominal construction and may help accelerate the use of a /thîi/ nominal.

From my data, /thîi/ as a relative marker occurred in the Mid-Ratanakosin period. Also, it is claimed that /thîi/ as a preposition also appeared at this time. This is supported by the fact that no evidence was found for the syntactic functions of /thîi/ in the Ayutthaya data. Thus, the appearance of a preposition /thîi/ and a relative clause of /thîi/ in the Sukhothai period is doubtful and the interpretation given in this article that they are occurrences of class noun is more likely.

The data in the Mid-Ratanakosin and Modern Thai periods illustrate that among the three relative markers, /ʔan/, /sûŋ/, and /thîi/, /thîi/ has become the most common relative marker. As has been said before, /thîi/ as a relative marker can be found in any one hundred-word passage of the modern time.

Lastly, /thîi/ as a classifier seems to be the most recent development of /thîi/. The data shows evidence of /thîi/ classifiers only in Modern Thai.

Below is a diagram that summarizes the chronological occurrences of /thîi/.

thîi		thîi		thîi		thîi		thîi		thîi
Simple	→	Class noun	→	Compound	→	Complementizer/	→	Nominalizer	→	Classifier
noun				noun		Relative marker		/ Preposition		

16.5.3. /thîi/ as an ordinal numeral marker

Table 16.4.4-1 shows that there was no occurrence of /thîi/ as an ordinal numeral marker in the Sukhothai or Ayutthaya period. It first appeared in the Ratanakosin period. K. Wulff (1934, cited in Egerod, 1976) in giving a list of Chinese and Thai words as evidences for a close relationship between Thai and Chinese, mentioned two Ancient Chinese words: **di** 'place' and **diei** 'number one' (the gloss for 'one' in a second word may probably be a convenient way for Wulff to convey the meaning of diei as a numeral). These two words share the same proto tone C2 which is equivalent to Proto Tai tone B2. In modern Chinese, **di** and **diei** have developed into a homophonous word /ti⁴/ (Prapin Manomaivibool, personal communication). The characters for the two words are still kept and thus, present a good evidence for the existence of two separate words in an earlier time.

In modern Thai as can be seen /thîi/ 'land' and /thîi/ 'ordinal numeral marker' are homophonous and homographic. There are at least two questions in connection with /thîi/ 'land' and /thîi/ 'ordinal numeral marker'. First, whether these two /thîi/s are two words borrowed from Chinese at different times. Evidences for saying that they were borrowed at different periods are from the fact that in Sukhothai and Ayuthaya periods, data do not show any occurrences of /thîi/, a numeral marker. It was first found in the Ratanakosin period. Also, the fact that /thîi/ 'a numeral marker' shares the same vowel as /thîi/ 'land' should prove they were borrowed at different times, otherwise /thîi/ 'a numeral marker' should have shown a

---

9   See also footnote 7.

different vowel. It is most likely that the numeral marker was borrowed late after **di** and **diei** have already merged into /ti⁴/ in Chinese. However, a second question can be posed: a numeral marker might not be borrowed from Chinese but developed from /thîi/ 'land' in the Ratanakosin period. To decide on one or the other needs a further study. Suffice it to note here that in most Black Tai dialects (Theraphan Luangthongkhum, Personal communication) and also in Shangsi Zhuang (See 6.2), there are two different words for land and a numeral marker while some other Tai dialects show one homophonous words for example, a Lao dialect in Mueang Hiam (See 6.1).

Since there is still a question whether /thîi/ as a numeral marker is a borrowed word or not, I decide not to put it in the line of development in the diagram above.

16.5.4. A comparison of a grammaticalization pathway and a historical study of /thîi/

Bisang (1996) stated that pathways of grammaticalization described the transitions of linguistic items from one category or one attractor position to another category or another attractor position. This is not, according to him, the historical development although there may be the coincidence between the two. It is this question of coincidence that will be dealt with first in the case of /thîi/.

If we compare the pathway of /thîi/ and the historical development of /thîi/ given in 5.3, we can see that the grammaticalization transition of noun to class noun and the historical development of a simple noun /thîi/ to a class noun /thîi/ coincide well. However, Bisang did not mention the /thîi/ compounds in his transition line. Here the historical study with the recognition of a /thîi/ compound can reveal the gradual semantic development of /thîi/ from a concrete meaning: land, a piece of land, place, to a more generalized and abstract meaning: person, instrument, state.

After a class noun Bisang gave the intermediate step of a nominalizer before the conjunctional noun or the relative marker. This transition step does not coincide with the historical study where the /thîi/ complementizer (what Bisang includes in the category of conjunctional noun) and /thîi/ relative marker seemed to occur before the /thîi/ nominalizer. Bisang quoted Bybee, Perkins and Pagliuca (1994: 11) that in order to trace the origin of grammatical meaning, one has to look at syntax and morphology of the source construction and not only at the referential meaning of the lexical items. This is what probably occurred in the case of the /thîi/ nominalizer. There are evidences that the /thîi/ nominalizer is more likely to occur because of the syntactic occurrence with the head noun /kaan/ rather than because of the extension of the /thîi/ class noun.

The development of /thîi/ preposition is also lacking from Bisang transition line. In the third type of pathways of grammaticalization, Bisang, however, mentioned the RELN or relational noun after the class noun. This seems to occur also in the case of /thîi/. Thus, in Bisang's second type of pathways of grammaticalization, the RELN step should be included in the transition line.

The last difference in the development of /thîi/,'land' in a grammaticalization process and a historical development is the lack of a /thîi/ classifier. As shown in the historical study, the /thîi/ classifier is found only in the modern Thai data.

16.6. THE EQUIVALENTS OF /thîi/ IN OTHER TAI LANGUAGES

Since /thîi/ 'land' in Thai has shown an interesting development as well as an interesting pathway of grammaticalization, a brief survey of two other Tai dialects are made to see whether there is a parallel development or not. These two dialects are a Lao dialect of Mueang Hiam and a Zhuang dialect of Shangsi.

16.6.1. /thîi/ in Mueang Hiam dialect

The Lao dialect of Mueang Hiam is spoken in a suburb of Luang Prabang. My consultant, Thong Phet Kingsada (personal communication, 2001) gave the following sentences:

(34) a. dek^{22} phuu^{35} *thii^{44}* sɔŋ^{24} mɛɛn^{44} luk^{22} khɔy^{35}

        child   *person*   *two*   *is*   *child* *I*

        'The second child is my child.'

   b. phuu^{35} *thii^{44}* maa^{33} han^{24} mɛɛn^{44} phɔɔ^{44} khɔɔŋ^{24} khɔy^{35}

        person   *come* *see* *is*   *father* *of*   *I*

        'The person who came to see me is my father.'

   c. (siŋ^{44})*thii^{44}* than^{44} waw^{35} maa^{33} khɔy^{35} bɔɔ^{44} sɯa^{44}

        thing   *you*   *say*   *come* *I*   *no*   *believe*

        What you said, I don't believe.

It can be seen from the above examples that this Lao dialect is similar to Thai in that the words for an ordinal numeral marker and for a relative marker are homophonous. However since Mueang Hiam Lao dialect has /din/ and not /thii/ for 'land' as in /mii^{33} din^{22} tɔɔn^{44} nɯŋ^{33} yuu^{4} nɔɔŋ^{24} khaay^{44}/ (have-a piece of land-classifier-one-stay -Nongkhai) '(I) have a piece of land in Nongkhai', one may wonder where /thii^{44}/ a relative marker comes from. Besides, no compound or a class noun with /thii/ equivalent to the Thai /thii^{42}/ is found. The Thai /thîi pə̀ət khùat/ 'an opener' is /ʔan^{22} pəət^{44}/ and the Thai /thîi yùu/ a residence, 'a place to live' is /bɔɔn^{44} yuu^{44}/ in Lao. This adds to the question of where /thii/ a relative marker comes from. A historical study of /thii^{44}/ in this dialect should be taken to reveal the development of /thii/ a relative marker and a numeral marker: which one is borrowed from Thai or both are, or none is. As to the question of whether there are two *thii*'s, the Lao dialect of Mueang Hiam does not show that there are two different words.

16.6.2. /thîi/ in Shangsi Zhuang

Shangsi Zhuang is a dialect of Southern Zhuang spoken in a town of the same name in Guangxi Autonomous region in China. Two words are given by my informant, You Hui Cai: /thow^{31}/ and /thaw^{31}/. The first word, /thow^{31}/ means 'land' as in /kaw^{33} mow^{22} thow^{31} naa^{22}/ (I-have-land-rice field) 'I own a rice field.' Unlike Thai, thow^{31}, does not show any further development. Where modern Thai uses a preposition /thîi/, Shangsi Zhuang does not need it, for example:

Thai:

(35) a. khǎw kin   khâaw thîi bâan   chǎn

        he   *eat*   *rice*   *at*   *house* *I*

        'He ate at my house.'

   b. mii   khon mâak thîi bâan   chǎn

        have *man* *many* *at*   *house* *I*

        'There are many men at my house.'

Zhuang:

(36) a. mən^{22} yaw^{35} lun^{22} kaw^{33} kən^{33} ŋaay^{22}

        He   *stay*   *house* *I*   *eat*   *meal*

        He ate at my house.'

b. yow^{35} lun^{22} kaw^{33} mow^{22} hon^{22} laay^{33}
    stay   *house* *I*   *have*   *man*   *many*
    'There are many men at my house.'

Besides, a complementizer or a relative clause marker are not needed to introduce the embedded clause:

(37) a. mən^{22} hun^{33}how^{22} ta:ŋ^{33} mən^{22} maa^{22} law^{22} lun^{22}
          he   *glad*   *time/when* *they*   *come*   *reach*   *house*
          'He was glad (at the time) when all come back home.'

      b. ʔoŋ^{33} lak^{22} phɔy^{22} ka:ŋ^{22}tɔn^{33} nɛ^{35}thak^{22} ʔaakɔy^{33} kaw^{33}
          clf   *man*   *speak*   *that*   *right*   *brother*   *I*
          'The man speaks, that man, is my brother'

For an ordinal numeral marker, Shangshi Zhuang uses /thay^{31}/ as in /thay^{31} ɬam^{33} tu^{33} kay^{35}/ (numeral marker-three-classifier-chicken) 'the third chicken'. It can be seen thus that the Shangsi Zhuang dialect has two different words for 'land' and 'an ordinal numeral marker' similar to Chinese although it does not show a homophonous word like Chinese. Also, there is no development of either word for other functions.

The above brief surveys of the words for land, a piece of land and an ordinal numeral marker in the two Tai dialects in comparison to Thai shows that the Thai /thîi/ has gone through a unique development. Also, whereas Thai and Laos have only one form, Zhuang shows two distinct words with two distinct forms. A further study however is needed to explain why there are two words of /thîi/ in some Tai dialects and only one word in others.

Another point to be made in connection with 'thii' in three Tai dialects is that Thai has shown a unique development of /thîi/ 'land', while Zhuang does not illustrate any development. It will be interesting to study further whether other South Western Tai dialects share the phenomenon as Thai or as Zhuang.

16.7. CONCLUSION

The historical study above reveals that /thîi/ 'land, a piece of land, place' has a unique and long history in Thai compared to some other Tai dialects. The historical development does not differ much from the grammatical pathway given by Bisang except, significantly, in the area of a nominalizer and a complementizer. The historical study clearly and interestingly shows the gradual semantic development over time. The abstract meaning of /thîi/ has become more frequent in the last two periods. Besides, it is evident that the derivation of /thîi/ into syntactic function words has been late, that is, only in the last two periods. These syntactic function words reveal Thai sentences which have become more complex with embedding and modifying constructions. This is evident in comparison to the Tai dialects such as Shangshi Zhuang.

REFERENCES

Bisang, Walter (1996) 'Areal Typology and Grammmaticalization: Processes of Grammaticalization Based on Nouns and Verbs in East and Mainland South East Asian Languages', *Studies in Language* 20.3: 519-597.
Bybee, Joan, Perkins, Revere and Pagliuca, William (1994) *The Evolution of Grammar: Tense, Aspect, and Modality in the Languages of the World*, Chicago and London: The University of Chicago Press.

Comrie, Bernard (1998) 'Attributive Clauses in Asian Languages: Towards an Areal Typology', in *Sprache in Raum und Zeit*, Tubingen: Gunter Warr Verlag Tubingen, 51-60.

CU Concordance (2000) Department of Linguistics, Faculty of Arts, Chulalongkorn University.

Diller, Anthony (2001) 'Grammaticalization and Tai Syntactic change', in M. R. Kalaya Tingsabadh and Arthur S. Abramson (eds) *Essay in Thai Linguistics*, Bangkok: Chulalongkorn University Press: 139-176.

Egrod, Soren (1976) 'Benedict's Austro-Thai Hypothesis and the Traditional View on Sino-Thai Relationship', *Computational Analyses of Asian and African Languages 6*: 51-60.

Fine Arts Department (1964) *Announcements in the Reign of King Rama V*, Bangkok: Phrachan Publishing House.

Fine Arts Department (1998) *Chumnun Phra Baromrachaathibaay Nai Pra Bat Somdet Phra Chom Klao Cawyuhua Lae Prachum Phra Ratchaniphon Nai Ratchakan Thi Sii*, Collections of King Rama IV's policies and His writings, reprint version by Chulalongkorn University Publishing House.

Fine Arts Department (1998) *Rama V's letters to the Queen*, the 7th reprinted version, Bangkok: Siriwathana Interprint Co.Ltd.

Hurford, James R. (1994) *Grammar: A Student's Guide*, Cambridge: Cambridge University Press.

Kullavanijaya, Pranee (2000) *Phasaa Tai Nuea [Tai Nuea Language]*, Bangkok: Faculty of Arts, Chulalongkorn University.

Luo, Yongxian (1999) *A Dictionary of Dehong, Southwest China*, Canberra: Pacific Linguistics, Australian National University.

National Library of Thailand (1983) *Charuek Samai Sukhothai (Sukhothai Inscription)*, Bangkok: Fine Art Department.

Prasithrathasint, Amara (1994) 'The Emergence and Development of Nominalization in Thai: Evidence of Thai Language Modernization', unpublished research report supported by Chulalongkorn University.

Thai Rath (2001) Thiim Kaan Sueksaa (Education Team), April 17.

The Committee of Thai Historical Documents (1987) *Prawat Kosapan Lae Banthuek Kaan Dern Thaang Pay Farangset [Kosapan Biography and his Memoirs of the Trip to France]*, Bangkok: The Secretariat Department.

CHAPTER SEVENTEEN

BIPOLAR DISTRIBUTION OF A WORD AND GRAMMATICALIZATION IN THAI: A DISCOURSE PERSPECTIVE

Shoichi Iwasaki

17.1. INTRODUCTION

The recent research on grammaticalization in Thai by Matisoff (1991), Bisang (1996), Diller (2001a), and others has greatly advanced our understanding of the diachronic linguistic process in this language. It is found repeatedly that Thai, an isolating language, shows many instances of transformation in which lexical words such as nouns and verbs have come to take on grammatical functions and have become, or are on the way to becoming, classifiers, auxiliaries, prepositions, complementizers, and conjunctions. Drawing on such previous research, this chapter attempts to provide a new perspective on grammaticalization by examining language changes that are observable in discourse and the actual language use of speakers. The discourse perspective is both possible and necessary. It is possible because language changes are always on-going and observable synchronically. It is necessary because changes in linguistic structures do not happen in a vacuum, but rather they proceed through actual deployment in discourse. This theoretical stance echoes the spirit of the 'usage-based model of language' (Langacker 1988, 2000; Kemmer and Balow 2000) and promotes the proposal that it is crucial to seriously take into account the language users' cognitive involvement in discourse in the study of language change. Based on such assumptions, the current paper concerns how discourse profiles of lexical items, or, more specifically, repeated patterns of their placement in discourse, lead to a structural reanalysis and to eventual grammaticalization into function words. The study first calls for attention to a particular distributional pattern of some words, termed here as the 'bipolar distribution of a word,' and presents the theoretical framework in which this pattern can be analyzed. It then examines in detail actual discourse environments for the bipolar distribution of two words, *hây* 'give' and *lɛ́ɛw* 'finish,' using the proposed framework.[1]

17.2. 'BIPOLAR DISTRIBUTION OF A WORD' AND THE THEORETICAL FRAMEWORK

This section first describes the 'bipolar distribution of a word' observable in Thai discourse, and then two theoretical notions, structural reanalysis and layered sentence structure, will be proposed to account for the phenomenon.

Examination of discourse profiles of certain Thai words reveals a pattern which may be termed as the 'bipolar distribution of a word.' In the bipolar distribution, the same word appears at the opposite ends of a linguistic unit (e.g., a sentence) with different functions. The following is intended to show this pattern schematically:

---

1   Parts of this paper were presented at Southeast Asian Linguistics Conferences (SEAL X in 2000 in Wisconsin and SEAL XI in 2001 in Bangkok).

(1-a) X1 ....

............X2

(1-b) X1 ....X2

In (1-a) X is a word, and it appears at the beginning of a unit as X1, and at the end of a unit as X2. As shown in (1-b), X1 and X2 may appear at the two poles of the same unit. When X1 and X2 have an identical shape (which is often the case), the different functions ascribed to them are defined exclusively by their positions. Words which show the bipolar distribution include *hây*, *léεw*, *lɔ́ɔy*, and *dây*. These words are function words of various sorts when they appear at a sentence's periphery, but they may also appear as verbs. Their meaning as verbs are *hây* = give; *léεw* = finish; *lɔ́ɔy* = pass, go beyond; and *dây* = get, obtain. What this means, in light of the general pattern of grammaticalization, is that the bipolarization is a consequence of a process whereby a lexical verb changes into a function word. Below are some examples of the bipolarization pattern.

(3) *hây* 'give' (CB #114: 163)

hây		mɔ̌ɔ	trùat	hây	chây	máy
CAU		doctor	examine	BEN	right	Q

'You had the doctor examine you, right?'

léεw 'finish' (CB #57: 11)

léεw		kûɯn	níi		pay	léεw	lǝǝ
CONJ		evening	this		go	ASP	Q

'And, did you already go (there) tonight?'

lɔ́ɔy 'pass' (CB #90: 45)

lɔ́ɔy		hây	kháw	tɔɔn	nán		lɔ́ɔy
CONJ		give	he	then	D.		MOD

'So, I gave (mangostins) to him then.'

dây 'get/obtain'

(CB   #105: 45)

kɔ̂ lǝǝy		mây	dây	fàak	phîi	nom	pay
so		NEG	AUX	leave	o.sister	(name)	go

'So I didn't get to leave it with Sister Nom.'

(CB #97: 35)

fàak		phîi	nom		mây	dây	lǝǝ
leave		o.sister	(name)		NEG	POT	SFP

'Can't you leave (it) with Sister Nom?'

As noted earlier, the words used in the above examples are not lexical verbs, though they may appear as verbs in some other contexts. According to a general tendency in grammaticalization, it is possible to assume that the words appearing here are later developments from a full-fledged verb. From the synchronic perspective, this situation is what Hopper (1991) calls 'layering' of older and newer functions of words. However, the functions associated with some words are extremely diverse and not simply explained as semantic extensions. Thus, a careful examination is necessary of how some words have come to end up in certain positions in a sentence and have assumed a variety of functions.

Two notions are relevant when analyzing the process of bipolarization as a symptom of grammaticalization: structural reanalysis and the layered structure of a language unit. Structural reanalysis is a process involved in many cases of grammaticalization in general, especially at its beginning stage. It is a process which deletes, adds, or shifts word boundaries, creating a new word and assigning a new function to an old word. Langacker (1977: 65) notes that boundary shift is less common than boundary loss (but more common than boundary creation). But many instances of grammaticalization described here are consequences of boundary shift. From the point of view of a usage based model, the structural reanalysis can be seen as a process in which a sequence of constituents is given a different structure from the originally intended one due to its ambiguous constituent arrangement, which allows different interpretations.

The second notion for the discussion of bipolarization is a view which assumes that a sentence consists of several concentric layers. A general model of layered structure has been proposed by Foley and van Valin (1984), and a specific model for Thai by Diller (2001b). The view adopted in this study is similar to Diller's model. Foley and van Valin recognize three layers of a clause in their model: 'nucleus,' 'core,' and 'peripheral.' The nucleus in most cases corresponds to the predicate; the core includes the subject and object, and the periphery contains secondary arguments and spatio-temporal expressing arguments.[2]

The model in (4) below shows how a sentence might be structured according to this view.

(4) [outer   [mid   [CORE]   mid   ] outer   ]

The organization of layers proposed here is slightly different from the Foley and van Valin model due largely to the fact that the current model takes the larger unit of a sentence as its descriptive scope rather than the more restricted unit of a clause found in Foley and van Valin's work. The 'core' in the current model refers to the most internal layer containing the semantic backbone of the unit. It may take a simple form consisting of a predicate and its associated arguments, or the complex form consisting, for example, of serialized verb phrases. In the 'mid layer' lies sentence modality and discourse salient information, represented by such words as sentence modals and left- and right-dislocated words. With these two layers a sentence expresses a discourse sensitive complete proposition, simple or complex. The 'outer layer' contains elements outside of the proposition. In particular, it hosts discourse markers, or conjunctives, and speech act related sentence final particles and other discourse modality expressions.

A structural reanalysis may occur within the most internal layer, often resulting in the creation of new prepositions and auxiliaries. It may occur across the boundaries between different layers, creating more discourse sensitive markers (e.g., benefactive sentence markers). Also, as discussed in detail later, a word may spill out from one part of a sentence to another part of a different sentence.

17.3. DATA

With the two notions of structural reanalysis and the layered structure of a sentence, the remainder of the chapter analyzes two specific words, *hây* 'give' and *léɛw* 'finish' in actual discourse contexts. Thus, it is in order at this point to describe the data used in this study. There are three major data sets. The first set (identified as CB = Child Birth) consists of 38 telephone conversations. These conversations were recorded at one household for a period of

---

2   Interestingly, a similar layered structural model has been also proposed in traditional Japanese linguistics, most notably by Tokieda (1973) and his students.

time in the late 1980's, during which one female member of the family was expecting a baby and finally delivered a baby boy. As a consequence, many people called to check if she had delivered her baby yet. These are very interactive speech activities. The second data set (identified as PN) is a collection of 21 Pear Story narratives. A speaker reports to an interviewer what they saw in a short video, entitled Pear Story, with only ambience noises but no speech (see Chafe 1980, for descriptions of this project). In this film, a number of participants come and go and participate in different activities involving pears. The narratives are in most part monologues with minimum interaction. The third data set (identified variously) consists of a miscellany of data, including the Northridge earthquake conversation data collected in Los Angeles in 1994 (see Iwasaki and Horie 1998), transcripts of radio talk show from the 1960's and other personal narratives.[3]

17.4. THE CASE OF *hây*

There are eleven different uses of *hây* identified in the data. The functions and their relationship with each other are summarized in Figure 17.4-1. Most of these instances of *hây* appear within the most inner, or core, layer, either at the anterior, posterior, or internal position; but two, (c) and (d) in the diagram, appears in the mid layer.

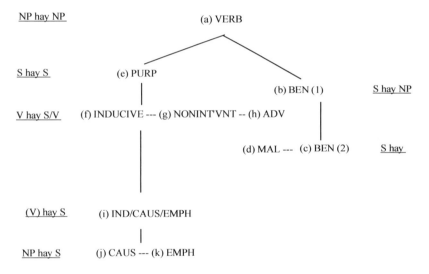

FIGURE 17.4-1: FUNCTIONS OF *hây*

Different functions along the vertical axis have different structural characteristics, as indicated on the left or right side of each horizontal line. Functions lined up on the same horizontal line are identical structurally but different on the basis of their semantic characteristics.

Following a typical pattern of grammaticalization, we assume that all instances of *hây* with grammatical functions, i.e., (b) through (k), are derived from the lexical verb *hây*, (a). When it is used as a lexical verb, *hây* is followed by either a Patient or Recipient NP. See (5).

---

3   Both the 'Child Birth' and 'Pear Story narrative' data were supplied by Supa Chotchoey. The radio talk show transcripts were supplied by Russell Campbell.

(5) VERB (NP *hây* NP)

(**hây** + PAT)	hây	námklɯa		lǝǝy	ná	nâ
	give	saline solution		SAdv	SFP	SFP

'(They should) give you saline solution.' (CB   #106: 12)

(**hây**+ REC)	hây	chán	lɔ́ǝ
	give	me	Q

'(Are you going to) give (it) to me?' (CB #108: 65)

In the development of the functions of *hây*, there are two distinct branches. One is the benefactive branch, (b) through (d), and the other the causative branch, (e) though (k). The benefactive branch will develop the posterior *hây* (i.e., after S), while the causative branch will develop the anterior *hây* (i.e., before S) via the centrally located *hây*.

The pathway for the benefactive meaning, especially from (a) to (b) is a common development across languages. In Thai, this process can be understood as a consequence of clause serialization, which involves a boundary loss, as schematically shown below.

(6) (i) Clause serialization

[[[phǒm sɯ́ɯ nǎŋsɯ̌ɯ] [()hây() lék]]]
I   buy   book   give   (name)
'I bought a book, and gave it to Lek.'

(ii) Reanalysis (boundary loss)

[[[phǒm sɯ́ɯ nǎŋsɯ̌ɯ hây lék]]]
I   buy   book   give (name)
'I bought a book for Lek.'

It is assumed that a clause boundary disappeared as the type of construction shown in (6-i) was used repeatedly. Notice that *hây* was near the anterior of the second clause in (6-i), but its relative position, after reanalysis with the boundary loss is closer to the posterior position in (6-ii). When this process proceeds, two things are bound to happen. First, the lexical meaning of *hây*, i.e., object transfer, becomes weakened, leading to a semantic extension of *hây* for a more abstract situation, as shown in (7).

(7)   BENEFACTIVE (1) (S *hây* NP: *hây* as a 'preposition-like' word)

[[[thambun   hây   khun taa]]]   (CB#59: 31)
make.merit   give   grandfather
'(We will) perform merit making for our grandfather.'

The other development is ellipsis of the Recipient NP after *hây*, leading to a further reanalysis, which pushes *hây* out of the inner core into the mid layer to become a sentence modal.

(8)   BENEFACTIVE (2) (S *hây*: *hây* as a sentence modal)

[[dǐaw ca   [bɔ̀ɔk]   hây]   ná] (CB#93: 38)
     soon MOD   tell   give   SFP
'(I'll) tell you in a moment.'

The structure represented by (8) has also acquired a different function, that of a malfactive meaning, as shown in (9).

(9)   MALEFACTIVE (S *hây*: *hây* as a sentence modal)
    [[[tòp   nâa]   **hây**]]   (Students)
         hit   face   give
    '(I) will slap your face.'

Thus, as seen above, in the benefactive branch, i.e., functions (b) through (d), *hây* moves towards the posterior of the core layer and finally moves out into the mid layer. In contrast, *hây* moves forward in the core layer in the causative branch, i.e., (e) through (k). As seen in Diagram 1, *hây* in the causative branch first develops the purposive *hây*. This is achieved through the process of amalgamation (*apo koinou*). Amalgamation is like a serialization but combines two clauses with one common element as a pivot. In the following schematic representation, the two clauses are amalgamated with *phûan* 'my friend' as the pivot.

(10) (i)   [[[phǒm sɯ́ɯ   nǎŋsɯ́ɯ maa **hây** phûan]   [phûan àan]]]
        I   buy   book   ASP give friend   friend read
        'I bought a book for a friend, and he read it.'

   (ii)   (Reanalysis: Boundary loss + Amalglamation)
      [[[phǒm sɯ́ɯ   nǎŋsɯ́ɯ maa **hây** phûan àan]]]
      I   buy   book   ASP give friend read
      'I bought a book for a friend to read.'

Let us examine an actual example of purposive *hây* in (11).

(11)   PURPOSIVE (S *hây* S)
    [[[fàak thúrian pay **hây** câw ûan   kin]]   nɔy] (CB#90: 169)
    leave durian   go give PFX(nick.name) eat   SFP
    'May I leave a durian (with you) for Fat Boy to eat?'

In this example, *câw ʔûan* is the pivot, with which two clauses are amalgamated. *hây* in this sentence still retains a good part of the meaning associated with the lexical verb *hây* 'give,' because this sentence means essentially that 'I leave a durian with you for the purpose of giving it to Fat Boy.'   However, as the grammaticalization process proceeds, the literal sense of giving will be weakened. Examples (12) and (13) are such cases.

(12)   PURPOSIVE/INDUCIVE (S *hây* S)
    [[shoo   **hây**   kháw   duu]]]   (Earthquake)
    show   give   he   see
    'I will show (something for) them to see.'

(13)   PURPOSIVE/INDUCIVE (S *hây* S)
    [mɔ̌ɔ   kháw [lâw **hây**   faŋ]]]   (CB#114: 170)
    doctor-   he   tell   give   listen
    'The doctor told (something for me) to listen to.'

In these examples, the first event ('show' and 'tell') is done for the purpose of the second event, and *hây* does not have the literal sense of giving some object to someone. It should also be noticed that when the lexical meaning of *hây* gets weakened, the purposive meaning also gets weakened, and in some cases *hây* can also be interpreted as the inducive marker, (f). So the examples above may be interpreted with the inducive sense: 'I will show something, and this action will induce the event of your seeing it' and 'the doctor told me something, and this action induced the event of my listening to it.' The next example of *hây* indicates the inducive meaning more strongly. That is, the speaker's calling Brother Chit on the phone will induce the event of Chit's calling the addressee in return.

(14) INDUCIVE (S *hây* S)   (CB #115: 48)

[[dǐaw [phǒm cǎ   pèklíŋ   hây   phîi chìt kháw   pék]   hây]   ná]
soon   I   MOD phone   give PFX-(name)-he   phone give   SFP
'I will call (him) so that Brother Chit will call you, okay?'

It is a well-known fact that the range of classes of words co-occurring with the target word in grammaticalization will increase over time. Thus, in a later development, *hây* can be preceded by a complement taking verb such as *bɔ̀ɔk* 'tell' *nát* 'make an appointment' *yɔɔm* 'allow' *sàŋ* 'order,' etc. It is also a well-known fact that it is the complement rather than the complement taking verb which is pragmatically more salient in this type of sentence, since complement taking verbs simply classify the type of communication process, while the complement informs the content of communication. In this structure with a complement taking verb, what follows *hây* is no longer a purpose for some other event, but rather a significant event which is, or will be, induced by an inducing event coded by a complement taking verb. In other words, the act of telling something will induce a certain result. Some examples of complement taking verbs preceding *hây* follow.

(15) INDUCIVE (S *hây* S)

kháw   bɔ̀ɔk   hây   thoo   pay   thăam   (CB#117: 14)
he   tell   give   phone go   ask
'He told me to call and ask.'

cà   yɔɔm   hây   klàp   pay   (earthquake)
ASP   allow   give   return go
'(They) would allow (us) to go back (to our rooms).'

mɔ̌ɔ   nát   hây   pay   ʔìik   lέεw   lǐ (CB#114:
                                                                          11)
doctor make.appointment give   go   again   ASP   Q
'Did the doctor make an appointment for you to go (to see her) again?'

There are two minor extensions of the inducive type of *hây* : non-interventive *hây* (g), and adverbial *hây* (h). With the non-interventive *hây*, the second event has a propensity to occur, and the first event is simply a process leading to the second event, as shown in (16) below. With the adverbial *hây*, the second part is a state which will be induced.

(16) NONINTERVENTIVE (S *hây* S)

tɔ̂ŋ   rɔɔ   hây   pùat   thɔ́ɔŋ   (CB#94: 23)
must   wait   give   hurt   stomach
'(You) have to wait till you have a contraction.'

(17) ADVERBIAL (S *hây* V)

    duu   hây   ríaprɔ́ɔy   (CB#58: 14)

    see   give   complete

    '(After) you finish seeing her, . . .'

A more significant development of *hây* is the development of the causative and emphatic *hây*. Both types of *hây* appear at the beginning of the inner layer.

(18) CAUSATIVE (NP *hây* S)

    hây   châŋ-   kháw   thamŋaan   (CB#114: 115)

    give   worker   he   work

    '(I will) have workers work.'

(19) EMPHATIC (NP *hây* S)

    hây   sòŋ   khàaw   maa   (CB#114: 183)

    give   send   news   come

    'Send us the news.'

Emphatic *hây* simply adds force to the following verb and can be omitted without altering any of the propositional meaning of a sentence. The causative meaning of *hây* is already detectable in some cases of the inducive *hây*. The importance of the inducing event becomes substantially weak as the saliency of the induced event becomes stronger, and the inducing event finally is no longer expressed.

    In the next excerpt, *hây* appears in two speakers' turns. This example indicates how structural reanalysis may proceed in actual discourse context.

(20) INDUCIVE/CAUSATIVE (S *hây* S)   (#CB106: 34-35)

    34A: kháw   bɔ̀ɔk   hây   laa   khrûn   wan

            she   tell   give   leave   half   day

            'She told me to request to leave work early.'

→   35 B: ʔɔ̌ɔ   châŷ   hây   maa   yùu   ka   nɔ́ɔy

            oh   yes   give   come   stay   with   (name)

            'Oh,   yes. So that you can stay with Noy.

Speakers A and B are sisters and they have another sister C. B is pregnant. In line 34, A uses the inducive *hây* with the complement taking *bɔ̀ɔk*. This sentence means that C told A to make a request so that she (A) could leave work early in order to assist Speaker B when she (B) goes to deliver her baby. Now on line 35, Speaker B reports that C also told her (B) that if A leaves work early she (A) can come to take care of her (B's) child at home when B goes to the hospital. Notice that line 35 conceptually includes Sister C as a producer of a sentence 'maa yùu ka nɔ́ɔy', but a noun phrase referring to C did not appear in the sentence. That is, structurally *hây* now appears at the beginning of a sentence, and simply signals that what follows is some event that is induced.

    Another clue to the process of obtaining the causative *hây* may be found in example (21). In this utterance, the inducing event of ordering is first expressed in a separate sentence, *kháw sàŋ ʔaw wáy* 'he ordered me,' and then the complement headed by *hây* is added as an independent segment. It is possible to analyze this *hây* as the inducive *hây*, or as the causative *hây*. This is part of the stage identified as (i) in Figure 17.4-1. These two possibilities for analysis are not only important for analysts, but significant for users of the language who assign a different structural analysis. In other words, this type of ambiguous situation will bring about a change in grammatical structure and the birth of new functions.

(21) INDUCIVE/CAUSATIVE (S *hây* S)   (CB #114: 47)

[[[kháw	sàŋ]	?aw wáy]]	[[hây	bɔ̀ɔk	kàp	payabaan	yaŋ	ŋíi]]]
he	order	ASP	give	tell	with	nurse	way	this

'He ordered me to tell the nurse this way.'

The next is a more extended discourse segment which also shows a possible trace of the development of the causative *hây*.

CB #114

16:B	léɛw	tɔn-níi	pay	trùat	thîi	khiinǐk	khaw-níi	kɔ̂
	CON	now	go	examine	at	clinic	Time this	HP

	trùat	?ik	thii	nùŋ	kháw	kɔ̂	lǝǝy	bɔ̂ɔk wâa
	examine	again	CLS	one	he	HP	CONJ	tell say

	nîa	dǐaw	khɯɯn	nía	hây	pay	sǎam	thûm
	DM	ADV	evening	this	give	go	three	hour

17:A	pay	nɔɔn	lǝǝy
	go	sleep	SAdv

18:B	sǎam	thûm	kwà	kwàa	hây	pay	nɔɔn
	three	hour	over	over	give	go	sleep

	léɛw	hây	bɔ̀ɔk	pùat	thɔɔŋ	pen	?aray	yaŋŋía
	CONJ	give	tell	hurt	stomach	be	what	SFP

	tè	ciŋ	ciŋ	?em	yaŋ	mây	pùat	lǝǝy
	but	real	real	(name)	yet	NEG	hurt	SAdv

	lakhɔɔn	lakhɔɔn	sǒŋsǎy
	act	act	I.think

19:A	hây ...	hây	bɔ̀ɔk	pùat	thɔ́ɔn
	give	give	tell	hurt	stomach

20:B	?ǝǝ	hây	bɔ̀ɔk	wâa	pùat	thɔ́ɔn	?aray	yaŋŋía
	INJ	give	tell	say	hurt	stomach	what	SFP

	kháw	ca	hây	?ɔ̀ɔk	phrûŋníi
	he	MOD	give	deliver	tomorrow

21:A	kháw	ca	<u>hây</u>	ʔɔ̀ɔk	phrûŋníi	
	he	MOD	give	deliver	tomorrow	

22:B	ʔəə					
	INJ					

23:A	kháw ca	ʔaw	ʔɔ̀ɔk	lɔ́		
	heMOD	take	deliver	Q		

24:B	ʔəə	kháw	<u>hây</u>	ʔem	ʔɔ̀ɔk	phrûŋníi	ŋay
	INJ	he	give	(name)	deliver	tomorrow	SFP
25:A	ʔəə						
	INJ						

(English translation)

16:B Then I went to the clinic to have them check me.

Now they checked it again.

So they said I would go there tonight at 9 PM.

17:A To stay there.

18:B Around 9 PM (they told me) to stay there

and (they told me) to say I have a contraction, or something like that.

but actually I don't have a contraction yet

Fake, fake, I think.

19:A (They told you) to say that you have a contraction?

20:B Yeah. (They told me) to tell them I have a contraction, or something like that.

They would have me deliver (the baby) tomorrow.

21:A They will make you deliver tomorrow?

22:B Yeah.

23:A Will they induce labor?

24:B They will make me deliver the baby tomorrow, you see?

25:A Yeah.

In the last line of 16, Speaker B sets up a speech quotation environment with *bɔ̀ɔk* 'tell.' Here, the doctor's act of 'telling' will induce an event of the speaker's 'going there at 9 PM.' Notice, however, that in the subsequent discourse other induced events are also expressed, 'going to sleep (in the hospital)' (line 18) and 'telling the nurse that you have a contraction' (lines 18-20). What needs to be emphasized here in these subsequent cases is that there is no explicit verb indicating the inducing event of 'telling,' making *hây* the first element in the sentence. That is, conceptually, each event can be understood as an event induced by the doctor's act of telling (i.e., the doctor told me to do …), but structurally the act of telling is not expressed and thus takes the form of a causative sentence. Such an ambiguous context is required for the structure to change.

This section has examined how the lexical verb *hây* 'give' develops various functions. Two branches of development which cause the bipolar distribution of this word were identified. Examination of actual discourse contexts clarified how some ambiguous situations lead to a reanalysis of this word. The development of different functions happen in most cases within the core of the sentence structure, but two functions, (c) and (d) in Figure 17.4-1 appeared when the word *hây* crossed the layer boundary and settled in the mid layer.

17.5. THE CASE OF *lɛ́ɛw*

The previous section examined the case of *hây* and analyzed mostly how a word may acquire different functions as it moves to the edge of the core layer. This section will consider the case of *lɛ́ɛw* and show that structural reanalysis may sometimes occur across a sentence boundary. More particularly, the *lɛ́ɛw* which appears toward the end of a sentence may be reanalyzed as an element at initial position of the following sentence. This process transforms the aspectual *lɛ́ɛw* into a discourse conjunctive *lɛ́ɛw*. First observe different functions of *lɛ́ɛw*.

(22)   Main Verb[4] (constructed)

lɛ́ɛw						rɯ	yaŋ
Finish						or	not yet

'Have you finished yet?'

(23)   Aspectual Auxiliary (Pear Story #19)

kháw						kɔ	thɨ̆ip	pay	lɛ́ɛw
He						HP	kick	go	ASP

'He has already gone with the bike.'

(24)   Pragmatic Particle (constructed)

taay	lá!?
die	PP

'Oh, my!'

(25)   Discourse Conjunctive (Typhoon Narrative, p. 10)

fǒn	man	kɔ̂	tòk	yàaŋ	nàk	lǝǝy
rain	it	HP	fall	ADV-	heavy	SA

lɛ́ɛw	chán	kɔ̂	wâa
CONJ	I	HP	think

ʔé	thammay	fǒn	màn	thɨ̆ŋ	tòk	phǐpòkkáti
uhm	why	rain	it	reach	fall	unusually

'It was raining very hard.

And I thought,

Uhm, why is it raining unusually (hard)?'

---

4   In Lao, *lɛ́ɛw* still functions as a full verb, which can be followed by the homophonous auxiliary as in *lɛ́ɛw lɛ́ɛw* (Carol Compton and Anthony Diller, personal communication, May 7th, 2000.)

(26)   Noun Phrase Conjunctive (Radio Talkshow #E from 1959-61)

yêɛk	ʔɔ̀ɔk	pen	khwaam	rák	dwây	hŭacay
divide	AUX	as	NOM	love	with	heart

lɛ́	khwaam	rák	dwây	samɔ̌ɔŋ
CONJ	NOM	love	with	head

'(We can) divide (love into) love with the heart and love with the head.'

Developments (22) through (24) will be described first. Though archaic to many speakers, *lɛ́ɛw* may still appear as a main verb. The change from a main verb meaning 'finish' to a completive aspectual auxiliary is well attested in many languages of the world (Bybee et al. 1994; Matisoff 1991: 436-7). Auxiliarization, a typical grammaticalization process for verbs in Thai (e.g., Matisoff 1991), is a result of verb serialization. That is, when *lɛ́ɛw* appears frequently after another verb to indicate that an action has completed, its full status as a verb becomes weakened. When *lɛ́ɛw* loses its verbal meaning, it moves out of the core layer and becomes a part of the mid layer appearing after the core. The layered structure is presented again below for review.

(27)   [outer   [mid   [CORE]   mid   ] outer   ]

When *lɛ́ɛw* appears in the mid layer frequently enough, it becomes susceptive to being reanalyzed as an element of the outer layer and becoming a sentence final particle. In fact, as *lɛ́ɛw* has acquired this pragmatic function, its phonological shape has been reduced to *laʔ/láʔ* (Cooke 1989: 11). In other words, an element of the mid layer attaches itself and settles in the outer layer.

Development from (25) to (26) can be explained as a functional extension from a clause conjunction to a nominal conjunction. This direction of development is supported because the former is realized either as the phonologically full form *lɛ́ɛw* or the reduced form *lɛ́ʔ*, while the latter appears only as the reduced form.

The above description of possible developments of functions associated with *lɛ́ɛw* produces two separate paths associated with this word.

(28)   Grammaticalization Paths for *lɛ́ɛw*

(a)   Verb > Aspect > Pragmatic particle
(b)   Discourse conjunctive > Noun phrase conjunctive

However, it is not immediately clear how these two pathways are related. It is proposed here that the discourse conjunctive developed from the aspectual function, so the proposed complete grammaticalization paths for this word can be summarized as follows:

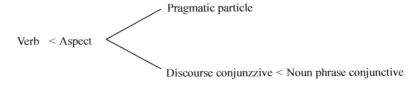

FIGURE 17.5-1: OVERVIEW OF GRAMMATICALIZATION PATH FOR *lɛ́ɛw*

Notice that the position of *lɛ́ɛw* in the pathway, Verb < Aspect < Pragmatic particle, is posterior, while it changes to anterior when the Aspectual *lɛ́ɛw* develops into the discourse conjunctive. This process can only be understood under an assumption that structural reanalysis may apply to units produced contiguously in discourse; that is, *lɛ́ɛw* as an aspectual marker that appears in the mid layer of one sentence may be reanalyzed as an initial element of the following sentence due to its ambiguous position in discourse (cf. Bisang 1996). The development process can still be seen in the way that *lɛ́ɛw* appears in certain cases of discourse, which are demonstrated immediately below.

In the next excerpt, *lɛ́ɛw* appears as the phrase *sèt lɛ́ɛw*. In this case, *lɛ́ɛw* is grammatically an aspectual marker attached to the verb *sèt* 'finish,' but the phrase as a whole serves the discourse conjunctive function of connecting the next utterance to the prior discourse. In other words, *lɛ́ɛw* is participating in dual functions.

(29) (Pear Story # 4)

```
36   (0.5) sèt lɛ́ɛw (0.4)dèk săam khon nîa
     finish  ASP   child    three CLS  TOP
```

```
37.  kɔ̂   mii  khon  nɯŋ kɔ̂  lên piŋpoŋ(0.3) kúk kúk kúk nîa
     HP   exist CLS   one  HP  play ping-pong   bonk bonk bonk TOP
```

'And then, (among) these three children
there is one child who is playing ping-pong ... bonk bonk bonk'

In the next excerpt, *lɛ́ɛw* appears twice in line 48. The first *lɛ́ɛw* appears in the same phrase just examined, so this *lɛ́ɛw* can be analyzed structurally as an aspectual marker. But *sèt lɛ́ɛw* as a whole has a conjunctive function as described above. The same word, *lɛ́ɛw*, appears again on the same line after a pause, functioning this time as the initial element of a sentence. (The sentence, however, was not completed.) Because it is detached from the verb *sèt* 'finish,' it is no longer an aspectual marker, and its conjunctive function is isolated. Here, a transition from an aspectual to a discourse marker can clearly be observed.

(30) (Pear Story #16)

```
48   (0.9) sèt   lɛ́ɛw (0.5) lɛ́ɛw dèk   săam   khon   kɔ̂
     finish       ASP       CONJ child three    CLS    HP
```

```
49   (0.8) dèk   nán     kɔ̂ ..  cuuŋ càkkayaan tɔɔ       pay
     child        that    HP     lead bicycle   continue  go
```

```
50   dèk        săam    khon kɔ̂  dəən    phàan   pay
     child       three   CLS  HP   walk    pass    go
```

'And then, and the three children then.
– that child continues walking with the bicycle –
the three children walk further.'

The next excerpt shows more examples of structurally ambiguous cases.

(31) (PearStory#5)

19 phɔɔ dây tem   krapǎw sɔ̌ɔŋ chɔ̂ŋ lɛ́ɛw
    when get full pocket two   CLS   ASP

    kháw kɔ̂ô .. loŋ   maa
    he   HP   descend come

20 (0.2) kháw mii banday tay   khûn   pay thîi tôn nî aná há
          He   have ladder climb ascend go   at   tree this PP   SLP

21 =>(0.4) sèt   lɛ́ɛw   kɔ̂ .   loŋ-maa
            finish ASP/CONJ   HP   descend-come

    ..loŋ-maa   lɛ́ɛw   kɔ̂   ʔaw
      descend-come ASP/CONJ   HP   get

22 (0.3) .. ʔaw ʔây-lûukpiich nîa   sày loŋ-pay   nay nay takrâa
             get PFX-peach   this put descent-go   in   in   basket

        'When he gets two pockets filled, he then comes down.
        He has a ladder to climb up the tree, OK?
        And then, he comes down. When he has come down, he takes,
        takes the peaches and puts them in a basket.'

Notice the first *lɛ́ɛw* in line 21 can be analyzed as an aspectual marker attached to the verb *sèt* 'finish,' and the sentence may end after *lɛ́ɛw*. However, this *lɛ́ɛw* is immediately followed by *kɔ̂* (an adverbial highlighting particle), and thus can be interpreted as the initial word of the second clause which follows (*loŋ-maa*). The second instance of *lɛ́ɛw* on the same line shows a parallel pattern. Schematically, these instances of *lɛ́ɛw* may be shown as follows:

Verb + *lɛ́ɛw* + *kɔ̂* – V

Two bracketing possibilities are:

[Verb + *lɛ́ɛw*] [*kɔ̂* – V   ]
[Verb] [*lɛ́ɛw* + *kɔ̂* – V]

Now observe the following utterance produced by a female narrator.

(32) (Train Accident)

2   phɔɔ ... <xx>chá?   rótfay
    when <unclearvhearing>   train

    phɔɔ ʔaw   khɔ̌ŋ khûn sàthaanii wátsúwan
    when take   thing up   station   Watsuwan

3   phɔɔ   khûn   sèt   lέεw   rótfay   ʔɔ̀ɔk   càak wátsúwan
    when   ascend   finish ASP/CONJ   train   depart   from Watsuwan.

'When the train … When (they) unloaded the stuff at Watsuan Station …
When (they) inished unloading, he train (started to) leave Watsuwan.'

The *lέεw* in line 3 again has a dual function. What is extremely interesting is that the person (native speaker of Thai) who transcribed this portion actually transcribed it as follows:

(32)' phɔɔ   khûn   sèt   lέεw   lέεw   rótfay   ʔɔ̀ɔk   càak   wátsúwa
       when   ascend   finish   ASP   CONJ   train   depart   from   Watsuwan

This clearly shows that this transcriber recognized the dual function and wrote, most likely unconsciously, *lέεw* twice to match the two functions.

This section has analyzed how *lέεw* may have developed different functions. Being a verb meaning 'finish,' it naturally developed into an aspect marker, then into a pragmatic particle. In this process, *lέεw* appears toward the end of a sentence. The same word with the discourse conjunction, on the other hand, appears at the beginning of a sentence. It as proposed that this development is a consequence of a reanalysis applied across two sentences.

17.6. CONCLUSION

This chapter put forward a proposal that lexical verbs acquire more grammatical functions as they change their positions within or across layers in a sentence, resulting eventually in a bipolar distribution of a word. The layers, as suggested in the chapter, work as machinery that processes and procreates linguistic materials. This idea is similar to that of 'attractor positions' proposed by Bisang (1996), which explains how verbs and nouns acquire different functions in the process of grammaticalization. While attractor positions are concerned with grammaticalization within the core, the layered structure proposed here is concerned with grammaticalization not only within the core but also between the different layers. In addition, some grammaticalization applies inter-sententially, i.e., between the mid or outer layer following the core of one sentence and the initial outer layer of the following sentence. This chapter considered actual discourse environments which promote the process of grammaticalization. As stated at the outset of the chapter, this perspective is essential in understanding language change, since language changes do not happen in a vacuum but are initiated in the actual use of language.

REFERENCE

Barlow, Michael and Kemmer, Suzanne (eds) (2000) *Usage Based Models of Language*, Stanford: CSLI.

Bisang, Walter (1996) 'Areal Typology and Grammaticalization: Process of Grammaticalization Based on Nouns and Berbs in East and Mainland South East Asian Languages', *Studies in Language* 20.3: 519-597.

Bybee, Joan, Perkins, Revere and Pagliuca, William (1994) *The Evolution of Grammar: Tense, Aspect, and Modality in the Languages of the World*, Chicago and London: The University of Chicago Press.

Cooke, Joseph R. (1989) *Thai Sentence Particles and Other Topics*, Canberra: The Australian National University.

Diller, Anthony (2001a) 'Grammaticalization and Tai Syntactic Change', in M. R. Kalaya Tingsabadh and Arthur S. Abramson (eds) *Essays in Tai Linguistics*, Bangkok: Chulalongkorn University Press, 139-175.

— (2001b) 'Nested Operations as Evidence for Thai Layered Clause Structure', paper presented at the Southeast Asian Linguistics Society Conference XI, May, Bangkok.

Foley, William A. and van Valin, Robert (1984) *Functional Syntax and Universal Grammar*, Cambridge/New York : Cambridge University Press.

Hopper, Paul J. (1991) 'On some principles of grammaticization', in Elizabeth Closs Traugott and Bernd Heine (eds) *Approaches to Grammaticalization*, Amsterdams: John Benjamins, vol. 1, 17–35.

Iwasaki Shoichi and Horie, Preeya Ingkaphirom (1998) 'The Northridge Earthquake Conversation: Floor Management and Turn-taking Behaviors in Thai and Japanese', *Discourse and Society* 9.4: 501-529.

Kemmer, Suzanne and Barlow, Michael (2000) 'Introduction: A Usage-based Conception of Language', in Michael Barlow and Suzanne Kemmer (eds), vii-xxviii.

Langacker, Ronald W. (1977) 'Syntactic Reanalysis', in Charles N. Li (ed.) *Mechanisms of Syntactic Change*, Austin and London: University of Texas Press.

— (1988) 'A Usage-based Model', in Brygida Rudzka-Ostyn (ed.) *Topics in Cognitive Linguistic*, Amsterdam: Benjamins, 127-61.

— (2000) 'A Dynamic Usage-based Model: Syntactic Reanalysis', in Michael Barlow and Suzanne Kemmer (eds), 1-63.

Matisoff, James A. (1991) 'Areal Universal Dimensions of Grammaticalization in Lahu', in E. Traugott and B. Heine (eds) *Approaches to Grammaticalization, No. 2*, Amsterdam: Benjamins, 383-453.

Chafe, Wallace (1980) *The Pear Stories: Cognitive, cultural, and linguistic aspects of narrative production*, Norwood, N.J.: Ablex Pub. Corp.

Tokieda Motoki (1973) *Gengo Honshitsuron*, Tokyo: Iwanami Shoten.

CHAPTER EIGHTEEN

DIRECTIONAL VERBS AS SUCCESS MARKERS IN THAI: ANOTHER GRAMMATICALIZATION PATH*

Kingkarn Thepkanjana and Satoshi Uehara

18.1. INTRODUCTION

Directional verbs refer to verbs which denote movements described in terms of their directionality with respect to a **Landmark**,[1] being directed towards or away from it. The landmark is not treated as the source nor the destination of a movement. Rather, the landmark is a known point in the path of movement and it may be construed as a possible source or destination if the movement were to be conceived as starting at one landmark and continuing to another landmark. Any physical entity may function as a landmark in specifying the direction of the movement. On this basis, directions may be specified as towards and away from such entities functioning as landmarks.

The Thai directional verbs to be examined in this paper are: *khɯ̂n* 'ascend', *loŋ* 'descend', *khâw* 'enter', *ʔɔ̀ɔk* 'exit', *pay* 'go', and *maa* 'come'. The verbs *khɯ̂n* 'ascend', and *loŋ* 'descend' denote directions with respect to the sky and the ground, which are salient entities in the environment. The verbs *khâw* 'enter'and *ʔɔ̀ɔk* 'exit' denote directions with respect to an enclosed space. The verbs *pay* 'go' and *maa* 'come' denote directions with respect to the speaker's center of attention. These six verbs can occur as single verbs in simple sentences, and as initial as well as non-initial verbs in serial verb constructions. When they occur as non-initial verbs in serial verb constructions, they may or may not be followed by a noun phrase object. It is generally known that directional verbs across languages are likely to grammaticalize into different types of grammatical markers, such as coverbs, postverbs, adpositions, adverbs, auxiliaries indicating tenses, aspects, and modalities. Most of the grammaticalized markers developed from directional verbs indicate meanings in spatial, temporal and attitudinal domains. This paper aims to introduce another type of grammaticalized marker which the six directional verbs evolve into. We will restrict our attention in this paper to the six directional verbs which appear in the following pattern: NP1

---

*   A part of this paper was presented at the 38th Meeting of the Chicago Linguistic Society, April 26th, 2002, the University of Chicago.

1   According to Talmy (1983) and Langacker (1987), the description of a location of an object involves the recognition of some kind of asymmetrical relation between the object we want to locate and the object with respect to which we locate it. We may recognize asymmetrical relations with respect to size, containment, support, orientation, order, direction, distance, motion, or a combination of these. In describing the asymmetrical relation between entities in a spatial situation, Talmy (1983) borrows the terms 'figure' and 'ground' from Gestalt Psychology (Köhler 1929, Koffka 1935) to label the object to be located (Figure) and the reference object (Ground), whereas Langacker (1987) introduces a different pair of terms, namely, Trajector and Landmark. In this study, Langacker's terms will be adopted.

TV NP2 DV (NP=noun phrase, TV=transitive verb, and DV=one of the six directional verbs), and which indicate a change of location of an entity crucially involved in an agent's action. The change of location of the entity entails that the agent is successful in performing the action. We will adopt the ad hoc label 'directional verbs' for these six directional words occurring as single verbs, and occurring both initially and non-initially in serial verb constructions until we reach section 18.3 of this paper. The sentences below illustrate the six Thai directional verbs which occur in the syntactic environment described above and which are used in this semantic function. It is noted that the directional verbs with this meaning are found to occur more frequently in negative and interrogative sentences than in affirmative, declarative sentences. Therefore, all examples given below are negative sentences for the sake of pragmatic felicity. (See section 18.2.3 for more details.)

(1) *khǎw*   *yók*   *klɔ̀ŋ*   *mây*   *khɯ̂n*
    he   lift   box   not   ascend
    'He tried to lift a box up but was not successful.'

(2) *khǎw*   *kòt*   *pùm*   *mây*   *loŋ*
    he   press   button   not   descend
    'He tried to push the button down but was not successful.'

(3) *khǎw*   *cɔ̀ʔ*   *kamphǽæŋ*   *mây*   *khâw*
    he   pierce   wall   not   enter
    'He tried to pierce the wall but was not successful.'

(4) *khǎw*   *láaŋ*   *khràap*   *sòkkapròk*   *mây*   *ʔɔ̀ɔk*
    he   wash   stain   dirty   not   exit
    'He tried to wash the stain out but was not successful.'

(5) *khǎw*   *khěn*   *rót*   *mây*   *pay*
    he   push   car   not   go
    'He tried to push the car away but was not successful.'

(6) *khǎw*   *taam*   *tamrùat*   *mây*   *maa*   *sàk*   *thii*
    he   call upon   police   not   come   even   time
    'He kept calling upon the police but they did not show up (even once).'

Specifically, this paper aims to:
(a) analyze semantic types of main verbs that co-occur with the six directional verbs functioning as success markers in the syntactic pattern described above;
(b) provide a semantic account which motivates the use of the six directional verbs to indicate success of the performance of the agent's actions;
(c) account for grammaticalization of the six directional verbs into success markers.

Section 18.2 deals with the first two objectives mentioned above. The grammaticalization process of these directional verbs is examined in section 18.3. Section 18.4 concludes the paper. The approach used in this study corresponds to what Traugott (1986) terms 'internal semantic reconstruction', which refers to the study of synchronic senses of a lexical item in order to hypothesize the historical order in which those senses arose. Therefore, the notion of polysemy plays a crucial role in the investigation of the grammaticalization of the directional verbs into success markers in this study.

18.2. MOTIVATION FOR USING THE SIX DIRECTIONAL VERBS AS SUCCESS MARKERS

In this section, we will examine semantic and pragmatic principles which motivate the use of the six directional verbs as success markers. We will first look into the inherent meanings of the six directional verbs when they are used in isolation in section 18.2.1. In section 18.2.2, we will discuss semantic properties of the verb phrases which co-occur with the directional verbs functioning as success markers in sentences. Such verb phrases are called in this paper 'the co-occurring verb phrases' for convenience. Section 18.2.3 will discuss a pragmatic constraint on the occurrence of the six success markers in sentences.

18.2.1. Inherent meanings of the six directional verbs

First, we will examine the semantics of the six directional verbs in detail since it plays a crucial role in accounting for the use of these verbs as success markers. As mentioned above, these verbs conflate motions and directions described with reference to certain landmarks. The conceptual core of the system for describing movement is the path, which usually has a distinctive beginning and end. Paths are the channels along which people move, such as streets, walkways, canals, rivers. They are generally conceived of as linear, one-dimensional entities (Miller and Johnson-Laird 1976: 378). Vertical and horizontal axes provide a conceptual frame of reference for path and directional descriptions. They represent internalized Landmarks anchoring judgements of direction and orientation. The verbs *khŵn* 'ascend' and *loŋ* 'descend' indicate directions of the path with reference to certain salient entities in the environment, namely, the sky and the ground. The former describes the direction of the path towards the sky whereas the latter describes that towards the ground. The effects of gravity enhance the salience of the ground since gravity results in movement towards it (Svorou 1994: 29). The directions of the path by these two directional verbs coincide with the vertical axis. The verbs *khâw* 'enter' and *ʔɔ̀ɔk* 'exit' describe the directions of the path with reference to an enclosure or containment. The former describes the direction of a movement into an enclosure relationship within another entity whereas the latter describes that out of an enclosure relationship.

The directions of the movement encoded by these two directional verbs can be along both the vertical as well as the horizontal axis. In other words, the axis of the path along which the movement traverses is not specified in these two verbs. The verbs *pay* 'go' and *maa* 'come' describe the directions of the movement with reference to the speaker's center of attention, which serves as the deictic center. The former expresses the direction away from the speaker's center of attention whereas the latter expresses the direction towards it. These two verbs are the only pair of directional verbs which are deictic; their interpretation must rely on the speech situation or the context of the utterance in which the two verbs are used. Like *khâw* 'enter' and *ʔɔ̀ɔk* 'exit', the directional verbs *pay* 'go' and *maa* 'come' can describe the direction of the movement either along the vertical or the horizontal axis.

Of all the three pairs of directional verbs, the directions indicated by *khŵn* 'ascend' and *loŋ* 'descend' are considered the most specific and the most constant for people since everybody is in the same gravitational field. These two verbs are thus physically anchored in the same way for everybody. The pair of deictic verbs *pay* 'go' and *maa* 'come' are considered the least semantically specific since the actual directions expressed by them when they are uttered in speech totally depend on the context of situation of the utterance containing them. In principle, they can coincide with the directions indicated by the other two pairs of verbs as long as they describe directions with respect to the speaker's center of attention. Note that the verbs *pay* 'go' and *maa* 'come', which are the least specific, are found to be used the least frequently as success markers in Thai. In short, the directional verbs enable us to identify dynamic locations, which arise from the movement of objects through many locations successively. The next question which we will address in the next section is what semantic properties the verb phrases that co-occur with the directional verbs have.

18.2.2. Semantic properties of the co-occurring verb phrases

As mentioned earlier, a predicate consisting of a transitive verb, its direct object argument and one of the six directional verbs functioning as a success marker expresses the meaning that an agent carries out a certain action which brings about an effect in an entity crucially involved in that action and which results in the change of location of that entity. The affected entity which tends to change its location as a result of the agent's action is not necessarily the entity denoted by the direct object argument although it is likely to be so. For example, the entity which changed the location in (3) above is not the entity named by the direct object, but rather the linguistically unexpressed instrument which is used by the agent in piercing the wall. On this basis, the sentences composed of a transitive verb, its direct object argument, and one of the six directional verbs, can be regarded as the resultative construction. The six directional verbs occurring in this construction are thus qualified to be called 'resultative phrases' or 'resultative predicates' since they indicate the changed location of an entity involved in an agent's action as a result of that particular action.

It is argued here that a verb phrase which co-occurs with one of the directional verbs functioning as a success marker must incorporate the notion of motion in some way. The motion may be transparent as in *yók klɔ̀ŋ* 'lift a box' and *khěn rót* 'push a car'. It may be merely implied as in *kin ʔaahǎan* 'eat food' and *plùuk tônmáy* 'plant a tree'. The notion of motion, which is transparently expressed or implied by the verb phrase, motivates its co-occurrence with one of the six directional verbs in a sentence.

The verb phrases which co-occur with the directional verbs functioning as success markers are semantically characterized by the fact that the agents of the actions named by these verb phrases have certain goals in mind in carrying out the actions. In other words, each co-occurring verb phrase consists of two main components, namely, (1) the agent's intended and executed action, and (2) the agent's further intention that this action lead to a particular desired result. In this case, the agent's goal is to set in motion an entity crucially involved in an agent's action so that the entity will be situated in a new location. There are varying degrees of intrinsicness of the agent's goal to the inherent semantics of the co-occurring verb phrase. In other words, the agent's goal may be weakly implicated or strongly implicated. It is more likely for the agent's goal in the latter case to be attained than that in the former case. Some Thai examples which illustrate the agent's goal which is weakly implicated in the semantics of the co-occurring verb phrase are given in (7)–(18). All of the examples are negative sentences for the sake of naturalness.

(7) *chǎn*   *tii*   *khày*   *mây*   *khɯ̂n*
     I   beat   egg   not   ascend
   'I tried to beat the eggs fluffy but was not successful.'

(8) *chǎn*   *khùt*   *din*   *mây*   *khɯ̂n*
     I   dig   soil   not   ascend
   'I tried to dig a hole but was not successful.'

(9) *chǎn*   *thúp*   *tapuu*   *mây*   *loŋ*
     I   hit down   nail   not   descend
   'I tried to hit the nail down but was not successful.'

(10) *chǎn*   *klɯɯm*   *nám*   *mây*   *loŋ*
     I   swallow   water   not   descend
   'I tried to swallow the water down but could not.'

(11) *chǎn* <u>*hàn*</u>   *nɯ́a*   *mây*   *khâw phrɔ́ʔ nǐaw mâak*
     I   cut   meat   not   enter because tough very
     'I tried to cut the meat but was not successful because it was very tough.'

(12) *chǎn* <u>*cɔ̂ʔ*</u>   *kamphǽæŋ*   *mây*   *khâw*
     I   pierce   wall   not   enter
     'I tried to pierce the wall but was not successful.'

(13) *chǎn* <u>*phàa*</u>   *tǽæŋmoo*   *mây*   *ʔɔ̀ɔk*
     I   cut in half   melon   not   exit
     'I tried to cut the melon in half but was not successful.'

(14) *chǎn* <u>*láaŋ*</u>   *khrâap*   *sòkkapròk* *mây* *ʔɔ̀ɔk*
     I   wash   stain   dirty   not   exit
     'I tried to wash the stain out but was not successful.'

(15) *khǎw* <u>*khěn*</u>   *rói*   *mây*   *pay*
     he   push   car   not   go
     'He tried to push the car away from him but was not successful.'

(16) *khǎw* <u>*lây*</u>   *mǽæw*   *mây*   *pay* *sàk* *thii*
     he   drive away, expel cat   not   go   even   time
     'He tried to drive the cat away from him but was not successful (even once).'

(17) *khǎw* <u>*rîak*</u>   *khonrápcháy* *mây*   *maa* *sàk* *thii*
     he   call   maid   not   come   even   time
     'He tried to call a maid but she did not come to him (even once).

(18) *khǎw* <u>*taam*</u>   *tamrùat*   *mây*   *maa* *sàk* *thii*
     he   call upon   police   not   come   even   time
     'He kept calling upon the police but they did not show up (even once).'

The motion is transparent in the meanings of the verb phrases in most examples above. Each of the co-occurring verb phrases expresses an action with the agent's goal that an entity involved in the agent's action changes its location as a result of his/her action. In each of the examples above except (11) and (12), the entity which was in motion is that denoted by the direct object argument. In (11) and (12), our real-world knowledge suggests that the entities in motion were a knife which was used to cut the meat and a drill which was used to pierce the wall, respectively. These two entities are not linguistically expressed in the sentence. Because we cannot tell from the inherent semantics of the co-occurring verb phrases if the agent's goal is attained or not, the goal is considered the weak implication. The following negated success markers serve to cancel the implication in the co-occurring verb phrases. Notice that it takes the whole verb phrase to convey the meaning that the agent has a certain goal in mind in performing an action. A single verb such as *tii* 'hit, beat' in (7) and *rîak* 'call' in (17) does not in itself convey such an implication.

The co-occurring verb phrases with the strong implication indicate that the agent's intention in setting an entity in motion is very likely to be fulfilled. Some examples of verb phrases with the strong implication are *khlɯ̂an (rói)* 'move (car),' *phlǐk (kràdàat)* 'turn over (paper),' *dàp (thian)* 'blow out (candle),' *cɔ̀ɔt (rói)* 'stop (car),' *pìt (pratuu)* 'close (door),' and *phaŋ (bâan)* 'demolish (house).' These transitive verbs correspond to what Thepkanjana

(2000: 265) called 'alternating transitive verbs', which are defined as transitive causative verbs which have identical intransitive variants. In other words, these verbs can appear in both transitive and intransitive constructions. When these verbs occur intransitively, they may express (a) activities, such as *(roî) khlɯ̂an* '(car) move', (b) processes or inchoativeness, such as *(thian) dàp* '(candle) go out', and (c) resulting states, such as *(kìŋmáy) hàk* '(twig) be broken'. Notice that some of the alternating transitive verbs are either motion or motion-implied verbs whereas some others are not. It should be noted that most alternating transitive verbs alone without their direct object noun phrases can indicate the implication that the agent's goal is very likely to be fulfilled. On the other hand, a non-alternating transitive verb refers to a transitive verb which does not have an intransitive form, such as *chìk* 'tear', *láaŋ* 'wash', *bòt* 'grind', *khâa* 'kill', *tàt* 'cut off', and *phàa* 'cut in half'. In the case of alternating transitive verbs, it is not possible to use their homophonous intransitive forms, which express the resulting states of the agent's actions expressed by the transitive verbs, to confirm the implication that the resulting states are very likely to occur because it will result in obvious redundancy. In the same vein, it is not possible either to use their negated homophonous intransitive forms to cancel such an implication. Examples (19) and (20) illustrate this point.

(19) *chǎn   hàk   kìŋmáy   hàk
     I   break   twig   broken

(20) *chǎn   khôon   tônmáy   mây   khôon
     I   fell   tree   not   collapse

However, it is possible to confirm (only in restricted contexts) and cancel the implication that the agent's intention has been fulfilled only by using appropriate directional verbs functioning as success markers. Only the examples with negated success markers are given below.

(21) *chǎn*   hàk   kìŋmáy   mâ   ʔɔ̀ɔk
     I   break   twig   not   exit
     'I tried to break the twig but was not successful.'

(22) *chǎn*   khôon   tônmáy   mây   loŋ
     I   fell   tree   not   descend
     'I tried to fell the tree but was not successful.'

Notice that the motions expressed in all examples above are of the physical type. It is also possible for the motion to be in the abstract realm as shown in the examples below.

(23) *chǎn khěn*   lûukchaay   mây   khɯ̂n   ciŋciŋ
     I   push   son   not   ascend   really
     'I tried to push my son to success but was not successful.'
     'I tried to push up my son but was not successful.' (Literal translation)

(24) *chǎn yúʔ*   phɯ̂an   mây   khɯ̂n
     I   convince someone to take action   friend   not   ascend
     'I tried to convince a friend to take an action but was not successful.'

(25) chǎn   àan   laaymɯɯ   khɔ̌ɔŋ khun   mây ʔɔ̌ɔk
     I   read   handwriting of   you   not exit
     'I tried to read your handwriting but was not successful.'

(26) chǎn   khít   khrooŋrɯ̂aŋ mây   ʔɔ̌ɔk
     I   think   plot   not   exit
     'I tried to think of a plot of the story but was not successful.'

(27) fàaykháan khôon   ráithabaan   mây   loŋ
     opposition turn upside down   government   not   descend'
     'The opposition tried to overthrow the government but was not successful.'

In sentences (23)–(27), there are nonphysical motions in the upward, outward and downward directions as a result of the agent's actions. The main verbs in (23) and (27), which roughly mean to set something in motion, are used in a metaphorical way which can be metaphorically interpreted as to make efforts to push someone to success and to overthrow (the government), respectively. We can see that the notion of motion is still transparent in both verbs. It is merely transferred to the abstract domain because the main verbs incorporating it are used in a metaphorical way. The situation is different in (24)–(26), in which the main verbs do not seem to involve the notion of motion at all. We would like to argue that metaphoric processes operate in a more complicated way in (24)–(26), which explains why motion is less transparent in these three sentences. In accounting for the metaphor at work in these three sentences, we will draw on the notion of metaphorical concept postulated by Lakoff and Johnson (1980). According to them, metaphor is not just a matter of language. 'On the contrary, human processes are largely metaphorical' (6). Metaphors for them do not refer to linguistic expressions, but to a person's conceptual system, which is metaphorical in nature. This motivates their postulation of the term 'metaphorical concept.' One type of metaphorical concepts discussed in their work which is pertinent to the issue in question is 'orientational metaphors', which give a concept of spatial orientation and which arise from our physical and cultural experience, for example, HAPPY IS UP; SAD IS DOWN; MORE IS UP; LESS IS DOWN. Orientational metaphors play an important role in human conceptualization because most of our fundamental concepts of human beings are claimed to be organized in terms of one or more spatialization metaphors. In (24), the metaphorical concept at work is TAKING ACTION IS UP, which is grounded in our experiential basis that taking an action is moving upward. The metaphorical concept which is operative in (25) is UNDERSTANDING IS OUT, which is based on our experience that if we understand something, we have the impression that the sense of that thing comes out and reaches us. The metaphorical concept at work in (26) is FIGURING OUT SOMETHING IS OUT. This metaphorical concept is based on the physical experience that when we try to come up with or to figure out something, our thinking takes place in our head. When we are successful in figuring it out, it will come out of our head and may be known to other people. In summary, the notion of motion in (23)–(27) arises from metaphorical processes but in different ways. In (23) and (27), the motion arises from the metaphorical use of the main verbs. In (24)–(26), the whole actions expressed by the verb phrases must be understood in a metaphorical way, which gives rise to the metaphorical concepts described above.

Notice that there is a particular direction inherent in the motion of an entity crucially involved in the agent's action. For example, in the egg-beating example in (7), since the eggs became fluffy as a result of the agent's beating them, the direction of the motion of the eggs must be upward. Therefore, it is argued that there must be semantic agreement between the direction of the motion associated with the verb phrase and that inherent in the directional verb functioning as the success marker. This is also true for the cases of pay 'go' and maa 'come' in (15)–(18) repeated here for convenience as (28)–(31), in which pay 'go' and maa 'come' are not interchangeable. However, when the verb phrases in (28)–(31) do not co-occur with *pay* 'go' and *maa* 'come'in the success reading, they do not exhibit any inherent direction. In other words, they do exhibit an inherent direction when they co-occur with the directional verbs *pay* 'go' and *maa* 'come' functioning as success markers.

(28) *khǎw*   *khěn*   *roí*   *mây*   *pay*
      he   push   car   not   go
      'He tried to push the car away from himself but was not successful.'

(29) *khǎw*   *lây*   *mææw*   *mây* *pay* *sàk* *thii*
      he   drive away,expel   cat   not   go   even time
      'He tried to drive the cat away from himself but was not successful (even once).'

(30) *khǎw*   *rîak*   *khonrápchaý* *mây* *maa* *sàk* *thii*
      he   call   maid   not   come even time
      'He tried to call a maid but she did not come to him (even once).'

(31) *khǎw*   *taam*   *tamrùat*   *mây* *maa* *sàk* *thii*
      he   call upon   police   not   come even time
      'He kept calling upon the police but they did not show up (even once).'

As we see here, the motions expressed by the main verbs and the direct object nouns occurring in (28)–(31) do have specific directions. The main verbs in (28) and (29) express the meanings that the agent tried to move the entities denoted by the direct object arguments away from him/her. On the other hand, the main verbs in (30) and (31) express the meanings that the agent tried to bring someone to where he/she was located. The directional verb *pay* in (28) and (29) cannot be replaced by *maa* and vice versa in (30) and (31) as shown in (32)–(35).

(32) **khǎw khěn roí mây maa*
      he   push car not come

(33) *khǎw lây   *mææw mây maa sàk thii*
      he   drive away, expel cat   not come even time

(34) *khǎw rîak   *khonrápchaý mây pay sàk thii*
      he   call   maid   not go even time

(35) *khǎw taam   *tamrùat*   *mây pay sàk thii*
      he   call upon police   not go even time

Notice that the speaker's center of attention in the two deictic verbs is replaced by the agent's in (28)–(31). In other words, these two deictic verbs have lost their deictic function when they are used as success markers. This explains why *pay* and *maa* are not interchangeable in the sentences above. This point will be fully discussed in section 18.3.

18.2.3. Pragmatic constraint on the occurrence of success markers

As seen in section 18.2.2, the verb phrases which co-occur with success markers convey the implication that the agent's intention in carrying out an action has been fulfilled, which entails that the agent has performed an action successfully. In this case, one might wonder why we would need to indicate the success of the agent's performance of an action by combining one of the six directional verbs with such verb phrases in the first place. Is such a success not expressed by default in the verb phrases? We want to argue in this study that those verb phrases in the normal state of affairs imply that the agent's goal in performing an action is attained, or, in other words, that a resulting state is incurred upon an affected entity. However, if the context of situation requires that the fulfillment or nonfulfillment of the agent's goal in performing the action be emphasized or highlighted, we can use the linguistic device of adding one of the directional verbs to the verb phrase in the sentence to obtain such a pragmatic effect. To highlight the success of the agent's performance of an action or the fulfillment of his/her goal in performing an action naturally requires a marked context since those verb phrases by default imply such a success on the part of the agent. According to Givón (1984: 323), the major function of declarative sentences in discourse is to convey new information. If any of the directional verbs functioning as success markers occur in sentences in an unmarked context, they will become redundant and the sentences in which they occur will be infelicitous since they do not provide new information. A marked context enables affirmative sentences with the directional verbs to provide new information, i.e. to emphasize the success of the agent's performance of an action. This 'new' information makes the occurrence of the directional verbs pragmatically appropriate. This explains why the use of directional verbs as success markers is not found frequently in affirmative (as opposed to negative) and declarative (as opposed to interrogative) sentences. Rather, these directional verbs functioning as success markers are more prevalent in negative sentences in which the directional verbs themselves are negated and in interrogative sentences. The negative variant of the declarative sentence is used to convey new information of a very different sort than the corresponding affirmative. In the negative sentence, the normal expectation or the presupposed presupposition, which is in this case the success of the performance of the agent's action, is denied, whereas it is questioned in the interrogative one. Since the negative sentence serves to provide new information and the interrogative one to question backgrounded information, they provide appropriate contexts in which the directional verbs can occur.

18.2.4. Summary

In section 18.2.2, we have investigated semantic and pragmatic principles which motivate the use of the six directional verbs as success markers. We have examined the inherent semantics of each directional verb when it occurs in isolation. The deictic verbs *pay* 'go' and *maa* 'come' are found to be the least specific semantically. We have found that the co-occurring verb phrases convey the implication that the agent's intention in carrying out an action has been fulfilled and that they must incorporate the notion of motion in some way. The motion can be either of the physical or abstract type. The abstract type of motion results from metaphorical processes which can operate either linguistically or conceptually. It is found that there must be semantic agreement in terms of direction between that inherent in the motion associated with the co-occurring verb phrase and that in the directional verb in a sentence. The success markers are found to be prevalent in negative and interrogative sentences because of their pragmatically marked nature. The next section will examine the grammaticalization process which derives success markers from their lexical sources. Some research works on the verbs in other languages which semantically correspond to the Thai directional verbs will be reviewed so that we will get a broader view of the Thai phenomenon being examined.

18.3. GRAMMATICALIZATION OF DIRECTIONAL VERBS INTO SUCCESS MARKERS

We will begin this section by reviewing how the verbs corresponding to the Thai directional verbs have been analyzed in other languages, especially Chinese. The previous analyses of these corresponding verbs in other languages will shed light on the Thai phenomenon under investigation.

18.3.1. Previous analyses of corresponding verbs in other languages

In studying the processes of grammaticalization of nouns and verbs in East and Southeast Asian languages, Bisang (1996) postulates six types of grammaticalized markers or, in his terms, six 'products of grammaticalization' of verbs, namely, resultative verbs, directional verbs, TAM (tense, aspect, modality) markers, coverbs, causative verbs, and conjunctional verbs. Three of the six products, i.e. directional verbs, TAM markers and coverbs, show a high degree of grammaticalization (Bisang 1996: 564). Note that Bisang makes distinctions between resultative verbs, directional verbs and TAM markers. It is found in his examples that the verbs which express directions when they occur in isolation in different languages can be grammaticalized into resultative verbs, directional verbs and TAM marker. Bisang's examples which illustrate resultative and directional verbs are quoted here as below.[2]

Some examples of resultative verbs given by Bisang (1996: 564–566)

(36) *tā   chī   bǎo-le*   (Chinese)
    s/he   eat   full-TAM
    'S/he has been eating his/her fill'

(37) *nó   tìm   du'o'c   vàng   o'   du'o'l sông* (Vietnamese)
    he   look-for get   gold   COV:be-at   down river
    'He found gold in the river.'

(38) *khǎw pìd   pratuu   (mâj)   lon*   (Thai)
    he   close   door   (NEG)   RES:go_down
    'He closed the door.' / ('He didn't close the door.')[3]

Some examples of directional verbs given by Bisang (1996: 565: 566).

(39) a.   *tā   pǎo   shàng   lái*   (Chinese)
        s/he   run   vdI:go_up   vdII:come
        'S/he runs up [towards the speaker].'

    b.   *tā   pǎo   xià   qù*   (Chinese)
        s/he   run   vdI:go_down vdII:go
        'S/he runs down [away from the speaker].'

(40) *kɔət lòːt   coh   cën   mɔ̀ːk*   (Cambodian)
    he   jump vdI:go_down vdII:go   _outvdIII:come
    'He jumps down and out towards the speaker/center of interest.'

Notice that sentence (38) contains one of our directional verbs functioning as a success marker.

---

2   The phonetic transcription, the glosses, and the sentence translation of the Bisang's examples are kept intact in this paper.

3   We would translate this sentence as 'He was trying to close the door but not successful.' This sentence translation implies that the agent has begun the action of closing the door but could not fulfill the task due to some reason. Bisang's translation of this sentence may be interpreted in such a way that the agent did not even begin the action of closing the door at all, which is not the accurate interpretation of this sentence.

Therefore, our six directional verbs functioning as success markers would be categorized as resultative verbs by Bisang since these verbs indicate resulting states of the affected entities involved in the agent's actions as pointed out earlier. These directional verbs are claimed in Thepkanjana and Uehara (to appear) to be a type of resultative predicate in the Thai resultative construction which indicates the change of location of an affected entity crucially involved in an agent's action. On the other hand, Bisang's category of directional verbs actually consists of the directional verbs which are used in their literal sense in the spatial domain only. It can be inferred from Bisang's separation of the resultative and directional verb categories from each other that there is no sense of direction involved in the verb *loŋ* 'go down' which is claimed by him to function as the resultative verb in sentence (38).

It is found that the Chinese verbs which semantically correspond to the Thai directional verbs have been treated in the literature on Chinese linguistics in a similar fashion as in Bisang (1996). Although the verbal constructions in question in Thai are structurally different from those in Chinese since the former are considered serial verb constructions with an intervening object argument whereas the latter are considered verb compounds, both types of verbal constructions in Thai and Chinese are comparable. Both types of constructions are composed of two verbs one of which serves to complement or modify the other. Furthermore, a large number of verbal complements or modifiers in Chinese verb compounds are claimed to add the resultative and the directional meanings to the main verbs, which is also true of a large number of serial verbs in Thai. In light of these facts, a review of analyses of Chinese verb compounds is relevant to the Thai phenomenon under investigation.

In studying resultative verb compounds in Mandarin Chinese, Thompson (1973) distinguishes between resultative verb compounds and directional ones and claims that they are derived by different means. Thompson's category of resultative verb compounds includes those which indicate a change of state or a change of location of an affected entity whereas the directional one includes those with directional suffixes having only a literal directional meaning. Some examples of Thompson's resultative verb compounds with directional suffixes having metaphorical meanings are quoted below (371).

(41) *xiǎng-chulai* 'think-come out' = 'think of a solution'

(42) *míngbai-guolai* 'understand-come past' = 'come to understand'

(43) *tīng-jinqu* 'hear-go in' = '"absorb" what is said'

If we apply Thompson's frame of categorization to the Thai verbal constructions containing directional verbs serving as success markers, most of the intantiations especially the ones with metaphorical meanings would be analyzed as resultative verb compounds. The Thai verbal constructions containing directional verbs used in their literal senses would fall under the directional verb compounds within Thompson's framework of analysis.

In studying the verb-verb construction in Mandarin, Lu (1977) also postulates a distinction between resultative and directional verb compounds in Mandarin. A resultative verb compound is defined as a 'V-V construction in a sentence where the second verb indicates a result caused by the action or the process represented by the first verb' (282). On the other hand, a directional verb compound is defined as a 'V-V construction in a sentence where the first verb indicates the manner of a motion verb and the second the direction in which that verb moves' (292). The former expresses a nonspatial change of the affected entity whereas the latter is used in the spatial domain. Lu also recognizes the third type of verb compound in Mandarin which displays a combination of features of the other two types of verb compound at the same time. The third type of verb compound is thus regarded ambiguous according to Lu. The example below belongs to Lu (1977: 300).[4]

---

4   Tone markers are missing in Lu's examples.

(44) *Ta ba   keren qing   shangqu le*
    he objectmarker guest invite goup   Asp
    'He invited the guest to go up and the guest did.'

Notice that sentence (44) is semantically analogous to the Thai sentences with the directional verbs functioning as success markers especially the verbs *pay* 'go' and *maa* 'come'. Since these Thai directional verbs are argued to be resultative predicates indicating a change of location of an affected entity, it is not surprising that their corresponding verbal constructions in Mandarin are claimed to be both resultative and directional at the same time. If we analyzed the Thai data in this frame, the Thai verbal constructions with the directional verbs used in the success reading would be put in Lu's third type of verb compound.

Yong (1997) is another piece of work which makes a distinction between resultative verbs and directional verbs, or in his terms, resultative verb complements (RVCs) and directional verb complements (DVCs). According to Yong (1997: 3), a large number of RVCs are realized as adjectives. The DVC category can be subclassified into the DVC with literal directional meaning and the DVC with nonliteral or little literal meaning. Some examples of the latter subtype of DVC cited by Yong belong to Teng (1977: 5–6), i.e. *ai-shang* 'love-up=fall in love', and to McDonald (1994: 329), i.e. *xing-guolai* 'wake-across towards=wake up'. In the light of Yong's analysis of Chinese data, the Thai directional verbs functioning as success markers might be categorized as the DVC type.

In summary, all of the works reviewed above aim at classifying verbal constructions consisting of two verbs into discrete types. The two types which appear in all works cited above are the resultative and directional types. All works make a distinction between resultative and directional verbal constructions. Some of them recognize the nonliteral and/or metaphorical uses of the directionals. The frames of analysis used in all of the works which study the comparable verbal constructions in other languages reviewed above are argued to be inadequate to account for the Thai phenomenon under investigation because the Thai directional verbs functioning as success markers arguably express resultative and directional meanings simultaneously. However, the directional meaning may not always be in the physical realm as shown above. These facts of Thai data would not be easy to account for within the previous frameworks of analysis used with data in other languages especially Chinese. In the next section, we will propose a new analysis of the Thai data in light of the findings that we have presented in section 18.2.

18.3.2. Grammaticalization of directional verbs into success markers

In this paper, we will propose a new analysis of the six directional verbs functioning as success markers in Thai. We argue that these six success markers are a 'product of grammaticalization' in Bisang's terms and have as their lexical sources full-fledged directional verbs which conflate both movement and direction. These verbs originally occurred as non-initial, serial verbs in the serial verb construction and have been grammaticalized into success markers. Our analysis is discussed in detail below. To prevent confusion about terminology, we will from now on use the term 'directional verbs' to refer to lexical sources of all grammaticalized forms derived from them. Therefore, the directional verbs, which are fully-fledged verbs, can either occur as single verbs in a sentence or initial verbs in the serial verb construction. We will use the term 'success markers' to refer to the grammaticalized forms of directional verbs which function as success markers in the Thai resultative construction. As mentioned earlier, the paper adopts the approach of studying synchronic senses of a lexical item in order to make a generalization about the historical order in which those senses arose, which is called by Traugott (1986) 'internal semantic reconstruction'.

It is well known that spatial words including nouns and verbs are cross-linguistically an important lexical source of grammatical forms which can be linguistically realized as adpositions, affixes, and case inflections (Svorou 1994: 64). These forms which are developed from spatial nouns and verbs are termed 'spatial grams' (Svorou 1994: 31).[5] These different forms of spatial grams represent different stages on a grammaticalization path and are used in other semantic domains than the spatial one.

According to the principles of grammaticalization set forth by Hopper and Traugott (1993), grammaticalization can be characterized by the following properties.

(a)   Lexical or content words are sources of grammaticalized forms.

(b)   Grammaticalized forms can be free or bound morphemes.

(c)   In some cases, lexical sources of grammaticalized forms and the grammaticalized forms themselves can coexist at the same time in a language, which constitutes a case of polysemy. In other cases, the former can disappear and only the latter remain.

(d)   The process of grammaticalization proceeds along a path which is a unidirectional cline. That is, it goes forward and does not go back, However, the path of grammaticalization does not necessarily reach the complete and final stage, which is typically morphologization of a lexical item into a bound grammatical morpheme.

(e)   Grammaticalization is typically accompanied by certain effects, namely, decategorization and semantic bleaching.

(f)   The grammaticalized forms can exhibit different degrees of lexical and grammatical status. They are not necessarily depleted of all lexical content and become 'completely' grammatical.

Returning to the phenomenon under investigation in this paper, the success markers in Thai synchronically coexist with their lexical sources, which are the homophonous full-fledged directional verbs which can occur in isolation and as initial verbs in the serial verb construction. This constitutes a case of polysemy according to Hopper and Traugott's principle (c). In order to argue that the six success markers in Thai are grammaticalized forms, or 'spatial grams' in Svorou's terms, which are developed from fully-fledged directional verbs, we have to rely on their syntactic and semantic properties since their morphological forms do not change. To find out how success markers differ syntactically and semantically from their lexical sources, we will try taking them out of the sentences in which they appear and combine them with the nouns denoting the entities which are in motion in those sentences to see how acceptable they are as below.

(45) a. *khǎw*   *yok*   *klɔ̌ŋ*   *mây*   *khûn*
        he   lift   box   not   ascend
        'He tried to lift a box up but was not successful.'

   b. **klɔ̌ŋ*   *mây*   *khûn*
        box   not   ascend

---

5   The term 'gram' was first used in Bybee (1986) to refer to grammatical morphemes. This term iconically reflects the typically small phonological size of grammatical morphemes as well as the fact that they are evolved from larger units.

(46) a. *chǎn   yúʔ   phɯ̂an   mây   khɯ̂n*
I   convince someone to take action friend   not   ascend
'I tried to convince a friend to take an action but was not successful.'

b. **phɯ̂an   mây   khɯ̂n*
friend   not   ascend

(47) a. *khǎw   kòt   pùm   mây loŋ*
he   press   button   not descend
'He tried to push the button down but was not successful.'

b. * *pùm   mây   loŋ*
button   not   descend

(48) a. *chǎn   <u>thúp</u>   tapuu   mây loŋ*
I   hit down   nail   not descend
'I tried to hit the nail down but was not successful.'

b. ?*tapuu   mây   loŋ*
nail   not   descend

(49) a. *khǎw   cɔ̀ʔ   kamphææŋ   mây khâw*
he   pierce   wall   not enter
'He tried to pierce the wall but was not successful.'

b. ? *sawàan mây   khâw*
drill   not   enter

(50) a. *chǎn   hàn   nɯ́a   mây khâw   phrɔ́ʔ   nǐaw   mâak*
I   cut   meat   not enter   because tough   very
'I tried to cut the meat but was not successful because it was very tough.'

b. **mîit   mây   khâw*
knife   not   enter

(51) a. *khǎw   láaŋ   khràap   sòkkapròk mây   ʔɔ̀ɔk*
he   wash   stain   dirty   not   exit
'He tried to wash the stain out but was not successful.'

b. *khràap sòkkapròk mây   ʔɔ̀ɔk*
stain   dirty   not   exit
'The stain did not go out.'

(52) a. *chăn*   *àan*   *laaymɯɯ*   *khɔ̆ɔŋ* *khun* *mây* *ʔɔ̀ɔk*
        I   read   handwriting   of   you   not   exit
        'I tried to read your handwriting but was not successful.'

     b. **laaymɯɯ*   *khɔ̆ɔŋ*   *khun*   *mây*   *ʔɔ̀ɔk*
        handwriting of   you   not   exit

(53) a. *khăw*   *khě n*   *roʻt*   *mây*   *pay*
        he   push   car   not   go
        'He tried to push the car away but was not successful.'

     b. ?*roʻt*   *mây*   *pay*
        car   not   go

(54) a. *khăw*   *lây*   *mææw*   *mây*   *pay*   *sàk*   *thii*
        he   drive away, expel cat   not   go   even   time
        'He tried to drive the cat away from himself but was not successful (even once).'

     b. *mææw*   *mây*   *pay*   *sàk*   *thii*
        cat   not   go   even   once
        'The cat did not go.'

(55) a. *khăw*   *rîak*   *khonrápcháy* *mây*   *maa*   *sàk*   *thii*
        he   call   maid   not   come   even   time
        'He tried to call a maid but she did not come to him (even once).'

     b. *khonrápcháy* *mây*   *maa*   *sàk*   *thii*
        maid   not   come   even   time
        'The maid did not show up.'

(56) a. *khăw*   *taam*   *tamrùat*   *mây*   *maa*   *sàk*   *thii*
        he   callupon   police   not   come   even   time
        'He kept calling upon the police but they did not show up (even once).'

     b. **tamrùat**   **mây**   **maa**   **sàk**   **thii**
        police   not   come   even   time
        'The police did not show up.'

Each of the (b) sentences above consists of two major components, i.e. (1) the subject noun phrase which was in motion and changed a location, which is an affected entity in the corresponding (a) sentence, and (2) the negated directional verb, which functions as the success marker in the corresponding (a) sentence. What we were trying to do with the (b) sentences above was to try using the success markers in the (a) sentences as full-fledged directional verbs in the (b) sentences with the noun phrases denoting entities which were in motion in the (a) sentences and see if they were acceptable in that syntactic context or not.

Therefore, it seems that each of the (b) sentences is a part of the corresponding (a) sentence. Some observations can be made based on the examples above as follows.

Some of the (b) sentences are acceptable; some are questionable; and some are not acceptable at all even though the noun phrases denoting the entities in motion are the same as those in the corresponding (a) sentences and even though they moved in the same directions in both (a)s and (b)s. The questionability and unacceptability of some of the (b) sentences above can be accounted for in terms of many factors. In some cases, certain subject noun phrases simply do not co-occur with certain directional verbs, such as in (45b), (46b), (47b), (50b), and (52b). There may be many reasons for the impossibility for them to co-occur. One reason may be that some of the directional verbs are likely to be used as main verbs with the subject noun phrases denoting animate entities which are capable of expressing volition only. The volitional element may be lost when directional verbs evolve into success markers. This explains why some of the (a) sentences, such as (45a), (47a), (48a), (49a), (50a), (52a), and (53a), in which success markers co-occur with inanimate noun phrases denoting the entities in motion, are acceptable, whereas their (b) counterparts, in which the directional verbs are used as main verbs, are either questionable or unacceptable. Another reason for the impossibility for some subject noun phrases to co-occur with some directional verbs may be that some of the directional verbs which co-occur with some subject noun phrases lack object ones. That means some directional verbs can be used with some subject noun phrases without any following direct object noun phrases only in some cases. In some other cases, if the same directional verbs co-occur with some other subject noun phrases, the sentences will become either questionable or unacceptable. It is thus obvious that each of the directional verbs may have idiosyncratic behaviors when they function as main verbs in sentences.

Some conclusions can be drawn from examples (45)–(56). First, although the (a) sentences and their (b) counterparts seem to contain roughly the same motion events, i.e. the same moving entities, the same motions, and the same directions of motions, the success markers in (a)s cannot be readily employed as the main verbs of motion in (b)s. This fact is reflected by the varying degrees of acceptability of the (b) sentences. It also indicates that the success markers in (a)s and the directional verbs in the corresponding (b)s have different syntactic and semantic properties. Even though the success markers in (a)s indicate motions in certain directions, we cannot take them out of their sentences along with the entities in motion and use the success markers and the entities in motion as main verbs and as subjects respectively in (b)s. It is argued here that the success markers in (a)s are grammaticalized forms of directional verbs, which are their lexical sources. In the grammaticalization process, the grammaticalized markers lost some of the properties which are present in the source verbs. This explains why they have different behaviors with regard to their potentiality to combine with various noun phrases denoting moving entities. The second conclusion to be drawn from the data above is that the success markers are not grammaticalized to the same degree. For example, *pay* 'go' and *maa* 'come' are arguably less grammaticalized than the other success markers since the former are more ready to be used as the main directional verbs in (b)s than the latter. This is shown by the acceptability of (54b), (55b) and (56b) and the questionability of (53b), in which *pay* 'go' and *maa* 'come' occur as main verbs. In contrast, the remaining (b) sentences, in which the other four directional verbs occur as main verbs, are mostly ungrammatical or questionable. Furthermore, different instantiations of the same success markers occurring in different sentences can be grammaticalized to different degrees. For example, the instantiations of the success marker *ɔ̀ɔk* 'exit' in (51a) and (52a) are not equally grammaticalized. It is argued that the one in (52a) is more grammaticalized since it is used in the metaphorical domain whereas that in (51a) is used in the concrete one. This explains why *ɔ̀ɔk* 'exit' in (51a) can be the main verb but that in (52a) cannot.

It is argued that the six directional verbs with full verbal meanings are lexical sources of success markers. These directional verbs are located at the starting point of a grammaticalization path. At an early stage, they were grammaticalized into forms which lost the movement aspect of the lexical content of the source verbs and retained only the relational aspect. This is the stage on a grammaticalization path which gave rise to the so-called 'directional verbs', 'directional adpositions', 'directional adverbs' or simply 'directionals' in linguistic literature. We will refer to the grammaticalized forms of directional verbs in which the movement aspect is depleted and in which the directional one is retained as 'directional markers' in this paper. The directional verbs that occur as serial verbs in the serial verb construction are lexical sources of grammaticalized directional markers. The tight link between grammaticalization and serialization is also noted by Bisang (1996: 563). The Thai examples below illustrate the directional markers, which are the grammaticalized forms at this stage of the grammaticalization path. The directional markers are underlined.

(57) *khǎw*   *sòŋ*   *nǎŋsɯ̌ɯ*   *pay*   *lǽæw*
    he   send   book   go   already
    'He already sent the book away.'

(58) *nok*   *bin*   *khɯ̂n*   *yàaŋrɯ́atrew*
    bird   fly   ascend   quickly
    'The bird flew up very quickly.'

(59) *hǎaycay*   *khâw*   *lɯ́klɯ́k*
    breathe   enter   deep
    'Breathe in deep!'

(60) *khǎw*   *lóm*   *loŋ*   *pay*
    he   collapse   descend   go
    'He collapsed (literally down and away from the speaker).'

Notice that the directional markers underlined in examples (57)–(60) are used to describe physical motions in the concrete domain. The movement aspect in these directional markers is still obvious. Directional markers become more and more grammaticalized as they progress along the grammaticalization path. As they become more grammaticalized, they are more and more abstract and metaphorical. This is the case which Yong (1997) refers to as directional verbs used in the 'nonliteral', 'abstract', or 'metaphorical' sense (see details in section 18.3.1). The examples below illustrate the use of more abstract and more metaphorical directional markers.

(61) *khǎw*   *plìan*   *pay*   *mâak*
    he   change   go   a lot
    'He has changed a lot.'

(62) *khǎ*   *kin*   *pay*   *rɯ̂ayrɯ̂ay*
    he   eat   go   continuously
    'He kept eating.'

(63) *khǎw*   *pùay*   *maa*   *sǎam*   *wa*   *lǽæw*
    he   besick   come   three   day   already
    'He has been sick for three days already.'

(64) *khǎw*   *thamŋaan*   *dii*   *khɯ̂n*   *mâak*
    he   work   good   ascend   alot
    'He worked much better than before.'

(65) khǎw   con   <u>loŋ</u>   mâak
     he   poor   descend   alot
     'He became much poorer.'

(66) thamŋaan   rewrew   <u>khâw</u>
     work   quick   enter
     'Hurry up with your work!'

(67) mùak   bay   nǐi   sǔay   <u>ʔɔ̌ɔk</u>
     hat   classifier this   pretty   exit
     'This hat is obviously pretty (contrary to what you think).'

The underlined directional markers in (61)–(67) are used in the abstract or metaphorical domain. In contrast with those in (57)–(60), the movement aspect of the directional verbs, which are the lexical sources, fades from these verbs. However, the directional sense, which is the relational part of the source verbs, is still retained. It can be concluded that the physical aspect of the meanings of the directional verbs fades more and more as they become more and more grammaticalized. What is left is the relational aspect of the verbs, which is the abstract part of their meanings. It is still debatable what specific meanings each of the directional markers in (61)–(67) expresses in addition to the directional meaning. We can see that some of the meanings expressed by these markers relate to the temporal, aspect, and modality (TAM) domains. It is not the objective of this paper to investigate the exact meanings or functions of these grammaticalized markers. It suffices for our purpose to point out that the directional markers in (61)–(67) are grammalicalized at a more advanced degree than those in (57)–(60). Note that the directional markers in Thai, which would be called 'directional verb compounds' by many researchers of Chinese linguistics, are arguably not located at one specific point on the grammaticalization path. Rather, they form a cluster and are distributed over a certain range on the path. Some directional markers in the cluster are more abstract than others.

We argue that the 'directional markers' which are fairly advanced on the grammaticalization path are likely to develop further into grammaticalized forms used primarily in the temporal domain,[6] namely, TAM (tense, aspect, modality) markers. Some of the directional markers in (61)–(67) can be argued to be TAM markers. The evolution of TAM markers from directional verbs has been extensively discussed in linguistic literature on grammaticalization. We want to point out that the TAM markers have to proceed via the stage of directional markers on the grammaticalization path. The mechanism which drives this evolution is metaphorization, which involves mapping between relevant aspects between distinct domains. The mapping structures our understanding of the more abstract domains in terms of our experientially based understanding of the more concrete domains. It has been suggested in the research works on metaphor that certain abstract and topological aspects of

---

6   According to Givón (1984), all of the TAM markers are associated with the notion of time in some way. He states that 'In one way or another, these three represent three different points of departure in our experience of time. Tense involves primarily — though not exclusively — our experience/concept of time as points in a sequence, and thus the notions of precedence and subsequence. Aspects of various kinds involve our notion of the boundedness of time-spans, i.e. various configurations of beginning, ending and middle points. .... Finally, modality encompasses among other things our notions of reality, in the sense of 'having factual existence at some real time' ("true"), 'having existence at no real time' ('false'), or 'having potential existence in some yet-to-be time' ("possible")' (Givón 1984: 272).

semantic structure are the aspects which must be preserved across metaphorical mappings (Sweetser 1990: 59). In this case, the directional aspect of the verbs is preserved as the verbs proceed along the grammaticalization path and, consequently, they become more and more metaphorical. We will not discuss the emergence of the TAM markers in detail because it is outside the scope of this paper. However, we want to point out that it is still debatable which tense, aspect or modality is actually indicated by which grammaticalized form. Even the status of the grammaticalized TAM markers is still debatable. Some say that they are aspect markers whereas others say they are merely quasi-aspect markers. In the former case, which aspect they indicate is still uncertain. It is noted that directional markers as illustrated in (57)–(60) still coexist with TAM markers in Thai although the latter are argued to develop from the former.

We want to argue in this paper that the directional markers evolve into success markers on a different grammatical path from the one that gives rise to TAM markers. These multiple paths of grammaticalization of directional verbs can be diagrammed in Figure 18.3.2-1.

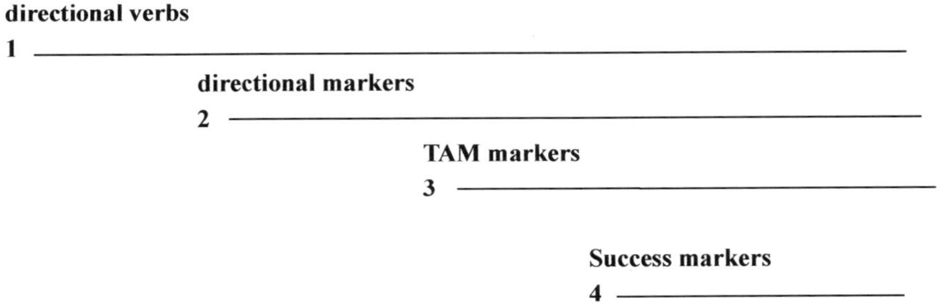

directional verbs

1 ————————————————————————————————

        directional markers

        2 ——————————————————————————

                TAM markers

                3 ——————————————————

                        Success markers

                        4 ——————————————

FIGURE 18.3.2-1: GRAMMATICALIZATION PATH OF DIRECTIONAL VERBS IN THAI

Figure 18.3.2-1 displays four lines. The first line, which is the longest, indicates that all grammaticalized forms, namely, directional markers, TAM markers, and success markers, are developed either directly or indirectly via directional markers from the directional verbs, which constitute the ultimate lexical sources. Since these three types of grammaticalized forms developed from the directional verbs still preserve the directional sense to a certain degree, we will use the term 'directional gram' in analogy with Svorou's (1994) term 'spatial gram' to refer to them as a homogeneous group of grammaticalized forms. The directional verbs, which conflate the movement and the directional aspect of the verbs and which are lexical sources of all types of directional grams, coexist with them. Their coexistence with the other directional grams is illustrated by the most length of the first line. At an early stage on the grammaticalization path, the directional verbs develop into 'directional markers' in which the material content of the verbs, i.e. the physical movement aspect of the semantics of the verbs, is lost. The less grammaticalized directional markers express more concrete meanings and are located closer to their lexical sources than the more grammaticalized ones. However, there may be a period of overlap between older and newer forms and/or functions of a morpheme. The grammaticalization path or cline should not be thought of as a line in which everything is in sequence (Hopper and Traugott 1993). Such an overlap is termed 'layering' by Hopper (1991: 22) and 'chaining' by Heine, Claudi, and Hünnemeyer (1991: 222). According to Hopper (1991: 22), 'Within a functional domain, new layers are continually emerging. As this happens, the older layers are not necessarily discarded, but may remain to coexist with and interact with the newer layers.' This is what happens in Figure 18.3.2-1. The directional verbs coexist with all directional grams developed from them. The directional markers, which are developed from the directional verbs and which emerge at the second layer, also coexist with TAM markers and success markers. Some of the directional markers evolve into TAM markers and emerge on the third layer. In examples (61)–(67), which illustrate the use of directional markers in the abstract domain, we can see that some directional markers are better viewed as TAM markers such as those in (64)–(67) whereas the remaining ones are at the borderline area between directional and TAM markers. However, this paper does not primarily aim to study the TAM markers. We only want to point out that success markers evolve on a different grammaticalization path from that of TAM markers. Since the grammaticalization path which gives rise to TAM markers and they themselves are still a matter of controversy, we use the dotted line to represent uncertainties and complexities revolving around them. The dotted line should not be taken as representing only one grammatical path leading to the development of TAM markers.

As argued earlier, the success markers have some syntactic and semantic properties which are distinct from directional verbs, which are their lexical sources. However, they still preserve the directional sense present in their lexical sources. It is found that some success markers are more grammaticalized than some others. The more grammaticalized ones seem to be the metaphorical ones, which are used in an abstract realm. We have argued in this section that success markers constitute a different type of directional gram from the other types and that they are developed on a distinct grammaticalization path. There are two issues regarding the development of success markers which we would like to point out before we end this section.

First, we would like to underscore one of Hopper and Traugott's (1993) principles that a lexical item is grammaticalized in a highly constrained syntagmatic context. Grammaticalization does not take place when a lexical item is in isolation. In our case, directional markers are grammaticalized into success markers if they occur in a specific syntactic context and co-occur with certain types of transitive verbs as discussed in section 18.2.2. Only in this context can directional markers evolve into success markers. The more grammaticalized or more abstract success markers also take place in certain contexts. Roughly speaking, they co-occur with verbs which do not express physical motions. This principle also holds true with the other types of directional grams.

The second thing which we will point out relates to the deictic property of *pay* 'go' and *maa* 'come' when they are grammaticalized into success markers. We have mentioned briefly in discussing the sentences with the success markers *pay* 'go' and *maa* 'come' in examples (28)–(31) in section 18.2.2 that the speaker's center of attention in the two deictic verbs is replaced by the agent's location in those examples. Those examples are repeated here for convenience as (68)–(71) below.

(68) *khǎw*   *khěn*   *roî*   *mây* *pay*
     he   push   car   not   go
     'He tried to push the car away from himself but was not successful.'

(69) *khǎw*   *lây*   *mææw*   *mây* *pay* *sàk* *thii*
     he   drive away, expel   cat   not   go   even time
     'He tried to drive the cat away from himself but was not successful (even once).'

(70) *khǎw*   *rîak*   *khonrápcháy*   *mây* *maa* *sàk* *thii*
     he   call   maid   not   come even time
     'He tried to call a maid but she did not come to him (even once).'

(71) khǎw   taam   tamrùat   mây   maa   sàk   thii
     he   call u'pon   police   not   come   even   time
     'He kept calling upon the police but they did not show up (even once).'

It was argued in section 18.2.2 that there must be semantic agreement between the direction of the motion associated with the verb phrase and that inherent in the success marker in a sentence. In (68) and (69), the direction inherent in the verb phrases is away from the agent's location whereas that in (70) and (71) is toward the agent's. The speaker's center of attention which was originally present in the deictic verbs, which are the lexical sources of these two success markers, is lost and replaced by the agent's location in the grammaticalization process. This explains why *pay* 'go' and *maa* 'come' cannot be interchangeable in the sentences above as illustrated by the ungrammaticality of the sentences below.

(72) *khǎw khěn   roî   mây maa
      he   push   car   not come

(73) *khǎw lây   mææw   mây maa sàk thii
      he   drive away, expel cat   not come even time

(74) *khǎw rîak   khonrápcháy mây pay sàk   thii
      he   call   maid   not go   even time

(75) *khǎw taam   tamrùat   mây pay sàk   thii
      he   callupon   police   not go   even time

The deixis can be regarded as a type of subjective element in linguistic expressions. Traugott has postulated an important principle in many of her works on grammaticalization that grammaticalization tends to give rise to increased subjectivity (Traugott 1982, 1988, 1991). In this paper, it is found that the case of the success markers *pay* 'go' and *maa* 'come' constitutes a counterexample to Traugott's principle regarding subjectification of grammaticalized linguistic elements. Therefore, further research on cases of 'objectification' in grammaticalization across languages is worth pursuing.

To summarize, the resultative meaning inherent in the success markers are not of the type that researchers on the resultative construction are familiar with. Based on research works on the resultative construction, those researchers seem to be more familiar with the change of state than the change of location. The point to be stressed here is that both TAM markers and success markers are argued to develop from directional markers but along different paths. This claim suggests that so-called 'directional verbs' in the research works which are reviewed in section 18.3.1, or alternatively directional markers in our terms, are not on a par with TAM makers nor success markers. The latter two are arguably later developments of the former. It is not necessary in principle that the final outcome of a grammaticalization path is a fully grammaticalized form, which is depleted of all or most semantic content. The semantic content may be still transparent to a certain degree in the final outcome of grammaticalization. In our case, the directional sense is still apparent to a certain degree in all directional grams including in the success markers. It may be even more obvious in some particular instantiations of success markers than some others. It is crucial to note that the abstract directional sense is present all the way throughout the grammaticalization path but may not be transparent to the same degree.

18.4. CONCLUSION

In this paper, we have examined one of the uses of six directional verbs in Thai, i.e. the use of directional verbs as the resultative predicate indicating success or failure of the agent's performance of an action in the transitive-based resultative construction. We have examined the semantics of the six directional verbs in detail, which motivates their use as success markers. It is found that the verb phrases which co-occur with the directional verbs functioning as success markers must be motion or motion-implied verbs. Furthermore, they must incorporate the implication that the agent has a goal in mind in performing an action and that the goal is more or less likely to take place. These directional verbs serve to highlight the success or failure of the agent's performance of an action and are thus used more frequently in negative and interrogative sentences. As success markers, they are argued to be grammaticalized forms which evolve from directional markers which are in turn grammaticalized from fully-fledged directional verbs, which conflate both physical movements and directions. As these directional verbs proceed further along the grammaticalization path, they will lose more and more of the movement aspect of their meanings but still keep the directional one. It is also argued that success markers develop along a different grammaticalization path from TAM markers. Both success and TAM markers are arguably grammaticalized from directional markers. In addition, it is found that success markers can express the resultative and directional meanings at the same time because they indicate the change of location of the affected entity. We hope that this paper not only contributes to the study of Thai linguistics but also sheds light on the areal phenomenon of verb serialization and on the theory of grammaticalization at large.

REFERENCES

Bisang, Walter (1996) 'Areal typology and grammaticalization: Processes of grammaticalization based on nouns and verbs in East and Mainland South East Asian languages', *Studies in Language* 20.3: 519–597.

Bybee, Joan L. (1986) 'On the nature of grammatical categories: A diachronic perspective', *Eastern States Conference on Linguistics* 2: 17–34.

Givón, Talmy (1984) *Syntax. A Functional Typological Introduction*, vol. I, Amsterdam: John Benjamins.

Heine, Bernd; Claudi, Ulrike and Hünnemeyer, Friederike (1991) *Grammaticalization: A Conceptual Framework*, Chicago: University of Chicago Press.

Hopper, Paul J. (1991) 'On some principles of grammaticization', in Elizabeth Closs Traugott and Bernd Heine (eds) *Approaches to Grammaticalization*, Amsterdams: John Benjamins, vol. 1, 17–35.

Hopper, Paul J. and Elizabeth Closs Traugott (1993) *Grammaticalization*, Cambridge: Cambridge University Press.

Koffka, Kurt (1935) *Principles of Gestalt Psychology*, New York: Harcourt Brace.

Köhler, Wolfgang (1929) *Gestalt Psychology*, New York: Liveright.

Lakoff, George and Johnson, Mark (1980) *Metaphors We Live By*, Chicago: University of Chicago Press.

Langacker, Ronald W. (1987) *Foundations of Cognitive Grammar, vol. I, Theoretical Prerequisites*, Stanford: Stanford University Press.

Lu, John H. T. (1977) 'Resultative verb compounds vs. directional verb compounds in Mandarin', *Journal of Chinese Linguistics* 5: 276–313.

McDonald, Edward (1994) 'Completive verb compounds in modern Chinese: A new look at an old problem', *Journal of Chinese Linguistics*, 22 2: 317–362.

Miller, George A. and Johnson-Laird, Philip N. (1976) *Language and Perception*, Cambridge: The Belknap Press of Harvard University Press.

Svorou, Soteria (1994) *The Grammar of Space*, Amsterdam: John Benjamins.

Sweetser, Eve E. (1990) *From Etymology to Pragmatics: The Mind-as-Body Metaphor in Semantic Structure and Semantic Change*, Cambridge: Cambridge University Press.

Talmy, Leonard (1983) 'How language structures space', in Herbert L. Pick and Linda P. Acredolo (eds) *Spatial Orientation: Theory, Research and Application*, New York: Plenum Press, 225–282.

Teng, Shou-hsin (1977) 'A grammar of verb-particles in Chinese', *Journal of Chinese Linguistics* 5.1: 1–25.

Thepkanjana, Kingkarn (2000) 'Lexical causatives in Thai', in Ad Foolen and Frederike van der Leek (eds) *Constructions in cognitive linguistics*, Amsterdam: John Benjamins, 259–281.

Thepkanjana, Kingkarn and Uehara, Satoshi (forthcoming) 'Semantic types of resultative predicates in Thai', *Proceedings of the 11th Annual Meeting of the Southeast Asian Linguistic Society*, May 16–18, 2001, Bangkok, Thailand.

Thompson, Sandra Annear (1973) 'Resulative verb compounds in Mandarin Chinese: A case for lexical rules', *Language* 49: 2: 361–379.

Traugott, Elizabeth Closs (1982) 'From prepositional to textual and expressive meanings: Some semantic-pragmatic aspects of grammaticalization', in Winfred P. Lehmann and Yakov Malkiel (eds) *Perspectives on Historical Linguistics*, Amsterdam: John Benjamins, 245–271.

—— (1986) 'From polysemy to internal semantic reconstruction', *Proceedings of the Twelfth Annual Meeting of the Berkeley Linguistics Society:* 539–550.

—— (1988) 'Pragmatic strengthening and grammaticalization', *Proceedings of the Fourteenth Annual Meeting Berkeley Linguistics Society:* 406–416.

—— (1991) 'The semantic-pragmatics of grammaticalization revisited', in Elizabeth Closs Traugott and Bernd Heine (eds) *Approach to Grammaticalization, Volume I*, Amsterdam: John Benjamin, 189–218.

Yong, Shin (1997) 'The grammatical functions of verb complements in Mandarin Chinese', *Linguistics* 35: 1–24.

PART 5

KAM-SUI LANGUAGES

CHAPTER NINETEEN

KAM[1]

Tongyin Yang and Jerold A. Edmondson

19.1. INTRODUCTION

The Kam are one of the fifty-five officially recognized minority ethnic groups of China. While they are referred to as 侗族 *Dongzu* in Chinese, their own designation or autonym is *Kam* or more explicitly [kɐm^{55}]. The population of the Kam was about 2.5 million according to the 1990 census, making it the fourteenth largest of China's ethnic groups. More than 90% of the Kam population is concentrated in a triangle overlapping SE Guizhou Province (1,410,000), Hunan Province (750,000) and the Guangxi-Zhuang Autonomous Region (290,000). A small group lives in a separated area in western Hubei Province (50,000) (Long and Zheng 1998 1: 11–12). There is also one Kam village in Vietnam's Tuyên Quang Province where a few people migrated about 150 years ago. A very few persons can still speak the language, but the language is utterly moribund and will die when these few speakers are gone (Edmondson 1998). The neighboring ethnic groups of the Kam include the Miao, Yao, Sui, Mulao, Zhuang, Buyi people, and, of course, the Han Chinese.

The Kam people generally reside in lowland terrain near rivers in the mountainous area south of the Central Plains. Small settlements may number only 10–30 houses; large settlements may have five hundred or more. They are considered masters of wood construction. The traditional dwelling of the Kam, for example, is the piled *ganlan* house of two or three stories with the main area one level above ground. In most of the southern Kam villages there is also a lofty drum tower, an eye-catching structure, serving as a landmark and the center of communal activity. Kam carpenters also build some exquisite bridges across the main rivers–called *tɕiu^{11} hwa^{35}* 'colorful bridge'; in Chinese they are called 风雨桥 *fengyu qiao*, 'bridges that shelter from wind and rain'. Amazingly, not a single nail or screw is used in any of their structures; only mortise and tenon joints with locking pegs find a place in their construction even when these reach ten stories in height or when the spans of the elegant bridges exceed 100 meters.

The Kam are also deservedly famous for their musical traditions. The importance of music is reflected in the Kam proverb, 'Food satisfies only the body, but song nourishes the soul.' In the pre-literate past Kam singing once constituted a feature essential to courting a prospective spouse, to toasting honored guests, and to preserving clan history. Even today this time-honored practice is fostered with singing contests and universal instruction for all young children. Kam multi-part choral songs surprised outsiders when in the 1980s Chinese folklorists first discovered it. The Guizhou Kam Chorus was even invited to perform in Paris.

The Kam are primarily subsistence farmers living on the products of wet paddy rice agriculture. Traditionally, glutinous rice has been the staple, because of its high nutritive value and ease of preservation. It is also a fundamental component of all societal rites and ceremonies. Nowadays, production of the hybrid japonica rice has outstripped glutinous rice, but each family nonetheless reserves part of its assigned acreage for growing glutinous rice. Daily activity centers upon the cycle of preparation, planting, cultivating, weeding, and harvesting. Another income source comes from logging and forestry. The Kam area coincides with one of China's eight largest forested zones. Thus, in the past, the Kam agricultural and

---

1 This chapter is based primarily on Tongyin Yang's MA thesis and part of his PhD dissertation at The University of Texas at Arlington.

forestry products allowed a largely self-supporting economy with enough surpluses to buy commercial good as was needed. But the situation has changed drastically today. Not only have the crop varieties been enlarged, but also many members of the younger generation have left the community and are seeking their fortunes in distant urban areas such as Guangzhou and Shanghai.

Kam is the native language of the Kam people. According to a survey conducted in 1995 (Chen 1995), the estimated number of Kam language speakers was 1.7 million. Among them, one million could not speak Chinese at all, 400,000 could speak Chinese in some form but not fluently; 300,000 were fluent Chinese speakers while Kam was still their native language; all others had shifted to local forms of Chinese completely (Chen 1995 1: 2–3). That means at least one-third of the Kam populace currently uses Chinese as their first language rather than Kam. Among the remaining two-thirds of the population, language use can be divided into two major subtypes according to geography and according to their degree of contact with Han Chinese. In the Southern areas – the boundary lies along a line running from Qimong, Jingping County, Guizhou and Lannichong, Jinzhou County, Hunan, where Kam, Miao, and Han Chinese live together – language use is more preservative. More archaic features are found in these isolated locations where the Kam make up the majority. By contrast, Northern Kam has been influenced more deeply by Chinese, not only in lexicon, but also in its phonological and grammatical structure.

Kam has been distinguished as an ethnic group since the sixteenth century (end of the Ming Dynasty, AD 1368–1644) but the earliest records of the Kam language appeared sporadically only after AD 1800 (Guangxi General Annals and Longsheng Ting Annals). The Kam of Tianzhu and Jinping Counties are mentioned in the Chinese Repository 1845 as planters of cotton and cultivators of silk. F. K. Li (1942) noted the Kam people and their language in his early work (Li 1942) but he published no detailed study of it.[2] The German ethnologist Inez de Beauclair visited Kam areas in September 1947 and described the people and their cultural setting in her original report to the Wenner Gren Foundation in 1948 (De Beauclair 1972). But formal systematic study of Kam did not start until the 1950s.

Kam is a part of the Kam-Tai language family. F. K. Li assigned it to the Kam-Sui subbranch (Li 1942), a classification that has, for the most part, been accepted by the international linguistic community. Linguistic study of Kam began in 1956 when the Chinese government responded to the need to create orthographies and to promote literacy for traditionally unlettered minority peoples throughout China. The plan was to begin by organizing broadly-based and detailed investigations in several field locations of the unstudied and understudied minority languages of the Chinese hinterlands. Kam was one of its first targets. The Kam Language Survey Group under the First Working Team of Chinese Academy of Sciences conducted a comprehensive field survey of Kam dialectology. As result, *Final Report Surveying Kam Dialects* was drafted in 1957. It provided the first comprehensive linguistic information about Kam with data from 20 survey locations and played a pivotal role in designing and legitimizing the Latin-based Kam orthography (promulgated 1959). This report became the foundation stone for all Kam linguistic research and members of the Survey Group became main forces in linguistic research about Kam. Among these pioneers were Professors Yang Quan and Zheng Guoqiao.

侗语简志 *A Brief Description of the Kam Language* (Liang Min 1980) was the first systematic published study on Kam in or outside of China. It provided a brief preliminary description of Kam phonology, morphology, grammar, lectal variation, and orthography. This work relied on the fieldwork carried out in 1950s.

The Institute of Nationality Studies of The Chinese Academy of Social Sciences, The Third Department of Minority Languages at the Central University of Nationalities, The Kam-Tai Research Units of Department of Chinese Language and Literature at Nankai University, and

---

2   He writes that he had worked on the Kam language of Rongjiang County, but that his notes were lost in the mail as a consequence of chaos accompanying the onset of war in the mid-1940's.

the Guizhou Institute of Nationalities have become the four most important research institutions engaged in the study of the Kam language. From results achieved in Liang (1980), scholars from these institutes have continued to deepen their analysis of Kam, exploring more aspects of the language, including questions about its tones, phonological variation, lexicon, grammar, dialectology, and sociolinguistic issues. Important scholars and their major works on the Kam language include the following: Yang Quan, a Kam native speaker, who classified the diachronic development of Kam tones, initials, and rhymes (Yang Quan 1988), Zheng Guoqiao, whose pedagogical work *Teaching Material on Kam Grammar* (1988) and *Teaching Material on Kam Dialectology* (1988) provided further enlightenment into Kam language structure and are highly regarded as Kam texts though they have remained unpublished. He later worked with Long Yaohong and they extended their views into the cultural environment. They combined efforts skillfully to produce *The Kam Language in Guizhou Province, China* (1998), which was the first lengthy description of the Kam language available in English, translated by D. Norman Geary. The native-speaker scholar Shi Lin studied Kam word categories (Shi Lin 1985, 1986). Also covered in his works are phonological variation, tones, dialectology and new Han borrowings (Shi Lin 1983, 1990, 1992, 1994). *The Sanjiang Kam language* is an excellent description of a local language practices by Shi and Xing Gongwan (1988). J. A. Edmondson treats Kam initials, tone quality and the interrelation between them (1988). He also has done tremendous translation work from Chinese to English and has made previous work available to researchers outside China. He, Yang Tongyin, and Somsonge Burusphat (2000) have collaborated to produce a 300-page multilingual dictionary, based upon the original meanings in Kam and not on translations of existing Kam-Chinese materials. A phonetic dictionary with meanings translated from Chinese glosses and transcriptions according to the conventions of Thai scholars has been prepared by Thomas Hudak (1999).

More has been done in Kam phonetic description, word compounding, sentence type and dialectology, but less research has been devoted to analyzing phrase structure, sentence patterns, and discourse structures.

19.2. PHONOLOGY

Kam is an isolating, analytic, tonal language, mostly made up of monosyllabic word forms, which means a syllable equals, in general, a word. Each syllable is composed of an initial consonant, a rhyme, and a tone.

The Kam consonant inventory is relatively simple in comparison to other Kam-Sui languages, such as Sui and Maonan. In comparison to Tai languages, it has fewer consonant phonemes as well. The number of its vowels is also relatively restricted. But the complex tonal system and the flexible combination of consonants and vowels within rhymes lead to an intricate syllable structure and result in a sound system with unique properties. It has been widely observed that in the Kam-Tai family there is a strong correlation among the three syllable units, *initial*, *rhyme*, and *tone*. In order to clarify and simplify these issues as much as possible, the consonant and vowel inventory will be mentioned only briefly. Primary attention will be paid to treating the three syllable units individually, and then the relationship among them. This method of presentation has proven to be an effective way in describing Kam-Tai family languages and is still in wide use today.

19.2.1. Consonants and syllable initial phonemes

There are 19 consonant initials in the standard Kam location of Rongjiang Zhanglu, Guizhou Province: /p ph t th tɕ tɕh k kh m n n̥ ŋ s ɕ h w l j/. Several features can be extracted from this consonant system. The first evident feature is the absence of a voicing contrast. That is, there are neither voiced obstruents, nor voiceless sonorants, in other words, [α sonorant] → [α voiced]. The second point is that Kam shows a well-balanced distribution of place and manner of articulation of consonants: from bilabial [p m], alveolar [t s], to velar [k ŋ] and glottal [ʔ h]; from plosive [ph], nasals [m n ŋ] to fricative [s ɕ] and lateral approximants [l]. Just as in the case of Sui, in the syllable initial position the dentals [t th] can be characterized as having the tongue tip in contact with the lingual surface of the upper central incisors and at the same time the blade of the tongue is in contact with the front part of the alveolar ridge. Such sounds are in actuality denti-alveolar (more precisely apico-dental lamino-alveolar). The Kam affricate sounds [tɕ tɕh] have a place of articulation that covers both the post-alveolar zone and the prepalatal zone simultaneously and are actually alveolo-palatals made with the blade of the tongue and the extreme anterior portion of the front part of the dorsum. These do not have the [i]-like or [y]-like offglides that the prepalatal affricates of Han Chinese [tɕ tɕh] have; these sound have often been transcribed in Chinese sources with [t̠ t̠h].

When some of the initial consonants appear in a syllable, secondary features (i.e., labialization, palatalization) can be added to them. Along with those initials without secondary articulations Kam initial phoneme system consists of the following segments:

TABLE 19.2.1-1: KAM INITIAL PHONEMES

	labial	alveolar	coronal	velar	glottal	palatal	labial
stop, unaspirated	p	t	tɕ	k	ʔ	pj	kw
stop, aspirated	ph	th	tɕh	kh		phj	khw
nasal	m	n	n̠	ŋ		mj	w
fricative		s	ɕ		h		
approximant	w		j			wj	
lateral		l				lj	

Notes on the Kam initials:

1. [tɕ tɕh] are voiceless lamino-alveopalatal affricates. The [tɕ] is articulated with a very short fricative release and a lengthened stop closure, while the [tɕh] has a longer fricative release and a shorter stop closure. The tongue positions for [tɕ tɕh n̠ ɕ] are similar to the cardinal consonant positions for these sounds.

2. Initial [t] and [th] are (denti-alveolar), whereas final /t/ is [ʔt], an apico-alveolar stop with near simultaneous glottal stop, a double articulation that is unreleased.

3. When [w] occurs before unrounded vowels, the back part of the tongue is raised, and friction is slight.

4. The [s] is lamino-alveolar with the blade approaching the front of the alveolar ridge.

5. [ʔj] is a preglottalized fronto-palatal approximant.

6. [tj], [thj], [ts], [tsh] and [f] occur only in modern Chinese loan words and are found exclusively in younger speakers (under 30 of age), so they are not included here. The older generations articulate them as [tɕ tɕh ɕ s h] correspondingly. The retroflex consonant series found in Modern Standard Chinese does not exist in Kam. The following are examples of Kam syllable initial phonemes:

TABLE 19.2.1-2: EXAMPLES OF KAM SYLLABLE INITIAL PHONEMES

Initial	Kam	Gloss	Initial	Kam	Gloss
p	pa^{55}	fish	ph	pha^{35}	grey
t	ta^{55}	eye	th	tha^{35}	elope
tɕ	$tɕa^{53}$	that	tɕh	$tɕha^{453}$	to climb

k	ka^{55}	leftover	kh	kha^{35}	ear
ʔ	ʔa^{11}	polite Pref.	pj	pja^{55}	large stone
phj	phja^{35}	feed (baby)	kw	kwe^{55}	cucumber
khw	khwan^{323}	manage	m	ma^{55}	vegetable
n	na^{35}	thick	ȵ	ȵa^{11}	you
ŋ	ŋa^{33}	gluttonous	mj	mja^{11}	hand
ŋw	ŋwa^{35}	dog	s	sa^{35}	twist
ɕ	ɕa^{55}	colic	h	ha^{11}	to scare
w	wa^{35}	picture	w	wa^{53}	dirty
j	ja^{11}	two	wj	wje^{11}	month
l	la^{11}	mushroom	j	ja^{453}	red
lj	lja^{11}	to lick			

19.2.2. Explanations about Kam vowels and syllables

1. Kam has six vowel phonemes: /ɐ e i o u ɑ/ in native Kam vocabulary.

2. Among them, /ɐ/ occurs only with codas (i.e. with /-p -t -k -i -u/). The segments /e i o u ɑ / can occur in a rhyme either with codas or alone.

3. The segment /i/ has two allophones: [i] and [ɨ]. The latter [ɨ] occurs when the coda is /u/, e.g. [pɨu^{55}] 'container made of a gourd' vs. [pjiu^{55}] 'to jump' or final /p t k/ e.g. [tɨp^{323}] 'to accept, receive (an object)'. The tongue position is lower and tends to be relatively open, cf. Long and Zheng (1998: 25).

4. The segment /o/ has two allophones: [o] and [ɔ]. The latter [ɔ] occurs in monophthongal rhyme and before syllable codas /-m -ŋ -p -k/, For example: *so*^{323} 'dry', *poŋ*^{11} 'float', and *mok*^{31} 'bird'. It is a little longer in articulation and lower in tongue position than [o]. The allophone [o] appears before codas /-i -n -t/, with an intervening [ɐ] glide between the main vowel and the syllable coda. For example: *ton*^{53} 'guess', *thot*^{323} 'take off (clothes)'.

5. The segment /o/ is fronted a bit after palatalization, /j/, and coronals, or whenever it is followed by codas /m n t/.

6. The nuclear vowels can combine with the vocalic codas /i u/, the three nasal codas /-m -n -ŋ/, and the three stop codas /-p –t -k/. The vowels /a/ and /ɑ/ contrast in vowel length and also in vowel quality; the former is usually IPA [ɐ] and the latter IPA [ɑ:]. Therefore, in the phonological system of Kam /ɑ/ is often called 'long a', while /ɐ/ is called 'short a'.

Rhymes

a	e	i	o	u		ə
ai			oi	ui	ɑi	əi
au	eu	iu			ɑu	əu
am	em	im	om	um	ɑm	əm
an	en	in	on	un	ɑn	ən
aŋ	eŋ	iŋ	oŋ	uŋ	ɑŋ	əŋ
ap	ep	ip	op	up	ɑp	əp
at	et	it	ot	ut	ɑt	ət
ak	ek	ik	ok	uk	ɑk	ək

Kam vowels and rhymes

Rhyme	Kam	Gloss	Rhyme	Kam	Gloss
a	ta^{55}	eye	e	kwe^{55}	cucumber
i	phji^{35}	to peel	ə	jə^{53}	really?
u	mu^{323}	later	o	so^{323}	dry
oi	moi^{55}	to skin	ai	pai^{55}	to go
ɑi	pɑi^{55}	to paste	ui	tɕui^{323}	ghost

au	pau⁵⁵	horn	əi	məi³¹	not yet
iu	miu¹¹	scissors	eu	çeu⁵⁵	to hoe
əu	məu⁵³	tadpole	au	lau³¹	to fool, cheat
em	mem⁵⁵	suddenly	am	lam¹¹	to forget
om	pom⁵⁵	bubble	im	lim³¹	(a) wedge
am	nam³¹	water	um	tum⁵³	blister
an	man³²³	yellow	əm	səm⁵³	soak
in	min¹³	mat	en	men³³	often
un	mun¹¹	fog	on	ton⁵³	to guess
ən	mən⁵³	(a) well	an	man⁵⁵	day
eŋ	meŋ⁵³	to crack	aŋ	maŋ⁵⁵	thin
oŋ	loŋ⁵⁵	forest	iŋ	miŋ⁵⁵	charcoal
aŋ	maŋ³¹	glad	uŋ	luŋ⁵⁵	cool
ap	lap³²³	thunder	əŋ	ləŋ³³	ice
ip	ɲip³²³	tongs	ep	pep³²³	to thrust into
up	sup³²³	to meet	op	kop³²³	just (a moment ago)
əp	məp⁵⁵	to sprout	ap	sap⁵⁵	to capture
et	pet³²³	eight	at	mat³²³	to cleanse
ot	lot³²³	to sin off	it	it³²³	grape
at	mat³⁵	to shake	ut	mut³¹	beard
ak	mak³¹	mud	ət	mət³¹	ant
ik	tik³²³	full	ek	mek³¹	vein
uk	muk³¹	mucus	ok	mok³¹	bird
ak	ljak³¹	to steal	ək	lək³¹	energy, strength

19.2.3. Tones

There are ten contrastive tones in Kam. If one tracks their historical origin and compares them to sister languages and with Chinese, and treats CVC and CVVC syllable shapes as different tones (as is the practice for Chinese and the languages of China), then the tone contrasts would number fifteen. For convenience, each tone is assigned a Tone Number as well as a Tone Value, as shown below.

TABLE 19.2.3-1: KAM TONES

ToneNo.	ToneValue	Example	
1	55	ma⁵⁵	'vegetable'
7	55	jak⁵⁵	'wet'
1'	35	ma³⁵	'tocome'
7'	35	mat³⁵	'flea'
2	11	ma¹¹	'tongue'
8	11	sak¹¹	'thief'
3	323	ma³²³	'cloud, soft'
9	323	mak³²³	'big'
3'	13	no¹³	'rat'
9'	13	phat¹³	'blood'
4	31	ma³¹	'horse'
10	31	mak³¹	'ink'
5	53	ja⁵³	'paddy, wetfield'
5'	453	ma⁴⁵³	'to soak (rice)'
6	33	pa³³	'rice husk'

Some notes about Kam tones:

1. Tone 2 has the lowest value while the peak of tone 5′ reaches the highest level.

2. The onset of tone 3 is higher than tone 6, but the end point of Tone 3 is a slightly lower than that of 6.

3. The 3′ tone is paired with tone 9′ in checked syllables; the 1′ tone is paired with 7′ in checked syllables, and the 5′ tone occurs only with aspirated initial consonants. The Tones 3′ and 9′ are not robustly distinguished in some kinds of Kam including Yang Tongyin's first language, Yutou Kam of Tongdao County, Hunan, Province. Only two minimal pairs are known: *kwaɲ^{323}* 'bowl' vs. *khwaɲ^{223}* 'wide', *pja^{323}* 'thunder' vs. *phja^{223}* 'cloth'.

4. There are no toneless vowels (such as in MSC Modern Standard Chinese).

19.2.4. Syllable structure and correlations among the units

Since Kam is a monosyllabic language without true clustered initials, the description of its syllable structure is relatively simple. The basic Kam syllable structure is: <u>initial + rhyme + tone</u>. If the phonetic elements vowel, consonant and tone are used to analyze and identify the syllable structure component further, then the structure can be generalized as follows (Here C=consonant, V=vowel, T=tone):

Syllable structure type	Example	Gloss
V-T	u^{55}	'above'
VC-T	ɐm^{323}	'lid'
VV-T	ui^{35}	'toflow'
CV-T	ta^{53}	'middle'
CVV-T	mau^{33}	's/he'
CVC-T	ton^{53}	'toguess'

Not all the vowels can be combined with all consonants in syllable construction, nor do all tones occur with all initials and rhymes. Some co-occurrence restrictions apply such as:

1. No diphthongs can be followed by a consonant coda, i.e. *aup, *aik, *uit.

2. Tone 1′, 3′, 5′, 7′, and 9′ can occur only with glide initials /w j/, with nasals and laterals /m mj n̠ ŋ ŋw l lj/ as well as with the aspirated stop initials /ph th kh phj khw/, and fricatives /h s/. They do not occur with plain voiceless stops.

3. Tone 5 and 6 cannot occur in checked syllables with stop codas /p t k/.

4. In the phonological system of vowels, /a e i/ count as being long vowels, and these only occur as simple vowels in open syllables and as nuclear vowels in checked rhymes and those with coda /i u/. The vowels /ɐ/ and /ə/ count in the phonological system as short, and, therefore, they occur as nuclear vowels for checked rhymes or with rhymes with codas /i u/. Thus, /a ɐ/ are contrastive in examples such as *pai^{55}* 'to go' vs. *pɐi^{55}* 'to paste'.

Thus, the phonology of Kam can be characterized as one that has elaborated its tonal contrasts at the expense of its initial consonants, though aspiration of stops is still found at most locations in the southern Kam speaking area. Vowels have also simplified considerably. Indeed, only the low vowels /a ɐ/ preserve a phonological contrast. All other nuclear vowels have lost this feature, though they show this or that allophone depending upon whether in open syllable or followed by codas /p t k m n ŋ i u/.

It is noteworthy that in some northern Kam locations phonological change is more advanced, so that even stops have lost aspiration displaying the carrier of the contrast from aspiration to tone. Moreover, in Shidong of Tianzhu County many voiceless stop codas are starting to decay yielding many examples of vocabulary that are distinguished by tone only, which has resulted in a tonal system that demonstrates five level tone trajectories (11, 22, 33, 44, and 55) in addition to three rising and one falling pitch shape. Thus Kam phonology can inform us about the history of Kam-Sui but also about the nature of sound change in general, especially as it relates to tonal development. One obvious fact, is that Kam at Rongjiang does not require that the cause of a change (aspiration) disappear before the change can be said to have been completed (Tones 1', 3', 5', 7', and 9'), which is required by the phonemic principle.

19.3. SYNTAX

Until recently there have been few sources of information about the morphological and syntactic structure of the Kam language. In 1984 Liang Min provided a sketch of the word categories, patterns of reduplication, monosyllabic vs. polysyllabic word forms, and basic sentence patterns of Kam. Long and Zheng (1998) provided a much more elaborate look at Kam grammar, including an introduction to Northern Kam structure. Yang (1999) in his MA thesis employs the X-bar model of phrase structure of Kam, concentrating on his own vernacular speech of Yutou, Tongdao, Hunan Province. It might be said to be the first 'theoretical' statement of Kam syntax. We have incorporated many aspects of Yang (1999) in this entry and recast it to capture the features of Rongjiang Kam, which is the standard on which the Kam writing system is based.

19.3.1. Noun phrases

Kam phrase structure is basically head-first. By looking at the simple Kam phrases:

(1) a.   le^{11} 'book' m̥a^{453} 'new' tça^{323} 'that'— 'that new book'
    b.   lau^{323} 'enter' kun^{53} 'before' — 'enter first'

One can recognize that Kam is a head-first language. That means that its phrase structure will be generated by the rules XP → X' Spec; X' → X' Adjunct AP; and X' → X Complement ZP in which Spec, Adjunct, and Complement elements appear on the right of the X' and X respectively. It will turn out that not all elements in phrases are as consistent in their left-headed ordering as these two examples. Kam will show itself to be a language that demonstrates predominantly head-first but also some head-final word order properties. Work also remains to be done in seeking the source of word order variations and its linguistic environments both historical and contextual.

The NP (noun phrase) is the constituent occupying the subject (or the object) position of a sentence. It is headed by a noun and may be augmented by other constituents such as complements, adjuncts, and specifier(s). The following tree diagram shows the basic structural characteristics of the first example mentioned above:

(2)

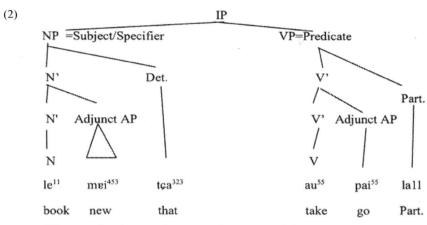

'That new book was taken away (by someone).'

In (2), except for IP, the specifiers and adjuncts follow their heads. This generalization extends not only to adjective phrases (AP), but also to many other phrasal categories—preposition phrases (PP), quantifier phrases (QP), pronouns, verb phrases (VP), and noun phrases themselves. In this section, only the *noun + single constituent* combination will be discussed out of considerations of simplicity and clarity.

First we consider the structure *noun + adjective*, a typical NP. The adjective ascribes attributes to the head noun through the process traditionally called *modification*. Usually that means mapping the head noun properties onto some proper subset of properties that are also those expressed by the attribute (restrictive or intersecting modification). So in (3) *wood* properties are mapped onto *dry wood* properties. See examples in (3):

(3) (a) mɐi³¹ so³²³   'dry wood'
       wood dry

   (b) jan¹¹ mɐi⁴⁵³   'new house'
       house new

   (c) tɕi⁵³ lai⁵⁵   'good idea'
       idea good

   (d) mɐi³¹ tɕa³²³   'the wood'
       wood that

   (e) jan¹¹ tɕa³²³   'the house'
       house that

   (f) jan¹¹ mɐi⁴⁵³ tɕa³²³   'the new house'
       house new that

The Kam adjuncts *so³²³*, *mɐi⁴⁵³*, *lai⁵⁵* in (3) a, b, c and specifier *tɕa³²³* in (3) d, e, and f must be placed after the head noun of the containing phrase. It is possible for an adjectival element to occur preceding the noun, but in such a case, the category of the combined phrase would no longer be taken as an NP but as a typical VP (see 3.2.1.1). Also personal pronouns are not treated as nouns in *pronoun + adjective* structures, but instead the structure belongs to the clause or sentence level. In other words, adjectives cannot modify a pronoun to form a 'pronoun' phrase.

It is, furthermore, to be noted that some elements can be inserted between the noun and the adjunct here (adverbs of degree or scope, negative markers, and adjective reduplication).

(4) (a) mɐi³¹   n̻ɐŋ³¹   so³²³   tɕa³²³   'the very dry wood'
        Wood   very   dry   that

(b) jan¹¹   tɕən⁵⁵   mɐi⁴⁵³   mɐi⁴⁵³   tɕa³²³ 'the pretty new-looking house'
        House very   new   new   that

(5)

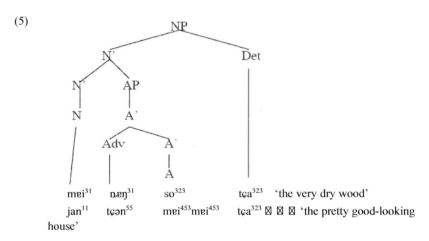

mɐi³¹   n̻ɐŋ³¹   so³²³   tɕa³²³ 'the very dry wood'
jan¹¹   tɕən⁵⁵   mɐi⁴⁵³mɐi⁴⁵³   tɕa³²³ ☒ ☒ ☒ 'the pretty good-looking house'

The adverb here needs help from a final demonstrative determiner such as *tɕa³²³* 'that', *nai³³* 'this', or interrogative determiner *nɐi³⁵* 'what, which' for the structure to be understood as an NP. If no determiner is present, the adverb will result in an interpretation requiring that the structure be taken as a complete sentence, IP, rather than as an NP. See (6) below:

(6)(a) mɐi³¹   n̻ɐŋ³¹   so³²³   'The wood is very dry'
        wood   very   dry

(b) jan¹¹   tɕən⁵⁵   mɐi⁴⁵³ 'The house is pretty new'
        house very   new

(7)

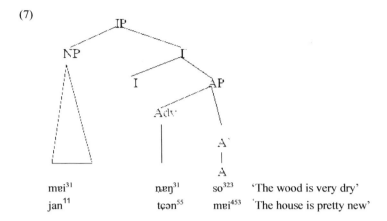

mɐi³¹	nɐŋ³¹	so³²³	'The wood is very dry'
jan¹¹	tɕən⁵⁵	mɐi⁴⁵³	'The house is pretty new'

Negation does not often occur in NPs with adjective modifiers, but it is acceptable, see (8a). Such negated adjuncts also require a determiner if they are to be understood as NPs and not to have the superficial form of a sentence (IP). The structure (8b) is unacceptable as an NP but acceptable as a sentence, IP.

(8) (a) NP: təm³³ məi³¹ ɕok³¹ tɕa³²³ 'the unripe fruit'
         fruit NEG ripe that

    (b) IP/*NP: təm³³ məi³¹ ɕok³¹   'The fruit is unripe.'

(9)

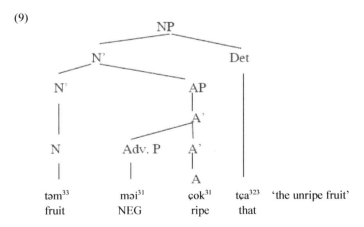

təm³³	məi³¹	ɕok³¹	tɕa³²³ 'the unripe fruit'
fruit	NEG	ripe	that

The modifying adjective phrase can be reduplicated to express emphasis and raise the degree of the specific properties the adjective adds to the containing phrase. Here the determiner is required. See examples in (10a) and (10b):

(10) (a) mja³¹ jai³³~ mja³¹ jai³³ jai³³ tɕa³²³ 'the very sharp knife'
         knife sharp   knife sharp sharp that

(b) n̥a⁵⁵ mak³²³~ n̥a⁵⁵ mak³²³ mak³²³ tɕa³²³ 'the very big river'
      river big   river big   big   that

Another way to emphasize the degree of an adjective is to add a special *intensifier* (INT) after the adjective. The INT is a lexical category (not found in English and other languages of Western Europe but a feature widely found in Asian languages, including Kam, Chinese, Thai, and others that usually co-occurs with adjectives, called 状语 *zhuangyu* in Chinese). These lexical items have no independent meaning, but cases of homophonous forms in other word categories do exists for some intensifiers; these might have independent meaning. An INT can only appear with (i.e., is subcategorized with) a particular adjective, and there is a very close lexical connection between an adjective and its own lexically determined intensifier. They remind one a little of English expressions intensified by similes, contrast, for example, Kam *nɐn⁵⁵ ɕuŋ³²³ ɕuŋ³²³* and English *pitch black*. Kam speakers simply know that *ɕuŋ³²³* (reduplicated or not) is the word form used to intensify *nɐn⁵⁵*, but unlike *pitch* Kam intensifiers are not lexical words otherwise in use. Thus, the question here is what structural position in the phrase does the INT fill, specifier, adjunct, or complement? No definitive answer will be given at this point, but the lexical closeness of the adjective and INT might suggest a complement relation. One further point is to be noticed. In some cases, such as the examples below, there is an optional particle *tɕa³³* that is perhaps the specifier of INT Phrases and functions something like English '-ly':

(11) (a) sik³²³   'bland'
        sik³²³ sik³²³ tɕa³²³ 'pretty bland'
        sik³²³ ɕem³²³ tɕa³²³ 'totally bland'

     (b) lɐk⁵⁵   'steep'
        lɐk⁵⁵ lɐk⁵⁵ tɕa³²³ 'very steep'
        lɐk⁵⁵ lem⁵⁵ tɕa³²³ 'as steep as one can imagine'

19.3.1.1. *Noun + possessive pronoun NP*

The pronoun is a [+N, -V] lexical category that can be used to express a possessive NP. The adjunct possessive pronoun construction follows the head noun. Note that the possessive is treated as an adjunct.

(12)

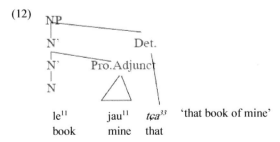

        le¹¹   jau¹¹ *tɕa³³* 'that book of mine'
        book   mine   that

19.3.1.1.1. *Personal pronouns*

The list of the personal pronouns in Kam that fill the possessive pronoun slot is very limited in number:

(13) jau¹¹   'I'   ɳa¹¹   'you (singular)'
    mau³³   's/he'   tau⁵⁵   'we' (inclusive)
    tɕiu⁵⁵⊠   'we'(exclusive)   ɕau³⁵   'you' (plural)
    tɕa³³mau³³ 'they'   si³³a⁵⁵   'self'
    tɕən¹¹/e³⁵ 'others'   tɕən¹¹tɕuŋ¹¹ 'everybody'

Each of the above pronouns can take the place of the Pronoun (Pro) in the *Noun + pronoun*
NP and defines the possessive status, the source of the noun, the object of the noun, or any
number of other relations between the head and the pronoun. Examples of the possessive are:

(14) səm³¹ jau¹¹ 'my room'
    li³¹ jən¹¹ tɕuŋ¹¹ 'gossip or views of people'

In Yutou Kam, unlike in the standard Rongjiang Kam, when the head noun here is a kinship
name that belongs to a higher generation than the speaker, only the plural pronouns can be put
into the Pronoun position. This lexical restriction is a consequence of social and cultural
customs and practices in this place. The singular pronouns are excluded from this NP type.
Thus, in a sense, YT Kam has a form of the *pluralis majestatis* construction that employs
plural forms to accord greater respect or social significance to elders. For example:

(15) nɐi³¹(mother) lau⁵⁵ (we/our)   'my/our mother'
    *nɐi³¹ (mother) jau¹¹ (I/my)
    koŋ³²³ maŋ³³ (ancestors) khe³⁵ (they)   'his, her/their ancestors'
    *koŋ³²³ maŋ³³ (ancestors) mau³³ (his/her)
    noŋ³¹(younger sibling) ɕau⁵⁵ (you. (pl.)) 'your (pl.) younger siblings'
    *noŋ³¹ (younger sibling) ɳa¹¹ (you. (sing.)) 'your (sing.) younger sibling(s)'

That means the plural pronoun can express not only a plural but also a singular possessive
meaning for a person. The *kinship name noun + singular pronoun* is unacceptable in a
pragmatic sense when the speaker belongs to a younger generation than the person addressed
or spoken of, except for one's spouse. So, one can say *mai³¹ jau¹¹* to refer to 'my wife' rather
than using *mai³¹ lau⁵⁵* (which means 'my brother's wife'); one can also say *lak³¹ jau¹¹* 'my
son' rather than *lak³¹ lau⁵⁵* (which means 'our descendents').

    This special restriction on kinship noun and personal pronoun combination will also be
included in 3.3 as example of lexical co-occurrence restrictions.

19.3.1.1.2. *The demonstrative and interrogative determiners*

The demonstrative and interrogative (abbreviated as DI hereafter) determiners can appear
with nouns directly to specify, limit, quantify, or ask the identity of the nouns. Kam has a set
of DIs to distinguish some subtle differences in spatial position.

(16) nai³²³   'this' (able to touch)
    tɕa³²³   'that' (previously mentioned)
    tɕa¹¹   'that, the' (specified, exactly that one)
    tɕa³³   'visible, within range'
    tɕa⁵³   'that' (visible but far away)
    ja⁴⁵³   'that, where' (invisible)
    nɐu³⁵/lɐu³⁵ 'which, what, whom, where'
    tɕak¹¹   'the (a definite description in some discourse setting)'

Examples are provided as follows (with CLF for animals tu^{11}):

(tu^{11}) ŋua^{35} nai^{33}	'this dog' (right beside the speaker)
(tu^{11}) ŋua^{35} tça^{323}	'that dog' (the one mentioned before)
(tu^{11}) ŋua^{35} tça^{11}	'the/that dog' (the identical or very one)
(tu^{11}) ŋua^{35} tça^{33}	'the dog over there'
(tu^{11}) ŋua^{35} tça^{53}	'that dog far over there'
(tu^{11}) ŋua^{35} nu^{35}	'which dog'

Other modifiers/adjuncts such as adjectives, personal pronouns or even an IP can be embedded between the noun and the DI, and the whole construction remains still an NP. If the same constituents should appear after the DI, then the structure can only be understood as a complete sentence. The following examples illustrate this difference:

(17) çe^{55} nai^{33} 'this coarse sand'   (NP)

çe^{55} man^{323}nai^{33} 'this yellow coarse sand'   (NP)

çe^{55} nai^{33} man^{323} 'this coarse sand is yellow' (IP)

If the personal pronoun is absent or appears outside the NP, then a headless NP construction with the specifier (determiner) ti^{55} '-s' is required in a structure that resembles the English form *ours*:

(18) (a) piu^{55} (gourd) mak^{323} (big) tau^{55} (our)   tça^{33} (that)

'our big gourd'

(b) piu^{55} (gourd) mak^{323} (big) tça^{33} (that) tau^{55} (our) ti^{55} (Part.)

'the big gourd is ours'

(19) (a)

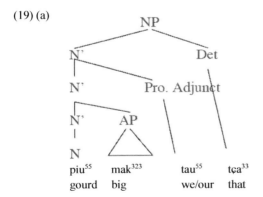

(b)

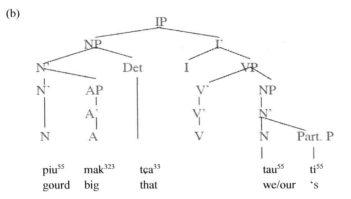

The grammar for the determiner of definite descriptions *tɕak³¹*, in meaning similar to English *the*, requires that it appear as the right-most element of the NP. An analysis of this particular construction will not be attempted here for lack of time.

19.3.1.2. *Noun + complement noun NP*

The head noun itself can be followed by another complement noun. In this case, the latter noun of the double NPs (i.e., the complement), expresses the quality, source, function, or shape of the noun. Examples are found in (20).

(20) (a) pa⁵⁵(fish)   ȵa⁵⁵(river)   'fish of the river'   — source
        vs. ȵa⁵⁵   pa⁵⁵   'the fish-abundant river'

     (b) təm⁵⁵   pa⁵³   pɐn⁵⁵ 'hat of bamboo leaves'   — quality
         hat   bamboo   leaf
         vs. pa⁵³   pɐn⁵⁵   təm⁵⁵ 'the bamboo leaf for making hats'

     (c) ɕoŋ¹¹(desk) məi³¹(wood)   'desk of wood'   — quality
         vs. məi³¹   ɕoŋ¹¹   'the wood for desk making'

     (d) ku¹¹(pot))   əu³¹(rice   'rice cooker'   — function
         vs. əu³¹   ku¹¹   'rice cooked in pot'

A simple tree is drawn for the contrastive pair in example a. as follows:

(21)

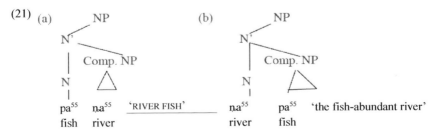

Prepositions such as *ɳau³³* 'at, on, in, with' and verbs can occur between the two nouns so that indicates that *pa⁵⁵ ɳa⁵⁵* is a part of phrase structure and that that *pa⁵⁵ɳa⁵⁵* is not just a compound noun. The NP lexical category of the phrase remains the same. Determiners can disambiguate the category of the phrase but are not necessarily required. For example:

(22) pa⁵⁵   ɳau³³ ɳa⁵⁵   tça³³ 'the fish that live in the river'
     fish   live, at river   that

     məi³¹ sau³³ çoŋ¹¹   tça¹¹ 'the wood for desks'
     wood make desk   that

     le¹¹ aŋ³²³ əm³²³   tça³³ 'the book about medicine'
     book speak medicine that

With the absence of the DIs, each of the three above NPs will overlap with a grammatically correct but applicationally wrong complete sentence.

(23) IP/*NP: pa⁵⁵ ɳau³³ ɳa⁵⁵   * 'the fish lives in river'
     IP/*NP: məi³¹sau³³ çoŋ¹¹   * 'the wood makes desk'
     IP/*NP: le¹¹ aŋ³²³ əm³²³   * 'the book speaks of medicine'

One further type of structure needs discussion, namely the topic that at first resembles the *Noun + Noun* and *Noun + Pronoun* NP morphologically but has a different derivational history. They can be distinguished in hierarchical organization. In (24) below the indicated portion of (24a) is an NP. In (24b) *mja¹¹* 'hands' has been topicalized and *jau¹¹* 'I' is the subject of the IP.

(24) (a) NP: [[mja¹¹ jau¹¹] çuk³²³ la¹¹] 'My hands are washed'
                hand   I   washed perf.
     (b) Topic: [[mja¹¹] [[jau¹¹] çuk³²³ la¹¹]] 'Speaking of hands, I have already washed
                                             them'
                hand   I   wash   perf.

(25)

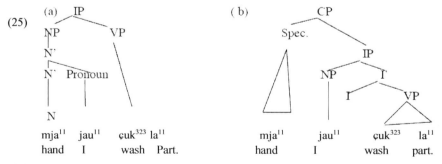

19.3.1.3. *Noun + localizer PP*

A localizer adjunct fixes the relative spatial position of the noun. Some most commonly used Kam localizers are: *u⁵⁵* 'above, up(on)', *te³²³* 'under, below', *au³¹* 'in, inside', *nuk³²³* 'outside', *phe³⁵* 'on the brim of', *pjin⁵⁵/ke⁵⁵* 'beside', *ta⁵³* 'in the middle of', *tiŋ⁵³* 'at the bottom of', *pan⁵³* 'half way', and *çut³²³* 'at the corner of'

The structure *localizer* + *noun* consists of a PP in which the localizer is a preposition describing the spatial relation between the noun and the reference identity. A determiner is helpful to parse the structure as an NP category but not required. See some examples:

(26) nɐm^{31}(water)   au^{31}(inside)   tau^{55}(pan)   tɕa^{33}(that) 'the water in the pan'
le^{11}(book)   u^{55}(on,above) ɕoŋ^{11}(desk) tɕa^{11}(that) 'the book on the table'
mau^{11}(fertilizer) ta^{53}(middle) ja^{53}(field) tɕa^{33}(that) 'fertilizer in the middle field'

It is clear that we are dealing here with an adjunct construction and not with specifiers or with complements, as the localizer phrase is restricted in occurrence and can be used widely with a large set of nouns.

19.3.1.4. *Noun + adjunct verb NP*

The head noun can also be modified by a verb with or without DI, as is seen in (27).

(27) (a) tɐŋ^{53} sui^{53}(tɕa^{33}) 'the bench for sitting'
     bench sit

(b) ma^{55} tuŋ^{55}(tɕa^{33}) 'the cooked dish'
     dish   cook

(c) ɲən^{11} pjiu^{55}(tɕa^{33}) 'the jumping person'
     person jump

The verb in (27) cannot be considered as the predicate of a sentence following a possible subject. In (27a) and (27b) it is clear that the bench itself cannot sit and the dish cannot cook. Even in (27c), if the verb here functions as a predicate, then it requires some other lexical and grammatical help from other constituents, such as VP marker (directional verb) *pai^{55}*, *taŋ^{55}*. The verb here is very much like a modifier whose functions will be discussed in 3.1.1.

There are some cases in which the relation between the noun constituents and the verb constituents is hard to define. They may be considered either as NP head and its modifier (28a), or as a subject and a predicate of a clause (28b):

(28) (a) As a NP: [[nok^{31} pən^{323}] [pai^{55} la^{11}]]. 'The flying bird has gone away'
                 bird   fly   go/away Part

(b) As a clause: [[nok^{31}] [pən^{323} pai^{55} la^{11}]]. 'The bird has flown away'

                 bird   fly   go/away Part.

(29) (a)   (b)

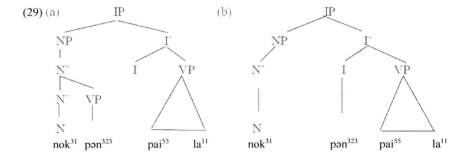

19.3.1.5. *Quantifier + noun NP*

Quantifier consists of *numeral + classifier*. There is co-occurrence between a Kam noun and its classifier; for each noun only one or two classifiers are compatible with a given noun. The interesting feature here is that the linear order of the noun and the quantifier does not obey the generalization that all phrase structure is head-first, as has been seen in all other NPs. The noun, which is head of the phrase, follows the classifier and numeral, and is thus not first in the phrase. See examples in (30):

(30)   sam⁵⁵   tu¹¹   meu³¹   'three cats'

       three   CLF   cat

       pet³²³   tɕɐk¹¹   tɕən¹¹   'eight people'

       eight   CLF   person

(31)

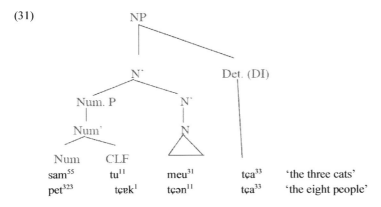

sam⁵⁵	tu¹¹	meu³¹	tɕa³³	'the three cats'
pet³²³	tɕɐk¹	tɕən¹¹	tɕa³³	'the eight people'

The relations expressed in the NP structure (31) above assume that the numeral phrase is an adjunct of the head noun and that the classifier is an adjunct of the numeral. There is, of course, lexical co-occurrence between the head noun and the classifier, but this dependency is lexical and not grammatical. Moreover, since any numeral can co-occur with a given classifier it must be assumed that there is no subcategorization relationship between CLF and NUM; thus the adjunct relation. There is also some gapping evidence to support this analysis. One can say *mau³³ li³²³ sam⁵⁵ tu¹¹ meu³¹, jau¹¹ li³²³ sɿ⁵³ tu¹¹ ti* 'he has three cats but I have four CLF e'. It is ungrammatical so say ... *jau¹¹ me¹¹ sɿ⁵³ tu¹¹ ti* '...I have four (no classifier)'. These data suggest that *sam⁵⁵-tu¹¹* is a constituent and *tu¹¹-meu³¹* is not. (But see 3.3. for a discussion of the matching relation between the noun and the classifier.)

    These inconsistent phenomena in NP linear order can perhaps be explained through contact with Chinese. In Chinese, the quantifier is placed before the modified noun in an order exactly the same as in Kam. The emergence of classifiers in Chinese is traceable. Before 200 BC there were no classifiers, and after the emergence of classifiers the quantifier and the classifier were placed after the noun. It is still true that in Kam traditional songs and poetry, the classifier can be omitted, and even more importantly the quantifiers with classifiers can, and often do occur after the noun. Other languages of the family may still show the original word order. For example, in Thai, numeral and classifier appear after the head noun (Haas 1942):

i)   mǎa sìi.tua   'dog four CLS   = 'four dogs'
ii) ajaan sǎam khon 'teacher three CLS   = 'three teachers'

Many languages show mixed typology by treating some phrase types as head-first and others as head-last. English is, of course, a well-known instance. One could try to impose consistency on the PS grammar by invoking movement rules, cf. i) below, or simply accept that languages can change their types over time, either from internal forces or from language contact. The case for change in Kam from head-first to partially head-last seems strong, cf. ii) below. It is noteworthy that the specifier determiner in Kam remains the last element of the NP. In some locations where northern Kam is spoken, for younger speakers however, the reversal of phrase structure of the NP has the possessive pronoun or even an attributive adjective before the head NP, just as in Chinese, cf. Edmondson 2003 and Zheng and Long 1998 for details.

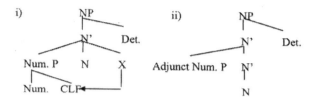

19.3.1.6. *X-bar schema*

All the NPs discussed in 3.1 are of the simplest NP type, but the linguistic data are far more complicated than these show. For example, the different modifiers and the complement constituents can combine to express more sophisticated and refined semantic relationships; an IP can also be inserted into an NP to restrict the Noun further. It is important and also interesting to extract more elaborate rules and principles determining NP organization.

In this section, the Kam NP X-bar schema, based on the analyses proposed in 18.3.1, will first be summarized. Then, the proposed scheme will be confronted with a variety of multiple modifiers and extended constructions in order to refine the proposal still more.

The X-bar format for Kam NPs can be generated with the following three schematic Rules:

(32) (a) NP → N', Det

(b) N' → N', Adjunct or   N'→ Adjunct, N' (because of the internal structure of the Numeral Phrase)

(c) N' → N, Complement

Simple examples produced by rules in (32) are given in (33) and (34):

(33)   pa^{55} mak^{323} au^{31} tɐm^{55} tɕa^{33} 'the big fish in the pond'
       fish   big   in   pond   that

(34)   lja^{33} je^{35} ji^{55} ləi^{323} 'casting nets (is easy).'
       cast   net   easy   PART

The structure of (33) can be shown in (33'):

(33')

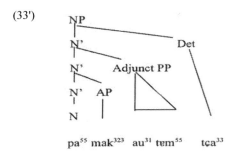

pa⁵⁵ mak³²³ au³¹ tɐm⁵⁵   tɕa³³

In (34) *lja³³ je³⁵* is the subject NP of the sentence; *lja³³* 'casting' takes as its complement NP *je³⁵* 'net' just as the corresponding sentence *lja³³ je³⁵* 'cast nets' the direct object NP *je³⁵*. To date we have not found other kinds of NP complement structures of the type so often discussed in the grammatical literature of English (such as *student of physics*, *farmer of rice*, *destruction of the city*, etc.) See Radford (1997).

19.3.1.7. *NP determiners*

The NP determiner refers to the lexical constituent those functions to specify the NP for definiteness, quantity, and other features. It may have semantic functions at the same time.

The previous discussion in this chapter indicated strongly that there are NP determiners in Kam. These need to be represented in the hierarchical organization. A summary of the NP markers list follows:

(35)   (a) determiners for definite description:

nai³³	'this'
tɕa⁵³	'that'
tɕa¹¹	'that'
tɕa³²³	'that'
nu³⁵	'which, whom, where'

(b) Conjunctions can also indicate that the around element(s) is/are NP:

ɲim³⁵	'and, (along) with'
toŋ¹¹	'and, (along) with'
tu⁵⁵	'though, even, further'
ju³³	'and, again; along'

The NP determiner role is to confirm and label the NP category of a phrase, even though the category of the NP phrase is not fully determined by the marker. They do, sometimes, not only help confirm the NP membership of the phrase, but also disambiguate the possible ambiguity between the topic structure and the NP. See examples in (36):

(36) (a) [le¹¹ jau¹¹] [au⁵⁵ pai⁵⁵ la¹¹]. (could be IP or topic)
        book my   take   go   Perf.
        — 'My book has been taken away'

(b) [le¹¹ jau¹¹ tɕa³³] [au⁵⁵ pai⁵⁵ la¹¹].   (IP, non-topic structure)
    book my   that   take go Perf.
    — 'My book has been taken away'

(c) [le¹¹ *tɕa³³*] [jau¹¹ au⁵⁵ pai⁵⁵ la¹¹].   (IP, topic structure)
    book that   I   take go Perf.
    — 'Speaking of the book, I have taken it away'

Xu and Langendoen (1985: 1) have a clear definition of the topic structure by saying 'By 'topic structure', we mean any grammatical configuration consisting of two parts: the topic, which invariably occurs first, and the comment, a clause which follows the topic and says something about it.' Kam topic structure is the same, but the ordering of the topic and the subject of the structure can overlap with a possible 'N + modifier N' NP.   In this case, the speaker can take advantage of the determiner's role to clarify the vagueness, when homonyms or multiple specifiers are involved in the structure. There can be several distinctive interpretations for (37), depending on parsing and intonation, as shown in (37).

(37)   si¹¹   man³²³   ɲa¹¹   tuŋ⁵⁵   lai⁵⁵   mi³¹?
       cake   yellow   you   steam   good   NEG

(a)   [si¹¹   man³²³   ɲa¹¹]   [tuŋ⁵⁵   lai⁵⁵   mi³¹]?
       — 'Is your yellow cake ready (to serve)?'

(b)   [si¹¹   man³²³   ɲa¹¹   tuŋ⁵⁵]   ]lai⁵⁵   mi³¹]?
       — 'Is the yellow cake you are supposed to bake already?'

(c)   [si¹¹   man³²³   ɲ a¹¹]   [tuŋ⁵⁵l   ai⁵⁵   mi³¹]?
       — 'Have you baked the yellow cake?'

(d)   [si¹¹   man³²³]   [ɲa¹¹   tuŋ⁵⁵   l   ai⁵⁵   mi³¹]?
       — 'Speaking of the yellow cake, have you baked it already?'

When an NP determiner appears, the interpretations become unambiguous. The above mentioned ambiguous sentence sets can then be disambiguated according for internal organization as:

(38) (a) NP1:   [le¹¹jau¹¹ tɕa¹¹] [au⁵⁵pai⁵⁵la¹¹.]
                  — 'My book has been taken away.'

         or even NP with an internal IP. Here the *au⁵⁵* 'buy' is a homonym of *au⁵⁵* 'take'.

     (b) NP2   [le¹¹ jau¹¹ au⁵⁵ tɕa¹¹] [pai⁵⁵ la¹¹].

                   — 'The book I bought is gone.'

     (c) Topic   sentence:
                   [le¹¹ tɕa¹¹] [jau¹¹ au⁵⁵ pai⁵⁵ la¹¹.]
                   — 'The book, I have taken that one away.'

The situation in (38) is a bit more complex due to its multiple modifiers but can be clarified as in (39).

(39) (a) NP1: [si^{11} man^{323} ṇa^{11} tɕa^{323}] [tuŋ^{55} lai^{55} mi^{31}]?

— 'Is your yellow cake right there baked already?'

(b) NP2: [si^{11} man^{323} ṇa^{11} tuŋ^{55} tɕa^{323}] [lai^{55} mi^{31}]?

— 'Is the yellow cake you baked ready?'

(c) Topic sentence:

[si^{11} man^{323} tɕa^{323}] [a^{11}] [tuŋ^{55} lai^{55} mi^{31}]?
— 'Regarding the yellow cake, have you baked it already?'

The situation in (38) is a bit more complex due to its multiple modifiers but can be clarified as in (39).

(39) (a) NP1: [si^{11} man^{323} ṇa^{11} tɕa^{323}] [tuŋ^{55} lai^{55} mi^{31}]?

— 'Is your yellow cake right there baked already?'

(b) NP2: [si^{11} man^{323} ṇa^{11} tuŋ^{55} tɕa^{323}] [lai^{55} mi^{31}]?

— 'Is the yellow cake you baked ready?'

(c) Topic sentence:

[si^{11} man^{323} tɕa^{323}] [a^{11}] [tuŋ^{55} lai^{55} mi^{31}]?
— 'Regarding the yellow cake, have you baked it already?'

It is very clear the NP determiner tɕa^{323} here works effectively to single the whole NP out, specifying its position and relationship with respect to other constituents, and clarifying the internal organization of the phrase. These Det's possess a special feature compared with their counterpart in many other languages, such as English and Chinese: its position is right after other NP constituents and marks the end of the NP structure. It indicates the NP boundary neatly and supports the idea that this may be considered as a marker of the whole NP. It is in this sense one might suggest separate the NP determiner from other phrase constituents and also from other possible roles such as Det's and homonyms.

Conjunction NP determiners work a little differently from the other determiners. For example, jən^{35} 'and, (along) with' can only occur between two equivalent NPs and cannot be used to separate multiple specifiers. The reason is that the functions of the adjuncts at different hierarchy levels are not equal.

Another point is that the conjoined NP determiner tu^{55} marks the NP status of the component, thus distinguishes it from otherwise verb/verb phrase like structures. At the same time, it can also mark an NP. See the examples in (40).

(40) (a) pjeu^{53} 'torun'

—   pjeu^{53} tu^{55} lam^{55} ki^{323} tɕha^{453}.

run   marker   chase   NEG   up   'Even running cannot catch that up'

(b) ne³²³ 'tocry'

   —   ne³²³   tu⁵⁵   wum⁵⁵ tɕən¹¹.

        cry   marker thin   person   'Even crying can make one lose weight'

An NP phrase is analyzed based on the above proposal in (41).

(41)

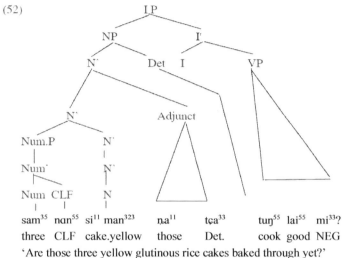

'Are those three yellow glutinous rice cakes baked through yet?'

In general, the determiners function nicely as NP markers.

19.3.2. Verb phrases

This chapter describes the main aspects of the more complex verb phrases. Since Kam is an isolating language, it adds on certain phrase elements and independent functional words such as *particles* and *conjunctions* to the structure rather than using inflections for *tense, aspect,* or *mood.* So a brief introduction to Kam verbs and functional word categories is first provided in 3.2.1.1. Then the structure of the VP will be discussed in 3.2.1.2. Some special extended topics, such as the *t əi¹¹ … V…* construction, *V + paⁱ⁵⁵/taŋ⁵⁵/ma³⁵* construction, and verbal serialization occupy the discussion in 3.2.3.

19.3.2.1. *Kam verb*

19.3.2.1.1. *Verb Categories*

Researchers divide the Kam verbs into four subcategories according to their semantic features (Liang 1984: 366):

(42) (a) *action* verbs(CV): describing movements or actions, for example:

            lam⁵⁵   'to chase'   mja¹¹   'to plant'

            tɕi⁵⁵   'to eat/drink'   mje³³   'to ponder'

(b) *stative* verbs(SV): stating the existence of something, for example:

tɕiŋ⁵³   'exactly be'   ɕi³³   'to be'

(c) *modal* verbs(MV): also called modal auxiliary verbs, for example:

ju⁵³   'want to'   ȵon³³   'be willing to'

ɕaŋ⁴⁵³   'want to'   tɕan¹¹   'be willing to'

(d) *directional* verbs(DV): reflect the direction of the movements or actions,   for
    example:

uk³²³   'to go or come out of a closed space'

lau³²³   'come or go into a closed space"

tɕha⁴⁵³ 'to go up/climb' lui³³   'go down/descend'

pai⁵⁵ 'to go'   ma³⁵/taŋ⁵⁵ 'to come'

One might wish to add a fifth class, the *predicate* noun. These are found only in Northern
Kam (Long and Zheng 1998: 120). Members of this new verb class are derived from
corresponding nouns and have some restrictions on occurrence. They have the same
morphological appearance as verbs (except different tone) but belong to the category noun.

Among the four Kam verb classes, the number of stative or copular verbs is very limited.
They can be omitted and the structure still remains grammatical, as is demonstrated in (43).

(43) (a)   mau³³ tɕaŋ³²³ ȵən¹¹   hu¹³ 'He is a poor man.'

           he   be   person big

=(b) mau³³ [0]   ȵən¹¹   hu¹³ 'He is a poor man.'

The copula *tɕaŋ³²³* is obligatory only when asserting against doubt, as, for example, when
speaker A says, A: *mau³³ aɪ³²³ tɕaŋ³²³ ȵən¹¹ hu¹³!* 'He's not a poor man' and then B replies:
mau³³ tɕaŋ³²³ȵən¹¹ hu¹³. 'He IS a poor guy!'

There are only a few modal verbs in Kam. They share some common features with
adjectives and can be placed into the adjective frame *ȵaŋ³¹* + *adj.* + *ȵaŋ¹¹* 'really/very +adj. +
really/very' and occupy the same position as adjectives. See (44a) and (44b):

(44) (a) le¹¹ ȵaŋ¹¹ ju⁵³   ȵaŋ¹¹ 'The book is desperately needed'

        book really want to really

    (b) e³⁵ ȵaŋ¹¹ lai⁵⁵   ȵaŋ¹¹ 'They are really nice'

        they really good   really'

It is still arguable whether the category modal verb is well supported or not.

Directional verbs are common verbs of motion that have taken on new functions in that
they occur frequently after other verbs giving the directional pathway along which the action
or movement take place as consequence. Directional verbs are the second verb of the clause.
Thus, one can say that it is important to separate the two different types of actions: one is the

action itself; the other is the spatial/quality shift of the action. In English this meaning is often expressed as a particle verb, such as *come out, go down*. See examples in (45):

(45) (a) ta⁵⁵man⁵⁵   uk³²³   ma³⁵   la¹¹.   'The sun has come out.'

      the Sun   appear come Perf.

      ta⁵⁵man⁵⁵   ləp⁵⁵   pai⁵⁵   la¹¹.   'The sun has gone down.'

      the Sun   hide   go   Perf.

    (b) lje³²³ ljau³⁵ wen³⁵ sɐk³⁵ la¹¹.   'The goat pushed down the fence.'

      goat push flip   fence Perf.

      lie³²³ ljau³³ wen³⁵ sak³⁵ pai⁵⁵ la¹¹   'The goat pushed down the fence

      goat push flip   fence go   Perf. (and) the fence is moved/changed.'

As the above discussion and examples show, the directional verb is tightly connected to the main verb complementing it with information about the actor along with the effect of the main verb action taking place. The tight connection between the two verbs prevents intervening elements. For instance, in the case of *lie³²³ ljau³³ wen³⁵ sak⁵⁵ pai⁵⁵ la¹¹* the final particle *la¹¹* cannot come before the directional complement (i.e., **lie³²³ liau³³ wen³⁵ sak⁵⁵ la¹¹ pai⁵⁵*). This behavior argues for treating directional verbs as complements. A similar case is seen in verbs of motion with complement of location (i.e., *mau³³ pai⁵⁵ Beijing ta¹¹.*) 'He's been to Beijing (once)', but not (except in northern areas) **mau³³ pai⁵⁵ ta¹¹ Beijing. 'He's been to Beijing.'* Moreover, the set of directional verb is limited in number. The most common ones are *pai⁵⁵* 'away from' and *ma³⁵/taŋ⁵⁵* 'toward the speaker'. This closeness and cooperation of the two verbs has led many to regard the directional verb as a complement and not an adjunct of the main verb.

19.3.2.1.2. *Functional words (FW)*

Functional words have grammatical function and thus appear only in construction and not in isolation. They occur at the end of a sentence expressing different moods. Their members are limited and can be listed exhaustively. They are divided into three classes: *structural* FW, *aspect* FW, and *modal auxiliary* FW.

    Structural FWs are used to set up special constructions, while adding extra semantic or even grammatical information. Three structural FWs are found:

1. *li³²³* — used after a verb or an adjective to express possibility, or capability, or permission. It is also a verb that means 'to get, obtain, have'. It is also used in the negative form of the *la¹¹* as in:

(46) (a) ma⁵⁵☒ ☒ nai³³☒ tçan⁵⁵☒ *li³³*   'This dish (of food) is edible'

      dish   this   eat   FW   or '(You are allowed) to eat this dish.'

    (b) mau³³   taŋ⁵⁵   la¹¹   mi³³? 'Has he arrived yet?'

    (c) taŋ⁵⁵   la¹¹   'Yes.'

If the answer is no, then *ai³¹ li³²³* 'No' (older speakers) or *mi³¹* (young speakers).

(46b) illustrates that a negative reply to the question involve li^{323} for some speakers. This structure is parallel to Chinese *meiyou* in answer to questions in *le*.

2. tau^{33}— used in sentences with passive-like meaning to introduce either the agent or the action if the agent is not mentioned. The position is right before the agent. It is also a verb that means 'to touch or suffer'.

(47) mau^{33} tau^{33} pjən^{55} çok^{11}. 'He got drenched.'

    he   FW   rain   whip

3. ti^{55}— used after an attribute or a verb or between a verb and its object to stress an element of the sentence. It turns a noun into an attributive structure. See (48).

(48) e^{35} ti^{55} ta^{323} 'their family's forest'

    they   FW   forest (Attribute)

    khai^{453} nai^{33} mau^{33} çem^{33} ti^{55} 'It is he who paneled this wood wall.'

    wall   this   he   panel   FW

Aspect FWs are used after verbs to indicate the sequence in time of given actions. Commonly used aspect FWs are:

1. to^{323}— indicates an action in progress or the continuity of the action. Its meaning is very similar to Chinese *guo*.

(49) na^{11} sui^{53} to^{323} 'you keep sitting/staying there'

    you   sit   FW

2. ta^{33}— indicates a completed/or experienced action. Example:

(50) (a) mau^{33} sui^{53} ta^{33}.   '(This tool) was used by him.'

    he   sit   FW

    (b) mau^{33} pai^{55} Changsha ta^{33}. 'He has been to Changsha (capital of Hunan Province).'

    he   go   Changsha FW

3. la^{11}/$ljeu^{31}$— indicates completion, change of state, or perfected events. Examples:

(51) ma^{55} çok^{11} leu^{31} 'The dish is cooked already'

    dish cooked FW

Modal FWs are used to express moods either at the end of a sentence, or at pauses after each serial phrase member in the middle of the sentence. For example:

(52) (a)   Question/interrogative:

    i)   na^{11} nan^{11} kwe^{11} han^{13} pai^{55} hi^{11}? 'You really don't want to go

        you   really NEG   willing go   FW   (I'm surprised)?'

ii) ŋa¹¹   ju⁵³   pai⁵⁵   mi³³?   'Do you want to go?'
   you   want   go   FW

(b) Prohibitive and imperative:

oŋ³³   we³¹   ho¹¹!   'You'd better not do that!'
don't   do   FW

(c) Exclamation:

mau³³   ɲɐŋ¹¹   phaŋ³⁵   lu³³   'He is really tall, as you told me!'
he   really tall   FW

(d) Listing miscellany:

le¹¹   a³³,   pjɔt⁵⁵   a³³,   mau³³   çet³²³   pe⁵⁵   li¹¹.   'He sells books and pens
book   FW1   pen   FW1   he   all   sell   FW2   (and stuff like that)'

19.3.2.2. *Verb phrase analysis*

The verb phrase consists of sentence parts other than the subject NP in a sentence. The I or inflection node in Kam is always unfilled, since Kam is an analytic language without overt inflectional morphology. The sentence in the X-bar theory has the following structure as in (53):

(53)

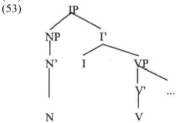

The head of VP is the verb. It is modified, specified, or supplemented by other constituents within the VP phrase. All the VP-internal constituents (including V itself) are layered not on equal footing but in an ordered organization. Discussion in this paragraph is intended to capture the internal hierarchy among the various constituents of the VP. The organizing relation between the verb and other complements is considered first, followed by the V-bar adjuncts and complements and the linear order in the multi-layered VP. Unlike the NP, VP complements are easy to find.

19.3.2.2.1. *Verb and its modifiers*

Kam is a head-first SVO language in its NP structures as shown in 3.1. So one would expect that the situation in VP would be the same, that is to say, 'VP → V', specifier; V' → V', adjunct; V' → V, complement.

19.3.2.2.1.1. 'Verb + NP complement' VP

The typical VP consists of verb and a noun acting as the direct object complement. Consider the examples in (54).

(54)

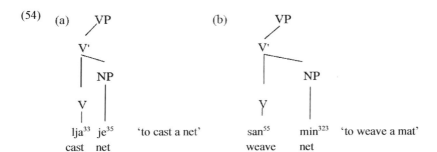

(a) VP / V' / V · NP / lja³³ je³⁵ · cast net · 'to cast a net'

(b) VP / V' / V · NP / san⁵⁵ min³²³ · weave net · 'to weave a mat'

The Kam direct object complement construction at first appearance shows no unusual features. The connection between verb and direct object complement is close and optional modifiers are not allowed to interrupt this sequence (e.g., *mau³³ lja³³ je⁵⁵ nɐm³¹* but unacceptable is **mau³³ lja³³ nɐm³¹ je³⁵* 'Cast the net into the water'). In this instance *nɐm³¹* cannot interrupt the sequence of verb + DO Complement.

There is one special feature of verbs and their direct object complements. Like other East Asian languages including Chinese, it is arguable whether there are any absolute intransitive verbs or not. It is difficult to find examples of absolute intransitives because it seems almost any verbs can take an object of some sort. For example, *tok⁵⁵*(drop) *pjən³⁵*(rain) 'to rain', *suɪ⁵³*(sit) *taŋ⁵³*(bench) 'to sit', *mau³³*(he) *tok⁵⁵*(drop) *pən⁵³*(sweat) *ljeu³¹*(Part). 'He dripped sweat'. It remains still to be investigated whether these examples involve true transitivity. Nonetheless, it is noteworthy that none of these 'transitive' sentences can be passivized. In any case, whether an NP is an obligatory or optional sister of V in many cases may be treatable as a lexical co-occurrence. For the moment, we may tentatively conclude that all Kam verbs are transitive or that at the least some kinds of nouns may appear in construction with the verb, perhaps as complements, perhaps as adjuncts, or perhaps as something else.

Another point that needs to be clarified is the concept *Predicate*. Not only the four classes of verbs mentioned above qualify as the head of a VP, but also adjective phrases and possibly NPs, which is a feature worthy of further exploration. Examples are:

(55) (nai³³) mja⁵³ ɲən¹¹   'it makes one sad   (eŋ⁵⁵) pəi¹¹ ŋu⁴⁵³   'let pig get fat

    this sad person /sadden'   food fat pig   /fatten'

Adjectives in Kam share many properties in common with verbs and function here as verbs, a phenomenon very similar to the English causative 'en-' or suffix '-en', even though the encoding is totally different from English affixes. Kam treats them as verbs and includes them in the VP. The analysis of the two above phrases is shown in (56):

(56)

VP / V' NP / V / mja⁵³ ɲən¹¹ · sad people

VP / V' NP / V / pəi¹¹ ŋu⁴⁵³ · fat pig

Other adjectives can also be verbs: *pak³¹* 'white'/'whiten', *kit³²³* 'painful'/ 'cause to pain', and so forth. It is reasonable to treat the adjective preceding a noun as a V. Compared with the reverse linear order of adjective and noun structure, as in a typical NP, it is obvious that the treatment of the same morphological form as adjective or verb according to its relation with other constituents is consistent. But, see 3.2.1. Let us now turn to other kinds of structures within the VP constituent.

19.3.2.2.1.2. "'Verb + adv. complement" and "adv. + tɕa³²³'' + verb' VP

Long & Zheng (1998: 132–133) divide adverbs into five classes:

(57) adverbs of degree:
    ȵaŋ¹¹ 'really'   the³⁵   'further'
    adverbs of scope:
    ɕet¹³ 'all'   pu³³   'also'
    adverbs of time:
    su³³   'then; atonce' wan¹¹   'already'
    adverbs of negation:
    kwe¹¹ 'do not have' ɔi³²³   'do not'
    adverbs of mood:
    ten³³ 'whenever'   hoŋ¹¹he¹¹ 'no matter what'

Adverbs in Kam as in other languages are used mainly to modify verbs, adjectives, or other adverbs. One expects them to follow the V head in a head-first language. And one does find examples very readily:

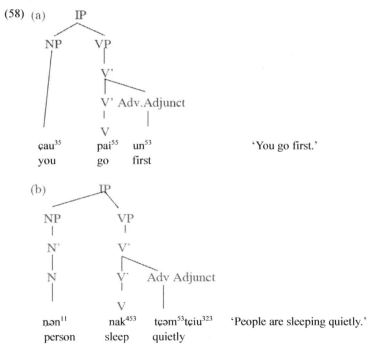

(58) (a)
çau³⁵ pai⁵⁵ un⁵³   'You go first.'
you go first

(b)
ȵən¹¹ nak⁴⁵³ tɕəm⁵³tɕiu³²³ 'People are sleeping quietly.'
person sleep quietly

In addition to the post-positive examples in (58), though, there are also cases in which members from the five adverb classes can be put before the verb in pre-positive position to modify it, for example:

(59) (a) nai³³ haŋ¹¹   çaŋ³³ lai⁵⁵ 'This will be better.'

         this   way   further good

    (b) mau³³ pən³²³   wo³¹   ne³²³ 'The only thing he knows is to cry.'

         he   only   know   cry

    (c) n̠a¹¹ naŋ⁵⁵   ju⁵³   e¹¹?   'Do you want some more?'

         you   still   want   NEG

    (d) jau¹¹ kwe¹¹   jiu⁵³ la¹¹   'I don't want anymore.'

         I   don't   want   Perf.

    (e) mau³³ weŋ¹¹si¹¹ ko⁵⁵   'He always smiles.'

         he   always   smile

Furthermore, the two head-first VP examples in (58) have close variants that show head-last VPs when they are accompanied by a conjunction or an adverb constituent *tɕa³²³* which has the same form with the NP determiner:

(60) (a) n̠a¹¹   ta³³   *kun⁵³* pai⁵⁵   'You go first'

         you   from   first   go

    (b) n̠ən¹¹ *tɕənr̠⁵³tɕiu³²³* tɕa³³ nak⁴⁵³ 'People are sleeping quietly'

         people quietly   DI   sleep

In (60b) the particle *tɕa³²³* is homophonous with the determiner. Notice though that other determiners cannot fill this slot (e.g., * *tɕənr̠⁵³ tɕiu³²³ nai³³*). Comparing (58b) and (60b) we see that adverbs can occur either before or after the V that they modify. If we assume that the pre-posed and the post-posed forms are related, then one of the positions could be taken as the result of movement. Another choice is to treat them as two independent elements that share no common derivational history. One would then take as evidence for their independence that they possess different positional characteristics. So no movement is needed to explain the surface facts. They are both adverbs, but they are different adverbs in a grammatical sense. The latter suggestion is preferred in this paper and detailed discussion will follow. We would note that adverbs are cross-linguistically a difficult category that in many languages fails to show consistent word order behavior.

    The advantages of categorizing different adverb as different types are obvious. First, it has just been shown that there are word order differences and second there are differences between the behaviors of these two types of adverb. Both of these facts support assuming two types of adverbs, namely the pre-head adverb labeled Adv1, and the post-head labeled Adv2, respectively. Their distinguishing characteristics can be tabulated as follows so they have different subcategorization.

1. Adv1 can never be put after the head V, while Adv2 can occur with no marking post-head or in pre-head position accompanied by the marker *tɕa³²³*.
2. post-head Adv2 describes the manner of the action, the way the action proceeds or is performed.
3. pre-head Adv2 with markers expresses a slightly different sense compared with the post-head Adv2. Consider the examples in (61):

(61) ne³²³   *hot³¹hot³¹*   'cried loudly' (emphasizes the scene or the situation)

     cry   Adv2

hot³¹hot³¹ tɕa³³   ne³²³ 'cried in a way to produce loud noise'
                         (emphasizes how the crying action is conducted)

Adv   DI   cry

pai⁵⁵   *kuŋ⁵³*   'go first' (emphasizes the fact/intention)

go   first

ta³³   *kuŋ⁵³*   pai⁵⁵ 'go from the first' (emphasizes the way how to go)

from   front   go

Post-posed adverbs in Kam seem semantically to map the verb meaning onto some part of the verb meaning; <u>running that is fast</u> or <u>crying that is loud,</u> for example. In other words, such adverbs are usually modal adverbs or manner adverbs. The pre-posed adverb, by contrast, does not modify the verb properties directly but seems to operate on more derived and indirect parts of the meaning. It is not easily characterized as to function. This difference suggests but, by no means, dictates that Adv2 is closer to the verb in syntactic representation than Adv1 (assuming that closeness of semantics is mirrored by closeness in syntax). Therefore, while awaiting additional evidence, we will assume that the phrase structure of the VP with both Adv1 and Adv2 is as illustrated in the following diagram.

62)

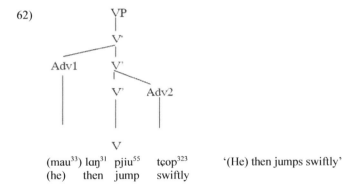

(mau³³) laŋ³¹ pjiu⁵⁵ tɕop³²³   '(He) then jumps swiftly'
(he)   then   jump   swiftly

19.3.2.2.1.3. "'Verb + adj. complement" and "adj. + verb"' VP

Consider the fact that adjectives and verbs share many features in Kam, for example, they can both function as the head of the predicate. It is possible that they can be confused sometimes, and difficulty arises in identifying them, especially when they are combined. Some examples in (63):

(63)

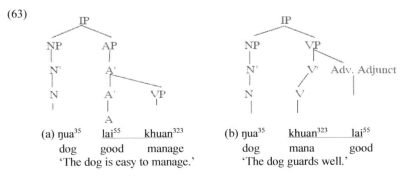

(a) ŋua³⁵   lai⁵⁵   khuan³²³   (b) ŋua³⁵   khuan³²³   lai⁵⁵
   dog   good   manage   dog   mana   good
'The dog is easy to manage.'   'The dog guards well.'

The adjective *laɨ⁵⁵* and verb *khuan³²³* are the heads of their respective phrases in (63a) and (63b). In (63a) *laɨ⁵⁵* is the main predicate – the dog is good, good at what? Being controlled. In (63b) *khuan³²³* is the main predicate and the adverb *laɨ⁵⁵*, equal in appearance to the adjective, modifies the preceding head – guarding how? Well. Despite this evidence let us consider some more examples in (64):

(64) mja⁵³   pai⁵⁵   'don't like to go'/'be sad about going'
     sad   go
     sai⁵³   pai⁵⁵   'go carefully'/'be careful in going'
     careful   go
     hoi⁴⁵³   pjeu⁵³   '(please) run quickly'/'be quick in running'
     fast   run

Adverbs behave as modifiers after their heads in VPs, but their functions are not so clear as the two English translations show. From the view of consistency, it would be better if the first element were treated as the head and the structure remaining grammatical with no significant semantic difference. The two contrasting analyses are shown here, using the *hoi⁵³ pjau⁵³* and a new *laɨ⁵⁵ (good) tçan⁵⁵ (eat)* 'delicious/good taste':

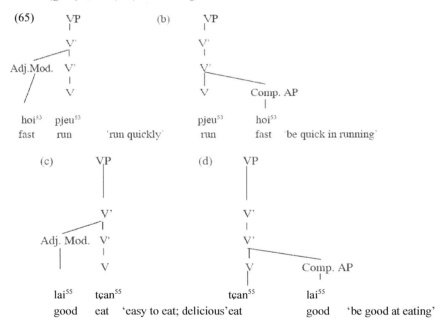

(65)

One very robust test for the head of a predicate phrase in Kam is the answer to a question. Kam structure allows the head element only as an answer, but adjuncts or complements alone are not permitted. Thus, the question in (66):

(66) mau³³ lja³³ je³⁵ kwe¹¹ ?   'Does he cast a net?'

can be answered *lja³³* 'casts' or *kwe¹¹ lja³³* 'doesn't cast.' So in this instance the sentence would be like (67):

(67) mau³³ pjau⁵³ hoi⁴⁵³ kwe¹¹? 'Does he/she run fast?'

The answer must be *hoi⁵³* 'fast' or *kwe¹¹ hoi⁵³* 'not fast'. The answers cannot be *pjeu⁵³ 'run' or *mi¹¹ pjeu⁵³* 'not run'. Therefore these data suggest that *hoi⁵³* is the head in the original sentence.

Chinese *pǎo* (run*) DE kuài (*fast*)* '(can) run fast' is a model to use in the analysis of Kam 'V + Adj.' structures. There are two possible analyses here too. One is to take the head as the first verb *pǎo* or the second *kuài*. Traditionally *pǎo DE kuài* is considered as a descriptive complement structure. James Huang (1988) summarizes the two treatments by saying that there are two hypothesis: P(rimary) P(redication), in which 'the second verb in a ... *V1*...*V2*... sequence is treated as the main verb of the sentence', while 'according to the S(econdary) P(redication) hypothesis the second V is treated as a complement of the first.' See the comparing diagrams based on P.P. and S.P. analysis in (68).

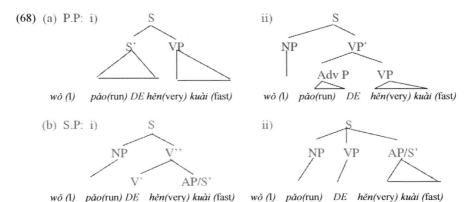

(68) (a) P.P: i)   S   ii)   S
       S'   VP   NP   VP'
                                                Adv P   VP
   *wǒ (*I*)   pǎo(*run*) DE hěn(*very*) kuài (*fast*)   wǒ (*I*)   pǎo(*run*) DE   hěn(*very*) kuài (*fast*)

   (b) S.P: i)   S   ii)   S
       NP   V''   NP   VP   AP/S'
           V'   AP/S'
   *wǒ (*I*)   pǎo(*run*) DE   hěn(*very*) kuài (*fast*)   wǒ (*I*)   pǎo(*run*) DE   hěn(*very*) kuài (*fast*)

Huang compares the P.P. and S.P. hypothesis and concludes 'that the traditional hypothesis taking V1 to be the main verb is more nearly correct' (i.e., he prefers the S.P. at the end). It is the way we chose in Kam in (65b) and (65d).

19.3.2.2.1.4. 'Verb + prepositional phrase' VP

Prepositional phrases (PP) can modify the verbs or adjectives that follow them, and are thus to be considered adjuncts.

(69) sok¹¹ khwən³⁵ səm³³   pai⁵⁵ 'search along the trail'
     along trail   search go
     n̠im³⁵ mau³³   khuan³¹   'talk with him'
     with him   talk

PPs can also occur after verbs or adjectives as complements of the preceding head, the predicted order of a head-first language. In (70) it is assumed that *kau³¹ tɕoŋ³³* and *ti⁵⁵ khe³⁵* are complements of their verbs as they are obligatory elements; they fill in meaning required by the verb. See (70):

(70) (a) liu⁵⁵   au³¹ pja¹¹   (b) au⁵⁵ ti⁵⁵ e³⁵
         throw in   bush   give to they
         'throw into the bushes'   'give to them'

(71)

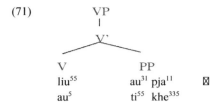

The same situation in which the modifier can be either after the head as a complement or before the head as an adjunct is confirmation that: firstly, it is not uncommon for languages not to be entirely consistent with regard to word order typology. The classification needs to be defined further and sub-classes need to be set up for each word class so they can determine the organizational patterns of the VP; or secondly the present classification of adverbs, adjectives, and prepositions is still preliminary. A new classification is necessary to define and identify the different modifiers. Afterwards, the inconsistency above will be resolved. English, for example, has *father's hat*, but also *center of earth*.

19.3.2.3. *X-bar and the multiple-modifier VP*

19.3.2.3.1. *VP X-bar scheme*

Summarizing the discussion above about the relations between the verb head and the modifiers in the VP, an X-bar scheme for Kam VPs is proposed as follows:

(72) (a) VP → V', XP

(b) V' → V'; YP{PP, AP, AdvP}

(c) V → V, ZP(NP, PP)

The linear order of V and NP Complement is consistent, but the linear order between the V and an adjunct modifier is variable, depending on the sub-class of the adverb, adjective and preposition modifiers.

19.3.2.3.2. *Multiple-modifier VP*

The VP head, either it is a typical verb itself, or an adjective that functions as a verb. Either can receive more than one attribution from different types of modifiers at the same time. It is also true that some modifiers cannot be used together to modify the same VP head. The linear order and the hierarchical organization among these different modifiers need to be studied in order to capture the nature of the VP phrases. Here is a complete sentence in which several VP head modifiers appear:

(73) mau³³ *ta³³*   *ȵin1 pɛ⁵⁵ su³³ kwe¹¹* tɕən³¹ tɕi⁵⁵   jen³⁵   taŋ⁵⁵ la¹¹.

he   from year last then NEG often smoke cigarette come Perf.

'He hasn't smoked so much since last year.'

A quick look at these different VP head modifiers indicates a linear order for them as:

PP + Adv1 + NEG Adv2 + V + NP + Perf. marker

All four modifiers (PP= *ta³³ ȵin¹¹ pɛ⁵⁵*, Adv1 = *su³²³*, NEG = *kwe¹¹*, Adv2 = tɕən³¹) precede the head V *tɕi⁵⁵*. See (74):

(74)

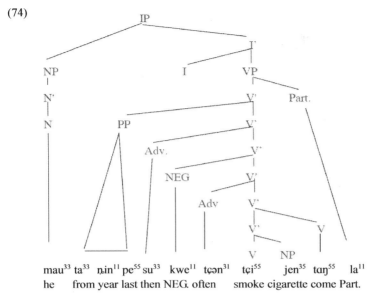

mau³³ ta³³ n̩in¹¹ pe⁵⁵ su³³ kwe¹¹ tɕən³¹ tɕi⁵⁵ jen³⁵ taŋ⁵⁵ la¹¹
he   from year last then NEG. often   smoke cigarette come Part.

The post-head modifier predictably occupies a position after the DO Complement and cannot be put in between the head V and the direct object complement NP. It must, as an adjunct, be put at the end of the VP, and it modifies the highest V'. This suggests that the direct object is a complement of V; the modifier, as an adjunct, cannot intervene.

(75) ai⁵³   tɕi⁵⁵ hoi⁴⁵³ '   'The chicken is eating fast.'
     chicken eat   fast
     ai⁵³   tɕi⁵⁵ nui¹¹ hoi⁴⁵³ 'The chicken eats the worms fast.'
     chicken eat   worm fast
     *ai⁵³   tɕi⁵⁵ hoi⁴⁵³ nui¹¹ 'The chicken eats the worms fast.'
     chicken eat   fast   worm

Clearly the modifier modifies the highest V', not just the head V, as shown in (76).

(76) VP

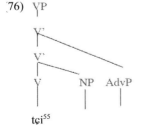

tɕi⁵⁵   nui
hoi⁴⁵³
eat   worm   fast

PP also can modify the VP along with other modifiers. See (77):

(77) mau³³ ljak¹¹ljak¹¹ tɕa³²³ soŋ⁵³ le¹¹ *au³¹   u⁵⁵ ɕoŋ¹¹* tɕa³²³
     he   quietly   DI   put book inside on desk DI
     'He put the book on the desk quietly.'

There is no doubt that the modifier is put outside the V and the possible object NP. This allows the demonstrated word order without any crossing of branches. The situation of pre-head modifiers is similar. For instance, the negation adverb modifies the head V and the possible object NP but not the head V alone. One can test the binding characteristic in question-and-answer context. The result is that either the head V or the head V with negation modifier can be used to satisfy the discourse function, depending on the truth of the situation. Consider examples in (78):

(78) (a) Q: e³⁵   pai⁵⁵ tɕən¹¹   mi³¹? 'Have they left for the fields?'
             they   go   mountain NEG

       A1: mi³¹   pai⁵⁵.   'Not yet.'
           NEG   go

       A2 :mi³¹   a¹¹.   'Not yet.'
           NEG   Part.

       A3: pai⁵⁵ la¹¹.   'Yes.'
           go   Perf.

     (b) Q: ɲaŋ¹¹ tok⁵⁵ pjən⁵⁵   a⁵⁵?   'Is it raining?'
            really fall rain   Part.

       A1 :kwe¹¹ ho⁵³.   'No, not at all.'
           NEG   Part.

       A2: tok⁵⁵ li³²³.   'Yes, it is.'
           rain   Part.

       A3 :ɲɐŋ¹¹ tok⁵⁵ li³²³.   'Yes, it is.'
           really rain Part.

It is rare that the 'V + NP' is used to answer the question either in confirming or denying the statement. This demonstrates again that the verb is the VP head and it is sufficient to use the negation marker with the head rather than the entire phrase. As the above cases show, only the head of the construction and the negation adverb are required. So a tree diagram is suggested in analysing the VP with preceding modifiers in (79):

(79)

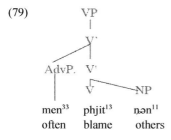

men³³ phjit¹³ ɲən¹¹
often blame   others

19.3.2.4. *Serial verb constructions*

For the purpose of simplification, everything considered in 3.2 and 3.3 is about the modification of a single headed V. Other possible complex constructions were left out temporarily. We now expand the range of data considering some other verb constructions such as the serial verb construction and 'V + *pai⁵⁵/ taŋ⁵⁵/ma³⁵*'.

19.3.2.4.1. *Classification of serial-verb constructions*

Serial-verb constructions (commonly abbreviated as SVCs) are found throughout Kam-Tai languages and beyond. SVCs are defined as constructions in which a series of one or more verbs follow the subject NP, and in which the actions may be connected in a temporal or cause-effect sequence. A classification of the SVC's is proposed here using the following categories of SVCs:

   1) modifying
   2) purposive
   3) object-raising
   4) coordinating

19.3.2.4.2. *Modifying serialization*

In modifying serialization, the first verb in the series acts somewhat adverbially, limiting or specifying the meaning of the later verb(s). See example (91):

(80) tə¹¹ le¹¹ pai⁵⁵ taŋ¹¹ hak³¹   'take books and go to school' or
    hold book go   place tell/inform 'go to school with books'

The two verbs are not equal. The meaning of the first verb is not so verb-like as the second one. It acts as a manner adverbial expressing the 'way (he) goes to school.'   It tells the way one goes to school. If there is no help from intonation and emphasis, the translation 'go to school with books' is more precise. Consider another example in (81).

(81) (mau³³) to³²³ a⁵⁵   lau³²³ nan³³   pau³¹.
    he   sing song enter valley Part.
    '(He) entered the valley, singing.'

Here the two actions (singing, entering) happen simultaneously but the second verb meaning is what the emphasis is on. The first one describes how the entering happens, or in what way it goes on. They are not equal, either. One more instance is:

(82) soŋ⁵³ pheu⁴⁵³ sip³²³ ȵən¹¹ məi⁴⁵³ 'greeting guest by firing firecracker'
    fireoff cracker greet people new

So in the hierarchical organization, these two verbs are not equal: the first one is the modifier, the second one is the head V. See the diagram in (83):

(83)

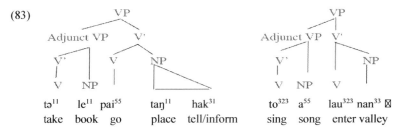

tə¹¹	le¹¹	pai⁵⁵	taŋ¹¹	hak³¹	to³²³	a⁵⁵	lau³²³	nan³³ ☒
take	book	go	place	tell/inform	sing	song	enter	valley

19.3.2.4.3. *Purposive serialization*

In purposive serialization, the first verb describes the action, while the second or latter verb specifies the purpose of the action denoted in the first verb as in (84).

(84) pai⁵⁵ so³¹ au⁵⁵ əu³¹ 'go to the barn to get rice '
   go   barn take rice

In this expression, the goal or purpose of going to the barn is to get the rice. The two verbs are not equal. The action of the first verb is the focus while the action of the second one is complementing or explaining. Examples are provided in (85):

(85) (a) tɕum⁵⁵   sin¹¹   tɕəi³²³ le¹¹   'accumulate money for book buying'
       accumulate money   buy   book
   (b) tat⁵⁵   tɕət⁵⁵   tuŋ⁵⁵   əu³¹   'split firewood for cooking'
       cut   firewood cook   dinner
   (c) tap³²³   mau¹¹   to³²³   ja⁵³   'carry manure for fertilizing paddy'
       carry   manure   apply   paddy

The first verb is the head. The second one identifies the purpose/goal/motivation of the action in the head V. The subject of the two IPs must be the same. The internal organization is shown in (86):

(86)

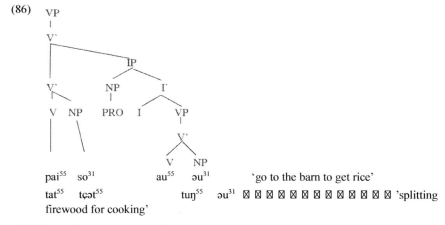

| pai⁵⁵ | so³¹ | | au⁵⁵ | əu³¹ | 'go to the barn to get rice' |
| tat⁵⁵ | tɕət⁵⁵ | | tuŋ⁵⁵ | əu³¹ ☒☒☒☒☒☒☒☒☒☒☒ | 'splitting firewood for cooking' |

19.3.2.4.4. *Object-raising serialization*

In object-raising serialization, the object of the first verb serves as the subject of the following second verb. Examples are offered in (87):

(87) hem^{31} noŋ^{31} ma^{35} jan^{11} 'call younger sibling to come back'
    call   sibling come home
    pau^{53} jau^{11} sui^{53} taŋ^{53} 'tell me to sit on the bench'
    tell   me   sit   bench

The first NP carries two functions: as the object of the first verb and the subject of the second verb. It is suggested that maybe there is another NP that is the duplication of the first noun but is omitted morphologically. Counter-evidence comes from the fact that retrieving the suggested omitted NP is very unnatural:

(88) *hem^{31} noŋ^{31} noŋ^{31} ma^{35} jan^{11} 'call sibling and sibling comes back home'
    call   sibling sibling come home
    *pau^{5} jau^{11} jau^{11} sui^{53} taŋ^{53} '(Someone) told me and I sat on the bench.'
    tell   me   me   sit   bench

The only way to make the above phrases in (88) grammatical is with two reduplicated NPs or by adding some adverbs, but the meaning will change somewhat:

(89) hem^{31} noŋ^{31} noŋ^{31} çu^{323} ma^{35} jan^{11}
    call   sibling sibling then   come home
    'call sibling, then sibling will come home'
    pau^{53} jau^{11} jau^{11} ha^{33} sui^{53} taŋ^{53}
    tell   me   me   only/after sit   bench
    '(Someone) told me, so I sat one the bench.'

The tense is changed and they can be considered as two complete sentences rather than constituents of one VP. So the idea of the omitted NP is not well supported and will not be preceded further. As a result, the hierarchy becomes hard to describe. The two actions are closely related in the sequence. They can be considered as origin/cause with result, and the interval between them is temporally very short. So they occur roughly contemporaneous. The problem is that two different AGENTs conduct them. If they are treated as two equal sub-VPs that form another VP, there is an obvious contradiction between the second member of the sub-VP and the subject of the VP:

(90)

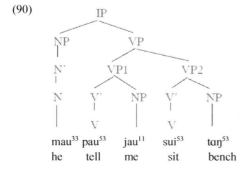

    mau^{33} pau^{53} jau^{11} sui^{53} taŋ^{53}
    he   tell   me   sit   bench

In order to overcome this dilemma, a new analysis is suggested in (91).

(91)

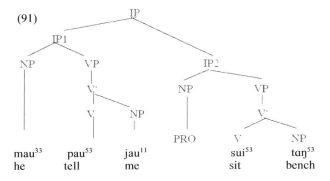

(92) (mau³³ pau⁵³ jau¹¹) sui⁵³ taŋ⁵³ çu³²³   mau³³
    he   tell   me   sit   bench wait   he
    '(He told me) to sit on the bench and wait for him/waiting for him by sitting on the
    bench'.

(92′)

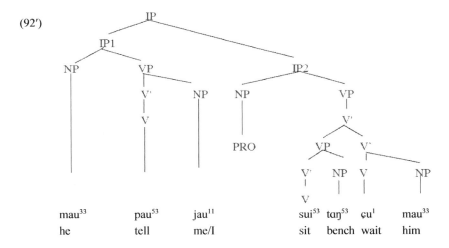

Some advantages of this extended IP are: the different AGENTs of different verbs are distinguished; the levels of the two IPs are slightly different; if there are any more serial verbs in the IP2, there is enough space left for them. For example, the IP2 can be extended as another modifying serialization (92).

19.3.2.4.5. *Coordinated serialization*

In coordinating serialization, several verbs are located at an equal grammatical level even though the actions may be in different steps/stages of a sequence or a process order. Usually adverbs or conjunctions are required to qualify the grammatical construction. Consider the examples in (93):

(93) a. pai^{55} tɕən^{11} tɕɨ^{55} təm^{33} au^{55} naŋ^{11}
          go   mountain   eat   fruit   take   bamboo shoots
          'look for fruits and bamboo shoots'

     b. wjen^{53} '   wa^{33} wjen^{53} ko^{55}
         while   speak   while   laugh
         'laugh and speak simultaneously'

     c. ju^{33} to^{323} ka^{55} ju^{33} kaŋ^{323} ku^{33}
         also   sing   song   also   speak   story
         'sing songs and tell stories'

Since the multi-coordinated serial verbs are of equal status, they will be treated simply as at the same level in the phrasal hierarchy.

19.3.3. Word order and variations

Word order typology has played a major role in the development of language typology. By the term 'word order', we are actually not concerned so much with the order of words as with the order of constituents. That way we can avoid the possible distraction coming from the fact that the word boundary in Kam is not clear-cut at all and hard to define.

Word order study of a language is a synchronic snapshot of how all the linguistic constituents are organized in certain linear orders. In functional-typological approach, the focus is how different grammatical functions are realized through linguistic methods and how different linguistic constituents are organized in language behavior. The three major parameters that have been used in recent typological literature (Comrie 1983) are:

a) The relative position between the major clausal constituents *Subject*, *Object*, and *Verb*;
b) Constituents' order in noun phrase (NP);
c) The order of head noun (N) and relative clause (Rel).

Word order also changes diachronically due to linguistic and social factors. As a language without literate history, it is very difficult to figure out what happened in Kam in the past. Fortunately, we have been witnessing some obvious changes in word order parameters in this language. In the following subsection, we will look at the three Kam major parameters in word order first, then the new variant candidates, and discuss further what may have triggered the changes; what may happen in the foreseeable future.

19.3.3.1. The three Kam major parameters in word order

1) Relative position between subject, object, and verb

Theoretically speaking, there are six possible combinations concerned with the order of the subject, object, and verb of a sentence: SVO, SOV, VOS, VSO, OSV, OVS (where S refers to *subject*, V to *verb* and O to *object*). According to preliminary statistical data, 44% of the languages in the world are SOV, 35% are SVO, 19% are VSO, and 2% are VOS. OSV and OVS are rare (Ohio State University 1991).

Kam is a *SVO* language with the subject preceding the verb and the object follows it. Examples:

(94) ləm^{11} səp^{31} təm^{55} pai^{55} la^{11} 'The wind blew the bamboo hat away.'
     wind blow bamboohat go   Perf.

(95) mau^{33} ljaŋ^{35} to^{323} a^{55}.   'He likes singing.'
     He   like   sing   song

The SVO order is consistent through almost all the types of sentence except in topicality in which the object is raised to the very beginning of a sentence. Examples:

(96) le^{11} jau^{11} to^{323} wən^{35} la$^{11.}$ 'As for the textbook, I have finished reading that.'

book   I   read   finish Perf.

(97) tu^{11} ɳa^{11} soŋ^{35} nɐm^{31} mi^{31}? 'Have you watered the ox?'

ox   you   release water Neg.

= ɳa^{11} soŋ^{35} nɐm^{31} tu^{11} mi^{31}?

you   release water   ox   Neg.

This kind of grammatical variation in word order is not considered here as it bears different grammatical meanings and fulfils special functions, compared with the common SVO. They may also be a product of language contact with Chinese initially, but they are very stable and used by all speakers.

2) Constituents within phrase: head-first or head-last?

An interesting fact about word order typology is that within phrasal categories languages tend to place the head of the phrase either consistently before its modifiers and complements or after its modifiers and complements. The head of a phrase is the central, obligatory member of the phrase, while the modifiers serve to modify the meaning of the head, or complements, which are other constituents occurring with the head. Obviously, Kam is a ***head-first*** language. Examples:

(98) VP: V(head) + Object
    (a) lam^{55} (hunt) sau^{35}(smell)   '(hunting dog) to track the smell'
    (b) pon^{11} (remove) jan^{11}(house)   'relocate, move'

(99) PP: P(head) + NP
    (a) u^{55}(on, above) çoŋ^{11}(table)   'on the table'
    (b) ta^{33}(from) nuk^{453} (outside) ma^{35}(come) 'comes from the outside'

(100) NP: NP(head) + relative clause
    (a) pən^{33} le^{11} jau^{11} ɳin^{11} pe^{55} tçəi^{323} tça^{323} ljeu^{31}
        CLF   book   I   year   last   buy   that   lost
    'The book that I bought last year is lost.'

    (b) mau^{33} lau^{323} jan^{11} li^{323} to^{55}tçiŋ^{55} tça^{323} pu^{31}.
        He   enter house   have gate   that   Part.
    'He went into the house with gate.'

(101) NP: N(head) + possessive NP
    (a) li^{31}(word)   mau^{33}(he, him)   'his words'
    (b) sin^{11}(money)   taŋ^{11} hak^{31}(school) 'school's money'

(102) NP: N(head) + AP
    (a) ma^{55} (dish)   ljan^{33}(hot, spicy)   'spicy dishes'
    (b) ɳin^{11}(person, people) lai^{55} (good)   'nice person'

3) The order of head noun (N) and relative clause (Rel)

Again the head (N) precedes the relative clause (Rel). See some samples here:

(103) tɕak^{31} ȵin^{11} mɛn^{55}ȵuŋ^{55} ma^{35} tɕɔi^{323} tu^{11} tɕa^{323} man^{55}nai^{33} ju^{33} ma^{35} la^{11}
      Cls   person yesterday come buy   ox   that   today   again come Perf.
      '*The person that came to buy the ox yesterday* comes back (to buy) today.'

(104) jau^1 jiu^{53} pən^{33} le^{11} e^{35} əi^{323} jiu^{53} pai^{55} tɕa^{323}.
      I   want Cls   book they abandon away Perf. that
      'I want to have *the book which they abandoned.*'

In summary, Kam is an SVO language where head precedes modifiers and complements within all major phrasal categories, and relative clauses.

19.3.3.2. *Word order variations*

By the term 'word order variations', we mean any constituent order at either phrasal, relative clausal, or clausal that is different from the description in part I. To exclude cases such as topic sentences, interrogative sentences, which bears extra grammatical functions, we define word order variation as situations in which the relative order of constituents varies from the above 3 parameters, yet has the same grammatical or semantic features as before.

There is no variation in basic SVO order so far, for the object raising cases are treated as a grammatical function of focusing or topicalization. Candidates are found mostly in phrasal categories and relative clause with the relative position between the head and the modifiers/complements, and between the head noun and the relative clause.

1) N(head) and possessive NP vs. possessive NP and N(head)

In the northern dialect, the modifier NP can be placed either before or after the head N. Examples:

(105) mau^{33} ko^{33} pai^{35} kui^{35}jan^{212} jaŋ^{31}
      he/his olderbrother go   Guiyan   Perf.
      'His older brother went to Guiyang.'   (Long and Zheng 1998: 201)

(106) tɕau^{212}le^{212} ljeu^{31} la^{212}.
      I/mybook   lose   Perf.
      'My book is lost.'

It is understandable that variation emerges in North dialect first, considering that the Chinese came from the north part and immigrated into Kam community after the Tang Dynasty, more than one thousand years ago. And in ancient Chinese, the possessive NP preceded the head noun, even though there was no *DE* between them at that time. For example, 'wo^3 mu^3' means 'my mother'. For educational and economic reason, more and more Kam people started to interact with Chinese and learn the Chinese language. And the usually rigid word order cracked a bit in this specific phrasal structure.

The Southern dialect area was harder to reach for outsiders in the past due to geographical conditions. Yet the population explosion and technological advancement in the past century led more Chinese people to spread and enter this far south area. And we witness the same phenomenon taking place as in Northern dialect. At least possessive NP other than pronouns can be placed before the modified head N, with the help of DE. Examples:

(107) a^{11} nəi^{31} ti^{55} uk^{323} 'mother's clothes'
        mother   DE clothes

(108) e^{35} ti^{55} tɕət^{55} 'their firewood'
        they/their DE firewood

But different from the Northern dialect, the pronoun modifiers cannot be put before the head N which is a person. Examples:

(109) *tau^{55} ti^{55} nəi^{31} 'my mother'   vs.   nəi^{31} tau^{55}

(110) *khe^{35} ti^{55} noŋ^{31} 'his/her younger siblings'   vs.   noŋ^{31} khe^{35}

Interestingly enough, in modern Chinese, the DE is still optional when the head N is a person. Examples:

(111) wo^3 ma^1-ma   = wo^3 DE ma^1-ma 'my mother'

(112) *wo^3 shu^1 but = wo^3 DE shu^1 'my book'

It can then be inferred that the relative order between different types of NP modifiers and their head N differs in some way. The degree of rigidity in pronoun NP is higher than other NPs.
    This may come from the fact that the DE type with pronoun has a strong meaning of possessing. Someone possesses something. So it makes sense that *a^{11}* (suffix) *nei^{31} (mother)* *ti^{55} (possessive marker) uk^{323} (clothes)* is acceptable in Southern Kam dialect, for the person can really possesses the referential entity of head N. On the contrary, when the head noun is also a person, it is hard to argue that the modifier pronoun can possess the one of the head noun. So '*ɕau^{55} ti^{33} nəi^{31}*' is ungrammatical, and one has to use the form '*nəi^{31} ɕau^{55}*'. Notice that in Southern dialect, the pronoun that modifies another pronoun must be a plural one. Examples:

(113) sa^{31}(grandmother)   tau^{55} (we/our/us)   'our grandmother'
        *sa^{31} jau^{11} 'my grandmother'
        tɕu^{11}(mother'syoungerbrother)   e^{35} 'their uncle'
        *tɕu^{11} mu^{11}(s/he)   'his/her uncle'
        noŋ^{31}(youngersibling)   ɕau^{35}(you, pl)   'your younger brothers and sisters'
        *noŋ^{31}(youngersibling) n̠a^{11}(you, sg)   'your younger brothers and sisters'

In its complicated addressing system, the cultural value makes it impossible to claim that one person is really only another one's uncle, for the reality is that he must be the uncle of many other people. A mother, in most cases, is mother of more than one child. Even parents with only one child are still referred as '*bux daol*' or '*neix daol*' in speech. So it makes perfect sense that the singular pronoun is excluded from being used as modifier of a head pronoun. That accords to the cultural environment in which the clan and family value is the core of the social system. Nothing is really single-personal owned or privileged in personal relationship. The cultural value behind the language keeps this specific type of modifiers from moving flexibly from its traditional position after the modified pronoun.

19.3.4. Passive structures

In passive structures, the grammatical subject is typically the recipient or 'goal' of the action denoted by the verb. See an instance in (114).

(114) tu^{11} lak^{31}un^{323} ça^{323} təu^{33} nəi^{31} e^{35} pjit^{323}.

   CLF kid   DI   by   mother they   scold

   'That little kid was scolded by his mother.'

In analytical languages, the passive voice cannot be expressed by the morpheme variations as European languages do. Instead, preposition and object-raising are applied to realize the grammatical purpose. 'THEME *təu^{323}* AGENT V (*pai^{55}/taŋ^{55}/ma^{35}*)' and 'AGENT *təi^{11}* THEME V (*pai^{55}/taŋ^{55}/ma^{35}*)' constructions are the most common passive constructions in Kam, corresponding to the *BEI construction* and *BA construction* in Chinese. The constructions in these two languages are very similar even though their functions are very different. For convenience, the Chinese BEI construction and BA construction are used to label the two similar Kam passive structures and will be shown one by one. See Audrey Li (1990) for details.

19.3.4.1. *BEI construction*

In BEI passive construction, the recipient is followed by the AGENT, linking through the *tau^{33}*, and then the head verb. In this construction, the action conducted by the AGENT affects the recipient (or the THEME). For example:

(115) je^{55} təu^{33} sui^{11} it^{31} 'The frog was bitten by the snake.'

   frog   by   snake   bite

   THEME BEI AGENT ACTION

The *tau^{33}* was originally a verb and can still be a common verb, which means 'to touch' or 'to look like', or 'to suffer'. But the verb sense has been bleached out and is very weak here. It is hard to connect its verbal meanings to its functions in the passive structure. Instead, it may be considered having been *grammaticalized* to a preposition. The active counterpart of the above passive construction would be:

(116) sui^{11} it^{31} je^{55} 'The snake bites the frog'

   snake   bite   frog

   AGENT ACTION THEME

It describes the quality of the action but doesn't emphasize which is the AGENT and/or which is the THEME. In order to highlight the AGENT, the object is actually raised to the beginning of the construction and the preposition *tau^{33}* is added to serve the pragmatic purpose. Now the PP headed by the *tau^{33}* functions somewhat as a modifier. The head V *hit^{31}* is actually not the same as it is in the active construction, even though the phonological form remains. The hierarchy analysis of this construction is drawn as follows:

(117)

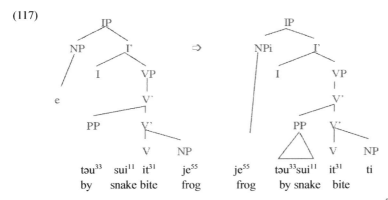

təu³³	sui¹¹	it³¹	je⁵⁵	je⁵⁵	təu³³sui¹¹	it³¹	ti
by	snake	bite	frog	frog	by snake	bite	

A variation of this BEI construction is to add a directional verb, such as *pai⁵⁵* 'go (away)', *ma³⁵* 'come (toward)', and *taŋ⁵⁵* 'come (toward)' right after the head V, and also a tense particle, usually at the end of the sentence. See examples in (118):

(118) (a)

mau³³	təu³³	e³⁵	əi³²³ju⁵³	pai⁵⁵	la¹¹	'He was fired by them.'
he	by	they	abandon	go	Perf.	

(b)

mau³³	təu³³	jau¹¹	kai¹¹	taŋ⁵⁵	la¹¹	'He was pulled here by me.'
he	by	me	pull	come	Perf.	

Here the sense of the directional verb *pai⁵⁵* and *taŋ⁵⁵* are not so strong as head Vs. They do help point the direction of the actions in some way, but it is still the head V that projects to the VP, and this construction is not an example of the SVC construction. Sentences with or without the directional verbs are different in meaning, at least in some way. When there is no DV after the verb and the final-particle, then the construction just states or describes a fact, a past action, who did what. But when DIs with end-particle are added, an extended continuous sequence is portrayed. Compare these two sentences in (119):

(119) (a)

uk³²³	təu³³	mau³³	ten³²³	pau³¹.
clothes	by	he	wear	Part.

'The clothes were worn by him.'

(b)

uk³²³	təu³³	mau³³	ten³²³	pai⁵⁵	pau³¹.
clothes	by	he	wear	go	Part.

'The clothes were donned (worn and taken) away by him.'

Sentence (119a) only states the fact that 'he wears the clothes', while sentence (119b) brings some extra aspects such that 'it results that the clothes have now been taken away with him and unavailable any more'. In the hierarchy diagram, the added elements can be placed outside the central V' but still within the VP. See (120).

(120)

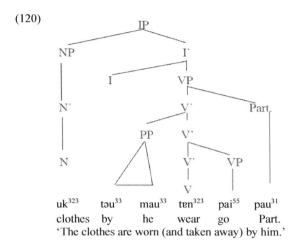

uk³²³   tou³³   mau³³   tɐn³²³   pai⁵⁵   pau³¹
clothes   by   he   wear   go   Part.
'The clothes are worn (and taken away) by him.'

19.3.4.2. *BA construction*

The Chinese BA construction has been called the disposal construction (Wang 1957; Chao 1968: 705), the ergative construction (Frei 1956), the executive construction (Hashimoto 1971), the accusative construction (Teng 1977), and simply the BA construction (Wang 1957) since then. It refers to sentences like (121):

(121)   wo   ba   shu   mai   le.

      I   BA   book   sell   ASP.

      'I sold that book.'

In Kam BA construction, the AGENT is followed by the recipient with a preceding *təi¹¹* and then the verb. A complement, or a minimum of the particle *la¹¹*, has to be added. It expresses how the AGENT handles/ treats the recipient. In Chinese many have suggested that the BA construction is allowed only if the DO complement is disposable. It is a construction that heightens transitivity (the opposite of passive). See examples in (122):

(122) (a) mau³³ təi¹¹ uk³²³   taŋ⁵⁵ pen⁵³ pai⁵⁵   la¹¹.

      he   BA clothes come throw go   Part.

      'He threw the clothes away.'

   (b) mau³³ təi¹¹ çoŋ¹¹   taŋ⁵⁵ tçin³¹ pai⁵⁵   la¹¹.

      he   BA table   come clear go/away Part.

      'He cleared the table away.'

It seems there are three verbs in each example. In fact, the *taŋ⁵⁵* before the head V is optional, but the adjunct *pai⁵⁵* after the head V is obligatory here. If *pai⁵⁵* and the end-particle are absent, then the tense changes immediately; *taŋ⁵⁵* is optional.

(123) (a) mau³³ təi¹¹ uk³²³   taŋ⁵⁵ pen⁵³

      he   BA clothes   come   throw

      'He is throwing/throws the clothes.'

(b) mau^{33} təi^{11} çoŋ^{11} taŋ^{55} tçin^{31}

   he   BA   table   come clear

   'He is clear/clearing the table.'

A treatment of this BA construction is suggested hereby:

(124)

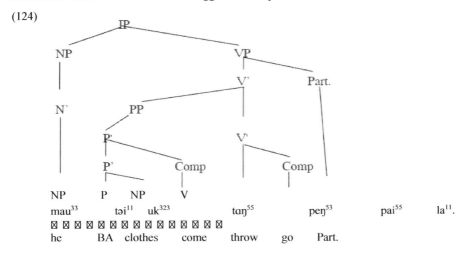

Note that word order here is fixed. Thus one cannot say *mau^{33}təi^{11} uk^{323}la^{11} taŋ^{55} peŋ^{53} paɪ^{55}.
To extract the rule, we suggest an X-bar analysis for this special structure as follows:

(125)

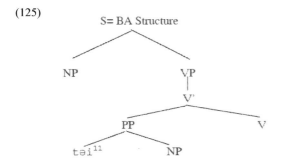

Audrey Li (1990: 181-197) has a detailed discussion of Chinese BA construction. She claims
that: firstly, the BA is not an inserted Case assigner; secondly, a *ba* NP is a PP, not an NP;
thirdly, *ba* here does not assign an argument theta-role to its object; fourthly, the object of *ba*
receives a theta-role from the verb or compositionally from the verb and its object; and so on.
She draws the same diagram for the Chinese BA construction as we do in 124. See Audrey Li
(1990: 192). The difference here is that in Kam a complement is required for the PP. So Li's
analysis of Chinese can be adopted for Kam after some adjustment is made.

   In this section, we have reviewed the types of Kam verbs, and then shifted the focus to
some special structures such as SVC, BEI construction, and BA construction. X-bar schemes
for the Kam VPs have been provided. The results show that the suggested X-bar framework is
helpful in clarifying the relations among the different phrase elements.

19.4. DISCOURSE PATTERNS AS REVEALED IN NARRATIVE

Discourse is one of the lesser-studied areas of the Kam language. Except for some Sanjiang folk stories by Shi Lin and Shi Feng (Xing 1988), even raw discourse data in the public domain are difficult to find, let alone any systematic analysis of discourse phenomena. Yet, recently some Kam narrative data and analysis have become available in the form of Tongyin Yang's dissertation on narrative discourse (Yang 2004). In this work note is taken of some reoccurring discourse patterns that have been observed, drawing mainly on Yang's latest discussion of Kam story-telling. We will specifically examine: a) the structural characteristics of Kam narrative discourse; b) sentence-final particles in discourse; and c) narrative as a channel of communication. A brief introduction to Kam storytelling event is provided to initiate the study.

19.4.1. Story-telling activity in Kam communities

Oral narration has been the main channel for transmitting Kam folklore across generations, since the communities lacked a writing system until the middle of the twentieth century. As one of the several genres of folk narrative, storytelling not only records and conveys the history of the people, but it also provides an important social occasion in the daily life of the community. It has a function that is both edifying and entertaining.

Storytelling is an indoor event for the evening hours, which may take place in a private home or in a public meeting place. The cast of performers includes narrators and decoys, a special group of adults whose main role is to acknowledge, react to, and comment on the developments in the ongoing story. There is also, of course, the audience, the gathered villagers, though in a sense, they are not there merely as passive listener-participants, as will become clear in the ensuing discussion. There are some additional rigid requirements placed upon a person who is to be the storyteller: the narrator must be male; in his fifties; he must have children, is ideally a grandfather; and is well respected in the community. There is no written rule but turn-taking in storytelling is occasioned either when the previous narrator signals an end to the just completed story and asks the next narrator to take a turn, or, sometimes, when the audience reminds the successor to step in and begin the next segment.

Data selected for the presentation here consists of two stories narrated by two storytellers from Xiyang of Yutou Township, Tongdao County, Hunan Province, on the same evening in December 2001: *Three Friends* (TF) by Jinlu Yang and *Repairing the Sky* (SR) by Zaiwei Yang. These two stories were recorded at Jinlu Yang's home. They are transcribed in Kam orthography rather than IPA for simplifying data presentation. The two stories can be viewed and searched at //ling.uta.edu/~jerry/index.html/3-friends.pdf/ and //ling.uta.edu/~jerry/index.html/ky-repair.pdf/.

19.4.2. The structural characteristics of Kam narrative discourse

19.4.2.1. *Labov's narrative framework*

Labov and Waletzky (1967) proposed a six-part model for naturally occurring narratives, and finalized and Labov formalized this treatment in his well-known study of Black English vernacular, Chapter 9 of his *Language in the Inner City* (1972).

The six components of his structure of narrative are: *abstract, orientation, complication, evaluation, resolution,* and *coda*. Some scholars labeled this personal experience narrative type PEN (personal experience narrative). Labov and Waletzky's hypothesis is that fundamental narrative structures are found in oral versions of personal experience. By exploring and revealing the true nature of ordinary narratives of ordinary speakers, they wished to identify and describe formal linguistic properties of narrative in regard to their functions, i.e., recapitulating of PEN. His definition of narrative is 'one method of recapitulating past experience by matching a verbal sequence of clauses to the sequence of events which (it is inferred) actually occurred' (Labov 1972: 359-360). He also specifies that 'a minimal narrative [is] a sequence of two clauses which are temporarily ordered ... a minimal narrative is defined as one containing a single temporal juncture' (Labov 1972: 361).

The current discussion of Kam narrative discourse can be related to Labov's well-defined model because, on the one hand, fundamental structures of narratives are supposed to be universal, and, on the other hand, it will be of interest to determine how different cultural environments and social functions of storytelling narrative among the Kam affect the structure itself.

Here is a more detailed definition of each of the six parts with brief examples as appropriate.

— *Abstract*: One or two clauses that the narrator uses to outline or advertise the whole story at the start of a narrative. For example, at the very beginning in Labov's 11th narrative, the subject responds to the question 'Were you ever in a situation where you thought you were in serious danger of being killed?' by saying 'I talked a man out of – Old Doc Simon I talked him out of pulling the trigger.'

— *Orientation*: Clauses or even paragraphs that introduce the participants and circumstances, especially of those of place and time, of the narrative, and are equivalent to what was called *setting* in the narratological chapters (Toolan 2001: 151). Some features of clauses in this section are that there occur a great many past progressive clauses in English as noticed by Labov: 'We was doing this 50-yard dash;' and clauses identifying persons, time, and place may not appear at the beginning of the narrative but must be placed at strategic points later on in narrative.

— *Complication*: Narrative clauses that recount a sequence of events leading up to their climax or peak, the point of maximum suspense. By referring to what happens in the story world and what happens in the narrating world, they create a tension that keeps the audience glued to their seats if not on their feet at all time.

— *Evaluation*: Clauses that occur right before the resolution that states or underscores the unusual or extraordinary characteristics of the events, why the audience should keep listening and allow the narrator to keep talking. They could be free clauses that comment on the on-goings of the story, the characters; clauses embedded in the narrative through scanning details of characters; 'correlatives' that decode what happens simultaneously; and explicatives that are appended to narrative clauses.

— *Resolution*: are clauses that release the tension and reveal what happened in the end.

— *Coda*: Signals the end of the narrative. These are also labeled closure in some literature (Abbott 2002: 188). This could be explicit declaring that the narrative proper is over. Some commonly used ways to do this include 'That is it', 'This is the end of my story', and 'OK. That is it, you know.' Often some codas have the property of bridging the gap between the moment of time at the end of the narrative proper and the present, that is, to bring the audience back to this world.

Kam narratives are of the same nature as Labov's in the sense that they also recapitulate what happened in the past, real or legendary. The difference is that in the Kam culture the narrators are 'invited' or customarily 'selected' to tell a folktale story that has been narrated many times before in a natural cultural setting, rather than 'interviewed' with the point of recapitulating only one's own personal experience, as in the case of Labov's stories. The intended audience is made up of fellow villagers, not 'strangers', though some guests may also be present on some occasions. Its main function is social, internal rather than talking to individual(s) and satisfying outside academic request. It is noteworthy that in order to 'obtain data on the most systematic form of language (the vernacular)...(and) how people speak when they are not being observed' (Labov 1972: xvii), Labov and his team developed contact with different preadolescent groups and conducted peer observation. It will be of interest to see how the two functions of narrative, i.e., *recapitulating* of PEN and *evaluating* – the point or worth of the narrative, as far as the speaker and the community jointly agree – are realized in Kam as opposed to Harlem African-American culture, two totally distinct communities in terms of both geography and time. How they share structural properties of narrative and how they differ in building their own structure will be the point of following discussion for a better and deeper understanding of Kam narrative. All these and other possible factors will be examined in further detail when a difference is observed and explanation is needed.

To begin the analysis, a brief anatomy of the two recorded narratives based on Labov's model is produced, followed by analysis of each of the six parts in Kam:

TABLE 19.4.2.1-1: THE SIX-PART ANATOMY OF THE KAM NARRATIVES

	SR	TF
Abstract	None	None
Orientation	#1-4	#1-14
Complication	#5-460	#39-363
Evaluation	#5-460	#39-363
Resolution	#461-466	#364-366
Coda	#467	#367-368

19.4.2.1.1. *Abstract*

There is an immediate difference between the Kam narratives and Labov's components; the Kam stories are missing the first or *abstract* part. In both stories, no such component occurs at the beginning to summarize what is coming next. The reason arises from the nature of storytelling; the *abstract* must not be a mandatory element. Its absence, in fact, will actually increase the level of curiosity of the audience and draw the attention of all participants. On the contrary, the *abstract* in PEN is the response conditioned by the interviewer's question. As the setting shifts, the very reason for an abstract becomes superfluous. Instead of an Abstract, the orientation will initiate the narrative as a result.

The situation here does not exclude the possibility of an abstract in other Kam narratives. Depending on the occasions, the use of abstracts may become an appeal. For instance, in Xing #3.3, 3.4, 3.10, and 3.12, a brief summary of what is coming is indeed presented in some cases. Though information of the physical settings within which the stories are narrated is missing, it is fairly safe to assume that one or more of the following situations may be true: a) the narrator has been asked by other participants to tell a story and any story will be welcomed. Under that circumstance, the narrator would search his mind and tell the audience the one that he has chosen. This is similar to Labov's PENs and is a reflective result of being asked. b) The narrator is taking a turn from a predecessor in a multi-narrator occasion. To separate his story from the others, a quick summary of the point of the story would be more than sufficient to serve the need.

19.4.2.1.2. *Orientation*

Just as in narratives of many other languages, the orientation part in Kam is rather brief, consisting of only a few clauses, i.e., 4 in SR and 14 in TF.

There are three characters in TF, the three 'brothers'. The information about their respective parents is so plain and simple that only SR16, 18, and 70 mention them. The same applies to the *lagx nuns* 'the (school) children' (in TF173, 174, 186, 186, 198, 210), along with sketchy references to their families. This does not mean that one can conveniently ignore these supporting players. On the contrary, they may figure significantly in developing events such as the *lagx nuns* in TF, who, in fact, do when they push the box down into the river to trigger the peak event in that story.

There is a familiar pattern to introduce the time, location, and characters in the two stories. The aperture *(dangl xul) xic jav* 'long, long ago' is the very first phrase to separate what will follow, the story, from the present world. The verb is the expected *meec* 'to have', the equivalent to the English 'there were' under this circumstance, followed by characters. The location part will appear right after the time indicator if needed, as TF is the case. The order of time-(location)-characters is as expected. Here in these two stories and 23 out of 33 stories in Xing's collection (1988), the narration begins with the time indicator *(dangl xul) xic jav* 'long, long ago'. The optional *dangl xul* 当初 is an old Chinese loan word that brings a sense of formality and authority to the narrative. This may well be a subtle symbol of power exercised by the narrator, since in the past a headmen and former official village head might well have used such expressions. This preliminary observation will be revisited later when the background of narrators becomes an issue. Also, a *four-syllable elaborate expression* echoes the trademark of Kam singing and poetic tradition since four-syllables, along with five and seven-syllable lines, are the most commonly used foot structures in Kam songs, proverbs, and other rhyme-oriented types of literature.

Once the time is fixed and the participants are introduced into the narrative world, the main characters are quickly identified to complete the introduction. If one remembers the 'Once upon a time...' in English or *congqian you yige* 从前有一个...in Chinese, then this reoccurring pattern of narrative aperture deserves to be considered as a candidate for a universal narrative initiation. The location of place is not mandatory, unlike time and characters, because it does not add that much to developing the story, especially when the story's historical nature is in doubt. The audience may care less where the event took place unless the place bears significance in the narrative world. By examining the available discourse data both from Yang (2004) and Xing (1988), it is obvious that among the significant qualities is firstly the proximity of the setting of the story, so the audience knows the location. In other words, they would be able to connect to that place through personal experience. See Xing #3.1, 3.10, 3.12, and 3.16. Such a connection would stimulate a sense of involvement among the participants to become involved in the narrative and raise their level of enthusiasm, an element of significance to draw the audience's attention and keep them in their seats. Secondly, the place itself is significant, as it is either known from the history of the Kam or of China or is found in Kam religious beliefs. In Xing #3.6, the *Xiangc Anl* 长安 was the fabled capital of the Tang Dynasty (618-907AD), and in TF1, the *Wangv Yeml* 'the nether world' is a significant concept in Kam native religion; c) historic significance of the figure(s) in the narrative. See Xing #3.1, 3.12, and 3.16. Location is covert in SR because it is a folkloric tale based on story of the great flood (deluge) that engulfed the whole world, a motif that is found widely among cultures. Where exactly the boy was from is without significance in the development of the plot.

19.4.2.1.3. *Complication and evaluation*

These two parts are the combined trunk of the narrative. While *complication* occupies the majority of the clause structures, and unfolds the plot in narrated order, it is the *evaluation* that glues them together. In the relatively short PENs, these two parts tend to be easy to identify and separate. As shown in the Table 19.4.2.1-1, this is not the case in the two Kam narratives. The *evaluation* part is so delicately infused into the *complication* throughout the course in both cases that the two become inseparable.

Taking the shorter TF as an example for discussion, evaluations can be found throughout the combined TF39-363 trunk, reaffirming Toolan's (2001: 151) observation that evaluation 'may take many forms and appear at almost any point in the telling', cf. TF9, 10, 14, 62, 154, and 186-188.

This feature of evaluation being infused over the complication has a lot to do with the genre of Kam narrative, setting the scene, and functions in society in general. As will be detailed in 4.3, it is apparent that as a form of interactive entertainment, Kam narrative in discussion requires the narrator to monitor the audience's comprehension closely and ensure that they comprehend the narrated events. In Labov's PENs, the interviewers ask or 'beg' the narrator to perform. So attention from the audience there is presupposed. No extra effort is needed to lure the listener(s). Unlike in PENs, a new narrator faces here the task to sustain his point and heighten the audience's interest throughout an otherwise lengthy and, perhaps, familiar narrative. Without exception these narratives last for 20 minutes, averaging 400 clauses respectively. Avoiding boredom and embarrassing silence in public are two peerless features of a good Kam narrative. To achieve that goal, it becomes necessary to invite the audience INTO the narrative. The narrator must constantly highlight and evaluate significant developments in this dynamic interactive process. He must also respond to their comments and answer their questions about the events as they unfold if he is to be regarded as a truly skilled storyteller. The audience will not feel marginalized or abandoned but will want to help in some way. Moreover, audience participation will also aid the narrator to focus on his agenda and make adjustments as needed. This is why evaluation can appear anywhere and everywhere (Labov 1972).

Evaluation itself is 'a temporary suspension of the action, a brief 'time out' from the telling of the story proper' (Toolan 2001: 153). It signals why the narrator is telling the story. In other words, it reveals why the events of the narrative are reportable or worthy of narrating. Two types of evaluations are distinguished: internal and external evaluations.

Externals evaluations are those appearing outside of the fixed-position clauses of narrative and may serve various roles at points. A fair classification of different subtypes of external evaluation is proposed here:

a. Summarizing the previous happening and being a starting point for the next event. See instances in TF9, 10, 11, 14, 36, and 50.

b. Responding to audience's questions and/or comments. A reliable marker of this subtype is the final particle *heek*, even though this may overlap with other subtypes in some cases. Also, the majority of these responses appear around the peak or climax of the events, indicating that the audience must be following and are getting more involved as the story reaches its resolution. See instances in TF10, 11, 170, 218, 222, 236, 240, 246, 256, 257, 256, 267, 364.

c. Self-questioning invites involvement of the audience. See instances in TF280, 218.

d. Commenting on details and developing of the events. See instances in TF29, 56, 63, 80, 94, 363.

e. Completely external evaluating, breaking the boundary between story and the world of the hearers to address the audience directly. See instances in TF62 and 149.

f. Explaining or analyzing the acts of characters in the story. See instances in 185-188, 204, 212-215, 235-240, and 268.

g. Supplementing information for listeners. See instances in 60, 84, 313-318.

h. Brief translation of Chinese quotations. See instances in 325-329.

The last type of external evaluation in TF is very important, since a Chinese couplet contest is invoked inside the narrative to decide who is to pay for a meal. In reality most or many of the participants do not know Chinese well if at all. To help them comprehend the developments in the story, it is vital to inform them what the Chinese couplet means. Usually the translation is condensed into a single or a few clauses to avoid interrupting the flowing of the narration.

Contrary to these subtypes, internal evaluations are those woven into the structure and composition of the core narrative clauses. They carry the central sequential *spine* of the narrative or along the *storyline* (Longacre 1996: 27) and fill the complicating mission and resolution sections in the model. Labov (1972: 370-375) identified four subgroups of internal evaluations and their counterparts are listed below:

a. *Intensifiers*, including expressive phonology, onomatopoeic, and intonational emphases. While *heek* is a reliable marker of external evaluations, *hix and ixhip* are good markers for internal evaluation. See a complete list at SR 67, 97, 102, 163, 178, 375, 409 for *hix* and 52, 60, 67, 87, 150, 177, 198, 283, 283, 302, 307, 328, 337, 342, 354, 375, 402, 408, 412, 419, and 442 for *ixhip*. Gestures/facial expressions also qualify as intensifiers.

b. *Comparators*: clauses mentioning what did not happen in the story.

c. *Correlatives*: operations that bring together events that have actually occurred so that they are conjoined in a single independent clause. This requires complex syntax usually and is a feature of articulate or mature narrators.

d. *Explicatives*: appended subordinate clauses which qualify, or give reasons for the main events narrated. Frequently they are introduced by *since, because, while, though*, and so on in English.

19.4.2.1.4. *Resolution*

The tension-releasing component is merely an instant in a sense, involving only three clauses in both stories. In SR 461-466 and TF354-456, the final resolution is that the poor brother pays nothing for his meal by standing his ground in a literacy contest in which he is expected to lose. This rather short resolution has something to do with folktale narration in Kam as a genre. First, besides being a way of transmitting traditional knowledge to younger generations, dramatized oral narrative is also entertainment for the community, a kind of artistic activity (Hymes 1972 and Wolfson 1982). To make a performance successful, performers will expend most of the time and space in complication and evaluation, delicately describing what happened, how it happened, and why. The point of resolution, the significance or the final result of the story is reached in a dramatic manner. These come rather rapidly and tersely. The brevity of the climax is set into sharp relief in comparison to the events that have led up to this ending and that adds surprise and profundity to the entire story. Extra commentary or explanation would only dilute or degrade the rhetorical skill narrator has just exhibited. Second, the fact that these two narratives were being recorded in a multiple-narrator setting may have also placed the storyteller under some pressure not to draw out the conclusion. A shortened resolution as an adjustment from the narrator is an acceptable sacrifice considering that shortening any other part, except the coda, would qualitatively damage the whole.

19.4.2.1.5. *Coda*

To seal off the telling of the specific story, the narrator clearly states that his story has now come to an end. In TF367-368, it is *xus, bens laih jagx. Wenp waeix lac, hux.* 'Well, this is all (that I would like to narrate this time), and I have finished this one already. Right.' The coda in SR is almost identical with a similar expression *huenp laeuc luh, bens hangc laeuc luh.* '(I) have finished and this is all (what I would narrate).' There are near-identical closures of narratives in many languages, even in the closings of radio and television news bulletins.

As usual, there are multiple narrators present in Kam storytelling settings. The next narrator will now step up to take his turn as the previous one finishes. To signal a clear break in proceedings and enforce the taking of a turn, a coda is required.

19.4.3. Sentence-final particles (SFP) in narrative discourse

19.4.3.1. *Introduction*

In his extensive description of the Lahu language, Matisoff (1973) dedicates over two hundred pages to the verb phrase, of which about eighty pages are devoted to *verb particles, universal unrestricted particles*, and *final unrestricted particles* (Person 2000: 64); these are to be the subject of the present section. They are all considered part as of the verb phrase in Lahu:

A verb-particle (Pv) is a word which cannot constitute an utterance by itself and which occurs always and only after members of the class of verbs (or after other verb-particles). Semantically, they serve to elucidate the meaning of the verb in a variety of ways, conveying notions of aspects, directionality, subjective attitudes towards the verbal event, etc. Conspicuously absent are any Pv's referring to tense. Tense concepts are foreign to the Lahu verbs, as they are for the Sino-Tibetan languages in general. (Matisoff 1973: 315)

Ever since the 1970's, scholars have contributed significant efforts to the study of these types of particles in Asian languages. It is surprising that such a commonly used part of speech existing in so many languages has been ignored for so long, even in MSC, one of the world's largest languages with a written tradition of more than two thousand years. On the one hand, it has something to do with the fact that the exact meaning of an SFP tends to be elusive and hard to specify outside of context; furthermore, SFPs predominantly occur in oral, narrative speech or *baihua* 白话, a linguistic genre considered until the early twentieth century in China to be informal and unrefined in comparison to the written language or *wenyan* 文言. Through the years, there are various terms referring to these particles, including *mood words* 语气词 in Chinese, *particles* (Chao 1968: 795), *utterance-final particles* (Bourgerie 1987), *auxiliary words* (Dai 1996, Long and Zheng 1998), auxiliary mood words 语气助词 (Liang 1984: 378), *sentence particles* (Cooke 1989, Hanson 1996), but *sentence-final particles* (SFPs) has emerged as the most general, well-accepted term among scholars since Li and Thompson's (1981) study.

SFPs are forms that are attached to the end of a sentence. Here the *sentence* is used in a loose sense, since in many instances the attached structure units may be clauses, an issue related the difficult question of how to determine sentence boundaries in MSC and other languages lacking TAM markers. Also zero anaphors in subject position are widespread in these languages, particularly in oral discourse, resulting in many VP or NP-like sentences. As well, the functions of these SFPs are mainly pragmatic, including expressions of request, question, assumption, endearment, and a simple statement with an undertone of relief.

However, more importantly, final particles convey speech act information, e.g., marking the attitude of the speaker toward what s/he is saying, marking an utterance as reported speech, or as a mild warning, etc. Generally speaking, the studies just cited investigate the specific speech act functions performed by individual particles, and the relationship between an utterance that ends with one of these particles and what has previously been said in a speech context (Law 1990: 1).

For all these reasons, SFPs have often been studied from the point of view of pragmatics or discourse, a tradition that the current research hopes to continue.

In this section, sentence-final particles in Kam are itemized based on the collected narrative data and other published resources. Each particle's main linguistic and pragmatic functions are illustrated briefly in subsection 19.4.3.2. Then in subsection 19.4.3.3, two very much less-explored areas in the study of SFPs, phonological and syntactic features of SFPs, become the focus. A special, super SFP *liax* will attract extra attention, since it has an unconventional distribution and a powerful role to play in construing storytelling narrative discourse.

19.4.3.2. *The inventory of Kam SFPs*

Kam SFPs are particles that appear at the end of a sentence to convey *attitudinal*, *textual*, *cognitive*, *interactional*, and *TAM* information about the speech act. According to this relatively loose definition, particles reflecting simply different tenses and aspects are also included in the current discussion SFPs. The primary reason for this inclusion is that even though some of the TAMs are particles functioning within the phrasal level, namely VPs, often they can also occupy the sentence final position in their respective clauses or sentences. Graphic representation of this syntactic feature of SFPs will be displayed in the syntactic analysis of SFPs later. Below is one of the most frequently encountered particle *lac* in TF13 as a demonstration example:

TF13

Wordform:	meec	il	lagx	dil	xus	laos	hangc	hangc	hangc
WfGloss:	have	one	child	pause	then	enter	kind; type	kind; type	kind; type
WfPOS:	v	num	com m	part	adv	v	CLS	CLS	CLS

nyads	jas	bail	lac
poor	that	go	PERF
adj int	mkr	v	asp

FT: (the other) one then entered a poor family.

In TF13 the *lac* here is a pure aspect indicator, qualifying the action of *laos* 'to enter, to be born into (a family)' by expressing that it is completed as scheduled or intended. Variants of *lac* include *laoc, laeuc, lax*, a group of SFPs that express similar TAMs but possess different attitudinal, cognitive, or interactional information of the speech act. In context, this sentence may also function as a sequential marker. Nevertheless, they manifest not only their semantic and syntactic functions, but also have pragmatic or discourse roles. So even if a particle occurs within the VP, it will still be included in the SFPs list as long as it could appear at the very end of a clause or sentence.

The various investigators have made slightly different arguments in many previous studies on SFPs such as Li and Thompson, Law, and Person's, but the result is the same. The current simple criteria of SFPs aid in the categorizing work of SFPs, and include their characteristic feature of operating at different levels from phrase to sentence to paragraph to discourse at the same time. By covering particles of TAMs such as *lac*, the scope of research on SFPs in the current study is broadened from the bottom to the top, so the intended goal of capturing the discourse function of sentence-final particles could be examined on a broader basis.

Here is a list of all the SFPs that appear in the two collected narratives in alphabetical order. SFPs from other sources such as Xing's, Long's, and the authors' other fieldwork notes, are incorporated and marked with an asterisk. They are included in the list below since the have been reported but the discussion of them will be limited in a sense, for many of these data are given in sources without context. It is evident that, as illustrated in the table below, some of the members have variants in context to express delicate and subtle attitudinal, textual, cognitive, or interactional differences. This long table spans a few pages.

TABLE 19.4.3.2-1: INDEXING OF THE KAM SFPS

No.	SFPs	Information conveyed	Instances
1	ac	Questioning, usually used as greeting;	SR392, TF59;
		Permitting, admitting pausing	SR24, TF108 TF7, 59
2	as	Pleasantly informing of others	SR203
3	ax	Strong questioning, seeking more information	SR83, TF115

4	bac*	Expressing uncertainty in negation Recommending or suggesting such as in *nyac bail bac* 'You'd better go.' Mild questioning, sometimes equals to greeting such as in *ac naeix bac*? On phone conversation 'Is this mom?/ how are you, mom?' Agreement soliciting	
5	daeux	Shortened form of 'daengl (DV) lac (PERF)', an aspect marker, also indicating new, unexpected information	SR65, TF48
6	dax	Shortened form of *daeux*	SR81, TF 28
7	dil	Unfinishing, pausing	SR69, TF22
8	eec	Closely questioning, interrogating	SR226, TF49
9	eel	Extended syllable of a previous *weex*, questioning	SR94, TF132
10	haeip	Shortened form of *haeix il*, *yes* or *no* question.	SR149, 176
11	has	Polite suggesting, 'would you...' Encouraging, comforting	SR204, F182
12	heec	Tag question	TF195
13	heep	Variation of *haeip*, *yes* or *no* questioning	SR32
14	heip	Strong appealing Great surprise with emotional overtones	SR128, 376
15	hic*	Mild reconfirmation seeking such as in *laih jagx hic?* 'Is this it?/Is this all? /OK'	
16	hix	Informing in a surprise, unexpected tone	SR55
17	hoc	Mildly surprised	TF289, 291
18	hox	Suddenly see the light; instant realization of a truth. I got it! self-independent clause such as in *Hox!* 'I see!'	
19	huc	Variation of *wuc*, for drawing attention suggesting	SR191, TF222
20	ic	Pausing	TF162, 170, 215
21	il	Strong questioning, doubting	SR115, 150
22	is	Appealing, begging	SR278, 293
23	jeec*	Tag question, more sure or confident of	
24	jeep*	Variation of *jeec*, less sure or confident of	
25	lac	Perfective. Indicating the completing of an act, especially in structures indicating sequence of actions.	TF12, 13, 15 SR147, 228
26	laeuc	Perfective. Variation of *lac*. Emphasizing the completion and implying expectation such as 'so what?'	TF31, 77 SR312, 431
27	lah*	Perfective. Variation of *lac*. Emphasizing the completion in a happy tone and implies 'how about it?'	
28	laoc*	Perfective. Variation of *lac*.	
29	las	Perfective. Variation of *lac*. Polite information seeking, in some cases a childish expression	SR388
30	leec	The truth is...like that, that is it	SR100, TF37
31	leep	Greatly disappointed or frustrated	SR102, TF33

32	lees	Admitting, conceding	TF339
33	liax	Universal discourse marker, communication operator. Seeking consensus from others as an SFP	SR60, TF2
34	lic	Committing; weak confirming, unsure of; asking for permission	SR298, TF61
35	lih	Fact revealing, confirming, told you so	TF409
36	lis	Fact revealing, confirming	TF95, 160
37	luc	Guessing, assuming	TF408
38	luh	Informing, agreeing	SR41, TF28
39	lus	Admonishing, Fact revealing, implies taking turns	SR119, TF131
40	lux	Strong recommending, alarming, warning	TF205
41	mac	Mild, polite suggesting, recommending	SR118, TF65
42	ngl	Questioning, wondering, reasoning	SR19, TF343
43	wuc	Drawing attention, serious questioning requiring answer	SR196, TF3

When *liax* is in bold, that is to draw attention to a special form of this SFP with unique status in discourse, when it is functioning as an SFP and a discourse marker simultaneously in many instances.

There are some SFPs clusters in which two SFPs appear at the end of a sentence to express multiple discourse meanings. The majority are made up of the perfective aspect marker *lac*, or its variants *laoc*, *laeuc*, *lah*, and *lax*, followed by another SFP. Theoretically the perfective aspect marker can combine with any other SFP, with the marker closer to the V, to form a cluster. A list of five clusters other than combinations with the perfective aspect marker(s) found in data is provided in the following table. Keep in mind that these several clusters can again combine with the perfective aspect marker to form a three-member cluster.

TABLE 19.4.3.2-2: SFP CLUSTERS WITHOUT THE PERF MARKER

No.	SFP clusters	Information conveyed	Instances
40	ac as	Variation of *ac has*, polite and mild form	SR203
41	ac has	Pausing for suggestions, recommendations, encouragement	SR130,TF217, 382
42	heip ic	Compassionately and seriously appealing	SR357
43	ic is	Pausing and questioning, doubting	SR177, 252
44	lic is	Curiously questioning, a response to surprise at what has happened	SR278

The phonological status of these SFP clusters is debatable. In other words, it is not conclusive, at this time, whether these SFP clusters are indeed two syllables as proposed here or actually just one extraordinarily lengthened syllable, though they make the impression of being two identifiable syllables. A cluster analysis is assumed here as a   working hypothesis that will still require additional argumentation and discussion. The category of SFP clusters in Table 19.4.3.2-2 offers strong evidence that the first syllable of the pair is decisive, hence suggesting that they may well be considered a variant of the individual SFP they follow. If there is any member that could possibly be considered to consist of two individual SFPs, that would be *heip ic*. The idea of treating *heip ic* as two obligatory members of one syllable pair rather than as one single syllable SFP is to avoid the potential burden of creating new tones. So unless there is another method to place the clearly lengthened linguistic components, for example intonation, the suggested SFP clusters seems the best analysis. In real narrative utterances, the length and tonal contour of a long syllable would have been different from any single syllable tone (note that Kam uses consonants at the end of a syllable as a marker of tone).

19.4.3.3. *Phonological and syntactic features of SFPs*

Phonological and syntactic aspects of SFPs have long been ignored despite the fact that there are many studies of SFPs in many languages of the region. While it is true that the major function of SFPs lies at the pragmatic and discourse level, and thus analyses in those two areas are well justified, it is also undeniable that better understanding of the phonological and syntactic features of SFPs will enhance the comprehension of SFPs. This is the very reason why Law (1990) concentrated all his efforts in his dissertation on the study of the syntax and phonology of Cantonese SFPs. His inspiring work shows the obvious and close relationship between particle systems and intonations. He examined whether individual particles have specific syntactic functions, what functions they perform, and what syntactic slots they occupy. The goal here is not to present an exhaustive study of the syntax and phonology of SFPs but to lay the ground in this subsection for further study.

19.4.3.3.1. *Tonal and other syllabic structural characteristics of SFPs*

It was noticed in the early transcriptional stages of the narrative texts in the present project that identifying the tones of some SFPs was difficult. On the one hand, intonation and tone interact in such a collaborative way. Subtle difference of tone can carry delicate distinctions of meaning. On the other hand, since the length and intensity of tone on an SFP can vary greatly according to the contextual environment, that could result in different syllabic parings. That is, is there only one tone-bearing-unit (TBU) within a single lengthened syllable or are there two? In many cases, the TBUs of the two clustered SFPs are identical except in the case of *heip ic*, a piece of evidence for the one TBU treatment. Or are there two TBUs and is the SFP the part occupied by the two separate syllables? The relative intensity can increase or decrease depending on the situational demand in communication. The adopted treatment here leads directly to the emergence of particle clusters in section 19.4.3.2, a practice favored, because it avoids introducing new tone categories into discussion.

As was mentioned previously in 19.2.3, there are nine distinct tones in unchecked syllables in Kam: high-level (1-'55'), high-rising (1'-'35'), low-level (2-'11'), mid-falling-rising (3-'323'), [low-rising (3'-'13')], mid-falling (4-'31'), high-falling (5-'53,'), high-rising-falling (5'-'453'), and mid-level (6-'33'). In checked syllables, there are six tones: high-level (7-'55'), high-rising (7'-'35'), low-falling (8-'21'), mid-falling-rising (9-'323'), [low-rising (9'-'13')], and mid-falling (10-'31'). The complexity of the Kam tonal system creates some unique difficulties for the expression of tone on SFPs and sentence intonation. First of all, variation of the sentence intonation is more constrained since the Kam tone space is already tightly packed by its nine contrasts in CV syllables. The possibilities for confusion looms large, since pragmatic sentence-level function and syllable-level tone contour may interfere. A resulting phenomenon is that length and intensity are applied more often to convey speech act information (even though intensity has not studied in current data transcription). Of the five SFP clusters, at least four could be combined and treated as a single particle if based on acoustic and phonetic evidence alone. The reason why a single SFP treatment is abandoned and the clustered SFP account has been adopted here is that that might lead to introduction new tones into the system, an issue that would be hard to justify. It will be simpler and more constrained to divide the lengthened SFP section into two separate particles. Fortunately, all the resulting individual SFPs except *as* have their counterpart in the list of single SFPs, further supporting the SFP cluster.

Secondly, checked syllables CV(V)C are not allowed to appear in SFPs. Of all the SFPs, none appears in the category with the three stop codas: /-p, -t, -k/. There are five checked Cantonese SFPs: ak^{33}, kak^{33}, lak^{33}, and $lək^{33}$, $t\int ek^{55}$ (Law 1990: 206), but Law provides no discussion of their phonological and syntactic features. Even though no specific analysis is provided by Law, one can assume that these SFPs must be different from the ones in unchecked syllables in some way. This reminds one of the dilemma for the conception of SFPs in the above discussion. That is, even though they might be single particles phonetically, treating them as clusters will not only avoid introducing new tone categories, but also the result of relating two SFPs to an existing SFPs. This reveals an interesting characteristic or quality of SFPs: the phonological structure allows it to be lengthened or extended, since the situation may require extra attitudinal, textual, cognitive, or interactional information to be coded through extension of a one-syllable SFP into a bi-syllabic cluster. An important phonological feature of Kam-Tai voiceless stop codas is that they are glottalized and unreleased (Liang 1984: 324), a well-known distinctive acoustic trait also found generally in SE Asian languages, many kinds of Chinese, and English. As noted, SFPs must be syllables without codas. An unreleased coda would make the extension or lengthening impossible. In the extreme, even nasal codas are disqualified in Kam. That leaves open syllables as the only valid rhyme candidates in SFPs.

The opposite observation has been made in earlier English. Brinton (1996) points out that 'shortness' is one of the properties of discourse markers: 'While the monosyllabic forms *hwæt* and *anon* and the aphetic form *gan* (<*on-/aginnan*) clearly meet the definition of phonetic shortness, as does *Þa*, which exists alongside the longer nonpragmatic form *Þanne/Þonne*, phrase such as *I gesse* and constructions such as *Þa gelamp Þt* and *then it bifel that* would not appear.' (Brinton 1996: 266).

Law notices that many Cantonese particles have the identical segmental shape and differ only in tone. 'When their meanings are taken into consideration, it becomes apparent that particles that are phonetically similar very often share a core meaning' (Law 1990: 82). His proposal is that these particles are underlyingly related. Regrouping, Kam SFPs partially confirms his account, as shown in the Figure 19.4.3.3.1-1, where tone –c (11) is the one that appears most frequently. And within a related group or set along the horizontal line, the one with this low-level tone (-c) tends to express a mild, polite type of speech act information such as making assumptions, guesses, suggestions, recommendations, and lukewarm confirmation. The mid-level tone (-h) conveys information in a relaxing, not-so-serious, neutral way. On the contrary, SFPs with falling tones – (-x) (31) tend to encode strong speech act information such as appealing, begging, criticizing, condemnations, and marking something as unusual. Also SFPs with high-rising (–p) (35) carry strong feelings such as great disappointment (e.g. *leep*) and a demand for a response (e.g. *heep*). To categorize the pragmatic difference among SFPs, a three-group classification is suggested: low-level tones are labelled as *weakeners*; mid-level ones *neutralizers*; and the ones with rising or falling tones *strengtheners*. These groupings will be considered in 4.3. This is a manifestation of how pitch and intensity, along with length of the syllable, can be applied in expressing discourse functions, an issue closely related to intonation. Remember that the sentence-final position is also a very important subpart of the entire sentence intonation contour. So in a sense, the study of intonation and the study of SFPs overlap often and complement one another. To draw a better picture of Kam intonation requires much a greater amount and more varieties of linguistic data including causal conversation and formal public speech, along with a proven model. Unfortunately neither prerequisite is currently available.

There is also evidence that not all the tones of SFPs are inherent. Out of context, many SFPs have no specific semantic meaning. Only in context would their meanings emerge and become comprehensible. In most cases, it is impossible to ask a subject what an SFP means as a headword in a glossary. And, another observation is that even in context, the meaning might still be unclear or vague to most native speakers. The transcription of narrative discourse data in Xing's is quite accurate and reliable. The only missing part is the semantic meaning of

SFPs from time to time, such as / ¹¹/ and / ¹¹/ (1988: 52), / ¹¹/ and / ¹¹/ (1988: 126), and / ¹¹/ and / ³¹/ (1988: 97). As Li and Thompson summarize the situation in Chinese SFPs: '(The SFPs') semantic and pragmatic functions are elusive, and linguists have had considerable difficulty in arriving at a general characterization of each of them' (1981: 238).

Weakener	Neutralizer	Strengthener
ac		ax as as, ac has
		daeux./dax
eec	eel	
		haeip
		heip, heip ic
		has
heec		heep
		heip
hic		hix
hoc		
ic		ic his, ic is
lac		las lax
laeuc		
leec		leep
		liax
lic	lih	lis, lic is
luc	luh	lux lus
mac		
wuc/huc		

FIGURE 19.4.3.3.1-1: GROUPING OF KAM SFPS

This leads to the subject of tonal operational territory. Unlike any other part of speech, SFPs are highly dependent on context. In other words, they are very discourse sensitive. Another observed trait of SFPs is that even in context, the tone on a specific SFP is not as clear or as stable as on other words, either because the tone is lexically indeterminant, or because it varies according to the emergent speech act information of the context. As a result, some scholars in the past simply marked them as untoned, while others have ignored them (Xing 1988). Similarly, most of the frequently used Chinese SFPs are de-stressed and have the neutral tone (Li and Thompson 1981: 238).

Contrary to the typologically widespread generalization of rising intonation in questions, Kam uses another system. Falling and level intonation appear frequently in questions. See an example sentence in TF319:

Wordform:	heek,	maoh	xus	baov	laeup	hangc	huc,	liax,
WfGloss:	exactly	3S	then	say	how	way	question	asking for response
WfPOS:	part	pro	adv	v	pro	n	part	part

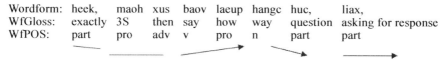

FT: 'Exactly', he asked then: 'What to do next?' something like that.

Until very recently, rising intonation was considered non-native in Yutou Kam. This has much to do with the fact that the vast majority of Kam SFPs bear either level or falling tones.

To alter the intonational shape from level or falling to rising would have been to change the tone of the SFPs themselves. As mentioned before, any change in tone contour in syllables has the potential to interfere with others since there are so many syllable-level tones in Kam. The fact that tone and intonation are intertwined so closely makes them inseparable, cf, Ross et al. 1986. As a result, tone variants that produce tone sandhi are highly restricted. In an isolating language such as Kam, the tone is lexically encoded with meaning. As long as the majority of the SFPs bear level and falling tones, the intonation pattern in questions will remain level or falling as determined predominately by the lexical pitch shape of the components.

From the 1990s onward, younger Kam speakers began to imitate the rising intonational pattern of MSC, since intensive language contact has occurred more and more through formal school education, TV broadcasts, and workplace language phenomena. The use of rising tone to express interrogation was first observed in the 1980s in the nearby Biicbac 琵琶 village. It had spread there from Wucgal, a Han island surrounded by Kam speakers. A notable majority of the residents of Wucgal can speak Kam, even though they kept their native local Chinese, including rising intonation in questions. Nowadays, the older generation has become more tolerant of the new speech norms even though they themselves are still reluctant to adopt them in their own speech.

19.4.3.3.2. *Syntactic characteristics of SFPs*

These particles are all located in the final position of a sentence, but they actually play different syntactic functions, and occupy specific syntactic positions. For example, question particles such as *bac*, *ax*, *eel*, *wuc* occur in specifier position (SPEC) of CP; other particles occupy the complementizer (COMP), as will be discussed in the following paragraphs. So, not only do SFPs have critical semantic and pragmatic roles, but also they affect the syntactic structure of a sentence. To illustrate this syntactic feature, one example is offered in Figure 19.4.3.3.2-1:

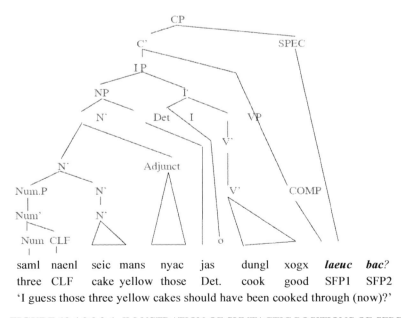

| saml | naenl | seic | mans | nyac | jas | dungl | xogx | *laeuc* | *bac?* |
| three | CLF | cake | yellow | those | Det. | cook | good | SFP1 | SFP2 |

'I guess those three yellow cakes should have been cooked through (now)?'

FIGURE 19.4.3.3.2-1: ILLUSTRATION OF SYNTACTIC POSITIONS OF SFPS

19.4.3.3.2.1. Question particles in SPEC position

The sample sentence in Figure 19.4.3.3.2-1 shows that the SFP *bac* occupies the specifier position of the CP. Within the highlighted SFP cluster, *laeuc* is the perfective marker for the VP, while the *bac* is one of the several question particles. It should be noted that questions in Kam lack the subject-object inversion or *wh* movement in syntax. The most common way of forming a question is using SFPs such as No. 3, 8, and 23 in Table 19.4.3.2-1, along with shifted intonation. The *lac* is considered as part of the VP, a feature that is widespread in languages such as Chinese, Kachin and Then (Bo 1997) in the area. In fact, the SFPs in Kachin reflect person, number, direction, focus, change-of-status, and mood. The SFPs could be formed by affixing, initial shifting, and root replacing (Dai 2002).

While *laeuc* strongly correlates with the verb, the final *bac* does not. In other words, *bac* relate to all the components of the clause/sentence. Since there is a well-studied counterpart *ba* 吧 in Chinese, the current study will refer to the previous research and see what the *bac* in Kam is and what semantic and syntactic function they play. Their discourse functions will be examined in the following section.

The *ba* 吧 in Chinese indicates 'suggestion', 'mild question', 'modesty', 'supposition', 'agreement', etc (Dow 1983: 151-2, Li et al. 1984: 428-9). Li and Thompson (1981: 307-311) assign a function of 'soliciting agreement'. These are all true in Kam as it is quite likely a Chinese loan word, as the *bac* in the above sentence also expresses 'mild question', 'modesty', and 'soliciting agreement'.

As for its syntactic characteristics, there are few accessible reference works. Obviously *bac*'s role reaches beyond the VP. To place the SFPs satisfactorily in the syntactic structure, Law (1990: 11) proposes that Cantonese question particles such as me^{55}, a^{13}, a^{11}, la^{33} $pɔ/wɔ^{33}$, $lɛ^{13}$, and ma^{33} actually occur in specifier (SPEC) position of the CP, as *wh* elements in other languages, with respect to FOCUS. One would then expect that a question particle could not contain a question element or FOCUS having wide scope, because the SPEC position cannot be doubly filled. His reasoning bases on the co-occurrence restrictions exhibited between question particles and other elements that are assumed to occur in SPEC in Logical Form. This SPEC of CP is to the right of C', contrary to the general assumption that SPEC is to the left of C' in Chinese (Henry 1988, Zhou 1988). In this section, Law's analysis of this position in Cantonese is adopted since the structure of questions and the list of SFPs in Kam closely parallel that in Cantonese. For example, 'ma^{33}'— *mac*, '$lɛ^{13}$' 13 —- *luc*, 'a^{13}' / 'a^{11}' — *ac/ax*, 'la^{33} $pɔ/wɔ^{33}$' — *lac bac*.

19.4.3.3.2.2. Other particles in COMP position

Chinese linguists have long disagreed about whether there are complementizers in MSC at all. Xu and Langendeon (1985) postulated that, since there are no lexical items that serve as sentence introducers, MSC sentences lack a COMP position entirely. The same can be said of Kam as well even though serious discussion of the matter is lacking. Huang (1988) argues convincingly that prepositions such as 跟 *gen* (with), 对 *dui* (towards), and conjunctions such as 因为 *yinwei* (because), 如果 *ruguo* (if) can be treated as pre-sentential COMPs since they can either take a sentence as object or precede a clause.

Now after placing question particles into the SPEC position, the remained non-question particles take the stage. Taking the frequently used *lic* as an example:

TF31

Wordform:	yuh	wanh	hangc	mienctangc	yuh	daengl	laeuc	**lic,**	liax
WfGloss:	also	change	kind; type	trick	also	come	PERF	**Confirming**	asking for response
WfPOS:	adv	v	CLS	comm	adv	v	part	**part**	Part

FT: They do new things in their life.

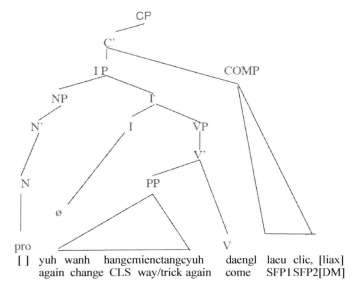

FIGURE 19.4.3.3.2.2-1: SFPS IN COMP POSITION

The *lic* here has the meaning of 'it is the case that...', 'the situation is that...', showing the speaker's commitment   to the truth of a claim or assertion. The SFP *lic* always ends a clause or a sentence. The **liax** after *lic* is a discourse marker, or a very special SFP at the most. So it is either a relative pronoun or a complementizer. Since there is no overt *wh* movement in Kam, the *relative pronoun* is ruled out immediately. It is more likely that the *lic* is a *complementizer*. In order to determine whether it occurs in the same SPEC position as *bac* or COMP at the end of the clause or sentence, a comparison between *lic* and the 'that' in 'that'- relatives in English is conducted.

As the only particle used with all types of relative clauses, *lic* can also accompany a clause with or without a gap. These properties are very similar to the 'that' in 'that' – relatives in English. Radford (1988) argues convincingly that the relative particle *that* is a complementizer, and not a relative pronoun. Also a genitive form of the relative particle cannot be formed by inserting the genitive marker immediately after '*lic*'. This is illustrated by example English (126) and example Kam in (127).

(126) *The car that's hood is damaged.

(127) *Yaoc jenl   liangp wenh leec naih dil   gaems lic
       1S   really like   CLS book this SFP GEN   cover
       * 'I like this book's cover very much.'

Since *lic* cannot be a relative pronoun, and exhibits many of the characteristics of 'that', we propose that *lic*, like 'that', is a complementizer, appearing to the right of the IP.

19.4.4. Communicational aspects of narrating

Undoubtedly Labov's work on narratives has been particularly influential in the English-speaking world. He is, however, by no means the only scholar interested in generalizing about the underlying formal and semantic structures of narratives and stories. For example, Schiffrin (1996) contributes her efforts to better understand how the structure of stories reflects the fact that stories perform social actions; Ochs et al (1989) and Norrick (1997) explore how the audience get involved into the developing of story; Goodwin (1982) touches on the 'instigating' in the discourse of urban African-American girls and demonstrates how the larger social context affects the way the story is told and comprehended.

It is the intention of the current study to look at narration from some new perspectives beyond Labov's to see how this will enrich and extend our understanding. The unique Kam narration-setting features as described in 4.1 point to an unexplored field in the discussion. Specifically, the interaction between the narrator and the audience will be covered in this section: How the narrating relationship is regulated; the functions of *decoys*, whose main role is to acknowledge, respond to, and comment on the narrator's story; how the input from other participants affects or changes the point in case or the direction of narration; and how the operator *liax* negotiates and lubricates the communication between the narrator and the audience.

19.4.4.1. *Narrating as communicational and social interaction*

Discourse structure can be accounted for in terms of syntax, semantics, stylistics, rhetoric, and in the study of specific genres such as those of argumentation and storytelling. In this section, another fundamental dimension of narrative discourse, namely its communicational and social aspects (van Dijk 1997: 2), will be focused on to see how this significant phenomenon is ordered and organized.

A brief introduction to the setting and context of Kam narratives is offered in 4.1, including the physical and social prerequisites. The social and cultural criteria for qualifying as public narrators are also discussed. It is now time to examine, in the described context, how different participants play out their roles and realize the many functions of storytelling. The nature of participant involvement, floor control, and decoy roles will come under scrutiny first to reveal some features in the relationship between discourse and (male) power; then input from non-narrators will be focused on to see what the nature of this interaction in Kam narrative is, how the narrator and audience interact, and what effects those inputs have on the developing of the discourse, both linguistically and communicationally.

19.4.4.1.1. *Monologue in which everyone can say something*

The Kam storytelling narratives represent primarily a monologic performance, as is the case in many other cultures. The narrator dominates the floor. Even though there are many social and cultural constraints on what and how he could narrate, it is basically a one-man show once it starts, in the sense that he has his will in regard to what he can tell the audience and how. That said, it also needs to be pointed out that it became quite evident during the transcription and video recording stages, there is a lot more going on besides pure 'monologic' activities. Temporary abbreviations in parenthesis will be adopted for convenience below in discussing bi-direction exchange.

a.   audience asking questions (AQ);

b.   commenting on developments in story or simply acknowledging the presented information (CM);

c.   greeting and informational exchange during the circulation of food and cigarette (GI);

d.   non-linguistic instant responses and reactions to actions by exclaiming, laughing, and body language (NL);

e.   reasoning or extensions along the lines presented by the narrator (RE);

f.   brief conversation among audience members concerning actions, including the rest of the audience's response to these (RR).

Narrative in Kam is not strictly a monologic act but a collective performance. It shares a lot of similarity with TV talk shows, in which the host performs while the audience is allowed to react. The difference is that both the physical setting and cultural setting equalize the status of narrator (host) and his audience to a far greater extent. The narrator sits among the audience and he himself will become an indistinguishable member of the audience once another narrator take over.

Originally, all of the above goings-on were not transcribed into the database linguistically even though they were recorded on tape. First their role as an integral part of the narrative was not realized; second, some of the reactions such as laughing and sighing are nonlinguistic. In order to identify them, and recover their functions in discourse, it is critical to check through and clarify their relation to the main action of the narrative. One clue is that most of these occurrences appear in the evaluation part. Here are some examples that occurred off the actions or storyline in the story in sequential order. Both linguistic and non-linguistic nature audience-reactions are noted here, no matter whether they were in or not in the in database and attached transcription:

In SR:

57-58	– NL
59	– NL
143	– GI
333	– CM

In TF:

1	– NL
6	– NL
10	– RE, CM
12	– CM
40	– CM
41	– CM
63	– RE
94	– CM

There are more instances of off storyline reaction from the audience in TF than in SR, an indicator that their participation in the narration was closer and more involved.

In a word, the narrator, the decoys, and the rest of participants can and do speak in one way or another, contributing to the formation and development of the narrative as a unit. In this sense Kam narrative is a monologue in which every participant can say something as long as they observe constraints within their own territories.

19.4.4.1.2. *The floor control and social power realization*

No designated order keeper is installed, but the host will exert his power to initiate such activity. He is the one that invites all participants and makes the activity possible. Once that is accomplished, it is up to the crowd to select one narrator at a time and formally start the storytelling.

Since the narrators belong to the elite group of people in the community, respect and admiration from the members will put the tacit order in place. With their position of age, life experience, and contribution to family and community, the audience is inclined to show them deference and attention. Moreover, they are also talented in speaking. A good narrator usually is also one of the headmen in the Kam community. Administration, whether that is official or just customary, brings with it authority. So the internal control of the floor is pretty much preset before the narrating even starts. Narration is one of the public activities in which an elite group of people can exert their power in such a covert way.

Once the narrating starts, a subtle collaborative takes over. Parents will keep an eye on their own children to ensure they do not break rules or embarrass anyone. The decoys will certainly help also. This will be looked at in the next subsection.

19.4.4.2. *Input from non-decoy audience*

Input from the audience is a mixture of various kinds of action. Outside input first shows the degree of audience involvement and proper comprehension of the development of the story. In TF148, when the audience expresses interest in details of the unusual box, commenting on its unique features, it sends a clear and positive message to the narrator that their curiosity level is high and they are interested in learning more about that. The appreciative narrator then calls to mind the distant image of the crafted wooden boxes they personally manufactured in 1960-70'. The encouraged narrator is rejuvenated constantly by these kinds of positive feedbacks and this keeps the narrating going.

Folktale narrative involves recounting preexisting events. A story may have been told many times before. To the elders, few folktales are completely novel. So when a narrator stutters or stumbles along the way, decoys will step up and help him overcome the hurdle. See instances between TF164-165.

The narrating clauses and various inputs from audience interleave and overlap subtly throughout the course of the story, and draw attention to a mixed type of narrative. In Polanyi's (1987: 109ff.) term, this is a 'diffuse story', 'in which a chunk of story is followed by a chunk of multi-party conversation glossing, clarifying, and amplifying aspects of the story chunk just told. In such a format, story evaluation can become a collaborative exercise' (Toolan 2001: 162-163). Apparently the degree of diffusion between narrating and audience input has not reached a level that one might need to treat the dispersed, inputs as the several sections of a single, over arching story. Nevertheless, these extremely introductory words and actions need to be included to see the rich, true picture of narrating in the Kam community. It offers clues to the covert fact that narrating is ultimately social interaction among all the participants, with narrating by the narrator(s) as the trunk or spine of the entity. Not only does the input aid or direct the narrating in some cases, but perhaps equally if not more importantly, it serves the purpose of reminiscence and social binding. In this regard, audience input is not necessarily limited to a supportive role any more. Rather it construes the picture of narrating activity in an organic way, perhaps more like collectively putting pieces of a jigsaw puzzle together.

19.4.4.3. *Communication operator liax*

In a narrative setting, the narrator leads in the information flow in a dominant way. Yet as observed in the previous discussion, this process is bi-directional, more so in Kam particularly. Not only does the narrator speak 'scheduled' vignettes, but also the audience responds spontaneously to what is unfolding through the course of the plot. To ensure that what he intends to convey reaches the audience and the outside input does not derail his progress, the speaker resorts to both linguistic and non-linguistic strategies. One of the most noticeable of the forms is the frequent usage of *liax*, an SFP and discourse marker with special status. The SFP *liax* can appear virtually at any position of the narrative:

a. At the end of an utterance, be that a clause or a sentence. This is the most common position for *liax*. Examples: TF1, TF268, SR34, SR60, etc.

b. Between two phrases or clauses. Examples: SR8, SR16, SR29, SR52, SR68, SR115, SR150, SR154, SR161, SR163, SR176, SR208, SR272, SR277, SR309, SR320, SR343, SR373, SR410, SR422, SR424, TF1, TF21, TF53, TF230.

c. In the middle of a phrase. Examples: SR17, SR33, SR41, SR201, SR222, SR254, SR321, SR361, SR371, SR399, SR400, SR408, SR447, SR451, TF136, TF156, TF185, TF283.

Rarely does *liax* initiate an utterance, reflecting the fact that its main function is to emphasize or draw the attention of the audience to what the speaker himself has just said. Immediate reaction is normally needed right on the spot. Any gap between the narrator's utterance of *liax* and late response from the audience would decrease the degree of attention and cohesion. A few exceptions are in TF325, 362, in which *liax* does, exceptionally, start a sentence. The unusual environment here is that the previous two sentences are couplets in Chinese produced by one of the contestants. It becomes then necessary to separate the character's oral couplets from the narrator's speech. Though *liax* is not completely inappropriate if placed at the end of the previous utterance, the pause between the couplets and *liax* is much shorter than the pause between the *liax* and the following components, thus supporting the parsing of *liax* as in a sentence initial rather final position.

19.4.4.3.1. *liax in sentence-final positions*

The *liax* is used most frequently to elicit acknowledgement, affirmation, agreement, and consensus from the addressees. For example, in TF254:

TF254

Wordform:	eex	heip,	baov	laenl	naih,	**liax,**
WfGloss:	sighing	surprised	say	object	this	**asking for response**
WfPOS:	part	part	v	CLS	dem	**part**

FT: Aha, saying: '(Look at) this!' let me tell you.

Here the *liax* signals the narrator's intention of emphasizing the details developing in the story, attracting the audience's attention to the direct quotation of the characters, and asking for input from them. Practically that is exactly what happens. Following the utterance of this *liax*, the audience expresses their strong reaction to the unexpected resolution, as the other two friends in the story unintentionally 'rescued' their poor friend. The narrator then reacts to their expressions and comments straight away in the next sentence. The particle *ngik* in TF255 symbolizes the narrator's intrusion into the story to convey his own regret, not just that of the two friends' in the story, similar to what the audience has expressed about the events in the story. This occurrence of *liax* also indicates compromise on the narrator's part to the audience's comments.

The *liax* functions slightly differently in causal conversation, since the speaker communicates with his/her interlocutor directly. The narrative setting does not exist anymore. In face-to-face personal interaction, *liax* still conveys the speaker's intention of seeking acknowledgement, affirmation, and consensus on the surface, but the underlying function is more of negotiating. Here the purpose of the utterance obviously differs from that in narrative. Instead of drawing the audience's attention to events in the story and helping them to comprehend the developments, the purpose is to express the truism that in real life convincing the other and reaching deals are practical and worthy objectives. Anyway, when appearing in the clause or sentence final positions, the absolute majority of *liax* occurrences serve to motivate and stimulate communication between the participants and carry the narrative forward.

To summarize, *liax* fulfills some modality functions realized usually through auxiliary words in other languages and carries abundant attitudinal, cognitive, and interactional information.

19.4.4.3.2. *liax in non-sentence-final positions*

In other instances, though, the usage of *liax* does not necessarily express a demand for overt response. The solicited acknowledgement, affirmation, agreement, and consensus from the addressees are not as strong as the previous cases. To put it another way, they are very mild requests and do not expect immediate responses. Rather they become an unconscious request for input often times and serve other discourse functions such as giving the narrator himself more time to paraphrase and, thus, promoting the audience's comprehension of the narrative and the communication between the narrator and audience. Apparently, occurrences of *liax* in non-final positions serve somewhat different purposes in discourse from the ones in sentence-final position. Let's take SR361 as an instance for documentation:

SR361

Wordform:	nuv	yaoc	weex	leis	taeuk	dil	yaoc	weengc	sic,
WfGloss:	if	1S	make, do	able	arrive, reach	in case of, if	1S	always	be
WfPOS:	conj	pro	v	part	v	conj	pro	adv	aux

liax,		**weengc**	**sic**	**tongcyiv**
asking for response		always	be	agree
part		adv	aux	v

FT: 'If I can do (it), I will, I will certainly agree (to do it).'

This *liax* occurs between the repeated *weengc sic* 'will always be'. While it intends to draw the audience's attention to the developing events in TF254, its main function is to pause and give the narrator sufficient time to choose just the right words for the occasion. In this case, repetition is adopted as a secondary means after *liax* to buy some time and provide the narrator a chance to regroup/recover. In other similar instances such as TF53, 156, 185, 230, 283, SR163, 222, 277, 321, and 400, the pausing aspect for the narrator himself is greater than for asking concrete and obvious consensus from the audience when single or multiple words are repeated after the pause.

Another subgroup of *liax* occurrences is used to initiate direct quotes such as in SR52, 309, 320, 343, 373, 410, 422. After specifying who the speaker is, *liax* is inserted and a direct quote follows right away. The main intention is to draw the audience's attention to the coming quotation. Just as viewpoint can shift from one pair of eyes to another through a narrative, so too can voice. Most frequently, this shift is accomplished by means of direct citation, indicated by the insertion of *liax*. In a language lacking of overt TAM representation, supplementary indicators such as *liax* certainly compensates to some degree. All these different uses of *liax* show that it serves multiple functions in discourse, as witnessed in its appearances at different sentential positions. It also reminds one that labeling all the occurrences of *liax* as particle 'asking for response' is an oversimplification. Its multi-faceted nature has not been detected or recorded until now.

19.4.4.4. *Time realization, narrator privilege, and metrical expedient*

Abbott concludes that 'narrative is the principal way in which our species organizes its understanding of time' (2002: 3). Interestingly, in Kam narrative itself, *liax* is used to realize the shift between the time of story and the time of narration. Whenever *liax* occurs, it not only strengthens the information communication between the narrator and the audience, but also acts as a time travel particle taking speaker and listeners back and forth between the two worlds. That is, it brings all the participants back to the present world. This shift usually is instantaneous, since the narrator can take the audience back to the story time right away. In an ideal narrative world, the audience would be fused completely into the story and lose their awareness of time, but in reality, realizing and acknowledging the time shift is essential to accomplish the narrative mission.

Another feature of *liax* that should not go unnoted is that it belongs to the narrator exclusively. Only the narrator has the privilege of using this operator. Never is there a case in which the audience uses *liax*, for that would have violated the rule of communication in narrative. The fact is that while other participants might have their fair share of the floor when invited, it is the individual narrator who ultimately manages the course and controls the narrative act as a whole. This brings back the issue of power and social control. The narrator's dominant role as narrator along with his elite role in the community is signified to a certain extent by his license to use *liax*.

The *liax* /lja^{31}/ is also a metrical or rhythmic expedient. A low falling tone requires less energy and is a nice break for the narrator to slow down, pause, and have a deep breath before going back to the narration. In fact, the tone is neutralized to zero in some cases to simply serve the role of a pause. This decreases the insistent tone and eases the impression that the narrator is 'forcing' others to listen. To call it a discourse lubricant is an underestimate of its power in connecting/gluing the audience to the story and the narrator himself. Rather it is labeled a *communication operator* to reflect better its critical role in information exchange between the narrator and audience.

In summary, to a great extent the spontaneously communicative nature of Kam narrative is expressed overtly in this *liax*. Kam narrative is typically viewed as an event sequence, but this notion needs to be supplemented with the notion that a core property of it is also that the audience's linguistic involvement is an integral part of the narrative itself. On the one hand, it avoids an absolute monologue from forming so all participants are motivated and can enjoy the experience; on the other hand, it allows the narrator to maintain full control over the plot. So linguistically *liax* is for representing various aspects of speech act other than the content of the story events narrated. Whenever it appears at the end of the sentence-final position, *liax* either seeks the audience's acknowledgement, affirmation, agreement, and consensus on developing details in the story, or provides for self-pausing. Communicationally, it connects the audience with the narrator and realizes the time frame shift of traveling from the time in narrated events to the present narrating momentarily. Socially, it is an unconscious way of expressing power and authority of the speaker over the listeners. In a word, *liax* fulfills multiple purposes or functions at the same time more often than not.

19.4.5. Summary

In this section, the discussion of narrative structure comes first, based on Labov's framework in PENs. Though the circumstances PEN and Kam narrative differ noticeably, the similarity or commonality between them is also apparent. The role of SFPs in discourse along with a complete list of Kam SFPs is added to the discussion. The study also examines the phonological and syntactic characteristics of the SFPs. After that, communicational aspects of the narrating are under scrutiny. Not only the relationship among different subgroups of participants is visited, but also how a very special group, the *yenc naemv guh* 'the decoys', functions in the narrative discourse was examined. Also different types of non-narrator input, of linguistic or non-linguistic nature, are sorted. Their effects on the developing of the story are viewed from a broader perspective. And finally, the communication operator *liax* occupied a subsection through which its multiple- roles of communicative nature were examined. Analyzing narrative in a sociolinguistic framework reveals the close relationships among the social settings, linguistic representations, and their respective functions as well.

19.5. SPEECH COMMUNITIES AND SOCIOLINGUISTIC ISSUES

Even though the Kam populace is spread across three provinces, Kam speech communities are, in fact, densely connected in terms of local topology and geography. Also Kam residents tend not to marry with other ethnic groups and also not within one's own village. So the community boundary among different ethnic groups in the area is, in general, relatively clear cut. Another fact that is noteworthy is that the Kam language has been exposed to Chinese influence since 700AD, and, at the same time, the Kam people have occupied relatively rich land in comparison to neighboring groups so as to develop economically and socially, which has led to a higher degree of self-esteem among the people. All these facts have collaborated longterm to promote the maintenance of Kam. As a result, Kam language has remained highly significant in people's daily lives.

19.5.1. Dialects

There are two Kam subdivisions: Southern Kam with four vernaculars, and Northern Kam with three vernaculars. The main isoglosses lie along the longitude from Datong to Qimeng in Jinping, Guizhou, where Kam, Hmong, and Han Chinese live together. The following is the detailed taxonomy of Kam varieties and their lects:

Southern subdivision:

a. The first lectal area includes Rongjiang Zhanglu, Liping Hongzhou, Jinping Qimeng in Guizhou, Tongdao in Hunan, Longsheng and Sanjiang Dudong in Guangxi.

b. The second lectal area includes Liping Shuikou, Congjiang Guandong, Rongjiang Pingjiang in Guizhou, and Sanjiang Heli in Guangxi.

c. The third lectal area includes Zhenyuan Baojing in Guizhou.

d. The fourth lectal area is in Rongshui, Guangxi (Long and Zheng 1998: 181).

Northern subdivision:

a. The first lectal area includes Tianzhu Shidong, Sansui Kuanchang, and Jianhe Xiaoguang in Guizhou.

b. The second lectal area includes Tianzhu Zhuxi in Guizhou.

c. The third area includes Jinping Datong in Guizhou.

The difference between the two main subdivisions is significant in the sense that intelligibility between Northern and Southern speakers is very low. Mainly differences of phonology and lexicon as well as some differences of syntax prevent understanding of running conversation: Northern Kam does not have vowel length contrast and the velar coda k of the south has either been dropped, or changed to the alveolar t or to glottal stop $?$. Some syntactic rules also differ. For example, the modifier possessive pronoun precedes the head noun in the north and there are phonetic changes in classifiers, some numerals, nouns, and verbs in the north. Recent research has shown, however, that at least one Southern location possesses similar phonetic changes (Yang 1999).

People from different lects within a subdivision can comprehend each other well, since the internal difference in phonology, lexicon, and syntax are relatively minor.

19.5.2. Language use

Kam is still the native and everyday language for most people in the southern area and for many in the northern villages such as in Tianzhu, Jinping, Zhenyuan, Jianhe, etc. as well. At the same time, more and more Kam have learned a local form of Chinese and the standard Putonghua through school education and interaction with other peoples. Long and Zheng (1998) have classified language use among the Kam into the following three types:

a. Kam people who can only speak Kam and no any other language(s). 'Most of these live in the southern dialect area or are old people, women, and children living in the mountain villages of the northern area far from Han Chinese centers. There are also some young men from these remote northern areas who have never attended schools, seldom leave their homes, and rarely come in contact with the outside world.' While these descriptions are still fairly precise nowadays, the evaluated 50% of the population seems too high. Of the 2.5 million Kam, 30–40% may fall into this group. As the society opens more and more to the outside world, the percentage goes down steadily.

b. Kam people who cannot speak Kam but Chinese only. Most of them are in northern, such as Yuping, Sansui, Tianzhu, etc. Of the 2.5 million Kam, over 30% may fall into this group.

c. Kam people who can speak both Kam and Chinese or other languages such as Hmong and Mien. Of the 2.5 million Kam, 30% may fall into this group. As the public school education in Kam area improves slowly and the interaction among peoples intensifies, both the total number of people in this group and the percentage among the populace will only go up.

Obviously there is a kind of gradient *diglossia* among the two languages. Although the exact number of speakers of the above three Kam groups may be hard to define, their domains in use are clearer. Within the villages where the old people and children cannot speak Chinese, all members use native Kam in daily life. Even government documents are interpreted into Kam for monolingual speakers. Speaking Chinese might be either just for entertaining outsiders or used to demonstrate one's knowledge of the 'outside world' and is regarded by the older generation as 'showing off'. Of course, Han is the language of the school classroom and professional government offices. Other exceptional uses of Han include speaking to non-Kam persons. It is interesting to observe that since the Kam show tenacious language maintenance in preferring their native language, many Han Chinese have learned some Kam in order to work with local people. For example, since almost all the daily fresh food supply is provided by Kam women in Shuangjiang township, Tongdao County, Hunan Province, many Han Chinese learn some basic Kam to help the trade process and get better deals in the markets.

19.5.3. Literacy effort

Kam did not have its own orthography until 1958. Some Kam intellectuals used Chinese characters to record Kam, the so-called 汉字记侗音 'Recording Kam in Chinese characters or demotic Chinese for recording Kam.' There are three ways of doing the recording (Long and Zheng 1998: 211):

a. Use Chinese characters with identical or similar pronunciations to Kam words. For example, 拣考 *jiankao* (literally 'pick-test') is used to record [tɕan^{55} ʔɐu^{31}] 'to eat (rice).

b. Use Chinese characters with identical meanings to Kam words. A sign is usually added around the character to indicate that this is Kam with the same meaning as the Chinese character but with different pronunciation. For example, 深 *shen* (literally 'deep') is used to record [jɐm^{55}] 'deep (water), hard to achieve'.

c. Use *fanqie* (反切), the Chinese tradition of combining the initial of the first character and the rhyme and tone of the second character to represent a word. For example, 尼亚 *níyà* to represent [na^{55}] 'river'.

Most of the works are transcripts of Kam custom law, literature, or personal notices. Since there was no accepted standard among the users, 'recording Kam in Chinese characters' was never publicly promoted or recognized as a true Kam orthography.

From December 1956 to February 1957, the Chinese government conducted the first extensive field survey of Kam language and planning of a Kam orthography in 22 locations, covering 14 counties in Guizhou, Hunan, and Guangxi. In August 1958, the designed draft *Kam Orthography* was adopted officially. This is an orthography written entirely in Roman letters. The southern subdivision was taken as the standard for grammar, style, and discourse and Rongjiang Zhanglu in Guizhou as the model for pronunciation. They are thirty-two initials, sixty-four rhymes, and nine tones.

The implementation of Kam orthography was very successful in Rongjiang, Liping, and other Kam areas under the guidance of the government until the Cultural Revolution broke out in 1966. Teachers were trained and assigned to different locations to teach others. Various reference books and reading materials were published during this period, including the *Kam-Chinese Dictionary, Chinese-Kam dictionary, and Kam Language Textbook*. In 1981, the implementation was resumed, as China opened to the outside world in a dramatic way and it spread to Hunan, and Guangxi Kam communities soon thereafter. Kam orthography played an important role in lowering illiteracy among Kam adults and was introduced into elementary schools in Guizhou as a help in learning *Putonghua* and *Pinyin*. More textbooks were published, and journals such as the *Journal of Kam Orthography* in Sanjiang, Guangxi were circulated. Not only did many illiterates learn to write in their own script after attending evening literacy classes for only 100 hours, but also the Kam language and orthography were studied in colleges such as the Central Institute of Nationalities in Beijing and the Guizhou Institute of Nationalities in Guiyang. By 1995, 857 classes of Kam orthography had been conducted in Qiandongnan Hmong and Kam Prefecture, Guizhou. The total enrollment reached 29,989. Of them 24,873 graduated and were considered officially literate. More than 140 college students majoring in *Kam language, literature, and culture* were graduated, including three graduate students (Chen 1995).

The momentum toward significant literacy among the Kam reversed in the middle of the 1990's. On the one hand, the government's financial support for the Kam orthography implementation decreased gradually. On the other hand, there developed a growing trend of marketing and looser residence restriction in China that triggered a great new *Völkerwanderung*. People, especially those of the younger generations, considered Kam orthography impractical and less useful than Chinese for finding employment and for rising economically.

19.5.4. New trends in migration, media exposure and family orientation

Historically, the Kam people, like other peoples of China, have been officially rooted in their traditional homelands and have thus not had the freedom to move around. The sedentary lifestyle was implemented with strict governmental residence policies. This regulation is one of the main reasons why the Kam language and culture have been fairly well preserved in the closed areas where they have traditionally lived. But in the 90's and perhaps a little earlier in some places, things began to change dramatically. People gained more freedom to choose a profession and a place of residence. More and more young Kam people 'immigrated' to towns in Han Chinese areas and cities along the east coast in Guangdong, Fujian, and Guangxi Provinces to seek their fortunes in the wider world of urban and suburban life. Young Kam of Guizhou Province have not yet been affected by this trend, but there is much impetus driving migration in many Kam communities of Hunan and Guangxi, so that today 70–80% of villagers in the age group 16–30 may be living away from their original homes. Left behind are old people and younger siblings, and also those without enough language or educational skills to allow them to make the occupational shift from agriculture to unskilled labor. Although these migration patterns are not yet permanent (usually they come back to visit their families during the Spring Festival for one to two weeks and then return to their work places again), the potential effects on the Kam language use among the younger generations and the cultural consequences are easy to discern. These 'little sisters and little brothers', as they are sometimes known, start to learn the language of the work place, especially Cantonese and Putonghua, and many Kam traditional cultural practices fall into disuse, i.e. they are not being transmitted or no longer being practiced by this more citified generation of new urban and semi-urban young, much to the concern and dismay of their parents and grandparents. Since most of them will return to their original Kam communities before they become 40, it will be interesting to see how the days they have spent in towns and cities will affect their language maintenance and language use in later life.

Another considerable input from outside comes from TV and advertising. Mass media and television are no longer taken to be exotic influences from the outside world but quite commonly observable even in remote villages. For example, in Yutou, a typical Kam village complex in Tongdao, Hunan with over 3000 people, around 500 households, there are more than 200 TV sets. These bring tremendous amounts of new exposure to Putonghua, even among the older generation, many of whom cannot speak or understand Chinese. All programs, of course, are in Chinese, and more and more of the traditional cultural gatherings are being replaced by communal watching of the 'boob tube'.

As society opens further, so does the family, the Kam family has noticeably decreased in size in the past two decades as well. On the one hand, this decrease has affected cross generational interaction between grandparents and grandchildren, and has led to a breakdown in traditional culture, including linguistic shift. On the other hand, old people have suffered economic erosion as well, in the sense that their position of social authority as purveyors of traditional cultural values has been downsized in favor of more centralized electronic media. Another important force for change is in the different family values portrayed in broadcast news and dramas and in the interaction with outside world.

All these new trends in Kam society contribute to accelerating changes in language use, many of which do not portend well for the future of the Kam language. These problems, however, have been loosed from many sources and are not in any way unique to the Kam or to China. They are the very same issues confronting hundreds of millions of people worldwide. How does one balance tradition with modernization, local traditions with global perspectives, and the agrarian grain cycles with an urban lifestyles? These large scale problems extend far beyond the Kam to many traditional cultures around the world and threaten, in the vast, vast majority of cases, the future of their languages.

REFERENCES

Abbott, Porter (2002) *The Cambridge Introduction to Narrative*, Cambridge: Cambridge University Press.

Bo, Wenze (1997) *Yanghuang Yu*, Shanghai: Far East Publishers.

Bourgerie, Dana (1987) 'Particles of Uncertainty: A Discourse Approach to the Cantonese Final Particles', unpublished MA thesis, Ohio State University.

Brinton, Laurel (1996) *Pragmatic Markers in English: Grammaticalization and Discourse Functions*, Berlin and New York: Mouton de Gruyter.

Chao, Yuen-Ren (1968) *A Grammar of Spoken Chinese*, Berkeley and Los Angeles: University of California Press.

Chen Dan (1995) *Surveying Report on the Designed Kam Orthography Practice*, unpublished manual, Beijing: Chinese Committee of National Minority Affairs and Chinese Academy of Social Sciences.

Chu, Chauncey C. (1998) *A Discourse Grammar of Mandarin Chinese*, New York: Peter Lang Publishing.

Comrie, Bernard (1983) *Language Universals and Linguistic Typology: Syntax and Morphology*, Oxford: Basil Blackwell.

Cooke, Joseph (1989) *Thai Sentence Particles and Other Topics* (Papers in South-East Asian Linguistics No. 12, Pacific Linguistics Series A-80), Canberra: The Australian National University.

Cumming, S. and Ono, T. (1997) 'Discourse and Grammar', in T. Dijk (ed.) *Discourse as Structure and Process*, Sage Publications.

Dai Qingxia (1996) 'Revisiting the Sentence-final Auxiliary Words in Kachin', *Minzu Yuwen* 4: 61-71.

Dai, Qingxia (2002) 'Jingpo yu "xing xiu ming" liangzhong yuxu dui bi [A comparative study between two word orders of nouns and their adjectives]', *Minzu Yuwen* 4: 12-20.

Dow, D.M. (1983) *Hanyu Yufa* [A Grammar of Mandarin Chinese], Edinburgh: University of Edinburgh, Department of Chinese.

De Beauclair, Inez (1972) 'Ethnographic Studies', in *A Miao Tribe of Southeast Kweichou and Its Cultural Configuration*, Taipei: Southern Material, 313-33.

Edmondson, Jerold A. (1998) *The Language Corridor: New Evidence from Vietnam, Proceedings of the International Conference on Tai Cultures outside Thailand*, Mahidol University, Bangkok.

Edmondson, Jerold A., and Samsong Burusphat (eds) (2000) *Kam-Mandarin-Thai-English Dictionary*, Bangkok: Mahidol University Press, Thailand.

Edmondson, Jerold. A., and Solnit, David (1988) *Comparative Kadai: Linguistics Beyond Tai*, Dallas: Summer Institute of Linguistics and The University of Texas at Arlington.

Frei, Henri (1956) 'The Ergative Construction in Chinese: Theory of Pekinese pa', *Gengo Kenkyu* 31: 22-50, 83–115.

Givón, Talmy (1984) *Syntax: A Functional-Typological Introduction*, Amsterdam: John Benjamin Publishing Company.

Goodwin, Marjorie (1982) '"Instigating": Storytelling as Social Process', *American Ethnologist* 9: 799-819.

Haas, Mary R. (1942) 'The Use of Numeral Classifiers in Thai', *Language* 18: 201-6.

Hanson, Inga-Lill (1996) 'The interplay between the verb particle 'ɔ' and the sentence particles in Akha', *Linguistics of the Tibeto-Burman Area* 19: 65-76.

Hashimoto, Anne Yue (1971) 'Mandarin syntactic structures', *Unicorn* 8: 1-146.

Henry, Alison (1988) 'Empty Categories in Chinese', unpublished PhD dissertation, University of Ulster.

Huang, C.-T. James (1988) 'Wǒ pǎo DE kuài and Chinese Phrase Structure', *Language* 64: 274-311.

Hudak, Thomas (1999) *Kam-Chinese Dictionary*, Tempe: Program for Southeast Asia Studies, Arizona State University.

Hymes, Dell (1972) 'Models of the Interaction of Language and Social Life', in John Gumperz, and Dell Hymes (eds) *Directions in Sociolinguistics*, New York: Holt, Rinehart, and Winston, 35-71.

Labov, William (1972) *Language in the Inner City: Studies in the Black English Vernacular*, Philadelphia: University of Pennsylvania Press.

Labov, William, and Waletzky, Joshua (1967) 'Narrative Analysis: Oral Versions of Personal Experience', in June Helm (ed.) *Essays on the Verbal and Visual Arts*, Seattle: University of Washington Press, 12-44.

Law Sam-Po (1990) *The Syntax and Phonology of Cantonese Sentence-final Particles*, unpublished PhD dissertation, Boston University.

Li, Charles and Thompson, Sandra (1981) *Mandarin Chinese: A Functional Reference Grammar*, Berkeley and Los Angeles: University of California Press.

Li, Fang-Kuei (1943) *Notes on the Mak Language*, Institute of History and Philology, Academia Sinica, Monograph Series A, No. 20.

Li, Yen-Hui Audrey (1990) *Order and Constituency in Chinese*, Dordrecht, Netherlands: Kluwer Academic Publishers.

Li, Ying-Che et al (1984) *Mandarin Chinese: A practical reference grammar for students and teachers*, Taipei: The Crane Publishing Co.

Linag, Min (1980) *Dong yu jianzhi* [Outline of the Dong language], Peking: Chinese Academy of Social Sciences.

— (1984) *A Brief Description of the Kam Language*, Beijing: Nationality Press.

Longacre, Robert (1996) *The Grammar of Discourse*, New York: Plenum Press.

Long, Yaohong and Zheng, Guoqiao (1998) *Language in Guizhou Province, China*. Dallas: SIL International and the University of Texas at Arlington Publications in Linguistics 126.

Matisoff, James (1973) *The Grammar of Lahu*, Berkeley: University of California Press.

Norrick, Neal (1997) 'Collaborative narration of familiar stories', *Language in Society* 26: 199-220.

Ochs, Elinor and Taylor, Carolyn (1989) 'Detective Stories at Dinner-time: Problem Solving through Co-narration', *Cultural Dynamics* 2: 238-57.

Ohio State University (1991) *Language Files: Materials for an Introduction to Languages and Linguistics*, Columbus, Ohio: Ohio State University.

Person, Kirk (2000) 'Sentence Final Particles in Bisu Narrative', unpublished PhD dissertation, The University of Texas at Arlington.

Polanyi, Livia (ed) (1987) *Structure of Discourse*, Norwood, NJ: Ablex Publisyhing Corporation.
Radford, Andrew (1988) *Transformational Grammar*. Cambridge: Cambridge University Press.
— (1997) *Syntactic Theory and the Structure of English, a Minimalist Approach*. Cambridge: Cambridge University Press.
Ross, Elliot, Edmondson, Jerold A. and Seibert, Burton (1986) 'The Effect of Affect on Various Acoustic Measures of Prosody in Tone and Non-tone Languages: A Comparison Based on Computer Analysis of Voice', *Journal of Phonetics* 14: 283-302.
Schiffrin, Deborah (1996) 'Narrative as Self-portrait: Social Linguistic Constructions of Identity', *Language in Society* 25: 167-203.
Shi Lin (1983) 'Phonetic Variations and Sandhi Phenomena in Kam', *Minzu Yuwen* 5: 61-71.
— (1985) 'Study of Kam Adjectives', *Journal of Guizhou Nationalities' Studies* 4: 128-140.
— (1986) *Analysis of Kam Pronouns*, Beijing: *Minzu Yuwen* 5: 40-46.
— (1990) 'Some Suggesting Adjustments in Boundaries of Kam Dialects', *Minzu Yuwen* 6: 52-57.
— (1992) 'Distinguishing Features of Kam Tones', *Minzu Yuwen* 3: 28-32.
— (1994) 'The Pronunciations of New Chinese Borrowing Words in Kam', *Minzu Yuwen* 5: 1-11.
Teng, Shou-hsin (1977) *A Semantic Study of Transitivity Relations in Chinese*, Taipei: Students Books.
Toolan, Michael (2001) *Narrative: A Critical Linguistic Introduction*, 2nd edition, London and New York: Routledge.
van Dijk, Teun (1997) 'Discourse as Interaction in Society', in Teun van Dijk (ed.) *Discourse as Social Interaction: Discourse Studies: A Multidisciplinary Introduction Volume 2*, London: Sage Publications, 1-17.
Wang Huan (1957) '*Bă zì jù hé bèi zì jù*' [*The BA sentences and BEI sentences*], Shanghai: Xin zhi shi Chubanshe. Translated into English in *Project on Linguistic Analysis* 4, edited by William S. Y. Wang, Columbus: Ohio University Department of Linguistics, 1963.
Wang Li (1957) *Zhongguo Yufa Lilun [Theory of Chinese Syntax]*, Beijing: Zhonghua Press.
Wolfson, Nessa (1982) *CHP, The Conversational Historical Present in American English and Narrative*, Cinnarmson: Foris Publication.
Xing Gongwan, Shi Lin, and Cui Jianxing (1988) *The Sanjiang Kam Language*, Tianjin: Nankai University Press.
Xu Liejong and Langendeon, Terence (1985) 'Topic Structures in Chinese', *Language* 61: 1-27.
Yang, Quan (1988) 'Developmental Tendencies in Kam Phonology', in Jerold Edmondson and David Solnit (eds) *Comparative Kadai: Linguistic Studies beyond Tai*, Summer Institute of Linguistics and University of Texas at Arlington.
Yang Tongyin (1988) 'Teaching Material on Kam Dialects', manuscript, Guiyang: Guizhou Institute of Nationalities.
— (1992) 'Phonetic Variation in Kam Classifiers', unpublished MA thesis, Central Institute of Nationalities (Beijing).
— (1993) 'Linguistic Recording of Chinese Minority Languages: Kam of Shuangjiang, Tongdao, Hunan Province', manuscript, Beijing: Research Center of Minority Languages, Chinese Academy of Social Sciences.
— (1999) *Aspects of Noun Phrase and Verb Phrase in Kam*, MA thesis, The University of Texas at Arlington.
— (2004) *Aspects of the Kam Language: As Revealed in its Narrative Discourse*, doctoral dissertation, The University of Texas at Arlington.
Zheng Guoqiao (1988) 'Teaching Material on Kam Grammar', manuscript, Guiyang: Guizhou Institute of Nationalities.
Zhou Xinping (1988) 'On the Head Movement Constraint', *Studies in the Linguistics Sciences* 18: 183-210.

CHAPTER TWENTY

SUI

James Wei and Jerold A. Edmondson

20.1. INTRODUCTON

The Sui people (in Chinese 水 *Shui* meaning 'water') constitute the second largest components of the Kam-Sui language grouping whose population according to the 1990 census was 346,000. But the Sui language has an importance far beyond its size, as this language has figured prominently in the history of research about the entire Kam-Tai family. It was namely the landmark investigations of Sui by Professor Li Fang Kuei in the 1930s and 1940s that proved a connection between Thai and some language groups of China. The Tai peoples are now thought to have once lived in this general area of China before departing for SE Asia. One important discovery Li made during his work was that the Sui language had preserved an inventory of sounds relatively rich and archaic in comparison to Tai groups of SE Asia. For example, the voiceless nasals of Sui /m̥ n̥/, are perhaps suggested in Thai spelling yet not pronounced voiceless today, but in Sui they are still truly voiceless nasals. For that reason lexical comparison with Sui is singularly helpful in understanding the nature of the parent from which it and the other Tai languages have sprung.

Despite its importance for comparative studies, Sui language and culture is much more than just a cornucopia of archaisms. The Sui perpetuates still today a vibrant and varied lifestyle in 三都水族自治县 Sandu Sui (Shui) Autonomous County of 贵州省 Guizhou Province and in the nearby counties of 荔波 Libo, 独山 Dushan, 平塘 Pingtang, 都匀 Duyun, 剑河 Jianhe, 榕江 Rongjiang, and 黎平 Liping. Indeed, ninty-three percent of the Sui population (322,000 people) reside in Guizhou Province, China. An additional 10,000 live in Guangxi-Zhuang Autonomous Region to the south at 融水苗族自治县 Rongshui Miao Autonomous County, in the far west of the county at 英洞 Yingdong Villages where there were 280 speakers in 1990 and in 南丹 Nandan County. A small number people of Sui migrated some decades ago to 富源 Fuyuan and 彝良 Yiliang Counties in Yunnan Province where they have adopted the Bouyei language (population 7,000) and also some Sui families left eight generations ago for Vietnam where 120 still speak Sui in Hồng Quang District of Tuyên Quang Province. But it is in Guizhou at Sandu Sui Autonomous County where the Sui population is most densely settled and which the Sui people rightly regard as their cultural and linguistic heartland.

The Sui people make up one element of a complex of Kadai peoples with whom they share a common history and also many common cultural practices. In Chinese annals and historical books it states that the Kam-Tai peoples originated from the ancient 越 Yue, who covered a large area in South China up to about 700 BC and who are accorded the ancestors of all the Kam-Tai people groups. Some scholars have suggested that Sui are directly descended from one branch, the 骆越 Luoyue (Zhou and Edmondson 1996: 6). There are today vestiges of common cultural practices of the Kam-Tai peoples in the shared vocabulary. For instance, Sui and the other Kam-Sui languages and cultures have cognate vocabulary and customs associated with wet paddy rice farming, e.g. *qui²* 'water buffalo', *ʔau⁴* 'rice', *ʔdoŋ³* 'winnowing basket' and *tap⁷* 'carrying pole' as well as with marriage practices. Among Kam-Sui peoples it was customary until some decades ago that a woman marry her father's sister's son (cross-cousin marriage), unless the age differences were too great. Some have suggested that cross-cousin bonds reflect an original clan-based social organization with the purpose of accumulating and preserving wealth and power within compact communities and villages. While there were advantages of a few hundred related by bloodlines, these practices ran counter to the Han Chinese custom of ancestor worship and patrilineal naming and inheritance. Over time the Han form of social organization gradually supplanted the Kadai one, but many traditions have persisted especially those regarding housing. So Sui villages, even today, are found in mountain hollows and display the stilted wooden house style.

The Sui people call themselves ai^{33} sui^{33}. The first element is a classifier element meaning '(male) person'and occurs widely in compounds with this interpretation. The origins of the autonym sui^{33} are more obscure. It has been suggested that Sui might refer to 'water' (resembling perhaps Chinese *shui*) in light of the propensity of the Sui people to settle near river banks. But this account seems flawed, as many other Tai and Kam-Sui groups have riverine cultures and, even more importantly, the Sui word for 'water' is nam^3, and does not approximate the Han Chinese word for water. To date no convincing account of the meaning of sui^{33} has emerged.

The closest linguistic relatives to the Sui are, perhaps, the 毛南族 Maonan population 90,000) who live separated from them to the south and west at 环江毛南族自治县 Huanjiang County in Guangxi Province. Other language groups in this same branch are 莫人 Mak and 佯爺人 T'en. And, just to the east of Sandu County are found the 侗族 Kam, the largest member of the Kam-Sui subbranch (population 2.5 million).

The Sui language is relatively homogenous from place to place and it is the language of wider communication among people living in Sui areas, as many people from other ethnic groups residing together with the Sui also can speak Sui. Just about everyone also can speak some form of local Chinese, as well. When Sui people live among other groups, only a few have shifted from their first language and adopted Chinese. These observations all testify to a strong tradition of language maintenance among the Sui people.

Although Sui does not vary greatly from place to place, that does not mean there are no internal divisions. From studies carried out in the 1950s, scholars have distinguished three vernacular types, based upon phonetic and lexical differences and some grammatical features. Much of the data sketched here has been taken from the 水语调查报告 Shuiyu Diaocha Baogao (ZSMYDBG 1956).

(1) Sandong vernacular, spoken in such areas as 三洞 Sandong, 水龙 Shuilong, 中和 Zhonghe, 苗草 Miaocao, 坝街 Bajie, Jiadao, Shiqi, 佳荣 Jiarong, 恒丰Hengfeng, 周覃 Zhouqin, 九仟 Jiuqian, 塘州 Tangzhou and 阳蒙 Yangmeng of Sandu Sui Autonomous County, 瑶庆 Yaoqing of Libo county, and Wenquan (Tianxing) of Dushan County, and in some other areas of 榕江 Rongjiang and 从江 Congjiang County of Guizhou Province. The people who speak Sandong vernacular make up 90% of the Sui population.

(2) Yang'an vernacular, spoken in such places as 阳安 Yang'an, 羊洛 Yangluo, 林桥 Linqiao in Sandu County and 董渺 Dongmiao in Dushan County of Guizhou Province.

(3) Pandong vernacular, spoken in 潘洞 Pandong, in Duyun City, and 翁台 Wengtai in Dushan County in Guizhou Province.

The phonological system of the Sui language described here is based on Sandong Miaocao vernacular, which representative of the kind of Sui spoken by the greatest number of speakers. The inventory of Sui initials is quite numerous. Initial consonants:

p	ph	mb	ʔb	m̥	ʔm	m	f	v	ʔw
t	th	nd	ʔd	n̥	ʔn	n	l		
ts	tsh	s	z						
tɕ	tɕh	ȵ̊	ʔȵ	ȵ	ɕ	j	ʔj		
k	kh	(g	ʔg)	ŋ̊	ʔŋ	ŋ	x	ɣ	ʔɣ
q	qh	(ɢ)	ʁ						

ʔ	h						
pj	phj	mbj	ʔbj	m̥j	mj	fj	vj
tj	thj	ndj	ʔdj	n̥j	ʔnj	lj	
tsj	tshj*	sj					
tw	dw						
tsw*	tshw*	ndw	ʔdw	lw	sw*		
kw	khw	ʔŋw					

Notes:

1) /mb/ and /nd/ are pronounced with slight pre-nasalization. Some specialists write them as [b] and [d].
2) The pronunciation of /tɕ tɕh/ is similar to MSC [tɕ tɕh] but don't have the [i-] or [y-] offglide of Chinese. Scholars in China often transcribe this sound as /ȶ/ and /ȶh/.
3) /v/ is sometimes pronounced as [w].
4) /pw tshj tshw tsw sw/ are found only in modern Chinese loan words.
5) The words we have found with initial consonants /ʔdw ʔŋw/ are few in number (less than 10).
6) /phw/ is only for spelling the family name Pan or for spelling this syllable in modern Chinese loan words.

p	pi² 'fat'	pɛ¹ 'sell'	pa³ 'father's older sister'
ph	pha¹ 'grey'		phja:t⁷ 'blood'
pj	pjen⁵ 'change'	pja⁴ 'oats'	pja⁶ 'weave'
phj	phjəi⁵ 'near'	phja³ 'once'	
mb	mbe¹ 'year'	mbiŋ³ 'expensive'	mba³ 'fawn on'
ʔb	ʔbən⁵ 'well, spring'	ʔba³ 'moth, butterfly'	ʔbən¹ 'sky'
ʔbj	ʔbja:n³ 'otter'	ʔbjək⁷ 'girl'	ʔbja:n³ 'shake, shiver'
ʔbw	ʔbwa:ŋ⁵ ʔu¹ 'exterior'	ʔbwa:i⁵ ȶa:i⁵ 'flank'	
m̥	m̥u⁵ 'pig'	m̥a¹ 'dog'	m̥ən³ 'maggot'
m	ma⁴ 'horse'	ma² 'tongue'	man² 'oil'
ʔm	ʔmi¹ 'bear'	ʔma¹ 'vegetable'	ʔmət⁷ 'blind'
mj	mja¹ 'hand'	mjn² 'blanket'	
f	fɔ⁶ ʔau⁴ 'husk'	fən¹ 'rain'	fa¹ 'right side'
fj	fjə³ 'rag'	fjap⁸ 'cave in'	fjen¹ 'garden'
ʔw	ʔwen⁵ 'blame'	ʔwa:ŋ⁵ te³ 'under'	
v	va⁵ 'write'	va:ŋ¹ 'high, tall'	va¹ 'be in estrus'
vj	vjan¹ 'tooth'	vjan¹ 'dream'	
t	ta:m¹ 'sick'	təi¹ 'die'	ta:p⁷ 'carrying pole'
th	tha:u³ 'search'	that⁷ 'kick, lunge'	thau⁵ 'arrive'
tj	fan¹ tjum³ 'white bamboo'	ʔai³ tjaŋ⁵ 'drunkard'	
thj	thjak⁷ la:k⁸	thjɔ² 'paste'	thjak⁷ 'wear'
tw	tsj¹ twa³ 'Double Ninth Festival'	twan⁴ 'most'	
nd	nda¹ 'eye'	ndən¹ 'body'	ndaŋ⁵ ha:n⁵ 'desert, flee'
ʔd	ʔde³ 'ladder'	ʔdi¹ 'far'	ʔdai³ 'gain'
ndj	ndjai³ 'buy'		ndjak⁷ 'grasshopper'
ʔdj	ʔdjə³ 'seedling'	ʔdja¹ 'beyond'	ʔdjam⁵ 'cloudy'
ndw	fe⁴ ndwɔ³ 'celebrate a Sui festival'		
ʔdw	ʔdwa¹ 'salt'		tsum² ha:i⁴ ʔdwɔ¹ 'navel'
n̥	n̥ak⁷ 'sleep'	n̥a³ 'bow'	n̥ai¹ 'shake'

n	nuk⁸ 'flower'	na:ŋ¹ 'bamboo shoot'	nui² 'insect'
ʔn	ʔna¹ 'thick'	ʔna³ 'face'	ʔnaŋ¹ 'have'
l	lɛ¹ 'book'	la:u⁴ 'big, great'	
lj	tjeu² ljen⁴ thje² 'spleen'		ljak⁷ 'steal'
lw	lwa⁵ 'to rest'	lwa¹ 'boat'	
ts	tsik⁷ 'ruler stick'	son¹ tsak⁷ 'heel of a shoe'	
tsh	thje² tsha:n⁶ 'spade'	tshu¹ 'vinegar'	
tsj	tsj¹ 'eat'	tsjə² 'tea'	tsjak⁷ 'guard'
tshj	tshjaŋ⁶ ʈe² 'rob'	sau⁶ tshja:ŋ³ 'pistol'	
tsw	tswən¹ 'brick'	tswaŋ¹ 'pretend'	
s	sa:u¹ 'pocket'	sa:i³ 'question'	sai⁶ 'matter, affair'
sj	sjɛn¹ 'fairy'		
sw	swan¹ miŋ⁶ 'tell fortune'		jin¹ swa² 'printing'
z	zən¹ 'person'		zən¹ 'heavy'
ʈ	ʈən¹ 'group of'	ʈən² 'caw, crow'	ʈən⁶ 'story'
ʈh	ʈhi¹ 'angry'	ʈhi¹ thi⁶ 'gas'	ʈhi³ 'bully'
ɲ̊	ɲ̊a⁵ 'pancreas'	ɲ̊am¹ 'adhesive'	ɲ̊au⁵ 'bad'
ɲ	ɲə² 'you'	ɲa⁵ 'foolish'	ɲat⁷ 'crack with the teeth'
ʔɲ	ʔɲam¹ 'grasp'	ʔɲam⁵ 'follow'	ʔɲam⁵ na:i⁶ 'tonight'
ç	çə¹ 'sharp'	çə³ 'wife'	çən¹ 'really'
j	ja⁴ 'grandmother'	ja¹ 'cogongrass'	
ʔj	ʔjə¹ 'cotton cloth'	ʔjək⁷ 'hunger'	ʔjam¹ 'deep'
k	ka¹ 'dragon'	tsiŋ⁵ ka:m³ 'branch'	
kh	kha:ŋ⁵ 'wind'	khiŋ³ 'sand'	
kw	kwa:n¹ 'axe'	kwə² 'country'	kwən⁵ 'picket, stake'
khw	khwan¹ 'road'	mai⁴ khwə² 'staff for herding chickens'	
ɣ	ɣəm⁴ 'drink'	ɣa² 'two'	ɣa¹ 'lick'
ʔɣ	ʔɣəm⁵ 'soak'	ʔɣa⁵ 'wet field'	ʔɣam¹ 'sink'
ŋ̊	ŋ̊ai¹ 'open'	ŋ̊ai⁵ 'hear'	ŋ̊am³ 'daze'
ŋ	ŋən¹ 'firm'	ŋa² 'duck'	ŋau⁶ 'goods'
ʔŋ	ʔŋaŋ⁵ 'move'	ʔŋe³ 'cry'	ʔŋok⁷ 'thrust upward'
ʔŋw	ʔŋwat⁷ 'nod head'	ʔŋwən³ 'cave'	ʔŋwa³ ku³ 'look up'
q	qa:i⁵ 'chicken'	qɛ⁵ 'excrement'	
qh	qha¹ 'ear'	qhak⁷ 'pickets, stakes'	qhan⁵ 'happy'
ʁ	ʁaŋ³ 'doorsill'	ʁa¹ 'fungus'	ʁa:ŋ⁵ 'female'
ʔ	ʔau⁴ 'paddy, rice'	ʔai³ 'classifier for persons'	ʔək⁷ 'burp'
h	hum⁵ 'earth'	həi¹ 'lime'	

20.2. RHYMES

The Sui rhyme system is as follows:

i	e	a		o	u	ə
		ai	a:i	oi	ui	
iu		au	a:u			
im	em	am	a:m	om	um	
in	en	an	a:n	on	un	ən

iŋ	eŋ	aŋ	aːŋ	oŋ	uŋ	əŋ
ip	ep	ap	aːp	op	up	
it	et	at	at	ot	ut	ət
ik	ek	ak	aːk	ok	uk	ək

Notes:

1) /i e a o u/ are long vowels when they appear without codas in a syllable. When they are followed by final vowels or consonants, only /a/ is contrastive in length, i.e. there are two contrastive segments /a/ and /aː/;
2) The tongue position for /a/ lies between [a] and [ʌ], and when followed by a final vowel [i], /a/ is pronounced close to [ʋ]; /ai/ is pronounced as /ei/;
3) No diphthongs are followed by final consonants;
4) The vowel [i] in modern Chinese loan words often has the true pronunciation of [ɪ].

i	ʔi¹ 'nose ring of ox'	khi³ ʔdaːŋ¹ 'dawn'	ʔmi¹ 'bear'
iu	ʔniu⁵ 'urine'	fiu⁵ 'to whistle'	kiu³ 'boil, cook'
im	sim³ 'claw, talon'	khim¹ 'crisp'	
in	pin⁵ 'cap, cover, lid'	tin² 'stone'	khin³ 'sandy soil'
iŋ	sə³ miŋ² 'wet leech'	si² miŋ⁴ 'dry season'	si³ miŋ² 'mourning'
ip	tip⁷ 'hay cutter, seam'	ʔyaːu³ çip⁸ 'accompany singer'	
it	ʔai³ tçit⁷ 'sick person'	ʔbən¹ çit⁷ 'early morning'	ʔbit⁷ 'pull, seize'
ik	ʔjik⁶ 'call to'	çik⁷ 'grass target'	ɲik⁸ 'soot'
ei	fei⁶ 'mother's younger sister'	mai⁴ ŋei³ 'lash, whip'	
em	mjen² tjem¹ 'cotton mat'	jem⁴ 'sickle'	qem¹ 'economize'
en	sən¹ jen³ 'nephritis'	sa⁵ njen² 'first ten days of a month'	
eŋ	seŋ¹ 'cattle'	sjeŋ⁵ 'support'	tək⁷ pjeŋ² 'level earth'
ep	thjep⁷ 'along'	tjep⁸ 'mortar'	ʔdjep⁷ 'lunch box'
et	ʔdjet⁷ ʔdjoŋ² 'tadpole'	tçhjet⁷ 'morning'	çet⁷ 'iron'
ek	yaːn² sjek⁷ 'rent'	fan² hek⁷ 'act as a matchmaker'	
aːi	faːi⁴ 'elder brother'	faːi⁵ 'cotton'	faːn⁶ paːi¹ 'go back'
aːm	fe⁴ ʔŋaːm¹ 'get angry'	fe⁴ vaːm⁶ 'offend'	fjaːm⁶ 'touch slowly'
aːn	fuː¹ taːn³ 'burden'	fwaːn² 'snore'	han⁴ haːan³ 'blood colored earthworm'
aːŋ	hau² saːŋ² 'bid'	haːŋ¹ 'root'	haːŋ⁵ 'bury'
aːp	haːp⁷ 'seal'	haːp⁷ tan² 'answer'	kaːp⁷ ʔaːu¹ 'forcibly occupy'
aːt	khaːt⁷ 'shovel'	khaːt⁷ 'all'	ko¹ kaːt⁷ 'rare'
aːk	kwaːk⁷ 'hoe'	kwaːn³ ŋaːk⁷ 'trigger'	
o	lam¹ ʔdo⁵ 'gall'	lam¹ lo² 'gardenia'	lam¹ qo⁶ 'throat'
oi	lu⁵ hoi¹ 'whitewash'	mai⁴ loi² 'small pestle'	mai⁴ toi⁵ 'chestnut'
om	mom⁶ 'fish'		ni⁴ tom² 'cormorant'
on	paːn³ kon⁵ 'elder'	pon² 'pan of a steelyard balance'	
oŋ	pu¹ joŋ⁵ 'arthritis'	pu⁵ toŋ² 'water pipe'	qaːm⁵ ʔdoŋ¹ 'wild orange'

op	qop^8 'valley'	tə^3 kop^7 'centipede'	tsop^7 'collect'
ot	ʔam^3 ʔot^7 'damp'	ʔda^3 ʔdot^7 'hard'	
ok	ʔdjok^7 'flirt'	ʔdok^7 'wick'	ʔdok^7 qha^1 'deaf'
u	ʔdu^1 'life'		m̥u^5 'pig'
ui	ʔdaːn^1 ʔui^5 'opposite riverbank'	ʔai^3 tui^2 çət^7 ˙blacksmith'	
um	ʔɣum^5 'swollen'	ʔɣum^1 'thin'	ɲ̊u^1 hum^3 'our'
un	ʔŋun^3 'rinse'	ʔai^3 qun^3 'widower'	ʔai^3 tu^3 ŋun^2 'estranged friends'
uŋ	ʔai^3 zuŋ^3 'humpback'	ʔbuŋ^3 'kind of thorn'	ʔbuŋ^5 'side'
up	hui^2 hup^8 'cobra'	hup^7 close	kə^3 ʔdjup^7 'ghost'
ut	lam^1 tut^8 'kind of wild fruit'	ljut^7 dribble lut^7 'come off, drop'	
uk	mai^4 fuk^7 'palm with hollow center'	man^2 luk^7 'sweet potato'	
ə	ʔdə^5 ʔdju^1 'just now'	ʔdjə^3 'seedling'	ʔjə^1 'cotton cloth'
ən	ʔjən^1 'cigarette'	ʔjən^5 'swallow (bird)'	tçən^1 'group of'
əŋ	çəŋ^1 'sun'	mbwəŋ^5 'cover'	ʔdjəŋ^5 'dark'
ət	ʔdjət^7 'firewood'	fe^4 hət^7 'loaf on the job'	hət^8 'tail'
ək	lam^1 ljək^7 'banana'	ʔbjək^7 'female, girl'	ljək^7 'lap, lick'

20.3. TONES

Sui, of course, is a tone language and displays the paramount features of Kam-Tai tonal systems. By tradition one distinguishes between tone category (number) and tone value (a phonetic pitch shape associated with the category). Tone category is a phonological concept, whereas tone value is a phonetic concept.

Tone number	Tone value
1	11 (some speakers appear to have the tone value 212)
2	31
3	33
4	51
5	35
6	24
7	35 with long vowels and 55 with short vowels
8	42 with long vowels and 31 with short vowels

Notes:
1) For tone number 6 Miaocao has tone value =24 but in Sandong there are two tone values for tone 6, namely, 24 for Sui native vocabulary, and 55 for modern Chinese loan words.
2) For tone number 7 and tone number 8, then the syllables is closed with final consonants -p, -t, or -k. Each of them has a long and a short tone value.

20.4. LANGUAGE VARIATION

As mentioned above, the Sui language does not show extreme variation from place to place. Still, the manifestation of various sounds allows a more complete view of how Sui descended from the parent language into various form of the language as spoken today.

In regard to the tones, there is only a narrow range of difference. Here are the tone values according to location:

	San-dong	Zhong-he	Jiu-qian	Yao-qing	Heng-feng	Shui-long	Pan-dong	Rong-jiang	Yang-an
1	13	13	13	13	12	13	13	13	13
2	31	31	31	31	31	31	31	31	31
3	33	33	33	33	33	33	33	33	33
4	53	53	53	53	53	53	53	42	53
5	35	35	35	35	35	35	35	34	35
6	55	24/55	55	55	24/55	24/55	55	55	24/55
7	55	55	55	55	55	55	55	55	55
8	35	35	35	35	35	35	35	35	35

There is also some variation in the manifestation of initial consonants. As mentioned earlier, according to the unpublished study of the Sui language of 1956, there are basically three vernacular types: Vernacular #1 represented by Shuilong, Vernacular #2 represented by Yang'an, and Vernacular #3 represented by Pandong (see above for the locations associated with these three types.).

The first kind of variation in the Sui language features the loss of preglottalization of initial consonants. Rules showing this loss are found in all series of initials: (a) voiced stops $\text{?b} > \text{b}$, $\text{?d} > \text{d}$; (b) nasals $\text{?m} > \text{m}$, $\text{?n} > \text{n}$, $\text{?ŋ} > \text{ŋ}$, $\text{?ɲ} > \text{ɲ}$, (c) fricatives $\text{?v} > \text{v}$, $\text{?ɣ} > \text{ɣ}$, $\text{?j} > \text{j}$.

Gloss	1	2	3
'fat'	pi²	fi²	pi²
'chicken louse'	mbjai¹	mbjai¹	mji²
'part'	mbja:ŋ⁵	mja:ŋ⁶	mja:ŋ⁶
'plant trees'	mbja¹	miək⁸	mja²
'day'	?bən¹	bən¹	mən¹
'woman'	?bja:k⁷	biək⁷	mja:k⁷
'ladle'	?bja:i⁵bi⁵		
'vegetable'	?ma¹	ma¹	ma¹
'new'	m̥ai⁵	hwãi⁵	hwãi⁵
'half old\new'	m̥ja:n⁵	m̥ja:n⁵	m̥ja:n⁵
'hand'	mja¹	mja¹	mja²
'bunch'	fiŋ⁵		piŋ⁵
'peach'	faŋ¹	waŋ¹	paŋ¹
'late'	vɛ¹	vɛ¹	
'stupid'	?va³*	—	—
'break law'	fa:m⁶	va:n⁶	va:m⁶
'false rice'	va:ŋ¹	xwaŋ¹	
'good'	?da:i¹	da:i¹	la:i¹
'bright'	?da:ŋ¹	da:ŋ¹	la:ŋ¹
'clothing'	?duk⁷\quk⁷	duk⁷	lik⁷
'raw'	?djup⁷	djup⁷	ljup⁷
'rice cake'	jut⁷	jut⁷	—
'green vegetable'	qa:t⁷	qa:t⁷	ka:t⁷
'mushroom'	ɢa¹	ga¹	ga¹
'carrying pole'	ɢa:n¹	ga:n¹	ga:n²

*The preglottalized form is found only at Jiuqian and Yaoqing

There are some clear generalizations visible in these data. The first observation is that on the peripheral of Sui territory (Yang'an and Pandong) there is DEPLOSIVIZATION, that is, preglottalized nasals /?m ?m ?n ?ɲ ?ŋ/ of area 1 tend to become plain nasals /m n ɲ ŋ/ in areas 2 and 3. In a similar development the prenasalized voiced stops /mb nd/ merge with original nasals /m n/ and those that evolved from preglottalized nasals. Secondly, there is onset softening, that is, the preglottalized voiced stops /ʔb ʔd ʔj/ become plain voiced stops /b d j/; in area 3 /ʔd/ becomes /l/. So even in sound change the preglottalized voiced stops and the preglottalized nasals are kept separate. The third observation to make is that the uvular voiced stop /ɢ/ become a plain voice velar stop /g/ in areas 2 and 3. Finally, voiceless nasals /m̥ n̥ ɲ̊ ŋ̊/ undergo a very interesting rule. The segmental features of these sounds are manifested in a voiceless glides and a non-segmental feature of nasalization on the following vowel, e.g. ma^1 varies with $hw\tilde{a}^1$ 'dog'.

20.5. WORD CATEGORIES

The Sui language resembles most other members of the Tai-Kadai subbranch in regard to parts of speech, word categories, and word building capacity. All of these languages, including Sui, differ from Chinese in many ways but also share some common features. Like Chinese, Sui is an analytic and isolating language, which means that its word forms do not show inflectional or paradigmatic variation for case, number, agreement, or the like. That is not to say that there are not rule-governed processes in the lexicon. As Packard 2000 has shown for Chinese, several differing word classes exist, some of which stand alone, some of which can enter into combination with others, and a few of which occur only in grammatical service. Using his terminology, we can call these types (free) root words, bound roots, affixes, and function words. Root words can combine to create new root words, e.g. ma^4 'horse' and $ʔan^1$ 'saddle' as well as $ʔa:n^1 ma^4$ saddle-horse 'horse saddle'. Examples of bound roots are intensifiers for adjectives, such as $ʔdum^1$ intensifier for black, which must be accompanied with the root word $ndjəŋ^5$ 'black'. The aspect particle for perfective aspect la^2 is a function word and ti^6 is an affix changing cardinal numerals into ordinal numerals. These examples all represent borrowings from Chinese, and indeed, there are few cases of native vocabulary in purely functional capacity.

One very obvious way Sui is unlike Chinese lies in its relative lack of bound form words. Modern Standard Chinese (MSC) possesses a lexicon that contains a high percentage of bound form words requiring combination with other bound forms, free words, affixes, or function words. Sui, by contrast, resembles older forms of Chinese in which a large percentage of the lexicon is made up of uncompounded free forms, perhaps a few bound forms (often borrowings from Chinese), and free forms in combination with bound forms, affixes, or function words. Sui is also unlike Chinese in regard to the HEADEDNESS PRINCIPLE. Headedness, as described by Packard (2000) is a property of MSC in which the identity of a gestalt or whole word 'confers an identity' on the components that make up that gestalt word. Thus, in a Sui form composed of two subparts [XA YB]A, if the category of the whole is a noun, verb, or adjective, then Sui morphology requires that XA also be a noun, verb, or adjective respectively. That means Sui is left-headed in its word construction, just as in its phrases. MSC is right-headed for gestalt nouns and left-headed for gestalt verbs. Some examples are: $ɲa^3 ɕen^2$ month-money 'interest (n.)', $ɲa^5 van^1$ soak-seedlings 'soak seedlings (v.)', $ɲen^5 qa:i^5$ insect-chicken 'chicken lice (n.)', $ɲu^5 ti^3$ pig-small 'piglet (n.)', $ndjəŋ^5 ndum^1$ black-intensely black 'black as pitch (adj.)', $zən^1 ʔɲam^1$ person-bad 'evil person, malefactor, villain (n.)', $zən^1 ʔda:i^1$ person-good 'good person (n.)', $zən^1 ʔnui^1$ person-snow 'snowman (n.)', $zən^1 ʔnuk^7$ person-outside 'stranger (n.)', $vin^5 mjə^1$ wave-hand 'wave (v.)'

The Sui language possesses the word categories: noun (n.), numeral classifier (CLS), pronoun (pro), numerals (num.), verbs (v.), adjectives (adj.), and adverbs (adv.). Nouns express the names of things, e.g. le^1 'book', $ɲən^3$ 'maggot', persons, e.g. ni^4 'mother', $zən^1 ti^2 zən^4$ 'enemy' places, e.g. $tu^3 vən^2$ 'Duyun County', times, e.g. $ʔɲam^5 ha:m^1 sup^8$ 'New Year's Eve', location, e.g. fa^1 'right', si^4 'left'. Nouns usually occur with numeral classifiers whenever the cardinality of a group is at issue, $ha:m^1 ai^3 zən^1$ three-CLS-person 'three men', $ɕi^5 to^2 tak^8 kui^1$ four-CLA-male-buffaloes 'four buffalo bulls'. Whenever the nouns express persons, then a classifier may be omitted $luŋ^2 ha:m^1$ paternal uncle-three 'three paternal uncles' or in the other order $ɣa^2 fa:i^4$ two-older brother 'two older brothers'. Nouns of location do not take classifiers or numerals, e.g. $te^3 te^4 tsa^5$ below-below-there 'way down below there'.

Classifiers include ai^3 for persons, to^2 for animals, ni^4 for trees, etc. Classifiers can be reduplicated to express every, each, as in lam^1 lam^1 'every (general classifier)'. Pronouns are divisible into personal pronouns ju^2 'I', $ndiu^1$ we exclusive, $nda.u^1$ we inclusive, a^2 you, $sa.u^1$ 'you pl', man^1 'he, she, it', he^1 'others'. Demonstrative pronouns are: $na.i^6$ 'this', tsa^5 'that', ui^5 'that (distant)', yo^2 'others', $he^4 ja^6$, ja^6 'this sort of', and $he^4 tsa^5$ 'that sort of'. Numerals are $la.u^3$ 'one', ya^2, ji^6 'two', $ha.m^1$ 'three', ci^5 'four', ηo^4 'five', $ljok^8$ 'six', $cət^7$ 'seven', $pa.t^7$ 'eight', tcu^3 'nine', and sup^8 'ten'.

There are also generalizations observable within families of words. One frequent pattern of variation within word families is the ablauting of a vowel, consonant, or tone in which changes of color, length, place/manner of articulation, or pitch trajectory, e.g. $?ni\eta^5$ $tcha.u^5$ vs. $?ni\eta^5$ $tha.u^5$ 'not condescending, not patronizing', $?niu^1$ 'urine puddle' vs. $?niu^5$ 'urine, urinate', and $?u^5$ tci^1 vs. $?u^6$ $tchi^1$ 'arms, armament, arms, weapon, weaponry'.

20.6. SYNTAX

The Sui language generally shows head-first typological properties. Attributes follow heads, specifier comes last in the NP. Indeed, most SE Asian languages have these properties. That attributive adjectives follow their heads is seen in: $?ep^7$ $ndiu^1$ 'duck-our' 'our duck', $\eta a^3 to\eta^2$ 'bow-bronze' 'bronze bow', wa^3 $?nam^1$ 'cloud-black' 'black clouds', $tjum^1$ $qa\eta^1$ 'hat-steel' 'hat of steel'. Adverbs follow adjectives they modify, as in: tun^1 lau^4 ljo^3 'hot-great-very' 'very very hot'. Numeral classifiers are also used in the NP: $ha.m^1$ ai^3 $zən^1$ 'three-CLS-person' 'three persons', pek^7ji^6 wan^1 ja^1 '100-2-CLS-grass' '120 kinds of grass', jen^1 i^6 wan^1 mai^4 '1000-2-CLS-tree' '1200 kinds of tree'. The verb in Sui can undergo a number of elaborations. It may be negated by means of a negator me^2. Questions can be made by adding a negation after a verb, e.g. fan^2 me^2 say-NEG 'say (or not)?'. There can also be reduplication according to the pattern AABB to indicate a general activity or concentrated activity, e.g. $pa.i^1$- $pa.i^1$- $ta\eta^1$-$ta\eta^1$ 'go-go-come-come' 'mill around'.

Example sentences:

(1) man^1 $?ai^3$ ka^4, me^2 $?ai^3$ sui^3 'He is Chinese, he is not Sui'.

(2) van^1 $na.i^6$ $sə^1$ ηo^4, van^1 $?mu^3$ $sə^1$ $ljok^8$ 'Today is the fifth day of the Lunar Year; tomorrow is the sixth.'

(3) fa^3 h^4 ni^4 $ma.\eta^2$ 'You are planning what = What are you planning?'

(4) ηa^2 $\eta a.u^6$ $djə\eta^3$ $\underset{\circ}{n}u^1$ $ta??$ 'You from where come = Where are you from?'

20.7. VARIATION IN WORD FORMS

One area of difference among the varieties of Sui is in the personal pronoun systems. Surprisingly, pronouns vary quite a lot from place to place.

	Sandong	Zhonghe	Jiuqian	Yaoqing	Hengfeng	Pandong	Yang'an
I	ju^2	$?ai^2$	$?iu^2$	ju^2	κai^2	$?ai^2$	jiu^2
You (s.)	$\eta ə^2$	$\eta ə^2$	$\eta ə^2$	$\eta ə^2$	$\eta iə^2$	$\eta iə^2$	η^2
He/she	man^1	man^1	man^1	man^1	man^1	man^1	mo^1
We (exc.)	$tcen^1diu^1$	$tcen^1diu^1$	diu^1 pi^2	$djeu^1$	$tcan^1da.u^1$	$xə^6da.u^1$	$da.u^1$
We (inc.)	$tcen^1$ $da.u^1$	$ya.n^1$ diu^1	$ya.n^1$ diu^1	$gan^1gə^6$ $da.u^1$	$gan^1xə^6$ $da.u^1$	gan^1 $da.u^1$	gan^1 $da.u^1$
You (pl.)	$tcen^1$ $sa.u^1$	$tcen^1$ $sa.u^1$	$sa.u^1$	pi^2 $cieu^1$	$tcen^1$	$xə^6$	siu^1
They	$tcen^1$ man^1	$kə^4$ man^1	$kə^4man^1$	pi^2 man^1	$tcen^1$ man^1	$qə^1$ man^1	$tcen^1$ $mə^6$

Also there are some slight differences in regard to whether the copula si^3 or si^1 is required in sentences such as Sandong $na.i^6$ $qa.i^5$; tsa^5 $?ep^7$ 'these are chickens; those are ducks' vs. Jiuqian $na.i^6$ si^1 $qa.i^5$; tsa^5 si^1 $?ep^7$.

20.8. RECORDING SYSTEM

The Sui are unique among Kam-Sui peoples in having a native system for recording in written form important things in their environment. The *le¹ shui³* or Shui Shu recording system was used for writing down important weather and religious phenomena. It was not a system of sufficient richness to serve as a true writing system, or was it a system that ordinary people learned, but was reserved to a few shamans and elite persons. The glyphs, about 100 in number, are based in part of Chinese; others seem to be pictographic in nature. Three categories of glyphs are distinguished. The first of these was for the Heavenly Stems and Earthly Branches, a part of Sui calendar and for numerals. Han characters were often the basis, some with altered shapes. The second was based on pictogram characters, using birds, fish, various demons and spirits. There is also a third category that belongs to neither of these two. Type one *le¹ shui³* glyphs are associated with Han readings for the characters. Type two forms sometimes have Sui pronunciation. Type three glyphs (very few in numbers) are usually given Han pronunciations as well. Some examples are:

Type 1:
∇	ꝛ	◯	厐	)(	)((	≡	示	巳
ta:p⁷	ŋwet⁸	ɲit⁸	sən¹	suji³	fa³	ha:m¹	ljoŋ²	ɲot⁸
Moon	Sun	Spring	water	fire	three	dragon	snake	

Type 2:
🐦	◎	○○	𓀀	𓀢	𓆰
nok⁸	qhu¹	nda¹	mon⁶	likeness of a	tree branch
bird	snail	eyes	monkey	dead person	

Type 3:
艹
tha:m¹
corrupt

20.9. CONCLUSION

The Sui language has many important archaic features. Notable is the complexity of its initials and its archaic vocabulary, some of which is not attested in other Kam-Sui and Tai languages.

REFERENCES

Edmondson, Jerold A., Esling, John H., Harris, Jimmy G. and Wei, James Xuecun (2004) 'A Phonetic Study of Sui Consonants and Vowels', *Mon-Khmer Studies* 34: 1-20.

Zhou Guoyan and Edmondson, Jerold A. (1996) 'An Introduction to the Kam-Tai (Zhuang-Dong) Group of Languages in China', in S. Burusphat (ed.) *Languages and Cultures of the Kam-Tai (Zhuang-Dong) Group: A Word List*, Bangkok: Institute of Language and Culture for Rural Development, Mahidol University at Salaya.

Li Fang Kuei (1943) 'The Hypothesis of a Series of Pre-glottalized Consonants in Primitive Tai', *Bulletin of the Institute of History and Philology*, Academia Sinica 2.2.

— (1944) 'The Influence of the Primitive Tai Glottal Stop and Preglottalized Consonants on the Tone System of Po-ai', *Bulletin of Chinese Studies* 4: 59-68.

— (1948) 'The Distribution of Initials and Tones in the Sui Language', Language 24: 160-67.

— (1977a) *A Handbook of Comparative Tai*, Honolulu: University of Hawaii Press.

— (1977b) *A Study of the Sui Language: Texts and Translations (I)*, Special Publication No. 79, Institute of History and Philology, Nankang, Taipei: Academia Sinica.

Packard, Jerome L. (2000) *The Morphology of Chinese*, Cambridge University Press.

Wang, Jun (ed.) (1984) *Zhuang-Dong yuzu yuyan jianzhi [Outline Grammar of the Kam-Tai Languages]*, Beijing: Minorities Publishing House.

Wei, Xuecun James and Edmondson, Jerold A. (2003) *Sui, Chinese, Thai, English dictionary*, Bangkok: Mahidol University Press.

Zeng Xiaoyu and Yao Fuxiang (1996) *Han-Sui Cidian [A Chinese-Sui Dictionary]*, Chengdu: Sichuan Minzu Chubanshe.

Zhang Junru (1980) *Shuiyu jianzhi [Sketch of the Sui language]*, Beijing: Minorities Publishing House.

ZSMYDBG = Zhongguo Shaoshu Minzu Yuyan Diaocha Bianyi Gongzuodui (1956) *Suiyu Diaocha Baogao* 'Guizhou, Guiyang', unpublished manuscript.

CHAPTER TWENTY-ONE

CHADONG, A NEWLY-DISCOVERED KAM-SUI LANGUAGE IN NORTHERN GUANGXI

Li Jinfang

Chadong is spoken mainly in the township of Chadong in Lingui County, southwest of the city of Guilin, with some spill-overs in several villages in the township of Liangjiang in the south and in the township of Longjiang in Yongfu County in the west. Chadong has approximately 20,000 speakers. Until recently, little has been known about this language, except a very brief sketch in the local *Gazetteer of Lingui County* (Liang, 1996).

Chadong township is the place of origin of mangosteen, a well-known local product of Guangxi. However, Chadong speakers were not the early inhabitants of this region. According to historical records, a garrison of some 2,000 men were stationed in Chadong (formerly called Chaodong) to control the rebellions of the Zhuang and the Yao of northern Guangxi during the Yuan Dynasty dynasty (1206–1368 AD). The inscriptions on the tablet of the Meng family of Chadong indicate that their ancestors were conscripted and relocated from Qingyuanfu in Nandan in northwest Guangxi. We believe that speakers of the Zhuang and other Kam-Tai languages around Chadong area probably migrated from Nandan and the surrounding counties.

Chadong speakers have a number of cultural traits that are identified with Kam-Sui. Their surnames typically include Xie, Lu, Meng, Yao, Long, Liang, Zhou, Wei, Qin, Wu, Huang, Yin and Su, all of which are common surnames of Kam-Sui speakers. Those with the surname Meng worship the King of Moliu, a tradition that is similar to that of the Maonan.

Before the 1950s, Chadong speakers were largely monolingual. Few spoke Chinese. Nowadays the majority of them are bilingual, fluent in southwestern Mandarin. A small number can speak Zhuang and Pinghua, a kind of local Chinese dialect with a lot of mixed elements. Those who have moved to Yao areas can speak Yao.

Chadong has a number of regional varieties. However, the differences between these varieties are quite slight, and thus do not constitute dialect differences, except for the speech of several villages in the south and in Liangjiang. This latter variety was influenced by Pinghua, southwestern Mandarin and Zhuang, which gives rise to a number of sound changes, such as voiceless nasals merging with plain nasals, bilabial nasal -m changing to velar -ŋ and the loss of final stops in a number of vocabulary items. On the whole, mutual intelligibility is characteristic of varieties of Chadong.

Linguistically, Chadong belongs to the Kam-Sui group of the Kadai language family, based on our fieldwork data. Chadong shares a number of phonological similarities and basic vocabularies with other languages of the Kam-Sui group. For example, like Sui and Mulam, Chadong has a set of voiceless nasals: [m̥], [n̥], and [n̥], as well as the palatal fricative [c]. Chadong sides with Mulao in having the voiceless lateral [l̥] and the mid low back vowel [ø].

In the area of basic vocabulary, Chadong has most in common with Sui and Maonan of the Kam-Sui group, particularly with Maonan:[1]

---

1   The following comparative material is from the Fifth Research Group (1985).

Gloss	Chadong	Maonan	Sui	Mulam	Kam
'the sun'	*-fai*^{5}	*-van*^{1}	*-wan*^{1}	*-fan*^{1}	*-man*^{1}
'sunlight'	*ka:ŋ*^{1}	*cha:ŋ*^{1}	*ɕa:ŋ*^{1}	–	*kha:ŋ*^{1}'
'star'	*zən*^{4}-	*zət*^{7}	*zət*^{7}	*-m̥ət*^{7}	*ɕət*^{7}
'body'	*lən*^{2}	*dən*^{2}	*dən*^{1}	*hɣən*^{1}	*ɕən*^{1}'
'do, make'	*fe*^{4}	*və*^{4}	*he*^{4}	*fə*^{4}	*we*^{4}
'deep'	*jam*^{1}	*ʔjam*^{1}	*ʔjam*^{1}	*jam*^{1}	*jam*^{1}
'clf. for human'	*ai*^{1}	*ai*^{1}	*ai*^{1}	*mu*^{6}	*muŋ*^{4}
'he'	*mən*^{2}	*man*^{2}	*man*^{1}	*mɔ*^{6}, *ki*^{3}	*qhe*^{1}'
'count'	*jai*^{5}	*ndai*^{5}	*jai*^{5}	*sɔ*^{3}	*ɕu*^{5}
'listen'	*ni*^{3}	*ʔni*^{3}	*ʔdi*^{3}	*theŋ*^{5}	*ʈhiŋ*^{5}'
'to feed'	*sa*^{1}	*sa*^{1}	*sa*^{1}	*n̥a:m*^{4}	*phja*^{1}'
'thick (soup)'	*tən*^{6}	*tən*^{6}	*ʔboŋ*^{5}	*cat*^{8}, *cak*^{7}	*nak*^{7}
'snow'	*cu*^{5}	*cu*^{5}	*ʔnui*^{1},*ʔnje*^{1}	*nui*^{1}	*nui*^{1}
'father'	*ti*^{1}	*tə*^{2}	*pu*^{4}	*pu*^{4}	*pu*^{4}
'sheep, goat'	*zø*^{2}	*zo*^{2}	*fa*^{2}	*cwa*^{2}	*lje*^{3}
'thatch grass'	*hi*^{1}	*hi*^{1}	*ja*^{1}	*ɕa:u*^{1}*fa*^{5}	*ʈa*^{1}
'to sprinkle (water)'	*fət*^{7}	*fət*^{7}, *phən*^{5}	*phin*^{5}	*hwon*^{5}	*phjən*^{5}'

In view of various common phonological and lexical features, as well as a number of ethnological traits discussed above, Chadong appears to be more closely related to Maonan than to the other languages of the Kam-Sui group. On the other hand, Chadong shares a number of lexical items with other members of Kam-Sui that are represented otherwise in Maonan.

Gloss	Chadong	Maonan	Sui	Mulam	Kam
'hand'	*m̥i*^{1}	*si:m*^{3}	*mja*^{2}	*nja*^{2}	*mja*^{2}
'fish'	*məm*^{6}	*mbjai*^{3}	*məm*^{6}	*məm*^{6}	*pa*^{1}
'to eat'	*tsə*^{1}	*na*^{4}	*tsjen*^{1}, *tsje*^{1}	*tsa:n*^{1}	*ʈa:n*^{1}, *ʈi*^{1}
'to give'	*θa:i*^{1}	*ʔna:k*^{7}	*ha:i*^{1}	*khɣe*^{1}	*sai*^{1}'
'scold'	*la*^{5}	*na:k*^{8}	*zja:i*^{6}, *ʔda*^{5}, *sje*^{6}	*ʔɣa*^{5}	*kwa*^{5}, *phjit*^{9}'
'cold'	*n̥o*^{1}, *n̥it*^{7}	*ja:m*^{5}	*ʔn̥it*^{7}, *ŋa:ŋ*^{5}	*n̥it*^{7}, *kak*^{7}	*ljak*^{7}', *leŋ*^{4}

Furthermore, Chadong has quite a number of native words that are not shared by any other member of the Kam-Sui group:

Gloss	Chadong	Maonan	Sui	Mulam	Kam
'neck'	*wan*^{1}	*dən*^{4}	*qo*^{4}	*lən*^{3}	*ɲən*^{6}
'breast'	*pu*^{6}	*sə*^{1}, *tsə*^{5}	*tju*^{4}	*me*^{6}	*mi*^{3}
'fingernail'	*-kai*^{4}	*dip*^{7}	*ʔdjap*^{7}-	*ɲəp*^{7}-	*ɲəp*^{7}-
'gourd'	*lu*^{1}	*kwa*^{1}	*pu*^{2}	*kwa*^{1}	*pu*^{2}
'self'	*pən*^{4}*ki*^{2}	*zi*^{6}	*si*^{3}	*ti*^{6}*ca*^{1}	*si*^{6}*qa*^{1}
'pull'	*ka:k*^{7}, *sai*^{2}	*pəŋ*^{2}, *la*^{1}, *thɔ*^{1}	*tin*^{6}, *tjət*^{8}	*la*^{1}	*ka:i*^{2},*khaŋ*^{5}
'flow'	*tshy*^{1}	*loi*^{1}	*lui*^{5}	*thoi*^{1}	*qhui*^{1}'
'discard'	*cha:u*^{5}	*vət*^{7}	*tu*^{5}, *peŋ*^{5}	*pət*^{8}	*liu*^{1}, *pan*^{5}
'forget'	*ju:ŋ*^{6}	*la:m*^{2}	*la:m*^{2}, *hoŋ*^{1}	*la:m*^{2}	*la:m*^{2}
'blind'	*muŋ*^{1}	*bu:t*^{8}	*ko*^{4}, *ʔmət*^{7}	*kha*^{1}	*pha*^{1}'
'sparsely spaced'	*pja:i*^{4}	*ca*^{4}, *ba:ŋ*^{2}	*ko*^{1}	*ʔwa:ŋ*^{1}	*ma:ŋ*^{1}

The data used in this study is from the variety of Chadong spoken in the village of Siji, about 3 kilometers from the township of Chadong.[2] The informant, Mr Meng Wanmei, was 66 years of age at the time of fieldwork in July, 2000. For most of his life he has lived in the village. Mr Meng is fluent both in Chadong and in Southwestern Mandarin.

21.1. THE SOUNDS OF CHADONG

21.1.1. Initials

Chadong has 28 simple initial consonants, 19 palatalized consonants and 7 labialized initials, as follows:

p	ph	m	m̥	f	w			
t	th	n	n̥	l	l̥	θ	s	z
ts	tsh	c	ch	n̠	n̠̥	ç	j	
k	kh	ŋ	ʔ	h				
pj	phj	mj	m̥j					
tj	thj	nj	n̥j	lj	l̥j	θj	sj	
tsj	tshj	n̠j						
kj	khj	ŋj	hj					
tw	thw	tsw	kw	khw	ŋw	hw		

Explanatory remarks:

(1) Nasals [m], [n], [n̠] and lateral [l] have contrastive voiceless counterparts. There is no voiceless velar nasal [ŋ].

(2) Historically preglottalized sounds [ʔb] and [ʔd], which are common in other Kam-Tai languages, are not found in Chadong. These have become [p] and [l] respectively, e.g. *pa:n⁴* 'village', *lo⁶* 'gall bladder' and *la:i⁴* 'good'. Sometimes, they become [b]/[d], e.g. *pi:k⁸/bi:k⁸* 'daughter', *bo²/do²* 'shallot, spring onion'.

(3) There is a voiceless dental fricative [θ] in Chadong, which is rare among the Kam-Sui group.

(4) Fricatives [ts] and [tsh] are realized as [tɕ] and [tɕh] before front vowels.

(5) Palatalization and labialization are not common. Palatalized and labialized sounds [kj] [θj] [thj] [n̠j] [thw] occur mainly in Chinese loans.

(6) [hj] is typically realized as [xj]. In fast speech, it sounds like [ç].

(7) Aspirated sounds rarely occur in native words.

(8) Nasals [m] and [n] have accompanying preglottalized effects when occurring in tone 1 (53) (Proto-Kam-Sui tone A1), tone 5 (45) (Proto tone B1) and tone 6 (35) (Proto tone B2). But these are not contrastive.

21.1.2. Finals

There are 9 simple vowels in Chadong, plus a syllabic [n̩], listed below:

a e ø i o u ə y ɯ n̩

2   The writer records his thanks to Mr Qin Youheng and Mr Yi Hongnan of the government of Lingui County for help in facilitating fieldwork. Thanks also go to two other informants, Mr Huang Shilian and Mr Meng Jiupeng, who shared their knowledge of their language.

There are 13 diphthongs:

a:i   ai   a:u   au   ua   eu   iu   oi   uo   u:i   ui   iə   uə

Simple vowels can take final nasals and final stops. Diphthongs do not, except /ua/, /ia/, and /ie/, which may take final nasal /n/. /ie/ may also take final /-m/. Below are the syllable combinations in Chadong:

a:m   am   a:n   an   a:ŋ   aŋ   a:p   ap   a:t   at   a:k   ak   ia:ŋ   uan
em   en   eŋ   ep   et   ek   iem   ien
øn   øŋ   øt   øk
i:m   im   i:n   in   i:ŋ   iŋ   i:p   ip   i:t   it   i:k   ik
om   on   oŋ   op   ot   ok
u:n   un   u:ŋ   uŋ   u:t   ut   u:k   uk
əm   ən   əŋ   əp   ət   ək
y:n   yn   yŋ   y:t   yt   y:k   yen
ɯŋ   ɯt

Remarks:
(1) /ø/ is phonetically realized as [œ]. [e] and [o] may sometimes be pronounced as [ɛ] and [ɔ] respectively, especially when used alone as finals. [ə] and [ɯ] are rarely used alone as simple finals. [u] often takes voiceless bilabial [ɸ-] when occurring as a simple final. For example, u^4 'rice' is realized as [ɸu⁴].
(2) Except when occurring as a simple final, rounded [ø] combines with only a limited number of consonants. High vowel [ɯ] has even less combining function.
(3) /a/, /i/, /u/, and /y/ have length contrasts when taking other final elements. Long /i:/ and /u:/ sound like [iə] and [uə].
(4) The first elements of /ua/, /uan/, /ia:ŋ/, /uo/,   /iem/ and /ien/ are not main vowels but vowel glides. These often occur with Chinese loans. /i/ and /u/ are the main vowels in /iə/ and /uə/, where [ə] is the vowel glide.
(5) Final /-k/ often has a very weak explosive effect.

21.1.3. Tones

Eight tones can be established for Chadong, which correspond to the tone categories in the Tai and Kam-Sui languages. Tones 1-6 are with unchecked syllables. Tones 7 and 8 are with checked syllables, each of which has an allotone, with length contrast.
    The tone values of Chadong are described below:

Tone	Tone value	Examples	
1	53	ma^1	'vegetable'
2	21	ma^2	'tongue'
3	31	ma^3	'soft'
4	23	ma^4	'horse'
5	45	ma^5	'carry on back'
6	35	mo^6	'hat'
7a (short)	45	pak^7	'north'
7b (long)	31	$pa{:}k^7$	'mouth'
8a (short)	21	lo^4pak^8	'turnip'
8b (long)	23	$la{:}k^8$	'offspring'

Remarks:
1) Odd-numbered tones have a higher tone pitch than even-numbered tones.
2) The tone pitch of tone 2 (21) is very close to that of tone 3 (31). Their tone range is very close too. Tones 4 (23) and 5 (45) are often pronounced as mid level (33) and high level (55) respectively in tone sandhi. The same is true of their corresponding checked tones, tones 7a and 8b.
3) Checked tones have length contrast. As a general rule, tone seven long lines with tone 3 (31), whereas tone seven short lines with tone 5 (45). Tone 8 long goes with tone 4 (23), while tone 8 short goes with tone 2 (21). There are exceptions where there are tonal flip-flops. Final /e/ and /o/ may combine freely with any tones in checked syllables as they have no length contrasts.
4) Aspirated initials mainly occur with odd-numbered tones. But Chinese loans, especially recent loans, also occur with even-numbered tones. Voiceless /m̥/, /n̥/, /ŋ̊/ and /l̥/ only occur in odd-numbered tones. Voiced sibilant initial /z/ only occurs in even-numbered tones.
5) Tone sandhi is a feature of Chadong. In disyllabic words, the first syllable undergoes tone change, with the second syllable unaffected, e.g. $tin^4(^1)kwa^1$ 'leg', $lən^3(^1)ti^4$ 'children' (citation forms are in brackets). This may be due to the prosody in Chadong, where the stress is in the second syllable.

21.2. LEXICON

21.2.1. Word formation

Chadong words can be formed through derivational prefixes and compounding.

21.2.1.1. *Derivation*

(1) Prefixes

A significant number of Chadong prefixes have derived from lexical items, which have been grammaticalized. For example, $mə^1$ (directional), $la:u^4$ (locative), ni^4 (female gender and diminutive). Other prefixes still preserve or are used side by side with lexical meanings. Some commonly-used prefixes are listed below.

ni^4 < 'mother, female': ni^4fai^5 'the sun', ni^4kwai^3 'frog'; ni^4pe^6 'roundworm', ni^4cai^6 'crab'; $ni^4na:ŋ^5$ 'prawn', ni^4mat^7 'louse', $ni^4ŋo^3$ 'mouse, rat', ni^4ma^4 'mare', $ni^4m̥u^5$ 'female pig'.

$la:k^8$ < 'offspring, fruit': $la:k^8 ni^1$ 'small stream', $la:k^8kin^1$ 'Mandarin speakers', $la:k^8lən^1ti^4$ 'baby', $la:k^8θo^1$ 'girl', $la:k^8yt^7$ 'pyramid shaped dumpling made of sticky rice', $la:k^8 ləŋ^2$ 'bell'.

na^3 < 'face': na^3tak^7 'chest', $na^3 pja:k^7$ 'forehead', $na^3θa:u^6$ 'kitchen', $na^3pu:k^8$ 'cymbals', na^3kun^5 'front, ahead';

$la:u^4$: $la:u^4ləŋ^1$ 'valley', $la:u^4hy^1$ 'market', $la:u^4ha:u^6$ 'inside', $la:u^4θam^1$ 'at heart', $la:u^4ca^3$ 'corner';

tak^8 < 'male': tak^8kwi^2 'bull', tak^8ma^4 'horse';

$mə^1$ < 'side': $mə^1θθ^4$ 'left', $mə^1ju^6$ 'right (side)', $mə^1nok^7$ 'outside'.

co^3 < 'head': co^3ko^6 'knee'; co^3chai^1 'blade of a plough', $co^4(^3)po^3$ 'cup for moxibulstion').

(2) Suffixes

Suffixes are few in Chadong. Only one example is found in our data: $θai^3$, which appears to be a Chinese loan *zi* 子 'offspring'. Examples: $zən^4(^1)θai^3$ 'star constellation', $θok^8θai^3$ 'nuts', $a^4(^3)θai^3$ 'mute'.

21.2.1.2. *Compounding*

Compounding takes the following forms, with modification being the most common:

(i) Modification

Modification takes the form of pre-modification and post-modification.

Pre-modification:

$tin^4(^1)jin^5$ $co^3la:i^1$

foot-trace   head-scalp

'trace'   'head scalp'

$pan^5\underset{\circ}{n}am^3$ $mi^2(^4)lu\eta^2$

splash-water   tree-forest

'spring'   'forest'

Post-modification:

kok^8phik^7 fa^3nam^1

grain not plump   cloud black

'(of grain) not plump' 'dark cloud'

$\underset{\circ}{l}\partial m^1\ l\partial k^8$ $f\partial n^1sa:m^6$

wind   big   rain flying

'strong wind'   'drizzle'

(ii) Verb + object:

$fe^4pu:n^4$ $sua^4\underset{\circ}{l}\partial m^1$

make-partner   play-wind

'companion'   'show off'

$kjau^4(^2)ts\partial^1$

beg-eat

'beggar, to beg'

(iii) Subject + predicate:

$p\partial n^2\ jim^1$ $p\partial n^2\ \underset{}{l}i\eta^3$

day-gloomy   day-sunny

'gloomy day' 'sunny day'

$la^3\ mu\eta^1$ $na^3\ ma^2$

Eye-blind   face-freckled

'blind'   'freckled face'

21.2.1.3. *Synonyms*

Chadong is particularly rich in synonyms. Some are native words, others are Chinese loans. Quite often, native words and loans form pairs, that is, they are used side by side with one another. Quite a number of concepts are expressed by Chinese loans. In some cases, loan words gain the upper hand, while in others, native words do. In a number of cases, native items became grammaticalized, giving way to loans or becoming subordinating elements of loan words. For example, the pair *toŋ⁴* and *ŋat⁸* both mean 'wobble, shake', the former is a Chinese loan, and the latter, a native word. *ŋat⁸* is rarely used alone now, but has become a descriptive element in the expression *toŋ⁴ ŋat⁸ ŋat⁸* 'loose, wobble'.

(i) Synonyms of native origin:

'hide, hidden': *pok⁸*; *tsam²*
'carry (water)': *tsau⁴*(with one hand), *pu³* (with two hands)
'pull (a rope)': *ka:k⁷*,   *sai²*
'pull (collar)': *ɲa¹*(gently), *kwa⁴*(suddenly and roughly)
'play': *loŋ⁶, fe⁴lø⁴*
'hurt (one's back)': *ljek⁷* (as result of being hit), *nək⁷*(as a result of being sprained)
'break': *eu³, khwek⁷*
'dark': *phu:ŋ³, phu:ŋ³ ḻap⁷*
'bathe': *luk⁷* (at home), a:p⁷ (in river)
'to cook': *tuŋ¹* (rice, food), *o¹* (for a long time)
'tired': *ne⁵, cak⁸*
'beautiful, handsome': *kho⁴*(of men), *hjuŋ¹* (of women)
'love': *maŋ⁴, kit⁸luŋ²*
'cold': *ɲo¹*(weather), *ɲit⁷*(water, food)
'(of water) fast flowing': *ɕaŋ³, tau³*
'squat': *ŋu⁵*(for a long time), *tsan³* (for a short while)

Quite often, synonym pairs involve both native words and Chinese loans. Examples:

chop (meat): *tsəŋ¹* — *te⁵* (Chinese *duo⁴* 剁)
hot: *tun¹* (water food) — *ɲi:t⁸* (weather) (from Ch. *re⁴* 热)
snore: *θu:n¹* — *tshe⁴lu³* (from Ch. dialect *che³ lu²* 扯炉¹)

to tread/tram on: *nap⁸*(gently) — *tsha:i³*(heavily) (from Ch. *chai³* 踩)
to hire to please: *lai⁵* — *tshən³*(Ch. *qing³* 请)
cut (tree): *nak⁷* — *te⁵* (Ch. *duo⁴* 剁)
play (with): *pjok⁷*(with a broken object) — *luŋ⁶* (play with) (Ch. *nong⁴* 弄)
new: *ṃi⁵* — *θan¹* (Ch. *xin¹* 新)
rotten: *mut⁷ ŋau⁵* — *la:n⁶* (Ch. *lan⁴* 烂)
clean/clear (water): *ḻiu¹* — *tshəŋ¹* (Ch. *qing¹* 清)
to air to dry: *sa⁵*(outside the house) — *la:ŋ⁵* (Ch. *liang⁴* inside the house)
aim: *leu⁵* — *mjeu³* (Ch. *miao³* 瞄)
take notice: *ø⁶* — *le⁶* (Ch. *li³* 理)
yellow: *ṃa:n²* — *wu:ŋ³* (Ch. huang² 黄)
tilted: *cuŋ³* — *cheu⁶* (Ch. *qiao⁴* 翘)
white: *kwa³* — *pek⁸* (Ch. *bai²* 白)
knock: *thak⁷* — *kha:u¹* (Ch. *qiao¹* 敲)
snatch loot: *pit⁷* — *θi:ŋ³* (Ch. *qiang³* 抢)
to shut (door): *cek⁸* — *sa:n¹* (Ch. *shuan¹* 闩)
winnow (grain): *ɕi:ŋ¹* — *ji:ŋ²* (Ch. *yang²* 扬)
press: *tjam²*(passive) — *ja:p⁷* (Ch. *ya¹* active)

(ii) Synonym pairs of Chinese origin:

pile: *tui¹* (Ch. *tui¹* 堆) — *tjep⁸* (Ch. *die²* 叠)
climb: *pha:n¹*(Ch. *pan¹* 攀) — *paŋ⁶* (Ch. *ping²* 凭)
jab: *thuŋ¹*(Ch. *tong³* 捅) — *tsok⁸* (Ch. *chuo¹* 戳)
tie: *ta:u²* (Ch. *tau⁴* 套) — *θuk⁸* (Ch. *su⁴* 束)

bald: *la:i⁶* (Ch *lai⁴* 癩)   *ku:ŋ¹* (Ch. *guang¹* 光)
take off: *thu:t⁷*(Ch. *tuo¹* 脱)   *tsi⁴* (Ch. *jie³* 解)

21.3. GRAMMAR

21.3.1. Word classes

21.3.1.1. *Nouns*

Nouns cannot be reduplicated except for those that can function as classifiers or measures. Examples: *wan¹wan¹* 'everyday, always', *pe⁴(¹)pe¹* 'every year, all years'.

When denoting a single entity, nouns may be modified by a bare measure word. Examples:

tsek⁸	u:n³	taŋ⁶	çu:ŋ¹	tsø⁶	paŋ³	me²	pa³.
CLF	bowl	and	pair	chopsticks	all	have	PART

'There is a bowl and a pair of chopsticks.'

(Without the classifiers *tsek⁸* and *çu:ŋ¹* the sentence would mean more than one bowl and more than one pair of chopsticks.)

Plurality is expressed with the use of nouns along with plural classifiers like *tsa:i³* 'group, flock' and *nit⁷* 'some'. For example:

tsa:i³	θam²tət⁸	pə¹	tok⁸	le̥¹	pa².
group	child	go	read	book	PART

'His children went to school.'

je²	la:u⁴	hja:n¹	θa:ŋ⁶	to²	nit⁷	ep⁷.
I	inside	house	feed, raise	ASP	some	duck

'I'm raising some ducks in my house.'

Some nouns may take the prefixes *ni⁴*, *lak⁴* to denote diminutive things (see 2.1. Derivation). *ni̥⁴* and *lak⁴* may also be used to indicate the sex of animals. Examples:

ni⁴m̥a¹	'bitch'	*tak⁸m̥a¹*	'male dog'
ni⁴ka:i⁵	'hen'	*tak⁸ka:i⁵*	'rooster'
θa:n³(¹)zø²tak⁸	'male goat'	*ljuŋ²tak⁸*	'dragon'

21.3.1.2. *Personal pronouns*

Chadong personal pronouns have both singular and plural forms. First person pronouns further distinguish between exclusive and inclusive forms.

Person	Singular	Plural
1st	*je²*	*la:u¹*(inclusive), *lje¹* (exclusive)
2nd	*ni̥²*	*çe¹*
3rd	*mən²*	*tje¹*

Demonstrative pronouns *na:i⁶* 'this' and *ka⁵* 'that' are most common. Other forms include: *kwa:i⁶* 'this', *ui⁶* 'that', *kui⁶* 'that'. *ui⁶* and *kui⁶* refer to entities that are further away from the speaker than *ka⁵*. These demonstrative pronouns have different syntactic properties with different distributions. Basically *na:i⁶ ka⁵ ui⁶* are placed after the nouns or classifiers they modify while *kwa:i⁶* and *kui⁶* go before the head word. Examples:

tsi^1 $na:i^6$ pit^7 OR: $kwa:i^6$ tsi^1 pit^7
CLF   this   pen   this   CLF   pen
'this pen (over here)'
tsi^1 ka^5 pit^7 OR: tsi^1 ui^6 pit^7 OR: kui^6 tsi^1 pit^7
CLF   that   pen   CLF   that pen   that CLF pen
'that pen (over there)'

21.3.1.3. *Interrogative pronouns*

Chadong interrogative pronouns are: $khau^1$ 'who', $t\vartheta^0m\vartheta^1$ (short form $tj\vartheta^1$) 'what'; there are multiple forms for 'where': $lo\eta^4$ ηau^1, $la:u^4\eta au^1$, and $ji:\eta^2\eta au^1$; $\eta au^1\theta ai^4$ 'how'; ki^1ta^1 'how many'. As can be seen, ηau^1 as a basic interrogative element displays some interesting distribution properties. It can occur before the head element as with 'where', or after the head element as with 'how'. Examples:

$k\vartheta^6$ ηi^3 $ha:m^3$ je^2 $p\vartheta^1$ $lo\eta^4\eta au^1$?
brother you call   me go   where
'Brother, where did you want me to go?'

$jy^2ku\vartheta^3$ $pien^3$ kua^6 ηau^1 θai^4 $ca:\eta^3$?
if   change   what   say?
If anything happens,   what would you say?'

21.3.1.4. *Classifiers*

The most common classifiers in Chadong are ai^1 for humans, and $kha\eta^6$ for both animate and inanimate things.
     Classifiers can be reduplicated, with the meaning of 'every', 'all'. For example:

$kwa:i^6$ $tsa:i^3$ po^4 $kha\eta^4(^6)$ $kha\eta^6$ $pa\eta^3$ pi^2.
this   flock   cow   CLF   CLF   all   fat
'Every cow in this flock is fat/All cows in this flock are fat.'

As with other Kam-Tai languages, Chadong classifiers can be used alone as subjects or objects. For example:

$la:u^1$ lo^4lo^4 $ta\eta^3(^1)$ $\theta a:i^1$ $lo^2(^4)la:k^8$, ai^1 $kha\eta^6$
we   everyone come   share fruit   CLF CLF
'We came and shared the fruits, and each of us got one.'

$kwa:i^6$ hja^1 ai^1 $l\vartheta n^1$, ai^1 $ts\vartheta^1$ $u:n^3$.
this   two CLF person CLF eat   bowl
'These two guys each had a bowl (of rice).'

Likewise, modifying phrases with classifiers as heads may function as subjects and objects. Examples:

$kwa:i^6$ $ts\vartheta k^7$ $n\vartheta n^2$, kui^6 $ts\vartheta k^7$ kwe^2 $n\vartheta n^2$.
this   CLF good   that CLF no   good
'This one is good, that one isn't.'

$je^2 ts\partial^1 \theta e^1$ $kwa{:}i^6$, $\underline{n}i^2 ts\partial^1 l\partial k^8 ko^6$
I   eat   small   this   you   eat   big   that
'I eat the small one, and you eat the big one.'

21.3.1.5. *Numerals*

21.3.1.5.1. *Cardinals and ordinals*

For the numbers from 1 to 10, see the Appendix at the end of the paper. In connected speech the numeral sap^8 'ten' is pronounced as $s\partial p^8$ or $s\partial^2$. The numbers for 'hundred', 'thousand' and 'ten thousand' are all borrowed from Chinese: pek^7 'hundred', θjen^1 'thousand', $wa{:}n^6$ 'ten thousand'. Ordinals take the ordinal prefix te^2, also a Chinese (Modern Chinese di^4). E.g. te^2jit^7 'first', te^2 $\underline{n}i^6$ 'second', te^2 $s\partial p^8$ jit^7 'eleventh', te^2 θi^5 sap^8 'fortieth'.

The numerals 'one' and 'two' each have two forms in Chadong. For numbers below ten, or for higher numbers like 'hundred', 'thousand', 'one' and 'two' are represented by ji^4 and hja^1 respectively. For numbers between eleven and twenty, jit^7 'one' and $\underline{n}i^6$ 'two' are used.

ji^4	'one',
hja^1	'two',
$\theta a{:}m^1$	'three'
$\underline{n}i^6sap^8$	'twenty'
$\underline{n}i^{4(6)}sap^8jit^7$	'twenty-one'
$\theta a{:}m^1sap^8\underline{n}i^6$	'thirty-two'
$ji^4pek^7l\partial\eta^2jit^7$	'one hundred and one'
hja^1 $wa{:}n^6$	'twenty thousand'

For ordinals, only jit^7 and $\underline{n}i^6$ are used. ji^4 and hja^1 cannot be used for ordinals.

When used as first digit with 'hundred, thousand, ten thousand', 'one' can be omitted. For example: $pek^7\underline{n}i^6$ 'one hundred and twenty'.

The native word $la{:}u^6$ 'one' appears to have given way to Chinese loans ji^4 and jit^7. $la{:}u^6$ is now used with the meaning 'the only one'. For example:

tje^1 kok^8 ni^4 tu^6 $tsi{:}k^8$ ηa^6 tai^1 tsi^2 pa^2,
they   CLF   mother also   pass. hungry die go PART
$s\partial\eta^6$ lui^4 $m\partial n^2$ $la{:}u^6$ ai^1 $l\partial n^1$.
remain below he   single CLF person

'His mother died of hunger and so he was left as an orphan.'

21.3.1.5.2. *Approximation, multiplication and fraction*

Approximation is expressed through the following elements: kak^7 'one (or two)' $t\partial t^7$ 'a bit', nit^7 'a little bit, some', ki^1 'several'.

The concept of 'fold, time' is expressed by poi^6 (from Chinese bei^4). For example:

hja^1 poi^6 'double, two folds'; $\theta a{:}m^1$ poi^6 'three times, three folds'.

Similarly, fractions are expressed through Chinese syntactic constructions, with the element zhi^1 'of' omitted, or replaced with $tsjem^1$, meaning 'take, occupy'. Examples:

$\theta a{:}m^1f\partial n^2jit^7$ 'one-third   (lit. three share one')
$pek^7f\partial n^2tsjem^{1(6)}sap^8\eta o^4$ 'fifteen one-hundredths'.

Cardinals cannot be reduplicated. But the approximation element *tət⁷* 'a bit' can. For example:

kwa:i⁶ khaŋ⁴ pa:n¹ ha:k⁸seŋ¹, tət⁷ tət⁷ ɕi⁴ la:k⁸ pi:k⁸.
this   CLF class student   bit bit be child female
'Of the students in this class, only a handful are girls.'

21.3.1.6. *Verbs*

A number of tense-aspect markers are found in Chadong. A reciprocal prefix is found which denotes reciprocal action. Directional verbs can be reduplicated to designate repetition of an action.

Most tense-aspect markers are derived from lexical items. Most of these lexical items are not fully grammaticalized, with their lexical meanings and lexical tones often retained.

21.3.1.6.1. *Completion*

Completion is expressed through *tsi⁴* and *pa²*. *tsi⁴* immediately follows the verb it modifies while *pa²* often occurs at the end of the sentence (very rarely in the middle of the sentence). For example:

je²   tsə¹   tsi⁴   tu⁶   pə¹.
I   eat   ASP   then   go
'I'll go after I have finished my meal.'

pe⁴(¹)ki⁶   kə⁰   nuŋ⁴   tok⁸   ḽe¹   pa².
last year   CLF   y. sibling   read   book   ASP
(*kə⁰* is the weak form of *kok⁸*, a general classifier for human being.)
'Younger brother started school last year'

mən²   phek⁷   tsi⁴   hja¹   cham²   m̥i¹   pa².
he   clap   ASP.   two   clf.   hand   ASP
'He clapped his hands twice.'

21.3.1.6.2. *Past/experiential*

The past/experiential can be expressed through the post-verbal marker *ta⁶*, which is derived from the lexical verb meaning 'to pass'. Sometimes, the element *tsi:k⁸* may also be used. For example:

mən²   taŋ¹   ta⁶   kwe⁴ljam²,   pe¹za²   aŋ⁵   taŋ¹.
he   come   ASP   Guilin   next year again come
'He's been here in Guilin before. He will come again next year.'

hja¹   pe¹   ji⁴θien²   je²   ḽaŋ¹   tsi:k⁸   mən²   ji⁴   to⁶.
two   year   before   I   see   ASP   3 sing.   one   time
'I saw him once two years ago.'

21.3.1.6.3. *Progressive/continuous*

The progressive/continuous aspect is expressed through the post-verbal marker *to³*, e.g.:

mən² θui⁶ to³ ɭaŋ¹ ɭe¹.
3 sing.   sit   ASP   read   book
'He was sitting (there) reading.'

21.3.1.6.4. *Temporary/transient*

Temporary/transient meaning is expressed through *paŋ⁴*, derived from the lexeme *paŋ⁴*, meaning 'a while, a little'. This item is not fully grammaticalized. For example:

θui⁶ paŋ⁴ tu⁶ lai⁴ tsə¹ pa².
sit   a while   then   can, able   eat   ASP
'Just sit for a little while and food will be ready (in a minute).'

21.3.1.7. *Reciprocal*

Reciprocal meaning is expressed through the preverbal reciprocal marker *tu⁴*. Example:

tje¹ hja¹ ai¹ paŋ⁵ tu⁴ wak⁷.
3. pl.   two   CLF   still   RECIP   hit
'The two of them are hitting one another.'

21.3.1.8. *Verb complement*

The word order for verb complement phrase in Chadong is V-C-O, which is different from that of other Kam-Tai dialects, where the order is V-O-C. For example:

mən² wak⁷ tai¹ tsi⁴ hja¹ kok⁸ tak⁸ məm⁴.
3 sing.   hit   dead   ASP   two   CFL   tiger
'He killed two tigers.'

However, when the complement involves directional verbs, the order may be either V-O-C or V-C-O. Thus, the sentence 'he brought a stick' can be said in Chadong in two ways:

(a) *mən² tsau⁴ ji⁴ tsi¹ mi⁴ taŋ¹.*
      he   take   one   CLF   stick   come
OR:
(b) *mən² tsau⁴ taŋ¹ ji⁴ tsi¹ mi⁴.*
      he   take   come   one   CLF   stick
      'He brought a stick.'

Directional verbs can be reduplicated, denoting repetition of the action.

ju¹ ca:i¹ lən¹ taŋ¹ taŋ¹ pə¹ pə¹.
on/above   street   people   come   come   go   go
'People come and go in the street.'

Quite a number of verbs take post-verbal descriptive elements to denote the state of the situation described by the verb in question. Most of these elements are disyllabic, some onomatopoeic, while others have specific expressive functions. Quite often, a verb may take several such descriptive elements to denote different meanings. For example:

khau^{6}	*ŋau*^{1}*ŋau*^{1}	*pa:i*^{3}	*n̥iu*^{5}*n̥iu*^{5}
bark	DESCRIP	wag	DESCRIP
'(of dogs)	to bark'	'to wag (the tail)'	

l̥aŋ^{6}	*ɲ̥aŋ*^{6} *ɲ̥aŋ*^{6}	*l̥aŋ*^{6}	*wa*^{3} *wa*^{3}
run	DESCRIP	run	DESCRIP
'to run (individually)'		'to run (in group)'	

l̥aŋ^{6}	*pi:u*^{1} *pi:u*^{6}	*l̥aŋ*^{6}	*kwe*^{3} *kwe*^{3}
run	DESCRIP	run	DESCRIP
'to run (fast)'		'to run (very fast), to dash'	

21.3.1.9. *Adjectives*

Most adjectives can be reduplicated. E.g.:

kwa:i^{6}	*tsi*^{1}	*khun*^{1}	*wa:n*^{1}	*wa:n*^{1}	*tsi:k*^{8}.
this	clf.	road	winding	winding	PART
'This road is extremely winding.'					

When used as modifiers, adjectives follow the head noun they modify. E.g.:

ja^{2}*(*^{1}*)*	*lək*^{8}	*ji*^{4}	*kjen*^{6}	*kuk*^{7}	*fa*^{1}	*m̥i*^{5}
field	big	one	clf.	garment	flower	new
'big field'		'a new patterned garment'				

The majority of adjectives take idiosyncratic expressive elements, indicating changes in degree or state. Such descriptive or expressive elements my be monosyllabic or disyllabic. Reduplicated monosyllabic descriptive elements may be used to describe the intensity of the sound, or the degree of a state. A small number of adjectives may have infixing elements.

The post-verbal descriptive/expressive element often shares the same phonetic series with the adjective it modifies. Apart from reduplication, these post-verbal elements may have similar initials and finals. The meaning of descriptive elements of this kind is often more difficult to pinpoint than those of verbs. Only a handful of adjectives may have differentiating suffixes in order to distinguish the subtle differences in meaning. For example:

nam^{1}	*ø*^{2} /	*kaŋ*^{2}	*nam*^{1}	*kə*^{0}*ly*^{2}*ty*^{3}
black,	dark	DESCRIP	dark	DESCRIP
'(of sky) dark'			'(of people) dark (skin)'	

ma:n^{5}	*mø*^{2}	*ma:n*^{5}	*mø*^{2}*mø*^{4}
slow	DESCRIP	slow	DESCRIP
'very slow'		'exceptionally slow'	

l̥an^{1}	*l̥uŋ*^{4}*l̥uŋ*^{6}	*tjaŋ*^{6}	*mek*^{8} *me*^{3}
red	DESCRIP	full, filled	DESCRIP
'very red'		'extremely full'	

pi²	*tam²nam²*	*pi*	*taŋ²naŋ⁶*
fat	DESCRIP	fat	DESCRIP

'(of a pig) fat (as a whole)'   'fat (esp. one with fat belly)'

Chadong adjectives generally modify nouns by following the head. However, they may occur before nouns when the structural particle *ti⁴* is used. This phenomenon is rare among the Tai-Kadai languages. Example:

na³ hja:n¹ me² ji⁴ kun⁶ wu:ŋ¹ chaŋ⁶   ti⁴   mi⁴.
front house have one CLF tall   DESCRIP PART tree
'There is a very tall tree in front of the house.'

21.3.1.10. *Adverbs*

As modifiers, adverbs often occur before verbs and adjectives, with a few exceptions. Among the most common postverbal adverbs are *kun⁵* 'before, first', *lim²* 'after(wards).' Note, that, the Chinese loan *θien¹* 'first, before' occurs pre-verbally.

ɲi² sa:m³ kun⁵.	Cf. *ɲi² θien¹ sa:m³.*
you walk/go before.	you before walk/go

'You go first.'

The negative adverb *kwe³* is often represented in its weak form *kə²* except when occurring in sentence initial position or when emphasized. Example:

ca:ŋ¹   tshu³   θa:i¹   kok⁸   kə⁴   la:i⁴   l̥aŋ¹.
speak   ugly   give   CLF   not   good   look
'I'm going to talk about something nasty to embarrass you.'

je² ə²   pə¹, ta:n⁴ɕi⁴ mən² kwe² pə¹.
I   also go but   he   not   go
'I am also going, but he isn't.'

21.3.1.11. *Prepositions*

The majority of prepositions in Chadong are derived from verbs. Some are borrowed from Chinese. Examples of some of the most common prepositions are: *θeu¹* 'taking (disposal)', *ɲa:u⁶* 'at, in (locative)',   *the⁵* 'for (beneficiary)',   *a:u¹* 'make' (causative), *ɲjeŋ⁶* (causative), *ta⁶⁄⁴* (across),   *tso⁴...* *thau⁶* 'from...to... (duration)' *θo⁴* 'from'. E.g.:

mən² θeu¹   la:m¹   tsau⁴ tsən²   taŋ¹.
he   taking basket take   ascend come
'He lifted the basket.'

tje¹ ku¹ a:u¹   mən²   wan¹ wan¹ l̥aŋ¹ po⁴.
3 pl. aunt make 3 sing.   day   day   herd cow
'His aunt makes him herd cows every day.'

21.3.1.12. *Conjunctions*

Common conjunctions include: *la:u¹ taŋ⁶* 'and, with', *ji⁴...tu⁶* 'as soon as...', 'no sooner... than...', *jyt⁸...jyt⁸...* 'the more... the more...', *hot⁸tse³, hop⁸so⁶* 'or'; *jin⁴wi⁶ ... so⁵ji⁵* 'because...therefore', *kə²ta:n¹...ə²tsje³* 'not only... but also' *jy²kuə²...tu⁶* ... 'if...then...'.

21.3.1.13. *Subordinators*

Two subordinators, *ti⁴/²* and *lai⁴*, are found in Chadong. Their usage is similar to that of the Chinese *de* (nominalizer) and *de²* (verb complementizer) respectively, with *ti⁴* corresponding to Chinese *de*, and *lai⁴* to Chinese *de²*. *Lai⁴* can also function as a lexical verb meaning 'get, obtain'. Examples:

ɲa:u⁶ məŋ²tsjeu²   ti⁴   ɕi²hau⁶, ...
at   Ming Dynasty SUB time
'During the Ming times,   ...'

na:i⁶ kwa:i⁶ ɕi⁴ ɲi² pən⁴ ki² ca:ŋ³ ti².
This CLF   be you self   say   NOM
'This is what you said.'

to²kuŋ¹   ḻaŋ¹   lai⁴   tsən²   mən².
shaman   look   SUB   up   3 sing.
'The shaman has great respect for him.'

21.3.1.14. *Discourse particles*

Like many Kam-Tai languages, Chadong is rich in discourse particles, which can express certain modal meanings. Common discourse particles in Chadong include *pa²* (assertive, which may also function as aspect marker, indicating completion; *ma⁶* (yes-no question particle); *kə²θaŋ³* (alternative question particle), *pa¹* (mild request), among others. For example:

pa⁵	*hja:n¹*	*ji⁴kin¹*	*θiu¹*	*nən²*	*pa².*
uncle	house	already	build	good	PART

'Uncle's house has been already been built.' / 'The construction of Uncle's house is completed.'

ɲi²	*pə¹*	*ta⁶*	*pak⁷kiŋ¹*	*ma⁶* ?
2 sing.	go	ASP	Beijing	PART

'Have you been to Beijing?'

mən²	*pə¹*	*tsi⁴*	*kə²θaŋ³?*
3 sing.	go	ASP	PART

'Has he left or not?'

ha:m³ mən²	*pə¹ kan¹ tje¹*	*ku¹ pa¹.*
tell   3 sing. go with 3 plural aunt PART

'Tell him to live with his aunt.'

21.4. WORD ORDER

The basic word order of Chadong is similar to that of other Tai-Kadai languages, that is, Subject-Verb-Object. Adjectives and adverbs may come before the head word, or after it, depending on their syntactic behaviours and semantic properties. Below we describe several common syntactic patterns that are characteristic of Chadong.

21.4.1. Modification of nouns and classifiers

Nouns are often modified by adjectives, pronouns, measure words, other nouns, numeral-classifier phrases or other modifier phrases. Classifiers take adjectives, pronouns, numerals and demonstratives as their modifiers.

Adjectives and demonstrative pronouns usually follow the head nouns (see PRONOUNS). Other modifiers normally precede the head noun.[3]   For example:

kuk^7	fa^1	
clothes	flowery	
'flowery clothes'		

$l\!\!\!,əm^1$	$lək^8$
wind	big
'strong wind'	

$ta{:}i^6$	kin^2
sister	skirt
'sister's skirt'	

tje^1	ku^1
they	aunt
'his aunt'	

$θa{:}m^1$	$ljuŋ^5$	ly^3
three	CLF	house
'three houses'		

$khaŋ^6$	pi^2	hja^1
CLF	fat	two
'two fat ones'		

Directional words such as ju^1 'above, upper', kha^3 'below, under', $la{:}u^4$ 'inside', na^3 'before, front', lim^2 'behind, back', $kuŋ^4$ 'side' take nouns as their heads, with the directional words preceding the nouns. For example:

ju^1	co^3
above	head
'above (one's) head	

kha^3	$ca{:}i^6$
below	world
'at the foot of the mountain'	

$la{:}u^4$	$mi^4luŋ^2$
inside	forest
'in the forest'	

na^3	$hja{:}n^1$
front	house
'in front of the house	

lim^2	$ta{:}i^2$
behind	table
'behind the table'	

$kuŋ^4$	$pa{:}n^4$
beside	village
'at the side of the village'	

When multiple modifications are involved, the order is: 'classifier – demonstrative pronoun – noun – adjective', or 'demonstrative pronoun – (numeral) classifier – noun – adjective'. For example:

ai^1	$na{:}i^6$	$lən^1$	$juŋ^1$
CLF	this	person	thin/skinny
'this skinny person'			

---

3   These may have been recent innovations, as in some compounds, modifiers typically follow the head. Cf. $ləm^4 la^1$ 'water-eye – tears', $ce^4 khja^1$ 'excrement-ear – ear wax'.

kwa:i[6]	khaŋ[6]	m̥u[5]	nam[1]
this	CLF	pig	black

'this black pig; the black pig over here'

tje[1]	hja[1]	ai[1]	lən[1]
3 plural	two	CLF	person

'the two of them'

ji[4]	kjen[6]	kuk[7]	m̥i[5]
one	CLF	clothes	new

'a new shirt/garment'

For numeral classifier constructions involving demonstrative pronouns, the structure may be either 'pronoun – numeral – classifier' or 'numeral – classifier – pronoun'. For example:

kwa:i[6]	(kui[6])	ŋo[4]	ai[1]	=	ŋo[4]	ai[1]	na:i[6]	(ka[5])
this	(that)	five	CLF		five	CLF	this	(that)

'these (those) five people'   'these (those) five people'

21.4.2. Double object constructions

In double object constructions, direct objects (thing) precede indirect objects (person). In sentences of this kind, the benefactive co-verb or preposition θa:i[1] 'for' (which is derived from the lexical verb θa:i[1] meaning 'to give') is compulsory to introduce the indirect object.

thaŋ[4] pek[8]	je[2]	θa:i[1]/tsau[4] hja[1] pan[3] ļe[1]	θa:i[1] n̥i[2].

wait a while I   give/bring two CLF book give you

'I'll give/bring you two books in a minute.'

In modern Chadong, the above sentence can be represented as:

thaŋ[4]	pek[8]	je[2]	θa:i[1]	n̥i[2]	hja[1]	pan[3]	ļe[1]
wait	a while	I	give	you	two	CLF	book

which is obviously an innovation influenced by Chinese grammar.

21.4.3. Comparative constructions

Comparative constructions are formed by using the comparative marker ta[6] to introduce the object of comparison. Example:

ni[4]fai[5]	lək[8]	ta[6]	njeŋ[2]ka:ŋ[1].
the sun	big	COMPAR	the moon

'The sun is bigger than the moon.'

Influenced by Chinese syntax, this sentence may also be said as:

ni[4]fai[5]	pi[3]	njeŋ[2]ka:ŋ[1]	lək[8]
the sun	compare	the moon	big

APPENDIX

Chadong basic vocabulary

alcohol	*kha:u³*
alive	*chu³*
all	*thuŋ⁴(¹) sən¹*
and, with	*la:u¹, taɪf⁶*
animal	*ja⁴na:n⁴*
ant	*ni⁴mət⁸*
ash	*fuk⁷*
back	*ta⁴ḷa:i¹*
back, behind	*lim²*
bad	*fa:i⁶*
bamboo	*fan¹*
bark (of tree)	*mi⁴pi²*
bean	*tau⁶*
bear (animal)	*kau⁴juŋ²*
beard	*nu:t⁸*
because	*jin⁴wi⁶*
bee	*mit⁸*
before, front	*na³*
belly, stomach	*luŋ²*
big	*lək⁸*
bird	*ɳok⁸*
bite	*cit⁸*
bitter	*kam¹*
black	*nam¹*
blood	*phja:t⁷*
blow	*tshy¹*
body	*lən²*
bone	*kut⁷*
boy	*la:k⁸hau²*
breast	*pu⁶*
breathe	*theu¹*
buffalo	*kwi²*
burn	*ta:u³*
butterfly	*ni⁴pa⁴*
catch	*θap⁷*
cave	*ŋa:m³*
chest	*na³tak⁷*
chicken	*ka:i⁵*
child	*lən³(¹)ti⁴*

chop	te^5, ηak^7
claw	$tsa{:}u^3$
cloth	i^1
cloud	fa^3
cockroach	$\theta o^4 ka{:}p^7$
cold	$\underset{\circ}{n}o^1$, $\textit{ni}t^7$
come	$ta\eta^1$
copper	$to\eta^2$
correct (adj.)	toi^5
count	jai^5
cow	po^4
crab	$ni^4 cai^6$
crack	$phik^7$
daughter	$la{:}k^8 pi{:}k^8$
day	wan^1
deep	jam^1
deer	$sa{:}n^4 pa^1$
die	tai^1
dig	$kwa{:}t^7$
dike	we^1
dirty	wa^5
dog	$\underset{\circ}{m}a^1$
drink	$ts\partial^1$, $su{:}k^7$
dry	hjo^1
duck	ep^7
dust	$phu\eta^5$
eagle	$lo^4 jiu^6$
ear	$pe^4 khja^1$
earthworm	$ne^4 zan^4$
eat	$ts\partial^1$
egg	cai^5
eight	$pa{:}t^7$
elder brother	$fa{:}i^4$
elder sister	$ta{:}i^6$
evening	$\underset{\circ}{n}am^5 lap^7$
excrement	ce^4
eye	la^1
face	na^3
fall, drop	tok^7
far	ci^1
fart	$t\partial t^7$
fat	man^2

father	ti^2
fear, afraid	$khwi^1$
fear, afraid	kwi^1
feather	$s\partial n^1$
female organ	ku^4tsi^6
fight	$sek^7kja^4\theta ai^2$
fire	wi^1
fish	$m\partial m^6$
fish gill	$njai^6$
five	ηo^4
float	$tshy^1$
flow	$tshy^1$
flower	fa^1
fly (n.)	$ni^4nju\eta^4$
fly (v.)	$pi\eta^3$
fog	$mu\eta^3lu^2ji{:}n^1$
foot	$ti{:}n^1$
forehead	$na^3pja{:}k^7$
forest	$mi^2\ (^4)lu\eta^2$
four	θi^5
freeze	$kau^6sy^3po^2lja{:}\eta^6$
frog	$k\partial p^7$ (big); $kwai^3$ (small)
fruit	$lo^4la{:}k^8$
full	tik^7
gallbladder	lo^6
girl	$la{:}k^8\theta o^1$
give	$\theta a{:}i^1$
gold	cim^1
good	$n\partial n^2$
gourd	lu^1
grandma	$pu\partial^2$
grandpa	$ku\eta^1$
grandson	$kha{:}n^1$
grass	$ca\eta^1$
green	$ljok^8$
hand	$\underset{\circ}{m}i^1$
he	$m\partial n^2$
head	co^3
head hair	$pjam^1$
hear	ni^3tsjek^8
heart	θam^4tau^2
heavy	lan^1

here	* n̥e⁶*
hill	*pja¹ (rocky), ca:i⁶ (earth)*
hit	*wak⁷*
home	*hja:n¹*
horn	*ŋa:u¹*
horse	*ma⁴*
hot	*ɲi:t⁸, tui¹*
how	*n̥au¹θai⁴*
hunt	*tsən⁴ (⁶)na:n⁴*
husband	*pa:n¹*
I	*je²*
ice	*θy³po²lja:ŋ ⁵*
if	*jy²kuə²*
insect	*ni⁴ta¹*
intestine	*θa:i³*
iron	*thjet⁷*
jab	*tsok⁸*
kill	*ha¹ (chicken), ha³ (people)*
knee	*co³ko⁶*
knife	*pja³*
know	*hjo⁴*
lake/pond	*toŋ̍²*
laugh	*cy¹*
leaf	*fa⁵*
leech	*ni⁴piŋ̍⁶*
left	*θø⁴*
less	*sjeu³*
level, flat	*peŋ̍²*
lie down	*lja:i³*
light (weight)	*la³*
liver	*tap⁷*
long	*ja:i³*
look for	*len¹*
louse	*nan²*
love	*maŋ⁴*
lower leg	*luŋ̍²kit⁸*
lung	*fe⁶*
male organ	*ku⁴ni⁶*
man	*ti²pa:n¹*
many, much	*cu:ŋ̍²*
marrow	*ŋwi²*
meat, flesh	*na:n⁴*

mend, sew	*fa:ŋ¹*
middle	*tu⁴ta⁵*
monkey	*ma⁴leu²*
month	*ŋwet⁸*
moon	*nje n̥²ka:ŋ¹*
mosquito	*ni⁴ta¹n̥e⁶*
mother	*ni⁴*
mouth	*pa:k⁷*
name	*la:n²*
narrow	*ça:p⁷*
near	*phjai⁵*
neck	*wan¹*
new	*m̥i⁵, θan¹*
nine	*cu³*
no, not	*kwe²*
nose	*naŋ¹*
old, aged	*la:u⁴*
one	*jit⁷, ji⁴*
path	*khun¹*
person	*lən¹*
pig	*m̥u⁵*
play	*loŋ⁶, fe⁴lø⁴*
pointed	*θim¹*
prawn	*ni⁴n̥a:ŋ⁵; ni⁴çy¹*
press	*a:p⁷,tjam²*
pull	*ka:k⁷, sai²*
rain	*fən¹*
rat	*ni⁴n̥o³*
red	*l̥an³*
rice	*u⁴*
rice field	*ja⁵*
rice seedling	*ce³*
right	*ju⁶*
river	*ni¹*
root	*tsha⁶*
rope	*la:k⁷*
rotten, rot	*map⁷*
round	*lu:n¹*
roundworm	*ni⁴pe⁶*
salt	*kø¹*
sand	*khiŋ³*
sea	*hai³*

see	$\underset{\underset{\circ}{l}}{} a \eta^{l} tsjek^{8}$
seed	$pən^{3}$
sesame	ηa^{l}
seven	$\theta ət^{7}$
shallow	lai^{6}
sheep	$zø^{2}$
shoe	$ha:i^{2}$
short	$lən^{4}$
shoulder	$co^{4}\ (^{3})ha^{l}$
silver	$ȵan^{2}$
sing	$tshi:tʃ^{6}$
sit	zui^{6}
six	$ljok^{8}$
skin	pi^{2}
sky	$pən^{2}$
sleep	$\underset{\circ}{ȵ}jak^{7}$
small	$\theta e^{5},\ ti^{5}$
smell	$nən^{4}$
smoke	$kwan^{2}$
snake	zy^{2}
snow	cu^{5}
soil	$khəm^{5}$
son, child, offspring	$la:k^{8}$
sour	θam^{3}
speak	$ca:\eta^{3}$
spicy, hot	$\underset{\underset{\circ}{l}}{}jen^{6}$
spider	$tak^{8}məm^{4}$
spit out	$phø^{3}$
stab	$tsok^{8}$
stand	jyn^{l}
star	$zən^{4}\theta ai^{3}$
stay, (to be) at	$ȵa:u^{6}$
stick	kun^{5}
stone	ty^{2}
straight	$\theta i:\eta^{2}$
stupid	pan^{6}
suck	$su:k^{7}$
sun	$ni^{4}fai^{5}$
sweet	$fa:n^{l}$
swim	θeu^{2}
swollen	fok^{7}
tail	$sət^{7}$

take	*tsau⁴*
taro	*i:k⁷*
ten	*səp⁸*
that	*ka⁵*
thatch grass	*hi¹*
there	*kui⁶ta:u³*
they	*tje¹*
thick	*na¹*
thin	*pa:ŋ²*
think	*θi:ŋ³*
this	*na:i⁶*
thorn	*lun¹*
three	*θa:m¹*
throw	*cha:u⁵*
thunder	*fa³kəm⁴*
tie up	*θuk⁸*
tiger	*tak⁸məm⁴*
tongue	*ma²*
tooth	*pjan¹*
tree	*mi⁴*
turn, spin	*tsy:n⁵*
two	*hja¹, ɲi⁶*
upland field	*hon⁴ti⁶*
upper garment	*kuk⁷*
vegetable	*ma¹*
village	*pa:n⁴*
vine	*taɲ²*
vomit	*løk⁷*
waist	*jiu¹*
walk	*sa:m³*
wash	*luk⁷*
water	*ṇam³*
we	*lje¹*
wet	*jak⁷*
what	*tə⁰mə⁵*
where	*loŋ⁴ṇau¹*
white	*kwa³, pek⁸*
who	*khau¹*
wide	*khu:t⁷*
wife	*ma:i⁴*
wind	*ḽəm¹*
wing	*hwa⁵*

wipe	$s \partial t^7$
woman	$ti^2pi:k^7$
yam, sweet potato	$wu:tf'su^2$
year	pe^1
yellow	$ma:n^3, wu:\eta^3$
you (pl.)	ϕe^1
you (sing.)	ni^2
younger brother	$nu\eta^4$
younger sister	mai^4

ACKNOWLEDGEMENTS

A shorter version of this chapter appeared in Chinese in Li (2001). The author has benefited from the insights of Wang et al (1984) in writing this chapter.

REFERENCES

Fifth Research Group, Minority Language Research Centre, Central University of Nationalities (1985) *A Comparative Lexicon of the Kam-Tai Languages*, Beijing: Central University of Nationalities Press.

Li, Jinfang (2001) 'Introduction to Chadong', *Minzu Yuwen* 127: 67-80.

Liang, Jinrong (1996) *Gazetteer of Lingui County* (chapter on languages), Beijing: Fangzhi Press.

Wang, Jun et al. (1984) *Outline Grammars of the Kam-Tai Languages*, Beijing: Ethnic Publishing House.

PART 6

HLAI (LI) AND KRA (KADAI) LANGUAGES

CHAPTER TWENTY-TWO

THE HLAI LANGUAGE

Weera Ostapirat

22.1. INTRODUCTION

The Hlai language group consists of several varieties that are spoken in the south-central part of Hainan island, China. Since 1952, this area has been designated the Hainan Li-Miao Autonomous Prefecture consisting of eight counties: Changjiang, Dongfang, Ledong, Yaxian, Lingshui, Baoting, Qiongzhong, and Baisha. With a population of over one million (1,110,900 people, according to the 1990 census), the ethnic Hlai constitute more than half of the overall inhabitants of the prefecture. Nowadays, they are also found in adjacent counties such as Danzhou, Wanning, Qionghai, Tunchang, and Ding'an in the north and east of the prefecture. Historically, Hlai people are believed to have lived on the island long before other ethnic groups such as the Miao (linguistically Mun or a Yao group), the Han (Chinese) and the Be (a Kra-Dai group) migrated to the island over the course of the last millennium.

The Hlai language belongs to the Kra-Dai language family, which includes related language groups such as Tai, Kam-Sui, and Kra. As most ethnic Kra-Dai people are found in southern China and mainland Southeast Asian areas, it is natural to think that the Hlai ancestors also once lived on the mainland. Yet it is difficult to determine when they migrated to Hainan. Nonetheless, from the fact that the Hlai languages show little of the early Chinese influence that overwhelmed the Tai and Kam-Sui groups as a consequence of the Qin-Han expansion into southern China (ca 3rd-2nd century BC), we may assume that, at least by that time, the Hlai people must have already crossed (or have started to cross) to the island. They probably arrived on the western/southern shores of Hainan from Northern Vietnam and adjacent coastal areas by traveling across the Gulf of Tonkin.

The central area of Hainan hosts clusters of mountain ranges including the Wuzhishan (Five Finger Mountain), the highest peaks on the island. From these mountains and hills, rivers radiate down toward the sea. Several Hlai centers are found along these river courses; for instance, Baoding on the bank of Changhua River in Ledong county, Baisha near the Nandu River in Baisha county, and Heitu near the Ningyuan river in Yaxian. Major Hlai expansions after this early history must have first followed along such river basins and valleys as well as across the coastal areas.

'Hlai' is a typable form of the autonym phonetically pronounced [ɬai]. This is the term used by the majority of Hlai people and may also mean 'men, people'. In China, this people group is known as 'Li'; the name is said to have been referred in Chinese historical records since the Han Dynasty two millennia ago (Henri 1886: 391). Several variants of the sort Lai, Loi, Le, are also attested in literature of the late 19th and early 20th centuries.[1] In the southern Hlai dialects, the autonym is pronounced [dai], e.g. in Savina's (1931) Ðay dialect and in Ouyang and Zheng's (1983) Heitu dialect. This initial d- of southern Hlai and ɬ- elsewhere is a regular correspondence. For example:

	Heitu	Baoding
Hlai	dai^{434}	$ɬai^{53}$
tongue	$diːn^{11}$	$ɬiːn^{11}$
blood	$daːt^{45}$	$ɬat^{55}$

---

1   Other more complex variants include s'lai, s'ai, b'lai, b'li, dli, k'lai, hiai, etc.

There were some early attempts to link the term 'Hlai [ɬai]' with other ethnic names in order to support a relationship between Hlai and those respective groups. For instance, Henri (1886: 482) noted that 'They (Les = Hlai) add a labial when speaking of themselves, and say b'lai, b'lay, etc.' He then related b'lai to Malay, the name of a well-known Austronesian group.[2] Benedict (1975: 336) further attempted to relate the term Hlai with almost all ethnic names under his Austro-Thai family. He linked Hlai not only to Malay but also to the terms Thai, Yay (Tai groups of Kd family), Kelao, Kabeo (Kra groups of Kd family), and various ethnonyms of the Miao-Yao language groups. As far as linguistic evidence is concerned, such linkages remain mere speculations.

The name 'Li' and its variants were sometimes also used to refer to the Be people and language in early references. This usage reflects the fact that, at times in the past, the ethnic Be were labeled in Chinese 熟黎 Shúlí 'the tamed Li', whereas the 生黎 Shēnglí 'the wild Li' referred to the ethnic Hlai.[3] For instance, the languages called K'iung-Shan Li (Parker 1890), Dam-Chiu Loi and Lim-Ko Loi (Jeremiassen 1892) are, in fact, the Be dialects spoken in those respective counties of present-day Qiongshan, Danzhou (or Danxian) and Lingao on the northern plains of Hainan. Though of the same stock, Hlai and Be constitute linguistically two separate groups within the Kra-Dai family. (For the lexical and phonological characteristics that define the Hlai group, see section 22.2.2)

22.2. HLAI PHONOLOGY AND LEXICONS

22.2.1. Hlai word structure

Hlai languages are monosyllabic and tonal. The canonical structure of a syllable consists of an initial consonant (C_i), a vowel (V), and a tone (T). The medial and final consonants (C_m and C_f) are optional.

$$T$$
$$C_i \, (C_m)V \, (C_f)$$

Examples:

	Baoding	Syllable forms
dog	pa^{53}	CV^T
uncover	pla^{55}	CCV^T
mouth	pom^{11}	CVC^T
house	ploŋ^{11}	CVC^T

22.2.1.1. *Tones*

A number of Hlai dialects have three tones in syllables that end with a vowel or a sonorant, plus another tone in syllables that end in a stop. These are reflexes of a system of three-plus-one tones in Proto-Hlai (PH), which can be symbolized as *A, *B, *C (non-stopped tones) and *D (stopped tone). Depending on the dialect, the pitch value of a stopped tone may be identical to the value of a non-stopped tone. Some Hlai dialects split

---

2   Since no Hlai varieties have the voiced aspirated stop [bh], what Henri wrote as b' probably represented [ph]. The form b'lai [phlai] can simply be the fusion of two syllables: [pha] 'male, men' and the ethnonym [ɬai]. Note the following Hlai phrases referring to 'person' where [pha] is often used [pha ɬoːk] 'deaf person', [pha plaːu] 'blind person', [pha ɬeːn̩] 'good person', etc.

3   Literally, *shú* = 'ripe/cooked' and *shēng* = 'raw'. These terms were often applied to ethnic names in China since ancient times and partially reflex the relative degrees of Chinese administrative controls over those ethnic groups. The groups that came under direct rule usually became *shú* or 'ripe'.

these proto tones into two series, which are normally indicative of the voicing of initial consonants at the time of tonal split in each dialect (voiceless initials with tones series 1 and voiced initials with tones series 2). Table 22.2.1.1-1 illustrates this system; Baoding represents a dialect with the original three-plus-one tones and Tongshi a dialect with further tonal splits.

TABLE 22.2.1.1-1: BAODING AND TONGSHI TONAL SPLIT SYSTEM

	Baoding	Tongshi	Tones
fish	$ɬa^{53}$	$ɬa^{33}$	A1
surplus	za^{53}	$ɬa^{11}$	A2
warm, a.	$ɬun^{55}$	$ɬun^{51}$	B1
snake	za^{55}	$ɬa^{121}$	B2
tongue	$ɬiːn^{11}$	$ɬiːn^{55}$	C1
neck	$zoŋ^{11}$	$ɬoŋ^{14}$	C2
enter	$luːt^{55}$	$ɬuːt^{55}$	D1
steal	zok^{55}	$ɬok^{13}$	D2

From Table 22.2.1.1-1, we can see that Tongshi initial _ɬ- corresponds to Baoding ɬ- and z-. Such loss of initial contrast in Tongshi (z- > ɬ-) resulted in a tonal split that doubled the numbers of original tones. The tonal correspondences between Baoding and Tongshi are summarized in Table 22.2.1.1-2.[4]

TABLE 22.2.1.1-2: TONAL CORRESPONDENCES BETWEEN BAODING AND TONGSHI

Tone category	Tone series	Tone value (Baoding)	Tone value (Tongshi)
*A	1	53	33
	2		11
*B	1	55	51
	2		121
*C	1	11	55
	2		14

---

4 Chinese scholars normally use raised numerals to symbolize tones. These numeral symbols, as used in Ouyang and Zheng (1983), typically correspond to Hlai tonal categories as follows:

Tones	A1	A2	B1	B2	C1	C2	D1	D2
no tone split		1		2		3		7
with tone split	1	4	5	2	3	6	7	8

Modern Hlai dialects have different numbers of tones, ranging from three to seven (in native words), but all these tones can be similarly traced back to the same PH system. The tonal correspondences of various Hlai dialects are provided in Appendix 1. This tonal system can also be related to those of Tai, Kam-Sui, Be, and Kra languages (Ostapirat 2000). Such connections provide important evidence that puts the whole family into a clear developmental system.

22.2.1.2. Initial consonants (C_i)

Modern Hlai inventories of initial consonants vary from dialect to dialect. Nonetheless, in native Hlai lexicons, a number of sounds overlap among varieties and the typical system of modern Hlai initial consonants may be generalized as follows.

1. Hlai dialects usually have glottalized/implosive stops /b/ and /d /, voiceless unaspirated stops and affricate /ts/, /k/, and a glottal stop /ʔ/. A set of voiceless aspirated obstruents /ph th tsh kh h/, nasals /m n ɳ ŋ/, liquids /l r/ and spirants /v z/ are also typical among dialects.[5]

b	d	ts	k	ʔ
ph	th	tsh	kh	h
m	n	ɳ	ŋ	
v	l,r	z		

Examples:

	Baoding	Yuanmen	Heitu
leaf	beɯ^1	beɯ^1	beɯ^1
face, nose	daŋ^1	dɔŋ^1	doŋ^1
sit	tsoŋ^3	tɔŋ^3	tsuŋ^3
early	kaːu^3	kaːu^3	kaːu^3
musk melon	ʔai^1	ʔai^1	ʔai^1
name	pheːɳ^1	phiaŋ^1	phaːɳ^1
short (not tall)	thaɯ^3	thaɯ^3	theɯ^3
tree	tshai^1	tshai^1	tshai^1
chicken	khai^1	khai^1	khai^1
excrement	haːi^3	huai^3	hai^3
hand	meɯ^1	meɯ^4	meɯ^1
thick	na^1	na^4	na^1
moon	ɳaːn^1	ɳuan^4	ɳaːn^1
liver	ŋaːn^1	ŋuan^4	ŋaːn^1
far	lai^1	lai^4	lai^1
star	raːu^1	raːu^4	raːu^1
shoulder	va^2	va^2	va^2
old	za^1	za^4	za^1

2. Lacking from the preceding example sets are p-, t- and voiceless fricative initials. These sounds are found across modern Hlai dialects but they do not often correspond one-to-one. For instance, stop initial reflexes in some varieties may correspond to nasals or fricatives in the others. These different reflexes among varieties are crucial to comparative phonology and dialect subgrouping (see Section 22.3 for more details). A few main types of such

---

5   Sibilant initials /ts/, /tsh/, and /z/, are pronounced as (pre-)palatal [tɕ], [tɕh], and [ɕ] in a number of dialects. Some dialects (e.g. Qiandui) may merge r- into l-.

correspondences are described below.

A. Nasal initials in some dialects may correspond to stops in the others (via prenasalized stops):

	Heitu	Baoding	Yuanmen
dog	ma^1	pa^1	pa^4
field, paddy	na^2	ta^2	ta^2
horse	ŋa^3	ka^3	ka^6

B. Fricative initials in some dialects may correspond to stops in the others:

	Xifang	Baoding	Heitu
fire	fei^1	fei^1	pei^1
tongue	ɬiŋ^3	ɬi:ŋ^3	di:n^3
thread, v.	sɔk^7	tok^7	tok^7

C. Voiced spirants in some dialects may be devoiced in others (e.g. v- > f-, z- > ɬ):

	Baoding	Yuanmen	Qiandui
raw	vi:p^7	fip^8	fi:p^8
ear	zai^1	tsai^4	ɬai^4
ask	ga:m^1	kham^1	ha:m^4

22.2.1.3. *Medial consonants (C$_m$)*

Hlai consonant clusters are rare. The only true cluster with medial -l- is pl-. The other complex initials have either -w- or -j- medials. The medial -w- may occur after velar (g- and ŋ-) or glottal (h- and ʔ-) initials while -j- is only found with glottal initials. Examples with ʔw- and ɟ- are few in number.

A number of Hlai dialects simplify initial clusters into simple initials. Either the initial or medial may drop (C$_i$ C$_m$ > C$_i$ or C$_i$ C$_m$ > C$_m$). For instance, in Heitu, pl- has become l- while all medials -w- and -j- are lost (gw- > g-, hj- > h-, etc). In Qiandui, the medial -l- is dropped (pl- > p-) while medials -w- and -j- were usually retained and became spirants (gw- > v-, hj- > z-, but ŋw- > ŋ-).

	Baoding	Heitu	Qiandui
hear	pleɯ^1	leɯ^1	peɯ^1
rotten	gwa:u^3	ga:u^3	va:u^6
straw	ŋwiŋ^3	ŋiŋ^3	ŋiŋ^6
ant	hwaɯ^3	heɯ^3	vaɯ^3
rise, get up	ʔwaɯ^2	ʔeɯ^2	vaɯ^5
thatch grass	hja^1	ha^1	za^1
swallow, v.	ʔjo:m^2	ʔo:m^2	zɔ:m^5

There are also two other reported clusters in modern Hlai: dr- and tl-. Ouyang and Zheng (1983) noted that what transcribed as /r-/ is sometimes variantly pronounced [dɽ], [ɽ], or [d]. This agrees with Savina's (1931) transcriptions of a southern Hlai dialect which shows the variants dr-/d- for the same sound. Recently, L-Thongkum (2001) reported dr- in a Bendi dialect which regularly correspond to r- in other varieties; for instance, /draw^{33}/ 'star', /drow^{33}/ 'knee' (Baoding /ra:u^{53}/ and /rou^{53}/ respectively). In general, there is no phonemic contrast between r- and dr- in the same dialect.

The cluster tl- appeared in   Savina's (1931) records of a central Hlai dialect and usually corresponds to /ɬ-/ in other records. This is compatible with Ouyang and Zheng's (1983) note that /ɬ/ is phonetically pronounced [tɬ] in some dialects. In the same dialect, Savina also recorded *tr-* in a couple of words corresponding to /ɬ-/. In the Vietnamese script (which Savina used in his records) the graph forms *tr-* represent a palatal affricate in Standard Vietnamese and was probably intended for [tɕ], the sound which is also reported for /ɬ/ in the Tongshi area (Ouyang and Zheng 1983: 14).

22.2.1.4. *Final consonants (C$_f$)*

The Hlai system of final consonants is relatively simple; a syllable may end with a nasal (-m, -n, -ɲ, -ŋ), or a stop (-p, -t, -ȶ, -k). These endings are fairly stable and often correspond one-to-one among the dialects. The palatal finals (-ɲ and -ȶ) are the most subject to change and are kept as such only in the Baoding dialect; in other dialects, they have usually merged with alveolars (-n and -t). Some northern-Hlai dialects (e.g. Xifang and Baisha) have adopted other changes such as -n > -ŋ and -t > -k, and several dialects show the weakening of *-k to -ʔ, especially after long vowels and diphthongs. With the exception of palatal endings, this Hlai system of final consonants is also typical among Kra-Dai languages.

	Baoding	Heitu	Baisha	
ask	ga:m[1]	ga:m[1]	xa:m[1]	*-a:m
moon	n̠a:n[1]	n̠a:n[1]	n̠a:ŋ[1]	*-a:n
take off	lan̠[3]	lan[3]	lan[3]	*-an̠
master	ve:ŋ[1]	va:ŋ[1]	viaŋ[1]	*-a:ŋ
carry on shoulder	tsha:p[7]	tsha:p[7]	tsha:p[8]	*-a:p
poor	va:t[7]	va:t[7]	va:ʔ[8]	*-a:t
blood	ɬa:ȶ[7]	da:t[7]	ɬa:t[8]	*-a:ȶ
banana	hwe:k[7]	va:ʔ[7]	veʔ[8]	*-a:k

There is another ending that may be posited as PH *-l. This final has become -l in a Baisha dialect (Wang and Qian 1951) and -ɯ in all other dialects. Its distribution is very limited, however; it occurs only after *-a-.

	Baoding	Heitu	Baisha (W)	
short (not tall)	thaɯ[3]	theɯ[2]	tha:l[3]	*-al
near	plaɯ[3]	leɯ[3]	pla:l[3]	*-al
nine	faɯ[3]	peɯ[3]	faa:l[3]	*-al

This ending is usually reflected as -ɯ (later >-i) in Tai, -i in Kam-Sui, and simply lost in Kra languages. For instance, 'near', Wuming /klaɯ/, Sui /phjai/, Laha /klaa/, etc.

22.2.1.5. *Vowels (V)*

Like initial consonants, modern Hlai vowel inventories differ from dialect to dialect. The typical vowel system that occurs in native vocabularies consists of six to seven monophthongs plus diphthongs, which may be described as follows:

Monophthongs:

i	ɯ	u
e	(ə)	o
	a	

In a number of Hlai dialects, vowels may be short or long. The long low vowels (a, e and o) are normally more open than their short counterparts (e.g. /eː/ and /oː/ are close to [ɛ] and [ɔ]). The long high vowels, on the other hand, are usually diphthongized (e.g. /iː/ and /uː/ are phonetically [ie ia] and [uo ua]).

The schwa [ə] is relatively rare among modern varieties. In most dialects, it occurs only before -ɯ, i.e. [əɯ]. (Because of this limited distribution, this rime is typically written as /eɯ/). In certain dialects such as Yuanmen, [ə] may be found before alveolar finals, e.g. -ən and -ət (historically from *un and *ut, etc.)

Diphthongs:

Diphthongs may be distinguished into two types. The first type consists of diphthongs that have a high vowel onset gliding down to a central low vowel:

    ia   ɯa   ua

These diphthongs seldom correspond one-to-one across dialects and may not be traced back to Proto-Hlai diphthongs. They do not occur in open syllables.

The other set of diphthongs all ends in a high vowel. Contrary to the first type, this type of diphthongs may not take a final consonant, i.e. they occur only in open syllables. Because of this constraint, these diphthongs may be synchronically interpreted as consisting of a vowel (monophthong) plus a glide ending (-j, -w, or -ɥ).

With ending -i

		ɯi, ɯi*	ui,uːi
ei			oi,oːi
		ai,aːi	

With ending -u

iu,iːu	
eu	ou
	au,aːu

With ending -ɯ

əɯ
aɯ

22.2.2. Hlai lexicons: Kra-Dai traits versus Hlai traits

The vocabularies of various Hlai dialects have been recorded since the late 19th century (for early materials, see especially Jeremiassen 1892, Savina 1931, and Stübel 1937). Their records show Hlai to be a tonal monosyllabic language which, similar to Tai and other Kd languages, hosts a set of nasal and stop finals such as -m, -n, -ŋ and -p, -t, -k. Such similar syllable structures, though not a guarantee of genetic relationship by itself, have facilitated lexical comparisons between Hlai and other Kd languages.[6]

The lexical connection between Hlai and other Kra-Dai languages is illustrated in Table 22.2.2-1. As we have noted, the Hlai tonal system has shown itself to be relatable to that of other Kd languages (Ostapirat 2000). These Kd tonal categories are shown in the last column.

---

6   Many languages of southern China and southeast Asia which belong to different language families have these similar kinds of syllable structure, e.g. the Yue dialects of Chinese (namely, Cantonese), Vietnamese, and a number of Yao dialects of Miao-Yao family.

TABLE 22.2.2-1: HLAI LEXICAL TRAITS OF KRA-DAI ORIGIN

	(Hlai)	(Tai)	(Kam-Sui)	(Kra)	
	Baoding	Siamese	Sui	Gelao	Tones
eye	tsha	taa	daa	tau	A
hand	meɯ	muɯɯ	mjaa	mpau	A
dog	pa	maa	m̥aa	mpau	A
bear, n.	mui	mii	ʔmii	mi (Lz)	A
fire	fei	fai	wii	pai	A
bitter	hoːm	khom	qam	qan	A
tooth	fan	fan	wjan	pan	A
drum	laŋ	klɔɔŋ	kuŋ (K)	lǝɯ	A
shoulder	va	baa	wie (Lk)	ʔbaa (By)	B
old	khau	kau	qaau	qa	B
excrement	hai	khii	qee	qɑ	C
water	nom	naam	nam	(ǝɯ)	C
fingernail	liːp	lep	ʔdjap	kle	D
fart	thuːt	tot	tǝt	tæ (Lz)	D
child, person	ɬuːk	luuk	laak	lei	D

On the other hand, the Hlai language group has lexical and phonological characteristics of its own.[7] Hlai dialects share among themselves a number of vocabulary items that differ from those of the other Kd groups. Examples in Table 22.2.2-2 are of two main types. The first set shows Hlai roots against pan-Kra-Dai etyma; the second set shows Hlai roots against Tai and Kam-Sui's, on the one hand, and Kra's, on the other.

TABLE 22.2.2-2: LEXICAL TRAITS OF HLAI LANGUAGES

	Hlai		Tai	Kam-Sui	Kra
	Baoding	Heitu	Siamese	Sui	Laha
liver	ŋaːn	ŋaːn	tap	tap	tap
ear	zai	zai	huu	qhaa	khlaa
fat	gwei	ruːi	man	man	mal
knee	rou	rou	khau	qu	qǝu (Lz)
bird	taƚ	tat	nok	nok	nok
sick	tshok	tshok	khai	saai (K)	khǝi
high	pheːk	phaːʔ	suuŋ	waaŋ	kwaaŋ
come	puːn	muːn	maa	m̥aa	maa
pluck	rou	rou	bit	ʔbit	bǝt
wind	hwoːt	vɔːt (Bc)	lom	lum	van
mouth	pom	mom	paak	paak	mul
forehead	daːu	daːu	phaak	pjaak	daŋ

---

7   One of the phonological characteristics of the Hlai language group is the aspiration of voiceless stops and affricate:

	Hlai		Tai	Kra
	Baoding	Heitu	Siamese	Laha
wing	phiːk	phiːʔ	piik	–
short (not tall)	thaɯ	theɯ	taai*	taa
pestle	tshaːk	tshaːʔ	saak	caak
chicken	khai	khai	kai	kɦi

* The Siamese form means 'below'.

flower	tshe:ŋ	tshe:ŋ	dɔɔk	nuk	baal
egg	zuu:m	zuu:m	khai	kai	tam
good	łeŋ.	din	dii	?da:i	?ai

In cultural perspective, it is worth noting that a number of Hlai rice terms are also distinct from other languages. (For these roots, Tai and Kam-Sui often share forms.)

	Hlai		Tai	Kam-Sui	Kra
	Baoding	Heitu	Siamese	Sui	Laha
rice	tha	tha	khaau	au	mlaa
rice seedlings	hwiu	viu	klaa	kaa	ta laa (By)
rice straw	ŋwiŋ	ŋiŋ	faaŋ	waaŋ	vaaŋ (Ph)
transplant[8]	dop	dup	dam	?dam	dam

Several material culture terms show similar distributions.

	Hlai		Tai	Kam-Sui	Kra
	Baoding	Heitu	Siamese	Sui	Laha
iron	go:i	ra:i	lek < *hl-	khɔt	kɛl
wine	bi:ŋ	bi:ŋ	lau < *hl-	khaau	pǝu
bow	vat	vat	naa< *hn-	ŋaa	—

Note that Chinese has related forms for the above Tai and Kam-Sui etyma: 'iron' *hlit < -k and 'crossbow' *na?. For the first root, the Old-Chinese voiceless lateral *hl- goes back at least to the Han period (ca. two thousand years ago) or earlier (*hl- later became th- in Middle Chinese). This suggests that the interaction between Chinese and Tai/Kam-Sui groups, that resulted in these shared forms, must have already occurred by that time. The word 'crossbow' is an areal root which is distributed widely across language families; it is also found as a typical root in Austroasiatic and Miao-Yao languages. The direction of loans for such roots is difficult to determine. However, the fact that Hlai (and Kra) did not adopt the terms possibly suggests that when these materials such as 'iron' and 'crossbow' spread throughout southern China and southeast asian areas, Hlai might have already left the mainland.

It is thus promising that thorough study of these kinds of vocabulary distributions will not only shed light on the history of Hlai but also bring us a clearer picture of the cultural history of the Kra-Dai people, the early migrations, as well as the interaction among various ethnic groups of the areas.

22.3. HLAI VARIETIES

Hlai dialects may be divided into northern, southern, central, and Jiamao groups, based on their phonological characteristics. In China, they are separated into five dialects: *ha*, *gei*, *hjuu:n*, *mo:i-fau*, and *tha:i*. The main reported varieties, including several dialects in early literatures, belong to the Hlai divisions as shown in Table 22.3-1.

TABLE 22.3-1: HLAI VARIETIES

Hlai branches	Ouyang and Zheng (1983)		Early sources
	Dialect groups	Vernaculars	
Northern	Xifang	*mo:i-fau*	Mefu (St)
	Baisha	*hjuu:n*	White Sand Loi (J);
	Yuanmen	(bendi)	Basadung (St); Baisha (W)

---

8   The Laha form /dam/ is probably a Tai loan. The word is not normally found in the Kra languages where *tam* C (Laha /tam/) 'plant' is used

Southern	Heitu	*ha*	Day (Sv)
			Lai of Yulinkan (Sw)
Central	Baoding		Small Cloth Loi (J)
	Zhongsha		Ha (St)
	Tongshi	*gei*	Shaved Head Loi (J);
	Baocheng		Double Cloth Loi (J);
	Qiandui		Hiai (Sv); Ki (St)
Jiamao	Jiamao	*thaːi*	Bupa (St)

Sw = Swinhoe 1871, J = Jeremiassen 1892, Sv = Savina 1931, St = Stübel 1937, W = Wang and Qian 1951

22.3.1. Southern Hlai (SH)

This variety is mainly distributed along the Ningyuan River valleys in Yaxian and adjacent areas of Ledong county. It is sometimes known as /bou[11] hiːm[11]/ and is included as one of the Ha vernaculars by Chinese scholars. A form of this dialect called Lai of Yulinkan was recorded as early as the late 19th century (Swinhoe 1871), but the few lexical items and vague transcriptions of the material made it less useful for serious linguistic purpose. Savina (1931) later published comprehensive lexicons of this variety (called 'southern Day') which contain more than 1,200 entries transcribed in quốc ngữ (romanized Vietnamese) scripts. The corpus surpassed all earlier word-lists on Hlai languages in both quantity and quality and remained the only source of southern Hlai forms until 1980s.

22.3.1.1.1. *Characteristics of the Southern Hlai varieties*

In the following comparisons, Heitu, Baoding, and Yuanmen varieties represent the southern (SH), central (CH), and northern (NH) groups of Hlai respectively.

1. SH has nasal initials in a set of words where other dialects have stops:

	(SH)	(CH)	(NH)
	Heitu	Baoding	Yuanmen
five	ma^1	pa^1	pa^4
long	naːu^3	taːu^3	taːu^6
firewood	ŋun^3	kun^3	kən^6

2. SH has d- in a set of words where others have ɗ-:

	(SH)	(CH)	(NH)
	Heitu	Baoding	Yuanmen
tongue	diːn^3	ɗiːn^3	ɗin^3
blood	daːt^7	ɗaːʈ^1	ɗuat^7

3. SH has p- in a set of words where other dialects have f-:

	(SH)	(CH)	(NH)
	Heitu	Baoding	Yuanmen
fire	pei^1	fei^1	fhei^1
rain	pun^1	fun^1	fhən^1

4. SH distinguishes *ɣ- and *R- (>r-) while others merge them:

	(SH)	(CH)	(NH)	
	Heitu	Baoding	Yuanmen	
ask	gaːm^1	gaːm^1	kham^1	*ɣ-
iron	raːi^1	goːi^1	khuːi^1	*R-

5. SH has -aː- before velars where others have fronted or diphthongized the vowel:

	(SH) Heitu	(CH) Baoding	(NH) Yuanmen	
name	phaːŋ[1]	pheːŋ [1]	phiaŋ[1]	*aːŋ
otter	naːʔ[7]	teːk[7]	tiaʔ[7]	*aːk

6. SH has -a- in a set of words where others have -oː- or -ua- (and its variants):

	(SH) Heitu	(CH) Baoding	(NH) Yuanmen
fruit	tsham[1]	tshoːm[1]	tshuam[1]
skin	naŋ[1]	noːŋ[1]	nuaŋ[4]
fish scale	lap[7]	loːp[7]	luap[8]

22.3.2. Northern Hlai (NH)

NH dialects include such dialects as Baisha, Yuanmen and Xifang, which are mainly distributed in Baisha and Dongfang counties. People speaking these dialects constitute about 10 percent of Hlai population. According to Chinese scholars, Baisha and Yuanmen belong to Bendi 'local' or [hjuːn] dialect group (Baisha county) and Xifang belongs to Mofu [moːi fau] group (Dongfang county).

22.3.2.1.1. Characteristics of the Northern varieties

1. NH dialects have palatal and velar (or labio-velar) nasal reflexes of PH *χj- and *χw- respectively. These NH nasal initials correspond to palatal and labio-velar glides (hj- and hw-) in such dialects as Baoding and Baocheng (-w- may be lost before certain vowels, namely, -u-). These glides may further lose yielding h- (e.g. in Heitu) or became spirants z- (<j) and v- (<w) (e.g. in Qiandui).

	NH			CH	SH
	Xifang	Baisha	Yuanmen	Baoding	Heitu
thatch grass	ɲa[1]	ɲa[1]	ɲa[1]	hja[1]	ha[1]
worm	ɲaŋ[2]	ɲaŋ[2]	ɲan[2]	hjan[2]	hen[2]
mountain	ŋo[3]	ŋo[3]	ɯo[3]	hwou[3]	hau[3]
hair (body)	ŋoŋ[1]	ŋoŋ[1]	ɯən[4]	hun[1]	hun[1]

2. NH dialects usually have fricative or affricate reflexes of PH *s-. This PH *s- has become t- in other dialect groups. The reconstruction of PH *s- thus relies mainly on NH reflexes.

	NH			CH	SH
	Xifang	Baisha	Yuanmen	Baoding	Heitu
wash	soːk[7]	tshoʔ	tshɔʔ[7]	toːk[7]	tak[7]
thread	sɔk[7]	tshɔk	tshɔk[7]	tok[7]	tok[7]
bird	sat[7]	tshat	–	tat[7]	tat[7]

3. NH dialects emphasize on vowel height distinction where other dialects show length distinction (phonetically diphthongized):

*i:

	NH			CH	SH
	Xifang	Baisha	Yuanmen	Zhongsha	Heitu
gift	xim^3	xim^3	khim^3	giːm^3	giːm^3
tongue	ɬiŋ^3	ɬiŋ^3	ɬin^3	ɬiːn^3	diːn^3
hang	riŋ^3	riŋ^3	rin^6	riːŋ^3	riːŋ^3
fingernail	lip^7	lip^8	lip^8	liːp^7	liːp^7
whip	fit^7	fit^8	fit^8	fiːt^7	phiːt^7
pole	fik^7	fit^7	fiʔ^7	fiːʔ^7	piːʔ^8

*i

	NH			CH	SH
	Xifang	Baisha	Yuanmen	Zhongsha	Heitu
forbidden	kem^3	kem^3	kem^3	kim^3	kim^3
fly, v.	ben^1	ben^1	ben^1	bin^1	bin^1
straw	ŋen^3	ŋen^3	ɱen^6	ŋiŋ^3	ŋiŋ^3
dog louse	tshep^7	tshep^8	tshep^7	tship^7	tship^7
spicy	xet^7	xet^8	khet^7	git^7	rit^7

*u:

	NH			CH	SH
	Xifang	Baisha	Yuanmen	Zhongsha	Heitu
body	ŋuŋ^1	ŋuŋ^1	ɱun^4	huːn^1	huːn^1
hole	tshuŋ^3	tshuŋ^3	tshuŋ^3	tshuːŋ^3	tshuːŋ^3
enter	ɬuk^7	ɬuk^7	ɬut^7	ɬuːt^7	duːt^7
termite	pluk^7	pluk^8	pluʔ^7	luːʔ^7	luːʔ^7

*u

	NH			CH	SH
	Xifang	Baisha	Yuanmen	Zhongsha	Heitu
hair	ŋoŋ^1	ŋoŋ^1	ɱən^4	hun^1	hun^1
neck	zoŋ^3	zoŋ^3	tsoŋ^6	zuŋ^3	zoŋ^3
ant	pot^7	pot^8	pət^8	puṭ^7	mut^7
stomach	pok^7	pok^8	pok^8	pok^7	mok^7

22.3.2.2. *Xifang or [moːɾ^{53} fau^{53}] dialect*

This variety is spoken by about 45,000 people who lived mainly in Xifang township and the southeastern part of Dongfang county. This area is located at the northwest periphery of Hlai settlement and little linguistic material had been available before 1980s. Among early studies on Hlai, only Stübel (1937) recorded some scores of vocabulary items from this dialect.

This dialect shows a unique modern reflex ɣ- which mainly corresponds to f- or v- in other Northern varieties.

	Xifang	Baisha	Yuanmen
ripe	ɣui^1	foi^1	fou^1
bone	ɣɯk^7	fɯk^8	fɯʔ^8
run	ɣou^2	vou^2	vou^5
rise	ɣəɯ^2	vaɯ^2	vaɯ^5

Alveolar codas usually change into velars (*-n > -ŋ and *-t > -k). On the other hand, early palatal codas have become alveolar (*-ɲ > -n and *-c > -t). These innovations are shared by Baisha variety and may suggest a close relationship between the two dialects. The Baoding forms (a CH dialect), which contrast alveolar and palatal endings, are provided as a point of reference.

*-n > -ŋ and *-t > -k

	Xifang	Baisha	Baoding	
stone	tshiŋ[1]	tshiŋ[1]	tshi:n[1]	*i:n
body	ŋuŋ[1]	ŋuŋ[1]	hu:n[1]	*u:n
rain	foŋ[1]	foŋ[1]	fun[1]	*un
grass	kaŋ[3]	kaŋ[3]	kan[3]	*an
moon	ɳa:ŋ[1]	ɳa:ŋ[1]	ɳa:n[1]	*a:n
nose	khak[7]	khak[7]	khat[7]	*at
poor	va:k[7]	va:ʔ[8] < -k	va:t[7]	*a:t

*-ɳ > -n and *-ȶ > -t

	Xifang	Baisha	Baoding	
blood	ɬo:t[7]	ɬa:ȶ[8]	ɬa:ȶ[7]	*a:ȶ
short	that[7]	that[8]	thaȶ[7]	*aȶ
ant	pot[7]	pot[8]	puȶ[7]	*uȶ
select	ɬan[1]	ɬan[1]	ɬaɳ[1]	*aɳ
fly, v.	ben[1]	ben[1]	beɳ[1]	*iɳ

Xifang has merged some pairs of rimes that end with -ɯ, -i, and -u. For instance, NH *aɯ merged with *əɯ, *iu with *eu, and *ui with *oi.

	Xifang	Baisha
short (not tall)	theɯ[3]	theɯ[3]
navel	ɣeɯ[1]	feɯ[1]
take	tshiu[3]	tshiu[3]
seedlings	viu[1]	veu[1]
cotton	bui[3]	bui[3]
bear, n.	mui[1]	moi[1]

22.3.2.3. *Baisha dialect*

Baisha varieties are spoken mainly in Baisha county, which has long been a gateway for excursions by Chinese and foreign travelers from the northern plain into Hlai territories. Different forms of Baisha have been recorded very early; for instance, White Sand Loi (Jeremiassen 1892), Basadung Li (Stübel 1937), and Baisha (Wang and Qian 1951).

Some features of Baisha varieties may be noted as follows.

1. Baisha shares with Xifang the changes of alveolar and palatal endings: *-n > -ŋ, *-t > -k, *-ɳ > -n and *-ȶ > -t (as mentioned above). However, Baisha alone has adopted the change -k > -t after the high front vowel -i-:

		NH		CH
	Baisha	Xifang	Yuanmen	Baoding
pole	fit[7]	fik[7]	fiʔ[7]	fi:k[7]
wing	phit[7]	phik[7]	phiʔ[7]	phi:k[7]

2. Baisha agrees with Yuanmen in having merged *s- and *ch- and in having diphthongs -ua-
and -ia- where Xifang has -o:- and -e:-:

	Baisha	Yuanmen	Xifang	
buffalo	tshoi³	tshou³	sui³	*s-
thread, v.	tshɔk⁷	tshɔk⁷	sɔk⁷	*s-
stone	tshiŋ¹	tshin¹	Tshiŋ¹	*ch-
hole	tshuŋ³	tshuŋ³	tshuŋ³	*ch-

	Baisha	Yuanmen	Xifang	
fruit	tshuam¹	tshuam¹	tsho:m¹	
skin	nuaŋ¹	nuaŋ⁴	no:ŋ¹	
fish scale	luap⁸	luap⁸	lo:p⁷	
master	viaŋ¹	viaŋ⁴	veŋ¹	

3. The Baisha vernacular recorded by Wang and Qian (1951) shows the unique final -l which
usually corresponds to -ɯ in other varieties:

	Baisha (W)	Baisha (O)	Yuanmen
near	pla:l³	plaɯ³	plaɯ³
nine	fa:l³	faɯ³	faɯ³
light, a.	kha:l³	khaɯ³	khaɯ³
short, a.	tha:l³	thaɯ³	thaɯ³

This same dialect shows voiceless unaspirated stops p- and t- for glottalized b- and d- in other
dialects:

	Baisha (W)	Baisha (O)	Yuanmen
fly, v.	pen¹	ben¹	ben¹
face, nose	taŋ¹	daŋ¹	dɔŋ¹

This dialect is spoken in the southeastern part of Baisha county. Yuanmen split PH tones into
two series conditioned by the voicing of initial consonants at the time of the tonal split.
Examples in Table 22.3.2.3-1 are all in PH tone *C category and show Yuanmen tones 44 (early
Yuanmen voiceless initials) and 13 (early Yuanmen voiced initials) corresponding to Baisha
tone 33 and Xifang tone 24 (the latter two varieties do not split tones).

TABLE 22.3.2.3-1: HLAI TONE C COMPARISONS

	Tone	Yuanmen	Baisha	Xifang	NH
male	C1	pha⁴⁴	pha³³	pha²⁴	*ph
short	C1	thaɯ⁴⁴	thaɯ³³	th«ɯ²⁴	*th
light, a.	C1	khaɯ⁴⁴	khaɯ³³	kɦ«ɯ²⁴	*kh
buffalo	C1	tshou⁴⁴	tshoi³³	sui²⁴	*s

		Yuanmen	Baisha	Xifang	NH
beard	C2	pum¹³ <b	pum³³	pum²⁴	*mp
long	C2	ta:u¹³ <d	ta:u³³	ta:u²⁴	*nt
grass	C2	kan¹³ <g	kaɳ³³	kaɳ²⁴	*ŋk
neck	C2	tsɔŋ¹³ <dz	zɔŋ³³	zɔŋ²⁴	*ʒ

22.3.3. Central Hlai (CH)

A majority of Hlai people (about three-fourth of Hlai population) speak the CH dialects, which includes most of the so-called Gei and Ha dialects (minus Heitu, which forms a southern Hlai dialect). The CH dialects are distributed in virtually all counties of Hlai territory, with dense concentration in big cities such as Tongshi (Baoting county) and Sanya (Yaxian). Most of Hlai varieties recorded in early literature belong to this CH group.

All CH dialects shows a set of stop (< nasal) consonants (which remain nasal in the SH dialect), like the NH group. On the other hand, they share with the SH group such changes as the occlusion of *s- > t- and demonstrate a length distinction (diphthongization) of early high vowels.

		(SH)		(CH)		(NH)
		Heitu		Baoding		Xifang
five	A	ma^1	/	pa^1		pa^1
long	C	na:u^3	/	ta:u^3		ta:u^3
firewood	C	ɳun^3	/	ꓘun^3		koɳ^3
bird	D	tat^7		tat̠^{7}	/	sat^7
thread v.	D	tok^7		tok^7	/	sɔk^7

In general, the CH dialects in the west and coastal areas (or the Ha group) do not split tones. This group is represented by such dialects as Baoding and Zhongsha. Baoding is located on the bank of the Changhua river in Ledong County and represents a vernacular sometimes known as Luohuo [lau^{55} hu:t^{55}]. It is distributed mainly in Ledong County and adjacent areas of Dongfang (eastern part), Changjiang (southern part), and Baisha (western part) Counties. Zhongsha represents a vernacular called [ha^{11} ʔeːm^{55}], which is scattered throughout the coastal areas from Dongfang in the northwest to Lingshui in the southeast of Hlai territory. About half of Hlai population are said to speak these varieties.

The other CH group (or the Gei group) is concentrated mainly to the east of the former, especially in Baoting and Qiongzhong Counties. This group is represented by such dialects as Tongshi (western areas of Baoting and Qiongzhong Counties), Qiandui (eastern area of Qiongzhong), and Baocheng (eastern area of Baoting). Speakers of these varieties constitute about one-fourth of Hlai population. All reported dialects of this group split tones.

Examples of tonal correspondences between the dialects that do not split tones (the western group, represented by Baoding) and the dialects that split tones (the eastern group) are shown in Table 22.3.3-1.

TABLE 22.3.3-1: EASTERN HLAI DIALECT TONE SPLIT

		Baoding	Tongshi	Qiandui	Baocheng	
sky	C1	fa^{11}	fa^{55}	fa^{35}	fa^{35}	*f
heart	C1	ɬa:u^{11}	ɬa:u^{55}	ɬa:u^{35}	ɬa:u^{35}	*ɬ
excrement	C1	ha:i^{11}	ha:i^{55}	ha:i^{35}	ha:i^{35}	*X
store (water)	C2	veːŋ^{11}	feːŋ^{14}	feːŋ^{213}	feːŋ^{213}	*v
neck	C2	zoŋ^{11}	ɬoŋ^{14}	ɬoŋ^{213}	ɬoŋ^{213}	*lʒ
grove	C2	goŋ^{11}	goŋ^{14}	hoŋ^{213}	huŋ^{213}	*ɣ

Some features of CH varieties may be further noted as follows:

A. Baoding is the only dialect that has palatal finals. These finals have merged with alveolar endings in other CH dialects.

	Baoding	Tongshi	Qiandui	Baocheng
blood	ɬaȶ^{55}	la:t^{55}	ɬa:t^{42}	ɬa:t^{53}
select	ɬaɲ^{53}	ɬan^{33}	ɬan^{33}	ɬan^{44}

B. Zhongsha has r- in a set of words where other CH dialects have labio-dental fricatives (Baoding v-, others (*v- >) f-).

	Zhongsha	Baoding	Tongshi	Qiandui	Baocheng
navel	reɯ^{53}	veɯ^{53}	feɯ^{11}	feɯ^{11}	feɯ^{22}
bone	rɯ:ʔ^{55}	vɯ:k^{55}	fɯ:ʔ^{13}	fɯaʔ^{21}	fɯ:ʔ^{31}

Zhongsha otherwise differs very little from Baoding dialect. The tonal reflexes are the same (*A=53, *B=55, *C=11, *D=55). In most cases, Zhongsha initial reflexes are simplified forms of Baoding's:

	Zhongsha	Baoding
straw	ŋiŋ^{11}	ŋwiŋ^{11}
head	gau^{11}	gwou^{11}
mountain	hau^{11}	hwou^{11}
thatch	ha^{53}	hja^{53}
seedlings	viu^{53}	hwiu^{53}
wasp	lou^{53}	plou^{53}

C. Baoding and Zhongsha share certain vowel reflexes that differ from the eastern dialects.

	Zhongsha	Baoding	Tongshi	Qiandui	Baocheng
many	ɬo:i^{1}	ɬo:i^{1}	ɬa:i^{1}	ɬa:i^{1}	ɬa:i^{1}
tomorrow	hau^{2}	hau^{2}	ho^{5}	ho^{5}	hɔ^{5}

D. Among the dialects that split tones (eastern dialects), early sonorant initials are treated differently with respect to tones. These initials all act as voiced initials and take tone series 2 in Qiandui (*A2=[11]), whereas in Baocheng they all take tone series 1 (*A1=[44]), indicating an early voiceless feature. Tongshi's reflexes split into two, showing tone series 1 (*A1=33) for nasal and lateral initials and tone series 2 (A2=[11]) for early glides.

	PH tones	Qiandui		Tongshi	Baocheng	
hand	A	meɯ^{11}	/	meɯ^{33}	meɯ^{44}	*m
thick	A	na^{11}	/	na^{33}	na^{44}	*n
liver	A	ŋa:n^{11}	/	ŋa:n^{33}	ŋa:n^{44}	*ŋ
far	A	lai^{11}	/	lai^{33}	lai^{44}	*l
master	A	ve:ŋ^{11}		fe:ŋ^{11}	/ ve:ŋ^{44}	*w
medicine	A	za^{11}		za^{11}	/ za^{44}	*y

E. Qiandui is the only dialect where early voiced stops have become voiceless aspirated.

		Qiandui	Tongshi	Baoding	
beard	C2	phuːm^{213}	puːm^{14}	puːm^{213}	*b < mp
long	C2	thaːu^{213}	taːu^{14}	thaːu^{213}	*d < nt
grass	C2	khan^{213}	kan^{14}	kan^{213}	*g < ŋk

Qiandui is also the only reported dialect that lost medial -l- in *pl-:

		Qiandui	Tongshi	Baocheng
near	C	pauɯ^{35}	plauɯ^{55}	plauɯ^{35}
hear	A	peuɯ^{33}	pleuɯ^{33}	pleuɯ^{44}

22.3.4. Jiamao

This variety, sometimes known as [thaːi^{11}], is spoken by about 70,000-80,000 people who live mainly in the Jiamao township, Baoting County, and in adjacent areas of Lingshui and Qiongzhong counties. It has long been understudied; the only early material on this dialect (called Bupali) is noted by Stübel (1937).

Jiamao is often considered the most aberrant among Hlai dialects.[9] The shared vocabulary between Jiamao and other Hlai dialects (around 550 words from among 1,630 vocabulary items) is only about half of the amount typically shared among other dialects (1,000+ words). Nonetheless, Jiamao appears to show clear lexical and phonological traits of the Hlai group. For instance, Jiamao has /ŋuən/ 'liver', which is a lexical item unique to Hlai languages (cf. Baoding Hlai /ŋaːn/, but Tai /tap/, etc.); moreover, Jiamao /khai/ 'chicken' shows the aspiration of stop initials typical of the Hlai group (cf. Baoding Hlai /khai/, but Tai /kai/, etc).

Jiamao hosts a number of phonological reflexes that are distinct from those of other Hlai dialects. Some of these features seem to suggest that Jiamao split off early from the rest of Hlai varieties (which we may call Hlai Proper). Details of phonological comparisons between Jiamao and other Hlai varieties are presented elsewhere (Ostapirat 2004).

1. Jiamao shows two kinds of stop initials, voiceless aspirated and glottalized or implosive, corresponding to the voiceless aspirated stops *ph- and *th- in other dialects.

	Jiamao	(NH) Yuanmen	(CH) Baoding	(SH) Heitu
name	phuu^{1}	phianꞈ^{1}	pheːn̩^{1}	phaːn̩^{1}
rice	thou^{1}	tha^{5}	tha^{2}	tha^{2}
sparrow	bat^{7}	phat^{7}	phat^{7}	phat^{7}
seven	dau^{1}	thou^{1}	thou^{1}	thu^{1}

2. Likewise, Jiamao has either voiceless unaspirated or glottalized/implosive stops corresponding to only one set of stops in other dialects.

	Jiamao	(NH) Yuanmen	(CH) Baoding	(SH) Heitu
leaf	pi^{1}	beuu^{1}	beuu^{1}	beuu^{1}
gall bladder	ti^{1}	dai^{1}	dai^{1}	dai^{1}
rice wine	biːŋ^{5}	biŋ^{5}	biːŋ^{2}	biːŋ^{2}
replant	dep^{7}	dap^{7}	dop^{7}	dup^{7}

---

9   Thurgood (1991a) considered it as a non-Hlai language.

3. Early nasal consonants which have become (prenasalized stops >) stops in some dialects also have two sets of reflexes in Jiamao.

	Jiamao	(NH) Yuanmen	(CH) Baoding	(SH) Heitu
dog	pou^4	pa^4	pa^1	ma^1
field, paddy	tou^4	ta^2	ta^2	na^2
needle	kuət^8	kət^8	kuʈ^7	ŋut^7
beard	mum^2	puɯm^6	puː:m^3	muː:m^3
six	nəm^4	tom^4	tom^1	nom^1
sleep	ŋɔ^4	kau^2	kau^2	ŋau^2

4. Jiamao distinguishes t- and tsh- where others have tsh-.

	Jiamao	(NH) Yuanmen	(CH) Baoding	(SH) Heitu
eye	tou^1	tsha^1	tsha^1	tsha^1
four	tiau^1	tshoa^3	tshau^1	tsha:u^3
tail	tshuət^7	tshət^7	tshuʈ^7	tshut^7
wear	tshɔ:t^a	tshat^7	tshat^7	tshet^7

5. On the other hand, Jiamao merges some early palatal and velar sounds which are distinguished in other dialects.

	Jiamao	(NH) Yuanmen	(CH) Baoding	(SH) Heitu	
sit	tsiəŋ^1	tɔŋ^3	tsoŋ^3	tsuŋ^3	*c
old	tso^1	za^4	za^1	za^1	*y
crocodile	kai^1	kai^3	kai^3	kai^3	*k
pile up	kəp^7	–	go:p^7	go:p^7	*ƭ

6. Jiamao lost early final *-k in some rimes, and thus the early checked syllables have become open syllables.

	Jiamao	(NH) Yuanmen	(CH) Baoding	(SH) Heitu
high	phɯ^5	phia?^{7}	phe:k^7	pha:?^{7}
otter	nɯ^2	tia?^{7}-t	te:k^7	na:?^{7}
wash	tsha^5	tshɔ?^{7}	to:k^7	tak^7
deep	ɬa^2	ɬo?^{7}	ɬo:k^7	dak^7

Jiamao also lost final *-ɯ and merged *əɯ and *aɯ (< al) into -a.

	Jiamao	(NH) Yuanmen	(CH) Baoding	(SH) Heitu
hand	ma^1	məɯ^4	məɯ^1	məɯ^1
dry, a.	kha^1	khaɯ^5	khaɯ^2	khəɯ^2

In sum, Jiamao shows a number of unique phonological developments which suggest that it split off early from the rest of Hlai. Jiamao evidence, once fully incorporated into the comparisons, will alter the picture of PH reconstruction. On the other hand, it is possible that some Jiamao aberrancies result from interlectal loans and recent historical contact that may not reflex the early Hlai sound system.

22.3.5. Other varieties

22.3.5.1. *Cun (Ngao Fon)*

The Cun language is spoken in Dongfang and Changjiang Counties, with the number of speakers estimated at between 45,000 to 60,000. These people have lived for generations among the Chinese of the area and are officially placed with the Han (Chinese) nationality in China. This is also reflected by the fact that the Cun people are usually called Moi [mo:i], the Hlai word designating ethnic Han, by the local Hlai people.

The word *Cun* in Chinese means 'village' and such terms as *Cun Hua* 'village language' and *Cun Ren* 'village people' refer respectively to the language and the people of this group. These are Chinese equivalents of the native forms [tshən^1 fɔn^1] 'language + village' and [ŋa:u^1 fɔn^1] 'people + village'.

The Cun language shows five tones in native words. These tones systematically reflex the PH tonal categories as shown in Table 22.3.5.1-1 (tone letters are as used in Ouyang (1998):

TABLE 22.3.5.1-1: CUN TONES IN HISTORICAL PERSPECTIVES

PH tones	A		B	C		D
Tone letter	1	4	5	3	4	2	4
Tone value	[35]	[13]	[21]	[42]	[13]	[33]	[13]

Examples:

	Cun	Yuanmen	Baoding	Heitu	Tones
name	phɛŋ^{35}	phiaŋ^{42}	phe:ŋ^{53}	pha:ŋ^{454}	A1
star	la:u^{13}	ra:u^{11}	ra:u^{53}	ra:u^{454}	A2
dry	khɔ^{21}	khauɯ^{51}	khauɯ^{55}	kheuɯ^{24}	B1
shoulder	vɔ^{21}	va^{131}	va^{55}	va^{24}	B2
water	nam^{42}	nam^{44}	nom^{11}	nom^{11}	C1
skirt	lin^{13}	rin^{13}	ri:n^{11}	ri:n^{11}	C2
full	thiək^{33}	thiʔ^{55}	thi:k^{55}	thi:ʔ^{45}	D1
centipede	lip^{13}	rip^{13}	ri:p^{55}	ri:p^{45}	D2

Some important phonological development in Cun can be noted as follows.

1. Cun shares a number of sound changes with Northern-Hlai varieties, including the nasal accretion from *χj- and *χw- to ɲ- and ŋ-:

		(NH)	(CH)	(SH)	
	Cun	Yuanmen	Baoding	Heitu	
thatch grass	ɲɔ^1	ɲa^4	hja^1	ha^1	*Xj-
worm	ɲan^5	ɲan^2	hjan^2	hen^2	*Xj-
mountain	ŋau^3	ɯo^6	hwou^3	hau^3	*Xw-

| hair (body) | ŋən¹ | ɯən⁴ | hun¹ | hun¹ | *Xw- |

Also similar to NH varieties, Cun often contrasts vowel height where CH and SH dialects distinguish vowel length:

		(NH)	(CH)	(SH)	
	Cun	Yuanmen	Zhongsha	Heitu	PH
centipede	lip⁴	rip⁸	ri:p⁷	ri:p⁷	*i:p
arm	khin¹	khin¹	khi:n¹	khi:n¹	*i:n
fly, v.	ben¹	ben¹	bin¹	bin¹	*in/n̻
spicy	het⁴	khet⁶	git⁷	rit⁷	*it/ʈ
hole	tshoŋ³	tshuŋ³	tshu:ŋ³	tshu:ŋ³	*u:ŋ
termite	lok⁴	plu?⁷	lu:?⁷	lu:?⁷	*u:k
neck	lɔŋ⁴	tsɔŋ⁶	zuŋ³	zoŋ³	*uŋ
stomach	bɔk⁴	pɔk⁸	puk⁷	mok⁷	*uk

PH *s- is reflexed as Cun *tθ-*. This *tθ-* becomes *tsh-* before the palatalized feature, which often developed secondarily from the influence of early palatal finals (e.g. *saʈ > tθiat > tshiat 'bird'). PH *s- usually becomes t- in CH and SH varieties.

		(NH)	(CH)	(SH)
	Cun	Yuanmen	Baoding	Heitu
thread, v.	tθɔk²	tshɔk⁷	tok⁷	tok⁷
wash	tθak2	tshɔ?⁷	to:k⁷	tak⁷
wart	tshuət²	tshut⁷	tu:ʈ⁷	tu:t⁷
bird	tshiat²	–	taʈ⁷	tat⁷

2. On the other hand, Cun has made a number of its own innovations. For instance, Cun has merged *s with *ɬ and *a with *aɯ (< al):

		(NH)	(CH)	(SH)	
	Cun	Yuanmen	Baoding	Heitu	
thread, v.	tθɔk²	tshɔk⁷	tok⁷	tok⁷	*s
wash	tθak²	tshɔ?⁷	to:k⁷	tak⁷	*s
blood	tθɔt²	ɬuat⁷	ɬa:ʈ⁷	da:t⁷	*ɬ
tongue	tθin³	ɬin³	ɬi:n³	di:n³	*ɬ

		(NH)	(CH)	(SH)	
	Cun	Yuanmen	Baoding	Heitu	PH
eye	hɔ¹	tsha¹	tsha¹	tsha¹	*a
thick	nɔ¹	na⁴	na¹	na¹	*a
dry	khɔ⁵	khaɯ⁵	khaɯ²	kheɯ²	*aʀ

| short (height) | thɔ³ | thauɯ³ | thauɯ³ | theuɯ³ | *aʀ |

3. Cun makes certain distinctions that are seldom found in other dialects. Cun shows two initial reflexes /h/ and /tsh/ corresponding to /tsh/ in other dialects. This distinction, which has to be reconstructed for PH, is also kept in Jiamao.

	Cun	Yuanmen	Baoding	Heitu	Jiamao
eye	hɔ¹	tsha¹	tsha¹	tsha¹	tou¹
four	hau³	tsho³	tshau³	tsha:u³	tiau¹
tail	tshɔt²	tshɔt⁷	tshuʈ⁷	tshut⁷	tshuɔt⁷
wear	tshat²	tshat⁷	tshat⁷	tshet⁷	tshɔ:t⁸

Cun has l- corresponding to fricatives (z- or ʐ-) or affricates (ts- < *dz-or *dʐ-) in other Hlai dialects. This suggests the reconstruction of PH palatal lateral fricative *ꞎ-:

	Cun	Yuanmen	Baoding	Heitu
neck	lɔŋ⁴	tsɔŋ⁶ < dz	zoŋ³	zoŋ³
ear	lai⁴	tsai⁴ < dz	zai¹	zai¹

In some words, Cun has palatalized reflexes where others have dental/alveolar initials:

	Cun	Yuanmen	Baoding	Heitu
rice	tshɔ⁵	tha⁵	tha²	tha²
face, nose	tseŋ¹	dɔŋ¹	daŋ¹	doŋ¹

To sum up, although having experienced enormous contact influence and borrowed a great amount of vocabulary from Chinese, Cun is linguistically a Hlai variety. It shares a number of phonological innovations with the Northern Hlai dialects. On the other hand, it shows certain developments that are not in evidence in other varieties. It remains to be seen whether Cun should be considered a primary subgroup that split off early from Proto-Hlai or one of the NH groups that was displaced early from the major areas of Hlai settlement and has since intermingled with the Chinese over a long period of time.

22.3.5.2. *Natou*

This variety is spoken in Dongfang county. Fu (1990) presented a list of around 70 words from this place; no new and substantial materials have been published since. The available data are thus very limited. Nonetheless, preliminary comparisons with other Hlai dialects seem to reveal that Natou possesses some characteristics of the Northern Hlai branch. The linguistic characteristics of Natou are described below.

1. Natou has four tones which correspond to PH tones as follows:

PH tones	A		B	C	D
Tone letter	1	4	2	3	7
Tone value	[11]	[21ʔ]	[42]	[25]	[21ʔ]

Examples:

	Natou	Yuanmen	Baoding	Heitu	Tones
seven	theu^{11}	thou^1	thou^1	thu^1	A1
dog	pa^{21} < b	pa^4 < b	pa^1	ma^1	A2
worm	ŋjen^{42}	ȵan^2	hjan^2	hen^2	B
black	dan^{25}	dam^3	dom^3	dom^3	C
blood	la$ʔ^7$	ɬuat^7	ɬa:t^7	da:t^7	D

2. Concerning final consonants, Natou shows more extensive changes than those of any other places. All proto stop finals (*-p, *-t, *-k), which have been preserved well in most Hlai dialects, have become glottal stop -ʔ and final *-m has merged to -n. These dramatic changes in final consonants are most likely to have arisen under influence of Chinese.

	Natou	Yuanmen	Baoding	Heitu	
worm	kɛʔ^7	kop^7	kɯp^7 (Ts)	kɯp^7	*-p
nose	khaʔ^7	khat^7	khat^7	khet^7	*-t
blood	laʔ^7	ɬuat^7	ɬa:t^7	da:t^7	*-ʈ
fall	thaʔ^7	thɔk^7	thok^7	thok^7	*-k
water	nan^3	nam^6	nom^3	nom^3	*-m
grass	kan^3	kan^6	kan^3	Nen^3	*-n
hang	liŋ^3	riŋ^6	ri:ŋ^3	ri:ŋ^3	*-ŋ

3. Natou shares Northern Hlai features such as the initial nasalization of PH *χj- and *χw-:

	(NH)	(CH)	(SH)	
	Natou	Yuanmen	Baoding	Heitu	
worm	ŋjen^2	ȵan^2	hjan^2	hen^2	*Xj-
hair (body)	ŋɛn^1	mjən^4	hun^1	hun^1	*Xw-
body	ŋun^1	mju:n^4	hu:n^1	hu:n^1	*Xw-

Also similar to NH varieties, Natou contrasts vowel height where CH and SH dialects distinguish vowel length:

	(NH)	(CH)	(SH)	
	Natou	Yuanmen	Baoding	Heitu	
fly, v.	ben^1	ben^1	benȵ^1	bin^1	*-iȵ
hang	liŋ^3	riŋ^6	ri:ŋ^3	ri:ŋ^3	*-i:ŋ
wing	phiʔ^7	phiʔ^7	phi:k^7	phi:ʔ^7	*-i:k
hair (body)	ŋɛn^1	mjən^4	hun^1	hun^1	*-un
body	ŋun^1	mjun^4	hu:n^1	hu:n^1	*-u:n

PH *s- has become f-. This PH *s- usually becomes *t- in CH and SH dialects.

	(NH)	(CH)	(SH)
	Natou	Yuanmen	Baoding	Heitu
buffalo	foi^3	tshou^3	tui^3	tui^3

4. On the other hand, Natou has experienced several changes of its own such as final consonant simplification described above. Other innovations include the following developments in initial consonants and vowels:

Velar/postvelar spirant initials become nasalized:

	Natou	Yuanmen	Baoding	Heitu	
ask	ŋan^4	kham^1	ga:m^1	ga:m^1	*ɣ
run	ŋeu^2	vou^2	gou^2	rou^2	*Rw

*pl- > pj-. This softening of medial -l- > -j- is known to occur in many Tai and Kam-Sui languages but is unique among Hlai dialects:

	Natou	Yuanmen	Baoding	Heitu
house	pjaŋ^3	ploŋ^3	ploŋ^3	–

*ɬ- > l-

	Natou	Yuanmen	Baoding	Heitu
blood	la?^{7}	ɬat^7	ɬa:ʈ^7	da:t^7
deep	lɔ?^{7}	ɬo?^{7}	ɬo:k^7	dak^7
many	lɔi^1	ɬu:i^1	ɬo:i^1	da:i^1

Natou has a central low vowel -a- where others have back rounded vowels (plus velars):

	Natou	Yuanmen	Baoding	Heitu	
fall	tha?^{7}	thɔk^7	thok^7	thok^7	*-uk
stomach	pa?^{7}	pɔk8	pok^7	mok^7	*-uk
house	pjaŋ^3	ploŋ^3	ploŋ^3	–	*-uŋ
neck	zaŋ^3	tsɔŋ^6	zoŋ^3	zoŋ^3	*-uŋ

In sum, Natou shows characteristics of the Northern Hlai branch, but more data are needed to confirm its place. The final consonants, which are relatively stable in most Hlai dialects, are drastically simplified in Natou; this reflects heavy contact with the Chinese.

22.4. OTHER LINGUISTICS FEATURES

22.4.1. Syntax

The study on the grammar and syntax of Hlai languages is still in its infancy. We may only note here some preliminary word order and typological features. Examples are from Baoding dialect unless indicated.

1. A sentence has a SVO order:

hou^1	tha:i^2	pa^1	'I beat the dog'
I	beat	dog	

2. A head noun precedes modifiers or adjuncts (including pronoun and demonstrative):

N + Adjective
pha³	len.¹	'good person'
person	good	

Noun + Demonstrative
tui³	nei²	'this buffalo'
buffalo	this	

N + Pronoun (possessive)
ploŋ³	hou¹	'my house'
house	I	

In dialects that have been heavily influenced from Chinese, the Chinese pattern may interfere. For instance, Cun has two ways to say 'my clothes'; the first type follows the N + Pronoun order to indicate possession and the second type shows the Chinese pattern Pronoun + di + Head N, where /di/ is a particle corresponding to Chinese 的 /de/.

vəŋ⁴	kə⁵	or	kə⁵	di²	vəŋ⁴
clothes	I		I	part.	clothes

3. A quantitative phrase usually has a classifier; the typical order is Numeral + Classifier + Head Noun:

ɬau³	laŋ¹	pa¹	'two dogs'
two	clf	dog	

4. A Head Verb may be preceded by an adverb (including directional verbs such as /hei¹/ 'go' and /puːn¹/ 'come'):

meu¹	khuːn²	hei¹		'you go first'
you	first	go		

meu¹	tai³	tai³	fei¹	'(you) walk slowly'
you	slow	slow	walk	

hou¹	hei¹	luːi¹	nom³	'I go down to the river'
I	dir.'go'	descend	river(water)	

5. Comparisons and experience. The morpheme /dua³/ (literally 'pass, cross over') may indicate a comparative degree when following a descriptive verb or adjective. When following certain groups of verbs, it may indicate experience.

meuu¹	phe:k⁷	dua³	hou¹		'You are taller than I'
you	tall	'pass'	I		

hou¹	la:i ³	dua³	meuu¹		'I have seen you'
I	see	'pass'	you		

Perfective may be indicated by using the morpheme /ba:i³/ (literally 'finish') before the verb. The final particle /ne¹/, similar to Chinese 了 /le/, is also usually added after the verb.

pai³	khai¹	ba:i³	zuu:m¹	ne¹
female	chicken	'finish'	(lay) egg	part.

'The hen has already laid an egg.'

6. Negation. The negative morpheme /ta¹/ precedes the verb or adjective:

ta¹	ɬo:i¹	'not much'
not	many	

hou¹	ta¹	hei¹	'I do not go'
I	not	go	

7. Prepositional phrases:

tsho:n ²	duu³	teuu¹	tsho¹	'put on the table'
put	part.'stay'	above	table	

tsoŋ³	duu³	fou¹	tshai¹	'sit under the tree'
sit	part.'stay'	under	tree	

22.4.2. Orthography

The orthography of the Hlai language was created in 1952, concurrent with the establishment of 'the Hainan Li-Miao Autonomous Prefecture'. This alphabetical system is partially modeled after the Pinyin or romanized system of Mandarin Chinese. Those who are familiar with Pinyin will notice the similar use of such graphs as b, d, g to represent IPA voiceless unaspirated stops /p t k/ while p, t, k are used to represent IPA voiceless aspirated stops /ph th kh/. A number of innovations were made, of course, since the sound inventories of the Hlai languages are different from those of Mandarin.

The Baoding dialect was selected as a standard for this system, though features in the other dialects were also taken into consideration. The phonetic values of the orthography in native words may be summarized as follows:

Consonants (initial)

bh	/ɓ/	dh	/ɗ/			gh	/g/
b	/p/	d	/t/	z,j*	/ts/	g	/k/
p	/ph/	t	/th/	c,q*	/tsh/	k	/kh/
f	/f/	hl	/ɬ/			h	/h/
m	/m/	n	/n/	ny	/ɲ/	ng	/ŋ/
v	/v/	r	/r/	dz	/z/		
w	/ʔw/	l	/l/	y	/ʔj/		

Notes:
*j and q are used for /ts/ and /tsh/ before the high front vowel -i-; elsewhere z and c are respectively used. For instance, jieu = /tsi:u/ 'savage, wild', zeeng = /tse:ŋ / 'ear of grain'; qien = /tshi:n/ 'stone', ca = /tsha/ 'eye'.

Complex initials are written by combining two graphs. For instance, bl = /pl/, hy = /hj/, hw = /hw/, ghw = /gw/, ngw = /ŋw/, etc.

Vowels

i	/i/*	uu	/ɯ/	u	/u/*
e	/e/			o	/o:/*
		a	/a/		

Notes:
*i is pronounced /e/ before /-ɲ,-ȶ/, e.g., bhin = /ɓeɲ/ 'to fly/, ghit = /geȶ/ 'spicy'.
*u is pronounced /o/ when followed by grave finals, e.g., um = /om/, up = /op/, ung = /oŋ/, uk = /ok/. Elsewhere it is pronounced /u/, e.g., un = /un/.
*o is pronounced /o/ only in the diphthong ou /ou/; elsewhere it represents /o:/.

Length is represented by adding the graph -e- after the vowels. For instance, a = /a/, ae = /a:/, i = /i/, ie = /i:/, etc.

Diphthongs are written by combining two graphs, e.g. ia = /ia/, ua = /ua/, ai = /ai/, auu = /aɯ/, etc.

Final consonants

-m	/m/	-n	/n ɲ/	-ng	/ŋ/
-p	/p/	-t	/t ȶ/	-k	/k/

The distinction between alveolar and palatal endings has been neutralized in the orthography. For instance, the form /dhat/ may represent either [dat] 'real' or [daȶ] 'insipid' in Baoding. Note also that the voiceless unaspirated stops [p t k] are written with the graphs -p, -t, -k when they occur as finals; when they occur as initials these stops are represented by b-, d-, g-.

Tones
In native words, Hlai tonal categories A, B, C, and D are represented by the symbols as shown in Table 22.4.2-1. The Hlai tonal categories B, and C are marked with the graphs -x and -s at the end of the forms; when nothing is added, the form indicates tone A. Tone D syllables are readily shown by stop endings.

TABLE 22.4.2-1: ORTHOGRAPHY OF HLAI TONES

Tonal categories	*A	*B	*C	*D
Graphs	zero	-x	-s	zero
Tonal values (Baoding)	[53]	[55]	[11]	[55]

Examples:

hlaeu	/ɬaːu⁵³/	burn, v.
hlaeux	/ɬaːu⁵⁵/	die
hlaeus	/ɬaːu¹¹/	heart
hlaet	/ɬaːɰ⁵⁵/	blood

ABBREVIATIONS

B	Be
By	Buyang
K	Kam
Kd	Kra-Dai
Lh	Laha
Lk	Lakkja
Lz	Laozhai (Gelao)
Ph	Paha
PH	Proto-Hlai
S	Sui

REFERENCES

Benedict, Paul K. (1942) 'Thai, Kadai, and Indonesian: A new alignment in Southeastern Asia', *American Anthropologist* 44: 576-601.

— (1975) *Austro-Thai Language and Culture, with a Glossary of Roots*, New Haven: HRAF Press.

Burusphat, Somsonge (ed.) (2003) *Hlai (Li)-Chinese-Thai-English dictionary*, Nakhonpathom: Mahidol University.

— (2004) 'Hlai orthography', paper presented at the 14th Southeast Asian Linguistics Society Conference, Bangkok.

Calder, J. (1882) 'Notes on Hainan and its aborigines', *China Review* 11: 42-50.

Edmondson, Jerold A. (1986) 'A computer-aided acoustic study of tones and initials in Kam, Lakkja, and Lhai', in Hartmann, J. and C. Compton (eds) *Tai Studies in Honor of the 77th Birthday of William J. Gedney*, Dekalb: Northern Illinois University, Program in Southeast Asian Studies.

Fu Zhennan (1983) 'The Cun speech on the west coast of Hainan island', *Minzu Yuwen* 4: 68-71. [In Chinese]

— (1990) 'Natou, a dialect island of Li', *Minzu Yuwen* 4: 14-18. [in Chinese]

Gao Daxian (1984) 'The Li people of Hainan island', in *China's Minority Nationalities* (1), Beijing: China Reconstructs.

Gedney, William J. (1967) 'Future directions in Tai linguistics', paper presented before the Thai-Lao group, UCLA.

Haudricourt, André G. (1984) 'La tonologie du Li de Hainan', *Minzu Yuwen* 4: 17-25.

Henri, BC (1883) 'The close of a journey through Hainan', *China Review* 12: 109-124.

— (1886) *Lingnam*, London: S.W. Partridge and Co.

Jeremiassen, Carl G. (1892) 'Loi aborigines of Hainan and their speech', *China Review* 20: 296-305.

L-Thongkum, Theraphan (2001) 'The Tai-Kadai peoples of Hainan island and their languages', in Tingsabadh K. and A. Abramson (eds) *Essays in Tai Linguistics, 189-204*, Bangkok: Chulalongkorn University Press.

Lacouperie, Terrain de (1887) *The Languages of China before the Chinese*, London: David Nutt.

Li Fang-Kuei (1965) 'The Tai and Kam-Sui languages', in G. B. Milner and E. J. Henderson (eds) *Indo-Pacific Linguistic Studies*, Amsterdam: North Holland Publishing Co., vol.1: 148-179.

Ma Yin (ed.) (1989) *China minority nationalities*, Beijing: Foreign Language Press.

Matisoff, James A. (1988) 'Proto-Hlai initials and tones: a first approximation', in J. A. Edmondson and D. B. Solnit (eds) *Comparative Kadai: Linguistic Studies beyond Tai*, Dallas: Summer Institute of Linguistics and the Univeristy of Texas at Arlington, 286-321.

Maspero, H. (1933) 'Review of Savina, Lexique day-français', *Bulletin de l'École Française d'Extrême-Orient* 34.3: 228-236.

Ostapirat, Weera (2000) 'Proto-Kra'. *Linguistics of the Tibeto-Burman Area 23.1* (monograph).

— (2004) 'Proto-Hlai Sound System and Lexicons', *Language and Linguistics Monograph Series* W-4, 121-75.

Ouyang Jueya (1998) *The Cun language*, Shanghai: Shanghai Yuandong Press. [in Chinese]

Ouyang Jueya and Fu Zhennan (1988) 'On the issue of the genetic classification of Cun speech in Hainan island', *Minzu Yuwen* 1: 8-17. [In Chinese]

Ouyang Jueya and Zheng Yiqing (1983) *Survey of the Li languages*, Beijing: Chinese Academy of Social Sciences. [In Chinese]

Parker, Edward H. (1889) 'Siamese words in Hainan and China', *China Review* 18: 198.

— (1890) 'The Li aborigines of K'iung-Shan', *China Review* 19: 383-387.

Savina, F. M. (1929) *Monographie de Hainan*, Hanoi: Imprimerie d'Extrême-Orient.

— (1931) 'Lexique day-français, accompagne d'un petit lexique français-day et d'un tableau des differences dialectales', *Bulletin de l'École Française d'Extrême-Orient* 31: 103-199.

Shafer, Robert (1957) 'Quelque equations phonetiques pour les langues li d'Hainan', *Rocznik Orientalistyczny* 21: 385-407.

Solnit, David B. (1982) 'The nasal and fricative initials of the Li languages: a new type of conditioning for tonal partition?', paper presented at the 15th International Sino-Tibetan Languages and Linguistics Conference, Beijing.

Stübel, Hans (1937) *Die Li-Stämme der Insel Hainan: ein Beitrag zur Volkskunde Süd-Chinas, unter Mitwirkung von P. Meriggi*, Berlin: Klinkhart und Biermann.

Swinhoe, Robert (1871) 'The aborigines of Hainan', *Journal of the Royal Asiatic Society, Northern China Branch* 7: 25-40.

Wang Jun (ed.) (1984) *Outline of the Kam-Tai languages*, Beijing: Nationalities Publishing House. [in Chinese]

Wang Li and Qian Sun (1951) 'Preliminary study of the White Sand Li language of Hainan', *Lingnan Science Journal* 2.11: 253-300.

Wen Mingying (1994) 'The cultural history of the Li', in Li Dezhu (ed.) *Cultural History of the Ethnic Minorities in China*, Liaoning People's Publishing House.

Zheng Yiqing and Ouyang Jueya (eds) (1990) *The Hlai-Chinese Dictionary*, Chengdu: Sichuan Nationality Press.

APPENDICES

A. TONAL CORRESPONDENCES AMONG HLAI DIALECTS

Tones	A		B		C		D	
Dialects	1	2	1	2	1	2	1	2
Heitu	454		24		11		45	
Baoding	53		55		11		55	
Zhongsha	53		55		11		55	
Tongshi	33	11	51	121	55	14	55	13
Qiandui	33	11	42	21	35	213	42	21
Baocheng	44	22	53	31	35	213	44, 53	31
Xifang	53		55		24		55	
Baisha	11		31		33		11	
Yuanmen	42	11	51	131	44	13	55	13
Cun	35	13	21		42	12	33	13
Natou	11	21	42		25		21	

* Baocheng's tonal split in the *D1 series is conditioned by vowel length: [44] for syllables with short vowels and [53] for syllables with long vowels.

B. MAP OF HAINAN ISLAND AND
THE HAINAN LI-MIAO AUTONOMOUS PREFECTURE

CHAPTER TWENTY-THREE

KRA OR KADAI LANGUAGES

Jerold A. Edmondson

23.1. INTRODUCTION

The Kra or Kadai language group is a relatively uncelebrated stock with small populations living in South China's Guizhou Province, Yunnan Province and Guangxi Zhuang Autonomous Region, as well as in Vietnam's Cao Bằng Province, Hà Giang Province, Lào Cai Province, and Sơn La Province.[1] Unlike the better known Kam-Tai Branch, the Kra data and history have been little discussed. In the listings below we have given their names in English, Chinese, and Vietnamese. There are seven languages in this group, which are listed in order of the number of speakers:

Lachi, 拉基, La Chi, 10,000 speakers
Gelao, 仡佬 Cơ Lao, in all countries, 7,900 speakers
Paha, 巴哈, Langjia 郎架, Ecun 峨村, Yalhong 雅郎 (collectively Buyang 布央), 2,000 speakers
Laha, 拉哈 La Ha, 1,400 speakers
Pubiao, 普标, Qabiao, Pu Peo, 700 speakers
En, 侬文, Nùng Vên, 250 speakers

The total number of speakers amounts perhaps to 22,000.

The Gelao ethnicity and some of their terms were mentioned in Chinese chronicles and gazetteers from a period well before the Tang Dynasty (618-907 AD). Scholars believe the Gelao precursors were those people recorded during Han times (206 BC to 220 AD) as the 濮 Pu and later the 僚 Lao. Many lexical items from the Lao find reflexes in some forms of the Gelao language, e.g. *lán-gān* 阑干. For example, the Book of the Latter Han Dynasty: Chapter on the SW Barbarians 後漢書 西南夷卷 Houhan Shu: Xinan Yijuan states that the Lao used densely woven flax (jute or linen), which in Gelao is still called la^{21} or lie^{33} (Zhang 1993: 3). Also the name *gānlán* 干兰 is used for a multistory house. Perhaps, these two characters were used to record this name according to the *qiēyùn* 切韵 'cut the rhyme' practice of that day in which the initial consonant of the first syllable is to be added to the rhyme and sometimes the entire second syllable so [k-an] + [lan] is a way transcribing *k+lan*. Ostapirat 2000 has recently provided detailed descriptions and reconstructions of this language group reconstructing 'house' as *kran^A and the form *klan* is a close approximation of that, as *l* and *r* are not clearly distinguished in this geographic area. The recorded history

1 The research reported on here has been sponsored by a 1995 grant NEH RT-21754-95 from the National Endowment for the Humanities and by the grants SBR 9511285 and SBR 9729043 from the National Science Foundation to the author and Dr Kenneth J. Gregerson all entitled 'Languages of the Vietnam-China Borderlands'. I wish also to acknowledge the assistance of Profs. Nguyễn Văn Lợi, Hoàng Văn Ma, and To Văn Thang, who arranged and accompanied me on the field trips that led to the data and analysis here. I also wish to thank Ms Shen Yu-May, who has provided me with data on several other kinds of Gelao from her own fieldwork elicitation.

of the the Lachi is not as long, as they are thought to have moved about 200-300 years ago into Chinese territory in Yunnan from locations in Vietnam called 麥布 Maibu,麥督 Maidu, and 麥哈 Maiha. Reports about the other Kra languages are of much more recent provenience. For example, the Buyang complex appeared in Liang 1990 with deeper studies by Li Jinfang 2000. The En or Nùng Vên language was reported only in Edmondson, Nguyễn, and Hoàng 1999. Indeed the data presented here for the first time on En is based on the author's own fieldwork investigations as well as my data on Qabiao, Laha, Lachi and Gelao; Buyang materials are taken from Li Jinfang, some Gelao material from my student Shen Yu-may, and some materials from Ostapirat 2000.

Ostapirat 2000 has also suggested a new name for the group Kra. He argues that the lexical item *kra C* 'person' in many of Kra languages is descended from *kraC 'people' in the parent language, comparing this root to Standard Thai *khaa Cl* 'slave, servant', which originally meant 'people, common people', who were in many cases vanquished during the Tai expansion over their territory. During my fieldwork on the Noong Lay Laha, Mr Sam, one of the local sages and an important informant for present and past fieldwork, noted that the *khla Cl* in *khla phlao* 'their autonym' meant 'slave' in the Black Thai of their surrounding neighbors.

23.2. KRA OR KADAI AND THE KAM-SUI BRANCH

While in the past there was some uncertainty whether this language group was related to Kam-Sui and Tai languages, that doubt has in recent years been definitely put to rest by Ostapirat (2000). The Kra or Kadai languages evidence several hallmark features that unequivocally confirm that Kra and Kam-Tai are descended from a common parent language. Some of the most important shared phonological and lexical features are:

I.   Kra and Kam-Tai languages have a similar tonal organization that enables the reconstruction of a common parent tonal system from which both are derived.

II.   Kra and Kam-Tai both have a special kind of glottal constriction at the end of a syllable that is found in vocabulary descended from the proto-C tone. This phenomenon is independent of the loss of coda in some Kra languages in items in the original D tone category, which also results in a glottal constriction.

III. Kra and Kam-Tai rhymes may be long or short when they are followed by a consonantal syllable coda /-p -t -k -m -n -ŋ -l -i -u/. Moreover, length is present before coda in the conservative Laha language of the village at Noong Lay, which has preserved a coda –l. This is also found in the Saek language of Nakhon Phanom at Ban Phay Lom, Thailand (Hudak 1993).

IV.   Kra and Kam-Tai share a great many lexical items, some in common with Tai, some in common with Kam-Sui, and some in common with both groups. There are also many etyma whose origins are unique to Kra languages and not belonging to the set it shares with Kam-Sui or Tai vocabulary.

V.   There is evidence in both Kra and Kam-Tai that original forms in the proto language may have included some sesqui-syllabics (weak first syllable plus strong second syllable) along with monosyllables.

The first of these important pieces of evidence connecting Kra with Kam-Tai is the tonal organization. Comparative evidence tells us that there were four original tones, called in

Kam-Tai studies *A, *B, *C, and *D. In Kra languages there are also these four tone categories. In both groups the *A, *B, *C, and *D tones often go on to split into high and low tone reflexes, depending upon whether the initial consonant was voiceless or voiced, respectively. Generally speaking, Kra languages tend to evidence fewer such tone splits than Kam-Tai. Moreover, despite many exact correspondences in A, B, C, and D tonal category between Kam-Tai and Kra, there are also many cases of presumed cognates that show conflicting tonal categories:

Gloss	Saek	Sui	En	Laha NL/TM	Proto-Kra
'fish'	pla^{A1}	pa^{A1}	pən^{A1} la^{A1}	bla^{A2}/ma^{A2} la^{A2}	*p-la^A
'ear'	rua^{A2}	qha^{A1}	khe^{53} ɾa^{33}	khla^{A2}/ka^{A2} ha^{A2}	*k-ra^A
'bone'		laak^{D1}	ʔdək^{D1}	dak^{D2}/thak^{D2}	*dək^D
'gallbladder'	ʔbli^{A1}	ʔdo^{B1}	ʔdi^{A1}	ʔdəi^{D1}/dəi^{D1}	*m-ʔdi^A
'navel'	ʔdua^{A1}	ʔdwɔ^{A1}	ʔdau^{A1}	dau^{A2}/thau^{A2}	*m-da?^{A}
'to forget'	–	–	ʔdap^{D1}	drap^{D2}/kɔ^{A2} thap^{D2}	*drap^D
'village'	ʔbaan^{C1}	ʔbaan^{C1}	–	ʔbaan^{C1}/faan^{C1} (ph>f)	–

The second common feature of Kra and Kam-Tai is glottal constriction in vocabulary descended from proto-C tone, a special characteristic connected with this tone category in ʔKra and Tai (Kam-Sui does not show it). We indicate this feature with a glottal stop placed after the numbers representing the pitch trajectory, e.g. Laha *ma$^{41?}$* 'horse'.

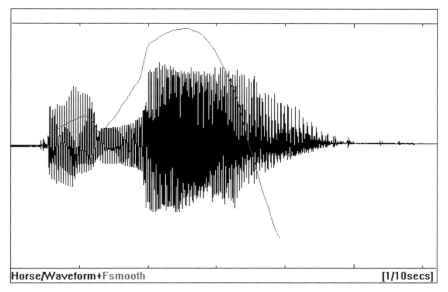

Horse/Waveform+Fsmooth   [1/10secs]

FIGURE 23.2-1: LALA NOONG LAY WAVEFORM AND PITCH TRACK *tu^{33}ma$^{41?}$* 'CLF-HORSE'

In Figure 23.2-1, one can see the rapidly decreasing waveform with a few very weak glottal vibrations at the end of the second syllable. Of course, *ma^{C2}* 'horse' is an example of a *Wanderwort* that appears widely in many families of E and SE Asia. But glottal constriction is also found in *C vocabulary not shared with Tai, cf. the example *ʔuŋ$^{41?}$* 'water'.

The third feature Kra and Kam-Tai share is vowel length contrast before codas. Many Kra languages have simplified their word structure shapes to permit only open syllables. However, Laha, Buyang, Qabiao, Paha, and En preserve codas and rhymes sufficiently to indicate that Kra languages once had a syllable coda as a possible word structure as well. Interestingly, there is evidence that vowels before final -*l* also distinguished length. One feature of Kra that is not found in Kam-Tai is the advanced state of atrophy of the right side of the syllable, especially in Gelao and Lachi, in which many final voiceless stops (though at times preserved as a final glottal catch) and even many of the nasals have disappeared through phonological change. The lack of codas has led to sound changes in the rhymes and probably the genesis of additional tones.

The common lexicon of Kra and Kam-Tai will be illustrated copiously below so I shall pass over this for the moment.

The fifth shared feature is the evidence for the reconstruction of prefixes or augmentative consonants before the stem, which may reflect a word structure composed of a weak syllable before a strong one. Ostapirat (2000) has reconstructed proto-Kra forms such as: *l-ma^A (*lal^A-ma^A) 'tongue', *k-ra^A 'ear', *x-ma^A 'dog', *x-mu^A 'pig', *p-la^A 'fish', *m-ɖjan^A 'moon', *d-la^C 'near', *k-li^A 'far', and *m-ru^A 'eight'. Kam-Tai also has this feature, which is most clearly seen in archaic Kam-Sui languages Sui and Lakkja (Lakkia). As was shown in Edmondson and Yang (1988), there is a systematic alternation between Sui and Lakkja forms such that Lakkja manifests a consonant with a nasalized vowel in the same places where Sui has a complex initial (cf. Edmondson and Yang 1988: 151, 152):

Proto-Form	Lakkja	Sui	Gloss	Lakkja	Sui	Gloss
*kh-ma^A	khwõ^1	m̥a^1	'dog'	kũːi^1	ʔmi^1	'bear' (n.)
*kh-mu^A	khũ^1	m̥u^1	'pig'	kjə^3	ʔna^3	'before, face'
*kh-ŋai^A	khjẽi^1	ŋ̊ai^1	'move'	kɔm^2	ʔŋam^1	'hold in mouth'
*kh-nep^D	khẽp^7	n̥ip^7	'stir fire'			

These examples should be compared to those without a prefix:

Lakkja	Sui	Gloss
mie^2	mja^1	'hand'

As these examples show, Lakkja has kh- plus nasalized vowel where Sui has a voiceless nasal, and Lakkja has k- plus nasalized vowel where Sui has a preglottalized nasal, suggesting perhaps the existence of an initial preconsonant, cf. proto-Kra 'dog' and 'pig' for similar structures.

Finally, it must be pointed out that Hlai, cf. Ostapirat (Chapter 22 of this volume), possesses features that would put it at a greater linguistic distance from Kra and Kam-Sui. It possesses the codas /n, t/, which must have disappeared in Kra and Kam-Tai. There are other differences: d ~ ł are not found in Kra or Kam-Sui. Also Hlai seems to have undergone a rather different tonal development than Kra and Kam-Tai. So it seems that the Hlai language must be accorded a place more distant from Kra and Kam-Tai.

Having tentatively located Kra within the wider family, I now turn to discussing the individual languages. In the following I will concentrate on examples of new data, as Ostapirat (2000) has done much to establish the relationship among members of this group. We now turn to examining information about the members of this group.

23.3. GELAO

The Gelao language has the largest number of speakers, perhaps numbering 7,900. The Gelao people are settled in territory from northern Guizhou Province to the border areas of northern Vietnam in Hà Giang Province. Mostly, they live today in mixed villages with other groups of the area and no longer have mono-ethnic settlements of their own. One of the consequences of this pattern is that there is today great diversity in the languages in various places. Usually, speakers from one village are unable to communicate with Gelao people from even nearby locations. Some varieties of Gelao are highly endangered.

23.3.1. Phonology and subdivisions

According to Ostapirat (2000: 26) there are three subvarieties of Gelao, which he labels *Southwestern* (represented in our data by Dồng Văn District Phố Là Village), *Central* (represented by Wanzi near Anshun City in Guizhou Province, China, autonym *klau*^{55}, data from He 1983), and *Northern*, represented here by Bigong. We include in our data as well examples from Red Gelao and *ha*^{53} *kei*^{33} Gelao at Sanchong in Guangxi Province (known as Green Gelao in Vietnam). During a visit to Hà Giang Province, Vietnam, May 25, 1997, Edmondson was able to gather data on a type then unreported in China. There are only two villages in Vietnam (Na Khê and Bìch Đich of Yên Minh District) where this language is still spoken by perhaps 50 people and one village in China at Fanpo in Malipo County of Yunnan Province, cf. Edmondson and Li 2003. Often brides are sent back and forth between these two non-contiguous places in order to ensure the continuation of the language and culture. These people call themselves *va*^{35} *nt ɯ*^{31}.

The differences among the three branches are quite large. The SW forms have retained voicing in A2, B2, C2, and D2 tone categories and have even developed prenasalization. The northern forms show a development of *t* to *z* (called *spirantal reflexes* by Ostapirat), e.g. 'eye' *ze*^{44} at Qiaoshang (N) and *zau*^{31} at Bigong (N) vs. *tau*^{33} at Laozhai (SW), and voiceless nasals to uvulars, e.g. 'dog' *^{N}qwau*^{31} at Qiaoshang (N) vs. *ɳ*^{45} at Laozhai (SW). The fricative initials in northern Gelao types are reflexes of retroflex initial of the parent language, cf. Ostapirat (2000: 26). This contrast has been merged in both SW and Central varieties and thus represents a shared innovation, suggesting perhaps that SW and C are slightly more closely related to one another than to the northern type. Another major Gelao type was left unclassified in Ostapirat, those varieties of Gelao with autonym *Hagei, Hoki*, etc. Sanchong is an example of this type, where they call themselves *ha*^{53} *kei*^{53}. Shen (2003) shows, however, that Sanchong undergoes the same changes as those found in Wanzi for the rhyme *-ak*, which in both places has become *-aŋ*. Some examples descended from *-ɔk are: 'bone' (in the table below), Sanchong *liaŋ*^{53} and Wanzi *laŋ*^{31} 'deep' from proto-Kra *(h)lɔk D2, Ostapirat (2000: 235), and Sanchong *ntʂaŋ*^{33} and Wanzi *tsaŋ*^{31} 'to hear', from proto-Kra *dʐɔk D2, Ostapirat (2000: 241). Therefore, it appears that the classification of the Green Gelao types has been solved; they are Central Gelao types.

As for the Red Gelao language exemplified below, it is indeed a piece of good fortune that we have been able to gather data on this smallest member of the Gelao complex while there are still some fluent speakers, though admittedly we possess at present only a limited word list. The Red Gelao people of call themselves *va*^{35} *ntə*^{31} Gelao-red with *va*^{35} representing a C1 tone and corresponding to *klau*^{55} of Wanzi; it probably represents a form derived from *vei*^{35} 'person' with assimilated final. It shares the feature of prenasalization of voiced stop initials, such as *nte*^{35} *xə*^{31} B1 'head' and *ma*^{35} *ndu*^{55} A1 'star'. Also, there are examples of retained voiceless nasals and laterals: *ma*^{13} *m̥a*^{31} 'flea', *qa*^{35} *n̥ua*^{31} 'nose', *ʔu*^{31} *ɬən*^{35} 'heart'. The development of voiceless nasals from the parent language into Red Gelao has taken some distinctive turns when velars are involved. Specifically, Red Gelao has evolved a rule of that moves a velar nasal or resonant such as /-r-/ in an initial consonant cluster with h- or x- to word final or coda position or perhaps. A more precise statement would be that the opening of the velic has been delay to the word final position. Consider the examples below (reconstructions from Ostapirat 2000): 'pig' *x-mu^{A} > foŋ^{44} or mɔŋ^{55}, 'belly' *hmok^{D} > fou$^{31?}$, 'dog' *xma^{A} > xaŋ^{44}, 'head' *krai^{B} > xɯ^{31}, 'road' *kron^{A} > xi^{44}, 'ripe' *hŋwu^{B} > xoŋ^{31}, 'wait' *hŋa(ɯ)^{A} > xiŋ^{44};

Red Gelao has some more conservative traits than SW Gelao in preserving final nasals (there are examples of both *-n* and *-ŋ*), e.g. *ɬən*^{35} C1 'heart', *ʔua*^{35} *hən*^{35} C1 'mushroom' and *fən*^{31} B1 'sticky', but *ʔu*^{55} *naŋ*^{55} A2 'salt', (though *pan 'teeth' A1 has become *poŋ*^{55} A1) while eliminating most initial clusters, e.g. *pl-* in favor of *p-*, cf. *pu^{35}* 'boil, ulcer'. Moreover, we noted that is has innovated a rule of nasal transportation and of vowel breaking from original *-a not found in SW Gelao types. It does not follow Central Gelao types in having reflexes of the original *-ak become *-aŋ* in some others: *ma^{13} ntua^{31}* 'bone' from *dək^{D} and *qai$^{13?}$* 'taro' from *p-ɣak^{D} (cf. Ostapirat 2000). Clearly Red Gelao is close to SW Gelao but seems to differ from it at the same time. Thus we will have leave open the question whether Red Gelao constitutes a separate branch of the parent proto-Gelao language. It seems to us likely instead that it is a distant sister to SW types such as White Gelao.

A view of Central and SW Gelao can be exemplified by the following set of data:

Gloss	Central	Southwestern	Red Gelao	Central
'autonym'	klau^{55} C1 (Wanzi)	te^{45} lə^{33} (Lz/PL)	va^{35} ntə^{31} (Na Khê)	ha^{53} kei^{33} (Sc)
'blood'	pla D1	plɑ^{31}/plɑ$^{31?}$ D1	pai$^{31?}$ D1	pla^{253} D1
'bone'	toŋ D2		ma^{35} ndua$^{31?}$D1	ta^{31} taŋ^{33} D2
'boil' (n.)	plau C1	plau^{33} C1	li^{44} pu^{35} C1	–
'face'	lau B2		ʔu^{55} le^{52} B2	mble^{33} B2
'ear'	zau A2	ʑi^{35}/ze^{35} A2	lo^{55} mlaŋ^{55} A2	tʂo^{35} A2
'head'	kla B1	ʔrə^{31}/ʔe^{31} B1	nde^{35} xɯ^{31} B1	bu^{33} ke^{53} B1
'intestine'	sai C1	çi^{33}/si^{33} C1	ʔa^{35} çi^{35} C1	sai^{33} C1
'leg'	qau A1		la^{55} qɯ^{55} A1	bu^{31} ko^{35} A1
'nose'	ɲtɕe D1	–/mæ$^{31?}$ D1	qa^{35} ɲuæ$^{31?}$ D1	n̥i^{53} D1
'dog'	mpau A1	m̥^{45}/hm^{55} A1	xaŋ^{55} A1	hm^{35} A1
'pig'	mpa A1	hỹ^{45}/hn̥^{55} A1	foŋ^{55} A1	mau^{35} A1
'fire'	pai A1	–/–	ʔa^{35} pi^{55} A1	pai^{35} A1
'star'	zoŋ A2	–/ndu^{55} A1	ma^{35} ndu^{55} A1	tʂa^{35} A1
'water'	ʔəɯ C2	–/ʔŋ^{33} C1	ʔaŋ^{35} C1	ʔm^{53} C1
'heavy'	xen A1	qo^{45}/ko^{45}	li^{55} koŋ^{55} A1	çe^{35} A1
'raw'	te D2	dæ^{31}/dæ$^{31?}$ D2	nte^{31} D2	nte^{31} ti^{35} D2
'drink' (v)	han C1	–/ndzɑ^{33}	Nqaŋ^{35} C1	haŋ^{53} C1
'one'	tsɿ C1	–/tɕi^{33} C1	tsə^{35} C1	sɿ^{53} C1
'two'	su A1	–/sæ^{33}	se^{55} A1	ʂa^{35} A1
'three'	ta A1	tɤu^{45}/tau^{45}	tua^{55} A1	tau^{35} A1
'four'	pu A1	pu^{45}/pu^{45}	pu^{55} A1	pu^{35} A1
'five'	mpu A2	mlen^{35}/mlæn^{35}	maŋ^{55} A2	mei^{31} A2
'six'	nan A1	–/–	łoŋ^{55} A1	ɳaŋ^{31} A2
'seven'	tu A1	–	te^{55} A1	tʂau^{35} A1
'eight'	vla A2	–	wu^{55} A2	zau^{31} A2
'nine'	səɯ B1	–	ʂe^{31} B1	ʂwo^{53} B1
'ten'	pe D1	–/–	kwe^{31} D1	sɿ^{53} pe^{53} D1

23.4. LACHI

The Lachi language was spoken by about 10,300 people, of which 7863 lived in Vietnam according to the 1990 census and 2500 in China according to a count taken in 1995 (Li 2000: 6). The Chinese Lachi live in Maguan County of Yunnan Province. We have data from two different locations. In China the Lachi call themselves *li^{35} pu^{44} ljo^{44}*, whereas in Vietnam the usual autonym is *qu^{32} te^{453}*. The etymon *qu^{32}* means 'person', probably from the root *khra C1, cf. Ostapirat (2000). In China the Flowery Lachi live at Jinchangzhen Zhongzhai 金厂中寨 and Sanjiajie 三家街; the Chinese Lachi live at Jiahanqing of Niulongshan 夹寒箐 (牛龙山), at Dujiaozhai 独脚寨, Qianchang 铅厂, Shi'er Daohe 十二道河, Laozhai 老寨, Renhezhen of Baishiyan 仁和镇 (白石岩), Shiqiao 石桥, and Huomuqing 火木箐; the Pocket Lachi live at Nanlaoxiang of Busu 南捞乡 (布苏), and the Red Lachi live at

Xiaobazizhen of Tianpeng 小坝子镇 (田棚) and Lajie 拉劫. In Vietnam the Lachi are an officially recognized minority group and live in Hà Giang Province, Hoàng Su Phì District at Xín Mần Township at Bản Phùng (Long Haired Lachi), Bản Pang, and Bản Máy (White Lachi), and Bản Dìu (Black Lachi). A large number of Lachi were resettled from the Vietnam-China border area to Bắc Quang near the southern border of Hà Giang Province. I was told that Vietnamese scholars are not able to find speakers of White Lachi any longer. The analysis here is based on Long Haired Lachi and Black Lachi.

Ostapirat (2000) suggests that Lachi might be divided into three types: the Northern, which includes the Chinese, or Flowery type, the Central or White Lachi, such as those at Bản Máy and Bản Pang, and the Southern or Long Haired and Black Lachi, which includes Bản Phùng and Bản Dìu. There is very little data available for the Central kinds (perhaps some vocabulary recorded by French colonial officials Bonifacy 1906 and Lajongière 1906, but we also agree that Bản Phùng and Bản Dìu are very similar and have important innovations not found in the Northern kinds. For comparison, consider this list of items from Ostapirat (2000) and our field data:

Kra	Northern Lachi			Central Lachi		Southern Bản Phùng	
*p	pje	A1	'fire'	pje	A1	pji	A1
*t	tje	B1	'ash'			te	B1
*ṭ	tā	A1	'egg'	tā	A1	tā	A1
*k	ko	D1S	'foot'	ko	D1S	qə	B1
	kho	D1S	'monkey'	ko	D1S	ko	D1S
	ku̱	C1		qu	C1	qu/qu	A1
*ʔ	ʔi	C1	'water'			ʔi	C1
*b	pɦu	B2	'shoulder'	pu	B2	phụ	B2
*d	tɦija̱	D2S	'bone'			thɔ$^{452?}$	
*ḍ	tɦije̱	D2	'raw'			thə$^{452?}$	
*dz	tɦijo	B2	'chopsticks'			thọ	B2
*s	su	A1	'two'			fu	A1
*ʃ	so	D1	'rope'			–	
*tʃ	sə	B1	'satisfied'				
*ts	tɕĩ	A1	'tobuy'			tɕĩ	A1
*ʒ	ʐɦo	B2	'y.brother'			jọ	B2
	tja	A1	'o.brother'	tja	A1	–	
*dʒ	ja	D2S	'tohear'			ʐọ	D2S
*ɟ	ʐɦu	C2	'grandmother'			ʐạ	C2
*dʐ	tɕɦi	A2	'mountain'			jọ	A2
*m	m	A2	'hand'			m̥	A2
*(ʔ)n	nɦĩ	A2	'six'			nị	A2
*ɳ	nɦijo	D2	'bird'	no$^{35?}$		nɔʔ	D2
*ṇ	n̥ɦijũ	A2	'salt'	ɳ̥ũ	A2		
*ŋ	ŋ̥	A2	'snake'			ŋ̥	A2
*hm	ma	D1	'flea'			maʔ	D1
*hŋ	ŋ	A1	'door'	ŋ	A1	ŋ	A1
*hl	lje	C1	'heart'	leʔ	C1	leʔ	C1
*l	lɦĩ	C2	'tosteal'	nụm	C2		
*ḷ	lɦiju	C2	'near'			lju	C2
*r	lɦu	A2	'ear'			lụ	A2
*v	vɦu	C2	'togo'			vụ	C2
*w	vɦã	A2	'sun'			ŋwã	A2
*pl	pjo	D1L	'blood'			pju	D1L
*pwl	pə̱	D1	'ten'			pwe	D1
*pr	phjo	B1	'silver'			phjo	B1

*pwr	phĩ	A1	'todie'			pe	A1
*bl	pɦii	D2	'tocarry'			phị?	D2
*tl	lje	C1	'waist'	la	C1		
kl	lə	D1	'fingernail'	lə	D1	lə	D1
kr	kho	A1	'house'	kho	A1	khu	A1
tr	to	C1	'nest'			to	C1
dt	tɕijã	A2	'b.louse'			thã	A2
kw	kwə	A1	'horn'	qə	A1	qə	A1
*kj	kei	C1	'iron'	qə	C1	qə	C1
*kӡ	ku	B1	'dry'	qhə	B1		
gj	kɦiu	C2	'skinny'				
ml	m̩	A2	'five'	m̩	A2		
mr	mɦei	A2	'ghost'				
hŋj	n̩a	D1	'nose'	n̩a	D1		
vj	vei	A2	'tall'				
wj	vã	A2	'tendon'				

Ostapirat (2000: 149) notes that in a few instances there is a velar initial with 'slight offglide' (kɦɣ-) as in *kɦɣei* C2 'ribs', which in Southern Lachi is *qɦɣei* C2 from Proto-Southwestern Kra *k-r-. Laha supports this analysis: Laha Noong Lay has *dak D khlaŋ C* and Laha Tamit has *thak le laŋ C*. Several differences between Northern and Southern Lachi are: (1) Central and Southern Lachi seems to have developed uvular reflexes for some consonants where Northern has velars, e.g. leg, excrement, iron, horn, dry, rib, etc; (2) Southern Lachi has labialized the initial *s* before *u* to *f* or *fw*, e.g. two, garlic, tail, etc. as well as some other initials, e.g. *ŋu B in *ɳɦii B2 to *ŋwi B2*; (3) the initial /l/ but not /hl/ l/ or C + l become /n/, e.g. steal, child, etc., and (4) Southern Lachi has simplified secondary articulations such the *tje B1 to *te* 'ash' and *kwə A1 to *qə 'horn'.

23.5. BUYANG AND EN

We now turn to the Buyang language group and En (also known as Nùng Vên). These Kra languages have been discovered only recently. They contribute important new perspectives on the family and its history.

Buyang was first reported by Liang Min (1990) though he states that he had encountered this people and language group in the 1950s. His data set was enriched by the work of Li Jinfang of The Central University of Nationalities in his doctoral dissertation (1999) and later in hisbook (1999). My data in this section were taken from this book.

The history of the En or [ain⁵³] language in the linguistic literature on this family is even shorter; its existence and status as a member of this group was discovered only in 1998. Before that this group had been named in *Các dân tộc ít ngời ở Viết Nam* (1978: 204), where it was treated in this largely anthropological work as a member of the Nùng subgroup of Central Tai languages called *Nùng Viển*. It is perhaps not surprising that the En (Nùng Vên) were grouped with the Nùng, since the Nùng group is a much larger minority. *Vên* or *Viển* in the *Nùng* language means 'earrings', perhaps signifying that the Nùng Vên women wear long, large, or distinctive ear ornamentation and they also are culturally influenced by their neighbors. By good fortune, Professor Hoàng Văn Ma of the Linguistic Institute of Vietnam, who is a Tày from Cao Bằng Province, Vietnam, heard this language on a trip to his home area and immediately recognized that En was not a Tai language but had no time to investigate it. A couple of years later in 1998, he accompanied us on our expedition to northern Cao Bằng, where we found them living in a single village called Nội Thun about 20 km northeast on foot from Hà Quảng City in Hà Quảng District, Cao Bằng Province at the location 22° 55' N, 106° 10' E. Mr Vường Văn Võ, our informant, 27 years of age, reported that the people do not have traditional accounts of their name, nor do they have any idea about where they once lived or how or when they arrived in Vietnam. This location is very near the China border at Jingxi County in southern Guangxi and lies less 100 km from Napo county seat (see below), where the Buyang live. In 2000 I visited Jingxi County in the area just opposite looking for other traces of the En without any success.

En will be treated with the Buyang languages for it is clear that they are all closely related. Indeed, Li Jinfang of The Central University of Nationalities in Beijing has told me that there are stories among the Buyang of Napo County in Guangxi that three brothers went their separate ways to escape from grinding poverty some generations ago. One brother went west from Napo into Yunnan Province; one stayed in Napo; and one went south into Vietnam. Perhaps, the En or Nung Ven represents the descendant of the third brother.

As for the Buyang languages themselves, Ostapirat considers one of the Buyang types to represent a separate language called *Paha*, which is spoken in Yunnan Province at Guangnan County 广南 at Diyu 底圩 Township Yangliancun Village 央连村. The other two described by Li Jinfang 1999 are: (1) *E-cun* and *Langjia* found respectively in Guangnan County 广南, Funing County 富宁, Gula 谷拉 Township at E-cun Village 峨村 and Langjia Village 郎架, and (2) *Yalhong* found in Guangxi in 那坡 Napo County. The isoglossic difference is that *r became z- and in Yalhong it developed further into a voiceless lateral ł-. Also, Yalhong has changed its rhymes dramatically.

Gloss	Yalhong	E-cun	En	Proto-Kra
'ear'	łou^{31}(A2)	ðaa^{44}	khe^{53}-ɽa^{33}	*k-ra A
'bee'	łaa^{53}	ðee^{44}	kə-ðe^{53}	*re A
'eye'	tau^{53}	taa^{24}	ta^{35}	*m-ṭa A
'two'	θau^{53}	θaa^{24}	ṣa^{35}	*sa A
'neck'	ẓaau^{31}	joo^{44}	kə-jau^{53}	*C-jo A
'dry'	qhɔ^{33}	haa45	hau^{54}	*kʒa B
'hand'	ɲiə31	ɲiak^{53}	ɲiik^{44}	
'excrement'	iə?53	?iak^{45}	?jik^{35}	*?ik D
'white'	uə?53	?ɔɔk^{53}	li-?uk^{35}	*r-?uk D

Ostapirat (2000) regards Paha as a language different enough from the others to warrant listing it as a separate language. Each of these languages differs in detail, especially in regard to the preglottalized series. Consider these correspondences:

Gloss	Paha	Yalang	Ecun	Langjia	En
'four'	pa^{322}	po^{53}	pa^{24}	pa^{54}	pa^{35}
'blind'	ma:u^{45}	?bi:u^{53}	?bu^{24}	?bon^{24}	?bun^{44}
'goat'	mi^{11}	?bɔ^{33}	?bəp^{55}	?bəp^{11}	?bəp^{44}
'leaf'	ren^{322}	?dia^{53}	?dja:ŋ^{24}	?dəŋ^{31}	?diŋ^{35}
'near'	ra^{322}	thu^{33}	θuɔ^{33}	thuɔ^{24}	thəu^{35}
'give'	na:k^{11}	–	na:k^{53}	–	na:k^{44}

As this chart makes clear, Paha differs from the others in regard to the preglottalized series /?b ?d/. Yalang, Ecun, Langjia, and En all show preglottalized stops, whereas Paha has nasals, plain voiced stops or breathy voiced stops in place of the preglottalized voiced stops. This feature suggests a division in Buyang separating Paha from the others, i.e. Paha-Yalang/Ecun/Langjia (Ostapirat 2000) and we would include En in the Yalang/Ecun/Langjia grouping. One other development in Paha/Buyang phonology deserves mention. The Laha language preserves final -*l*. In most other languages this coda develops into -n, but in Buyang it is occasionally realized as -*t*. En partakes in this diagnostic development.

Gloss	Laha	Paha	Yalang	Ecun	Langjia	En
rain	dʑaal⁴⁴ʔ	ʑin³¹	ʐuut³¹	ʐuut⁵⁵	ʑiit⁵⁵	jit⁴⁴
new	maal⁴⁴ʔ	maːil⁴¹	maːt³¹	maːn³³	maːn³¹²	maːn⁵²
yellow	ŋil⁴¹ʔ	ŋaːn⁴⁵	ŋaːt³¹	ŋaːn¹¹	ŋaːn¹¹	
sweet	thəl¹³²	–	iːt³³	ʐən³³	ən²⁴	jin⁴³ʔ
louse	maɖral⁴⁴	–	ʔdɔt⁵³	tən³³	tən³¹²	ʔdan³⁵

Both lexically and phonologically En and the Buyang group share much in common. Much work is still needed on En as this language has only a small population of speakers. Encouragingly, it was reported to us that children are still learning En as their first language.

23.6. QABIAO

The Qabiao language is often referred to in Chinese language materials as Pubiao 普标, cf. Zhang Junru's (1990) treatment. This is also the term used by Ostapirat (2000). The people call themselves *qa°biau³³* with a very short toneless syllable preceding the main syllable. They live directly on the China-Vietnam border in Yunnan Province, Guangnan Prefecture in Malipo County and in territory just opposite this place in Vietnam's Hà Giang Province in Đồng Văn District in the villages of Phố Là and Sùng Chéng and perhaps in a few neighboring places in Yên Minh and Mèo Vạc Districts. No one knows the exact meaning of this name Qabiao today. There about 380 in Vietnam and perhaps an equal number in China today; the *Ethnologue* (2001) gives a total population of 689. This language is highly endangered and the situation of the people themselves is unstable because of a lack of nearby potable water in this area.

The Qabiao language has a large inventory of disyllabic vocabulary in which the first or weak syllble has no real tonal contour.

Qabiao tones:

A1 tee⁴² 'eye'   B1 kə°mii⁴²³ 'hand'   C1 qaa³³ʔ 'blood'   D1 ʔək³³ 'excrement'
A2 kə°rfiɔɔ³³ 'ear'   B2 mfiaau²¹⁴ 'face'   C2 muum³⁵ 'beard'   D2 pa°nuk²⁵ 'bird'

We have listed a number of examples here in their full forms as we recorded them. At times these also differ insignificantly from the forms recorded by Ostapirat (2000). In other cases the full disyllabic forms of Qabiao and En (see above) are supportive of his reconstructions.

A1	kə°mfijəə⁴² 'bear'	m̥aa⁴² 'dog'	m̥uu⁴² 'pig'
	pa°ka°taau⁴² 'head louse'	pa°ka°nan⁴² 'body louse'	kən⁴² 'to eat'
	lam⁴² 'black'		
A2	ka°mfiaauŋ³³ 'frost'	pfijaau³³ 'stone'	ne°wfiən³³ 'sun'
	nfiii³³ 'name'	kfiaai³³ 'far'	rfiuuu³³ 'eight'
	ka°rfiooi³³ 'bee'	pakə°n̥aaŋ³³ 'mosquito'	
B1	yɯɯa⁴²³ 'wing'	tau⁴²³ 'ashes'	phjɔ⁴²³ 'silver'
	tsee⁴²³ 'to go'	ŋhaau⁴²³ 'pus'	
B2	mfiiiŋ²¹⁴ 'left'	mfiuu²¹⁴ 'to smell'	ŋən²¹⁴ 'heart'
	saa²¹⁴ 'slow'		
C1	ʔaŋ³³ʔ 'water'	pa³³ qaaŋ³³ʔ 'chin'	ʔjau³³ʔ 'meat'
	ʔbin³³ʔ 'to cut with scissors'	kə°toŋ³³ʔ 'nose'	
C2	jiŋ³⁵ 'to rest'	mfiaai³⁵ 'mother'	pa³³ laaŋ³⁵ 'eagle'
D1	rɔɔk³³ 'monkey'	pa³³ ljet³³ 'barking deer'	ʔuət³³ 'earth'
	lap³³ 'to forget'	laak³³ 'bone'	

D2   pa^{33} karaat^{25} 'crab'   rfiɔk^{25} mbjaat^{25} 'sour'
ram^{25} 'to bite'   panuk^{25} 'bird'

The Qabiao of Vietnam differs from the data presented in Ostapirat (2000) especially in regard to the preglottalized series of initials.

23.7. LAHA

The Laha are one of Vietnam's officially recognized minority groups. The total population in 1989 was 1,400. They live in two separated locations in Northern Vietnam, one area in Lào Cai Province, Than Uyên District, Nậm Cần, Ta Mit, and Pha Mu Villages and one location in Sơn La Province at Chiềng Xòm, Noong Lay, Liệp Tè, Nam Ét, as well as those at Mường La District in the communes of Nậm Giôn, Chiềng Xàng, Chiềng Dong, Pi Toong, and Mường Bú.

In Edmondson and Gregerson (1997), we presented data from Ta Mit Laha. The Ta Mit Laha data were gathered in the summer of 1996 at Sa Pa District in Lào Cai Province from Mr Hoàng Văn Phòm, who was 26 years of age at the time. He told us that there were eight Laha settlements mostly along the eastern bank of the Nậm Mu River, a secondary waterway that flows southward into the Sông Đà or Black River in Sơn La Province (22° 05' N, 103° 50' E). The Ta Mit Laha live with Black Thai and a few Hmong neighbors. In this paper we augment our previous analysis with data from the Laha of Noong Lay and Nặt Ét Communes in Sơn La Province about 80-90 km to the south. The second study site was at Noong Lay Commune, pop. 700, which is located about 25 km northwest of Sơn La City, Sơn La Province in northern Vietnam. Specifically, if one follows National Route 6 northwest from Sơn La City to a place where the road forks and then proceeds along Route 107 for 10 km to the next main market and turns right off the road into a lane that leads 8 km to the commune center (21° 30' N, 103° 45' E). The commune is about 10 km from the Sông Đa or Black River, which descends from Lai Châu Province to the west and flows easterly to the great lake created above the dam at Hoa Bình City. The landscape is determined by a rich fertile basin several kilometers wide along the banks of a relatively large river with high mountains to the west separating Sơn La from Lai Châu Province. Most of the people in the village are Khmu. There are two or three Black Thái families and recently some Vietnamese have moved there. The wider area is, however, mostly inhabited by Black Thái wet paddy rice farmers, who are concentrated in this part of Vietnam in 500,000 strength, along with Khmu, Kháng, and Ksongmul peoples. It is reported in Solntseva N.B. and Hoang Van Ma 1986 that another group of Laha speakers is found in Phù Yên on the north bank of the Sông Đa about 80 km to the southeast of the Noong Lay community. We were unable to study this group.

It is notable that the Laha language at these two locations differs considerably and the two groups have not been in contact for a long time (according to Mr Lò Văn Sám of Noong Lay.) The linguistic data from the two locations also demonstrate several distinctive features that confirm a considerable time depth of independent development. Basically, Noong Lay possesses initial consonant clusters, whereas Ta Mit shows dissyllabic word structure. We give a listing of Laha initials as found in Noong Lay in the table below.

Laha initials

p	pa^{423}	'four'				
ph	phaai^{132}	'cloth'				
?b	?baan^{354}	'harrow'	?bik^{24}	'carry on shoulder'		
b	baal$^{44?}$	'flower'				
m	ma^{23}	'dog'	pa^{254}ma$^{44?}$	'hand'	ma°na^{41}	'buffalo'

w	$wəl^{41}$	'mat of rice straw'	wa^{132}	'to go'	wan^{354}	'wind'
t	$ken^{354}ta^{423}$	'eye'	tai^{354}	'to bite'	$təu^{423}$	'three'
th	$maak^{354}thai^{354}$	'plow'	$theel^{354}$	'sweet'		
ʔd	$ʔduut^{24}$	'red'	$ʔdrəi^{423}$	'gall'	$ʔdrəu^{423}$	'urine'
d	$da^{44ʔ}$	'boat'	ta^{254} $dan^{44ʔ}$	'moon'		
ʑ	$ʑa^{354}$	'grandmother'	$ʑa^{423}$	'medicine'		
n	$na^{44ʔ}$	'wet plot'	na^{132}	'bow'	$nəi^{44ʔ}$	'ox'
l	$laal^{41}\ lat^{24}$	'lightning'	nam^{423} lul^{132}	'heart'	$mu^{44ʔ}$ $laal^{41}$	'arrow'
tɕ	$tɕam^{132}$	'one'	$tɕok^{45}$	'rice mortar'		
ɳ	$ɳan^{354}$	'short'				
k	$ʔuŋ^{41ʔ}\ kul^{423}$	'saliva'				
kh	$khan^{354}$	'shrimp'	kha^{354}	'dry'	kha^{132}	'lightweight'
ŋ	$ŋa^{44ʔ}$	'snake'	$ŋiil^{41}$	'yellow'	$ŋiip^{45}$	'bat'
h	ha^{41}	'dry field'	ha^{132}	'five'		
ʔ	$ʔaai^{41}$	'father'	$ʔuŋ^{132}$	'water'		
pl	$plaat^{24}$	'blood'	$pliŋ^{354}$	'black'	$pluuŋ^{354}$	'wet leech'
phl	$phla^{354}$	'knife'				
bl	$tu^{44ʔ}\ bla^{44ʔ}$	'fish'	$bli^{44ʔ}$	'needle'		
ml	mla^{41}	'rice'	$mləi^{44ʔ}$	'bride'		
tr	$trai^{132}$	'back basket'				
dʑ	$dʑaŋ^{41}$	'rest, to'	$dʑal^{44ʔ}$	'rain'		
dr	$draal^{44ʔ}$	'body louse'				
kl	$klun^{44ʔ}$	'star'	$kləi^{44ʔ}$	'far'	kla^{41}	'near'
khl	$khla^{44ʔ}$	'ear'	$khlaat^{45}$	'crab'		
kw	$kwaaŋ^{44ʔ}$	'sambar deer'				
hw	$kau^{354}hwaaŋ^{354}$	'eagle'				

As this table shows, Laha has two series of voiced stops, a preglottalized series /ʔb ʔd/ and a series of plain voiced stops /b d/. In Noong Lay the contrast is /ʔb ʔd/ vs. /b d/. In Ta Mit the two series also have different reflexes, but the contrast is /b d/ vs. /f th/ (f is derived from ph). Thus, we find these developments:

Kra	*ʔb	*ʔd	*b	*d
NoongLay	ʔb	ʔd	b	d
TaMit	b	d	ph	th

as in the examples:

	'harrow'	'red'	'village'	'boat'
Noong Lay	$ʔbaan^{354}$	$ʔdut^{24}$	$baan^{354}$	$da^{44ʔ}$
Ta Mit	$baan^{343}$	dut^{35}	$faan^{243}$	tha^{343}

The two series of voiced stops in Laha suggests two original series, which in all the remaining languages have merged in Gelao and Lachi to /b d/ and in the others to /ʔb ʔd/, thereby reducing the contrasts.

Laha has a vowel length contrast before the codas /-p -t -k -m -n -ŋ -l -i -u/. This feature is one it shares with all Kam-Tai languages, as mentioned at the beginning. Some good examples are $sau^{354}saau^{41}$ 'rope', $mai^{423}maai^{354}$ 'widow', and sal^{354} 'sputum' vs. $saal^{423}$ 'unhusked rice', though the vowel length contrast is today not as robust as it once must have been. The system is Tai-like in a second sense that the proto-Tai mid vowels, /e ə o/, when long, developed into the open reflex, i.e. -ɔɔC,-əəC, and -ɛɛC, but when short, demonstrate the more closed reflex, i.e. -oC, -ɯC, and -eC cf. Li points out, the Tai languages show today a wide variety of long and short vowel possibilities. Laha is unlike Tai languages, though, in the sense that in CV syllables the open reflex is usually found, e.g. $tɕɔ^{423}$ 'wife' and $mɛ^{44ʔ}$ 'bear'. There are also the diphthong $ɯa$, as in $ɳɯa^{423}$ 'big'. There are only a very few examples in our corpus of Ci and Cu syllables, however, as the word shapes in Laha Noong Lay have undergone an innovation, not unlike in the history of English, creating outgliding diphthongs $Cəi$ and $Cəu$ from these sources, as in: mu^{423} 'pig', ki^{423} 'chicken', pi^{423} 'fire' dri^{423} 'gall'. It is one of the two or three remaining languages with a lateral coda. The following is a list of vocabulary with final -l coda.

Gloss	Noong Lay	Ta Mit	Gloss	Noong Lay	Ta Mit
'anus'	$lol^{41ʔ}$	–	'arrow'	$mu^{354}\ laal^{41}$	$ma^{33}\ an^{24}$
'below'	$ɳuul^{41}$	–	'buy'	$tɕɔɔl^{423}$	$tɕɯn^{343}$
'carry midpole'	$khɔɔl^{41}$	$haam^{343}$	'comb'	$kaal^{354}$	$si^{41ʔ}$
'difficult'	$ʔdau^{423}\ khaal^{354}$	$kɛɛn^{31}$	'iron/hard'	$kɛɛl^{354}$	$kɛɛn^{31}$
'dry in sun'	$haal^{423}$	–	'fishy'	$kaal^{423}$	$kaan^{24}$
'flower'	$baal^{44ʔ}$	$ʔbɔk^{21}$	'to fly'	$pɔl^{354}$	$hɯn^{343}$
old or yellow'	$ɲiil^{41ʔ}$	–	'heart'	$nam^{23}\ lul^{354}$	$ma^{343}\ lun^{212}$
'heavy'	$khaal^{423}$	xan^{343}	'lizard'		$ŋa^{44}\ lal^{44}$
'body louse'	$ma°dral^{44}$	$ma^{33}\ than^{33}$	'old thing'	$maal^{44ʔ}$	–
'mouth'	$muul^{41ʔ}$	$mɔn^{24}$	'rag'	$si^{423}\ baal^{41ʔ}$	–
'sticky rice'	$wɔl^{41ʔ}$	–	'unhusked rice'	$saal^{423}$	$saan^{343}$
'saliva'	$ʔuŋ^{132}\ kuul^{423}$	$ma^{33}\ khun^{24}$	'fat'	mal^{44}	man^{33}
'slick'	tal^{423}	$thi^{31}\ than^{24}$	'rice spike'	$kal^{423}\ hɔi^{44}$	–
'sputum'	sal^{354}	–	'stone'	$nuul^{423}$	$ʔdun^{343}$
'sweet, honey'	$thɔl^{132}$	–	'taro'	$maal^{44ʔ}\ haak^{45}$	$man^{33}\ haak^{24}$
'yellow wasp'	tel^{423}	–	'forest'	pal^{423}	–

23.8. COMPARISION OF THE SYNTACTIC FEATURES

Kra language speakers have had small populations in comparison to neighboring minorities and the majority groups for quite a long time. As a consequence, many of these Kra speakers know other languages of wider communication: Han Chinese, Vietnamese, Nùng, Tày, Zhuang, Miao, Yao, Thái (Black and White Thai) etc. Our impression is that the language having the greatest influence on them has been Guanhua Chinese (SW Mandarin), as this language is more widely spoken in the borderlands area than, for example, Vietnamese or Modern Standard Chinese. In fact, it was a curiosity that many of our informants were not able to speak Vietnamese well nor do they participate much in the larger Vietnamese world, which necessitated using Guanhua, Miao, or Tày. Our Red Gelao informant, though a citizen of Vietnam, could not speak Vietnamese but did know Red Gelao, Miao, Kim Mun Yao, and Tày, so he brought along a Kim Mun neighbor to help interpret into Vietnamese. That said, I was impressed at the lack of Vietnamese borrowings in these languages; generally the lexical borrowings were more likely to Guanhua Chinese forms. That said, the sentence patterns of Kra languages were strongly SVO and conformed strongly to the trans-regional and and trans-typological norms.[2] For the NP that meant an order of elements *numeral (NUM)-classifier (CLS)-N-specifier (SPEC)*; for the VP the order is V-NP (direct object). There are examples of the Chinese-like *ba* construction in some of these languages NP$_1$-take-NP$_2$-VP such as Pingba Gelao:

(1)   *su^{33} u^{24}*   *hau^{13}*   *la^{55} tɛ^{55}*   *pə^{13}*   *hu^{33}*   *tsu^{33}*   *ni^{21}*

    s/he   take   bowl   put- on   top   table-   this

    'S/he put the bowl on the table.'

Adverbial modifiers with meaning 'very, excessive' are often placed after the adjective or adverb. Chinese *hěn* precedes and Vietnamese *lắm* follows but *rất* precedes. Eg.

(2)   plei^{33} ni^{21} ɯ^{55} mei^{33} zau^{55} ŋkau^{21} ŋkau^{21} tei^{13} ŋkə^{42} (Pingba Gelao)

    year   this   water   rain   excessive   ADV   ADV   much   PERF

      'This year's rain has been excessively much!'

The syntactic structure of these languages largely matches those of the area except for one dramatic exception, the position of the negative. Nearly all the Kra languages share the common feature that the negative element (negator) in the sentence comes last, even after direct objects. The fact is that all share this position. It seems likely that the parent language differed from Kam-Tai sister languages in this regard.

    With this brief introduction we now turn to some illustrations of these syntactic patterns.

23.8.1. Word order

All the Kra languages show SVO word order typology.

(3) Gelao   (Bigong)
    zəɯ^{35} qo^{33} ju^{31} tjo^{31} qan^{31} qo^{33} qa^{33} pai^{35} qhju^{31}
    farm   worker   person   must   farm   work   then   can   eat
    'A farmer must work in order to eat.'

    Lachi
    a^{44} ȵe^{44} ĩ^{55} pi^{44} vua^{35}
    here   be   hot   very
    'It is very hot here.'

    Laha
    then^{432} dʑal$^{44?}$
    sky   rain
    'It's raining.'

---

2   Data from Zhang Jimin 张济民 (1993), He Jiashan 贺嘉善 (1983), Li Yunbin 李云兵 (2000), Li Jinfang 李锦芳 (1999) as well as Solntseva and Hoang Van Ma (1986). Some examples also come from my field notes on the languages or from Ms Shen Yu-May.

ai^{523}	dʑen^{354}	taŋ^{354}	lon^{44ʔ}
father	1S	lives	home

'My father lives at home.

bla^{44ʔ}	loi^{44ʔ}	kluŋ^{354}	ʔuŋ^{354},	nok^{55}	pəl^{354}	nuk^{35}	then^{423}
fish	swim	in	water,	birds	fly	above	sky

'Fish swim in the water, and birds fly in the sky'

Langjia Buyang:

ku^{54}	pa:ŋ^{33}	ma^{312}
I	help	you

'I'll help you.'

En:

ʔbaau^{35}	le^{232}	tɕa^{323ʔ}	ki^{54}
I	NEG	know	him

'I don't know him'

Modifiers, adjuncts, and complements all follow heads (head-first) in NP structures. Examples from Pingba Gelao are: *la*^{42} *tu*^{21} ground-level 'level ground', *mpau*^{33} *laŋ*^{55} pig-black 'black pig', *luŋ*^{55} *zɒ*^{13} *sɛ*^{13} vegetable-insect-plant 'bugs'; Langjia Buyang (Li 1999: 78) *uə*^{24} *qai*^{54} meat-chicken 'chicken (meat)' and *ma ̊ŋa*^{11} *ɔk*^{11} horse-white 'white horse', and Laha has *lon*^{44ʔ} *mal*^{44ʔ} house-new 'new house'.

Prepositions and not post-postitions are employed, cf. Pingba Gelao *hu*^{33} *tsu*^{33} on-table 'on the table' and *tsen*^{21} *thɒ*^{55} below-bed 'under the bed'. Laha *kluŋ*^{354} *ʔuŋ*^{354} in-water 'in the water'.

In Wanzi Gelao (He 1983: 30-50) the head of the construction comes first as in: (1) head-in situ interrogative adjective *i*^{24} *an*^{33} *t'ɒ*^{55} *nu*^{31} duck-at-place-where 'Where is the duck?',

In Kra the order is numeral-classifier-head noun-specifier (Gelao) *lɒ* ^{44} *ni*^{31} bowl-this 'this bowl', *mɒ*^{13} *ts'a*^{44} *ni*^{31} CLS-mountain-this 'this mountain', and Laha *tu*^{44ʔ} *ma ̊na*^{41ʔ} *ʔe*^{354} CLS-buffalo-those 'those buffalos' and *təu*^{423} *tu*^{44ʔ} *nok*^{55} three-CLS-bird 'three birds'. The possessive adjective follows the head noun as in Gelao *tau*^{33} *i*^{33} book-my 'my book' and *luŋ*^{44} *mu*^{44} *i*^{44} *nɒ*^{55} *sen*^{44} *sen*^{33} clothing-new-my-yesterday-buy 'I bought my new clothes yesterday'.

Adverbs follow adjectives:

(4) Lachi

a^{44} ȵe^{44}	ĩ^{55}	pi^{44}	vua^{35}
here	be	hot	very

Laha

thau^{354}	əi^{44}
old	very

The pronominal system of Gelao shows several features quite unlike those of other members of the Kam-Tai group. Pronouns are distinctive for singular and plural. In the singular there is a long and short form. Regular plurals are distinct from the pronominal form for 'family, household, clan'. These are portrayed below:

(5) Gelao Pronouns

i^{42} or su^{33} i^{42} 'I'   su^{33} ta^{33} 'we'   qa^{33} qei^{42} 'my household'
mu^{21} or su^{33} mu^{21} 'you sg.'   su^{33} sa^{33} 'you pl.'   a^{33} mu^{21} 'your household'
u^{42} or su^{33} u^{42} 'he, she, it'   pə^{42} nu^{42} 'they'   qa^{33} qu^{42} 'his/her household'

(6) Lachi pronouns

	Singular	Plural
1st person	ki^{51}	la^{44} tei^{51}, tha^{51} tei^{51}, thai^{51} tei^{51}
2nd person	m̩^{51}	la^{44} m̩^{44} tei^{51}
3rd person	kje^{31}	tha^{51} kje^{31}

Plural forms of the household pronoun are identical to the usual plurals. Some examples are:

(7) a. su^{33} san^{33} mpi^{32} ni^{21} tshu^{55} qa^{33}su^{33}qu^{55} li^{33} ə^{42}.
    two   CLF   goat this   be   clan house's   POSS   NEG
    'This goat is not ours.'

   b. ma^{21} thau^{33} ni^{21} tshu^{55} qa^{33} su^{33} sa^{33} li^{33}.
    CLF   knife   this   be   clan   2PL   POSS
    'This knife is your (household)'s.'

   c. ma^{21} i^{44} tshu^{55} mu^{21} li^{33} vu^{55}
    mother 1SG   be   2SG   POSS maternal aunt
    'My mother is your maternal aunt.'

   d. a^{33} tau^{33} i^{42} xa^{33} a^{55} mpau^{33} ə^{42}
    POL m. granddad   1SG   eat   meat   dog   NEG
    'My maternal grandfather does not eat dog.'

   e. qa^{33} ua^{55} tɕa^{55}
    clan   Wang   house
    'The Wang family house(hold)'

Interrogative pronouns. Gelao uses its own interrogative forms for questions. 'What' is *sa^{33} tsaŋ^{13}*, 'how' is *aŋ^{33} na^{21}*, 'how much' is *xen^{13} na^{21}*.

Numerals and classifiers. Gelao and the other Kra languages have their own number system (except when items have been borrowed from Chinese or other languages.) Ostapirat (2000) has reconstructed the numerals as *tʂəm C 'one', *sa A 'two', *tu A 'three', *pə A 'four', *r-ma A 'five', *x-nəm A 'six', *t-ru A 'seven', *m-ru A 'eight', *s-ɣwa B 'nine', and *pwlot D 'ten'. The system of classifiers is very rich. So, for example, Gelao at Pingba has distinct classifiers for a number of long narrow objects that are all rendered by *tiao* in Chinese, i.e.: sๅ^{33} qan^{13} qen^{33} 'one-CLF- road', sๅ^{33} san^{13} ŋkau^{55} 'one-CLF-snake', sๅ^{33} la^{55} en^{55} 'one-CLF-skirt', sๅ^{33} nen^{33} thau^{55} 'one-CLF-boat', and sๅ^{33} tshuu^{33} ten^{55} 'one-CLF- blanket'.

Demonstrative pronouns. Gelao at Pingba distinguishes only proximal and distal forms in its demonstrative system, but at other Gelao locations three forms are the norm as in Tai and Kam-Sui languages. In the NP the position for demonstratives or specifiers is at the end of the NP. Examples are:

(8) a.   su^{33} u^{42} hau^{13} la^{55} tɛ^{55} pə^{13} hu^{33} tsu^{33} ni^{21}

s/he   take   bowl   pu on   top   table   this

'S/he put the bowl on this table.'

b.   nen^{33} ni^{21} a^{33},   nen^{33} nu^{42} a^{33} ə^{24}

CLF   this   good   CLS   that   good   NEG

'This is good, but that is bad.'

c.   sๅ^{33} tsa^{21} mpə^{21} ni^{21} kuu^{21} a^{33}

one   meal   rice   this   full   good

Lachi

d.   saŋ^{55} ɲɛ^{44} a^{55},   saŋ^{55} pje^{44} a^{55} ljo^{31}

CLF   this   good   CLF   that   good   NEG

'This one (animal) is good, but that one is not good.'

Family names, such as Wang, Huang, Long, etc., are rendered into Gelao with the word corresponding to that meaning. Thus *Long* 'dragon' is *zau^{55}*; *Wen* is *ven^{21}*, etc.

Negation is one aspect of this subgrouping that is quite unlike other Kam-Tai languages. Negation always comes at the end of the sentence (also in questions, which are of the V-V-NEG 'are you, or are you not' type. Examples are:

Gelao

(9) a.   su^{33}ta^{33} vu^{13} a^{33} (Wanzi)

we   go   NEG

'We are not going.'

b.   tjo^{31} lie^{31},   pai^{35} qhju^{31} tou^{35} o^{33}.   (Bigong Gelao)

plant   late   obtain   eat   arrive   NEG

'If you plant late, you won't be able to eat.'

c. $(qo^{33}ju^{31})$ le^{35} te^{31} o^{33}
   a farmer   lazy   can   NEG
   '(A farmer) cannot be lazy.'

Laha
d. $in^{41?}$ $an^{44?}$ $si^{41?}$
   I   have comb
   'I have a comb.'

d'. $in^{41?}$ $an^{44?}$ $si^{41?}$ $tou^{41?}$
    I   have comb   NEG
    'I don't have a comb.'

Buyang resembles the other Kra languages in another important and distinctive feature: negation. For example. van^{54} ni^{11} qa° $\textit{?bot}^{11}$ $laai^{11}$ day-this-cold-NEG 'Today it is not cold' and $k\varepsilon^{54}$ $tin^{11}la\,^{\circ}vi^{312}qhn^{54}laam^{11}$ s/he-can-walk-road-not yet 'S/he can walk yet.' Paha is exceptional in the position of negation by having it precede the verb. The meaning 'No one knows him' can be rendered in Buyang dialects as (10).

(10) a. Paha:
       pa^{33} nau^{33} ko^{33} pi^{45} θaai^{45} θa^{31} ko^{55}
       who   also   NEG   know   3sg

   b. Yalang:
      va^{31} ni^{12} jo^{53} ka^{33} ki^{33} la^{31}
      who   also   know   3sg   NEG

   c. Ecun:
      $vaai^{33}$ no^{33} ko^{33} $?de^{55}$ ke^{24} $naai^{53}$
      who   also   know   3sg   NEG

   d. Langjia:
      ma° no^{11} ko^{54} tin^{11} ko^{54} $laai^{11}$
      who   also know   3sg   NEG

Data on the Kra languages are only just beginning to emerge. They are giving us a glimpse into a language and culture of great interest, great antiquity, and surprising sophistication. They have not only their own number system but also unique vocabulary for metalworking (silver, gold, iron) and handicrafts (needlework). They do not appear to have been involved in the central occupation of the Kam-Tai group of wet paddy rice cultivation or at least did not share its unique vocabulary. We look forward to seeing much more about this important group.

REFERENCES

Benedict, Paul K (1942) 'Tai, Kadai, and Indonesian: A new alignment in Southeast Asia', *American Anthropologist* n.s.44: 576-601.

— (1975) *Austro-Thai: Language and Culture with a Glossary of Roots*, New Haven: HRAF.

Bonifacy, Auguste (1905) 'Étude sur les langues parlées par les populations de la haute Rivière Claire', *BEFEO* 5: 306-27.

Bonifacy, Auguste (1906) 'Étude sur les coutumes et la langue des La-ti', *BEFEO* 6: 271-78.

Bonifacy, Auguste (1908) 'Étude sur les coutumes et la langue des Lolo et des La-quea du Haut Tonkin', *BEFEO* 8: 531-58.

Các dân tộc ít ngời ở Viêt Nam(1978) *Hà Nội: Nhà Xuất Bản Học Xã Hội*.

Edmondson, Jerold A. and Gregerson, Kenneth J. (1997) 'Outlying Kam-Tai: Notes on the Ta Mit Laha', *Mon Khmer Studies* 27: 257-69.

Edmondson, Jerold A. and Li Jinfang (1996) 'The language corridor', *Proceedings of the Pan-Asiaticc Linguistics III*, Bangkok: Mahidol University.

Edmondson, Jerold A. and Li Jinfang (2003) 'Red Gelao, the most endangered form of the Gelao language', paper presented at International Conference on Sino-Tibetan Languages and Linguistics, La Trobe University, Melbourne, Australia.

Edmondson, Jerold A., Nguyễn Văn Lợi, and Hoàng Văn Ma (1999) 'Nùng Vên (Ênh): Một ngôn ngữ thuộc nhóm Ka Đai mới được phát hiện. (Nung Ven (Ênh): a newly discovered language of the Kadai (outlier) group)', *Ngôn Ngữ* 5: 12-21.

Edmondson, Jerold A. and Yang Quan (1988) 'Word initial preconsonants and the history of Kam-Sui resonants', in Jerold A Edmondson and David Solnit (eds) *Comparative Kadai: Linguistic Studies Beyond Tai*, Dallas: SIL and UTA Series in Linguistics, 143-66.

贺嘉善 He Jiashan (1983) 仡佬语简志 *Gelaoyu jianzhi*, Beijing. Minzu Chubanshe.

Hoàng Văn Ma and Vũ Ba Hùng (1992) *Tiếng Pu Péo (The Pubiao language)*, Hà Nội: Nhà Xuất Bản Khoa Học Xã Hội.

Hudak, Thomas John (1993) *William J. Gedney's The Saek language: Glossary, Texts, and Translations*, Ann Arbor: Michigan Papers on South and Southeast Asia.

李锦芳和周國炎 Li Jinfang and Zhou Guoyan (1999) *Studies on Outlier Kam-Tai*, Beijing: 中央民族大学出版社 Zhongyang Minzu Daxue Chubanshe.

李锦芳 Li Jinfang (1996) 布央语研究 *[Studies on the Buyang Language]*, unpublished PhD dissertation, Central University of Nationalities 中央民族大学, Beijing.

— (1999) 布央语研究 *Buyangyu Yanjiu [Studies on the Buyang Language]*, Beijing: 中央民族大学出版社 Zhongyang Minzu Daxue Chubanshe (revised edition of the author's 1996 dissertation).

李云兵 Li Yunbin (2000) 拉基语研究*Lajiyu Yanjiu [Studies on the Laji Language]*. Beijing: 中央民族大学出版社 Zhongyang Minzu Daxue Chubanshe.

Lajongière, Étienne E. Lunet de (1906) *Ethnographie du Tonkin septentrional*, Paris: Leroux.

梁敏 Liang Min (1990) 'The Buyang Language', *Kadai* 2: 13-21.

Nguyễn Văn Lợi and Edmondson, Jerold A. (1999), 'Tiếng La Chì thượng nguồn Sông Lô (The La Chi language of the Upper Reaches of the Clear River)', *Ngôn Ngữ* 5: 1-11.

Ostapirat, Weera (2000) 'Proto-Kra', *LTBA* 23.1: 1-251.

Robert, J. (1913). 'Notice sur les Lati', *Revue d'Ethnographie et de Sociologie* 4: 338-52.

Shen Yu-May (2003) Phonology of Sanchong Gelao, unpublished MA Thesis, University of Texas at Arlington.

Solntseva, N. B. and Hoang Van Ma, (eds) (1986). Язык Лаха: Материалы советско-вьетнамской лингвистической экспедиции 1979 года *[The Laha Language. Materials of the Soviet-Vietnamese linguistic expedition in 1979]*, Moscow: Nauka.

张济民 Zhang Jimin (1993)仡佬语研究 *Gelaoyu yanjiu [Studies on the Gelao Language]*, Guiyang: Guizhou Natinalities Publishing House.

张均如 Zhang Junru (1990) 'The Pubiao language', *Kadai* 2: 23-33.

APPENDIX: LANGUAGE MAPS

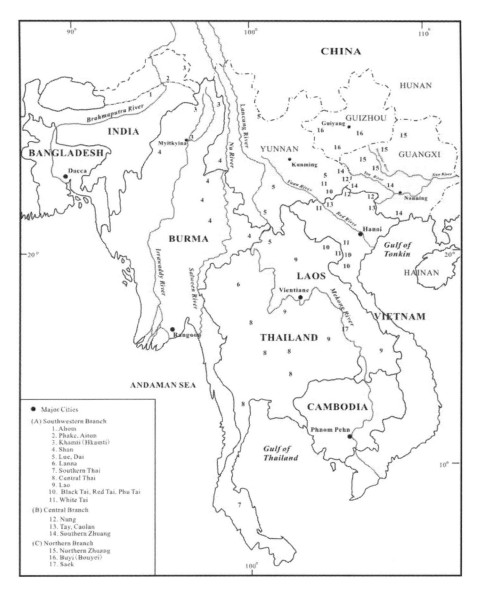

MAP AP-1: DISTRIBUTION OF TAI

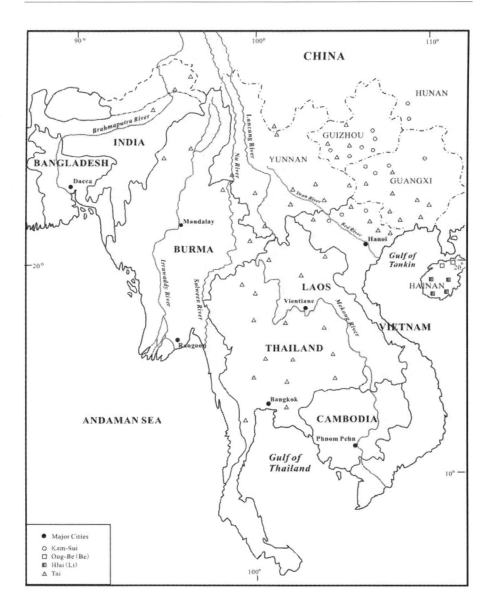

MAP AP-2: DISTRIBUTION OF KAM-TAI

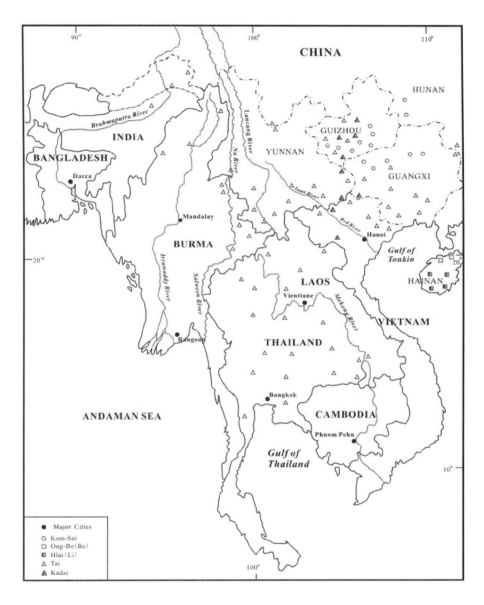

MAP AP-3: DISTRIBUTION OF TAI-KADAI

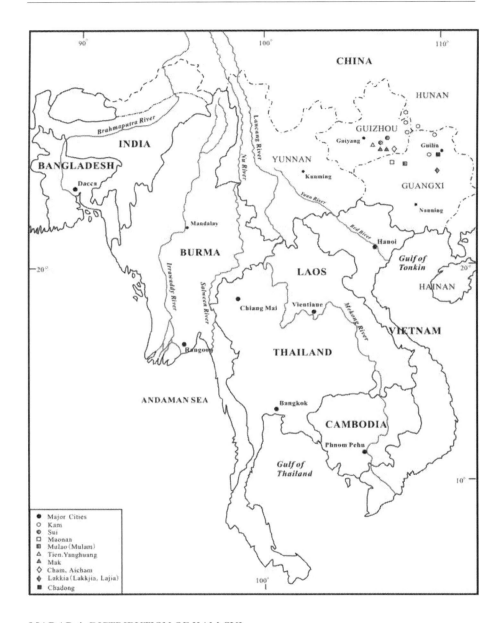

MAP AP-4: DISTRIBUTION OF KAM-SUI

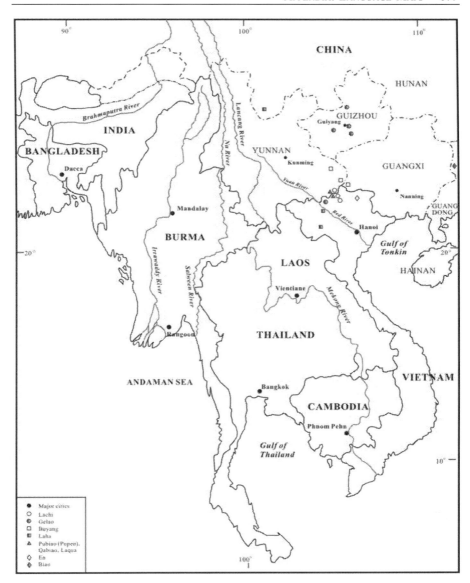

MAP AP-5: DISTRIBUTION OF GELAO, BUYANG AND OTHER KADAI

INDEX

Printed in Poland
by Amazon Fulfillment
Poland Sp. z o.o., Wrocław

11220137R00394